Shooter's Bible

107TH EDITION

Shooter's Bible

107TH EDITION

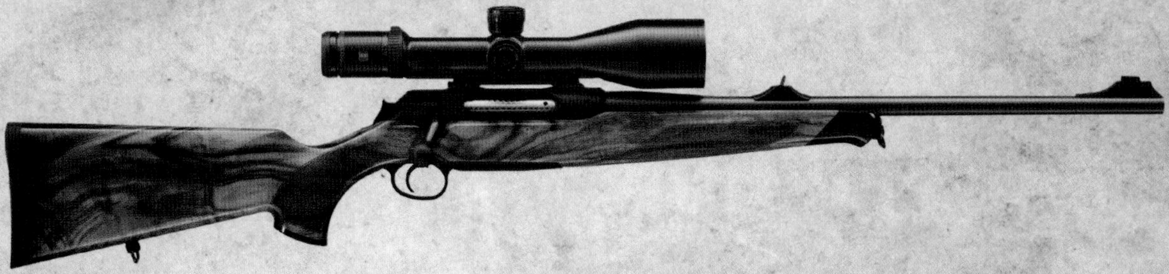

SKYHORSE PUBLISHING

Skyhorse Publishing books may be purchased in bulk at special discounts for sales promotion, corporate gifts, fund-raising, or educational purposes. Special editions can also be created to specifications. For details, contact the Special Sales Department, Skyhorse Publishing, 307 West 36th Street, 11th Floor, New York, NY 10018 or info@skyhorsepublishing.com.

Visit our website at www.skyhorsepublishing.com.

10 9 8 7 6 5 4 3 2 1

Cover design by Brian Peterson

Print ISBN: 978-1-63450-588-8
Ebook ISBN: 978-1-5107-0192-2
ISSN: 0080 9365

Printed in Canada

Note: Every effort has been made to record specifications and descriptions of guns, ammunition, and accessories accurately, but the Publisher can take no responsibility for errors or omissions. The prices shown for guns, ammunition, and accessories are manufacturers' suggested retail prices (unless otherwise noted) and are furnished for information only. These were in effect at press time and are subject to change without notice.

CONTENTS

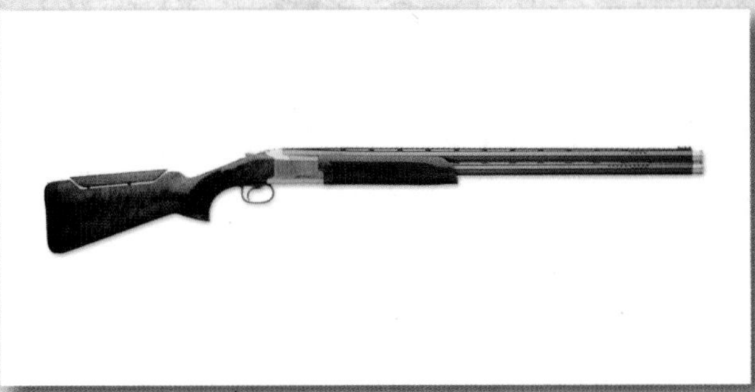

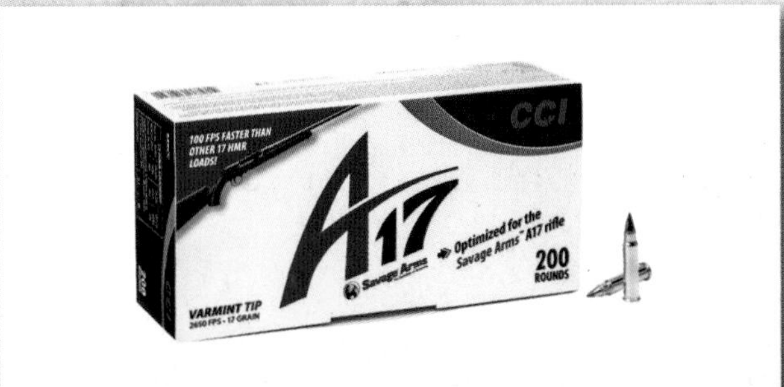

INTRODUCTION 1

GUNS, OPTICS, AND AMMO 2016 5

HANDGUN BUYER'S GUIDE 13

PUTTING IT IN ITS PLACE 19

NEW PRODUCTS 23

RIFLES 24

AIR RIFLES 52

SHOTGUNS 54

HANDGUNS 67

BLACK POWDER 89

OPTICS 90

RANGE FINDERS 100

AMMUNITION 101

MZ BULLETS 105

BULLETS 106

CURRENT PRODUCTS 107

RIFLES 107

AIR RIFLES 231

SHOTGUNS 246

HANDGUNS 297

BLACK POWDER 391

OPTICS 409

AMMUNITION 477

REFERENCE 547

BALLISTICS 547

DIRECTORY OF MANUFACTURERS & SUPPLIERS 595

GUNFINDER INDEX 597

INTRODUCTION

Yes, another year has indeed gone by and yes, it is time for the newest edition of the *Shooter's Bible*, in this case the 107th.

Despite pressure from certain sectors, the gun industry as a whole had another banner year in 2015 and, by all accounts, the coming year should be just as prosperous, with arms manufacturers everywhere ramping up their production to meet the insatiable demand of the gun-buying public. Many companies have come out with new and exciting firearms this year. Both Glock and SIG have come out with 10mm pistols built specifically for hunting. On the rifle front, Mossberg has a new flagship centerfire rifle in the Patriot, with four short action calibers and seven long action calibers. (I'm taking their new synthetically stocked .300 Win. Mag. on an elk hunt in Idaho this fall, and I can't wait! Range work has been easy, and accurate.) And there is more, of course. Ruger has a semiautomatic AR-556 chambered in 5.56 NATO, while Sako has an 85 Carbonlight, its lightest rifle featuring a carbon fiber stock and fluted stainless steel barrel in .22-250, .243 Win., .60 Rem., 7mm-08 Rem., and .308 Win. In shotguns, Beretta has a new high-end 12-gauge over-and-under in its new 690 Field III, while Legacy has a new Escort M87 Pump in 12 or 20 gauge, adult or youth model.

For a full report on what's new for 2016, check out "Guns, Optics, and Ammo 2016" by Robert Sadowski, starting on page 5. You'll be amazed at the wide array of new firearms that is now available. Sadowski hits the highlights, but you find much more in the New Products sections, right after his feature. Then you'll move on to the meat of the *Shooter's Bible*, the existing products section, starting on page 107. Here is where you'll find every gun in production on the planet, with totally up-to-date prices and specs. I'm guessing that everyone reading this book owns some firearms that are in this section. (If you own a gun that isn't in this section, it is probably out of production, in which case you need to pick up a copy of another Skyhorse Publication, the *Gun Trader's Guide*.) Optics, ammunition, and accessories are also covered in the *Shooter's Bible*, as they are every year.

If this is first time you have picked up a copy of the *Shooter's Bible*, you should know that the *Shooter's Bible* has a long and storied past. The first numbered

Here I check out another new firearm at the Mossberg booth.

edition of the *Shooter's Bible* was published in 1925; it's been published annually, and in some cases bi-annually, ever since. More than seven million copies have been sold in that time, and it continues to be the ultimate reference book for millions of people who want information on new guns, ammunition, optics, and accessories, as well as up-to-date prices and specs for thousands of in-production firearms.

The Skyhorse staff is proud of this newest edition of the *Shooter's Bible*, a book that has been continually updated and fact-checked for the past twelve

When I attended the Shooting-Hunting-Outdoor-Trade (SHOT) show in Las Vegas last January, I had the chance to check out Mossberg's new Patriot rifle. For more on these rifles, see page 5.

Aimpoint came out with the new Micro H-2 sight.

John Lazzeroni with one of his newer models. Lazzeroni rifles are known for their high quality and spot-on accuracy.

months. Not content to rest on our laurels, however, we have also continued to produce more and more *Shooter's Bible* guidebooks. In the past year, we have added a number of new volumes to our growing lineup, including the *Shooter's Bible Guide to Tactical Firearms*, also by Robert Sadowski. A guide we did a few years ago, the *Shooter's Bible Guide to AR-15s*, by Doug Howlett, did so well that Howlett is now busy updating and revising that book. The second edition includes a totally new product section, more AR-15 companies (and there are a ton of them!), and more accessories. That will be out in fall 2016, as will another *Shooter's Bible* guidebook, the *Shooter's Bible Guide to Handloading*, by Wayne van Zwoll. For a full list of all of the *Shooter's Bible* guidebooks, as well as our *Gun Trader's Guide* and the *Gun Trader's Guide* guidebooks (new this year—the *Gun Trader's Guide to Shotguns*), please go to www.skyhorsepublishing.com.

What does the future hold? No one can predict that. But what we do know is that the *Shooter's Bible* and all of its offshoot guidebooks will be available each and every year, with revised editions, new topics, and complete coverage.

Jay Cassell
Editorial Director
Skyhorse Publishing

Researcher Lindsey Breuer holds her Benelli Ultra Light 28-gauge in preparation for a snowy day on the clays course in Ohio.

Researcher Andres Dietz-Chavez looks through a thermal scope mounted on a silenced DPMS Panther Arms Model A-15 while hog hunting in Georgia. Photo courtesy of Gary Frye at Happy Acres Expeditions.

ALSO AVAILABLE FROM SKYHORSE PUBLISHING

The Shooter's Bible Guide to Firearms Assembly, Disassembly, and Cleaning
The Shooter's Bible Guide to Combat Handguns
The Shooter's Bible Guide to Planting Food Plots
The Shooter's Bible Guide to Bowhunting
The Shooter's Bible Guide to Home Defense
The Shooter's Bible Guide to Optics
The Shooter's Bible Guide to Knives
The Shooter's Bible Guide to Bowhunting
The Shooter's Bible Guide to Tactical Firearms
The Shooter's Bible Guide to Whitetail Strategies
The Shooter's Bible Guide to Handloading
The Shooter's Bible Guide to Rifle Ballistics
The Shooter's Bible Guide to Cartridges
The Shooter's Bible Guide to AR-15s
The Shooter's Bible Guide to Extreme Iron
The Shooter's Bible Guide to Concealed Carry
The Shooter's Bible Guide to the Hunting Rifle and Its Ammunition

GUNS, OPTICS, AND AMMO 2016

By Robert A. Sadowski

Rifle manufactures are creating some accurate long guns in both rimfire and centerfire calibers to suit the hunter, sniper, target shooter, and just plain plinker. A variety of shotguns in all types of actions—from single-shot break open to semiautomatic—are making the hunting bird population very nervous. Clay shooters can also find a wide variety of new shotguns. The big news in handguns this year is powerful 10mm. Both Glock and SIG are offering pistols purpose but for hunting. New rifle and handgun cartridges and shotgun shells introduced this year are purpose built to hunt, train, or defend. For optics, the two trends that continue this year are optics for AR platforms and long range shooting optics.

MOSSBERG BLAZE-47

RIFLES

Ashbury Precision Ordnance (ashburyprecisionordnance.com)

The SPR-308 (MSRP: $5,650) bolt action uses a Saber-Forsst chassis system and a 20-in. Pinnacle series fluted barrel chambered in .308 Win.

Browning (browning.com)

The AB3 (MSRP: $739) bolt-action series is now available in short action calibers like .243 Win., 7mm-08, and .308 Win. An Eclipse Varmint (MSRP: $1,069) and Eclipse Target (MSRP: $1,069) are the newest additions to the X-Bolt line with thumbhole laminates stocks.

CMMG (cmmginc.com)

The MK47 Mutant T (MSRP: $1,450) is a combination AR and AK. The Mutant uses an AR style direct impingement system and feeds off of 7.62x39mm ammo from AK magazines. The MK47 Mutant AKM (MSRP: $1,650) features Magpul furniture.

CZ USA (cz-usa.com)

The Sonoran (MSRP: $3,199) was designed for flat-trajectory and long-range shooting. Chambered in 26 Nosler with a Manners carbon stock. The CZ 455 Training rifle (MSRP: $399) offers a 24.8-in. barrel chambered in .17 HMR. The CZ 455 Ultra Lux (MSRP: $449) features a premium wood stock and is chambered in .22 LR.

Legacy Sports International (legacysports.com)

The Howa Mini Action (MSRP: $652) is nearly an inch shorter than a short bolt action and is available in .223 Rem. and .204 Ruger.

Magnum Research (magnumresearch.com)

The Magnum Lite .22 LR (MSRP: $824) and .22 WMR (MSRP: $941) semiautomatic rimfires have been upgraded with Barracuda American Black Walnut stocks in three finishes: Pepper, Nutmeg, and Forest Camo.

Mossberg (mossberg.com)

The new flagship of Mossberg's centerfire rifles, the Patriot (MSRP: $320/synthetic, $350/scope package) line of bolt-action rifles come in four short action calibers and seven long action calibers. The new Blaze (MSRP: $99–$175) rimfire rifles are semiautomatic and come in a variety of stock configurations, but they all feature a 16.5-in barrel. The Blaze-47 (MSRP: $290) looks like an AK-47.

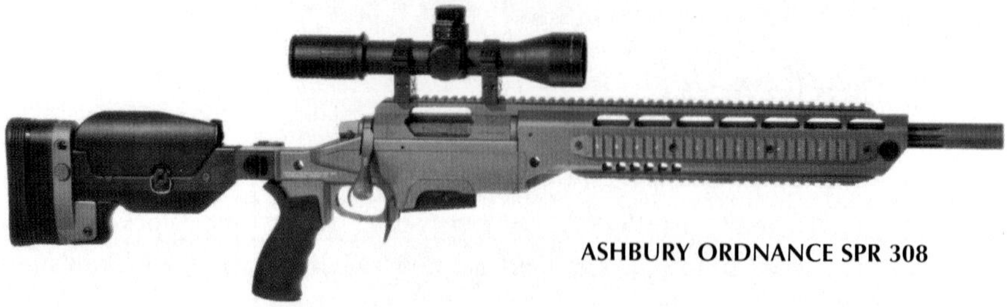

ASHBURY ORDNANCE SPR 308

CZ-USA 455 ULTRA LUX

Ruger (ruger.com)

The semiautomatic AR-556 (MSRP: $749) uses a traditional direct impingement system and comes chambered in 5.56 NATO. The American rifles series now offers a Ranch (MSRP: $499) model with 16.12-in. barrel as well as left hand models (MSRP: $459).

Savage (savagearms.com)

The A17 is a semiautomatic chambered in .17 HMR (MSRP: $465), yes .17 HMR. The A17 uses a delayed blowback system to handle the increased pressure of the .17 HMR. Got a hankering for the swamp and crocs? Then the Model 93 Landry (MSRP: $424) bolt-action rimfire is all set up for the bayou. The economical AXIS rifle series has added a Heavy Barrel model (MSRP: $386) in varmint calibers.

Sako (sako.fi)

The 85 Carbonlight (MSRP: $2,848) is Sako's lightest rifle featuring a carbon fiber stock and fluted stainless steel barrel in .22-250, .243 Win., .260 Rem., 7mm-08, and .308 Win.

Thompson/Center Arms (tcarms.com)

The Venture goes small with a 20-in. barrel Compact (MSRP: $458). It comes with a black synthetic stock.

Winchester (winchesterguns.com)

The new XPR (MSRP: $550) centerfire bolt-action rifle offers a polymer stock, detachable magazine, MOA triggers system and a button rifled barrel. The Model 73 gets a case hardened finish in the 24-in. barrel Sporter (MSRP: $1,740) and 20-in. Short Rifle (MSRP: $1,580).

BENELLI 828U

SHOTGUNS

Benelli (benelliusa.com)

The 828U is as striking over-and-under with adjustable stock in either a nickel (MSRP: $2,999) or black-anodized (MSRP: $2,499) finish and a walnut stock.

Beretta (beretta.com)

The new high-end 690 Field III (MSRP: $3,495) is an over-and-under chambered for 12-gauge and 3-inch shells. The new 692 over-and-under series incorporates the Beretta Steelium Plus barrel system with lengthened forcing cones to produce better pattern performance, improved recoil reduction, and a decrease in muzzle rise. Models include 692 Sporting (MSRP: $3,520) and 692 Skeet (MSRP: $3,870). The 486 Parallelo (MSRP: $5,350) is a new side-by-side built on a round-body action.

Browning (browning.com)

The Citori 725 series has expanded with a Pro Sporting (MSRP: $4,000) and Pro Trap (MSRP: $4,000) with 30- or 32-in. barrels.

Chiappa (chiappafirearms.com)

The C6-12 Youth Model (MSRP: $270) pump gun is chambered in 20 gauge for less recoil and comes with a camo finished stock and forend.

BROWNING CITORI 725 PRO TRAP

CZ USA (cz-usa.com)

The CZ 812 (MSRP: $699) was designed for duck work and features a recoil-operated system and in Realtree Max-4 camo. The Sharp-Tail (MSRP: $1,022) is a small lightweight side-by-side with casehardened finish boxlocks.

Legacy Sports International (legacysports.com)

The new Escort Pump Shotgun (MSRP: $349) is available in 12- or 20-gauge and in adult or youth model. The new Pointer Slug Combo (MSRP: $755) is a two-barrel set available in either pump or semiautomatic actions with a 28-in. smooth bore barrel and three choke tubes and 24-in. rifled slug barrel with scope mount. The Break-Action (MSRP: $188) single shot shotgun is available in either 12, 20, or .410 and features a black synthetic stock with a fixed modified choke.

Mossberg (mossberg.com)

Designed for left-handed shooters, the Model 500, 590, and 590A1 Special Purpose shotguns are available in version suitable for lefties.

Remington (remington.com)

The Versamax evolves with the V3 (MSRP: $895 synthetic; $995 walnut/camo) with a more refined gas system that reduces recoil.

Weatherby (weatherby.com)

Weatherby is back offering quality over-and-under shotguns. The Orion I (MSRP: $1,099) features a walnut stock and a blued finish. The Element Deluxe is a semiautomatic, inertia operated shotgun chambered in either 12 or 20 gauge (MSRP: $1,099) or 28 gauge (MSRP: $1,149).

MAGNUM RESEARCH DESERT EAGLE 1911 GSS

HANDGUNS

Browning (browning.com)

The 1911-380 (MSRP: $670) is a 1911 style platform chambered in .380 featuring a 4.25-inch barrel and matte black finish.

Charter Arms (charterfirearms.com)

The Pitbull is now chambered in America's favorite big bore cartridge the .45 ACP (MSRP: $489).

HECKLER & KOCH HK 45 CERAKOTE

Cimarron (cimarron-firearms.com)

Cowboy action shooters can get an edge with Short Stroke variants on many of Cimarron's single action model revolvers. The shorter hammer stroke means the revolvers are easier to cock (MSRP: $714–$974).

Glock (glock.com)

Glock's long slide models—G34, G35, G41—are now available in MOS configuration that allows easy mounting of a red for sight. The new G40 in 10mm features a 6-in. barrel and is also in MOS configuration. Compact and powerful describes the G43, a single stack 9mm made for conceal carry (MSRP: $529).

Heckler & Koch (hk-usa.com)

The USP9 Tactical features all of HK's tactical pistols features: threaded barrel with an O-ring, match trigger with adjustable trigger stop, and adjustable target sights. The HK45 and HK45 Compact, both in .45 ACP, are now available in matching Cerakote colored frame and slide finishes in Sand and Green with contrasting black operating controls (MSRP: $1199).

Kahr Arms (kahr.com)

The newest addition to the value-priced CT series is the CT380 chambered in .380 ACP that weighs just 11 ounces unloaded (MSRP: $419).

Magnum Research Inc. (magnumresearch.com)

The iconic Desert Eagle is now made in a 400 series stainless steel barrel and frame as well as stainless steel slide, plus a bottom Picatinny rail to mount accessories (MSRP: $599). A Desert Eagle chambered in .357 Magnum with black finish and integral muzzle brake is also new this year (MSRP: $710). Also new are three stainless steel 1911 pistols: the full size 1911GSS (MSRP: $904), the commander sized 1911CSS (MSRP: $904), and a compact 1911USS with a 3-in. (MSRP: $1019) barrel.

SMITH AND WESSON M&P 9
SHIELD CRIMSON TRACE

Ruger (ruger.com)

The LCRx (MSRP: $545) revolver series now comes in a three-inch barrel model with adjustable sights. The GP100 Match Champion (MSRP: $929) is now available with a rear adjustable sight. The SR1911 Lightweight Commander (MSRP: $899) features a lightweight aluminum frame and stainless slide in .45 ACP. The compact LC9s (MSRP: $449) is a single-stack 9mm with a striker fire system and polymer frame. The 22/45 Lite (blue) (MSRP: $515) features a light blue finished receiver with radical cooling grooves. The rimfire 22 Charger (MSRP: $309–$409) is back with enhanced ergonomics and new BX-15 magazine.

SIG Sauer (sigsauer.com)

The P220 is now available in the powerful 10mm. All models feature a five-inch barrel to maximize the internal ballistics of the 10mm round and are designed for duty carry, personal defense, or hunting. The P320 series of modular pistols now is available in .45 ACP and in a subcompact version.

Smith and Wesson (smith-wesson.com)

The standard M&P9 Shield is now available factory equipped with a Green Crimson Trace Laser sight (MSRP: $589). A carbon fiber finish on full size and compact M&P9 (MSRP: $599) and M&P40 is now available (MSRP: $599).

LEUPOLD VX-6 SERIES

OPTICS

Aimpoint (aimpoint.com)

The economical ACO (MSRP: $393) is designed to mount out of the box on an AR platform and provides absolute co-witness with iron sights. The Micro T-2 (MSRP: $849) has be revamped with a new housing that allows use of flip covers and beefed up turret protection.

BSA (bsaoptics.com)

The Tactical Weapon Illuminated Sight (MSRP: $100) offers four red/green illuminated reticle options. The 10–50x56mm Long Range Scope (MSRP: $310) is built with a 30mm tube.

Bushnell (bushnell.com)

The Elite 4.5–18x44mm (MSRP: $2,100) Long Range Hunting Scope (LRHS) features a first focal plane G2H or G2M reticle and RevLimiter zero stop elevation turret. The Rimfire Optics 4–12x40mm (MSRP: $188) riflescope is calibrated to the .17 WSM with a holdover up to 350 yards.

Leupold (leupold.com)

The Z-shaped D-EVO (MSRP: $1875) is mounted behind a reflex, holographic or red dot sight without obstructing the view. Shooters can shift their focus from the 1x view of red dot to a 6x precision optic. The 1x LCO (MSRP: 1250) red dot sight delivers a wider field of view than other red dots with an 1 MOA aiming dot.

Nightforce Optics (nightforceoptics.com)

The afordable SHV line has ad added 3–10x42mm SHV (MSRP: about $900) with two reticle options and side pallax adjustment. the ACTAR line now includes a high-magnification 5–25x56mm F1 ATACR (MSRP: $2800) scope with a first focal plane reticle configuration with several reticle options. The 4–16x42mm F! ATACR (MSRP: $2400) offers extreme performance in a compact package.

Nikko Stirling (legacysports.com)

The Panamax Series features a 3–9x40mm, 3–9x50mm, and 4–12x50mm AO (MSRP: beginning at $119) all a one piece

AIMPOINT MICRO H-2

tube, Microlux ETE Gen III lens coatings and dual red/green illuminated Half Mil Dot reticle. The Diamond Series has six new models: 1–4x24mm, 1.5–6x42mm, 3–9x42mm, 3–12x42mm, 3–12x56mm, and 3–12x162mm (MSRP: beginning at $219) all with 30mm tubes, low profile turrets, dual color red/green Illuminated reticle.

Simmons (simmonsoptics.com)

Designed for AR hunters the 1–6x24mm Predator/Varmint (MSRP: $260) scope has an illuminated Strike Zone 223 reticle calibrated for 5.56 NATO/.223 Rem. loads.

FEDERAL PREMIUM 3RD DEGREE

AMMUNITION

Barnes Precision (barnesbullets.com)

New Precision Match Ammunition line features two 5.56x45mm loads (69- and 85-gr. OTM BT), a .308 Win. (175-gr. OTM BT), a .300 Win. Mag. (220-gr. OTM BT), and for long range a .338 Lapua Mag. (300-gr. OTM BT). Barnes Range AR line has a new 5.56mm and .300 AAC Blackout. The VOR-TX line of all-copper bullets now includes two 5.56x45mm cartridges (62- and 70-gr. TSX bullet) a .300 ACC BLK load (120-gr. TAC-TX) and a .338 Lapua Magnum (280-gr. LRX).

CCI (cci-ammunition.com)

The A17 Varmint Tip rimfire is a 17 HMR cartridge specifically designed to work in the semiautomatic Savage A17 rifle.

Federal Premium (federalpremium.com)

Using a three-stage payload 3rd Degree turkey loads are made to deliver lethal patterns at any range—close, medium, and out to past 40 yards. Radical new Trophy Copper Muzzleloading Bullets use a polymer cup called a B.O.R. Look MZ system in stead of a sabot.

Hornady (hornady.com)

Full Boar ammo uses monolithic copper alloy GMX bullets for deep penetration on though pigs and is available in .223 Rem., .243 Win., 6.8mm, .270 Win., 7mm Rem. Mag., .308 Win., .30-06, and .300 Win. Mag. The American Whitetail line now offers a 12-gauge rifled slug constructed of a tough lead-alloy core and with a muzzle velocity of 1,600 fps. Hornady's 17 Win Super Mag is loaded with a 20-gr. V-Max bullet that delivers 3,000 fps velocity. American Gunner handgun ammunition uses XTP bullets to create a versatile and economical round for target shooting, competition or defense in .380, 9mm, .357 Mag., .38 Spl, .40 S&W and .45 ACP. The juiced up Superformance line now offers a .243 Win. (75-gr. V-Max) load. Hornady Match now loads a .338 Lapua Magnum cartridge (285-gr. A-Max) that delivers 2745 muzzle velocity. Critical Defense Lite in 9mm (100-gr. FTX) offers a reduced recoil option for lightweight, compact pistols and for shooters who are sensitive to recoil. The new Critical Duty .357 Mag. (135-gr. Flexlock) meets the established FBI protocol standards for penetration and terminal performance.

Remington (remington.com)

Nitro Steel ups the velocity ante in steel shot in 10, 12, 16 and 20 gauge in shot sizes ranging from BBB, BB, 1, 2, 3, and 4.

Winchester (winchester.com)

The W Train & Defend .45 ACP ammo is a training and defense system of cartridges with a 230-gr. FMJ practice round paired with 230-gr. HP defense round. Both rounds are ballistically matched. Long Beard XR extends the lethal turkey range for turkey out to 60 yards with two new 12 gauge loads; a 3-inch shell loaded with 1 7/8 ounces of shot and a 3 ½-inch shell loaded with 2 1/8 ounces of shot. Expect knock power on white tails with Deer Season XP that uses a new Extreme Point polymer tip bullet that creates massive impact wound and expansion; available in .243 Win., .270 Win., .270 WSM, 7mm Rem. Mag., .308 Win., .30-06, .300 Win. Mag., and .300 WSM.

Clay shooters will find the TrAAcker 12-gauge shells can help improve scores through the use of black wad for clear sky backgrounds or florescent orange for overcast days that allows a shooter to tracks the shot string. Winchester AA Steel Target loads in 12-gauge offer lead performance but with an eco-friendly steel payload load.

Jeff Steele is a longtime shooter, and he owns and operates a gun shop near Cincinnati, Ohio. Experienced shooters like Jeff can help you make important decisions when purchasing a firearm, and they have a finger on the pulse of the industry so they can make suggestions on new products.

HANDGUN BUYER'S GUIDE: How to Make Informed Decisions When Buying Your Next Firearm

By Brad Fitzpatrick

An increase in CCW permits has created great demand for compact, easy-to-carry defensive firearms like this Taurus revolver. Many handgun companies now offer firearms that are designed specifically for concealed carry, so there are numerous options to fit your individual needs.

The market for new handguns is expanding rapidly, and that's good news for consumers. Each year more and more new models break cover, and there has never been a better time to be in the market for a new handgun, whether you're a recreational shooter, a concealed carry permit holder, a hunter, or a serious competitive shooter. Today's handguns offer superb machining and utilize some of the most technologically advanced alloys, polymers, and finishes to help make the current crop of handguns lightweight, accurate, durable, and affordable. This increase in product offerings stems from new interest in handguns, primarily as a result of nationwide issuance of concealed carry permits. As laws have been enacted that protect the rights of gun owners and defend our personal liberties, more and more new shooters are showing up on the range. But first-time shooters and new concealed carry permit holders are not the only segment of the handgun market that is seeing growth and interest. Pistol competitions have become more popular and more advanced, evolving from slow-fire matches at local gun clubs to modern IPSC, IDPA, and 3-gun competitions. Today more and more shooters are enjoying these events and are putting themselves to the test mentally and physically, and although not everyone can win these competitions, they are a fantastic way to introduce new shooters to the sport and sharpen skills, the same skills that may one day save your life. In recent years a number of gun companies have introduced new rimfire versions, which may be similar in design and structure to their centerfire guns or totally unique product offerings. The rise in the number of rimfire handguns is a good thing; it shows that there is growing interest in rimfire shooting and it also provides a wide array of options for those looking to purchase a low-recoiling handgun with less muzzle blast.

While the handgun market has grown over the past several years, a new crop of innovative accessories has also come onto the scene, everything from pleasant-smelling, nontoxic cleaning liquids to biometric safes. One of the largest expansions in the realm of handgun accessories has come in the form of optics. Only a few years ago, handgun optics were a highly specialized items that only a handful of shooters relied on for competitive and recreational shooting, defense, and hunting. Today, however, the market for handgun optics has expanded tremendously, and there is a wide variety of different lasers, red dot sights, holographic sights, and scopes that serve a number of different purpos-

Many handguns offer accessory rails for mounting optics, lights, and lasers. This Glock is outfitted with a Crimson Trace laser, a popular and effective sighting option.

es. As more and more people exercise their right to carry concealed firearms for defense, companies have responded by developing new accessories that are designed to meet the needs of shooters, whether that's safely storing items in a vehicle or carrying a handgun while performing strenuous activities like jogging or hiking.

Today, most hunters and defensive shooters realize that selecting a bullet that is properly designed and constructed is extremely important, perhaps even more so than caliber selection. Buying the right ammunition or loading the proper bullets makes a big difference, and recent advancements in bullets, powders, reloading equipment, and loaded ammunition make it very easy to find what you need. Recently, Nosler and SIG Sauer both introduced new lines of defensive handgun ammunition, and Winchester, Remington, Hornady, Federal, and other companies are also providing bullets that have been thoroughly tested and evaluated to determine their effectiveness, either as a big game bullet or a defensive bullet. Reloading equipment continues to improve, making the process simpler and safer than ever before.

Another great product that is largely overlooked in the handgun world is educational classes that will help you achieve your goals, whether that is to become an Olympic shooter, to learn to safely defend yourself with a handgun, or anywhere in between. The number of new shooting schools and courses continues to grow, and with so many options there is likely to be a class that meets your needs and will serve to help you advance to the next level. Today's trainers have a wide variety of background experience; some are former law enforcement or military personnel, others are competitive shooters, and still others simply have a long history of shooting and a proven track record as firearms educators. Finding a reputable school and attending courses will likely improve your shooting.

WHAT'S IMPORTANT IN A HANDGUN?

Part of the reason why the modern handgun market is so diverse is because there are a wide variety of shooters who rely on their guns to perform a variety of tasks. Some guns are slanted more toward serious competition shooters, and in this book we will examine some of the newest models for that discipline. Other guns are designed for self-defense, a huge and growing market that encompasses everything from inexpensive pocket pistols that provide a level of security without breaking the bank all the way to high-end custom guns that are built one at a time on bench to customer specifications. Some are military and law enforcement designs, guns that must be relied upon to provide lifesaving backup in the very worst situations imaginable. Still others are hunting handguns that are built with the intention of taking big or small game. Many guns are simply designed for backyard target practice, and they provide hours of enjoyment and fun. Finding the right gun for you can be tricky, and everyone's needs and budgets are a little different.

Recently, I conducted a poll of concealed carry weapon (CCW) carriers and asked them what they were looking for in a concealed carry gun. This is perhaps the widest and most diverse of all markets, including shooters of every background and skill set from rank beginners who are purchasing their very first firearm to serious competitors looking for the perfect pocket gun. The results of the test show that different shooters have different concerns when buying a firearm, so understanding your needs and where you fit in this spectrum may help shed some light on which gun is best for you.

Of the dozens of shooters polled for this survey, trends began to appear. The individual with the least experience were still planning to obtain a CCW permit and had only recently begun looking at firearms to purchase with very

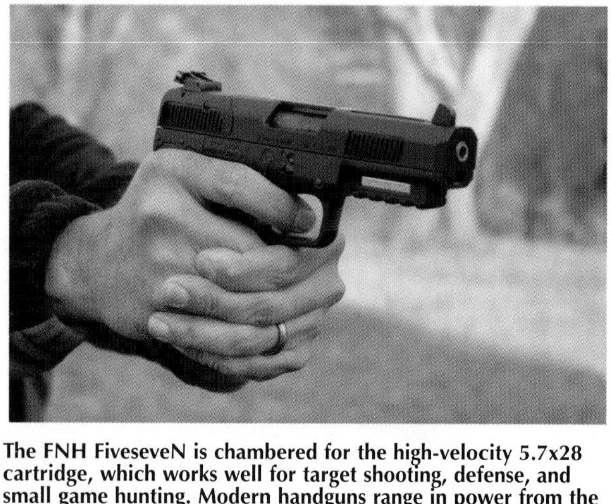

The FNH FiveseveN is chambered for the high-velocity 5.7x28 cartridge, which works well for target shooting, defense, and small game hunting. Modern handguns range in power from the lighter rimfires to powerful magnums, so consumers have a lot of options.

The FNH FNS is an example of a striker fire semiauto. The striker fire design has grown in popularity over the last two decades because it is a lightweight, reliable firing system. FNH also offers a compact version of the gun specifically designed for concealed carry.

little idea of what they wanted or needed. The most experienced shooter had over fifty years of experience with firearms and had shot several thousand rounds in their life. Obviously, they were far apart in both their practical shooting knowledge and their experience with firearms.

NEW SHOOTERS VERSUS EXPERIENCED SHOOTERS

New shooters, those who had shot fewer than 500 rounds and had their permit less than a year (or didn't have it at all) reported that what they were looking for in a firearm was price, ease of use, and comfort. They weren't well-versed in the current trends, they relied heavily on the opinions of experienced shooters to make their decisions, and almost all had a budget. That means that they were looking for a gun they felt was easy to use, inexpensive to purchase, and was comfortable to shoot and carry. These shooters universally had a budget, usually $500 or less, and they weren't particularly interested in brand name or accuracy tests so long as the gun was reliable and easy to use. Most were open to the idea of attending a shooting school, but very few ever had and didn't know where to find a good school. Only one of the respondents stated that they had been to a national convention, the annual NRA convention, where they had a chance to see several manufacturers and speak with company representatives first hand. Almost invariably, they planned to use whatever sight came with the firearm, whether that was iron sights or a pre-mounted laser, and over 80 percent stated that they made their choices on ammunition for their defensive firearm based on price. The vast majority did not have a "set" carry method but either used a holster that was inexpensive and comfortable or were actively looking for a method of carry that suited them. Less than 20 percent stated that they planned to carry their firearm every day. The vast majority of them stated that they relied on an "experienced" shooter, either a friend or a salesperson in a gun shop, to help guide their decisions. Some new shooters had multiple firearms, but the majority stated that they own or plan to own three guns or less.

More experienced shooters, those who had fired over 500 rounds (and many who had fired over 10,000), had a very different set of needs and wants when purchasing a concealed carry handgun. Price was still an important consideration, although most experienced shooters were willing to pay more for a gun they knew or liked very much, and some were even willing to consider paying the extra money to have a custom gun built for them. Brand loyalty was an important consideration, and many responded that they had a favorite gun maker that they trusted and would make their decision based on reputation and brand name. The bulk of experienced

No matter whether you are a new shooter or a seasoned competitor, practice is critical. The good news is that there are shooting schools around the country designed to help you improve as a shooter regardless of your skill level.

The classic single-action revolver is a favorite of reenactors, and today there are a number of companies that are building classic guns using advanced machining. This is an Uberti replica of the 1873 Colt Single Action Army, popular with cowboy action shooters and those who appreciate the look and feel of a historical revolver.

The Kimber Solo is a great choice for concealed carry. It's compact, reliable, and accurate. These guns are also available with grip lasers, as shown here—a great option for a concealed carry gun.

shooters owned multiple guns, some as many as forty, and they were almost invariably in the market for a new gun if something that interested them came along. The major difference between experienced shooters and novices, largely a by-product of time spent at the range, is that they had their own opinions on various firearms and were less likely to seek the advice and assistance of someone else in the purchase of a new gun. Over 50 percent said that they kept abreast of the newest designs and products through Internet searches and magazine articles on the subject. Experienced shooters generally carry more often, with about half of the respondents to the survey stating that they carry a firearm every day or most days. Most have tried different carry methods, read up on the subject, and have shopped around, and over half say that they normally attend gun shows or have attended large conventions. They are also more well-versed in the purchase of accessories, and many are familiar with different brands of safes, holsters, lasers, and ammunition. They are also more likely than

Practice is key, but where can you shoot? The NSSF offers a list of available ranges, or, if you have the land, you can build your own range. If you're relying on a handgun to protect you in a dangerous encounter, plan on shooting it at least weekly. That level of familiarity can save your life.

new shooters to accessorize their guns with aftermarket lights and lasers, though that trend may be changing with the increase in the number of new sighting systems and more widespread availability. Most have never had formal training outside of a military or law enforcement background or CCW training, but the majority were responsive to the idea of attending shooting classes provided that the content was not basic. This survey provided some very important insight into firearms purchasers, what they deem important in purchasing a firearm, and where they go for insight into the world of guns. It's a very good example of why there are so many different firearms and accessories for different shooters. It's also important to note that much of the information coming to new shooters is being presented to them from "experienced" shooters, a term that was used to describe just about anyone who had a reasonable level of experience with guns. Many of the new shooters also said that they based their decisions largely upon the recommendations of the person who taught their CCW class.

IN THE MARKET

The above survey results indicate that there is a wide variety of shooters who are in the market for a new handgun. Some simply want a small, inexpensive carry gun, while others may be looking to add to an already extensive collection with the acquisition of a brand-new custom gun that they've wanted for years. In short, there are many options. To make an informed decision and buy the handgun that's right for your needs, no matter what your level of experience, you'll need to familiarize yourself with what's on the market. The *Shooter's Bible* can help.

EDITOR'S NOTE
This chapter was excerpted, with edits, from Brad Fitzpatrick's new book, *Handgun Buyer's Guide*. The book is broken down by both gun types and disciplines, including revolvers, semiautos, competition guns, hunting guns, rimfires, concealed carry firearms, and custom guns. There are also chapters that examine storage options, holsters, reloading, ammunition, and after-market sighting systems, as well as a section on shooting school. To order a copy of this book, go to www.skyhorsepublishing.com

PUTTING IT IN ITS PLACE: On the Importance of Proper Shot Placement

By Thomas McIntyre

Some years ago—never mind how long precisely (very long)—a Super Cub on big balloon "tundra" tires dropped me on a ridge in Alaska's Chugach Mountains where my young Dall sheep guide was waiting for me. As the Super Cub took off behind us, the guide's nearly first words were about hunt etiquette. Two things in particular he emphasized: a) should a grizzly attack him and pull him down, I was not to run away like some ninnyhammer but was to shoot the bear off him, preferably without hitting him, the guide; and b) while in camp, he made it a practice never to enter into discussions about religion, politics, or ballistics.

Next to ballistics, shot placement probably generates the most heated arguments among hunters. Shot placement is, to begin with, a little awkward to discuss, especially in print, because it highlights the fact that killing is an integral part of hunting. So we rather unctuously refer to "taking" or even, heaven forbid, "harvesting" instead of shooting or killing. But if we are going to hunt, we do want to know the swiftest, most humane way of killing.

There is certainly no swifter way to kill an animal than to find its brain. I am not going to say you should never try for this kind of shot placement, or any of the others I will discuss, but am just going to offer some thoughts about it. Unless you are at extremely close range, and know exactly where to aim, the brain is a very small target to hit. An animal, like a deer, is also moving its head almost constantly, even when standing in one place, compounding the difficulty in aiming true. (If an animal is a buck or bull, it has antlers or horns covering its head, potentially capable of deflecting a shot; and who wants

A well-placed shot equals a good gemsbok

Do what you need to shoot accurately. Here the author uses a shooting stick.

Doubles aren't all magnums. Here is a classic Greener double in the classic 318 Westley Richards caliber.

to risk blowing up the trophy on an animal.) Missing the brain can leave an animal fatally wounded but still capable of running off and not being recovered. When it comes to the placement of any shot, the main consideration should be: what offers the highest odds of recovering that animal?

Moving down the game animal anatomy, the neck-shot is also considered to be extremely swift. A hunting friend once told me that, as his father had told him, if you aim for the neck you get either an instant kill or a clean miss—proving that most of us have a lot to unlearn when it comes to the accepted wisdom of elders. Once, when I was hunting mule deer over in South Dakota, I came over a ridge and saw antlers above the buffalo grass. I went into my sneak mode and seemed to be getting closer and closer without the buck detecting me, I was that good—until I could see that it was lying dead. A cursory examination showed a rather neat bullet hole through the throat, allowing the deer to get away before bleeding out. Unless you can absolutely, positively hit the spine in an animal's neck, you risk having it vanish over the horizon.

You will see, especially on outdoor cable shows, something called the "high shoulder shot." This has the supposed advantage of dropping the animal in its tracks (very good for television broadcast standards); but if you are an inch or two too high, and don't hit the spine, you generally only shock the animal briefly, and it will gather itself up and head for the tall timber in a blink. Also, if you know, tell me where the "high shoulder" is on a bear? Another oft-recommended place for a shot is the shoulder itself, on the theory that you will "break down" an animal, ignoring

Only accurate rifles are interesting.

the fact that game can move very fast, very far on no more than three legs.

Bringing me to my "best" for shot placement, because no animal can survive without an intact heart and/or lungs. You do need to have a working knowledge of the animal's anatomy (a bison, for instance, carries its heart very low in its chest cavity); but once you do, you have the largest vital area on an animal. In general, holding along the first crease behind the front leg, just above the elbow—about a third of the way up from the brisket, and aiming through its body for the front leg on the animal's other side, will generally result in recovery within fifty yards or less. As with any shot, though, it's all about having the experience, skill, and practice to place it right where it needs to be. Colonel Townsend Whelen said, "Only accurate rifles are interesting." And the same goes for hunters, in spades.

Thomas McIntyre's a contributing editor to Sports Afield and Field & Stream *magazines and the author of the novel,* The Snow Leopard's Tale, *available from Bangtail Press, http://www.bangtailpress.com/the-snow-leopards-tale-by-thomas-mcintyre/, as well as* The Shooter's Bible Guide to Optics, *available at www.skyhorsepublishing.com. His collection of 40 years of safari stories,* Augusts in Africa, *is scheduled to be published in 2016 by Skyhorse. Follow Tom on Twitter @mcintyrehunts.*

Proper bullet placement starts at the firing range.

A SIGHTING-IN SECRET

Putting a shot on target depends on your scope being properly sighted in, and that begins with proper scope mounting. One of the factors in insuring that, is making sure the screws in your scope mount's bases and rings are torqued the correct amount. The scope-mount manufacturer will have a recommended amount of torque, usually listed in "inch-pounds," for the base and ring screws; and if you're going to follow those recommendations, there is no alternative but to invest in a torque driver, a useful tool that few of us own but that can repay its cost in what you save in mounting your scopes yourself, rather than paying a gunsmith to do them.

Torque drivers can start with the relatively inexpensive, such as the Wheeler FAT Wrench (www.battenfeldtechnologies.com), to a $249 Torque Limiting Screwdriver found in the Brownells catalog (www.brownells.com). The more expensive, the more accurate, generally; and it's ultimately a matter of how precise you want to be. Precise inch-pounds, though, are less important than consistent torque all the way around, without screwing rings and bases down too tight or too loose.

After torquing down the base screws on the mount, and setting up the rings, adjust the scope to the right eye relief for you, and make sure the reticle is aligned with the rifle's bore (does the vertical post of the sight run directly perpendicular to the axis of the bore?). The "trick" to using a torque driver is to tighten the screws to the proper torque the way you would the lug nuts on a wheel when changing a tire: Crisscross back and forth so that the pressure remains evenly distributed throughout the process. With that, the scope should be ready for bore-sighting and zeroing in on a target with live ammunition.

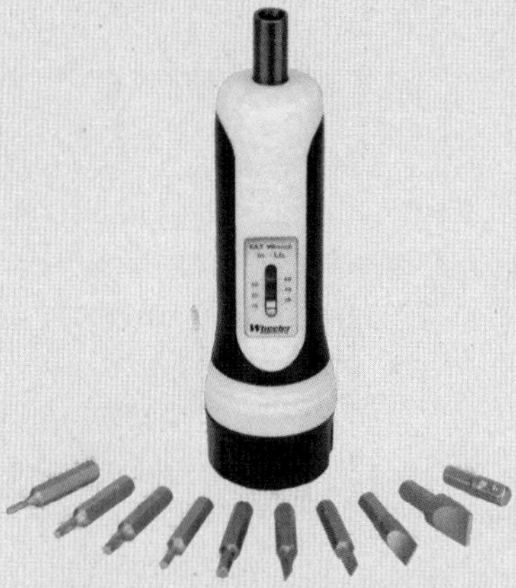

A FAT wrench with a ten-bit set, from Wheeler Engineering

NEW PRODUCTS 2015–2016

24 Rifles
52 Air Rifles
54 Shotguns
67 Handguns
89 Black Powder
90 Optics
100 Range Finders
101 Ammunition
105 MZ Bullets
106 Bullets

AMERICAN TACTICAL OMNI HYBRID MAXX

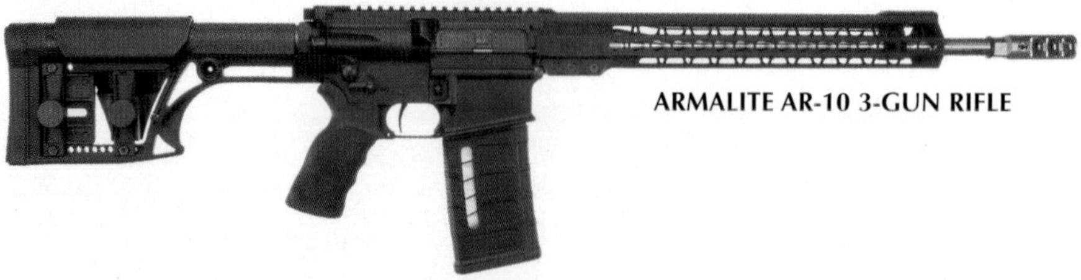

ARMALITE AR-10 3-GUN RIFLE

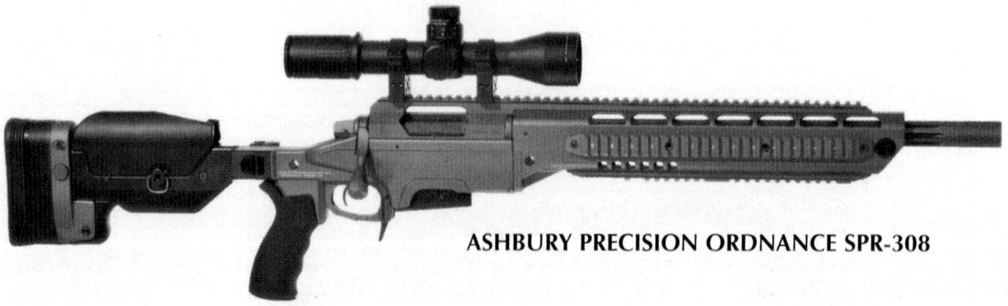

ASHBURY PRECISION ORDNANCE SPR-308

AMERICAN TACTICAL OMNI HYBRID MAXX

Action: Semiautomatic
Stock: Synthetic
Barrel: 16 in.
Sights: None
Weight: 6 lb. 4 oz., 6 lb. 8 oz.
Caliber: .223 Rem./5.56 NATO, .300 AAC
Magazine: Detachable box, 30 round
Features: Retractable stock; metal-reinforced polymer lower and upper receiver; Picatinny rail
MSRP. . . . .$600–$645

ARMALITE AR-10 3-GUN RIFLE

Action: Semiautomatic
Stock: Synthetic
Barrel: 16 in., 18 in.
Sights: None
Weight: 8 lb. 3 oz, 8 lb. 14 oz.
Caliber: .308 Win./7.62 NATO
Magazine: Detachable box, 25 rounds
Features: Picatinny rail; Armalite tunable brake pinned and welded; 12-in. free-floating handguard; stock adjustable for length-of-pull and comb height; ambidextrous safety and charging handle
MSRP. $2099

ASHBURY PRECISION ORDNANCE SPR-308

Action: Bolt
Stock: Synthetic
Barrel: 20 in.
Sights: None
Weight: 11 lb. 3 oz.
Caliber: .308 Win.
Magazine: Detachable box
Features: The latest innovation in the patented SABER-FORSST modular rifle chassis system (MRCS), an interlocking action/chassis design; SPR precision rifles are ideal for law enforcement agencies seeking to enhance their tactical long gun capabilities or practical rifle shooters requiring a versatile ergonomic precision rifle platform with modular upgradeability; overall length of 39 3/8 inches extended, and a compact folded length of 29 5/8 inches
MSRP. $5650

BROWNING AB3

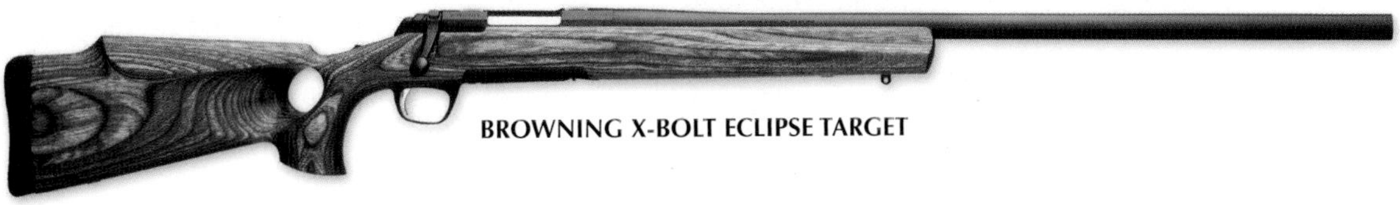

BROWNING X-BOLT ECLIPSE TARGET

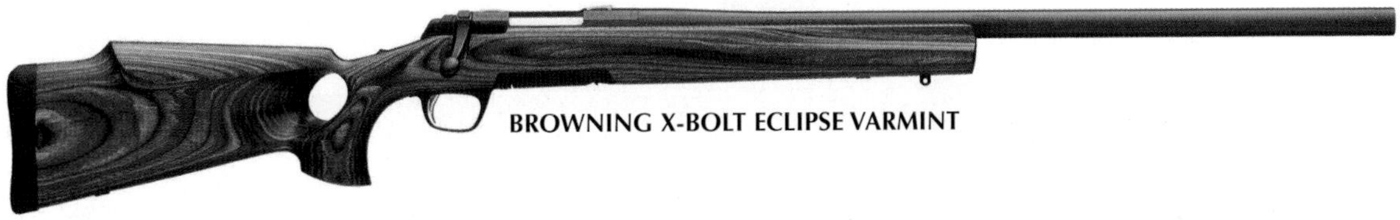

BROWNING X-BOLT ECLIPSE VARMINT

BROWNING AB3 HUNTER

Action: Bolt
Stock: Satin
Barrel: 22 in.
Sights: Drilled and tapped for sights
Weight: 6 lb. 13 oz.
Caliber: .243 Win.
Magazine: Detachable box
Features: 5-round mag capacity; steel barrel; polished finish
MSRP. $670

BROWNING X-BOLT ECLIPSE TARGET

Action: Bolt
Stock: Satin
Barrel: 28 in.
Sights: None
Weight: 10 lb.
Caliber: .308 Win.
Magazine: Detachable box
Features: Steel barrel; short action; drilled and tapped for scope
MSRP. $1070

BROWNING X-BOLT ECLIPSE VARMINT

Action: Bolt
Stock: Satin
Barrel: 26 in.
Sights: None
Weight: 9 lb. 6 oz.
Caliber: .204 Ruger
Magazine: Detachable box
Features: Steel barrel; super short action; steel barrel
MSRP. $1070

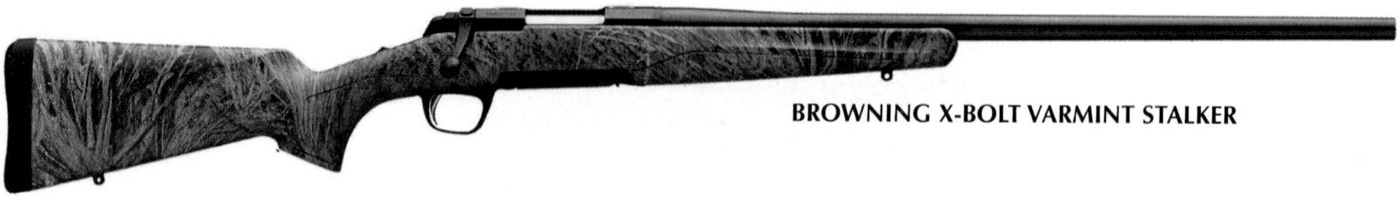

BROWNING X-BOLT VARMINT STALKER

BUSHMASTER C-22 CARBINE

BUSHMASTER XM-15 QUICK RESPONSE CARBINE (QRC)

BROWNING X-BOLT VARMINT STALKER

Action: Bolt
Stock: Synthetic
Barrel: 24 in., 26 in.
Sights: None
Weight: 6 lb. 13 oz.–7 lb. 2 oz.
Caliber: .204 Ruger, .22-250 Rem., .223 Rem., .243 Win., .308 Win.
Magazine: Detachable box, 4 rounds
Features: Available in a variety of calibers and twist rates intended to take advantage of lighter bullets and faster velocities; sporter contour barrel; standard style X-Bolt stock
MSRP $940

BUSHMASTER C-22 CARBINE

Action: Semiautomatic
Stock: Synthetic
Barrel: 18.5 in.
Sights: None
Weight: 8 lb. 12 oz.
Caliber: .22 LR
Magazine: Detachable box, 25 rounds
Features: 416 stainless melonite barrel; standard six-position M4 stock; accepts .223 upper receivers and various aftermarket attachments
MSRP $499

BUSHMASTER XM-15 QUICK RESPONSE CARBINE (QRC)

Action: Semiautomatic
Stock: Synthetic
Barrel: 16 in.
Sights: Mini red-dot
Weight: 6 lb.
Caliber: 5.56 NATO
Magazine: 30 rounds
Features: Superlight 4150 barrel, FNC treated for durability and longevity; forged 7075 lower receiver with six-position collapsible M4 stock; forged 7075 Lightweight flat top receiver with shell deflector
MSRP $769

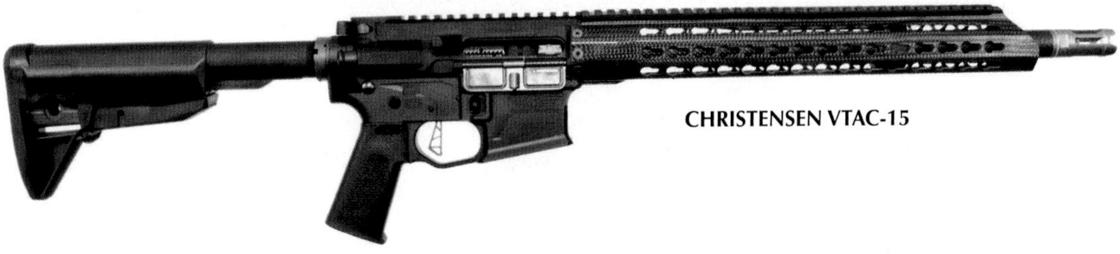

CHRISTENSEN VTAC-15

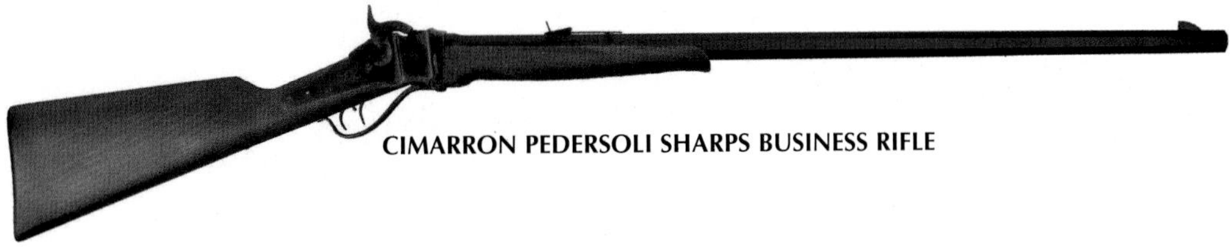

CIMARRON PEDERSOLI SHARPS BUSINESS RIFLE

CMMG MK47 MUTANT AKM

CHRISTENSEN VTAC-15

Action: Semiautomatic
Stock: Synthetic
Barrel: 16 in.
Sights: None
Weight: 5 lb. 5 oz.–5 lb. 8 oz.
Caliber: 5.56 NATO
Magazine: Detachable box
Features: Flared magwell; Picatinny rails; steel fluted barrel or carbon wrapped barrel; flash hider; 1:8-inch barrel twist
MSRP. . . . . $2650–$2850

CIMARRON PEDERSOLI SHARPS BUSINESS RIFLE

Action: N/A
Stock: Wood
Barrel: 32 in.
Sights: Adjustable
Weight: 11 lb. 14 oz.
Caliber: .45-70 Govt.
Magazine: N/A
Features: Octagonal barrel; color case hardened framel; walnut stock and fore-arm; standard blue finish; double set triggers
MSRP. $1450

CMMG MK47 MUTANT AKM

Action: Semiautomatic
Stock: Synthetic
Barrel: 16.1 in.
Sights: None
Weight: 7 lb. 3 oz.
Caliber: 7.62x39mm
Magazine: Detachable box
Features: Combining the accuracy and modularity of the AR-15 with the reliability of the AK47, the Mk47 features all new mid-sized receivers based on a Mk3 platform carved from billet 7075-T6 aluminum; designed to harness the power and reliability of the 7.62x39mm cartridge utilizing a robust bolt; unique Mk47 lower receiver readily accepts all standard AK magazines; equipped with a MOE pistol grip, SV muzzle brake, 30rd AK PMAG, and lifetime quality guarantee
MSRP. $1650

CMMG MK47 MUTANT T

CMMG MK47 MUTANT T

Action: Semiautomatic
Stock: Synthetic
Barrel: 16.1 in.
Sights: None
Weight: 7 lb.
Caliber: 7.62 Warsaw
Magazine: Detachable box, 30 rounds
Features: Features all new mid-sized receivers based on a Mk3 platform carved from billet 7075-T6 aluminum; designed to harness the power and reliability of the 7.62 Warsaw cartridge utilizing a robust bolt; unique Mk47 lower receiver readily accepts all standard AK magazines; equipped with a MOE pistol grip, and SV muzzle brake
MSRP $1500

COLT COMPETITION COLT "MARKSMAN" MODEL CRX-16E

Action: Semiautomatic
Stock: MAGPUL MOE
Barrel: 16 in.
Sights: Scope
Weight: 7 lb.
Caliber: .223 Rem.
Magazine: 30 Round Magpul mag
Features: Match-grade; chrome-moly-steel barrel
MSRP $1399

COLT COMPETITION COLT "MARKSMAN" MODEL CRX-16E

CZ–USA 455 TRAINING

CZ–USA 455 ULTRA LUX

CZ–USA "WESTERN SERIES" 550 SONORAN

CZ–USA 455 TRAINING

Action: Bolt
Stock: Beechwood with Schnabel
Barrel: 24.8 in.
Sights: Tangent adjustable
Weight: 6 lb. 5 oz
Caliber: .17 HMR
Magazine: Detachable box
Features: 5 or 10 round magazine
MSRP $399

CZ–USA 455 ULTRA LUX

Action: Bolt
Stock: Beechwood, European with cheekpieace
Barrel: 26.6 in.
Sights: Tangent adjustable
Weight: 6 lb. 13 oz.
Caliber: .22 LR
Magazine: Detachable box
Features: Long barreled rimfire; tangent rear sight; 10-round magazine
MSRP $449

CZ–USA "WESTERN SERIES" 550 SONORAN

Action: Bolt
Stock: Carbon Fiber
Barrel: 26 in.
Sights: None
Weight: 7 lb. 13 oz.
Caliber: .26 Nosler
Magazine: Hinged Floorplate
Features: Magnum chamberings; fluted barrel; 100 percent carbon fiber
MSRP $3199

DANIEL DEFENSE DDM4V11 PRO

DEL-TON DTI EXTREME DUTY 316

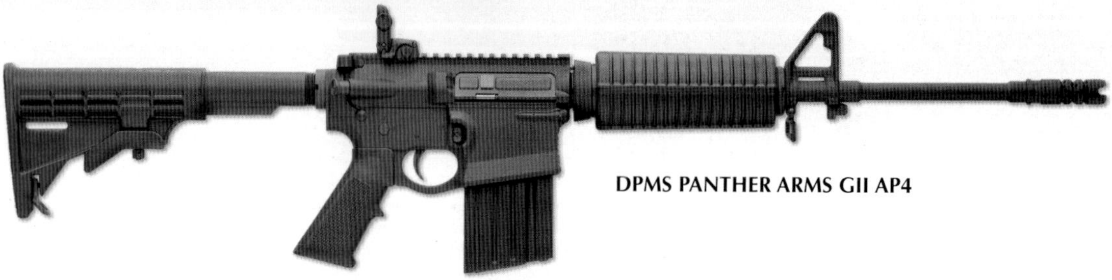

DPMS PANTHER ARMS GII AP4

DANIEL DEFENSE DDM4V11 PRO

Action: Semiautomatic
Stock: Synthetic
Barrel: 18 in.
Sights: None
Weight: 7 lb. 8 oz.
Caliber: 5.56 NATO
Magazine: Detachable box, 30 rounds
Features: Picatinny rails; muzzle climb mitigator; freefloat rail; Geissele automatics super dynamic 3-gun trigger; flared magazine well
MSRP $1849

DEL-TON DTI EXTREME DUTY 316

Action: Semiautomatic
Stock: M4 reinforced fiber
Barrel: 16 in.
Sights: Samson quick flip dual aperture rear sight
Weight: 6 lb. 6.4 oz.
Caliber: 5.56 NATO
Magazine: Detachable box
Features: Hammer forged CMV chrome-lined barrel; H-buffer
MSRP $1100

DPMS PANTHER ARMS GII AP4

Action: Semiautomatic
Stock: M4 6 position collapsible
Barrel: 16 in.
Sights: F marked front sight base
Weight: 7 lb. 4 oz.
Caliber: 7.62 NATO
Magazine: Detachable box
Features: A2 pistol grip; cancellation brake; 34.25 in. collapsed
MSRP $1499

DPMS PANTHER ARMS GII RECON

DPMS PANTHER ARMS GII SASS

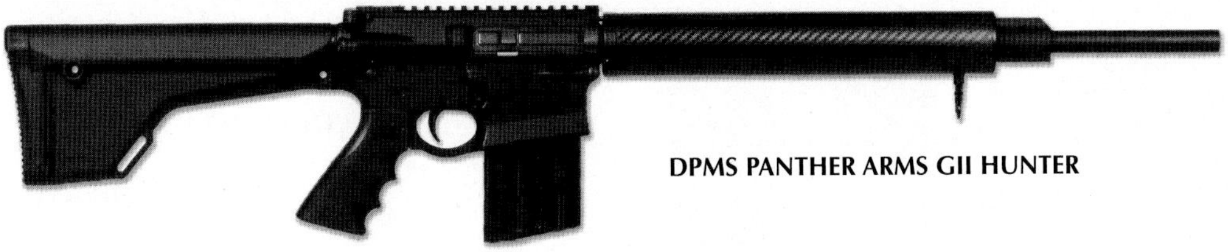

DPMS PANTHER ARMS GII HUNTER

DPMS PANTHER ARMS GII RECON

Action: Semiautomatic
Stock: MOE 6 position collapsible
Barrel: 16 in.
Sights: Front and rear BUIS
Weight: 8 lb. 8 oz.
Caliber: 7.62 NATO
Magazine: Detachable box
Features: 416 stainless steel barrel; bead blasted-mid length glass
MSRP $1759

DPMS PANTHER ARMS GII SASS

Action: Semiautomatic
Stock: PRS rifle
Barrel: 18 in.
Sights: Front and rear BUIS
Weight: 10 lb. 8 oz.
Caliber: 7.62 NATO
Magazine: Detachable box
Features: 416 stainless steel barrel; teflon coated; fluted bull barrel; mid length glass
MSRP $2379

DPMS PANTHER ARMS GII HUNTER

Action: Semiautomatic
Stock: MOE rifle
Barrel: 20 in.
Sights: None
Weight: 7 lb. 12 oz.
Caliber: 7.62 NATO
Magazine: Detachable box
Features: 416 stainless steel barrel; teflon coated
MSRP $1699

DPMS PANTHER ARMS GII BULL

DPMS PANTHER ARMS GII MOE

FNH FN 15 1776

DPMS PANTHER ARMS GII BULL

Action: Semiautomatic
Stock: A2
Barrel: 24 in.
Sights: None
Weight: 10 lb.
Caliber: 7.62 NATO
Magazine: Detachable box
Features: 416 stainless steel bull barrell
MSRP $1759

DPMS PANTHER ARMS GII MOE

Action: Semiautomatic
Stock: MOE carbine
Barrel: 16 in.
Sights: F marked front sight base
Weight: 7 lb. 4 oz.
Caliber: 7.62 NATO
Magazine: Detachable box
Features: Lightweight 4150 chrome-lined
MSRP $1599

FNH FN 15 1776

Action: Semiautomatic
Stock: Polymer
Barrel: 16 in.
Sights: None
Weight: 6 lb. 10 oz.
Caliber: 5.56 NATO
Magazine: Detachable box, 30 rounds
Features: Alloy steel, button-broached barrel; six-position collapsible stock; A2-style compensator; sling attachments; Picatinny rail
MSRP $899

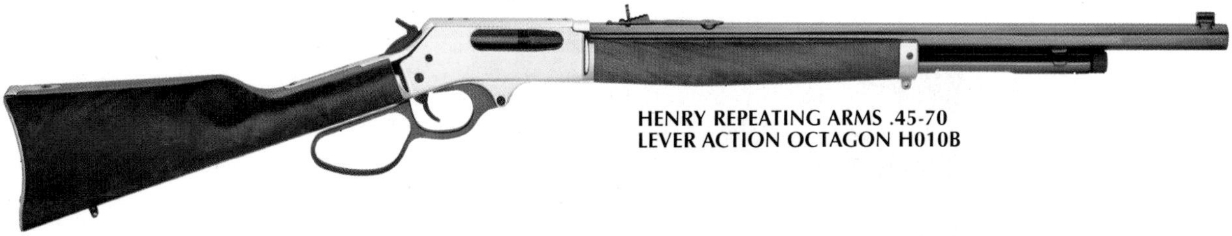

HENRY REPEATING ARMS .45-70
LEVER ACTION OCTAGON H010B

HI-POINT FIREARMS 4095TS

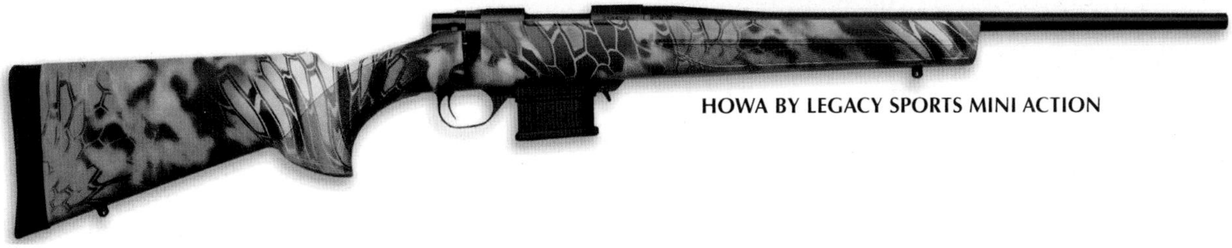

HOWA BY LEGACY SPORTS MINI ACTION

HENRY REPEATING ARMS .45-70 LEVER ACTION OCTAGON

Action: Lever
Stock: Wood
Barrel: 22 in.
Sights: Adjustable
Weight: 8 lb. 2 oz.
Caliber: .45-70 Govt.
Magazine: 4 rounds
Features: Straight-grip American Walnut stock with brass buttplate; fully adjustable semi-buckhorn rear, and brass beaded front sight; brass drilled and tapped for a Weaver 63B mount
MSRP $950

HI-POINT FIREARMS 4095TS

Action: Semiautomatic
Stock: Polymer
Barrel: 17.5 in.
Sights: Adjustable
Weight: 7 lb.
Caliber: .45 ACP
Magazine: 9 rounds
Features: All-weather; black polymer skeletonized stock sling; swivels and scope base internal recoil buffer in stock weaver style rails; fully adjustable sights ("ghost ring" rear peep and post front); quick on/off thumb safety Grip-mounted clip release
MSRP . . . . $315–$461

HOWA BY LEGACY SPORTS MINI ACTION

Action: Bolt
Stock: Synthetic
Barrel: 20 in., 22 in.
Sights: None
Weight: 5 lb. 11 oz.–6 lb. 10 oz.
Caliber: .223 Rem., .204 Ruger
Magazine: Detachable box, 10 rounds
Features: Available in black, highlander, and green finishes; steel barrel; three position safety; H.A.C.T. two-stage trigger
MSRP . . . . $608–$681

JARRETT RIFLES SHIKAR SERIES

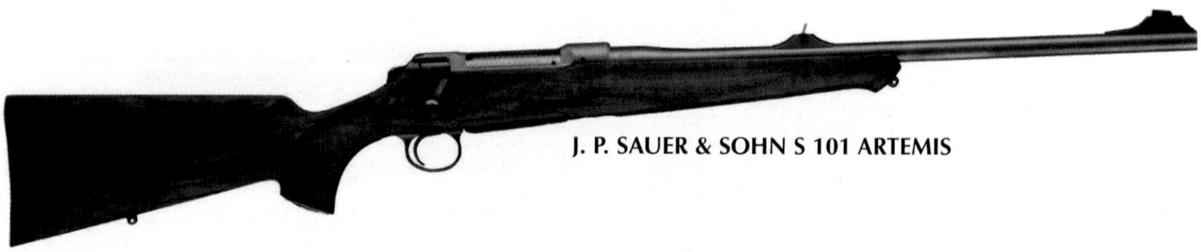

J. P. SAUER & SOHN S 101 ARTEMIS

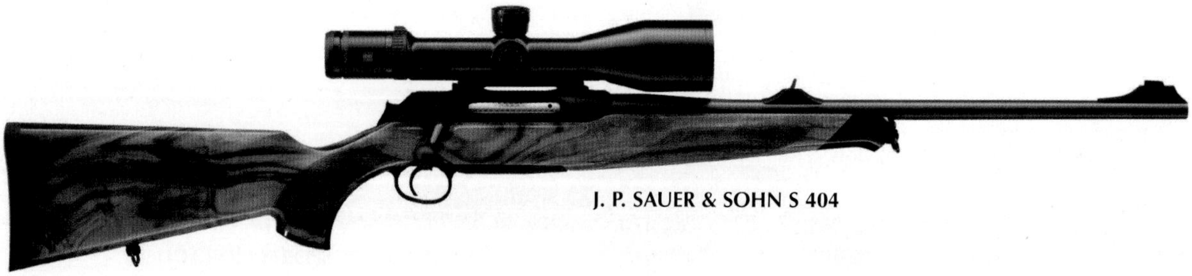

J. P. SAUER & SOHN S 404

JARRETT RIFLES SHIKAR SERIES

Action: Bolt
Stock: Wood
Barrel: N/A
Sights: None
Weight: 8 lb.
Caliber: Any long action, standard or magnum caliber
Magazine: N/A
Features: Muzzle brake; decelerator pad; hand checkering; trap door plate; Shilen or Jewell trigger; aged American black walnut stock; Jarrett Tri-Lock left or right hand receiver
MSRP $9640

J. P. SAUER & SOHN S 101 ARTEMIS

Action: Bolt
Stock: Wood
Barrel: 20 in.
Sights: Adjustable
Weight: 6 lb. 6 oz.
Caliber: .243 Win., .270 Win., .308 Win., 7x64 Brenneke, .30-06 Spfd., 8x57IS, 9.3x62 Mauser
Magazine: 5+1 rounds
Features: Designed for individuals with small hands and frames; walnut ERGO MAX stock; laserline stock grain; exclusive jeweled bolt; DURA SAFE direct firing pin safety; walnut bolt knob; super crisp 2-lb. trigger pull; fully adjustable iron sights
MSRP $1969

J. P. SAUER & SOHN S 404

Action: Bolt
Stock: Wood
Barrel: 20–24.4 in.
Sights: Adjustable
Weight: 7 lb.–7 lb. 3 oz.
Caliber: .243 Win., 6.5x55 Swedish, .270 Win., 7x64 Brenneke, .308 Win., .30-06 Spfd., 8x57IS, 9.3x62 Mauser, 7mm Rem. Mag., .300 Win. Mag., 8x68 S, .338 Win. Mag., .375 H&H Mag.
Magazine: 2–3 rounds
Features: ERGO LUX stock in grade-5 figured walnut; aviation-grade high-alloy aluminum receiver; perfectly placed ergonomic manual cocking slide on the bolt shroud; easily replaceable bolt head makes switching from standard to magnum calibers a snap; twin ejectors for a precisely perpendicular ejection pattern; 6-lug bolt locks directly into the barrel; jeweled bolt body; SAUER Quattro trigger with choice of four trigger pull weights: 550 g (1.2 lbs), 750 g (1.7 lbs), 1000 g (2.2 lbs) and 1250 g (2.7 lbs); infinitely adjustable trigger blade with 8 mm (0.3 in) adjustment range for length of pull and a left-to-right swivel range of 5 degrees; SAUER Universal Mount (SUM) integral to with receiver for an extremely low build height; SAUER universal key (SUS) integrated into the front sling swivel for forend and buttstock removal, barrel removal or replacement, and selection of trigger pull weight; MagLock magazine safety
MSRP . . . . $3200–$3900

MAGNUM RESEARCH .22LR BARRACUDA NUTMEG

MAGNUM RESEARCH .22WMR BARRACUDA FOREST CAMO

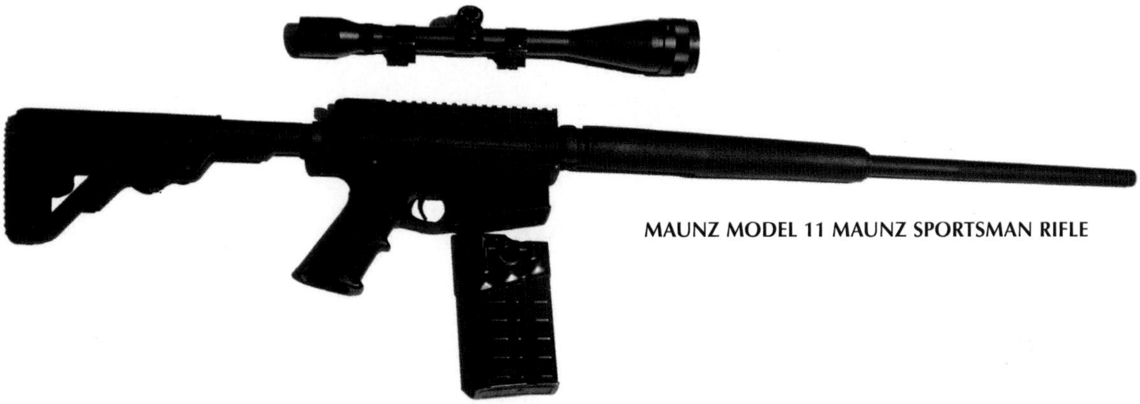

MAUNZ MODEL 11 MAUNZ SPORTSMAN RIFLE

MAGNUM RESEARCH .22LR BARRACUDA NUTMEG

Action: Bolt
Stock: Barracuda American black walnut
Barrel: 17 in.
Sights: Rail for weaver style rings on receiver
Weight: 4 lb. 5 oz.
Caliber: .22 LR
Magazine: One 10 round magazine
Features: Patented graphite barrel; light weight; great accuracy
MSRP $824

MAGNUM RESEARCH .22WMR BARRACUDA FOREST CAMO

Action: Bolt
Stock: Barracuda forest camo
Barrel: 19 in.
Sights: Rail for weaver style rings on receiver
Weight: 6 lb. 10 oz.
Caliber: .22 Win Mag
Magazine: One 9 round
Features: Gas-assisted blowback; graphite or stainless steel barrel
MSRP $935

MAUNZ MODEL 11 MAUNZ SPORTSMAN RIFLE

Action: Semiautomatic
Stock: Custom made wood; left or right hand
Barrel: 20 in.
Sights: Iron or scope available, not included
Weight: 9 lb.
Caliber: .22-250, .243, 7mm, .308, .40 Maunz, .45 Maunz
Magazine: 5- or 10-round HK magazine
Features: Modeled after the AR-10 frame; ammunition available for custom rifles at a reasonable cost as well as reloading equipment
MSRP $1500

MAUNZ MODEL 97 MAUNZ SPORTSMAN CARBINE

MOSSBERG PATRIOT SERIES

MAUNZ MODEL 97 MAUNZ SPORTSMAN CARBINE

Action: Semiautomatic
Stock: Custom made wood; left or right hand
Barrel: 20 in.
Sights: Iron or scope available, not included
Weight: 8 lb.
Caliber: .223, 6 mm Maunz, .30 Maunz, .40 Maunz, .45 Maunz
Magazine: 5- or 10-round magazine
Features: Ammunition available for custom rifles at a reasonable cost as well as reloading equipment
MSRP $1500

MOSSBERG PATRIOT SERIES

Action: Bolt
Stock: Wood, synthetic, or laminate
Barrel: 20 in., 22 in.
Sights: Fixed
Weight: 6 lb. 8 oz.–8 lb. 12 oz.
Caliber: .243 Win., .22-250 Rem., 7mm-08 Rem., .308 Win., .25-06 Rem., .270 Win., .30-06 Spfd., 7mm Rem. Mag., .300 Win. Mag., .338 Win. Mag., .375 Ruger
Magazine: Detachable box, 4–5 rounds
Features: Twin-lug, push-feed machined-steel action which is fed from a lightweight polymer, flush box magazine with 4 or 5-round total capacity (magnum and standard calibers respectively); button-rifled, standard contour, free-floating 22-inch barrels (20-inch barrels on Bantam/ Super Bantam) are constructed of carbon steel, feature straight-edge fluting (375 Ruger versions have non-fluted barrels) and recessed crowns; metal finishes include a choice of Matte Blue or Mossberg's Marinecote protective finish; every Patriot rifle also features Mossberg's LBA (Lightning Bolt Action) Adjustable Trigger System for consistent shot placement and is user-adjustable from 2 to 7 pounds; standard features include distinctive, spiral-fluted bolts; receiver-mounted, weaver-style scope bases; adjustable, fiber optic sights (select calibers); and sling swivel studs
Patriot bolt-action: . . . . $386–$584
Scoped combos: . . . . . . $386–$584
Deer Thug scoped combos: . . . . $386–$584
Bantam: . . . . $386–$584
Super Bantam: . . . . $386–$584
Vortex Optics scoped combo: $552
Patriot Night Train tacticals: . . . . $634–$811

MOSSBERG BLAZE SERIES

MOSSBERG BLAZE-47

MOSSBERG MVP LC (LIGHT CHASSIS) SERIES

MOSSBERG BLAZE SERIES

Action: Semiautomatic
Stock: Synthetic
Barrel: 16.5 in.
Sights: Fixed
Weight: 3 lb. 8 oz.
Caliber: .22LR
Magazine: Detachable box, 11–26 rounds
Features: All Blaze rifles feature free-floating 16.5-inch barrels with fixed front sight; 1:16 twist rate; 3/8-inch dovetail for ease of scope mounting; and blue metal finishes; optional sight systems include adjustable rifle rear sight for windage and elevation; barrel-mounted, top Picatinny rail to easily add the optic of your choice; or as a field-ready option, scoped combos come with a rail-mounted, Dead Ringer Green Dot adjustable sight featuring four optional reticle configurations; synthetic stocks feature vented forends and choice of black or camo-dipped finishes (Kryptek Highlander, Muddy Girl or Wildfire Camouflage patterns); the Blaze Bantam, available in black synthetic, features a shortened, 12-inch length-of-pull (LOP) to comfortably fit a younger shooter or any adult requiring a reduced LOP; Blaze 10- and 25-round magazines and top Picatinny rails are available

Blaze rimfire: . . . . $187–$270
Dead Ringer green dot: $252
Bantam: $187

MOSSBERG BLAZE-47

Action: Semiautomatic
Stock: Wood or synthetic
Barrel: 16.5 in.
Sights: Adjustable
Weight: 4 lb. 8 oz.–4 lb. 12 oz.
Caliber: .22LR
Magazine: Detachable box, 11–26 rounds
Features: Adjustable fiber optic rear sight and raised front rifle sights; choice of fixed wood stocks with 13 ½-inch length-of-pull (LOP) or lever-activated, 6-position adjustable LOP synthetic stock (11 ¼–14 inch); optional 10 or 25- round capacity magazines; FLEX TLS System on the synthetic-stocked versions of the Blaze 47: with the simple push of the integrated TLS latch, the recoil pad can be easily interchanged for other sizes of FLEX recoil pads, no tools required

MSRP . . . .$329–$375

MOSSBERG MVP LC (LIGHT CHASSIS) SERIES

Action: Bolt
Stock: Synthetic
Barrel: 16.25 in., 18.5 in.
Sights: None
Weight: 8 lb.–10 lb.
Caliber: 5.56 NATO, 7.62 NATO
Magazine: Detachable box, 11 rounds
Features: Housed in an aluminum, tan-finished, light chassis stock designed by MDT that provides a modular, ergonomic base; free-floating, medium bull barrel is threaded and comes with a SilencerCo Saker muzzle brake, utilizing the Trifecta quick-detach mounting system (thread cap included); the barrels, constructed of carbon steel, are button-rifled with 16.25-inch length and 1:7 twist rate in the 5.56 NATO (.223 Rem.) chambering and the 7.62 NATO (.308 Win.) sports an 18.5-inch barrel with a 1:10 twist rate; both barrels feature a matte blue finish on all metalwork; Mossberg's Lightning Bolt Action (LBA) Trigger System is user-adjustable from 3 to 7 pounds and is machined from aircraft-grade aluminum and hard-coat anodized to military spec; spiral fluted bolt; oversized tactical-style bolt handle; Picatinny top rail; adjustable bipod; Magpul P-Mag 10-round magazines standard

MVP LC rifle: $1438
Vortex HS-T scoped combo: . $2102

MOSSBERG MVP LR (LONG RANGE) SERIES

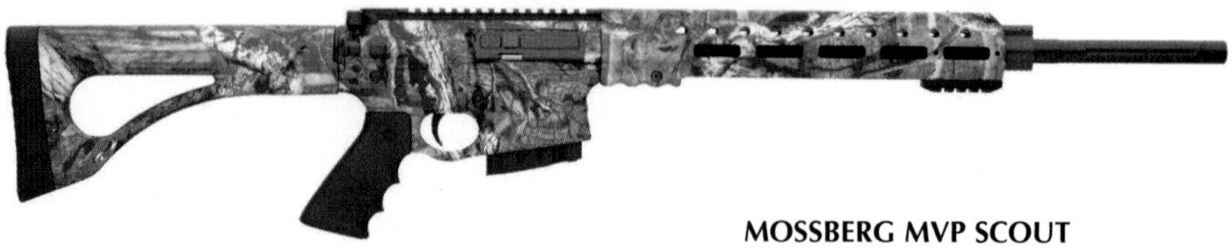

MOSSBERG MVP SCOUT

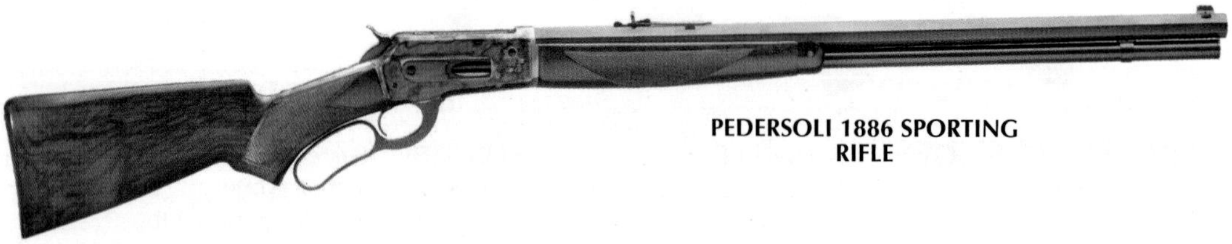

PEDERSOLI 1886 SPORTING RIFLE

MOSSBERG MVP LR (LONG RANGE) SERIES

Action: Bolt
Stock: Synthetic
Barrel: 16.25 in., 20 in.
Sights: None or fixed
Weight: 7 lb.–8 lb.
Caliber: 5.56 NATO, 7.62 NATO
Magazine: Detachable box, 11 rounds
Features: MVP-LR feature a benchrest-style Mosscote stock with ergonomically-designed pistol grip with palm swell and deeply-relieved area behind the pistol grip; 20-inch fluted, medium bull barrels with 1:7 (5.56 NATO/.223 Rem.) and 1:10 (7.62 NATO/.308 Win.) twist rates; and dual front and single rear sling swivel studs; MVP-LR Tactical feature a classically-styled, Mosscote stock; 16.25-inch medium bull barrel with respective twist rates as above; adjustable fiber optic sights; and single front and rear sling swivel studs
MVP LR rifle: $996
Tactical: $996

MOSSBERG MVP SCOUT

Action: Bolt
Stock: Synthetic
Barrel: 16.25 in.
Sights: Fixed
Weight: 6 lb. 12 oz., 8 lb. 12 oz.
Caliber: 7.62 NATO
Magazine: Detachable box, 11 rounds
Features: Has an 11-inch receiver/barrel-mounted Picatinny rail; an integrated, rail-mounted, Ghost Ring rear sight is paired with a barrel-mounted, fiber optic front sight; two Picatinny side rails, located near the front of the forend; a compact 16 ¼-inch medium bull, carbon steel button-rifled, threaded barrel with an A2-style suppressor, with a 1:10 twist rate; a protective thread cap is provided; an adjustable, rifle sling; scoped combo features a UTG AccuShot 1–4x28mm scope with extended eye relief (6 to 9 inches)
MVP Scout rifle: $777
Scoped combo: $940

PEDERSOLI 1886 SPORTING RIFLE

Action: Lever
Stock: Wood
Barrel: 26 in.
Sights: Adjustable rear, fixed front
Weight: 9 lb. 13 oz.
Caliber: .45-70 Govt.
Magazine: N/A
Features: PMG quality barrel; forged and CNC machined frame; American selected walnut stock; blade front sight and adjustable rear sight; drilled and tapped to assemble the aperture bolt sight
MSRP $2049

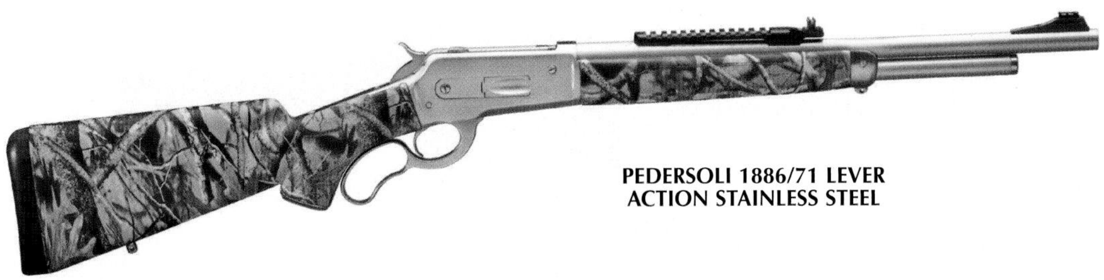

PEDERSOLI 1886/71 LEVER ACTION STAINLESS STEEL

PEDERSOLI ROLLING BLOCK MISSISSIPPI CLASSIC

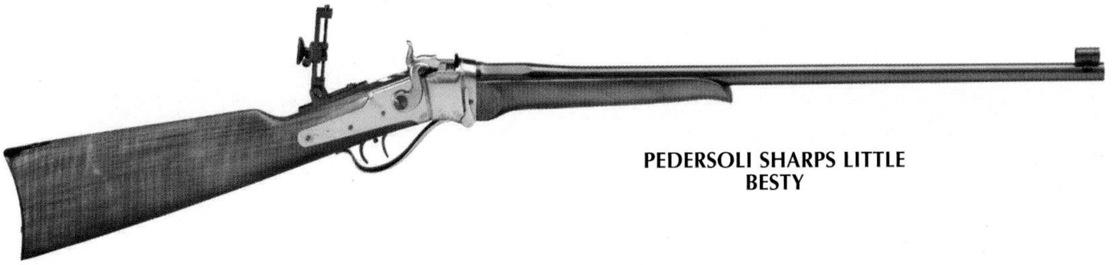

PEDERSOLI SHARPS LITTLE BESTY

PEDERSOLI 1886/71 LEVER ACTION STAINLESS STEEL

Action: Lever
Stock: Synthetic
Barrel: 19 in.
Sights: Adjustable rear, fixed front
Weight: 7 lb. 15 oz.
Caliber: .45-70 Govt.
Magazine: N/A
Features: PMG barrel, broach rifled; fiber optic front sight and Weaver/ Picatinny base with integrated rear sight; stock is made of American walnut covered with a camouflage film; microcell thick butt plate and swivel stud
MSRP. $2687

PEDERSOLI ROLLING BLOCK MISSISSIPPI CLASSIC

Action: N/A
Stock: Wood
Barrel: 26 in.
Sights: Adjustable rear, fixed front
Weight: 7 lb. 8 oz.
Caliber: .357 Mag.
Magazine: N/A
Features: High carbon steel barrel is broach rifled; alloy frame is embellished with a engraving; old silver colour finishing; equipped with a blade front sight and an adjustable rear sight, drilled to assemble the Creedmoor sight; stock and forend are made of American walnut with brass fittings
MSRP. . . . . $889–$1046

PEDERSOLI SHARPS LITTLE BETSY

Action: N/A
Stock: Wood
Barrel: 24 in.
Sights: Adjustable
Weight: 7 lb. 10 oz.
Caliber: .17 HRM
Magazine: N/A
Features: Forged and CNC machined frame features a floral engraving; stock is made of American walnut; barrel PMG quality features a matt blue finish; sights includes a tunnel front sight and the folding Creedmoor sight; with double set trigger
MSRP. . . . . $1860–$2032

PTR INDUSTRIES GEN 2 PTR-32

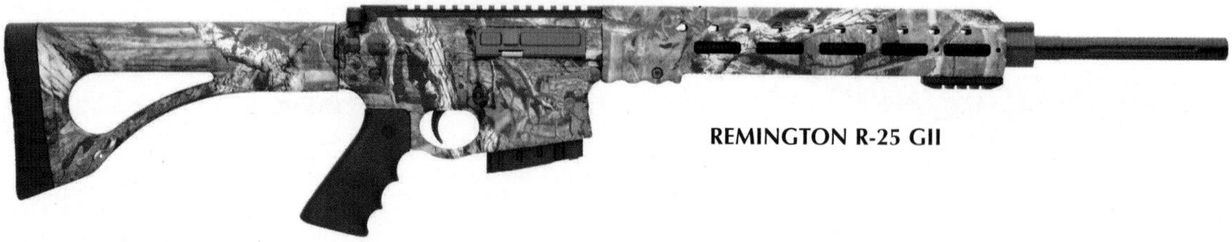

REMINGTON R-25 GII

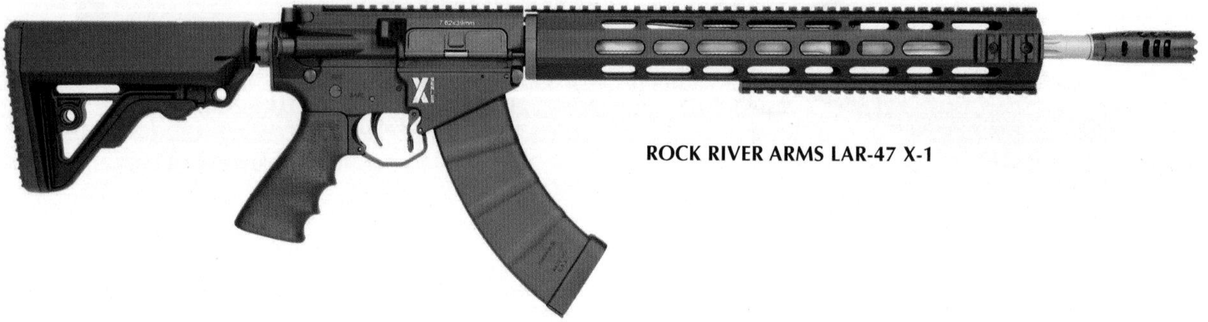

ROCK RIVER ARMS LAR-47 X-1

PTR INDUSTRIES GEN 2 PTR-32

Action: Semiautomatic
Stock: Synthetic, telescoping
Barrel: 16 in.
Sights: Fixed
Weight: 11 lb.
Caliber: 7.62 Warsaw
Magazine: Detachable, 30 rounds
Features: Delayed blowback roller-lock action; Picatinny rails; flash hider; HK 93 length handguard and cocking tube; black powdercoat finish; welded scope mount
MSRP . . . . $1029–$1249

REMINGTON R-25 GII

Action: Semiautomatic
Stock: Synthetic
Barrel: 18 in.
Sights: None
Weight: 7 lb. 10 oz.
Caliber: .243 Win., .260 Rem., 7mm-08 Rem., .308 Win.
Magazine: 4 rounds
Features: Stainless steel, Teflon-coated barrel, target crown muzzle; fixed, light-weight stock with SuperCell Recoil pad, available in Mossy Oak Breakup Infinity; Hogue pistol grip; carbon fiber vented free float hand-guard; two stage match trigger
MSRP $1697

ROCK RIVER ARMS LAR-47 X-1

Action: Semiautomatic
Stock: Synthetic
Barrel: 18 in.
Sights: None
Weight: 8 lb. 3 oz.
Caliber: 7.62 Warsaw
Magazine: Detachable box
Features: Available in black or tan; RRA Operator A2 Stock; RRA Beast muzzle brake
MSRP . . . . $1600–$1650

ROCK RIVER ARMS LAR-300 AAC BLACKOUT

RUGER 10/22 COLLECTOR'S SERIES

RUGER AMERICAN RIFLE RANCH

ROCK RIVER ARMS LAR-300 AAC X-1

Action: Semiautomatic
Stock: Synthetic
Barrel: 18 in.
Sights: None
Weight: 7 lb. 14 oz.
Caliber: .300 AAC
Magazine: Detachable box
Features: Stainless steal cryo treated barrel; RRA two stage trigger; RRA beast muzzle break
MSRP. $1585

RUGER 10/22 COLLECTOR'S SERIES

Action: Semiautomatic
Stock: Synthetic
Barrel: 18.5 in.
Sights: Adjustable
Weight: 5 lb.
Caliber: .22 LR
Magazine: Detachable rotary, 10 rounds
Features: Picatinny rail; adjustable rear sight; 1:16 in. barrel twist; stain black finish; exclusive Collector's Series bolt marking and a Collector's Series box with a Ruger decal; Collector's Series pin, a reprint of the "Father's Advice" ad, and a limited-edition Ruger Collector's Series street sign
MSRP. $349

RUGER AMERICAN RIFLE RANCH

Action: Bolt
Stock: Synthetic
Barrel: 16.1 in.
Sights: None
Weight: 6 lb.–6 lb. 8 oz.
Caliber: .223/5.56 NATO, .300 AAC
Magazine: Detachable rotary, 5 rounds
Features: Ruger Marksman Adjustable trigger offers a pull weight that is adjustable between 3 and 5 pounds; ergonomic, lightweight flat dark earth composite stock with modern forend contouring and grip serrations and swivel studs; soft rubber recoil pad; Power Bedding positively locates the receiver and free-floats the barrel for outstanding accuracy; threaded barrel is cold hammer-forged; tang safety; rotary magazine; factory installed one-piece aluminum scope rail
MSRP. $499

RUGER AR-556

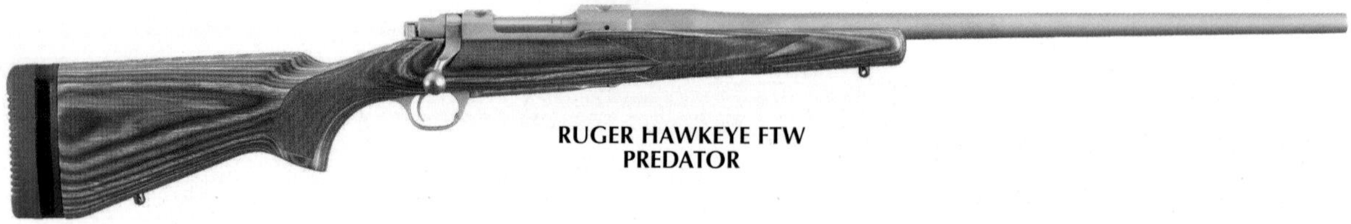

RUGER HAWKEYE FTW PREDATOR

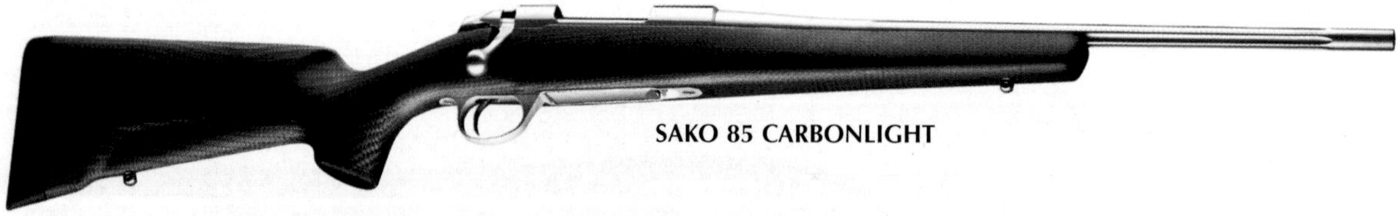

SAKO 85 CARBONLIGHT

RUGER AR-556

Action: Semiautomatic
Stock: Synthetic
Barrel: 16.1 in.
Sights: Adjustable
Weight: 6 lb. 8 oz.
Caliber: .223 Rem./5.56 NATO
Magazine: Detachable box, 30 rounds
Features: The milled gas block is located at a carbine length (M4) position; multiple attachment points include a QD socket and bayonet lug; front sight post is elevation adjustable, and a front sight tool is included; A-2 Style F-Height allows co-witness with many optics; Ruger Rapid Deploy folding rear sight provides windage adjustability; six-position telescoping M4-style buttstock and Mil-Spec buffer tube; barrel is cold hammer-forged; Ruger flash suppressor; matte black oxide finish on the exterior of the bolt carrier
MSRP $749

RUGER HAWKEYE FTW PREDATOR

Action: Bolt
Stock: Laminate
Barrel: 22 in., 24 in.
Sights: None
Weight: 8 lb., 8 lb. 2 oz.
Caliber: .308 Win., 6.5 Creedmor
Magazine: 4 rounds
Features: Non-rotating, Mauser-type controlled round feed extractor; hinged solid-steel floorplate; cold hammer-forged barrel; patented integral scope mounts
MSRP $1099

SAKO 85 CARBONLIGHT

Action:Bolt
Stock: Carbon fiber
Barrel: 20 in.
Sights: None
Weight: 5 lb. 5 oz.
Caliber: .22-250 Rem., .243 Win., .260 Rem., 7mm-08 Rem., .308 Win.
Magazine: Detachable box, 5 rounds
Features: Fluted barrel; stainless steel action; stainless steel barrel; single stage trigger; single set trigger available
MSRP $2859

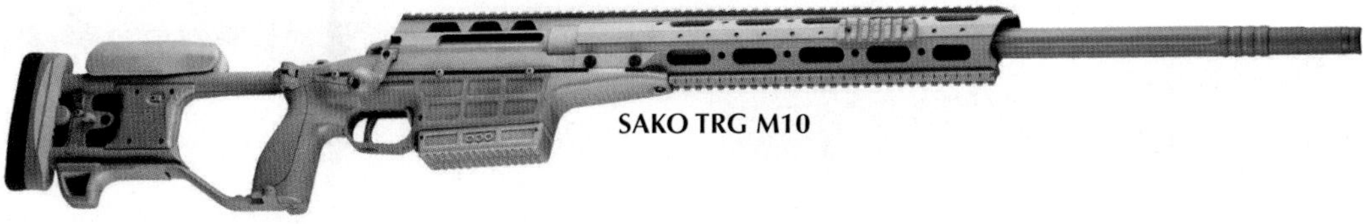

SAKO TRG M10

SAVAGE ARMS 10 FCP-SR

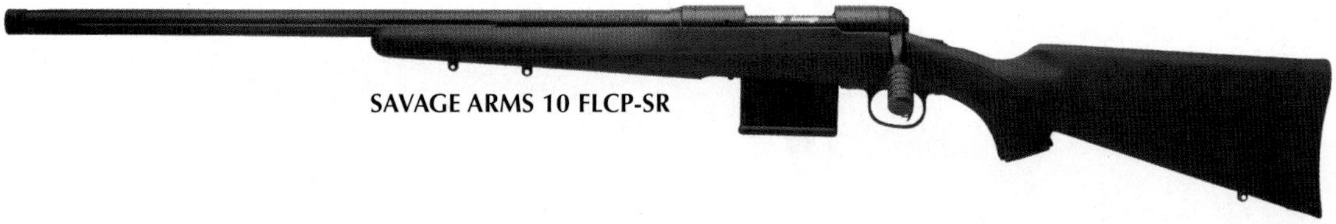

SAVAGE ARMS 10 FLCP-SR

SAKO TRG M10

Action: Bolt
Stock: Synthetic
Barrel: 20–27 in.
Sights: None
Weight: 13 lb. 4 oz.–14 lb. 5 oz.
Caliber: .308 Win., .338 Lapua Mag.
Magazine: Detachable box, 8 or 11 rounds
Features: Threaded muzzle; muzzle break available; phosphatized steel parts; stainless steel barrel; double stage trigger; Picatinny or Weaver rail; fully adjustable rear stock; ambidextrous controls
MSRP. $10500

SAVAGE ARMS 10 FCP-SR

Action: Bolt
Stock: Synthetic
Barrel: 20 in.
Sights: None
Weight: 8 lb. 12 oz.
Caliber: .308 Win.
Magazine: Detachable box
Features: Carbon steel barrel; matte barrel finish
MSRP. $761

SAVAGE ARMS 10 FLCP-SR

Action: Bolt
Stock: Synthetic
Barrel: 24 in.
Sights: None
Weight: 9 lb.
Caliber: .308 Win.
Magazine: Detachable box
Features: Carbon steel barrel; matte barrel finish
MSRP. $761

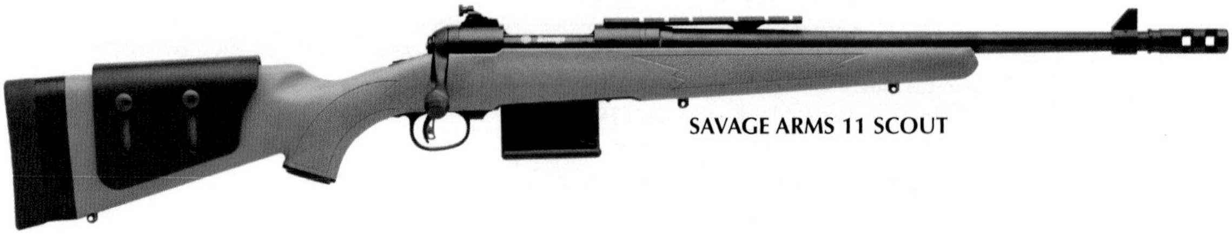

SAVAGE ARMS 11 SCOUT

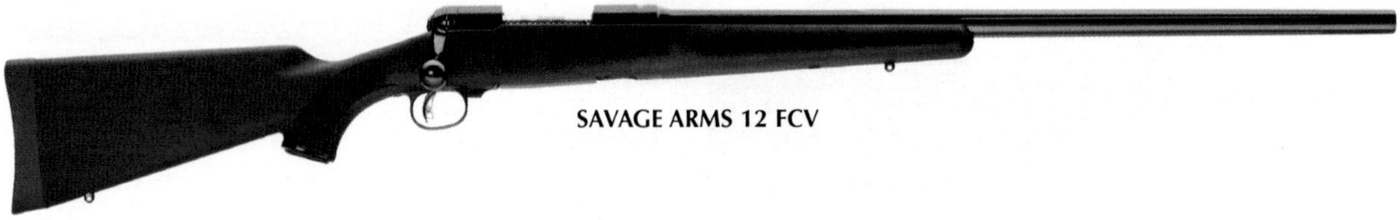

SAVAGE ARMS 12 FCV

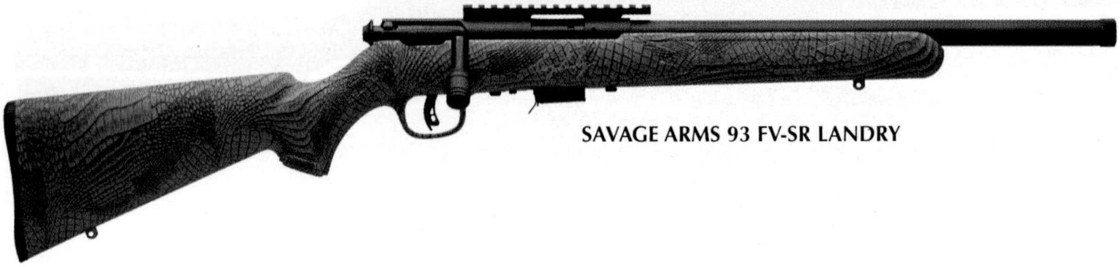

SAVAGE ARMS 93 FV-SR LANDRY

SAVAGE ARMS 11 SCOUT

Action: Bolt
Stock: Synthetic
Barrel: 18 in.
Sights: Front fixed
Weight: 7 lb. 13 oz.
Caliber: .308 Win.
Magazine: Detachable box
Features: Carbon steel barrel; matte barrel finish
MSRP $794

SAVAGE ARMS 12 FCV

Action: Bolt
Stock: Synthetic
Barrel: 26 in.
Sights: None
Weight: 9 lb.
Caliber: .204 Ruger
Magazine: Detachable box
Features: Carbon steel barrel; matte barrel finish
MSRP $781

SAVAGE ARMS 93 FV-SR LANDRY

Action: Bolt
Stock: Synthetic
Barrel: 16.5 in.
Sights: None
Weight: 5 lb. 8 oz.
Caliber: .22 WMR
Magazine: Detachable box
Features: Carbon steel barrel; matte barrel finish
MSRP $424

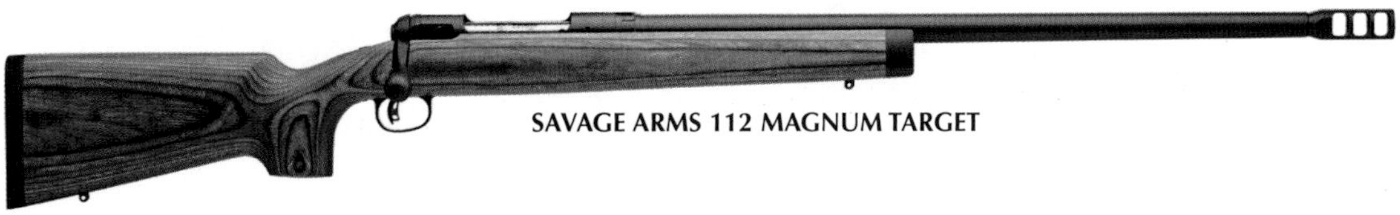

SAVAGE ARMS 112 MAGNUM TARGET

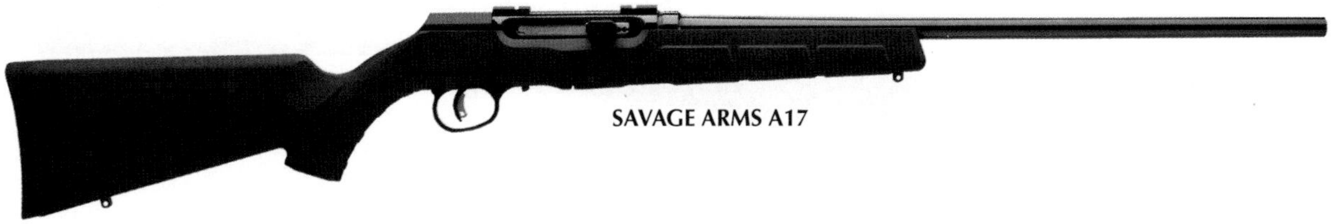

SAVAGE ARMS A17

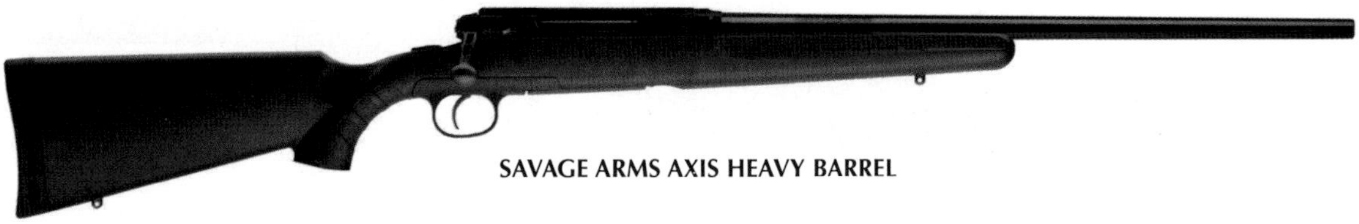

SAVAGE ARMS AXIS HEAVY BARREL

SAVAGE ARMS 112 MAGNUM TARGET

Action: Bolt
Stock: Wood laminate
Barrel: 26 in.
Sights: None
Weight: 12 lb.
Caliber: .338 Lapua Mag.
Magazine: Single shot
Features: Carbon steel barrel; matte barrel finish
MSRP $1177

SAVAGE ARMS A17

Action: Semiautomatic
Stock: Synthetic
Barrel: 22 in.
Sights: Drilled and tapped for scope mounts
Weight: 5 lb. 7 oz.
Caliber: .17 HMR
Magazine: Detachable rotary
Features: Carbon steel barrel; high luster barrel finish; Delayed Blowback Action, Hard Chromed Bolt with Dual Controlled Round Feed, Case Hardened Receiver, Button-Rifled Barrel
MSRP $465

SAVAGE ARMS AXIS HEAVY BARREL

Action: Bolt
Stock: Synthetic
Barrel: 22 in.
Sights: None
Weight: 8 lb.
Caliber: .22-250 Rem., .223 Rem., .243 Win., .308 Win.
Magazine: Detachable box, 4 rounds
Features: Drilled and tapped for scope mounts; matte black finish; carbon steel barrel
MSRP $382

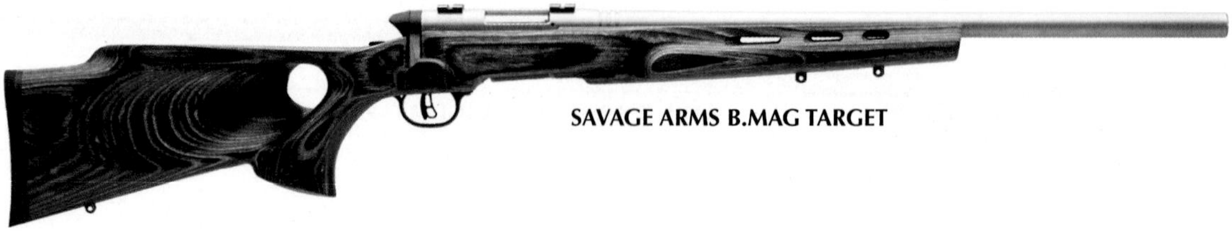

SAVAGE ARMS B.MAG TARGET

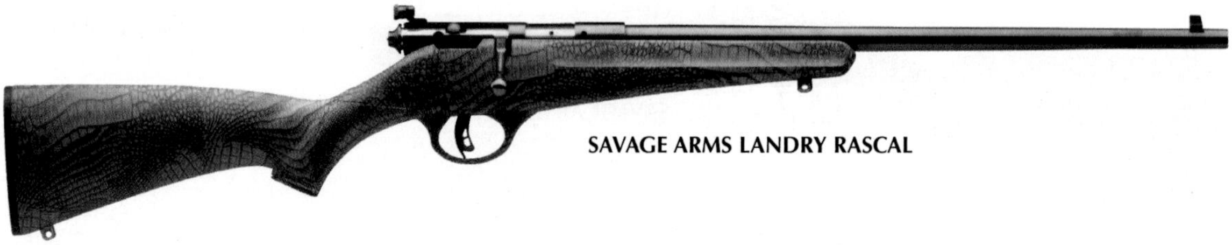

SAVAGE ARMS LANDRY RASCAL

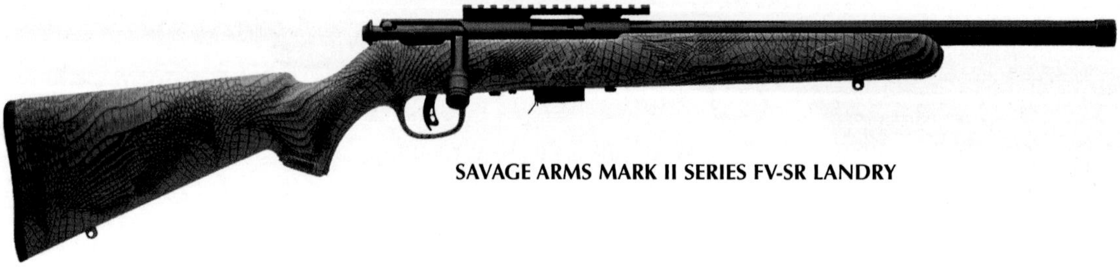

SAVAGE ARMS MARK II SERIES FV-SR LANDRY

SAVAGE ARMS B.MAG TARGET

Action: Bolt
Stock: Synthetic
Barrel: 22 in.
Sights: None
Weight: N/A
Caliber: .17 WSM
Magazine: Detachable rotary, 8 rounds
Features: Stainless steel barrel; matte barrel finish
MSRP $566

SAVAGE ARMS LANDRY RASCAL

Action: Bolt
Stock: Synthetic
Barrel: 16 in.
Sights: Adjustable peep
Weight: 2 lb. 11 oz.
Caliber: .22 LR
Magazine: Single shot
Features: Carbon steel barrel; satin barrel finish
MSRP $233

SAVAGE ARMS MARK II SERIES FV-SR LANDRY

Action: Bolt
Stock: Synthetic
Barrel: 16.5 in.
Sights: None
Weight: 5 lb. 8 oz.
Caliber: .22 LR
Magazine: Detachable box
Features: Carbon steel barrel; matte barrel finish
MSRP $461

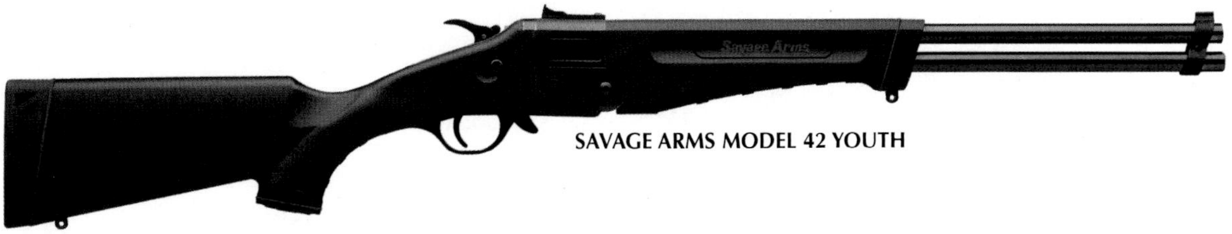

SAVAGE ARMS MODEL 42 YOUTH

SMITH & WESSON M&P10

SPRINGFIELD ARMORY LOADED M1A

SAVAGE ARMS MODEL 42 YOUTH

Action: Over/under
Stock: Synthetic
Barrel: 20 in.
Sights: Adjustable
Weight: 6 lb.
Caliber: .22 LR, .410
Magazine: 2 rounds
Features: Carbon steel barrel; matte barrel finish; break-open combination gun, .22 LR over .410
MSRP $485

SMITH & WESSON M&P10

Action: Gas-operated semiautomatic
Stock: Synthetic
Barrel: 18 in.
Sights: None
Weight: 7 lb. 11 oz.
Caliber: .308 Win., 7.62 NATO
Magazine: Detachable box, 20 rounds
Features: Ambidextrous magazine catch, bolt catch; reversible, ambidextrous safety selector; S&W enhanced flash hider; gas block with integral Picatinny rail; QD sling swivel attachment point (bottom of gas block); 5R rifling
MSRP $1619

SPRINGFIELD ARMORY LOADED M1A

Action: Semiautomatic
Stock: Synthetic
Barrel: 22 in.
Sights: Adjustable
Weight: 11 lb. 4 oz.
Caliber: 7.62 NATO
Magazine: 10 rounds
Features: 1:11 inch barrel twist; match grade aperture with ½ MOA adjustment for windage and 1 MOA for elevation; FDE precision adjustable stock
MSRP . . . . $1774–$1981

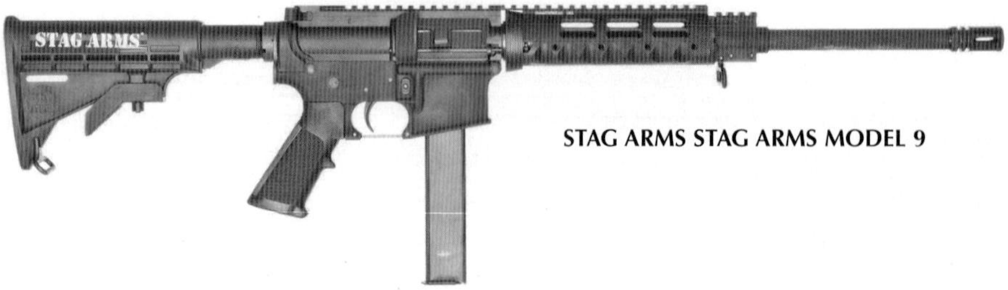

STAG ARMS STAG ARMS MODEL 9

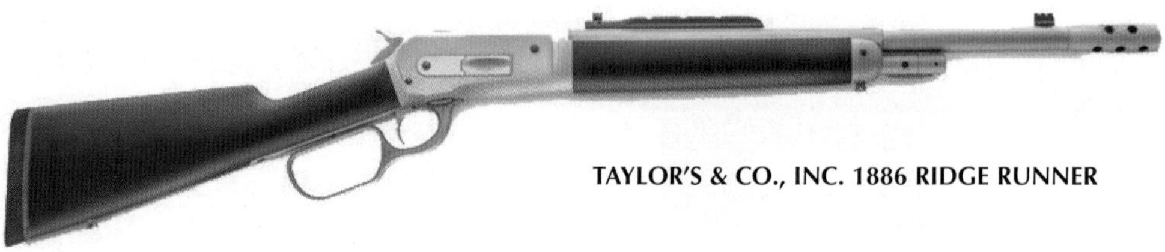

TAYLOR'S & CO., INC. 1886 RIDGE RUNNER

THOMPSON/CENTER VENTURE COMPACT

STAG ARMS STAG ARMS MODEL 9

Action: Semiautomatic blowback
Stock: Plastic
Barrel: 16 in.
Sights: Front Sight Picatinny Railed Gas Block, Back Sight None
Weight: 6 lb. 13 oz.
Caliber: 9mm
Magazine: 32 round
Features: Doesn't need mag block; very customizable; right safety
MSRP $990

TAYLOR'S & CO., INC. 1886 RIDGE RUNNER

Action: Lever
Stock: Wood or synthetic
Barrel: 18. in., 26 in.
Sights: Fixed
Weight: 7 lb. 13 oz.–9 lb.
Caliber: .45-70 Govt.
Magazine: 4, 8 rounds
Features: Full or half octagonal barrel; case hardened frame or chrome or blued frame; fixed fiber optic sights available; Picatinny rail; muzzle break
MSRP . . . . $1461–$1669

THOMPSON/CENTER VENTURE COMPACT

Action: Bolt
Stock: Composite
Barrel: 20 in.
Sights: None
Weight: 6 lb. 12 oz.
Caliber: .22-250 Rem., .243 Win., .308 Win., 7mm-08 Rem.
Magazine: Detachable box, 3+1 rounds
Features: Adjustable trigger; included spacer and buttpad; Hogue traction inlays; Melanite coated bolt; two position safety
MSRP $537

WALTHER HK G36 RIMFIRE

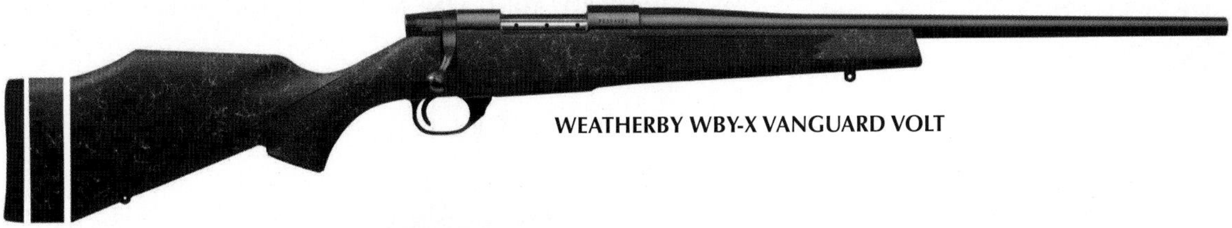

WEATHERBY WBY-X VANGUARD VOLT

WILSON COMBAT .308 SUPER SNIPER

WALTHER HK G36 RIMFIRE

Action: Semiautomatic
Stock: Synthetic, telescoping
Barrel: 18 in.
Sights: Fixed front, adjustable back
Weight: 6 lb. 12 oz.
Caliber: .22 LR
Magazine: Detachable box, 20 rounds
Features: Ambidextrous safety; Picatinny rail; 10- and 30-round magazines available
MSRP $599

WEATHERBY WBY-X VANGUARD VOLT

Action: Bolt
Stock: Synthetic
Barrel: 20 in.
Sights: None
Weight: 6 lb. 12 oz.
Caliber: .22-250 Rem., .223 Rem., .243 Win., 7mm-08 Rem., .308 Win.
Magazine: Detachable box, 5+1 rounds
Features: Injection-molded, composite Monte Carlo stock features bright green spiderweb accents; adjustable length of pull with stock spacer (included); matte bead blasted blue finish; #1 contour cold hammer forged barrel
MSRP $749

WILSON COMBAT .308 SUPER SNIPER

Action: Semiautomatic
Stock: Synthetic, telescoping
Barrel: 20 in.
Sights: None
Weight: 10 lb. 11 oz.
Caliber: .308 Win.
Magazine: 10 rounds, 20 rounds
Features: Barrel is precision button rifled from 416-R stainless steel; 1:10 twist; Picatinny rail; BILLet-AR machined aluminum upper and lower receivers; 12 inch or 14 inch free-floating TRIM rail; available with a fluted or non-fluted barrel
MSRP . . . . $3095–$3195

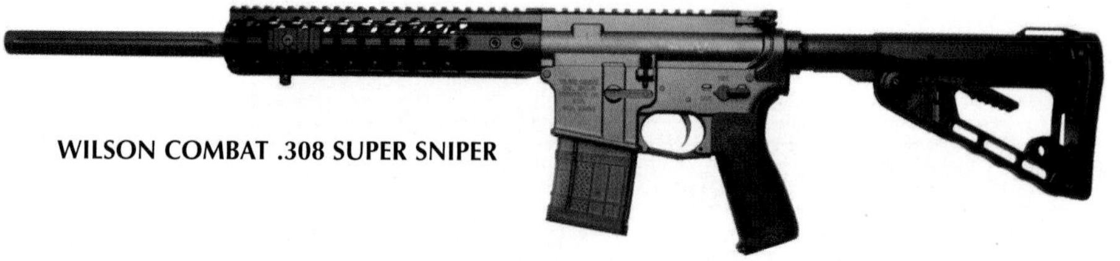

WILSON COMBAT .308 SUPER SNIPER

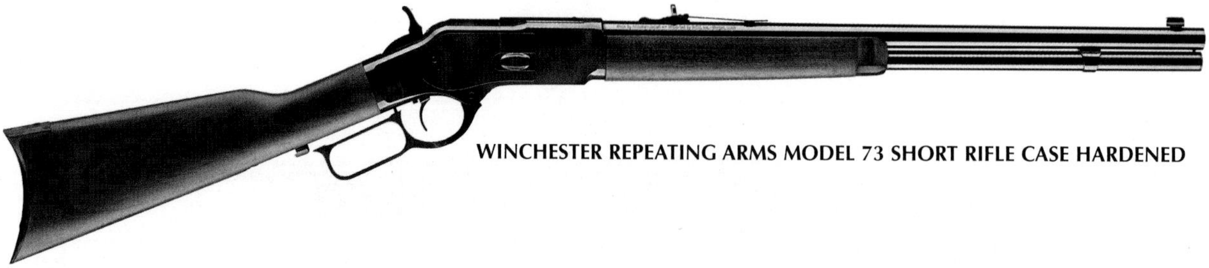

WINCHESTER REPEATING ARMS MODEL 73 SHORT RIFLE CASE HARDENED

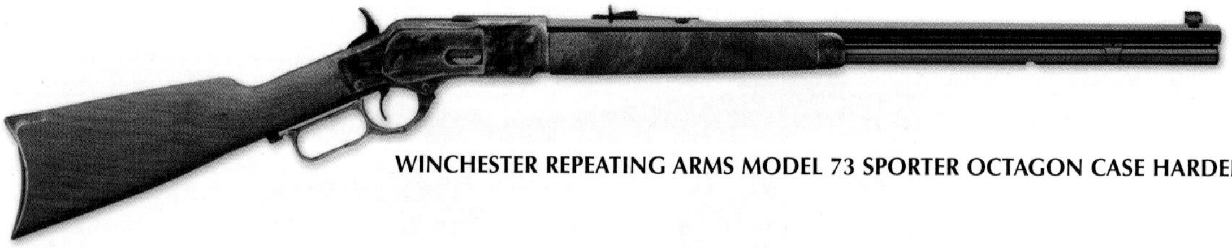

WINCHESTER REPEATING ARMS MODEL 73 SPORTER OCTAGON CASE HARDENED

WILSON COMBAT URBAN SUPER SNIPER

Action: Semiautomatic, mid-length gas system with low-profile gas block
Stock: Synthetic, telescoping
Barrel: 18 in.
Sights: None
Weight: 7 lb. 5 oz.
Caliber: .223 Wylde, .223 Rem./5.56 NATO
Magazine: 10, 20, or 30 rounds
Features: Medium heavy-weight, fluted, stainless steel premium match-grade barrel; 1:8 twist; Picatinny rail; 10.4 inch free-floating TRIM rail
MSRP $2225

WINCHESTER REPEATING ARMS MODEL 73 SHORT RIFLE CASE HARDENED

Action: Lever
Stock: Wood
Barrel: 20 in.
Sights: Adjustable
Weight: 7 lb. 4 oz.
Caliber: .357 Mag., .38 Spl., .44-40 Win., .45 Colt
Magazine: 10–11 rounds
Features: Steel receiver, color case hardened; steel loading gate; rear tang is drilled and tapped for scope mount; steel barrel, polished blued finish; full-length magazine tube; grade II/III walnut stock; straight grip; classic rifle-style forearm; steel forend cap; semi-buckhorn rear sight; Marble's gold bead front sight; color case hardened crescent buttplate, lever, forend cap, and loading gate
MSRP $1580

WINCHESTER REPEATING ARMS MODEL 73 SPORTER OCTAGON CASE HARDENED

Action: Lever
Stock: Wood
Barrel: 24 in.
Sights: Adjustable
Weight: 7 lb. 8 oz.
Caliber: .357 Mag., .38 Spl., .44-40 Win.
Magazine: 13–14 rounds
Features: Steel reciver, color case hardened; steel loading gate; rear tang is drilled and tapped for scope mount; full octagon barrel, polished blued finish; full-length magazine tube; grade II/III walnut stock; straight grip; classic rifle-style forearm; steel fore-end cap; semi-buckhorn rear sight; Marble's gold bead front sight; color case hardened crescent buttplate, lever, fore-end cap, and loading gate; production limited to 250 units
MSRP $1740

WINCHESTER REPEATING ARMS MODEL 73
SPORTER OCTAGON CASE HARDENED

WINDHAM WEAPONRY 300 BLACKOUT

WINCHESTER REPEATING ARMS XPR BOLT ACTION RIFLE

Action: Bolt
Stock: Composite polymer
Barrel: 24 in., 26 in.
Sights: None
Weight: 7 lb.
Caliber: .270 Win., .30-06 Spfd., .300 Win. Mag., .338 Win. Mag.
Magazine: Detachable box, 3 rounds
Features: Chromoly steel barrel; matte blue finish; hardened steel components; recessed target-style crown; Inflex recoil pad
MSRP $550

WINDHAM WEAPONRY 300 BLACKOUT

Action: Semiautomatic gas impingment system
Stock: Synthetic, telescoping
Barrel: 16 in.
Sights: None
Weight: 7 lb.
Caliber: .300 BLK, 7.62x35
Magazine: Detachable box, 30+1 rounds
Features: Hogue six-position telescoping buttstock; 1:7 inch twist; Diamondhead VRS-T 13.5 inch free-float forend; two quick detachable sling swivels included; Hogue beavertail pistol grip; hardcoat black anodize receiver finish; Picatinny rail; chrome-lined barrel with Diamondhead T brake
MSRP $1680

NEW Products: Air Rifles

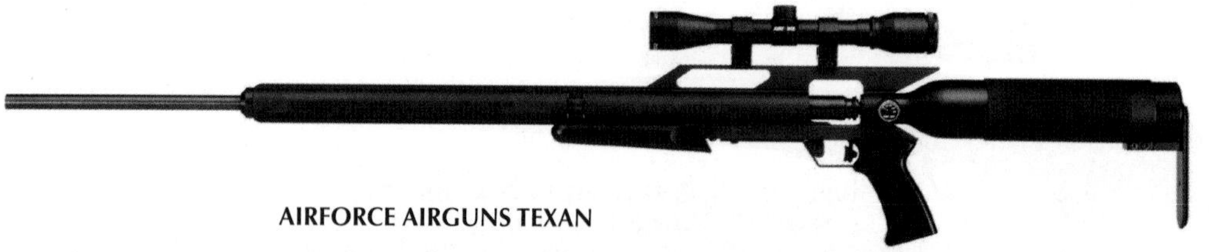

AIRFORCE AIRGUNS TEXAN

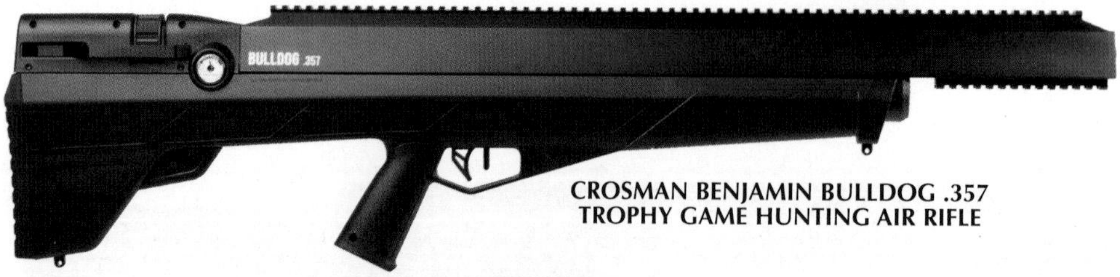

CROSMAN BENJAMIN BULLDOG .357
TROPHY GAME HUNTING AIR RIFLE

CROSMAN BENJAMIN ARMADA

CROSMAN BENJAMIN ARMADA
MAGPUL EDITION

CROSMAN BENJAMIN ARMADA

Power:Multi-shot pneumatic, bolt
Stock: Synthetic
Overall Length: 42 in.
Sights: None
Weight: 7 lb. 5 oz.
Caliber: .177, .22, .25
Features: Modular, versatile design; backwards compatible with Mil-Spec AR-15 grips and stocks; machined receiver featuring 5 inches of Picatinny rail space; delivers over 30 consistent shots per fill (up to 16 in .25 cal); bolt action is reversible; integrated resonance dampener; 10-round magazine delivers fast follow up shots (8-rd magazine in .25 cal); rifled barrel, choked and shrouded; optics and bipod not included
MSRP. $650

AIRFORCE AIRGUNS TEXAN

Power:Compressed air
Stock: Synthetic
Overall Length: 48 in.
Sights: Open or optical
Weight: 8 lb.
Caliber: .45
Features: With the ability to launch .45 caliber projectiles at over 1000 feet per second and generating energy levels of over 500 foot pounds, the Texan takes its place as the world's most powerful production air rifle. Easy to load and simple to use, this Big Bore air rifle will let you focus on hunting with the knowledge you have enough power to get the job done.
MSRP. $1055

CROSMAN BENJAMIN BULLDOG .357 TROPHY GAME HUNTING AIR RIFLE

Power:Multi-shot pneumatic, bolt
Stock: Synthetic
Overall Length: 36 in.
Sights: None
Weight: 7 lb. 11 oz.
Caliber: 0.357
Features: Bullpup configuration; 26 inches of picatinny rail; Baffle-less SoundTrap shroud for big bore sound suppression; sidelever bolt reversible for left hand shooters; intuitive, easy to load 5-shot magazine; reversible bolt; 10 shots per fill
MSRP. $1000

CROSMAN BENJAMIN ARMADA MAGPUL EDITION

Power: Multi-shot pneumatic, bolt
Stock: Synthetic
Overall Length: 42 in.
Sights: 4–16x56mm scope included
Weight: 8 lb. 3 oz.
Caliber: 0.22
Features: The Magpul Edition includes an M-LOK licensed aluminum handrail with picatinny rails and Magpul MOE grip; Magpul MOE 6-position stock with cheek riser; CenterPoint 4-16x56mm scope with co-witness rings and sunshade; bipod adjustable from 6 in. to 9 in.
MSRP. $1000

GAMO USA COYOTE PCP

GAMO USA MACH1 PIGMAN EDITION

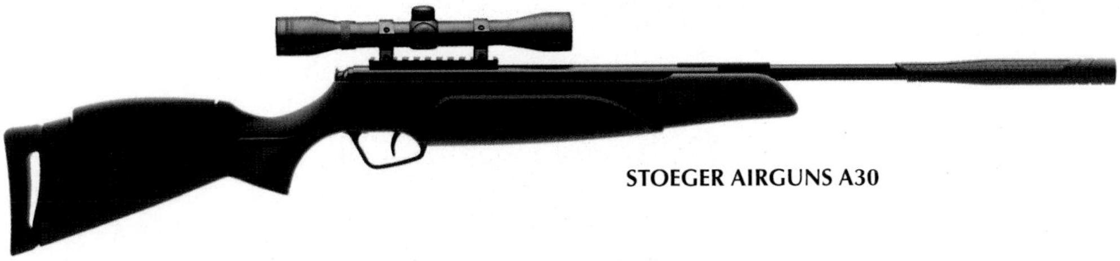

STOEGER AIRGUNS A30

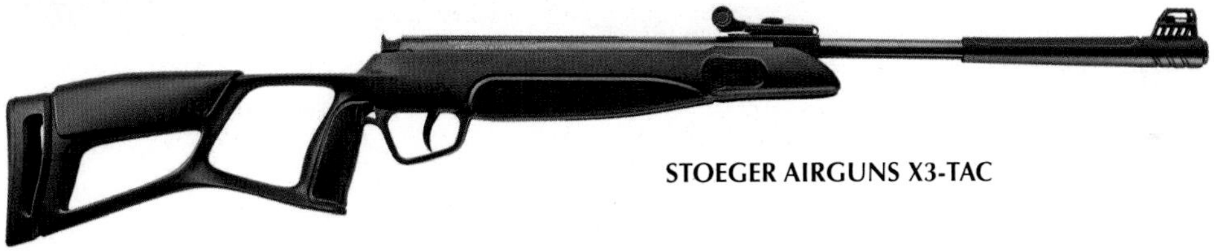

STOEGER AIRGUNS X3-TAC

GAMO USA COYOTE PCP

Power:Multi-shot pneumatic
Stock: Beechwood
Overall Length: 38.5 in.
Sights: None
Weight: 6 lb. 10 oz.
Caliber: .177, .22
Features: Multishot mechanism; 10 pellet rotary clip; hammer forged rifled barrel; bolt action; working pressure 3365 psi (1000 fps, 30 shots)
MSRP **$660**

GAMO MACH1 PIGMAN EDITION

Power:Single shot/spring piston
Stock: Synthetic
Overall Length: 43 in.
Sights: Fiber optic front and rear; 3-9x40 scope
Weight: 6 lb. 8 oz.
Caliber: .177, .22
Features: Fluted polymer jacketed rifled steel barrel; up to 1420 FPS; 33 mm cylinder, high power plant; rubberized grips; Whisper Fusion technology
MSRP **$370**

STOEGER AIRGUNS A30

Power:Gas operated
Stock: Synthetic
Overall Length: 42.5 in.
Sights: Fiber optic sights and 4x32 scope
Weight: 8 lb. 5 oz.
Caliber: .177, .22
Features: Gas-Ram Technology system, or GRT; fully CNC machined precision breech; velocities are up to 1,200 fps for .117 cal and up to 1,000 fps for .22 cal
MSRP **$199**

STOEGER X3-TAC

Power:Air-operated break action
Stock: Synthetic
Overall Length: 36 in.
Sights: Fiber optic sights
Weight: 5 lb. 5 oz.
Caliber: .177
Features: Features a single-shot air rifle chambered for .177-caliber pellets; powered by a fast break-action, spring-and-piston mechanism that requires only 16 pounds of force to cock; incorporates an ambidextrous automatic safety located at the rear of the receiver; features a skeletonized tactical-style black synthetic stock; has an 11 ¾″ length of pull
MSRP **$99**

AYA, AGUIRRE Y ARANZABAL CENTENARY

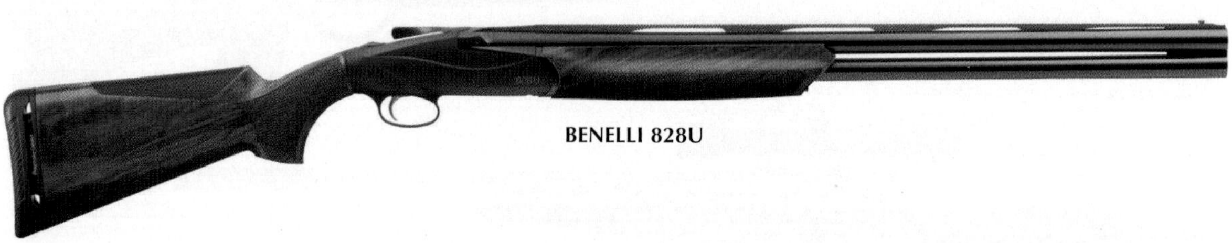

BENELLI 828U

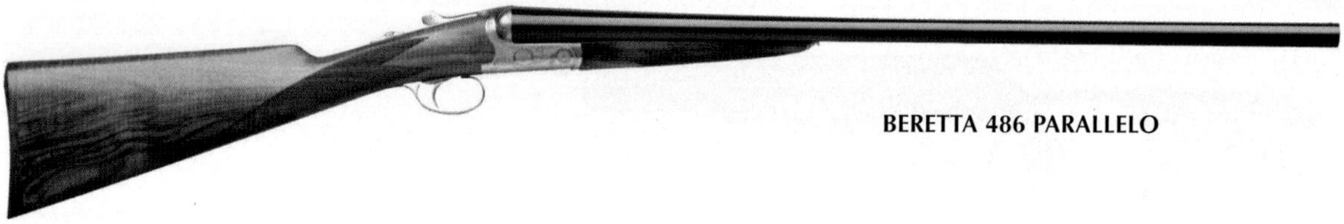

BERETTA 486 PARALLELO

AYA, AGUIRRE Y ARANZABAL CENTENARY

Action: Side-by-side
Stock: Wood
Barrel: 28 in.
Chokes: N/A
Weight: 6 lb. 12 oz.
Bore/Gauge: 12, 16, 20, 28, .410
Magazine: 2 shells
Features: Forged steel action with double locking mechanism and gas vents; hardened steel intercepting safety sears; gold lined cocking indicators; double trigger with hinged front trigger; optional selective or non-selective single trigger; chopper lump steel barrels; concave rib; straight hand, finely chequered oil finished walnut stock; exhibition wood; custom Centenary engraving, gold inlays; initial oval; automatic safety
MSRP $15145

BENELLI 828U

Action: Over/under
Stock: Wood
Barrel: 26 in., 28 in.
Chokes: C, IC, M, IM, F, wrench
Weight: 6 lb. 8 oz.
Bore/Gauge: 12
Magazine: 2 shells
Features: Patented steel locking system and plate; easily removable trigger group receiver; adjustable drop and cast; ergonomic opening lever; impulse activated ejectors
MSRP . . . . $2499–$2999

BERETTA 486 PARALLELO

Action: Side-by-side
Stock: Wood
Barrel: 28 in., 30 in.
Chokes: Fixed, Optima-Choke
Weight: 7 lb.
Bore/Gauge: 12
Magazine: 2 shells
Features: Round action with lavish scroll engraving; new leaf springs, trigger group, barrel technology
MSRP $5350

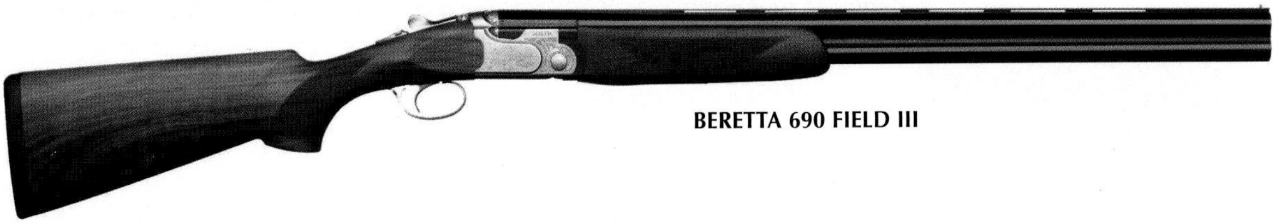

BERETTA 690 FIELD III

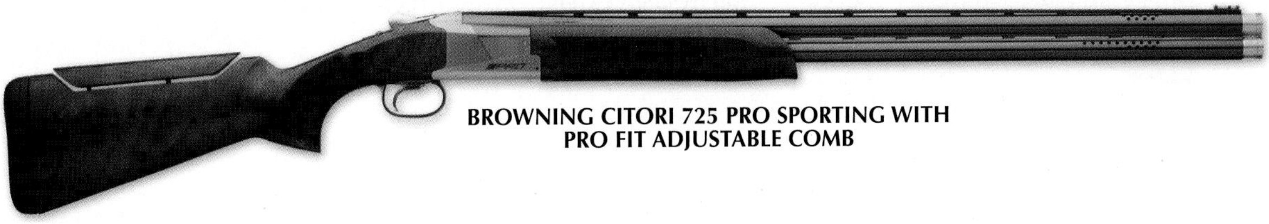

BROWNING CITORI 725 PRO SPORTING WITH PRO FIT ADJUSTABLE COMB

BROWNING CITORI 725 PRO TRAP WITH PRO FIT ADJUSTABLE COMB

BERETTA 690 FIELD III

Action: Over/under
Stock: Wood
Barrel: 28 in.
Chokes: Optima-Choke
Weight: 7 lb. 6 oz.
Bore/Gauge: 12
Magazine: 2 shells
Features: Micro Core recoil pad; adjustable Extraction-ejection; double top receiver and shoulder design
MSRP $3475

BROWNING CITORI 725 PRO SPORTING WITH PRO FIT ADJUSTABLE COMB

Action: Over/under
Stock: Wood
Barrel: 30 in., 32 in.
Chokes: F, IM, M, IC, S
Weight: 7 lb. 5 oz.–7 lb. 13 oz.
Bore/Gauge: 12, 20
Magazine: 2 shells
Features: Polished blue barrel finish; grade III/IV black walnut stock with gloss oil finish; HiViz ProComp sights; vented ribs; drilled and tapped for scopes
MSRP $4000

BROWNING CITORI 725 PRO TRAP WITH PRO FIT ADJUSTABLE COMB

Action: Over/under
Stock: Wood
Barrel: 30 in., 32 in.
Chokes: F, LF, M, 2IM
Weight: 8 lb. 8 oz., 8 lb. 11 oz.
Bore/Gauge: 12
Magazine: 2 shells
Features: Polished blue barrel finish; grade III/IV black walnut stock with gloss oil finish; HiViz ProComp sights; vented ribs; drilled and tapped for scopes
MSRP $4000

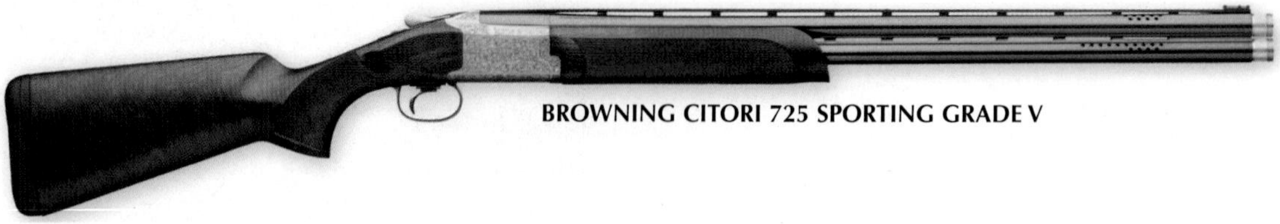

BROWNING CITORI 725 SPORTING GRADE V

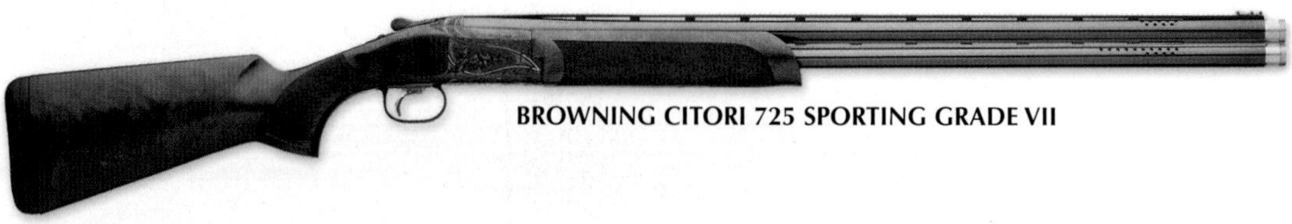

BROWNING CITORI 725 SPORTING GRADE VII

BROWNING CYNERGY MICRO MIDAS

BROWNING CITORI 725 SPORTING GRADE V

Action: Over/under
Stock: Wood
Barrel: 30 in., 32 in.
Chokes: F, IM, M, IC, S
Weight: 7 lb. 8 oz.–7 lb. 10 oz.
Bore/Gauge: 12
Magazine: 2 shells
Features: Polished blue barrel finish; grade IV/V black walnut stock with gloss oil finish; HiViz ProComp sights; large Inflex 2 recoil pad
MSRP **$5340**

BROWNING CITORI 725 SPORTING GRADE VII

Action: Over/under
Stock: Wood
Barrel: 30 in., 32 in.
Chokes: F, IM, M, IC, S
Weight: 7 lb. 8 oz.–7 lb. 10 oz.
Bore/Gauge: 12
Magazine: 2 shells
Features: Polished blue barrel finish; grade VI/VII black walnut stock with gloss oil finish; HiViz ProComp sights; large Inflex 2 recoil pad
MSRP **$6270**

BROWNING CYNERGY MICRO MIDAS

Action: Over/under
Stock: Wood
Barrel: 24 in., 26 in.
Chokes: F, M, IC
Weight: 6 lb.–6 lb. 2 oz.
Bore/Gauge: 20
Magazine: 2 shells
Features: Matte blued barrel finish; grade I/II black walnut stock with satin finish; ivory bead front sight; Cynergy Inflex recoil pad
MSRP **$1870**

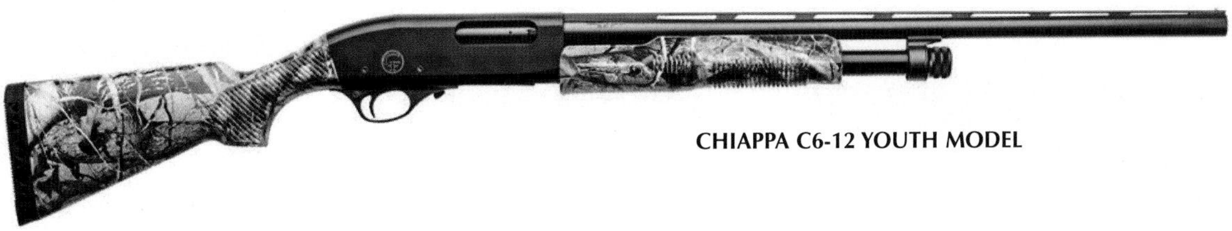

CHIAPPA C6-12 YOUTH MODEL

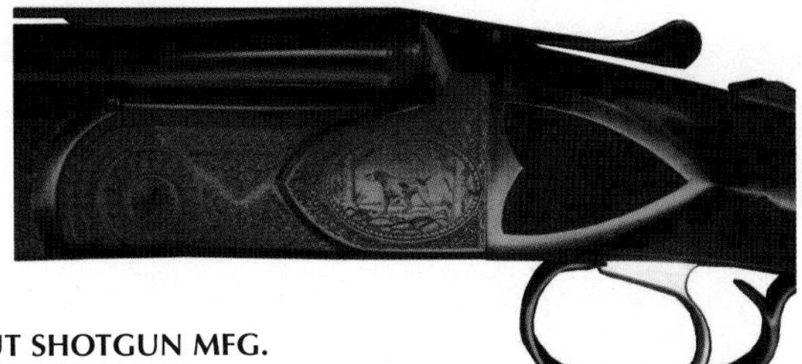

CONNECTICUT SHOTGUN MFG. CO. CSMC MODEL 21

CZ–USA 712 G2

CHIAPPA C6-12 YOUTH MODEL

Action: Pump
Stock: Synthetic
Barrel: 22 in.
Chokes: MC-1 M
Weight: 5 lb.
Bore/Gauge: 20
Magazine: 5+1 shells
Features: Polymer pistol grip, stock, and forearm; matt black with Next G1 camo stock and forend; push button safety at rear of trigger guard
MSRP . . . . N/A

CONNECTICUT SHOTGUN MFG. CO. CSMC MODEL 21

Action: Sidelock over/under
Stock: American black walnut
Barrel: 28 in.
Chokes: 5 included
Weight: 7 lb. 9 oz.
Bore/Gauge: .16
Magazine: 2 shells
Features: Pistol grip; automatic ejectors; fully engraved skeleton butt; solid matte rib
MSRP $21500

CZ–USA 712 G2

Action: Semiautomatic
Stock: Turkish walnut
Barrel: 26 in., 28 in.
Chokes: 5 included
Weight: 7 lb. 5 oz.–7 lb. 6 oz.
Bore/Gauge: 12
Magazine: 4+1 shells
Features: Accepting 2¾ and 3-inch shells, it is an all-arounder, a great choice for upland game, waterfowl, or clays; barrel is chrome-lined and has a matte black hard chrome exterior that will resist corrosion for many seasons in the field; G2 stock adds new laser-engraved checkering, right-hand palm swell as well as a barrel lock-ring to make assembly easier
MSRP $499

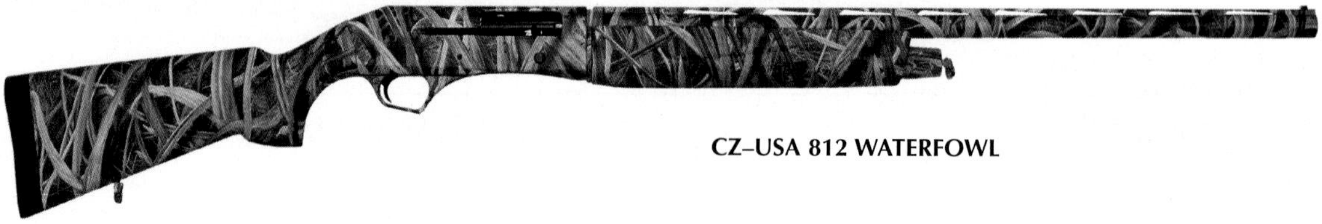

CZ–USA 812 WATERFOWL

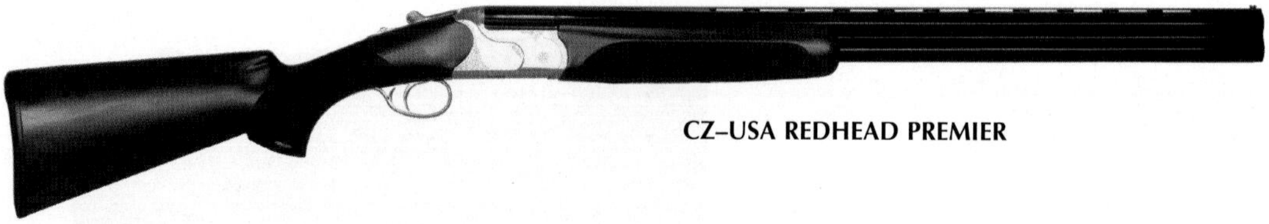

CZ–USA REDHEAD PREMIER

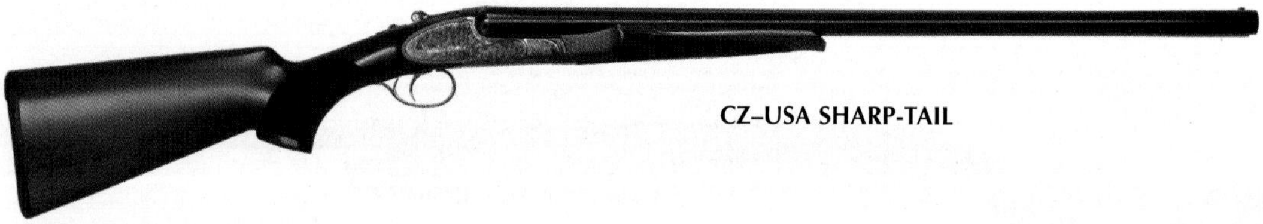

CZ–USA SHARP-TAIL

CZ–USA 812 WATERFOWL

Action: Semiautomatic
Stock: Synthetic
Barrel: 28 in.
Chokes: 5 extended black
Weight: 6 lb. 11 oz.
Bore/Gauge: 12
Magazine: 4+1 shells
Features: Stock and barrel finished in waterfowl camo; 8mm flat rib vent; crossbolt safety behind trigger; 3-inch chamber
MSRP. $699

CZ–USA REDHEAD PREMIER

Action: Over/under
Stock: Turkish walnut
Barrel: 26 in., 28 in.
Chokes: 5 flush-mount
Weight: 6 lb. 14 oz.
Bore/Gauge: 12, 20
Magazine: 2 shells
Features: The tried-and-true Redhead also gets CZ's new 1-piece CNCed receiver; laser-cut checkering, solid mid-ribs, pistol grip, and a classy white bead; silver receiver and ejectors that kick out the spent shells automatically, hard plastic case included
MSRP. $959

CZ–USA SHARP-TAIL

Action: Side-by-side
Stock: Wood
Barrel: 28 in.
Chokes: 5 flush interchangeable
Weight: 6 lb.– 7 lb. 5 oz.
Bore/Gauge: 12, 20, 28, .410
Magazine: 2 shells
Features: Black hard chrome barrel finish; color case hardened receiver finish; semi-beavertail forend; extractor; manual safety
MSRP. . . . . $1022–$1229

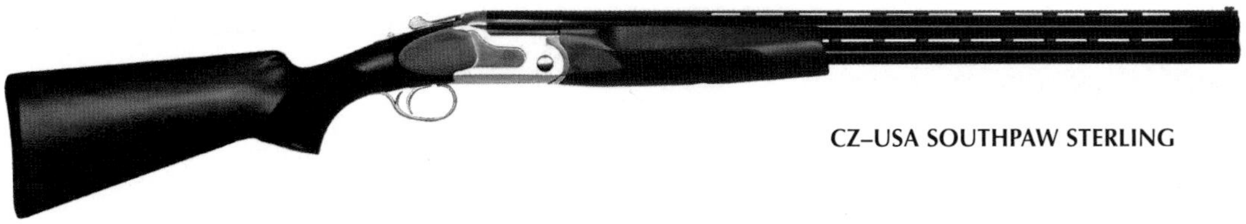

CZ-USA SOUTHPAW STERLING

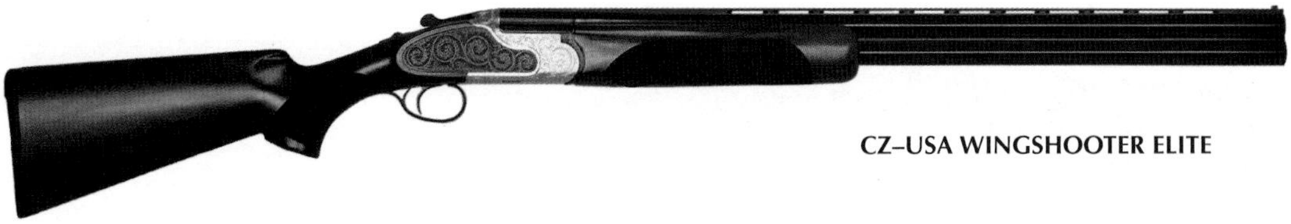

CZ-USA WINGSHOOTER ELITE

ESCORT BY LEGACY SPORTS M87

CZ-USA SOUTHPAW STERLING

Action: Over/under
Stock: Turkish walnut with laser stippling
Barrel: 29 in.
Chokes: 5 flush-mount
Weight: 7 lb. 8 oz.
Bore/Gauge: 12
Magazine: 2 shells
Features: Cast on for left-handed shooters; shares most of the other features of the Upland Sterling, but with a more universal 29-inch barrel; a mechanical trigger and safety with selectable barrels; a regular right-handed top lever latch; plastic case
MSRP $999

CZ-USA WINGSHOOTER ELITE

Action: Over/under
Stock: Turkish walnut
Barrel: 28 in.
Chokes: 5 flush-mount
Weight: 7 lb. 6 oz.
Bore/Gauge: 12, 20
Magazine: 2 shells
Features: Replaces the Wingshooter; new CNCed 1-piece receiver; fully hand-engraved side-plates, reminiscent of custom-grade Super Scroll; single selectable trigger, solid mid-ribs, ejectors, and two-tone chromed finish; laser-cut checkering, solid mid-ribs, pistol grip stock, white bead; hard plastic case
MSRP $1059

ESCORT BY LEGACY SPORTS M87

Action: Pump
Stock: Wood
Barrel: 22–28 in.
Chokes: Multi-3
Weight: 5 lb. 13 oz.–6 lb. 13 oz.
Bore/Gauge: .12, 20
Magazine: 4 +1 shells
Features: Available in youth; all come with 3-inch chambers
MSRP $350

ESCORT BY LEGACY SPORTS PUMP ACTION

FABARM AXIS RS12 SPORTING

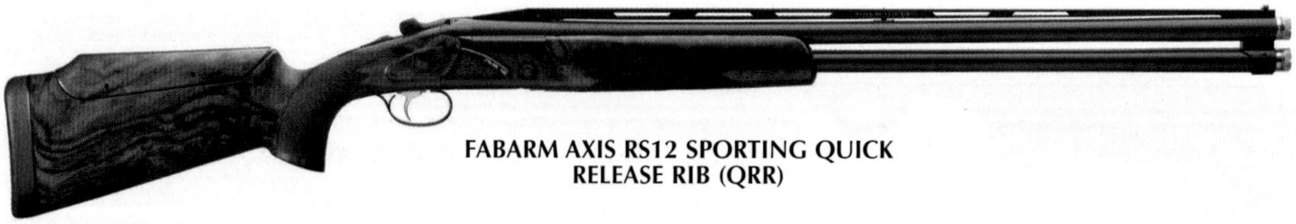

FABARM AXIS RS12 SPORTING QUICK RELEASE RIB (QRR)

ESCORT BY LEGACY SPORTS PUMP ACTION

Action: Pump
Stock: Synthetic
Barrel: 22–28 in.
Chokes: Multi-3
Weight: 5 lb. 13 oz.–7 lb. 6 oz.
Bore/Gauge: .12, 20
Magazine: N/A
Features: Raised sight rib and fiber-optic front sights; top of the receiver milled with 3/8-inch dovetail for accessory sights
MSRP . . . .$379–$393

FABARM AXIS RS12 SPORTING

Action: Over/under
Stock: Wood
Barrel: 32 in.
Chokes: 5 Exis HP
Weight: 8 lb. 4 oz.
Bore/Gauge: 12
Magazine: 2 shells
Features: Axis free-floating barrels feature Tribore HP tapered bores that lower recoil and reduce the need for excessively long forcing cones; blued action; Fabarm Micro Metric adjustable comb and left hand stocks available
MSRP $3150

FABARM AXIS RS12 SPORTING QUICK RELEASE RIB (QRR)

Action: Over/under
Stock: Wood
Barrel: 30–32 in.
Chokes: 5 Exis HP
Weight: 8 lb. 6 oz.
Bore/Gauge: 12
Magazine: 2 shells
Features: Quick Release Rib design allows configuration for varying shooting styles and disciplines; standard offering includes two 10mm high ramp style ribs—one with a 50/50 percent point-of-impact and a second for a higher 65/35 percent; includes Tribore free floating barrels for improved balance and performance; 97mm Exis HP hyperbolic choke tubes; integrated recoil reducer; adjustable trigger; Triwood enhanced stock finish; Micro Metric adjustable stock comb
MSRP $4195

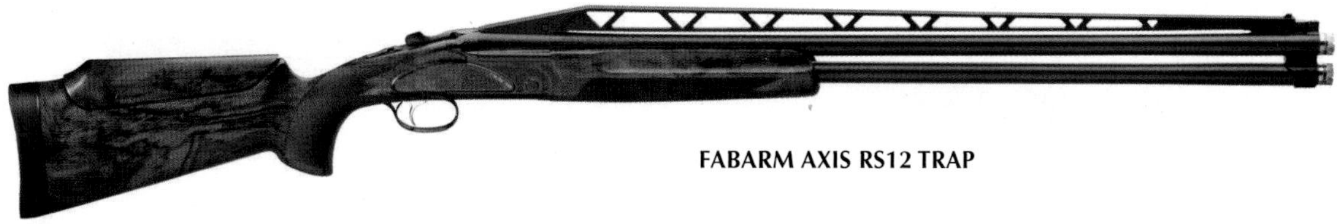

FABARM AXIS RS12 TRAP

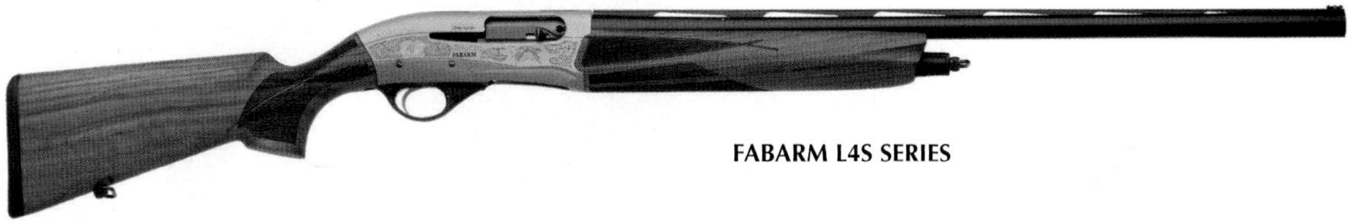

FABARM L4S SERIES

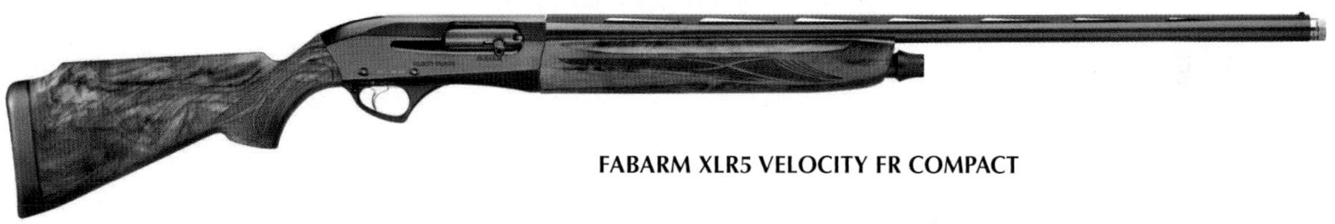

FABARM XLR5 VELOCITY FR COMPACT

FABARM AXIS RS12 TRAP

Action: Over/under
Stock: Wood
Barrel: 32 in., 34 in. (unsingle)
Chokes: 5 Exis HP
Weight: 8 lb. 14 oz.
Bore/Gauge: 12
Magazine: 1 or 2 shells
Features: Free-floating over-and-under barrels; adjustable ribs on all barrels; tapered bores; integrated recoil reducer; adjustable comb; optional release triggers; 97mm Exis HP hyperbolic choke tubes; adjustable trigger; Triwood enhanced stock finish
MSRP . . . . $4195–$5775

FABARM L4S SERIES

Action: Semiautomatic
Stock: Wood
Barrel: 26 in., 28 in.
Chokes: 3 Inner HP
Weight: 6 lb. 5 oz.–6 lb. 13 oz.
Bore/Gauge: 12
Magazine: 4 shells
Features: Stock shim system for adjusting fit; Tribore HP tapered barrels; available in three grades: Initial Hunter (black action), Grey Hunter (silver action with game scene), and Deluxe Hunter (silver action with detailed game scene with gold inlays and upgraded wood)
MSRP . . . . $1250–$2100

FABARM XLR5 VELOCITY FR COMPACT

Action: Semiautomatic
Stock: Wood
Barrel: 28 in., 30 in.
Chokes: 5 Exis HP
Weight: 7 lb. 6 oz.
Bore/Gauge: 12
Magazine: 5 shells
Features: Tapered Tribore HP barrel; oversized bolt handle; oversized bolt release; three optional magazine cap weights to adjust the balance point; barrel features a tapered top rib; stock features Triwood enhanced finish
MSRP . . . . $1990–$2165

NEW Products: Shotguns

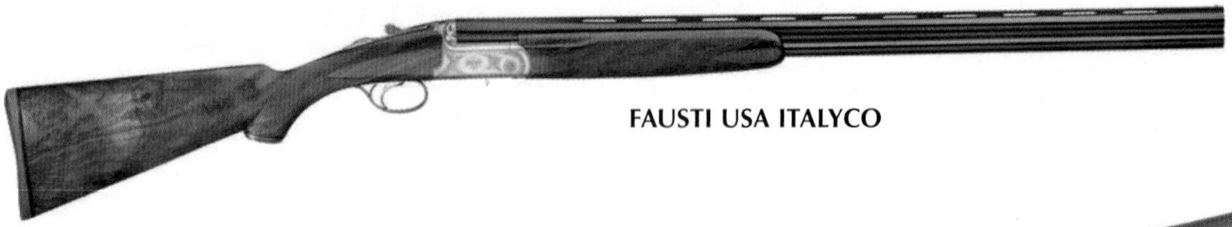

FAUSTI USA ITALYCO

KEL-TEC KSG

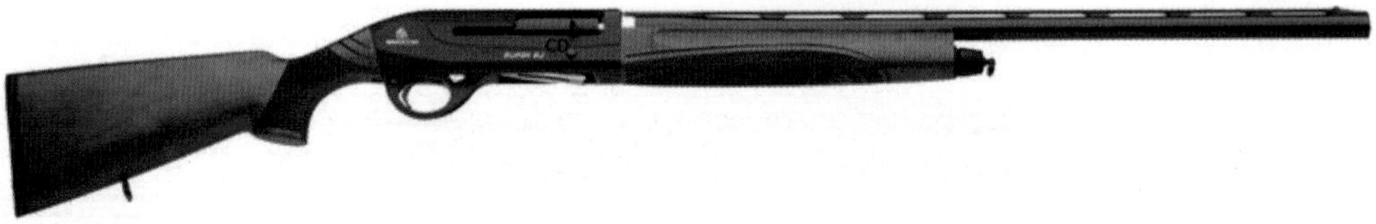

MOSSBERG 500 L SERIES

FAUSTI USA ITALYCO

Action: Over/under
Stock: Wood
Barrel: 23–32 in.
Chokes: Fixed
Weight: N/A
Bore/Gauge: 12 (2 ¾ in., 3 in.), 16 (2 ¾ in.), 20 (2 ¾ in., 3 in.), 28 (2 ¾ in.), .410 (3 in.)
Magazine: 2 shells
Features: Single selective trigger (double trigger available); automatic ejector (manual ejector available); box lock round body; pistol grip with steel grip cap or Prince of Wales or English
MSRP $8960

KEL-TEC KSG

Action: Pump
Stock: Glass reinforced nylon
Barrel: 18.5 in.
Chokes: Cylinder bore
Weight: 6 lb. 14.4 oz.-8 lb. 8 oz.
Bore/Gauge: 12 gauge (3 in.)
Magazine: 6+6+1
Features: KSG receiver is made from hardened steel and includes the magazine tubes which have been welded in place; pump action feeds from either the left or right tube
MSRP $990

MAROCCHI SUPER SJ

Action: Semiautomatic
Stock: Wood or synthetic
Barrel: 28 in., 30 in.
Chokes: Various
Weight: 6 lb. 13 oz.
Bore/Gauge: 12
Magazine: 4+1 shells
Features: Inertia operated; five chokes, chokes key, and distance pieces to change the angle of stock; available in standard, camo, or nickel; Complus version for reduced recoil available
MSRP $1495

MOSSBERG 500 L SERIES

Action: Pump
Stock: Wood or synthetic
Barrel: 18.5 in.–28 in.
Chokes: Accu-Set, fully rifled, XX-Full, cylinder bore
Weight: 6 lb. 12 oz.–7 lb. 8 oz.
Bore/Gauge: 12, 20
Magazine: 6 or 8 shells
Features: Feature black synthetic stocks; fully-camouflaged Mossy Oak Break-Up Infinity (Turkey) and Realtree MAX-4 (Waterfowl) synthetic stocks with complementing camo barrels and receivers; non-binding twin action bars; positive steel-to-steel lock-up and anti-jam elevator; dual extractors; anodized aluminum receiver; versatile vent rib Accu-Choke barrel (excluding Slugster and Tactical models); ambidextrous top-mounted safety
MSRP . . . .$518–$745

MOSSBERG 500 FLEX ALL PURPOSE L SERIES

MOSSBERG 590 L SERIES

MOSSBERG 590A1 L SERIES

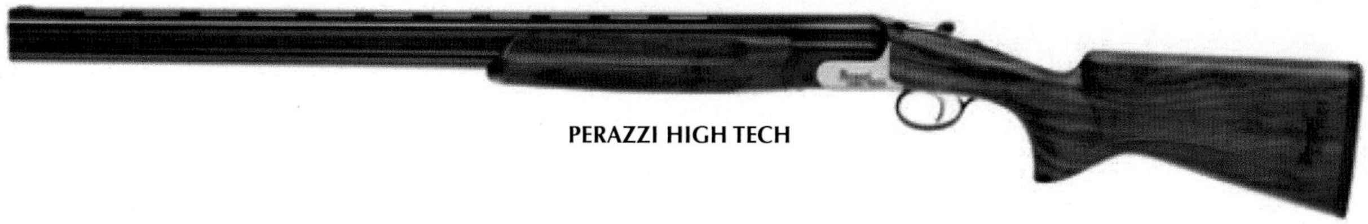

PERAZZI HIGH TECH

MOSSBERG 500 FLEX ALL PURPOSE L SERIES

Action: Pump
Stock: Synthetic
Barrel: 28 in.
Chokes: Accu-Set
Weight: 7 lb. 8 oz.
Bore/Gauge: 12
Magazine: 6 shells
Features: Feature black synthetic stocks; non-binding twin action bars; positive steel-to-steel lock-up and anti-jam elevator; dual extractors; anodized aluminum receiver; versatile vent rib Accu-Choke barrel (excluding Slugster and Tactical models); ambidextrous top-mounted safety
MSRP $668

MOSSBERG 590 L SERIES

Action: Pump
Stock: Synthetic
Barrel: 20 in.
Chokes: Cylinder bore
Weight: 7 lb. 4 oz.
Bore/Gauge: 12
Magazine: 9 shells
Features: Feature black synthetic stocks; non-binding twin action bars; positive steel-to-steel lock-up and anti-jam elevator; dual extractors; ambidextrous top-mounted safety
MSRP $691

MOSSBERG 590A1 L SERIES

Action: Pump
Stock: Synthetic
Barrel: 20 in.
Chokes: Cylinder bore
Weight: 7 lb.
Bore/Gauge: 12
Magazine: 9 shells
Features: Feature black synthetic stocks; non-binding twin action bars; positive steel-to-steel lock-up and anti-jam elevator; dual extractors; ambidextrous top-mounted safety
MSRP $942

PERAZZI HIGH TECH

Action: Over/under
Stock: Wood
Barrel: 27–31 in.
Chokes: Can be specified or made interchangeable
Weight: N/A
Bore/Gauge: 12
Magazine: 2 shells
Features:High Tech has a sporty and futuristic look; a large logo engraved in black smoke color on both sides of the receiver, under clear varnish, in contrast to the rest of the receiver; hinge pins are engraved with a checkered design; action is two-tone and varnished "in the white" only in the areas where the logo appears; frame has a greater weight than other Perazzi models and it is distributed within the median line between the grip of the hands, which both improves the fluidity of handling and further reduces recoil; divergent rib that goes from 7mm wide at the action to 10mm at the front end of the barrels allows you to greatly speed up your perception of the target and also expands your field of vision.
MSRP $12900

POINTER BY LEGACY SPORTS BREAK-ACTION

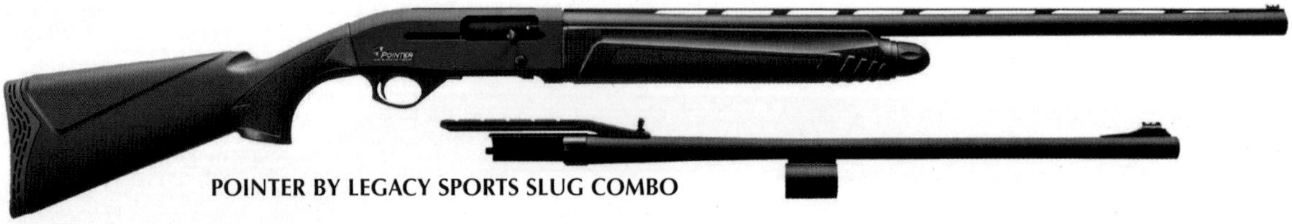

POINTER BY LEGACY SPORTS SLUG COMBO

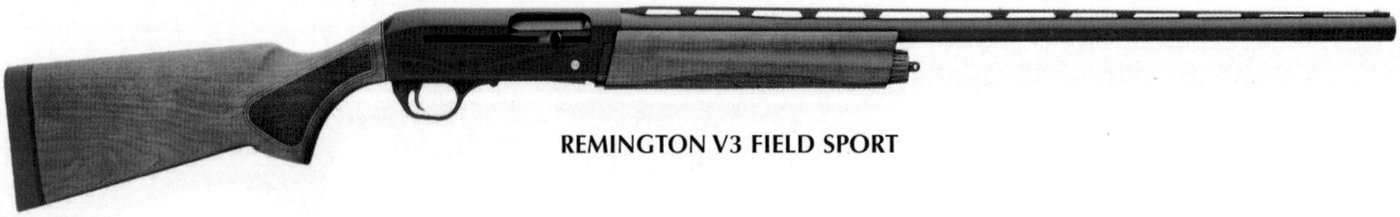

REMINGTON V3 FIELD SPORT

POINTER BY LEGACY SPORTS BREAK-ACTION

Action: Break action
Stock: Synthetic
Barrel: 28 in.
Chokes: Fixed
Weight: 4.8–5.4 lb.
Bore/Gauge: 12, 20, .410
Magazine: 1 shell
Features: Fixed, modified choke; matte black finish; black synthetic stock and forend; brass bead sight; manual safety, hammer safety and transfer bar safety
MSRP $188

POINTER BY LEGACY SPORTS SLUG COMBO

Action: Semiautomatic or pump
Stock: Synthetic
Barrel: 24 in., 28 in.
Chokes: Multi-5
Weight: 6–6.8 lb.
Bore/Gauge: 12, 20
Magazine: 5+1 shells
Features: Slug guns come as semiautos or pumps; both actions come with chrome lined 28 inch field barrels and 24 inch slug barrels
MSRP . . . . $620–$755

REMINGTON V3 FIELD SPORT

Action: Semiautomatic
Stock: Wood or synthetic
Barrel: 26 in., 28 in.
Chokes: Modified
Weight: 7 lb 3 oz.
Bore/Gauge: 12
Magazine: 3+1 shells
Features: Reliably cycles 12-gauge rounds from 2 ¾″ to 3″ magnum; Versaport gas system regulates cycling pressure based on shell length; light contoured barrel with ventilated rib; twin bead sights; synthetic and synthetic camo available
MSRP . . . . $895–$995

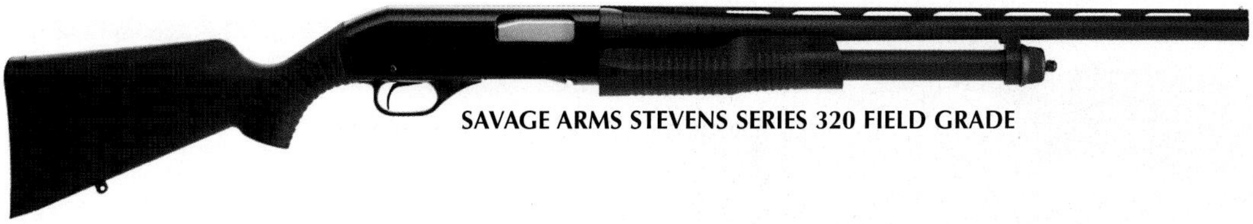

SAVAGE ARMS STEVENS SERIES 320 FIELD GRADE

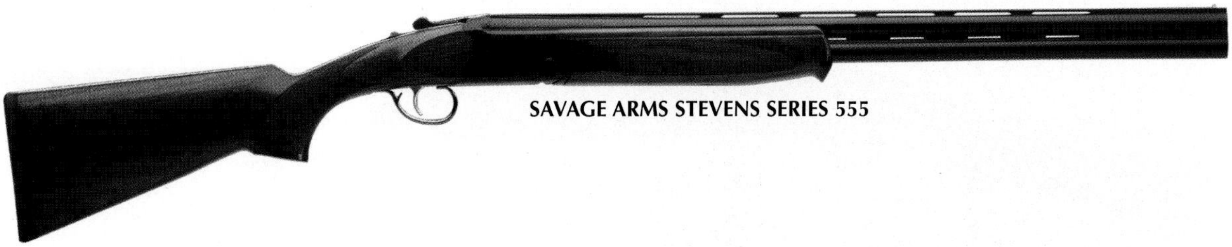

SAVAGE ARMS STEVENS SERIES 555

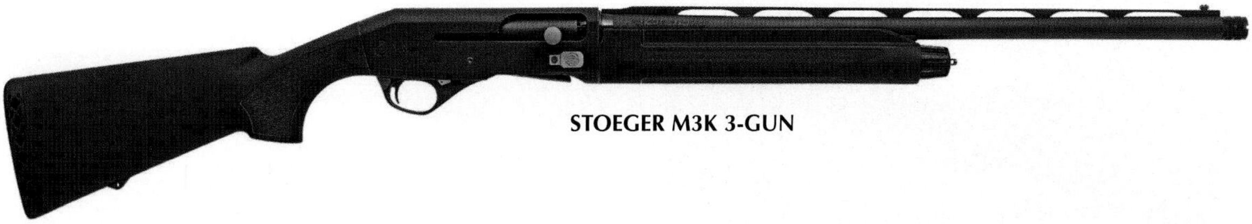

STOEGER M3K 3-GUN

SAVAGE ARMS STEVENS SERIES 320 FIELD GRADE YOUTH

Action: Pump
Stock: Synthetic
Barrel: 22 in.
Chokes: N/A
Weight: 7 lb.
Bore/Gauge: 20
Magazine: 2 shells
Features: Carbon steel barrel; compact size and light recoil make it the ideal shotgun for introducing young people to the shooting sports
MSRP. $235

SAVAGE ARMS STEVENS SERIES 555

Action: Over/under
Stock: Wood
Barrel: 28 in.
Chokes: 5 interchangeable chokes
Weight: 6 lb.
Bore/Gauge: 12, 20, 28, .410
Magazine: 2 shells
Features: Lightweight alloy receiver, Turkish walnut stock & forearm, single selective trigger, mechanical triggers, extractors, manual safetys
MSRP. $692

STOEGER M3K 3-GUN

Action: Semiautomatic, inertia-driven
Stock: Synthetic
Barrel: 24 in.
Chokes: XC, IC, M
Weight: 7 lb. 5 oz.
Bore/Gauge: 12
Magazine: 4+1
Features: Fiber optic sights; based on the M3000 line of shotguns; 3-gun ready; oversized anodized aluminum bolt release, oversized safety, and extended tactical-style anodized aluminum bolt handle; elongated carrier and enlarged, beveled loading port for quicker and easier reloading
MSRP. $699

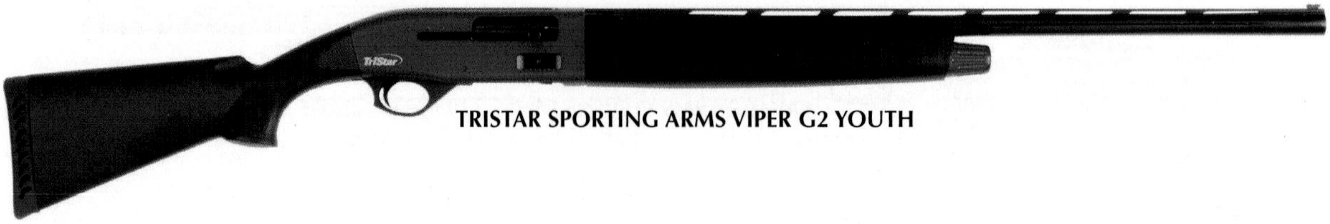

TRISTAR SPORTING ARMS VIPER G2 YOUTH

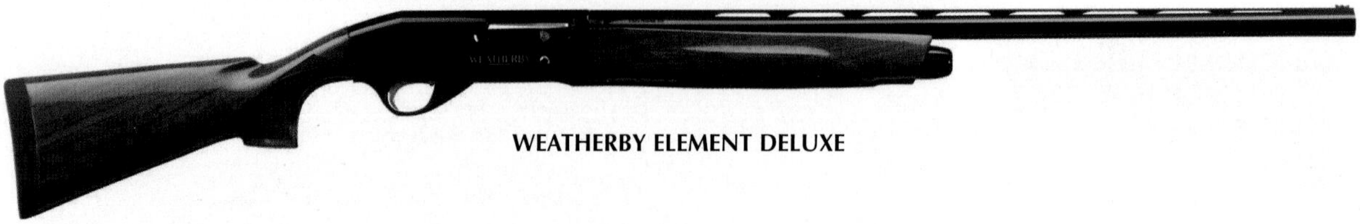

WEATHERBY ELEMENT DELUXE

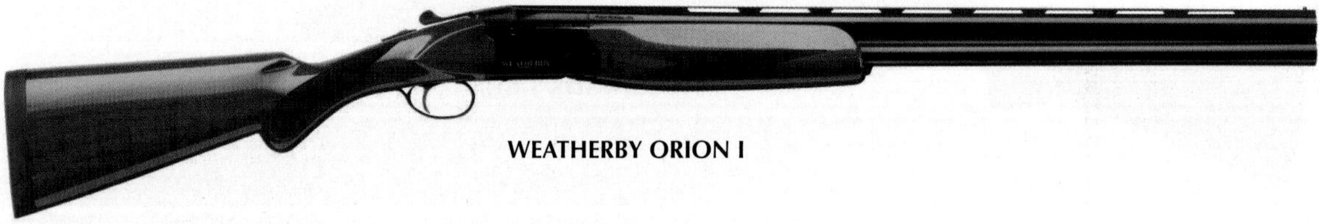

WEATHERBY ORION I

TRISTAR SPORTING ARMS VIPER G2 YOUTH

Action: Semiautomatic, gas-operated
Stock: Synthetic
Barrel: 26 in.
Chokes: SK, IC, M, F
Weight: 6 lb. 3 oz.
Bore/Gauge: 20
Magazine: 5 shells
Features: Manual E-Z Load magazine cut-off; raised target rib w/ matted sight plane; middle bead and fiber pptic sight; quick shot plug removal; chrome-lined chamber and barrel; adjustable comb
MSRP $549

WEATHERBY ELEMENT DELUXE

Action: Semiautomatic
Stock: Walnut
Barrel: 26 in., 28 in.
Chokes: IC, M, F
Weight: 6 lb.–6 lb.12 oz.
Bore/Gauge: 12, 20, 28
Magazine: 3+1 or 4+1 shells
Features: Fiber optic front sight; "AA" grade American walnut stock; aircraft grade aluminum; chrome-lined bores; drop-out trigger system; dual purpose bolt release; chrome-plated bolt; inertia-operated action; chrome-lined barrel; ventilated top rib; integral multi choke system with three application specific tubes (IC, Mod, Full)
MSRP $1099

WEATHERBY ORION I

Action: Over/under
Stock: Walnut
Barrel: 26 in., 28 in.
Chokes: IC, M, F
Weight: 7 lb.
Bore/Gauge: 12
Magazine: 2 shells
Features: Brass front sights; ambidextrous top tang safety; automatic ejectors; low profile receiver; chrome-lined bores; matte ventilated top rib with brass bead front sight; traditional boxlock action; integral multi choke system with three application specific tubes (IC, Mod, Full)
MSRP $1099

ANDERSON RIFLES AM15-7.5 PISTOL

BERSA BP40CC (BPCC9MM DUO-TONE SHOWN)

BERSA BP380CC (BPCC9MM MATTE SHOWN)

BROWNING 1911-380

ANDERSON RIFLES AM15-7.5 PISTOL

Action: Semiautomatic
Grips: Synthetic
Barrel: 7.5 in. extended barrel
Sights: None
Weight: 4 lb. 14 oz.
Caliber: .223 Rem./5.56 NATO
Capacity: Detachable box, 30 rounds
Features: Picatinny rail; Anderson Knight Stalker flash hider; Magpul grip; available treated with proprietary no lube RF85 treatment
MSRP. N/A

BERSA BP40CC

Action: Semiautomatic
Grips: Synthetic
Barrel: 3.3 in.
Sights: Fixed
Weight: 21.5 oz.
Caliber: .40 S&W
Capacity: 7+1 rounds
Features: Interchangeable Sig Sauer–type front sight; interchangeable Glock-type rear sights; short reset DOA; integral locking system, firing pin, and trigger; available in duotone or matte black finishes
MSRP. . . . . $430–$440

BERSA BP380CC

Action: Semiautomatic
Grips: Synthetic
Barrel: 3.3 in.
Sights: Fixed
Weight: 21.5 oz.
Caliber: .380 ACP
Capacity: 8+1 rounds
Features: Interchangeable Sig Sauer–type front sight; interchangeable Glock-type rear sights; short reset DOA; integral locking system, firing pin, and trigger; available in duotone or matte black finishes
MSRP. . . . . $423–$440

BROWNING 1911-380

Action: Semiautomatic
Grips: Synthetic
Barrel: 4.25 in.
Sights: Fixed
Weight: 18 oz.
Caliber: .380 ACP
Capacity: 8 rounds
Features: Combat sights; matte black finish; single-stack magazine
MSRP. $670

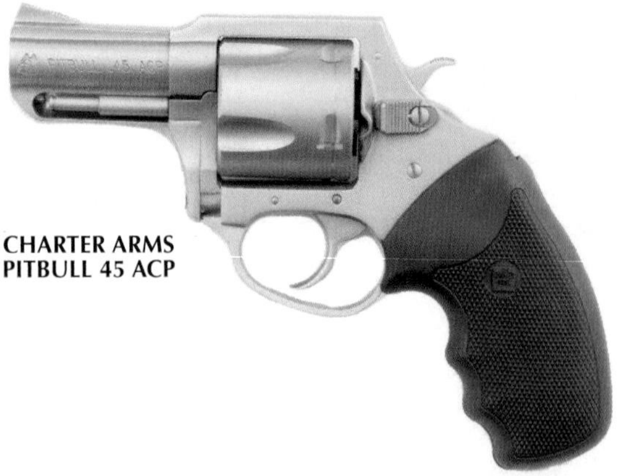

CHARTER ARMS PITBULL 45 ACP

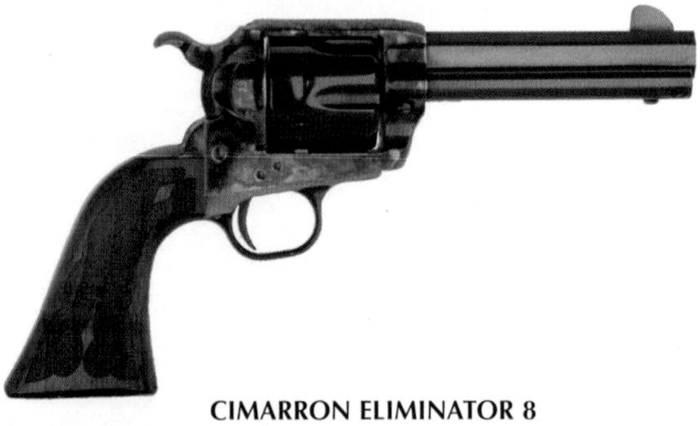

CIMARRON ELIMINATOR 8

CIMARRON ELIMINATOR C

CIMARRON ELIMINATOR TS

CHARTER ARMS PITBULL 45 ACP

Action: DA/SA
Grips: Rubber
Barrel: 2.5 in.
Sights: Fixed
Weight: 22 oz.
Caliber: .45 ACP
Capacity: 5 rounds
Features: Unique design provides a dual coil spring assembly located in the extractor which allows for the insertion and retention of rimless .45 ACP caliber cartridge in each chamber of the revolver's cylinder
MSRP. $489

CIMARRON ELIMINATOR 8

Action: SA
Grips: Wood
Barrel: 4.75 in.
Sights: Fixed
Weight: N/A
Caliber: .357 Mag., .38 Spcl., .45 LC
Capacity: N/A
Features: Octagonal barrel; short stroke; checkered walnut Army grip; Cimarron low wide hammer; US action job; case hardened pre-war frame; standard blue finish;
MSRP. $779

CIMARRON ELIMINATOR C

Action: SA
Grips: Wood
Barrel: 4.75 in.
Sights: Fixed
Weight: N/A
Caliber: .357 Mag., .38 Spcl., .45 LC
Capacity: N/A
Features: Short stroke; checkered walnut grip; Cimarron Cowboy Comp US action job; standard hammer; frame available in stainless steel pre-war and color case hardened pre-war
MSRP. . . . . $714–$974

CIMARRON ELIMINATOR TS

Action: SA
Grips: Wood
Barrel: 3.5 in., 4.75 in.
Sights: Fixed
Weight: N/A
Caliber: .45 LC
Capacity: N/A
Features: Short stroke; checkered Army-style grips; Cimarron Cowboy Comp US action job; standard hammer; frame available in stainless steel pre-war and color case hardened pre-war
MSRP. . . . . $758–$974

CIMARRON FRONTIER

CZ–USA 75 SP-01 SHADOW TARGET II

CZ–USA 805 BREN PS1 PISTOLI

CIMARRON FRONTIER

Action: SA
Grips: Ivory
Barrel: 4.75 in., 7.5 in.
Sights: Fixed
Weight: 4 lb. 8 oz.
Caliber: .45 Colt
Capacity: N/A
Features: Old silver frame; standard blue finish; laser engraved; nickel frame and finish available
MSRP. $714

CZ–USA 75 SP-01 SHADOW TARGET II

Action: DA/SA
Grips: Thin aluminum checkered
Barrel: 4.61 in.
Sights: Adjustable target rear, fiber optic front
Weight: 38.4 oz.
Caliber: 9mm Luger
Capacity: 18 rounds
Features: Competition-ready Pre-B style SP-01 Shadow, featuring a CZ Custom trigger job with the new short reset single-action trigger, fully-adjustable rear sight, fiber optic front sight, stainless steel guide rod, lighter springs for competition (11 lb recoil and 13 lb main springs), extended magazine release, drop-free magazines and checkered aluminum grips; created by champion shooter Angus Hobdell's CZ Custom Shop to have trigger pulls of 3.0-4.0 lbs in SA and 7.5-8.5 lbs in DA
MSRP. $1600

CZ–USA 805 BREN PS1 PISTOL

Action: Semiautomatic
Grips: Polymer
Barrel: 11 in.
Sights: Low-profile, adjustable, 4 rear aperture sizes
Weight: 6 lb. 11 oz.
Caliber: .223/5.56
Capacity: 10 rounds, 30 rounds
Features: The first civilian-legal form of CZ's 805 Bren; STANAG magazine used in the AR-15/M16; one-piece aluminum upper receiver with a monolithic Picatinny rail; multipurpose rear mounting point, fit from the factory with a single-point sling attachment; accessory arm brace adapter coupled with the effective factory-equipped two-port brake
MSRP. $1982

NEW Products: Handguns

CZ–USA 85 COMBAT

CZ–USA SCORPION EVO 3 S1 PISTOL

CZ–USA 1911 A1

CZ–USA 85 COMBAT

Action: DA/SA
Grips: Plastic
Barrel: 4.61 in.
Sights: Adjustable three-dot
Weight: 35.4 oz.
Caliber: 9mm Luger
Capacity: 10 rounds, 16 rounds
Features: Extended magazine release, drop-free magazine and overtravel adjustment on the trigger; Combat designation comes from the lack of a firing pin block safety, allowing the replacement of the firing pin without tools; ambidextrous features include safety levers, slide stop levers and a reversible magazine release; lack of a firing pin safety gives the 85 Combat a slight advantage in the trigger pull department, making it a long-time favorite of competition shooters
MSRP. $664

CZ–USA 1911 A1

Action: SA
Grips: Checkered walnut
Barrel: 5 in.
Sights: Post and notch, dovetailed
Weight: 38.7 oz.
Caliber: .45 ACP
Capacity: 7+1 rounds
Features: The CZ 1911 A1 is an homage to the past, a 5-in. government sized model built as a modern incarnation of the original 1911 A1; CZ's version makes several small improvements, swapping the checkered plastic grips for checkered walnut, adding serrated slide stop, magazine catch and mainspring housing and using a stainless steel barrel; built with much tighter slide-to-barrel and slide-to-frame tolerances than vintage models, the result is much improved accuracy without compromising reliability; bubilt without a trigger safety, the trigger itself is aluminum, with pull specified at 5 lbs., give or take a pound; a forged carbon steel frame and slide are finished in a black oxide and it ships with two 7-round magazines
MSRP. $849

CZ–USA SCORPION EVO 3 S1 PISTOL

Action: SA
Grips: Polymer
Barrel: 7.72 in.
Sights: Low-profile fully adjustable aperture and post, 4 rear aperture sizes
Weight: 5 lb.
Caliber: 9mm Luger
Capacity: 10+1 rounds, 20+1 rounds
Features: Scorpion sub-gun, imported as a pistol; blowback-operated; sights ride on an 11-in. Picatinny rail perfect for mounting optics; ambidextrous controls; non-reciprocating charging handle is swappable and reach to the trigger is adjustable; arm brace adapter quickly and easily adds an AR-style pistol buffer tube to the rear of the action, enabling the use of an arm brace for added stability
MSRP. $849

GLOCK G40 GEN4

GLOCK G43 SINGLE STACK

GLOCK G40 GEN4

Action: Semiautomatic
Grips: Synthetic
Barrel: 6.02 in.
Sights: Fixed
Weight: 28.15 oz.
Caliber: 10mm
Capacity: 15 rounds
Features: Right hand, hexagonal barrel rifling; capable of taking down game such as whitetail deer, Russian boar and feral hogs
MSRP $699

GLOCK G43 SINGLE STACK

Action: Semiautomatic
Grips: Synthetic
Barrel: 3.39 in. Sights: Fixed
Weight: 17.95 oz.
Caliber: 9mm
Capacity: 6 rounds
Features: Right hand, hexagonal barrel rifling; single stack pistol; large magazine catch
MSRP $529

HECKLER & KOCH HK45 CERAKOTE

HECKLER & KOCH HK45 COMPACT CERAKOTE

HECKLER & KOCH P30SK

HECKLER & KOCH HK45 CERAKOTE

Action: Semiautomatic
Grips: Synthetic
Barrel: 4.46 in.
Sights: Fixed
Weight: 31.2 oz.
Caliber: .45 ACP
Capacity: 10 rounds
Features: Picatinny rail molded into the polymer frame dust cover; ergonomic grip profiles with user replaceable grip panels; ambidextrous controls with dual slide releases and enlarged magazine release; uses the proven modified Browning linkless recoil operating system; O-ring barrel for precise barrel-to-slide lockup; polygonal rifling for longer barrel life and better accuracy; improved ergonomic control levers (safety and/ or decocking); low profile drift adjustable 3-dot sights; contoured and radiused slide with forward slide (grasping) grooves and anti-glare longitudinal ribs
MSRP. $1199

HECKLER & KOCH HK45 COMPACT CERAKOTE

Action: Semiautomatic
Grips: Synthetic
Barrel: 3.94 in.
Sights: Fixed
Weight: 28.48 oz.
Caliber: .45 ACP
Capacity: 8 or 10 rounds
Features: Picatinny rail molded into the polymer frame dust cover; slim-line grip profiles with user replaceable grip panels; ambidextrous controls with dual slide releases and enlarged magazine release; uses the proven modified Browning linkless recoil operating system; O-ring barrel for precise barrel-to-slide lockup and better accuracy; polygonal rifling for longer barrel life and increased accuracy; improved ergonomic control levers (safety and/or decocking); low profile drift adjustable 3-dot sights; contoured and radiused slide with forward slide (grasping) grooves and anti-glare longitudinal ribs; black polymer frame
MSRP. $1199

HECKLER & KOCH P30SK

Action: Semiautomatic
Grips: Rubber
Barrel: 3.27 in.
Sights: Fixed
Weight: 23.99 oz.
Caliber: 9mm
Capacity: 10 rounds
Features: Picatinny rail; interchangeable backstraps and lateral grip panels; available in multiple trigger firing modes including HK's enhanced double action only Law Enforcement Modification (LEM); trigger modes include conventional double action/ single action (DA/SA)
MSRP. . . . .$719–$819

HECKLER & KOCH USP9 TACTICAL

HECKLER & KOCH VP40

KAHR ARMS CT380

HECKLER & KOCH USP9 TACTICAL

Action: Semiautomatic
Grips: Synthetic
Barrel: 4.86 in.
Sights: Adjustable
Weight: 28.16 oz.
Caliber: 9mm
Capacity: 10 or 15 rounds
Features: High profile target sights; target sights with micrometer adjustment for windage and elevation; one piece machined, nitro-carburized steel slide; can be converted to any of nine trigger firing modes; patented HK recoil reduction system; corrosion resistant "Hostile Environment" blued finish; corrosion proof fiber-reinforced polymer frame; oversized trigger guard for use with gloves; choice of flat and extended floorplate magazines; universal mounting grooves for installing accessories; ambidextrous magazine release lever; extended slide release; extractor doubles as a loaded chamber indicator; patented Lock-Out Safety device
MSRP . . . . $1349–$1449

HECKLER & KOCH VP40

Action: Semiautomatic
Grips: Rubber
Barrel: 4.09 in.
Sights: Fixed
Weight: 26.56 oz.
Caliber: .40 S&W
Capacity: 10 or 13 rounds
Features: Ergonomic handgun grip design that includes three changeable backstraps and six grip side panels; ambidextrous controls; charging supports—simple components that are mounted on each side of the rear of the slide and provide better gripping leverage for racking the slide rearward; extended Picatinny rail molded into the polymer frame; captive flat recoil spring
MSRP . . . . $719–$819

KAHR ARMS CT380

Action: Semiautomatic
Grips: Synthetic
Barrel: 3 in.
Sights: Fixed
Weight: 11.44 oz.
Caliber: .380 ACP
Capacity: 7+1 rounds
Features: Textured polymer grips; trigger cocking DAO; lock breech; Browning-type recoil lug; passive striker block; no magazine disconnect; drift adjustable white bar-dot combat rear sight; pinned in polymer front sight
MSRP $419

MAGNUM RESEARCH DESERT EAGLE 1911GSS

MAGNUM RESEARCH DESERT EAGLE 1911GSS

MAGNUM RESEARCH DESERT EAGLE 1911USS

MAGNUM RESEARCH DESERT EAGLE 1911CSS

Action: Semiautomatic
Grips: Wood
Barrel: 4.33 in.
Sights: Adjustable rear
Weight: 33.9 oz.
Caliber: .45 ACP
Capacity: 8 rounds
Features: Ships with two eight round magazines; skeletonized hammer; extended magazine release; extended thumb safety; checkered, flat mainspring housing made from aluminum; stainless steel full-length guide rod; bushingless barrel
MSRP.................... $904

MAGNUM RESEARCH DESERT EAGLE 1911GSS

Action: Semiautomatic
Grips: Wood
Barrel: 5.05 in.
Sights: Adjustable rear
Weight: 36.2 oz.
Caliber: .45 ACP
Capacity: 8 rounds
Features: Ships with two eight round magazines; skeletonized hammer; extended magazine release; extended thumb safety; checkered, flat mainspring housing made from aluminum; stainless steel full-length guide rod; bushingless barrel
MSRP.................... $904

MAGNUM RESEARCH DESERT EAGLE 1911USS

Action: Semiautomatic
Grips: Wood
Barrel: 3 in.
Sights: Adjustable rear
Weight: 25.8 oz.
Caliber: .45 ACP
Capacity: 6 rounds
Features: Ships with two eight round magazines; skeletonized hammer; extended magazine release; extended thumb safety; checkered, flat mainspring housing made from aluminum; stainless steel full-length guide rod; bushingless barrel
MSRP.................... $1019

MAGNUM RESEARCH BABY DESERT EAGLE III SERIES

MAGNUM RESEARCH DESERT EAGLE .357 MAGNUM W/ INTEGRAL MUZZLE BREAK (DE50AE SHOWN)

MAGNUM RESEARCH MR40 EAGLE

MAGNUM RESEARCH BABY DESERT EAGLE III SERIES

Action: Semiautomatic
Grips: Rubber
Barrel: 3.85 in., 4.43 in.
Sights: Fixed
Weight: 25 oz.–37.9 oz.
Caliber: 9mm, .40 S&W, .45 ACP
Capacity: 10 or 13 Rounds
Features: Polymer or steel frame; available in full size or semi-compact; Weaver rail; double action/single action; ambidextrous, slide-mounted safety and decocker; three dot combat sights
MSRP . . . . $646–$691

MAGNUM RESEARCH DESERT EAGLE .357 MAGNUM W/ INTEGRAL MUZZLE BREAK

Action: Semiautomatic
Grips: Rubber
Barrel: 6 in.
Sights: Fixed
Weight: 4 lb. 8.8 oz.
Caliber: .357 Mag.
Capacity: 9 rounds
Features: High quality carbon steel barrel, frame and slide w/ full Weaver style accessory rail and integral muzzle brake; gas-operated, rotating bolt semiautomatic; fixed combat sights
MSRP $1710

MAGNUM RESEARCH MR40 EAGLE

Action: Semiautomatic
Grips: Rubber
Barrel: 4.5 in.
Sights: Adjustable rear
Weight: 26.4 oz.
Caliber: .40 S&W
Capacity: 10 or 11 rounds
Features: Manual decocker/striker block; safety decocker button; internal striker drop plunger; internal trigger safety; textured polymer frame; matte stainless slide w/ laser engraved markings; locked breech semiautomatic
MSRP $559

NIGHTHAWK CUSTOM PREDATOR T5

NIGHTHAWK CUSTOM WAR HAWK COMPACT

NIGHTHAWK CUSTOM WAR HAWK GOVERNMENT

NIGHTHAWK CUSTOM PREDATOR T5

Action: Semitautomatic
Grips: Synthetic
Barrel: 5 in.
Sights: Fixed
Weight: 40.3 oz.
Caliber: 9mm, 10mm, .45 ACP
Capacity: N/A
Features: Stainless steel frame standard; black nitride finish; Nighthawk two-piece magwell; tritium dot front sight; Heinie Slant Pro Straight Eight Tritium rear sight; stainless steel barrel; single-side safety; thinned cocobolo with double diamond checkering
MSRP. $3795

NIGHTHAWK CUSTOM WAR HAWK COMPACT

Action: Semitautomatic
Grips: Synthetic
Barrel: 4.25 in.
Sights: Fixed
Weight: 34.7 oz.
Caliber: 9mm, .45 ACP
Capacity: N/A
Features: Unique tri-cut slide with bold angles; serrated arrow style slide top; heavy bevel on bottom of slide; hand serrated rear of slide; barrel is crowned and beveled with the bushing; one-piece fully machined 20 LPI checkered mainspring housing/magwell; high-cut front strap; hightweight solid aluminum match grade trigger; thin G10 in hyena brown; Heinie Slant Pro Straight Eight Tritium night sights; Nighthawk Custom/Marvel EVERLAST recoil system; War Hawk logo engraved on slide; stainless steel frame standard; black nitride finish
MSRP. $3895

NIGHTHAWK CUSTOM WAR HAWK GOVERNMENT

Action: Semitautomatic
Grips: Synthetic
Barrel: 5 in.
Sights: Fixed
Weight: 39.6 oz.
Caliber: 9mm, .45 ACP
Capacity: N/A
Features: Unique multi-faceted slide; serrated arrow style slide top; heavy bevel on bottom of slide; hand serrated rear of slide; barrel is crowned and beveled with the bushing; one-piece fully machined 20 LPI checkered mainspring housing/magwell; high-cut front strap; lightweight aluminum medium solid match trigger; aggressive G10 hyena brown grips; red fiber optic front sights; Tritium dot front sight upgrade available; Jardine Hook rear sight; tactical magazine catch; Nighthawk Custom/Marvel EVERLAST recoil system; War Hawk logo engraved on slide
MSRP. $3895

NIGHTHAWK CUSTOM WAR HAWK RECON

REMINGTON RM380

ROCK ISLAND ARMORY BABY ROCK STANDARD CS

NIGHTHAWK CUSTOM WAR HAWK RECON

Action: Semitautomatic
Grips: Synthetic
Barrel: 5 in.
Sights: Fixed
Weight: 39.6 oz.
Caliber: 9mm, .45 ACP
Capacity: N/A
Features: Integrated recon accessory rail; unique multi-faceted slide; serrated arrow style slide top; heavy bevel on bottom of slide; hand serrated rear of slide; barrel is crowned and beveled with the bushing; one-piece fully machined 20 LPI checkered mainspring housing/magwell; high cut front strap; lightweight aluminum medium solid match trigger; aggressive G10 hyena brown grips; red fiber optic front sight; Tritium dot front sight upgrade available; Jardine rear hook sight; extended tactical mag catch; Nighthawk Custom/Marvel EVERLAST recoil system; War Hawk logo engraved on slide
MSRP $3995

REMINGTON RM380 SUBCOMPACT

Action: Semiautomatic
Grips: Synthetic
Barrel: 2.9 in.
Sights: Fixed
Weight: 12.2 oz.
Caliber: .380 ACP
Capacity: 6+1 rounds
Features: Fully functional slide stop; all metal construction; DOA trigger; ambidextrous magazine release; checkered front strap and undercut trigger guard; optimized grip handle; 8–9-pound trigger pull
MSRP . . . . $417–$450

ROCK ISLAND ARMORY BABY ROCK STANDARD CS

Action: Semiautomatic
Grips: Rubber
Barrel: 4 in.
Sights: Fixed
Weight: 1 lb. 8 oz.
Caliber: .380 ACP
Capacity: 7 rounds
Features: Parkerized frame; front post, Novak-style rear sight
MSRP $462

ROCK ISLAND ARMORY GI STANDARD FS HI-CAP

ROCK ISLAND ARMORY GI STANDARD MS

ROCK ISLAND ARMORY PRO MATCH ULTRA

ROCK ISLAND ARMORY GI STANDARD FS HI-CAP

Action: Semiautomatic
Grips: Rubber
Barrel: 5 in.
Sights: Fixed
Weight: 2 lb. 9 oz.
Caliber: .45 ACP
Capacity: 14 rounds
Features: Parkerized frame; 1:16 in. twist; 4–6 lb. trigger pull
MSRP $618

ROCK ISLAND ARMORY GI STANDARD MS

Action: Semiautomatic
Grips: Wood
Barrel: 4.25 in.
Sights: Fixed
Weight: 2 lb. 6 oz.
Caliber: .45 ACP
Capacity: 8 rounds
Features: Parkerized frame; 1:16 in. twist; 4–6 lb. trigger pull
MSRP $546

ROCK ISLAND ARMORY PRO MATCH ULTRA

Action: Semiautomatic
Grips: Rubber or wood
Barrel: 6 in.
Sights: Fixed
Weight: 2 lb. 8 oz.
Caliber: 10mm, .45 ACP
Capacity: 8 rounds
Features: Parkerized frame; orange fiber-optic front sight, tactical adjustable rear sight; comes with 9mm conversion kit; 1:16 twist; 4–6 lb. trigger pull; ambidextrous safety; combat hammer; extended beavertail
MSRP . . . . $981–$1187

ROCK ISLAND ARMORY PRO MATCH ULTRA HC

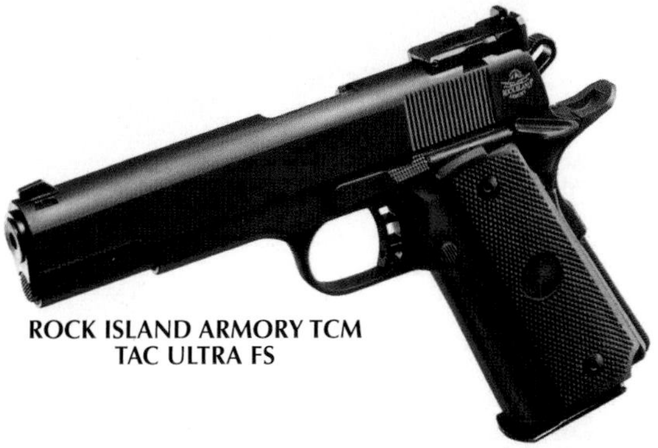

ROCK ISLAND ARMORY TCM TAC ULTRA FS

ROCK ISLAND ARMORY TCM TAC ULTRA MS

ROCK ISLAND ARMORY PRO MATCH ULTRA HC

Action: Semiautomatic
Grips: Rubber
Barrel: 5 in.
Sights: Fixed
Weight: 2 lb. 14 oz.
Caliber: .40 S&W
Capacity: 16 rounds
Features: Parkerized frame; orange fiber-optic front sight, tactical adjustable rear sight; comes with 9mm conversion kit; 1:16 twist; 4–6 lb. trigger pull; ambidextrous safety; combat hammer; extended beavertail
MSRP $1095

ROCK ISLAND ARMORY TCM TAC ULTRA FS

Action: Semiautomatic
Grips: Rubber
Barrel: 5 in.
Sights: Fixed
Weight: 3 lb.
Caliber: .22 TCM
Capacity: 10 rounds
Features: Parkerized frame; orange fiber-optic front sight, tactical adjustable rear sight; comes with 9mm conversion kit; 1:16 twist; 4–6 lb. trigger pull; ambidextrous safety; combat hammer; extended beavertail
MSRP . . . .$812–$867

ROCK ISLAND ARMORY TCM TAC ULTRA MS

Action: Semiautomatic
Grips: Rubber
Barrel: 4.25 in.
Sights: Fixed
Weight: 2 lb. 8 oz.
Caliber: .22 TCM
Capacity: 10 rounds
Features: Parkerized frame; orange fiber-optic front sight, tactical adjustable rear sight; comes with 9mm conversion kit; 1:16 twist; 4–6 lb. trigger pull; ambidextrous safety; combat hammer; extended beavertail
MSRP . . . .$832–$882

ROCK ISLAND ARMORY TCM TAC ULTRA MS HC

ROCK ISLAND ARMORY XT 22 MAGNUM

ROSSI MODEL R98104

ROSSI MODEL R98106

ROCK ISLAND ARMORY TCM TAC ULTRA MS HC

Action: Semiautomatic
Grips: Rubber
Barrel: 4.25 in.
Sights: Fixed
Weight: 2 lb. 8 oz.
Caliber: .22 TCM
Capacity: 17 rounds
Features: Parkerized frame; orange fiber-optic front sight, tactical adjustable rear sight; comes with 9mm conversion kit; 1:16 twist; 4–6 lb. trigger pull; ambidextrous safety; combat hammer; extended beavertail
MSRP $914

ROCK ISLAND ARMORY XT 22 MAGNUM

Action: Semiautomatic
Grips: Rubber
Barrel: 5 in.
Sights: Fixed
Weight: 2 lb. 3 oz.
Caliber: .22 Mag.
Capacity: 22 rounds
Features: Parkerized frame; single action
MSRP $609

ROSSI MODEL R98104

Action: DA/SA
Grips: Rubber
Barrel: 4 in.
Sights: Adjustable
Weight: 29 oz.
Caliber: .22 LR
Capacity: 8 rounds
Features: Adjustable rear sight, fixed fiber-optic front sight; hammer block; blued finish
MSRP $408

ROSSI MODEL R98106

Action: DA/SA
Grips: Rubber
Barrel: 6 in.
Sights: Adjustable
Weight: 29.5 oz.
Caliber: .22 LR
Capacity: 8 rounds
Features: Adjustable rear sight, fixed fiber-optic front sight; hammer block; blued finish
MSRP $408

RUGER 22/45 LITE

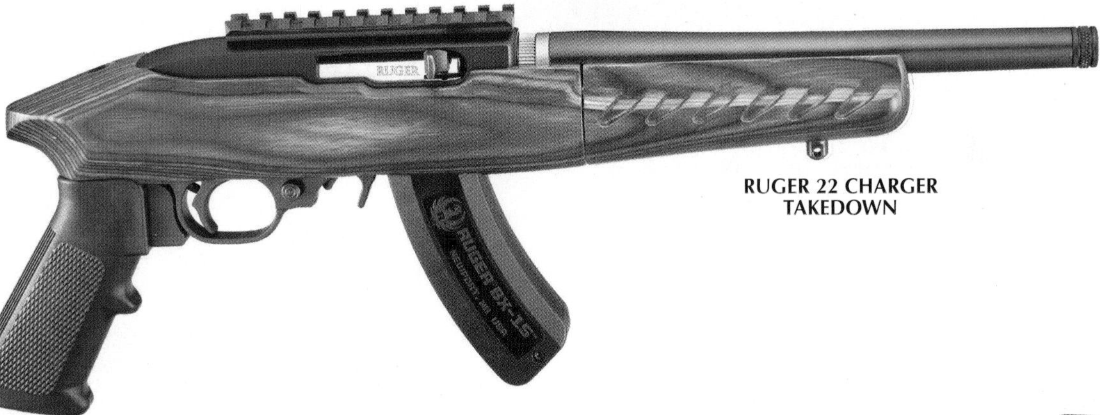

RUGER 22 CHARGER TAKEDOWN

RUGER GP100 MATCH CHAMPION

RUGER 22/45 LITE

Action: Semiautomatic
Grips: Synthetic
Barrel: 4.4 in.
Sights: Adjustable
Weight: 22.7 oz.
Caliber: .22 LR
Capacity: 6 rounds
Features: Zytel polymer grip frame; threaded barrel; ccontoured ejection port; loaded chamber indicator
MSRP $515

RUGER 22 CHARGER TAKEDOWN

Action: Semiautomatic
Grips: Synthetic
Barrel: 10 in.
Sights: None
Weight: 3 lb. 4 oz.
Caliber: .22 LR
Capacity: 15 rounds
Features: Cold hammer-forged barrel; threaded barrel; Picatinny rail; A2-style grip; adjustable bipod
MSRP $409

RUGER GP100 MATCH CHAMPION

Action: Double action
Grips: Wood
Barrel: 4.2 in.
Sights: Fixed or adjustable
Weight: 38 oz.
Caliber: .357 Mag.
Capacity: 6 rounds
Features: Hogue stippled hardwood; fiber optic front sight; triple-locking cylinder; easy takedown; features a slab-sided, half-lug barrel
MSRP $929

RUGER LC9

RUGER LCP CUSTOM

RUGER LCR

RUGER LC9

Action: Semiautomatic
Grips: Synthetic
Barrel: 6 in.
Sights: Adjustable
Weight: 17.2 oz.
Caliber: 9mm
Capacity: 7+1 rounds
Features: Dovetailed, high-visibility 3-dot sight system with windage adjustable rear sight and fixed front sigh; striker fire; includes finger grip extension floorplate; blued, alloy steel barrel; integrated trigger safety, manual safety, magazine disconnect, inert magazine for safe disassembly, and a visual inspection port
MSRP. $449

RUGER LCP CUSTOM

Action: Semiautomatic
Grips: Synthetic
Barrel: 2.75 in.
Sights: Fixed
Weight: 9.75 oz.
Caliber: .380 ACP
Capacity: 6+1 rounds
Features: Photoluminescent front and drift adjustable rear sights; blued, alloy steel barrel; 1:16 in. twist
MSRP. $419

RUGER LCR

Action: DA/SA
Grips: Rubber
Barrel: 3 in.
Sights: Adjustable
Weight: 15.7 oz.
Caliber: .38 Spcl. +P
Capacity: 5 rounds
Features: Hogue Tamer monogrip; adjustable black blade rear sight; Ionbond Diamondblack cylinder finish
MSRP. $545

RUGER REDHAWK

RUGER SR1911

RUGER SP101

RUGER REDHAWK

Action: DAO
Grips: Wood
Barrel: 4.2 in.
Sights: Fixed
Weight: 2 lb. 12 oz.
Caliber: .45 ACP, .45 Colt
Capacity: 6 rounds
Features: Stainless steel construction; triple-lock cylinder; single spring mechanism; adjustable rear sight
MSRP. $1029

RUGER SR1911

Action: Semiautomatic
Grips: Wood
Barrel: 4.25 in.
Sights: Fixed
Weight: 1 lb. 12 oz.
Caliber: .45 ACP
Capacity: 7+1 rounds
Features: Anodized aluminum frame; stainless steel barrel; standard recoil guide system and flat mainspring housing; rear slide serrations allow for positive grip
MSRP. $899

RUGER SP101

Action: DA/SA
Grips: Wood and rubber
Barrel: 4.2 in.
Sights: Fixed
Weight: 1 lb. 13 oz.
Caliber: .327 Fed. Mag.
Capacity: 6 rounds
Features: Features a light-gathering front sight, windage and elevation adjustable rear sight; triple-locking cylinder; easy takedown
MSRP. $719

SMITH & WESSON MODEL 460 XVR BONE COLLECTOR

SMITH & WESSON MODEL 460 XVR BONE COLLECTOR

Action: SA/DA
Grips: Synthetic
Barrel: 7.5 in.
Sights: Front fiber optic green, rear adjustable
Weight: 4 lb. 13 oz.
Caliber: .460 S&W Mag.
Capacity: 5 rounds
Features: Highest muzzle velocity of any production revolver on earth; XVR stands for X-treme Velocity Revolver; muzzle brake; chrome teardrop hammer; limited edition; ChromeTrigger; gun rug and sling included
MSRP $1680

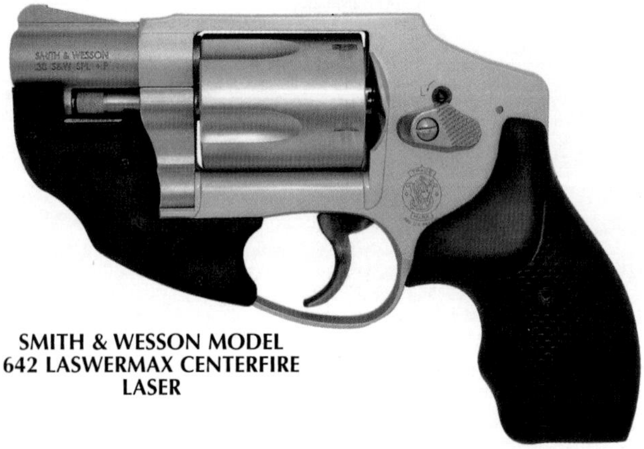

SMITH & WESSON MODEL 642 LASWERMAX CENTERFIRE LASER

SMITH & WESSON MODEL 642 LASERMAX CENTERFIRE LASER

Action: DAO
Grips: Synthetic
Barrel: 1.88 in.
Sights: Fixed front, integral rear
Weight: 15.5 oz.
Caliber: .38 S&W Special +P
Capacity: 5 rounds
Features: Enables positive target acquisition and enhances accuracy in low-light conditions; no-snag, hammerless design; rapid target acquisition of the LaserMax sighting system; matte silver finish
MSRP $539

SMITH & WESSON M&P9 SHIELD CRIMSON TRACE GREEN LASERGUARD

SMITH & WESSON M&P9 SHIELD CRIMSON TRACE GREEN LASERGUARD

Action: Semiautomatic
Grips: Synthetic
Barrel: 3.1 in.
Sights: Fixed
Weight: 19 oz.
Caliber: 9mm
Capacity: 7 or 8 rounds
Features: Striker fire action; white dot front sight; stainless steel slide and barrel
MSRP $589

SMITH & WESSON M&P9
CARBON FIBER FINISH

SMITH & WESSON M&P40
CARBON FIBER FINISH

SPRINGFIELD ARMORY 1911
LOADED BLACK OPERATOR

SMITH & WESSON M&P9 CARBON FIBER FINISH

Action: Semiautomatic
Grips: Synthetic
Barrel: 4.25 in.
Sights: Fixed
Weight: 24 oz.
Caliber: 9mm
Capacity: 17+1 rounds
Features: Three interchangeable palmswell grip sizes; ambidextrous controls; 18-degree grip angle; white dot front sight; stainless steel barrel and slide

MSRP $599

SMITH & WESSON M&P40 CARBON FIBER FINISH

Action: Semiautomatic
Grips: Synthetic
Barrel: 4.25 in.
Sights: Fixed
Weight: 24.25 oz.
Caliber: .40 S&W
Capacity: 15+1 rounds
Features: Three interchangeable palmswell grip sizes; ambidextrous controls; 18-degree grip angle; white dot front sight; stainless steel barrel and slide

MSRP $599

SPRINGFIELD ARMORY 1911 LOADED BLACK OPERATOR

Action: Semiautomatic
Grips: Synthetic
Barrel: 5 in.
Sights: Fixed
Weight: 43 oz.
Caliber: .45 ACP
Capacity: 8 rounds
Features: Forged steel; integral accessory rail; black Armory Kote; low profile combat, 3-dot tritium; GI style recoil system

MSRP $1399

SPRINGFIELD ARMORY 1911
MARINE CORPS OPERATOR

SPRINGFIELD ARMORY 1911
RANGE OFFICER CHAMPION

SPRINGFIELD ARMORY XD MOD.2
SUB-COMPACT WITH GRIP ZONE

SPRINGFIELD ARMORY 1911 MARINE CORPS OPERATOR

Action: Semiautomatic
Grips: Synthetic
Barrel: 5 in.
Sights: Fixed
Weight: 43 oz.
Caliber: .45 ACP
Capacity: 7 rounds
Features: Forged steel; integral accessory rail; olive drab Armory Kote; low profile combat, 3-dot tritium; GI style recoil system
MSRP. $1299

SPRINGFIELD ARMORY 1911 RANGE OFFICER CHAMPION

Action: Semiautomatic
Grips: Wood
Barrel: 4 in.
Sights: Fixed
Weight: 30 oz.
Caliber: .45 ACP
Capacity: 7 rounds
Features: Grips are Cross Cannon double diamond cocobolo; fiber optic front and low profile combat rear; dual spring recoil system with full length guide rod
MSRP. $899

SPRINGFIELD ARMORY XD MOD.2 SUB-COMPACT WITH GRIP ZONE

Action: Semiautomatic
Grips: Rubber
Barrel: 3–3.3 in.
Sights: Fixed
Weight: 26–27 oz.
Caliber: 9mm, .40 S&W, .45 ACP
Capacity: 9 or 13 rounds
Features: Captive recoil spring with full length guide rod; fiber optic front and low profile combat rear
MSRP. . . . .$565–$629

STI INTERNATIONAL DVC OPEN

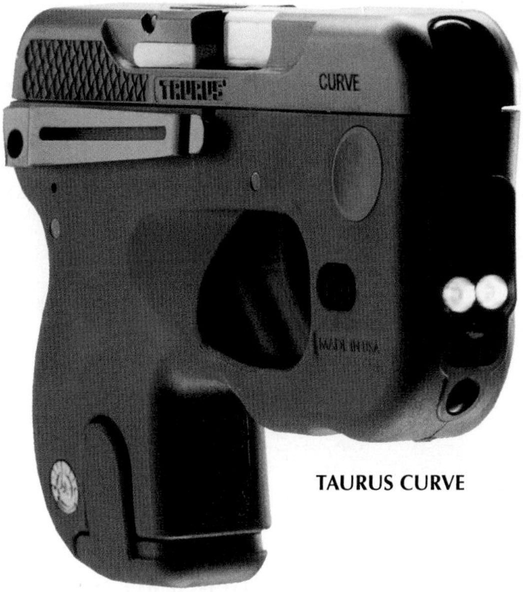

TAURUS CURVE

TAURUS MILLENIUM G2

STI INTERNATIONAL DVC OPEN

Action: Semitautomatic
Grips: Synthetic
Barrel: 5 in.
Sights: None
Weight: 48 oz.
Caliber: .38 Super, 9mm
Capacity: 15, 17, 20, 26 rounds
Features: 2.5 lb. trigger; Dawson tool-less guide rod; hard chrome finish; titanium nitride finish barrel and compensator; reversible, dual detent slide racker; mounted C-More 6 MOA dot sight
MSRP $3699

TAURUS CURVE

Action: DAO
Grips: Polymer
Barrel: 2.5 in.
Sights: None
Weight: 10.2 oz.
Caliber: .380 ACP
Capacity: 6+1 rounds
Features: Curved form; features Taurus Security System (TSS); light and laser built in
MSRP $392

TAURUS MILLENIUM G2

Action: Semiautomatic
Grips: Polymer
Barrel: 3.2 in.
Sights: Adjustable
Weight: 22 oz.
Caliber: 9mm
Capacity: 12+1 rounds
Features: Loaded chamber indicator; blue finish; Taurus Security System; accessory rail
MSRP $317

TRISTAR ARMS P-100

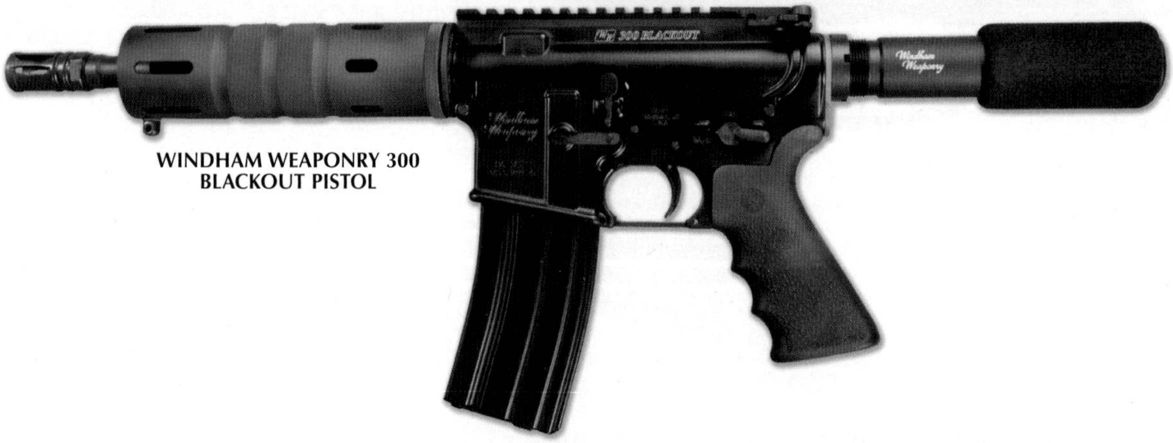

WINDHAM WEAPONRY 300 BLACKOUT PISTOL

TRISTAR ARMS P-100

Action: Semiautomatic
Grips: Polymer
Barrel: 3.7 in.
Sights: Fixed front, rear dovetail
Weight: 2 lb. 5 oz.
Caliber: 9mm, .40 S&W
Capacity: Detachable box, 11–15 rounds
Features: Steel frame and steel slide; double/single action; rear snag free dovetail sights and fixed blade front sight; Picatinny rail built into frame; Cerakote finish and black polymer checkered grips
MSRP. $489

WINDHAM WEAPONRY 300 BLACKOUT PISTOL

Action: Semiautomatic gas impingment system
Grips: Rubber
Barrel: 9 in.
Sights: None
Weight: 4 lb. 14 oz.
Caliber: .300 BLK
Capacity: Detachable box, 30+1 rounds
Features: Quick-detach swing swivel; 1:7 inch twist; Picatinny rail; hardcoat black anodize reciever finish with laser caliber identification; chrome-Lined barrel with A2-type flash suppressor
MSRP. $1160

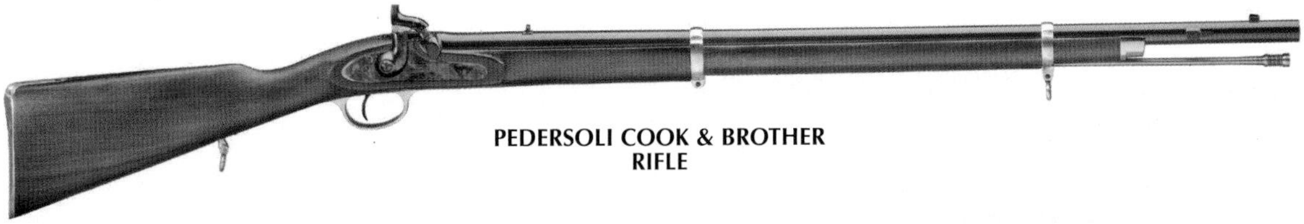

PEDERSOLI COOK & BROTHER RIFLE

PEDERSOLI HAWKEN HUNTER RIFLE

PEDERSOLI TRADITIONAL HAWKEN TARGET RIFLE

TRADITIONS FIREARMS PURSUIT G4 ULTRALIGHT

PEDERSOLI COOK & BROTHER RIFLE

Lock: Muzzleloading
Stock: Wood
Barrel: 33 in.
Chokes: IC, M, F
Sights: Fixed
Weight: 8 lb. 10 oz.
Bore/Gauge: .58
Features: Brass garnitures; brown colour barrel; walnut stock
MSRP $1195

PEDERSOLI HAWKEN HUNTER RIFLE

Lock: Muzzleloading
Stock: Wood
Barrel: 28.4 in.
Chokes: IC, M, F
Sights: Adjustable rear, fixed front
Weight: 8 lb. 10 oz.
Bore/Gauge: .50
Features: Blade front sight and a dovetail slot to equip it with the rear sight; ghost ring aperture sight is mounted to the tang; American walnut stock features a micro-cell thick butt plate; double set triggers
MSRP . . . . $727–$783

PEDERSOLI TRADITIONAL HAWKEN TARGET RIFLE

Lock: Muzzleloading
Stock: Wood
Barrel: 28.4 in.
Chokes: IC, M, F
Sights: Adjustable rear, fixed front
Weight: 8 lb. 10 oz.
Bore/Gauge: .50
Features: Double set trigger; adjustable buckhorn rear sight; American walnut stock is enriched with a brass patch box; left-handed version available
MSRP . . . . $644–$696

TRADITIONS FIREARMS PURSUIT G4 ULTRALIGHT

Lock: Muzzleloading
Stock: Synthetic
Barrel: 26 in.
Chokes: IC, M, F
Sights: Fixed front, adjustable rear
Weight: 5 lb. 12 oz.
Bore/Gauge: .50
Features: Wider forend for better grip and hand position; Accelerator Breech Plug; Ultralight Chromoly Tapered, Fluted Barrel with Premium CeraKote Finish; LT-1 Alloy Frame; dual safety system - internal hammer block safety and trigger block safety; speed load system; Quick-T Ramrod Handle; soft touch camo stocks; Quick Relief Recoil Pad; Williams Fiber Optic Metal Sights; fast action release button; 1:28″ twist rifling; extended ambidextrous hammer extension; drilled and tapped for a scope; sling swivel studs; 209 shotgun primer ignition; solid aluminum ramrod
MSRP $344

NEW Products: Optics

SCOPES

BUSHNELL BANNER RIMFIRE

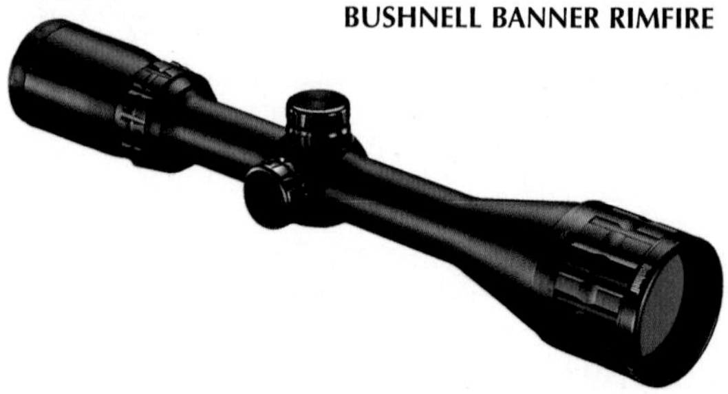

BUSHNELL ELITE LONG RANGE HUNTER

LEATHERWOOD/HI-LUX OPTICS M1200 ART

BUSHNELL RIMFIRE SERIES

Weight: 20.4 oz., 20 oz., 15 oz., 15 oz., 20.3 oz.
Length: 12.2 in., 12 in., 12.5 oz., 12 in., 12.4 in.
Power: 3–9x, 3–12x, 3.5–10x, 4–12x, 6–18X
Obj. Dia.: 40mm, 40mm, 36mm, 40mm, 40mm
Main Dia.: 1 in.
Exit Pupil: 13–4.4mm, 13–7mm, 10.3–3.6mm, 10–3.3mm, 6.6–2.2mm
Field of View @ 100 Yds: 31–9.4 ft, 33–10 ft, 30–10.4 ft, 29–11 ft, 18–5.5 ft
Twilight Factor: 10.95–18.97, 10.95–21.91, 11.23–20.78, 12.65–21.91, 15.49–26.83
Eye Relief: 3.9 in., 3.9 in., 3.4 in., 3.3 in., 3.9 in.
Features: Second focal plane; adjustable objective; multi-coated lenses; Multi-X reticle
MSRP. N/A

BUSHNELL ELITE LONG RANGE HUNTER SERIES

Weight: 24.4 oz., 26.5 oz.
Length: 13.4 in., 14.2 in.
Power: 4.5–18x
Obj. Dia.: 44mm
Main Dia.: 30mm
Exit Pupil: 12.1–3.7mm, 9.2–2.5mm
Field of View @ 100 Yds: 24.9–8.96 ft, 23.5–6 ft
Twilight Factor: 11.49–22.98, 14.07–28.14
Eye Relief: 3.74 in., 3.94 in.
Features: Fully multi-coated and ultra wide band coating; first focal plane; G2H mil or G2M MOA
MSRP. N/A

LEATHERWOOD/HI–LUX OPTICS M1200 ART

Weight: 29 oz.
Length: 15.5 in.
Power: 6–24X
Obj. Dia.: 50mm
Main Dia.: 30mm
Exit Pupil: 8.5–2mm
Field of View @ 100 Yds: 12–4 ft
Twilight Factor: 17.32–34.64
Eye Relief: 3.25 in.
Features: Auto-ranging trajectory; multi-coated lenses; second focal plane; nitrogen gas filled; waterproof; ZRO-LOK system
MSRP. $649

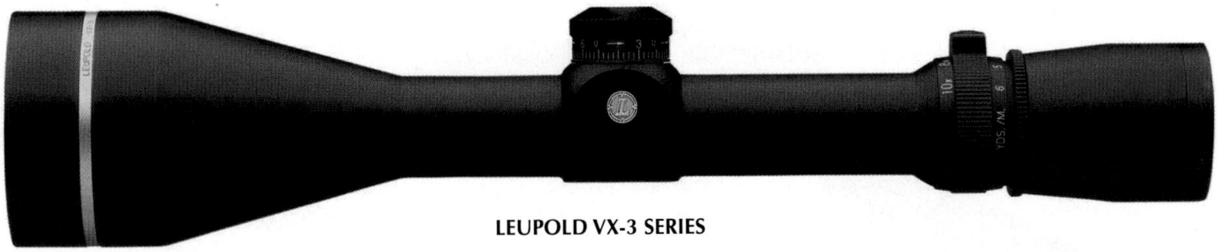

LEUPOLD VX-3 SERIES

LEUPOLD VX-3L SERIES

LEUPOLD VX-3 SERIES

Weight: 13.1 oz., 15.2 oz., 13.5 oz., 17 oz.
Length: 12.6 in., 12.3 in., 12.6 in., 12.2 in.
Power: 3.5–10X, 3.5–10X, 4.5–14X, 4.5–14X
Obj. Dia.: 40mm, 50mm, 40mm, 50mm
Main Dia.: 1 in.
Exit Pupil: N/A
Field of View @ 100 Yds: 29.8–11 ft, 29.8–11 ft, 19.9–7.4 ft, 19.1–7.4 ft
Twilight Factor: 11.83–20, 13.23–22.36, 13.42–23.66, 15–26.46
Eye Relief: 3.6–4.4 in., 3.6–4.5 in., 3.7–4.4 in., 3.6–4.4 in.
Features: Adjustable objective model available; 30mm main diameter with side focus models available; water- and fogproof; DiamondCoat 2; Xtended Twilight Lens System; Quantum Optical System
MSRP . . . . $690–$1065

LEUPOLD VX-3L SERIES

Weight: 15.2 oz, 17 oz., 22.8 oz.
Length: 12.3 in., 12.2 in., 13.1 in.
Power: 3.5–10X, 4.5–14X, 4.5–14X
Obj. Dia.: 50mm, 50mm, 56mm
Main Dia.: 1 in., 1 in., 30mm
Exit Pupil: N/A
Field of View @ 100 Yds: 29.8–11 ft, 19.1–7.4 ft, 25.5–6.8 ft
Twilight Factor: 13.23–22.36, 15–26.46, 15.88–28
Eye Relief: 3.6–4.5 in., 3.6–4.4 in., 3.3–4.4 in.
Features: Water- and fogproof; DiamondCoat 2; Xtended Twilight Lens System; Quantum Optical System; 30mm version has side focus; 3:1 zoom ratio; twin bias spring erector system
MSRP . . . . $875–$1315

NIKKO STIRLING PANAMAX SERIES

LEUPOLD VX-6 SERIES

NIGHTFORCE OPTICS ATACR F1 SERIES

LEUPOLD VX-6 SERIES

Weight: 14.6 oz., 17.8 oz., 19.2 oz., 20.7 oz.
Length: 10.7 in., 13 in., 13.5 in., 1.5 in.
Power: 1–6X, 2–12X, 3–18X, 3–18X
Obj. Dia.: 24mm, 42mm, 44mm, 50mm
Main Dia.: 30mm
Exit Pupil: N/A
Field of View @ 100 Yds: 116–19 ft, 57–10 ft, 38–7 ft, 38–7 ft
Twilight Factor: 4.9–12, 9.17–22.45, 11.49–24.14, 12.25–30
Eye Relief: 3.8 in., 3.8 in., 3.7–3.8 in., 3.7–3.8 in.
Features: Custom Dial System (CDS) for quickly dialing elevation to different sight-in ranges with a custom adjustment matched to specific ballistics information; water- and fogproof; DiamondCoat 2; Xtended Twilight Lens System; Quantum Optical System; 6:1 zoom ratio; FireDot illumination models available; side focus and illuminated side focus models available
MSRP . . . . $1375–$2500

NIGHTFORCE OPTICS ATACR F1 SERIES

Weight: 30 oz., 38 oz.
Length: 12.6 in., 15.37 in.
Power: 4–16X, 5–25X
Obj. Dia.: 42mm, 56mm
Main Dia.: 34mm
Exit Pupil: 10.3–2.7mm, 8.3–2.3mm
Field of View @ 100 Yds: 26.9–6.9 ft, 18.7–4.92 ft
Twilight Factor: 12.96–25.92, 16.73–10.58
Eye Relief: 3.35–3.54 in.
Features: Front focal plane; illumianted; multicoated lenses; eyepiece features enhanced engraving, an integrated Power Throw Lever (PTL) and an XtremeSpeed thread for making a fast diopter adjustment; adjustments are standard with the patented Nightforce Hi-Speed ZeroStop, and available in .1 Mrad (12 Mils per revolution) or .25 MOA (30 MOA per revolution) increments
MSRP . . . . $2900–$3400

NIKKO STIRLING PANAMAX SERIES

Weight: 13.1 oz., 16.6 oz., 19.6 oz.
Length: 12 in., 12.1 in., 12.5 in.
Power: 3–9X, 3–9X, 4–12X
Obj. Dia.: 40mm, 50mm, 50mm
Main Dia.: 1 in.
Exit Pupil: N/A
Field of View @ 100 Yds: 44.1–14.7 ft, 44.1–14.7 ft, 32.9–10.9 ft
Twilight Factor: 10.95–18.97, 12.25–21.21, 14.15–24.49
Eye Relief: 3.1 in.
Features: ¼ MOA Increments (7mm @ 100m); centerfire, rimfire and airgun rated; AO models available - adjustable objective from 10 yards up to infinity; half mil dot reticle; fast eye focus, illuminated reticle models available; shock- and waterpoof; nitrogen filled; multicoated lenses
MSRP . . . . N/A

NIKKO STIRLING PANAMAX
LONG RANGE SERIES

NIKKO STIRLING ULTIMAX
SERIES

SCHMIDT & BENDER
POLAR T96

NIKKO STIRLING PANAMAX LONG RANGE SERIES

Weight: 23.6 oz., 24 oz.
Length: 14.1 in., 14.5 in.
Power: 6–18X, 8–24X
Obj. Dia.: 50mm
Main Dia.: 1 in.
Exit Pupil: N/A
Field of View @ 100 Yds: 22–7.3 ft, 16.5–5.5 ft
Twilight Factor: 17.32–30, 20–34.64
Eye Relief: 3.1 in.
Features: 1/4 MOA Increments (7mm @ 100m); centerfire, rimfire and airgun rated; AO models - adjustable objective from 10 yards up to infinity; IR models - illuminated reticle models features red/green illumination; half mil dot reticle; illuminated models features glass etched reticles; fast eye focus; shock- and waterproof; nitrogen filled; multicoated lenses
MSRP . . . . N/A

NIKKO STIRLING ULTIMAX SERIES

Weight: 16.7 oz., 22.2 oz., 24.6 oz.
Length: 10.9 in., 14 in., 14.1 in.
Power: 1–6X, 2.5–10X, 3–12X
Obj. Dia.: 24mm, 50mm, 56mm
Main Dia.: 30mm
Exit Pupil: N/A
Field of View @ 100 Yds: 117.6–19.5 ft, 45.6–11.8 ft, 35.7–9.8 ft
Twilight Factor: 4.9–12, 11.18–22.36, 12.96–25.92
Eye Relief: 3.5 in., 2.8–3.1 in., 3–3.7 in.
Features: 4A illuminated reticles; fiber illumination technology for brightest and crisp dot; precise small center dot for accurate shooting; matte black finishing; 1/4 MOA (7mm @ 100m) clicks; shock- and waterpoof; nitrogen filled; multicoated lenses
MSRP . . . . N/A

SCHMIDT & BENDER POLAR T96

Weight: 22.9 oz.
Length: 13.2 in.
Power: 2.5–10x
Obj. Dia.: 50mm
Main Dia.: 34mm
Exit Pupil: 15–5mm
Field of View @ 100 Yds: 49–12.3 ft
Twilight Factor: 11.18–22.36
Eye Relief: 3.5 in.
Features: Waterproof; front or rear focal plane; illuminated; exterior parts made of anodized aluminum
MSRP . . . . N/A

SIMMONS (BY BUSHNELL) PREDATOR/VARMINT SERIES

STEINER T5XI SERIES

SWAROVSKI OPTIK X5(I)

SIMMONS (BY BUSHNELL) PREDATOR/VARMINT SERIES

Weight: 20.5 oz.
Length: 10.7 in.
Power: 1–6x
Obj. Dia.: 24mm
Main Dia.: 30mm
Exit Pupil: 11–4mm
Field of View @ 100 Yds: 105–18 ft
Twilight Factor: 4.9–12
Eye Relief: 3.9 in.
Features: Strike Zone 223 Reticle is calibrated for common .223/5.56 hunting loads; 11 illumination settings for low-light predator hunting; fully multi-coated optics provide bright, high-contrast images; SureGrip rubber on all adjustments surfaces
MSRP. $360

STEINER T5XI SERIES

Weight: 19.4 oz.; 29.8 oz.; 33 oz.
Length: 11.3 in.; 13.1 in.; 16.6 in.
Power: 1–5x; 3–15x; 5–25x
Obj. Dia.: 24mm; 50mm; 56mm
Main Dia.: 30mm; 34mm; 34mm
Exit Pupil: 11–4.8mm; 12–3.4mm; 11.2–2.3mm
Field of View @ 100 Yds: 108–21 ft; 36–7.3 ft; 21.5–4.3 ft
Twilight Factor: 4.9–10.95, 12.25–27.39, 16.73–37.42
Eye Relief: 3.5–4.3 in.
Features: The 1-5–24 is designed as a close-combat scope; medium-range 3–15x50 and long-range 5–25x56 scope come with illuminated etched glass featuring the new Special Competition Reticle (SCR) and Second Rotation Indicator that shows each mil of elevation through the indication window on the elevation turret; front focal plane
MSRP. . . . . $1610–$2300

SWAROVSKI OPTIK X5(I)

Weight: 32.1 oz.
Length: 14.8 in.
Power: 5–25x
Obj. Dia.: 56mm
Main Dia.: 30mm
Exit Pupil: 9.5–2.3mm
Field of View @ 100 Yds: 21–4.5 ft
Twilight Factor: 15.5–37.4
Eye Relief: 3.7 in.
Features: The X5(i) from SWAROVSKI OPTIK redefines accuracy; new spring retention system and turrets are part of the total package promoting accuracy and offering across the entire adjustment range an accurate impact point adjustment of ¼ or 1/8 MOA in terms of both elevation and windage (X5/X5i 5-25x56 P), even in the most extreme situations; use the SUBZERO function to go below the sight-in distance
MSRP. N/A

TRIJICON ACCUPOINT
1–6X24

TRIJICON ACCUPOINT
2.5-12.5X42

TRIJICON ACCUPOWER SERIES

TRIJICON ACCUPOINT 1–6X24

Weight: 19.2 oz.
Length: 11 in.
Power: 1–6x
Obj. Dia.: 24mm
Main Dia.: 30mm
Exit Pupil: 12–4.1mm
Field of View @ 100 Yds: 117.5–18.8 ft
Twilight Factor: N/A
Eye Relief: 3.9 in.
Features: Waterproof; illuminated; fiber optic reticle dot; several reticle options; rear focal plane
MSRP $1599

TRIJICON ACCUPOINT 2.5-12.5X42

Weight: 22.4 oz.
Length: 13.8 in.
Power: 2.5–12.5x
Obj. Dia.: 42mm
Main Dia.: 30mm
Exit Pupil: 10.6–3.3mm
Field of View @ 100 Yds: 41.3–8.3 ft
Twilight Factor: N/A
Eye Relief: 3.9 in.
Features: Waterproof; illuminated; fiber optic reticle dot; several reticle options; adjustable parallax; rear focal plane
MSRP $1399

TRIJICON ACCUPOWER SERIES

Weight: 16.2 oz; 17 oz.; 23.6 oz; 23.3 oz.
Length: 10.2 in.; 12.3 in.; 13.8 in.; 14.2 in.
Power: 1–4x; 3–9x; 2.5–10x; 4–16x
Obj. Dia.: 24mm; 40mm; 56mm; 50mm
Main Dia.: 30mm; 1 in.; 30mm; 30mm
Exit Pupil: 15–5mm; 13.3–4.4mm; 16.5–5.6mm; 9.3–3.1mm
Field of View @ 100 Yds: 97.5–24.2 ft; 35.5–11.8 ft; 37.9–10.2 ft; 25.8–6.4 ft
Twilight Factor: N/A
Eye Relief: 3.5 in.; 3.7–3.5 in.; 4 in.; 3.6–3.7 in.
Features: Waterproof; illuminated; several reticle options; adjustable parallax; rear focal plane
MSRP $999

NEW Products: Optics

VORTEX STRIKE EAGLE

Weight: 17.6 oz.
Length: 10.5 in.
Power: 1–6x
Obj. Dia.: 24mm
Main Dia.: 30mm
Exit Pupil: N/A
Field of View @ 100 Yds: 116.5–19.2 ft @ 100 yds
Twilight Factor: N/A
Eye Relief: 3.5 in.
Features: Fully multi-coated lens; illuminated, glass etched, rear focal plane reticle; water-, fog-, and shock-proof; hard anodized finish; fast focus eyepiece
MSRP. $429

VORTEX STRIKE EAGLE

SIGHTS

AIMPOINT AIMPOINT CARBINE OPTIC

AIMPOINT MICRO H-2

AIMPOINT AIMPOINT CARBINE OPTIC (ACO)

Weight: 7.8 oz.
Length: 5.1 in.
Power: 1X
Field of View @ 100 Yds: N/A
Eye Relief: N/A
Features: Developed with the modern sporting rifle owner in mind, the ACO is ready to mount and shoot directly out of the box; 30mm aluminum alloy sight tube is paired with a rugged fixed height mount designed to provide absolute co-witness with AR-15 backup iron sights; 2 MOA red-dot to allow maximum target acquisition speed and accuracy at all distances; exclusive ACET technology allows for up to one year of constant-on use from a single DL1/3N battery; completely waterproof housing.
MSRP. $393

AIMPOINT MICRO H-2

Weight: 4.8 oz.
Length: 2.7 in.
Power: 1X
Field of View @ 100 Yds: N/A
Eye Relief: N/A
Features: Advanced optical lenses for even better light transmission; can be used on shotguns, rifles, handguns or archery tackle; transparent front and rear flip-up lens covers are included; reinforced protection of the turrets for even greater ruggedness; 12 daylight settings; available in 2 MOA dot size; can be "piggybacked" on larger magnifying optics using an adapter.
MSRP. $780

BSA TACTICAL WEAPON ILLUMINATED SIGHT

BSA STEALTH TACTICAL ILLUMINATED SIGHT

LEUPOLD DELTAPOINT PRO

BSA TACTICAL WEAPON ILLUMINATED SIGHT

Weight: 22 oz.
Length: 8.75 in.
Power: 1X
Field of View @ 100 Yds: 3.7–19.3 ft
Eye Relief: 2 in.
Features: Fully multicoated optics; easy one-piece mounting; 5/8-inch Weaver-style rail; illuminated red dot; rubber eye guard; output power: 5mW; wave length: 650 nm
MSRP $100

BSA STEALTH TACTICAL ILLUMINATED SIGHT

Weight: 5 oz.
Length: 5.4 in.
Power: 1X
Field of View @ 100 Yds: 65 ft
Eye Relief: Unlimited
Features: Glass fully multicoated; multi-purpose twist-cap technology; 5/8-inch Weaver-style rail; illuminated red dot
MSRP $135

LEUPOLD DELTAPOINT PRO

Weight: 1.95 oz.
Length: 1.82 in.
Power: 1X
Field of View @ 100 Yds: N/A
Eye Relief: Unlimited
Features: Water- and fogproof; DiamondCoat; removable, adjustable rear sight; tool-less, spring actuated battery compartment; illuminated reticle available
MSRP $750

LEUPOLD D-EVO

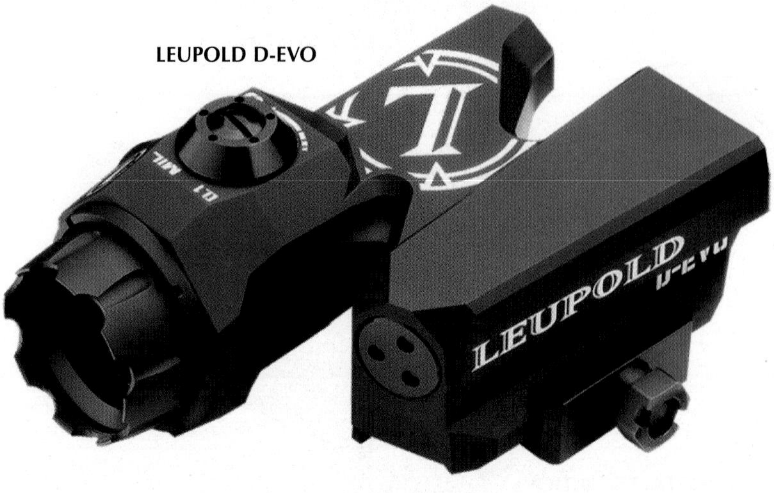

LEUPOLD LEOPOLD CARBINE OPTIC (LCO)

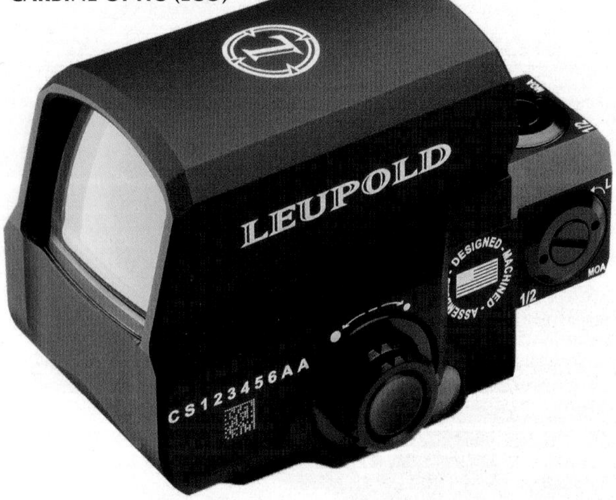

STEINER (BY BURRIS) MICRO REFLEX SIGHT (MRS)

LEUPOLD D-EVO

Weight: 13.8 oz.
Length: 4.6 in.
Power: 6X
Obj. Dia.: 20mm
Field of View @ 100 Yds: 15.7 ft
Eye Relief: 3.4 in.
Features: Bullet drop compensation; water- and fogproof; 1/10th MIL click adjustment; 6061-T6 aircraft quality aluminum
MSRP $1875

LEUPOLD LEOPOLD CARBINE OPTIC (LCO)

Weight: 9.5 oz.
Length: 3.6 in.
Power: 1X
Obj. Dia.: 32mm
Field of View @ 100 Yds: N/A
Eye Relief: Unlimited
Features: Nitrogen filled; water- and fogproof; ½ MOA field click; 6061-T6 aircraft quality aluminum
MSRP $1250

STEINER (BY BURRIS) MICRO REFLEX SIGHT (MRS)

Weight: 2.5 oz.
Length: N/A
Power: 1X
Field of View @ 100 Yds: N/A
Eye Relief: Unlimited
Features: Picatinny mount; waterproof; holographic sight; adjustable for windage and elevation; illuminated
MSRP . . . . N/A

VORTEX VENOM

VORTEX VIPER

VORTEX VENOM

Weight: 1.1 oz.
Length: 1.9 in.
Power: 1X
Field of View @ 100 Yds: N/A
Eye Relief: Unlimited
Features: Bright red dot; Picatinny mount; 3 MOA dot; machined aluminum housing
MSRP $329

VORTEX VIPER

Weight: 1.37 oz.
Length: 1.8 in.
Power: 1X
Field of View @ 100 Yds: N/A
Eye Relief: Unlimited
Features: Bright red dot; Picatinny mount; 6 MOA dot
MSRP $329

NEW Products: Rangefinders

HALO OPTICS XTANIUM 600

HALO OPTICS XTANIUM 1000

HALO OPTICS XTANIUM 600

Weight: N/A
Power: 8X
Obj. Dia.: N/A
Range: up to 600 yd
Features: OLED display for easy use (organic light emitting diode); AI Technology accounts for slope to the target; scan mode allows for constant ranging; precise to +/- 1 yard; water resistant
MSRP $275

HALO OPTICS XTANIUM 1000

Weight: N/A
Power: 8X
Obj. Dia.: N/A
Range: up to 1000 yd
Features: OLED display for easy use (organic light emitting diode); AI Technology accounts for slope to the target; scan mode allows for constant ranging; precise to +/- 1 yard; water resistant
MSRP $330

BARNES BULLETS RANGEAR

Features: Higher velocity, flatter trajectory, and ultimate accuracy at an affordable price; first quality factory-fresh brass paired with a lead-free, copper-jacketed, zinc core OTFB (Open Tip Flat Base) projectile; zinc core provides excellent performance in ARs with quick twist barrels; specialized propellants optimized for ARs ensure that RangeAR offers superior performance in these high performance platforms of any barrel length

Available in: 5.56x45mm, .300 AAC BLK

Box 200: . . . . N/A

BARNES BULLETS RANGEAR

CCI AMMUNITION A17 VARMINT TIP

Features: Optimized for feeding and function in the Savage Arms A17 semiautomatic rifle and can be fired through bolt-action .17 HMR firearms; 100 fps faster than other .17 HMR loads of the same weight; Varmint Tip bullet provides rapid expansion; CCI-made and primed case

Available in: .17 HMR

Box 200: $67

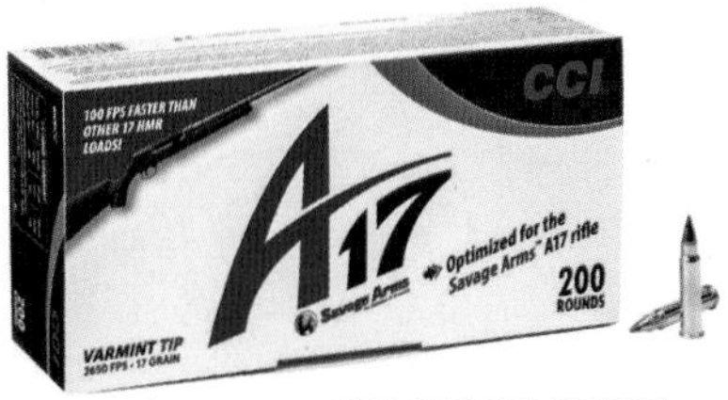

CCI AMMUNITION A17 VARMINT TIP

FEDERAL PREMIUM 3RD DEGREE

Features: Uses a multi-shot, three-stage payload and the exclusive FLITECONTROL¬Æ wad to deliver forgiving, lethal patterns; FLITECONTROL wad is designed for use with standard choke tubes

Available in: 12 (3 in., 3 ½ in.); Shot sizes: 5, 6, 7

Box: . . . . N/A

GECO RIMFIRE AMMUNITION

Features: Target shooters can always depend on the cartridges perfect functioning, consistent performance and good precision.; reliable rimfire ammunition to guarantee required standards of accuracy at a favorable price

Available in: .22 LR Rifle, .22 LR Semi-Auto

Box 50:. . . . . $5–$8

FEDERAL PREMIUM 3RD DEGREE

GECO SUPER MATRIX AMMUNITION

Features: The entire line of GECO Super Matrix for pistols, shotguns and rifles, retains the same point of impact, along with the same perceived recoil and muzzle flash as standard duty rounds. By micro-pulverizing into a fine powder upon impact, GECO Super Matrix frangible bullets, buckshot, and slugs will not harm steel targets or other valuable range equipment. By eliminating back splatter, 100% bullet containment in indoor ranges is guaranteed.

Available in: .223 Win. , .308 Win, 9mm, .38 Special, .357 Sig, .40, .45, 12 ga. slug, 12 ga. pellet

Box 50:. . . . . $8–$26

HORNADY 17 WINCHESTER SUPER MAGNUM

Features: 20 grain V-Max bullet that provides tack-driving accuracy; muzzle velocity of 3,000 feet per second; fills the gap between the rimfire 17 HMR and centerfire 17 Hornet

Available in: .17 WSM (20 gr.)

Box 50:. $22

GECO RIMFIRE AMMUNITION

GECO SUPER MATRIX AMMUNITION

HORNADY 17 WINCHESTER SUPER MAGNUM

HORNADY AMERICAN GUNNER

HORNADY AMERICAN WHITETAIL RIFLED SLUG

HORNADY CRITICAL DEFENSE LITE

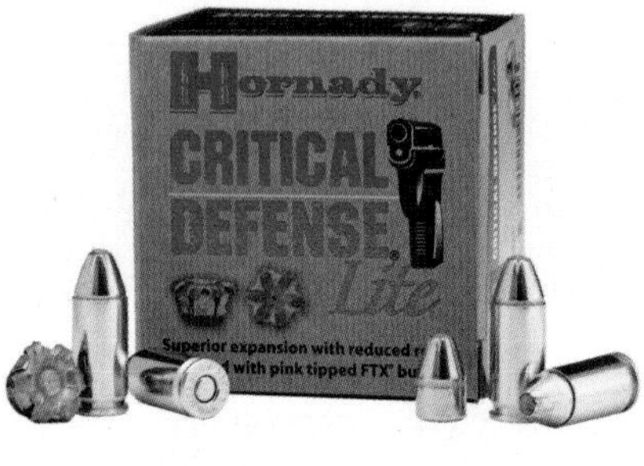

HORNADY AMERICAN GUNNER

Features: XTP (eXtreme Terminal Performance) bullets are exceptionally accurate and deliver excellent versatility and superior ballistic performance; propellants are matched to each load to ensure optimal pressure, velocity, volume and consistency from lot to lot; high quality primers and Hornady cases combine to deliver consistent shooting in the field

Available in: .380 ACP (90 gr.), 9mm (115 gr.), 9mm+P (124 gr.), .38 Spl. (125 gr.), .357 Mag. (125 gr.), .40 S&W (180 gr.), .45 ACP (185 gr.)

Box 20–25: $22

HORNADY AMERICAN WHITETAIL RIFLED SLUG

Features: Rifled slug for smooth-bore barrels; 12 gauge 1-ounce rifled, foster style slug; hollow point, tough lead-alloy core; 1,600 feet per second

Available in: 12 Ga.

Box 5:. $11

HORNADY CRITICAL DEFENSE LITE

Features: Highly effective reduced recoil load for all shooters; 27 percent reduction in recoil; 10-inch penetration through FBI heavy clothing test with .550–.590-inch expansion; cycles in semiautomatics; excellent choice for compact, lightweight handguns; same point of aim/point of impact as standard Critical Defense loads; PINK Flex Tip—portion of the proceeds go to help fund breast cancer research

Available in: 9mm (100 gr.)

Box 25:. $28

HORNADY FULL BOAR

Features: Hard hitting Hornady GMX bullets for deep penetration and maximum weight retention; monolithic, copper alloy bullets deliver controlled expansion and 95+ percent weight retention; excellent fit, feed and function in ARs and other semi-autos; California compatible and approved for use in other areas requiring the use of non-traditional bullets

Available in: .223 Rem. (50 gr.), .243 Win. (80 gr.), 6.8 SPC (100 gr.), .270 Win. (130 gr.), 7mm Rem. Mag. (139 gr.), .308 Win. (165 gr.), .30-06 Spfd. (165 gr.), .300 Win. Mag. (165 gr.)

Box 20: . . . . $29–$57

WINCHESTER AMMUNITION AA STEEL

Features: Steel shot; high-strength hull; AA wads

Available in: 12 (2¾ in.); Shot sizes: 7.5, 8

Box: . . . . N/A

WINCHESTER AMMUNITION BLIND SIDE MAGNUM PHEASANT

Features: High Packing density for increased powder charge with hinged wad results in 1675 fps; high velocity HEX Shot allows reduced leads and increased pellet energy; diamond cut wad design provides choke responsiveness for increased kill zone; Drylok Super Steel System keeps your powder dry

Available in: 12 (2 ¾ in., 3 in.)

Box: . . . . N/A

HORNADY FULL BOAR

WINCHESTER AMMUNITION AA STEEL

WINCHESTER AMMUNITION BLIND SIDE MAGNUM PHEASANT

WINCHESTER AMMUNITION BLIND SIDE MAGNUM WATERFOWL

Features: High Packing density for increased powder charge with hinged wad results in 1675 fps; high velocity HEX Shot allows reduced leads and increased pellet energy; diamond cut wad design provides choke responsiveness for increased kill zone; Drylok Super Steel System keeps your powder dry

Available in: 12 (2 ¾ in., 3 in., 3 ½ in.), 20 (3 in.)

Box: .... N/A

WINCHESTER AMMUNITION ROOSTER LOK'D & LETHAL XR

Features: Protects shot during in-bore acceleration; shot launches from barrel near perfectly round for extremely tight long-range patterns; greater penetration over standard lead loads beyond 50 yards; devastating terminal on-target performances

Available in: 12 (2 ¾ in., 3 in.)

Box: .... N/A

WINCHESTER AMMUNITION DEER SEASON XP

Features: Large diameter polymer tip accelerates bullet expansion; built specifically for deer hunting and taking down big bucks; alloyed leather core; contoured jacket

Available in: .243 Win., .270 Win., 270 WSM, .30-06 Spfd., .300 Win. Mag., .300 WSM, .308 Win., 7mm Rem. Mag.

Box: .... N/A

WINCHESTER AMMUNITION BLIND SIDE MAGNUM WATERFOWL

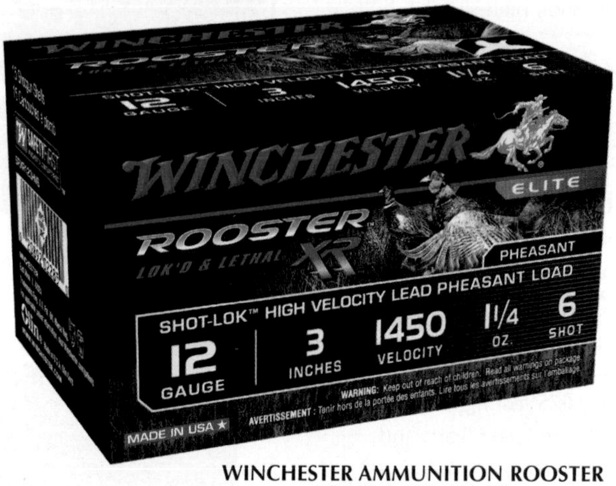

WINCHESTER AMMUNITION ROOSTER LOK'D & LETHAL XR

WINCHESTER AMMUNITION DEER SEASON XP

SWIFT A-FRAME MUZZLELOADING BULLETS

Features: Muzzleloader and heavy revolver A-Frame bullets are one in the same; initiate expansion at 950 feet per second, expand to .65x their original caliber, and maintain 97% of their weight; virtually indestructible at velocities in excess of 3000 feet per second
Available in: .50 (240, 300 gr.); .54 (265, 325 gr.)
Box: S18

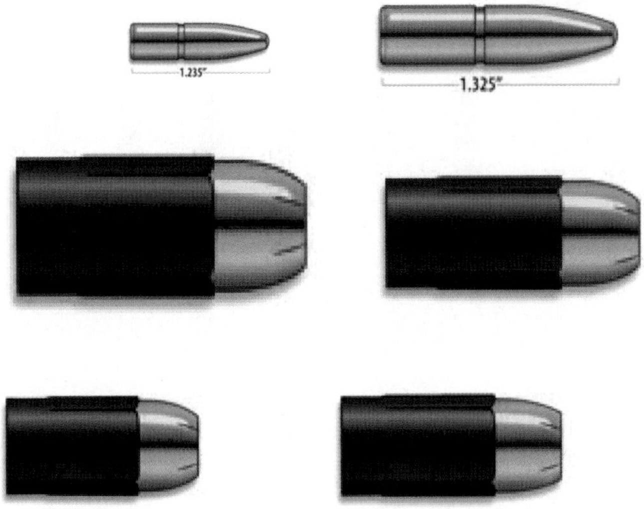

SWIFT A-FRAME MUZZLELOADING BULLETS

SIERRA BULLETS TIPPED MATCHKING

Features: The acetal resin tip reduces drag, produces a more favorable ballistic coefficient, and helps reliable feeding in magazine fed firearms; having heavier jackets than Sierra's Hornet or Blitz line of bullets, these bullets will not provide the same explosive expansion on small varmints

Available in: .224 (69, 77 gr.); .308 (125, 155, 168, 175 gr.)

Box: . . . . $31–$46

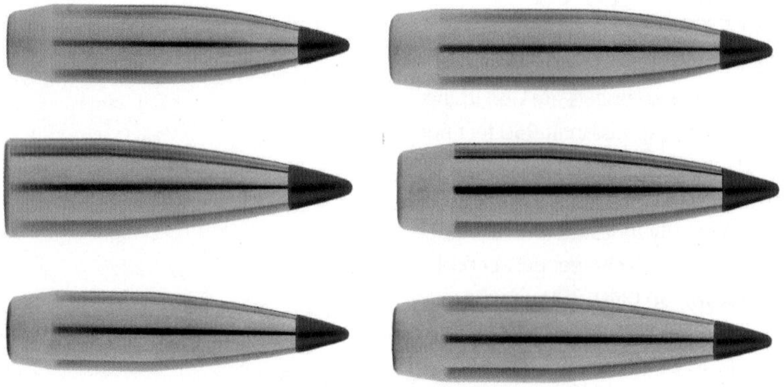

SIERRA BULLETS TIPPED MATCHKING

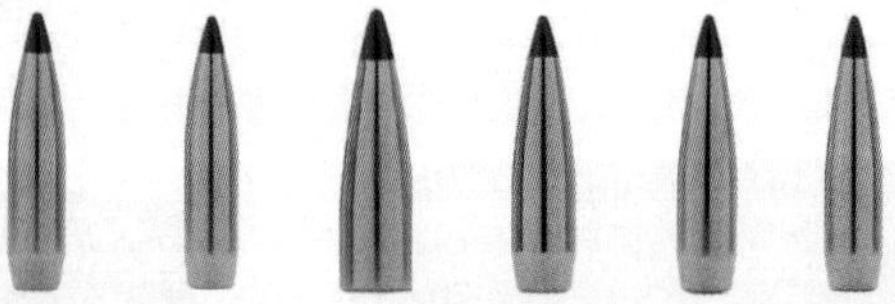

MATCHKING

Caliber & Description	224	224	308	308	308	308
Diameter, Inches	.224	.224	.308	.308	.338	.308
Weight, Grains	69	77	125	155	168	175
Density	.169	.219	.188	.233	.253	.264
Ballistic Coefficient						
Catalog Number	7169	7177	7725C	7755	7768	7775

08 Adcore Defense
08 Advanced Armament Corp.
09 American Tactical
09 J. G. Anschütz
11 ArmaLite
14 Arsenal Firearms
14 Arsenal, Inc.
16 Auto-Ordnance
17 Barrett
18 Benelli USA
18 Beretta USA
18 Blaser USA
20 Browning
24 Bushmaster Firearms Internat'l
27 Century International Arms
128 C&H Precision
129 Chiappa Firearms
30 Chipmunk Rifles
31 Christensen
31 Cimarron Firearms Co.
33 Citadel by Legacy Sports
33 Colt's Manufacturing Company
35 Connecticut Valley Arms (CVA)
36 Cooper Firearms
38 CZ-USA (Ceska Zbrojovka)
142 Dakota Arms
143 Daniel Defense
144 Del-ton
144 Dixie Gun Works
145 DPMS Panther Arms
150 E.M.F. Company
151 E.R. Shaw
151 Excel Arms
152 FNH USA
153 Heckler & Koch
154 Henry Repeating Arms
157 High Standard
157 Hi-Point Firearms
157 Howa by Legacy Sports
159 H-S Precision
159 I.O. Inc.
160 Jarrett Rifles
160 J.P. Sauer & Sohn
161 Kel-Tec
162 Kimber
164 Krieghoff
164 Kriss
165 K-VAR
165 Lazzeroni Rifles
166 Les Baer Custom
167 Magnum Research
168 Marlin
170 MasterPiece Arms
170 Maunz Match Rifles
172 Mauser
172 McMillan
173 Merkel
174 Montana Rifles
175 Mossberg
177 Nesika
178 New Ultra Light Arms
178 Noreen
179 Nosler
180 Noveske
180 Olympic Arms
180 Patriot Ordnance
181 Pedersoli
182 Primary Weapons Systems
182 Purdey
183 Remington Arms
189 Rifles Inc.
190 Rock River Arms
193 Rossi
196 Ruger
200 Sako
204 Savage Arms
208 Sig Sauer
209 Smith & Wesson
212 Springfield Armory
213 Stag Arms
214 Steyr Arms
215 Szecsei & Fuchs Fine Guns
216 Tactical Rifles
216 Taurus
217 Taylor's & Co. Firearms
218 Thompson/Center
219 Tikka
220 Troy Defense
220 Turnbull Manufacturing Co.
221 Uberti
224 Volquartsen Custom
224 Weatherby
228 Wilson Combat
228 Winchester Repeating Arms

RIFLES

Adcor Defense

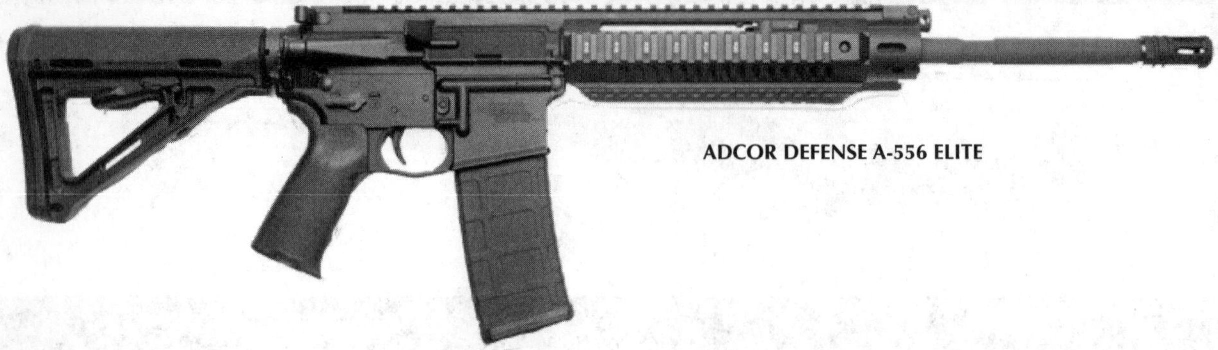

ADCOR DEFENSE A-556 ELITE

A-556 ELITE
Action: Semiautomatic
Stock: Synthetic
Barrel: 10.5 in.–20 in.
Sights: None
Weight: 6 lb. 7 oz.–7 lb. 13 oz.
Caliber: 5.56 NATO
Magazine: Detachable box, 30 rounds
Features: Custom rifle stock; custom ergonomic rifle grip with aggressive texturing; forward placed, reversible/ambidextrous charging handle; gas piston system with multi-position regulator; free-floating barrel; ejection port dust wiper; two-piece keyed quad-rail system; tool-free field strip design
MSRP. $2295

Advanced Armament Corp.

ADVANCED ARMAMENT CORP. MULTI PURPOSE WEAPON (MPW)

MULTI PURPOSE WEAPON (MPW)
Action: Semiautomatic
Stock: Magpul CTR
Barrel: 9 in., 12.5 in., 16 in.
Sights: None
Weight: N/A
Caliber: 7.62x35mm (300 BLK)
Magazine: Detachable box, 30 rounds
Features: Bolt carrier features a proprietary design with a modified cam path and nickel-boron finish to enhance reliability and ease of cleaning; bolt machined from Carpenter 158 steel; freefloating forearm; lower receiver features a Geissele two-stage trigger; six-position Mil-Spec collapsing stock
MSRP. $1600

American Tactical

AMERICAN TACTICAL GSG MP-40 CARBINE

GSG MP-40 CARBINE

Action: Semiautomatic
Stock: Metal
Barrel: 17.2 in.
Sights: Fixed
Weight: 9 lb.
Caliber: .22LR
Magazine: Detachable box, 10 or 28 rounds
Features: Bakelite support under the barrel; adjustable iron sights; simple safety features; all metal construction; blued finish
MSRP. $500

AMERICAN TACTICAL OMNI HYBRID 5.56

OMNI HYBRID 5.56

Action: Semiautomatic
Stock: Synthetic
Barrel: 16 in.
Sights: None
Weight: 7 lb.
Caliber: 5.56 NATO
Magazine: Detachable box, 10 or 30 rounds
Features: Picatinny rail; retractable stock
MSRP. $645

J. G. Anschütz

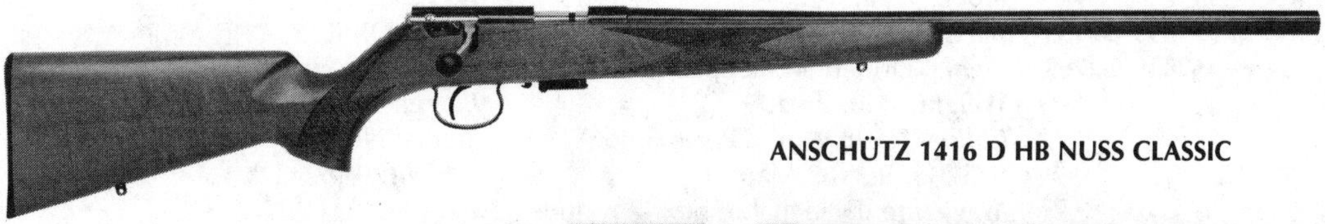

ANSCHÜTZ 1416 D HB NUSS CLASSIC

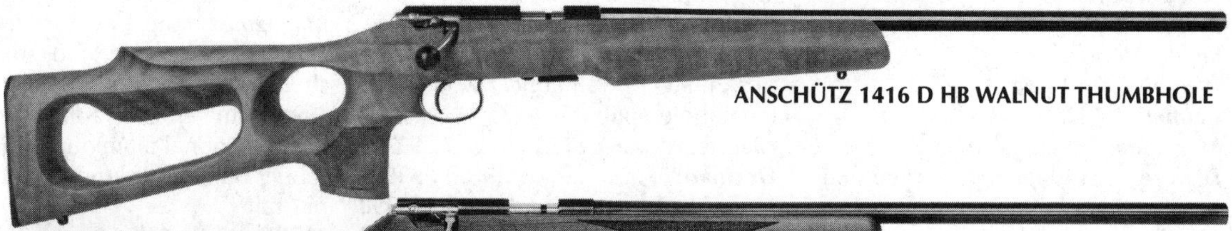

ANSCHÜTZ 1416 D HB WALNUT THUMBHOLE

ANSCHÜTZ 1517 D HB NUSS CLASSIC

1416 D HB

Action: Bolt
Stock: Walnut
Barrel: 23 in.
Sights: None
Weight: 6 lb. 7 oz.
Caliber: .22LR
Magazine: Detachable box, 5 rounds
Features: Heavy barrel; lacquered walnut wood stock (optional beaver-tail); pistol grip; black buttplate; studs for sling swivel; lateral sliding safety
MSRP. $1099

1416 D HB WALNUT THUMBHOLE

Action: Bolt
Stock: Walnut
Barrel: 23 in.
Sights: None
Weight: 6 lb. 7 oz.
Caliber: .22 LR
Magazine: Detachable box, 5 rounds
Features: Luxus repeating rifle; single-stage trigger; black buttplate; carved German checkering on the pistol grip; sling swivel studs; wave-style V-block dovetail rail for telescopic sight
MSRP. $1517

1517

Action: Bolt
Stock: Walnut, hardwood
Barrel: 22 in.
Sights: None
Weight: 6 lb. 2 oz.–8 lb. 9 oz.
Caliber: .17 HMR
Magazine: Detachable box, 4 rounds
Features: Single- or two-stage adjustable trigger; optional beavertail stock
MSRP. . . . . $1079–$1429

J. G. Anschütz

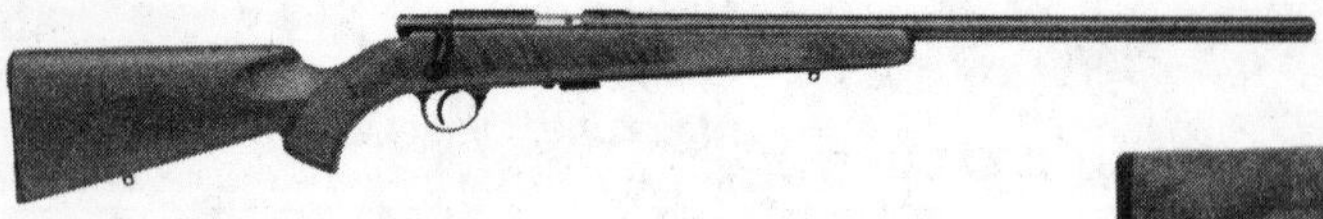

ANSCHÜTZ 1710 D HB NUSS CLASSIC

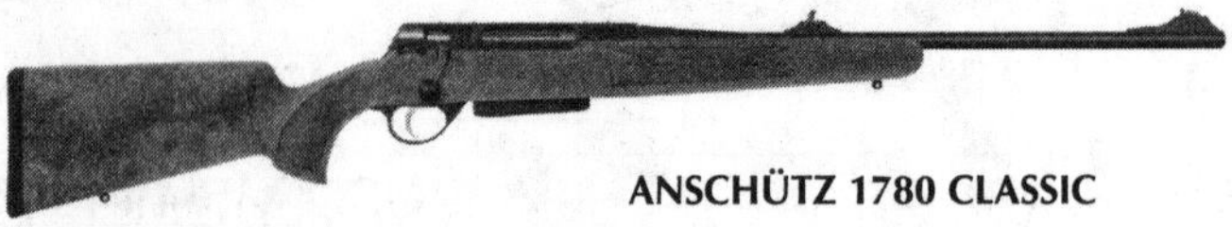

ANSCHÜTZ 1780 CLASSIC

ANSCHÜTZ 1727F

ANSCHÜTZ 1903 TARGET SMALL BORE RIFLE

ANSCHÜTZ 1827 FORTNER SPRINT

ANSCHÜTZ 1907 IN 1914 STOCK

1710

Action: Bolt
Stock: Walnut
Barrel: 23 in.
Sights: Open
Weight: 7 lb. 8 oz.
Caliber: .22LR
Magazine: Detachable box, 5 rounds
Features: Drilled and tapped for scope mounts; sliding safety catch; two-stage or single-stage trigger; adjustable folding leaf sights and pear front adjustable ramp; Meistergrade has engraved forestock and trigger guard; black plastic buttplate
Classic: . . . . $1899–$2159
Monte Carlo: . . . . $2039–$2269

1727F

Action: Lever
Stock: Walnut German stock
Barrel: 22 in.
Sights: None
Weight: 7 lb. 11 oz.
Caliber: .17 HMR
Magazine: Internal, 4 rounds
Features: Two-stage trigger; precision barrel; rubber buttplate
MSRP $3409

1770

Action: Bolt
Stock: Walnut
Barrel: 22 in.
Sights: Drilled and tapped for scopes
Weight: 7 lb. 11 oz.
Caliber: .223 Rem.
Magazine: Detachable, 3-shot, in-line
Features: Six locking lug action for strength and reliability; adjustable, single-stage match trigger; hand checkered stock with oval cheekpiece and rubber buttpad; detachable sling swivel studs
MSRP $2499

1780

Action: Bolt
Stock: Walnut
Barrel: 23 in.
Sights: Drilled and tapped for scopes
Weight: 7 lb. 2 oz.
Caliber: .308 Win., .30-06 Spfd., 8x57 IS, 9.3x62 Mauser
Magazine: Detachable box, 5 rounds
Features: Single-stage trigger; fast acquisition sight; sliding safety catch; stock made of walnut heartwood, thumbhole optional
Classic: $2757
German: $3077
Thumbhole: $3398
Monte Carlo: $3495

1827 FORTNER SPRINT

Action: Bolt
Stock: Biathlon, walnut
Barrel: 22 in.
Sights: None
Weight: 8 lb. 2 oz.
Caliber: .22LR
Magazine: Detachable box, 5 rounds
Features: Combination of an extra light 1827 Fortner barreled action with the stock of the 1827 model; lacquered walnut stock with stippled checkering; heavy, cylindrical match barrel; match stage two or single trigger
MSRP $3398

1903 TARGET SMALL BORE RIFLE

Action: Bolt
Stock: Hardwood
Barrel: 26 in., heavy
Sights: None
Weight: 9 lb. 11 oz.
Caliber: .22LR
Magazine: None
Features: A match rifle for small bore shooters; anatomically perfect walnut stock with vertically adjustable cheek piece; optional aluminum, hook, or rubber buttplate; aluminum accessories rail
MSRP $1282

1907 IN 1914 STOCK

Action: Bolt
Stock: Walnut
Barrel: 32.28 in.
Sights: None
Weight: 10 lb. 12 oz.
Caliber: .22LR
Magazine: None
Features: Match 54 action; heavy, cylindrical barrel; match two-stage or single-stage trigger; safety signal pin
MSRP $3013

J. G. Anschütz

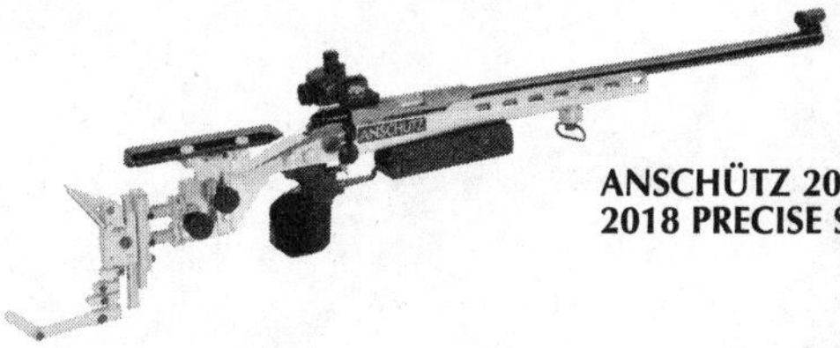

ANSCHÜTZ 2013/690 WITH 2018 PRECISE STOCK

ANSCHÜTZ MSR RX 22 BLACK

2013/690 WITH 2018 PRECISE STOCK

Action: Bolt
Stock: Aluminum
Barrel: 32 in., 33 in.
Sights: None
Weight: 13 lb., 13 lb. 10 oz.
Caliber: .22LR
Magazine: None
Features: Single loader; two-stage trigger; optional buttplate; new backend offers large range of adjustment for small shooters
MSRP $4296

MSR RX 22

Action: Semiautomatic
Stock: Laminated wood, plastic
Barrel: 16.5 in.
Sights: None
Weight: 7 lb.
Caliber: .22LR
Magazine: Detachable box, 10 rounds
Features: Folding stock; aluminum grooved Picatinny rail for accessories; six possible positions for cocking lever; optional buttplate and sight set; black, desert, aluminum colors available
Precision, Precision Black: . . . $995
Black Hawk, Desert: $895

ArmaLite

ARMALITE AR-10A A4 CARBINE

ARMALITE AR-10 SUPER SASS

AR-10A A4 CARBINE

Action: Semiautomatic
Stock: Synthetic
Barrel: 16 in.
Sights: Front
Weight: 7 lb. 14 oz.
Caliber: 7.62 NATO, .308 Win.
Magazine: Detachable box, 20 rounds
Features: Functionally identical to the AR-10B family, the AR-10A family is designed to accept early ArmaLite AR- 10 "Waffle" magazines and good quality magazines copied from them, including Magpul PMAG 20LR, Knight's Armament, and DPMS; gas block with Picatinny rail; black synthetic stock; sling, hard case, and sling swivel mounts included
MSRP $1571

AR-10 SUPER SASS

Action: Semiautomatic
Stock: Synthetic
Barrel: 20 in.
Sights: Adjustable front
Weight: 11 lb. 13 oz.
Caliber: 7.62 NATO, .308 Win.
Magazine: Detachable box, 20 rounds
Features: Functionally identical to the AR-10B family, the AR-10A family is designed to accept early ArmaLite AR- 10 "Waffle" magazines and good quality magazines copied from them, including Magpul PMAG 20LR, Knight's Armament, and DPMS; adjustable gas block front sight; black synthetic stock; sling, hard case, and sling swivel mounts included
MSRP $3099

ArmaLite

ARMALITE AR-10A SUPER SASS CARBINE

ARMALITE AR-30A1 STANDARD RIFLE

ARMALITE AR-30A1 TARGET RIFLE

RIFLES

AR-10A SUPER SASS CARBINE

Action: Semiautomatic
Stock: Synthetic
Barrel: 16 in.
Sights: None
Weight: 9 lb.
Caliber: .308 Win., 7.62 NATO
Magazine: Detachable box, 20 rounds
Features: Quad-rail Picatinny handguard; triple lapped, 416R stainless steel match barrel
MSRP $3100

AR-30A1 STANDARD RIFLE

Action: Bolt
Stock: Aluminum
Barrel: 24 in., 26 in.
Sights: None
Weight: 12 lb. 13 oz.–13 lb. 6 oz.
Caliber: .300 Win. Mag., .338 Lapua
Magazine: Detachable box, 5 rounds
Features: Cheekpiece is at the optimum height for viewing through a telescopic sight; buttstock is ergonomically correct; steel magazine; ambidestrous magazine catch; fixed stock; detachable sight rail, hard case, and sling included
MSRP . . . . $3264–$3404

AR-30A1 TARGET RIFLE

Action: Bolt
Stock: Aluminum
Barrel: 24 in., 26 in.
Sights: None
Weight: 14 lb. 8 oz.–15 lb. 5 oz.
Caliber: .300 Win. Mag., .338 Lapua
Magazine: Detachable box, 5 rounds
Features: MOA Picatinny rail over receiver and barrel; cheekpiece vertically adjustable; adjustable buttstock; 1913 accessory rail at the bottom of the buttstock; buttpad is adjustable for height
MSRP . . . . $3460–$3599

ARMALITE AR-31

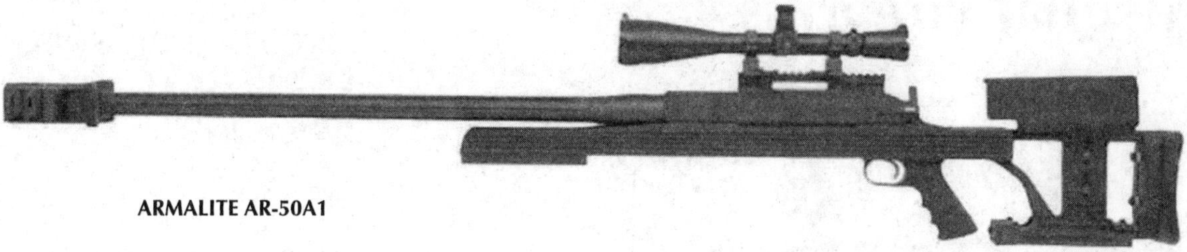

ARMALITE AR-50A1

ARMALITE M-15 A4 CARBINE

AR-31

***Action*: Bolt**
Stock: Synthetic
Barrel: 24 in.
Sights: None
Weight: 14 lb.
Caliber: .308 Win.
Magazine: Detachable box, 10 rounds
Features: Can use 5, 10, 15, 20, and 25 round magazines
MSRP $3460

AR-50A1

Action: Bolt
Stock: Synthetic
Barrel: 33 in.
Sights: None
Weight: 33 lb. 3 oz.
Caliber: .50 BMG
Magazine: None
Features: Chromoly barrel; muzzle-brake; 15 minute rail; single-stage trigger
MSRP $3359

M-15 A4 CARBINE

Action: Semiautomatic
Stock: Synthetic
Barrel: 16 in.
Sights: None
Weight: 6 lb. 7 oz.
Caliber: 7.62x39 Warsaw
Magazine: Detachable box, 10 rounds
Features: Forged flattop with Picatinny rail; forged aluminum receiver; tactical two-stage trigger; A2 flash suppressor; sling; black case; black or green stock
MSRP $1073

ArmaLite

ARMALITE SPR MOD 1 CARBINE

SPR MOD 1 CARBINE

Action: Semiautomatic, short gas system
Stock: Synthetic
Barrel: 16 in.
Sights: 3 detachable rails
Weight: 6 lb. 8 oz.
Caliber: .223 Rem., 6.8 SPC, 7.62x39 Warsaw
Magazine: Detachable box, 30 rounds
Features: Muzzle flash suppressor; black synthetic tactical stock; aluminum handguard; tactical two-stage trigger, sling; black case
MSRP $1589

Arsenal Firearms

ARSENAL FIREARMS SPECIAL PURPOSE RIFLE (SPR-1)

SPECIAL PURPOSE RIFLE (SPR-1)

Action: Bolt
Stock: Synthetic
Barrel: 24 in.
Sights: None
Weight: 11 lb. 8 oz.
Caliber: .300 Win., .308 Win. Mag., 6.5-284 Norma
Magazine: Detachable box, 3, 5, or 10 rounds
Features: Fluted barrel; protected muzzle thread for flash hider/suppressor; Picatinny rails; stock with adjustable cheek piece and adjustable rubber shoulder pad, available in Black, Olive Drab or Desert Tan (solid colours) or three variants of Desert Camo, Multi Terrain Camo and Arctic Camo
MSRP $3950

Arsenal, Inc.

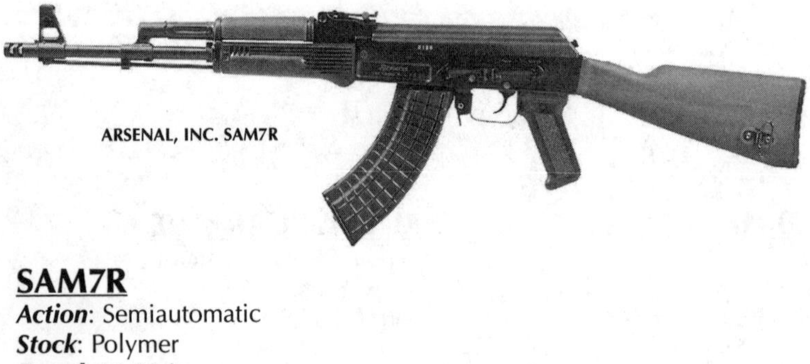

ARSENAL, INC. SAM7R

SAM7R

Action: Semiautomatic
Stock: Polymer
Barrel: 16.25 in.
Sights: Scope rail
Weight: 8 lb.
Caliber: 7.62x39 Warsaw
Magazine: Detachable box, 10 rounds
Features: Milled receiver; chrome-lined, hammer-forged barrel; muzzle brake; cleaning rod; intermediate length US-made 10 in. trapdoor buttstock
MSRP $1299

SAM7UF

Action: Semiautomatic
Stock: Metal underfolding
Barrel: 16.25 in.
Sights: Adjustable
Weight: 7 lb. 8 oz.
Caliber: 7.62x39 Warsaw
Magazine: Detachable box, 10 rounds
Features: Milled and forged receiver; chrome lined hammer forged barrel; muzzle nut, bayonet/accessory lug; reinforced underfolding buttstock; black polymer pistol grip and handguards; stainless steel heat shield
MSRP $1299

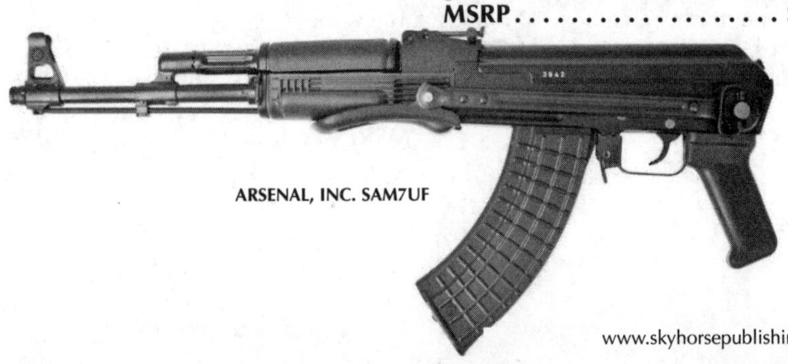

ARSENAL, INC. SAM7UF

RIFLES

SA RPK-3R

ARSENAL SA RPK-3R

Action: Gas-operated semiautomatic
Stock: Black polymer or blond wood
Barrel: 23.2 in.
Sights: Open
Weight: 10 lb. 8 oz.
Caliber: 5.45x39 Warsaw
Magazine: Detachable box, 45 rounds
Features: RPK heavy barrel; milled receiver; U.S.-made; paddle style buttstock and scope rail; includes sling, oil bottle, and cleaning kit
MSRP.................................... $2500

SLR-104FR

Action: Semiautomatic
Stock: Synthetic
Barrel: 16.25 in.
Sights: Adjustable
Weight: 6 lb. 2 oz.
Caliber: 5.45x39 Warsaw
Magazine: Detachable box, 30 rounds
Features: Left-sided folding stock; muzzle brake; bayonet and accessory lugs; scrope rail; sling; two-stage trigger; available in 5.56 NATO and 7.62x39 Warsaw
MSRP.................................... $1099

SLR-104UR

Action: Semiautomatic
Stock: Synthetic
Barrel: 16.25 in.
Sights: Fixed
Weight: 6 lb.
Caliber: 5.45x39 Warsaw
Magazine: Detachable box, 30 rounds
Features: Stamped receiver; short gas system; front sight block/gas block combination; black polymer furniture; stainless steel heat shield; left-side folding polymer stock; two stage trigger; scope rail
MSRP.............................$1299

SLR-106F

Action: Semiautomatic
Stock: Synthetic
Barrel: 16.25 in.
Sights: Scope rail
Weight: 7 lb. 5 oz.
Caliber: 5.56 NATO
Magazine: Detachable box, 5 rounds
Features: Stamped receiver; chrome-lined, hammer-forged barrel; bayonet lug; stainless steel heat shield handguards; left-side folding buttstock; also available in desert sand color
MSRP.............. $1049

ARSENAL, INC. SLR-104FR

ARSENAL, INC. SLR-104UR

ARSENAL, INC. SLR-106F

Auto-Ordnance

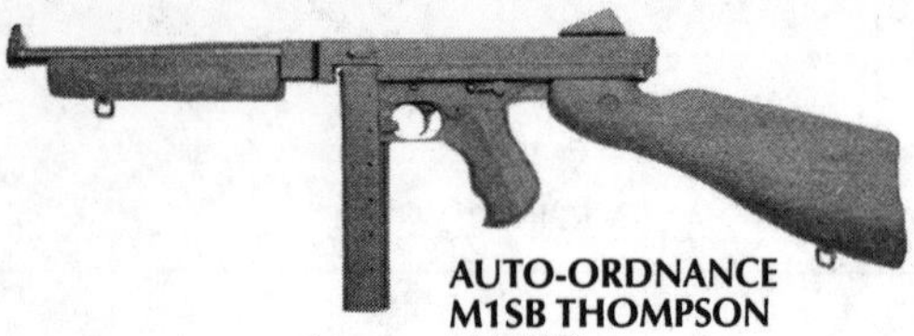

AUTO-ORDNANCE M1SB THOMPSON M1 SBR

AUTO-ORDNANCE AOM150

AUTO-ORDNANCE T1 THOMPSON 1927 A-1

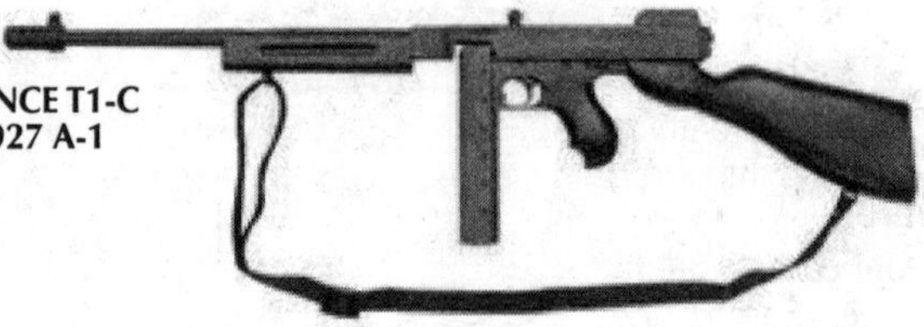

AUTO-ORDNANCE T1-C THOMPSON 1927 A-1 COMMANDO

AUTO-ORDNANCE T1SB THOMPSON 1927 A-1 SBR SHORT BARREL RIFLE

AUTO-ORDNANCE TM1 THOMPSON M1 CARBINE

AOM150

Action: Semiautomatic
Stock: Walnut; handguard
Barrel: 18 in.
Sights: Blade front; flip style rear
Weight: 5 lb. 6 oz.
Caliber: .30
Magazine: Detachable stick, 15 rounds
Features: Folding stock; Parkerized finish
MSRP $933

M1SB THOMPSON M1 SBR

Action: Semiautomatic
Stock: Walnut, vertical foregrip
Barrel: 10.5 in.
Sights: Blade front, fixed battle rear
Weight: 10 lb. 8 oz.
Caliber: .45 ACP
Magazine: Detachable stick, 30 rounds
Features: Will not accept drum magazines; frame and receiver made from solid steel
MSRP $2027

T1 THOMPSON 1927 A-1

Action: Semiautomatic
Stock: Walnut, vertical foregrip
Barrel: 16.5 in.
Sights: Blade front, open rear adjustable
Weight: 13 lb.
Caliber: .45 ACP
Magazine: Detachable stick, 30 rounds
Features: Frame and receiver made from solid steel; compensator; optional 50-round drum magazine
MSRP $1461

T1-C THOMPSON 1927 A-1 COMMANDO

Action: Semiautomatic
Stock: Black finish stock and forend
Barrel: 16.5 in.
Sights: Blade front, open rear adjustable
Weight: 13 lb.
Caliber: .45 ACP
Magazine: Detachable stick, 30 rounds
Features: Frame and receiver made from solid steel; compensator; black nylon sling
MSRP $1393

T1SB THOMPSON 1927 A-1 SBR SHORT BARREL RIFLE

Action: Semiautomatic
Stock: Walnut, vertical foregrip
Barrel: 10.5 in.
Sights: Blade front, open rear adjustable
Weight: 12 lb.
Caliber: .45 ACP
Magazine: Detachable stick, 30 rounds
Features: Frame and receiver made from solid steel; blued steel finish
MSRP $2114
Detachable butt stock: $2630

TM1 THOMPSON M1

Action: Semiautomatic
Stock: Walnut, vertical foregrip
Barrel: 16.5 in.
Sights: Blade front, fixed battle rear
Weight: 8 lb., 11 lb. 8 oz.
Caliber: .45 ACP
Magazine: Detachable stick, 30 rounds
Features: Side bolt action; frame and receiver made from solid steel; lightweight model features a frame and receiver made from solid aluminum
MSRP $1329

Barrett

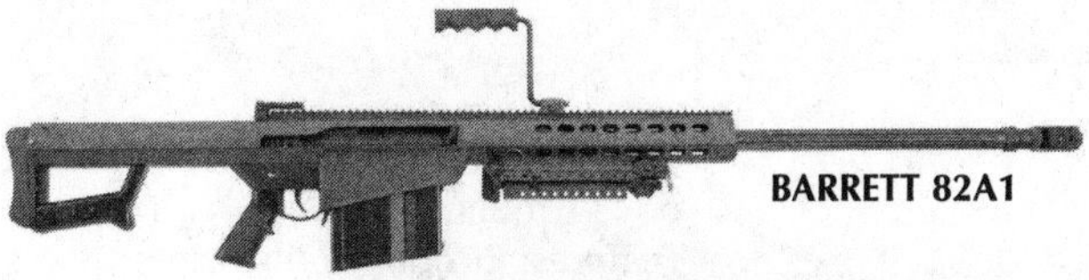
BARRETT 82A1

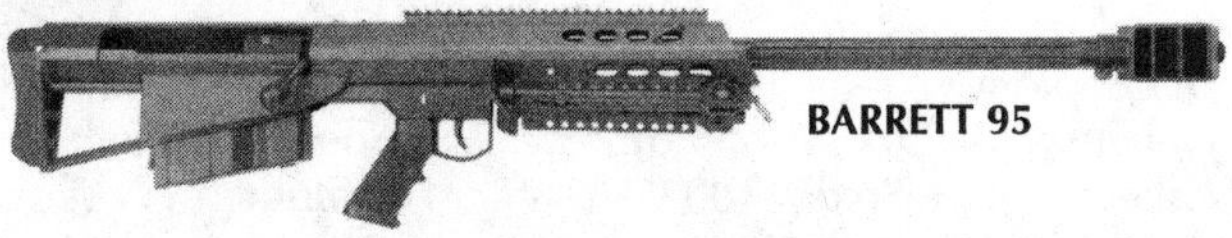
BARRETT 95

BARRETT 98B

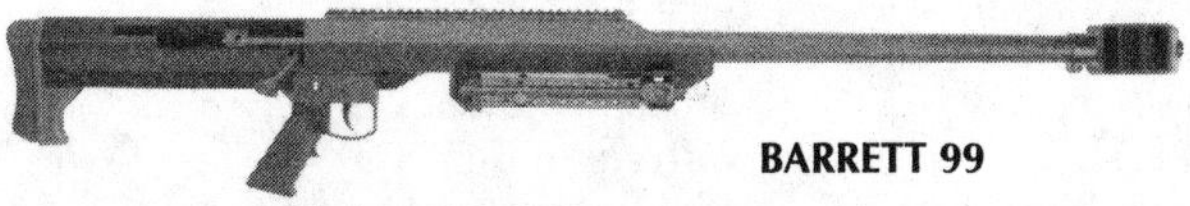
BARRETT 99

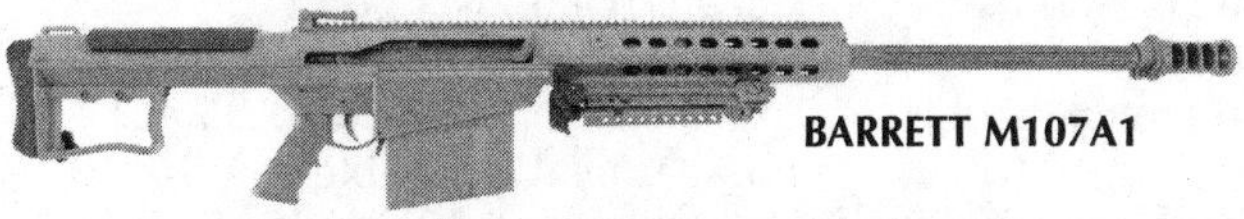
BARRETT M107A1

BARRETT MRAD

BARRETT REC7 GEN II

MODEL 82A1

Action: Semiautomatic
Stock: Synthetic
Barrel: 20 in., 29 in.
Sights: Flip-up iron sights or Leupold scope
Weight: 30 lb. 14 oz.
Caliber: .416, .50 BMG
Magazine: Detachable box, 10 rounds
Features: Pelican case; detachable adjustable bipod legs; cleaning kit; carry handle; muzzlebrake; Picatinny rail; chrome-lined barrel
MSRP. . . . . $9119–$9323

MODEL 95

Action: Semiautomatic
Stock: Synthetic
Barrel: 29 in.
Sights: Flip-up iron sights
Weight: 25 lb.
Caliber: .50 BMG
Magazine: Detachable box, 5 rounds
Features: Pelican case; detachable adjustable bipod legs; cleaning kit; Picatinny rail
MSRP. $6671

MODEL 98B

Action: Bolt
Stock: Synthetic
Barrel: 20 in., 26 in.
Sights: None
Weight: 13 lb. 8 oz.
Caliber: .338 Lapua Mag.
Magazine: Detachable box, 10 rounds
Features: Ergonomic pistol grip; muzzlebrake; heavy or fluted barrel; Harris bipod; monopod; cleaning kit; side accessory rail; air/watertight hard case; black stock
MSRP. . . . . $4927–$4980

MODEL 99

Action: Bolt
Stock: Synthetic
Barrel: 29 in., 32 in.
Sights: None
Weight: 25 lb.
Caliber: .416, .50 BMG
Magazine: None
Features: Picatinny rail; pelican case; detachable adjustable bipod; cleaning kit
MSRP. . . . . $3967–$4222

M107A1

Action: Semiautomatic
Stock: Synthetic
Barrel: 20 in., 29 in.
Sights: Flip-up iron sights
Weight: 30 lb. 14 oz.
Caliber: .50 BMG
Magazine: Detachable box, 10 rounds
Features: Chrome-lined barrel, Flat Dark Earth stock finish; suppressor-ready muzzlebrake; pelican case; M1913 optics rail; detachable adjustable lightweight bipod legs; lightweight monopod
MSRP. $12281

MRAD

Action: Bolt action repeater
Stock: Synthetic
Barrel: 17 in.–22 in.
Sights: None
Weight: 14 lb. 13 oz.
Caliber: .300 Win. Mag., .308 Win. Mag., .338 Lapua Mag.
Magazine: Detachable box, 10 rounds
Features: Fluted or heavy barrel; multi-role brown finish stock; folding stock; adjustable cheekpiece and buttplate; includes two 10-round magazines, two sling loops, and three adjustable accessory rails
MSRP. . . . . $6000–$6154

REC7 GEN II

Action: Semiautomatic
Stock: Synthetic
Barrel: 9.25 in.–18 in.
Sights: Adjustable
Weight: 6 lb.–7 lb. 3 oz.
Caliber: 5.56 NATO, 6.8 SPC
Magazine: Detachable box, 30 rounds
Features: Forged 7075 aluminum upper and lower receivers are Type 3 hard-coat anodized; free-floated, hammer-forged, chrome-lined barrel with M4 feed ramps machined into the receiver and the barrel extension; mil-spec A2 flash hider protects the muzzle
MSRP. . . . . $2835–$3159

Benelli USA

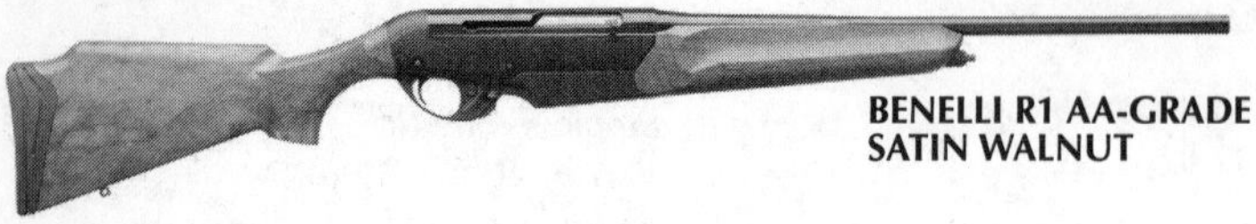

BENELLI R1 AA-GRADE SATIN WALNUT

R1

Action: Semiautomatic
Stock: AA-grade satin walnut, synthetic or Realtree APG
Barrel: 22 in., 24 in.
Sights: None
Weight: 7 lb. 2 oz.–7 lb. 5 oz.
Caliber: .30-06 Spfd., .300 Win. Mag., .338 Win. Mag.
Magazine: Detachable box, 3+1 or 4+1 rounds
Features: Picatinny rail; synthetic and APG finish come with GripTight coating; raised comb; auto-regulating gas-operated system
Walnut: $1019
ComforTech: . . . . $1139–$1249

Beretta USA

BERETTA USA ARX100

BERETTA CX4 STORM

ARX100

Action: Semiautomatic
Stock: Telescopic folding
Barrel: 12 in., 16 in.
Sights: Removable back-up sights
Weight: 6 lb. 13 oz.
Caliber: 5.56 NATO (other barrels available)
Magazine: Detachable box, 30 rounds
Features: Cold hammer forged barrel can be replaced with barrels in different lengths and calibers; case ejection switches from right to left at a button push; completely ambidextrous; technopolymer receiver; contains no pins and can be disassembled without the use of tools; optional .300 Black Out kit available
MSRP. $1950

CX4 STORM

Action: Single-action
Stock: Synthetic
Barrel: 16.6 in.
Sights: Front sight post
Weight: 5 lb. 12 oz.
Caliber: 9mm, .40 S&W, .45 ACP
Magazine: Detachable box, 10, 15, 17, 20 (9mm); 10, 11, 12, 14, 17 (40 S&W); 8 (.45 ACP) rounds
Features: Picatinny rail; allows for reverse ejection and extraction; ideal for left-handed shooters; adjustable length-of-pull; easy to accessorize
MSRP. . . . .$800–$915

Blaser USA

BLASER USA CLASSIC SPORTER

BLASER USA K95 STUTZEN BARONESSE

K95 STUTZEN BARONESSE

Action: Single shot
Stock: Walnut
Barrel: 19.75 in.
Sights: None
Weight: 5 lb. 11 oz.
Caliber: .222 Rem., 5.6R Mag., .243 Win., 6.5x57R, 7x57 R, .308 Win., .30-06 Spfd., 8x57 IRS
Magazine: None
Features: Octagonal barrel standard, barrels are interchangeable; available from grade Lexus; split forearm for continuous precision even in extreme weather; black forearm tip; range of ornamentation and game engravings
MSRP. $16931

R8 CLASSIC SPORTER

Action: Bolt
Stock: Turkish walnut
Barrel: Variable
Sights: None
Weight: Variable
Caliber: Variable
Magazine: Variable
Features: Manual cocking bolt; interchangeable caliber system; trigger magazine housing combination; Prince of Wales grip
MSRP. $4495

Blaser USA

BLASER R8 JAEGER

BLASER R8 PROFESSIONAL

BLASER R8 PROFESSIONAL SUCCESS

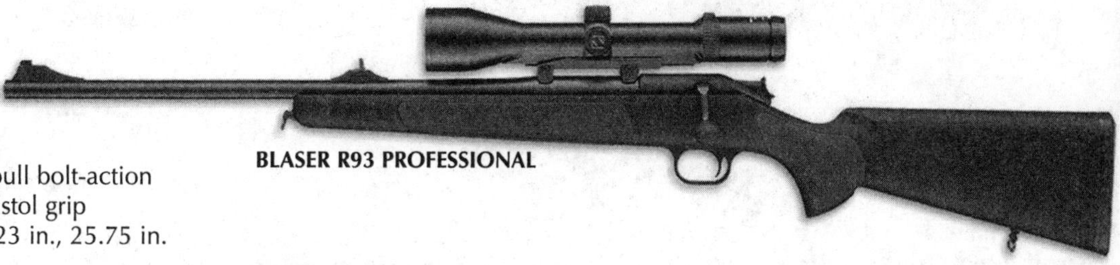

BLASER R93 PROFESSIONAL

R8 JAEGER

Action: Straight-pull bolt-action
Stock: Walnut, pistol grip
Barrel: 20.5 in., 23 in., 25.75 in.
Sights: None
Weight: 6 lb. 6 oz.
Caliber: .222 Rem. to .338 Win. Mag.
Magazine: Detachable box, 3 rounds with lock
Features: Cold-hammer-forged barrels and chambers; black forearm tip; synthetic stock in dark green or walnut, straight comb; manual cocking system; integrated trigger/magazine unit; original Blaser saddle mount
MSRP $4195

R8 PROFESSIONAL

Action: Straight-pull bolt-action
Stock: Matte dark green synthetic stock, pistol grip
Barrel: 20.5 in., 23 in., 25.75 in.
Sights: None
Weight: 6 lb. 6 oz.
Caliber: .222 Rem. to .338 Win. Mag.
Magazine: Detachable box, 3 rounds with lock
Features: Shatter-proof, synthetic dark green stock; detachable magazine/trigger unit; single-stage trigger; quick-release scope mount; ergonomically optimized pistol grip; kickstop optional; precision trigger; black forearm tip; integrated receiver
MSRP $3623

R8 PROFESSIONAL SUCCESS

Action: Bolt
Stock: Synthetic
Barrel: 22.8 in., 25.6 in.
Sights: Open
Weight: 7 lb.
Caliber: .222 Rem., .204 Ruger, .223 Rem., .22–250 Rem., .243 Win., 6XC, 6.5x55 Swedish, 6.5x57, 6.5x65 RWS, .270 Win., 7x64 Brenneke, .308 Win., .30-06 Spfd., 8x57 IS, 8.5x63, 9.3x57, 9.3x62 Mauser, 6.5x68, 7.5x55 Suisse, 8x68 S, .257 Wby. Mag., .270 Wby. Mag., .270 WSM, 7mm Blaser Mag., 7mm Rem. Mag., .300 Blaser Mag., .300 Win. Mag., .300 Wby. Mag., .300 WSM, .338 Blaser Mag., .338 Win. Mag., .375 Blaser Mag., .375 H&H
Magazine: 3+1, 4+1, 5+1 rounds
Features: Blaser precision trigger; radial locking system; ergonomically optimized stock in dark green or dark brown and elastomer grips; double loading option; leather model available
MSRP $4148
Leather: $5198

R93 PROFESSIONAL

Action: Straight-pull bolt-action
Stock: Synthetic
Barrel: 25.50 in. (Magnum), 25.59 (Ultra Magnum); 27.56 in. (Swiss Kaliber)
Sights: None
Weight: 6 lb. 6 oz.–6 lb. 13 oz.
Caliber: .222 Rem., .223 Rem., .22-250 Rem., .243 Win., 6x62 Freres, .25-06 Rem., 6.5x55 Swedish, 6.5x57, 6.5-284 Norma, 6.5x65 RWS, .270 Win., .280 Rem., 7x57, 7mm-08 Rem., 7x64, .308 Win., .30-06 Spfd., 8x57IS, 8x64 S, 8.5x63, 9.3x62 Mauser, 6.5x68, 7.5x55, 8x68 S, .257 Wby. Mag., .270 Wby. Mag., 7mm Rem. Mag., .300 Win. Mag., .300 Wby. Mag., .338 Win. Mag., .375 H&H Mag., 7mm STW, .300 Rem. Ultra Mag., 1.3x60 R
Magazine: In-line box, 2, 3, 4 rounds
Features: Anodized barrel; quick-release scope mount; shatter-proof stock comes in natural stone, slate gray, dark green, Mossy Oak camo; left-handed version optional
MSRP $3145
Left-hand versions add. $459

Blaser USA

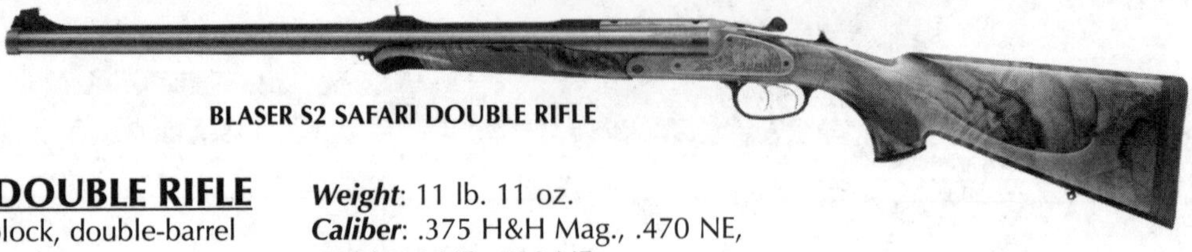

BLASER S2 SAFARI DOUBLE RIFLE

S2 SAFARI DOUBLE RIFLE

Action: Tilting block, double-barrel
Stock: Grained walnut
Barrel: 24.4 in.
Sights: None
Weight: 11 lb. 11 oz.
Caliber: .375 H&H Mag., .470 NE, .500/.416 NE, .500 NE
Magazine: None
Features: Straight Safari stock with Monte Carlo cheekpiece; kickstop; rubber recoil pad; half-beavertail forend
MSRP $11060

Browning

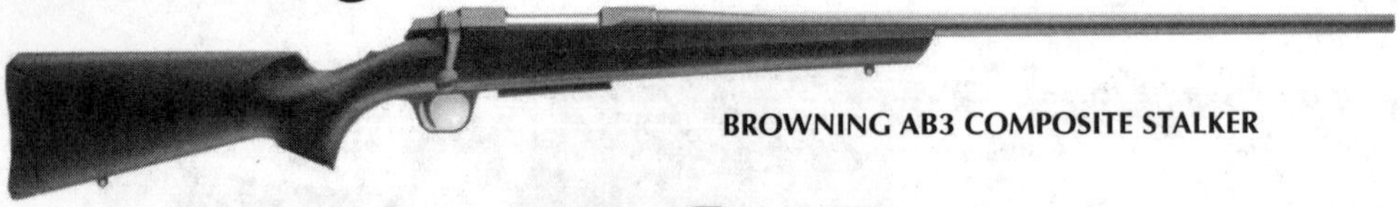

BROWNING AB3 COMPOSITE STALKER

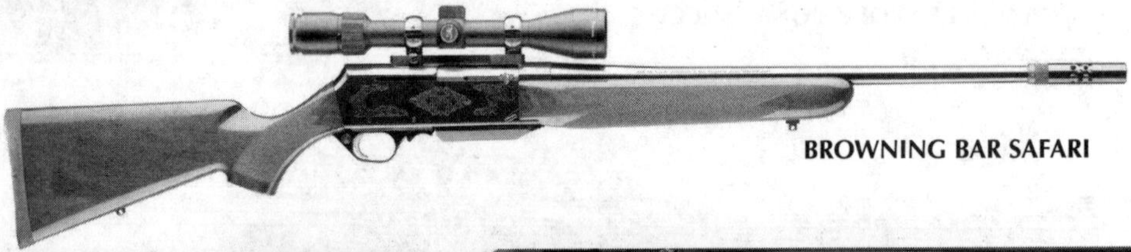

BROWNING BAR SAFARI

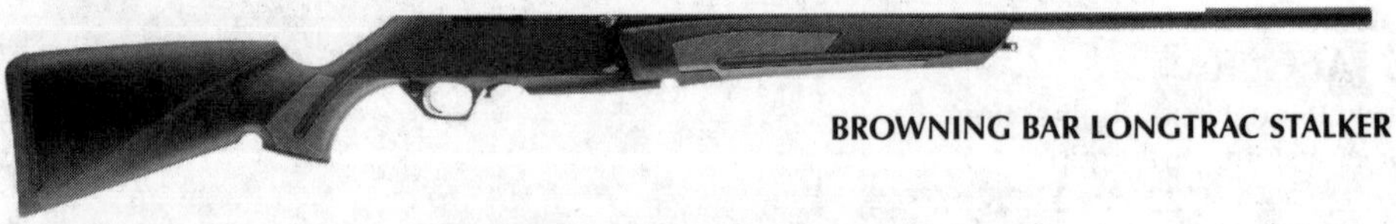

BROWNING BAR LONGTRAC STALKER

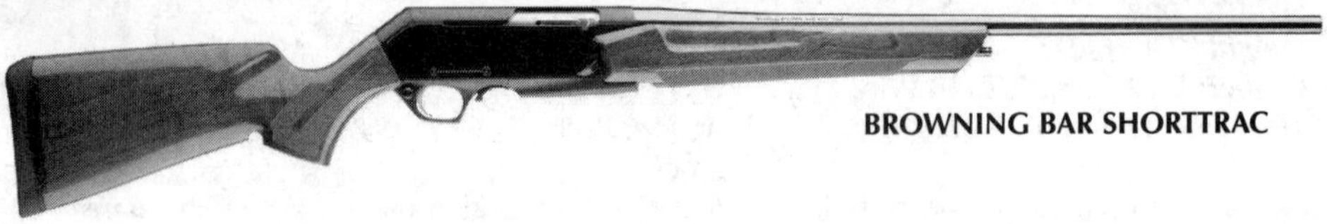

BROWNING BAR SHORTTRAC

AB3 COMPOSITE STALKER

Action: Bolt
Stock: Synthetic
Barrel: 22 in., 26 in.
Sights: None
Weight: 6 lb. 13 oz.
Caliber: .243 Win., .270 WSM, .30-06 Spfd.; 7mm Rem. Mag., .300 Win. Mag., .300 WSM, . 308 Win., 7mm-08 Rem.
Magazine: Detachable box, 4 rounds
Features: Inflex Technology recoil pad; top tang safety; blued barrel and action
MSRP $600

BAR LONGTRAC STALKER

Action: Gas-operated semiautomatic
Stock: Composite
Barrel: 22 in., 24 in.
Sights: None
Weight: 6 lb. 15 oz.–7 lb. 8 oz.
Caliber: .270 Win., .30-06 Spfd., 7mm Rem. Mag., .300 Win. Mag.
Magazine: Detachable box
Features: Aircraft-grade alloy receiver with matte blued finish; drilled and tapped for scope mounts; hammer-forged; multi-lug rotary bolt; composite stock in matte black finish; gripping panels; recoil pad; composite trigger guard and floor plate
MSRP . . . .$1260–$1340

BAR SAFARI

Action: Gas-operated semiautomatic
Stock: Walnut
Barrel: 22 in., 23 in., 24 in.
Sights: None
Weight: 7 lb. 6 oz.–8 lb. 6 oz.
Caliber: .243 Win., .308 Win., .25-06 Rem., .270 Win., .30-06 Spfd., 7mm Rem. Mag., .300 Win. Mag., .338 Win. Mag., .270 Win. (BOSS), 7mm Rem. Mag. (BOSS), .300 Win. Mag. (BOSS), .338 Win. Mag. (BOSS), .300 WSM (BOSS), .270 WSM (BOSS), 7mm WSM (BOSS)
Magazine: Detachable box
Features: Checkered, select gloss finish walnut stock; steel receiver with blued finish and scroll engraving; drilled and tapped for scope mounts; multi-lug rotary bolt; recoil pad BOSS and BOSS-CR option; sling swivel studs installed
MSRP . . . .$1230–$1500

BAR SHORTTRAC

Action: Gas-operated semiautomatic
Stock: Walnut
Barrel: 23 in.
Sights: None
Weight: 6 lb. 10 oz.–7 lb. 4 oz.
Caliber: .243 Win., 7mm-08 Rem., .308 Win., .300 WSM, .270 WSM, 7mm WSM, .325 WSM
Magazine: Detachable box
Features: Oil finish walnut stock with stylized forearm; aircraft-grade alloy receiver with blued finish; drilled and tapped for scope mounts; interchangeable recoil pad
MSRP . . . .$1230–$1340

BROWNING BAR SHORTRAC HOG STALKER REALTREE MAX-1

BROWNING BAR SHORTTRAC, LEFT-HAND

BROWNING BLR LIGHTWEIGHT '81

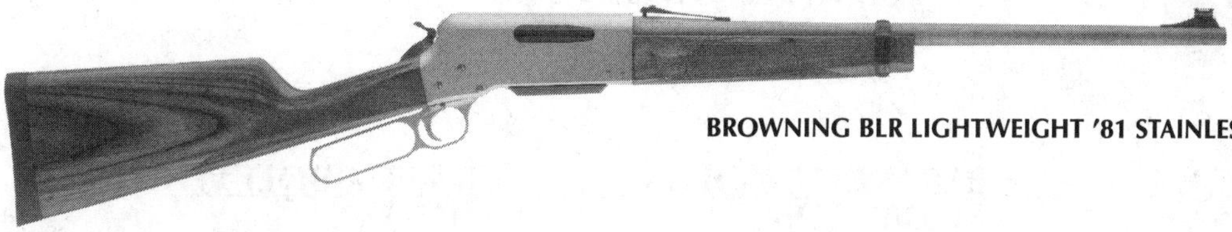

BROWNING BLR LIGHTWEIGHT '81 STAINLESS TAKEDOWN

BAR SHORTRAC HOG STALKER REALTREE MAX-1

Action: Gas-operated semiautomatic
Stock: Composite Realtree Max-1
Barrel: 20 in.
Sights: None
Weight: 9 lb. 5 oz.
Caliber: .308 Win.
Magazine: Detachable box, 10 rounds
Features: Aircraft-grade alloy receiver; drilled and tapped for scope mount; three interchangeable cheekpieces and recoil pads for different fit options; ambidextrous magazine release
MSRP $1670

BAR SHORTTRAC, LEFT-HAND

Action: Gas-operated semiautomatic
Stock: Walnut
Barrel: 22 in., 23 in.
Sights: None
Weight: 6 lb. 10 oz.–7 lb. 4 oz.
Caliber: .243 Win., 7mm-08 Rem., .308 Win., .300 WSM, .270 WSM, 7mm WSM, .325 WSM
Magazine: Detachable box
Features: Aircraft-grade alloy receiver; drilled and tapped for scope mounts; hammer-forged barrel; grade II walnut stock with oil finish; stylized, checkered forearm; sling swivel studs installed; interchangeable recoil pad
MSRP $1360

BLR LIGHTWEIGHT '81

Action: Lever
Stock: Walnut, straight grip
Barrel: 20 in., 22 in., 24 in.
Sights: None
Weight: 6 lb. 8 oz.–7 lb. 12 oz.
Caliber: .223 Rem., .22-250 Rem., .243 Win., 7mm-08 Rem., .308 Win., .358 Win., .270 Win., .30-06 Spfd., 7mm Rem. Mag., .300 Win. Mag., .300 WSM, .270 WSM, 7mm WSM, .450 Marlin, .325 WSM
Magazine: Detachable box
Features: Aircraft-grade alloy receiver; drilled and tapped for scope mounts; crowned muzzle; adjustable sights; gloss finish walnut stock; recoil pad
MSRP . . . . $960–$1040

BLR LIGHTWEIGHT '81 STAINLESS TAKEDOWN

Action: Lever-action
Stock: Laminate, straight grip
Barrel: 20 in., 22 in., 24 in.
Sights: Open
Weight: 6 lb. 8 oz.–7 lb. 12 oz.
Caliber: .223 Rem., .22-250 Rem., .243 Win., 7mm-08 Rem., .308 Win., .358 Win., .270 Win., .30-06 Spfd., 7mm Rem. Mag., .300 Win. Mag., .300 WSM, .270 WSM, 7mm WSM, .450 Marlin, .325 WSM
Magazine: Detachable box
Features: Aircraft-grade alloy receiver; drilled and tapped for scope mounts; stainless steel barrel with matte finish; gray laminate wood stock in satin finish; recoil pad; separates for storage or transportation; optional Scout-style scope mount; TRUGLO/Marble's fiber optic front sight
MSRP . . . . $1230–$1300

Browning

BROWNING BLR LIGHTWEIGHT STAINLESS

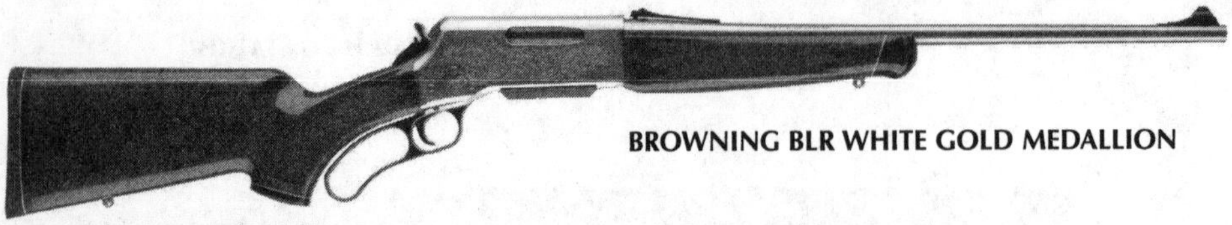

BROWNING BLR WHITE GOLD MEDALLION

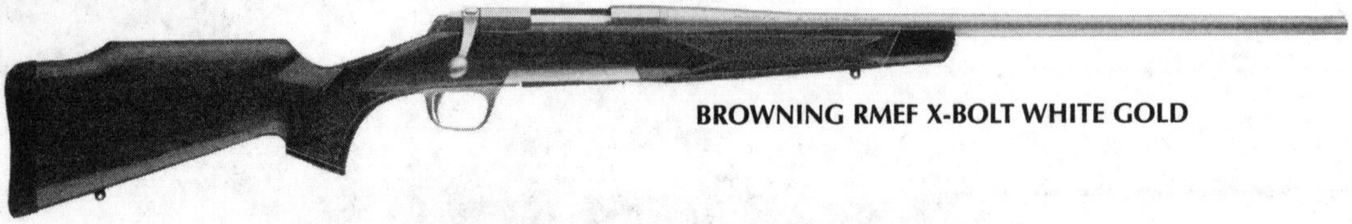

BROWNING RMEF X-BOLT WHITE GOLD

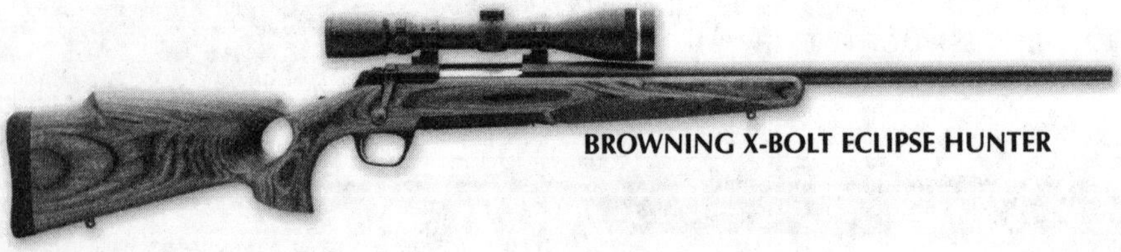

BROWNING X-BOLT ECLIPSE HUNTER

RIFLES

BLR LIGHTWEIGHT STAINLESS

Action: Lever-action
Stock: Walnut, pistol grip
Barrel: 20 in., 22 in., 24 in.
Sights: None
Weight: 6 lb. 8 oz.–7 lb. 12 oz.
Caliber: .223 Rem., .22-250 Rem., .243 Win., 7mm–08 Rem., .308 Win., .358 Win., .270 Win., .30-06 Spfd., .300 Win. Mag., .300 WSM, .270 WSM, 7mm WSM, .450 Marlin, .325 WSM
Magazine: Detachable box
Features: Aircraft-grade alloy receiver; drilled and tapped for scope mounts; steel barrel with matte finish; crowned muzzle; adjustable sights; gloss finish walnut stock with pistol grip; sling swivel studs installed; recoil pad
MSRP . . . . $1100–$1180

BLR WHITE GOLD MEDALLION

Action: Lever-action
Stock: Walnut, pistol grip
Barrel: 20 in., 22 in.
Sights: Open
Weight: 6 lb. 8 oz.–6 lb. 12 oz.
Caliber: .243 Win., 7mm-08 Rem., .308 Win., .300 WSM, .270 WSM
Magazine: Detachable box
Features: Aircraft-grade aluminum receiver with nickel finish; high-relief engraving on receiver; drilled and tapped for scope mounts; crowned muzzle; stainless steel barrel; stock comes in grade IV/ V walnut with a checkered pistol grip and forearm; rosewood forend cap; silver pistol grip cap; adjustable sights; recoil pad; sling swivel studs installed
MSRP . . . . $1470–$1550

RMEF X-BOLT WHITE GOLD

Action: Bolt
Stock: Walnut
Barrel: 23 in.
Sights: None
Weight: 7 lb. 3 oz.
Caliber: .325 WSM
Magazine: Detachable rotary box
Features: Monte Carlo stock; stainless steel barrel and receiver, receiver etched in gold; raised cheekpiece; Inflex technology recoil pad; adjustable feather trigger; top-tang safety with bolt unlock button
MSRP $1540

X-BOLT ECLIPSE HUNTER

Action: Bolt
Stock: Wood laminate
Barrel: 22 in., 23 in., 24 in., 26 in.
Sights: None
Weight: 6 lb. 7 oz.–7 lb. 8 oz.
Caliber: .25-06 Rem., .243 Win., .270 Win., .270 WSM, .30-06 Spfd., .300 Win. Mag., .300 WSM, .308 Win., 7mm Rem. Mag., 7mm-08 Rem.
Magazine: Detachable box, 4 rounds
Features: Inflex Technology recoil pad
MSRP . . . . $1020–$1060

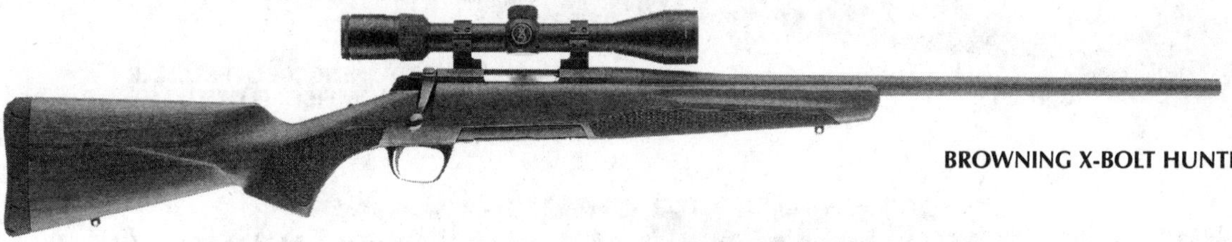

BROWNING X-BOLT HUNTER

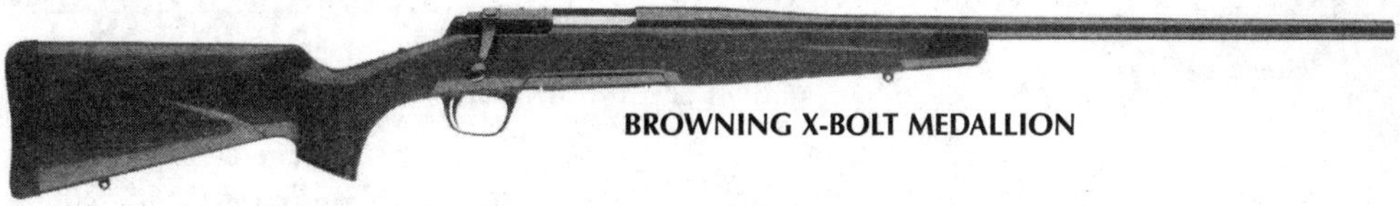

BROWNING X-BOLT MEDALLION

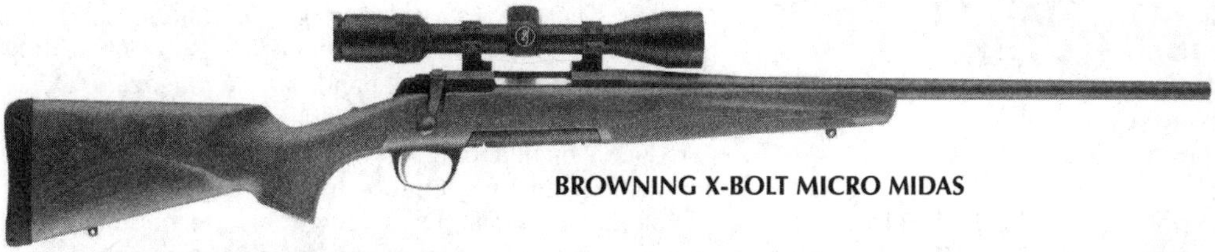

BROWNING X-BOLT MICRO MIDAS

BROWNING X-BOLT STAINLESS STALKER

X-BOLT HUNTER

Action: Bolt
Stock: Satin finish walnut stock
Barrel: 22 in., 23 in., 24 in., 26 in.
Sights: None
Weight: 6 lb. 13 oz.–7 lb.
Caliber: .243 Win., 7mm-08 Rem., .308 Win., .25-06 Rem., .270 Win., .280 Rem., .30-06 Spfd., 7mm Rem. Mag., .388 Win. Mag., .300 WSM, .270 WSM, 7mm WSM, .325 WSM, .223 Rem., .22-250 Rem.
Magazine: Detachable rotary box
Features: Adjustable feather trigger; top-tang safety with bolt unlock button; sling swivel studs installed; Inflex technology recoil pad
MSRP . . . . $900–$950

X-BOLT MEDALLION

Action: Bolt
Stock: Walnut
Barrel: 22 in., 23 in., 24 in., 26 in.
Sights: Open
Weight: 6 lb. 6 oz.–7 lb.
Caliber: .223 Rem., .22-250 Rem., .243 Win., .308 Win., .25-06 Rem., .270 Win., .280 Rem., .30-06 Spfd., 7mm Rem. Mag., .300 Win. Mag., .338 Win. Mag., .300 WSM, .270 WSM, 7mm WSM, .325 WSM
Magazine: Detachable rotary box
Features: Gloss finish walnut stock, rosewood forend grip and pistol cap; Inflex technology recoil pad; adjustable feather trigger; drilled and tapped for scope mounts; left-hand option
MSRP . . . . $1040–$1080
Left-hand: . . . . $1070–$1100

X-BOLT MICRO MIDAS

Action: Bolt
Stock: Walnut
Barrel: 20 in.
Sights: None
Weight: 6 lb. 1 oz.
Caliber: .243 Win., 7mm-08 Rem., .308 Win., .22-250 Rem.
Magazine: Detachable rotary magazine
Features: Drilled and tapped for scope mounts, low-luster blued finish, free-floating barrel; adjustable feather trigger; top-tang safety; left-hand option
MSRP $860

X-BOLT STAINLESS STALKER

Action: Bolt
Stock: Composite
Barrel: 22 in., 23 in., 24 in., 26 in.
Sights: None
Weight: 6 lb. 3 oz.–6 lb. 13 oz.
Caliber: .243 Win., 7mm-08 Rem., .308 Win., .25-06 Rem., .270 Win., .280 Rem., .30-06 Spfd., 7mm Rem. Mag., .300 Win. Mag., .388 Win. Mag., .300 WSM, .270 WSM, 7mm WSM, .325 WSM, .223 Rem., .22-250 Rem.
Magazine: Detachable rotary box
Features: Composite stock in matte black with textured gripping surfaces; Dura-Touch armor coating; adjustable feather trigger; top-tang safety; bolt unlock button; palm swell
MSRP . . . . $1140–$1800

Browning

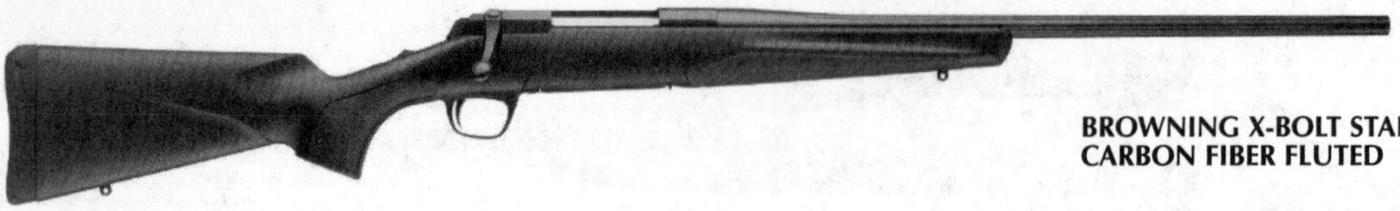

BROWNING X-BOLT STALKER CARBON FIBER FLUTED

BROWNING X-BOLT VARMINT SPECIAL STAINLESS

X-BOLT STALKER CARBON FIBER FLUTED

Action: Bolt
Stock: Composite
Barrel: 22 in., 23 in., 26 in.
Sights: None
Weight: 6 lb. 3 oz.–6 lb. 11 oz.
Caliber: .308 Win., .270 Win., .30-06 Spfd., .300 Win. Mag., .300 WSM, .270 WSM
Magazine: Detachable rotary
Features: Matte blued receiver glass bedded; drilled and tapped for scope mounts; matte blued barrel; hand chambered; target crown; eight flutes to reduce weight and increase cooling; adjustable feather trigger; top-tang safety; bolt unlock button; Dura-Touch® armor coating; Inflex technology recoil pad; sling swivel studs installed
MSRP. . . . . $999–$1020

X-BOLT VARMINT SPECIAL STAINLESS

Action: Bolt
Stock: Altamont Paladin, black laminated
Barrel: 24 in., 26 in.
Sights: None
Weight: 8 lb. 8 oz.–8 lb. 11 oz.
Caliber: .223 Rem., .22-250 Rem., .308 Win., .300 WSM
Magazine: Detachable rotary box
Features: Stainless steel, free-floating barrel; adjustable feather trigger; top-tang safety; bolt unlock button; Inflex technology recoil pads; sling swivel studs installed
MSRP. $1070

Bushmaster Firearms Internat'l

300 AAC BLACKOUT

Action: Semiautomatic
Stock: Magpul ACS stock
Barrel: 16 in.
Sights: None
Weight: 6 lb. 9 oz.
Caliber: 300 BLK
Magazine: Accepts all AR-types
Features: A compact 30-caliber solution for the AR platform; sound and flash suppression; use existing AR magazines; low-profile milled gas block; Magpul MOW grip; quad rail; Magpul enhanced trigger guard
MSRP. $1471

.308 HUNTER

Action: Semiautomatic
Stock: Synthetic
Barrel: 20 in.
Sights: None
Weight: 8 lb. 6 oz.
Caliber: .308 Win., 7.62 NATO
Magazine: Detachable box, 5 rounds
Features: Two riser blocks, A2 grip on Vista; free-floating, vented aluminum forend; MOE trigger guard for gloved finger
MSRP. $1685

BUSHMASTER 300 AAC BLACKOUT

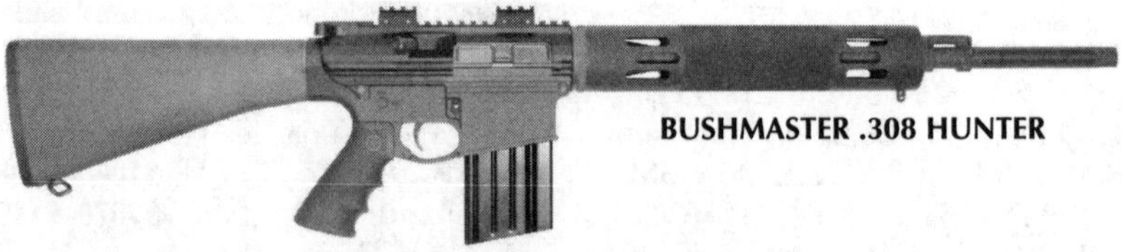

BUSHMASTER .308 HUNTER

BUSHMASTER .308 ORC

.308 ORC

Action: Semiautomatic
Stock: Synthetic
Barrel: 16 in. (carbine), 20 in. (rifle)
Sights: None
Weight: 7 lb. 12 oz.
Caliber: .308 Win., 7.62 NATO
Magazine: Detachable box, 20 rounds
Features: Milled gas block; heavy, chrome-lined barrel; A2 Birdcage flash hider; receiver-length Picatinny rail with two .5-in. optic raisers; heavy oval hand guards; six-position telescoping stock; shipped in lockable hard case with yellow safety block; black web sling included
MSRP. $1403

Bushmaster Firearms Internat'l

BUSHMASTER .450 RIFLE & CARBINE

BUSHMASTER ACR BASIC FOLDER COMBINATION

BUSHMASTER ACR DMR

BUSHMASTER A-TACS PREDATOR

BUSHMASTER M4 TYPE CARBINE

.450 RIFLE & CARBINE

Action: Semiautomatic
Stock: Synthetic, A2 pistol grip
Barrel: 16 in. (carbine), 20 in. (rifle)
Sights: None
Weight: 8 lb. 2 oz. (carbine), 8 lb. 8 oz. (rifle)
Caliber: .450 Bushmaster
Magazine: Detachable box, 5 rounds
Features: Chromoly steel barrels; free-floating aluminum forends; forged aluminum receivers; solid A2 buttstock with trapdoor storage compartment; Pictatinny rail; black web sling included; shipped in lockable hard plastic case with orange safety block
Rifle: $1485
Carbine: $1500

ACR BASIC FOLDER COMBINATION

Action: Semiautomatic
Stock: Synthetic
Barrel: 10.5 in., 14.5 in., 16.5 in.
Sights: None
Weight: N/A
Caliber: .223 Rem./5.56 NATO to 6.8mm Rem. SPC
Magazine: 30-round PMAG
Features: Cold-hammer-forged barrel with melonite coating; A2 birdcage-type hider; toolless quick-change barrel system; quick and easy multi-caliber bolt carrier assembly; free-floating Picatinny top rail for optic mounting; high-impact composite hand guard with heat shield; ambidextrous controls; composite stock comes in black or coyote
MSRP. $2552

ACR DMR (DESIGNATED MARKSMAN RIFLE)

Action: Semiautomatic
Stock: Synthetic
Barrel: 18.5 in.
Sights: None
Weight: 8 lb. 12 oz.
Caliber: 5.56 NATO
Magazine: Detachable box, 30 rounds
Features: Magpul PRS stock and MIAD grip; AAC 51T Blackout flash hider; Geissele enhanced trigger; Picatinny rail
MSRP. $2799

A-TACS PREDATOR

Action: Semiautomatic
Stock: Synthetic
Barrel: 20 in.
Sights: None
Weight: 8 lb.
Caliber: 5.56 NATO, .223 Rem.
Magazine: Detachable box, 5 rounds
Features: Coated in A-Tacs digital camouflage; fluted extra-heavy barrel with competition muzzle crown; two-stage competition trigger
MSRP. $1519

M4 TYPE CARBINES

Action: Semiautomatic
Stock: Synthetic
Barrel: 16 in.
Sights: Open
Weight: 6 lb. 3 oz.
Caliber: 5.56 NATO, .223 Rem.
Magazine: Detachable box, 30 rounds (accepts all M16/ AR15 type)
Features: Six-position telestock; "Izzy" flash suppressor; hard chrome-lined barrels are designed to accept M203 grenade launcher; A2 receiver has 300–800 meter rear sight system; shipped in lockable hard case with orange safety block
A2: $1368

Bushmaster Firearms Internat'l

MOE 308 ENHANCED ORC

Action: Semiautomatic
Stock: Synthetic
Barrel: 16 in.
Sights: None
Weight: 9 lb.
Caliber: .308 Win., 7.62 NATO
Magazine: Detachable box, 20 rounds
Features: Magpul PRS stock and MIAD grip
MSRP. $1599

BUSHMASTER MOE 308 ENHANCED ORC

BUSHMASTER MOE 308 MID-LENGTH

BUSHMASTER PREDATOR

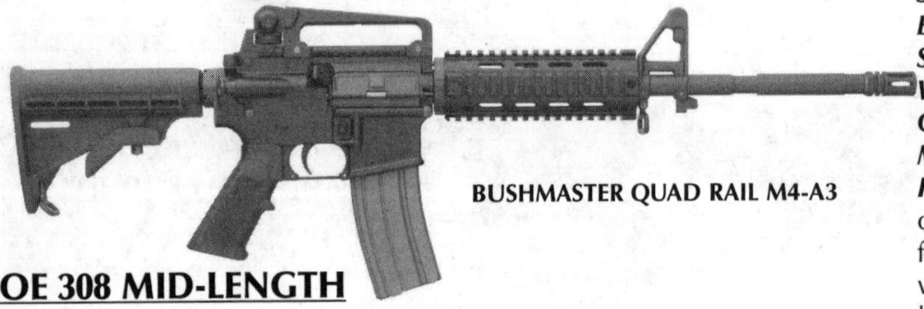

BUSHMASTER QUAD RAIL M4-A3

MOE 308 MID-LENGTH

Action: Semiautomatic
Stock: Synthetic
Barrel: 16 in.
Sights: Magpul MSBUS rear flip sight
Weight: 6 lb. 2 oz.
Caliber: .308 Win., 7.62 NATO
Magazine: Detachable box, 20 rounds
Features: Receiver length Picatinny rail; Magpul MOE polymer mid-length handguard; Magpul MOE adjustable buttstock with strong A-frame design; rubber buttplate; Magpul MOE vertical grip; MOE enhanced trigger guards; shipped in lockable hard case with yellow safety block; stock comes in black, Flat Dark Earth, or OD green
MSRP. $1599

PREDATOR

Action: Semiautomatic
Stock: Synthetic, ambidextrous pistol grip
Barrel: 20 in.
Sights: None
Weight: 8 lb.
Caliber: 5.56 NATO, .223 Rem.
Magazine: Detachable box, 5 rounds (accepts all M16/AR 15 type)
Features: Steel lined fluted barrel; two-stage competition trigger; vented tubular aluminum free-floater forend with bipod stud; shipped with safety block in lockable, foam-padded hard case
MSRP. . . . . $1344–$1518

QUAD RAIL M4-A3

Action: Semiautomatic
Stock: Synthetic
Barrel: 16 in.
Sights: None
Weight: 8 lb. 5 oz.
Caliber: 5.56 NATO, .223 Rem.
Magazine: Detachable box, 30 rounds
Features: Chrome-lined barrel; A2 birdcage-type suppressor; free-float quad rail forend; six-position telestock for light weight and quick handling; ships with lockable hard case and yellow safety block
A3:. $1391

TARGET MODEL RIFLES

Action: Semiautomatic
Stock: Synthetic
Barrel: 20 in
Sights: None
Weight: 8 lb. 7 oz.
Caliber: 5.56 NATO, .223 Rem.
Magazine: Detachable box, 30 rounds (accepts all M16 / AR15 type)
Features: A2 upper receiver 300–800 meter rear sight system; chromoly steel or polished stainless steel barrels; shipped in a lockable hard case with orange safety block
A2:. . . . . $1204–$1266

BUSHMASTER TARGET MODEL RIFLE A2

RIFLES

Bushmaster Firearms Internat'l

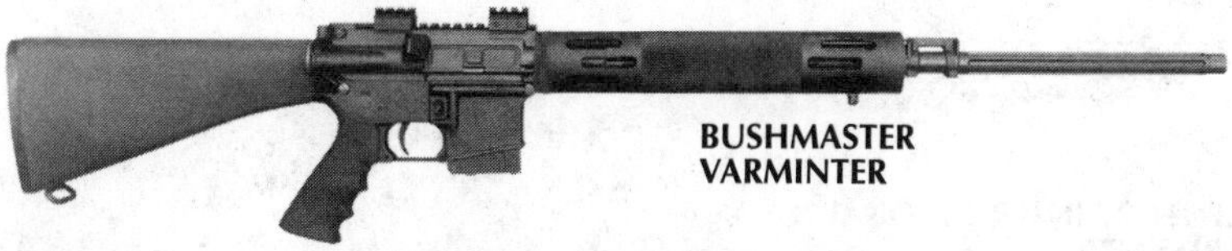

BUSHMASTER VARMINTER

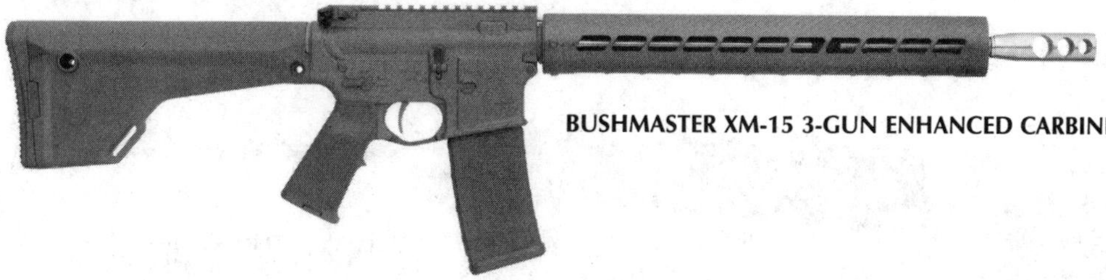

BUSHMASTER XM-15 3-GUN ENHANCED CARBINE

VARMINTER

Action: Semiautomatic
Stock: Synthetic, ambidextrous pistol grip
Barrel: 24 in.
Sights: None
Weight: 8 lb. 6 oz.
Caliber: 5.56 NATO, .223 Rem.
Magazine: Detachable box, 5 rounds (accepts all M16/AR 15 type)
Features: Competition crowned muzzle; chromoly vanadium steel barrel with full-length fluting; two-stage competition trigger; twelve cooling vents in forend; bipod stud installed on forend; black stock with rubberized, non-slip surface; shipped in hard plastic, lockable storage case complete with orange safety block
MSRP. $1359

XM-15 3-GUN ENHANCED CARBINE

Action: Semiautomatic
Stock: Synthetic
Barrel: 16 in.
Sights: None
Weight: 7 lb. 12 oz.
Caliber: 5.56 NATO
Magazine: Detachable box, 30 rounds
Features: Rolling Thunder compensator; Magpul MIAD grip and MOE stock
MSRP. $1750

Century International Arms

CENTURY INTERNATIONAL ARMS CENTURION 39 SPORTER

CENTURION 39 SPORTER

Action: Semiautomatic
Stock: Synthetic
Barrel: 16.5 in.
Sights: Front post, adjustable rear
Weight: 8 lb. 3 oz.
Caliber: 7.62x39 Warsaw
Magazine: Detachable box, 30 rounds
Features: Milled receiver machined from an 11-pound block of 4140 ordnance quality steel; rear sight adjustable for windage and elevation; high visibiliy from sight post; buttstock 1-in. longer than military-style stocks; upper and lower handguard have four Picatinny rails; two 30 round magazines included; 100 percent American made
MSRP. $799

Century International Arms

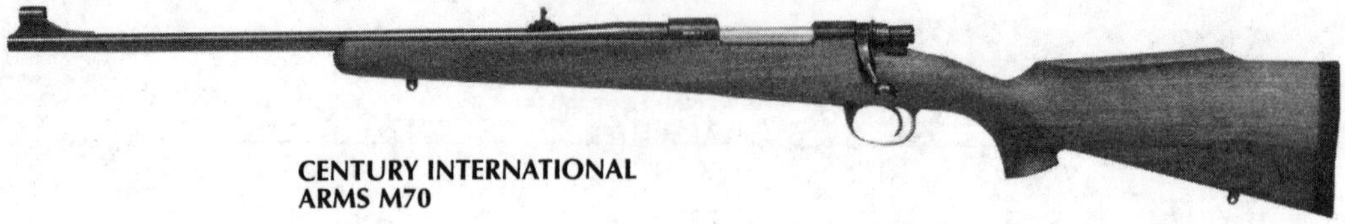

CENTURY INTERNATIONAL ARMS M70

CENTURY INTERNATIONAL ARMS M85 MINI MAUSER

M70 STANDARD/ MAGNUM

Action: Bolt
Stock: Walnut
Barrel: 23.6 in.
Sights: Adjustable
Weight: 7 lb. 11 oz.
Caliber: .30-06 Spfd., .270 Win., .308 Win., .243 Win., 7mm Rem. Mag., .300 Win. Mag.
Magazine: 5 rounds
Features: New rifle from the famous Zastava factory in Serbia; oiled European walnut stock; adjustable sights; modernized thumb actuated safety; cold forged chrome-vanadium steel
MSRP . . . . $519–$549

M85 MINI MAUSER

Action: Bolt
Stock: Walnut
Barrel: 20.07 in., 22.04 in.
Sights: Adjustable
Weight: 6 lb. 2 oz.–6 lb. 6 oz.
Caliber: .223 Rem., 7.62x39 Warsaw, .22 Hornet
Magazine: 5 rounds
Features: New rifle from the famous Zastava factory in Serbia; oiled European walnut stock; adjustable sights; modernized thumb actuated safety; cold forged chrome-vanadium steel
MSRP $549

C&H Precision USMC

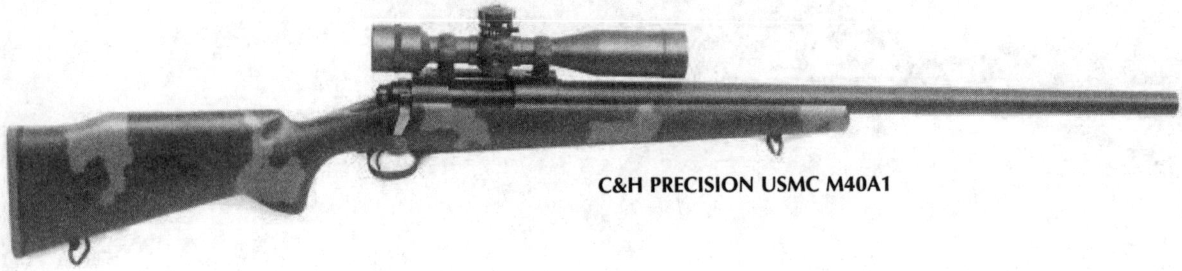

C&H PRECISION USMC M40A1

M40A1

Action: Bolt
Stock: Synthetic
Barrel: 25 in.
Sights: None
Weight: N/A
Caliber: .308 Win., 7.62 NATO
Magazine: N/A
Features: USMC stainless steel countour barrel; McMillan M40A1-HTG stock in forest camo; USMC spec. trigger guard custom made from Winchester model 70 steel trigger guard and floor plate; matte black finish
MSRP $3250

C&H Precision USMC

C&H PRECISION USMC M40A3

C&H PRECISION USMC M40A5

M40A3

Action: Bolt
Stock: Synthetic
Barrel: 25 in.
Sights: None
Weight: N/A
Caliber: .308 Win., 7.62 NATO
Magazine: N/A
Features: USMC stainless steel countour barrel; McMillan A4 stock with adjustable saddle cheek and spacer system in olive drab green; DD Ross trigger guard; matte black finish
MSRP $3650

M40A5

Action: Bolt
Stock: Synthetic
Barrel: 25 in.
Sights: None
Weight: N/A
Caliber: .308 Win., 7.62 NATO
Magazine: Detachable box, 5 rounds
Features: USMC stainless steel countour barrel with Surefire muzzle brake/suppressor adapter; McMillan A4 stock with adjustable saddle cheek, spacer system, and PGW PVS-22 night vision mount, in olive drab green; Badger Ordnance M5 DBM with five round magazine; matte black finish
MSRP $4100

Chiappa Firearms

CHIAPPA FIREARMS AK-22

AK-22

Action: Semiautomatic
Stock: Wood or synthetic
Barrel: 17.25 in.
Sights: Adjustable
Weight: 6 lb.
Caliber: .22LR
Magazine: Detachable box, 10 rounds
Features: Steel blued receiver and barrel
MSRP . . . . $429–$464

Chiappa Firearms

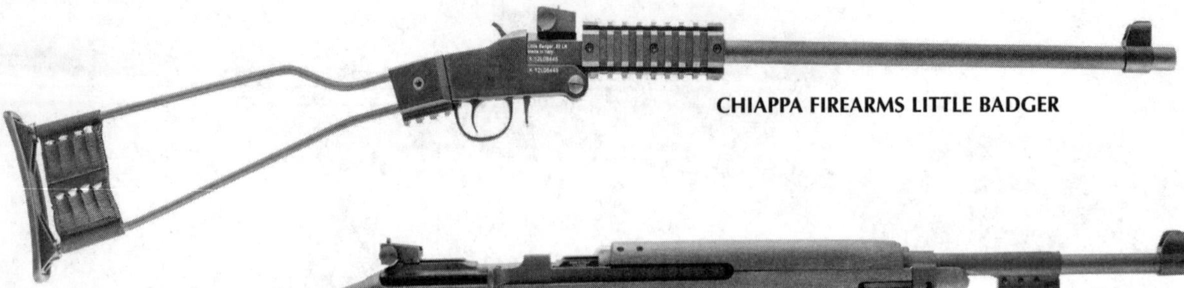

CHIAPPA FIREARMS LITTLE BADGER

CHIAPPA FIREARMS M1-22

CHIAPPA FIREARMS MODEL 39

LITTLE BADGER

Action: Single shot
Stock: Metal foldable
Barrel: 16.5 in.
Sights: Adjustable rear
Weight: 3 lb. 8 oz.
Caliber: .22LR
Magazine: None
Features: Single barrel; foldable rifle; extremely light for comfortable carry; folds to 16.5 in. total length; nylon carry bag and special cartridge holder available
MSRP. . . . . $180–$182

M1-22

Action: Semiautomatic
Stock: Wood or black synthetic
Barrel: 18 in.
Sights: Adjustable rear
Weight: 5 lb. 8 oz.
Caliber: .22LR
Magazine: Detachable box, 10 rounds
Features: The M1 carbine is a lightweight, easy-to-use semiautomatic carbine that became a standard firearm for the U.S. military during World War II, the Korean War, and the Vietnam War, and was produced in several variants
Synthetic: $349
Wood: $399

MODEL 39

Action: Lever
Stock: Wood or synthetic
Barrel: 18.5 in.
Sights: Adjustable
Weight: 5 lb.
Caliber: .22LR
Magazine: Internal, 15 rounds
Features: Blued barrel; take down; drilled and tapped for Marlin sights
MSRP. . . . . $419–$459

Chipmunk Rifles

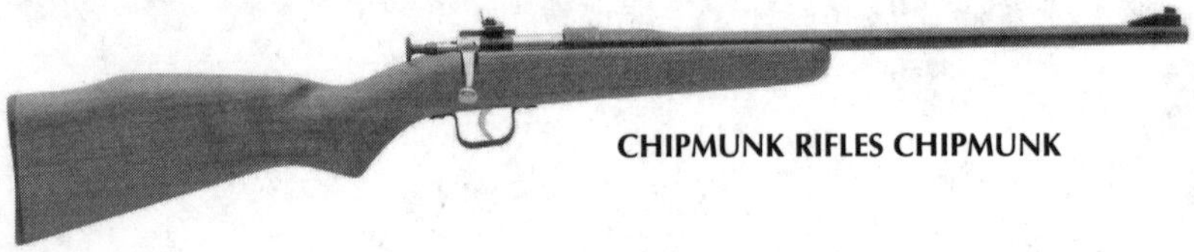

CHIPMUNK RIFLES CHIPMUNK

CHIPMUNK

Action: Bolt
Stock: Walnut, laminated
Barrel: 16.125 in.
Sights: Target
Weight: 2 lb. 8 oz.
Caliber: .22LR
Magazine: None
Features: Designed with younger shooters in mind; single-shot; manual-cocking action; receiver-mounted rear sights; metal with blued finish or stainless steel; post sight on ramp front, fully adjustable peep rear; adjustable trigger; extendable buttplate and front rail; available in black, walnut, deluxe walnut, camo laminate, and brown laminate
MSRP. . . . . $166–$219
Barracuda. . . . . $208–$233

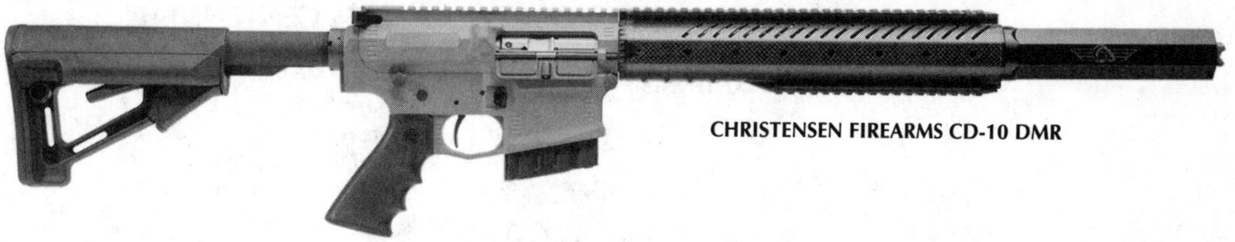

CHRISTENSEN FIREARMS CD-10 DMR

CHRISTENSEN CD-15 RECON

CD-10 DESIGNATED MARKSMAN RIFLE (DMR)

Action: Semiautomatic
Stock: Synthetic
Barrel: 24 in.
Sights: None
Weight: 8.2 lb.
Caliber: .243 Win., .308 Win., 6.5 Creedmoor
Magazine: Detachable box
Features: Picatinny rail; OSS suppressor; ambidextrous magazine release; Magpul stock; various finishes available
MSRP. . . . . N/A

CD-15 RECON

Action: Semiautomatic
Stock: Synthetic
Barrel: 24 in.
Sights: None
Weight: 7.3 lb.
Caliber: .223 Wylde, 5.56 NATO
Magazine: Detachable box
Features: Picatinny rail; OSS suppressor; ambidextrous magazine release; Magpul stock; various finishes available; optional .204 Ruger, .223 Rem., 300 BLK, 6.5 Grendel, and 6.8 SPC
MSRP. . . . . N/A

Cimarron Firearms Co.

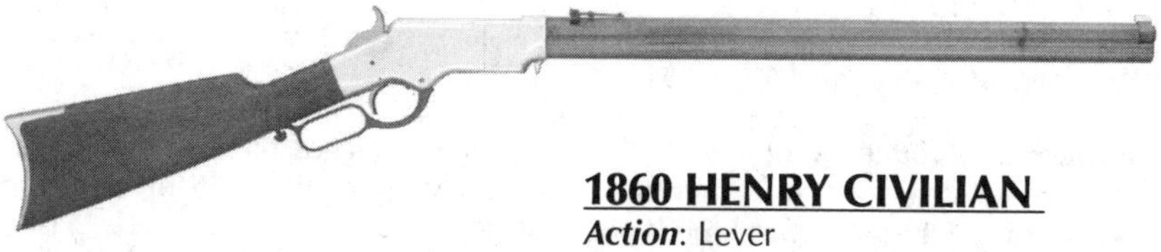

CIMARRON 1860 HENRY CIVILIAN

1860 HENRY CIVILIAN

Action: Lever
Stock: Walnut
Barrel: 24 in.
Sights: Open
Weight: 9 lb. 1 oz.–9 lb. 2 oz.
Caliber: .45 LC, .44 WCF
Magazine: Under-barrel tube, 12 rounds
Features: Reproduction of 1860 Civil War Henry rifle; includes military sling swivels; frame comes in charcoal blue or original finish
MSRP: . . . . $1460–$1593

1873 SADDLE SHORTY

1873 SADDLE SHORTY

Action: Lever
Stock: Wood
Barrel: 18 in.
Sights: Open
Weight: N/A
Caliber: .357 Mag., .38 Spl., .45 Colt, .44 WCF
Magazine: Fixed tube
Features: Full octagon barrel; straight stock with checkered forearm and stock
MSRP. $1351

Cimarron Firearms Co.

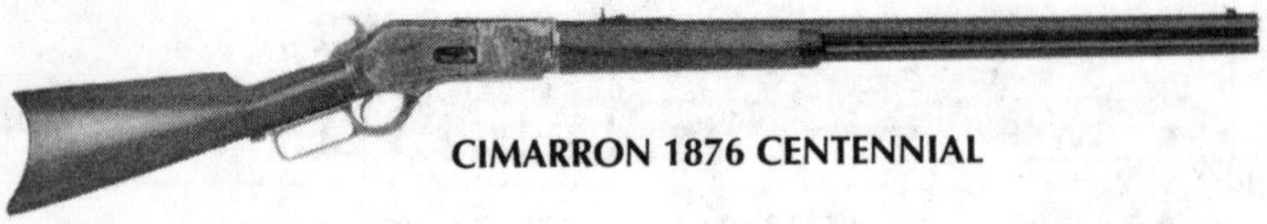

CIMARRON 1876 CENTENNIAL

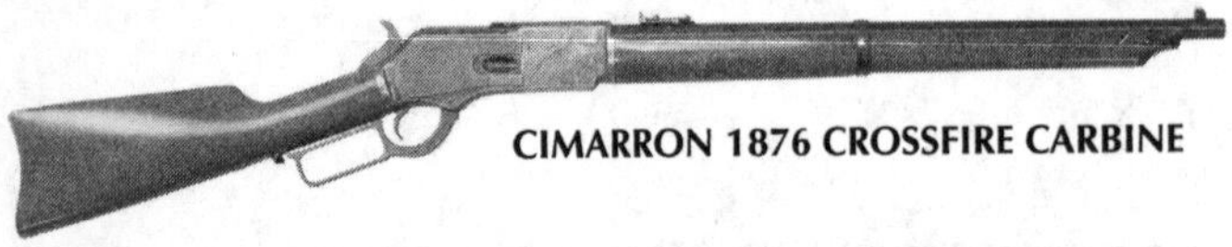

CIMARRON 1876 CROSSFIRE CARBINE

CIMARRON 1876 N.W.M.P. CARBINE

CIMARRON 1885 HIGH WALL SPORTING RIFLE

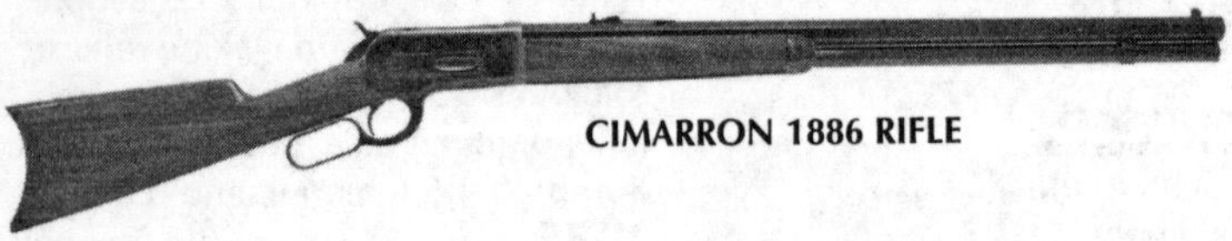

CIMARRON 1886 RIFLE

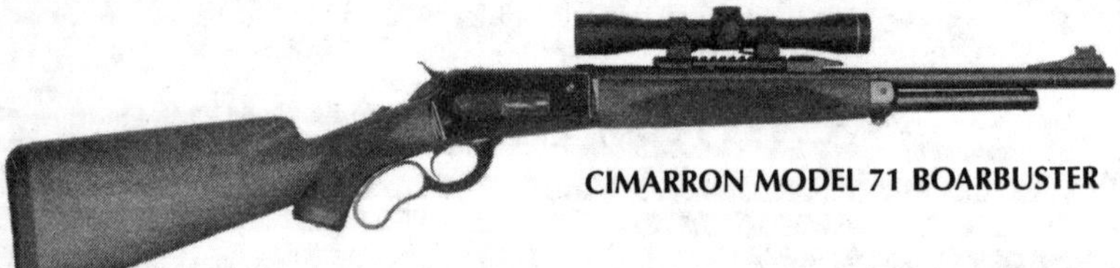

CIMARRON MODEL 71 BOARBUSTER

1876 CENTENNIAL

Action: Lever
Stock: Walnut
Barrel: 28 in.
Sights: Open
Weight: 9 lb. 15 oz.–10 lb. 2 oz.
Caliber: .45-60, .45-75, .40-60, .50-95
Magazine: Under-barrel tube, 12 rounds
Features: The favorite rifle of Teddy Roosevelt. Reproduction of 1876 Civil War Henry rifle; includes military sling swivels; frame comes in charcoal blue or original finish
MSRP $1689

1876 CROSSFIRE CARBINE

Action: Lever
Stock: Walnut
Barrel: 22 in.
Sights: None
Weight: 8 lb. 15 oz.
Caliber: .45-60, .45-75
Magazine: Under-barrel tube, 8 rounds
Features: Gun was glorified in the movie *Crossfire Trail;* case-hardened stock with standard blued finish
MSRP $1853

1876 N.W.M.P. (NORTH WEST MOUNTED POLICE) CARBINE

Action: Lever
Stock: Walnut
Barrel: 22 in.
Sights: None
Weight: 8 lb. 15 oz.
Caliber: .45-60, .45-75
Magazine: Under-barrel tube, 8 rounds
Features: Available in walnut stock and all blued metal; reproduction of popular firearm used by mounted police in 1870s
MSRP $1819

1885 HIGH WALL SPORTING RIFLE

Action: Dropping block
Stock: Walnut, pistol grip
Barrel: 30 in.
Sights: Open
Weight: 9 lb. 4 oz.–10 lb. 6 oz.
Caliber: .45-70 Govt., .40-65, .38-55, .45-90, .30-40 KRAG, .405 Win.
Magazine: None
Features: Reproduction of the Winchester single-shot hunting rifle popular in 1880s; standard blued finish on octagonal barrel; single- or double- set triggers
MSRP . . . . $1068–$1416

1886 RIFLE

Action: Lever
Stock: Walnut
Barrel: 22 in., 26 in.
Sights: None
Weight: 8 lb.–9 lb.
Caliber: .45-70 Govt.
Magazine: Under-barrel tube, 7+1, 8+1 rounds
Features: Made by Armi Sport in Italy; color case-hardened receiver and buttplate; octagonal barrel; standard blued finish; carbine version available
MSRP $1559

MODEL 71 BOARBUSTER

Action: Lever
Stock: Walnut
Barrel: 19 in.
Sights: Fiber optic
Weight: N/A
Caliber: .45-70 Govt.
Magazine: Fixed tube
Features: Carbine model; scout rail; pistol grip stock
MSRP $1846

Cimarron Firearms Co.

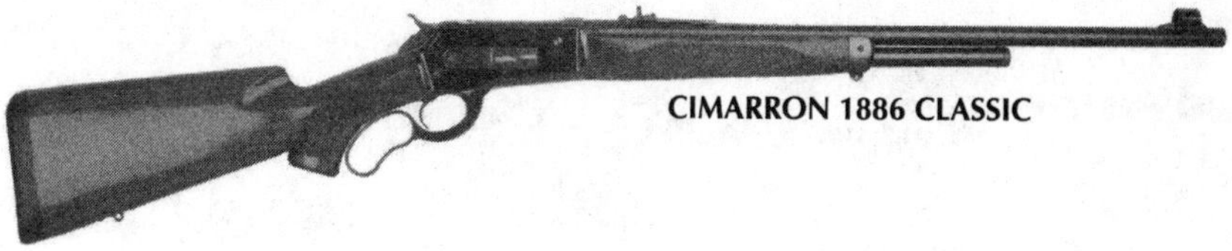

CIMARRON 1886 CLASSIC

MODEL 71 CLASSIC

Action: Lever
Stock: Walnut
Barrel: 26 in.
Sights: Open
Weight: N/A
Caliber: .45-70 Govt.
Magazine: Fixed tube
Features: Blued receiver; pistol grip stock
MSRP. $1846

Citadel by Legacy Sports

CITADEL M1 9MM CARBINE

M1 9MM CARBINE

Action: Semiautomatic
Stock: Wood or synthetic
Barrel: 18 in.
Sights: Adjustable
Weight: 5 lb. 13 oz.
Caliber: 9mm
Magazine: Detachable box, 10 or 17 rounds
Features: Blow-back action semiautomatic comes with two Beretta style 92FS ten round magazines
MSRP. . . . .$539–$642

Colt's Manufacturing Company

COLT COMPETITION CRX-16

COLT COMPETITION CRP-18

COMPETITION MARKSMAN CRX-16

Action: Semiautomatic
Stock: M4 carbine-style
Barrel: 16 in.
Sights: None
Weight: 6 lb. 7 oz.
Caliber: .223 Rem.
Magazine: Detachable box, 30 rounds
Features: Match-grade chrome-moly steel barrel; twin-port muzzle brake; vented modular float-tube handguard; low profile gas block; charging handle with extended tactical latch; match-target trigger coated with nickel-Teflon
MSRP. $1399

COMPETITION PRO CRP-18

Action: Semiautomatic
Stock: Magpul CTR adjustable
Barrel: 18 in.
Sights: None
Weight: 7 lb. 3 oz.
Caliber: .223 Rem.
Magazine: Detachable box, 30 rounds
Features: Match-grade, polished 416 stainless steel barrel; gas-operated, original direct-impingement system; triple port muzzle brake; Picatinny top handguard rail and accessory rail; Magpul MOE grip with extended back-strap; low profile adjustable gas block
MSRP. $2019

Colt's Manufacturing Company

COLT LE901-16S

COLT LE6940

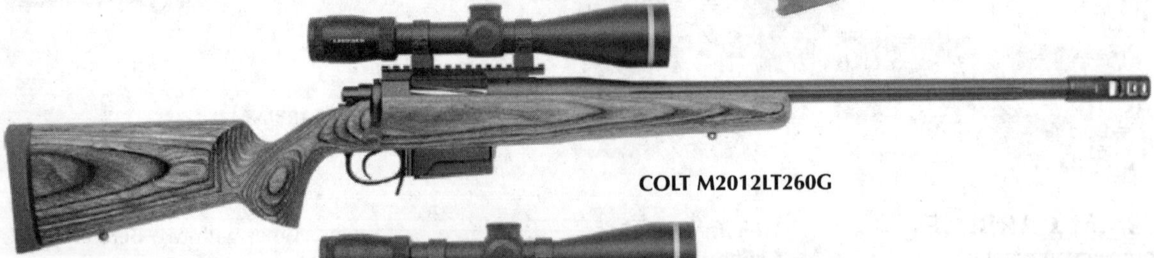

COLT M2012LT260G

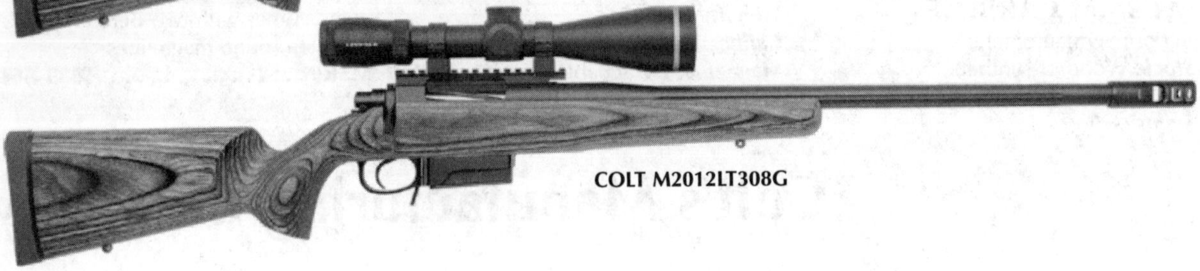

COLT M2012LT308G

LE901-16S

Action: Semiautomatic
Stock: Combat-style, synthetic
Barrel: 16.1 in.
Sights: Flip-up front, adjustable post, flip-up rear
Weight: 9 lb. 6 oz.
Caliber: .308 Win.
Magazine: Detachable box, 20 rounds
Features: Matte black, monolithic upper receiver; .308 Winchester upper receiver group can be swapped out for Mil-Spec Colt upper in 5.56 NATO; ambidextrous controls on magazine release, bolt catch and safety selector; back up iron sights; full floated barrel; bayonet lug and flash hider
MSRP $1399

LE6940, LE6920 CARBINES

Action: Semiautomatic
Stock: Combat-style, synthetic
Barrel: 16.1 in.
Sights: Flip-up front, adjustable post, flip-up rear
Weight: 6 lb. 13 oz.–7 lb.
Caliber: 5.56 NATO
Magazine: Detachable box, 20, 30 rounds
Features: Chrome-lined barrel; direct gas or articulating link piston system with locking bolt; Magpul MOE handguards, MOE carbine stock, MOE pistol grip, MOE vertical grip, and a Magpul back-up sight; flip-up front sight with adjustable post for elevation; flip-up rear sight adjustable for both windage and elevation; matte black finish; additional models available: LE6920MP-FDE, LE6920MP-B, LE6920SOCOM, LE6940P, LE6920CA, LE6940CA, LE6920CMP-B
MSRP . . . . $999–$1399

M2012LT260G

Action: Bolt
Stock: Wood
Barrel: 22 in.
Sights: None
Weight: 8 lb. 8 oz.
Caliber: .260 Rem.
Magazine: Detachable box, 5 or 10 rounds
Features: Timney single stage adjustable trigger; match grade barrel; custom Cooper Firearms muzzle brake; custom stock
MSRP $2795

M2012LT308G

Action: Bolt
Stock: Wood
Barrel: 22 in.
Sights: None
Weight: 8 lb. 8 oz.
Caliber: .308 Win.
Magazine: Detachable box, 5 or 10 rounds
Features: Timney single stage adjustable trigger; match grade barrel; custom Cooper Firearms muzzle brake; custom stock
MSRP $2795

Colt's Manufacturing Company

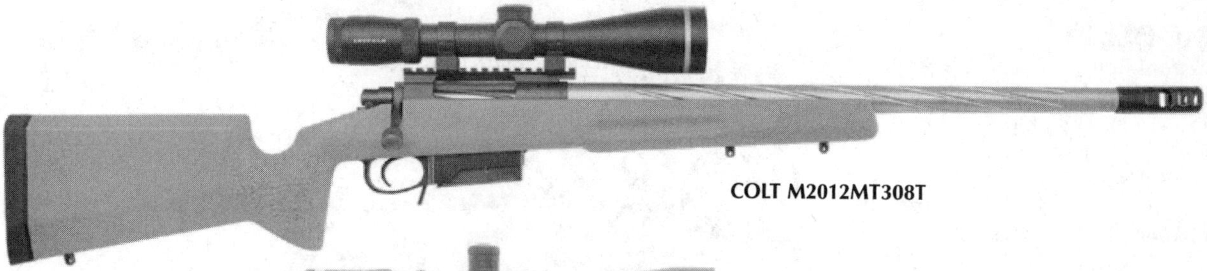

COLT M2012MT308T

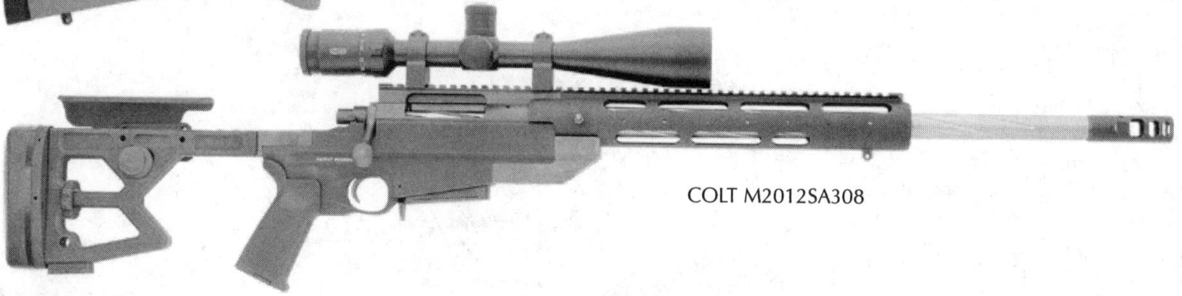

COLT M2012SA308

M2012MT308T

Action: Bolt
Stock: Synthetic
Barrel: 22 in.
Sights: None
Weight: 10 lb. 4 oz.
Caliber: .308 Win.
Magazine: Detachable box, 5 or 10 rounds
Features: Timney single stage adjustable trigger; match grade barrel; custom Cooper Firearms muzzle brake; custom stock
MSRP $2795

M2012SA308

Action: Bolt
Stock: Aluminum
Barrel: 22 in.
Sights: None
Weight: 13 lb. 3 oz.
Caliber: .308 Win.
Magazine: Detachable box, 5 or 10 rounds
Features: Timney single stage adjustable trigger; match grade barrel; custom Cooper Firearms muzzle brake; custom stock
MSRP $2795

Connecticut Valley Arms (CVA)

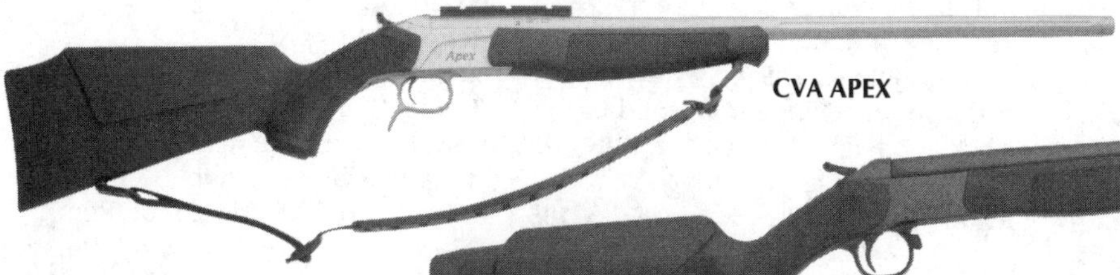

CVA APEX

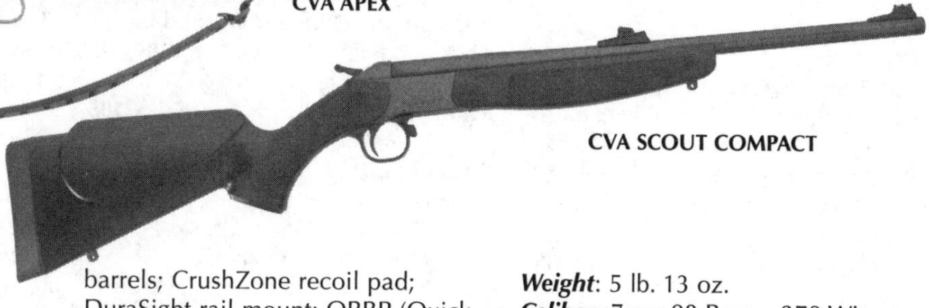

CVA SCOUT COMPACT

APEX

Action: Break-action centerfire
Stock: Synthetic
Barrel: 25 in.
Sights: None
Weight: 7 lb. 8 oz.
Caliber: .45-70 Govt., 7mm-08 Rem., .308 Win., .30-06 Spfd., .300 Win. Mag., .35 Whelen, .270 Win., .243 Win., .223 Rem., .222 Rem., .22-250 Rem.
Magazine: None
Features: Ambidextrous synthetic stock with rubber grip panels; comes in black or Realtree APG camo; stainless steel, fluted Bergara barrel; adjustable trigger; interchangeable barrels; CrushZone recoil pad; DuraSight rail mount; QRBP (Quick Release Breech Plug); reversible hammer spur; Quake Claw Sling; also available in muzzleloading models
MSRP . . . .$651–$731

SCOUT

Action: Centerfire, single shot
Stock: Synthetic
Barrel: 20 in. (compact), 22 in. (standard fluted barrels)
Sights: None
Weight: 5 lb. 13 oz.
Caliber: 7mm-08 Rem., .270 Win., .30-06 Spfd., .35 Whelen, .243 Win. (compact only)
Magazine: None
Features: Stainless steel or blued barrel; ambidextrous black synthetic stock; DuraSight Dead-On integral scope rail; CrushZone recoil pad; reversible hammer spur; compact and alternate length stocks available
MSRP . . . .$413–$480

Cooper Firearms

COOPER FIREARMS MODEL 21
VARMINT EXTREME

COOPER FIREARMS MODEL 21
VARMINT LAMINATE

COOPER FIREARMS MODEL 38
JACKSON VARMINTER

COOPER FIREARMS MODEL 51

MODEL 21

Action: Bolt
Stock: 1, 2, 3, 4, 10, 11, 12, 13, 14, 15, 17 (see key on page 135)
Barrel: 22 in., 24 in.
Sights: None
Weight: 6 lb. 8 oz.–7 lb. 8 oz.
Caliber: .17 Rem., .19-223, Tactical .20, .204 Ruger, .222 Rem., .222 Rem. Mag., .223 Rem., .223 Rem. Al., 6x45, 6x47, 6.8 SPC, .17 Fireball, .20 VarTarg, .221 Fireball
Magazine: None
Features: Three-front locking lug bolt action single shot; Sako style extraction machined from solid bar stock; plunger style ejector machined from solid bar; fully adjustable single-stage trigger
MSRP $2195

RIFLES

MODEL 22

Action: Bolt
Stock: 1, 2, 3, 4, 10, 11, 13, 14
Barrel: 24 in., 26 in.
Sights: None
Weight: 7 lb. 8 oz.–8 lb. 4 oz.
Caliber: .22-250 Rem., .22-250 Rem. Al., .220 Swift, .25-06 Rem., .25–06 Rem. Al., .243 Win., .243 Rem. Al., .250 Savage, .250 Savage Al., .22BR, 6BR, .257 Roberts, .257 Roberts Al., .284 Win., 7mm-08 Rem., 6mm Rem., .260 Rem., 6x284, 6.5x284, 6.5x55 Swedish, 6.5 Creedmoor, 7x57 Mauser, .308 Win.
Magazine: None
Features: Three-front locking lug bolt action single-shot; Sako style extraction machined from solid bar stock; plunger style ejector machined form solid bar; fully adjustable single-stage trigger
MSRP $2195

MODEL 38

Action: Bolt
Stock: 1, 2, 3, 4, 10, 11, 13, 14
Barrel: 22 in., 24 in.
Sights: None
Weight: 6 lb. 8 oz.–7 lb. 8 oz.
Caliber: .17 Squirrel, .17 Ackley Hornet, .17 He Bee, .19 Hornet, .22 Hornet, .22 K-Hornet, .22 Squirrel, .218 Bee, .218 Mashburn Bee
Magazine: None
Features: Three-front locking lug bolt action single-shot; Sako style extraction machined from solid bar stock; retractable tab ejector; fully adjustable single-stage trigger
MSRP $2195

MODEL 51

Action: Bolt
Stock: Classic, Custom Classic, Western Classic, Schnabel, Mannlicher, Jackson Game, Jackson Hunter, Excaliber
Barrel: 22 in., 24 in.
Sights: None
Weight: 6 lb. 4 oz.–7 lb. 4 oz.
Caliber: .17 Rem., .19-223, Tactical .20, .204 Ruger, .222 Rem., .222 Rem. Mag., .223 Rem., .223 Rem. Al, 6x45, 6x47, 300 BLK
Magazine: None
Features: Longer barrel standard on all varmint models; fully adjustable single-stage trigger; Sako style extraction machined from solid bar stock
MSRP $2275

MODEL 52

Action: Bolt
Stock: 1, 2, 3, 4, 5, 6, 8, 9
Barrel: 22 in., 23 in., 24 in.
Sights: None
Weight: 7 lb. 8 oz.–8 lb.
Caliber: .30-06 Spfd., .25-06 Rem., .25-06 Rem. Al., 6.5x284, 6.5-06, .270 Win., .284 Win., .280 Rem., .280 Rem. Al., .338-06, .35 Whelen
Magazine: 3 rounds
Features: Three-rear locking lug bolt action magazine fed repeater; centerfire action, also available in stainless steel; Sako style extraction machined from solid bar stock; retractable tab ejector machined from solid bar; fully adjustable single-stage trigger
MSRP $2275

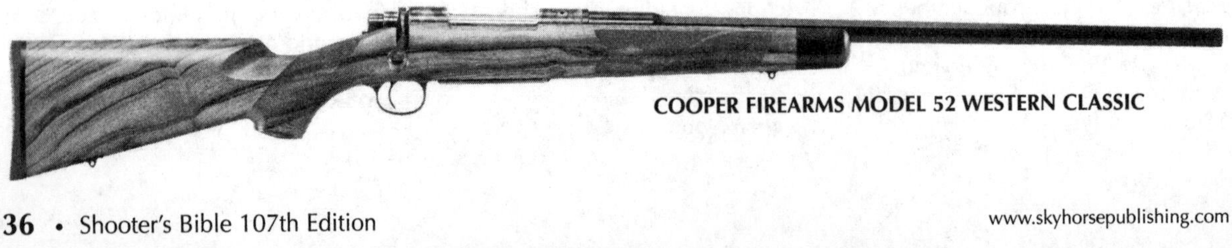

COOPER FIREARMS MODEL 52 WESTERN CLASSIC

Cooper Firearms

COOPER FIREARMS MODEL 57M CLASSIC

COOPER FIREARMS MODEL 57 LIGHT VARMINT TARGET - LVT

COOPER FIREARMS EXCALIBUR

MODEL 54

Action: Bolt
Stock: 1, 2, 3, 4, 5, 6, 8, 9, 10, 11, 13, 14
Barrel: 22 in., 23 in., 24 in.
Sights: None
Weight: 6 lb. 8 oz.–8 lb.
Caliber: .22-250 Rem., .22-250 Rem. Al., .220 Swift, .243 Win., .243 Rem. Al., 6mm Rem., .250 Savage, .250 Savage Al., .257 Roberts, .257 Roberts Al., 7mm-08, .260 Rem., 6.5 Creedmoor, 6.5x47 Lapua, .308 Win.
Magazine: 3 rounds
Features: Three-rear locking lug bolt action magazine fed repeater; center-fire action, also available in stainless steel; Sako style extraction machined from solid bar stock; plunger style ejector machined form solid bar; fully adjustable single-stage trigger
MSRP $2275

MODEL 57M

Action: Bolt
Stock: 1, 2, 3, 4, 5, 7, 9, 12, 15, 16
Barrel: 22 in., 24 in.
Sights: None
Weight: 6 lb.–8 lb.
Caliber: .17 Mach 2, .22LR, .22 WMR, .17 HMR
Magazine: 4, 5 rounds
Features: Three-rear locking lug bolt action magazine fed repeater; twin extractor claw; fixed ejector; feed block; fully adjustable single-stage trigger
MSRP $2275

1. CLASSIC
AA Claro walnut; steel grip; four-panel hand checkering; oil finish; matte metal finish; no options

2. CUSTOM CLASSIC
AAA Claro walnut; steel grip and stock metal; ebony tip; western-fleur wrap-around hand checkering; oil finish; 4140 blued steel match barrel; gloss metal finish; all options

3. WESTERN CLASSIC
AAA Claro walnut; steel grip and stock metal; Doug Turnbull case color metal; octagon barrel; matte metal finish; wrap-around western-fleur hand checkering; oil finish; ebony tip; 4140 blued steel match barrel; all options

4. MANNLICHER
AAA Claro walnut; shadowline beaded cheek piece; African ebony tip; multi-point wrap around hand checkering; oil finish; Pachmayr pad; standard sling swivel studs; steel grip cap; chromoly premium match grade barrel; high gloss finish on metalwork; all options available

5. SCHNABEL
Available in models 52, 54, 56, and 57; AA+ Claro walnut; raised comb; slim taper forearm; multi-point two panel hand checkering; oil finish; standard grade sling swivel studs; Pachmayr pad; steel grip cap; chromoly premium match grade barrel; metal work is matte finished; all options available

6. EXCALIBUR
Synthetic copy of the Classic; M52 only

7. JACKSON SQUIRREL
AA Select walnut; roll-over cheekpiece; fluted forearm; hand checkering; oil finish; steel grip cap

8. JACKSON GAME
Characteristics of Jackson Squirrel stock with a North American Hunting rifle (M52); some options

9. JACKSON HUNTER
Synthetic version of Jackson Squirrel in M57; in M52, this is a version of the Jackson Game

10. VARMINTER
AA Claro walnut; stainless match barrel; hand checkering; hand oil finish; matte metal finish; no options

11. MONTANA VARMINTER
AA Select Claro walnut; steel grip cap; cooling vents; stainless match barrel; hand checkering and hand oil finish; matte metal finish; all options

12. LIGHT VARMINT TARGET
AA Select Claro walnut; steel grip cap; cooling vents; stainless match barrel; hand checkering and hand oil finish; matte metal finish; all options

13. VARMINT EXTREME
AAA Claro walnut; steel grip and stock metal; stainless match barrel; hand checkering with cross-over grip pattern; hand oil finish; egg shell matte metal finish; all options

14. PHOENIX
Synthetic in flat black and brown spider-web finish; stainless match barrel; aluminum bedding block; cooling vents; matte metal finish; no options

15. VARMINT LAMINATE
Laminated hardwood stock; oil finish; Pachmayr pad; steel grip cap; ventilated forearm; stainless steel, striaght taper, premium grade match barrel; sling swivel studs available upon request

16. TRP-3
Benchrest style; synthetic BR stock; straight stainless match barrel; matte metal finish; some options

CZ-USA (Ceska Zbrojovka)

CZ 455 AMERICAN

CZ-USA 455 AMERICAN SYNTHETIC SUPPRESSOR READY

CZ 455 FS

CZ 455 LUX

CZ-USA 455 TACTICOOL SUPRESSOR READY

CZ-USA 455 TRAINING RIFLE

455 AMERICAN

Action: Bolt
Stock: Walnut, black polymer
Barrel: 20.5 in.
Sights: None
Weight: 5 lb. 13 oz.–6 lb. 2 oz.
Caliber: .17 HMR, .22LR, .22 WMR, Combo .22LR with .17 HMR replacement barrel
Magazine: Detachable box, 5 rounds
Features: Cold hammer-forged barrel; blued receiver and barrel finish; integrated dovetail scope base; interchangeable barrel system; adjustable trigger
MSRP . . . . $385–$557

455 AMERICAN SYNTHETIC SUPPRESSOR READY

Action: Bolt
Stock: Synthetic
Barrel: 16.5 in.
Sights: None
Weight: 5 lb. 8 oz.
Caliber: .22LR
Magazine: Detachable box, 5 rounds
Features: High, flat comb for scope; suppressor not included
MSRP $421

455 FS

Action: Bolt
Stock: Walnut
Barrel: 20.6 in.
Sights: Adjustable iron sights
Weight: 6 lb. 6 oz.
Caliber: .22LR, .17 HMR
Magazine: Detachable box, 5 rounds
Features: Action machined from bar stock; adjustable trigger; detachable feed magazine; cold-hammer-forged barrels; standard 11mm optic-mounting dovetail; full length Mannlicher walnut stock; adjustable iron sights
MSRP . . . . $514–$540

455 LUX

Action: Bolt
Stock: Walnut
Barrel: 20.6 in.
Sights: Open
Weight: 6 lb. 2 oz.
Caliber: .22LR, .22 WMR
Magazine: Detachable box, 5 rounds
Features: Interchangeable barrel system; adjustable trigger; hammer-forged barrel and billet machined receiver; adjustable iron sights; lux pattern walnut stock
MSRP . . . . $440–$469

455 TACTICOOL SUPRESSOR READY

Action: Bolt
Stock: Laminate
Barrel: 16.5 in.
Sights: None
Weight: 6 lb. 10 oz.
Caliber: .22LR
Magazine: Detachable box, 5 rounds
Features: Suppressor not included
MSRP $549

455 TRAINING RIFLE

Action: Bolt
Stock: Beechwood
Barrel: 24.8 in.
Sights: Adjustable
Weight: 6 lb. 5 oz.
Caliber: .22LR
Magazine: Detachable box, 5 rounds
Features: Ability to swap the barrel and/or stock; single-shot adapter and 10 round magazine are available
MSRP $374

CZ-USA (Ceska Zbrojovka)

CZ 455 VARMINT

CZ-USA 455 VARMINT TACTICOOL

CZ 455 VARMINT EVOLUTION

CZ-USA 455 VARMINT PRECISION TRAINER

CZ 512 RIMFIRE

455 VARMINT

Action: Bolt
Stock: Walnut
Barrel: 20.5 in.
Sights: Optic mounting dovetail
Weight: 7 lb. 1 oz.
Caliber: .22LR, .22 WMR, .17 HMR
Magazine: Detachable box, 5 rounds
Features: Action machined from bar stock; adjustable trigger; detachable feed magazine; cold-hammer-forged barrels; standard 11mm optic-mounting dovetail; heavier and stiffer barrel for enhanced accuracy; accepts all accessory barrels for the 455 models
MSRP . . . . $440–$469

455 VARMINT WITH SS EVOLUTION STOCK

Action: Bolt
Stock: Laminate
Barrel: 20.5 in.
Sights: Optic mounting dovetail
Weight: 7 lb. 2 oz.
Caliber: .17 HMR, .22LR
Magazine: Detachable box, 5 rounds
Features: Action machined from bar stock; adjustable trigger; detachable feed magazine; cold-hammer-forged barrels; standard 11mm optic-mounting dovetail; sky blue/gray laminated stock; ambidextrous; free floated barrel; accepts all accessory barrels for the 455 models
MSRP . . . . $538–$565

455 VARMINT PRECISION TRAINER

Action: Bolt
Stock: Carbon fiber
Barrel: 20.5 in.
Sights: None
Weight: 7 lb. 13 oz.
Caliber: .22LR
Magazine: Detachable box, 5 rounds
Features: Camo stock; blued finish
MSRP $940

455 VARMINT TACTICOOL

Action: Bolt
Stock: Black laminate
Barrel: 20.5 in.
Sights: None
Weight: 7 lb. 6 oz.
Caliber: .22LR
Magazine: Detachable box, 5 rounds
Features: Built as a tactical trainer with a number of ergonomic features; stock has ambidextrous palm swells on its pistol grip and an especially high Monte Carlo to accommodate larger scopes; beavertail forend is great for riding bags or affixing bipod; cold hammer-forged barrel; interchangeable barrel system; adjustable trigger
MSRP $549

512 RIMFIRE RIFLE

Action: Semiautomatic
Stock: Lacquered beech wood
Barrel: 20.7 in.
Sights: Adjustable
Weight: 5 lb. 14 oz.
Caliber: .22LR, .22 WMR
Magazine: Detachable box, 5 rounds
Features: Aluminum alloy upper receiver and fiberglass reinforced polymer lower half; dual guide rods; hammer-forged CZ barrel; integral 11mm dovetail for mounting optics
MSRP . . . . $480–$510

CZ-USA (Ceska Zbrojovka)

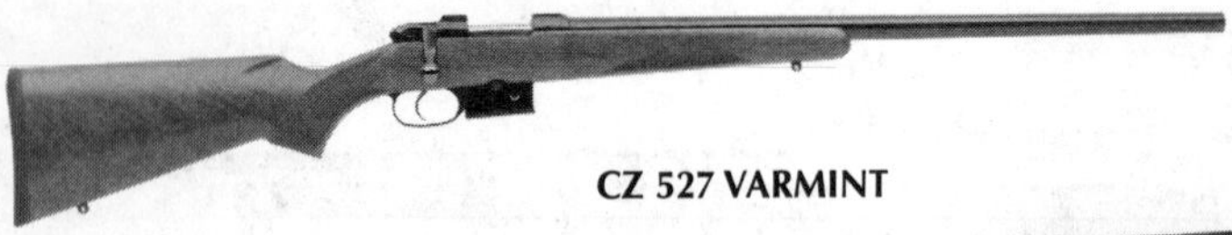

CZ 527 VARMINT

CZ 550 CARBINE

CZ-USA 550 BADLANDS

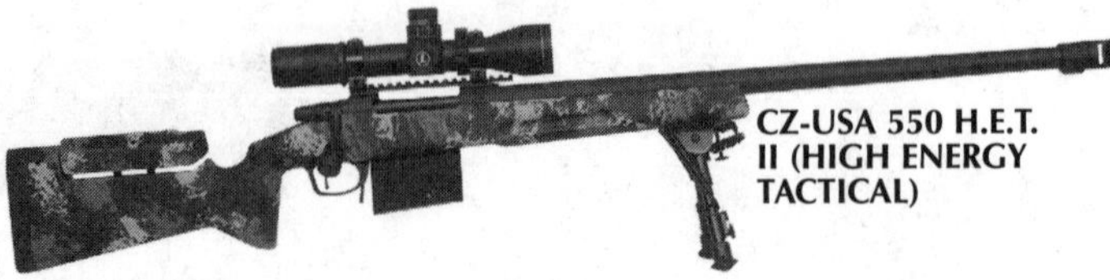

CZ-USA 550 H.E.T. II (HIGH ENERGY TACTICAL)

CZ 550 SAFARI MAGNUM

527

Action: Bolt
Stock: Walnut
Barrel: 18.5 in.–24 in.
Sights: Open
Weight: 5 lb. 14 oz.–7 lb. 13 oz.
Caliber: .222 Rem., .223 Rem., .22 Hornet; American: .17 Hornet .204 Ruger, .221 Fireball; Carbine: 7.62x39 Warsaw; Varmint Target: .204 Ruger
Magazine: Detachable box, 5 rounds
Features: Hammer-forged barrel; controlled round feed; single-set trigger; each model comes in a variety of calibers and a different stock; Turkish walnut stock in Bavarian pattern on Lux model; Varmint model comes in walnut, Kevlar, or laminated; left-hand version available in American model
American: . . . . $733–$787
Carbine: $733
FS: $784
Lux: . . . . $733–$778
Varmint:. . . . . $725–$775

550

Action: Bolt
Stock: Walnut, Kevlar
Barrel: 20.5 in., 23.6 in.
Sights: Open
Weight: 7 lb.–7 lb. 10 oz.
Caliber: .22-250 Rem., .243 Win., .270 Win., .30-06, .308 Win.; 6.5x55 Swedish, 9.3x62 Mauser; (Medium Lux): 6.5x55 Swedish
Magazine: Detachable box, 4, 5 rounds
Features: Adjustable single-set trigger; detachable magazine optional; full stocked model (FS) available; American model includes Pachmayr recoil pad; carbine has Kevlar stock
Carbine: . . . .$1080–$1129
FS: . . . . $890–$939

550 BADLANDS

Action: Bolt
Stock: Kevlar
Barrel: 25 in.
Sights: None
Weight: 9 lb. 3 oz.
Caliber: .338 Lapua
Magazine: Internal, 4 rounds
Features: Blued finish; muzzle break
MSRP $2599

550 H.E.T. II (HIGH ENERGY TACTICAL)

Action: Bolt
Stock: Carbon fiber
Barrel: 25 in.
Sights: None
Weight: 14 lb.
Caliber: .338 Lapua
Magazine: Detachable box, 5 rounds
Features: Adjustable cheekpiece; molded-in midnight camo; low-mount Picatinny rail; Badger Ordinance FTE muzzle brake
MSRP $3929

550 SAFARI MAGNUM

Action: Bolt
Stock: Walnut
Barrel: 25 in.
Sights: Express sights
Weight: 9 lb. 6 oz.
Caliber: .375 H&H Mag., .416 Rigby, .458 Win. Mag.
Magazine: Fixed, 3 (.416 Rigby), 5 rounds
Features: Known worldwide as the 602 BRNO; hammer-forged barrel; single-set trigger; controlled round feed and fixed ejector make the rifle reliable enough for heavy and dangerous game; express sights (1 standing, 2 folding); select Trukish walnut stock with classic safari shape
MSRP . . . . $1215–$1318

CZ-USA (Ceska Zbrojovka)

CZ-USA 550 SONORAN

CZ 550 ULTIMATE HUNTING RIFLE

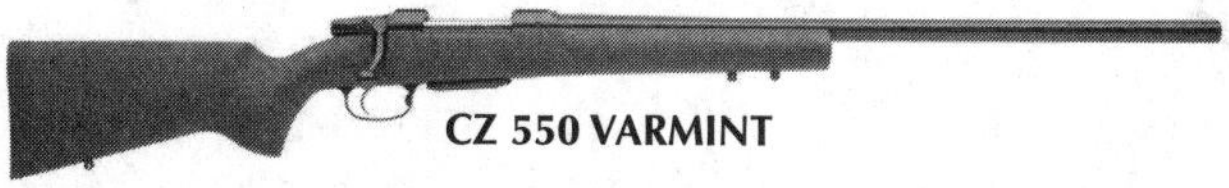

CZ 550 VARMINT

CZ-USA 550 VARMINT TACTICOOL

CZ-USA 557 CARBINE

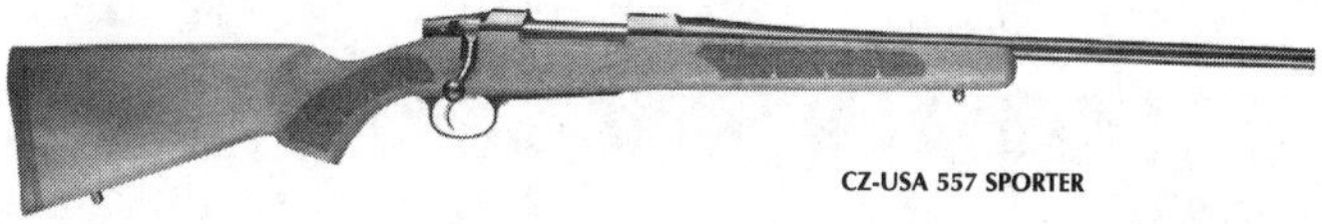

CZ-USA 557 SPORTER

550 SONORAN

Action: Bolt
Stock: Carbon fiber
Barrel: 24 in., 26 in. (Mag.)
Sights: None
Weight: 7 lb. 10 oz., 7 lb. 13 oz. (Mag.)
Caliber: .30-06 Spfd., .270 Win., .300 Win. Mag., 7mm Rem. Mag.
Magazine: Internal, 5 or 3 (Mag.) rounds
Features: Fluted barrel; high corrosion and wear resistence
MSRP $3199

550 ULTIMATE HUNTING RIFLE

Action: Bolt
Stock: Walnut, Kevlar
Barrel: 23.6 in.
Sights: Open
Weight: 7 lb. 11 oz.
Caliber: .300 Win. Mag.
Magazine: Fixed, 3 rounds
Features: Hammer-forged, blued barrel; single-stage trigger
MSRP $1361
Kevlar: $1497

550 VARMINT

Action: Bolt
Stock: Walnut
Barrel: 25.6 in.
Sights: Open
Weight: 9 lb. 11 oz.
Caliber: .22-250 Rem., .308 Win.
Magazine: Detachable box, 4 rounds
Features: Heavy barreled, two position manual safety; firing-pin-block and bolt lock
MSRP $924

550 VARMINT TACTICOOL

Action: Bolt
Stock: Laminate
Barrel: 25.6 in.
Sights: None
Weight: 10 lb. 12 oz.
Caliber: .308 Win.
Magazine: Detachable box, 4 rounds
Features: Foliage green stock; blued finish; available in walnut
MSRP $924

557 CARBINE

Action: Bolt
Stock: Walnut
Barrel: 20.5 in.
Sights: Fixed
Weight: 7 lb. 4 oz.
Caliber: .30-06 Spfd., .243 Win., .308 Win., .270 Win., 6.5x55 Swedish
Magazine: Internal, 4 rounds
Features: Integral 19mm dovetails
MSRP $812

557 SPORTER

Action: Bolt
Stock: Walnut
Barrel: 20.5 in.
Sights: None
Weight: 7 lb. 4 oz.
Caliber: .30-06 Spfd., .243 Win., .308 Win., .270 Win., 6.5x55 Swedish
Magazine: Internal, 4 rounds
Features: Integral 19mm dovetails
MSRP $792

CZ-USA (Ceska Zbrojovka)

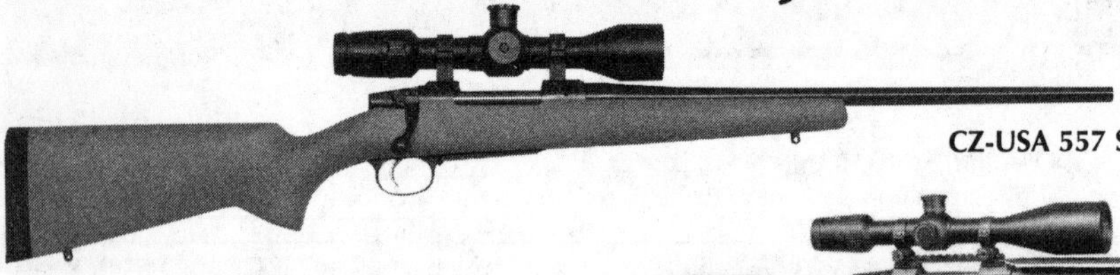

CZ-USA 557 SPORT MANNERS

CZ 750 SNIPER

557 SPORTER MANNERS

Action: Bolt
Stock: Carbon fiber
Barrel: 20.5 in.
Sights: None
Weight: 6 lb. 11 oz.
Caliber: .30-06 Spfd., .270 Win., 6.5x55 Swedish
Magazine: Internal, 4 rounds
Features: Fiber optic front sight
MSRP $1268

750 SNIPER

Action: Bolt
Stock: Synthetic thumbhole
Barrel: 26 in.
Sights: Open
Weight: 11 lb. 14 oz.
Caliber: .308 Win.
Magazine: Detachable box, 10 rounds
Features: Adjustable comb; underside of forend is fitted with a 220mm-long rail for bipod attachment; muzzle-brake; thread protector; mirage shield; blued barrel; single-stage trigger
MSRP $1999

Dakota Arms

DAKOTA MODEL 10

DAKOTA MODEL 76 CLASSIC

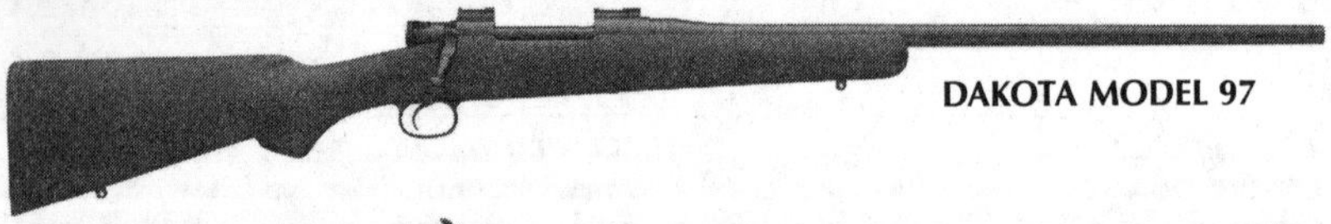

DAKOTA MODEL 97

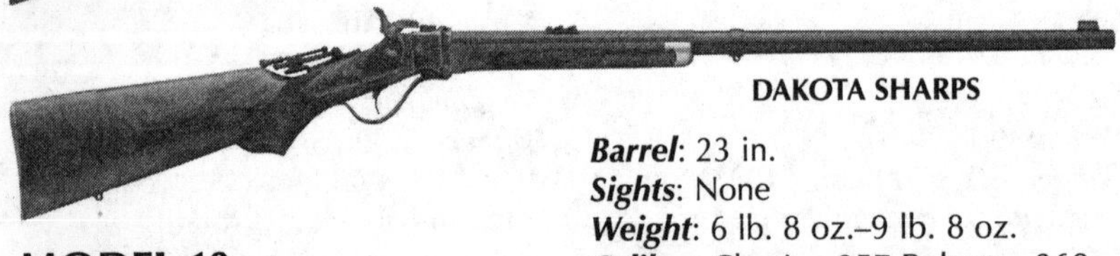

DAKOTA SHARPS

MODEL 10

Action: Falling block
Stock: Walnut
Barrel: 23 in.
Sights: None
Weight: 6 lb.–7 lb.
Caliber: .22LR to .300 Win., .338 to .375 H&H Mag.
Magazine: None
Features: Point wrap checkering; scope ring bases installed; custom length of pull; barrel break in
MSRP . . . . .from $5260
Deluxe: . . . . .from $6690

MODEL 76 CLASSIC

Action: Bolt
Stock: Walnut
Barrel: 23 in.
Sights: None
Weight: 6 lb. 8 oz.–9 lb. 8 oz.
Caliber: Classic: .257 Roberts, .260 Rem., .270 Win., .280 Rem., .30-06 Spfd., .300 Dakota, .300 Win. Mag., .300 WSM, .308 Win., .330 Dakota, .416 Rem., 7mm Rem. Mag., 7mm-08 Rem.; Safari: .300 H&H, .375 Dakota, .416 Rem., 7mm Dakota; African: .338 Win. Mag., .375 H&H, .416 Rem., .404 Jeffery, .416 Rigby, .450 Dakota, .458 Lott
Magazine: Box, 4 rounds
Features: Barrel break in; custom length of pull; optional engraving; point panel checkering; Dakota swivel studs; 1-inch recoil pad; straddle floor plate; right- or left-hand configurations; Safari model has front island sight with flip-up night sight; African model has quarter rib sights with banded front sights and flip-up night sights
Classic: . . . . .from $6030
Safari: . . . . .from $8010
African: . . . . .from $8890

MODEL 97

Action: Bolt
Stock: Fiberglass, composite, walnut
Barrel: 22 in. (short action), 25 in. (long action)
Sights: None
Weight: 7 lb.
Caliber: All-Weather: .30-06 Spfd., .338 Win. Mag., .375 H&H, 7mm Rem. Mag., 7mm-08 Rem.; Long Range: .280 Rem., .338 Win. Mag., 7mm Rem. Mag., 7mm-08 Rem.
Magazine: Blind box
Features: Stainless Douglas barrel; black composite stock with two inletted Ken Howell swivel studs; stainless trigger bow
All-weather: . . . . .from $4050
Deluxe: . . . . .from $4820
Long Range: . . . . .from $3720

SHARPS

Action: Falling block
Stock: Walnut
Barrel: 26 in.
Sights: Open
Weight: 8 lb. 4 oz.
Caliber: .17 HMR, .22 Hornet, .30-30 Win., .30-40 Krag., .375 H&H
Magazine: None
Features: Octagon barrel; steel butt-plate; single blade rear sight with front bead; matte blued metal finish
Sharps: . . . . .from $4490
Miller: . . . . .from $5590

Dakota Arms

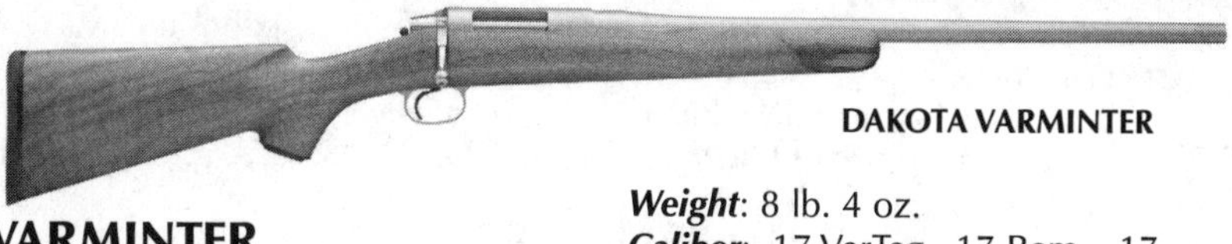

DAKOTA VARMINTER

VARMINTER

Action: Bolt
Stock: Walnut
Barrel: 22 in.
Sights: None
Weight: 8 lb. 4 oz.
Caliber: .17 VarTag, .17 Rem., .17 Tactical, .20 PPC, .204 Ruger, .221 Rem. Fireball, .22 PPC, .223 Rem., 6mm PPC, 6.5 Grendel
Magazine: None
Features: Available in walnut sporter-style stock or XXX walnut varmint style stock with semi-beavertail forend; checkered grip; recessed target crown; vapor hone matte bead blast finish on stainless; stainless steel barrel
MSRP . . . . from $2840
All-weather: . . . . from $3390
Deluxe: . . . . from $3390
Heavy: . . . . from $2840

Daniel Defense

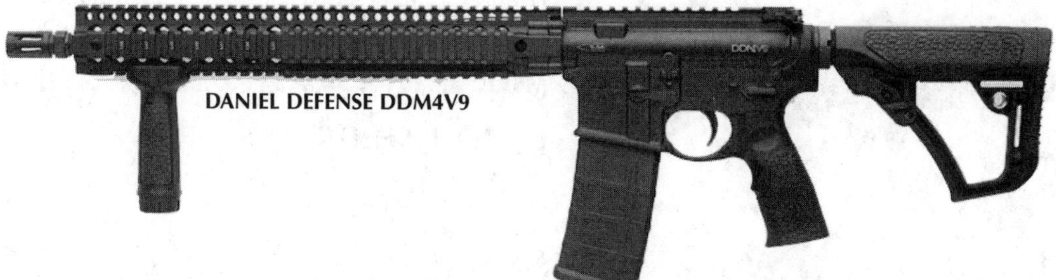

DANIEL DEFENSE DDM4V9

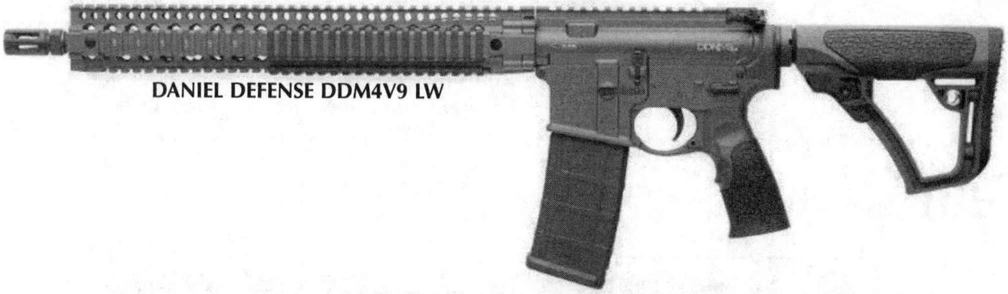

DANIEL DEFENSE DDM4V9 LW

DANIEL DEFENSE DDM4V9 S2W

DDM4V9

Action: Semiautomatic
Stock: Synthetic
Barrel: 16 in.
Sights: None
Weight: 6 lb. 10 oz.
Caliber: 5.56 NATO
Magazine: Detachable box, 30 rounds
Features: Daniel Defense stock, pistol and vertical grips, flash suppressor, and M4 rail
MSRP $1689

DDM4V9 LW

Action: Semiautomatic
Stock: Synthetic
Barrel: 16 in.
Sights: None
Weight: 6 lb. 6 oz.
Caliber: 5.56 NATO
Magazine: Detachable box, 30 rounds
Features: Daniel Defense stock, pistol and vertical grips, flash suppressor, and M4 rail; Daniel Defense Tornado Cerakote finish; available in black finish
MSRP $1819

DDM4V9 S2W

Action: Semiautomatic
Stock: Synthetic
Barrel: 18 in.
Sights: None
Weight: 7 lb. 8 oz.
Caliber: 5.56 NATO
Magazine: Detachable box, 30 rounds
Features: Daniel Defense stock, pistol and vertical grips, flash suppressor, and M4 rail
MSRP $1689

Del-Ton

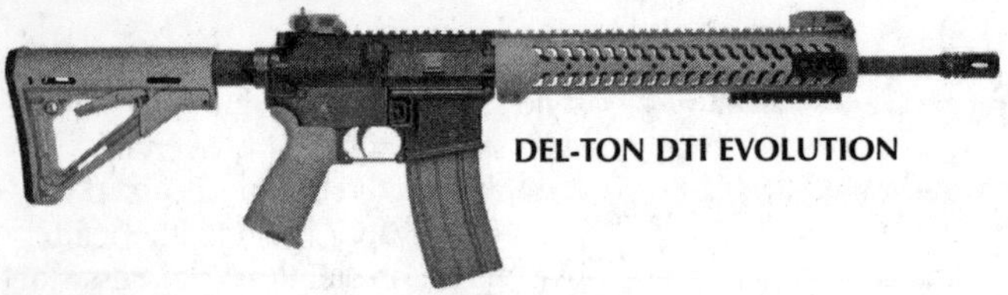

DEL-TON DTI EVOLUTION

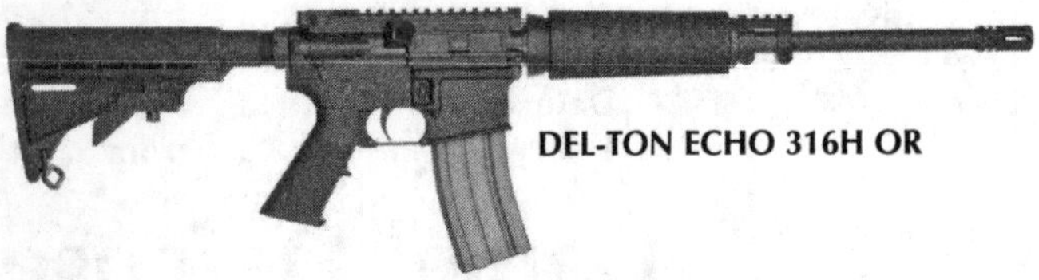

DEL-TON ECHO 316H OR

DEL-TON DT SPORT OR

RIFLES

DT SPORT OR

Action: Semiautomatic
Stock: M4 six-position
Barrel: 16 in.
Sights: None
Weight: 5 lb. 13 oz.
Caliber: 5.56 NATO
Magazine: Detachable box, 30 rounds
Features: Low profile gas block; six-position M4 stock; CAR handguards with single heat shields; A2 flash hider; anodized receiver; gun lock included
MSRP $707

DTI EVOLUTION

Action: Semiautomatic
Stock: Magpul CTR Mil-Spec
Barrel: 16 in.
Sights: Folding front, flip rear
Weight: 7 lb. 3 oz.
Caliber: 5.56 NATO
Magazine: Detachable box, 30 rounds
Features: Chrome-lined barrel; Samson Evolution free-float rail; Quick Flip Dual Aperture rear sight; Magpul MOE+ grip
MSRP $1299

ECHO 316H OR

Action: Semiautomatic
Stock: M4 five-position
Barrel: 16 in.
Sights: None
Weight: 6 lb. 10 oz.
Caliber: 5.56 NATO
Magazine: Detachable box, 30 rounds
Features: Single rail gas block; CAR handguards with single heat shields; A2 flash hider; forged 7075 T6 aluminum upper and lower receivers
MSRP $859

Dixie Gun Works

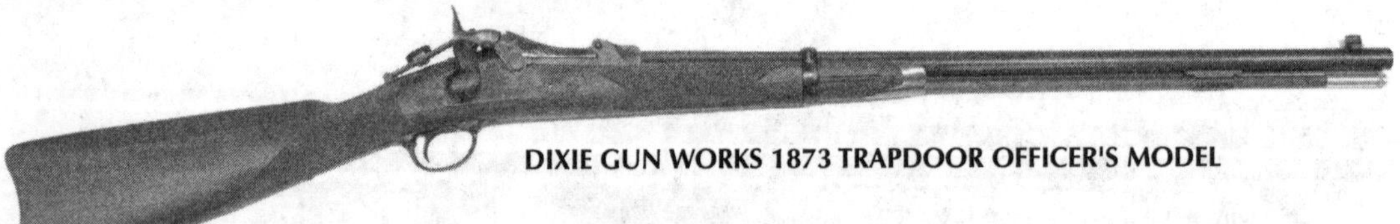

DIXIE GUN WORKS 1873 TRAPDOOR OFFICER'S MODEL

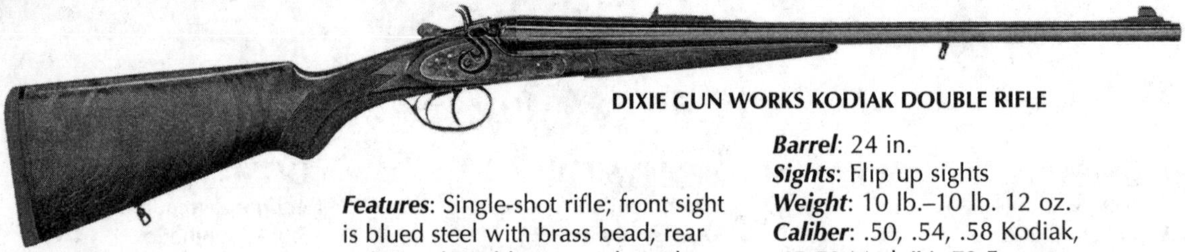

DIXIE GUN WORKS KODIAK DOUBLE RIFLE

1873 TRAPDOOR OFFICER'S MODEL BY PEDERSOLI

Action: Breechloading
Stock: Walnut
Barrel: 26 in.
Sights: Adjustable
Weight: 8 lb.
Caliber: .45-70 Govt.
Magazine: None
Features: Single-shot rifle; front sight is blued steel with brass bead; rear sight is adjustable tang sight; color case-hardened steel furniture, pewter nose cap; single set trigger; chambered for black powder cartridges or factory-loaded smokeless ammo
MSRP $1950

KODIAK DOUBLE RIFLE BY PEDERSOLI

Action: Lever
Stock: Walnut, pistol grip
Barrel: 24 in.
Sights: Flip up sights
Weight: 10 lb.–10 lb. 12 oz.
Caliber: .50, .54, .58 Kodiak, .45-70 Mark IV, .72 Express
Magazine: None
Features: Express has dovetail, steel ramp with brass bead as front sight; blued barrels; external hammers are rebounding style; double triggers; sling is included; English walnut buttstock and forearm are checkered; rubber recoil pad; chambered for black powder cartridges or factory-loaded smokeless ammo
MSRP . . . . $1250–$1525

DPMS Panther Arms

.22 BULL BARREL

Action: Semiautomatic
Stock: Fixed A2 synthetic
Barrel: 16 in.
Sights: None
Weight: 7 lb. 5 oz.
Caliber: .22LR
Magazine: Detachable box, 10 rounds
Features: Capable of accepting after-market stocks, grips, fire control components; integral feed ramp; fixed ejector
MSRP $1029

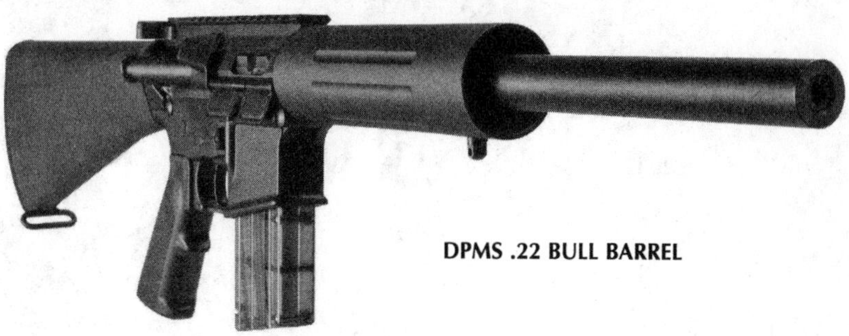

DPMS .22 BULL BARREL

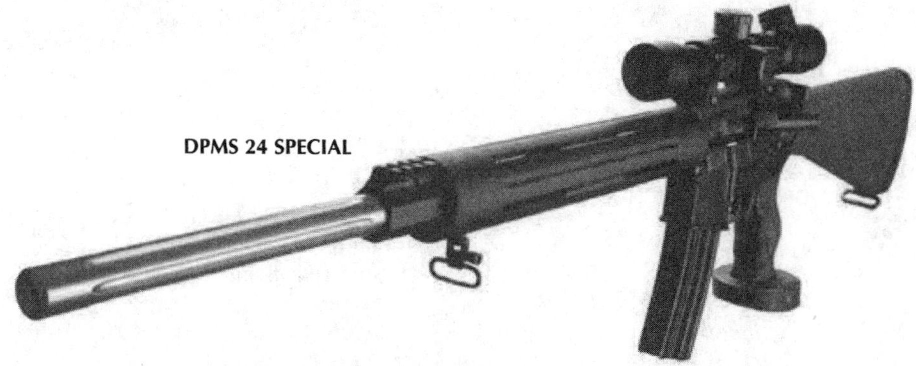

DPMS 24 SPECIAL

DPMS 3G2

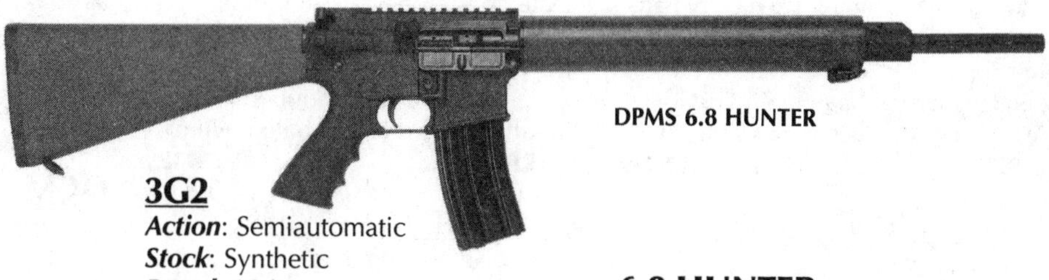

DPMS 6.8 HUNTER

24 SPECIAL

Action: Semiautomatic
Stock: Synthetic; pistol grip
Barrel: 24 in.
Sights: None
Weight: 10 lb. 4 oz.
Caliber: .233 Rem
Magazine: Detachable box, 30 rounds
Features: Aircraft aluminum alloy, A3 style flattop receiver coated in black Teflon; aluminum trigger guard; black standard A2 Zytel Mil-Spec stock with Panther Tactical grip; aluminum ribbed free-float tube; nylon web sling included; adjustable buttplate
MSRP $1229

3G2

Action: Semiautomatic
Stock: Synthetic
Barrel: 16 in.
Sights: Magpu Gen 2 BUS
Weight: 7 lb. 1.6 oz.
Caliber: 5.56 NATO
Magazine: Detachable box, 30 rounds
Features: Stainless lightweight barrel with Miculek compensator; full length M111 handguard allows for the placement of back-up sights either on the top rail or on a 45-degree angle for rapid close-range target acquisition; Ergo grip and Magpul STR stock round out this range-ready carbine; pistol grip stock
MSRP $1239

6.8 HUNTER

Action: Semiautomatic
Stock: A2-style
Barrel: 20 in.
Sights: N/A, optics ready
Weight: 7 lb. 2 oz.
Caliber: 6.8 SPC
Magazine: Detachable box, 25 rounds
Features: Carbon-fiber free-float tube handguard; flattop upper; fluted teflon coated barrel; two-stage match fire control
MSRP $1269

DPMS Panther Arms

DPMS A2 CLASSIC

DPMS AP4 CARBINE

DPMS CARBINE 16

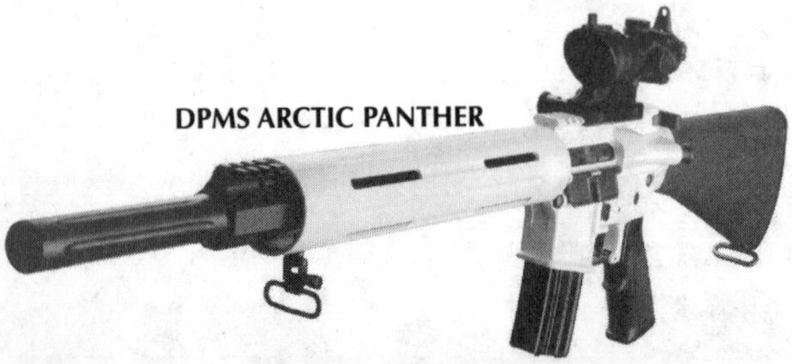
DPMS ARCTIC PANTHER

DPMS DCM

DPMS COMPACT HUNTER

A2 CLASSIC

Action: Semiautomatic
Stock: Synthetic
Barrel: 20 in.
Sights: Open
Weight: 9 lb.
Caliber: 5.56 NATO
Magazine: Detachable box, 30 rounds
Features: Chromoly steel barrel with A2 flash hider; forged aircraft aluminum alloy receiver with A2 fixed carry handle; black standardized A2 black style Mil-Spec stock; standard A2 round handguards; dual aperture adjustable rear sights, Mil-Spec front sight post
MSRP $869

AP4 CARBINE

Action: Semiautomatic
Stock: Synthetic
Barrel: 16 in.
Sights: Open
Weight: 7 lb. 2 oz.
Caliber: 5.56 NATO
Magazine: Detachable box, 30 rounds
Features: Chromoly steel barrel with A2 Flash hider; A3 aircraft aluminum alloy receiver with detachable carrying handle; adjustable rear sight and A2 front sight assembly; black AP4–6 position, telescoping fiber reinforced polymer stock; oval, carbine length GlacierGuards
MSRP $959

ARCTIC PANTHER

Action: Semiautomatic
Stock: Synthetic
Barrel: 20 in.
Sights: None
Weight: 9 lb.
Caliber: .223 Rem.
Magazine: Detachable box, 30 rounds
Features: Fluted and black Teflon coated barrel; aircraft aluminum alloy, A3 style flattop receiver coated in white; standard A2 black Zytel Mil-Spec stock; aluminum ribbed free-float handguard tube (coated white)
MSRP $1129

CARBINE 16

Action: Semiautomatic
Stock: Synthetic
Barrel: 16 in.
Sights: Open
Weight: 6 lb. 14 oz.
Caliber: 5.56 NATO
Magazine: Detachable box, 30 rounds
Features: Chromoly steel barrel with flash hider; A3 aircraft aluminum alloy receiver with detachable carrying handle; adjustable rear sight and A2 front sight assembly; DPMS Pardus black stock; oval, carbine length GlacierGuards
MSRP $859

COMPACT HUNTER

Action: Semiautomatic
Stock: Synthetic
Barrel: 16 in.
Sights: None
Weight: 7 lb. 12 oz.
Caliber: .308 Win.
Magazine: Detachable box, 4, 10, 20 rounds
Features: Designed for smaller statures and suitable for youth, female, and hunters who prefer a compact firearm; Teflon-coated stainless steel barrel; carbon fiber free-float tube; Hogue pistol grip; B5 Systems-Special Operations Peculiar Modification (SOPMOD) stock
MSRP $1499

DCM

Action: Semiautomatic
Stock: Synthetic
Barrel: 20 in.
Sights: Adjustable NM
Weight: 9 lb. 6 oz.
Caliber: .233 Rem.
Magazine: Detachable box, 30 rounds
Features: National Match dual aperture rear sight, NM front sight post; A2 fixed carry handle; forged aircraft aluminum alloy receiver; receiver coated in Teflon; aluminum trigger guard; standard black A2 style Mil-Spec stock with trap door assembly; DCM free-float handguard system
MSRP $1213

DPMS Panther Arms

DPMS PANTHER ARMS GII AP4

DPMS PANTHER ARMS GII BULL

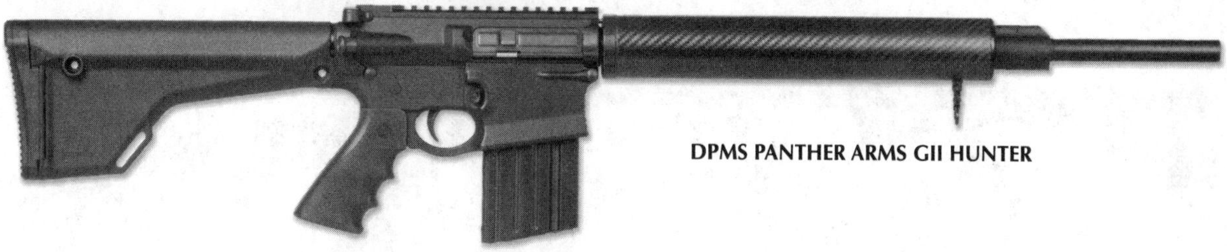

DPMS PANTHER ARMS GII HUNTER

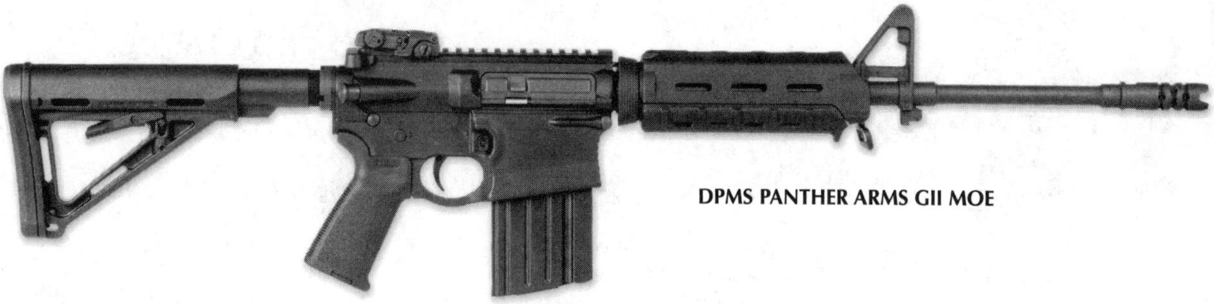

DPMS PANTHER ARMS GII MOE

GII AP4

Action: Semiautomatic
Stock: Synthetic
Barrel: 16 in.
Sights: Adjustable
Weight: 7 lb. 4 oz.
Caliber: .308 Win., 7.62 NATO
Magazine: Detachable box, 20 rounds
Features: Front F-marked sight, rear Magpul Gen 2 BUS; six-position collapsible stock; muzzle brake; receiver mounted Picatinny rail
MSRP. $1499

GII BULL

Action: Semiautomatic
Stock: Synthetic
Barrel: 24 in.
Sights: None
Weight: 10 lb.
Caliber: .308 Win., 7.62 NATO
Magazine: Detachable box, 20 rounds
Features: A2 Mil Spec buttstock; receiver mounted Picatinny rail
MSRP. $1759

GII HUNTER

Action: Semiautomatic
Stock: Synthetic
Barrel: 20 in.
Sights: None
Weight: 7 lb. 12 oz.
Caliber: .308 Win., 7.62 NATO
Magazine: Detachable box, 20 rounds
Features: Magpul MOE RIfle stock; receiver mounted Picatinny rail
MSRP. $1699

GII MOE

Action: Semiautomatic
Stock: Synthetic
Barrel: 16 in.
Sights: Adjustable
Weight: 7 lb. 4 oz.
Caliber: .308 Win., 7.62 NATO
Magazine: Detachable box, 20 rounds
Features: Front F-marked sight, rear Magpul Gen 2 BUS; six-position collapsible stock; muzzle brake; receiver mounted Picatinny rail
MSRP. $1599

RIFLES

DPMS Panther Arms

DPMS PANTHER ARMS GII RECON

DPMS PANTHER ARMS GII SASS

DPMS LITE LR-308

DPMS LR-204

DPMS LO-PRO CLASSIC

GII RECON

Action: Semiautomatic
Stock: Synthetic
Barrel: 16 in.
Sights: Adjustable
Weight: 8 lb. 8 oz.
Caliber: .308 Win., 7.62 NATO
Magazine: Detachable box, 20 rounds
Features: Magpul Gen 2 front and rear BUS; six position collapsible stock; Advanced Armament 51T Blackout flash hider; handguard and receiver mounted Picatinny rails
MSRP. $1759

GII SASS

Action: Semiautomatic
Stock: Synthetic
Barrel: 18 in.
Sights: Adjustable
Weight: 10 lb. 8 oz.
Caliber: .308 Win., 7.62 NATO
Magazine: Detachable box, 20 rounds
Features: Magpul Gen 2 front and rear BUS; MagPul PRS stock; Panther flash hider; Harris bipod; handguard and receiver mounted Picatinny rails
MSRP. $2379

LITE LR-308

Action: Semiautomatic
Stock: Synthetic
Barrel: 24 in.
Sights: None
Weight: 10 lb. 4 oz.
Caliber: .308 Win.
Magazine: Detachable box, 4, 10, 20 rounds
Features: 416 stainless steel lightweight fluted barrel; improved 2012 carbon fiber free-float tube; A3 receiver
MSRP. $1499

LO-PRO CLASSIC

Action: Semiautomatic
Stock: Synthetic
Barrel: 16 in.
Sights: None
Weight: 7 lb. 12 oz.
Caliber: 5.56 NATO
Magazine: Detachable box, 30 rounds
Features: Chromoly steel barrel; flattop Lo-Pro, extruded receiver made of aircraft aluminum alloy; semiauto trigger group; standard A2 black Zytel Mil stock with trap door assembly; GlacierGuards
MSRP. $769

LR-204

Action: Semiautomatic
Stock: Synthetic
Barrel: 24 in.
Sights: None
Weight: 10 lb. 4 oz.
Caliber: .204 Ruger
Magazine: Detachable box, 30 rounds
Features: Fluted barrel; standard A2 black stock; aluminum ribbed free-float tube; aircraft aluminum alloy, Teflon coated, forged A3 style receiver; nylon web sling included
MSRP. $1213

DPMS Panther Arms

DPMS LR-243H

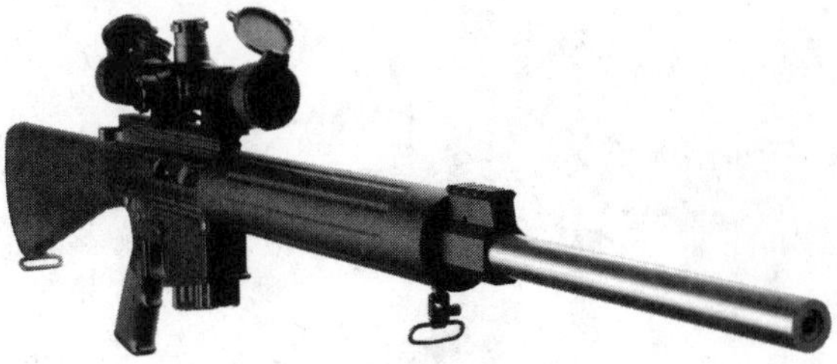

DPMS LR-308

DPMS RECON

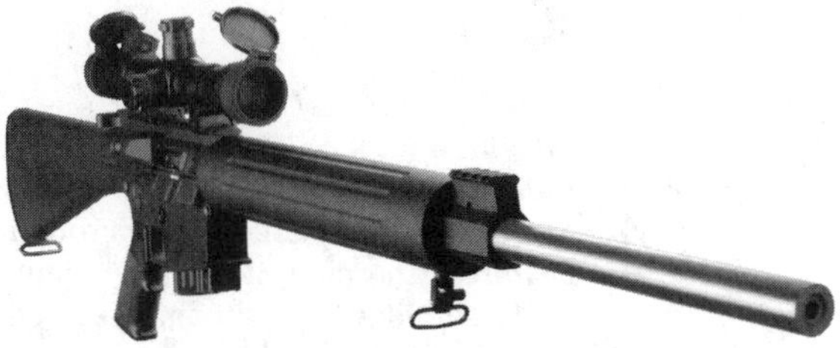

DPMS LR-260

DPMS REPR

LR-260/LR-65

Action: Semiautomatic
Stock: Synthetic
Barrel: 24 in.
Sights: None
Weight: 11 lb. 4 oz.
Caliber: .260 Rem.
Magazine: Detachable box, 19 rounds
Features: 416 Stainless steel bull barrel; A3 style flattop receiver made of thick walled aluminum; standard AR-15 trigger group; standard A2 black style Mil-Spec stock with trap door assembly; standard length ribbed free-float handguard tube
MSRP. $1239

LR-308

Action: Semiautomatic
Stock: Synthetic
Barrel: 24 in.
Sights: None
Weight: 11 lb. 3 oz.
Caliber: .308 Win.
Magazine: Detachable box, 19 rounds
Features: 416 Stainless steel bull barrel; thick walled aluminum receiver coated with Teflon; internal trigger guard; raised Picatinny rail for easy scope mounting; standard A2 Black Zytel Mil-Spec stock
MSRP. $1199

PRAIRIE PANTHER CAMO

Action: Semiautomatic
Stock: Synthetic
Barrel: 20 in.
Sights: None
Weight: 7 lb. 2 oz.
Caliber: .223 Rem.
Magazine: Detachable box, 20 rounds
Features: Target crowned, stainless steel heavy barrel; A3 flattop aircraft aluminum alloy receiver; Magpul winter trigger guard; King's Desert Shadow camo, King's Snow Shadow camo, or Mossy Oak Brush camo stock; receiver features durable ceramic over coat in either type of camo; nylon web sling included
MSRP. $1289

RECON

Action: Semiautomatic
Stock: Synthetic
Barrel: 16 in.
Sights: Magpul BUIS
Weight: 9 lb.
Caliber: 5.56 NATO
Magazine: Detachable box, 30 rounds
Features: Bead-blasted stainless, mid length gas system; semi-auto trigger group; Magpul MOE stock in Teflon black
MSRP. $1129

REPR

Action: Semiautomatic
Stock: Synthetic
Barrel: 20 in.
Sights: None
Weight: 9 lb. 12 oz.
Caliber: 7.62 NATO
Magazine: Detachable box, 19 rounds
Features: Two-stage match grade trigger; dark earth Magpul PRS stock; Hogue rubber grip with finger grooves; A3 style flattop; ambi-selector installed; milled from solid billet of aluminum; AAC flash hider/suppressor adapter
MSRP. $2589

DPMS Panther Arms

DPMS SWEET 16

DPMS TACTICAL 16

SWEET 16, BULL 20, BULL 24

Action: Semiautomatic
Stock: Synthetic
Barrel: 16 in., 20 in., 24 in.
Sights: None
Weight: 7 lb. 14 oz.–9 lb. 13 oz.
Caliber: .223 Rem.
Magazine: Detachable box, 30 rounds
Features: Aircraft aluminum alloy, A3 style flattop receiver coated in black Teflon; aluminum trigger guard; black standard A2 Zytel Mil-Spec stock; aluminum ribbed free-float tube; Nylon web sling included
Bull Sweet 16: $939
Bull 20:. $969
Bull 24:. $999

TACTICAL 16

Action: Semiautomatic
Stock: Synthetic
Barrel: 16 in.
Sights: Open
Weight: 8 lb. 3 oz.
Caliber: 5.56 NATO
Magazine: Detachable box, 30 rounds
Features: Chromoly steel barrel with A3 Flash hider; A2 front and rear sight assembly; forged aircraft aluminum alloy receiver coated in Teflon; black standard A2 style mil stock; nylon web sling included
MSRP $859

E.M.F. Company

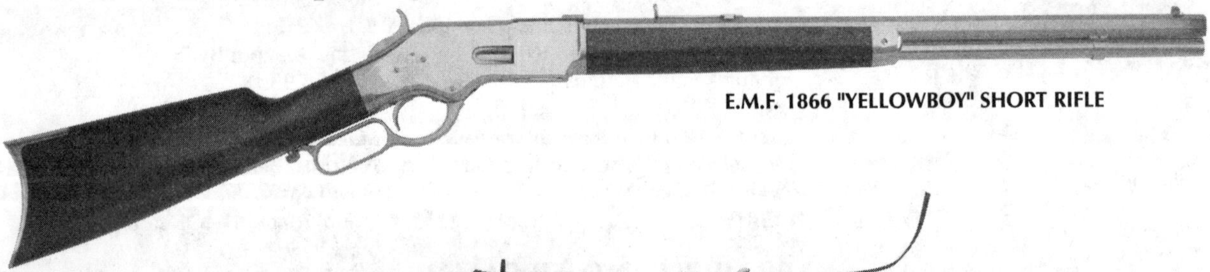

E.M.F. 1866 "YELLOWBOY" SHORT RIFLE

E.M.F. ROSSI 1892 TRAPPER CARBINE

1866 "YELLOWBOY" SHORT RIFLE

Action: Lever
Stock: Walnut
Barrel: 20 in.
Sights: Open
Weight: 8 lb. 3 oz.
Caliber: .38 Spl., .45LC
Magazine: Under-barrel tube, 10+1 rounds
Features: First true cowboy lever-action rifle; loading gate passes cartridges through side of the receiver; SASS badge engraved on both sides
MSRP $1175

ROSSI 1892 TRAPPER CARBINE

Action: Lever
Stock: Hardwood
Barrel: 16 in.
Sights: Fixed
Weight: 4 lb. 13 oz.
Caliber: .44 Mag.
Magazine: Under-barrel tube, 8+1 rounds
Features: Stainless steel frame; round stainless steel barrel; hardwood forend and buttstock; fast western-style lever; crescent buttplates
MSRP $585

E.R. Shaw

MARK VII CUSTOM

Action: Bolt
Stock: Walnut, laminate wood, or synthetic
Barrel: 16.25 in.–26 in.
Sights: None
Weight: Depending on specifications
Caliber: 75 caliber choices from .17 Rem. to .458 Lott
Magazine: Fixed magazine
Features: Right- or left-hand actions; stainless receivers; contour barrels; polished or matte blued finish; recoil pads and swivel studs; choice of two barrel contours, stainless steel or blued chromoly steel
Base price:. . . . . $775–$1250

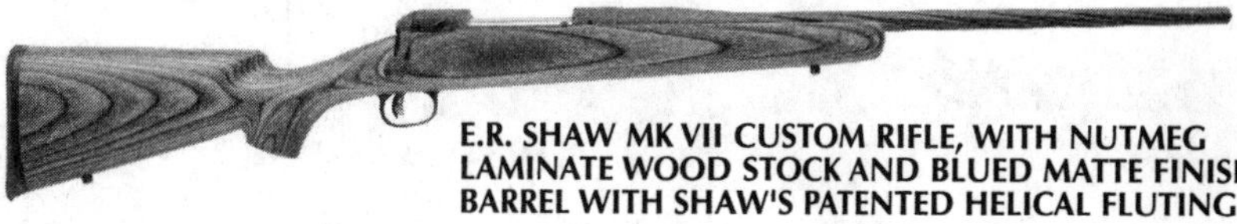

E.R. SHAW MK VII CUSTOM RIFLE, WITH NUTMEG LAMINATE WOOD STOCK AND BLUED MATTE FINISH BARREL WITH SHAW'S PATENTED HELICAL FLUTING

Excel Arms

EXCEL ARMS ACCELERATOR RIFLE

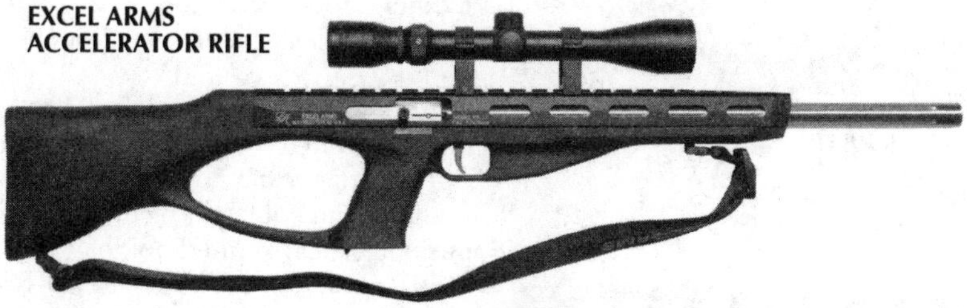

EXCEL ARMS X-5.7R

EXCEL ARMS X-22R

ACCELERATOR RIFLE

Action: Semiautomatic
Stock: Polymer composite, pistol grip
Barrel: 18 in.
Sights: Standard includes Red/Green dot optic
Weight: 8 lb.
Caliber: .22 WMR, .17 HMR
Magazine: Detachable box, 9 rounds
Features: Weaver rail for scope, sights, and optics; pin-block safety; stainless steel barrel; polymer composite stock available in black or silver shroud
MR-22: . . . .$538–$670
MR-5.7: . . . .$672–$805

X-5.7R

Action: Semiautomatic
Stock: Synthetic
Barrel: 18 in.
Sights: None
Weight: 6 lb. 4 oz.
Caliber: 5.7x28mm
Magazine: Detachable box, 25, 10 rounds
Features: CNC-machined aluminum; Picatinny rail; tactical AR styling; collapsible stock; tapped holes in the hand guard for mounting accessory rails
MSRP $795
Iron sights: $916

X-22R RIFLE

Action: Semiautomatic
Stock: Synthetic
Barrel: 18 in.
Sights: None
Weight: 4 lb. 12 oz.
Caliber: .22LR HV
Magazine: Detachable box, 25 rounds, (10 rounds optional)
Features: CNC-machined aluminum frame; optional 3–9x40 scope; tapped holes in hand guard for mounting accessory rails; integral weaver base to mount scopes, sights, and optics
Basic: $504
Scoped: $594
10 RD: $504

FNH USA

FNH BALLISTA

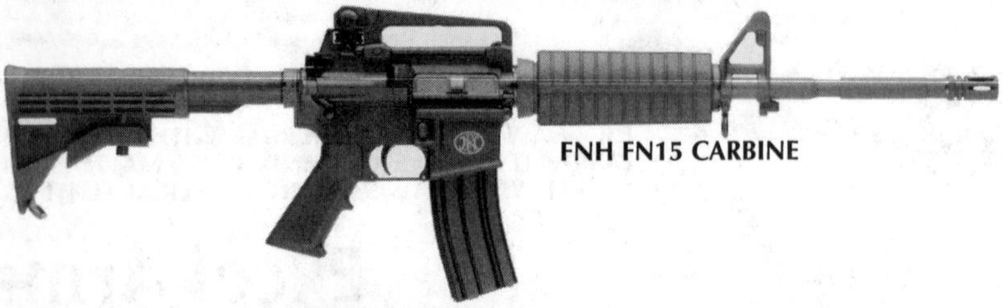
FNH FN15 CARBINE

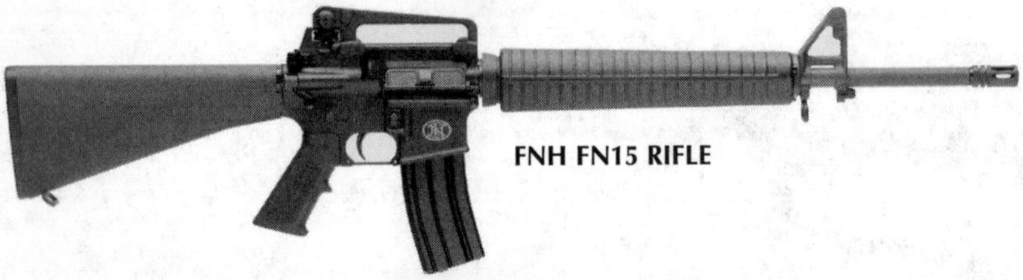
FNH FN15 RIFLE

FNH FN SPR A5M XP

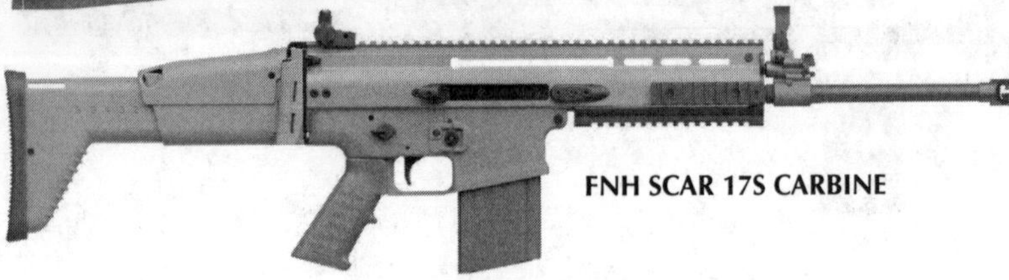
FNH SCAR 17S CARBINE

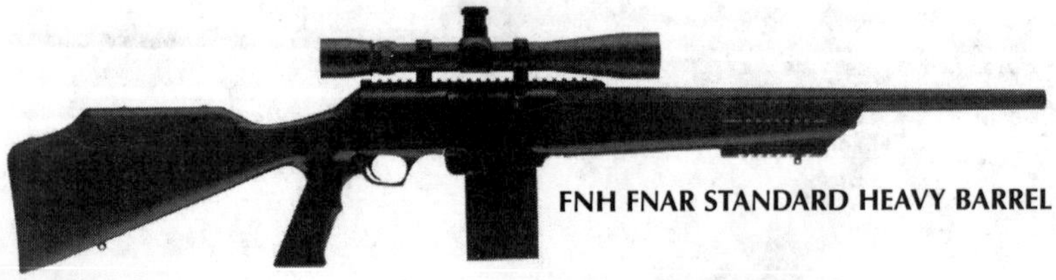
FNH FNAR STANDARD HEAVY BARREL

BALLISTA

Action: Bolt
Stock: Collapsible
Barrel: 26 in.
Sights: N/A, scope compatible
Weight: 15 lb.
Caliber: .308 Win., .300 Win. Mag., .338 Lapua Mag.
Magazine: Detachable box, 8 or 15 rounds (.308 Win.), 6 or 10 rounds (.300 Win. Mag.), 5 or 8 rounds (.338 Lapua)
Features: Modular, multi-caliber designed for long-range precision work; aluminum alloy receiver; adjustable trigger; ambidextrous stock; vibration-isolated aluminum alloy receiver; Picatinny rail
MSRP $6999

FN15 CARBINE

Action: Semiautomatic
Stock: Synthetic
Barrel: 16 in.
Sights: Fixed
Weight: 7 lb.
Caliber: 5.56 NATO, .223 Rem.
Magazine: Detachable box, 30 rounds
Features: Fixed front sights, a removable rear carrying handle; six position collapsible stock; A2-style compensator
MSRP $1149

FN15 RIFLE

Action: Semiautomatic
Stock: Synthetic
Barrel: 20 in.
Sights: Fixed
Weight: 8 lb.
Caliber: 5.56 NATO, .223 Rem.
Magazine: Detachable box, 30 rounds
Features: Fixed front sights, a removable rear carrying handle; A2-style compensator
MSRP $1149

FN SPR A5M XP

Action: Bolt
Stock: McMillan fiberglass
Barrel: 20 in., 24 in.
Sights: None
Weight: 11 lb. 5 oz.–11 lb. 13 oz.
Caliber: .300 WSM, .308 Win.
Magazine: Detachable box, 4 or 5 rounds
Features: Threaded tactical bolt knob; barrel threaded muzzle; Picatinny rail; external claw extractor with controlled round feeding; integral recoil lug; three-position safety; knurled bolt handle
MSRP . . . . $1999–$2899

FNAR STANDARD

Action: Gas-operated semiautomatic
Stock: Synthetic
Barrel: 16 in., 20 in. standard fluted, 20 in. heavy fluted
Sights: Receiver mounted rail
Weight: 8 lb. 13 oz.–10 lb.
Caliber: .308 Win., 7.62 NATO
Magazine: Detachable box, 10, 20 rounds
Features: Extended bolt handle, hammer-forged barrel with crown; comes with one magazine, three interchangeable recoil pads, three comb inserts and shims for adjusting for cast-on, cast-off, and drop at comb; stock is matte black synthetic with pistol grip and adjustable comb
MSRP . . . . $1199–$1767

SCAR 17S CARBINE

Action: Gas-operated semiautomatic
Stock: Polymer
Barrel: 16.25 in.
Sights: Adjustable, folding, removable
Weight: 8 lb.
Caliber: .308 Win., 7.62 NATO
Magazine: Detachable box, 10, 20 rounds
Features: Fully adjustable stock; Picatinny rail plus three accessory rails for attaching a variety of sights and lasers; free-floating, cold-hammer-forged barrel; available in black or Flat Dark Earth tactical, telescoping, side-folding polymer stock
MSRP . . . . $2995–$3349

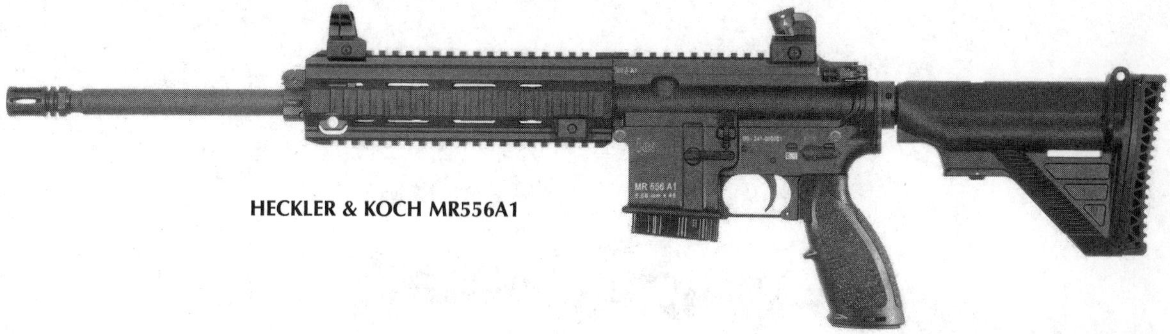

HECKLER & KOCH MR556A1

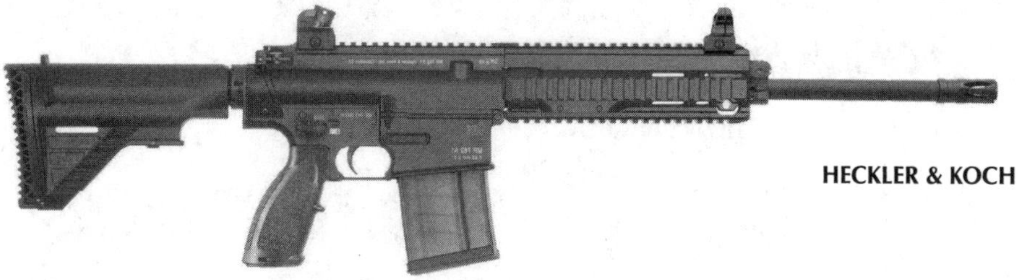

HECKLER & KOCH MR762A1

HECKLER & KOCH MR762A1 (LRP)

MR556A1

Action: Semiautomatic
Stock: Synthetic
Barrel: 16.5 in.
Sights: Adjustable
Weight: 8 lb. 10 oz.
Caliber: 5.56 NATO, .223 Rem.
Magazine: Detachable box, 30 rounds
Features: Free-floating Picatinny rail; gas operated piston system
MSRP $3295

MR762A1

Action: Semiautomatic
Stock: Synthetic
Barrel: 16.5 in.
Sights: None
Weight: 9 lb. 15 oz.
Caliber: 7.62 NATO
Magazine: Detachable box, 10, 20 rounds
Features: Match rifle features; direct descendant of HK416/417 series, but made for civilians; uses a piston and a solid operating "pusher" rod in place of the common gas tube normally used in AR-style rifles; cold-hammer-forged barrel; adjustable stock
MSRP $3995

MR762A1 (LRP)

Action: Semiautomatic
Stock: Synthetic
Barrel: 16.5 in.
Sights: 3–9x40mm scope
Weight: 9 lb. 15 oz.
Caliber: 7.62 NATO
Magazine: Detachable box, 10, 20 rounds
Features: Rifle; Leupold 3–9 VX-R Patrol scope and mount; HK G28 buttstock; LaRue Tactical BRM-S bipod; ERGO Pistol Grip; Blue Force Gear sling; Manta rail covers; OTIS cleaning kit; a 10- and 20-round magazine; Model 1720 Pelican case
MSRP . . . . $6399–$6899

Henry Repeating Arms

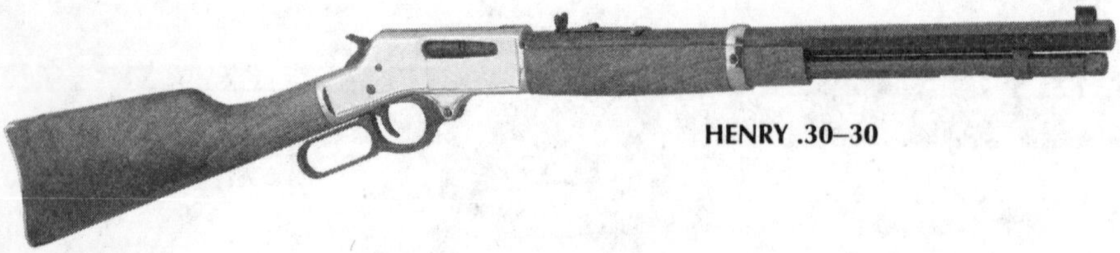

HENRY .30–30

HENRY .45-70 LEVER ACTION

HENRY BIG BOY

HENRY GOLDEN BOY DELUXE

.30-30

Action: Lever
Stock: Walnut
Barrel: 20 in.
Sights: Open
Weight: 7 lb.
Caliber: .30-30 Win.
Magazine: Under-barrel tube, 5 rounds
Features: Steel round barrel: deluxe checkered American walnut with rubber buttpad; XS Ghost Rings sights; blued steel receiver, drilled and tapped for easy scope mounting. Brass octagon barrel: straight-grip American walnut with buttplate; marble fully adjustable semi-buckhorn rear sight, with diamond insert, beaded front sight; brass receiver, drilled and tapped for easy scope mounting
Steel:. $850
Brass:. $950

.45-70 LEVER ACTION

Action: Lever
Stock: Walnut
Barrel: 18.43 in.
Sights: Closed rear, blade front
Weight: 7 lb. 1 oz.
Caliber: .45-70 Govt.
Magazine: Under-barrel tube, 4 rounds
Features: Pistol-grip American walnut with buttplate; blued steel drilled and tapped for easy scope mounting; XS Ghost Rings rear sight with blade front
MSRP. $850

BIG BOY

Action: Lever
Stock: Walnut
Barrel: 20 in.
Sights: Open
Weight: 8.68 lb.
Caliber: .44 Mag., .45 Colt, .357 Mag.
Magazine: Under-barrel tube, 10 rounds
Features: Adjustable marble semi-buckhorn rear with white diamond insert and brass beaded front sight; solid top brass receiver, brass buttplate and brass barrel band; straight-grip American walnut stock; octagonal barrel
MSRP. $900

GOLDEN BOY DELUXE ENGRAVED II

Action: Lever
Stock: Walnut
Barrel: 20 in.
Sights: Open
Weight: 6 lb. 12 oz.
Caliber: .22
Magazine: Under-barrel tube, 16 rounds (LR), 21 rounds (Short)
Features: American walnut stock; adjustable buckhorn rear sight, beaded front sight; brasslite receiver, brass buttplate, and blued barrel
MSRP. $1585

Henry Repeating Arms

HENRY LEVER ACTION .22

HENRY LEVER OCTAGON FRONTIER

HENRY MARE'S LEG

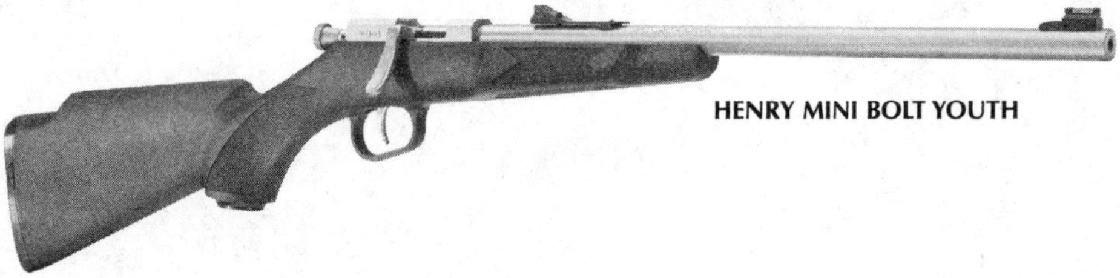

HENRY MINI BOLT YOUTH

LEVER ACTION .22

Action: Lever
Stock: Walnut
Barrel: 16.13 in. (carbine, youth), 18.25 in.
Sights: Open
Weight: 4 lb. 8 oz. (carbine, youth), 5 lb. 4 oz., 5 lb. 8 oz. (Mag.)
Caliber: .22, .22L, .22LR
Magazine: Under-barrel tube, 11 rounds (.22 Mag.), 15 rounds (.22LR), 17 rounds (.22L), 18 rounds (.22S), 21 rounds (.22)
Features: Straight-grip American walnut stock; deluxe checkered American walnut stock (.22 Magnum); adjustable rear, hooded front sight; blued round barrel and lever
Rifle, Youth, Carbine: . . .$360–$375
Magnum: $500

LEVER OCTAGON FRONTIER

Action: Lever
Stock: Walnut
Barrel: 20 in.
Sights: Open
Weight: 6 lb. 4 oz.
Caliber: .22LR, .22S, .17 HMR
Magazine: Under-barrel tube, 21 rounds (.22S), 16 rounds (.22LR); 12 rounds (.22 Mag.); 11 rounds (.17 HMR)
Features: American walnut; marble fully adjustable semi-buckhorn rear with reversible white diamond insert and brass beaded front sight; blued barrel and lever
.22LR, .22S: $450
.22 Mag.: $550
.17 HMR: $550

MARE'S LEG

Action: Lever
Stock: Walnut
Barrel: 12.9 in.
Sights: Open
Weight: 4 lb. 7 oz. (.22S/L/LR), 5 lb. 7 oz. (.45 Colt)
Caliber: .22S/L/LR, .45 Colt
Magazine: Under-barrel tube, 10 rounds (.22 S/L/LR); 5 rounds (.45 Colt)
Features: .45 Colt: American walnut; marble fully adjustable semi-buckhorn rear with reversible white diamond insert and brass beaded front sights; brasslite receiver, brass buttplate, and blued barrel; .22 S/L/LR: American walnut; fully adjustable rear, with hooded front sight; blued metal barrel and lever
.22 Magnum. $450
.22 S/L/LR: $440
.45 Colt, .44 Mag., .357 Mag.: . .$975

MINI BOLT YOUTH

Action: Bolt
Stock: Synthetic
Barrel: 16.25 in.
Sights: Open
Weight: 3 lb. 4 oz.
Caliber: .22LR, .22S
Magazine: None
Features: Single-shot; one-piece fiberglass synthetic stock in orange or black; Williams fire sights; stainless steel receiver and barrel
MSRP. $275

RIFLES

Henry Repeating Arms

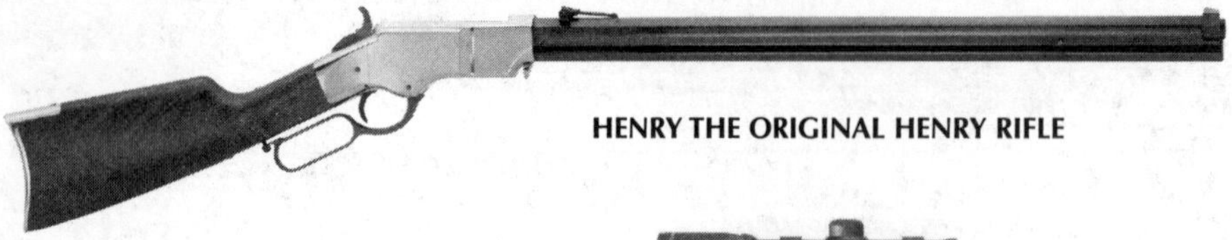

HENRY THE ORIGINAL HENRY RIFLE

HENRY PUMP ACTION OCTAGON

HENRY U.S. SURVIVAL AR-7

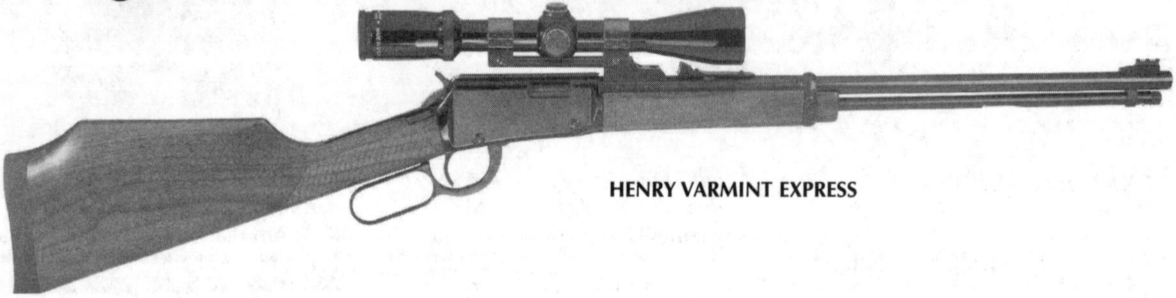

HENRY VARMINT EXPRESS

THE ORIGINAL HENRY RIFLE

Action: Lever
Stock: Walnut
Barrel: 24.5
Sights: Folding ladder rear
Weight: 9 lb.
Caliber: .44-40
Magazine: Under-barrel tube, 13+1 rounds
Features: True to original specifications; first time the Original Henry has been offered in the U.S. by an American manufacturer in 150 years
MSRP $2300

PUMP ACTION OCTAGON

Action: Pump
Stock: Walnut
Barrel: 19.75 in.
Sights: Open
Weight: 6 lb.
Caliber: .22LR, .22S, .22Mag
Magazine: Under-barrel tube, 15 rounds (.22LR, .22S), 12 rounds (.22 Mag.)
Features: American walnut stock; adjustable rear, beaded front sight; blued octagonal barrel
MSRP $550
Magnum: $590

U.S. SURVIVAL AR-7

Action: Semiautomatic
Stock: ABS Plastic
Barrel: 16 in.
Sights: Open
Weight: 2 lb. 4 oz.
Caliber: .22LR
Magazine: Detachable box, 8 rounds
Features: ABS plastic in black; adjustable rear sight, blade front sight; Teflon coated receiver and coated steel barrel
Black: $290
Camo: $350

VARMINT EXPRESS

Action: Lever
Stock: Walnut
Barrel: 20 in.
Sights: Open
Weight: 5 lb. 12 oz.
Caliber: .17 HMR
Magazine: Under-barrel tube, 11 rounds
Features: Checkered American walnut stock; Williams fire sights; blued round barrel and lever
MSRP $540

High Standard

ENFORCER

Action: Semiautomatic
Stock: Synthetic
Barrel: 16 in.
Sights: Flip-up
Weight: 7 lb. 6 oz.
Caliber: 5.56 NATO
Magazine: Detachable box, 30 rounds
Features: A2 flash hider; YHM quad rail with smooth side; YHM same plane flip-up sights; ergonomic grip; two-stage match trigger
MSRP $1050

HIGH STANDARD ENFORCER

Hi-Point Firearms

MODEL 995TS

Action: Blow-back semiautomatic
Stock: Black, skeleton-style, all-weather molded polymer
Barrel: 16.5 in.
Sights: Adjustable
Weight: 7 lb.
Caliber: 9mm, .40 S&W, .45 ACP
Magazine: Detachable box, 10 rounds
Features: Sling, swivels, and base mount included; last round lock-open latch; multiple Picatinny rails; internal recoil buffer
MSRP . . . . $297–$449

HI-POINT FIREARMS MODEL 995TS

Howa by Legacy Sports

HOWA CLASSIC LAMINATE THUMBHOLE VARMINTER

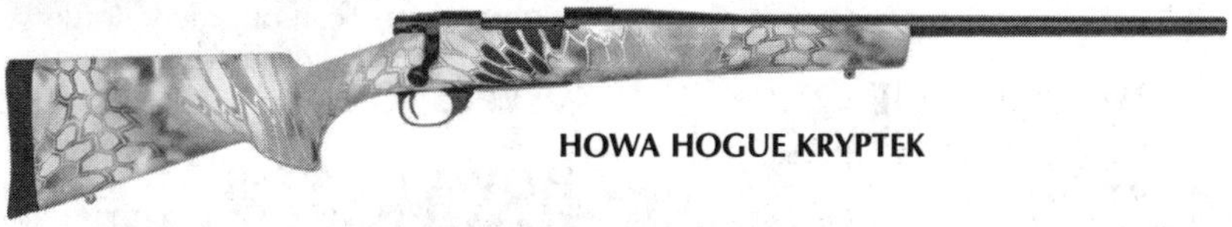
HOWA HOGUE KRYPTEK

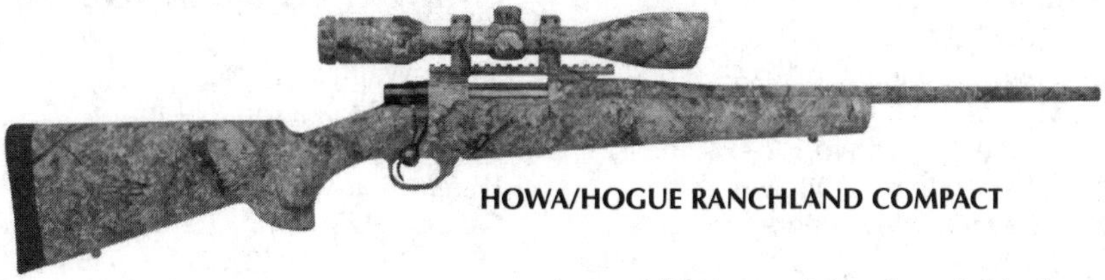
HOWA/HOGUE RANCHLAND COMPACT

CLASSIC LAMINATE VARMINTER

Action: Bolt
Stock: Laminate
Barrel: 24 in.
Sights: None
Weight: 9 lb. 14 oz.
Caliber: .223, .204 Ruger, .22–250 Rem., .243 Win., .308 Win.
Magazine: Internal box, 5 rounds
Features: Nutmeg or Pepper stock color; optional thumbhole stock; heavy blued or stainless barrel; black recoil pad; sling swivel studs
Blued barrel $869
Stainless barrel. $985

HOGUE KRYPTEK

Action: Bolt
Stock: Synthetic
Barrel: 20 in., 22 in., 24 in.
Sights: None
Weight: 7 lb. 12 oz.–8 lb.
Caliber: .22-250 Rem., .25-06 Rem., .204 Ruger, .223 Rem., .243 Win., .270 Win., .30-06 Spfd., .300 Win. Mag., .308 Win., .338 Win. Mag., .375 Ruger, 6.5x55 Swedish, 7mm Rem. Mag.
Magazine: Internal
Features: Available in three different stock patterns: Highlander, Typhon, and Raid
MSRP . . . . $626–$762

HOWA/HOGUE RANCHLAND COMPACT

Action: Bolt
Stock: Synthetic
Barrel: 20 in.
Sights: None
Weight: 7 lb. 2 oz.–8 lb. 12 oz.
Caliber: .223 Rem., .204 Ruger, .22-250 Rem., .243 Win., .308 Win., 7mm-08 Rem.
Magazine: Internal box
Features: Black, green, or sand overmolded stock; includes one-piece scope rail; color match combo option includes Nikko Stirling 3–10x42 Nighteater scope; rings and one-piece base; full camo packages include Desert Camo Stock
MSRP $652

Howa by Legacy Sports

HOGUE RIFLE

HOWA/TALON SNOWKING

HOWA HOGUE ZEISS PACKAGE

TARGETMASTER COMBO

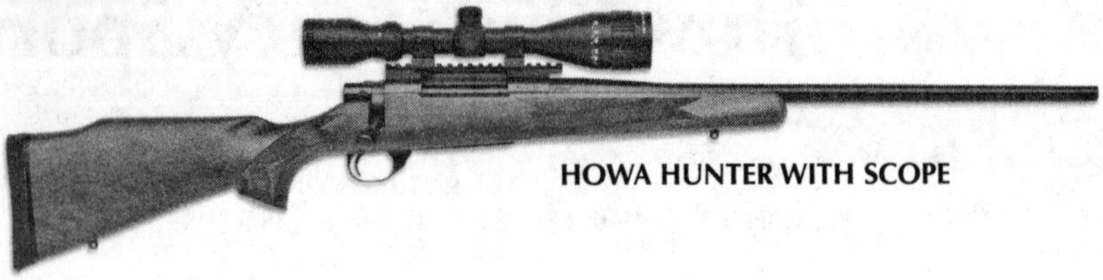

HOWA HUNTER WITH SCOPE

HOWA/HOGUE RIFLES

Action: Bolt
Stock: Synthetic
Barrel: 20 in., 22 in., 24 in.
Sights: None
Weight: 7 lb. 12 oz.
Caliber: Standard Blue, Stainless: .223 Rem., .204 Ruger, .22-250 Rem., .243 Win., .308 Win., 7mm–08, 6.5x 55 Swedish, .25-06 Rem., .270 Win., .30-06 Spfd.; Magnum Blue, Stainless: .300 Win. Mag., .375 Ruger, .338 Win. Mag, 7mm Rem. Mag.
Magazine: Internal box
Features: Stainless or blued barrel; synthetic stock comes in black, sand, or green with matching Hogue Soft Grip; recoil pad; hinged floor plate; sling; swivel studs
Standard:. . . . .$570–$678
Magnum:. . . . .$599–$704
Varmint:. . . . .$631–$717

HOWA/HOGUE OR TALON SNOWKING

Action: Bolt
Stock: Synthetic
Barrel: 22 in.
Sights: Mounted 4–16x44 scope
Weight: 9 lb. 6 oz.
Caliber: .223 Rem., .243 Win., .22-250 Rem., .308 Win.
Magazine: 4+1 rounds
Features: HACT 2-stage trigger system; 3 position safety; Blackhawk Talon or Hogue overmolded stock in Kings Snow Shadow Camo; Nikko Stirling Gameking 4–16x44 scope with LRK Range-finding Reticle; color matched scope, rings, and one-piece base; limited edition and limited availability only through Bill Hicks & Co.
Hogue: $799
Talon:. $1136

HOGUE ZEISS PACKAGE

Action: Bolt
Stock: Synthetic
Barrel: 22 in., 24 in.
Sights: Scope
Weight: 9 lb. 6 oz.–9 lb. 9 oz.
Caliber: .22-250 Rem., .25-06 Rem., .204 Ruger, .223 Rem., .243 Win., .270 Win., .30-06 Spfd., .300 Win. Mag., .300 Win. Mag. Fluted, .308 Win., .338 Win. Mag., .375 Ruger, 6.5x55 Swedish, 7mm Rem. Mag.
Magazine: Internal
Features: Zeiss Terra 3–9x42 scope; available in green and black stocks; walnut package available
MSRP . . . . $1182–$1359

HOGUE/TARGETMASTER COMBO

Action: Bolt
Stock: Synthetic
Barrel: 20 in.
Sights: Mounted 4–16x44 scope
Weight: 9 lb. 13 oz.
Caliber: .223 Rem., .22-250 Rem., .308 Win.
Magazine: 4+1 rounds
Features: Fluted barrels and heavy standard barrels available; black or OD green Hogue overmolded stocks; Nikko-Stirling Targetmaster 4–16x44 scopes; HACT two-stage trigger system; three-position safety; forged flat-bottomed receiver
MSRP . . . .$844–$913

HOWA HUNTER GAMEKING PACKAGE

Action: Bolt
Stock: Walnut
Barrel: 20 in., 22 in., 24 in.
Sights: Optional mounted scope
Weight: 7 lb. 7 oz.
Caliber: .223 Rem., .204 Ruger, .22-250 Rem., .243 Win., 6.5x55 Swedish, .25-06 Rem., .270 Win., .308 Win., .30-06 Spfd., .300 Win. Mag., .338 Win. Mag., 7mm Rem. Mag., .375 Ruger
Magazine: 4+1 rounds
Features: Blued or stainless steel barrels; one-piece high grade walnut stock; checkering at forend and pistol grip; Monte Carlo cheekpiece; rubber recoil pad; sling swivel studs; scopes optional on blued models
MSRP . . . .$762–$944

H-S Precision

H-S PRECISION HTR

H-S PRECISION PHR

HTR (HEAVY TACTICAL RIFLE)

Action: Bolt
Stock: Synthetic
Barrel: 20 in., 22 in., 24 in., 26 in., 28 in.
Sights: None
Weight: 10 lb. 12 oz.–11 lb. 4 oz.
Caliber: Any standard SAAMI, LR calibers
Magazine: Detachable box, 3, 10 rounds
Features: Pro-Series 2000; fully adjustable synthetic stock comes in a wide range of colors combinations including sand, black, olive, gray, and spruce green; heavy fluted barrel
MSRP $5995

PHR (PROFESSIONAL HUNTER RIFLE)

Action: Bolt
Stock: Synthetic
Barrel: 20 in., 22 in., 24 in., 26 in., 28 in.
Sights: None
Weight: 7 lb. 12 oz.–8 lb. 4 oz.
Caliber: All popular magnum calibers up to .375 H&H and .338 Lapua
Magazine: Detachable box, 3, 4 rounds
Features: Pro-Series 2000; cheekpiece and built-in recoil reduction system; steel barrel; optional muzzlebrake; synthetic stock comes in a wide range of color combinations including sand, black, olive, gray, and spruce green; left-hand available for additional cost
MSRP $3695

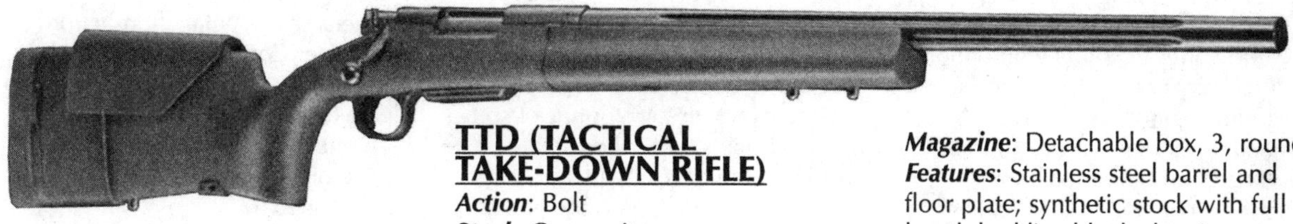

H-S PRECISION TTD

TTD (TACTICAL TAKE-DOWN RIFLE)

Action: Bolt
Stock: Composite
Barrel: 22 in., 24 in.
Sights: None
Weight: 11 lb. 4 oz.–11 lb. 12 oz.
Caliber: Available in all standard SA SAAMI and LR calibers
Magazine: Detachable box, 3, rounds
Features: Stainless steel barrel and floor plate; synthetic stock with full length bedding block chassis system; metal parts are finished in matte black Teflon; wide variety of stock colors including sand, black, olive, gray, and spruce green
MSRP $5995

I.O. Inc.

I.O. INC. M214

M214

Action: Semiautomatic
Stock: Synthetic
Barrel: 16 in.
Sights: Adjustable
Weight: N/A
Caliber: 7.62x39 Warsaw
Magazine: Detachable box, 30 rounds
Features: Americanized version of the AK-47; Phantom flash hider; gas block/front sight combo; recoil buffer; nitrided barrel; optional folding stick
MSRP $540

Jarrett Rifles

JARRETT BEANFIELD

JARRETT PROFESSIONAL HUNTER

JARRETT WIND WALKER

BEANFIELD

Action: Bolt
Stock: Synthetic
Barrel: Various lengths available
Sights: None
Weight: Varies depending on options
Caliber: Any popular standard or magnum chambering
Magazine: Comes with 20 rounds
Features: Can build rifle on any receiver provided; optional caliber, stock style, color, muzzlebrake, barrel size, and taper; includes load data and 20 rounds of custom ammo
MSRP. . . . . .starting at $5380

PROFESSIONAL HUNTER

Action: Bolt
Stock: Synthetic or walnut
Barrel: Various lengths available
Sights: None
Weight: Varies depending on options
Caliber: .375 H&H, .416 Rem., .416 Rigby, .450 Rigby
Magazine: Comes with 40 rounds
Features: Includes 40 rounds of soft pointed bullets and solids created custom for each gun; ballistics printout and last three targets the gun shot also provided; optional scopes; .416 Rem. comes with Jarrett Tri-Lock receiver
MSRP. . . . . .starting at $10400

WIND WALKER

Action: Bolt
Stock: Synthetic
Barrel: Up to 24 in.
Sights: None
Weight: 7 lb. 8 oz.
Caliber: Any popular short-action
Magazine: Comes with 20 rounds
Features: Jarrett Tri-Lock action; muzzlebrake; Tally scope mounting system; phenolic resin metal finish with choice of stock colors; ballistic print out included
MSRP. . . . . starting at $7380

J.P. Sauer & Sohn

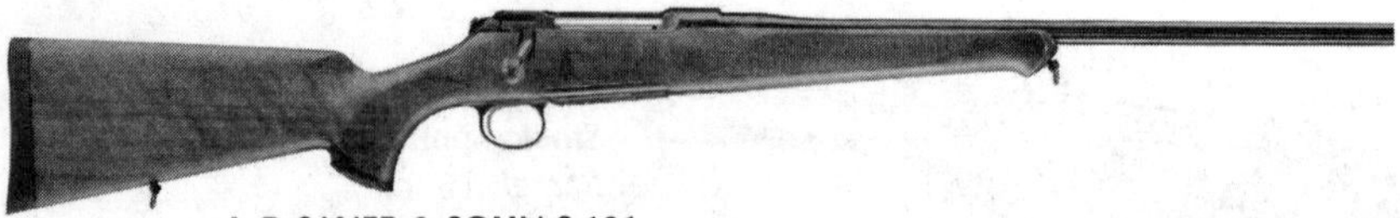

J. P. SAUER & SOHN S 101

S 101

Action: Bolt
Stock: Walnut
Barrel: 22 in., 24 in.
Sights: Adjustable open sights optional
Weight: 6 lb. 12 oz.
Caliber: .22-250 Rem., .243 Win., .270 Win., .308 Win., .30-06 Spfd., 6.5x55 Swedish, 7x64 Brenneke, 8x57IS, 9.3x62 Mauser, 7mm Rem. Mag., .300 Win. Mag., .338 Win. Mag.
Magazine: 5+1 rounds (standard), 4+1 rounds (magnum)
Features: 60-degree bolt lift; six locking lugs; available in standard and magnum calibers; matte black finish; DURA SAFE firing pin safety; EVER REST action bedding; ambidextrous stock
MSRP. . . . .$1499–$1699

J.P. Sauer & Sohn

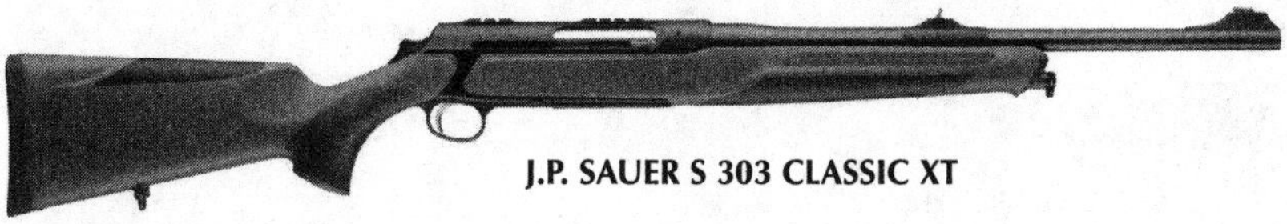

J.P. SAUER S 303 CLASSIC XT

S 202 CLASSIC BOLT ACTION RIFLE

Action: Bolt
Stock: Walnut
Barrel: 24 in.
Sights: None
Weight: 7 lb. 11 oz.
Caliber: .22, .22 Mag.
Magazine: Detachable box, 5 rounds
Features: Features stable, dark tan walnut heartwood; Monte Carlo stock with cheek-piece; luxury wood tip on the forend and pistol grip; polymer-coated steel surface; round bolt handle
MSRP $3509
Left-hand: $4192

S 303 CLASSIC XT

Action: Semiautomatic
Stock: Synthetic with anti-slip elastomer inlays
Barrel: 20 in., 22 in.
Sights: Yellow triangle rear sight; red-dot front sight
Weight: 7 lb. 5 oz.
Caliber: .30-06 Spfd., .300 Win. Mag.
Magazine: Detachable box, 2, 5 rounds
Features: Light-metal receiver; manual cocking safety; straight comb stock for either left- or right-handed shooters; rust protection with Nitrobond-X finish
MSRP $3352

S 303 ELEGANCE

Action: Semiautomatic
Stock: Walnut
Barrel: 20 in., 22 in.
Sights: High contrast
Weight: 7 lb. 3 oz.–7 lb. 6 oz.
Caliber: .30-06 Spfd., .300 Win. Mag.
Magazine: Detachable box, 2, 5 rounds
Features: Manual cocking at the upper wrist; crisp single-stage trigger; four bolt lugs engage directly into the barrel; free-floating barrel
MSRP $4752

Kel-Tec

KEL-TEC RFB

KEL-TEC SUB-2000

RFB

Action: Semiautomatic
Stock: Synthetic
Barrel: 18 in., 24 in., 26 in., 32 in.
Sights: None
Weight: 8 lb. (carbine), 11 lb. 5 oz. (target)
Caliber: 7.62 NATO
Magazine: Detachable box, 10 or 20 rounds
Features: Picatinny rail; short-stroke gas piston operation; A2-style flash hider
MSRP $1930

SUB-2000

Action: Semiautomatic
Stock: Polymer
Barrel: 16.1 in.
Sights: Target
Weight: 4 lb.
Caliber: 9mm, .40 S&W
Magazine: 10+1 rounds
Features: Self-loading carbine for pistol cartridges; by rotating the barrel upwards and back, it can be reduced to a size of 16x7 inches to facilitate secure storage
MSRP $500

Kimber

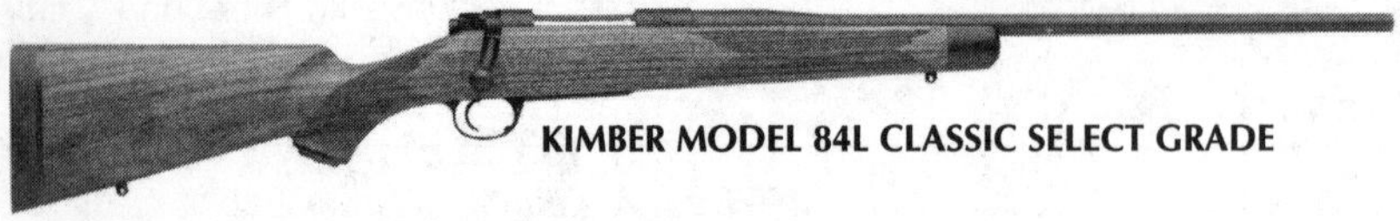
KIMBER MODEL 84L CLASSIC SELECT GRADE

KIMBER MODEL 84M ADIRONDACK

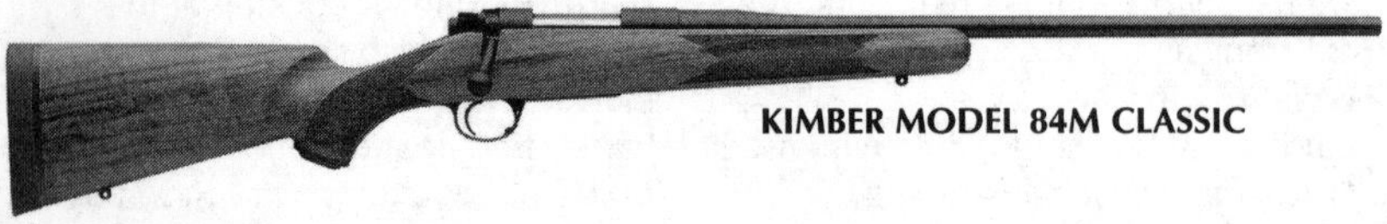
KIMBER MODEL 84M CLASSIC

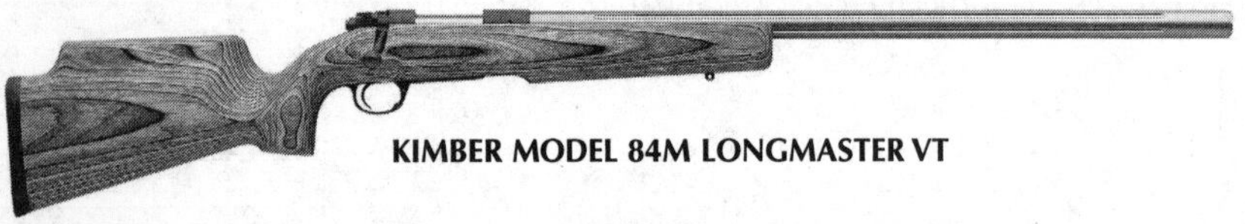
KIMBER MODEL 84M LONGMASTER VT

KIMBER MODEL 84M MONTANA

MODEL 84L SERIES

Action: Bolt
Stock: Walnut, synthetic
Barrel: 24 in.
Sights: None
Weight: 5 lb. 5 oz.–6 lb. 3 oz.
Caliber: .270 Win., .30-06 Spfd., .25-06 Rem., .280 Ackley Improved
Magazine: Internal box, 5 rounds
Features: Full-length Mauser claw exactor; 1-in. Pachmayr recoil pad; full-length match-grade barrel with pillar and glass bedding; match-grade trigger and three-postion wing safety; Classic Select has French walnut stock with ebony forend tip; Montana has Kevlar/carbon fiber stocks
Classic: $1223
Classic Select Grade: $1427
Montana: $1359

MODEL 84M ADIRONDACK

Action: Bolt
Stock: Synthetic
Barrel: 18 in.
Sights: None
Weight: 4 lb. 13 oz.
Caliber: .308 Win., 7mm-08 Rem.
Magazine: Internal, 4 rounds
Features: Kevlar/carbon fiber stock with Optifade Forrest finish; recoil pad; fluted barrel threaded for muzzle break/suppressor
MSRP $1768

MODEL 84M CLASSIC

Action: Bolt
Stock: Walnut
Barrel: 18 in., 22 in., 24 in.
Sights: None
Weight: 5 lb. 9 oz.–5 lb. 13 oz.
Caliber: .243 Win., .7mm-08 Rem., .308 Win.
Magazine: Internal box, 5, 6 rounds
Features: A-grade walnut stock with checkering panel, or AA walnut with ebony forend on Select Grade; recoil pad; sling swivel studs; steel matte blued or satin stainless steel finish; front locking repeater
Classic: $1223
Classic Select Grade: $1427

MODEL 84M LONGMASTER

Action: Bolt
Stock: Laminate
Barrel: 26 in.
Sights: None
Weight: 7 lb. 5 oz.–10 lb.
Caliber: Classic: .223 Rem., .308 Win.; VT: .22-250 Rem.
Magazine: Internal box, 5 rounds
Features: A-grade walnut with oil finish on Classic or gray laminated stock on VT model; sling swivel stud or front swivel stud for bipod; recoil pad; stainless steel barrel with satin finish; steel action with matte blued finish
Classic: $1291
VT: $1427

MODEL 84M SERIES

Action: Bolt
Stock: Walnut, laminate, Kevlar/carbon fiber
Barrel: 22 in.
Sights: None
Weight: 4 lb. 13 oz.–8 lb. 5 oz.
Caliber: 7mm-08 Rem., .308 Win., .204 Ruger, .22-250 Rem., .204 Ruger, .223 Rem., .243 Win., .257 Roberts, .338 Federal (among the various models)
Magazine: Internal box, 4, 5, 6 rounds
Features: A-grade walnut on Varmint; AAA-grade walnut stock with checkering panel on SuperAmerica; gray laminate on ProVarmint and SVT; Kevlar/carbon fiber on Montana; recoil pad; stainless steel barrel and action; front locking repeater; adjustable trigger
Montana: $1359
ProVarmint: $1427
SuperAmerica: $2240
SVT: $1427
Varmint: $1291

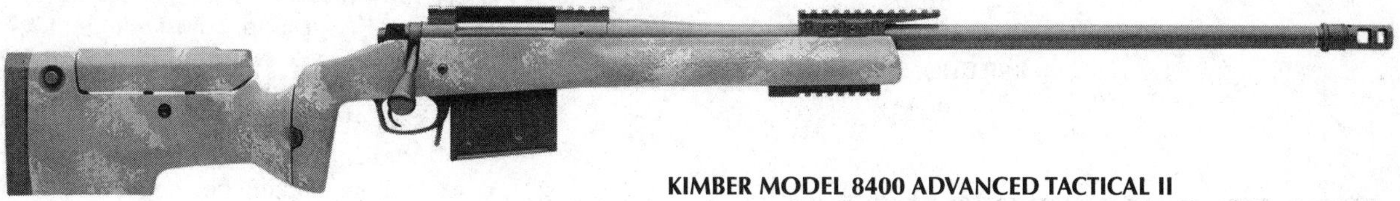

KIMBER MODEL 8400 ADVANCED TACTICAL II

KIMBER MODEL 8400 ADVANCED TACTICAL SOC

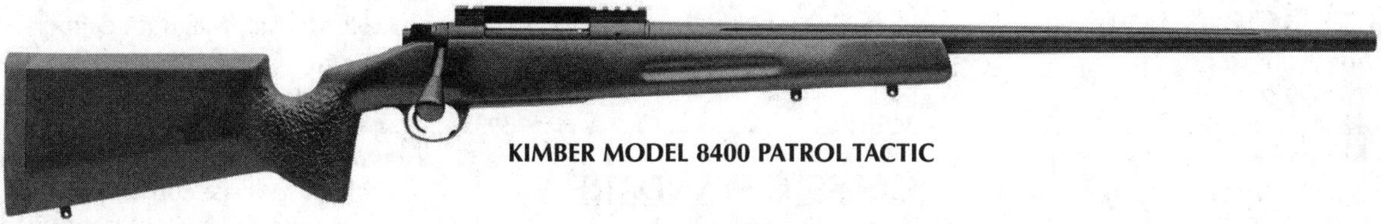

KIMBER MODEL 8400 PATROL TACTIC

KIMBER MODEL 8400 WSM CLASSIC

MODEL 8400 ADVANCED TACTICAL II

Action: Bolt
Stock: Synthetic
Barrel: 22 in.
Sights: None
Weight: 10 lb. 10 oz.
Caliber: .300 Win. Mag., .308 Win.
Magazine: Detachable box, 5 rounds
Features: Manners MCS-TF4 folding stock with adjustable comb; fluted barrel with muzzle brake/suppressor thread; adjsutable trigger
MSRP $4351

MODEL 8400 ADVANCED TACTICAL SOC

Action: Bolt
Stock: Synthetic
Barrel: 22 in.
Sights: None
Weight: 11 lb. 6 oz.
Caliber: .300 Win. Mag., .308 Win.
Magazine: Detachable box, 5 rounds
Features: Fluted barrel threaded and fitted with SureFire muzzle break/ suppressor adapter; Picatinny rails; side folding stock; Harris bipod adapter included
MSRP $4419

MODEL 8400 PATROL TACTIC

Action: Bolt
Stock: Synthetic
Barrel: 24 in., 26 in.
Sights: None
Weight: 8 lb. 12 oz.
Caliber: .300 Win. Mag., .308 Win.
Magazine: Internal, 5 rounds
Features: Manners MCS-T6 reinforced carbon fiber stock; sling swivel studs; front swivel stud for bipod; recoil pad
MSRP $2447

MODEL 8400 WSM

Action: Bolt
Stock: Walnut, synthetic
Barrel: 24 in.
Sights: None
Weight: 6 lb. 3 oz.–6 lb. 10 oz.
Caliber: .270 WSM, .300 Swam, .325 Swam; SuperAmerica: .270 WSM, .300 WSM
Magazine: Internal box, 3 rounds
Features: Stock options: A-grade walnut with checkered panels, A-grade French walnut with checkered panels, gray synthetic Kevlar/carbon fiber stock; sling swivel studs; recoil pad; steel barrel with matte blued finish or stainless steel satin finish; front locking repeater; Mauser claw extractor
Classic: $1223
Classic Select Grade: $1427
SuperAmerica: $2240
Montana: $1359

Krieghoff

KRIEGHOFF CLASSIC BIG FIVE

KRIEGHOFF CLASSIC STANDARD

KRIEGHOFF SEMPRIO THUMBHOLE

CLASSIC BIG FIVE

Action: Hinged breech
Stock: Walnut
Barrel: 23.5 in.
Sights: Open
Weight: 9 lb. 8 oz.–10 lb. 8 oz.
Caliber: .375 H&H Mag., .375 Flanged Magnum N.E., .450/.400 NE, .500/.416 N.E., .470 N.E., .500 N.E.
Magazine: None
Features: Double triggers; V-shaped rear sight with a white, vertical middle line and a pearl front sight; optional Super-Express sight; Monte Carlo style cheekpiece; European walnut stock with small game scene engraving; steel trigger and floor plate; straight comb and large recoil pad
MSRP $13995

CLASSIC STANDARD

Action: Hinged breech
Stock: Walnut
Barrel: 23.5 in.
Sights: Open
Weight: 7 lb. 4 oz.–8 lb. 4 oz.
Caliber: 7x57R, 7x65R, .308 Win., .30-06 Spfd., 8X57JRS, 8x75RS, 8.5x75RS, 9.3x74R
Magazine: None
Features: European walnut stock with conventional rounded cheekpiece and Kaiser Grip; adjustable, removable muzzle wedge integrated in the front sight ramp; Universal-Trigger-System; Combi-cocking device; ergonomically shaped "Kickspanner" manual cocking device
MSRP $10995

SEMPRIO

Action: Hinged breech
Stock: Walnut
Barrel: 21.5 in., 25 in.
Sights: Open
Weight: 7 lb. 8 oz.
Caliber: .223 Rem., .243 Win., 6.5x55 Swedish, 6.5x57, .270 Win., 7x64 Brenneke, .308 Win., .30-06 Spfd., .338 Win. Mag., 8x57JS, 9.3x62 Mauser; Magnum calibers: 7mm Rem. Mag., .300 Win. Mag., .375 Ruger
Magazine: Detachable box
Features: Barrels are plasma nitrated and blued to resist corrosion; open sights feature fluorescent front bead and rear sight, designed for target acquisition in low light conditions; accepts various types of scope-mounts; Turkish walnut stock available with or without the Semprio cheekpiece; rubber recoil pad; sling swivels; optional BreaKO recoil reducer; includes fitted case
Standard Caliber: $4690
Magnum Caliber: $4990

Kriss

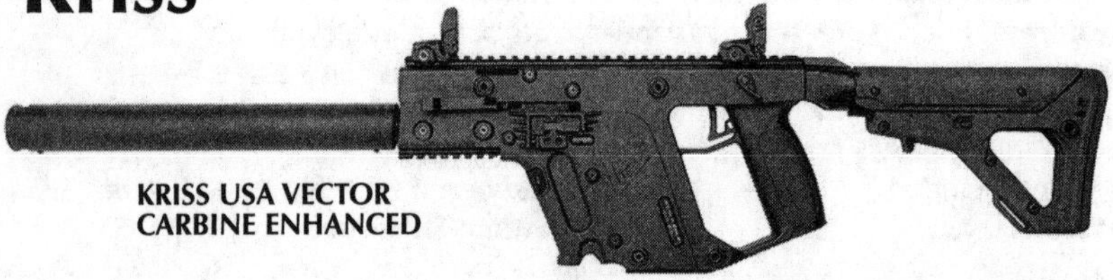

KRISS USA VECTOR CARBINE ENHANCED

KRISS VECTOR SBR

VECTOR CARBINE ENHANCED

Action: Semiautomatic
Stock: Synthetic
Barrel: 16 in.
Sights: Adjustable
Weight: 8 lb. 3 oz.
Caliber: .45 ACP
Magazine: Detachable box, 13, 21, or 30 rounds
Features: Ambidextrous fire and safety settings; closed bolt, delayed-blowback patented KRISS Super V system; Picatinny rails
MSRP $1995

VECTOR SBR

Action: Semiautomatic
Stock: Polymer
Barrel: 5.5 in.
Sights: Custom flip-up iron
Weight: 5 lb. 10 oz.
Caliber: .45 ACP
Magazine: Detachable stick, 13 rounds
Features: Also available in Carbine and Special Duty Pistol configurations; adjustable folding stock; Picatinny rails; ambidextrous F/S controls; foregrip; cable lock
MSRP $1895

K-Var

K-VAR SGL 31–95

SGL 31–95

Action: Semiautomatic
Stock: Mil-Spec black polymer
Barrel: 16.3 in.
Sights: Rear leaf
Weight: 7 lb. 5 oz.
Caliber: 5.45x39.5mm
Magazine: Detachable box, 30, 45 rounds
Features: Manufactured at the Izhmash Factry in Russia; authentic Russian polymer side-folding butt-stock; chrome-lined, hammer-forged barrel; scope rail; accessory lug
MSRP $1349

Lazzeroni Rifles

LAZZERONI L2012LLT LONG MAGNUM LITE

LAZZERONI L2012SP-XTLR LONG MAGNUM SPORTER

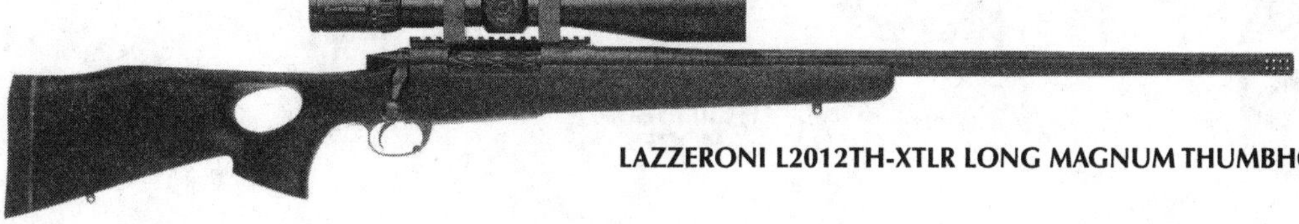

LAZZERONI L2012TH-XTLR LONG MAGNUM THUMBHOLE

L2012LLT LONG MAGNUM LITE

Action: Bolt
Stock: Graphite/composite
Barrel: 26 in.
Sights: None
Weight: 7 lb. 5 oz.
Caliber: 7.82 (.308) Warbird, 7.21 (.284) Firebird
Magazine: 4 rounds
Features: All new precision CNC-machined chromoly receiver; one-piece diamond-fluted bolt shaft; stainless steel match-grade button-barrel; custom molded hand-bedded graphite/composite stock designs; precision-machined aluminum alloy floor plate/trigger guard assembly; jewel competition trigger; Vais muzzlebrake; Limbsaver recoil pad
MSRP $5500

L2012SP-XTLR LONG MAGNUM SPORTER

Action: Bolt
Stock: Graphite/composite
Barrel: 28 in.
Sights: None
Weight: 8 lb. 13 oz.
Caliber: 7.82 (.308) Warbird, 7.21 (.284) Firebird, 8.59 (.338) Titan
Magazine: Detachable box, 4 rounds
Features: Heavy barrel contour; recoil reducing roll-over cheekpiece incorporated into stock design; 20 MOA Picatinny rail; 34mm or 30mm rings
MSRP $7000

L2012TH-XTLR LONG MAGNUM THUMBHOLE

Action: Bolt
Stock: Graphite/composite
Barrel: 25 in.
Sights: None
Weight: 7 lb. 11 oz.
Caliber: 7.82 (.284) Warbird, 7.21 (.284) Firebird, 8.59 (.338) Titan
Magazine: 4 rounds
Features: 20 MOA Picatinny style rail; 34mm or 30mm ring sets; right hand only
MSRP $6700

RIFLES

LES BAER .308 SEMI-AUTO MATCH RIFLE

LES BAER AR .223 SUPER VARMINT

LES BAER MID-LENGTH MONOLITH .308 SEMI-AUTO SWAT MODEL

.308 SEMI-AUTO MATCH RIFLE

Action: Semiautomatic
Stock: Synthetic
Barrel: 18 in. or 20 in.
Sights: None
Weight: 11 lb. 3 oz.
Caliber: .308 Win.
Magazine: Detachable box, 20 round
Features: No forward assist; Picatinny style flat top rail; LBC carrier, chromed; chromed precision bolt; Geissele two-stage trigger group; steel gas block; LBC Custom grip; Harris bipod; DuPont S coating on barrel; enforcer muzzlebrake; Magpul stock
MSRP $3640

AR .223 SUPER VARMINT

Action: Semiautomatic
Stock: Synthetic
Barrel: 20 in. (optional 18 in., 22 in., 24 in.)
Sights: None
Weight: 9 lb.
Caliber: .223 Rem.
Magazine: Detachable box, 20 rounds
Features: Includes targets; LBC forged and precision machined upper and lower receivers; Picatinny style flat top rail; LBC National Match chromed carrier; LBC chromed bolt; LBC extractor; Geissele two-stage trigger group; adjustable free-float handguard with locking ring; aluminum gas block; stainless steel barrel; Versa Pod installed
MSRP $2640

MID-LENGTH MONOLITH .308 SEMI-AUTO SWAT MODEL

Action: Semiautomatic
Stock: Synthetic
Barrel: 16 in.
Sights: Optional scope and rings
Weight: 11 lb. 5 oz.
Caliber: .308 Win.
Magazine: Detachable box, 20 rounds
Features: LBC carrier, chromed; LBC precision chromed bolt; Geissele two-stage trigger group; LBC steel gas block with Picatinny rail; LBC bench rest 416R stainless steel barrel with rifling; Magpul PRS stock; two twenty-round Magpul magazines
MSRP $3940

Les Baer Custom

LES BAER MONOLITH .308 SEMI-AUTO SWAT

MONOLITH .308 SEMI-AUTO SWAT

Action: Semiautomatic
Stock: Synthetic
Barrel: 20 in. (optional 18 in., 24 in.)
Sights: None
Weight: 9.04 lb.
Caliber: .308 Win.
Magazine: Detachable box, 20 round
Features: Geissele two-stage trigger group; LBC Steel gas block with Picatinny rail on top; LBC bench rest, stainless steel barrel; Magpul PRS stock in black; special Versa Pod and adapter; DuPont S coating in barrel
MSRP. $4390

Magnum Research

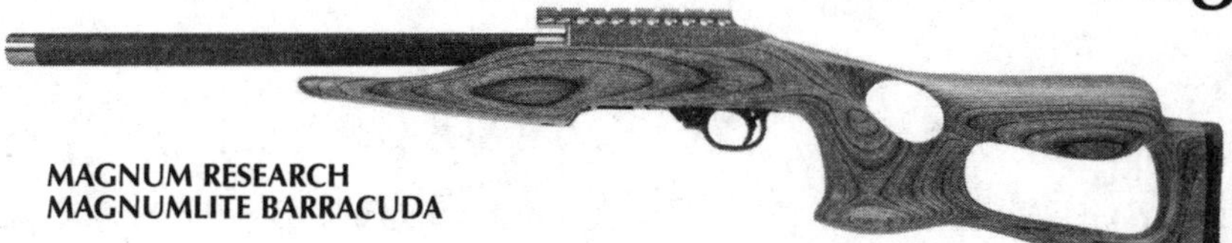

MAGNUM RESEARCH MAGNUMLITE BARRACUDA

MAGNUM RESEARCH MAGNUMLITE ULTRA BARREL

MAGNUM RESEARCH MOUNTAIN EAGLE MAGNUMLITE GRAPHITE

MAGNUMLITE BARRACUDA

Action: Semiautomatic
Stock: Wood, composite, or laminate
Barrel: 17 in.
Sights: None
Weight: 4 lb. 7 oz.–7 lb. 5 oz.
Caliber: .22LR, .22 Win. Mag.
Magazine: Box, 9, 10 rounds
Features: 17 in., 19 in. models have graphite barrels; 18 in. barrels come in stainless steel; .22 Win. Mag. version has patented gas-assisted blowback operation; CNC receivers machined from aircraft aluminum; include integral Weaver type rail for optics; heat treated steel with tight bolt face depth tolerances
MSRP. . . . . $819–$941

MAGNUMLITE ULTRA BARREL

Action: Semiatuomatic
Stock: Synthetic
Barrel: 17 in.
Sights: None
Weight: 4 lb. 4 oz.
Caliber: .22LR
Magazine: 10+1
Features: Ambidextrous lightweight thumbhole stock made of polypropylene with fiber additives; semi palm swell on both sides of the pistol grip; molded-to-fit hard rubber buttplate attached with screws; graphite bull barrel with uni-directional graphite fibers parallel to the bore axis; full floating barrel; French gray anodized finish
MSRP. . . . . $569–$625

MOUNTAIN EAGLE MAGNUMLITE GRAPHITE

Action: Bolt
Stock: Composite
Barrel: 24 in., 26 in.
Sights: None
Weight: 7 lb. 4 oz.–9 lb. 2 oz.
Caliber: .30-06 Spfd., .223 Rem., .308 Win., .280 Rem., 7mm Rem. Mag., .300 Win. Mag., .22-250 Rem., .300 WSM, 7mm WSM
Magazine: Box, 4, 5 rounds
Features: Adjustable trigger; Kevlar-graphite stock in H-S Precision or Hogue Overmolded; open grip; free-floating match-grade barrel; hinged floor plate of solid steel; recoil pad; sling swivel studs; left-hand available for most calibers; action has been drilled and tapped for scope
MSRP. . . . . $2173–$2475

Marlin

MARLIN 60

MARLIN 70PSS

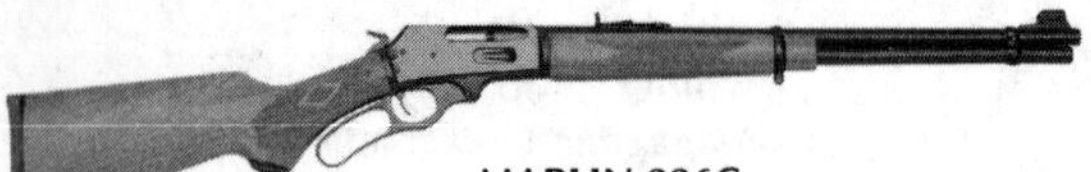
MARLIN 336C

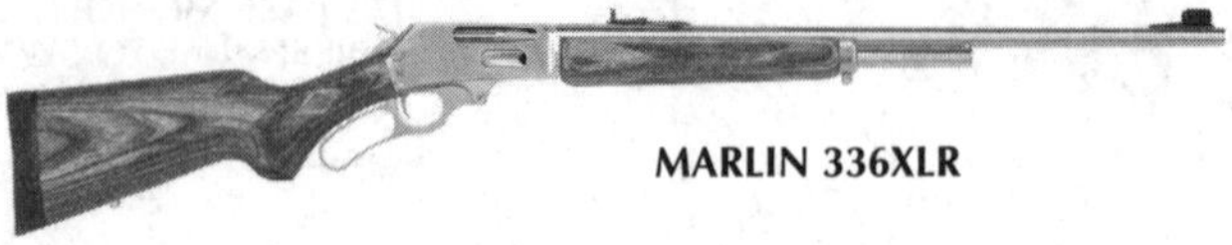
MARLIN 336XLR

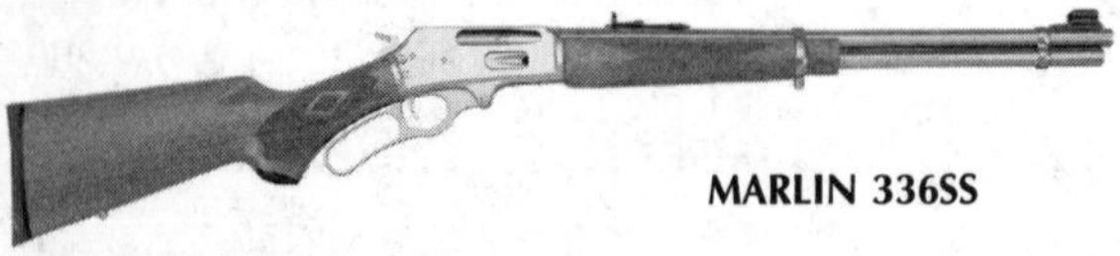
MARLIN 336SS

MARLIN 795SS

60

Action: Semiautomatic
Stock: Laminated hardwood
Barrel: 19 in.
Sights: Open
Weight: 5 lb. 8 oz.
Caliber: .22LR
Magazine: Under-barrel tube, 14 rounds
Features: Manual and automatic "last-shot" bolt hold-opens; receiver top has serrated, non-glare finish; cross-bolt safety; steel charging handle; Monte Carlo walnut-finished laminated hardwood; M60C comes with camouflage patterned Monte Carlo hardwood stock; full pistol grip; tough Mar-Shield finish; adjustable open rear sight, front ramp sight

60: $208
60C: $246
60SB: $265

70PSS

Action: Semiautomatic
Stock: Synthetic
Barrel: 16.25 in.
Sights: Open
Weight: 3 lb. 4 oz.
Caliber: .22LR
Magazine: Detachable clip, 7 rounds
Features: Automatic "last-shot" bolt hold-open; manual bolt hold-open; Monte Carlo black fiberglass-filled synthetic stock with abbreviated forend; nickel plated swivel studs; molded-in checkering; adjustable open rear sight; front ramp sight with high visibility orange post and cut-away wide-scan hood

MSRP $345

336C

Action: Lever
Stock: Walnut
Barrel: 20 in.
Sights: Open
Weight: 7 lb.
Caliber: .30-30 Win., .35 Rem.
Magazine: Under-barrel tube, 6 rounds
Features: Deeply blued surfaces; hammer block safety; American black walnut stock with pistol grip and checkering

MSRP $629

336SS

Action: Lever
Stock: Walnut
Barrel: 20 in.
Sights: Open
Weight: 7 lb.
Caliber: .30-30 Win., .35 Rem.
Magazine: Under-barrel tube, 6 rounds
Features: Stainless steel receiver, barrel, lever, and trigger guard; hammer block safety; American black walnut pistol grip stock with fluted comb and cut checkering; rubber rifle buttpad; adjustable semi-buckhorn folding rear, ramp front sight with brass bead and wide-scan hood; solid top receiver tapped for scope mount; offset hammer spur for scope use

MSRP $771

336XLR

Action: Lever
Stock: Laminated hardwood
Barrel: 24 in.
Sights: Open
Weight: 7 lb.
Caliber: .30-30 Win.
Magazine: Under-barrel tube, 5 rounds
Features: Stainless steel receiver, barrel, lever, and trigger guard plate; black/gray laminated hardwood stock with pistol grip and checkering; deluxe recoil pad; nickel plates swivel studs; adjustable semi-buckhorn folding rear sight and brass bead front sight with wide-scan hood; receiver tapped for scope mount

MSRP $959

795

Action: Semiautomatic
Stock: Synthetic
Barrel: 18 in.
Sights: Open
Weight: 4 lb. 8 oz.
Caliber: .22LR
Magazine: Detachable clip, 10 rounds
Features: Automatic "last-shot" bolt hold-open, manual bolt hold-open; cross-bolt safety; Monte Carlo black fiberglass-filled synthetic stock with swivel studs and molded in checkering; adjustable open rear sight and front ramp sight; receiver grooved for scope mount

795: $183
795SS: $262

MARLIN 1894 COWBOY

MARLIN 1895GBL

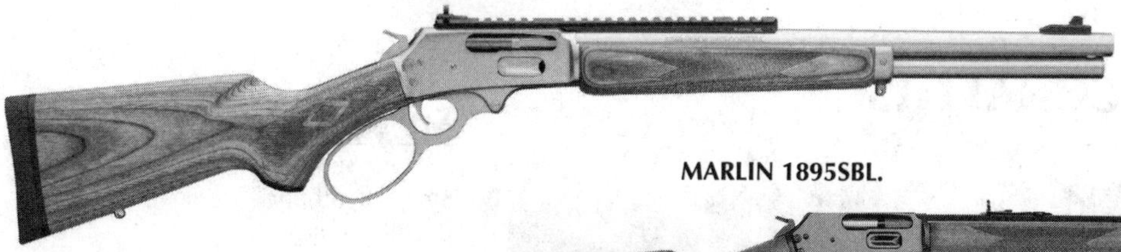

MARLIN 1895SBL.

MARLIN CLASSIC 1895

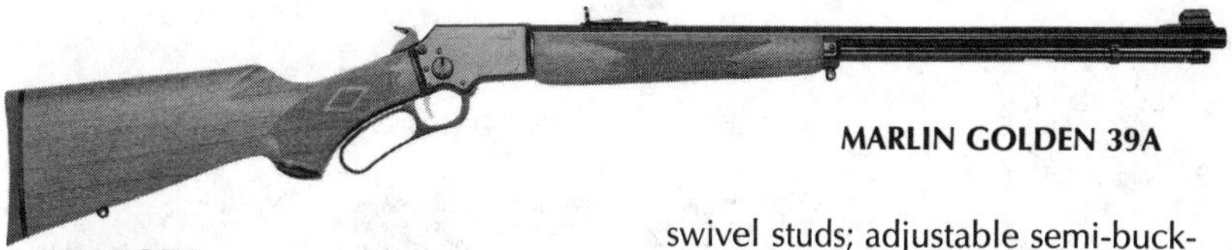

MARLIN GOLDEN 39A

1894 COWBOY

Action: Lever
Stock: Walnut
Barrel: 20 in.
Sights: Open
Weight: 6 lb. 8 oz.
Caliber: .45 Colt, .357 Mag./.38 Spl., .44 Mag./.44 Spl.
Magazine: Under-barrel tube, 10 rounds
Features: Lever action with squared finger lever; deeply blued metal surfaces; straight-grip American black walnut stock; hard rubber buttplate; tough Mar-Shield finish; blued steel forend cap; tapered octagon barrel; adjustable marble semi-buckhorn rear sight and marble carbine front sight; solid top receiver tapped for scope mount

MSRP $766

1895GBL

Action: Lever
Stock: Laminate
Barrel: 18.5 in.
Sights: Open
Weight: 7 lb.
Caliber: .45-70 Govt.
Magazine: Full length tubular magazine, 6 rounds
Features: Lever action with big loop finger lever; deeply blued metal surfaces; hammer block safety; American pistol grip two-tone brown laminate stock with cut checkering; ventilated recoil pad; tough Mar-Shield finish; swivel studs; adjustable semi-buckhorn folding rear sight and ramp front sight with brass bead; receiver tapped for scope mount; offset hammer spur for scope use

MSRP $713

1895SBL

Action: Lever
Stock: Laminated hardwood
Barrel: 18.5 in.
Sights: Open
Weight: 8 lb.
Caliber: .45-70 Govt.
Magazine: Under-barrel tube, 6 rounds
Features: Lever action with big loop finger lever; deeply blued metal surfaces; stainless steel barrel and receiver; black/gray laminated hardwood with pistol-grip stock and cut checkering; fluted comb; deluxe recoil pad; compact version available

MSRP $1039

CLASSIC 1895

Action: Lever
Stock: Walnut
Barrel: 22 in.
Sights: Open
Weight: 7 lb. 8 oz.
Caliber: .45-70 Govt.
Magazine: Under-barrel tube, 4 rounds
Features: Deeply blued metal surfaces; hammer block safety; American black walnut pistol grip with fluted comb and cut checkering; rubber rifle buttpad; tough Mar-Shield finish; swivel studs; adjustable semi-buckhorn folding rear sight and front ramp sight with brass bead and wide-scan hood; model 1985 G has 18.5-in. barrel and straight grip; model 1985 Cowboy has a 26-in. octagonal barrel and straight grip

Classic 1895: $730
1895G: $735
1895GS: $878

GOLDEN 39A

Action: Lever
Stock: Walnut
Barrel: 24 in.
Sights: Open
Weight: 6 lb. 8 oz.
Caliber: .22S, L, LR
Magazine: Under-barrel tube, holds 26 Short, 21 L or 19 LR rounds
Features: Rebounding hammer; hammer safety block; one-step takedown; deeply blued metal surfaces; gold plated steel trigger; genuine American black walnut with full pistol grip and forend; blued steel forend cap; swivel studs; rubber rifle buttpad; tough Mar-Shield finish; adjustable semi-buckhorn folding rear sight and front ramp sight with brass bead and wide-scan hood

MSRP $709

Marlin

MARLIN XT-22

XT-22

Action: Bolt
Stock: Hardwood
Barrel: 22 in.
Sights: Open
Weight: 6 lb.
Caliber: .22LR
Magazine: Detachable clip, 7 rounds
Features: Pro-Fire adjustable trigger; Micro-Groove rifling; blued bolt action; thumb safety; red cocking indicator; Monte Carlo walnut-finished hardwood with swivel studs; full pistol grip; tough Mar-Shield finish; adjustable rear sight and front ramp sights; receiver grooved for scope mount, drilled and tapped for scope bases
MSRP . . . .$220–$265

MasterPiece Arms

MASTERPIECE ARMS MPAR 556 RIFLE

MASTERPIECE ARMS MPAR 6.8

MPAR 6.8

Action: Semiautomatic
Stock: Synthetic
Barrel: 16 in.
Sights: None
Weight: N/A
Caliber: 6.8 SPC
Magazine: Detachable box, 30 rounds
Features: Side folding telescoping stock; short stroke piston; Vista Camo hydrographics; Picatinny rails; available in black
MSRP . . . . $1029–$1103

MPAR 556 RIFLE

Action: Semiautomatic
Stock: Synthetic
Barrel: 16 in.
Sights: None
Weight: 7 lb. 13 oz.
Caliber: 5.56 NATO, .223 Rem.
Magazine: Detachable box, 30 rounds
Features: Short stroke piston design; lightweight, free-floating, two-piece aluminum handguard; user located Picatinny rails; side-folding collapsible stock; full length top rail
MSRP $750

RIFLES

Maunz Match Rifles

MODEL 007 MAUNZ RIFLE

Action: Semiautomatic
Stock: Custom made wood or Kevlar; left or right hand
Barrel: 28 in.
Sights: Iron or scope available, not included
Weight: 11 lb.
Caliber: .22-250, .243, 6.5-06, 7mm, .308, .30-06, .338-06, .40 Maunz Long, .45 Maunz Long
Magazine: 5- or 10-round HK magazine
Features: Ammunition available for custom rifles at a reasonable cost as well as reloading equipment
MSRP $1650

MODEL 007 MAUNZ RIFLE

Maunz Match Rifles

MODEL 11 MAUNZ SPORTSMAN RIFLE

MODEL 77 MAUNZ SERVICE MATCH RIFLE

MODEL 97 MAUNZ MATCH RIFLE

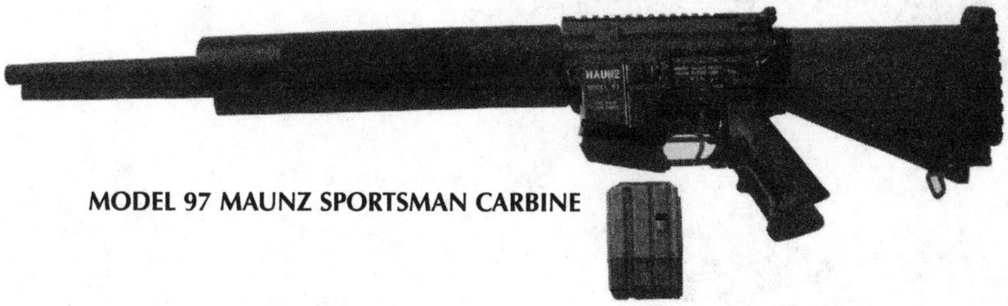

MODEL 97 MAUNZ SPORTSMAN CARBINE

MODEL 97 MAUNZ MATCH RIFLE

Action: Semiautomatic
Stock: Custom fit wood; left or right hand
Barrel: 24 in., 28 in.
Sights: Iron or scope available,not included
Weight: 11 lb.
Caliber: .22-250, .243, 6.5-06, 7mm, .308, .40 Maunz, .45 Maunz
Magazine: 5- or 10-round magazine
Features: Maunz Rifles were manufactured in Toledo and Maumee, Ohio, from the 1960s until 1987 by Karl Maunz for high-end military, law enforcement, and competition customers; modeled after the AR-10 frame; ammunition available for custom rifles at a reasonable cost as well as reloading equipment
MSRP **$2500**

MODEL 97 MAUNZ SPORTSMAN CARBINE

Action: Semiautomatic
Stock: Custom made wood; left or right hand
Barrel: 20 in.
Sights: Iron or scope available, not included
Weight: 8 lb.
Caliber: .223, 6 mm Maunz, .30 Maunz, .40 Maunz, .45 Maunz
Magazine: 5- or 10-round magazine
Features: Ammunition available for custom rifles at a reasonable cost as well as reloading equipment
MSRP **$1500**

MODEL 11 MAUNZ SPORTSMAN RIFLE

Action: Semiautomatic
Stock: Custom made wood; left or right hand
Barrel: 20 in.
Sights: Iron or scope available, not included
Caliber: .22-250, .243, 7mm, .308, .40 Maunz, .45 Maunz
Magazine: 5- or 10-round HK magazine
Weight: 9 lb.
Features: Modeled after the AR-10 frame; ammunition available for custom rifles at a reasonable cost as well as reloading equipment
MSRP **$1500**

MODEL 77 MAUNZ SERVICE MATCH RIFLE

Action: Semiautomatic
Stock: Wood or fiberglass
Barrel: 22 in.
Sights: ½ National Match (NM/2A) front; .062 ½ min. rear; special removable front globe sight
Caliber: 7.62 NATO, .308 Win., other chambering on custom orders
Magazine: 5- or 10-round magazine
Weight: 10 lb. (standard medium barrel), 13 lb. (heavy barrel)
Features: Ammunition available for custom rifles at a reasonable cost as well as reloading equipment
MSRP **$2850**

Mauser

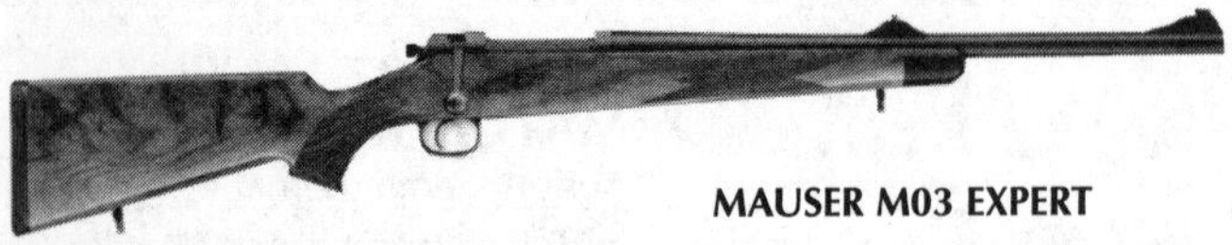

MAUSER M03 EXPERT

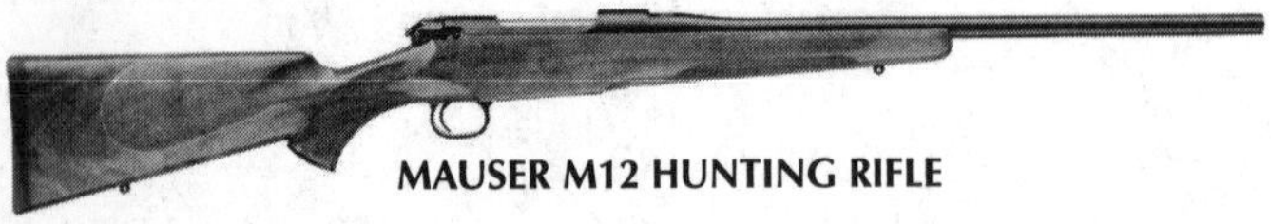

MAUSER M12 HUNTING RIFLE

M03 EXPERT

Action: Bolt
Stock: Wood or synthetic
Barrel: 20.5 in., 23.5 in. (Mag.)
Sights: Fixed
Weight: 8 lb.
Caliber: .30-06 Spfd., .300 Win. Mag., 8x57IS, 9.3x62 Mauser, .308 Win., .338 Blaser Mag., 8x68S
Magazine: Internal, 5+1 or 4+1 (Mag.) rounds
Features: Muzzle-Safe and Mag-Safe; three-dot sight
MSRP $6822

M12 HUNTING RIFLE

Action: Bolt
Stock: Wood, Synthetic
Barrel: 22 in., 24.5 in.
Sights: None
Weight: 7 lb.
Caliber: .22-250 Rem., .243 Win., 6.5x55 Swedish, .270 Win., 7x64 Brenneke, .308 Win., .30-06 Spfd., 8x57 IS, 9.3x62 Mauser, 7mm Rem., .300 Win. Mag., .338 Win. Mag.
Magazine: 5+1 rounds
Features: 60-degree bolt lift; detachable magazine; open sights available; drilled and tapped for scopes; stock extension available
MSRP $1799
Extreme: $1499

McMillan

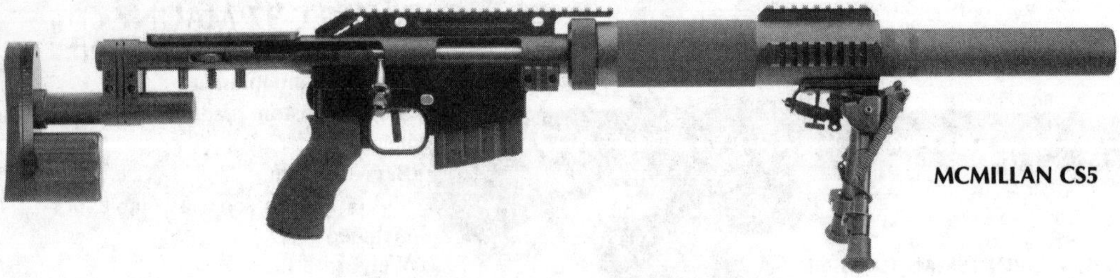

MCMILLAN CS5

MCMILLAN CUSTOM HUNTING RIFLE - LEGACY

CS5

Action: Semiautomatic
Stock: Synthetic
Barrel: 12.5 in., 18.5 in.
Sights: None
Weight: 10 lb. 10 oz., 11 lb. 10 oz.
Caliber: .308 Win.
Magazine: Detachable box, 10, 20 rounds
Features: Concealable Subsonic/Supersonic Suppressed Sniper System; available in "Stubby" suppressed configuration for military and law enforcement use; with buttstock and suppressor detached, will fit in backpack; adjustable buttstock; tactile safety button can be operated without moving your trigger finger
MSRP $6500
Standard: $5500

CUSTOM HUNTING RIFLES - LEGACY

Action: Bolt
Stock: Synthetic
Barrel: 22 in., 24 in.
Sights: None
Weight: 6 lb. 10 oz.–7 lb.
Caliber: .222 Win., .243 Win., .260 Rem., .308 Win., .300 WSM
Magazine: Fixed
Features: McMillan classic sporter fiberglass stock with shadow line cheekpiece; McMillan G30 custom action in long or short; match-grade stainless steel barrel, with a matte finish and target crown; custom machined one-piece aluminum hinged floor plate; custom Jewell trigger; includes scope base and travel case with rollers
MSRP $6235

McMillan

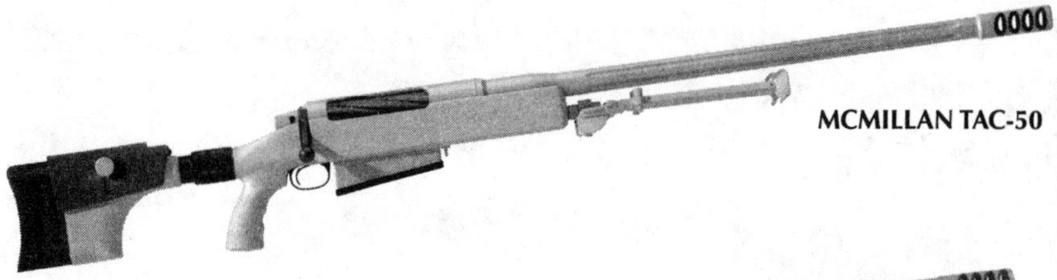

MCMILLAN TAC-50

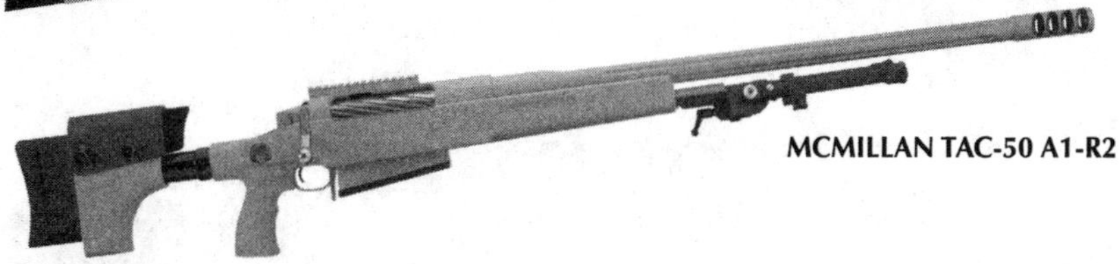

MCMILLAN TAC-50 A1-R2

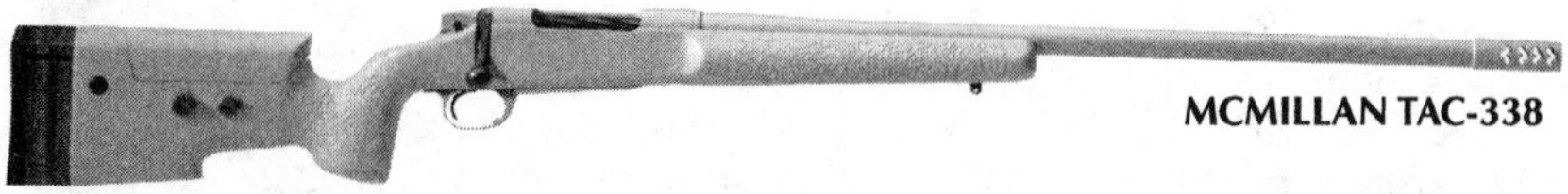

MCMILLAN TAC-338

TAC-50 A1

Action: Semiautomatic
Stock: Synthetic
Barrel: 29 in.
Sights: Drilled and tapped for scopes
Weight: 26 lb.
Caliber: .50 BMG
Magazine: Detachable box, 5 rounds
Features: Take-down fiberglass stock with a longer forend that moves the balance point for the bipod forward; integral cheekpiece; monopod on the buttstock; smaller pistol grip; lighter, sturdier bipod; positive, self-locking magazine latch; magazine release lever repositioned ahead of trigger bow; match grade free floating barrel
MSRP. $9990

TAC-50 A1-R2

Action: Semiautomatic
Stock: Synthetic
Barrel: 29 in.
Sights: Drilled and tapped for scopes
Weight: 26 lb.
Caliber: .50 BMG
Magazine: Detachable box, 5 rounds
Features: New hydraulic recoil mitigation system reducing peak recoil by 90 percent; take-down fiberglass stock with a longer forend that moves the balance point for the bipod forward; integral cheekpiece; monopod on the buttstock; smaller pistol grip; lighter, sturdier bipod; positive, self-locking magazine latch; magazine release lever repositioned ahead of trigger bow; match grade free floating barrel
MSRP. $11990

TAC-338

Action: Bolt
Stock: Composite
Barrel: 26.5 in.
Sights: None
Weight: 11 lb.
Caliber: .338 Alpha Mag., .338 Norma Mag.
Magazine: Detachable box, 1 to 5 rounds
Features: G30 McMillan Long Action; hinged floor plate system; metal finish (to match stock)—black, olive, gray, tan, or dark earth; Vanguard Case; adjustable cheekpiece; tight benchrest tolerances; square-surfaced recoil lugs; threaded cap provided; match grade, stainless steel barrel with matte finish
MSRP. $6895

RIFLES

Merkel

MERKEL AFRICAN SAFARI SERIES DOUBLE RIFLE MODEL 140AE

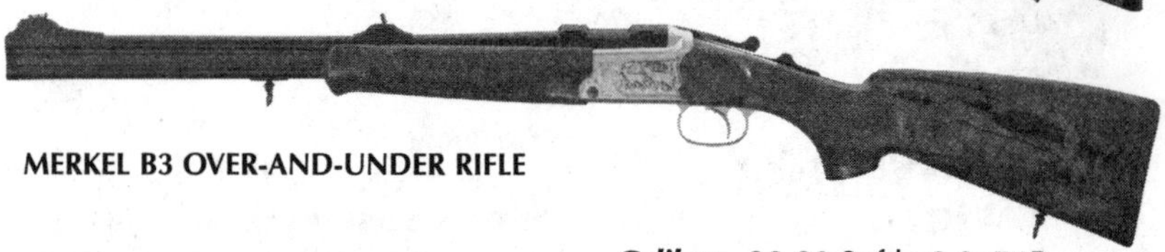

MERKEL B3 OVER-AND-UNDER RIFLE

AFRICAN SAFARI SERIES DOUBLE RIFLE MODEL 140AE

Action: Boxlock
Stock: Walnut
Barrel: 23.6 in.
Sights: Bead front, four-leaf express rear
Weight: 10 lb. 8 oz.
Caliber: .375 H&H, .450/400 NE, .470 NE, .500 NE
Magazine: None
Features: Classic styling with cheekpiece, half luxus Turkish walnut; hand-engraved, English-style arabesque, gold relief Cape buffalo; tapered, octagonal barrel with rust blued finish
MSRP. $18995

B3 OVER-AND-UNDER RIFLE

Action: Over/under
Stock: Checkered walnut
Barrel: 21.6 in.
Sights: Driven-hunt sight with integrated light elements
Weight: 6 lb. 6 oz.
Caliber: .30-06 Spfd., 9.3x74R
Magazine: None
Features: Short, light, and responsive; manual cocking mechanism; tilting breech block can be removed without tools; adjustable single trigger; pistol grip; cheekpiece and hogback comb; rubber buttpad
Hunting: . . . . $5495–$6495

Merkel

MERKEL RX HELIX EXPLORER

MERKEL RX HELIX

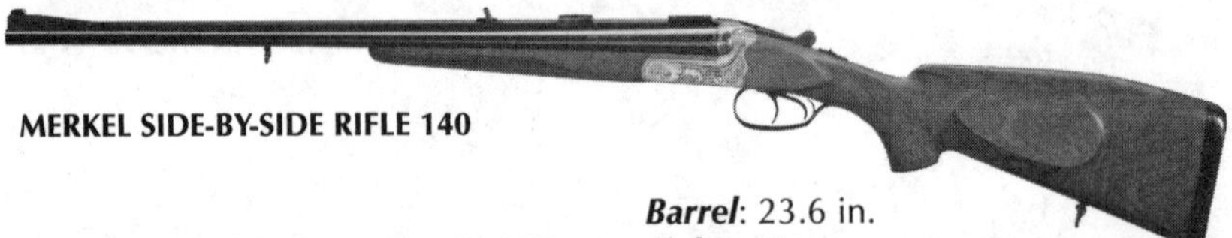
MERKEL SIDE-BY-SIDE RIFLE 140

RX HELIX EXPLORER

Action: Straight-pull bolt
Stock: Synthetic
Barrel: 20 in., 22 in., 24 in.
Sights: Fixed fiber optic
Weight: 6 lb.–6 lb. 3 oz.
Caliber: .222 Rem., .223 Rem., 6.5x55 Swedish, .270 Win., 7x64 Brenneke, .308 Win, .30-06 Spfd., 8x57 IS, 9.3x62 Mauser, 7mm Rem. Mag., .300 Win. Mag.
Magazine: Detachable box, 3, 5 rounds
Features: Fully enclosed action with integral rail; interchangeable barrels and mags for tool-free caliber change in 60 seconds; tang-mounted safety; aluminum action; Weaver rail; manual cocking system; Elastomer recoil pad
MSRP. $3295

RX HELIX

Action: Straight-pull bolt
Stock: Walnut
Barrel: 20 in., 22 in., 24 in.
Sights: Fixed fiber optic
Weight: 6 lb. 6 oz.
Caliber: .222 Rem., .223 Rem., .243 Win., .270 Win., .300 Win. Mag., .308 Win., 6.5x55 Swedish, 7mm Rem. Mag., 7x64 Brenneke, 7x65R, .30-06 Spfd., .30R Blaser, 8x57 IS, 9.3x62 Mauser
Magazine: Detachable box, 3, 5 rounds
Features: Fully enclosed action with integral rail; interchangeable barrels and mags for tool-free caliber change in 60 seconds; tang-mounted safety; aluminum action; Weaver mounting rail; European walnut stock; manual cocking system; Elastomer recoil pad; checkering on forend and pistol grip
Standard:. . . . .$3795–$10495

SIDE-BY-SIDE RIFLE 140

Action: Hinged breech
Stock: Wood
Barrel: 23.6 in.
Sights: None
Weight: 7 lb. 8 oz.
Caliber: .375 H&H, .416 Rigby, .450/400 NE, .470 NE, .500 NE
Magazine: None
Features: Interchangeable barrel options; Anson & Deeley locks; steel action; Greener-style cross-bolt and double bottom bite; double trigger with front set trigger, optional single trigger; automatic trigger safety; optional with ejectors; hard soldered barrels with muzzle adjustment; engraving English arabesque or game scene "JAGD"; rubber buttplate; pistol grip; cheekpiece and hogback comb
MSRP. . . . .$11995–$13995

Montana Rifles

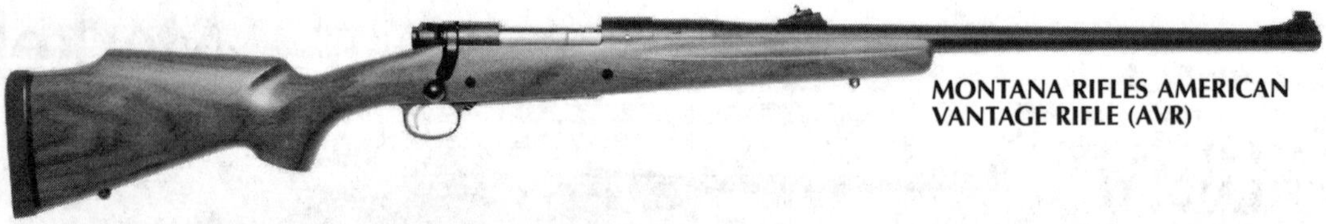
MONTANA RIFLES AMERICAN VANTAGE RIFLE (AVR)

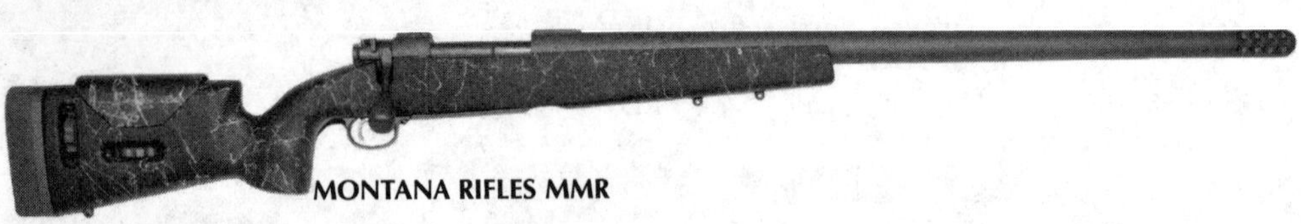
MONTANA RIFLES MMR

AMERICAN VANTAGE RIFLE (AVR)

Action: Bolt
Stock: Walnut, Synthetic
Barrel: 24 in.
Sights: Marble replaceable front and rear
Weight: 9 lb.
Caliber: .35 Whelen, .375 H&H, .375 Ruger, .416 Rem. Mag., .416 Ruger, .458 Lott, .458 Win. Mag.
Magazine: N/A
Features: Matte blued chrome moly steel or stainless steel barreled actions; available in right or left hand configurations
MSRP. $1616

MONTANA MARKSMAN RIFLE (MMR)

Action: Bolt
Stock: Synthetic
Barrel: 22 in.–26 in.
Sights: None
Weight: 13 lb.
Caliber: .300 Win. Mag., .300 WSM, .308 Win., 6.5-284 Norma
Magazine: N/A
Features: Long-range tactical rifle; fluted and nitrided barrel; detachable muzzle brake; adjustable stock
MSRP. $2990

Montana Rifles

MONTANA RIFLES SCR

SEVEN CONTINENT RIFLE (SCR)

Action: Bolt
Stock: Synthetic
Barrel: 24 in.–26 in.
Sights: None
Weight: 9 lb.–10 lb.
Caliber: .338 Lapua, .338 Norma Mag., .378 Wby Mag., .416 Rigby, .460 Wby Mag.
Magazine: N/A
Features: Staineless steel barrel
MSRP $2204

Mossberg

MOSSBERG 464 LEVER-ACTION RIFLE

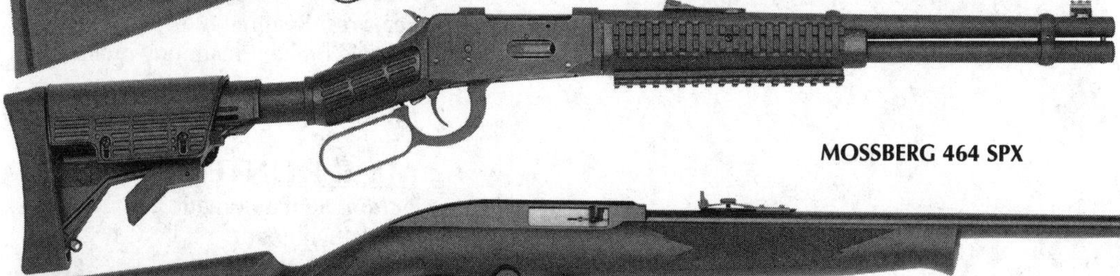

MOSSBERG 464 SPX

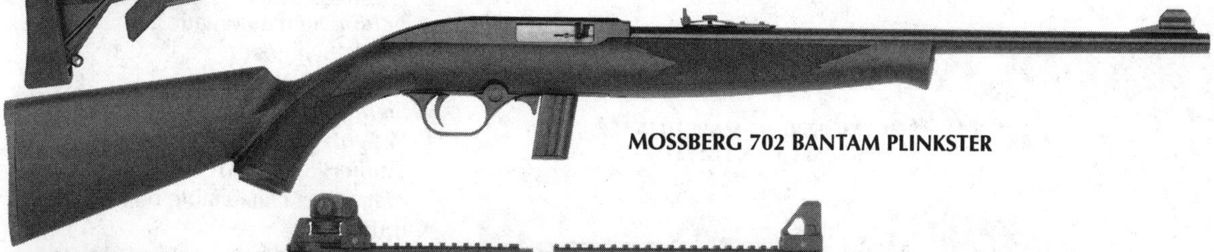

MOSSBERG 702 BANTAM PLINKSTER

MOSSBERG 715T TACTICAL FLAT TOP

464 LEVER-ACTION RIFLE

Action: Lever
Stock: Walnut
Barrel: 20 in.
Sights: Adjustable rifle sights
Weight: 6 lb. 12 oz.
Caliber: .22LR, .30-30 Win.
Magazine: Under-barrel tube, 7 rounds
Features: Adjustable rifle sights; 18 in. model has dovetail receiver; drilled and tapped for scope; walnut stock with optional pistol grip
18 in.: $497
20 in.: . . . .$530–$569

464 SPX

Action: Lever
Stock: Synthetic
Barrel: 16.25 in., 18 in.
Sights: Open
Weight: 6 lb.–6 lb. 8 oz.
Caliber: .22LR, .30-30 Win.
Magazine: Under-barrel tube, 14, 6 rounds
Features: 6-position adjustable stocks; tri-rail forends with rail covers; adjustable fiber optic sights; optional flash suppressor and muzzlebrake; top-tang safety; dovetail receiver rifle sights or fiber optic 3-dot sights
MSRP . . . . $530–$569

702 BANTAM PLINKSTER

Action: Semiautomatic
Stock: Synthetic or wood
Barrel: 18 in.
Sights: Rear sight
Weight: 4 lb. 2 oz.
Caliber: .22LR
Magazine: Detachable box, 10 rounds
Features: Fold down rear sight; synthetic stock comes in black or pink; blued finish on barrel and metal
MSRP . . . . $187–$230

715T TACTICAL FLAT TOP

Action: Semiautomatic
Stock: Synthetic
Barrel: 16.25 in.
Sights: Adjustable
Weight: 5 lb. 4 oz.
Caliber: .22LR
Magazine: Detachable box, 11, 26 rounds
Features: Fixed stock or six-position adjustable stock versions available; stock finish is black matte or Mossy Oak Brush camo; red-dot combo package; optional 10 round or 25 round magazine; flat top receiver with full-length Picatinny top rail; free-floating barrels with matte blued finish; removable rear and front adjustable sights; pistol grip
MSRP $375

Mossberg

MOSSBERG 802 PLINKSTER BOLT-ACTION

MOSSBERG 817 BOLT-ACTION

MOSSBERG DUCK COMMANDER 715T

MOSSBERG MMR HUNTER - MOSSY OAK TREESTAND

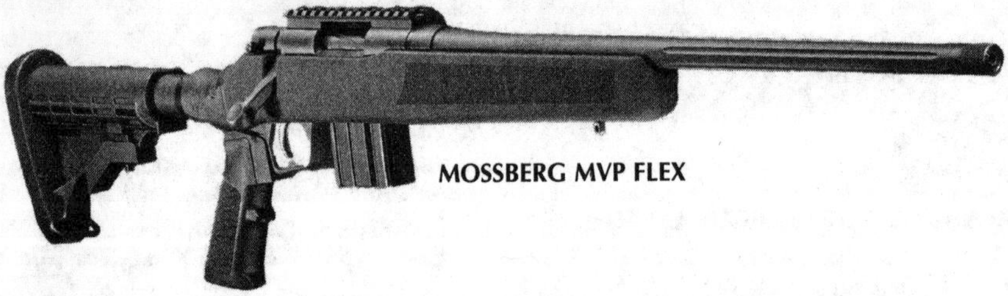

MOSSBERG MVP FLEX

802 PLINKSTER BOLT-ACTION

Action: Bolt
Stock: Synthetic or wood
Barrel: 18 in., 21 in.
Sights: Adjustable rifle sights
Weight: 4 lb. 2 oz.–4 lb. 10 oz.
Caliber: .22LR
Magazine: Detachable box, 11 rounds
Features: Stock comes in black, pink, or marble pink finish; receiver grooved to accept .375-inch scope mounts; cross-bolt safety and magazine release buttons; free-float barrel with blued or brushed chrome finish; includes free gun lock
MSRP . . . . $187–$230

817 BOLT-ACTION

Action: Bolt
Stock: Synthetic or wood
Barrel: 21 in.
Sights: None
Weight: 4 lb. 8 oz.–5 lb.
Caliber: .17 HMR
Magazine: Detachable box, 5 rounds
Features: Factory-mounted Weaver-style scope bases; cross-bolt safety and magazine release buttons; free gun lock included; stock available in black synthetic or wood; metal finishes include blued or brushed chrome; optional scope; optional muzzlebrake
MSRP . . . . $219–$279

DUCK COMMANDER 715T

Action: Semiautomatic
Stock: Synthetic
Barrel: 16.25 in.
Sights: Adjustable
Weight: 5.5 lb.
Caliber: .22LR
Magazine: Detachable box, 26 rounds
Features: Realtree Max-4 camo; muzzle brake; Picatinny quad-rail forearm
MSRP $509

MMR HUNTER

Action: Semiautomatic
Stock: Synthetic
Barrel: 20 in.
Sights: None
Weight: 7 lb. 8 oz.
Caliber: 5.56 NATO
Magazine: Detachable box, 5+1 rounds
Features: Carbon steel barrel with black phosphate finish; black synthetic, Mossy Oak Treestand, or Mossy Oak Brush stocks; single-stage trigger; oversized trigger guard for use with gloves; integral Picatinny rail
Black: $1028
Mossy Oak: $1127

MVP FLEX

Action: Bolt
Stock: Synthetic
Barrel: 18.5 in., 20 in.
Sights: Adjustable
Weight: 7 lb.
Caliber: 5.56 NATO, 7.62 NATO
Magazine: Detachable box, 10+1 rounds
Features: Lightning Bolt trigger system; compatible with all FLEX buttstocks featuring the tool-less locking system; fluted medium bull barrel or sporter barrel; threaded, removable A2-style flash suppressor and thread protector included on bull barrel model; Picatinny rail
MSRP . . . . $764–$1018

Mossberg

MOSSBERG MVP PATROL

MOSSBERG MVP SERIES PREDATOR

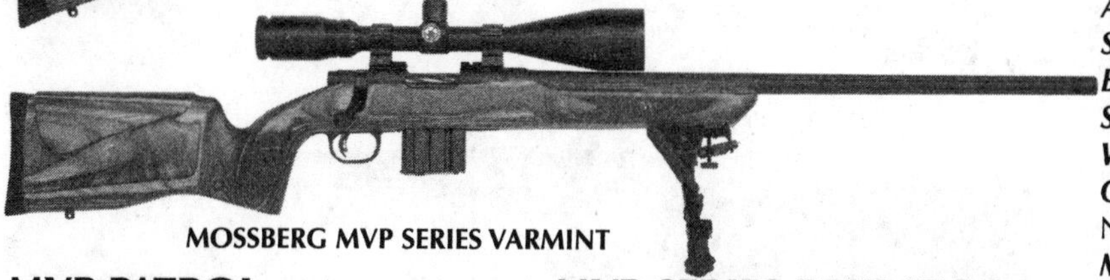

MOSSBERG MVP SERIES VARMINT

MVP PATROL

Action: Bolt
Stock: Synthetic
Barrel: 16.25 in.
Sights: Adjustable
Weight: 7 lb.
Caliber: 5.56 NATO, 7.62 NATO
Magazine: Detachable box, 10+1 rounds
Features: Picatinny rail; threaded barrel for flash suppressor; Lightning Bolt action adjustable trigger system
MSRP . . . .$732–$748

MVP SERIES PREDATOR

Action: Bolt
Stock: Laminate
Barrel: 18.5 in., 20 in.
Sights: Weaver-style bases
Weight: 7 lb. 8 oz.
Caliber: 5.56 NATO
Magazine: Detachable box, 11 rounds
Features: Mossberg Varmint Predator series; gray laminate sporter-style stock; optional compact barrel lengths; scoped combo package available; Weaver-style bases for adding optics; carbon steel barrels; varmint style muzzle crown; helically-fluted bolt and barrel fluting; metalwork has durable, non-reflective matte blued finish; front and rear sling swivel studs
MSRP . . . . $732–$748

MVP SERIES VARMINT

Action: Bolt
Stock: Laminate
Barrel: 24 in.
Sights: Weaver-style bases
Weight: 7 lb. 8 oz.
Caliber: 5.56 NATO, .204 Ruger, 7.62 NATO
Magazine: Detachable box, 10+1 rounds
Features: Mossberg Varmint Predator series; Weaver-style bases for optics customization; button-rifled medium bull barrel; varmint style crown; fluting on the barrel; helically-fluted bolt; metalwork has matte blued finish; gray laminate benchrest stock with pistol grip
MSRP . . . .$754–$770

RIFLES

Nesika

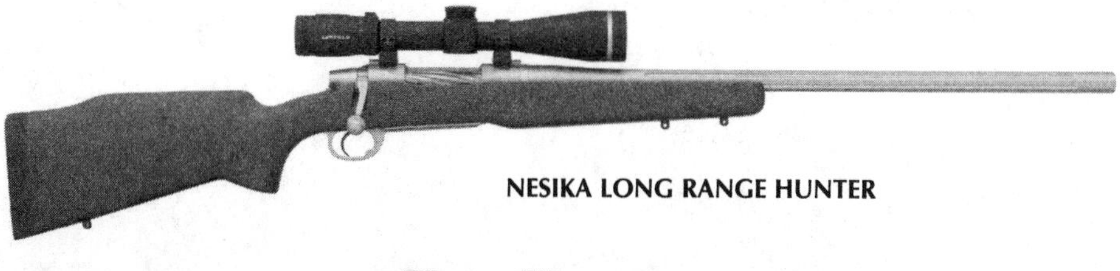

NESIKA LONG RANGE HUNTER

NESIKA SPORTER

LONG RANGE HUNTER

Action: Bolt
Stock: Synthetic
Barrel: 26 in.
Sights: None
Weight: 9 lb. 12 oz.
Caliber: .300 Win. Mag., 7mm Rem. Mag.
Magazine: Internal
Features: Nesika stainless Hunter action; receiver made from 15-5 stainless steel; one-piece bolt from 4340 CM steel; Douglas air-gauged stainless steel barrel; fluted Varmint contour; Timney trigger set at a 3 lbs.; Leupold QRW bases
MSRP $3999

SPORTER

Action: Bolt
Stock: Synthetic
Barrel: 24 in., 26 in.
Sights: None
Weight: 8 lb.
Caliber: .30-06 Spfd., .280 Rem., .300 Win. Mag., .308 Win., 7mm Rem. Mag., 7mm-08 Rem.
Magazine: Internal
Features: Nesika stainless Hunter action; receiver made from 15-5 stainless steel; one-piece bolt from 4340 CM steel; Douglas air-gauged stainless steel barrel; fluted Varmint contour; Timney trigger set at a 3 lbs.; Leupold QRW bases
MSRP $3499

Nesika

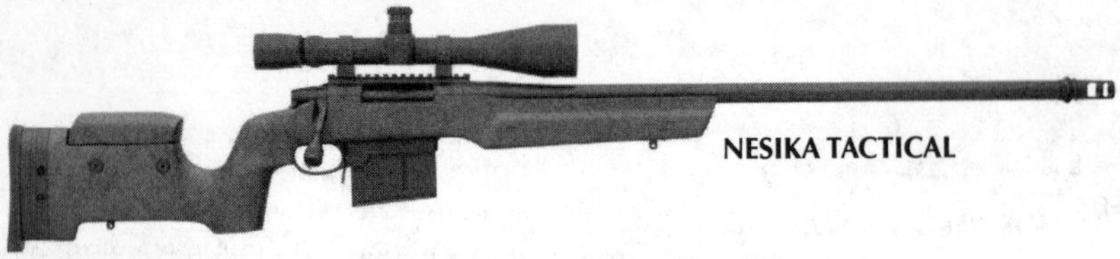

NESIKA TACTICAL

TACTICAL

Action: Bolt
Stock: Synthetic
Barrel: 26 in., 28 in.
Sights: None
Weight: 13 lb. 12 oz.
Caliber: .300 Win. Mag., .338 Lapua
Magazine: Detachable box, 5 rounds
Features: Picatinny rail; all metal coated with Cerakoted matte black finish; tactical hand laid-up composite stock with aluminum bedding block, spacer adjuster system, and adjustable cheekpiece; Timney trigger set at 3 lbs.
MSRP $4499

New Ultra Light Arms

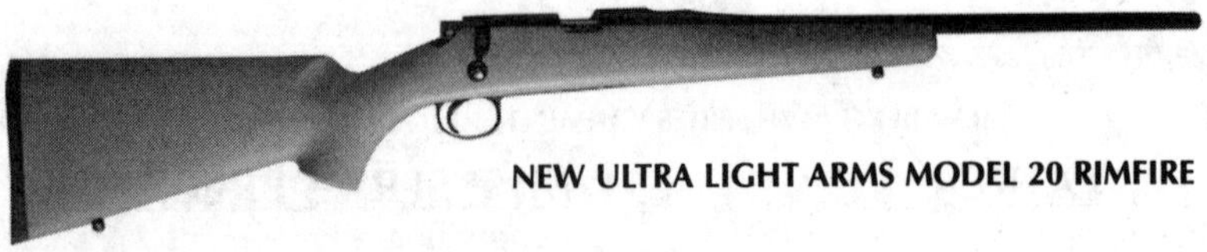

NEW ULTRA LIGHT ARMS MODEL 20 RIMFIRE

NEW ULTRA LIGHT ARMS MODEL 20 ULTIMATE MOUNTAIN RIFLE

MODEL 20 RIMFIRE

Action: Bolt
Stock: Kevlar/graphite composite
Barrel: 22 in.
Sights: None
Weight: 5 lb. 4 oz.
Caliber: .22LR
Magazine: None or detachable box, 5 rounds
Features: Single-shot or repeater; drilled and tapped for scope; recoil pad; sling swivels; color stock options; left-hand models available for no extra charge
Single shot: $1800
Repeater: $1850

MODEL 20 ULTIMATE MOUNTAIN RIFLE

Action: Bolt
Stock: Kevlar/graphite composite
Barrel: 22 in.
Sights: None
Weight: 5 lb.
Caliber: .308 Win., .243 Win., 6mm Rem., .257 Roberts, 7mm-08, .284 Win.
Magazine: Detachable box
Features: Available in left-hand; choice of stock colors; 20-oz. action; two-position safety
MSRP $3500
Left-handed: $3600

Noreen

BN36

Action: Semiautomatic
Stock: Synthetic
Barrel: 22 in.
Sights: None
Weight: 8 lb.
Caliber: .25-06 Rem., .30-06 Spfd., .270 Win.
Magazine: Detachable box, 5, 10, or 20 rounds
Features: Picatinny rail; direct gas impingement, side charging semiautomatic; Mil-Spec or optional match trigger
MSRP . . . . $1700–$2000

NOREEN BN36

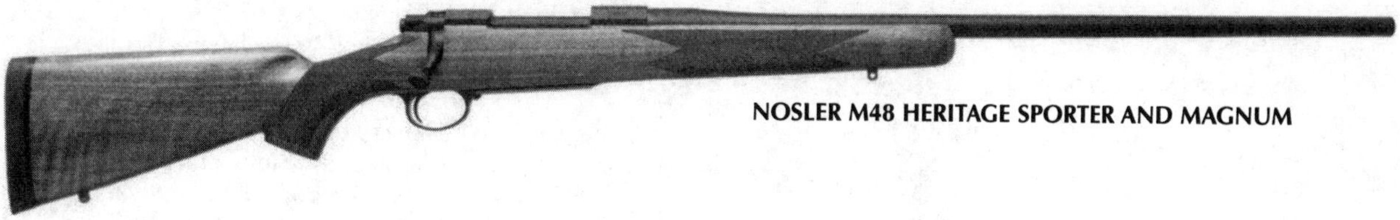

NOSLER M48 HERITAGE SPORTER AND MAGNUM

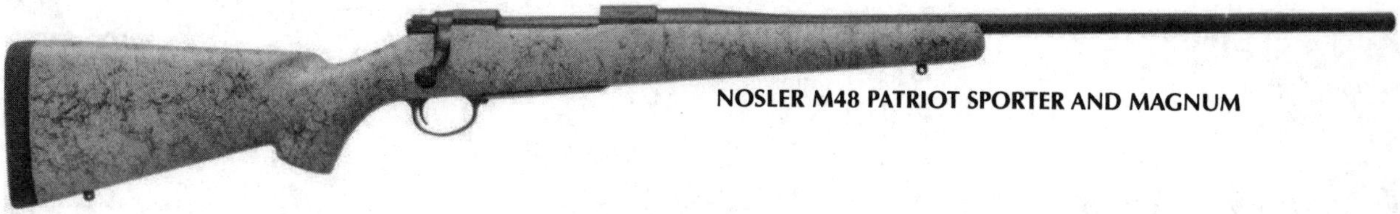

NOSLER M48 PATRIOT SPORTER AND MAGNUM

NOSLER CUSTOM RIFLE

M48 HERITAGE MAGNUM

Action: Bolt
Stock: Wood
Barrel: 24 in.–26 in.
Sights: None
Weight: 7 lb. 12 oz.
Caliber: .26 Nosler, .280 Ack. Imp., .35 Whelen, .300 WSM, .300 Win. Mag., .325 WSM, .338 Win. Mag., 7mm Rem. Mag., 9.3x62 Mauser
Magazine: N/A
Features: Nosler Model 48 Custom action; stainless match-grade barrel; fancy walnut stock with heckering; hinged floor-plate; two-position Rocker safety; Cerakote all-weather finish
MSRP $1895

M48 HERITAGE SPORTER

Action: Bolt
Stock: Wood
Barrel: 24 in.
Sights: None
Weight: 7 lb. 4 oz.
Caliber: .22-250 Rem., .243 Win., .260 Rem., .270 Win., .270 WSM, .30-06 Spfd., .308 Win., 7mm-08 Rem., 7x57 Mauser
Magazine: N/A
Features: Nosler Model 48 Custom action; stainless match-grade barrel; fancy walnut stock with heckering; hinged floor-plate; two-position Rocker safety; Cerakote all-weather finish
MSRP $1895

M48 PATRIOT MAGNUM

Action: Bolt
Stock: Synthetic
Barrel: 24 in.–26 in.
Sights: None
Weight: 7 lb.–7 lb. 10 oz.
Caliber: .26 Nosler, .280 Ack. Imp., .35 Whelen, .300 WSM, .300 Win. Mag., .325 WSM, .338 Win. Mag., 7mm Rem. Mag.
Magazine: N/A
Features: Nosler Model 48 Custom action; stainless match-grade barrel; lightweight aramid fiber reinforced composite stock; glass and aluminum pillar bedding; hinged floor-plate; two-position Rocker safety; Cerakote all-weather finish
MSRP $1695

M48 PATRIOT SPORTER

Action: Bolt
Stock: Synthetic
Barrel: 24 in.
Sights: None
Weight: 6 lb. 12 oz.–7 lb.
Caliber: .22-250 Rem., .243 Win., .260 Rem., .270 Win., .270 WSM, .30-06 Spfd., .308 Win., 6.5-284 Norma, 7mm-08 Rem., 7x57 Mauser
Magazine: N/A
Features: Nosler Model 48 Custom action; stainless match-grade barrel; lightweight aramid fiber reinforced composite stock; glass and aluminum pillar bedding; hinged floor-plate; two-position Rocker safety; Cerakote all-weather finish
MSRP $1695

NOSLER CUSTOM RIFLE

Action: Bolt
Stock: Walnut
Barrel: 24 in., 24.75 in.
Sights: Open
Weight: 8 lb. 4 oz.–8 lb. 12 oz.
Caliber: .300 WSM, .280 Ack. Imp., .338 Win. Mag.
Magazine: Internal, 3, 4 rounds
Features: Leupold Custom Shop; match-grade stainless, fully free-floated hand lapped barrel; three-stage safety; glass pillar-bedded fancy walnut stock; custom case cruzer by Pelican; custom leather sling
MSRP $3795

Noveske

NOVESKE GEN 3 SERIES

GEN 3 SERIES

Action: Semiautomatic
Stock: Synthetic
Barrel: 10.5 in.–18 in.
Sights: Adjustable
Weight: N/A
Caliber: 300 BLK, 5.56 NATO
Magazine: Detachable box, 30 rounds
Features: Picatinny rail; adjustable stock; Cerakote coating; Switchblock, Thunder Ranch, and Shooting Team models available
MSRP. . . . . $2505–$2930

Olympic Arms

OLYMPIC ARMS GAMESTALKER

GAMESTALKER

Action: Gas-operated semiautomatic
Stock: ACE Skeleton stock in camo
Barrel: 22 in. stainless fluted
Sights: None
Weight: 7 lb. 8 oz.
Caliber: .243 WSSM, .25 WSSM, .300 OSSM
Magazine: Detachable box, 5 rounds
Features: Flat-top upper receiver; free-floating aluminum handguard; ERGO grip; Picatinny rail
MSRP. $1364

OLYMPIC ARMS UMAR

ULTIMATE MAGNUM AR (UMAR)

Action: Gas-operated semiautomatic
Stock: Synthetic
Barrel: 24 in.
Sights: None
Weight: 9 lb. 6 oz.
Caliber: .22-250 Rem., .223 WSSM, .243 WSSM, .25 WSSM, .300 OSSM
Magazine: Detachable box, 5 rounds
Features: Aluminum forged receiver machined by Olympic Arms; black matte anodized receiver, Parkerized steel parts; flat top with Picatinny rails; heavy match grade bull barrel; side-sling mount or bi-pod mount
MSRP. $1559

Patriot Ordnance

P15 PURITAN

Action: Semiautomatic
Stock: Synthetic
Barrel: 16.5 in.
Sights: None
Weight: 6 lb. 11 oz.
Caliber: 5.56 NATO, .223 Rem., 7.62 Warsaw
Magazine: Detachable box, 30 rounds
Features: Picatinny flattop gas block, bayonet mount, and QD sling mount; black anodized finish; the ejection port is embellished with the words God Bless America and the American flag
MSRP. $1500

PATRIOT ORDNANCE FACTORY P15 PURITAN

PEDERSOLI 1874 SHARPS OLD WEST

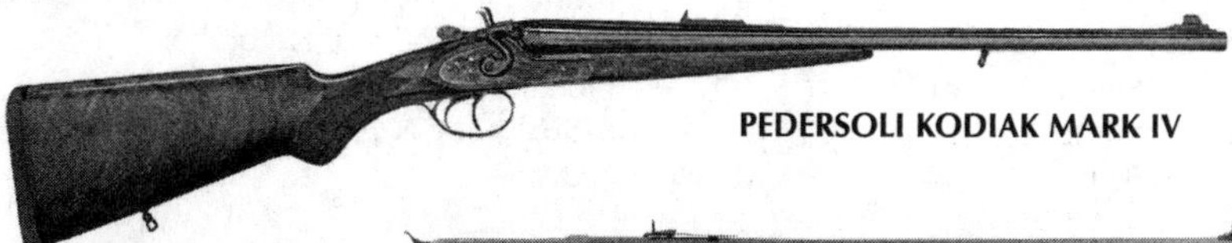

PEDERSOLI KODIAK MARK IV

PEDERSOLI MODEL 86/71 LEVER ACTION CLASSIC

PEDERSOLI MODEL 86/71 LEVER ACTION BOARBUSTER CAMO

PEDERSOLI MODEL 86/71 LEVER ACTION WILDBUSTER

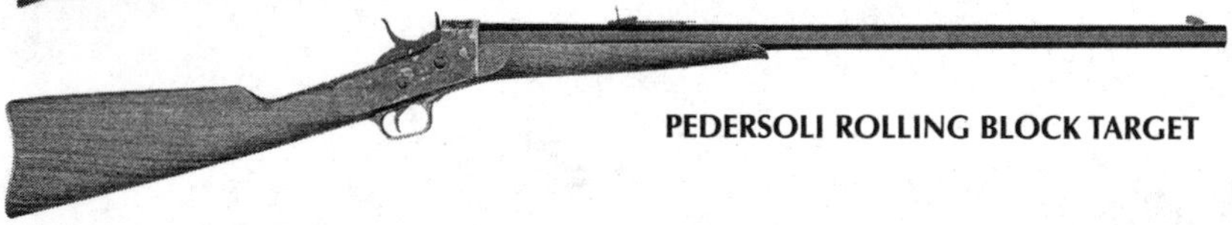

PEDERSOLI ROLLING BLOCK TARGET

1874 SHARPS OLD WEST MAPLE

Action: Dropping block
Stock: Maple
Barrel: 30 in.
Sights: None
Weight: 11 lb. 7 oz.
Caliber: .45-70 Govt.
Magazine: None
Features: Optional Creedmoor and tunnel sights; brass plate on right side of butt stock can be personalized; forend has wedge plates; pistol grip cap is made of hardened steel
MSRP **$2279**

KODIAK MARK IV

Action: Breech loading
Stock: Walnut
Barrel: 22 in., 24 in.
Sights: Open
Weight: 9 lb. 11 oz.–10 lb. 5 oz.
Caliber: .45-70 Govt. 8x57JRS, 9.3x74R
Magazine: None
Features: Double-leave rear sight in a dovetail; tapered round barrels made of blued steel; select walnut stock with checkering and oil finish
MSRP **$6009**

MODEL 86/71 LEVER ACTION BOARBUSTER

Action: Lever
Stock: Walnut
Barrel: 19 in.
Sights: Drilled and tapped for scopes
Weight: 7 lb. 4 oz.
Caliber: .444 Marlin, .45-70 Govt.
Magazine: 5 rounds
Features: Barrel equipped with European Picatinny style base with integral rear sight; half cock safety on hammer; safety slide catch at the rear of the frame; checkered pistol grip stock and forend are made from walnut; also available in soft touch orange camo color; metal parts are blued; drilled and tapped for sights
MSRP **$1771**

MODEL 86/71 LEVER ACTION CLASSIC

Action: Lever
Stock: Walnut
Barrel: 24 in.
Sights: Drilled and tapped for scopes
Weight: 8 lb. 3 oz.
Caliber: .45-70 Govt.
Magazine: 5 rounds
Features: Last "big frame" rifle for Winchester; drilled and tapped for scopes; broach rifled barrel and magazine are blued finished; checkered walnut pistol grip; frame is forged and CNC-machined, with a blued finish on the standard version and case-hardened frame and buttcap on the Premium model with select walnut stock and forend
MSRP **$1771**

MODEL 86/71 LEVER ACTION WILDBUSTER

Action: Lever
Stock: Walnut
Barrel: 24 in.
Sights: Drilled and tapped for scopes
Weight: 8 lb. 3 oz.
Caliber: .45-70 Govt.
Magazine: 5 rounds
Features: Ramp rear sight; walnut forend and pistol grip stock with checkered buttplate; blued finish on metal parts; drilled and tapped for scopes
MSRP **$1709**

ROLLING BLOCK TARGET

Action: Dropping block
Stock: Walnut
Barrel: 30 in.
Sights: Open
Weight: 10 lb. 9 oz.
Caliber: .357 Mag., .45–70 Govt.
Magazine: None
Features: Octagonal, conical blued barrel; case-hardened color frame is equipped with ramp rear sight adjustable in elevation; steel buttplate and trigger guard; straight stock and forend made of walnut with oil finish
MSRP **$1151**

Primary Weapons Systems

MK216
Action: Semiautomatic
Stock: Synthetic
Barrel: 16 in.
Sights: Adjustable
Weight: 8 lb. 12 oz.
Caliber: .308 Win., 7.62 NATO
Magazine: Detachable box, 10 or 20 rounds
Features: FSC muzzle brake and suppressor; Picatinny rail; adjustable stock
MSRP. $2600

MK220
Action: Semiautomatic
Stock: Synthetic
Barrel: 20 in.
Sights: Adjustable
Weight: 9 lb. 8 oz.
Caliber: .308 Win., 7.62 NATO
Magazine: Detachable box, 10 or 20 rounds
Features: PRC muzzle brake; Picatinny rail; adjustable stock
MSRP. $2900

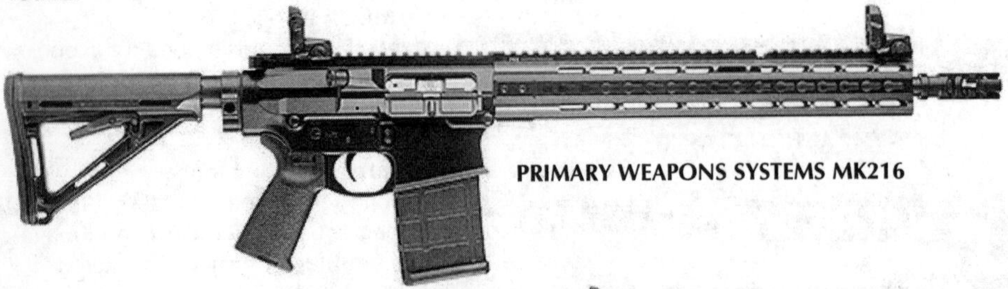

PRIMARY WEAPONS SYSTEMS MK216

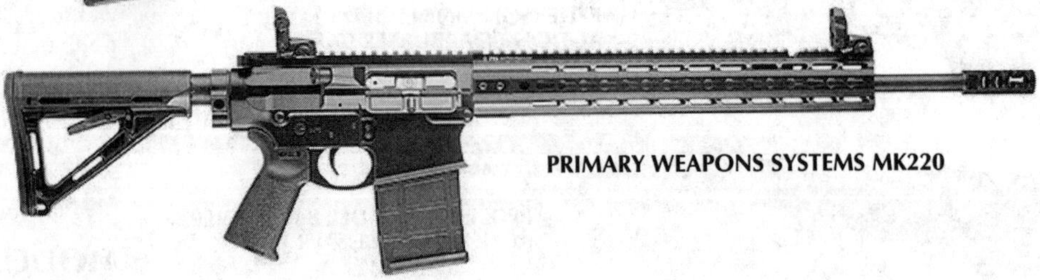

PRIMARY WEAPONS SYSTEMS MK220

RIFLES

Purdey

PURDEY BOLT ACTION RIFLE

PURDEY DOUBLE RIFLE

BOLT ACTION RIFLES
Action: Bolt
Stock: Walnut
Barrel: 25 in.
Sights: Open
Weight: 10 lb. 8 oz.
Caliber: .375 H&H, 7mm Mag.
Magazine: None
Features: Original Mauser '98 or modern Mauser type magnum square bridge; model 70 type safety catch for use with telescopic sights; quick detachable claw or Purdey rail mounts depending on the type of action and telescopic sight chosen; Purdey's rail mount system with integral recoil bar; Turkish walnut stock with pistol grip; cheekpiece and rubber recoil pad; single trigger
Original Mauser Action: . . . $46195
Magnum Square Bridge Action (.375 caliber & above): $46195

DOUBLE RIFLES
Action: Self-Opening
Stock: Walnut
Barrel: 23 in.–26 in.
Sights: Open
Weight: 12 lb. 4 oz.
Caliber: .375, .416, .470, .475, .500, .577, .600
Magazine: None
Features: Hinged front trigger; bolted non-automatic safety catch; sling swivels optional; full pistol grip; cheekpiece and leather covered recoil pad; chopper lump barrel construction; express rear sights with bead foresight with flip-up moon sight; optional beavertail forend and telescopic sights
.375 or smaller: $156248
.416, .470, .475, .500: $156248
.557, .600: $165755

Remington Arms

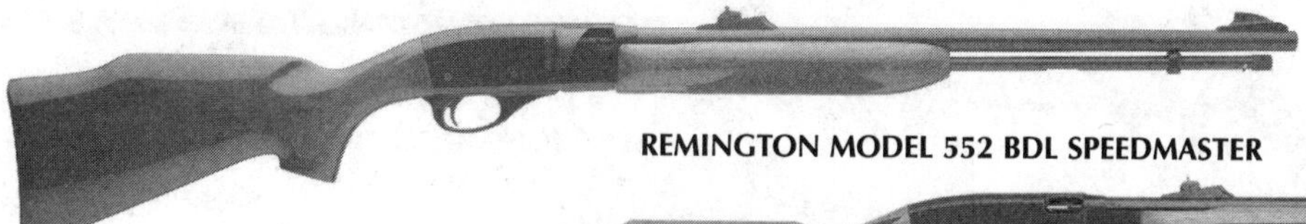

REMINGTON MODEL 552 BDL SPEEDMASTER

REMINGTON MODEL 572 BDL FIELDMASTER

REMINGTON MODEL 597 WITH SCOPE

REMINGTON MODEL 597 HB

REMINGTON MODEL 597
HEAVY BARREL A-TACS CAMO

MODEL 552 BDL SPEEDMASTER

Action: Semiautomatic
Stock: Walnut
Barrel: 22 in.
Sights: Open
Weight: 5 lb. 12 oz.
Caliber: .22S, L, LR
Magazine: Under-barrel tube
Features: Adjustable iron sights for open sight plinking; grooved receiver for scope mounts; high-gloss American walnut stock and forend checkering; richly blued carbon-steel barrel; positive cross-bolt safety
MSRP $650

MODEL 572 BDL FIELDMASTER

Action: Pump
Stock: Walnut
Barrel: 21 in.
Sights: Open
Weight: 5 lb. 12 oz.
Caliber: .22S, L, LR
Magazine: Under-barrel tube
Features: Smooth classic side action; high-gloss American walnut stock and forend with cut checkering; richly blued carbon-steel barrel; adjustable iron sights for open slight plinking; receiver grooved for scope mounts; positive cross-bolt safety
MSRP $665

MODEL 597

Action: Semiautomatic
Stock: Synthetic
Barrel: 22 in.
Sights: Open
Weight: 5 lb. 8 oz.
Caliber: .22LR, .22 WMR
Magazine: Detachable clip, 10 rounds
Features: Bolt-guidance system features twin, tool-steel guide rails; sear and hammer are Teflon/nickel-plated; non-glare matte finish; adjustable big game iron sights; last-shot "hold open" bolt for added safety
MSRP $204

MODEL 597 HEAVY BARREL

Action: Semiautomatic
Stock: Synthetic
Barrel: 22 in.
Sights: None
Weight: 5 lb. 12 oz.
Caliber: .22 LR
Magazine: Detachable clip, 10 rounds
Features: Heavy barrel with rugged green synthetic stock; bolt-guidance system features twin tool-steel guide rails; Teflon nickel plated sear and hammer; patented drop-out staggered stack, detachable metal magazine; last-shot "hold open" bolt; scope rail
MSRP $249

MODEL 597 HEAVY BARREL A-TACS CAMO

Action: Semiautomatic
Stock: Synthetic
Barrel: 22 in.
Sights: None
Weight: 5 lb. 12 oz.
Caliber: .22 LR
Magazine: Detachable box, 10 rounds
Features: Heavy barrel with A-TACS camo synthetic stock; bolt-guidance system features twin tool-steel guide rails; Teflon nickel plated sear and hammer; patented drop-out staggered stack, detachable metal magazine; last-shot "hold open" bolt; scope rail
MSRP $349

Remington Arms

REMINGTON MODEL 700 BDL

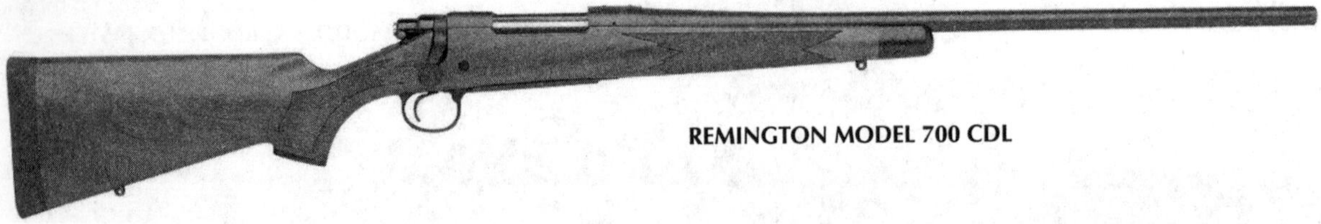

REMINGTON MODEL 700 CDL

REMINGTON MODEL 700 LONG RANGE

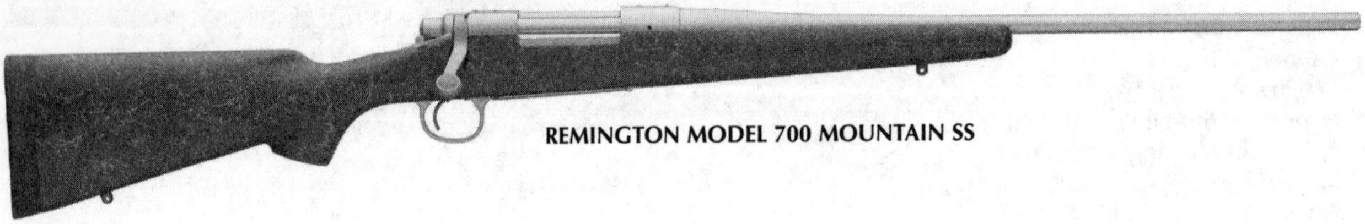

REMINGTON MODEL 700 MOUNTAIN SS

MODEL 700 BDL

Action: Bolt
Stock: Walnut
Barrel: 22 in., 24 in., 26 in.
Sights: Open
Weight: 7 lb. 4 oz.–7 lb. 10 oz.
Caliber: .243 Win., .270 Win., .30-06 Spfd., 7mm Rem. Mag., .300 Rem. Ultra Mag.
Magazine: Internal
Features: Adjustable X-Mark Pro Trigger system; walnut stock with black forend cap; Monte Carlo comb with raised cheekpiece and skipline cut checkering; hinged magazine floor plate; sling swivel studs; hooded ramp front sight and adjustable rear sight; cylindrical receiver machined from solid-steel bar
MSRP $994

MODEL 700 CDL

Action: Bolt
Stock: Walnut
Barrel: 24 in., 26 in.
Sights: None
Weight: 7 lb. 5 oz.–7 lb. 10 oz.
Caliber: .243 Win., .270 Win., 7mm-08 Rem., .300 Win. Mag., .300 Rem. Ultra Mag.
Magazine: Internal
Features: Adjustable X-Mark Pro Trigger system; cylindrical receiver machined from solid-steel bar stock; walnut stock with oil finish
MSRP $1029

MODEL 700 LONG RANGE

Action: Bolt
Stock: Synthetic
Barrel: 26 in.
Sights: None
Weight: 9 lb.
Caliber: .25-06 Rem., .30-06 Spfd., .300 Ren. Ultra Mag., .300 Win. Mag., 7mm Rem. Mag.
Magazine: Internal, 4 or 3 (Mag.) rounds
Features: Bell and Carlson M40 tactical stock; heavy varmint barrel with matte finish; X-Mark Pro externally adjustable trigger system
MSRP $829

MODEL 700 MOUNTAIN SS

Action: Bolt
Stock: Synthetic
Barrel: 22 in.
Sights: Drilled and tapped for scopes
Weight: 6 lb. 8 oz.
Caliber: .25-06 Rem., .270 Win., .280 Rem., .30-06 Spfd., 7mm-08 Rem., .308 Win.
Magazine: Internal
Features: Bell & Carson aramid fiber reinforced stock; X-Mark Pro trigger system; cylindrical receiver design; sling swivel studs; stainless steel barrel and action; hinged magazine floor plate
MSRP $1135

REMINGTON MODEL 700 SENDERO SF II

REMINGTON MODEL 700 SPS LEFT-HAND

REMINGTON MODEL 700 SPS CAMO

REMINGTON MODEL 700 SPS TACTICAL

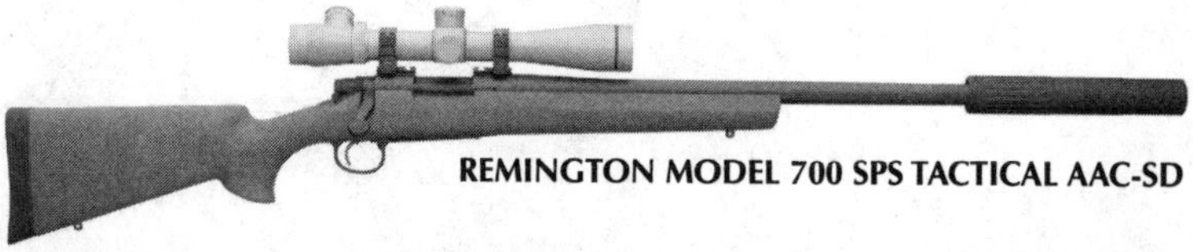

REMINGTON MODEL 700 SPS TACTICAL AAC-SD

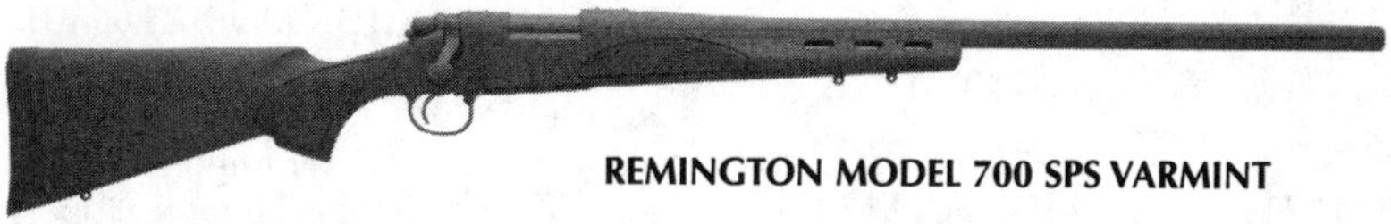

REMINGTON MODEL 700 SPS VARMINT

MODEL 700 SENDERO SF II

Action: Bolt
Stock: Composite
Barrel: 26 in.
Sights: None
Weight: 8 lb. 8 oz.
Caliber: 7mm Rem. Mag., .300 Win. Mag., .300 Rem. Ultra Mag.
Magazine: Internal
Features: Composite stock in black with gray webbing, reinforced with aramid fibers; features contoured beavertail forend with ambidextrous finger grooves and palm swells; heavy contour barrels are fluted for rapid cooling; full-length aluminum bedding stocks; twin front swivel studs for sling and bipod; concave target-style barrel crown
MSRP $1465

MODEL 700 SPS

Action: Bolt
Stock: Synthetic
Barrel: 24 in., 26 in.
Sights: None
Weight: 7 lb.–7 lb. 10 oz.
Caliber: .270 WSM, .300 WSM, .223 Rem., .243 Win., 7mm-08 Rem., .308 Win., .270 Win., .30-06 Spfd., .300 Win. Mag., .300 Rem. Ultra Mag., 7mm Rem. Mag.
Magazine: Internal box
Features: Black ergonomic synthetic stock; carbon steel sight drilled and tapped for scope mounts; exterior metal-work features matte blued finish; hinged floor plate; swivel studs
MSRP $724

MODEL 700 SPS CAMO

Action: Bolt
Stock: Synthetic
Barrel: 20 in., 22 in., 24 in.
Sights: None
Weight: 7 lb.–7 lb. 6 oz.
Caliber: .270 Win., .30-06 Spfd., 7mm Rem. Mag., .300 Win. Mag., .243 Win., 7mm-08 Rem.
Magazine: None
Features: Hammer-forged barrel; X-Mark Pro externally adjustable trigger system; SuperCell recoil pad; synthetic stock in Mossy Oak Break-Up Infinity pattern; Hogue over-molded grips; receivers tapped and drilled
MSRP $809

MODEL 700 SPS TACTICAL

Action: Bolt
Stock: Synthetic
Barrel: 20 in.
Sights: None
Weight: 7 lb. 4 oz.–7 lb. 11 oz.
Caliber: .223 Rem., .308 Win.
Magazine: Detachable box
Features: Ergonomic tactical stock in black; sling swivel studs; carbon steel barrel is drilled and tapped for sights; metal features blued finish; X-Mark Pro adjustable trigger; SuperCell recoil pad; semi-beavertail forend; hinged floor plate
MSRP $788

MODEL 700 SPS TACTICAL AAC-SD

Action: Bolt
Stock: Synthetic
Barrel: 20 in.
Sights: None
Weight: 7 lb. 5 oz.
Caliber: .308 Win.
Magazine: Internal box
Features: Heavy barrel with threaded muzzle; accepts AAC and other threaded flash hiders, muzzlebrakes and suppressors; Hogue overmolded hillier green pillar bedded stock; X-Mark Pro adjustable trigger; optional Leupold Mark IV scope
MSRP $833

MODEL 700 SPS VARMINT

Action: Bolt
Stock: Synthetic
Barrel: 26 in.
Sights: None
Weight: 8 lb. 8 oz.
Caliber: .204 Ruger, .223 Rem., .22-250 Rem., .243 Win., .308 Win.
Magazine: Internal
Features: Ergonomic black synthetic stock has a vented beavertail forend; non-reflective matte blued finish on barrel and receiver; hinged floor plate; sling swivel studs; drilled and tapped for scope mounts
MSRP $761

Remington Arms

REMINGTON MODEL 700 SPS WOOD TECH

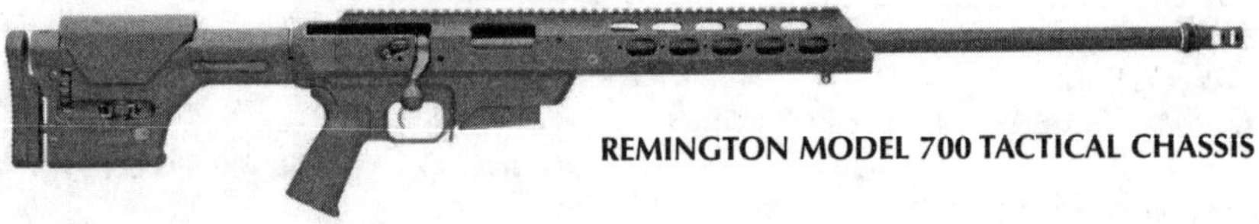

REMINGTON MODEL 700 TACTICAL CHASSIS

REMINGTON MODEL 700 TARGET TACTICAL WITH SCOPE

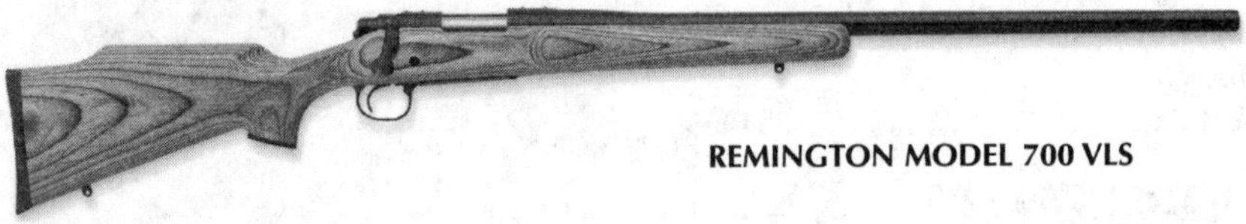

REMINGTON MODEL 700 VLS

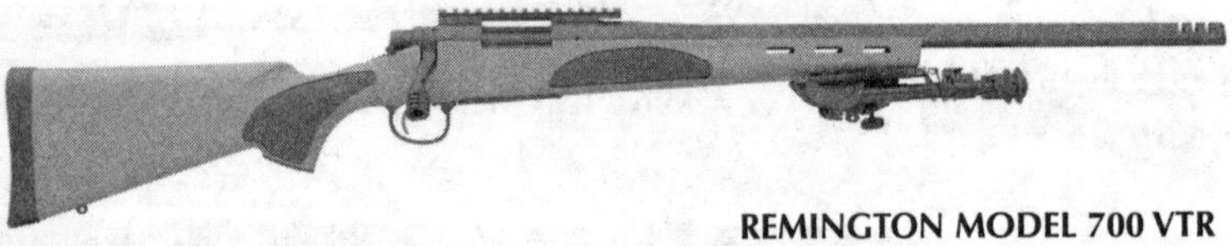

REMINGTON MODEL 700 VTR

MODEL 700 SPS WOOD TECH

Action: Bolt
Stock: Synthetic walnut finish
Barrel: 22 in., 24 in.
Sights: None
Weight: 7 lb. 6 oz.–7 lb. 10 oz.
Caliber: .270 Win., 30-06 Spfd., .300 Win., 7mm Rem. Mag.
Magazine: 4 rounds
Features: Hammer-forged barrel; X-Mark Pro externally adjustable trigger ensures peak shot control; overmolded grip panels on stock; SuperCell recoil pad
MSRP: $809

MODEL 700 TACTICAL CHASSIS

Action: Bolt
Stock: Synthetic
Barrel: 24 in., 26 in.
Sights: None
Weight: 11 lb. 12 oz.–12 lb. 4 oz.
Caliber: .300 Win. Mag., .308 Win., .338 Lapua
Magazine: Detachable box
Features: MDT TAC21 tactical chassis constructed out of aluminum anodized to Mil-Spec Type III; top full-length Picatinny rail; stainless steel barreled action with black cerakote finish; Magpul MAG307 PRS adjustable stock and pistol grip; target tactical bolt handle; AAC 51-T ratchet mount muzzle brake; X-Mark Pro externally adjustable trigger
MSRP $2900

MODEL 700 TARGET TACTICAL

Action: Bolt
Stock: Synthetic
Barrel: 26 in.
Sights: Target
Weight: 11 lb. 12 oz.
Caliber: .308 Win.
Magazine: Internal
Features: Triangular VTR barrel configuration; Bell & Carson Medalist varmint/tactical stock in black; 5-R hammer-forged tactical target rifling; adjustable length of comb and pull; tactical style bolt knob; X-Mark Pro adjustable trigger
MSRP $2138

MODEL 700 VLS

Action: Bolt
Stock: Laminate
Barrel: 26 in.
Sights: Target
Weight: 9 lb. 6 oz.
Caliber: .204 Ruger, .22-250 Rem., .223 Rem., .243 Win., .308 Win.
Magazine: Internal
Features: Varmint laminated stock; Monte Carlo cheekpiece; beavertail shape forend; blued, satin finish metal; concave target-style barrel crown
MSRP $1056

MODEL 700 VTR

Action: Bolt
Stock: Synthetic
Barrel: 22 in.
Sights: None
Weight: 7 lb. 10 oz.
Caliber: .22-250 Rem., .223 Rem., .260 Rem., .308 Win.
Magazine: Internal
Features: Integral muzzle brake; Picatinny rail; detachable bipod; stainless steel barrel available
MSRP . . . .$930–$980

REMINGTON MODEL 750 WOODSMASTER

REMINGTON MODEL 770

REMINGTON MODEL 770 STAINLESS CAMO

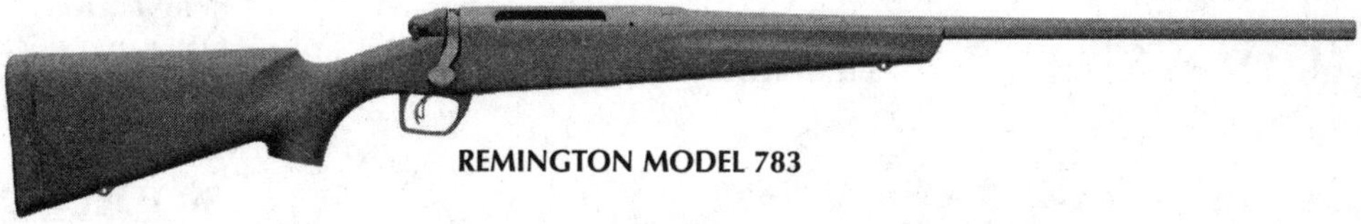

REMINGTON MODEL 783

MODEL 750 WOODSMASTER

Action: Semiautomatic
Stock: Walnut, synthetic
Barrel: 22 in.
Sights: Open
Weight: 7 lb. 8 oz.
Caliber: .270 Win., .30-06 Spfd., .308 Win., .243 Win.
Magazine: None
Features: American walnut or black synthetic stock and forend; iron sights; receiver drilled and tapped for model 7400 scope mounts; rotary-bolt lock-up; sling swivel studs
MSRP. $1004

MODEL 770

Action: Bolt
Stock: Synthetic
Barrel: 22 in.
Sights: Boresighted 3–9x40mm scope
Weight: 8 lb. 8 oz.–8 lb. 10 oz.
Caliber: .243 Win., 7mm-08 Rem., .270 Win., .30-06 Spfd., 7mm Rem. Mag., .300 Win. Mag., .308 Win.
Magazine: Detachable box, standard 4 rounds, magnum 3 rounds
Features: Button rifling; ergonomically contoured stock with a raised cheekpiece; textured grips; black synthetic stock; blued or stainless barrel with nickel-plated action and bolt; easy-camming 60 degree bolt; stainless steel barrel
MSRP. $383

MODEL 770 STAINLESS CAMO

Action: Bolt
Stock: Synthetic
Barrel: 22 in., 24 in.
Sights: Boresighted 3–9x40mm scope
Weight: 8 lb. 8 oz.
Caliber: .270 Win., .30-06 Spfd., 7mm Rem. Mag., .300 Win. Mag.
Magazine: Detachable box, standard 4 rounds, magnum 3 rounds
Features: Realtree AP HD camo synthetic stock design; molded swing swivel studs; stainless barrel with nickel-plated action and bolt; easy-camming 60 degree bolt
MSRP. $467

MODEL 783

Action: Bolt
Stock: Black synthetic
Barrel: 22 in., 24 in.
Sights: None
Weight: 7 lb.–7 lb. 4 oz.
Caliber: .270 Win., .30-06 Spfd., .308 Win., 7mm Rem. Mag.
Magazine: 4 rounds
Features: CrossFire trigger system; carbon steel magnum contour button rifled barrel; pillar-bedded stock and free-floated barrel; SuperCell recoil pad
MSRP. $451

Remington Arms

REMINGTON MODEL 7600

REMINGTON MODEL 7600 SYNTHETIC

REMINGTON MODEL R-15 450 BUSHMASTER WITH SCOPE

REMINGTON MODEL SEVEN CDL

REMINGTON MODEL SEVEN SYNTHETIC

MODEL 7600

Action: Pump
Stock: Wood
Barrel: 22 in.
Sights: Open
Weight: 7 lb. 8 oz.
Caliber: .243 Win., .270 Win., .30-06 Spfd., .308 Win.
Magazine: Detachable box, 4 rounds
Features: Free-floated barrel; Monte Carlo walnut stock with satin finish as standard; metal work has black non-reflective finish; iron sights and drilled and tapped receiver for scope mounts; rotary-bolt lock-up
MSRP. $918

MODEL 7600 SYNTHETIC

Action: Pump
Stock: Synthetic
Barrel: 22 in.
Sights: Open
Weight: 7 lb. 8 oz.
Caliber: .243 Win., .270 Win., .30-06 Spfd., .308 Win.
Magazine: Detachable box, 4 rounds
Features: Fiberglass-reinforced synthetic stock and forend; free-floated barrel; metal work has black non-reflective finish; iron sights and drilled and tapped receiver for scope mounts; rotary-bolt lock-up
MSRP. $771

MODEL R-15 450 BUSHMASTER

Action: Gas-operated semiautomatic
Stock: Synthetic
Barrel: 18 in., 22 in.
Sights: None
Weight: 7 lb. 8 oz.–7 lb. 12 oz.
Caliber: .450 Bushmaster, .30 Rem. AR
Magazine: Detachable box, 4 rounds
Features: Free-floated, fluted barrel; clean-breaking single-state trigger; receiver-length Picatinny rail; aluminum receiver; synthetic full Mossy Oak camo stock with ergonomic pistol grip; lockable hard case included
MSRP. $1631

MODEL SEVEN CDL

Action: Bolt
Stock: Walnut
Barrel: 20 in.
Sights: Open
Weight: 6 lb. 8 oz.
Caliber: .243 Win., .260 Rem., 7mm-08 Rem., .308 Win.
Magazine: Internal box
Features: SuperCell recoil pad; American walnut CDL stock with satin-finished barrel; compact design for fast handling; cylindrical receiver; available in Rem. short-action magnum and Winchester short magnum
MSRP. $1039

MODEL SEVEN SYNTHETIC

Action: Bolt
Stock: Synthetic
Barrel: 18 in., 20 in.
Sights: None
Weight: 6 lb. 2 oz.–6 lb. 8 oz.
Caliber: .223 Rem., .243 Win., .260 Rem., 7mm-08 Rem., .308 Win.
Magazine: Internal
Features: Synthetic black stock; compact design for fast handling; cylindrical receiver design
MSRP. $731

RIFLES INC. CANYON

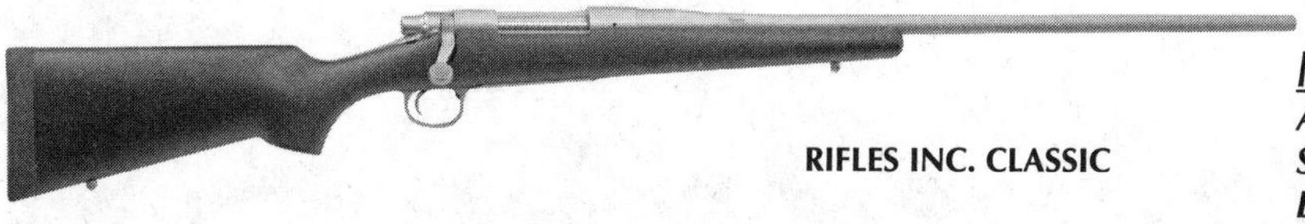

RIFLES INC. CLASSIC

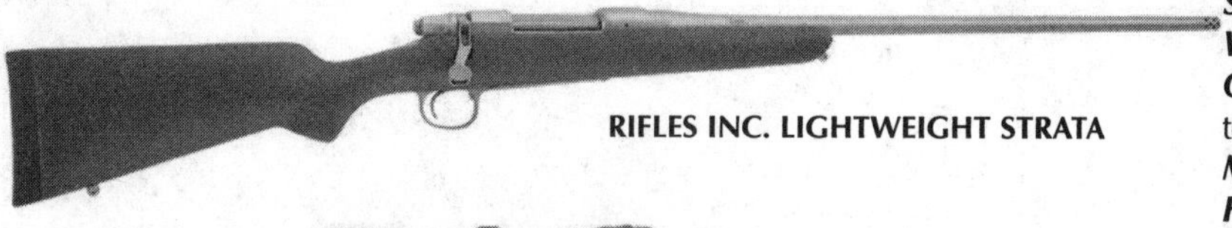

RIFLES INC. LIGHTWEIGHT STRATA

RIFLES INC. MASTER'S SERIES

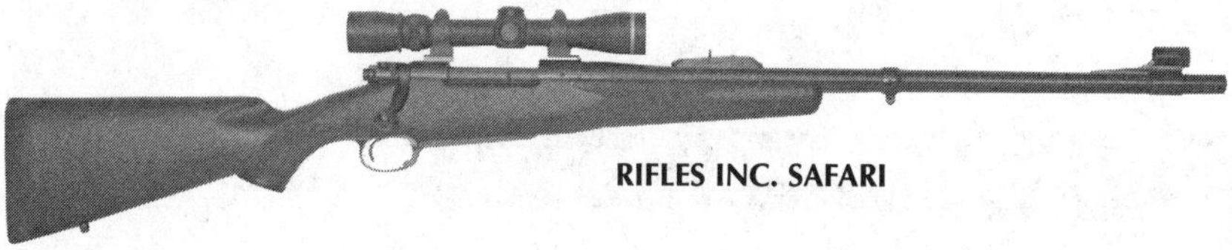

RIFLES INC. SAFARI

CANYON

Action: Bolt
Stock: McMillan HTG
Barrel: 24 in.
Sights: None
Weight: 10 lb.
Caliber: Most popular calibers
Magazine: Internal
Features: Blind or hinged floor plate; customer-supplied Rem. 700 action; match grade stainless steel Lilja number 6 barrel; optional muzzlebrake; matte stainless metal finish, optional black Teflon; adjustable cheekpiece; custom buttpad
MSRP $3500

CLASSIC

Action: Bolt
Stock: Laminated fiberglass
Barrel: 24 in.–26 in.
Sights: None
Weight: 6 lb. 8 oz.
Caliber: All popular chamberings up to .375 H&H
Magazine: Internal
Features: Customer-supplied Rem. 700 action; match grade stainless steel Lilja barrel; blind or hinged floor plate; matte stainless metal finish, optional Black Teflon finish; black laminated fiberglass, pillar glass bedded stock
MSRP $2900

LIGHTWEIGHT STRATA

Action: Bolt
Stock: Laminate
Barrel: 22 in.–26 in.
Sights: None
Weight: 4 lb. 8 oz.–5 lb. 12 oz.
Caliber: All popular chamberings up to .375 H&H
Magazine: Internal
Features: Customer-supplied Rem. 700 action; match grade stainless steel Lilja barrel; fluted bolt and hollowed-handle; blind or hinged floor plate; matte stainless metal finish, optional black Teflon finish; hand-laminated blend of Kevlar/graphite and boron, pillar glass bedded stock; Titanium Strata has hand-laminated graphite stock with pillar glass bedded; custom buttpad; Quiet Slimbrake II muzzlebrake
Lightweight Strata: $3200
Lightweight 70: $3100
Titanium Strata: $3500

MASTER'S SERIES

Action: Bolt
Stock: Laminated fiberglass
Barrel: 24 in.–27 in.
Sights: None
Weight: 7 lb. 12 oz.
Caliber: All popular chamberings up to .375 H&H
Magazine: Internal
Features: Customer-supplied Rem. 700 action; match grade stainless steel Lilja number 5 barrel; hinged floor plate; matte stainless metal finish, optional black Teflon finish; black laminated fiberglass, pillar glass bedded stock; optional muzzlebrake
MSRP $3200

SAFARI

Action: Bolt
Stock: Laminated fiberglass
Barrel: 23 in.–25 in.
Sights: Optional Express Sights
Weight: 8 lb. 8 oz.
Caliber: .375 H&H, .416 Rem. Mag., and other large game cartridges
Magazine: 4 rounds
Features: Customer-supplied Winchester Model 70 Classic action; lapped and face trued bolt; match grade stainless steel Lilja barrel; Quiet Slimbrake II muzzlebrake; hinged floor plate or optional drop box; matte stainless finish, optional black Teflon; double laminated fiberglass, pillar glass bedded stock; Pachmayr decelerator; optional barrel band
MSRP $3500

Rock River Arms

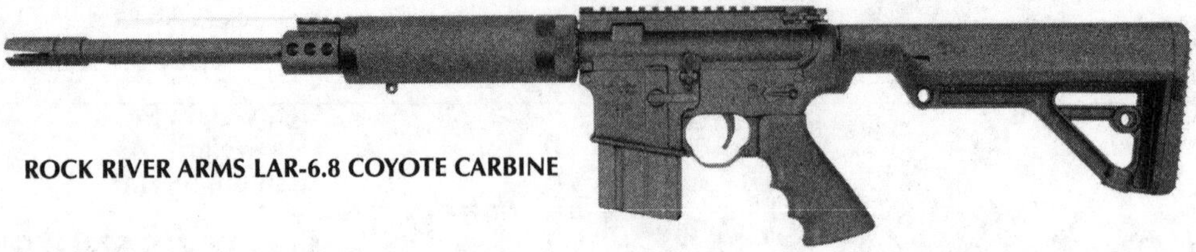

ROCK RIVER ARMS LAR-6.8 COYOTE CARBINE

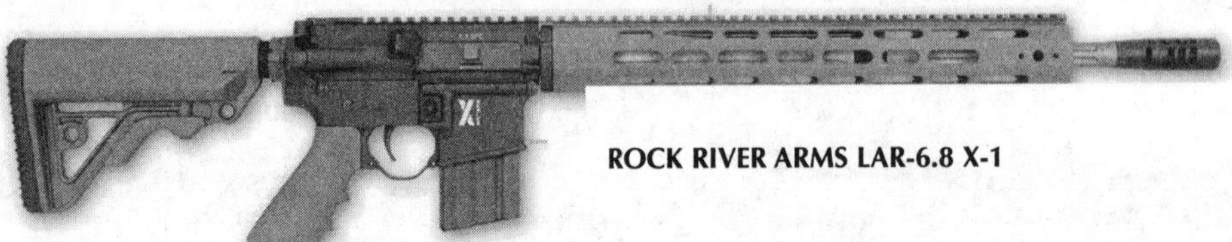

ROCK RIVER ARMS LAR-6.8 X-1

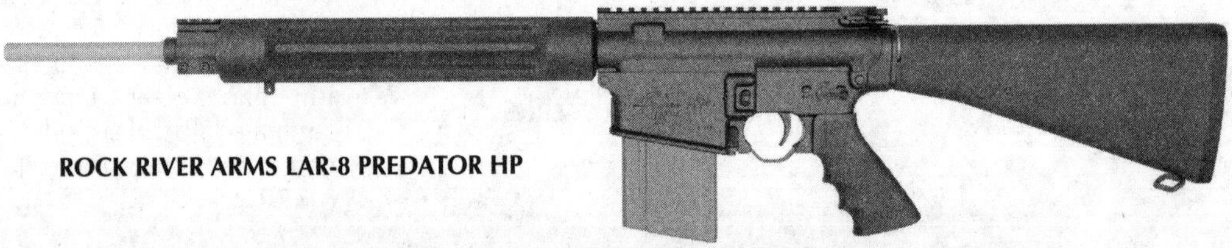

ROCK RIVER ARMS LAR-8 PREDATOR HP

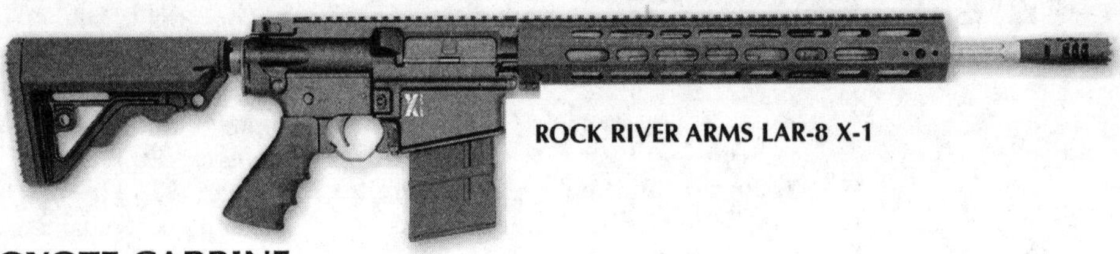

ROCK RIVER ARMS LAR-8 X-1

LAR-6.8 COYOTE CARBINE

Action: Semiautomatic
Stock: Synthetic
Barrel: 16 in.
Sights: None
Weight: 7 lb.
Caliber: 6.8 SPC II
Magazine: 1 round
Features: Smith Vortex flash hider; chromoly barrel; RRA two-stage match trigger
MSRP $1310

LAR-6.8 X-1

Action: Semiautomatic
Stock: Synthetic
Barrel: 18 in.
Sights: None
Weight: 7 lb. 13 oz.
Caliber: 6.8 SPC II
Magazine: Detachable box, 25 rounds
Features: RRA Beast of Hunter muzzle brake; available in black or tan; available with A2 or CAR stocks
MSRP . . . . $1550–$1600

LAR-8 PREDATOR HP

Action: Semiautomatic
Stock: Synthetic
Barrel: 20 in.
Sights: None
Weight: 8 lb. 10 oz.
Caliber: .308 Win., 7mm-08 Rem., .243 Win.
Magazine: Detachable box
Features: Forged A4 receiver with forward assist and port door; stainless steel barrel; gas block sight Base; two-stage trigger; Hogue rubber grip; RRA aluminum free-float tube; A2 buttstock or operator stock
MSRP . . . . $1690–$1740

LAR-8 X-1

Action: Semiautomatic
Stock: Synthetic
Barrel: 18 in.
Sights: None
Weight: 9 lb. 8 oz.
Caliber: .308 Win., 7.62 NATO
Magazine: Detachable box, 20 rounds
Features: RRA Beast of Hunter muzzle brake; available in black or tan; available with A2 or CAR stocks
MSRP . . . . $1800–$1850

RIFLES

ROCK RIVER ARMS LAR-15 DELTA CAR/DELTA MID-LENGTH

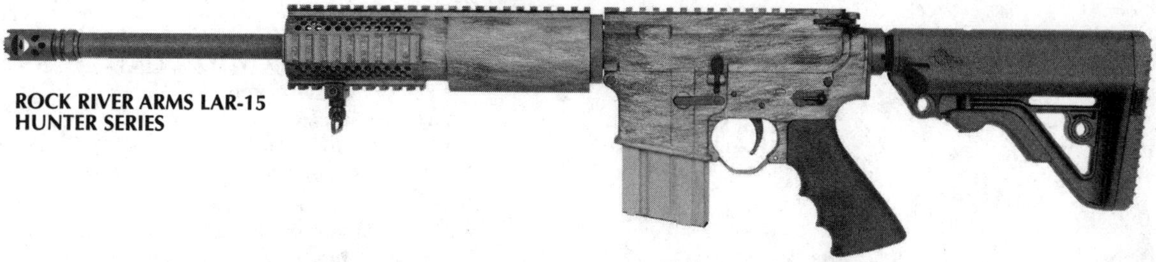

ROCK RIVER ARMS LAR-15 HUNTER SERIES

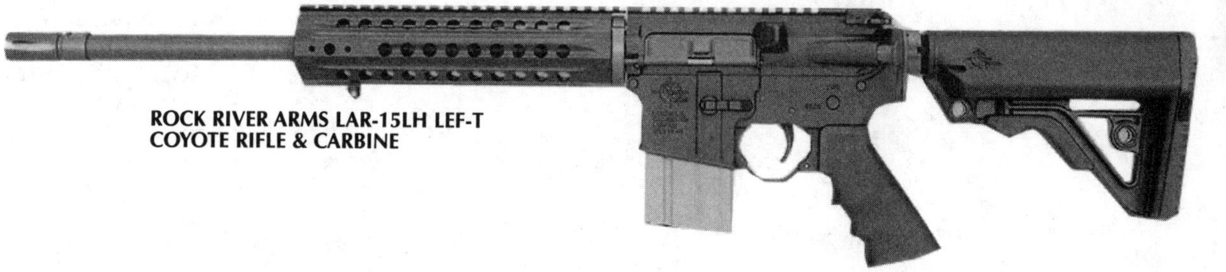

ROCK RIVER ARMS LAR-15LH LEF-T COYOTE RIFLE & CARBINE

LAR-15 DELTA CAR/DELTA MID-LENGTH

Action: Semiautomatic
Stock: Synthetic
Barrel: 16 in.
Sights: None
Weight: 7 lb.–7 lb. 4.8 oz.
Caliber: 5.56 NATO, .223 Rem.
Magazine: Detachable box, 30 rounds
Features: Delta Quad Rail two piece drop-in and gas system, available in CAR or Mid-length; low profile gas block; Ergo SureGrip; two stage trigger
MSRP . . . . $1085–$1100

LAR-15 HUNTER SERIES

Action: Semiautomatic
Stock: Synthetic
Barrel: 16 in.
Sights: None
Weight: 7 lb. 10 oz.
Caliber: 5.56 NATO, .223 Rem.
Magazine: Detachable box, 20 rounds
Features: Finish in choice of WYL-Ehide or PRK-Ehide, digitalized imagery of real coyote or wild hog; finish is in the hardcoat anodizing, not a film dip or applique; camo anodized to the lower receiver, upper receiver, charging handle, trigger guard, and RRA half quad rail handguard; Hogue rubber pistol grip; low profile gas block; RRA operator CAR stock
MSRP $1550

LAR-15LH LEF-T COYOTE RIFLE & CARBINE

Action: Semiautomatic
Stock: Synthetic A2
Barrel: 16 in., 20 in.
Sights: None
Weight: 7 lb.-8 lb. 6.4 oz.
Caliber: 5.56 NATO, .223 Rem.
Magazine: Detachable box, 20 rounds
Features: Smith Vortex Flash Hider; Hogue free float tube; Hogue grip; two stage trigger
Carbine: $1445
Rifle: $1490

Rock River Arms

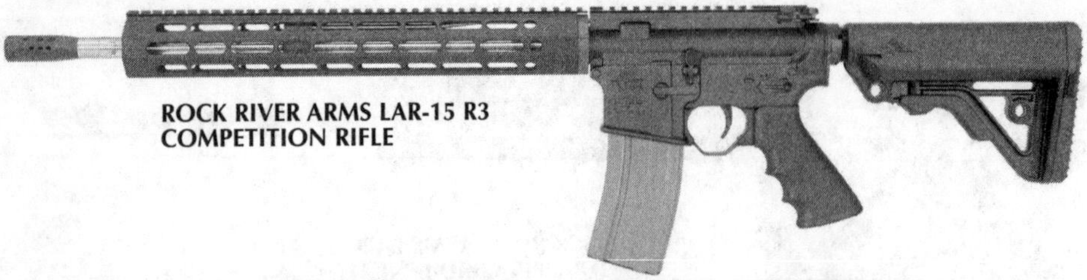

ROCK RIVER ARMS LAR-15 R3 COMPETITION RIFLE

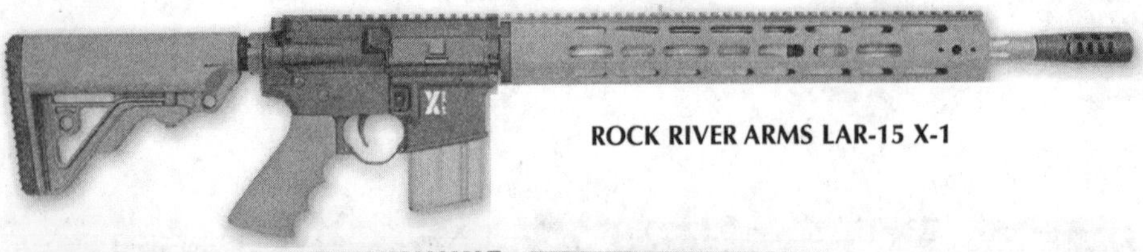

ROCK RIVER ARMS LAR-15 X-1

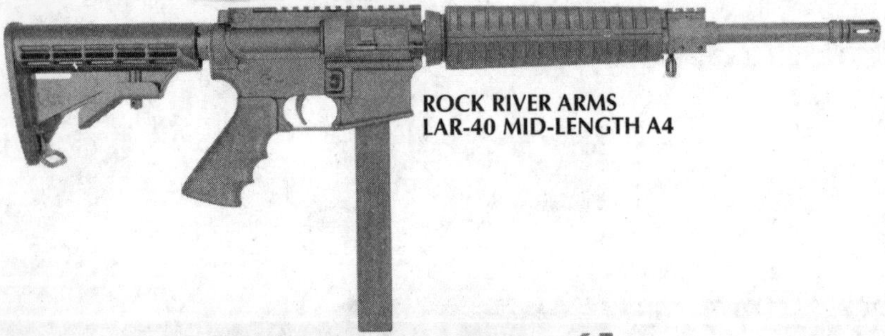

ROCK RIVER ARMS LAR-40 MID-LENGTH A4

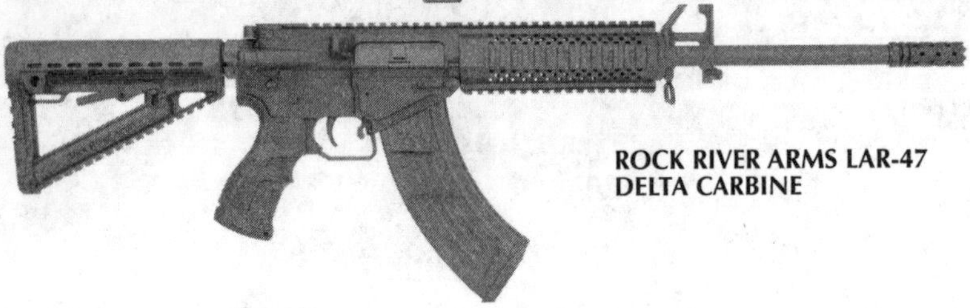

ROCK RIVER ARMS LAR-47 DELTA CARBINE

ROCK RIVER ARMS LAR-47 CAR A4

LAR-15 R3 COMPETITION RIFLE

Action: Semiautomatic
Stock: Synthetic A2 or CAR
Barrel: 18 in.
Sights: None
Weight: 7 lb. 9.6 oz.
Caliber: 5.56 NATO, .223 Rem.
Magazine: Detachable box, 30 rounds
Features: RRA tuned and ported muzzle brake; low profile gas block; two stage trigger; Hogue Rubber grip
MSRP $1355

LAR-15 X-1

Action: Semiautomatic
Stock: Synthetic
Barrel: 18 in.
Sights: None
Weight: 7 lb. 13 oz.
Caliber: 5.56 NATO, .223 Rem.
Magazine: Detachable box, 30 rounds
Features: RRA Beast of Hunter muzzle brake; available in black or tan; available with A2 or CAR stocks
MSRP . . . . $1450–$1500

LAR-40 MID-LENGTH A4

Action: Semiautomatic
Stock: Synthetic
Barrel: 16 in.
Sights: None
Weight: 7 lb. 2 oz.
Caliber: .40 S&W
Magazine: Detachable clip
Features: Flash hider; single-stage trigger; RRA tactical CAR stock with Hogue grip
A4: $1260

LAR-47 CAR A4

Action: Semiautomatic
Stock: Synthetic
Barrel: 16 in.
Sights: None
Weight: 6 lb. 6 oz.
Caliber: 7.62x39 Warsaw
Magazine: Detachable box, 30 rounds, standard AK-47 mag
Features: RRA 6-postion tactical CAR stock; A2 pistol grip; CAR handguards; RRA two-stage trigger; A2 flash hider; ambidextrous mag release
MSRP $1270

LAR-47 DELTA CARBINE

Action: Semiautomatic
Stock: Synthetic
Barrel: 16 in.
Sights: None
Weight: 7 lb. 12 oz.
Caliber: 7.62x39 Warsaw
Magazine: Detachable box, 30 rounds, standard AK-47 mag
Features: RRA 6-position delta CAR stock; RRA delta pistol grip; RRA 2-piece quad rail; RRA delta muzzlebrake; RRA two-stage trigger; ambidextrous mag release
MSRP $1545

Rock River Arms

ROCK RIVER ARMS LAR-458 CAR A4

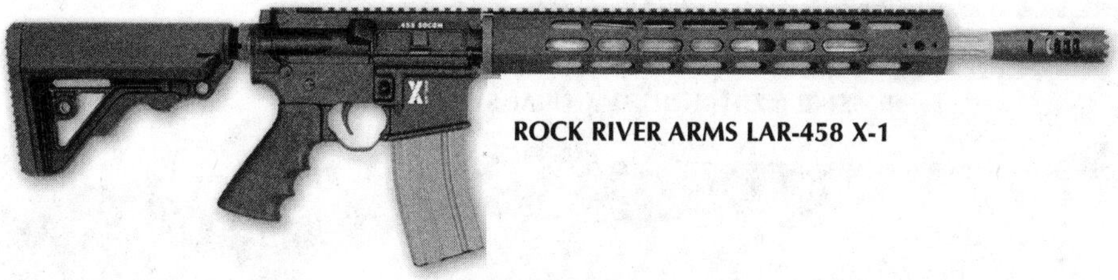

ROCK RIVER ARMS LAR-458 X-1

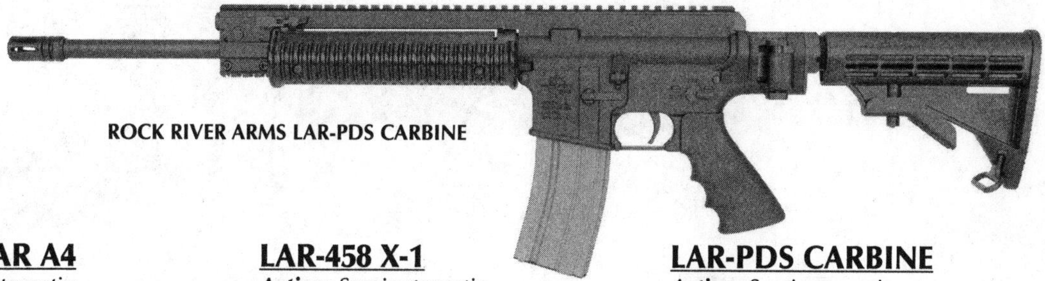

ROCK RIVER ARMS LAR-PDS CARBINE

LAR-458 CAR A4

Action: Semiautomatic
Stock: Synthetic
Barrel: 16 in.
Sights: None
Weight: 7 lb. 10 oz.
Caliber: .458 SOCOM
Magazine: Detachable box
Features: Forged A4 receiver; A2 flash hider; chromoly bull barrel; varmint gas block with sight rail; RRA two-stage trigger; RRA aluminum free-float tube; A2 pistol grip; A2 buttstock
MSRP $1220

LAR-458 X-1

Action: Semiautomatic
Stock: Synthetic
Barrel: 18 in.
Sights: None
Weight: 8 lb. 12 oz.
Caliber: .458 SOCOM
Magazine: Detachable box, 30 rounds
Features: RRA Beast of Hunter muzzle brake; available in black or tan; available with A2 or CAR stocks
MSRP . . . . $1550–$1600

LAR-PDS CARBINE

Action: Semiautomatic
Stock: Synthetic
Barrel: 16 in.
Sights: None
Weight: 7 lb. 6 oz.
Caliber: .223 Rem.
Magazine: Detachable box
Features: Ambidextrous non-reciprocating charging handle; A2 flash hider; RRA two-stage trigger; Hogue rubber grip; tri-rail handguard available
MSRP . . . . $1595–$1750

Rossi

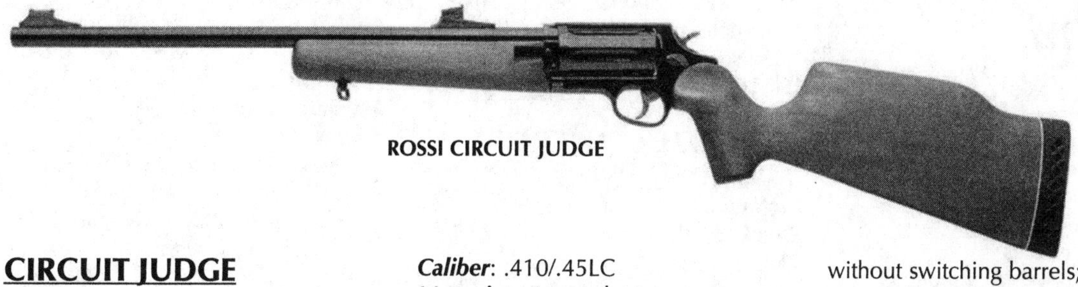

ROSSI CIRCUIT JUDGE

CIRCUIT JUDGE

Action: DA Revolver
Stock: Hardwood
Barrel: 18.5 in.
Sights: Fiber optic front sight
Weight: 5 lb. 5 oz.
Caliber: .410/.45LC
Magazine: 5 rounds
Features: Shotgun/rifle crossover allows you to fire .410 3-in. magnum shotshells, .410 2.5-in. shotshells, and .45 Colt ammunition in any order without switching barrels; available in smooth-bore shotgun or rifled barrel shotgun; yoke detent; transfer bar; Taurus Security System
MSRP $669

Rossi

ROSSI CIRCUIT JUDGE .44 MAG.

ROSSI CIRCUIT JUDGE CONVERTIBLE

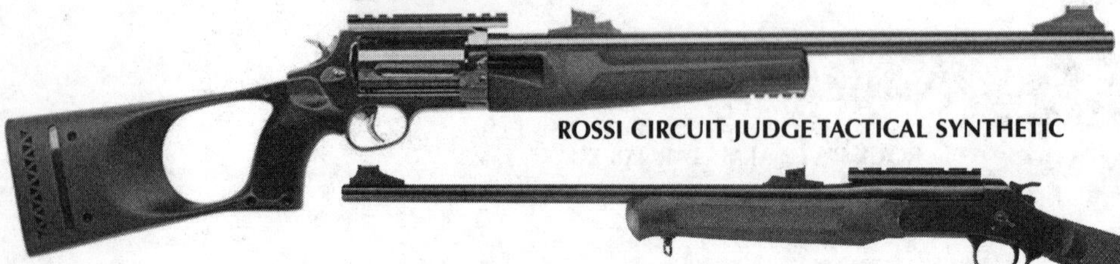

ROSSI CIRCUIT JUDGE TACTICAL SYNTHETIC

ROSSI FULL SIZE CENTERFIRE MATCHED PAIR

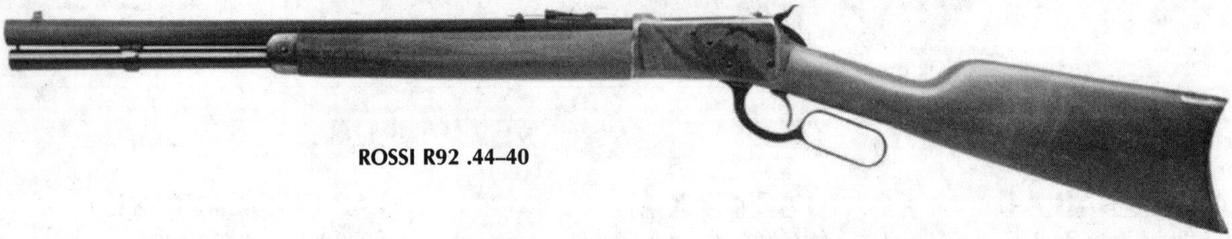

ROSSI R92 .44–40

CIRCUIT JUDGE .44 MAG.

Action: SA/DA
Stock: Hardwood
Barrel: 18.5 in.
Sights: Red fiber optic front
Weight: 5 lb. 3 oz.
Caliber: .44 Mag.
Magazine: 6 rounds
Features: Yoke detent; transfer bar; Taurus Security System
MSRP $669

CIRCUIT JUDGE CONVERTIBLE

Action: SA/DA
Stock: Synthetic
Barrel: 18.5 in.
Sights: Red fiber optic front
Weight: N/A
Caliber: .22LR, .22 Mag.
Magazine: 6 rounds
Features: Removable cylinder to change easily from .22LR to .22 Mag.; blued finish
MSRP $716

CIRCUIT JUDGE TACTICAL SYNTHETIC

Action: Revolver
Stock: Synthetic
Barrel: 18.5 in.
Sights: Red fiber optic front sight
Weight: 4 lb. 11 oz.
Caliber: .45 LC, .410
Magazine: 5 rounds
Features: Can fire .410 Ga 3-in. magnum shotshells, .410 2.5-in. shotshells, and .45 Colt ammunition in any order, without switching barrels; includes modern features like yoke detent, transfer bar, and the Taurus Security System.
MSRP $668.61

FULL SIZE CENTERFIRE MATCHED PAIR

Action: Break Open, single-shot
Stock: Synthetic
Barrel: 23 in., 28 in.
Sights: Adjustable sights
Weight: 5 lb. 4 oz.–6 lb. 4 oz.
Caliber: 20 Ga./.243 Win., 12 Ga./.243 Win., 20 Ga./.223 Rem., 12 Ga./.223 Rem.
Magazine: None
Features: Quick-interchangeable rifle and shotgun barrels; single shot; recoil pad; sling swivels; black synthetic stock; steel barrel with matte blued finish; button rifled barrel
MSRP $344.98

R92 .44-40

Action: Lever
Stock: Wood
Barrel: 20 in., 24 in.
Sights: None
Weight: 7 lb.
Caliber: Most popular calibers: .38/.357 Mag., .44 Mag., .45 Colt, .44-40 Win.
Magazine: Under-barrel tube, 12+1 rounds
Features: Octagonal barrel with a variety of metal finishes: blued, blued/case-hardened, blued/brass, and stainless; curved buttplate
MSRP . . . .$624–$689

R92 CARBINE .45 COLT STAINLESS

Action: Lever
Stock: Wood
Barrel: 20 in.
Sights: Open
Weight: 5 lb.
Caliber: .45 Colt
Magazine: Under-barrel tube,, 10+1 rounds
Features: Stainless steel or blued round barrel; crescent buttplates and extended front sight; for brush hunting and wilderness packing; recoil absorbing buttpad
MSRP $650

RIO GRANDE

Action: Lever
Stock: Hardwood
Barrel: 20 in.
Sights: Open
Weight: 5 lb. 13 oz.–7 lb.
Caliber: .30-30 Win., .45-70 Govt., .410
Magazine: Under-barrel tube, 6+1 rounds
Features: Blued or stainless steel barrel; authentic buckhorn sights; Taurus Safety System
MSRP $673

SINGLE SHOT RIFLE

Action: Break-open, single-shot
Stock: Synthetic
Barrel: 23 in.
Sights: Adjustable fiber optic front
Weight: 6 lb. 4 oz.–7 lb.
Caliber: .243 Win., .44 Mag.
Magazine: None
Features: Steel barrel in matte blued finish; equipped with scope rail and hammer extension that accommodates all popular optics; black synthetic stock with removable cheekpiece; soft recoil pad; white line spacer; button rifled barrels; sling swivels
MSRP $312.93

YOUTH SIZE CENTERFIRE MATCHED PAIR

Action: Break-open, single-shot
Stock: Synthetic
Barrel: 22 in.
Sights: Adjustable fiber optic front (rifle barrels), brass bead front (shotgun)
Weight: 5 lb., 6 lb. 4 oz.
Caliber: 20 Ga./.44 Mag., 20 Ga./.243 Win., 20 Ga./.223 Rem.
Magazine: None
Features: Quick-interchangeable rifle and shotgun barrels in youth size; matte blued finish
MSRP $352

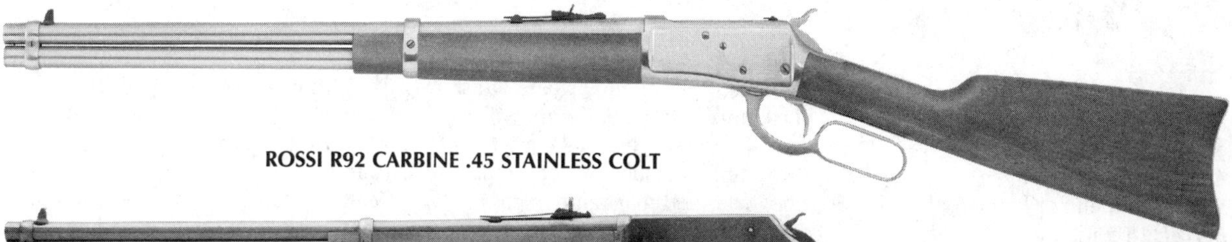

ROSSI R92 CARBINE .45 STAINLESS COLT

ROSSI RIO GRANDE

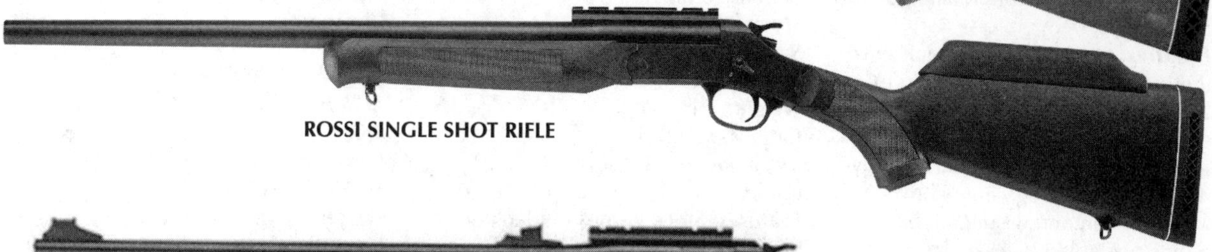

ROSSI SINGLE SHOT RIFLE

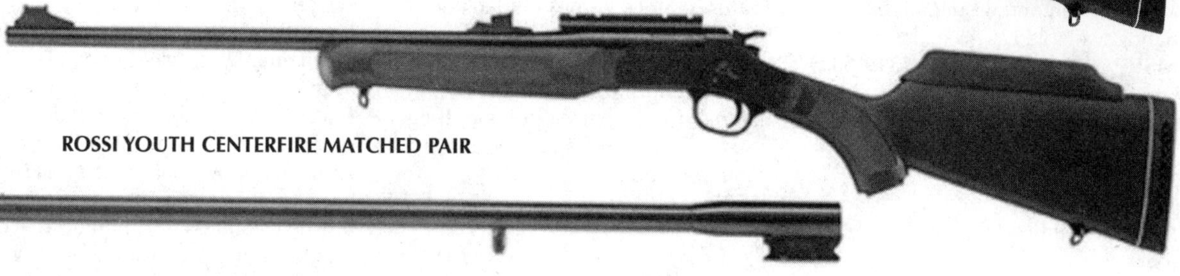

ROSSI YOUTH CENTERFIRE MATCHED PAIR

Ruger

RUGER 10/22 CARBINE

RUGER 10/22 TAKEDOWN

RUGER 10/22 TARGET

RUGER 77/17

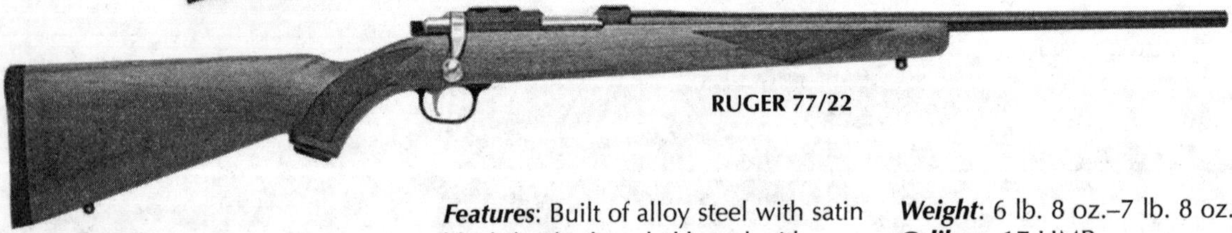

RUGER 77/22

10/22 CARBINE

Action: Semiautomatic
Stock: Synthetic or hardwood
Barrel: 18.5 in.
Sights: Gold bead front sight, adjustable rear
Weight: 5 lb.
Caliber: .22LR
Magazine: Detachable rotary, 10 rounds
Features: Stock comes in black synthetic and hardwood; extended magazine release; push-button manual safety; combination scope base adapter; hammer-forged barrel; polymer trigger housing; aluminum receiver; contoured buttpad; barrel band; available LaserMax laser
MSRP . . . . $319–$339

10/22 TAKEDOWN

Action: Semiautomatic
Stock: Black synthetic
Barrel: 16.6 in.
Sights: Gold bead front, adjustable rear
Weight: 4 lb. 10.7 oz.
Caliber: .22LR
Magazine: Detachable rotary, 10 rounds
Features: Built of alloy steel with satin black finish; threaded barrel with flash suppressor; easy takedown and reassembly; detachable rotary magazine; extended magazine release; combination scope base adapter; push-button manual safety
MSRP $477

10/22 TARGET

Action: Semiautomatic
Stock: Laminate
Barrel: 20 in.
Sights: None
Weight: 7 lb. 8 oz.
Caliber: .22LR
Magazine: Detachable rotary, 10 rounds
Features: Stock comes in black or brown laminate; extended magazine release; push-button manual safety; combination scope base adapter; hammer-forged barrel; polymer trigger housing; aluminum receiver; target trigger; flat buttplate
MSRP . . . . $550–$589

77/17

Action: Bolt
Stock: Walnut or laminate
Barrel: 22 in., 24 in.
Sights: None
Weight: 6 lb. 8 oz.–7 lb. 8 oz.
Caliber: .17 HMR
Magazine: Detachable rotary, 9 rounds
Features: Stock options include American walnut with blued finish or black laminate with target gray finish; alloy steel or stainless steel barrel; integral scope mounts; three-position safety; sling swivel stud mounts
Walnut: $939
Laminate: $999

77/22

Action: Bolt
Stock: Laminate, walnut, synthetic
Barrel: 20 in., 24 in.
Sights: None
Weight: 6 lb.–7 lb. 8 oz.
Caliber: .22LR, .22 Mag., .22 Hornet
Magazine: Detachable rotary, 6, 9, 10 rounds
Features: Stock options include black synthetic, American walnut, or brown laminate; alloy steel or stainless steel barrel in target gray, blued, or brushed stainless finish; integral scope mounts; three-position safety; sling swivel studs
Walnut, Synthetic: $939

Ruger

RUGER 77/44

RUGER AMERICAN RIFLE

RUGER GUIDE GUN

RUGER GUNSITE SCOUT RIFLE

RUGER M77 HAWKEYE

77/44

Action: Bolt
Stock: Vista Camo, synthetic
Barrel: 18.5 in.
Sights: Front bead sight, adjustable rear
Weight: 5 lb. 4 oz.
Caliber: .44 Mag.
Magazine: Detachable rotary, 4 rounds
Features: Stock options include Next G1 Vista Camo or black synthetic; stainless steel barrel with brushed steel finish; integral scope mounts; three-position safety; sling swivel studs
Vista Camo: $1060
Synthetic: $999

AMERICAN RIFLE

Action: Bolt
Stock: Synthetic
Barrel: 22 in.
Sights: Drilled and tapped for scopes
Weight: 6 lb. 2 oz.–6 lb. 4 oz.
Caliber: .22-250 Rem., 7mm-08 Rem., .243 Win., .270 Win., .30-06 Spfd., .308 Win.
Magazine: Detachable rotary, 4 rounds
Features: Ruger Marksman adjustable trigger; ergonomic, lightweight stock; soft rubber recoil pad; three-lug 70 degree bolt; Power Bedding positively locates the receiver and free-floats the barrel; hammer-forged barrel; tang safety; round rotary magazine
MSRP $369

GUIDE GUN WITH MUZZLE BRAKE SYSTEM

Action: Bolt
Stock: Green Mountain laminate
Barrel: 20 in.
Sights: Bead front, adjustable rear
Weight: 8 lb.-8 lb. 2 oz.
Caliber: .300 RCM, .300 Win. Mag., .30-06 Spfd., .338 RCM, .338 Win. Mag., .375 Ruger
Magazine: 3 rounds (4 rounds in .30-06 Spfd.)
Features: LC6 Trigger; Mauser-type extractor; muzzle brake system; three-position safety; manner-forged barrel; integral scope mounts; stainless steel bolt; swivel studs;
MSRP $1199

GUNSITE SCOUT RIFLE

Action: Bolt
Stock: Laminate
Barrel: 16.50 in.
Sights: Post front sight, adjustable rear
Weight: 7 lb.
Caliber: .308 Win.
Magazine: Detachable box, 10 rounds
Features: Flash suppressor, Picatinny rail; recoil pad; accurate sighting system; integral scope mounts; Mauser-type extractor; developed with Gunsite and features their logo
MSRP . . . . $1075–$1139

M77 HAWKEYE

Action: Bolt
Stock: Walnut
Barrel: 22 in., 24 in.
Sights: None
Weight: 7 lb.–8 lb. 4 oz.
Caliber: .204 Ruger, .22-250 Rem., .223 Rem., .243 Win., 6.5 Creedmoor, .257 Roberts, .270 Win., 7mm Rem. Mag., 7mm-08 Rem., .300 RCM,
.30-06 Spfd., .300 Win. Mag., .308 Win., .338 RCM, .338 Win. Mag.
Magazine: 5 rounds
Features: American walnut stock; alloy steel, satin blued barrel; LCG Trigger; positive floor plate latch; integral scope mounts; three-position safety
MSRP $939

Ruger

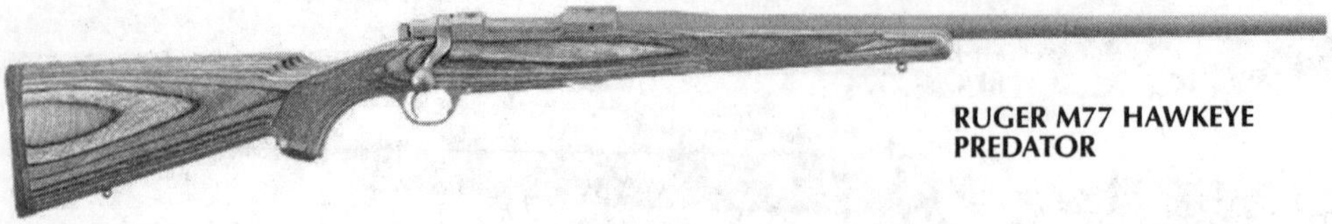

RUGER M77 HAWKEYE PREDATOR

RUGER MINI-14 RANCH RIFLE

RUGER MINI-14 TACTICAL

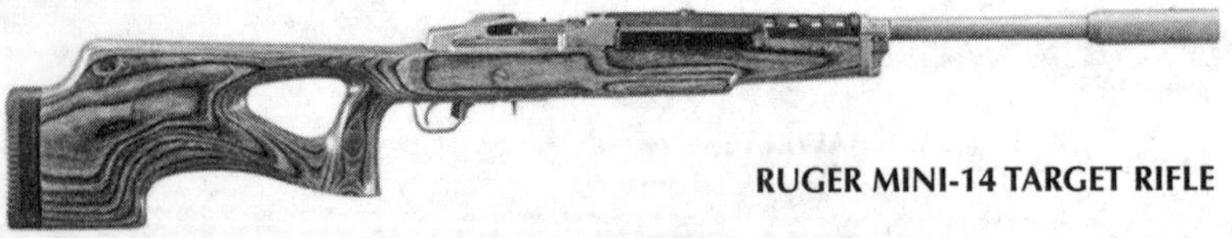

RUGER MINI-14 TARGET RIFLE

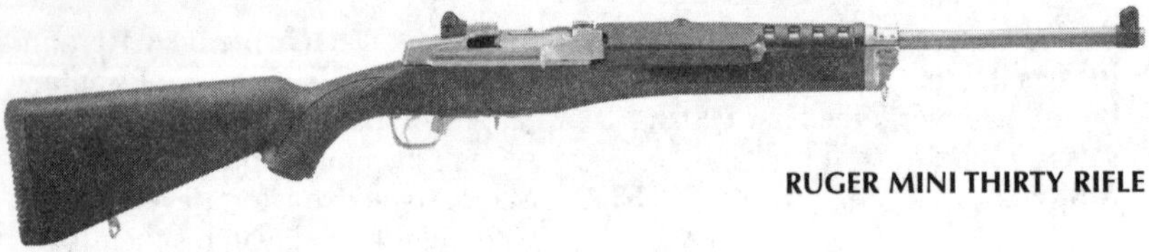

RUGER MINI THIRTY RIFLE

M77 HAWKEYE PREDATOR

Action: Bolt
Stock: Green Mountain Laminate
Barrel: 22 in., 24 in.
Sights: None
Weight: 7 lb. 12 oz.–8 lb.
Caliber: .204 Ruger, .22-250 Rem., .223 Rem., 6.5 Creedmoor, .308 Win.
Magazine: 4, 5 rounds
Features: Hawkeye matte stainless steel finish on barrel; two-stage adjustable target trigger; non-rotating, Mauser-type controlled round feed extractor; hinged solid-steel floor plate; three-position safety; integral scope mounts; sling swivel studs
MSRP $1069

MINI-14 RANCH RIFLE

Action: Semiautomatic
Stock: Hardwood, synthetic
Barrel: 18.5 in.
Sights: Blade front sight, adjustable rear
Weight: 6 lb. 12 oz.–7 lb.
Caliber: 5.56 NATO, .223 Rem., 6.8 SPC
Magazine: 5 rounds, or detachable box, 20 rounds
Features: Stock comes in hardwood or black synthetic; Garand style action; hammer-forged barrel; sighting system; integral scope mounts; flat buttpad; integral sling swivels on hardwood or black synthetic stocks
MSRP . . . . $939–$1099

MINI-14 TACTICAL

Action: Semiautomatic
Stock: Synthetic
Barrel: 16.1 in.
Sights: Adjustable
Weight: 6 lb. 12 oz.–7 lb. 4 oz.
Caliber: 5.56 NATO, .223 Rem.
Magazine: Detachable box, 5, 20 rounds
Features: Black synthetic stock; blued barrel with a flash suppressor; adjustable ghost ring rear sight, non-glare protected-post front sight
MSRP $1019

MINI-14 TARGET RIFLE

Action: Semiautomatic
Stock: Laminate or Hogue overmolded
Barrel: 22 in.
Sights: None
Weight: 8 lb. 8 oz.–9 lb. 8 oz.
Caliber: .223 Rem.
Magazine: 5 rounds
Features: Black laminate with thumb hole stock or Black Hogue overmolded stock; matte stainless finish on stainless steel barrel; Garand style action; hammer-forged barrel; integral scope mounts; harmonic dampener; sling swivel studs
MSRP $1199

MINI THIRTY RIFLE

Action: Semiautomatic
Stock: Synthetic
Barrel: 16.12 in., 18.5 in.
Sights: Blade front sight, adjustable rear
Weight: 6 lb. 12 oz.
Caliber: 7.62x39 Warsaw
Magazine: 5 rounds, or detachable box, 20 rounds
Features: Garand style action, hammer-forged barrel; sighting system; integral scope mounts; black synthetic stock; sling swivels; stainless steel or alloy steel barrel in matte or blued finish
MSRP $999

Ruger

RUGER NO. 1 LIGHT SPORTER

RUGER NO. 1 VARMINTER

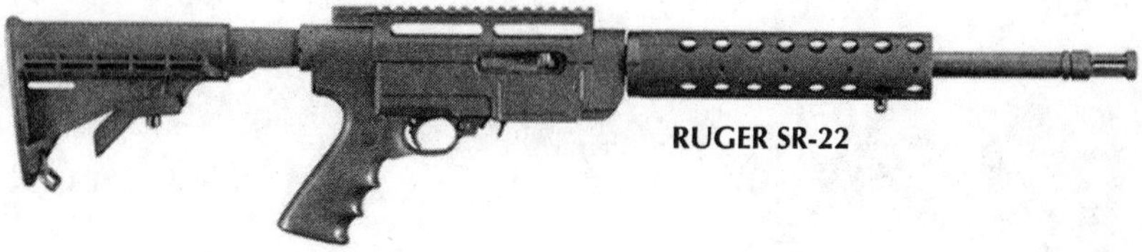

RUGER SR-22

RUGER SR-556

NO. 1 LIGHT SPORTER

Action: Falling block, single-shot
Stock: Walnut
Barrel: 22 in.
Sights: Front bead sight, adjustable rear
Weight: 7 lb. 4 oz.
Caliber: .222 Rem.
Magazine: None
Features: Falling block breech mechanism, sliding tang safety; sculptured receiver; Ruger scope mounting system; Alexander Henry-style forend; sporting style buttpad; grip cap and sling swivel studs; American walnut stock
MSRP $1449

NO. 1 VARMINTER

Action: Falling block, single-shot
Stock: Walnut
Barrel: 26 in.
Sights: None
Weight: 8 lb. 8 oz.
Caliber: 6.5 Creedmoor, .22-250 Rem., .223 Rem., .25-06 Rem.
Magazine: None
Features: Falling block breech mechanism, sliding tang safety; sculptured receiver; Ruger scope mounting system; Alexander Henry-style forend; sporting style buttpad; grip cap and sling swivel studs; American walnut stock
MSRP $1449

SR-22

Action: Semiautomatic
Stock: Synthetic
Barrel: 16.12 in.
Sights: None
Weight: 6 lb. 8 oz.–6 lb. 14 oz.
Caliber: .22LR
Magazine: Detachable rotary, 10 rounds
Features: Black laminate stock in standard or collapsible; AR-style ergonomic Hogue Monogrip and six-position telescoping buttstock; hammer-forged barrel; round handguard; barrel support block
MSRP $669

SR-556

Action: Semiautomatic
Stock: Synthetic
Barrel: 16.12 in.
Sights: Folding BattleSights
Weight: 7 lb. 15 oz.
Caliber: 5.56 NATO, .223 Rem., 6.8 SPC
Magazine: Detachable box, 10 or 30 rounds
Features: Stock options include black synthetic standard or collapsible; two-stage piston with adjustable regulator; chrome-lined gas block; quad rail handguard; Troy Industries Sights; telescoping buttstock; hammer-forged barrel; pistol grip stock; rail covers and soft case
MSRP $2049

SR-556VT

Action: Semiautomatic
Stock: Black synthetic
Barrel: 20 in.
Sights: None
Weight: 8 lb. 8 oz.
Caliber: 5.56 NATO
Magazine: Detachable box, 5 rounds
Features: Two-stage piston with adjustable regulator; handguard; target-style trigger; hammer-forged barrel; pistol grip; charging handle; chrome-plated bolt
MSRP $1995

RUGER SR-556VT

SAKO 85 BAVARIAN

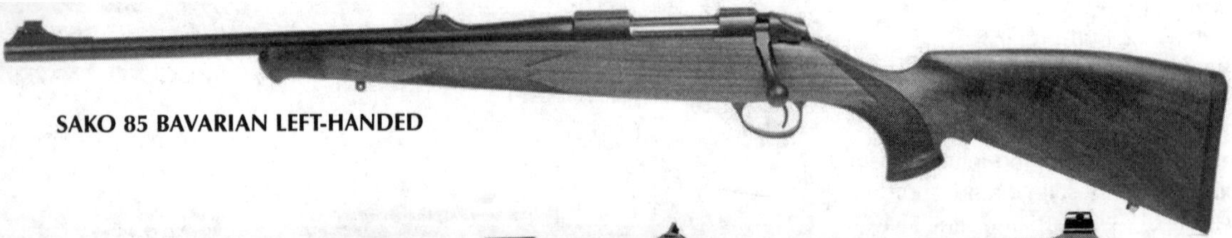

SAKO 85 BAVARIAN LEFT-HANDED

SAKO 85 BLACK BEAR

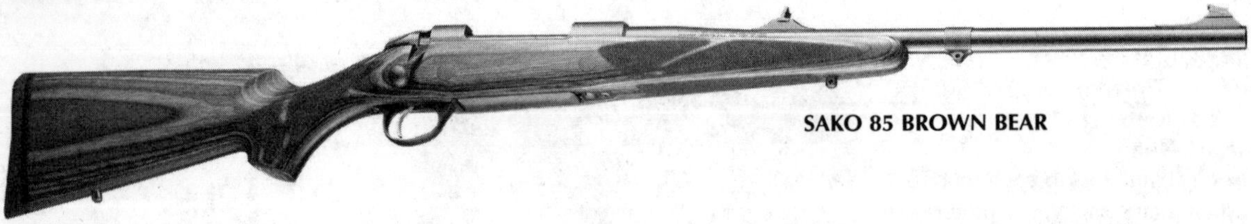

SAKO 85 BROWN BEAR

85 BAVARIAN

Action: Bolt
Stock: Walnut
Barrel: 22 in., 24 in.
Sights: None
Weight: 7 lb.–7 lb. 8 oz.
Caliber: .308 Win., .270 Win., .30-06 Spfd., .300 Win. Mag., .270 WSM, .300 WSM, 6.5x55 Swedish, 7mm-08 Rem., 7mm Rem. Mag.
Magazine: 4, 5 rounds
Features: High grade walnut stock in traditional European style; single-set trigger
MSRP $2225

85 BAVARIAN LEFT-HANDED

Action: Bolt
Stock: Wood
Barrel: 20–22.4 in.
Sights: Fixed
Weight: 7 lb.–7 lb. 4 oz.
Caliber: .25-06 Rem., .30-06 Spfd., .270 Win., 6.5x55 Swedish, 7x64 Brenneke, 8x57IS, 9.3x62 Mauser
Magazine: Detachable box, 5+1 rounds
Features: Oil finished walnut stock with Schnabel-type forend and pistol grip endplate in rosewood
MSRP $2275

85 BLACK BEAR

Action: Bolt
Stock: Black composite
Barrel: 21.25 in.
Sights: Adjustable Express "V" rear, white bead front and integral dovetail for scope mounts
Weight: 6 lb. 13 oz.–7 lb.
Caliber: .308 Win., .338 Fed., .30-06 Spfd., 8x57IS, 9.3x62 Mauser, 9.3x66 Sako
Magazine: Detachable box, 5 rounds
Features: Purpose built weapon for bear and wild boar hunters; adjustable single-stage trigger; adjustable shallow "V" Express style rear sight with white bead front sight for fast target acquisition and a barrel band for front swivel; patented Total Control Magazine Latch (TCL) prevents accidental release of the stainless steel magazine under the heaviest recoil or harshest hunting conditions
MSRP $1850

85 BROWN BEAR

Action: Bolt
Stock: Brown laminate
Barrel: 21.25 in.
Sights: Adjustable open rear, blade style front and integral dovetail for scope mounts
Weight: 7 lb. 15 oz.
Caliber: .338 Win. Mag., .375 H&H Mag.
Magazine: Detachable box, 4 rounds
Features: Open adjustable rear sight and blade style front sight; short free-floated bull barrel has a band type front swivel; forged one-piece bolt with three locking lugs offers fast, smooth cycling with controlled round feed and mechanical case ejection; patented Total Control Magazine Latch (TCL) prevents accidental release of the stainless steel magazine
MSRP $2500

SAKO 85 BROWN BEAR XL

SAKO 85 CLASSIC

SAKO 85 FINNLIGHT

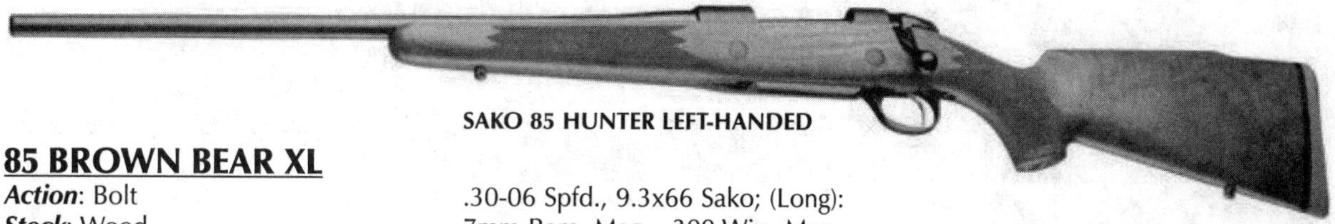

SAKO 85 HUNTER LEFT-HANDED

85 BROWN BEAR XL

Action: Bolt
Stock: Wood
Barrel: 22 in.
Sights: Adjustable
Weight: 9 lb. 8 oz.
Caliber: .416 Ridgby, .450 Ridgby, .500 Jeffery
Magazine: Detachable box, 4+1 rounds
Features: Brown laminated hardwood, straight classic stock, black action and 540mm semi heavy barrel; purpose built weapons for bear and bruise hunters; adjustable special fast target acquisition iron sights; detachable staggered two-row steel magazine; can be top-loaded; integral Dovetail rails for secure scope mounting
MSRP $2295

85 CLASSIC

Action: Bolt
Stock: Walnut
Barrel: 22.4 in., 24.4 in.
Sights: Open
Weight: 7 lb.–7 lb. 12 oz.
Caliber: (Short): .243 Win., .260 Rem., 7mm-08 Rem., .308 Win., .338 Federal; (SM) .270 Win. S Mag., .300 Win. S Mag.; (Medium) .25-06 Rem., 6.5x55 Swedish, .270 Win., .30-06 Spfd., 9.3x66 Sako; (Long): 7mm Rem. Mag., .300 Win. Mag., .338 Win. Mag., .375 H&H Mag.
Magazine: Detachable box, S/M 6 rounds, SM/L 5 rounds
Features: Comes in short actions Extra Short (XS), Short (S) and Short Magnum (SM), medium action (M), and long action (L); straight, classic walnut stock with rosewood forend tip and pistol grip cap; integral rails for scope mounts; free-floating barrel is cold-hammer-forged; adjustable single-stage trigger
MSRP $2275

85 FINNLIGHT

Action: Bolt
Stock: Synthetic
Barrel: 20.25 in., 22.4 in.
Sights: None
Weight: 6 lb. 3 oz.–6 lb. 13 oz.
Caliber: (Short): .22-250 Rem., .243 Win., .260 Rem., .7mm-08 Rem., .308 Win.; (SM) .270 Win. Short Mag., .300 Win. Short Mag.; (Medium): .25-06 Rem., 6.5x55 Swedish, .270 Win., .30-06 Spfd.; (Long) 7mm Rem. Mag., .300 Win. Mag.
Magazine: Detachable box, S/M 6 rounds, SM/L 5 rounds
Features: Comes in short actions Short (S) and Short magnum (SM), Medium action (M), and Long action (L); single-stage trigger; two-way Sako safety locks both trigger and bolt handle; black synthetic stock with soft gray grip areas; pistol grip stock; integral rails for scope mounts; free-floating barrel is cold-hammer-forged of stainless steel
MSRP $1800

85 HUNTER LEFT-HANDED

Action: Bolt
Stock: Wood
Barrel: 24.4 in.
Sights: None
Weight: 7 lb. 12 oz.
Caliber: .300 Win. Mag., .338 Win. Mag., .375 H&H Mag., 7mm Rem. Mag.
Magazine: Detachable box, 4+1 rounds
Features: High-grade walnut stock and satin-like blued finish on the barrel and receiver
MSRP $2125

SAKO 85 KODIAK

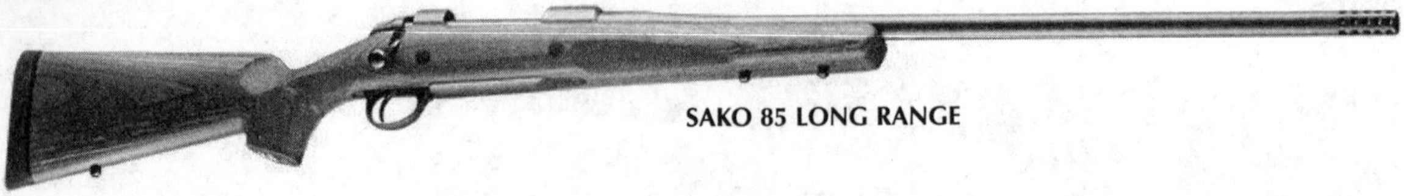

SAKO 85 LONG RANGE

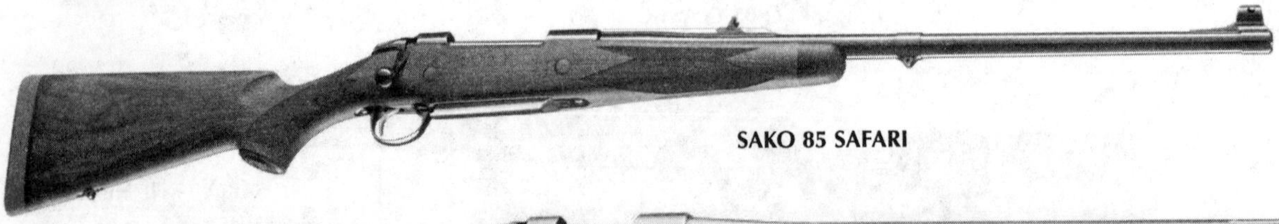

SAKO 85 SAFARI

SAKO 85 SYNTHETIC BLACK

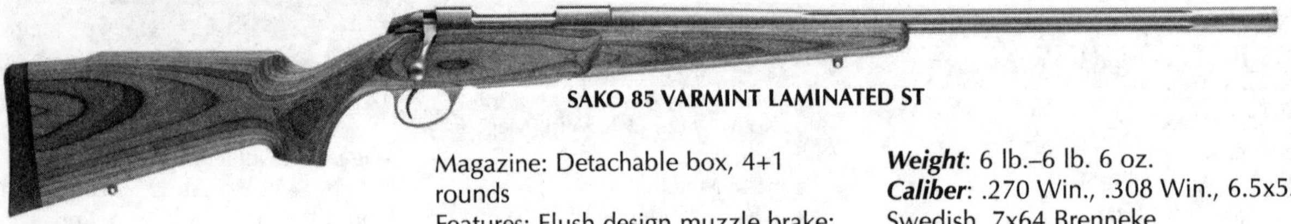

SAKO 85 VARMINT LAMINATED ST

85 KODIAK

Action: Bolt
Stock: Laminated hardwood
Barrel: 12.25 in.
Sights: Open
Weight: 7 lb. 15 oz.
Caliber: .338 Win. Mag., .375 H&H Mag.
Magazine: Detachable box, 5 rounds
Features: Adjustable single-stage trigger; barrel band for front swivel; integral dovetail rails for secure scope mounting; straight stock made of gray matte-lacquered laminated hardwood and reinforced with two cross-bolts; free-floating "bull" barrel
MSRP. $1950

85 LONG RANGE

Action: Bolt
Stock: Wood
Barrel: 26 in.
Sights: None
Weight: 9 lb. 12 oz.
Caliber: .300 Win. Mag., .338 Lapua Mag.
Magazine: Detachable box, 4+1 rounds
Features: Flush design muzzle brake; designed for long range hunting
MSRP. $2865

85 SAFARI

Action: Bolt
Stock: Walnut
Barrel: 24.2 in.
Sights: Front bead, adjustable iron sights rear
Weight: 9 lb.
Caliber: .375 H&H Mag.
Magazine: Detachable box, 6 rounds
Features: Free-floating barrel; ergonomic walnut stock with checkering; staggered, two-row magazine with total control latch; single-set adjustable trigger; steel trigger guard; two-way Sako safety locks both trigger and bolt handle; Pachmayr recoil pad; limited models imported to U.S.
MSRP. . . . . $10000–$10500

85 SYNTHETIC BLACK

Action: Bolt
Stock: Synthetic
Barrel: 22.4 in.
Sights: None
Weight: 6 lb.–6 lb. 6 oz.
Caliber: .270 Win., .308 Win., 6.5x55 Swedish, 7x64 Brenneke
Magazine: Detachable box, 5+1 rounds
Features: Matte black, fluted barrel
MSRP. $1895

85 VARMINT LAMINATED STAINLESS

Action: Bolt
Stock: Laminated hardwood
Barrel: 20 in., 23.6 in.
Sights: None
Weight: 8 lb. 10 oz.–9 lb.
Caliber: (XS) .204 Ruger, .222 Rem., .223 Rem.; (Short) .22-250 Rem., .243 Win., .260 Rem., 7mm-08 Rem., .308 Win., .338 Federal
Magazine: Detachable box, XS 7 rounds, S 6 rounds
Features: Comes in short actions Extra Short (XS) and Short (S); single-set trigger; two-way Sako safety locks both trigger and bolt handle; straight stock with wide forend is made of brown matte laquered laminated hardwood; integral rail for scope mounts
MSRP. $2025

SAKO A7 ROUGHTECH PRO

SAKO A7 ROUGHTECH RANGE

SAKO FINNFIRE II

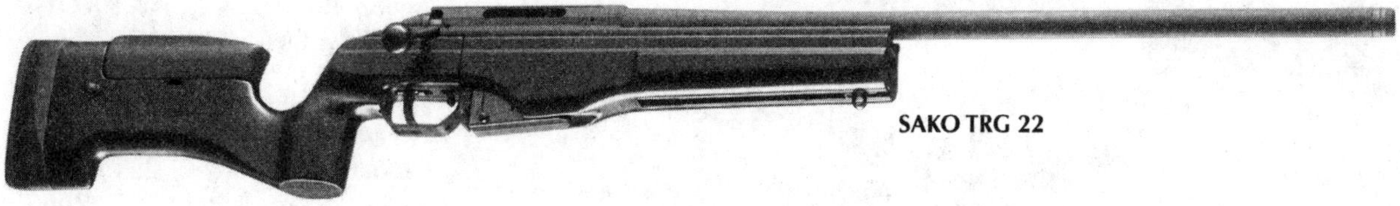

SAKO TRG 22

A7 ROUGHTECH PRO

Action: Bolt
Stock: Synthetic
Barrel: 24.4 in.
Sights: None
Weight: 6 lb. 13 oz.
Caliber: .30-06 Spfd., .243 Win., .270 Win., .300 Win. Mag., .300 WSM, .308 Win., 7mm Rem. Mag.
Magazine: Detachable box
Features: Stocks are coated with rough surface texture to offer a solid grip in all weather conditions, have a full integrated aluminum bedding; stocks are equipped with advanced high energy dissipation recoil pad and come with two 5mm spacers for length of pull adjustment; mounting rail
MSRP $1200

A7 ROUGHTECH RANGE

Action: Bolt
Stock: Synthetic
Barrel: 26 in.
Sights: None
Weight: 8 lb.
Caliber: .25-06 Rem., .300 Win. Mag., .300 WSM, .308 Win., 7mm Rem. Mag.
Magazine: Detachable box
Features: Stocks are coated with rough surface texture to offer a solid grip in all weather conditions, have a full integrated aluminum bedding; stocks are equipped with advanced high energy dissipation recoil pad and come with two 5mm spacers for length of pull adjustment; mounting rail
MSRP $1200

FINNFIRE II

Action: Bolt
Stock: Wood
Barrel: 22 in.
Sights: None
Weight: 6 lb. 3 oz.
Caliber: .17 HMR, .22LR
Magazine: Detachable box, 5+1 rounds
Features: Oiled stock; single stage trigger; muzzle thread
MSRP $1095

TRG 22

Action: Bolt
Stock: Synthetic
Barrel: 20 in., 26 in., 27.1 in.
Sights: None
Weight: 10 lb. 4 oz.–10 lb. 12 oz.
Caliber: .308 Win, .300 Win. Mag., .338 Lapua Mag.
Magazine: Detachable box, 5, 7, 10 rounds
Features: Double-stage trigger; two-way Sako safety locks both trigger and bolt handle; base of stock is made of polyurethane with aluminum skeleton; adjustable cheekpiece and buttplate; Ambidextrous stock in green or desert tan color; includes integral dovetail on receiver and is drilled and tapped for Picatinny rail mounting
MSRP: . . . . $3500–$7100

Savage Arms

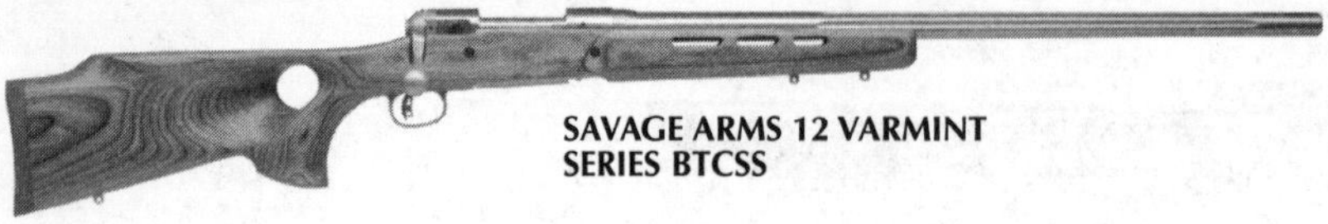

SAVAGE ARMS 12 VARMINT SERIES BTCSS

SAVAGE ARMS 14/114 AMERICAN CLASSIC

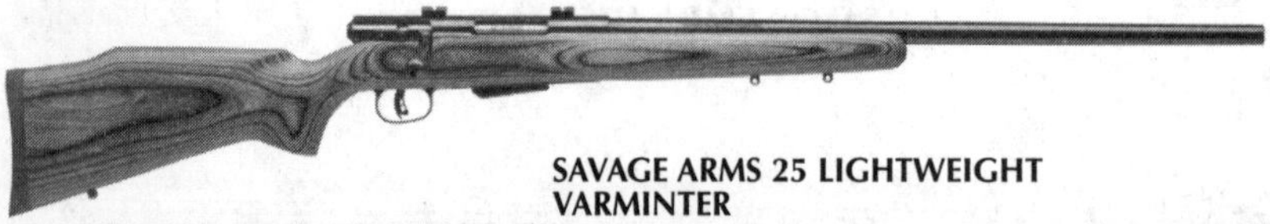

SAVAGE ARMS 25 LIGHTWEIGHT VARMINTER

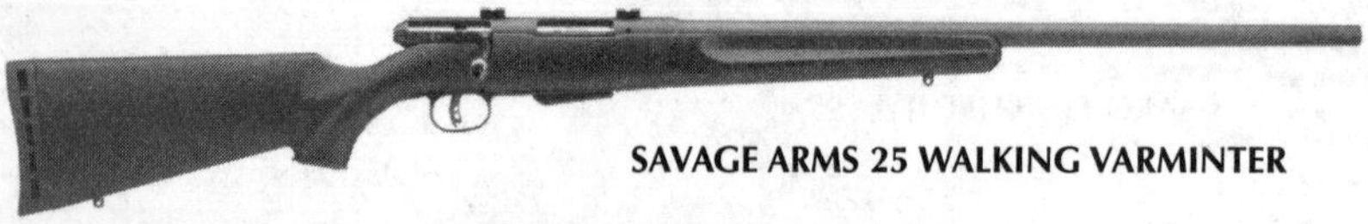

SAVAGE ARMS 25 WALKING VARMINTER

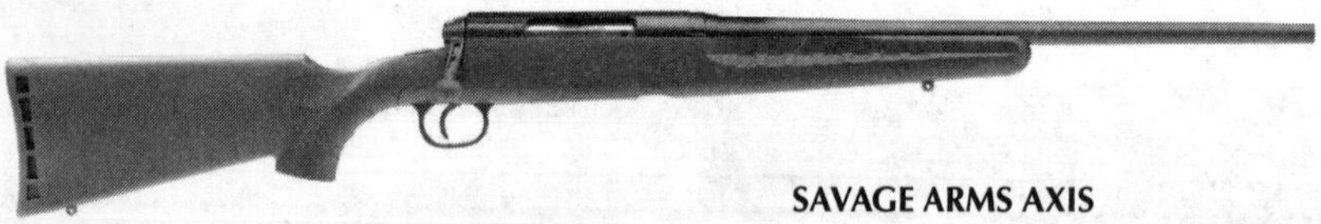

SAVAGE ARMS AXIS

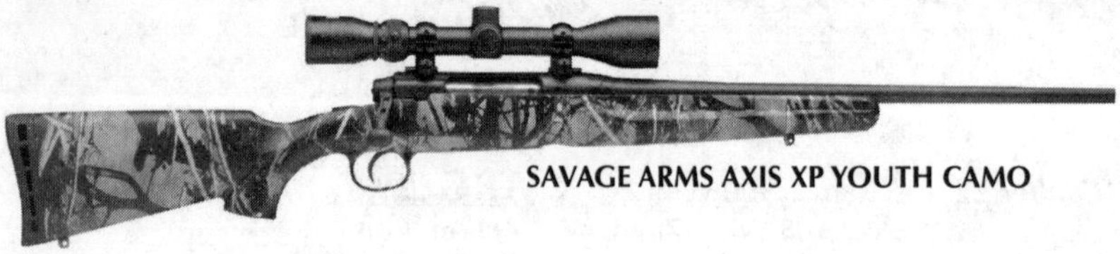

SAVAGE ARMS AXIS XP YOUTH CAMO

12 VARMINT SERIES BTCSS

Action: Bolt
Stock: Laminate
Barrel: 26 in.
Sights: None
Weight: 10 lb.
Caliber: .204 Ruger, .223 Rem., .22-250 Rem.
Magazine: Detachable box, 4 rounds
Features: Drilled and tapped for scope mounts; stainless steel barrel with high luster finish; AccuTrigger; wood laminate with thumbhole and satin finish
MSRP $1255

14/114 AMERICAN CLASSIC

Action: Bolt
Stock: Wood
Barrel: 22 in., 24 in.
Sights: None
Weight: 7 lb. 4 oz.–7 lb. 12 oz.
Caliber: .243 Win., .250 Sav., .270 Win., .300 WSM, .30-06 Spfd., .300 Win. Mag., .308 Win., 7mm Rem. Mag., 7mm-08 Rem.
Magazine: Hinged floor plate, 2, 4 rounds
Features: Drilled and tapped for scope mounts; carbon steel barrel with matte blued finish; short action; AccuTrigger; satin finish wood stock
MSRP $949

25 LIGHTWEIGHT VARMINTER

Action: Bolt
Stock: Wood laminate
Barrel: 24 in.
Sights: None
Weight: 8 lb. 4 oz.
Caliber: .17 Hornet, .204 Ruger, .22 Hornet, .223 Rem.
Magazine: Detachable box, 4 rounds
Features: Drilled and tapped for scope mounts; carbon steel barrel with blued satin finish; wood laminate stock with satin finish
MSRP $772

25 WALKING VARMINTER

Action: Bolt
Stock: Synthetic
Barrel: 22 in.
Sights: None
Weight: 6 lb. 14 oz.
Caliber: .17 Hornet, .204 Ruger, .22 Hornet, .222 Rem., .223 Rem.
Magazine: Detachable box, 4 rounds
Features: Matte black synthetic stock; matte black carbon steel barrel; AccuTrigger
MSRP $620

AXIS

Action: Bolt
Stock: Synthetic
Barrel: 22 in.
Sights: None
Weight: 6 lb. 8 oz.
Caliber: .22-250 Rem., .223 Rem., .243 Win., .25-06 Rem., .270 Win., .30–06 Spfd., .308 Win., 7mm-08 Rem.
Magazine: Detachable box, 4 rounds
Features: New modern design, smooth bolt operation; drilled and tapped for scope mounts; carbon steel barrel with black matte finish; synthetic stock with matte black finish
MSRP $362

AXIS XP YOUTH CAMO

Action: Bolt
Stock: Synthetic
Barrel: 20 in.
Sights: Scope included
Weight: 6 lb. 13 oz.
Caliber: .223 Rem., .243 Win., 7mm-08 Rem.
Magazine: Detachable box, 4 rounds
Features: Made with cooperation from the Youth Shooting Sports Alliance; carbon steel barrel with matte black finish; stock comes in camo or muddy girl
MSRP $475

Savage Arms

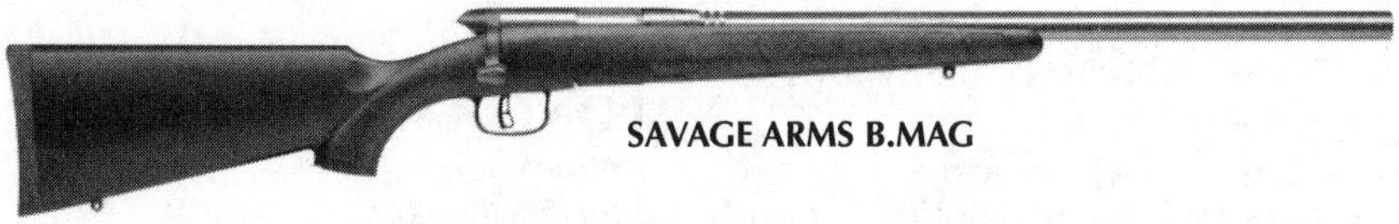

SAVAGE ARMS B.MAG

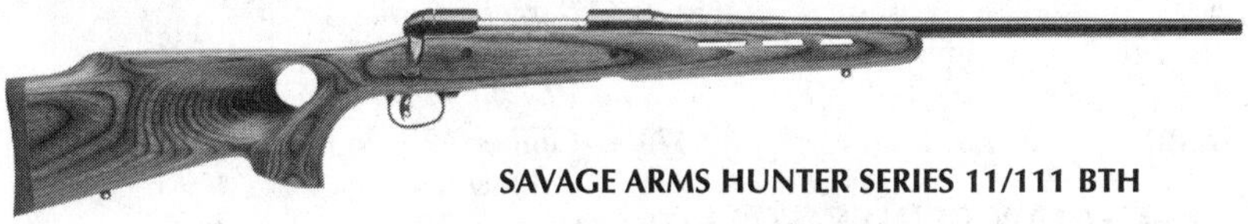

SAVAGE ARMS HUNTER SERIES 11/111 BTH

SAVAGE ARMS LAW ENFORCEMENT SERIES 110 BA LEFT HAND MODEL

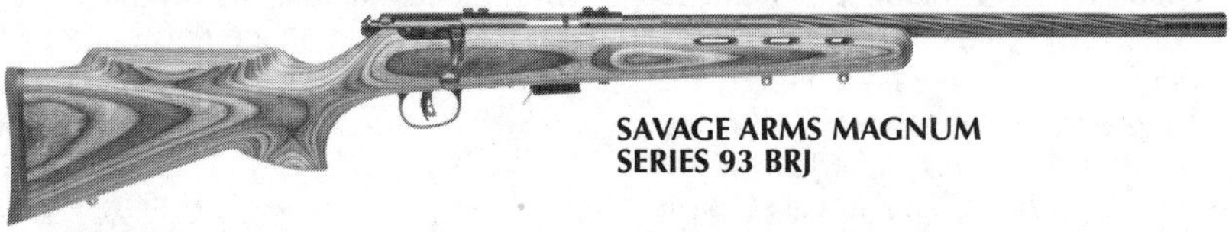

SAVAGE ARMS MAGNUM SERIES 93 BRJ

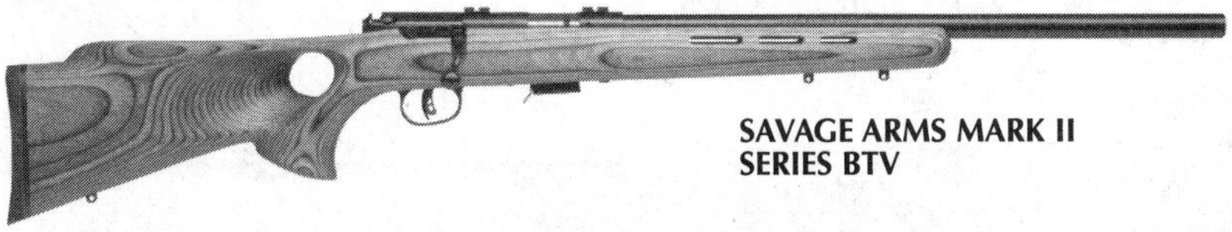

SAVAGE ARMS MARK II SERIES BTV

SAVAGE ARMS RASCAL SINGLE SHOT

B.MAG

Action: Bolt
Stock: Synthetic
Barrel: 22 in.
Sights: None
Weight: 5 lb.
Caliber: .17 WSM
Magazine: Detachable box, 8 rounds
Features: Drilled and tapped for scope mounts; AccuTrigger; stainless steel barrel with matte finish
MSRP $372

HUNTER SERIES 11/111 BTH

Action: Bolt
Stock: Wood laminate
Barrel: 22 in.
Sights: None
Weight: 6 lb. 12 oz.–7 lb.
Caliber: .22-250 Rem., .243 Win., .223 Rem., .25-06 Rem., .270 Win., .30-06 Spfd., .308 Win.
Magazine: Hinged floor plate, 4 rounds
Features: Drilled and tapped for scope mounts; carbon steel barrel with blued satin finish; AccuTrigger; wood laminate stock with thumbhole in satin finish
MSRP $954

LAW ENFORCEMENT SERIES 110 BA LEFT HAND MODEL

Action: Bolt
Stock: Aluminum
Barrel: 26 in.
Sights: Drilled and tapped for scope
Weight: 15 lb. 12 oz.
Caliber: .300 Win. Mag., .338 Lapua Mag.
Magazine: Detachable box, 5 rounds
Features: Also available in right hand model; AccuTrigger; matte black carbon steel barrel; 20 MOA scope rail
MSRP $2638

MAGNUM SERIES 93 BRJ

Action: Bolt
Stock: Wood laminate
Barrel: 21 in.
Sights: None
Weight: 7 lb.
Caliber: .22 WMR
Magazine: Detachable box, 5 rounds
Features: Carbon steel barrel in blued satin finish; wood laminate stock; AccuTrigger
MSRP $542

MARK II SERIES BTV

Action: Bolt
Stock: Wood laminate
Barrel: 21 in.
Sights: None
Weight: 6 lb. 8 oz.
Caliber: .22LR
Magazine: Detachable box, 5 rounds
Features: Carbon steel barrel with blued satin finish; wood laminate stock with thumbhole; AccuTrigger
MSRP $461

RASCAL SINGLE SHOT

Action: Bolt
Stock: Synthetic, hardwood
Barrel: 16.125 in.
Sights: Adjustable
Weight: 2 lb. 10 oz.–2 lb. 15 oz.
Caliber: .22LR
Magazine: None
Features: Matte synthetic stock available in seven colors; adjustable peep sights; drilled and tapped for scope mounts; AccuTrigger; carbon steel barrel with satin blued finish
MSRP $238

Savage Arms

SEMI-AUTOMATIC SERIES 64 F

Action: Semiautomatic
Stock: Synthetic
Barrel: 20.5 in.
Sights: Open
Weight: 5 lb.
Caliber: .22LR
Magazine: Detachable box, 10 rounds
Features: Drilled and tapped for scope mounts; carbon steel barrel with satin blued finish; synthetic matte black stock
MSRP $175

SPECIALTY SERIES 11/111 HOG HUNTER

Action: Bolt
Stock: Synthetic
Barrel: 20 in.
Sights: Adjustable
Weight: 7 lb. 4 oz.–8 lb.
Caliber: .223 Rem., .308 Win., .338 Win.
Magazine: Internal box, 4 rounds
Features: Green composite synthetic stock; matte black carbon steel barrel; LPA adjustable sights; threaded barrel; AccuTrigger
MSRP $578

SPECIALTY SERIES 11/111 LADY HUNTER

Action: Bolt
Stock: Wood
Barrel: 20 in.
Sights: None
Weight: 6 lb.–6 lb. 8 oz.
Caliber: .22-250 Rem., .223 Rem., .243 Win., .270 Win., .30-06 Spfd., .308 Win., 6.5 Creedmoor, 7mm-08 Rem.
Magazine: Detachable box, 4 rounds
Features: Oil-finish American walnut stock with ladies-specific geometry; carbon steel barrel in matter black
MSRP $899

SPECIALTY SERIES 11/111 LONG RANGE HUNTER

Action: Bolt
Stock: Synthetic
Barrel: 26 in.
Sights: None
Weight: 8 lb. 6 oz.
Caliber: .25-06 Rem., .260 Rem., .300 Win. Mag., .300 WSM, .308 Win., .338 Lapua Mag., 6.5 Creedmoor,
6.5-284 Norma, 7mm Rem. Mag.
Magazine: Hinged floor plate, 2, 4 rounds
Features: Drilled and tapped for scope mounts; carbon steel barrel with black matte finish; synthetic stock with black matte finish; AccuTrigger
MSRP $1136

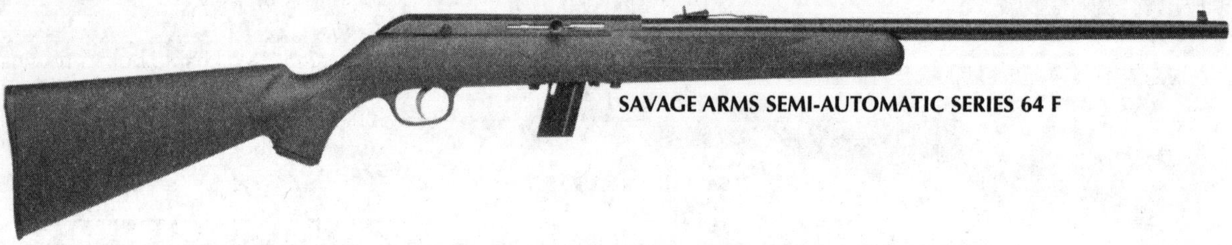

SAVAGE ARMS SEMI-AUTOMATIC SERIES 64 F

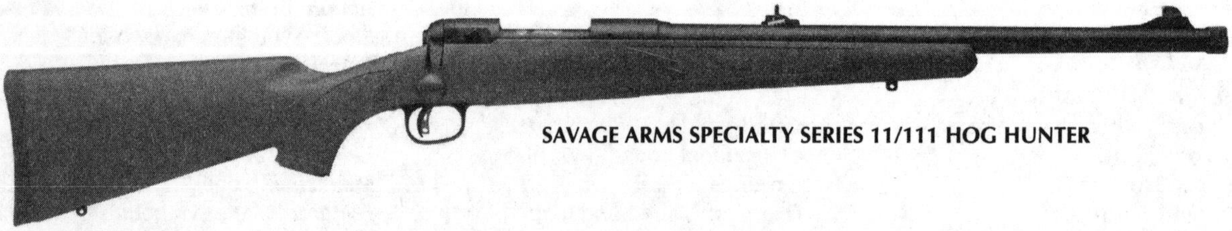

SAVAGE ARMS SPECIALTY SERIES 11/111 HOG HUNTER

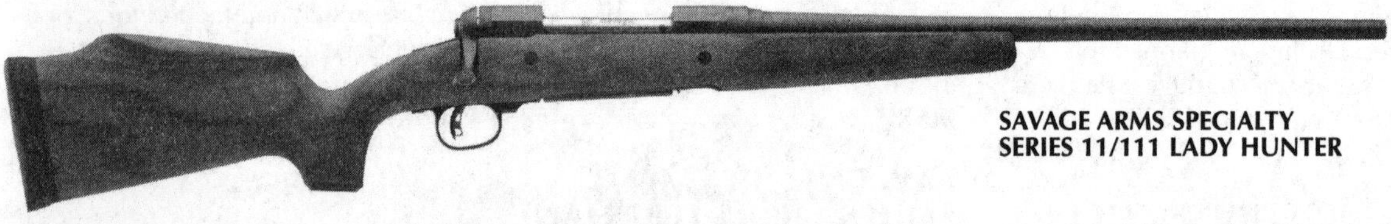

SAVAGE ARMS SPECIALTY SERIES 11/111 LADY HUNTER

SAVAGE ARMS SPECIALTY SERIES 11/111 LONG RANGE HUNTER

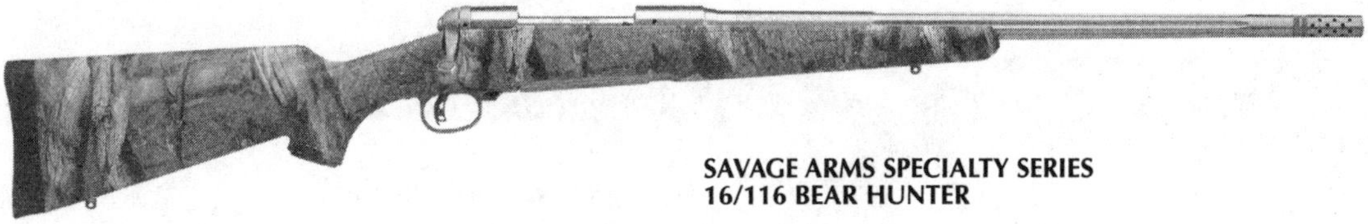

SAVAGE ARMS SPECIALTY SERIES 16/116 BEAR HUNTER

SAVAGE ARMS SPECIALTY SERIES MODEL 42

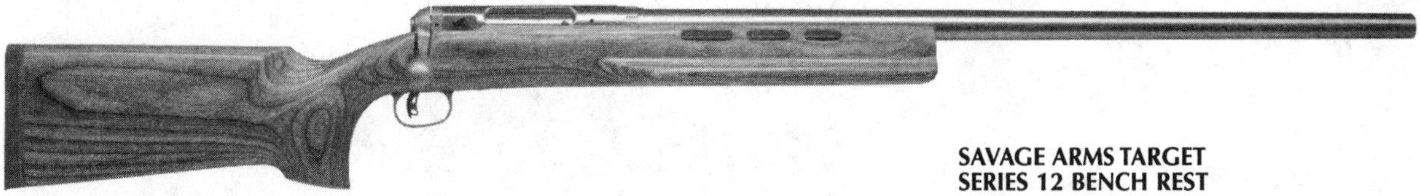

SAVAGE ARMS TARGET SERIES 12 BENCH REST

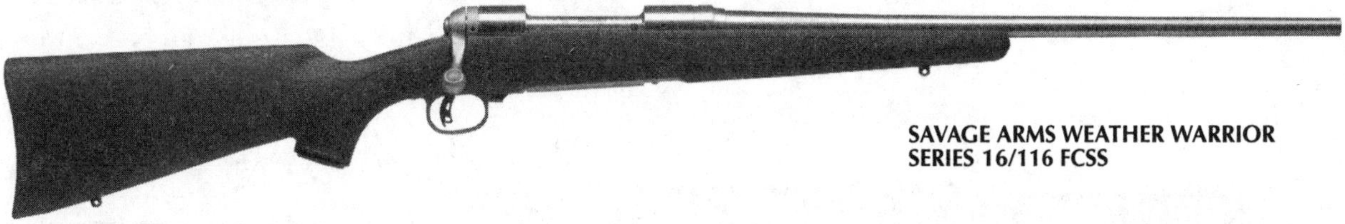

SAVAGE ARMS WEATHER WARRIOR SERIES 16/116 FCSS

SPECIALTY SERIES 16/116 BEAR HUNTER

Action: Bolt
Stock: Synthetic
Barrel: 23 in.
Sights: None
Weight: 7 lb. 8 oz.
Caliber: .300 Win. Mag., .300 WSM, .325 WSM, .338 Win. Mag., .375 Ruger
Magazine: Hinged floor plate, 2 rounds
Features: Drilled and tapped for scope mounts; adjustable muzzle-brake; stainless steel barrel; synthetic stock with matte camo finish; AccuTrigger; AccuStock
MSRP....................$1066

SPECIALTY SERIES MODEL 42

Action: Break-action
Stock: Synthetic
Barrel: 20 in.
Sights: Adjustable
Weight: 6 lb. 2 oz.
Caliber: .22LR, .22 WMR
Magazine: None
Features: Rifle-shotgun combo; break-open combination gun over 410 bore; carbon steel matte black barrel; matte black synthetic stock;
MSRP....................$485

TARGET SERIES 12 BENCH REST

Action: Bolt, single shot
Stock: Wood laminate
Barrel: 29 in.
Sights: None
Weight: 12 lb. 12 oz.
Caliber: .308 Win., 6.5-284 Norma, 6 Norma BR
Magazine: None
Features: Drilled and tapped for scope mounts; stainless steel barrel with high luster finish; wood laminate stock with satin finish; AccuTrigger
MSRP....................$1678

WEATHER WARRIOR SERIES 16/116 FCSS

Action: Bolt
Stock: Synthetic
Barrel: 22 in., 24 in.
Sights: None
Weight: 6 lb. 14 oz.–7.15 lb.
Caliber: .204 Ruger, .22-250 Rem., .223 Rem., .243 Win., .25-06 Rem., .260 Rem., .270 WSM, .270 Win., .30-06 Spfd., .300 WSM, .300 Win. Mag., .308 Win., .308 Win. Mag., .375 Ruger, 6.5 Creedmoor, 6.5-284 Norma, 7mm Rem. Mag., .7mm-08 Rem.
Magazine: Detachable box, 2, 4 rounds
Features: Drilled and tapped for scope mounts; stainless steel barrel with high luster finish; synthetic stock with black matte finish; AccuTrigger
MSRP....................$911

Sig Sauer

SIG SAUER SIG516 CARBON

SIG SAUER SIG516 PATROL

SIG SAUER 522 COMMANDO

SIG SAUER SIG556XI RUSSIAN

SIG516 CARBON

Action: Semiautomatic
Stock: Synthetic
Barrel: 16 in.
Sights: Adjustable
Weight: 7 lb.
Caliber: 5.56 NATO
Magazine: Detachable box, 30 rounds
Features: Locking flip-up front/rear sights; Picatinny rail; carbon fiber fixed A1 length stock; two-stage match trigger
MSRP $2004

SIG516 PATROL

Action: Semiautomatic
Stock: Tactical synthetic
Barrel: 16 in.
Sights: None
Weight: 7 lb. 5 oz.
Caliber: 5.56 NATO
Magazine: Detachable box, 30 rounds
Features: Gas piston operating system; three-position gas regulator; free-floating military grade chrome-lined barrel; Picatinny flat top upper; aircraft grade aluminum upper and lower receiver with hard coat anodize finish
MSRP $1885

SIG522 COMMANDO

Action: Semiautomatic
Stock: Tactical synthetic
Barrel: 16 in.
Sights: Mini red-dot
Weight: 6 lb. 2 oz.
Caliber: .22LR
Magazine: Detachable box, 10 or 25 rounds
Features: Removable inert training suppressor; anodized alloy upper receiver and Picatinnyrail; folding telescopic stock
MSRP $600

SIG556XI RUSSIAN

Action: Semiautomatic
Stock: Synthetic
Barrel: 16 in.
Sights: Adjustable
Weight: 7 lb.
Caliber: 5.56 NATO
Magazine: Detachable box, 30 rounds
Features: Caliber convertible to 7.62x39 Warsaw and 300 BLK; three-position adjustable gas piston operating system with rotating bolt; swiss-style folding stock with removable cheek riser; ambidextrous controls; locking flip-up front and rear sights
MSRP . . . . $1466–$1599

Sig Sauer

SIG SAUER SIG716 PATROL RIFLE

SIG SAUER SIG M400

SIG SAUER M400 ENHANCED CARBINE

SIG716 PATROL RIFLE

Action: Semiautomatic
Stock: Tactical synthetic
Barrel: 16 in.
Sights: None
Weight: 9 lb. 5 oz.
Caliber: 7.62 NATO
Magazine: Detachable box, 20 rounds
Features: Short stroke pushrod operating system; Picatinny rail; free-floating barrel; aluminum quad rail forend; telescoping stock
MSRP. $2399

SIG M400

Action: Semiautomatic
Stock: Synthetic
Barrel: 16 in.
Sights: Adjustable front post, dual aperture
Weight: 5 lb. 10 oz.
Caliber: 5.56 NATO
Magazine: Detachable box, 30 rounds
Features: Military grade, chrome-lined barrel, flat top upper with Picatinny rail
MSRP. $1313

SIG M400 ENHANCED

Action: Semiautomatic
Stock: Magpul MOE
Barrel: 16 in.
Sights: None
Weight: 6 lb. 11 oz.
Caliber: 5.56 NATO
Magazine: Detachable box, 30 rounds
Features: SIG's first direct gas impingement system; taking the enhancements of the 516 platform into a traditional Stoner design; 1:7 chrome lined barrel; ambi selector & mag release; integral QD sling swivel mounts machined into lower; upper/lower tension adjustment device; offered in traditional configuration with removable carry handle with poly or Picatinny quad rail; offered as 'enhanced' variants with Magpul MOE furniture in black, FDE, and OD; new variants also include a Sight Ready Platform (SRP), a lightweight with contoured barrel
MSRP. $1234

Smith & Wesson

SMITH & WESSON M&P10

M&P10

Action: Semiautomatic
Stock: Synthetic
Barrel: 18 in.
Sights: None
Weight: 7 lb. 12 oz.
Caliber: .308 Win., 7.62 NATO
Magazine: Detachable box, 20 rounds
Features: Ambidextrous magazine catch and bolt catch; reversible, ambidextrous safety selector; patented S&W enhanced flash hider; gas block with integral Picatinny rail
MSRP. . . . . $1619–$1729

Smith & Wesson

SMITH & WESSON M&P15

SMITH & WESSON M&P15-22 RIFLE

SMITH & WESSON M&P15 300 WHISPER

SMITH & WESSON M&P15 MOE MID

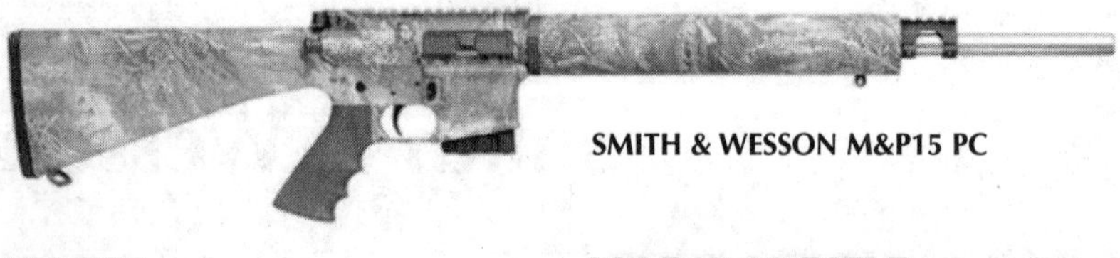

SMITH & WESSON M&P15 PC

M&P15

Action: Semiautomatic
Stock: Synthetic
Barrel: 16 in.
Sights: Troy adjustable front post, folding rear battle sight
Weight: 6 lb. 12 oz.
Caliber: 5.56 NATO, .223 Rem.
Magazine: Detachable box, 30 rounds
Features: Six-position telescopic black stock; chrome-lined gas key and bolt carrier; flash suppressor compensator; two-position safety lever
MSRP. $1249

M&P15-22 RIFLE

Action: Semiautomatic
Stock: Synthetic
Barrel: 18 in.
Sights: Adjustable A2 front post, adjustable dual aperture
Weight: 5 lb. 6 oz.
Caliber: .22LR
Magazine: Detachable box, 25 rounds
Features: Six-position collapsible stock; functioning charging handle; two-position receiver mounted safety selector; cartridge case deflector; bolt catch; recessed magazine release button; match grade precision, threaded barrel
MSRP. $559

M&P15 300 WHISPER

Action: Semiautomatic
Stock: Synthetic
Barrel: 16 in.
Sights: None
Weight: 6 lb. 6 oz.
Caliber: .300 Whisper, 300 BLK
Magazine: Detachable box, 10 rounds
Features: Sub-sonic and super-sonic capabilities; 4140 chromoly steel barrel; forged 7075 aluminum receivers coated with Realtree APG finish; gas-operated rifle; single-stage trigger; integral one-piece trigger guard; six-position collapsible CAR stock; optics ready
MSRP. $1119

M&P15 MOE MID

Action: Semiautomatic
Stock: Synthetic
Barrel: 16 in.
Sights: M4-A2 post front, folding Magpul rear
Weight: 6 lb. 8 oz.
Caliber: 5.56 NATO
Magazine: Detachable box, 30 rounds
Features: Mid-length operating system, patent-pending flash hider; available in black and dark earth finish; Magpul designed forged lower receiver with flared magazine; one-piece integrated trigger guard; Melonite finish on barrel; MOE six-position collapsible buttstock
MSRP. $1259

M&P15 PC

Action: Semiautomatic
Stock: Synthetic
Barrel: 20 in.
Sights: None
Weight: 8 lb. 2 oz.
Caliber: 5.56 NATO, .223 Rem.
Magazine: Detachable box, 10 rounds
Features: Hogue Green pistol grip; A2 buttstock; two-stage trigger; Realtree Advantage Max-1 Camo finish stock; chromed gas key and bolt carrier
Black:. $1549
Camo: $1589

M&P15 SPORT

Action: Semiautomatic
Stock: Synthetic
Barrel: 16 in.
Sights: Adjustable A2 front post, adjustable dual aperture
Weight: 6 lb. 8 oz.
Caliber: 5.56 NATO
Magazine: Detachable box, 10 or 30 rounds
Features: Six-position telescopic black stock or fixed stock; chrome-lined gas key and bolt carrier; flash suppressor compensator; two-position safety lever
MSRP $739

M&P15T

Action: Semiautomatic
Stock: Synthetic
Barrel: 16 in.
Sights: Folding Magpul
Weight: 6.85 lb.
Caliber: 5.56 NATO
Magazine: Detachable box, 30 rounds
Features: 10-in. patent-pending, anti-twist, free-floating quad rail; melonite barrel; chromed bolt carrier and gas key; gas operated; single-stage trigger
MSRP $1159

M&P15 VTAC II

Action: Semiautomatic
Stock: Synthetic
Barrel: 16 in.
Sights: None
Weight: 6 lb. 4 oz.
Caliber: 5.56 NATO
Magazine: Detachable box, 30 rounds
Features: Mid-length operating system, patent-pending flash hider; 4150 CMV steel barrel with Melonite finish; VTAC/Troy Extreme TRX handguard that reduces heat transfer; packaged with 2-inch adjustable Picatinny rails; Geissele Super V trigger
MSRP $1949

RIFLES

SMITH & WESSON M&P15 SPORT

SMITH & WESSON M&P15T

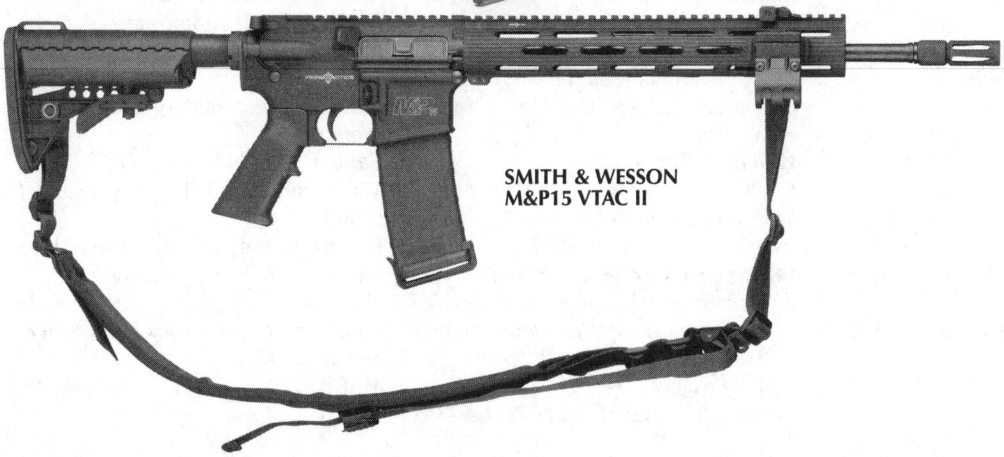

SMITH & WESSON M&P15 VTAC II

Springfield Armory

SPRINGFIELD ARMORY M1A SOCOM 16

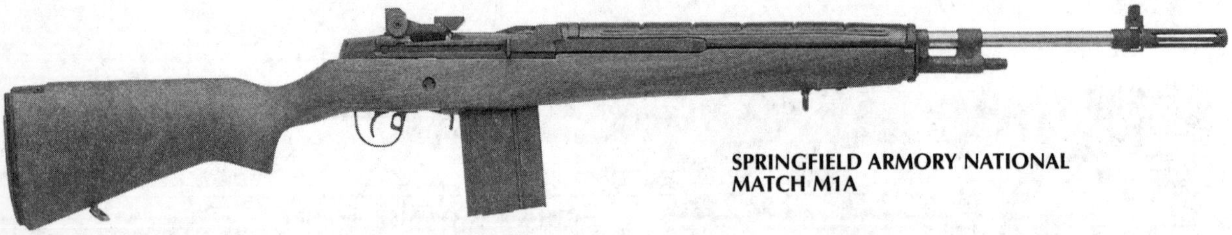

SPRINGFIELD ARMORY NATIONAL MATCH M1A

SPRINGFIELD ARMORY SCOUT SQUAD

M1A SOCOM 16

Action: Semiautomatic
Stock: Composite
Barrel: 16.25 in.
Sights: Tritium front sight
Weight: 8 lb. 13 oz.
Caliber: 7.62 NATO, .308 Win
Magazine: Detachable box, 10 rounds
Features: Muzzlebrake; forward mounted scope base; two-stage military trigger; composite black or green stock
MSRP. . . . . $1761–$1921

NATIONAL MATCH M1A

Action: Semiautomatic
Stock: Walnut
Barrel: 22 in.
Sights: National Match front military post sight; rear National Match hooded aperture
Weight: 9 lb. 13 oz.
Caliber: 7.62 NATO, .308 Win.
Magazine: Detachable box, 10 rounds
Features: Glass bedded; NM gas cylinder; NM recoil spring guide; NM flash suppressor; walnut stock; stainless steel or carbon barrel; two-stage military trigger
MSRP. . . . . $2291–$2345

SCOUT SQUAD

Action: Semiautomatic
Stock: Walnut, composite
Barrel: 18 in.
Sights: National Match front military post sight; rear military aperture
Weight: 9 lb. 5 oz.
Caliber: 7.62 NATO, .308 Win.
Magazine: Detachable box, 10 rounds
Features: Mounted optical sight base; muzzle stabilizers; black or green fiberglass composite, American walnut stock or Mossy Oak camo stock; two-stage military trigger
MSRP. . . . . $1776–$1909

Springfield Armory

SPRINGFIELD ARMORY STANDARD M1A

STANDARD M1A

Action: Semiautomatic
Stock: Composite or walnut
Barrel: 22 in.
Sights: National Match military front post, adjustable rear aperture sight
Weight: 9 lb. 5 oz.
Caliber: 7.62 NATO, .308 Win.
Magazine: Detachable box, 10 rounds
Features: Black fiberglass with rubber buttplate, Mossy Oak stock with metal buttplate or American walnut with original military buttplate; two-stage military trigger
MSRP . . . . $1621–$1718

Stag Arms

STAG ARMS MODEL 3G

STAG ARMS MODEL 8

STAG ARMS MODEL 8T

MODEL 3G

Action: Semiautomatic
Stock: Synthetic
Barrel: 18 in.
Sights: None
Weight: N/A
Caliber: 5.56 NATO, .223 Rem.
Magazine: Detachable box, 30 rounds
Features: A2 flash hider; Picatinny rail; Magpul ACS buttstock; enhanced semiauto with a manganese phosphate coating
MSRP $1459

MODEL 8

Action: Gas-operated piston semiautomatic
Stock: Synthetic
Barrel: 20 in.
Sights: Midwest Industries front and rear flip-up
Weight: 6 lb. 14 oz.
Caliber: 5.56 NATO
Magazine: Detachable box, 30 rounds
Features: Right and left-hand available; six-position collapsible stock; chrome-lined barrel
MSRP $1145

MODEL 8T

Action: Semiautomatic
Stock: Synthetic
Barrel: 16 in.
Sights: Adjustable
Weight: N/A
Caliber: 5.56 NATO, .223 Rem.
Magazine: Detachable box, 30 rounds
Features: A2 flash hider; Picatinny rail; six-position stock; piston bolt carrier with a manganese phosphate coating
MSRP $1275

RIFLES

Steyr Arms

STEYR ARMS AUG/A3 SA USA

STEYR ARMS DUETT COMBO

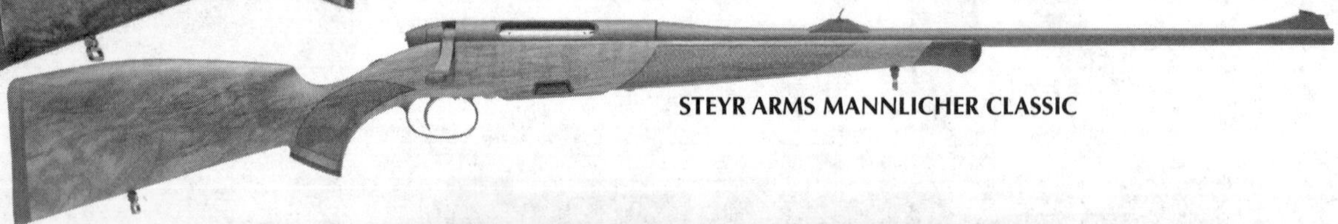

STEYR ARMS MANNLICHER CLASSIC

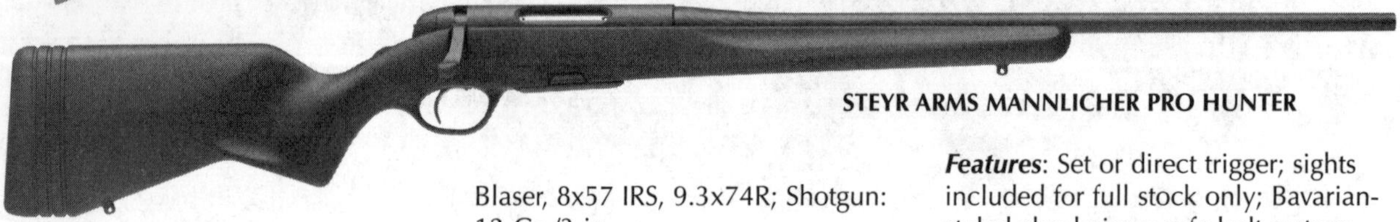

STEYR ARMS MANNLICHER PRO HUNTER

AUG/A3 SA USA

Action: Semiautomatic
Stock: Synthetic
Barrel: 16 in.
Sights: None
Weight: 8 lb. 2 oz.
Caliber: 5.56 NATO, .223 Rem.
Magazine: Detachable box, 30 rounds
Features: Synthetic black stock; lateral push-through type, locks trigger; Picatinny rail; changeable barrel; includes factory AUG sling and cleaning kit that fits inside butt stock
MSRP $2099

DUETT HUNTING COMBINATION RIFLE/ SHOTGUN

Action: Break-action
Stock: Walnut
Barrel: 23.6 in.
Sights: Open sights, 11mm prismatic scope mount rail
Weight: 6 lb. 6 oz.
Caliber: Rifle: .222 Rem., .243 Win., .308 Win., 7x65R, .30-06 Spfd., .30R Blaser, 8x57 IRS, 9.3x74R; Shotgun: 12 Ga./3-in.
Magazine: None
Features: Break-action over-under combination rifle/shotgun; dual gold-plated single-stage triggers; free-floated cold-hammer-forged barrels, Mannox finish; tang-mounted manual cocking lever; 5 models available; manual cocking system; European walnut stock; checkered forend and pistol grip
Standard: . . . . $3995–$7495

CLASSIC

Action: Bolt
Stock: European Walnut
Barrel: 20 in., 23.6 in., 25.6 in.
Sights: Open
Weight: 7 lb. 5 oz.
Caliber: .222 Rem., .223 Rem., .243 Win., 6.5x55 Swedish, .270 Win., 7x64 Brenneke, .25-06 Rem., .308 Win., .30-06 Spfd., 8x57 JS, 9.3x62 Mauser, 6.5x57
Magazine: Detachable box, 3 or 4 rounds
Features: Set or direct trigger; sights included for full stock only; Bavarian-styled cheekpiece; safe bolt system; case hardening surface finish on European walnut stock
MSRP: $2895

PRO HUNTER

Action: Bolt
Stock: Synthetic
Barrel: 20 in., 23.6 in., 25.6 in.
Sights: None
Weight: 7 lb. 5 oz.–8 lb. 3 oz.
Caliber: .222 Rem., .223 Rem., .243 Win., 6.5x55 Swedish, .25-06 Rem., .270 Win., 7x64 Brenneke, 7mm-08 Rem., .308 Win., .30-06 Spfd., 9.3x62 Mauser, .338 Fed. Mag. Magnum Caliber: .300 Win. Mag., 7mm Swam, .270 WSM, .300 WSM
Magazine: Detachable box
Features: Direct trigger, optionally set trigger; durable synthetic stock adjusted by spacers; Mannotm metal surface finish protects against corrosion; three-position safety
MSRP $1150
Stainless: $1250

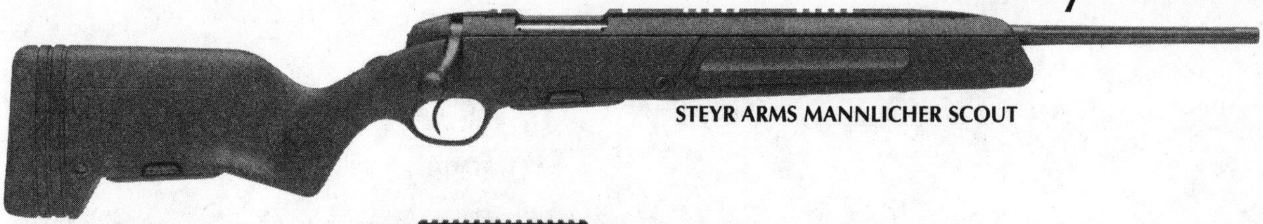

STEYR ARMS MANNLICHER SCOUT

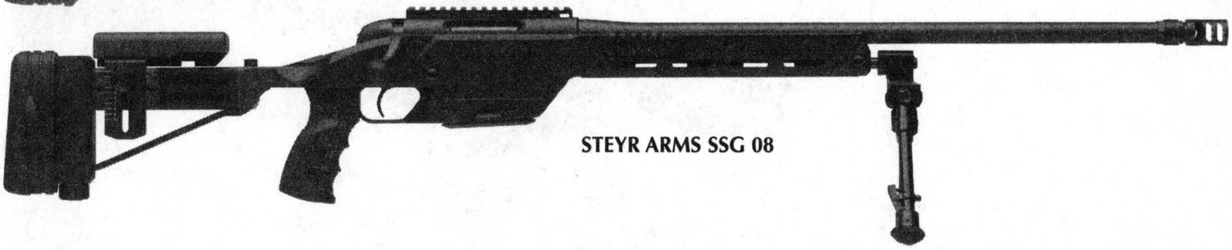

STEYR ARMS SSG 08

SCOUT

Action: Bolt
Stock: Synthetic
Barrel: 19 in.
Sights: None
Weight: 6 lb. 10 oz.
Caliber: .223 Rem., .243 Rem., 7mm-08 Rem., .308 Win.
Magazine: Detachable box, 5 rounds (optional 10 round magazine)
Features: Weaver scope mounting rail; set trigger or direct trigger; synthetic stock in black or gray wood imitation; optional bipod integrated into forearm; matte black or stainless steel finish on barrel
MSRP . . . . $1799–$2399

SSG 08

Action: Bolt
Stock: Synthetic
Barrel: 20 in., 23.6 in.
Sights: None
Weight: 5 lb. 8 oz.–5 lb. 11 oz.
Caliber: .300 Win. Mag., .308 Win.
Magazine: Detacable box, 10 rounds
Features: Direct trigger; Mannox TM system; high grade aluminum folding stock; adjustable cheekpiece and buttplate with height marking; ergonomic exchangeable pistol grip; UIT rail and Picatinny rail; muzzlebrake; Versa-Pod
MSRP . . . . $5895–$6795

Szecsei & Fuchs Fine Guns

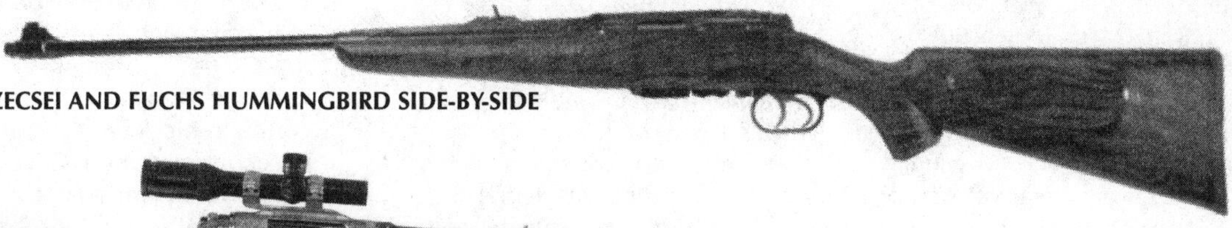

SZECSEI AND FUCHS HUMMINGBIRD SIDE-BY-SIDE

SZECSEI AND FUCHS AFRICAN QUEEN

DOUBLE-BARREL BOLT ACTION REPEATING RIFLE

Action: Double-barrel bolt
Stock: Hand selected, exclusive grade, Turkish walnut
Barrel: 20 in.–24 in.
Sights: Options of scopes or open sights
Weight: Small caliber rifles: approx. 7 lb. 8 oz.; Large caliber rifles: 9 lb. 12 oz.–12 lb.
Caliber: Available in many popular calibers, starting with .17 HMR all the way up to large game calibers, like Szecsei & Fuchs' custom .700 SSS
Magazine: Detachable box, 4+2 rounds
Features: The DBR, only ever custom built to personal taste, is crafted with great care and handiwork from the finest materials. Incorporating a design remarkable for its cleverness, the six-shot magazine feeds two rounds simultaneously, both of which can be fired by two quick pulls of the trigger. The triggers have integrated, noiseless double firing safety catches, the barrels may be requested in either octagon or round profile, and a one-piece bolt reloads two rounds with each cycle of the action. Starting with the selection of either side-by-side or over-and-under, the rifle can be personalized with exquisite custom engravings, optics, mounts and rings, extra magazines, and custom leather-bound cases. *As these rifles are custom order only, and with the fluctuation of the U.S. dollar, it is best to contact the sales representative listed in back to obtain a firm quotation. Average product delivery currently 16 months.
MSRP . . . . . . Small caliber rifles are $25000 and up. Large caliber rifles are approximately $100000 and up. Both small and large calibers are available in side-by-side and over/under rifle configurations (African Queen $190k as shown).

Tactical Rifles

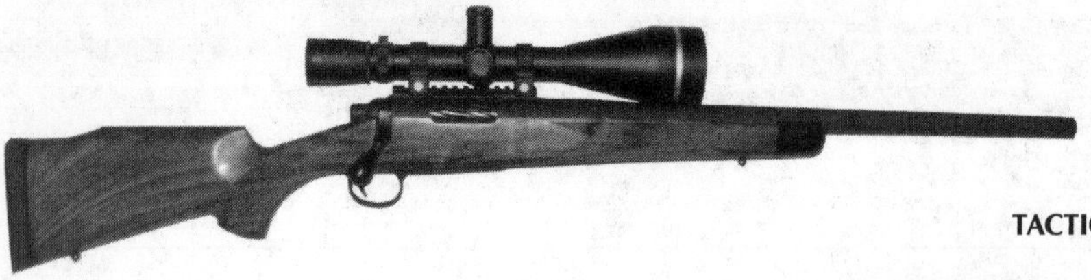

TACTICAL RIFLES CLASSIC SPORTER

TACTICAL RIFLES SPG

TACTICAL RIFLES TACTICAL L.R.

CLASSIC SPORTER

Action: Chimera bolt
Stock: Walnut
Barrel: 22 in.
Sights: None
Weight: 8 lb. 14 oz.
Caliber: .308 Win., .260 Rem., 6.5 Creedmoor and Lapua, .243 Win., 7mm-08 Rem. (short action); .30-06 Spfd., .270 Win., .300 Win. Mag., 7mm Rem. Mag. (long action)
Magazine: 4+1 rounds
Features: Chimera action is constructed from stainless steel with a hand-fitted spiral-groove bolt and "Magnum" extractor; Picatinny rail; XXX grade English walnut stock with 22 lpi checkering at grip and forearm; extreme environment matte black finish
MSRP $5895

SPECIAL PURPOSE GRENDEL (SPG)

Action: Semiautomatic
Stock: Magpul PRS
Barrel: 20 in.
Sights: None
Weight: 10 lb. 8 oz.
Caliber: 6.5 Grendel, .264 Les Baer Custom
Magazine: Detachable box, 17+1 rounds
Features: Stainless steel match grade barrel; SureFire muzzlebrake; enhanced upper and lower receivers; Magpul MOE pistol grip; Picatinny rail
MSRP $3195

TACTICAL L.R.

Action: Bolt, 700 Rem.
Stock: Synthetic
Barrel: 18 in.-26 in.
Sights: None
Weight: 12 lb.–13 lb. 6 oz.
Caliber: 7.62 NATO, .308 Win.
Magazine: Detachable box, 5 or 10 rounds
Features: Ergonomic thumbhole stock comes in black or green; raised cheekpiece; free-floating chromoly match grade barrel; ambidextrous sling swivel studs; soft rubber recoil pad; Picatinny rail; aluminum block chassis stock system; optional bipod
MSRP $3450

Taurus

TAURUS CTG29 CARBINE

CTG29 CARBINE

Action: Semiautomatic
Stock: Synthetic
Barrel: 16 in.
Sights: Adjustable
Weight: 6 lb. 10 oz.
Caliber: 9mm
Magazine: Detachable box, 10 rounds
Features: Close quarter carbine platform with a blowback-operated system that fires from the closed-bolt position; fixed front, adjustable rear sights; Picatinny rail; ambidextrous charging handle
MSRP $879

Taurus

TAURUS CTG240 CARBINE

CTG240 CARBINE

Action: Semiautomatic
Stock: Synthetic
Barrel: 16 in.
Sights: Adjustable
Weight: 6 lb. 10 oz.
Caliber: .40 S&W
Magazine: Detachable box, 10 rounds
Features: Close quarter carbine platform with a blowback-operated system that fires from the closed-bolt position; fixed front, adjustable rear sights; Picatinny rail; ambidextrous charging handle
MSRP $879

Taylor's & Co. Firearms

TAYLOR'S & CO. 1860 HENRY LEVER ACTION RIFLE

TAYLOR'S & CO. 1873 RIFLE - CHECKERED STRAIGHT STOCK

TAYLOR'S & CO. ALASKAN TAKE-DOWN MODEL

TAYLOR'S & CO. LIGHTNING SLIDE ACTION RIFLE

1860 HENRY LEVER ACTION RIFLE

Action: Lever
Stock: Walnut
Barrel: 24.25 in.
Sights: Open
Weight: 9 lb. 3 oz.
Caliber: .44-40 Win.
Magazine: Under-barrel tube, 9–13 rounds
Features: Brass frame; octagonal barrel with blued finish; includes sling swivels
MSRP . . . . $1411–$1723

1873 RIFLE - CHECKERED STRAIGHT STOCK

Action: Lever
Stock: Walnut
Barrel: 20 in.
Sights: Open
Weight: 8 lb. 8 oz.
Caliber: .357 Mag., .45 LC
Magazine: Under-barrel tube, 10+1 rounds
Features: Case-hardened frame; straight stock with checkering; available with full octagon barrel
MSRP $1318

1892 ALASKAN TAKE-DOWN MODEL

Action: Lever
Stock: Synthetic
Barrel: 16 in., 20 in.
Sights: Skinner rear
Weight: 6 lb. 10 oz.
Caliber: .44RM, .45 LC
Magazine: Under-barrel tube, 10 rounds
Features: Matte chrome finish; soft touch stock
MSRP $1366

LIGHTNING SLIDE ACTION RIFLE

Action: Slide
Stock: Walnut
Barrel: 24.25 in., 26 in.
Sights: Open
Weight: 6 lb. 3 oz.–6 lb. 8 oz.
Caliber: .45 LC, .44-40, .357 Mag.
Magazine: Under-barrel tube
Features: Case-hardened frame; walnut stock with checkered forend; octagonal barrel
MSRP . . . . $1645–$1992

Thompson/Center

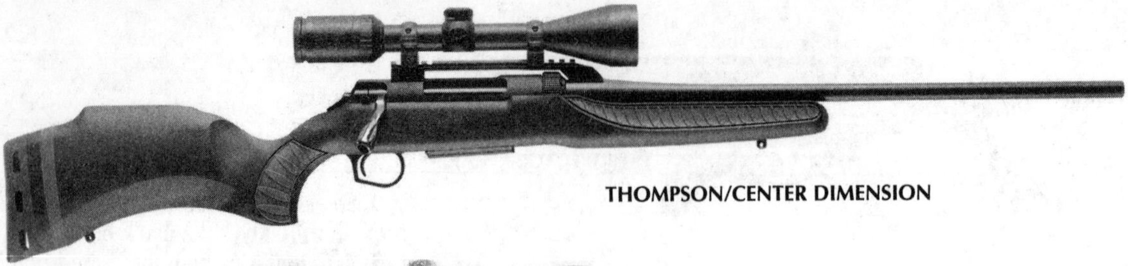

THOMPSON/CENTER DIMENSION

THOMPSON/CENTER PROHUNTER PREDATOR

THOMPSON/CENTER VENTURE COMPACT

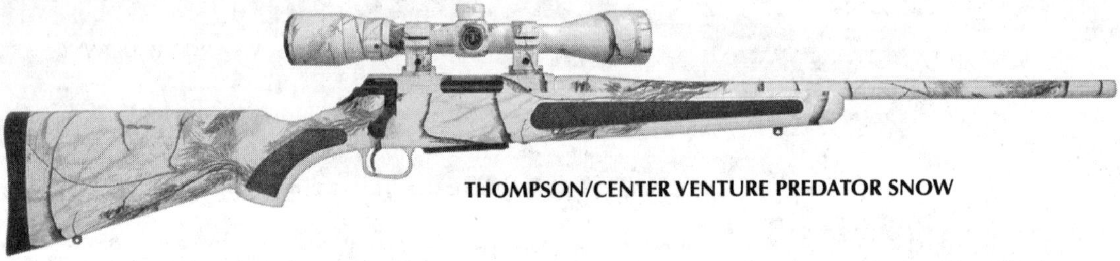

THOMPSON/CENTER VENTURE PREDATOR SNOW

RIFLES

DIMENSION

Action: Bolt
Stock: Composite
Barrel: 22 in., 24 in.
Sights: None
Weight: 7 lb.
Caliber: .204 Ruger, .223 Rem., .22-250 Rem., .243 Win., 7mm-08 Rem., .308 Win., .270 Win., .30-06 Spfd., 7mm Rem. Mag., .300 Win. Mag.
Magazine: Detachable box, 3 rounds
Features: A bolt action platform you can build on season after season; switch out barrels, bolts, magazines, and and other components such as scopes and mounts
MSRP $689

PROHUNTER PREDATOR

Action: Single-shot, break-open
Stock: Composite
Barrel: 28 in.
Sights: None
Weight: 7 lb. 12 oz.
Caliber: .204 Ruger, .223 Rem., .22-250 Rem., .308 Win.
Magazine: None
Features: Realtree MAX-1 camo composite stock and barrel; FlexTech; mounted and drilled for scopes
MSRP $882

VENTURE COMPACT

Action: Bolt
Stock: Composite
Barrel: 20 in.
Sights: None
Weight: 6 lb. 12 oz.
Caliber: .22-250 Rem., .243 Win., .308 Win., 7mm-08 Rem.
Magazine: Detachable box, 3+1 rounds
Features: Adjustable trigger; included spacer and buttpad; Hogue traction inlays; Melanite coated bolt; two position safety
MSRP $537

VENTURE PREDATOR SNOW

Action: Bolt
Stock: Composite
Barrel: 22 in., 24 in.
Sights: Bases for mounting scopes
Weight: 6 lb. 12 oz.
Caliber: 7mm-08 Rem., .243 Rem., .22-250 Rem., .308 Win.
Magazine: Detachable box, 3+1 rounds
Features: Adjustable trigger; Hogue rubber inlays; sling swivel studs; Weather Shield bolt handle
MSRP $638

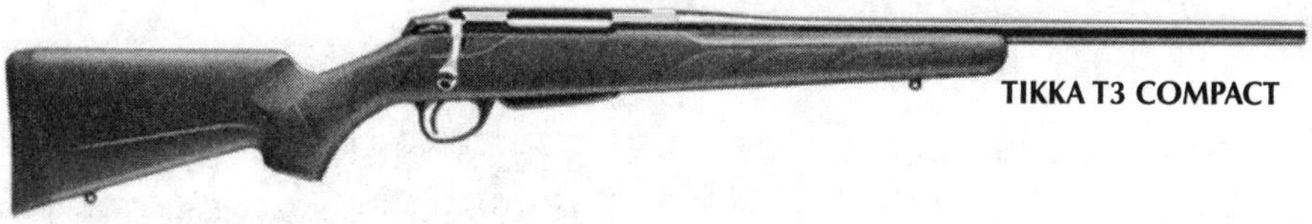

TIKKA T3 COMPACT

TIKKA T3 CTR

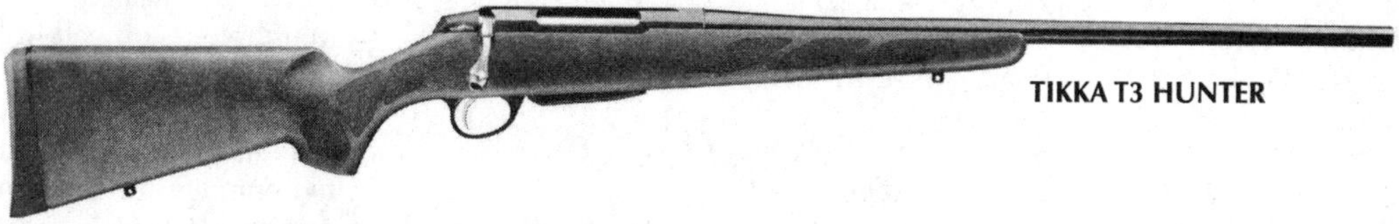

TIKKA T3 HUNTER

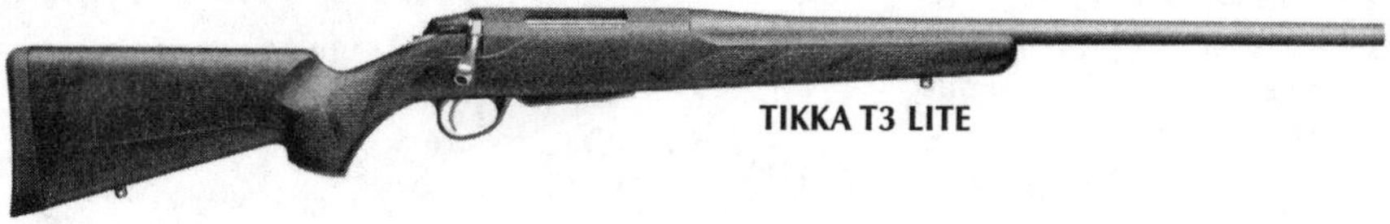

TIKKA T3 LITE

T3 COMPACT

Action: Bolt
Stock: Synthetic
Barrel: 20.1 in.
Sights: None
Weight: 6 lb. 10 oz.
Caliber: .22-250 Rem., .204 Rem., .222 Rem., .223 Rem., .243 Win., .308 Win., 7mm-08 Rem.
Magazine: 3–6 rounds
Features: Comes with 30mm spacer and larger recoil pad to enable longer length of pull; optional magazine; muzzle threaded for silencer on some calibers
MSRP $675

T3 CTR

Action: Bolt
Stock: Synthetic
Barrel: 20.1 in.
Sights: None
Weight: 7 lb. 8 oz.
Caliber: .260 Rem., .308 Win.
Magazine: Detachable box, 10 rounds
Features: Muzzle threaded for silencer; Picatinny rail; aluminium trigger guard where the magazine release lever has been positioned to enable fast magazine change
MSRP $1095

T3 HUNTER

Action: Bolt
Stock: Walnut
Barrel: 20 in., 22.4 in., 24.4 in.
Sights: None
Weight: 6 lb. 10 oz.–7 lb.
Caliber: .204 Ruger, .222 Rem, .223 Rem., .22-250 Rem., .243 Win., .260 Rem., 7mm-08 Rem., .308 Win., .338 Federal, .25-06 Rem., 6.5x55 Swedish, .270 Win., 7x64 Brenneke, .30-06 Spfd., 8x57IS, 9.3x62 Mauser, 7mm Rem. Mag., .300 SM, .338 Win. Mag., .270 WSM, .300 WSM
Magazine: Detachable box, 4 or 5 rounds
Features: Sling swivels; free-floating cold-hammer-forged barrel; two locking Lug T3 action; two-stage safety; single-set trigger; walnut stock in oil finish and optional matte lacquered stock; integral scope mounts
MSRP $775

T3 LITE

Action: Bolt
Stock: Synthetic
Barrel: 20 in., 22.4 in., 24.4 in.
Sights: None
Weight: 6 lb.–6 lb. 6 oz.
Caliber: .204 Ruger, .222 Rem., .223 Rem., .22-250 Rem., .243 Win., .260 Rem., 7mm-08 Rem., .308 Win., .338 Federal, .25-06 Rem., 6.5x55 Swedish, .270 Win., 7x64 Brenneke, .30-06 Spfd., 8x57IS, 9.3x62 Mauser, 7mm Rem. Mag., .300 Win. Mag., .338 Win. Mag., .270 WSM, .300 WSM
Magazine: Detachable box, 4 or 5 rounds
Features: Stainless steel bolt; two-stage safety; single-set trigger; fiberglass synthetic stock in black; Weaver scope mount bases; free-floating, cold-hammer-forged barrel
MSRP . . . . $675–$725
Stainless: . . . . $775–$825
Stainless, LH: $845

Tikka

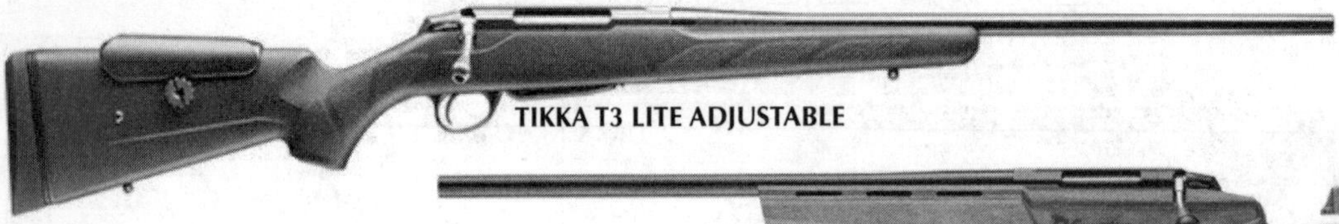
TIKKA T3 LITE ADJUSTABLE

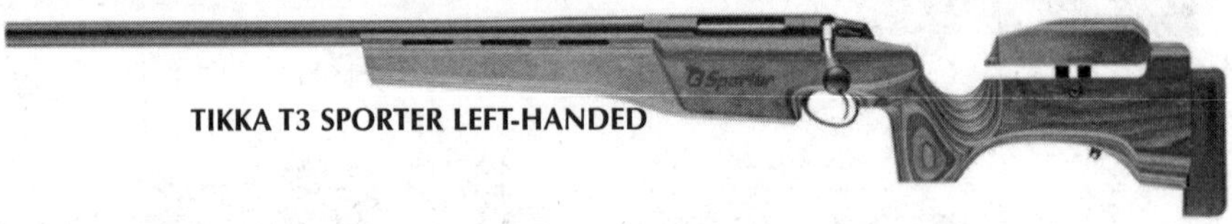
TIKKA T3 SPORTER LEFT-HANDED

T3 LITE ADJUSTABLE

Action: Bolt
Stock: Synthetic
Barrel: 20.1 in.–24.4 in.
Sights: None
Weight: 6 lb.–6 lb. 6 oz.
Caliber: .22-250 Rem., .25-06 Rem., .30-06 Spfd., .204 Rem., .222 Rem., .223 Rem., .243 Win., .260 Rem., .270 Win., .270 WSM, .300 Win. Mag., .300 WSM, .308 Win., .338 Fed., .338 Win. Mag., 6.5x55 Swedish, 7mm Rem. Mag., 7mm-08 Rem., 7x64 Brenneke, 8x57IS, 9.3x62 Mauser
Magazine: 3–6 rounds
Features: Adjustable cheek piece; left-handed available; optional magazine; muzzle threaded for silencer on some calibers
MSRP. $775

T3 SPORTER

Action: Bolt
Stock: Laminated wood, oiled
Barrel: 20 in., 24 in.
Sights: Scope rail and threads for Weaver-type scope rail
Weight: 9 lb.–9 lb. 11 oz.
Caliber: .222 Rem., .223 Rem., 6.5x55 Swedish, .260 Rem., .308 Win.
Magazine: 5 or 6 rounds
Features: Adjustable cheekpiece; adjustable recoil pad in length and height; various rail placements that allow rifle to be carried in biathlon style; metal parts are matte blued; limited number of left-handed models imported to U.S.
MSRP. $1595
Left-handed: $1755

Troy Defense

M7A1 PDW

Action: Semiautomatic
Stock: Synthetic
Barrel: 7.5 in.
Sights: Adjustable
Weight: 5 lb. 13 oz.
Caliber: 5.56 NATO
Magazine: Detachable box, 30 rounds
Features: Ambidextrous safety selector; nickel boron PDW bolt carrier group; Picatinny rail
MSRP. . . . . $1749–$1849

TROY DEFENSE M7A1 PDW

Turnbull Manufacturing Co.

TURNBULL MFG. CO. TAR-15

TAR-15

Action: Semiautomatic
Stock: Black Walnut
Barrel: 16 in.
Sights: None
Weight: 8 lb. 8 oz.
Caliber: .223 Rem.
Magazine: Detachable box, 5 or 10 rounds
Features: AR-15 gas impingement system; 8620 carbon steel receivers; color case hardened steel; oversized integral trigger guard; picatinny rail; screw on muzzle brake; also available in 7.62x39 Warsaw and 300 BLK
MSRP. $2750

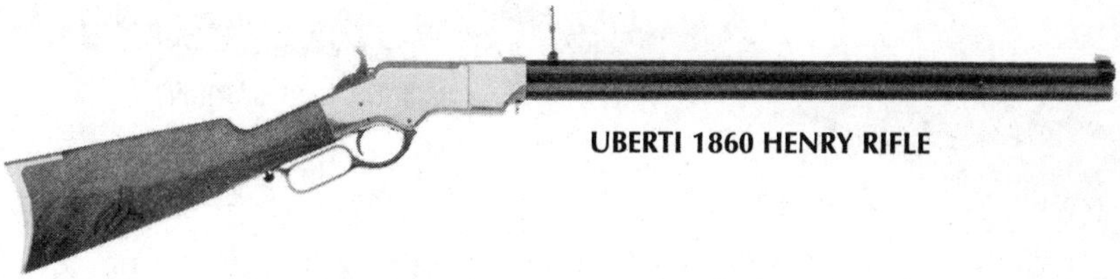
UBERTI 1860 HENRY RIFLE

1860 HENRY RIFLE

Action: Lever
Stock: Walnut
Barrel: 18.5 in., 24.5 in.
Sights: Adjustable
Weight: 9 lb.
Caliber: .45 Colt, .44-40 Win.
Magazine: Under-barrel tube, 8+1 or 13+1 rounds
Features: Blued or standard buttplate; case-hardened lever and frame; A-grade walnut stock; octagonal barrel
MSRP . . . . $1429–$1459

UBERTI 1866 YELLOWBOY

1866 YELLOWBOY

Action: Lever
Stock: Walnut
Barrel: 19 in., 20 in., 24.25 in.
Sights: Adjustable
Weight: 8 lb. 3 oz.
Caliber: .45 Colt, .44-40 Win., .38 Spl.
Magazine: Under barrel tube, 10+1 or 13+1 rounds
Features: Brass forend nose cap; solid brass crescent buttplate; case-hardened lever; brass frame and buttplate
MSRP . . . . $1119–$1169

UBERTI 1871 ROLLING BLOCK HUNTER CARBINE

UBERTI 1871 ROLLING BLOCK HUNTER RIMFIRE

1871 ROLLING BLOCK HUNTER CARBINE

Action: Rolling block
Stock: Walnut
Barrel: 22 in.
Sights: Fixed
Weight: 4 lb. 8 oz.
Caliber: .38-55, .30-30 Win., .45-70 Govt.
Magazine: None
Features: Rubber buttpad; case-colored receiver
MSRP $799

1871 ROLLING BLOCK HUNTER RIMFIRE

Action: Rolling block
Stock: Walnut
Barrel: 22 in.
Sights: Adjustable
Weight: 4 lb. 8 oz.
Caliber: .22LR, .22 Mag., .17 HMR
Magazine: None
Features: Round blued barrel; brass trigger guard; case-hardened frame; A-grade walnut stock with rubber buttpad
MSRP $709

1873 COMPETITION

Action: Lever
Stock: Wood
Barrel: 20 in.
Sights: Adjustable
Weight: 8 lb.
Caliber: .357 Mag., .45 Colt
Magazine: Under-barrel tube, 10+1 rounds
Features: Octagonal barrel; A-grade walnut; lever lock; side loading gate for ease of loading
MSRP $1499

UBERTI 1873 COMPETITION

Uberti

UBERTI 1873 CARBINE

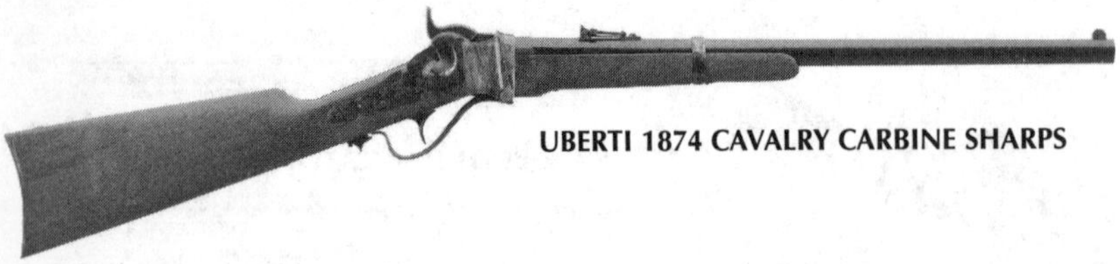

UBERTI 1874 CAVALRY CARBINE SHARPS

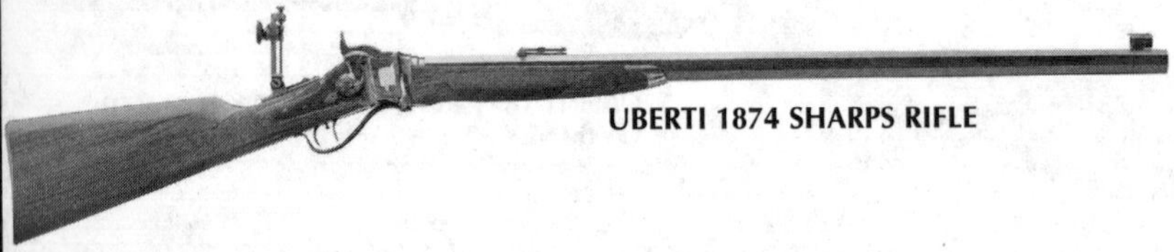

UBERTI 1874 SHARPS RIFLE

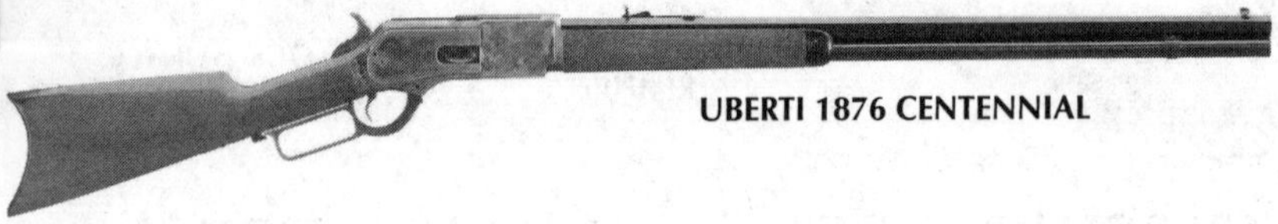

UBERTI 1876 CENTENNIAL

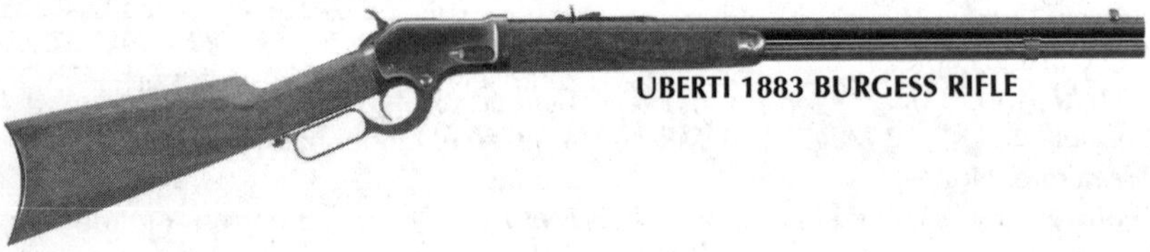

UBERTI 1883 BURGESS RIFLE

1876 CENTENNIAL

Action: Lever
Stock: Walnut
Barrel: 28 in.
Sights: Adjustable
Weight: 10 lb.
Caliber: .45-60, .45-75, .50-95
Magazine: Under-barrel tube, 11+1 rounds
Features: Case-hardened frame and lever; blued buttplate; octagonal barrel; straight stock
MSRP. $1609

1883 BURGESS RIFLE & CARBINE

Action: Lever
Stock: Walnut
Barrel: 20 in. (carbine), 25.5 in. (rifle)
Sights: Fixed
Weight: 7 lb. 10 oz.–8 lb. 2 oz.
Caliber: .45 Colt
Magazine: Under-barrel tube, 10 or 13 rounds
Features: Case-hardened, round barrel; straight grip
MSRP. $1499

1873 RIFLE & CARBINE

Action: Lever
Stock: Walnut
Barrel: 16.1 in., 18 in., 19 in., 20 in., 24.5 in.
Sights: Adjustable
Weight: 7 lb. 3 oz.–8 lb. 3 oz.
Caliber: .45 Colt, .357 Mag., .44-44
Magazine: Under-barrel tube, 9+1, 10+1 or 13+1 rounds
Features: Octagonal barrel on rifle; round barrel on carbine and trapper; A-grade walnut with checkered pistol grip and forend
Trapper: $1219
Rifle: $1259
Carbine: . . . . $1219–$1309
Sporting: $1259

1874 CAVALRY CARBINE SHARPS

Action: Falling block
Stock: Walnut
Barrel: 22 in.
Sights: Creedmoor Sight
Weight: 8 lb.
Caliber: .45-70 Govt.
Magazine: None
Features: Round blued barrel; case-hardened levers and blued buttplate
MSRP. $1809

1874 SHARPS RIFLE

Action: Falling block
Stock: Walnut
Barrel: 32 in., 34 in.
Sights: Creedmoor Sight
Weight: 10 lb. 4 oz.–11 lb.
Caliber: .45-70 Govt.
Magazine: None
Features: Blued octagonal barrel; checkered walnut stock; case-hardened, except Extra Deluxe model; double-set trigger; pewter forend cap
Special: $2019
Deluxe: $3129
Down Under:. $2539
Buffalo Hunter: $2539
Extra Deluxe: $4999

UBERTI 1885 HIGH-WALL SINGLE-SHOT SPECIAL SPORTING MODEL

UBERTI LIGHTNING

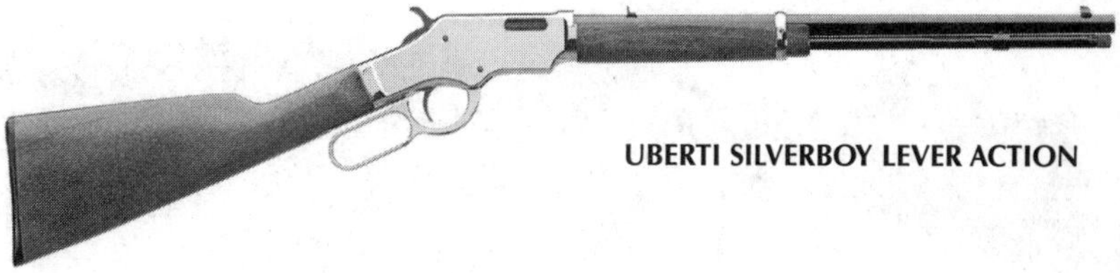

UBERTI SILVERBOY LEVER ACTION

UBERTI SPRINGFIELD TRAPDOOR CARBINE

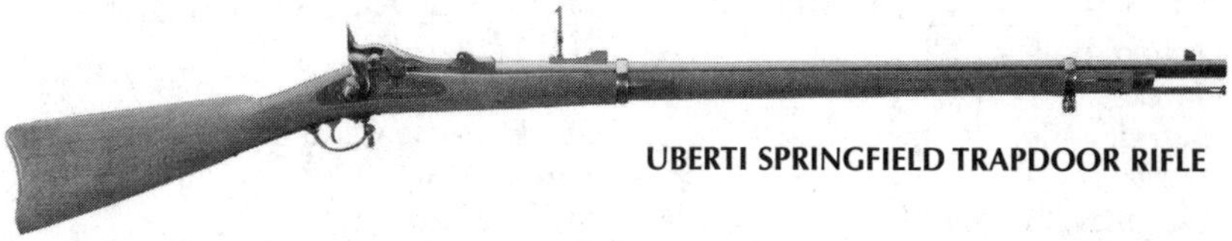

UBERTI SPRINGFIELD TRAPDOOR RIFLE

1885 HIGH-WALL SINGLE-SHOT

Action: Falling block
Stock: Walnut
Barrel: 28 in., 30 in., 32 in.
Sights: Adjustable
Weight: 9 lb. 5 oz. (carbine), 10 lb.
Caliber: .45-70 Govt., .45-90, .45-120
Magazine: None
Features: Case-hardened frame and lever; blued buttplate; octagonal barrel; carbine model has round barrel; carbine and sporting rifle have straight stock
Carbine: $1009
Sporting Rifle: . . . . $1009–$1139
Special Sporting . . . . . . $1009–$1279

LIGHTNING

Action: Pump
Stock: Walnut
Barrel: 20 in., 24.25 in.
Sights: Adjustable
Weight: 6 lb. 3 oz.–6 lb. 8 oz.
Caliber: .45 Colt, .357 Mag.
Magazine: Under-barrel tube, 10+1 round (short rifle), 13+1 rounds (standard)
Features: Case-hardened frame and trigger guard; octagonal barrel
MSRP $1319

SILVERBOY LEVER ACTION

Action: Lever
Stock: Walnut
Barrel: 19 in.
Sights: Fixed
Weight: 5 lb. 13 oz.
Caliber: .22LR, .22 Mag.
Magazine: Under-barrel tube, 15+1 rounds
Features: Chrome-plated alloy reciever; walnut straight stock; cartridge-control mechanism allows controlled-round-feed; blued barrel
MSRP . . . . $559–$599

SPRINGFIELD TRAPDOOR CARBINE

Action: Hinged breech
Stock: Walnut
Barrel: 22 in.
Sights: Adjustable
Weight: 7 lb. 5 oz.
Caliber: .45-70 Govt.
Magazine: None
Features: Blued steel, case-hardened breechblock and buttplate; fitted with sliding ring and bar for cavalryman to carry it clipped to carbine sling
MSRP $1669

SPRINGFIELD TRAPDOOR RIFLE

Action: Hinged breech
Stock: Walnut
Barrel: 32.5 in.
Sights: Adjustable
Weight: 8 lb. 13 oz.
Caliber: .45-70 Govt.
Magazine: None
Features: Blued steel, case-hardened breechblock and buttplate
MSRP $1669

Volquartsen Custom

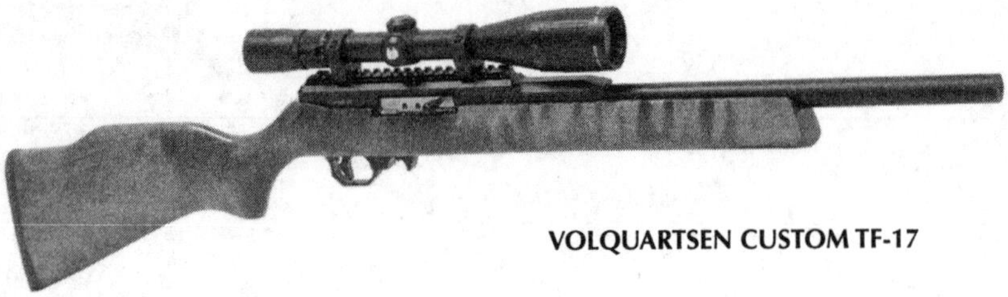

VOLQUARTSEN CUSTOM TF-17

TF-17 & TF-22

Action: Semiautomatic
Stock: Ambidextrous birch
Barrel: 18.5 in.
Sights: Picatinny rail
Weight: 8 lb. 8 oz.
Caliber: .17 HMR, .22 WMR
Magazine: Rotary mag, 9 rounds
Features: Blowback design, TG2000 trigger unit with 2.25-lb. pull; black stainless barrel
MSRP. $1200

RIFLES

Weatherby

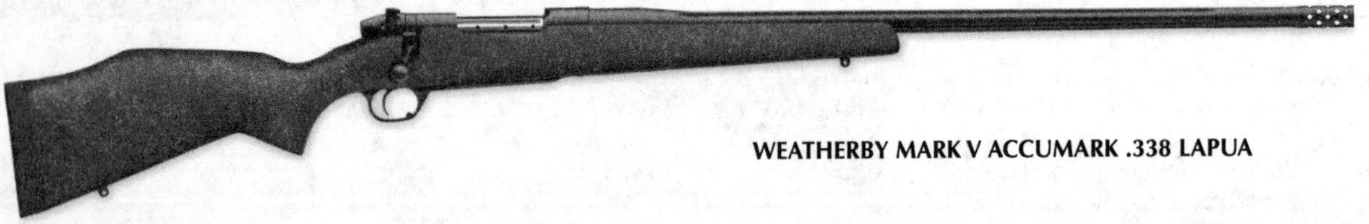

WEATHERBY MARK V ACCUMARK .338 LAPUA

WEATHERBY MARK V ACCUMARK RC RIFLE

MARK V ACCUMARK

Action: Bolt
Stock: Composite
Barrel: 24 in., 26 in., 28 in.
Sights: None
Weight: 7 lb. 4 oz.–9 lb.
Caliber: .270 Win., .208 Win., .257 Wby. Mag., .270 Wby. Mag., 7mm Rem. Mag., 7mm Wby. Mag., .300 Win. Mag., .300 Wby. Mag., .30-378 Wby. Mag., .340 Wby. Mag., .247 Wby. Mag, .338 Lapua Mag.
Magazine: 2+1, 3+1 or 5+1 rounds
Features: Adjustable trigger; hand-laminated raised comb; Monte Carlo composite stock with matte gel coat finish and spider web accents; Pachmayr decelerator pad; button rifled; CNC-machined 6061 T-6 aluminum bedding plate; cocking indicator; fluted bolt body
MSRP. $2100

MARK V ACCUMARK RC RIFLE

Action: Bolt
Stock: Monte Carlo composite
Barrel: 24 in., 26 in., 28 in.
Sights: None
Weight: 7 lb. 4 oz.–9lb.
Caliber: .240 Wby. Mag., .270 Win., .308 Win., .30-06 Spfd., .257 Wby. Mag., .270 Wby. Mag., 7mm Rem. Mag., 7mm Wby. Mag., .300 Win. Mag., .300 Wby. Mag., .30-378 Wby. Mag., .338-378 Wby. Mag., .340 Wby. Mag., .338 Lapua
Magazine: 5+1, 3+1, or 2+1 rounds
Features: "Range Certified" model comes with a SUB-MOA guarantee; button-rifled stainless steel barrel; free floated barrel with a recessed target crown; Pachmayr Decelerator pad
MSRP. . . . .$2400–$2700

WEATHERBY MARK V DELUXE

WEATHERBY MARK V FIBERMARK

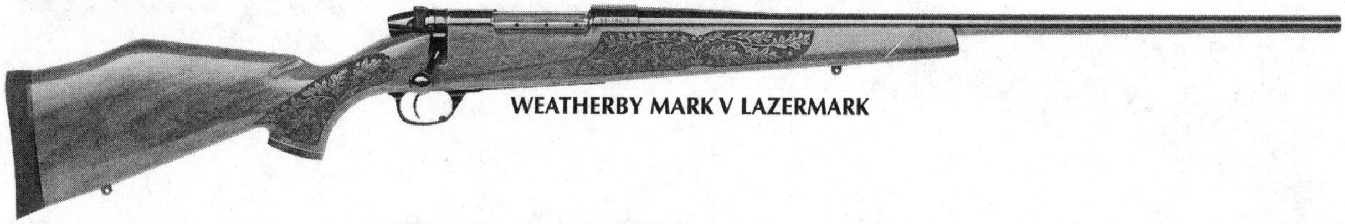

WEATHERBY MARK V LAZERMARK

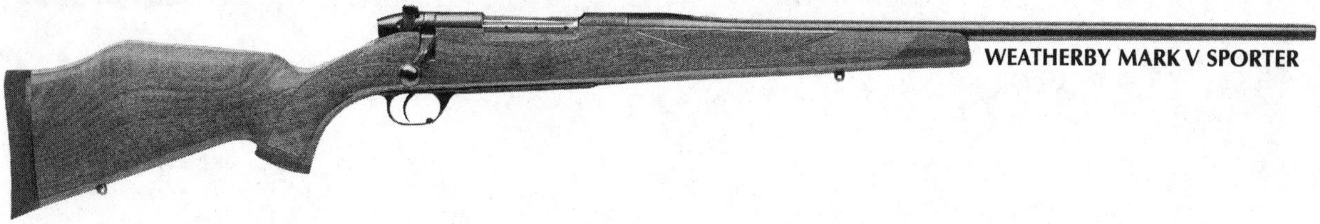

WEATHERBY MARK V SPORTER

MARK V DELUXE

Action: Bolt
Stock: Walnut
Barrel: 24 in., 26 in., 28 in.
Sights: None
Weight: 6 lb. 12 oz.–10 lb.
Caliber: .270 Win., .308 Win., .30–06 Spfd., .257 Wby. Mag., .270 Wby. Mag., 7mm Wby. Mag., .300 Wby. Mag., .340 Wby. Mag., .378 Wby. Mag., .416 Wby. Mag., .460 Wby. Mag.
Magazine: 2+1, 3+1, 5+1 rounds
Features: Adjustable trigger; walnut Monte Carlo stock with rosewood forend and pistol grip cap and maplewood spacers; blued metalwork in high luster finish; Pachmayr decelerator pad
MSRP $2400

MARK V FIBERMARK

Action: Bolt
Stock: Composite
Barrel: 24 in., 26 in., 28 in.
Sights: None
Weight: 6 lb.–8 lb. 8 oz.
Caliber: .240 Wby. Mag., .270 Win., .30-06 Spfd., .257 Wby. Mag., .270 Wby. Mag., 7mm Rem. Mag., 7mm Wby. Mag., .300 Win. Mag., .300 Wby. Mag., .30-378 Wby. Mag., .340 Wby. Mag., .375 H&H Mag.
Magazine: 2+1, 3+1 rounds
Features: Adjustable trigger; pillar-bedded, hand-laminated raised comb Monte Carlo composite stock with strategically placed bedding points assures consistent, repeatable accuracy
MSRP $1500

MARK V LAZERMARK

Action: Bolt
Stock: Walnut
Barrel: 26 in.
Sights: None
Weight: 8 lb. 8 oz.
Caliber: .257 Wby. Mag., .270 Wby. Mag., 7mm Rem. Mag., 7mm Wby. Mag., .300 Win. Mag., .300 Wby. Mag.
Magazine: 3+1 rounds
Features: Adjustable trigger; hand-selected, raised comb Monte Carlo stock with laser-carved oak leaf pattern; blued metalwork in high luster finish; Pachmayr decelerator pad
MSRP $2600

MARK V SPORTER

Action: Bolt
Stock: Walnut
Barrel: 24 in., 26 in.
Sights: None
Weight: 8 lb.
Caliber: .257 Wby. Mag., .270 Wby. Mag., 7mm Rem. Mag., 7mm Wby. Mag., .300 Win. Mag., .300 Wby. Mag., .340 Wby. Mag.
Magazine: 3+1 rounds
Features: Adjustable trigger; raised comb Monte Carlo walnut stock with satin finish; features fine line diamond point checkering and rosewood forend and grip cap; bead blasted, blued metalwork with low luster finish; Pachmayr decelerator pad
MSRP $1600

Weatherby

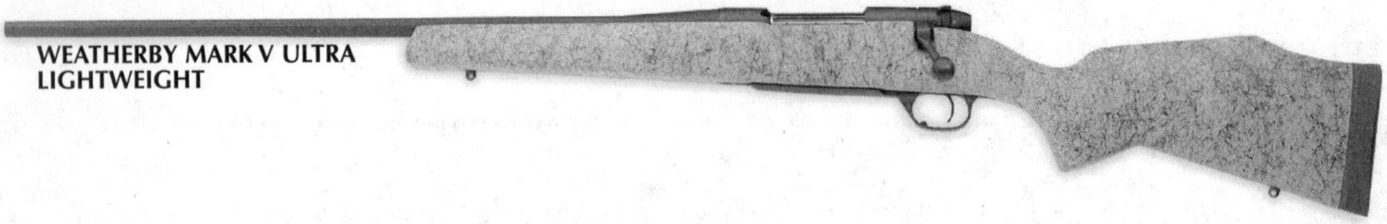

WEATHERBY MARK V ULTRA LIGHTWEIGHT

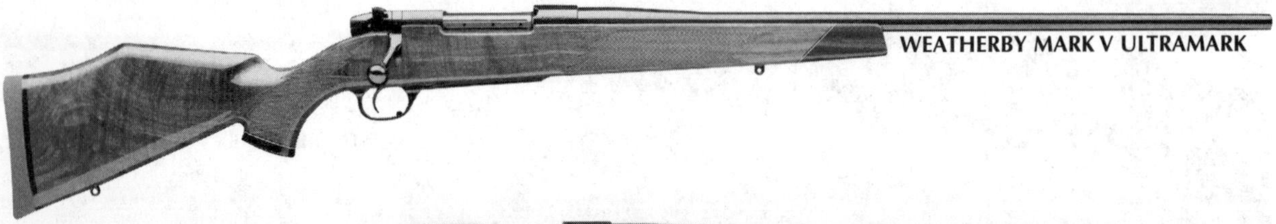

WEATHERBY MARK V ULTRAMARK

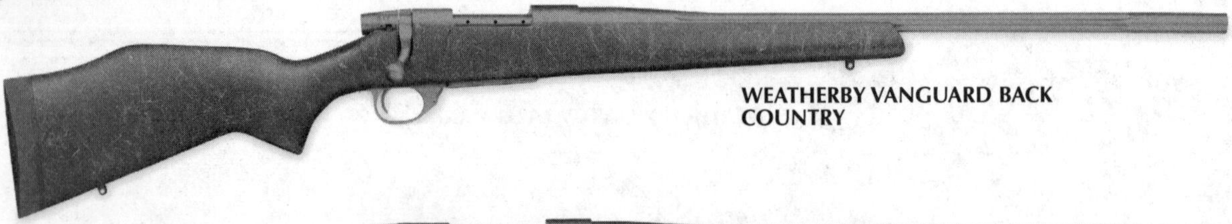

WEATHERBY VANGUARD BACK COUNTRY

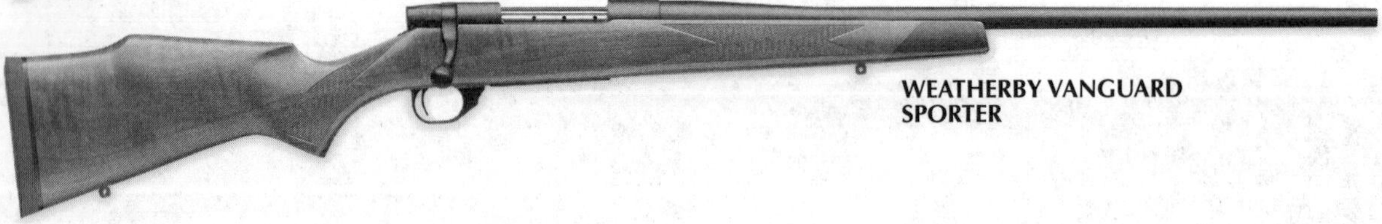

WEATHERBY VANGUARD SPORTER

MARK V ULTRA LIGHTWEIGHT

Action: Bolt
Stock: Composite
Barrel: 24 in., 26 in.
Sights: None
Weight: 5.75 lb.–6.75 lb.
Caliber: .243 Win., .240 Wby. Mag., .25-06 Rem., .270 Win., 7mm-08 Rem., .308 Win., .30-06 Spfd., .257 Wby. Mag., 7mm Rem. Mag., 7mm Wby. Mag., .300 Win. Mag., .257 Wby. Mag., .300 Wby. Mag.
Magazine: 3+1, 5+1 rounds
Features: Adjustable trigger; contoured fluted stainless steel barrel, blackened to reduce glare; Bell & Carlson composite stock with spider web accents; CNC-machined 6061 T-6 aluminum bedding plate; one-piece forged bolt; Pachmayr decelerator pad
MSRP $2100

MARK V ULTRAMARK

Action: Bolt
Stock: Walnut
Barrel: 26 in.
Sights: None
Weight: 8 lb. 8 oz.
Caliber: .257 Wby. Mag., .300 Wby. Mag.
Magazine: 3+1 rounds
Features: Adjustable trigger; hand-selected, AAA fancy exhibition grade walnut stock; features 20 lpi checkering, maplewood/ebony spacers and rosewood forend and grip caps; blued metalwork in high luster finish; Pachmayr decelerator pad
MSRP $3200

VANGUARD BACK COUNTRY

Action: Bolt
Stock: Monte Carlo composite
Barrel: 24 in.
Sights: None
Weight: 6 lb. 12 oz.
Caliber: .240 Wby. Mag., .270 Win., .257 Wby. Mag., .30-06 Spfd., .300 Win. Mag., .300 Wby. Mag.
Magazine: 5+1 or 3+1 rounds
Features: SUB-MOA guarantee; chrome moly metalwork with Cerakote Tactical Grey finish; pillar-bedded stock; two-stage trigger; 3-position safety; auxiliary trigger sear; Pachmayr Decelerator pad
MSRP $1429

VANGUARD SPORTER

Action: Bolt
Stock: Walnut
Barrel: 24 in.
Sights: None
Weight: 7 lb. 4 oz.–7 lb. 8 oz.
Caliber: .223 Rem., .22-250 Rem., .243 Win., .25-06 Rem., .270 Win., 7mm-08 Rem., .308 Win., .30-06 Spfd., .257 Wby. Mag., .270 WSM, 7mm Rem. Mag., .300 Win. Mag., .300 WSM, .300 Wby. Mag., .338 Win. Mag.
Magazine: 3+1, 5+1 rounds
Features: Two-stage trigger; raised comb, Monte Carlo stock with satin urethane finish; hand-selected A fancy grade Turkish walnut; rosewood forend; low luster, matte blued metalwork; fine line diamond point checkering; low density recoil pad
MSRP $849

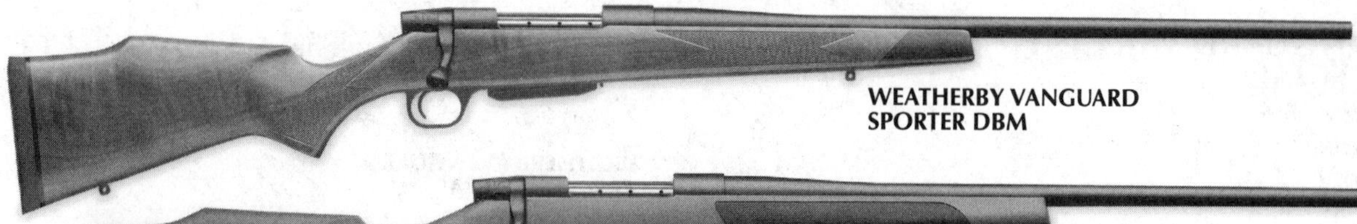

WEATHERBY VANGUARD SPORTER DBM

WEATHERBY VANGUARD SYNTHETIC

WEATHERBY VANGUARD SYNTHETIC PACKAGE

WEATHERBY VANGUARD SYNTHETIC DBM

VANGUARD SPORTER DBM

Action: Bolt
Stock: Walnut Monte Carlo
Barrel: 24 in.
Sights: None
Weight: 7 lb. 4 oz.
Caliber: .25-06 Rem., .270 Win., .30-06 Spfd.
Magazine: Detachable box, 3 rounds
Features: Rosewood forend; raised comb; satin urethane finish; matte blued metalwork; adjustable trigger
MSRP $929

VANGUARD SYNTHETIC

Action: Bolt
Stock: Synthetic
Barrel: 24 in.
Sights: None
Weight: 7 lb. 4 oz.
Caliber: 6.5 Creedmoor
Magazine: Internal, 6+1 rounds
Features: Lightweight, composite Monte Carlo Griptonite stock; matte bead blasted blued finish; three-position safety; also available in .25-06 Rem., .30-06 Spfd., .223 Rem., .240 Wby. Mag., .243 Win., .257 Wby. Mag.; .300 Wby. Mag., .300 Win. Mag., .308 Win., .338 Win. Mag., 7mm Rem. Mag., and 7mm-08 Rem.
MSRP $649

VANGUARD SYNTHETIC PACKAGE

Action: Bolt
Stock: Synthetic
Barrel: 24 in.
Sights: 3–9x42mm Redfield Revenge scope
Weight: 8 lb. 4 oz.–8 lb. 8 oz.
Caliber: .223 Rem., .22-250 Rem., .243 Win., .25-06 Rem., .270 Win., 7mm-08 Rem., .308 Win., .30-06 Spfd., .257 Wby. Mag., 7mm Rem. Mag., .300 Win. Mag., .300 Wby. Mag., .338 Win. Mag.
Magazine: 5+1 or 3+1 rounds
Features: SUB-MOA guarantee; mounted and boresighted Redfield scope with matte finish and 4-plex reticle; Talley-designed mounts; adjustable nylon sling; injection-molded scoped rifle case
MSRP $999

VANGUARD SYNTHETIC DBM

Action: Bolt
Stock: Injection-molded Monte Carlo
Barrel: 24 in.
Sights: None
Weight: 7 lb. 4 oz.
Caliber: .25-06 Rem., .270 Win., .30-06 Spfd.
Magazine: Detachable box, 3 rounds
Features: Matte bead blasted blued metalwork; low density recoil pad; two-stage trigger
MSRP $749

Weatherby

VANGUARD VARMINT SPECIAL

Action: Bolt
Stock: Composite
Barrel: 22 in.
Sights: None
Weight: 8 lb. 12 oz.
Caliber: .223 Rem., .22-250 Rem., .308 Win.
Magazine: 5+1 rounds

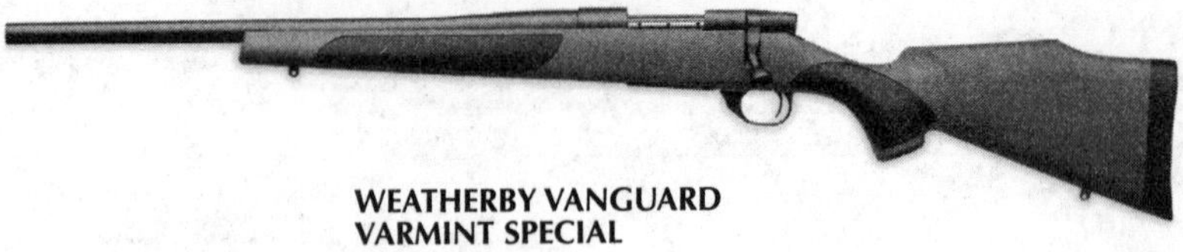

WEATHERBY VANGUARD VARMINT SPECIAL

Features: Adjustable trigger; Monte Carlo composite stock in Griptonite; matte bead blasted blued metalwork; features recessed target crown to enhance accuracy and protect rifling
MSRP $849

Wilson Combat

RECON TACTICAL

Action: Semiautomatic
Stock: Synthetic tactical
Barrel: 16 in.
Sights: Optional rail
Weight: 7 lb.
Caliber: 5.56 NATO, 6.8 SPC, 300 BLK, 7.62x40WT, .458 SOCOM
Magazine: Detachable box, 30 rounds
Features: Match grade medium weight stainless steel barrel; forged 7075 upper (flat top) and lower receiver; mid-length gas system with low-profile gas block; Wilson Combat T.R.I.M. rail; ergo pistol grip
MSRP $2300

WILSON COMBAT RECON TACTICAL

Winchester Repeating Arms

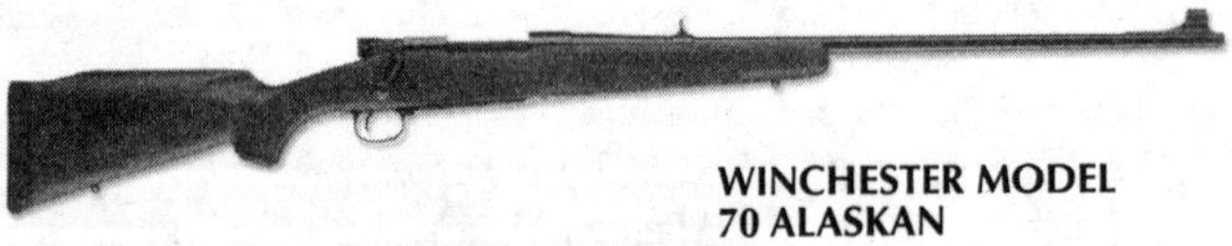

WINCHESTER MODEL 70 ALASKAN

WINCHESTER MODEL 70 COYOTE LIGHT

WINCHESTER MODEL 70 FEATHERWEIGHT COMPACT

MODEL 70 ALASKAN

Action: Bolt
Stock: Walnut
Barrel: 25 in.
Sights: Open
Weight: 8 lb. 8 oz.
Caliber: .30-06 Spfd., .300 Win. Mag. .338 Win. Mag., .375 HH Mag.
Magazine: None
Features: Satin finish Monte Carlo walnut stock with cut checkering; folding adjustable rear sight with hooded gold bead front sight; recessed target crown
MSRP . . . . $1340–$1380

MODEL 70 COYOTE LIGHT

Action: Bolt
Stock: Composite
Barrel: 24 in.
Sights: None
Weight: 7 lb. 8 oz.
Caliber: .22-250 Rem., .243 Win., .308 Win., .300 WSM, .270 WSM, 325 WSM
Magazine: 3 rounds
Features: Bipod mounting studs; matte-blued receiver and medium-heavy fluted stainless barrel mount; Pachmayr Decelerator
MSRP . . . . $1200–$1240

MODEL 70 FEATHERWEIGHT COMPACT

Action: Bolt
Stock: Walnut
Barrel: 20 in.
Sights: None
Weight: 6 lb. 8 oz.
Caliber: .22-250 Rem., .243 Win., 7mm-08 Rem., .308 Win.
Magazine: 5 rounds
Features: Pachmayr decelerator recoil pad; action is drilled and tapped for optics
MSRP $940

Winchester Repeating Arms

WINCHESTER MODEL 70 SAFARI EXPRESS

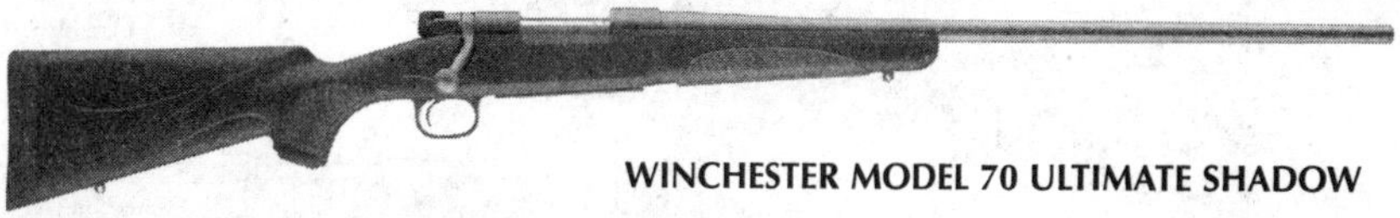

WINCHESTER MODEL 70 ULTIMATE SHADOW

WINCHESTER REPEATING ARMS MODEL 70
ULTIMATE SHADOW HUNTER SS

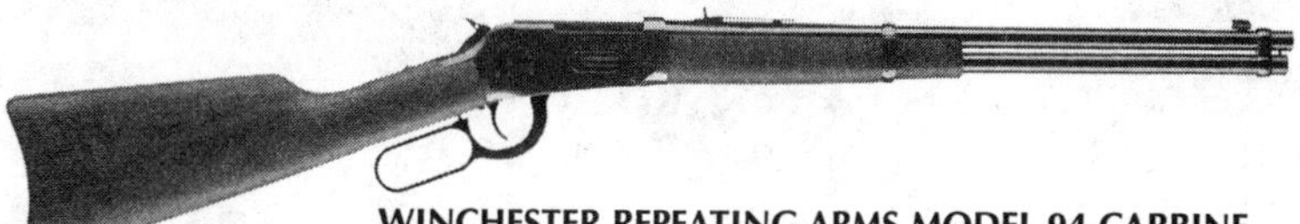

WINCHESTER REPEATING ARMS MODEL 94 CARBINE

WINCHESTER MODEL 94 SHORT RIFLE

MODEL 70 SAFARI EXPRESS

Action: Bolt
Stock: Satin-finished checkered walnut with deluxe cheekpiece
Barrel: 24 in.
Sights: Hooded-blade front and express-style rear
Weight: 9 lb.
Caliber: .375 H&H Mag., .416 Rem. Mag., .458 Win. Mag.
Magazine: 3 rounds
Features: Pre-'64 type claw extractor; Pachmayr decelerator recoil pad; barrel band front swivel base; dual recoil lugs and three-position safety; MOA trigger system; matte blued finish; two steel cross-bolts and one-piece steel trigger guard and hinged floor plate
MSRP $1500

MODEL 70 ULTIMATE SHADOW

Action: Bolt
Stock: Composite
Barrel: 22 in., 24 in., 26 in.
Sights: None
Weight: 6 lb. 12 oz.–7 lb. 4 oz.
Caliber: .300 WSM, .270 WSM, .243 Win., 7mm-08 Rem., .308 Win., .25-06 Rem., .270 Win., .30-06 Spfd., .7mm Rem. Mag., .300 Win. Mag., .338 Win. Mag., .325 WSM
Magazine: 3 rounds
Features: Features integrated, rubberized oval-dot gripping surfaces; pistol grip; controlled round feed action
MSRP . . . . $800–$840

MODEL 70 ULTIMATE SHADOW HUNTER SS

Action: Bolt
Stock: Synthetic MO Break-Up Infinity Camo
Barrel: 22 in., 24 in., 26 in.
Sights: None
Weight: 6 lb. 12 oz.–7 lb. 4 oz.
Caliber: .243 Win., 7mm-08 Rem., .308 Win., .270 Win., 30-06 Spfd., .300 Win. Mag., .338 Win. Mag., .300 WSM, .270 WSM, .325 WSM
Magazine: 3 rounds
Features: Gray overmolded rubberized gripping surfaces; matte metal; alloy one-piece bottom metal; pre-'64 style controlled round feed with claw extractor; three-position safety; free-floating stainless steel barrel; recessed target crown; blade-type ejector; M.O.A. Trigger System; available in blued and stainless steel
MSRP . . . . $1100–$1140

MODEL 94 CARBINE

Action: Lever
Stock: Walnut
Barrel: 20 in.
Sights: Adjustable semi-buckhorn rear, Marble Arms front
Weight: 6 lb. 8 oz.
Caliber: .30-30 Win., .38-55 Win.
Magazine: Under-barrel tube
Features: Triple-checked button rifled barrel; round locking bolt trunnions; top-tang safety; rebounding hammer; bolt relief cut; steel loading gate; articulated cartridge stop; available knurled hammer spur extension
MSRP $1200

MODEL 94 SHORT RIFLE

Action: Lever
Stock: Walnut
Barrel: 20 in.
Sights: Front, adjustable rear
Weight: 6 lb. 12 oz.
Caliber: .30-30 Win., .38-50 Win.
Magazine: Under-barrel tube, 7 rounds
Features: Straight grip; rifle-style forearm and black grip cap; semi-buckhorn rear sights, Marble Arms gold-bead front sight; drilled and tapped for optics
MSRP $1230

Winchester Repeating Arms

WINCHESTER MODEL 94 SPORTER

WINCHESTER MODEL 94
TRAILS END TAKEDOWN

WINCHESTER REPEATING ARMS MODEL 1873 SHORT RIFLE

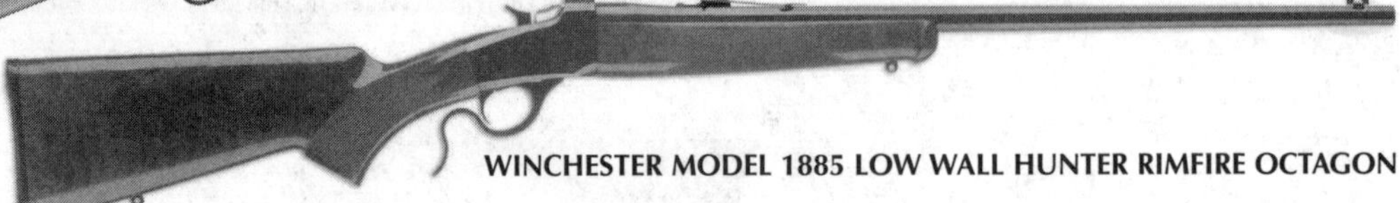

WINCHESTER MODEL 1885 LOW WALL HUNTER RIMFIRE OCTAGON

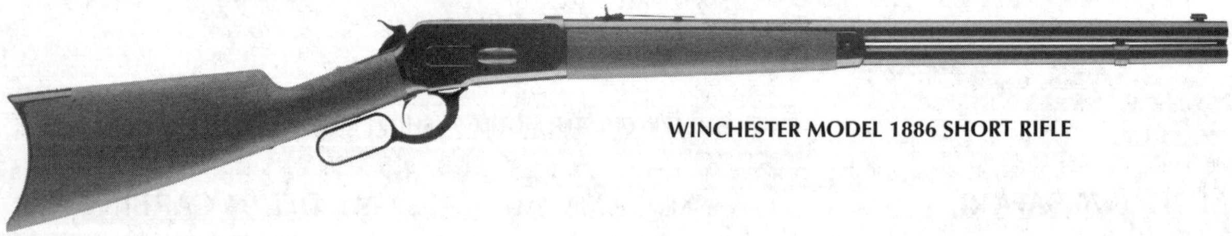

WINCHESTER MODEL 1886 SHORT RIFLE

MODEL 94 SPORTER

Action: Lever
Stock: Walnut
Barrel: 24 in.
Sights: Marble Arms front, adjustable rear
Weight: 7 lb. 8 oz.
Caliber: .30-30 Win., .38-55 Win.
Magazine: Under-barrel tube, 8 rounds
Features: Half-round, half-octagon blued barrel; straight grip stock with a crescent butt and finely checkered blued-steel buttplate with double-line bordering; drilled and tapped for optics
MSRP $1400

MODEL 94 TRAILS END TAKEDOWN

Action: Lever
Stock: Walnut
Barrel: 20 in.
Sights: Adjustable
Weight: 6 lb. 12 oz.
Caliber: .30-30 Win., .38-55 Win., .450 Marlin
Magazine: Under-barrel tube, 6 rounds
Features: Walnut stock and forearm with satin finish and straight-grip styling; blued steel receiver and barrel; Marble Arms front sight with semi-buckhorn rear sight; Pachmayr Decelerator recoil pad (450 model)
MSRP $1460

MODEL 1873 SHORT RIFLE

Action: Lever
Stock: Wood
Barrel: 20 in.
Sights: Adjustable
Weight: 7 lb. 4 oz.
Caliber: .44-40 Win.
Magazine: Under-barrel tube, 10 rounds
Features: Walnut straight grip stock with satin oil finish; classic rifle style forearm with blued steel cap; semi-buckhorn rear sight with Marble Arms gold bead front sights; steel loading gate; receiver rear tang drilled and tapped for optional tang-mounted rear sight
MSRP $1300

MODEL 1885 LOW WALL HUNTER RIMFIRE OCTAGON

Action: Lever
Stock: Walnut
Barrel: 24 in.
Sights: Semi-buckhorn rear, gold bead front
Weight: 7 lb. 8 oz.
Caliber: .22LR, .22 WMR, .17 HMR, .17 WSM
Magazine: Single shot
Features: Gloss blued steel receiver; octagon barrel; pistol grip buttstock; Pachmayr rubber butt pad; sling swivel studs
**MSRP . . . .
$1470**

MODEL 1886 SHORT RIFLE

Action: Lever
Stock: Walnut
Barrel: 20 in., 24 in.
Sights: Front with brass bead, adjustable rear
Weight: 8 lb. 6 oz.
Caliber: .45-70 Govt.
Magazine: Under-barrel tube, 8 rounds
Features: Deeply blued receiver and lever; end cap and steel crescent buttplate; straight grip
MSRP $1340

AIR RIFLES

232 AirForce Airguns
234 J. G. Anschütz
235 Beeman Precision Airguns
237 Crosman
240 Daisy
242 Gamo USA
244 RWS
245 Stoeger Airguns

AirForce Airguns

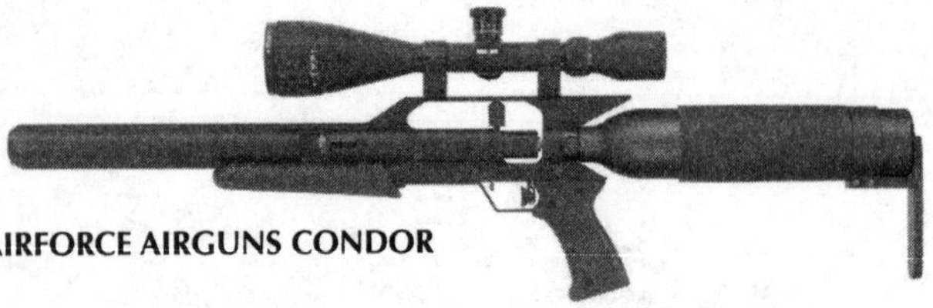

AIRFORCE AIRGUNS CONDOR

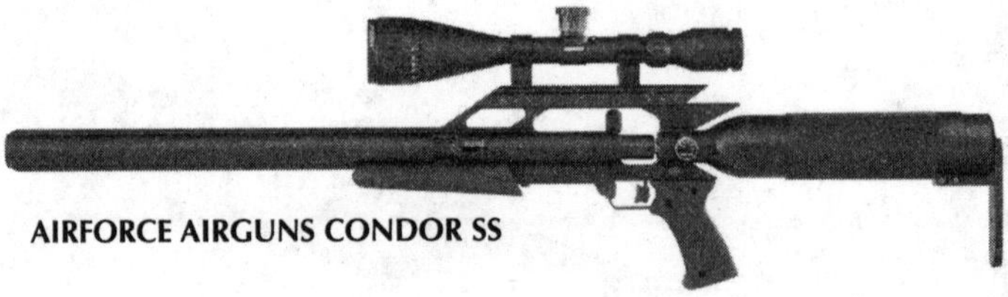

AIRFORCE AIRGUNS CONDOR SS

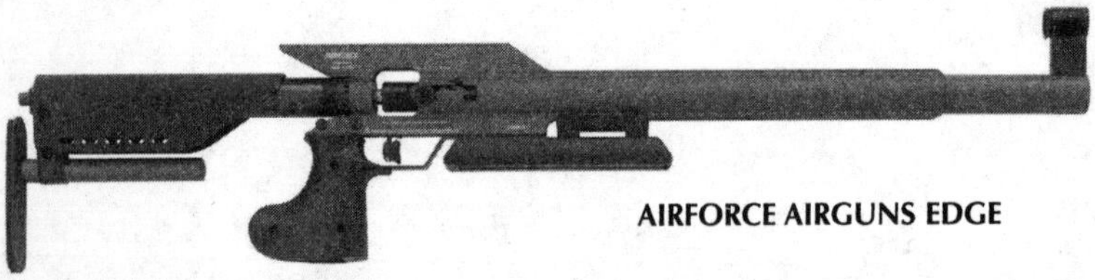

AIRFORCE AIRGUNS EDGE

AIRFORCE AIRGUNS ESCAPE

CONDOR

Power: Pre-charged pneumatic, user adjustable
Stock: Composite
Overall Length: 38.7 in.
Sights: None
Weight: 6 lb. 8 oz.
Caliber: .25, .22, .20, .177
Features: Black, red, or blue composite stock; integral extended scope rail; detachable air tank; Lothar Walther barrel; pressure relief device; adjustable power; scopes optional
Quick-Detach: $710
Spin-Loc: $730

CONDOR SS

Power: Compressed air
Stock: Composite
Overall Length: 38.125 in.
Sights: Open or optical may be installed
Weight: 6 lb. 2 oz.
Caliber: .177, .20, .22, .25
Features: CondorSS combines the major attributes of the TalonSS's quiet operation and the Condor's high power levels; new sound reduction technology; 18-inch barrel blue, red, or original black; 600–1300 fps; two-stage trigger; single shot
Quick-Detach: $740
Spin-Loc: $760

EDGE

Power: Pre-charged pneumatic
Stock: Composite
Overall Length: 35–40 in.
Sights: TS1 peep sight system
Weight: 6 lb. 2 oz.
Caliber: .177
Features: Ambidextrous cocking knob; regulated air system; adjustable length of pull; adjustable forend; hooded front sight only or front and rear sight available; two-stage adjustable trigger; composite stock in red or blue finish; scopes optional
Front sight: $546
Rear & front sights: $680

ESCAPE

Power: Compressed air
Stock: Synthetic
Overall Length: 34.5 in.–39 in.
Sights: Open or optical
Weight: 5 lb. 4.8 oz
Caliber: .22, .25
Features: Lothar Walther Barrels; Quick-Detach or Spin-Loc air tanks; lightweight and compact; geared for survival situations; user adjustable length
Quick-Detach: $660
Spin-Loc: $680

AirForce Airguns

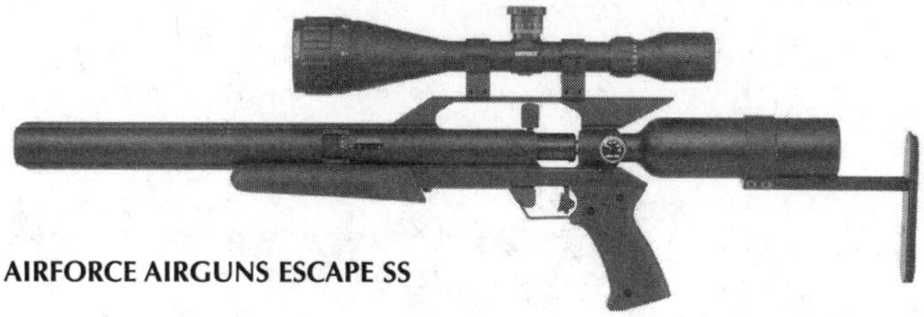

AIRFORCE AIRGUNS ESCAPE SS

AIRFORCE AIRGUNS ESCAPE UL

AIRFORCE AIRGUNS TALON SS

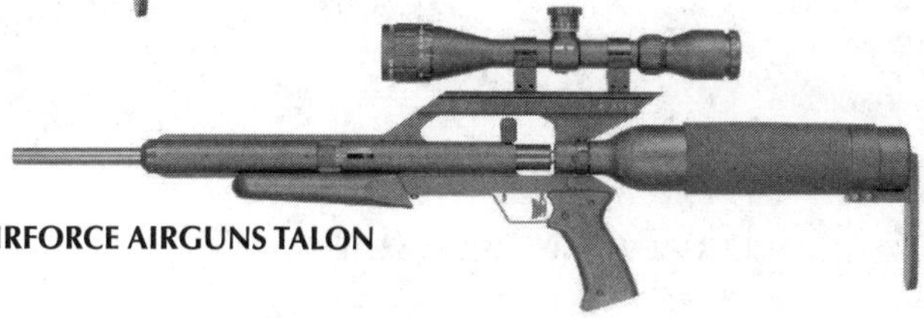

AIRFORCE AIRGUNS TALON

ESCAPE SS

Power: Compressed air
Stock: Synthetic
Overall Length: 27.75 in.–32.25 in.
Sights: Open or optical
Weight: 4 lb. 4.8 oz
Caliber: .22, .25
Features: Lothar Walther Barrels; Quick-Detach or Spin-Loc air tanks; lightweight and compact; geared for survival situations; user adjustable length; Sound-Loc sound reduction technology installed
Quick-Detach: $650
Spin-Loc: $670

ESCAPE UL

Power: Compressed air
Stock: Synthetic
Overall Length: 28.5 in.–33 in.
Sights: Open or optical
Weight: 4 lb. 4 oz
Caliber: .22, .25
Features: Lothar Walther Barrels; Quick-Detach or Spin-Loc air tanks; lightweight and compact; geared for survival situations; user adjustable length
Quick-Detach: $610
Spin-Loc: $630

TALON

Power: Compressed air
Stock: Composite
Overall Length: 32.6 in.
Sights: None
Weight: 5 lb. 8 oz.
Caliber: .25, .22, .20, .177
Features: Lothar Walther barrel; pressure relief device; adjustable power; detachable air tank; black composite stock; scopes optional
Quick-Detach: $580
Spin-Loc: $600

TALON P

Power: Compressed air
Stock: Composite
Overall Length: 24 in.
Sights: None
Weight: 3 lb. 8 oz.
Caliber: .25
Features: Designed to deliver over 50 ft.-lbs. of energy with a .25-caliber hunting pellet; integral extended scope rail; Lothar Walther barrels; scopes optional
Quick-Detach: $450
Spin-Loc: $470

AIRFORCE AIRGUNS TALON P

TALON SS

Power: Compressed air
Stock: Composite
Overall Length: 32.7 in.
Sights: None
Weight: 5 lb. 4 oz.
Caliber: .25, .22, .20, .177
Features: Improved sound reduction; Lothar Walther barrel; pressure relief device; adjustable power; detachable air tank; black, red, or blue composite stock; multiple mounting rails; two-stage trigger; innovative muzzle cap that strips away air turbulence and reduces discharge sound levels; scopes optional
Quick-Detach: $620
Spin-Loc: $640

J. G. Anschütz

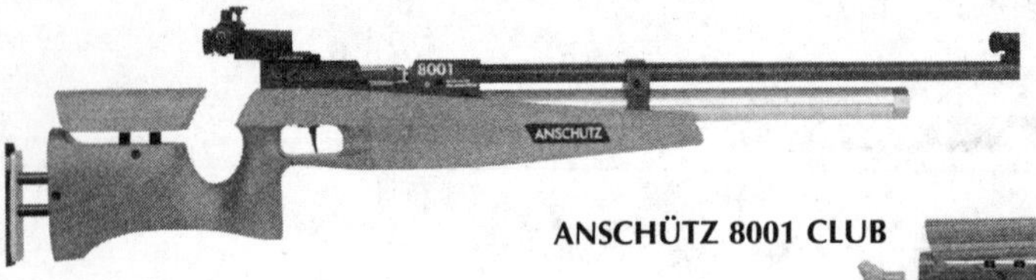

ANSCHÜTZ 8001 CLUB

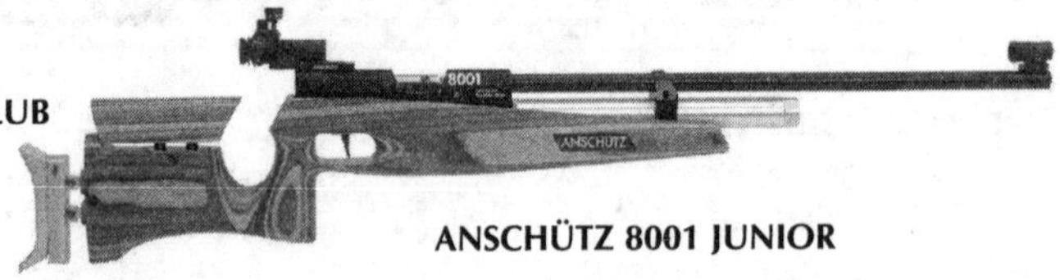

ANSCHÜTZ 8001 JUNIOR

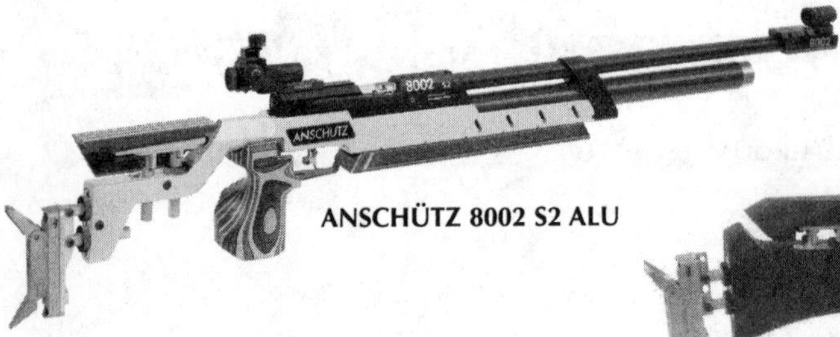

ANSCHÜTZ 8002 S2 ALU

ANSCHÜTZ 8002 S2 BLACK AIR

ANSCHÜTZ 9003 PREMIUM S2 ALU

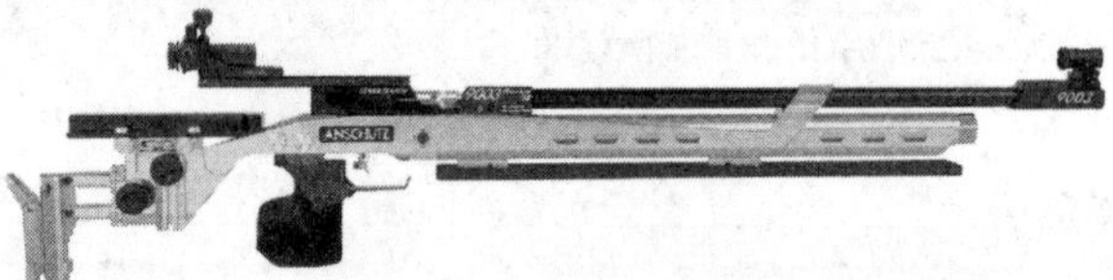

ANSCHÜTZ 9003 PREMIUM S2 BENCHREST PRECISE

8001 CLUB

Power: Compressed air
Stock: Walnut
Overall Length: 42.1 in.
Sights: Open, includes sight set 6834
Weight: 8 lb. 6 oz.
Caliber: .177
Features: Walnut stock with stippled checkering and non-stained aluminum or rubber buttplate; adjustable trigger; match grade barrel
MSRP. $1730

8001 JUNIOR

Power: Compressed air
Stock: Laminate
Overall Length: 37.4 in.
Sights: Open, includes sight set 6834
Weight: 8 lb. 2 oz.
Caliber: .177
Features: Laminated wood in blue and orange with aluminum buttplate stock; cylindrical match grade barrel; comes with accessory box
MSRP. $1859

8002 S2 ALU

Power: Compressed air
Stock: Aluminum and synthetic pistol grip or laminated wood pistol grip
Overall Length: 42.1 in.
Sights: Open, includes sight set 6834
Weight: 10 lb. 2 oz.
Caliber: .177
Features: Aluminum stock in silver and blue with laminated wood or synthetic pistol grip; blue air cylinder; ProGrip cheekpiece and forend; includes accessory box; aluminum accessory rail
Aluminum: $2564
Wood: $2244

8002 S2 BLACK AIR

Power: Compressed air
Stock: Plastic
Length: 43.3 in.
Sights: Rear, turnable front
Weight: 9 lb. 8 oz.
Caliber: .177
Features: IWA special edition equipped with new Anschütz SOFT-Grip stock, combining the vibration damping and recoil absorbing characteristics of a naturally grown wooden stock with the characteristics of an easy-care and weather-proof plastic stock; match barrel; aluminum buttplate; cheekpiece; two-stage trigger
MSRP. $2308

9003 PREMIUM S2 PRECISE

Power: Compressed air
Stock: Aluminum
Overall Length: 43.7 in.
Sights: Open, includes sight set 6834
Weight: 9 lb. 15 oz.
Caliber: .177
Features: Silver/black aluminum stock pistol grip; Soft Link shock absorber pads; adjustable forend stock, cheekpiece, and buttplate; includes plastic rifle case; steel match barrel; aluminum accessory rail on stock
MSRP. $4040

9003 PREMIUM S2 BENCHREST PRECISE

Power: Compressed air
Stock: Aluminum
Length: 39.96 in.
Sights: Open, includes sight set 6834
Weight: 11 lb. 11 oz.
Caliber: .177
Features: Aluminum stock with wedge-shaped design; pistol grip; Soft Link shock absorber pads; adjustable forend stock, cheekpiece and buttplate; includes plastic rifle case; valve and valve body coated with gold; steel match barrel; aluminum accessory rail on stock
MSRP. $4040

Beeman Precision Airguns

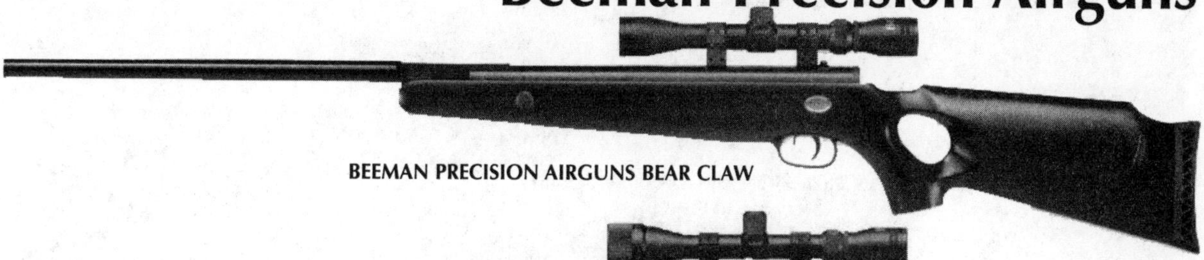

BEEMAN PRECISION AIRGUNS BEAR CLAW

BEEMAN PRECISION AIRGUNS ELKHORN

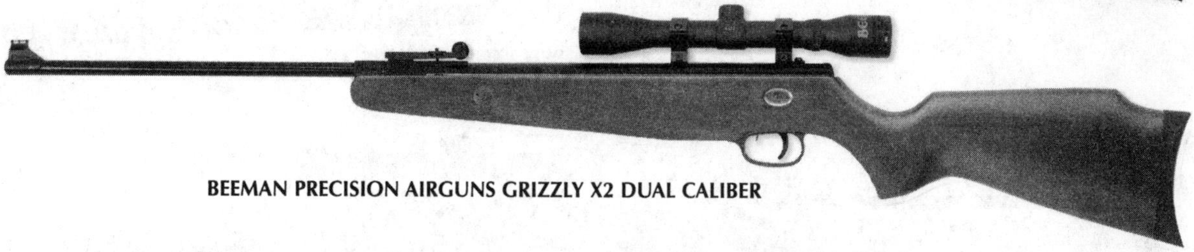

BEEMAN PRECISION AIRGUNS GRIZZLY X2 DUAL CALIBER

BEEMAN PRECISION AIRGUNS MACH 12.5

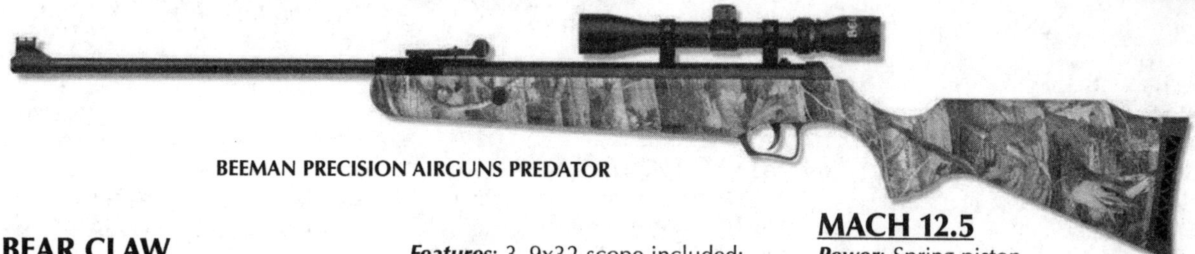

BEEMAN PRECISION AIRGUNS PREDATOR

BEAR CLAW

Power: Spring piston
Stock: Wood
Overall Length: 45.5 in.
Sights: Scope
Weight: 8 lb. 8 oz.
Caliber: .177
Features: 3–9x32 scope included; break barrel action; available as dual caliber version
MSRP . . . . **$240–$260**

ELKHORN

Power: Spring piston
Stock: Wood
Overall Length: 46.5 in.
Sights: Scope
Weight: 9 lb.–10 lb
Caliber: .177, .22
Features: 3–9x32 scope included; break barrel action; fluted barrel
MSRP **$250**

GRIZZLY X2 DUAL CALIBER

Power: Spring piston
Stock: Wood
Overall Length: 45.5 in.
Sights: Fixed and scope
Weight: 8 lb. 8 oz.
Caliber: .177, .22
Features: 4x32 scope and fiber optics sights; break barrel action; interchangeable barrels; available with case
MSRP . . . . **$180–$196**

MACH 12.5

Power: Spring piston
Stock: Wood
Overall Length: 46.5 in.
Sights: Scope
Weight: 10 lb.
Caliber: .177, .22
Features: 3–9x40 scope included; break barrel action; muzzle break
MSRP **$300**

PREDATOR

Power: Spring piston
Stock: Synthetic
Overall Length: 45.5 in.
Sights: Fixed and scope
Weight: 8 lb. 8 oz.
Caliber: .177
Features: 3–9x32 scope and fiber optic sights; break barrel action
MSRP **$212**

Beeman Precision Airguns

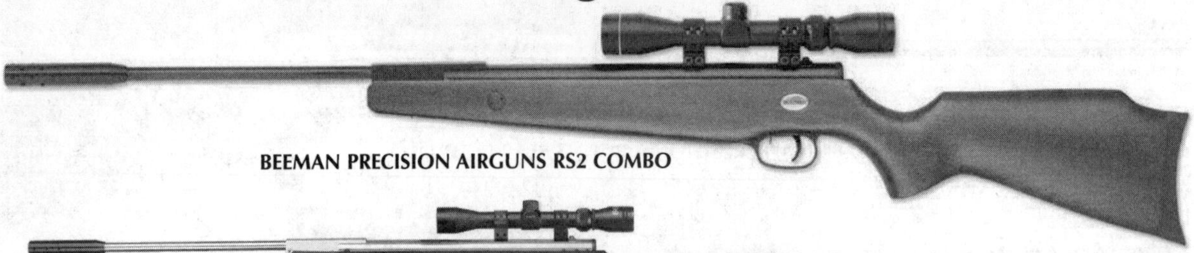

BEEMAN PRECISION AIRGUNS RS2 COMBO

BEEMAN PRECISION AIRGUNS
SILVER KODIAK X2 DC

BEEMAN PRECISION AIRGUNS
SILVER PANTHER

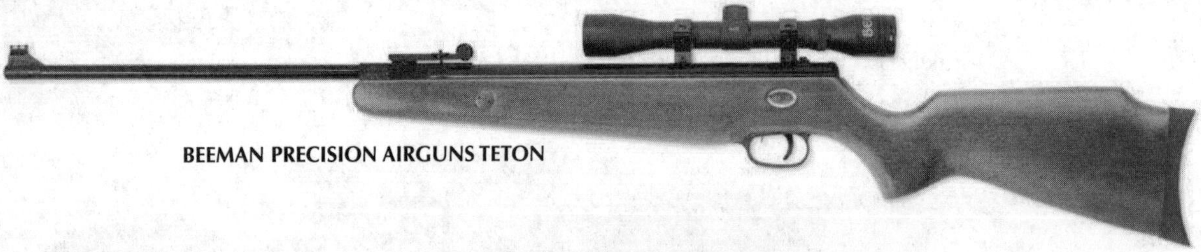

BEEMAN PRECISION AIRGUNS TETON

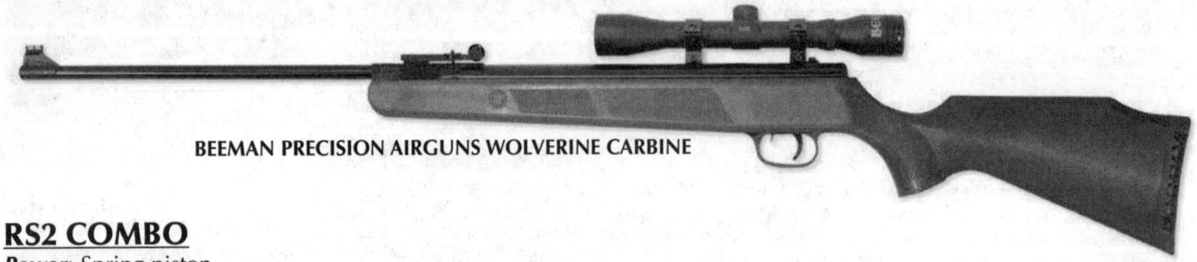

BEEMAN PRECISION AIRGUNS WOLVERINE CARBINE

RS2 COMBO

Power: Spring piston
Stock: Wood
Overall Length: 46.5 in.
Sights: Scope
Weight: 10 lb.
Caliber: .177, .22
Features: 3–9x32 scope inlcuded; break barrel action; rifled barrel
MSRP. $196

SILVER KODIAK X2 DC

Power: Break action, spring piston
Stock: All-weather synthetic
Overall Length: 47.5 in.
Sights: 3–9x32 or 4x32 scope
Weight: 8 lb. 12 oz.
Caliber: .177, .22
Features: Two airguns in one; satin nickel plated barrel and receiver; ported muzzle brake; 1000 fps max velocity
MSRP. $205

SILVER PANTHER

Power: Break action, spring piston
Stock: All-weather synthetic
Overall Length: 47.5 in.
Sights: 4x32 scope
Weight: 8 lb. 12 oz.
Caliber: .177, .22
Features: Satin nickel plated barrel and receiver; ported muzzle brake; 1000 fps max velocity
MSRP. $150

TETON

Power: Spring piston
Stock: Wood
Overall Length: 44.5 in.
Sights: Fixed and scope
Weight: 9 lb.
Caliber: .177, .22
Features: 4x32 scope and fiber optic sights; break barrel action; rifled barrel
MSRP. . . . . $130–$150

WOLVERINE CARBINE

Power: Spring piston
Stock: Synthetic
Overall Length: 45.5 in.
Sights: Fixed and scope
Weight: 8 lb. 8 oz.
Caliber: .177, .22
Features: 4x32 scope and fiber optic sights; break barrel action; rifled barrel; rubber recoil pad
MSRP. $150

Crosman

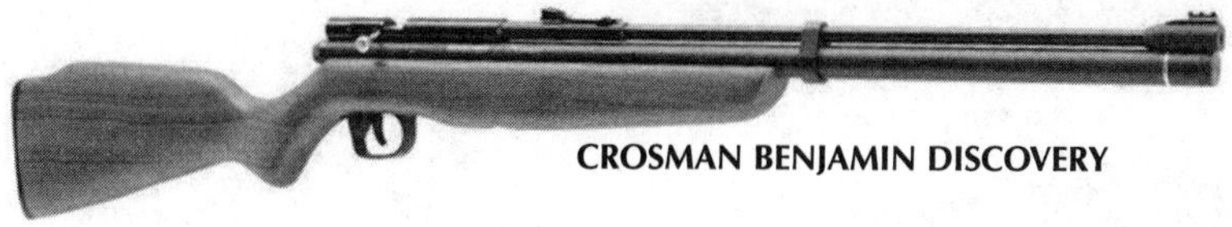

CROSMAN BENJAMIN DISCOVERY

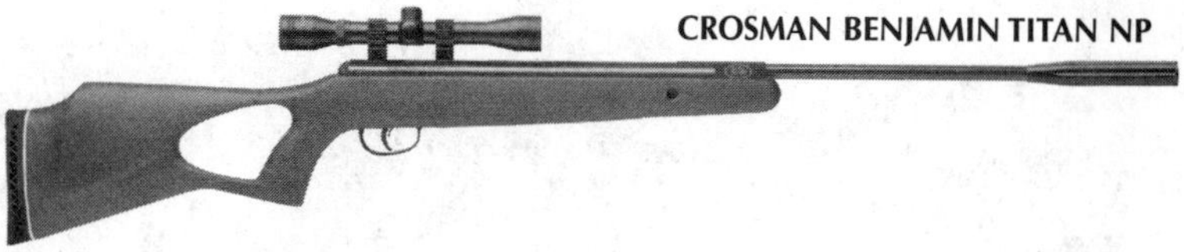

CROSMAN BENJAMIN TITAN NP

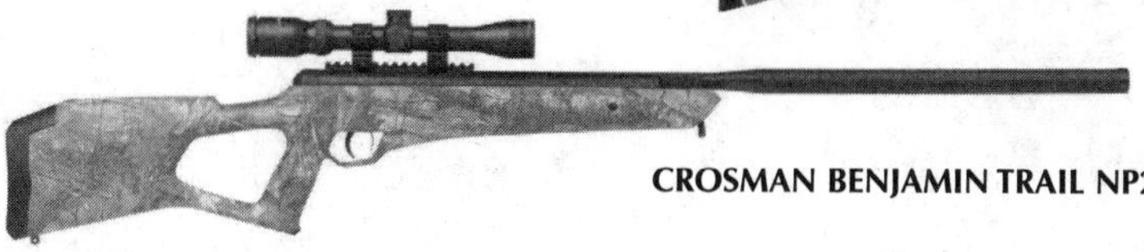

CROSMAN BENJAMIN TRAIL NP2

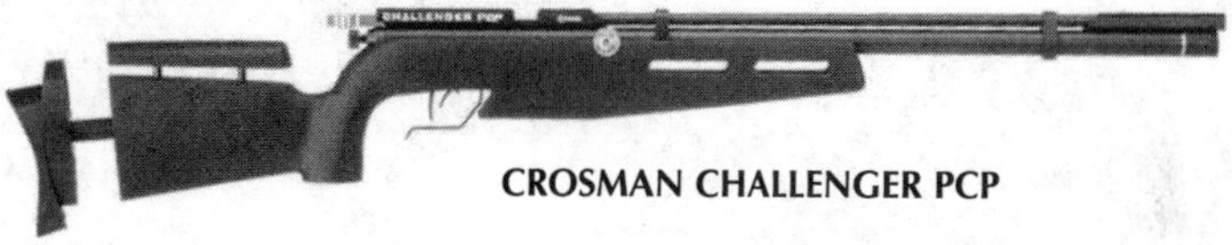

CROSMAN CHALLENGER PCP

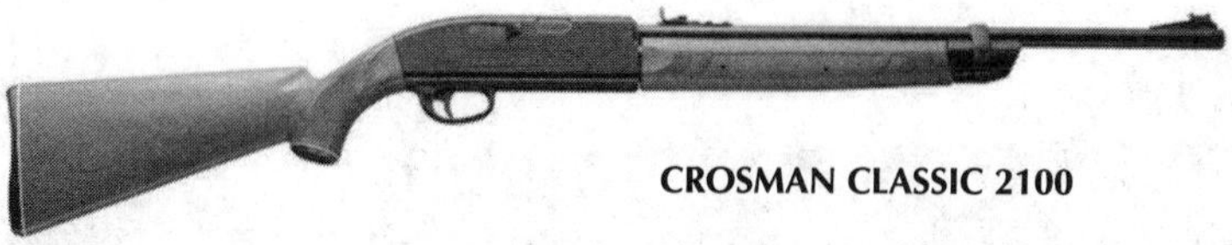

CROSMAN CLASSIC 2100

BENJAMIN DISCOVERY

Power: Dual fuel compressed air
Stock: Walnut
Overall Length: 39 in.
Sights: Fiber optic front, adjustable rear
Weight: 5 lb. 2 oz.–5 lb. 3 oz.
Caliber: .22, .177
Features: Rifled steel barrel; velocity up to 900 fps; cross-bolt safety; built-in pressure gauge; high pressure pump included
MSRP $455

BENJAMIN TITAN NP

Power: Nitro piston
Stock: Hardwood
Length: 43 in., 44.5 in.
Sights: 4x32mm scope included
Weight: 6 lb. 10 oz.–6 lb. 14 oz.
Caliber: .177, .22
Features: Powered by Nitro Piston technology; delivers velocities up to 1200 fps (.177) with alloy pellets; included 4x32mm scope; ambidextrous hardwood stock with thumbhole; two-stage adjustable trigger; ventilated rubber recoil pad
MSRP $180

CROSMAN BENJAMIN TRAIL NP2

Power: NP2 nitro piston
Stock: Synthetic or wood
Overall Length: 46.25 in.
Sights: CenterPoint 3–9x32mm scope
Weight: 8 lb. 5 oz.
Caliber: .177, .22
Features: Break barrel; first to feature new NP2 power system; enhanced Clean Break Trigger; integrated sound suppression system; shoots up to 1200 fps alloy, 900 fps pellet; .22 available in hardwood, synthetic, and Realtree Xtra
Hardwood: $260
Synthetic: $260
Realtree: $295

CHALLENGER PCP

Power: Pneumatic pump and CO2
Stock: Synthetic
Overall Length: 41.5 in.
Sights: Open
Weight: 7 lb. 2 oz.
Caliber: .177
Features: Two-stage match grade adjustable trigger; Lothar Walther barrel; adjustable cheekpiece and buttpiece; black synthetic stock; 11mm scope mount rails; ambidextrous
MSRP $530

CLASSIC 2100

Power: Pneumatic pump
Stock: Synthetic
Overall Length: 39.75 in.
Sights: Visible impact front, adjustable rear
Weight: 4 lb. 13 oz.
Caliber: .177
Features: Cross-bolt safety; BB up to 755 fps, pellet up to 725 fps
MSRP $70

Crosman

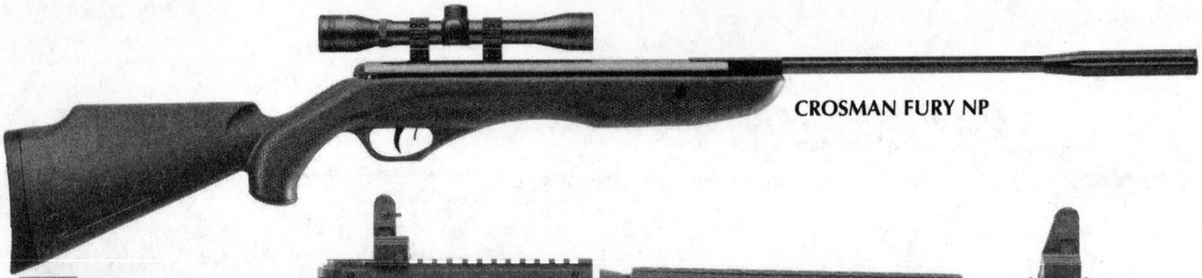

CROSMAN FURY NP

CROSMAN M4-177

CROSMAN MARAUDER

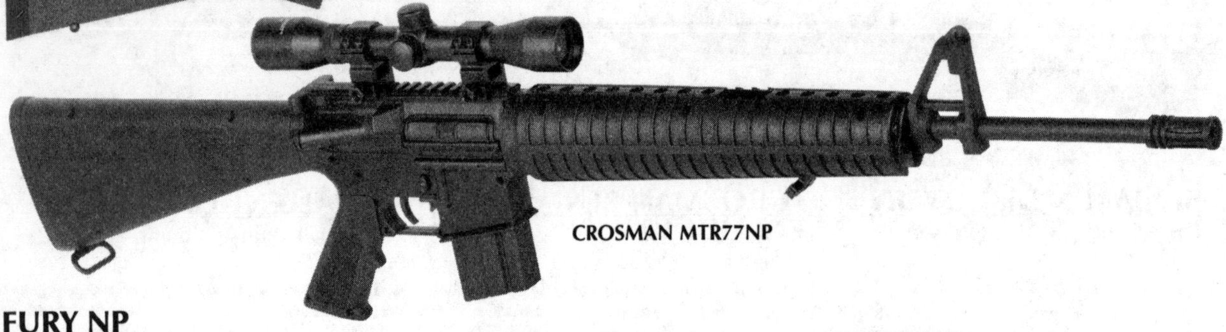

CROSMAN MTR77NP

FURY NP

Power: Break action Nitro Piston
Stock: Synthetic all-weather
Overall Length: 45 in.
Sights: 4x32mm scope
Weight: 6 lb. 6 oz.
Caliber: .177
Features: Velocities up to 1200 fps; rifled steel barrel; adjustable two-stage trigger; Nitro Piston technology delivers smooth cocking, reduced vibration and shoots with 70 percent less noise
MSRP $140

M4-177 RIFLE

Power: Multi-pump pneumatic
Stock: Synthetic
Length: 34 in.
Sights: Adjustable front and rear
Weight: 3 lb. 9 oz.
Caliber: .177
Features: Rifled steel barrel; shoots both pellets and BBs; variable pump action easy to use for right- or left-handed shooters; Picatinny rails; front and rear sights and stock are removable for upgrades; adjustable stock; velocities up to 660 fps with BBs
and 625 fps with 7.9gr, .177 caliber pellets
MSRP $80

MARAUDER

Power: Compressed air
Stock: Wood
Overall Length: 42.8 in.
Sights: None
Weight: 8 lb. 3 oz.
Caliber: .177, .22, .25
Features: Bolt action; ten round magazine; reversable bolt; dovetail mounting rail
MSRP $700

MTR77NP

Power: Break action Nitro Piston
Stock: Synthetic all-weather
Overall Length: 40 in.
Sights: 4x32mm scope
Weight: 6 lb. 2 oz.
Caliber: .177
Features: Nitro Piston technology delivers smooth cocking, reduced vibration and shoots with 70 percent less noise; sling mounts; storage in false magazine; up to 1200 fps; carry handle available
MSRP $200

Crosman

CROSMAN OPTIMUS

CROSMAN PHANTOM 1000

CROSMAN PUMPMASTER 760

CROSMAN RECRUIT

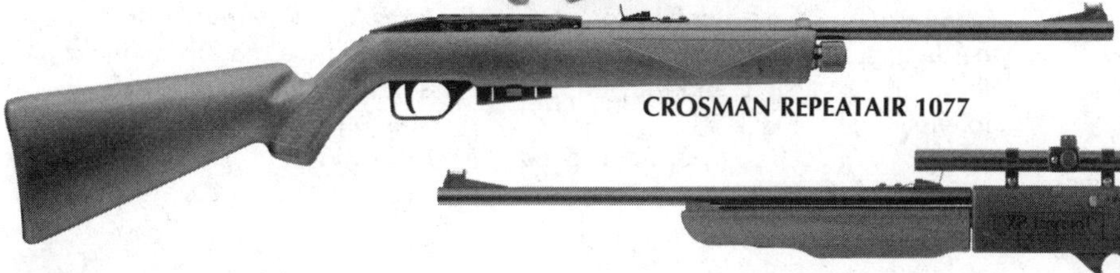

CROSMAN REPEATAIR 1077

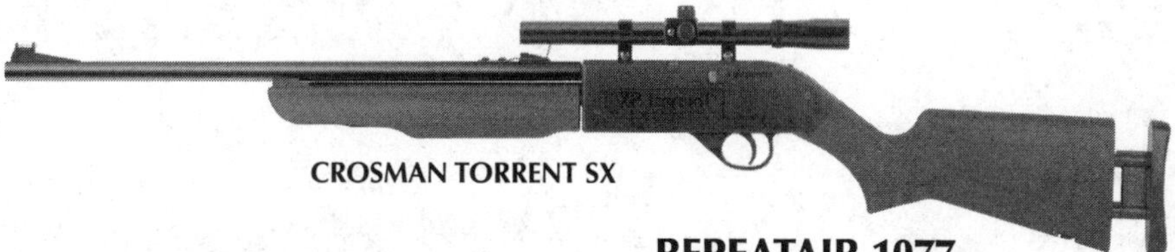

CROSMAN TORRENT SX

OPTIMUS

Power: Break action
Stock: Hardwood
Overall Length: 43 in.
Sights: 4x32mm CenterPoint scope
Weight: 6 lb. 8 oz.
Caliber: .177, .22
Features: Ambidextrous hardwood stock; relatively light cocking force and a two-stage adjustable trigger; velocities of up to 1200 fps with alloy pellets; barrel incorporates a micro-adjustable rear sight and fiber optic front sight
MSRP $139

PHANTOM 1000

Power: Spring piston
Stock: Synthetic
Overall Length: 44.5 in.
Sights: Fiber optic front, adjustable rear
Weight: 6 lb.
Caliber: .177
Features: All-weather, synthetic black stock and forearm; checkered grip and forearm; velocity up to 1000 fps; rifled steel barrel; two-stage adjustable trigger
MSRP $100

PUMPMASTER 760

Power: Pneumatic pump
Stock: Synthetic
Overall Length: 33.5 in.
Sights: Fiber optic front, adjustable rear
Weight: 2 lb. 12 oz.
Caliber: .177
Features: Cross-bolt safety; BB up to 625 fps; pellet up to 600 fps
MSRP $50

RECRUIT

Power: Pneumatic pump
Stock: Synthetic
Overall Length: 38.25 in.
Sights: Scope
Weight: 2 lb. 15 oz.
Caliber: .177
Features: Adjustable buttstock; adjustable synthetic stock; 11mm dovetail scope rail; cross-bolt safety
MSRP $80

REPEATAIR 1077

Power: CO2
Stock: All-weather, synthetic
Overall Length: 36.88 in.
Sight: Fiber optic front, adjustable rear
Weight: 3 lb. 11 oz.
Caliber: .177
Features: Exclusive 12-shot rotary pellet clip lets you shoot longer; maximum velocity 625 fps; cross-bolt safety
MSRP $90

TORRENT SX

Power: Variable pump
Stock: Synthetic
Overall Length: 36.75 in.
Sights: Fiber optic front, adjustable rear
Weight: 2 lb. 15 oz.
Caliber: .177
Features: Lightweight, variable pump BB/pellet rifle; adjustable stock; customized length of pull; up to 695 fps; five-shot clip; olive-drab stock and forearm
MSRP $50

Crosman

CROSMAN TR77

CROSMAN VANTAGE NP

CROSMAN VARMINT POWER PACK

TR77 NPS

Power: Nitro piston
Stock: Synthetic
Length: 41.5 in.
Sights: Fiber optic front, adjustable rear
Weight: 6 lb.
Caliber: .177
Features: Tactical break air rifle with military styling and all-weather tactical, synthetic stock; two-stage adjustable trigger; pistol grip; includes CenterPoint 4x32mm scope; velocities up to 1000 fps
MSRP. $160

VANTAGE NP

Power: Break action
Stock: Hardwood
Length: 45 in.
Sights: Fiber optic front, adjustable rear 4x32mm scope included
Weight: 7 lb. 2 oz.
Caliber: .177
Features: Crosman's own version of the Bantage NP; hardwood stock; fiber optic front sight and fully adjustable rear sight
MSRP. $160

CROSMAN VARMINT POWER PACK

Power: Nitro piston
Stock: Synthetic
Overall Length: 44.5 in.
Sights: CenterPoint 4x32mm scope
Weight: 7 lb. 6 oz.
Caliber: .22
Features: Break barrel; 90 lumen LED flashlight with a red flip-up filter; red, class III fast acquisition laser with push on/off or remote tape switch
MSRP. $250

Daisy

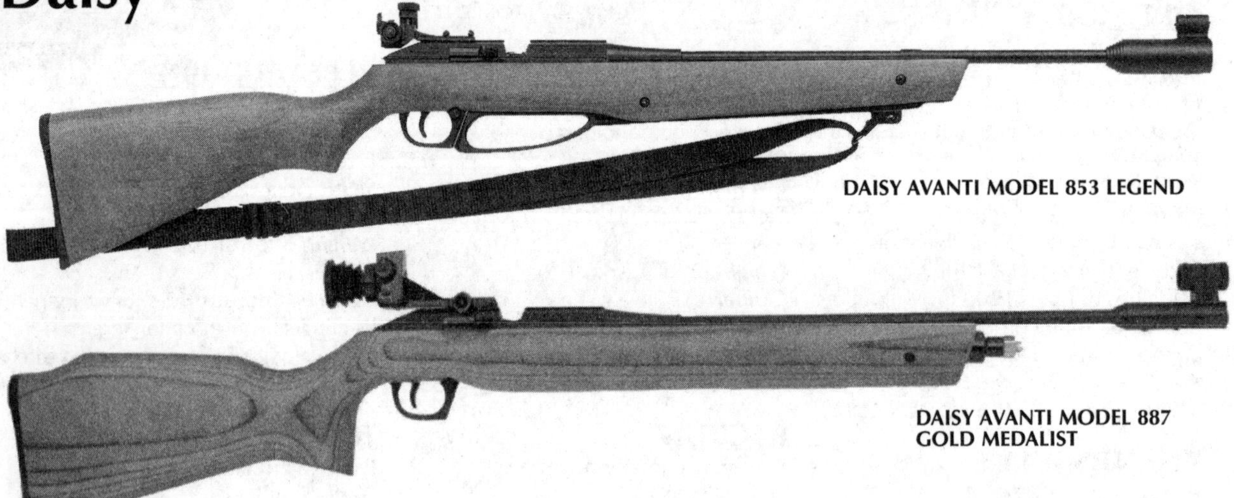

DAISY AVANTI MODEL 853 LEGEND

DAISY AVANTI MODEL 887 GOLD MEDALIST

AVANTI MODEL 853 LEGEND

Power: Single-pump pneumatic
Stock: Hardwood
Overall Length: 38.5 in.
Sights: Hooded front with interchangeable aperture inserts, micrometer adjustable rear
Weight: 5 lb. 8 oz.
Caliber: .177
Features: Diecast receiver with dovetail scope mount; Lothar Walther rifled high-grade steel barrel; full-length, sporter-style hardwood with adjustable length
MSRP. $400

AVANTI MODEL 887 GOLD MEDALIST

Power: CO2 single shot bolt
Stock: Laminated hardwood
Overall Length: 39.5 in.
Sights: Front globe with changeable aperture inserts, rear diopter with micrometer
Weight: 7 lb. 5 oz.
Caliber: .177
Features: Laminated hardwood stock; Lothar Walther rifled high-grade steel barrel; manual, cross-bolt trigger block; includes scope rail adapter
MSRP. $500

Daisy

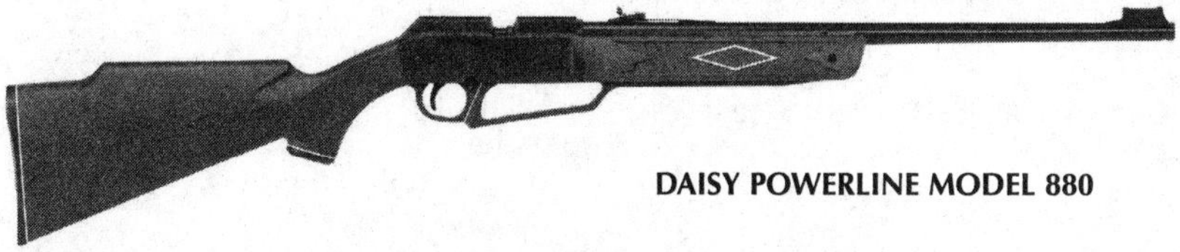

DAISY POWERLINE MODEL 880

DAISY POWERLINE MODEL 901

DAISY POWERLINE TARGETPRO 953

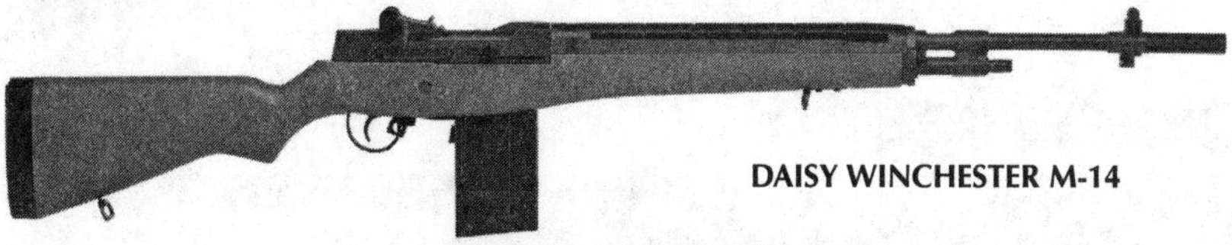

DAISY WINCHESTER M-14

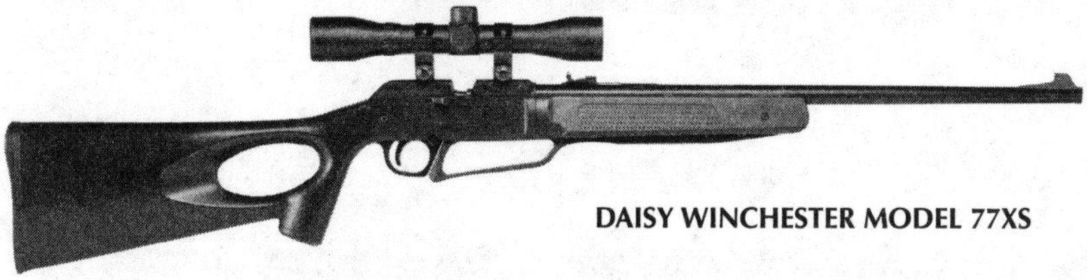

DAISY WINCHESTER MODEL 77XS

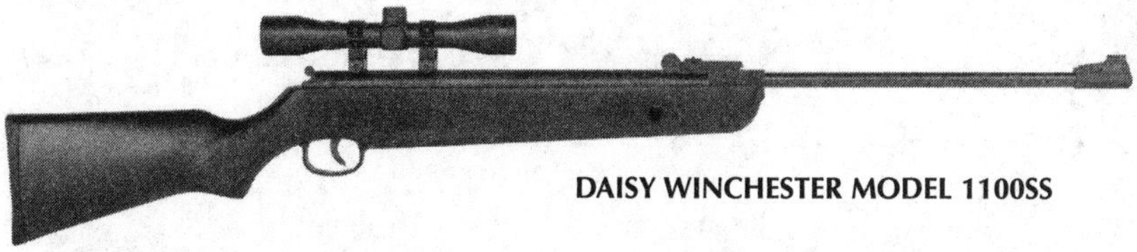

DAISY WINCHESTER MODEL 1100SS

POWERLINE MODEL 880

Power: Multi-pump pneumatic
Stock: Molded wood grain
Overall Length: 37.6 in.
Sights: TruGlo fiber optic front, adjustable rear
Weight: 3 lb. 11 oz.
Caliber: .177
Features: Wood-grained, Monte Carlo stock and forearm; rifled steel barrel; cross-bolt trigger block; velocity up to 750 fps; engineering resin with dovetail mount for scope
MSRP $50

POWERLINE MODEL 901

Power: Multi-pump pneumatic
Stock: Composite
Overall Length: 37.5 in.
Sights: Fiber optic front, adjustable rear
Weight: 3 lb. 11 oz.
Caliber: .177
Features: Rifled steel barrel; black advanced composite stock; dovetail mounts for optics
MSRP $70

POWERLINE TARGETPRO 953

Power: Pneumatic single-pump cocking lever
Stock: Composite
Overall Length: 37.75 in.
Sights: Front and rear fiber optic
Weight: 6 lb. 6 oz.
Caliber: .177
Features: Full-length, match-style black composite stock; rifled high-grade steel barrel; diecast metal receiver; manual cross-bolt trigger block with red indicator
MSRP $120

WINCHESTER M-14

Power: CO2 semiautomatic
Stock: Composite
Length: 44.5 in.
Sights: Blade front, adjustable rear
Weight: 4 lb. 6 oz.
Caliber: .177
Features: Dual ammo BB or pellet rifle; rifled steel barrel; adjustable rear sight, fixed front sight; brown composite stock; 700 fps maximum velocity
MSRP $100

WINCHESTER MODEL 77XS

Power: Multi-pump pneumatic
Stock: Composite
Length: 37.6 in.
Sights: TruGlo fiber optic front, adjustable rear
Weight: 3 lb. 2 oz.
Caliber: .177
Features: Rifled steel barrel; TruGlo fiber optic front, adjustable rear sight; 4x32mm air rifle scope included; black composite stock; 800 fps maximum velocity
MSRP $130

WINCHESTER MODEL 1100SS

Power: Break action/spring piston
Stock: Composite
Overall Length: 46.25 in.
Sights: Blade front, micro-adjustable rear
Weight: 6 lb. 10 oz.
Caliber: .177
Features: Rifled steel barrel; 1100 fps with alloy pellets; single shot; thumb safety engages when rifle is cocked
MSRP $130

Daisy

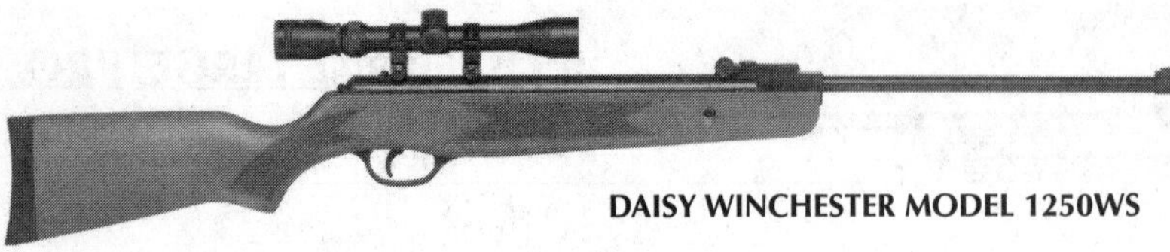

DAISY WINCHESTER MODEL 1250WS

WINCHESTER MODEL 1250WS

Power: Break action/spring piston
Stock: Hardwood
Overall Length: 46.25 in.
Sights: Fiber optic front, 3–9x32mm scope
Weight: 6 lb. 10 oz.
Caliber: .177
Features: Rifled steel barrel; 1250 fps; thumb safety engages when cocked
MSRP $180

Gamo USA

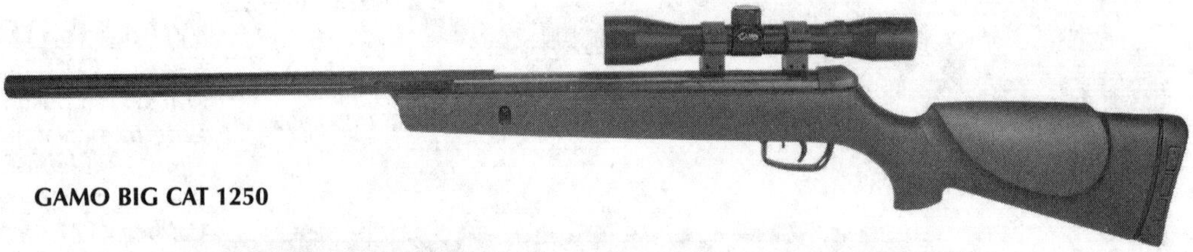

GAMO BIG CAT 1250

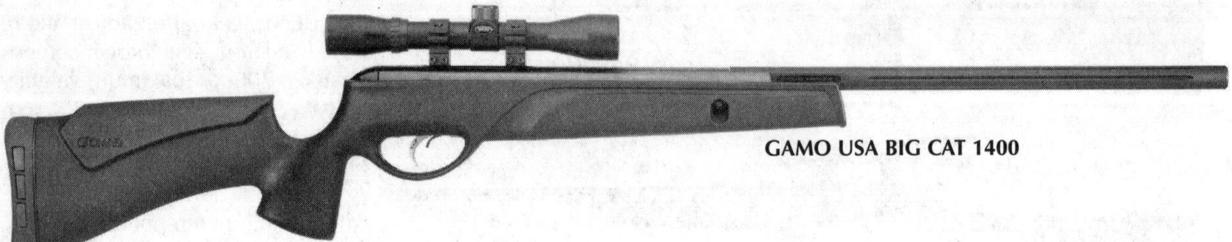

GAMO USA BIG CAT 1400

GAMO USA LITTLE CAT

AIR RIFLES

BIG CAT 1250

Power: Break action/spring piston
Stock: Synthetic
Overall Length: 43.3 in.
Sights: 4x32mm scope
Weight: 6 lb. 2 oz.
Caliber: .177
Features: Tough all-weather molded synthetic stock; ventilated rubber pad for recoil; twin cheekpads; non-slip texture design on grip and forearm; manual trigger system; fluted barrel; two-stage adjustable trigger
MSRP $200

BIG CAT 1400

Power: Break action/spring piston
Stock: Synthetic
Overall Length: 43.3 in.
Sights: 4x32 scope
Weight: 6 lb. 2 oz.
Caliber: .177
Features: 33mm power plant enabling it to shoot at up to 1,400 fps with PBA Platinum Ammo; Smooth Action Trigger to maximize pinpoint accuracy; all-weather synthetic stock with rubberized grips; Shock Wave Absorber recoil pad
MSRP $230

LITTLE CAT

Power: Break action/spring piston
Stock: Beechwood
Overall Length: 36 in.
Sights: Front, rear fiber optics
Weight: 5 lb. 10 oz.
Caliber: .177
Features: Newest addition to the Youth Precision Airguns family from Gamo; 525 fps with Match Lead Pellets and up to 750 fps with PBA Platinum; metal barrel; grooved cylinder for optional scope mounting
MSRP $110

Gamo USA

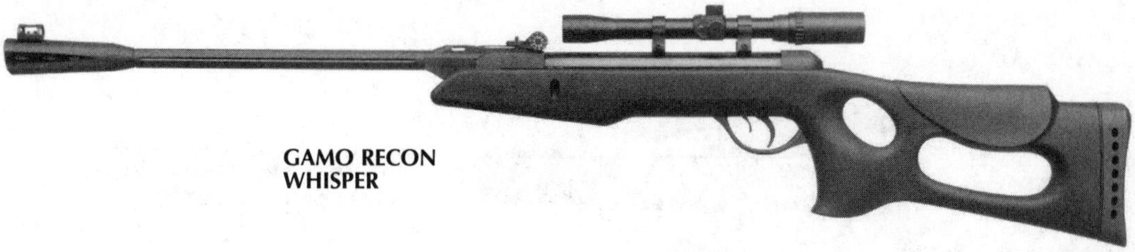

GAMO RECON WHISPER

GAMO VARMINT HUNTER HP 177

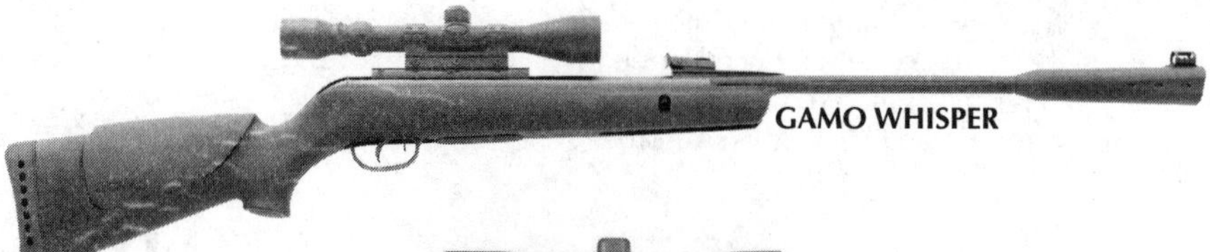

GAMO WHISPER

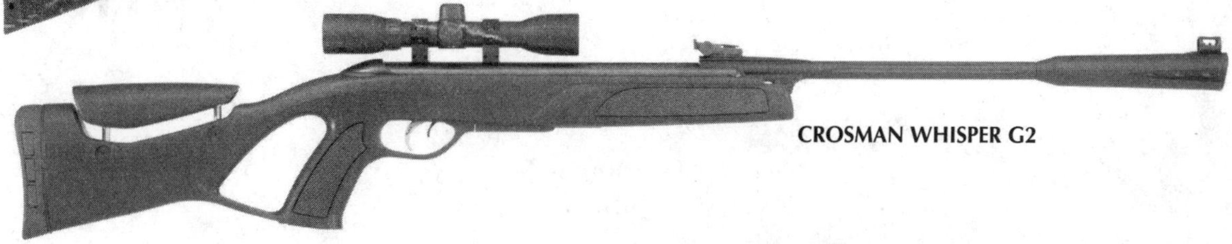

CROSMAN WHISPER G2

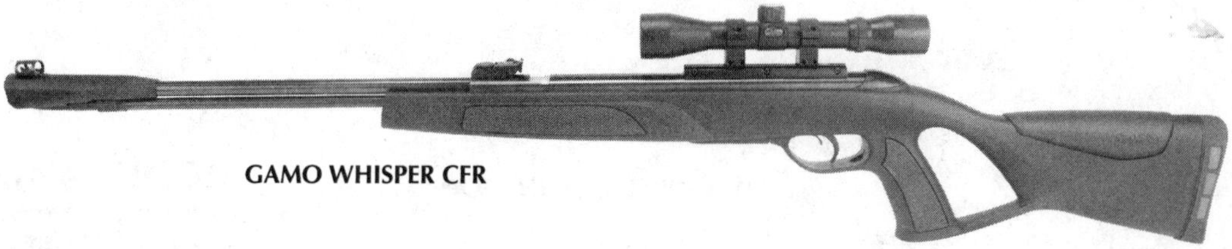

GAMO WHISPER CFR

RECON WHISPER

Power: Break action/spring piston
Stock: Synthetic
Overall Length: 37.2 in.
Sights: 4x20mm scope
Weight: 4 lb. 10 oz.
Caliber: .177
Features: All-weather black molded synthetic stock; ventilated rubber buttpad; twin cheekpads; automatic cocking safety system; 525 fps maximum velocity
MSRP. $120

VARMINT HUNTER HP 177

Power: Break action/spring piston
Stock: Synthetic
Length: 43.78 in.
Sights: 4x32mm scope
Weight: 6 lb. 10 oz.
Caliber: .177
Features: Lightweight synthetic stock; match grade fluted barrel; 1400 fps maximum velocity; 4x32mm air rifle scope with laser sight and flashlight; break barrel single cocking system
MSRP. $290

WHISPER

Power: Break action/spring piston
Stock: Synthetic
Overall Length: 37.2 in.
Sights: Mounted scope with rings
Weight: 4 lb. 10 oz.
Caliber: .177
Features: Raised rail scope mount with 39x40mm scope; two-stage adjustable trigger; manual safety; non-removable noise dampener; black synthetic all-weather stock; ventilated rubber buttplate; non-slip checkering on grip and forearm
MSRP. $270

WHISPER G2

Power: Compressed air
Stock: Synthetic
Overall Length: 46 in.
Sights: 4x32mm scope
Weight: 8 lb.
Caliber: .177, .22
Features: Single shot, break barrel action; fiber optic sights front and rear
MSRP. $270

WHISPER CFR

Power: Single shot/spring piston
Stock: Synthetic
Length: 46.85 in.
Sights: Fiber optic sights, mounted 4x32 standard reticle scope
Weight: 8 lb.
Caliber: .177
Features: First Whisper Air Rifle with a fixed barrel; integrated ND52 noise dampener system; fixed rifled steel barrel; capable of 1100 fps; newly designed recoil pad with 74 percent more recoil absorbing pressure; all-weather synthetic molded stock with thumbhole
MSRP. $300

Gamo USA

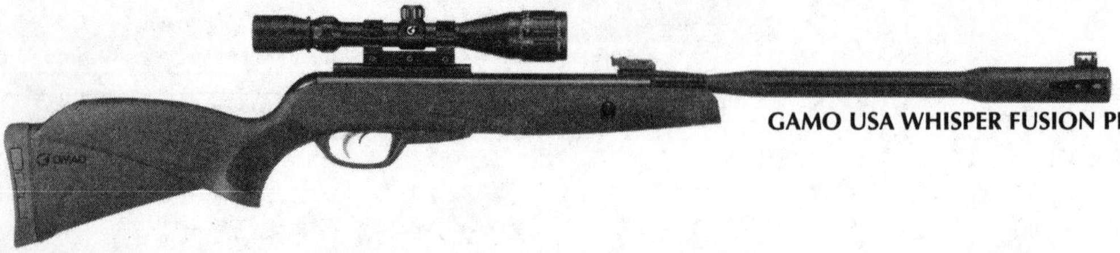

GAMO USA WHISPER FUSION PRO

WHISPER FUSION PRO

Power: Break action/spring piston
Stock: Synthetic
Overall Length: 43 in.
Sights: 3–9x40 adjustable objective scope
Weight: 8 lb.
Caliber: .177
Features: Includes the latest noise dampening technology developed exclusively by Gamo that is integrated in the barrel; noise is reduced by up to 89.5 percent; Smooth Action Trigger; new recoil pad Shock Wave Absorber that is able to absorb the recoil up to 74 percent; rubberized grips; all-weather black stock with adjustable cheekpiece; max velocity 1400 fps
MSRP $330

RWS

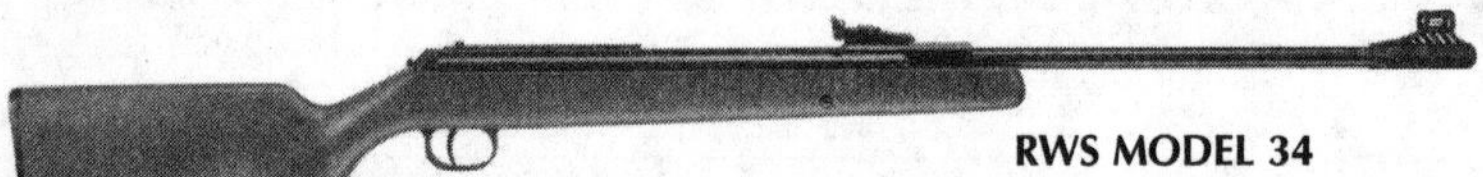

RWS MODEL 34

RWS MODEL 48 WITH SCOPE

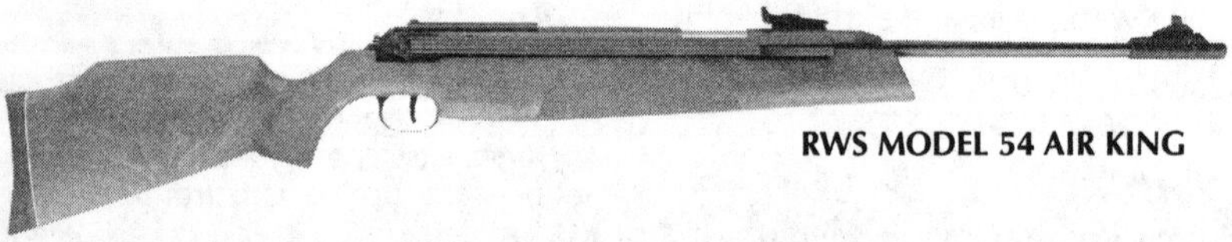

RWS MODEL 54 AIR KING

RWS MODEL 350 MAGNUM

MODEL 34

Power: Break action/spring piston
Stock: Hardwood, synthetic
Overall Length: 45 in.
Sights: 4x32mm scope
Weight: 7 lb. 8 oz.–8 lb.
Caliber: .177, .22
Features: Polished with blued metalwork; full-sized hardwood stock; two-stage adjustable trigger; automatic safety; finely rifled barrel; 34 Pro large muzzlebrake
MSRP $339
With scope: $395

MODEL 48

Power: Side lever/spring piston
Stock: Hardwood
Overall Length: 42.5 in.
Sights: Adjustable rear
Weight: 8 lb. 8 oz.
Caliber: .177
Features: Extended breech stock to reduce recoil; fixed barrel system; adjustable trigger; automatic safety; optional RWS 4x32mm scope and mounts
MSRP $575
With scope: $636

MODEL 54 AIR KING

Power: Side lever/spring piston
Stock: Hardwood
Overall Length: 43.75 in.
Sights: Adjustable rear
Weight: 9 lb.
Caliber: .177, .22, .25
Features: Adjustable trigger; scope rail; Monte Carlo hardwood stock with cheekpiece and checkering; automatic safety; 1100 fps maximum velocity
MSRP $847
With scope: $897

MODEL 350 MAGNUM

Power: Break action/spring piston
Stock: Hardwood
Overall Length: 48.3 in.
Sights: 4x32mm scope
Weight: 8 lb. 3 oz.
Caliber: .177, .22
Features: Two-stage trigger; mounted scope rail
MSRP . . . . $471–$565
With scope: $626

Stoeger Airguns

STOEGER AIRGUNS ATAC SUPPRESSOR

STOEGER X-5 SYNTHETIC

STOEGER X-20 SUPPRESSOR

STOEGER X-50 AIR RIFLE COMBO

AIR RIFLES

ATAC SUPPRESSOR

Power: Break action/gas-operated
Stock: Synthetic
Overall Length: 42.5 in.
Sights: 4–16x40mm scope
Weight: 8 lb. 14 oz.
Caliber: .177, .22
Features: Airflow control technology and dual-stage noise reduction system; automatic ambidextrous safety; black tactical stock; up to 1200 fps with alloy pellets (.177); adjustable length of pull; integral Picatinny rails
MSRP $299

X-5

Power: Break action/spring piston
Stock: Hardwood, black synthetic
Overall Length: 41 in.
Sights: Hooded front with red, fiber optic insert; rear fiber optic
Weight: 5 lb. 11 oz.
Caliber: .177
Features: Automatic, ambidextrous safety mounted on back of receiver; Monte Carlo-style stock; integral dovetail scope rail on receiver
MSRP $109

X-20 SUPPRESSOR

Power: Break action/spring piston
Stock: Black synthetic
Overall Length: 43 in.
Sights: 4x32mm illuminated red green scope
Weight: 7 lb.
Caliber: .177
Features: Air Flow Control system; adjustable two-stage trigger; integral dovetail scope rail on receiver; non-slip, deluxe rubber recoil pad; Monte Carlo-style, black synthetic stock with checkering; rifled, blued steel barrel
MSRP $249

X-50

Power: Break action/spring piston
Stock: Black synthetic
Overall Length: 50 in.
Sights: 3–9x40mm parallax adjustable scope with rings
Weight: 9 lb. 14 oz.
Caliber: .177
Features: Ergonomic cocking grip; rifled blued steel barrel; synthetic Monte Carlo-style stock; ambidextrous automatic safety
MSRP $319

SHOTGUNS

247 American Tactical
247 AYA (Aguirre y Aranzabal)
248 Benelli USA
251 Beretta USA
254 Bernardelli
254 Blaser USA
255 Browning
260 Caesar Guerini
262 Century International Arms
262 Charles Daly
262 Chiappa Firearms
264 Cimarron Firearms Co.
264 Connecticut Shotgun Mfg. Co.
264 CZ-USA (Ceska Zbrojovka)
269 Escort by Legacy Sports
270 Fabarm
271 Fausti USA
271 Federal Armament
272 Flodman Guns
272 Franchi
274 Ithaca Gun Company
275 Krieghoff
276 Ljutic
277 Marocchi
277 Merkel
278 Mossberg
281 Perazzi
281 Pointer by Legacy Sports
282 Purdey
282 Remington
286 Rossi
286 Ruger
286 Savage Arms
287 SRM Arms
287 Stoeger
290 Taylor's & Co.
290 Thompson/Center
290 Tristar Sporting Arms
292 UTAS
292 Weatherby
294 Winchester Repeating Arms

American Tactical

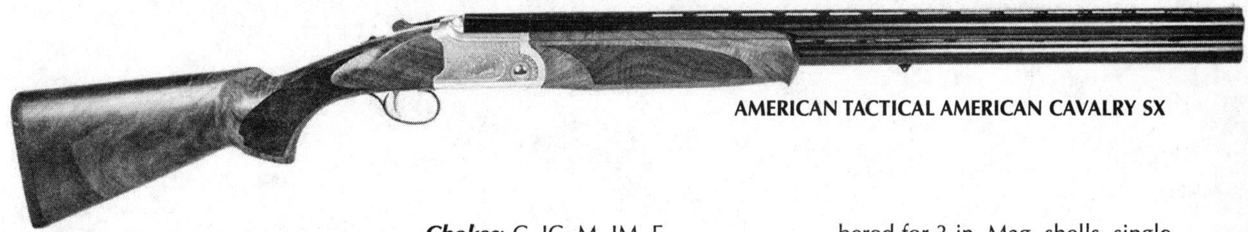

AMERICAN TACTICAL AMERICAN CAVALRY SX

CAVALRY SX OVER/UNDER

Action: Over/under
Stock: Turkish Walnut
Barrel: 26 in., 28 in.
Chokes: C, IC, M, IM, F
Weight: N/A
Bore/Gauge: 12, 20, 28, .410
Magazine: 2 shells
Features: Brass front bead sights, available with auto ejector, chambered for 3-in. Mag. shells, single selective trigger
MSRP . . . . $500–$560

AYA (Aguirre y Aranzabal)

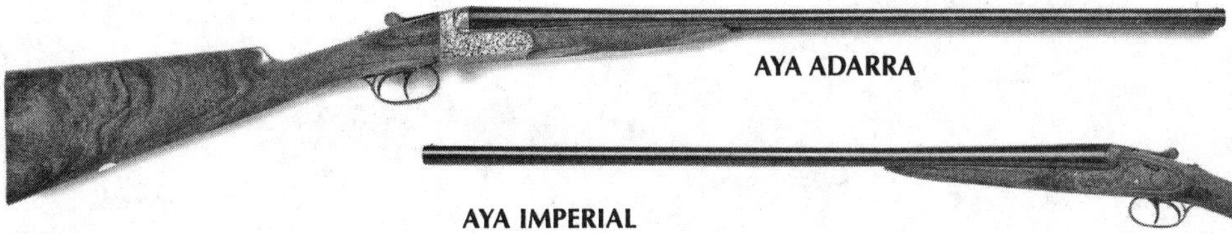

AYA ADARRA

AYA IMPERIAL

AYA MODEL NO. 4/53

ADARRA

Action: Side-by-side hammerless boxlock ejector shotgun
Stock: Walnut
Barrel: 28 in., with other lengths to order
Chokes: Screw-in tubes
Weight: 6 lb. 10 oz.
Bore/ Gauge: 12, 16, 20, 28, .410
Magazine: None
Features: Double locking mechanism with replaceable hinge pin; disc set firing pins; double trigger;
MSRP $5280

IMPERIAL

Action: Side-by-side hammerless sidelock
Stock: Walnut
Barrel: 28 in., with other lengths to order
Chokes: Screw-in tubes
Weight: 6 lb. 12 oz.
Bore/Gauge: 12, 16, 20, 28, .410
Magazine: None
Features: Forged steel action with double locking mechanism and gas vents; gold washed internal lock parts; gold lined cocking indicators; optional selective or non-selective single trigger; concave rib; straight hand, finely checkered walnut stock; gold initial oval
From $34385

MODEL NO. 4/53

Action: Side-by-side hammerless boxlock ejector
Stock: Walnut
Barrel: 28 in., with other lengths to order
Chokes: Screw-in tubes
Weight: 6 lb. 10 oz.
Bore/Gauge: 12, 16, 20, 28, .410
Magazine: None
Features: Double locking mechanism with replaceable hinge pin; disk set firing pins; double trigger; chopper lump barrels with concave rib; light scroll engraving; metal finish available in hardened, old silver, or white finish; automatic safety
From $7880

MODEL NO. 37

Action: Over/under sidelock
Stock: Walnut
Barrel: 28 in.
Chokes: Screw-in tubes
Weight: 7 lb. 8 oz.
Bore/Gauge: 12
Magazine: None
Features: Double underlocking lugs and double crossbolt; chopper lump chrome nickel steel barrels; hardened steel intercepting safety sears; gold line cocking indicators; gold washed internal lock parts; double trigger with hinged front trigger; fine rose and scroll, game scene, or bold relief engraving on action plates; full pistol grip walnut stock
From . . . . $16500–$17490

Benelli USA

AYA MODEL NO. 37

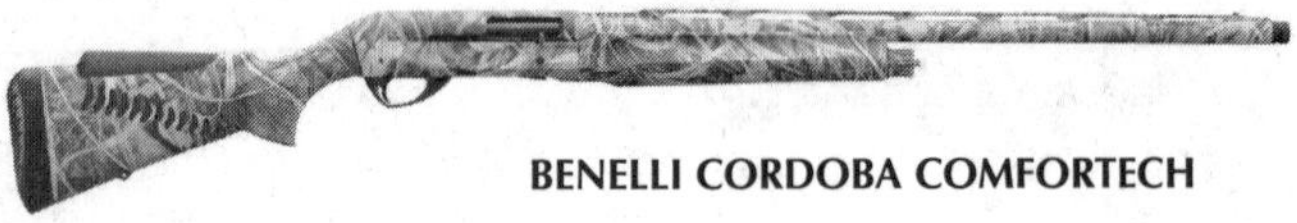

BENELLI CORDOBA COMFORTECH

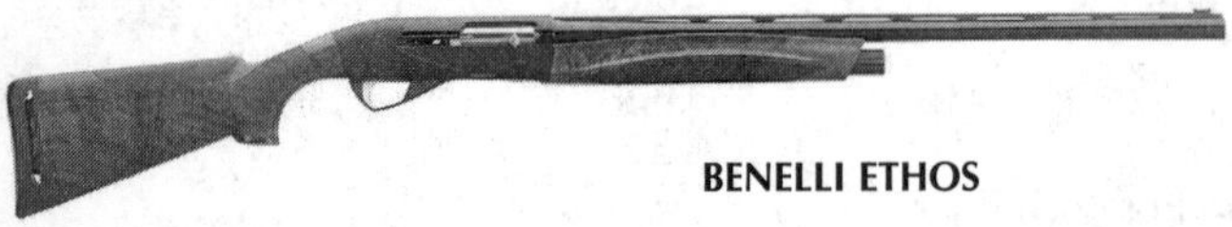

BENELLI ETHOS

BENELLI LEGACY

BENELLI LEGACY SPORT

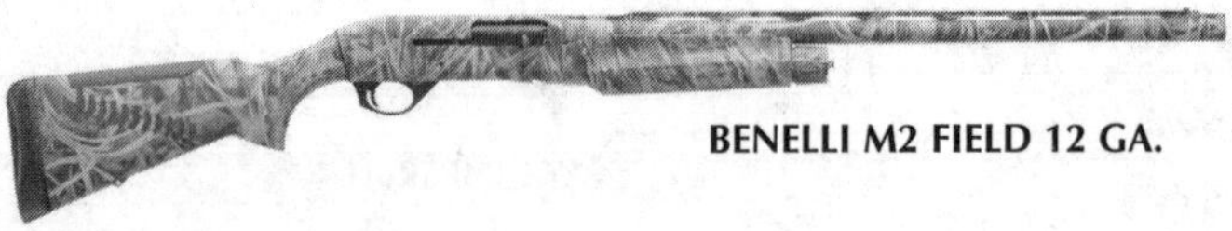

BENELLI M2 FIELD 12 GA.

BENELLI M2 FIELD 20 GA.

CORDOBA COMFORTECH

Action: Inertia operated semiautomatic
Stock: Synthetic
Barrel: 28 in., 30 in.
Chokes: Extended Crio Chokes
Weight: 7 lb.
Bore/Gauge: 12, 20
Magazine: 4+1 shells
Features: Black synthetic stock with GripTight; Crio ported barrels; ComforTech gel recoil pad and comb insert; heavy duty magazine cap
MSRP . . . . $2069–$2099

ETHOS

Action: Inertia-operated semiautomatic
Stock: Walnut
Barrel: 26 in., 28 in.
Chokes: C, IC, M, IM, F
Weight: 6 lb. 6 oz.–6 lb. 8 oz.
Bore/Gauge: 12
Magazine: 4+1 shells
Features: Progressive Comfort recoil reduction system; two-part carrier latch for easy reloading; interchanger-able fiber optic sights
MSRP . . . . $1999–$2199

LEGACY

Action: Inertia operated semiautomatic
Stock: Walnut
Barrel: 24 in., 26 in., 28 in.
Chokes: Crio Choke (C, IC, M, IM, F); 28 gauge: (C & M)
Weight: 4 lb. 14 oz.–7 lb. 6 oz.
Bore/Gauge: 12, 20, 28
Magazine: 4+1, 28 Ga.: 2+1 shells
Features: Satin walnut with Weathercoat or AA-grade stock; classic game scene etchings on receiver; red front sight and metal bead mid sight
MSRP . . . . $1799–$2039

LEGACY SPORT

Action: Inertia operated semiautomatic
Stock: Walnut
Barrel: 28 in., 30 in.
Chokes: Extended Crio Chokes (C, CI, M, IM, F)
Weight: 7 lb. 6 oz.–7 lb. 8 oz.
Bore/Gauge: 12
Magazine: 4+1 shells
Features: Acid-etched game scenes on receiver plates; AA-grade walnut stock; red front sight and metal bead mid sight
MSRP $2439

M2 FIELD 12 GA.

Action: Inertia operated semiautomatic
Stock: Synthetic, Realtree APG
Barrel: 21 in., 24 in., 26 in., 28 in.
Chokes: Crio Chokes (IC, M, F)
Weight: 6 lb. 14 oz.–7 lb. 3 oz.
Bore/Gauge: 12
Magazine: 3+1 shells
Features: ComforTech gel recoil pad and comb insert; ComforTech shim kit; red bar front sight; stock comes in black synthetic, Realtree APG, and Realtree MAX-4 Camo
Synthetic: $1449
Realtree APG: $1549

M2 FIELD 20 GA.

Action: Inertia operated semiautomatic
Stock: Synthetic
Barrel: 24 in., 26 in.
Chokes: Crio Chokes (IC, M, F)
Weight: 5 lb. 13 oz.–6 lb. 8 oz.
Bore/Gauge: 20
Magazine: 3+1 shells
Features: ComforTech gel recoil pad and comb insert; ComforTech shim kit; red bar front sight; synthetic stock in Realtree Max-4 Camo or matte black finish
Synthetic $1499
Realtree APG $1599

Benelli USA

BENELLI M2 FIELD COMPACT

BENELLI MONTEFELTRO BLACK SYNTHETIC

BENELLI NOVA PUMP TACTICAL

BENELLI PERFORMANCE SHOP SUPER BLACK EAGLE II TURKEY EDITION

BENELLI M2 PERFORMANCE SHOP 3-GUN

BENELLI SPORT II

BENELLI SUPER BLACK EAGLE II

M2 FIELD COMPACT

Action: Inertia operated semiautomatic
Stock: Black synthetic
Barrel: 24 in., 26 in.
Chokes: C, IC, M, IM, F
Weight: 5 lb. 10 oz.–7 lb.
Bore/ Gauge: 12, 20
Magazine: 3+1 shells
Features: M2 Field now in compact model; ComforTech gel recoil pad and comb insert; ComforTech shim kit; red bar front sight
MSRP . . . .$1449–$1499

MONTEFELTRO BLACK SYNTHETIC

Action: Semiautomatic
Stock: Black synthetic
Barrel: 26 in.
Chokes: IC, M, F
Weight: 6 lb. 14 oz.
Bore/ Gauge: 12
Magazine: 4 +1 shells
Features: Now with a black synthetic stock; red bar front sight; black rubber ventilated recoil pad; hard case included
MSRP $1139

NOVA PUMP TACTICAL

Action: Pump
Stock: Synthetic
Barrel: 18.5 in.
Chokes: Fixed cylinder choke
Weight: 7 lb. 3 oz.
Bore/Gauge: 12
Magazine: 4+1 shells
Features: Available with ghost-ring or open rifle sights; push-button shell stop; grooved grip surface stocks in black synthetic stock
MSRP . . . . $419–$459

PERFORMANCE SHOP SUPER BLACK EAGLE II TURKEY EDITION

Action: Inertia operated semiautomatic
Stock: Synthetic
Barrel: 24 in.
Chokes: Custom XTF extended choke
Weight: 7 lb. 2 oz.
Bore/Gauge: 12
Magazine: 3+1 shells
Features: Burris FastFire sight; ComforTech gel recoil pad and comb insert; larger trigger guard for use with gloves; EDM ported Crio barrel; ComforTech synthetic stock with Realtree APG finish
MSRP $2949

SPORT II

Action: Inertia operated semiautomatic
Stock: Walnut
Barrel: 28 in., 30 in.
Chokes: Extended Crio Chokes (C, CI, M, IM, F)
Weight: 6 lb. 5 oz.–7 lb. 5 oz.
Bore/Gauge: 12, 20
Magazine: 4+1 shells
Features: Red bar front sight and metal bead mid sight; Crio ported barrels; ComforTech gel recoil pad and comb insert; heavy duty magazine cap
MSRP $1899

SUPER BLACK EAGLE II

Action: Inertia operated semiautomatic
Stock: Walnut, synthetic, Realtree APG, Mossy Oak
Barrel: 24 in., 26 in., 28 in.
Chokes: Crio Choke (C, IC, M, IM, F)
Weight: 7 lb. 2 oz.–7 lb. 5 oz.
Bore/Gauge: 12
Magazine: 3+1 shells
Features: Red bar front sight and metal bead mid sight; ComforTech gel recoil pad and comb insert; larger trigger guard for use with gloves; stock in black synthetic, Realtree Max-4 camo, Realtree APG camo, or walnut
MSRP . . . . $1569–$1999

Benelli USA

SUPERNOVA FIELD

Action: Pump
Stock: Synthetic
Barrel: 24 in., 26 in., 28 in.
Chokes: Standard choke (IC, M, F)
Weight: 7 lb. 13 oz.–8 lb.
Bore/Gauge: 12
Magazine: 4+1 shells
Features: Stock comes in black synthetic, Realtree APG camo, or Realtree Max-4 camo; receiver drilled and tapped for scope mounting; standard chokes; vented recoil pad
ComforTech Stock: . . . . $549–$669
SteadyGrip Stock: $669

SUPERSPORT

Action: Inertia operated semiautomatic
Stock: Synthetic
Barrel: 28 in., 30 in.
Chokes: Extended Crio Chokes(C, IC, M, IM, F)
Weight: 6 lb. 5 oz.–7 lb. 5 oz.
Bore/Gauge: 12, 20
Magazine: 4+1 shells
Features: Stock comes in black SuperSport carbon fiber finish; red bar front sight and metal bead mid sight; Crio ported barrels; ComforTech gel recoil pad and comb insert
MSRP $2199

SUPER VINCI

Action: Inertia operated semiautomatic
Stock: Synthetic, Realtree APG
Barrel: 26 in., 28 in.
Chokes: Crio Chokes (C, IC, M, IM, F)
Weight: 6 lb. 14 oz.–7 lb.
Bore/Gauge: 12
Magazine: 3+1 shells
Features: In-line inertia driven system; enlarged trigger and trigger guard for use with gloves; ComforTech Plus recoil pad; QuadraFit shim kit; drilled and tapped for scopes; synthetic stock in black, Realtree APG camo, or Realtree MAX-4 camo
MSRP . . . . $1799–$1899

ULTRA LIGHT

Action: Inertia operated semiautomatic
Stock: Walnut
Barrel: 24 in., 26 in.
Chokes: Crio Chokes (IC, M, F)
Weight: 5 lb. 3 oz.–6 lb. 2 oz.
Bore/Gauge: 12, 20, 28
Magazine: 2+1 shells
Features: Weather-coated walnut stock; red bar front sight and metal bead mid sight; gel recoil pad; option of checkered Montefeltro forend or ultra light forend
MSRP . . . . $1669–$1799

VINCI

Action: Inertia operated semiautomatic
Stock: Synthetic
Barrel: 24 in., 26 in., 28 in.
Chokes: Crio Chokes (C, IC, M, IM, F)
Weight: 6 lb. 13 oz.–6 lb. 14 oz.
Bore/Gauge: 12
Magazine: 3+1 shells
Features: Stock in black, Realtree APG, Realtree APG HD SteadyGrip, or Realtree MAX-4 camo; red bar front sight and metal bead mid sight; drilled and tapped for scope mounting; ComforTech Plus recoil pads
MSRP . . . .$1359–$1629

BENELLI SUPERNOVA FIELD

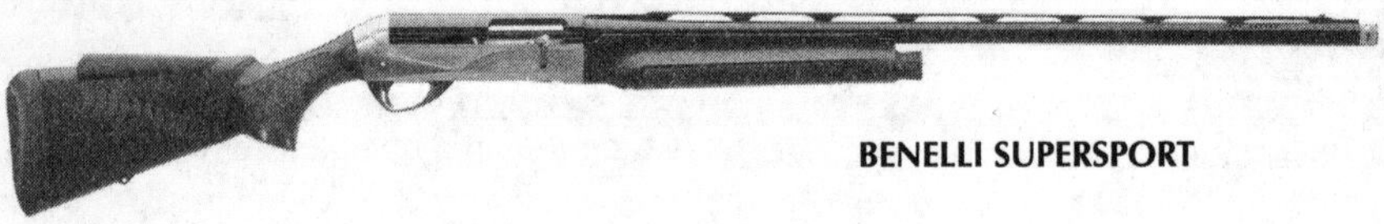

BENELLI SUPERSPORT

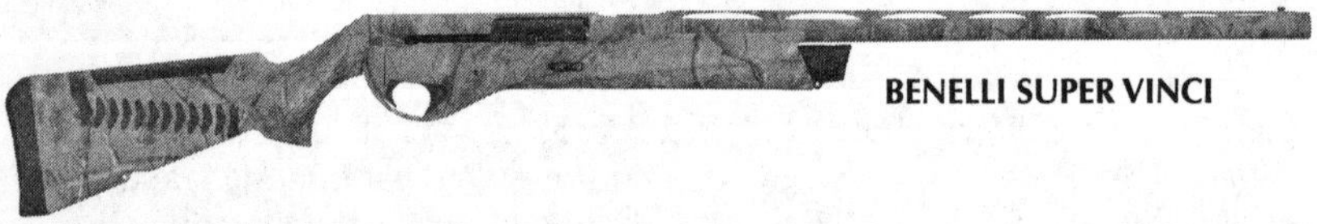

BENELLI SUPER VINCI

BENELLI ULTRA LIGHT

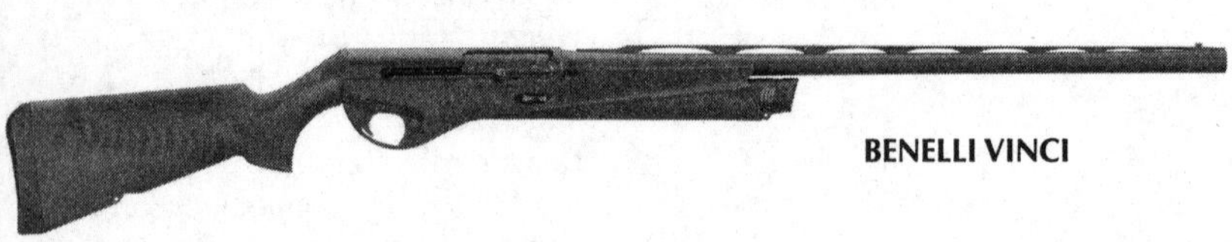

BENELLI VINCI

Beretta USA

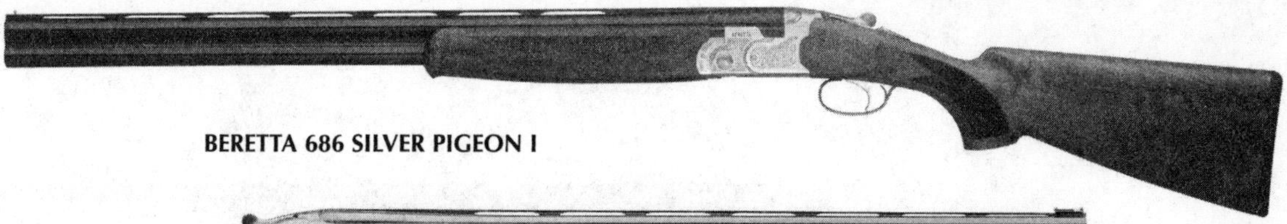

BERETTA 686 SILVER PIGEON I

BERETTA 687 SILVER PIGEON V

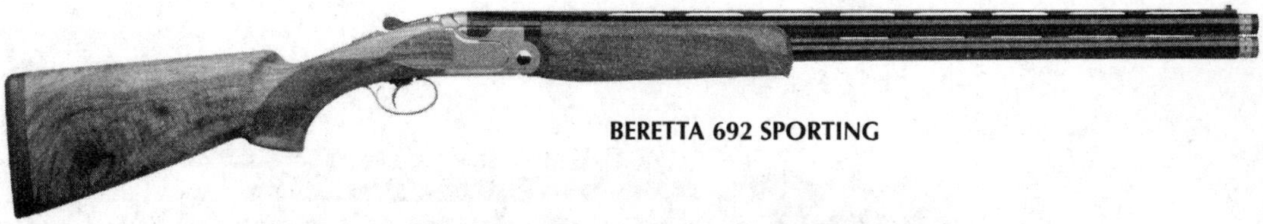

BERETTA 692 SPORTING

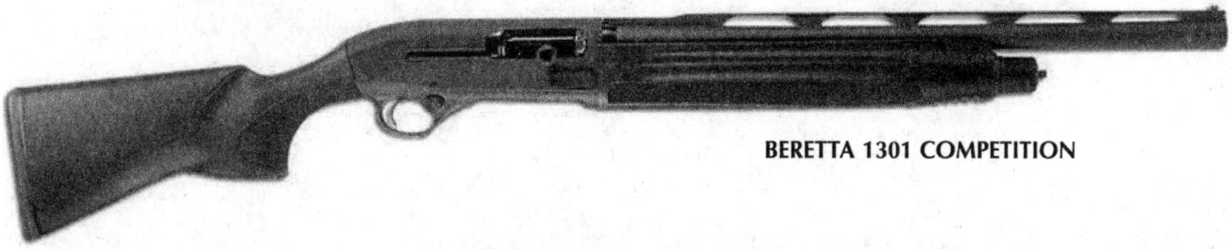

BERETTA 1301 COMPETITION

BERETTA 1301 TACTICAL

686 SILVER PIGEON I

Action: Over/under
Stock: Walnut
Barrel: 26 in., 28 in., 30 in.
Chokes: MC
Weight: 6 lb. 13 oz.
Bore/Gauge: 12, 20, 28, .410
Magazine: 2 shells
Features: Extensive but refined floral and scroll decoration on the frame; dual-conical locking mechanism; automatic safety; oil finish on checkered walnut stock and forend; metal bead sight
MSRP. $2350

687 SILVER PIGEON V

Action: Over/under
Stock: Walnut
Barrel: 28 in.
Chokes: Screw-in tubes
Weight: 6 lb. 13 oz.
Bore/Gauge: 12, 20, 28, .410
Magazine: 2 shells
Features: Oil-finished walnut stock detailed with gold game bird inlays and a gold Beretta medallion underneath; color-case finish; single selective trigger; 3-inch chambers; available with English stock or standard stock with pistol grip
MSRP. . . . . $4800–$5275

692 SPORTING

Action: Over/under
Stock: Walnut
Barrel: 30 in., 32 in.
Chokes: 5 OCHP
Weight: 7 lb. 11 oz.
Bore/ Gauge: 12
Magazine: 2 shells
Features: Steelium Plus barrels; longer forcing cone; Beretta Fast Adjustment System Technology; Adjustable Balance System; adjustable trigger
MSRP. . . . .$4800–$5275

1301 COMPETITION

Action: Gas-operated semiautomatic
Stock: Synthetic
Barrel: 21 in., 24 in.
Chokes: IC
Weight: 7 lb. 2 oz.
Bore/Gauge: 12
Magazine: 5+1 shells
Features: Fiber optic sights; oversized bolt release and handle; Optima Bore HP interchangable choke system
MSRP. $1275

1301 TACTICAL

Action: Gas-operated semiautomatic
Stock: Synthetic
Barrel: 18.5 in.
Chokes: F
Weight: 7 lb. 2 oz.
Bore/Gauge: 12
Magazine: 5+1 shells
Features: Ghost ring sight; front blade sight; Picatinny rail; oversized bolt release and handle; fixed cylinder choke
MSRP. $1075

Beretta USA

BERETTA A300 OUTLANDER

BERETTA A400 XPLOR ACTION

BERETTA A400 XPLOR LIGHT

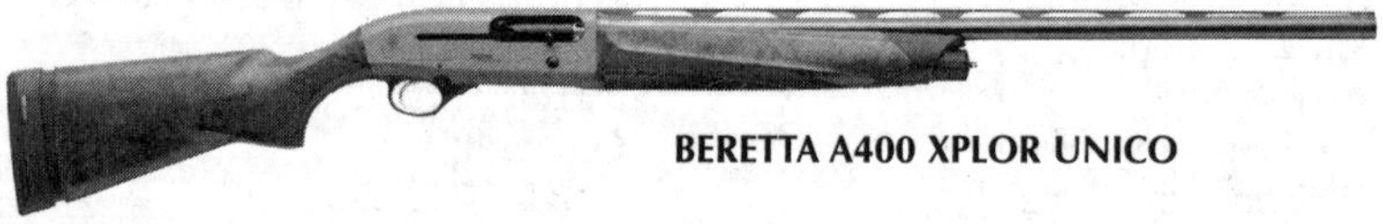

BERETTA A400 XPLOR UNICO

A300 OUTLANDER

Action: Gas-operated semiautomatic
Stock: Synthetic, camo, walnut
Barrel: 28 in.
Chokes: MC3
Weight: 7 lb. 10 oz.
Bore/Gauge: 12
Magazine: 3+1 shells
Features: Gas operation with compensating exhaust valve and self-cleaning piston; adjustable shim system on stock; aluminum alloy receiver; crossbolt safety with ergonomics; front metal bead sight; black synthetic, camo, or oiled wood stock finish
Synthetic: $775
Wood: $875
Camo: . . . . $845 –$875

A400 XPLOR ACTION

Action: Gas-operated semiautomatic
Stock: Walnut
Barrel: 26 in., 28 in.
Chokes: F
Weight: 5 lb. 8 oz.
Bore/Gauge: 28
Magazine: 3+1 shells
Features: Fiber optic sights; Gun Pod shell counter, cartridge tester, and temperature display; Kick-Off recoil reduction system; Optima Bore interchangable bore system
MSRP. . . . . $1600–$1700

A400 XPLOR LIGHT 12 GA.

Action: Semiautomatic
Stock: Walnut and polymer
Barrel: 26 in., 28 in.
Chokes: OptimaChoke screw-in tube
Weight: 6 lb. 3 oz.–6 lb. 10 oz.
Bore/Gauge: 12
Magazine: 3+1 or 2+1 shells
Features: Steelium barrel design, walnut stock with polymer forend insert, trigger guard and kick-off interface; 3-in. chamber; blink operating system; Micro-Core recoil pad; available with kick-off damper system
MSRP. $1600

A400 XPLOR UNICO

Action: Semiautomatic
Stock: Walnut or polymer
Barrel: 26 in., 28 in.
Chokes: OptimaChoke screw-in tube
Weight: 6 lb. 10 oz.–7 lb.
Bore/Gauge: 12
Magazine: 3+1 or 2+1 shells
Features: Single-selective trigger; green receiver; walnut stock with polymer forend insert, trigger guard and kick-off interface; 3.5-in. chamber; metal bead front sight; camo or green anodized available
MSRP. . . . . $1750–$1850

Beretta USA

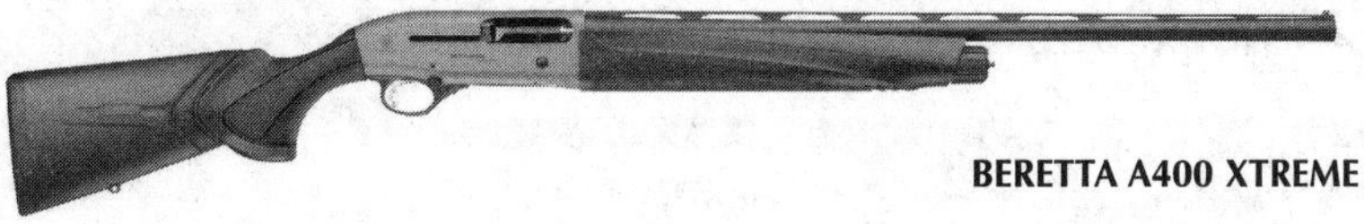

BERETTA A400 XTREME

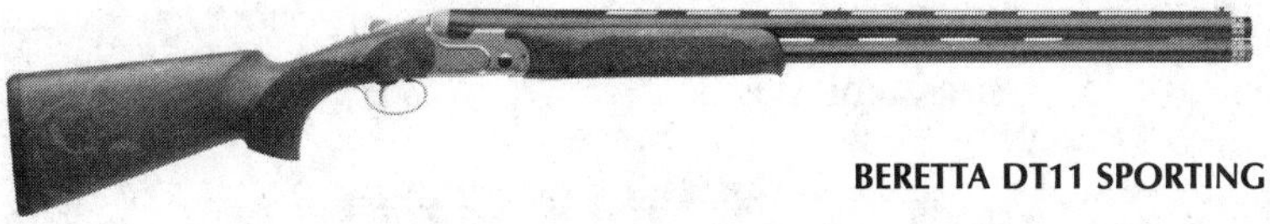

BERETTA DT11 SPORTING

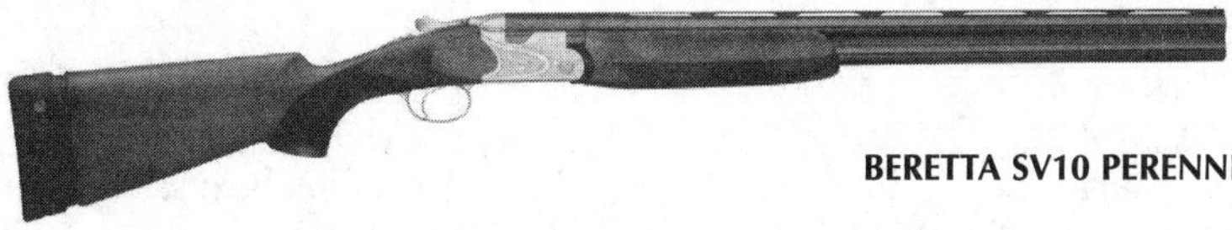

BERETTA SV10 PERENNIA I

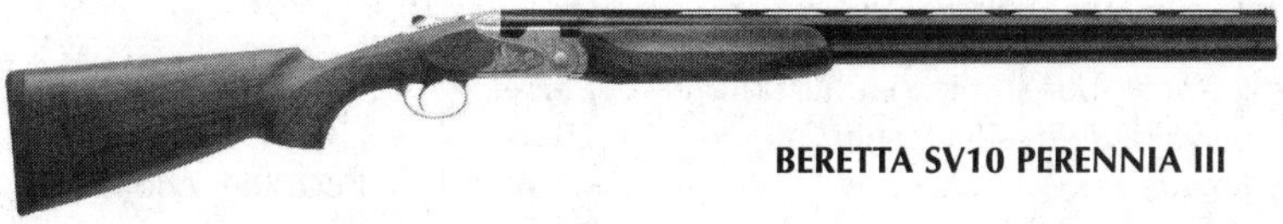

BERETTA SV10 PERENNIA III

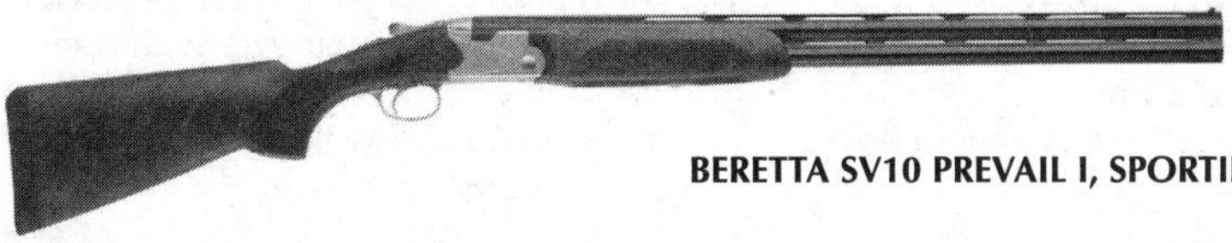

BERETTA SV10 PREVAIL I, SPORTING

A400 XTREME

Action: Semiautomatic
Stock: Synthetic or camo
Barrel: 26 in., 28 in.
Chokes: Optima Bore HP (C, Mod, Full)
Weight: 7 lb. 10 oz.
Bore/Gauge: 12
Magazine: 4+1 or 3+1 shells
Features: Advanced Kick-Off Mega recoil system; Micro-Core recoil pad; overmolded grip panels; Aqua Technology's corrosion proof barrier; synthetic black or MAX4 camo.
Synthetic: $1750
MAX4: $1895

DT11 SPORTING

Action: Over/under
Stock: Walnut
Barrel: 30 in., 32 in.
Chokes: OCHPe
Weight: 9 lb.
Bore/ Gauge: 12
Magazine: 2 shells
Features: Steelium Pro barrel; top rib with hollowed bridges; ergonomic top lever; safety selector switch; increased receiver side wall thickness; select high-quality walnut wood finished in oil; stock and forend can be fitted to customer's measurement; pistol grip and forend are hand-checkered; B-Fast adjustable stock available
MSRP . . . . $8650–$12999

SV10 PERENNIA I

Action: Over/under
Stock: Walnut or synthetic
Barrel: 26 in., 28 in., 30 in.
Chokes: Optima-Choke HP
Weight: 7 lb.
Bore/Gauge: 12, 20
Magazine: 2 shells
Features: Nano-Ceramic forend iron reduces wear and corrosion; choice between automatic ejection and mechanical extraction; floral engraving; Kick-Off recoil system available; Micro-Core recoil pad.
Standard: $2895
KO: $3295

SV10 PERENNIA III

Action: Over/under
Stock: Walnut
Barrel: 26 in., 28 in.
Chokes: OptimaChoke HP Extended
Weight: 7 lb. 5 oz.
Bore/Gauge: 12, 20
Magazine: 2 shells
Features: Optional Kick-Off hydraulic dampening reduction system; sling swivels; plastic pad; Optima-bore high-performance cold, hammer-forged barrels; automatic safety; chrome-lined bore and chamber
MSRP . . . . $3620–$3945

SV10 PREVAIL I

Action: Over/under
Stock: Walnut
Barrel: 30 in., 32 in.
Chokes: Optima Bore HP Extended
Weight: 7 lb. 13 oz.
Bore/Gauge: 12
Magazine: 2 shells
Features: Kick-Off, extraction/ejection selection system; easy-removable trigger group; Xtra-Grain walnut checkered stock with oil finish; manual safety; white front bead with steel mid-bead sights; available in sporting and trap versions
MSRP . . . . $2900–$3450

Bernardelli

BERNARDELLI HEMINGWAY DELUXE

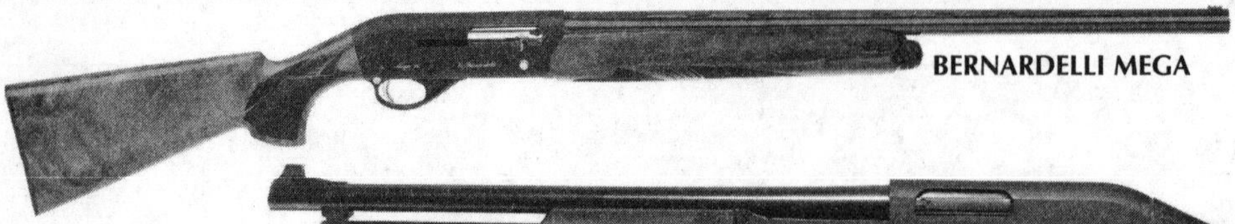
BERNARDELLI MEGA

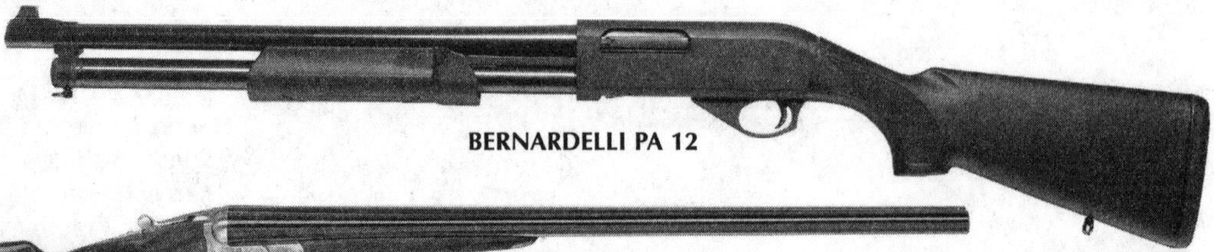
BERNARDELLI PA 12

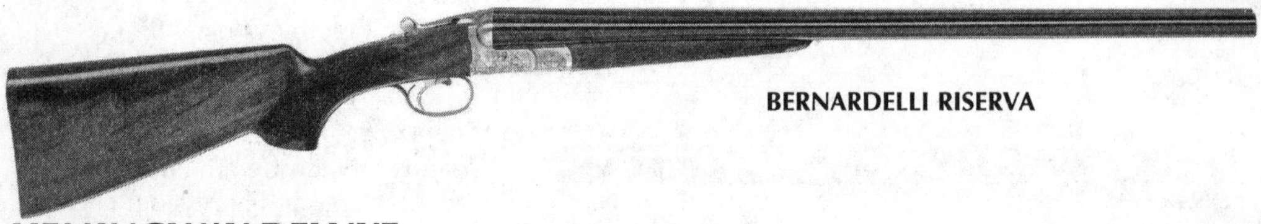
BERNARDELLI RISERVA

HEMINGWAY DELUXE

Action: Side-by-side
Stock: Walnut
Barrel: 24 in., 26 in., 27 in., 28 in., 29 in.
Chokes: Fixed cylinder chokes
Weight: 6 lb. 2 oz.–6 lb. 3 oz.
Bore/Gauge: 12, 20
Magazine: 2 shells
Features: Simple or automatic extractors; double trigger or single trigger with selector; beavertail buttstock; forged steel frame; English walnut stock with pistol grip
MSRP. $5887

MEGA

Action: Semiautomatic
Stock: Walnut or synthetic
Barrel: 24 in., 26 in., 28 in., 30 in.
Chokes: 5 tubes
Weight: 5 lb. 14 oz.
Bore/ Gauge: 20
Magazine: 5+1 shells
Features: Gas-operated system with partial autocompensator for a more uniform action bar speed; plasma technology to increase corrosion resistance; four shims to adjust drop; also available in silver, sporting, and synthetic
MSRP Available upon request

PA 12

Action: Pump
Stock: Synthetic
Barrel: 20 in.
Chokes: Steel cylinder chokes
Weight: 6 lb.
Bore/Gauge: 12
Magazine: 6+1 shells
Features: Synthetic black matte stock; shipped in carton box; steel barrel
MSRP. $596

RISERVA

Action: Side-by-side
Stock: Walnut
Barrel: 24 in., 26 in., 27 in., 28 in., 29 in.
Chokes: Fixed cylinder chokes
Weight: 6 lb. 13 oz.
Bore/Gauge: 12
Magazine: 2 shells
Features: Forged steel frame; double trigger or single trigger with selector; simple or automatic extractor; English walnut stock with pistol grip; beavertail buttstock
Standard:. $5069
De Luxe: $5646

Blaser USA

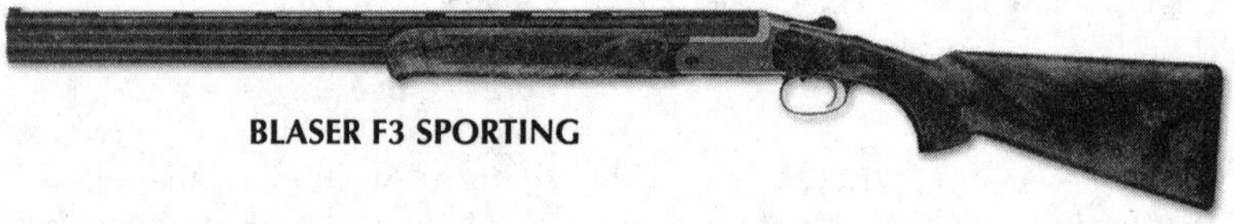
BLASER F3 SPORTING

F3 SPORTING

Action: Over/under
Stock: Walnut
Barrel: 28 in., 30 in., 32 in., 34 in.
Chokes: Briley Spectrum chokes (SK, IC, M., IM, F)
Weight: 7 lb. 5 oz.
Bore/Gauge: 12, 20, 28, .410
Magazine: 2 shells
Features: Sporting stock, forearm with Schnabel; internal block system; ergonomically optimized, adjustable trigger blade; Triplex Bore design; ejection-ball-system; balancer
Standard:. $7613
Luxus: $9340
Grand Luxus: $12233
Super Luxus: $13913
Baronesse:. $15010
Exclusive:. . . . . . . Price on request
Super Exclusive:. . Price on request
Imperial: . . . . Price on request

BROWNING A5 HUNTER

BROWNING A5 STALKER

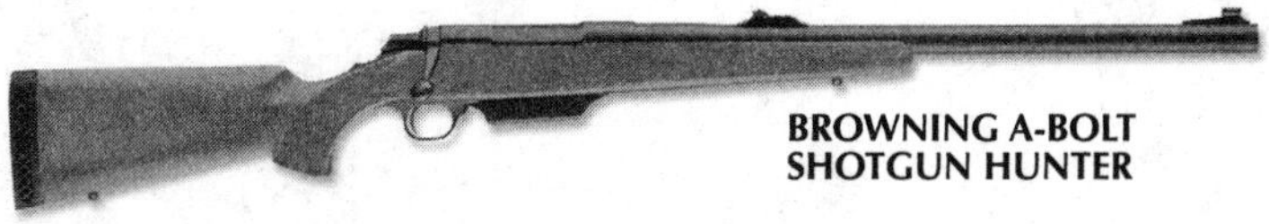

BROWNING A-BOLT SHOTGUN HUNTER

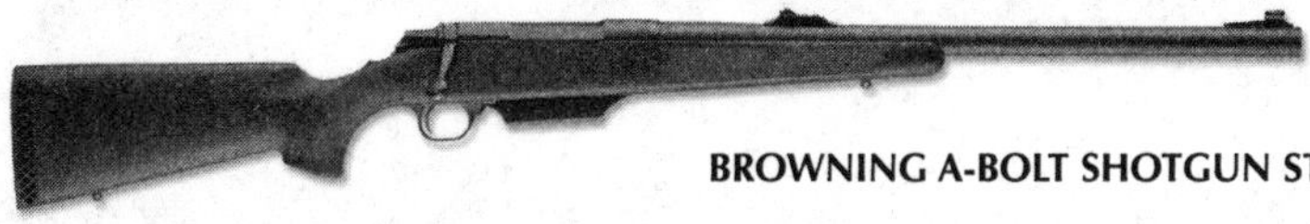

BROWNING A-BOLT SHOTGUN STALKER

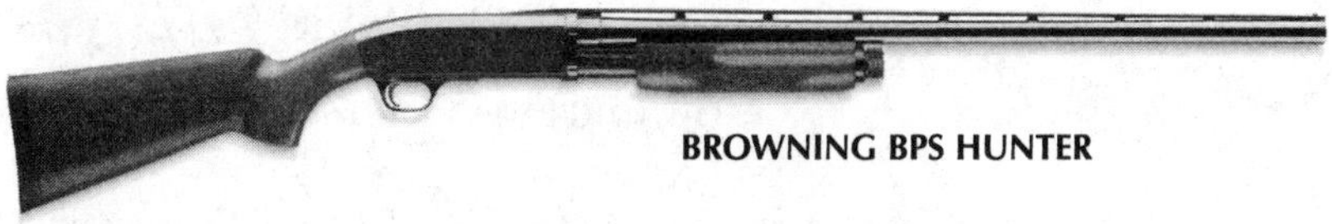

BROWNING BPS HUNTER

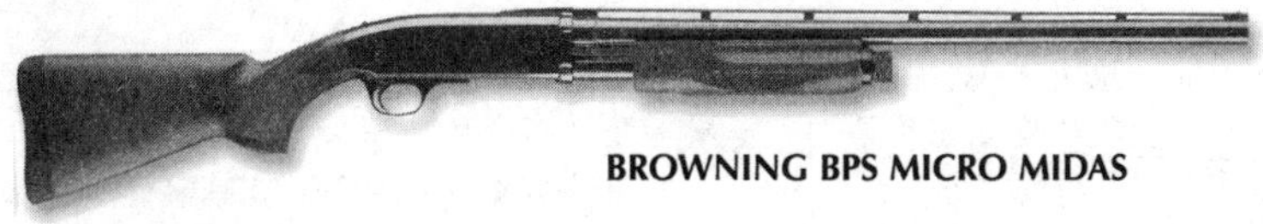

BROWNING BPS MICRO MIDAS

A5 HUNTER

Action: Semiautomatic
Stock: Walnut
Barrel: 26 in., 28 in., 30 in.
Chokes: Invector-DS
Weight: 6 lb. 15 oz.
Bore/Gauge: 12
Magazine: None
Features: Strong, lightweight aluminum alloy; black anodized bi-tone finish; flat, ventilated rib; recoil operated Kinematic Drive is ultra-reliable and cycles a wide range of loads; gloss finish walnut with close radius pistol grip; 22 lines-per-inch checkering; shim adjustable for length of pull, cast and drop; Vector Pro lengthened forcing cone; three invector-DS™ choke tubes; Inflex II technology recoil pad; brass front bead sight; ivory mid-bead sight; included ABS case
MSRP . . . . $1500–$1630

A5 STALKER

Action: Semiautomatic
Stock: Composite
Barrel: 26 in., 28 in., 30 in.
Chokes: Invector-DS
Weight: 7 lb. 3 oz.–7 lb. 7 oz.
Bore/Gauge: 12
Magazine: None
Features: Strong, lightweight aluminum alloy; flat, ventilated rib; recoil operated Kinematic Drive is ultra-reliable and cycles a wide range of loads; composite with close radius pistol grip; textured gripping surfaces; shim adjustable for cast and drop; matte black finish; Dura-Touch armor coating; Vector Pro lengthened forcing cone; Inflex II technology recoil pad; fiber-optic front sight; included ABS case
MSRP . . . . $1629–$1760

A-BOLT SHOTGUN HUNTER

Action: Bolt
Stock: Walnut
Barrel: 22 in.
Chokes: None
Weight: 7 lb. 2 oz.
Bore/Gauge: 12
Magazine: Detachable, 2+1 shells
Features: Sling swivel studs; satin finish walnut stock with checkered forearm; low-luster blued finish, steel receiver; drilled and tapped for scope mounts
MSRP $1280

A-BOLT SHOTGUN STALKER & INFINITY CAMO

Action: Bolt
Stock: Composite
Barrel: 22 in.
Chokes: None
Weight: 7 lb.
Bore/Gauge: 12
Magazine: Detachable, 2+1 shells
Features: Black composite (Stalker model); Mossy Oak Break-Up Infinity composite (Infinity Camo Model); textured gripping surfaces; Dura-touch armor coating; sling swivel studs installed; recoil pad; Truglo/Marble's fiber optic front sight, adjustable rear sight
Stalker: $1150
Infinity Camo: $1300

BPS HUNTER

Action: Pump
Stock: Walnut
Barrel: 26 in., 28 in.
Chokes: Three Invector-Plus choke tubes with 12 and 20 gauges; Standard Invectors with 16, 28, and .410
Weight: 6 lb. 15 oz.–7 lb. 11 oz.
Bore/Gauge: 12, 16, 20, 28, .410
Magazine: None
Features: Satin finish walnut stock; forged and machined steel receiver; ventilated rib barrel; top-tang safety
MSRP . . . . $700–$730

BPS MICRO MIDAS

Action: Pump
Stock: Walnut
Barrel: 24 in., 26 in.
Chokes: 3 Invector-Plus (12, 20 Ga.), 3 Standard Invector (28, .410 Ga.)
Weight: 6 lb. 15 oz.–7 lb. 10 oz.
Bore/ Gauge: 12, 20, 28, .410
Magazine: None
Features: Ventilated rib barrel; dual steel action bars; top-tang safety; scaled down for smaller shooters; Inflex Technology recoil; silver colored front bead sight; stock spacers
MSRP . . . . $700–$730

Browning

BPS RIFLED DEER HUNTER
Action: Pump
Stock: Walnut
Barrel: 22 in.
Chokes: Screw-in tubes
Weight: 7 lb. 4 oz.–7 lb. 10 oz.
Bore/Gauge: 12, 20
Magazine: None
Features: Satin finish walnut stock; forged and machined steel receiver; thick-walled barrel for slug ammunition only; dual steel action bars
MSRP . . . . $830–$840

BPS TRAP
Action: Pump
Stock: Walnut
Barrel: 30 in.
Chokes: Three Invector-Plus choke tubes
Weight: 8 lb. 2 oz.
Bore/Gauge: 12
Magazine: None
Features: Satin finish walnut stock with raised comb; forged and machined steel receiver with engraving; dual steel action bars; top-tang safety; magazine cut-off; HiViz ProComp fiber optic sight with mid-bead
MSRP $840

BT-99
Action: Pump
Stock: Walnut
Barrel: 32 in., 34 in.
Chokes: Screw-in tubes
Weight: 8 lb. 3 oz.–8 lb. 5 oz.
Bore/Gauge: 12
Magazine: None
Features: Satin finish walnut stock with beavertail forearm; steel receiver with blued finish; high-post ventilated rib
MSRP $1430

BT-99 MICRO MIDAS
Action: Pump
Stock: Walnut
Barrel: 28 in., 30 in.
Chokes: 1 Invector-Plus
Weight: 7 lb. 11 oz
Bore/ Gauge: 12
Magazine: None
Features: Blued finish; high-post ventilated rib barrel; beavertail forearm; scaled down for smaller shooters; Vector-Pro lengthed forcing cone; recoil pad; ivory front and mid-bead sights
MSRP $1430

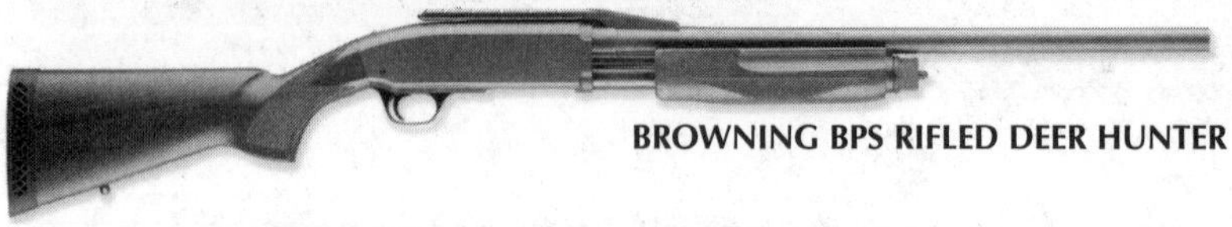
BROWNING BPS RIFLED DEER HUNTER

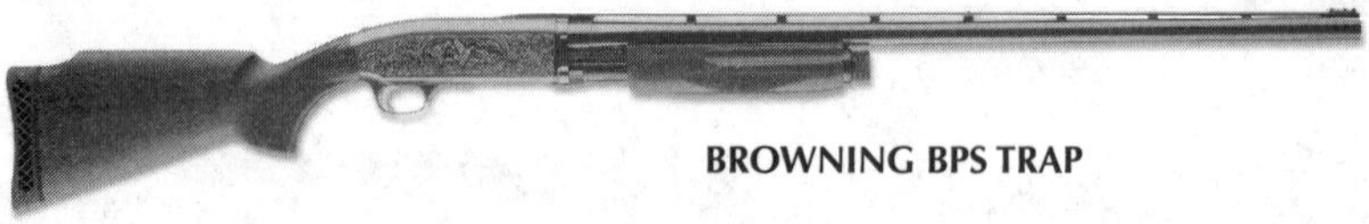
BROWNING BPS TRAP

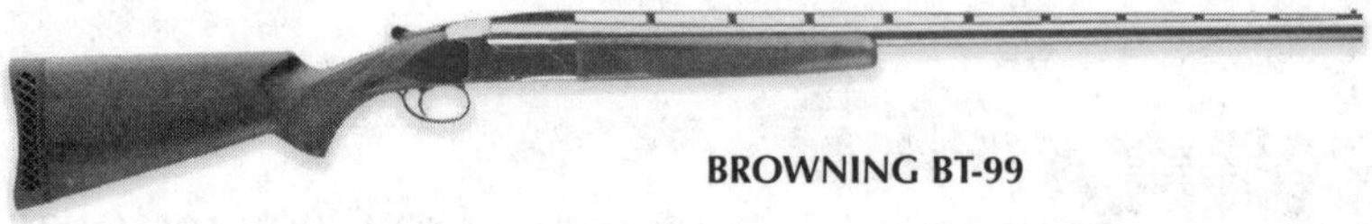
BROWNING BT-99

BROWNING BT-99 MICRO MIDAS

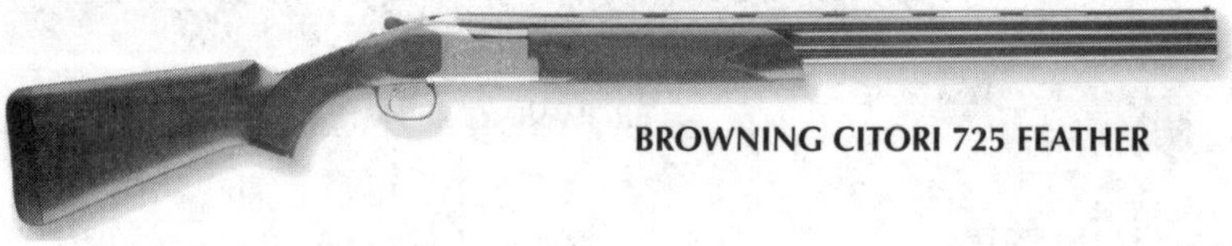
BROWNING CITORI 725 FEATHER

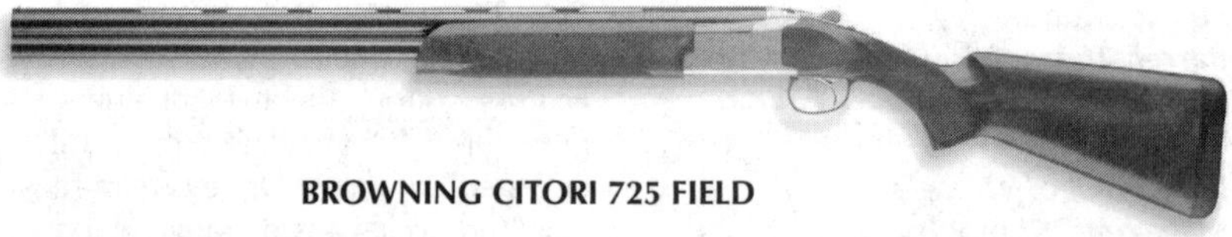
BROWNING CITORI 725 FIELD

CITORI 725 FEATHER
Action: Over/under
Stock: Walnut
Barrel: 26 in., 28 in.
Chokes: 3 Invector-DS
Weight: 6 lb. 7 oz.
Bore/ Gauge: 12
Magazine: 2 shells
Features: Lightweight alloy receiver; low-profile; silver nitride finish; ventilated top rib barrel; Fire Lite Mechanical Trigger system; hammer ejectors; ivory front and mid-bead sights
MSRP $2550

CITORI 725 FIELD
Action: Over/under
Stock: Walnut
Barrel: 26 in., 28 in.
Chokes: Invector-DS
Weight: 7 lb. 4 oz.–7 lb. 6 oz.
Bore/Gauge: 12
Magazine: 2 shells
Features: Steel receiver with silver nitride finish; accented, high-relief engraving; ventilated top rib action; mechanical trigger system; hammer ejectors; top-tang barrel selector/safety; gloss oil finish Grade II/III walnut with close radius pistol grip; Vector Pro lengthened forcing cones; ivory front and mid-bead sights
MSRP . . . . $2470 –$2540

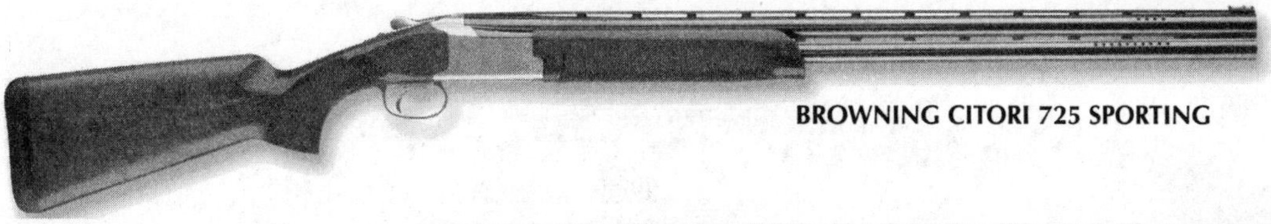

BROWNING CITORI 725 SPORTING

BROWNING CITORI 725 SPORTING ADJUSTABLE COMB

BROWNING CITORI 725 TRAP ADJUSTABLE COMB

BROWNING CITORI LIGHTNING

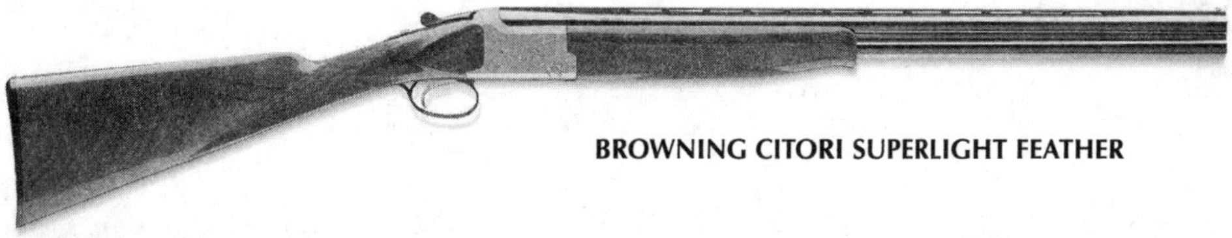

BROWNING CITORI SUPERLIGHT FEATHER

CITORI 725 SPORTING

Action: Over/under
Stock: Walnut
Barrel: 28 in., 30 in., 32 in.
Chokes: Invector-DS
Weight: 7 lb. 6 oz.–7 lb. 10 oz.
Bore/Gauge: 12
Magazine: 2 shells
Features: Steel receiver with silver nitride finish; gold accented engraving; ventilated top and side rib action; mechanical trigger system; hammer ejectors; top-tang barrel selector/safety; gloss oil finish Grade III/IV walnut with close radius pistol grip; Vector Pro lengthened forcing cones; five Invector-DS choke tubes; HiViz Pro-Comp sight and ivory mid-bead
MSRP . . . . $3140–$3200

CITORI 725 SPORTING ADJUSTABLE COMB

Action: Over/under
Stock: Wood
Barrel: 32 in.
Chokes: F, IM, M, IC, S
Weight: 7 lb. 13 oz.
Bore/Gauge: 12
Magazine: 2 shells
Features: Steel low-profile receiver with silver nitride finish and gold accented engraving; ventilated barrel with top and side ribs; Fire Lite mechanical trigger system; top-tang barrel selector/safety; gloss oil finish Grade III/IV walnut stock with close radius pistol grip and adjustable comb; HiViz Pro-Comp sight and ivory mid-bead
MSRP $3600

CITORI 725 TRAP ADJUSTABLE COMB

Action: Over/under
Stock: Wood
Barrel: 32 in.
Chokes: F, IM, M
Weight: 8 lb. 11 oz.
Bore/Gauge: 12
Magazine: 2 shells
Features: Steel low-profile receiver with silver nitride finish and gold accented engraving; ventilated barrel with top and side ribs; Fire Lite mechanical trigger system; top-tang barrel selector/safety; gloss oil finish Grade III/IV walnut stock with close radius pistol grip and Monte Carlo or adjustable straight comb; HiViz Pro-Comp sight and ivory mid-bead
MSRP $3340

CITORI LIGHTNING

Action: Over/under
Stock: Walnut
Barrel: 26 in., 28 in.
Chokes: Three Invector-Plus choke tubes on 12 and 20, three standard Invector tubes on 28 and .410
Weight: 6 lb. 7 oz.–8 lb. 2 oz.
Bore/Gauge: 12, 20, 28, .410
Magazine: 2 shells
Features: Walnut stock with pistol grip; ventilated rib; single selective trigger; hammer ejectors; top-tang barrel selector/safety; ivory front bead sight
MSRP . . . . $1990–$2070

CITORI SUPERLIGHT FEATHER

Action: Over/under
Stock: Walnut
Barrel: 26 in.
Chokes: Invector-Plus
Weight: 5 lb. 11 oz.–6 lb. 4 oz.
Bore/Gauge: 12, 20, 28, .410
Magazine: 2 shells
Features: Lightweight alloy receiver with steel breech face and hinge pin; high-relief engraving; single selective trigger; hammer ejectors; top-tang barrel selector/safety; gloss finish walnut, English-style straight grip stock, Schnabel forearm; three Invector-Plus choke tubes
MSRP $2390

Browning

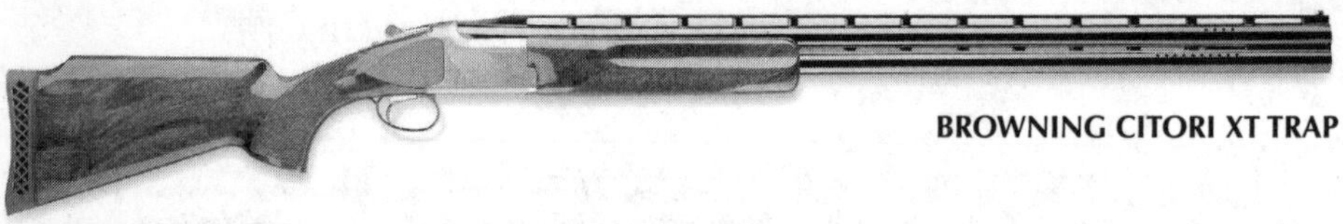

BROWNING CITORI XT TRAP

BROWNING CYNERGY CLASSIC TRAP UNSINGLE COMBO WITH ADJUSTABLE COMB

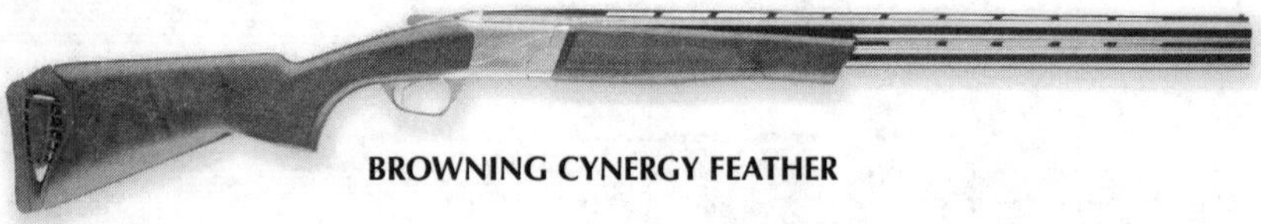

BROWNING CYNERGY FEATHER

BROWNING CYNERGY FIELD

CITORI XT TRAP

Action: Over/under
Stock: Walnut
Barrel: 30 in., 32 in.
Chokes: Three Invector-plus choke tubes
Weight: 8 lb. 6 oz.–8 lb. 8 oz.
Bore/Gauge: 12
Magazine: 2 shells
Features: Triple-trigger system; HiViz Pro-Comp sight; steel receiver with gold accented engravings; ventilated barrel; walnut stock with close radius pistol grip and right-hand palm swell; semi-beavertail forearm with finger grooves
MSRP. $2650

CYNERGY CLASSIC TRAP UNSINGLE COMBO WITH ADJUSTABLE COMB

Action: Single shot and over/under
Stock: Walnut
Barrel: 30 in., 32 in.
Chokes: Four Invector-Plus Midas Grade choke tubes
Weight: 8 lb. 13 oz.–8 lb. 15 oz.
Bore/Gauge: 12
Magazine: 1 or 2 shells
Features: Steel receiver with MonoLock hinge; double- and single-barrel sets included; reverse striker ignition system; impact ejectors; top-tang barrel selector/safety; gloss finish Monte Carlo grade III/IV walnut stock with right-hand palm swell
MSRP. $4270

CYNERGY FEATHER

Action: Over/under
Stock: Walnut
Barrel: 26 in., 28 in.
Chokes: Three Invector-Plus choke tubes on 12 and 20, Standard Invector on 28 and .410
Weight: 5 lb. 12 oz.–6 lb. 10 oz.
Bore/Gauge: 12, 20
Magazine: 2 shells
Features: Lightweight alloy receiver; gold enhanced grayed finish; MonoLock hinge; reverse striker ignition system; top-tang barrel selector/safety; Inflex technology recoil pad system; ivory front and mid-bead sights
MSRP. . . . . $2140–$2200

CYNERGY FIELD

Action: Over/under
Stock: Walnut
Barrel: 26 in., 28 in.
Chokes: Three Invector-Plus choke tubes on 12 and 20; Standard Invector on 28 and .410
Weight: 6 lb. 1 oz.–7 lb. 11 oz.
Bore/Gauge: 12, 20, 28, .410
Magazine: 2 shells
Features: Steel receiver with MonoLock hinge; reverse striker ignition system; impact ejectors; oil finish walnut stock; ivory front and mid-bead sights
MSRP. . . . . $1870–$1940

Browning

BROWNING CYNERGY SATIN FIELD

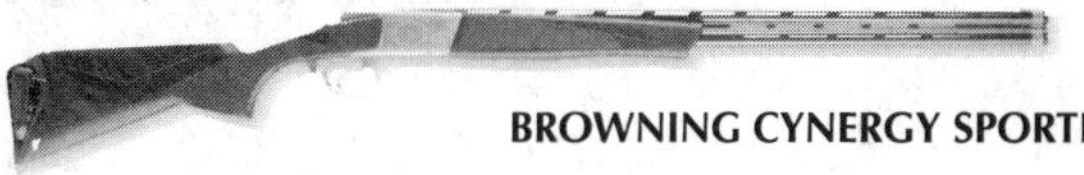

BROWNING CYNERGY SPORTING

BROWNING GOLD LIGHT 10 GA., MOSSY OAK DUCK BLIND

BROWNING MAXUS HUNTER

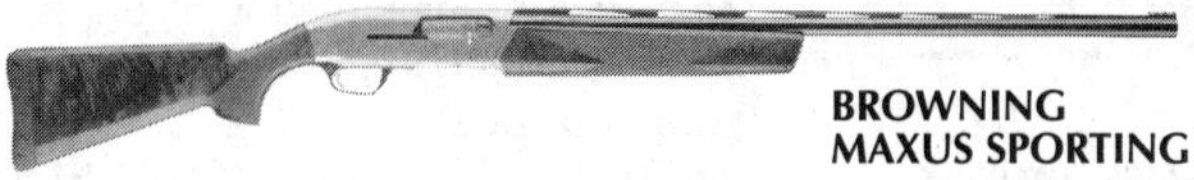

BROWNING MAXUS SPORTING

BROWNING MAXUS SPORTING GOLDEN CLAYS

CYNERGY SATIN FIELD

Action: Over/under
Stock: Wood
Barrel: 28 in.
Chokes: F, M, IC
Weight: 7 lb. 11 oz.
Bore/Gauge: 12
Magazine: 2 shells
Features: Inflex recoil pad; Reverse Striker mechanical trigger; Grade I wood stock
MSRP. $1740

CYNERGY SPORTING

Action: Over/under
Stock: Walnut
Barrel: 30 in., 32 in.
Chokes: Three Invector-Plus choke tubes
Weight: 6 lb. 4 oz.–8 lb. 1 oz.
Bore/Gauge: 12
Magazine: 2 shells
Features: Reverse striker ignition system; impact ejectors; top-tang barrel selector/safety; gloss oil finish on grade III/IV walnut; steel receiver; Inflex technology recoil pad system; HiViz Pro-Comp fiber optic sight
MSRP. $2400

GOLD LIGHT 10 GA.

Action: Gas-operated semiautomatic
Stock: Composite
Barrel: 26 in., 28 in.
Chokes: Three Standard Invector choke tubes
Weight: 9 lb. 9 oz.–9 lb. 10 oz.
Bore/Gauge: 10
Magazine: 4+1 shells
Features: Aluminum alloy receiver; ventilated rib barrel; composite stock and forearm in MO Break-Up Infinity or MO Shadow Grass Blades; DuraTouch armor coating
MSRP. . . . .$1740–$1870

MAXUS HUNTER

Action: Gas-operated semiautomatic
Stock: Composite
Barrel: 26 in., 28 in., 30 in.
Chokes: Three Invector-Plus
Weight: 6 lb. 15 oz.–7 lb. 1 oz.
Bore/Gauge: 12
Magazine: None
Features: Aluminum alloy receiver with durable satin nickel finish; laser engraving of pheasant and mallard on receiver; Inflex technology recoil pad; ivory front bead sight
MSRP. . . . . $1550–$1700

MAXUS SPORTING

Action: Gas-operated semiautomatic
Stock: Walnut
Barrel: 28 in., 30 in.
Chokes: Five Invector-Plus choke tubes
Weight: 7 lb. 3 oz.–7 lb. 4 oz.
Bore/Gauge: 12
Magazine: None
Features: Aluminum alloy receiver with durable satin nickel finish; laser engraving of game birds transforming into clay birds; speed lock forearm; ivory mid bead sight, HiVix Tri-Comp fiber optic front sight
MSRP. $1760

MAXUS SPORTING GOLDEN CLAYS

Action: Gas-operated semiautomatic
Stock: Walnut
Barrel: 28 in., 30 in.
Chokes: 5 Invector-Plus
Weight: 7 lb. 3 oz.
Bore/ Gauge: 12
Magazine: None
Features: Gold-enhanced engraving; lightweight aluminum alloy; flat, ventilated rib; 3 in. chamber; Power Drive Gas System; Speed Lock Forearm; Vector Pro lengthened forcing cone; HiViz Pro-Comp fiber optic front sight
MSRP. $2070

Browning

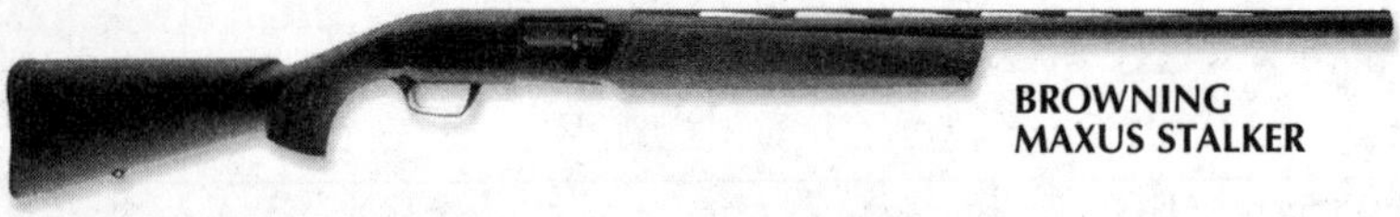

BROWNING MAXUS STALKER

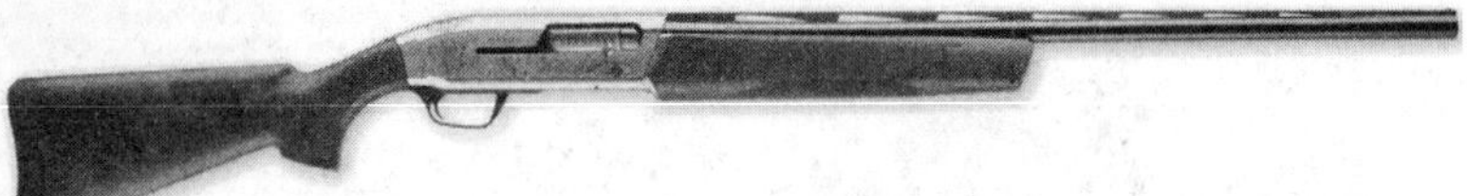

BROWNING MAXUS ULTIMATE

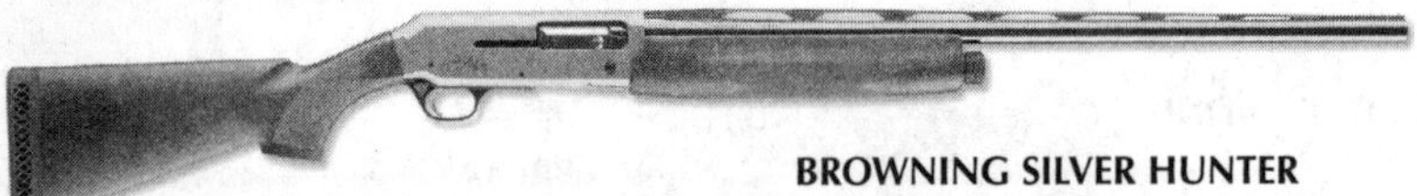

BROWNING SILVER HUNTER

BROWNING SILVER HUNTER MICRO MIDAS

MAXUS STALKER

Action: Gas-operated semiautomatic
Stock: Composite
Barrel: 26 in., 28 in.
Chokes: Three Invector Plus choke tubes
Weight: 7 lb.–7 lb. 2 oz.
Bore/Gauge: 12
Magazine: None
Features: Magazine cut-off, matte black composite stock with pistol grip; speed lock forearm; textured gripping surfaces; Dura Touch armor coating; Inflex technology recoil pads; lightning trigger system; ventilated rib
MSRP. . . . . $1380–$1550

MAXUS ULTIMATE

Action: Gas-operated semiautomatic
Stock: Walnut
Barrel: 26 in., 28 in., 30 in.
Chokes: Invector Plus (F, M, IC)
Weight: 7 lb. 1 oz.–7 lb. 4 oz.
Bore/Gauge: 12
Magazine: None
Features: Strong, lightweight aluminum alloy receiver; durable satin nickel finish; laser engraved (pintails on the left-hand side and pheasants on the right); gloss blued finish; ventilated rib; gloss oil finished grade III walnut with close radius pistol grip; speed lock forearm; shim adjustable for length of pull, cast, and drop; Inflex technology recoil pad; brass bead front sight; ABS case included
MSRP. $1940

SILVER HUNTER

Action: Gas-operated semiautomatic
Stock: Walnut
Barrel: 26 in., 28 in., 30 in.
Chokes: Three Invector-Plus choke tubes
Weight: 6 lb. 5 oz.–7 lb. 9 oz.
Bore/Gauge: 12, 20
Magazine: None
Features: Aluminum alloy receiver; ventilated rib barrel; satin finish walnut stock
MSRP. . . . . $1200–$1360

SILVER HUNTER MICRO MIDAS

Action: Gas-operated semiautomatic
Stock: Walnut
Barrel: 24 in., 26 in.
Chokes: Three Invector-Plus choke tubes
Weight: 6 lb.–7 lb. 5 oz.
Bore/Gauge: 12, 20
Magazine: None
Features: Semi-humpback receiver design with silver finish; ivory front bead sight
MSRP. $1200

Caesar Guerini

CAESAR GUERINI CHALLENGER ASCENT

CHALLENGER ASCENT

Action: Over/under
Stock: Hand-rubbed oil
Barrel: 30 in., 32 in.
Chokes: 6 MAXIS competition chokes
Weight: 8 lb. 6 oz.–8 lb. 8 oz.
Bore/ Gauge: 12
Magazine: 2 shells
Features: 10mm high tapered top rib is designed to shoot at 50/50 percent point-of-impact; White Bradley style front sight, with brass center bead; DTS trigger system; manual safety
MSRP. $6175

ELLIPSE

Action: Round body
Stock: Hand-rubbed oil on walnut
Barrel: 28 in.
Chokes: 5 nickel plated, flush fitting
Weight: 6 lb. 1 oz.–7 lb. 4 oz.
Bore/ Gauge: 12, 20, 28
Magazine: 2 shells
Features: Engraving pattern coated with Invisalloy; brass front bead sight; single (selective optional) trigger; manual safety; tapered, solid top rib
MSRP. . . . . $4325–$6175

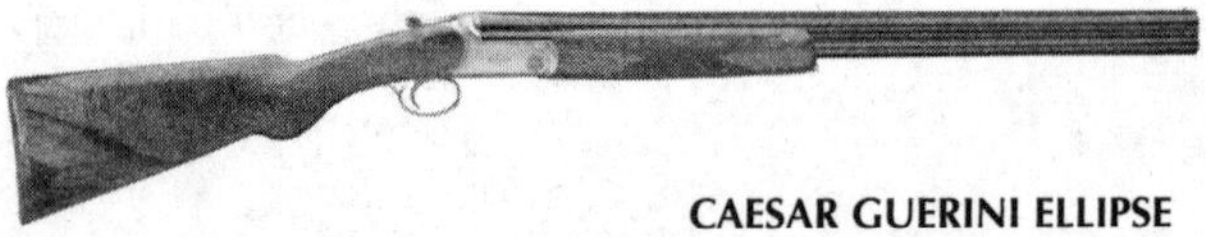

CAESAR GUERINI ELLIPSE

Caesar Guerini

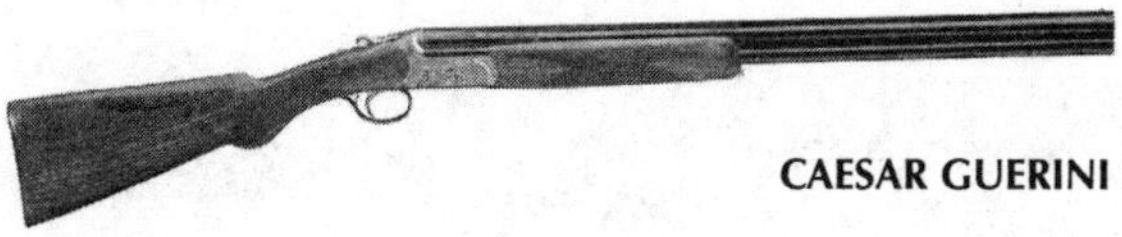

CAESAR GUERINI ELLIPSE EVO

CAESAR GUERINI INVICTUS I SPORTING

CAESAR GUERINI MAGNUS SPORTING

CAESAR GUERINI MAXUM IMPACT

CAESAR GUERINI TEMPIO FIELD GUN

CAESAR GUERINI WOODLANDER

ELLIPSE EVO

Action: Over/under
Stock: Walnut
Barrel: 28 in.
Chokes: 5 choke tube options
Weight: 6 lb.–7 lb.
Bore/Gauge: 12, 20, 28
Magazine: None
Features: Single trigger; rounded forend; chrome-lined barrel; non-ventilated center rib; hand-polished coin finish receiver with Invisalloy protective finish
MSRP . . . . $6150–$8115

CAESAR GUERINI INVICTUS I SPORTING

Action: Over/under
Stock: Wood
Barrel: 30 in., 32 in.
Chokes: 6 MAXIS competition chokes
Weight: 8 lb. 1 oz.–8 lb. 3 oz.
Bore/Gauge: 12
Magazine: 2 shells
Features: White Bradley style front silver center bead; manual safety (automatic optional); DTS-2 trigger system with two trigger pull weight options, take up, over travel and length of pull adjustments
MSRP $6750

MAGNUS SPORTING

Action: Over/under
Stock: Hand-rubbed oil on walnut
Barrel: 30 in., 32 in., 34 in.
Chokes: 6 CCP competition chokes (6 MAXIS for 12 Ga. models)
Weight: 7 lb. 6 oz.–8 lb. 2 oz.
Bore/ Gauge: 12, 20, 28, .410
Magazine: 2 shells
Features: Single selective trigger; manual safety; ventilated center rib; available 20/28 gauge combo and 20/28/.410 gauge combo
MSRP $5150
Combo gauges: . . . . . . $7005–$9035

MAXUM IMPACT

Action: Over/under
Stock: Checkered walnut with adjustable cheekpiece
Barrel: 30 in., 32 in., 34 in.
Chokes: Maxis choke system
Weight: 7 lb. 11 oz.–8 lb. 7 oz.
Bore/Gauge: 12, 20
Magazine: 2 shells
Features: Engraved receiver; 17mm-tall D.T.S. rib for more upright shooting; 5 in. dual conical forcing cones; selective and non-selective triggers available; left-hand available
MSRP . . . . $8450–$10800

TEMPIO FIELD GUN

Action: Over/under
Stock: Turkish walnut
Barrel: 26 in., 28 in., 30 in.
Chokes: 5 nickel plated, flush fitting chokes
Weight: 6 lb.–7 lb.
Bore/Gauge: 12, 20, 28, .410
Magazine: 2 shells
Features: Designed to be a sleek and fast pointing shotgun in the field; perfect companion for upland game hunters; low-profile receiver matched with a trim stock, classic Prince-of-Wales grip and schnabel forend make the gun a perfect match for fast game birds; contemporary style of "ornato" style scroll with tasteful gold accents; Invisalloy protective coating
MSRP . . . . $3350–$7575

WOODLANDER

Action: Over/under
Stock: English walnut
Barrel: 26 in., 28 in., 30 in.
Chokes: Five precision patterned flush chokes (CYL, IC, M, IM, F)
Weight: 6 lb.–7 lb.
Bore/Gauge: 12, 20, 28, .410
Magazine: 2 shells
Features: Gun reflects passion for fall coverts, autumn foliage, wet gun dogs, and the smell of wood; understated elegance of color case hardening and nicely figured, oil-finished English walnut that speaks of quality from a bygone era; a superior-handling upland game gun that's perfect for tight cover and fast-flushing birds
MSRP . . . .$3350–$6975

Century International Arms

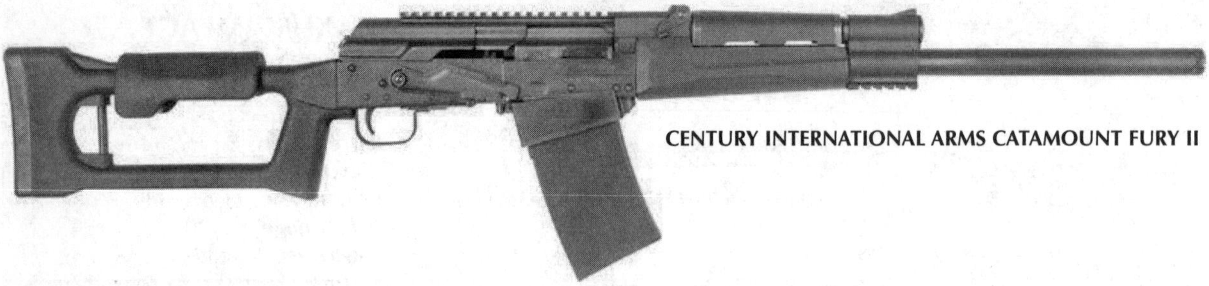

CENTURY INTERNATIONAL ARMS CATAMOUNT FURY II

CATAMOUNT FURY II
Action: Gas-operated semiautomatic
Stock: Synthetic
Barrel: 20.125 in.
Chokes: F, M, C
Weight: 8 lb. 11 oz.
Bore/Gauge: 12
Magazine: Detachable box, 5 shells
Features: Gas system is adjustable for both high and low pressure ammunition; accepts both 2 ¾-in. and 3-in. shells; magazine locks in and drops free more like an M16 style magazine
MSRP $586

Charles Daly

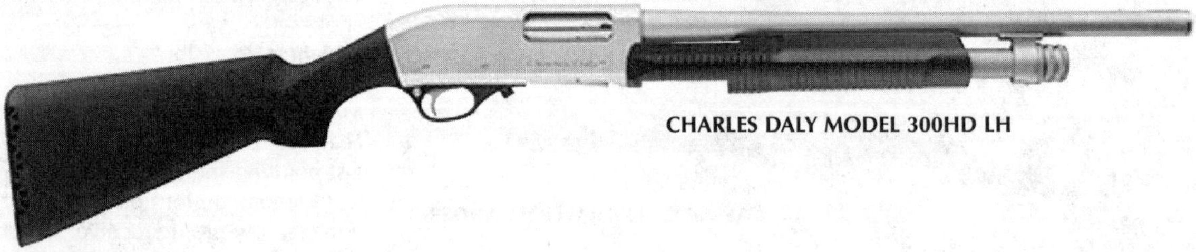

CHARLES DALY MODEL 300HD LH

MODEL 300 HOME DEFENSE LEFT-HANDED
Action: Pump
Stock: Synthetic
Barrel: 18.5 in.
Chokes: C
Weight: 5 lb. 8 oz.
Bore/Gauge: 12
Magazine: 5+1 shells
Features: Bead sight; push button safety at rear of trigger guard; ventilated rib; black oxide blued finish
MSRP $387

Chiappa Firearms

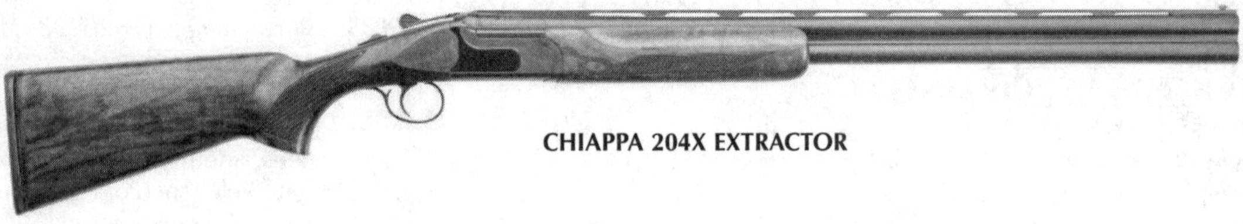

CHIAPPA 204X EXTRACTOR

204X EXTRACTOR
Action: Over/under
Stock: Walnut
Barrel: 26 in., 28 in.
Chokes: Skeet, IC, MOD, IM, F
Weight: 6 lb. 6 oz.–6 lb. 13 oz.
Bore/Gauge: 20, 12
Magazine: 2 shells
Features: Fiber optic sights; matte black receiver
MSRP $846

Chiappa Firearms

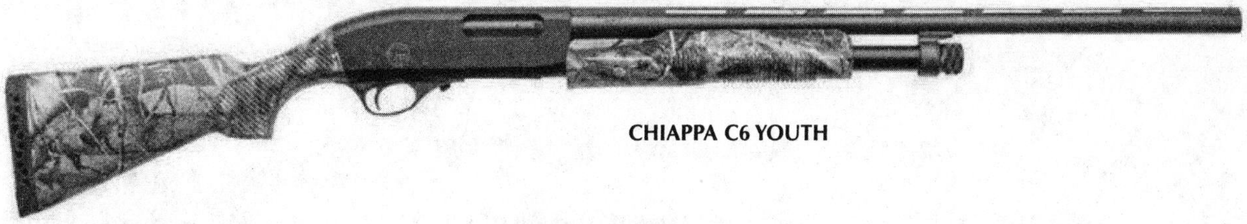

CHIAPPA C6 YOUTH

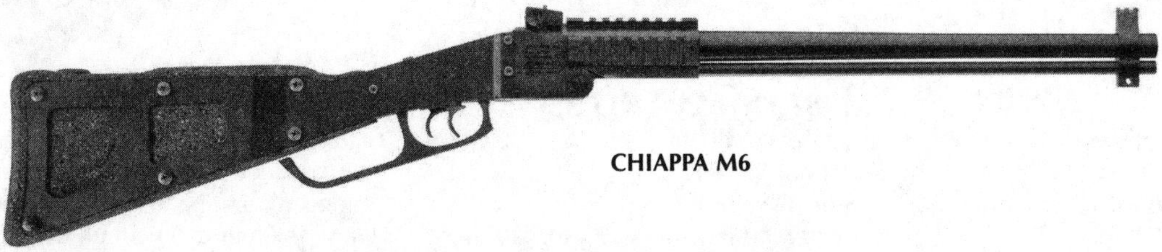

CHIAPPA M6

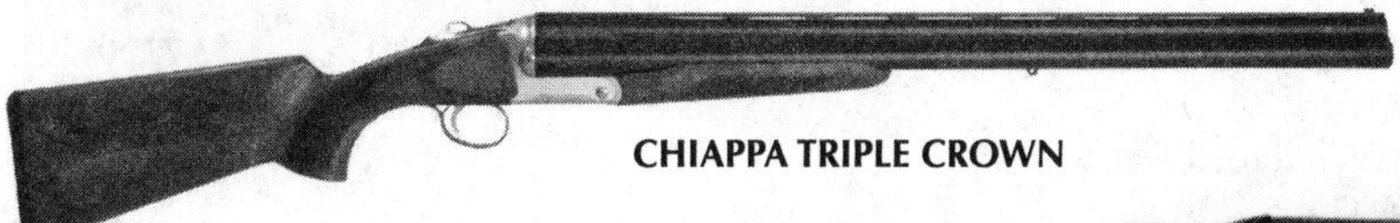

CHIAPPA TRIPLE CROWN

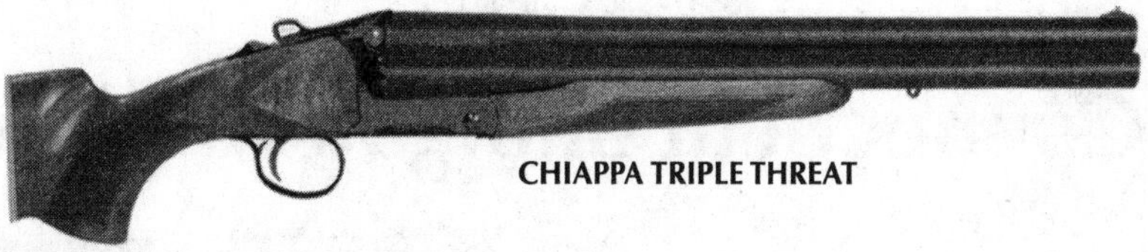

CHIAPPA TRIPLE THREAT

CHIAPPA X-CALIBER

C6 YOUTH

Action: Pump
Stock: Synthetic
Barrel: 22 in.
Chokes: RemChoke MOD
Weight: 5 lb.
Bore/Gauge: 20
Magazine: 5+1 shells
Features: Black receiver, camo stock and forend
MSRP $374

M6

Action: Over/under
Stock: Foam and steel
Barrel: 18.5 in.
Chokes: N/A
Weight: 6 lb.
Bore/Gauge: 20 Ga., .22LR
Magazine: 2 shells
Features: Three Picatinny rails; cleaning kit included in stock; folds for transportation; top tang manual safety; adjustable iron type with fiber optics
MSRP $459

TRIPLE CROWN

Action: Break-action
Stock: Wood
Barrel: 28 in.
Chokes: Rem-choke in all barrels
Weight: 8 lb. 11 oz.
Bore/ Gauge: 12
Magazine: 3 shells
Features: Side-by-side and middle arrangement sporting model with three shotgun barrels; chokes in all three barrels; sling swivel studs
MSRP $1632

TRIPLE THREAT

Action: Break-action
Stock: Wood
Barrel: 18.5 in.
Chokes: Rem-choke in all barrels
Weight: 8 lb.
Bore/ Gauge: 12
Magazine: 3 shells
Features: Side-by-side and middle arrangement defense model with three shotgun barrels; chokes in all three barrels; sling swivel studs; wooden stock can be partly disassembled
MSRP $1632

X-CALIBER

Action: Over/under
Stock: Foam and steel
Barrel: 18.5 in.
Chokes: N/A
Weight: 5 lb. 13 oz.
Bore/Gauge: 12 Ga., .22LR
Magazine: 2 shells
Features: Three Picatinny rails; cleaning kit included in stock; folds for transportation; top tang manual safety; adjustable iron type with fiber optics; included barrel adapters allow eight calibers (.380 ACP, 9mm, .357 Mag/.38 Spl., .40 S&W, .44 Mag., .45 ACP, .410/.45 Colt, 20 Ga.)
MSRP $749

Cimarron Firearms Co.

CIMARRON 1878 COACH GUN

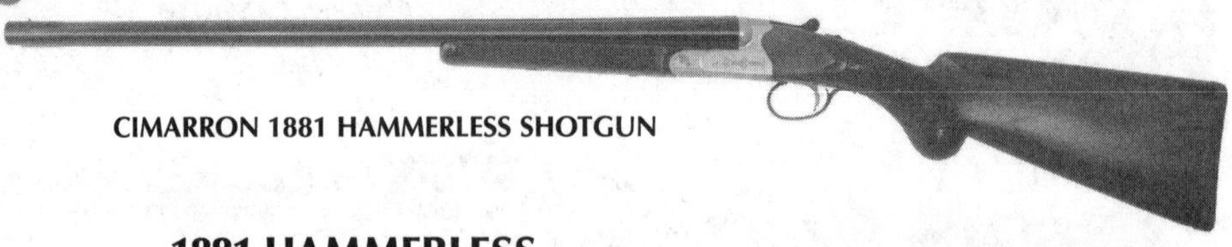

CIMARRON 1881 HAMMERLESS SHOTGUN

1878 COACH GUN

Action: Side-by-Side
Stock: Wood
Barrel: 20 in., 26 in.
Chokes: Open
Weight: 8 lb.–8 lb. 15 oz.
Bore/ Gauge: 12
Magazine: 2 shells
Features: 3 in. blue steel real working hammers; available in standard blue, original finish, or USA finish
MSRP . . . . $597–$880

1881 HAMMERLESS SHOTGUN

Action: Side-by-side
Stock: Walnut
Barrel: 20 in., 22 in., 26 in., 28 in., 30 in.
Chokes: Double Barrel STD
Weight: N/A
Bore/Gauge: 12
Magazine: 2 shells
Features: Authentic frontier styling; manual ejectors; threaded for interchangeable choke tubes; stock and forend is American walnut; deluxe stock available
MSRP . . . . $722–$761

Connecticut Shotgun Mfg. Co.

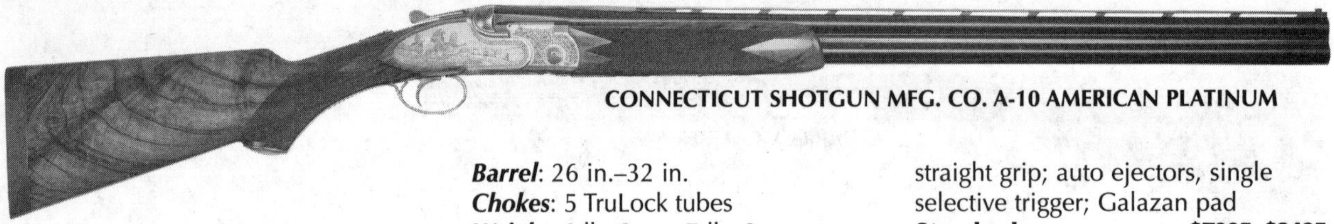

CONNECTICUT SHOTGUN MFG. CO. A-10 AMERICAN PLATINUM

A-10 AMERICAN

Action: Sidelock over/under
Stock: Checkered American black walnut
Barrel: 26 in.–32 in.
Chokes: 5 TruLock tubes
Weight: 6 lb. 8 oz.–7 lb. 8 oz.
Bore/Gauge: 12, 20, 28
Magazine: 2 shells
Features: Finely engraved, cut checkering; ventilated rib; pistol grip or straight grip; auto ejectors, single selective trigger; Galazan pad
Standard: . . . . $7995–$8495
Deluxe: . . . . $8995–$9495
Rose & Scroll: . . . . . $10000–$10500
Platinum: $21500

CZ-USA (Ceska Zbrojovka)

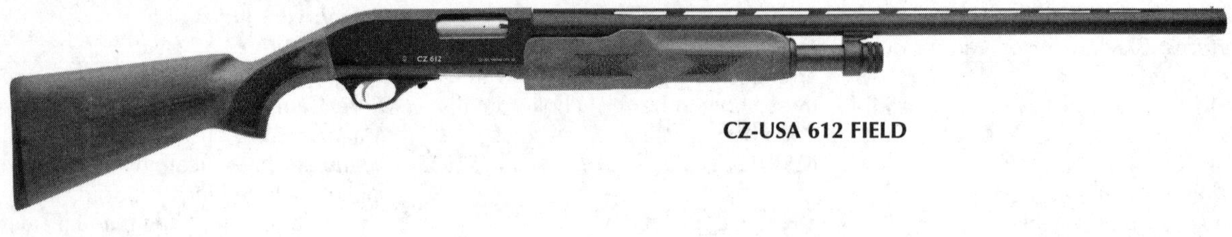

CZ-USA 612 FIELD

612 FIELD

Action: Pump
Stock: Walnut
Barrel: 28 in.
Chokes: 3 chokes
Weight: 6 lb. 3 oz.
Bore/Gauge: 12
Magazine: 4+1 shells
Features: Satin chrome finish; capable of shooting 2 ¾-in. and 3-in. shells; supplied with three chokes
MSRP $389

CZ-USA (Ceska Zbrojovka)

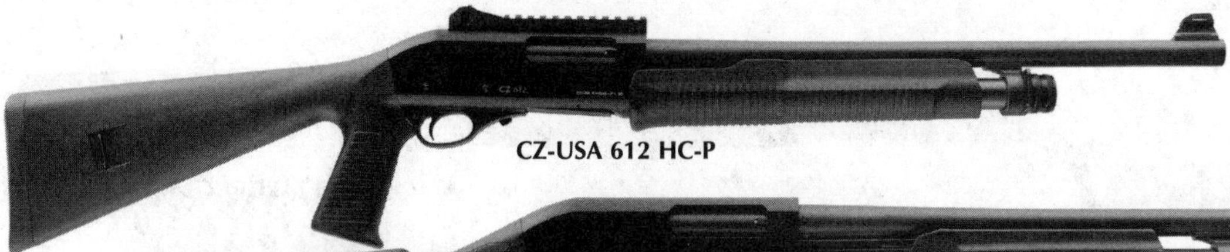
CZ-USA 612 HC-P

CZ-USA 612 HOME DEFENSE

CZ-USA 620 BIG GAME

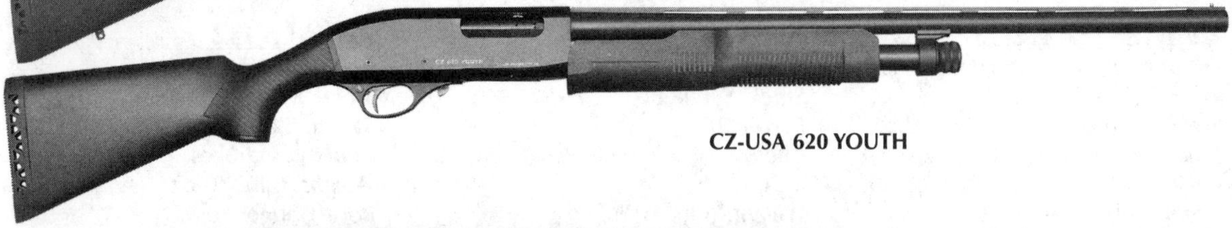
CZ-USA 620 YOUTH

CZ 712 ALS

CZ-USA 712 PRACTICAL G2

612 HC-P

Action: Pump
Stock: Black polymer
Barrel: 20 in.
Chokes: Removable cylinder
Weight: 6 lb. 8 oz.
Bore/ Gauge: 12
Magazine: None
Features: Full-length pistol grip stock; ghost ring sights with glow fiber dots for fast zombie target acquisition; full-length pump forend; barrel accepts CZ choke tubes and ships with one cylinder choke
MSRP. $369

612 HOME DEFENSE

Action: Semiautomatic
Stock: Polymer
Barrel: 18.5 in.
Chokes: Fixed cylinder
Weight: 6 lb.
Bore/ Gauge: 12
Magazine: 5+1 shells
Features: Cylinder-bore barrel; a 26-inch vent-rib barrel is available for purchase that easily converts the 612 Home Defense into a field gun
MSRP. . . . . $304–$409

620 BIG GAME

Action: Pump
Stock: Synthetic
Barrel: 22 in.
Chokes: 1 chokes
Weight: 5 lb. 3 oz.
Bore/Gauge: 20
Magazine: 4 shells
Features: Weaver rail
MSRP. $399

620 YOUTH

Action: Pump
Stock: Synthetic
Barrel: 24 in.
Chokes: 3 chokes
Weight: 5 lb. 3 oz.
Bore/Gauge: 20
Magazine: 4 shells
Features: Brass bead sight; capable of shooting 2 ¾-in. and 3-in. shells; supplied with three chokes
MSRP. $349

712 ADJUSTABLE LENGTH STOCK G2

Action: Gas-operated semiautomatic
Stock: Polymer
Barrel: 28 in.
Chokes: Interchangeable chokes (F, M, IC)
Weight: 7 lb. 13 oz.
Bore/Gauge: 12
Magazine: 4+1 shells
Features: Polymer ATI adjsutable stock; fiber optic front sight; adjustable length of pull from 12 to 14 inches
MSRP. $579

712 PRACTICAL G2

Action: Semiautomatic
Stock: Synthetic
Barrel: 22 in.
Chokes: 5 chokes
Weight: 8 lb. 2 oz.
Bore/Gauge: 12
Magazine: 9 shells
Features: Designed specifically for 3-Gun competition; brass bead sight; six position carbine style adjustable butt stock adjusts from 11.25 to 15 inches; ATI fluted magazine extension gives 9+1 rounds of firepower and extends just past the 22-in. 12-Ga. barrel to help protect the muzzle; five flush choke tubes; ejector
MSRP. $699

CZ-USA (Ceska Zbrojovka)

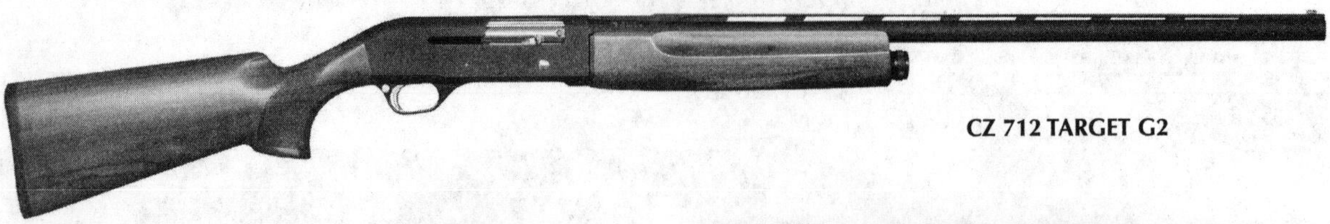

CZ 712 TARGET G2

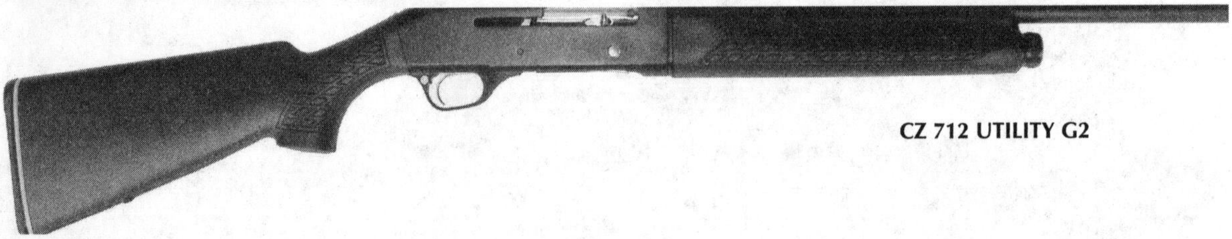

CZ 712 UTILITY G2

712 TARGET G2

Action: Gas-operated semiautomatic
Stock: Walnut
Barrel: 30 in.
Chokes: Interchangeable chokes (F, M, IC)
Weight: 7 lb. 10 oz.
Bore/Gauge: 12
Magazine: 4+1 shells
Features: Gas operated aluminum alloy action with target-grade enhancements; chrome-lined barrel; fiber optic front sight on a 10mm stepped rib; Schnabel forend; smooth rounded heel; Monte Carlo buttstock
MSRP. $680

712 UTILITY G2

Action: Semiautomatic
Stock: Synthetic
Barrel: 20 in.
Chokes: Screw-in chokes (F, IM, M, IC, C)
Weight: 6 lb. 10 oz.
Bore/Gauge: 12
Magazine: 4+1 shells
Features: 3-in. chamber cross-bolt safety; black synthetic stock; matte chrome black barrel
MSRP. $499

720 ALS G2

Action: Semiautomatic
Stock: Synthetic
Barrel: 24 in.
Chokes: 3 chokes
Weight: 6 lb. 10 oz.
Bore/Gauge: 20
Magazine: 4 shells
Features: Fully-adjustable ATI Akita stock; capable of shooting 2 ¾-in. and 3-in. shells; ejector
MSRP. $599

912 SEMIAUTO

Action: Recoil-operated semiautomatic
Stock: Walnut
Barrel: 28 in.
Chokes: 5 interchangeable choke tubes
Weight: 7 lb. 5 oz.
Bore/Gauge: 12
Magazine: 4+1 shells
Features: Fiber optic front bead; features a gloss black finish on metalwork; cross-bolt safety; chrome-lined barrel; aluminum frame
MSRP. $544

CZ-USA 720 ALS G2

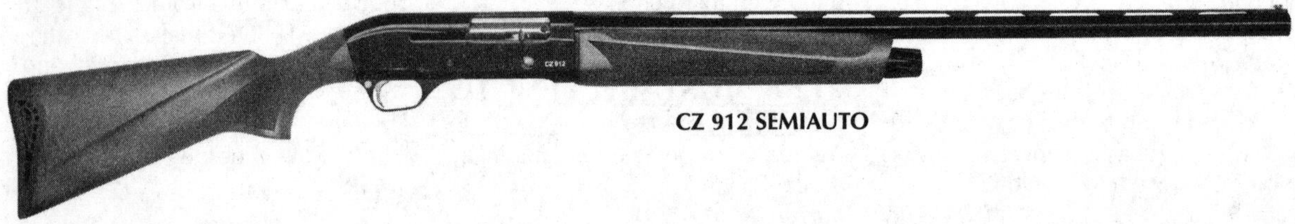

CZ 912 SEMIAUTO

CZ-USA (Ceska Zbrojovka)

CZ-USA CANVASBACK GOLD

CZ-USA LADY STERLING

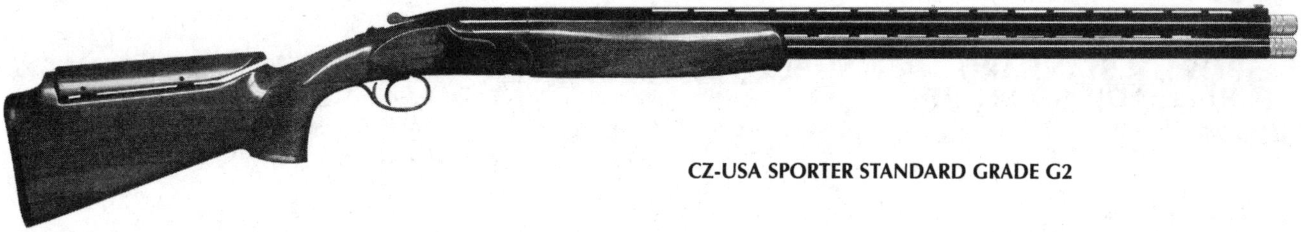

CZ-USA SPORTER STANDARD GRADE G2

CANVASBACK GOLD

Action: Over/under
Stock: Turkish walnut
Barrel: 26 in., 28 in.
Chokes: C, IC, M, IM, F
Weight: 6 lb.–7 lb. 8 oz.
Bore/Gauge: 12, 20, 28, .410
Magazine: 2 shells
Features: Single selectable trigger and extractor that lifts the shells partially out of the chamber on opening
MSRP . . . .$827–$959

LADY STERLING

Action: Over/under
Stock: Turkish walnut
Barrel: 28 in.
Chokes: 5 chokes
Weight: 7 lb. 8 oz.
Bore/Gauge: 12
Magazine: 2 shells
Features: Capable of shooting both 2 ¾-in. and 3-in. shells
MSRP $1281

SPORTER STANDARD GRADE G2

Action: Over/under
Stock: Grade 2 Turkish walnut
Barrel: 30 in.
Chokes: 6 Kicks extended SS
Weight: 8 lb. 8 oz.
Bore/ Gauge: 12
Magazine: 2 shells
Features: Designed specifically with the sporting clay enthusiast in mind; single selectable trigger system; Grade 2 Monte Carlo sporting stock with adjustable comb and right-hand palm swell; ships with a set of 6 Kicks stainless steel extended choke tubes
MSRP $1899

CZ-USA (Ceska Zbrojovka)

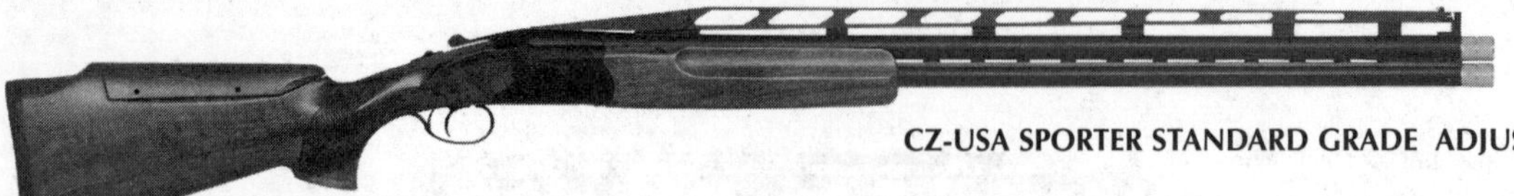

CZ-USA SPORTER STANDARD GRADE ADJUSTABLE RIB

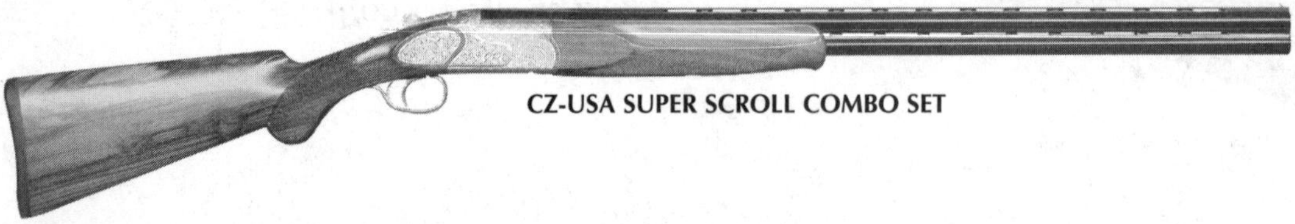

CZ-USA SUPER SCROLL COMBO SET

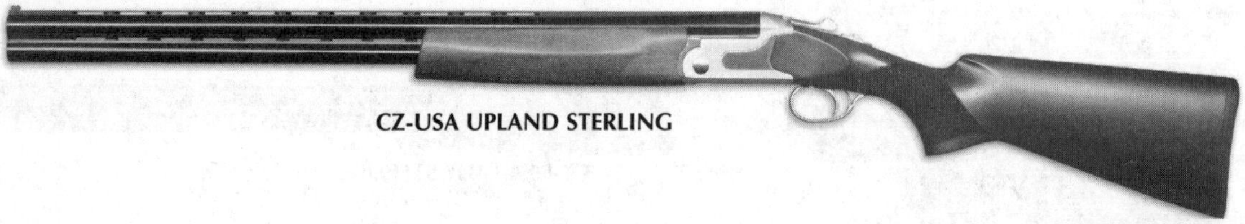

CZ-USA UPLAND STERLING

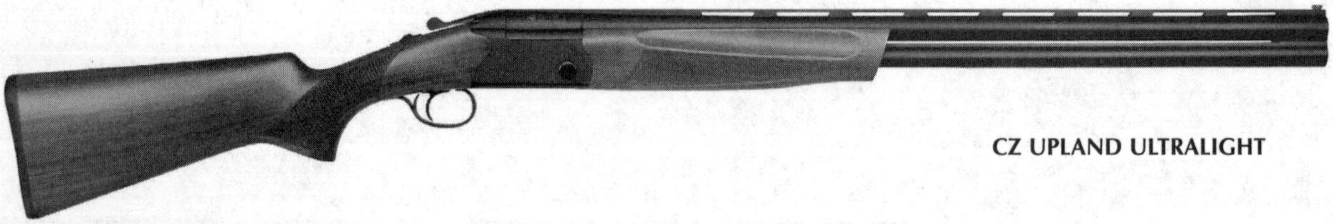

CZ UPLAND ULTRALIGHT

SPORTER STANDARD GRADE ADJUSTABLE RIB

Action: Over/under
Stock: Grade II wood
Barrel: 30 in., 32 in.
Chokes: 6 chokes
Weight: 8 lb. 8 oz.–8 lb. 11 oz
Bore/Gauge: 12
Magazine: 2 shells
Features: Equipped with Moneymaker Guncraft's famous adjustable rib and a factory four-way adjustable parallel comb; comes with a six tube set of Kicks Tom Mack series stainless steel choke tubes
MSRP. $3122

SUPER SCROLL COMBO SET

Action: Over/under
Stock: Grade 5 Turkish walnut
Barrel: 30 in.
Chokes: 5 per gauge
Weight: 6 lb. 11 oz.
Bore/ Gauge: 20, 28
Magazine: 2 shells
Features: Intended for the hunter or sporting clays shooter who wants to carry an absolutely gorgeous shotgun; ornate hand-engraved scrollwork on receiver, faux sideplates, trigger guard and mono-block; both barrel sets are equipped with ejectors; five chokes per gauge and a full grip, making it an excellent crossover gun between clay and feather
MSRP. $3899

UPLAND STERLING

Action: Over/under
Stock: Turkish walnut
Barrel: 28 in.
Chokes: 5 screw-in
Weight: 7 lb. 8 oz.
Bore/ Gauge: 12
Magazine: 2 shells
Features: Built on a new platform featuring a CNC-milled steel receiver, resulting in mechanical components that operate with clockwork precision and consistency; Turkish walnut stock features a stippled grip area on the wrist and forend rather than the traditional checkering
MSRP. $999

UPLAND ULTRALIGHT

Action: Over/under
Stock: Turkish Walnut
Barrel: 26 in., 28 in.
Chokes: F, IM, M, IC, C
Weight: 6 lb.
Bore/Gauge: 12
Magazine: 2 shells
Features: Lightweight, black alloy receiver; vent rib
MSRP. $762

Escort by Legacy Sports

AIMGUARD, MARINEGUARD HOME DEFENSE

Action: Pump
Stock: Synthetic
Barrel: 18 in.
Chokes: Cylinder bore
Weight: 6 lb. 4 oz.
Bore/Gauge: 12
Magazine: 5 shells
Features: Rifle-style front sight; black synthetic stock; AimGuard has black metal finish, MarineGuard has water resistant nickel finish; sling swivel studs; dovetail receiver for mounting accessory sights
AimGuard: $312
MarineGuard: $380

EXTREME MAGNUM SEMI-AUTO

Action: Semiautomatic
Stock: Synthetic
Barrel: 24 in., 26 in., 28 in.
Chokes: 5+1 chokes
Weight: 7 lb.–7 lb. 10.4 oz.
Bore/Gauge: 12, 20
Magazine: 5+1 shells
Features: Non-slip grip pads on the forend and pistol grip; SMART Valve gas pistons; HiVis MagniSight fiber optic, magnetic sight; available in Realtree MAX-4, Realtree AP Camo, Realtree AP Camo Turkey, and black synthetic
Black:. . . . . $551–$650
Realtree: . . . . $736–$816
Realtree Turkey:. $663

EXTREME AND SUPREME LEFT HANDED ACTIONS

Action: Semiautomatic
Stock: Black synthetic, Realtree camo (Supreme model only), or Wood
Barrel: 26 in., 28 in.
Chokes: F, M, IM, IC, Skeet (Extreme Camo models also come with MR Waterfowl)
Weight: 6 lb. 8 oz.–7 lb. 10 oz.
Bore/ Gauge: 12, 20
Magazine: 5+1 shells
Features: Available in Magnum and Supreme Magnum models; cycle rate of 3 shots/second with 7/8oz. loads; true left-handed action and receiver; SMART valve cycling for blowback; nickel chrome moly lined barrel; ventilated rib and fiber optic front sight; magazine cut-off for quick load changes
MSRP . . . . $551–$816

GLADIUS HOME DEFENSE SHOTGUN

Action: Pump or semiautomatic
Stock: Synthetic
Barrel: 18 in.
Chokes: C
Weight: 6 lb. 13 oz.
Bore/Gauge: 20
Magazine: 5+1 shells
Features: Fiber optic front sight with elevation adjustment; ghost ring rear sight with full adjustment; Picatinny rails; muzzle break; forend pistol grip; built-in holder for two extra shells
Pump: $485
Semiautomatic: $579

ESCORT MARINEGUARD HOME DEFENSE

ESCORT EXTEME MAGNUM SEMI-AUTO, REALTREE AP CAMO

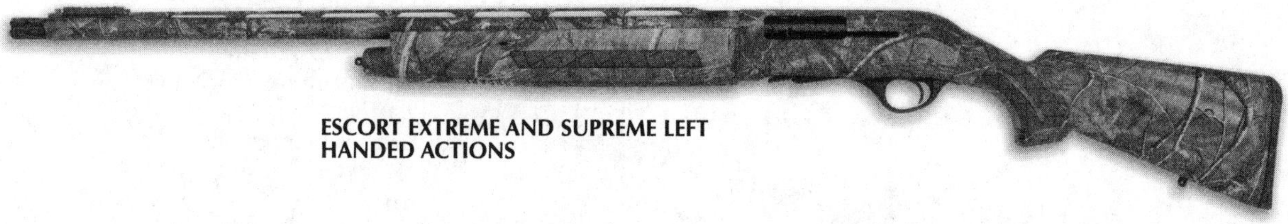

ESCORT EXTREME AND SUPREME LEFT HANDED ACTIONS

LEGACY SPORTS ESCORT GLADIUS SA

SHOTGUNS

Escort by Legacy Sports

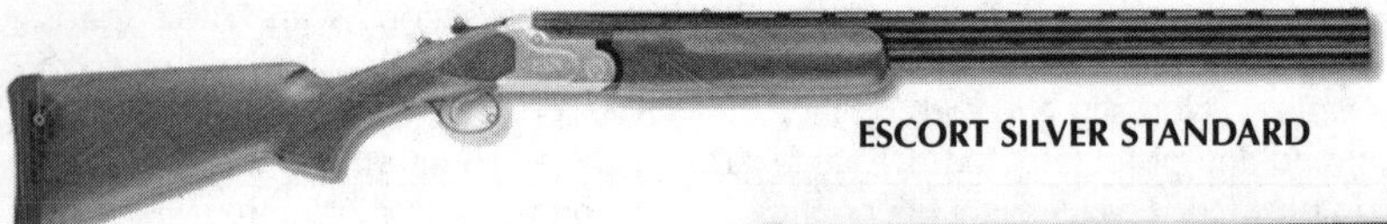

ESCORT SILVER STANDARD

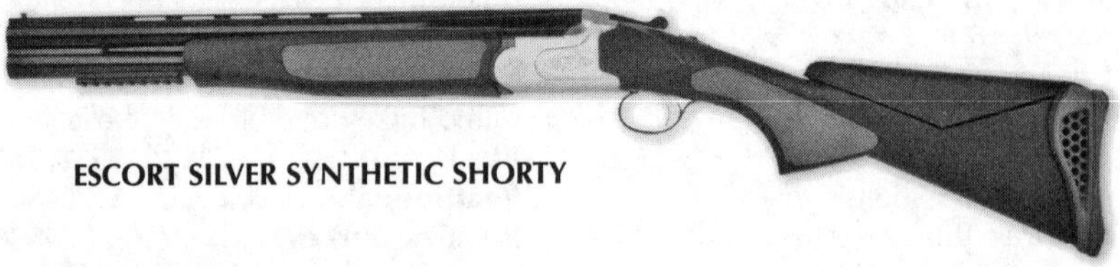

ESCORT SILVER SYNTHETIC SHORTY

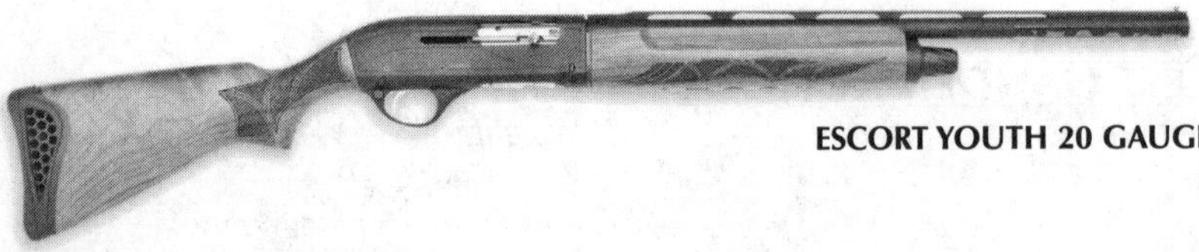

ESCORT YOUTH 20 GAUGE

SILVER STANDARD

Action: Over/under
Stock: Walnut, synthetic
Barrel: 28 in.
Chokes: Choke tubes (M, IC, F, IM, Skeet)
Weight: 7 lb. 10 oz.–8 lb. 3 oz.
Bore/Gauge: 12
Magazine: 2 shells
Features: 3-in. chamber; Turkish walnut stock; trio recoil pad; blued tang lever; barrel selector switch and trigger guard; auto safety; nickel plated receiver; blued barrel
MSRP. . . . . $641–$694

SILVER SYNTHETIC SHORTY

Action: Over/under
Stock: Synthetic
Barrel: 18 in.
Chokes: Choke tubes (M, IC, F, IM, Skeet)
Weight: 7 lb.
Bore/Gauge: 12
Magazine: 2 shells
Features: Nickel plated receiver; adjustable comb; auto safety; blued tang lever, barrel selector switch, and trigger guard; soft rubber grey synthetic stock with cobblestone grip inserts
MSRP. $653

YOUTH 20 GAUGE

Action: Semiautomatic
Stock: Wood, Black Synthetic, Realtree Max4 and AP camo, and Moon Shine Muddy Girl camo
Barrel: 22 in., 26 in. (Ladies Muddy Girl)
Chokes: Multi-3
Weight: 6 lb. 6 oz.
Bore/ Gauge: 20
Magazine: Cut-off for single round loading
Features: TRIO recoil pad; top of receiver milled with 3/8 in. dovetail for sights; raised, ventilated sight rib with fiber optic sight; nickel chrome moly lined barrel
Synthetic $512
Wood. $524
Camo $553

Fabarm

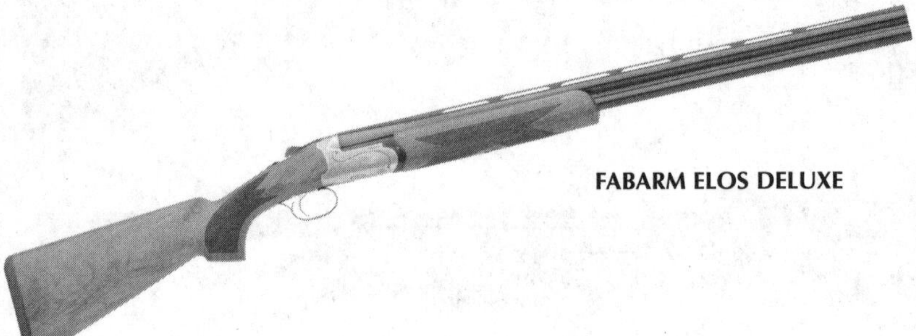

FABARM ELOS DELUXE

ELOS DELUXE

Action: Over/under
Stock: European walnut
Barrel: 28 in.
Chokes: 5 Inner HP
Weight: 5 lb. 14 oz.–7 lb. 1 oz.
Bore/ Gauge: 20
Magazine: 2 shells
Features: Round action and trim stock provide speed in keeping up with wild birds; Fabarm Tribore HP tapered bore; steel or aluminum frame
MSRP. . . . .$2995–$3120

Fausti USA

FAUSTI USA CALEDON

FAUSTI USA CLASS

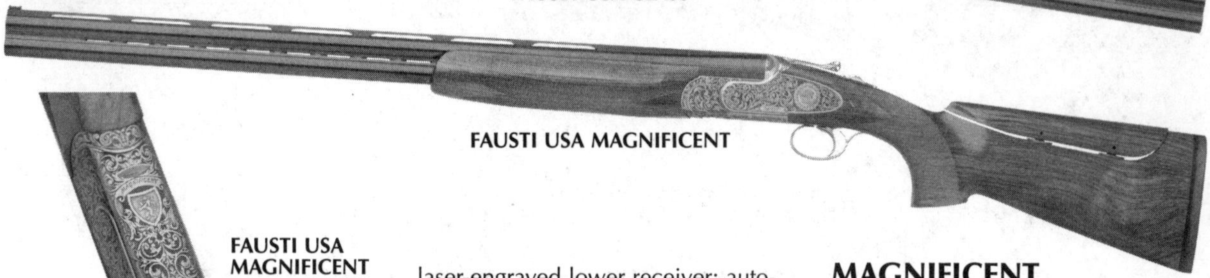

FAUSTI USA MAGNIFICENT

FAUSTI USA MAGNIFICENT

CALEDON

Action: Over/under
Stock: Walnut
Barrel: 26 in., 28 in., 30 in.
Chokes: Fixed or interchangeable choke tubes
Weight: 5 lb. 12 oz.–7 lb. 4 oz.
Bore/Gauge: 12, 16, 20, 28, .410
Magazine: 2 shells
Features: Single selectable trigger; A+ Turkish walnut stock with oil finish; laser-engraved lower receiver; automatic ejectors; metallic bead sight
MSRP. . . . .$1999–$2569

CLASS

Action: Over/under
Stock: Walnut
Barrel: 26 in., 28 in., 30 in.
Chokes: Fixed or interchangeable choke tubes
Weight: 5 lb. 12 oz.–7 lb. 5 oz.
Bore/Gauge: 12, 16, 20, 28, .410
Magazine: 2 shells
Features: Features automatic ejectors; metallic bead; single-selectable trigger; 14–3/8-in. length of pull; timeless AA walnut oil-polished stock; Prince of Wales style stock; receiver laser-engraved with flushing quail
MSRP. . . . . $2449–$2999

MAGNIFICENT

Action: Over/under
Stock: Walnut
Barrel: 26 in., 28 in., 30 in.
Chokes: Fixed or interchangeable choke tubes
Weight: 5 lb. 12 oz.–7 lb. 6 oz.
Bore/Gauge: 12, 16, 20, 28, .410
Magazine: 2 shells
Features: AAA+ walnut stock with oil finish; precision scroll engraving accompanies Aphrodite, the Greek goddess of love and beauty, on the receiver; the Crest of the city of Brescia, Italy, where all Fausti shotguns are produced, is on the underside of the receiver; single selectable trigger; automatic ejectors; metallic bead sight
MSRP. . . . .$4999–$5559

Federal Armament

FEDERAL ARMAMENT UZKON BR-99

UZKON BR-99

Action: Gas-operated semiautomatic
Stock: Synthetic
Barrel: 20 in.
Chokes: Choke set
Weight: 7 lb. 3 oz.
Bore/Gauge: 12
Magazine: 5+1 shells
Features: Ergonomic grips and cheekrest; removable chokes; Picatinny rails
MSRP. $569

Flodman Guns

FLODMAN SHOTGUN

Action: Over/under
Stock: Walnut
Barrel: 28 in.–34 in.
Chokes: Multichoke
Weight: 6 lb. 3 oz.–8 lb. 6 oz.
Bore/Gauge: 12, 20
Magazine: 2 shells
Features: Boxlock offered in any standard gauge or rifle/shotgun combination; walnut stock with pistol grip available; auto or manual safety; Combi stainless steel barrel
From: $23000
Extra double rifle barrels: . . . $18500

FLODMAN SHOTGUN

Franchi

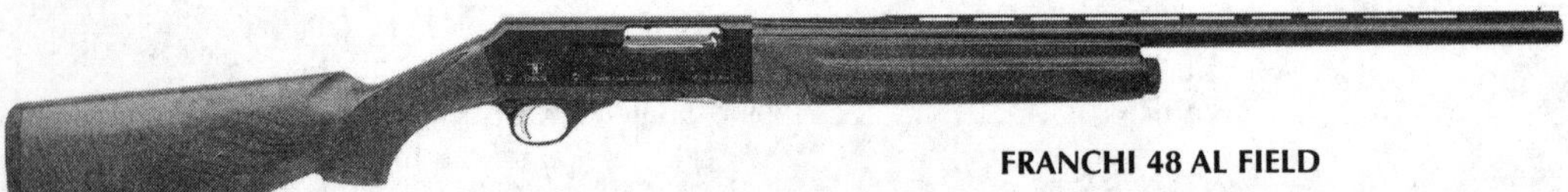

FRANCHI 48 AL FIELD

FRANCHI AFFINITY 20 GA. - REALTREE APG

FRANCHI AFFINITY COMPACT

FRANCHI ASPIRE

48 AL

Action: Semiautomatic
Stock: Walnut
Barrel: 24 in., 26 in., 28 in.
Chokes: Screw-in tubes Standard (IC, M, F, wrench), optional (C, IC, M, IM, F)
Weight: 5 lb. 6 oz.–5 lb. 10 oz.
Bore/Gauge: 20, 28
Magazine: 4+1 shells
Features: Matte blue steel barrel; polished steel barrel on deluxe model; satin walnut stock on Field model; A-grade satin walnut on Deluxe model; optional custom-fitted hard case
Field: . . . . $899–$999
Deluxe: . . . .$1199–$1249

AFFINITY

Action: Inertia driven semiautomatic
Stock: Black synthetic, Realtree Max-4, Realtree APG
Barrel: 24 in., 26 in., 28 in., 30 in.
Chokes: Interchangeable (IC, M, F)
Weight: 5 lb. 8 oz.–6 lb. 12 oz.
Bore/Gauge: 12, 20
Magazine: 4+1 shells
Features: Red fiber optic bar; durable synthetic stock impervious to all-weather elements as well as gun solvents and lubricants; newly designed recoil pad; aluminum alloy receiver strengthened with steel inserts
Black: . . . . $729–$849
Realtree: $949
Compact: . . . . $899–$999
Sporting: $1159

AFFINITY COMPACT

Action: Semiautomatic
Stock: Synthetic
Barrel: 26 in.
Chokes: IC, M
Weight: 6 lb. 5 oz.
Bore/Gauge: 12
Magazine: 4+1 shells
Features: Fiber optic red-bar fron sight; available in black or Realtree MAX-5 camo
MSRP . . . .$899–$999

ASPIRE

Action: Over/under
Stock: Walnut
Barrel: 28 in.
Chokes: IC, M, F
Weight: 5 lb. 13 oz.
Bore/ Gauge: 28, .410
Magazine: 2 shells
Features: Slim, round-action receiver; color-case hardened receiver; automatic safety with built-in barrel selector
MSRP $2299

FRANCHI INSTINCT L 12 GA.

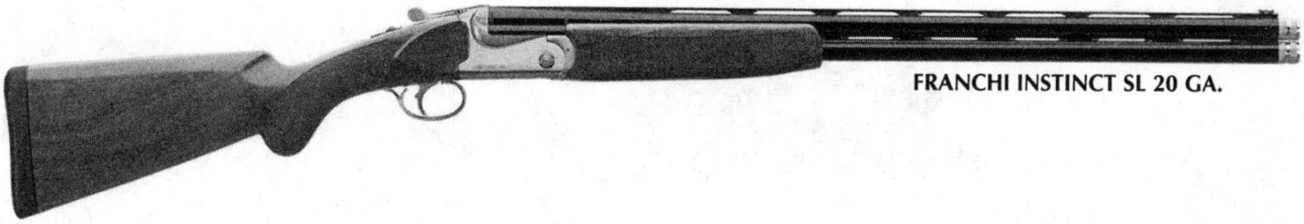

FRANCHI INSTINCT SL 20 GA.

FRANCHI INTENSITY

INSTINCT L

Action: Over/under
Stock: Walnut
Barrel: 26 in., 28 in.
Chokes: Interchangeable (IC, M, F)
Weight: 6 lb. 2 oz.–6 lb. 6 oz.
Bore/Gauge: 12, 20
Magazine: 2 shells
Features: Ventilated raised rib; red fiber optic front sight; blued and color-case-hardened finish on the receiver, with gold inlay; A-grade walnut stock in Prince-of-Wales style with cut checkering on the forend and pistol grip; satin oil finish; single gold-plated trigger; chrome-lined barrels proofed for steel shot; hard-shell custom-fitted gun case included
MSRP $1349

INSTINCT SL

Action: Over/under
Stock: Walnut
Barrel: 26 in., 28 in.
Chokes: Interchangeable (IC, M, F)
Weight: 5 lb. 6 oz.–5 lb. 11 oz.
Bore/Gauge: 12, 20
Magazine: 2 shells
Features: Vent rib; red fiber optic front bead; aluminum alloy receiver; blued barrels; AA-grade satin walnut stock in Prince-of-Wales style with cut checkering and oil finish; tang-mounted automatic safety; custom-fitted, hard-shell gun case included
MSRP $1699

INTENSITY

Action: Inertia driver semiautomatic
Stock: Black synthetic, Realtree Max4, Realtree APG, Bottomlands
Barrel: 26 in., 28 in., 30 in.
Chokes: IC, M, F
Weight: 6 lb. 11 oz.
Bore/ Gauge: 12
Magazine: 4+1 shells
Features: Inertia Driven system; recoil spring encircles the magazine tube forward the receiver; stepped, ventilated-rib, red fiber optic front sight; three extended choke tubes
MSRP . . . . $1099–$1199

Ithaca Gun Company

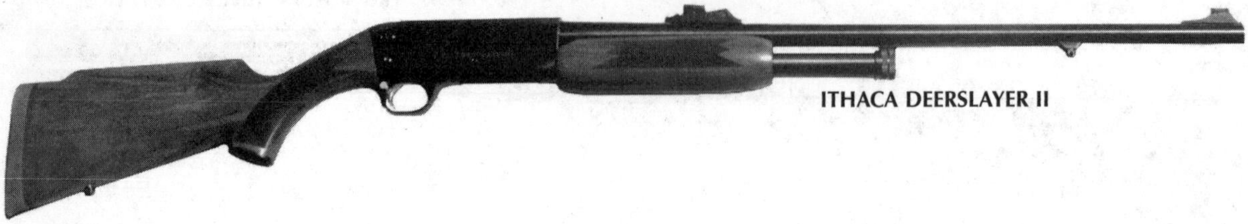

ITHACA DEERSLAYER II

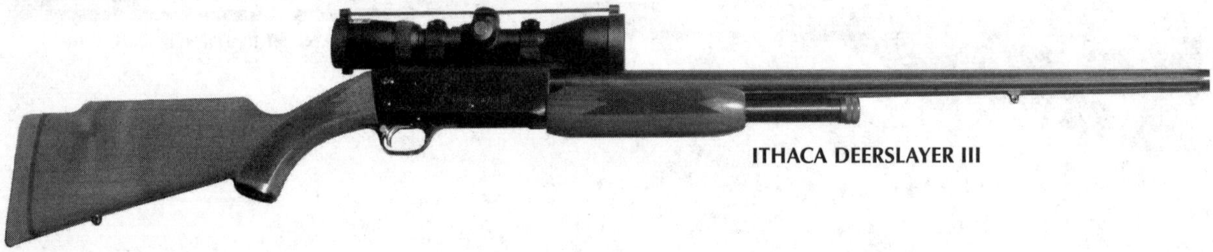

ITHACA DEERSLAYER III

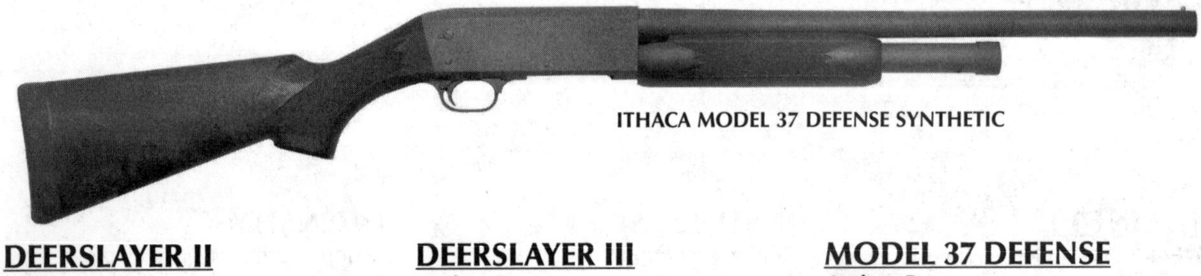

ITHACA MODEL 37 DEFENSE SYNTHETIC

DEERSLAYER II

Action: Pump
Stock: Walnut
Barrel: 24 in.
Chokes: None
Weight: 6.8 lb.–8 lb. 6 oz.
Bore/Gauge: 12, 20
Magazine: 4+1 shells
Features: Solderless barrel system; thumbhole or standard black walnut Monte Carlo stock; fat deluxe checkered forend; sling swivel studs; Pachmayr 750 Decelerator recoil pad; matte blued finish on barrel; gold-plated trigger; Marble Arms rifle sights; drilled and tapped for Weaver #62 scope rail
MSRP. $1150

DEERSLAYER III

Action: Pump
Stock: Walnut
Barrel: 20 in., 26 in., 28 in.
Chokes: None
Weight: 8.1 lb.–9 lb. 8 oz.
Bore/Gauge: 12, 20
Magazine: 4+1 shells
Features: Heavy-walled, fluted, fixed barrel in blue matted finish; walnut Monte Carlo stock with optional thumbhole; Pachmayr 750 Decelerator recoil pad; sling swivel studs; gold-plated trigger; Weaver #62 rail pre-installed on receiver
MSRP. $1350

MODEL 37 DEFENSE

Action: Pump
Stock: Synthetic or walnut
Barrel: 18.5 in., 20 in.
Chokes: None
Weight: 6.5 lb.–7 lb. 2 oz.
Bore/Gauge: 12, 20
Magazine: 4+1 or 7+1 shells
Features: Choice of walnut or black synthetic stock; 3 in. chamber; matte blued finish barrel; Pachmayr decelerator recoil pad
MSRP. . . . .$880–$910

Ithaca Gun Company

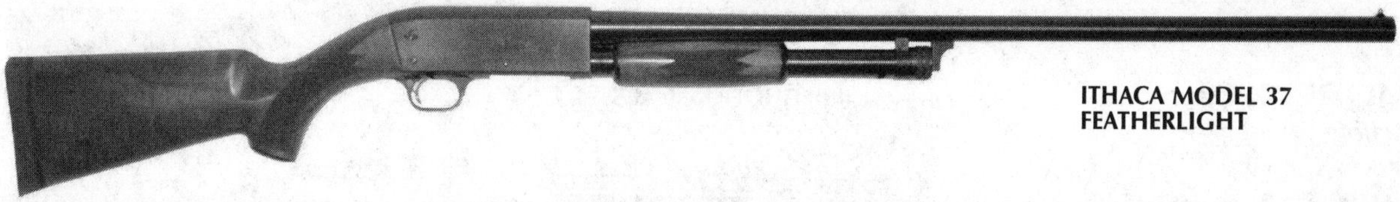

ITHACA MODEL 37 FEATHERLIGHT

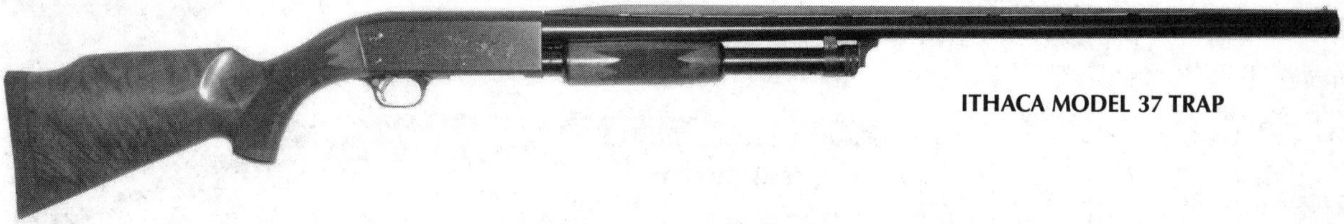

ITHACA MODEL 37 TRAP

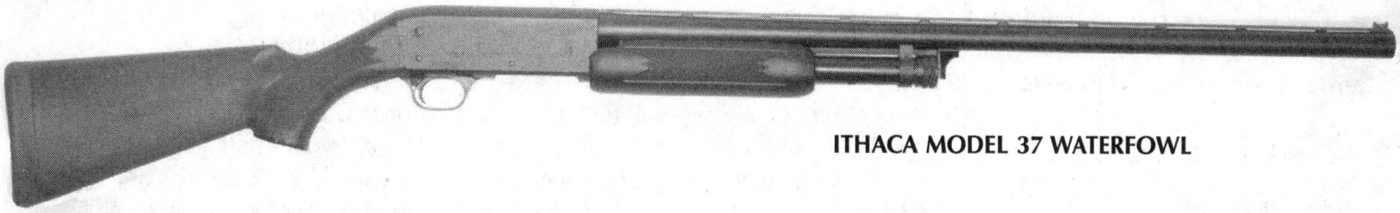

ITHACA MODEL 37 WATERFOWL

MODEL 37 FEATHERLIGHT

Action: Pump
Stock: Walnut
Barrel: 26 in., 28 in., 20 in.
Chokes: 3 Briley Choke tubes (F, M, IC, and wrench)
Weight: 6.1 lb.–7 lb. 10 oz.
Bore/Gauge: 12, 16, 20, 28
Magazine: 4+1 rounds
Features: Solderless shells system; classic game scene engraving; black walnut stock with semi-pistol butt stock; TruGlo red front sight; Pachmayr 752 Decelerator recoil pad
MSRP. $999

MODEL 37 TRAP

Action: Pump
Stock: Walnut
Barrel: 30 in.
Chokes: Briley Choke tubes
Weight: 7 lb. 13 oz.
Bore/Gauge: 12
Magazine: 4+1 shells
Features: Bottom ejection; 3 in. chamber; gold plated tubes; walnut Monte Carlo stock; vent rib barrel; classic game scene engraving
MSRP. $1050

MODEL 37 WATERFOWL

Action: Pump
Stock: Camo, synthetic black
Barrel: 28 in., 30 in.
Chokes: Briley choke tubes
Weight: 7 lb. 3 oz.–7 lb. 6 oz.
Bore/ Gauge: 12, 20
Magazine: 4+1 shells
Features: 3 in. chamber; gold plated trigger; gamescene engraving; perma-guard protection
MSRP. $999

Krieghoff

KRIEGHOFF K-20

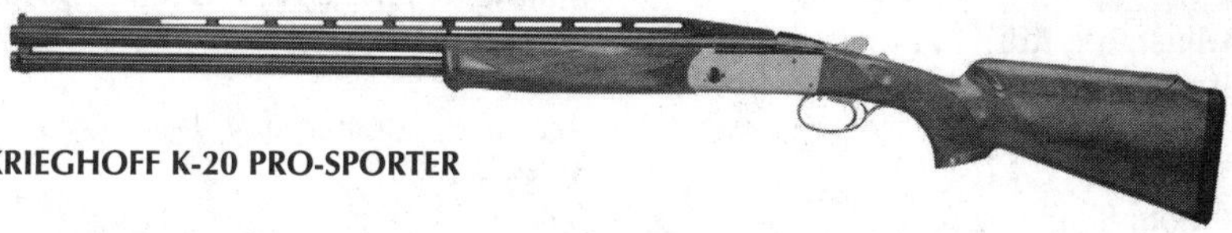

KRIEGHOFF K-20 PRO-SPORTER

MODEL K-20

Action: Over/under
Stock: Walnut
Barrel: 30 in., 32 in.
Chokes: 5 choke tubes (C, S, IC, LM, M, LIM, IM, F)
Weight: 7 lb. 8 oz.
Bore/Gauge: 20, 28, .410
Magazine: 2 shells
Features: Top-tang push safety button; classic scroll engraving; white pearl front bead and metal center bead; single-selective mechanical trigger; hand-checkered select European walnut stock with satin epoxy finish
20 Ga.:. $11395
28 Ga.:. $11495
.410:. $11495
20/28 Ga. Set:. $15890
Set of 3:. $20405

K-20 PRO-SPORTER

Action: Over/under
Stock: Walnut
Barrel: 30 in., 32 in.
Chokes: Titanium choke tubes
Weight: 8 lb.
Bore/Gauge: 20, 28, .410
Magazine: 2 shells
Features: Higher rib and stock allows shooter to keep their head more erect, increasing sight range, allowing for quicker target acquisition, reduced neck fatigue, and perceived recoil; high rib easily adjustable
MSRP. . . . . $11695–$11795
20/28 Ga. Set:. $16390
3 Ga. Set:. $21105

Krieghoff

KRIEGHOFF K-80 ACS

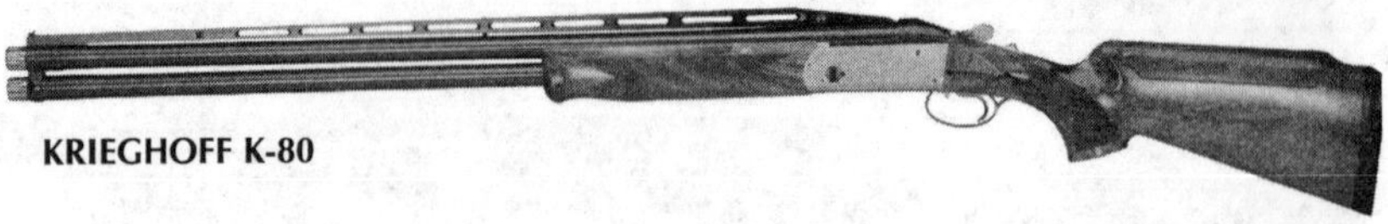

KRIEGHOFF K-80

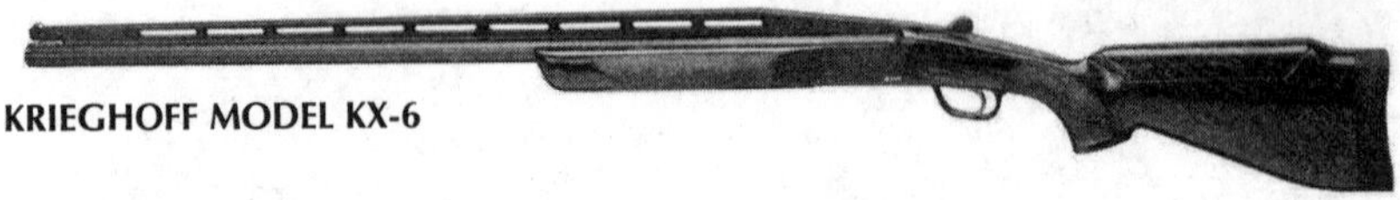

KRIEGHOFF MODEL KX-6

MODEL K-80

Action: Over/under
Stock: Walnut
Barrel: 30 in., 32 in., 34 in.
Chokes: Steel or Titanium choke tubes (C, S, IC, LM, M, LIM, IM, F, SF)
Weight: 8 lb. 4 oz.
Bore/Gauge: 12
Magazine: 2 shells
Features: White pearl front sight and metal center bead; nickel plated steel receiver with satin grey finish; single select trigger; top-tang push button safety; fine-checkered Turkish walnut
Standard Models: . . $10595–$13000

MODEL K-80 ACS

Action: Single barrel
Stock: Walnut
Barrel: 30 in., 32 in., 34 in.
Chokes: 8 factory steel choke tubes
Weight: 8 lb. 12 oz.
Bore/Gauge: 12
Magazine: 2 shells
Features: White pearl front bead and metal center bead sight; case-hardened action, nickel-plated steel receiver with nitride silver finish; single selective trigger; over/under available
From: $17370

MODEL KX-6

Action: Single-shot trap
Stock: Walnut
Barrel: 34 in.
Chokes: IM, LIM, F
Weight: 8 lb. 12 oz.
Bore/ Gauge: 12
Magazine: 1 shell
Features: White pearl front sight and metal center bead; case hardened, long lasting black nitro carbonized finish; semiautomatic ejector; adjustable tapered rib; available choke tubes: CY, SK, IC, M, SF
MSRP $5490

Ljutic

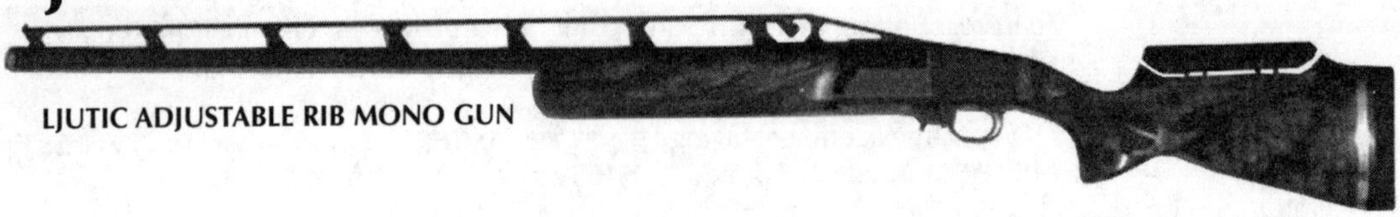

LJUTIC ADJUSTABLE RIB MONO GUN

LJUTIC MONO GUN

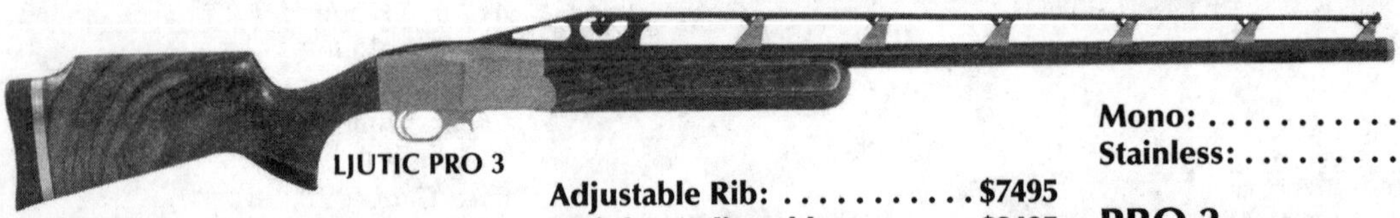

LJUTIC PRO 3

ADJUSTABLE RIB MONO GUN

Action: Single barrel
Stock: Walnut
Barrel: 34 in.
Chokes: Fixed or Ljutic SIC
Weight: 10 lb.
Bore/Gauge: .740, 12
Magazine: 1 shell
Features: "One Touch" adjustable rib allows you to change your point-of-impact; adjustable comb stock
Adjustable Rib: $7495
Stainless Adjustable: $8495

MONO GUN

Action: Single barrel
Stock: Walnut
Barrel: 32 in.–34 in.
Chokes: Optional screw in chokes (Fixed, Ljutic SIC, Briley SIC)
Weight: 10 lb.
Bore/Gauge: .740, 12
Magazine: 1 shell
Features: Comes with American walnut wood; optional roll over combs and cheek pieces; various upgrades available
Mono: $7495
Stainless: $8495

PRO 3

Action: Single barrel
Stock: Walnut
Barrel: 34 in.
Chokes: 4 Briley Series 12 chokes
Weight: 9 lb.
Bore/Gauge: .740, 12
Magazine: 1 shell
Features: Aluminum baseplate; interchangeable two-pad system; adjustable comb; English or American walnut stock; screw in hinge pin; stainless or blued barrel
Blued barrel: $8495
Stainless: $8995

Marocchi

FINNCLASSIC 612

Action: Over/under
Stock: Wood
Barrel: 24 in., 28 in., 30 in.
Chokes: 5 choke tube Maxi 70 plus key
Weight: 6 lb. 8 oz.
Bore/ Gauge: 12
Magazine: 2 shells
Features: 3-in. chamber; available Maxi 90 choke tubes; special steel, proof tested by the Italian National Proof House; scroll work
MSRP $1375

MAROCCHI FINNCLASSIC 612

Merkel

MERKEL MODEL 47E

MERKEL MODEL 303E

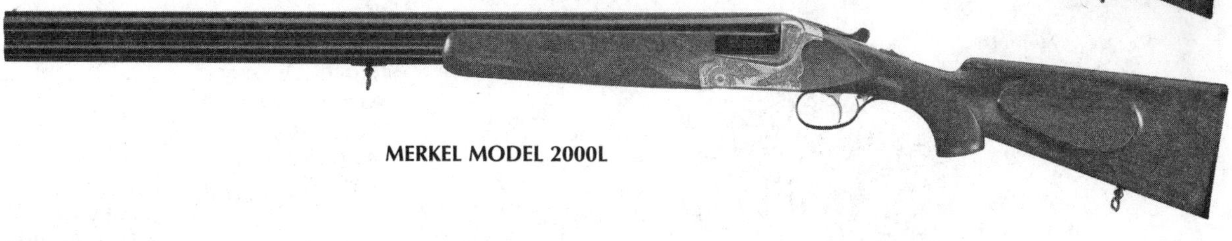

MERKEL MODEL 2000L

MODEL 47E, 147E, 147EL

Action: Side-by-side
Stock: Wood
Barrel: 27 in., 28 in.
Chokes: Steel-shot proofed chokes
Weight: 6 lb. 3 oz.
Bore/Gauge: 12, 20
Magazine: None
Features: English stock finished with fine hand-cut checkering at buttplate; silver monogram plate; steel action is gray nitrated; Anson & Deeley locks; Greener-style cross bolt and double bottom bite; double trigger; automatic safety
47E: $4595
147E: $5795
147EL: $7195

MODEL 303E

Action: Over/under
Stock: Wood
Barrel: 27 in., 28 in.
Chokes: Steel-shot proofed chokes
Weight: 6 lb. 13 oz.
Bore/Gauge: 12, 20
Magazine: 2 shells
Features: Sidelocks with V-springs; Kersten cross-bolt with double conventional bottom bite; double trigger; front trigger articulated; optional selective single trigger; engraving English arabesque; luxury grade walnut stock with pistol grip; optional English-styled stock
MSRP $27995

MODEL 2000L

Action: Over/under
Stock: Wood
Barrel: 27 in., 28 in.
Chokes: 2 interchangeable chokes steel-shot proofed
Weight: 6 lb. 13 oz.
Bore/Gauge: 12, 20
Magazine: 2 shells
Features: Disconnectable ejectors; arabesque engraving; Anson & Deeley locks in steel receiver; Kersten cross-bolt; selective single trigger, adjustable in length; manual safety; wood stock with pistol grip and cheekpiece
MSRP $10995

Mossberg

MOSSBERG 500 CLASSIC ALL-PURPOSE FIELD

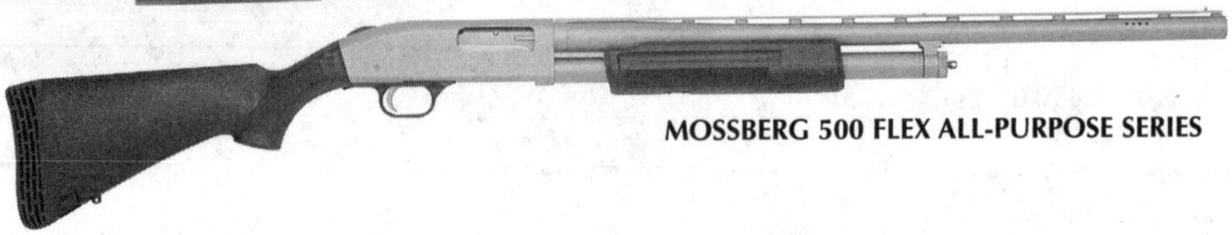

MOSSBERG 500 FLEX ALL-PURPOSE SERIES

500 CLASSIC ALL-PURPOSE FIELD

Action: Pump
Stock: Walnut, synthetic
Barrel: 28 in.
Chokes: Interchangeable Accu-Choke tubes
Weight: 7 lb. 8 oz.
Bore/Gauge: 12
Magazine: 6 shells
Features: High-gloss walnut stock and forend; fine checkering on the pistol grip and wrapping around the underside of the forend; classic red recoil pad with white Pachmayr line spacer; distinctive jeweled bolt, gold trigger, and high polished blued metal finish; non-binding twin action bars; anodized aluminum receiver; vent rib Accu-Choke barrel; ambidextrous top-mounted safety; available in MO Break-up Infinity
MSRP **$491**

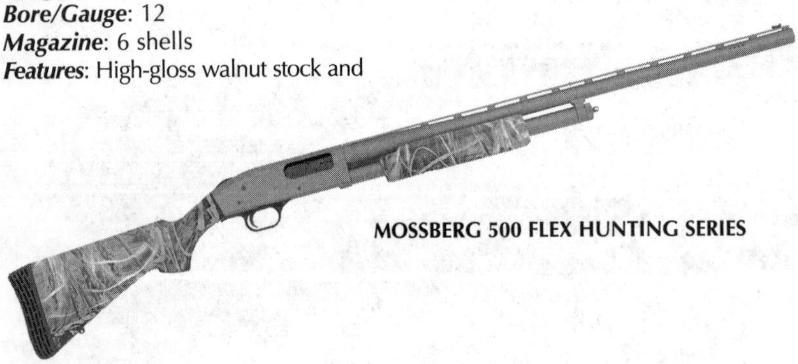

MOSSBERG 500 FLEX HUNTING SERIES

MOSSBERG 500 JIC FLEX

500 FLEX ALL-PURPOSE SERIES

Action: Pump
Stock: Synthetic
Barrel: 26 in., 28 in.
Chokes: Accu-Set
Weight: 7 lb. 8 oz.
Bore/Gauge: 12
Magazine: 6 shells
Features: Matte metal finishes or Marinecote finish; stock with medium recoil pad; stock and forend constructed of synthetic with black matte finish; twin bead sights
MSRP . . . . **$649–$708**

500 FLEX HUNTING SERIES

Action: Pump
Stock: Synthetic
Barrel: 24 in.
Chokes: Accu-Set
Weight: 7 lb. 8 oz.
Bore/Gauge: 12, 20
Magazine: 6 shells
Features: OD green, coyote tan, Mossy Oak Break-Up Infinity, or Realtree Max-4 cam receiver finishes; standard stocks and forends feature Infinity or Realtree Max-4 camo finishes
MSRP . . . . **$484–$908**

500 JIC FLEX

Action: Pump
Stock: Synthetic
Barrel: 18.5 in.
Chokes: C
Weight: 5 lb. 8 oz.
Bore/Gauge: 12
Magazine: 6 shells
Features: Bead sights; FLEX pistol grip; 3-in. barrel with matte black finish
MSRP **$518**

Mossberg

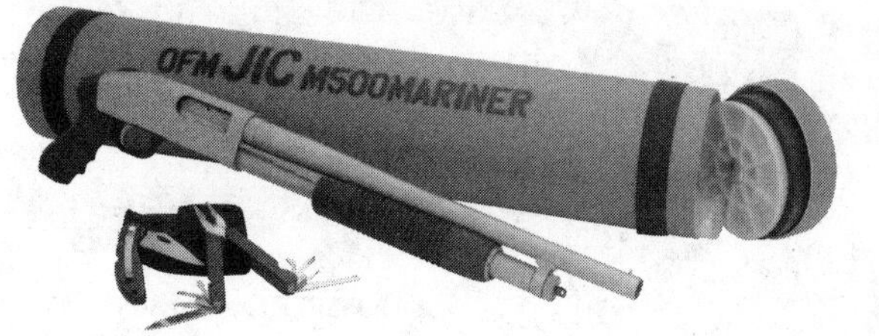

MOSSBERG 500 JIC MARINER

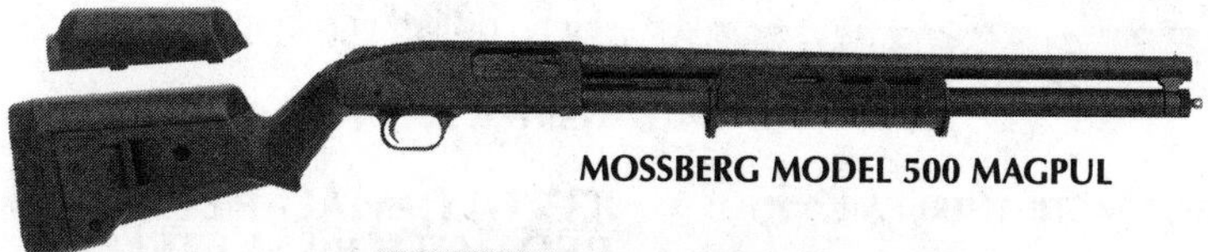

MOSSBERG MODEL 500 MAGPUL

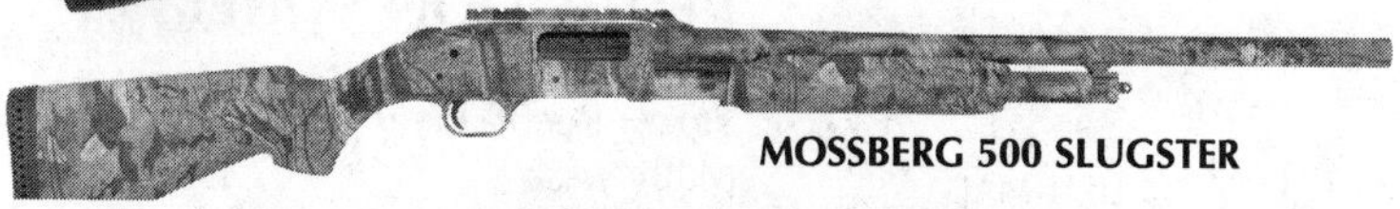

MOSSBERG 500 SLUGSTER

MOSSBERG 500 SUPER BANTAM SLUGSTER

MOSSBERG 500 SUPER BANTAM TURKEY

MOSSBERG 500 TURKEY

500 JIC MARINER

Action: Pump
Stock: Synthetic
Barrel: 18.5 in.
Chokes: Cylinder bore chokes
Weight: 5 lb. 8 oz.
Bore/Gauge: 12
Magazine: 6 shells
Features: Bead sight; Marinecote metal finish; comes with multi-tool, survival knife and cordura carrying case; gun lock; swivel studs; black synthetic stock; only pump-action shotguns to pass all U.S. Military Mil-Spec 3443 standards
MSRP $661

500 MAGPUL

Action: Pump
Stock: Synthetic
Barrel: 18.5 in.–20 in.
Chokes: C
Weight: 7 lb.
Bore/Gauge: 12
Magazine: 6–8 shells
Features: Magpul SGA stocks and MOE forends designed specifically for tactical shotguns; SGA stock features a spacer system for LOP adjustment; improved grip ergonomics; recoil-reducing buttpad; optional cheek riser for use wtih mounted optics or raised sights
MSRP . . . .$602–$655

500 SLUGSTER

Action: Pump
Stock: Synthetic
Barrel: 24 in.
Chokes: None
Weight: 6 lb. 12 oz.–7 lb. 4 oz.
Bore/Gauge: 12, 20
Magazine: 6 shells
Features: Fully-rifled bore; integral scope base; ported barrel; ambidextrous thumb-operated safety; available in MO Break-up Infinity
MSRP . . . . $428–$525

500 SUPER BANTAM SLUGSTER

Action: Pump
Stock: Synthetic
Barrel: 24 in.
Chokes: None
Weight: 5 lb. 4 oz.
Bore/Gauge: 20
Magazine: 6 shells
Features: Fully-rifled bore; adjustable synthetic stock; Blued or Realtree AP finish; drilled and tapped for scopes; ported barrels; adjustable rifle sights
MSRP $428

500 SUPER BANTAM TURKEY

Action: Pump
Stock: Synthetic
Barrel: 22 in.
Chokes: Interchangeable Accu-Choke (X-full and wrench)
Weight: 5 lb. 4 oz.
Bore/Gauge: 20
Magazine: 6 shells
Features: Adjustable synthetic stock in Mossy Oak Break-Up Infinity camo or Hardwoods HD Green camo; adjustable fiber optic sights; drilled and tapped for scopes; gun lock
MSRP $496

500 TURKEY

Action: Pump
Stock: Synthetic
Barrel: 24 in.
Chokes: Accu-Choke tubes (XX-Full)
Weight: 7 lb. 4 oz.–8 lb. 4 oz.
Bore/Gauge: 12
Magazine: 6 or 7 shells
Features: Adjustable front sight; synthetic finish in Mossy Oak Break-Up Infinity camo; ported barrel; ambidextrous thumb-operated safety; includes gun lock; LPA (Lightning Pump Action) trigger system providing creepfree rifle-like trigger available
MSPR . . . . $496–$538

Mossberg

MOSSBERG 510 MINI ALL PURPOSE

MOSSBERG 510 MINI CAMO

MOSSBERG 590A1 ADJUSTABLE TACTICAL TRI-RAIL 9 SHOT

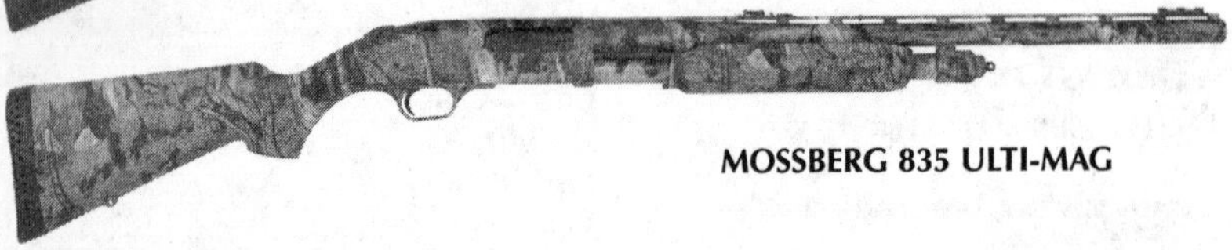

MOSSBERG 835 ULTI-MAG

510 MINI ALL PURPOSE

Action: Pump
Stock: Synthetic
Barrel: 18.5 in.
Chokes: Accu-set in 20 Ga., Fixed-Mod. in .410 bore
Weight: 5 lb.
Bore/Gauge: 20, .410
Magazine: 3 (.410) or 4 (20 Ga.) shells
Features: Good choice for petite or younger shooter; adjustable synthetic stock in black; blued barrel finish; dual bead sights
MSRP . . . . $428–$481

510 MINI CAMO

Action: Pump
Stock: Synthetic
Barrel: 18.5 in.
Chokes: Interchangeable Accu-Choke tubes
Weight: 5 lb.
Bore/Gauge: 20, .410
Magazine: 3 or 4 shells
Features: Dual bead sights; synthetic stock comes in Mossy Oak Infinity camo
MSRP $481

590A1 ADJUSTABLE TACTICAL TRI-RAIL 9 SHOT

Action: Pump
Stock: Synthetic
Barrel: 18.5 in., 20 in.
Chokes: Cylinder bore
Weight: 7 lb. 8 oz.
Bore/Gauge: 12
Magazine: 9 shells
Features: Six-position adjustable stock with a tri-rail forend; ghost ring sights; Parkerized finish; speedfeed, black stock; heavy barrel wall; Blackwater logo
MSRP $898

835 ULTI-MAG

Action: Pump
Stock: Synthetic
Barrel: 20 in., 24 in.
Chokes: Ulti-full tube chokes
Weight: 7 lb. 4 oz.
Bore/Gauge: 12
Magazine: 6 shells
Features: Overbored, ported barrel; synthetic stock comes in woodlands, Mossy Oak Break-Up Infinity, Hardwoods HD Green Camo, or blued; ambidextrous, thumb-operated safety; drilled and tapped for scope mounts
MSRP . . . . $676–$717

835 ULTI-MAG-RECOIL REDUCTION SYSTEM

Action: Pump
Stock: Recoil Reduction System/ Mathews
Barrel: 24 in., 28 in.
Chokes: Accu-Mag set, Modified tube, or Ulti-full tube
Weight: 8 lb. 8 oz.
Bore/ Gauge: 12
Magazine: 6 shells
Features: Exclusive stock incorporating Mathews Harmonic Damper Technology; two interchangeable low and high profile combs; 3.5 in. chamber; ported barrels; free gun lock and 10-year limited warranty
MSRP $670

930 DUCK COMMANDER SIGNATURE MODEL

Action: Semiautomatic
Stock: Synthetic
Barrel: 28 in.
Chokes: Accu-Set
Weight: 7 lb. 12 oz.
Bore/Gauge: 12
Magazine: 5 shells
Features: Realtree Max-5 camo; Tru-Glo, Tru-Bead dual color front fiber optic sight; Duck Commander logo and "Happy Happy Happy" engraved on the mag cap
MSRP $928

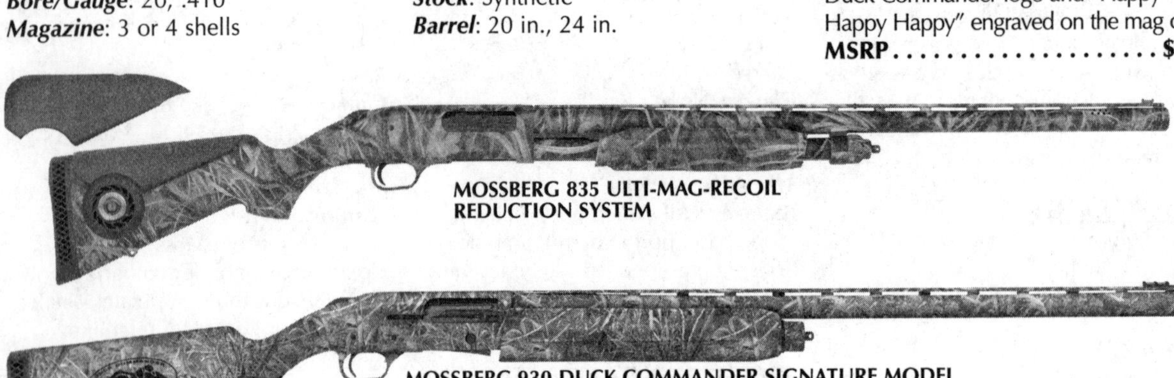

MOSSBERG 835 ULTI-MAG-RECOIL REDUCTION SYSTEM

MOSSBERG 930 DUCK COMMANDER SIGNATURE MODEL

Mossberg

MOSSBERG 935 MAGNUM TURKEY

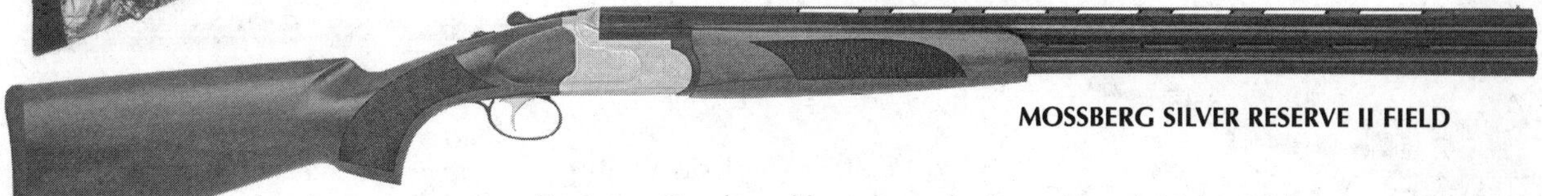

MOSSBERG SILVER RESERVE II FIELD

935 MAGNUM TURKEY

Action: Semiautomatic
Stock: Synthetic
Barrel: 24 in.
Chokes: Ulti-full tube chokes
Weight: 7 lb. 8 oz.
Bore/Gauge: 12
Magazine: 5 shells
Features: Overbored barrel; synthetic stock in Mossy Oak Break-Up Infinity or Hardwoods HD Green camo; quick-empty magazine button; adjustable fiber optic sights; wide ventilated rib
MSRP . . . . $866–$983

SILVER RESERVE II FIELD

Action: Over/under
Stock: Walnut, satin
Barrel: 26 in., 28 in.
Chokes: 5, Field set
Weight: 7 lb. 8 oz.
Bore/ Gauge: 12, 20, 28, .410
Magazine: 2 736
Features: Bead front sight; 3 in. chamber; blued barrels with silver receiver and scroll engraving; 12 Ga. model features shell ejectors
MSRP . . . . $736–$848

Perazzi

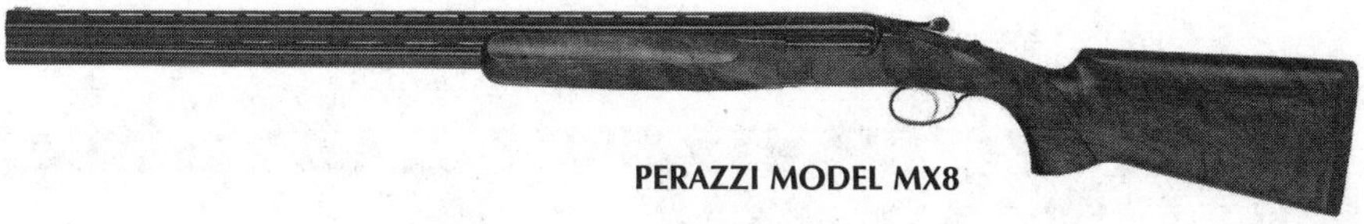

PERAZZI MODEL MX8

MX8 SPORTING CLAYS

Action: Over/under
Stock: Walnut
Barrel: 29 in., 30 in., 31 in.
Chokes: Interchangeable chokes
Weight: 7 lb. 5 oz.
Bore/Gauge: 12, 20
Magazine: 2 shells
Features: Custom walnut stock with beavertail forend; half-ventilated side ribs on barrel; removable trigger with flat or coil springs; blue or nickel plating; Sporting, Skeet and Trap models; 28 Ga. and .410 models also available
MSRP $10460

Pointer by Legacy Sports

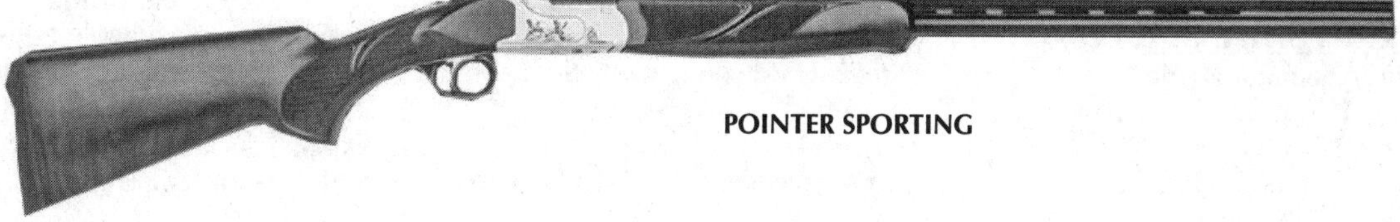

POINTER SPORTING

SPORTING SERIES

Action: Over/under
Stock: Wood
Barrel: 26 in.–28 in.
Chokes: Multi-5
Weight: 6 lb.–7 lb 8 oz.
Bore/Gauge: 12, 20, 28, .410
Magazine: 2 shells
Features: Ventilated raised rib; carbon steel barrel with chrome moly lined bore; brass bead sight; comes with five choke tubes (.410 Ga. is fixed); satin blued barrel finish; high luster Turkish walnut stock
MSRP $664

Purdey

PURDEY OVER AND UNDER GUN

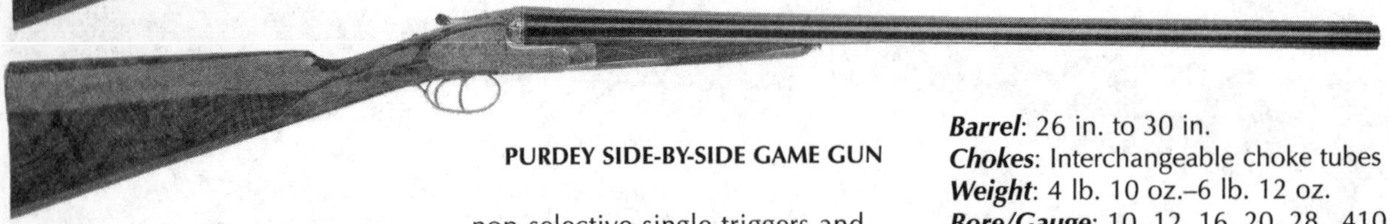

PURDEY SIDE-BY-SIDE GAME GUN

OVER AND UNDER GUN

Action: Over/under
Stock: Walnut
Barrel: 26 in.–30 in.
Chokes: Interchangeable choke tubes
Weight: 4 lb. 14 oz.–7 lb. 8 oz.
Bore/Gauge: 12, 16, 20, 28, .410
Magazine: 2 shells
Features: Available in round, square, or ultra-round action shapes; available with double or non-selective single triggers and automatic safety catch; demi-bloc construction; solid game rib with hand matted finish; Turkish walnut with straight, semi, or full pistol grip; gold oval or inlaid gold letters; sporter scroll engraving
Starting at:............. $131181
Sporter:................. $43545

SIDE-BY-SIDE GAME GUN

Action: Side-by-side
Stock: Walnut
Barrel: 26 in. to 30 in.
Chokes: Interchangeable choke tubes
Weight: 4 lb. 10 oz.–6 lb. 12 oz.
Bore/Gauge: 10, 12, 16, 20, 28, .410
Magazine: 2 shells
Features: Built on self-opening system; available with double or non-selective single triggers and automatic safety catch; Turkish walnut in straight, semi or full pistol grip; gold oval or inlaid gold letters; sporter scroll engraving; traditional splinter or beavertail forend available
Starting at:............. $106686

Remington

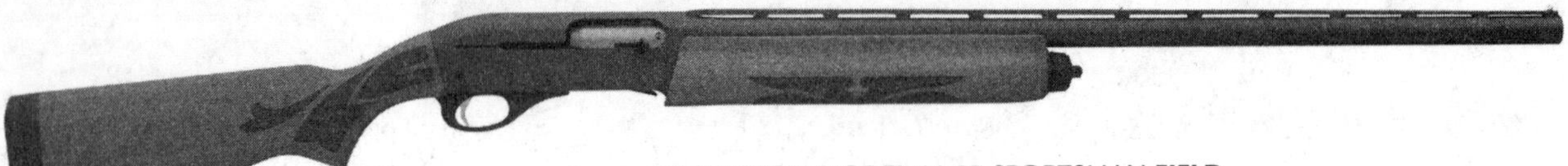

REMINGTON MODEL 11-87 SPORTSMAN FIELD

REMINGTON MODEL 870 EXPRESS

MODEL 11-87 SPORTSMAN FIELD

Action: Semiautomatic
Stock: Walnut
Barrel: 26 in., 28 in.
Chokes: Rem. modified choke
Weight: 7 lb. 4 oz.–8 lb. 4 oz.
Bore/Gauge: 12, 20
Magazine: None
Features: Solid walnut stock and forend with satin finish and fleur-de-lis checkering; nickel-plated bolt and gold-plated trigger; vent rib with dual bead sights
MSRP................... $845

MODEL 870 EXPRESS

Action: Pump
Stock: Hardwood, synthetic, laminate, or camo
Barrel: 18 in.–28 in.
Chokes: Modified Remington choke, extra full Rem.
Weight: 6 lb.–7 lb. 4 oz.
Bore/Gauge: 12, 20
Magazine: 2–7 shells depending on model
Features: Single bead sight; standard express finish on barrel and receiver; rubber recoil pad; twin action bars ensure smooth, reliable non-binding action; solid steel receiver; optional thumbhole stock in some models
Express:..................$417
Syn. 7-round:..............$443
Syn. Deer:.................$463
Turkey Camo: $492

SHOTGUNS

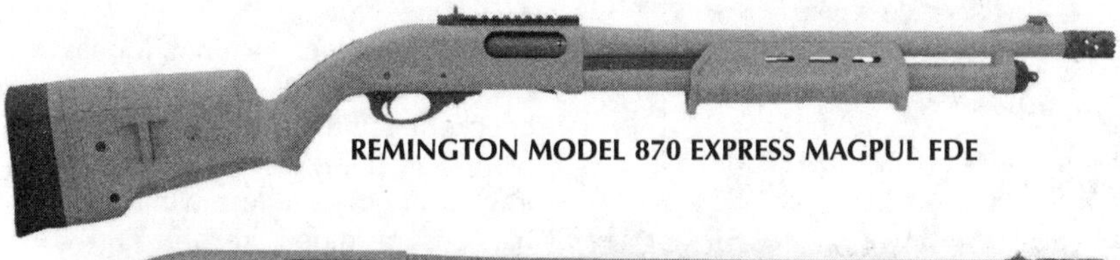

REMINGTON MODEL 870 EXPRESS MAGPUL FDE

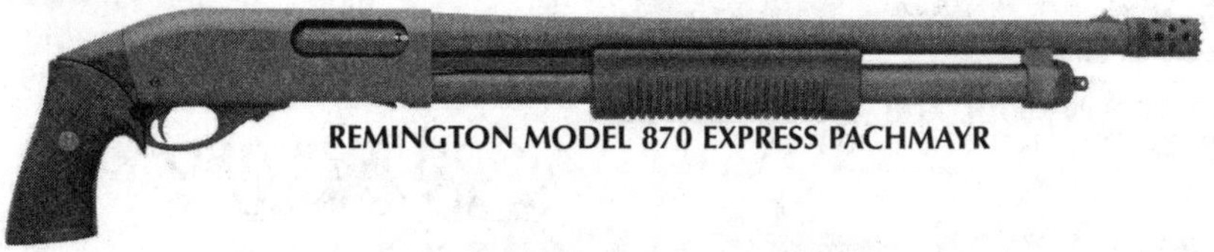

REMINGTON MODEL 870 EXPRESS PACHMAYR

REMINGTON MODEL 870 EXPRESS SUPER MAGNUM TURKEY WATERFOWL

REMINGTON MODEL 870 EXPRESS TACTICAL A-TACS CAMO

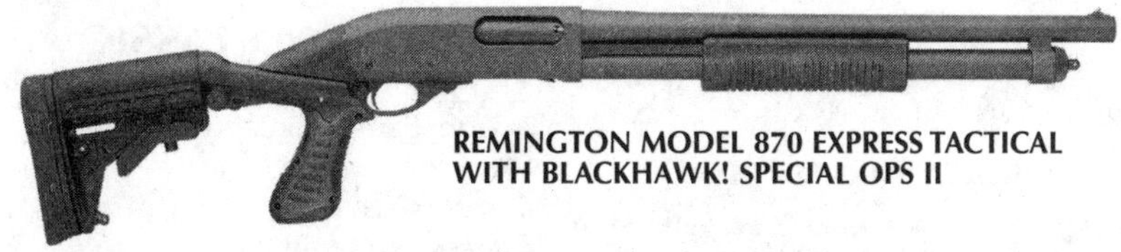

REMINGTON MODEL 870 EXPRESS TACTICAL WITH BLACKHAWK! SPECIAL OPS II

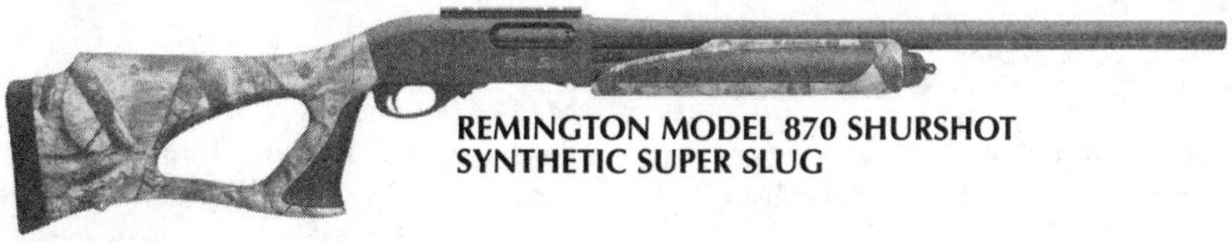

REMINGTON MODEL 870 SHURSHOT SYNTHETIC SUPER SLUG

MODEL 870 EXPRESS MAGPUL FDE

Action: Pump
Stock: Synthetic
Barrel: 18.5 in.
Chokes: Rem. Choke
Weight: 7 lb. 8 oz.
Bore/Gauge: 12
Magazine: 6+1 shells
Features: Picatinny rail; receiver and barrel features weather resistant FDE Cerakote coating; Magpul SGA stock and MOE fore-end in FDE; one piece magazine tube; fully adjustable XS Ghost Ring sight rail with removable white bead front sight; available in black synthetic
MSRP $898

MODEL 870 EXPRESS PACHMAYR PISTOL GRIP

Action: Pump
Stock: Synthetic
Barrel: 18.5 in.
Chokes: Rem. Choke
Weight: 7 lb. 8 oz.
Bore/Gauge: 12
Magazine: 6+1 shells
Features: Tactically proven Model 870 receiver milled from solid steel; 18.5-in. barrel with extended tactical ported choke tube; one-piece high strength magazine tube; Pachmayr pistol grip; ships with standard black synthetic stock in box
MSRP $497

MODEL 870 EXPRESS SUPER MAGNUM

Action: Pump
Stock: Hardwood, synthetic, or camo
Barrel: 26 in.
Chokes: Wingmaster HD Waterfowl and Turkey Extra Full Rem chokes
Weight: 7 lb. 4 oz.
Bore/Gauge: 12
Magazine: None
Features: Synthetic stock in full Mossy Oak Bottomland camo; HiVix fiber-optics; SuperCell recoil pad; drilled and tapped receiver
Express Super Mag: $469
Synthetic: $469
Turkey/Waterfowl: $629
Waterfowl Camo: $629

MODEL 870 EXPRESS TACTICAL

Action: Pump
Stock: Synthetic
Barrel: 18.5 in.
Chokes: Screw-in tube
Weight: 7 lb. 8 oz.
Bore/Gauge: 12
Magazine: None
Features: Synthetic stock available in A-tacs digitized camo; Tactical Rem. choke SpeedFeed IV; pistol grip stock; SuperCell recoil pad; adjustable XS Ghost Ring sight rail with removable with bead front sight; Picatinny-style rail
Express Tactical: $601
A-Tacs Camo: $720

MODEL 870 EXPRESS TACTICAL WITH BLACKHAWK! SPECIAL OPS II

Action: Pump
Stock: Synthetic
Barrel: 18 in.
Chokes: Screw-in tube
Weight: 7 lb.
Bore/Gauge: 12
Magazine: 6+1 shells
Features: Plain barrel with front bead; 7 position LOP adjustment; recoil reduction system; enhanced pistol grip; sling mount; drilled and tapped receiver; SuperCell recoil pad; Blackhawk Ops II buttstock features built-in recoil reduction system and is adjustable over several increments of length of pull
MSRP $638

MODEL 870 SHURSHOT SYNTHETIC

Action: Pump
Stock: Synthetic
Barrel: 25 in.
Chokes: Screw-in tubes
Weight: 7 lb. 13 oz.
Bore/Gauge: 12
Magazine: None
Features: Ambidextrous Shurshot pistol-grip synthetic stock; rubberized overmolding; SuperCell recoil pad; receiver is drilled and tapped; Weaver rail; sling swivels
Turkey: $536
Cantilever: $571

Remington

Bore/Gauge: 12
Magazine: None
Features: American walnut, Monte Carlo stock; forend with deep cut checkering and a high-gloss finish; twin bead sights; three specialized trap Rem. choke tubes; twin action bars ensure smooth, reliable non-binding action; choke vent rib barrel
MSRP **$1098**

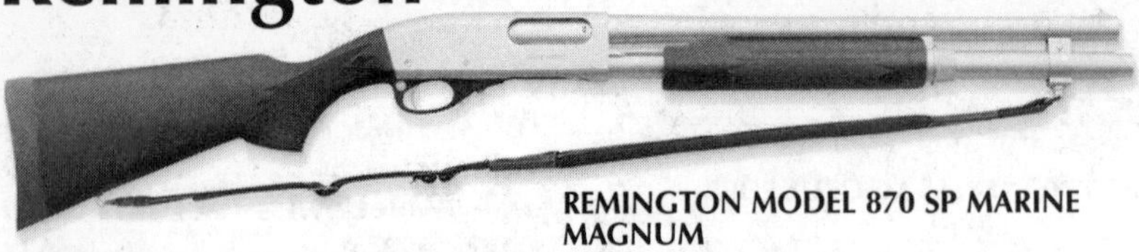

REMINGTON MODEL 870 SP MARINE MAGNUM

REMINGTON MODEL 870 SPS SHURSHOT SYNTHETIC TURKEY

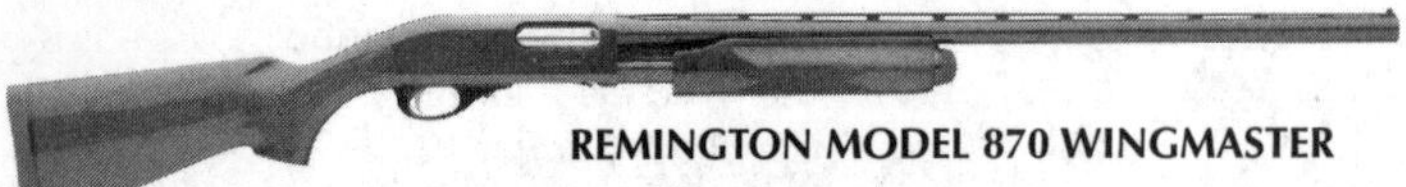

REMINGTON MODEL 870 WINGMASTER

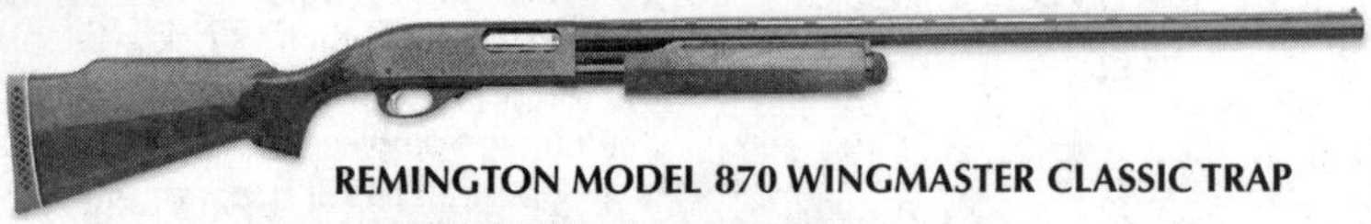

REMINGTON MODEL 870 WINGMASTER CLASSIC TRAP

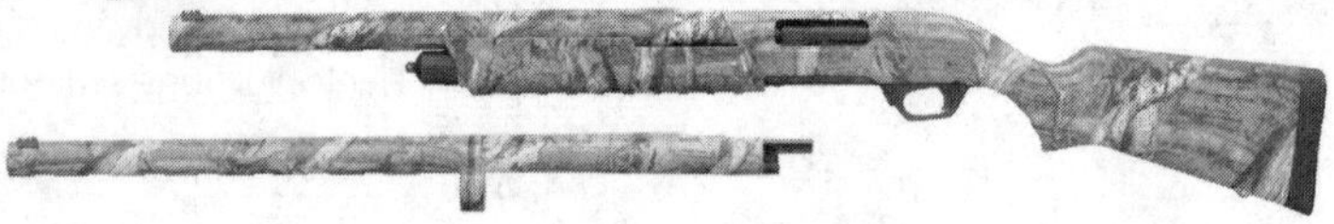

REMINGTON MODEL 887 NITRO MAG CAMO COMBO

REMINGTON MODEL 1100 CLASSIC TRAP

REMINGTON MODEL 1100 COMPETITION SYNTHETIC

MODEL 870 SP MARINE MAGNUM

Action: Pump
Stock: Synthetic
Barrel: 18 in.
Chokes: Cylinder chokes
Weight: 7 lb. 8 oz.
Bore/Gauge: 12
Magazine: 6 shells
Features: Single-bead front sight; padded Cordura; sling swivels; electroless nickel plating covers all metal; twin action bars ensure smooth, reliable non-binding action
MSRP **$841**

MODEL 870 SPS SHURSHOT SYNTHETIC

Action: Pump
Stock: Synthetic
Barrel: 23 in.
Chokes: Wingmaster HD extended Rem Choke
Weight: 7 lb. 8 oz.
Bore/Gauge: 12
Magazine: None
Features: Realtree APG HD camo; features ShurShot synthetic pistol grip stock; adjustable TruGlo fiber-optic sights; receiver drilled and tapped for scope mounts
Turkey: **$681**
Super Slug: **$829**

MODEL 870 WINGMASTER

Action: Pump
Stock: Walnut
Barrel: 25 in.
Chokes: Screw-in tubes
Weight: 6 lb.–6 lb. 4 oz.
Bore/Gauge: 12, 20, 28, .410
Magazine: None
Features: Twin action bars for non-binding action; receiver machined from solid billet of steel; highly polished and richly blued receiver; wide array of barrel and choke options
MSRP **$830**

MODEL 870 WINGMASTER CLASSIC TRAP

Action: Pump
Stock: Walnut
Barrel: 30 in.
Chokes: Screw-in tube, Rem. Choke
Weight: 8 lb. 4 oz.

MODEL 887 NITRO MAG CAMO COMBO

Action: Semiautomatic
Stock: Synthetic
Barrel: 22 in., 28 in.
Chokes: Screw-in tubes
Weight: 7 lb.–7 lb. 4 oz.
Bore/Gauge: 12
Magazine: None
Features: Synthetic camo stock with ArmorLkt coating; SuperCell recoil pad; HiViz front sight; contoured grip panels; sling swivel
MSRP **$728**

MODEL 1100 CLASSIC TRAP

Action: Semiautomatic
Stock: Walnut
Barrel: 30 in.
Chokes: Screw-in tubes
Weight: 8 lb. 4 oz.
Bore/Gauge: 12
Magazine: None
Features: American walnut stock with cut-checkering; bead blasted top and bottom radius; blued finish on receiver and barrel; gold triggers and gold embellishments on receiver
MSRP **$1308**

MODEL 1100 COMPETITION SYNTHETIC

Action: Semiautomatic
Stock: Synthetic
Barrel: 30 in.
Chokes: 5 extended Briley (Target) choke tubes (Skeet, IC, LM, M, Full)
Weight: 8 lb. 2 oz.
Bore/Gauge: 12
Magazine: None
Features: Nickel-Teflon finish on receiver and all internal parts; barrel has 10mm target-style rib; adjustable comb and cast adjustment options; high-gloss blued barrel; fully adjustable target-style stock with recoil reduction; synthetic polymer stock and forend finished with carbon graphite appearance; twin target-style bead sights
MSRP **$1279**

REMINGTON VERSA MAX MO DUCK BLIND

REMINGTON VERSA MAX COMPETITION TACTICAL

REMINGTON VERSA MAX SPORTSMAN

REMINGTON VERSA MAX TACTICAL

REMINGTON VERSA MAX WOOD TECH

VERSA MAX

Action: Semiautomatic
Stock: Synthetic
Barrel: 26 in., 28 in.
Chokes: 5 Flush Mount Pro Bore chokes (F, M, IM, LB, IC)
Weight: 7 lb. 8 oz.–7 lb. 11 oz.
Bore/Gauge: 12
Magazine: 3+1 or 2+1 shells
Features: Remington patented gas-piston system; synthetic stock and forend with gray overmolded grips, comes in black or a Mossy Oak Duck blind camo; drilled and tapped receiver; enlarged trigger guard opening and larger safety for easier use with gloves; TriNyte Barrel and nickel Teflon plated internal components
Black:. $1427
Camo: $1630

VERSA MAX COMPETITION TACTICAL

Action: Semiautomatic
Stock: Synthetic
Barrel: 22 in.
Chokes: IC, M, IM, LM, F
Weight: 8 lb.
Bore/Gauge: 12
Magazine: 8 shells
Features: Enlarged feeding port; "welded" style carrier; enlarged bolt closure button, safety and cocking handle; adjustable XS rear rifle sight; two-shot carbon fiber extension (10+1 shells); QD sling swivel cups on stock and forend
MSRP $1699

VERSA MAX SPORTSMAN

Action: Semiautomatic
Stock: Synthetic
Barrel: 22 in., 26 in., 28 in.
Chokes: Modified Pro Bore Flush Mount; Pro Bore Wingmaster Turkey TXF Extended
Weight: 7 lb. 8 oz.
Bore/ Gauge: 12
Magazine: 3+1 or 2+1 shells
Features: VersaPort Gas System; 4140 Hammer-Forged barrel; available in Mossy Oak Camo, Realtree AP Camo, and black oxide; SuperCell Recoil Pad; ivory front bead sights, steel mid bead
MSRP $1045

VERSA MAX TACTICAL

Action: Semiautomatic
Stock: Synthetic
Barrel: 22 in.
Chokes: IC and Tactical ProBore tube
Weight: 7 lb. 12 oz.
Bore/Gauge: 12
Magazine: 8+1 shells
Features: Ventilated rib; fiberoptic HiViz front sight; receiver is drilled and tapped for optics; Picatinny rail; recoil pad; size bolt-release button; oversized trigger guard for easy operation when wearing gloves
MSRP $1427

VERSA MAX WOOD TECH

Action: Semiautomatic
Stock: Synthetic
Barrel: 28 in.
Chokes: IC, M, IM, LM, F
Weight: 7 lb. 12 oz.
Bore/Gauge: 12
Magazine: 3+1 or 2+1 shells
Features: Versaport gas system regulates cycling pressure based on shell length; synthetic stock and forend with overmolded grips and Wood Tech finish; drilled and tapped receiver; enlarged trigger guard opening and larger safety for easier use with gloves; TriNyte barrel and nickel teflon plated internal components for extreme corrosion resistance
MSRP $1630

Rossi

ROSSI FIELD GRADE SHOTGUN

ROSSI RIFLED
BARREL SLUG GUN

FIELD GRADE SHOTGUN

Action: Single-shot, break-open
Stock: Synthetic
Barrel: 28 in.
Chokes: Modified screw-in chokes
Weight: 3 lb. 12 oz.–5 lb. 4 oz.
Bore/Gauge: 12, 20, .410
Magazine: 1 shell
Features: Steel receiver; black synthetic stock with grips; blue finish metal; transfer bar safety action
Full size: $171
Youth 22-in. barrel: $171

RIFLED BARREL SLUG GUN

Action: Single shot, break open
Stock: Synthetic
Barrel: 23 in.
Chokes: Screw-in tubes
Weight: 6 lb. 4 oz.
Bore/Gauge: 12
Magazine: 1 shell
Features: Steel receiver; black synthetic stock with grips; blued matte finish on metal; removable cheekpiece; Trifecta three-barrel youth gun includes either .243 Win. or 44 Mag. barrel with fiber optic sights or .22 LR barrel with adjustable fiber optics and 20 Ga. shotgun barrel with brass bead front sight
MSRP $322

Ruger

RUGER RED LABEL

RED LABEL

Action: Over/under
Stock: Wood
Barrel: 26 in.–30 in.
Chokes: IC, M, F, Skeet
Weight: 7 lb. 8 oz.–7 lb. 14 oz.
Bore/Gauge: 12
Magazine: 2 shells
Features: Automatic, two-position tang safety/barrel selector; finely polished, stainless steel receiver; single mechanical trigger; blued alloy steel, cold hammer-forged barrels made of high-strength chrom molyb steel; ¼-in. dovetailed, free-floating, ventilated rib with brass bead front sight; cut-checkered American Walnut stock features a traditional pistol grip, tapered, slim forend and a stainless steel latch release; soft Pachmayr buttpad
MSRP $1399

Savage Arms

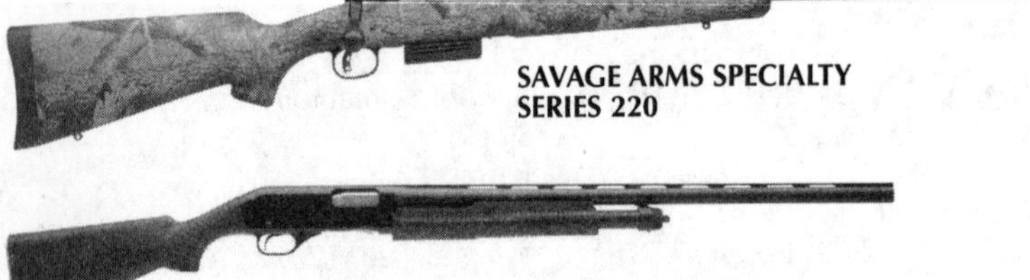

SAVAGE ARMS SPECIALTY
SERIES 220

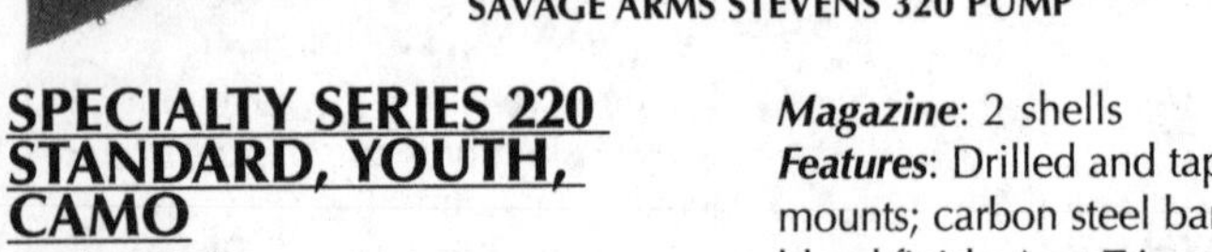

SAVAGE ARMS STEVENS 320 PUMP

SPECIALTY SERIES 220 STANDARD, YOUTH, CAMO

Action: Bolt
Stock: Synthetic
Barrel: 22 in.
Sights: None
Weight: 7 lb. 8 oz.
Caliber: 20 Ga.
Magazine: 2 shells
Features: Drilled and tapped for scope mounts; carbon steel barrel with matte blued finish; AccuTrigger; synthetic stock in matte black finish or camo
Standard: $601
Camo: $666
Youth: $601

STEVENS 320 PUMP

Action: Pump
Stock: Synthetic
Barrel: 18.5 in.
Chokes: None
Weight: 7 lb.
Bore/Gauge: 12
Magazine: 5 shells
Features: Proven rotary bolt design; dual side bars; carbon steel barrel with matte black finish; optional pistol grip, front bead, rifle sights, or ghost ring sights on some models
MSRP . . . . $234–$274

Savage Arms

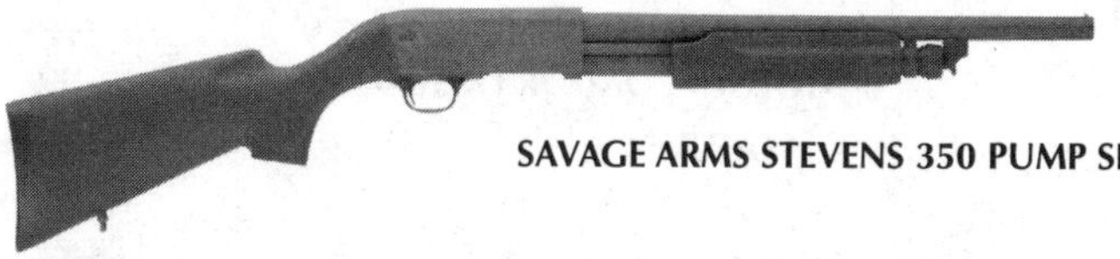

SAVAGE ARMS STEVENS 350 PUMP SECURITY

STEVENS 350 PUMP SECURITY

Action: Pump
Stock: Synthetic
Barrel: 18.25 in.
Chokes: None
Weight: 7 lb. 10 oz.
Bore/Gauge: 12
Magazine: 5 shells
Features: Bead sights; carbon steel barrel with matte blued finish; synthetic stock in matte black finish
MSRP. $276

SRM Arms

SRM ARMS GEN 2 MODEL 1216

GEN 2 MODEL 1216

Action: Semiautomatic
Stock: Synthetic
Barrel: 18 in.
Chokes: N/A
Weight: 7 lb. 4 oz.
Bore/Gauge: 12
Magazine: 16 shells
Features: Picatinny rail combined with a three face handguard rail; ambidextrous receiver and controls; quad-tube, revolving detachable magazine
MSRP. $2400

Stoeger

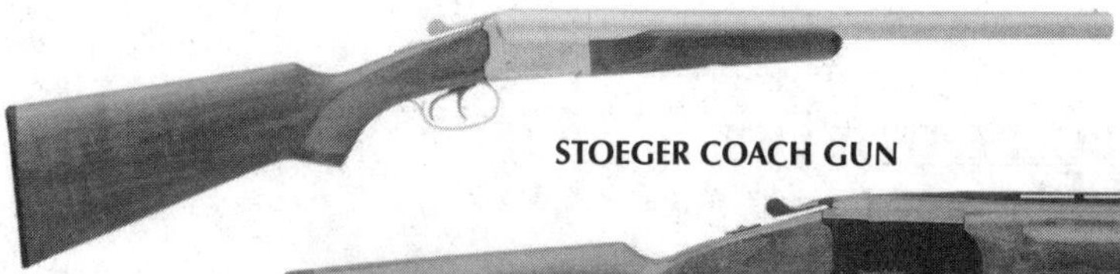

STOEGER COACH GUN

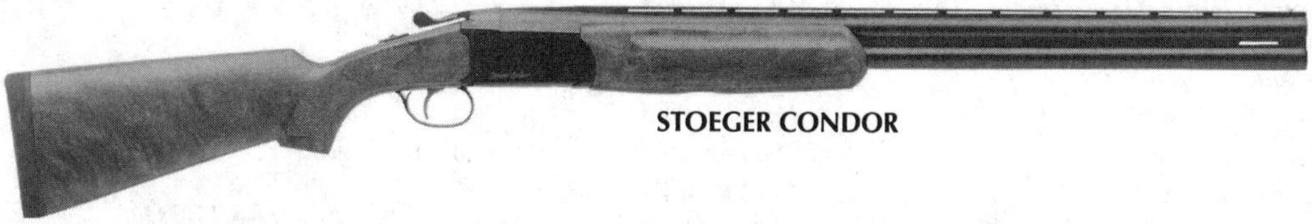

STOEGER CONDOR

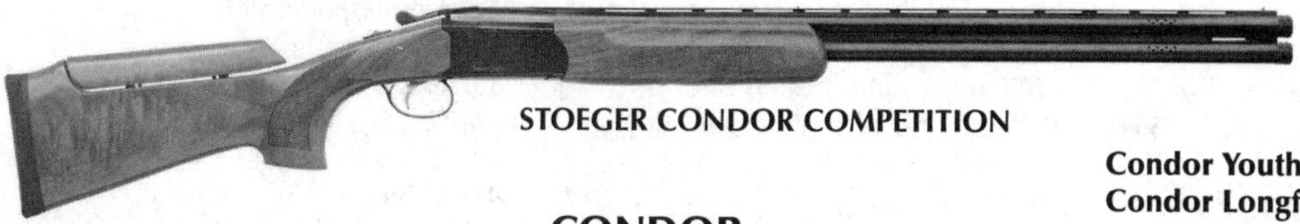

STOEGER CONDOR COMPETITION

COACH GUN

Action: Side-by-side
Stock: Walnut, hardwood
Barrel: 20 in.
Chokes: Fixed chokes (IC, M)
Weight: 6 lb. 5 oz.–7 lb.
Bore/Gauge: 12, 20, .410
Magazine: 2 shells
Features: A-grade satin or black finished hardwood stock; brass bead sights; nickel or blued metal finish
MSRP. . . . . $449–$549

CONDOR

Action: Over/under
Stock: Walnut
Barrel: 22 in., 24 in., 26 in., 28 in.
Chokes: Screw-in and fixed chokes on 12 Ga., 20 Ga., 28 Ga. (IC, M), 16 Ga. (M, F), .410 (F&F)
Weight: 5 lb. 8 oz.–7 lb. 6 oz.
Bore/Gauge: 12, 16, 20, 28, .410
Magazine: 2 shells
Features: Walnut stock; brass bead sight; single trigger; auto-ejectors
Condor Field: $449
Condor Supreme: $649
Condor Youth:. $499
Condor Longfowler: $499

CONDOR COMPETITION

Action: Over/under
Stock: Walnut
Barrel: 30 in.
Chokes: Screw-in (IC, M, F)
Weight: 7 lb. 5 oz.–7 lb. 13 oz.
Bore/Gauge: 12, 20
Magazine: 2 shells
Features: Walnut stock; brass bead with silver mid-bead sight; single selective trigger; automatic ejector; ported barrel
MSRP. $679

Stoeger

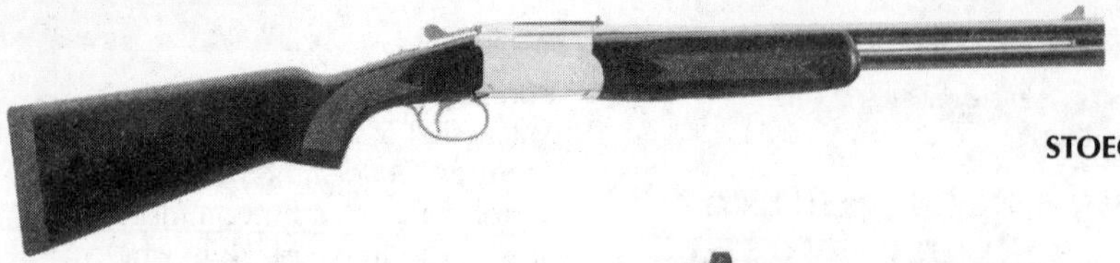

STOEGER CONDOR OUTBACK

STOEGER DOUBLE DEFENSE OVER/UNDER

STOEGER DOUBLE DEFENSE

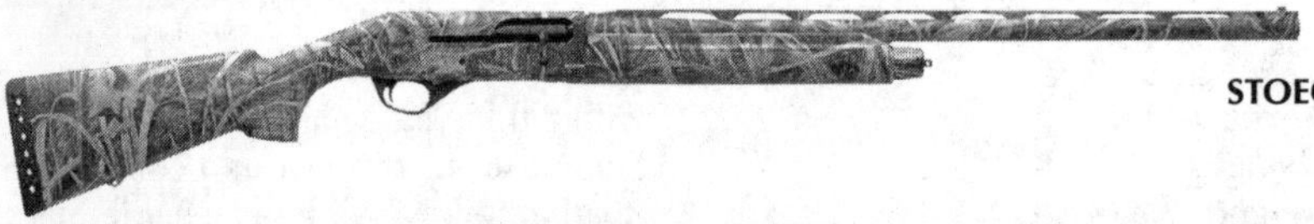

STOEGER MODEL 3000

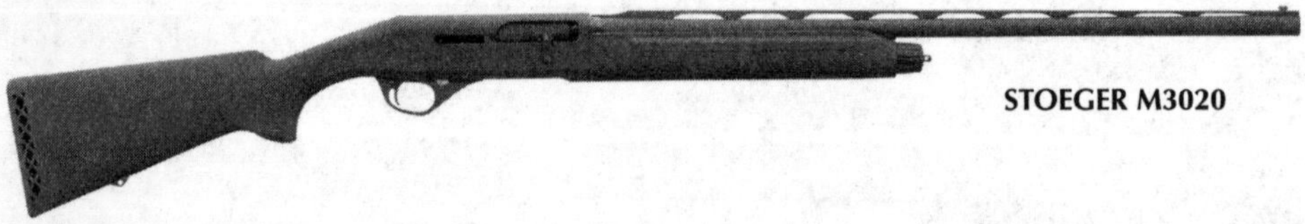

STOEGER M3020

CONDOR OUTBACK

Action: Over/under
Stock: Walnut, hardwood
Barrel: 20 in.
Chokes: Screw-in (IC, M)
Weight: 6 lb. 8 oz.–7 lb.
Bore/Gauge: 12, 20
Magazine: 2 shells
Features: Notched rear sight and fixed blade front sight; shell extractor; single trigger; A-grade satin walnut or black finished hardwood
MSRP. $549

DOUBLE DEFENSE OVER/UNDER

Action: Over/under
Stock: Hardwood
Barrel: 20 in.
Chokes: Screw-in chokes (IC/IC fixed)
Weight: 6 lb. 3 oz.–6 lb. 8 oz.
Bore/Gauge: 12, 20
Magazine: 2 shells
Features: Black hardwood stock; green fiber optic front sight; ported barrels; two Picatinny rails; single trigger design; tang-mounted automatic safety
MSRP. $479

DOUBLE DEFENSE SIDE-BY-SIDE

Action: Side-by-side
Stock: Hardwood
Barrel: 20 in.
Chokes: Screw-in chokes (IC/IC fixed)
Weight: 6 lb. 8 oz.
Bore/Gauge: 12, 20
Magazine: 2 shells
Features: Black hardwood stock; fiber optic front sight; ported barrels; two Picatinny rails; single trigger design; tang-mounted automatic safety
MSRP. $499

MODEL 3000

Action: Semiautomatic
Stock: Black synthetic, Realtree APG, Realtree APG SteadyGrip
Barrel: 24 in.
Chokes: IC, M, XFT, wrench
Weight: 7 lb. 5 oz.
Bore/ Gauge: 12
Magazine: 4+1 shells
Features: Intertia Driven; red-bar front sight; drilled and tapped; shim kit; 3 in. loads
MSRP. . . . . $599–$679

M3020

Action: Semiautomatic
Stock: Synthetic
Barrel: 26 in., 28 in.
Chokes: IC, M, XFT
Weight: 5 lb. 12 oz.
Bore/Gauge: 20
Magazine: 4 shells
Features: Ideal for waterfowl, turkey and upland game; handles a full range of loads, from 2 ¾-in. to 3-in. magnum; barrels are fitted with a ventilated, stepped rib and fiber-optic front sight; available in black, Realtree APG, or Realtree Max-5
MSRP. . . . .$599–$649

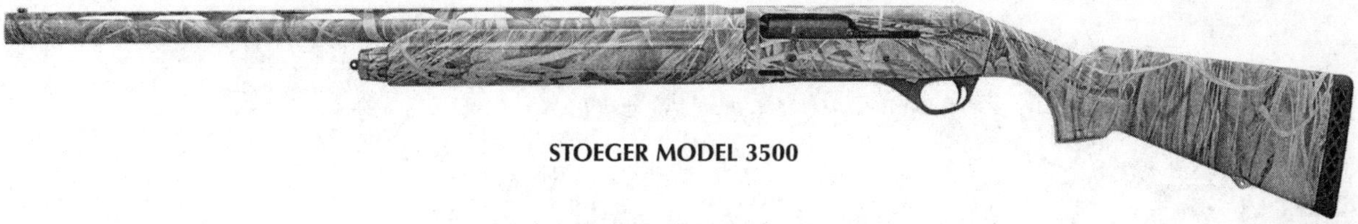

STOEGER MODEL 3500

STOEGER P350 PUMP

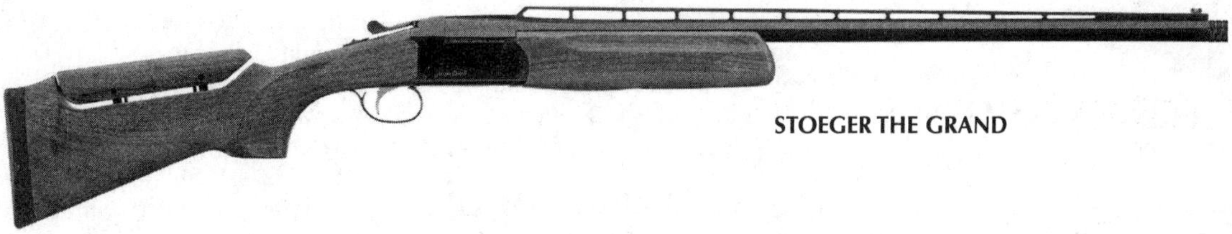

STOEGER THE GRAND

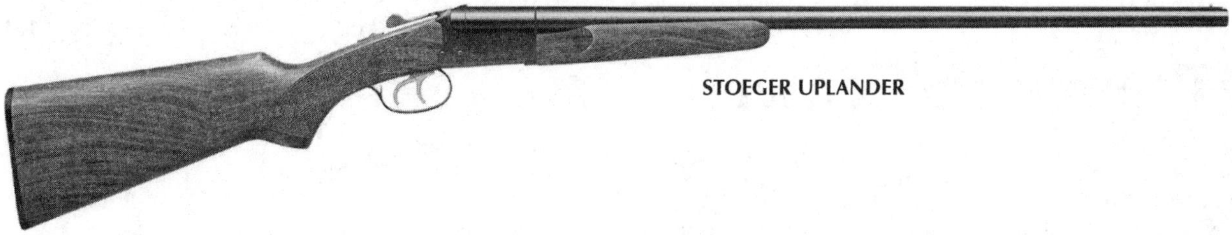

STOEGER UPLANDER

MODEL 3500

Action: Semiautomatic
Stock: Synthetic
Barrel: 24 in., 26 in., 28 in.
Chokes: Screw-in choke tubes (C, IC, M, F, XFT) and wrench
Weight: 7 lb. 7 oz.–7 lb. 10 oz.
Bore/Gauge: 12
Magazine: 4+1 shells
Features: Synthetic stock comes in black or camo finish in Advantage Max-4, Realtree APG, inertia drive system; recoil reducer; red-bar front sight; Weaver scope base; includes shim kit
Black synthetic: $679
Realtree: $799

P350 PUMP

Action: Pump
Stock: Walnut
Barrel: 18.5 in., 24 in., 26 in., 28 in.
Chokes: Screw-in (C, IC, M, F, XFT)
Weight: 6 lb. 6 oz.–6 lb. 14 oz.
Bore/Gauge: 12
Magazine: 4+1 shells
Features: Red bar front sight and metal bead mid-sight; shipped with limiter plug installed; synthetic stock comes in black, Realtree APG, or Realtree Max-4 HD; ergonomic forend
Synthetic: $349
Realtree: $449
Realtree APG Steady Grip: $479

THE GRAND

Action: Break-action
Stock: Wood
Barrel: 30 in.
Chokes: M, IM, F
Weight: 9 lb.
Bore/Gauge: 12
Magazine: 1 shell
Features: Single-barrel target gun designed for shooting trap; stepped ventilated rib and fiber optic front sight; automatic safety that engages when the lever is activated to open the action
MSRP $679

UPLANDER

Action: Side-by-side
Stock: Walnut
Barrel: 22 in. (youth), 26 in., 28 in., 28 in.
Chokes: Screw-in and fixed tubes
Weight: 6 lb. 8 oz.–7 lb. 8 oz.
Bore/Gauge: 12, 16, 20, 28, .410
Magazine: 2 shels
Features: Brass bead sights; A-grade satin walnut stock; tang-mounted safety; single or double triggers; extractors included
Uplander: $499
Uplander Supreme: $549
Uplander Youth: $499
Uplander Longfowler: $499

SHOTGUNS

Taylor's & Co.

TAYLOR'S & CO. 1887
T-SERIES PISTOL

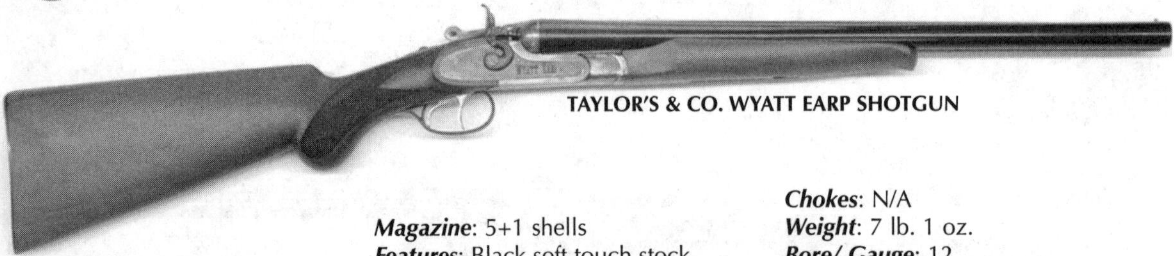

TAYLOR'S & CO. WYATT EARP SHOTGUN

1887 T-SERIES PISTOL

Action: Lever
Stock: Synthetic
Barrel: 18.5 in.
Chokes: None
Weight: 7 lb.
Bore/Gauge: 12
Magazine: 5+1 shells
Features: Black soft touch stock, matte blued finish; Bootleg Model
MSRP . . . . $1168–$1189

WYATT EARP SHOTGUN

Action: Side-by-side
Stock: Walnut checkered pistol grip
Barrel: 20.06 in.
Chokes: N/A
Weight: 7 lb. 1 oz.
Bore/ Gauge: 12
Magazine: 2 shells
Features: Easily opened with one hand for fast shell loading; case-hardened frame stamped with 'Wyatt Earp'; chromed barrel bores with blued finish
MSRP $1647

Thompson/Center

THOMPSON/CENTER PRO HUNTER TURKEY

PRO HUNTER TURKEY

Action: Hinged-breech single-shot
Stock: AP camo with Flextech
Barrel: 24 in. or 26 in.
Chokes: T/C extra full
Weight: 6 lb. 4 oz.–6 lb. 12 oz.
Bore/Gauge: 12, 20
Magazine: 1 shell
Features: Fiber optic sights; 14 in. length pull
MSRP $892

Tristar Sporting Arms

TRISTAR SPORTING ARMS COBRA FIELD PUMP

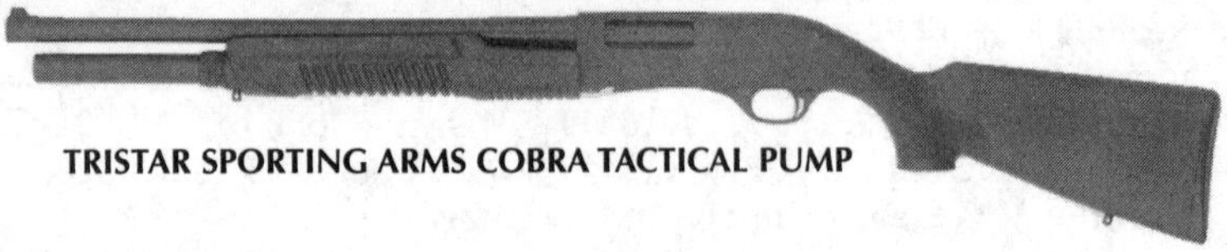

TRISTAR SPORTING ARMS COBRA TACTICAL PUMP

COBRA FIELD PUMP

Action: Pump
Stock: Synthetic
Barrel: 24 in., 26 in., 28 in.
Chokes: 1 Berretta-style choke (M)
Weight: 5 lb. 10 oz.–7 lb.
Bore/Gauge: 12, 20
Magazine: None
Features: Fiber optic front sight; extended forearm to keep out dirt; sling swivel studs
MSRP . . . . $339–$349
Camo: . . . . $429–$489

COBRA TACTICAL PUMP

Action: Pump
Stock: Synthetic
Barrel: 20 in.
Chokes: Screw-in tubes
Weight: 6 lb. 5 oz.
Bore/Gauge: 12
Magazine: 5+1 shells
Features: Faux extended magazine tube; spring-loaded forearm; synthetic stock in matte black; 3-in. chamber
MSRP . . . . $319–$369

Tristar Sporting Arms

TRISTAR SPORTING ARMS HUNTER EX LT

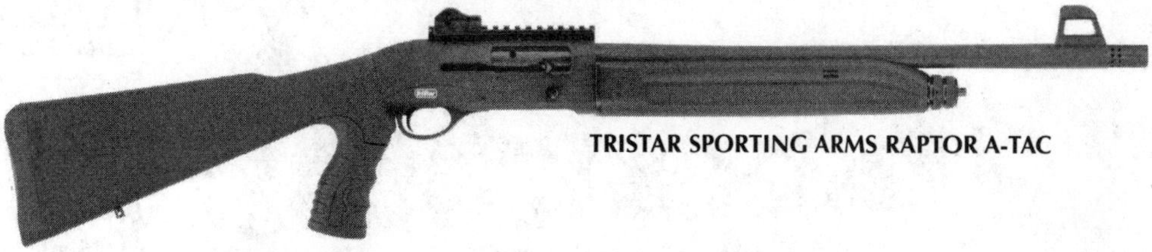

TRISTAR SPORTING ARMS RAPTOR A-TAC

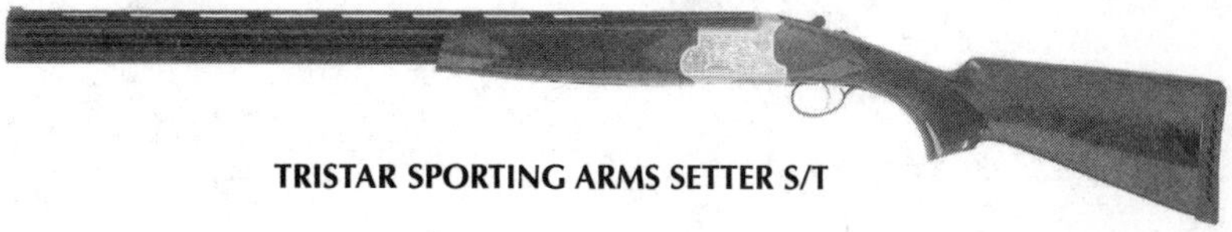

TRISTAR SPORTING ARMS SETTER S/T

HUNTER EX LT

Action: Over/under
Stock: Wood
Barrel: 26 in.
Chokes: SK, IC, M, IM, F
Weight: 5 lb. 6.4 oz.
Bore/ Gauge: 20
Magazine: 2 shells
Features: Aluminum alloy receiver; steel hinge and firing pins; chambered for 3 in.; fiber optic sight
MSRP. $669

RAPTOR A-TAC

Action: Semiautomatic
Stock: Synthetic
Barrel: 20 in.
Chokes: N/A
Weight: 7 lb.
Bore/Gauge: 12
Magazine: 5 shells
Features: Gas-operated; bridge-front sight with fiber optic bead; Picatinny rail mounted on of the receiver with a ghost ring sight installed; fixed pistol grip stock, swivel studs, and a tactical style operating handle; comes with an Extended Tactical Beretta/Benelli style choke; available in Kryptec Typhon and digital camo finishes
MSRP. . . . .$429–$489

SETTER S/T

Action: Over/under
Stock: Walnut
Barrel: 26 in., 28 in.
Chokes: 3-Beretta style tubes (IC, M, F)
Weight: 6 lb. 5 oz.–7 lb. 3 oz.
Bore/Gauge: 12, 20
Magazine: 2 shells
Features: Fiber optic front sight; high-gloss wood; single selective trigger; extractors; ventilated rib
MSRP. $529

TEC 12

Action: Pump or semiautomatic
Stock: Black synthetic
Barrel: 20 in.
Chokes: External Ported Cylinder choke
Weight: 7 lb. 6.4 oz.
Bore/ Gauge: 12
Magazine: N/A
Features: Capable of operating in pump or semiautomatic mode; 3 in. chamber; picatinny rail; ghost ring sight; raised front bridge sight with fiber optic bead; fixed rubber pistol grip; military sling swivels and swivel studs
MSRP. $689

VIPER G2 LH

Action: Semiautomatic
Stock: Synthetic
Barrel: 28 in.
Chokes: IC, M, F
Weight: 6 lb. 14.4 oz.
Bore/ Gauge: 12
Magazine: N/A
Features: Chrome lined chambers; barrels threaded for Beretta/Benelli style choke tubes; 3 in. chambers
MSRP. . . . . $579–$669

VIPER G2 YOUTH CAMO

Action: Semiautomatic
Stock: Camo synthetic
Barrel: 24 in.
Chokes: Beretta/Benelli style chokes (IC, M, F)
Weight: 5 lb. 11 oz.
Bore/Gauge: 20
Magazine: 5+1 shells
Features: Now in Realtree Advantage Timber stock; manual E-Z load magazine cut-off; vent rib with matted sight plane; fiber optic front sight; chrome-lined chamber and barrel; soft touch stock
MSRP. $609

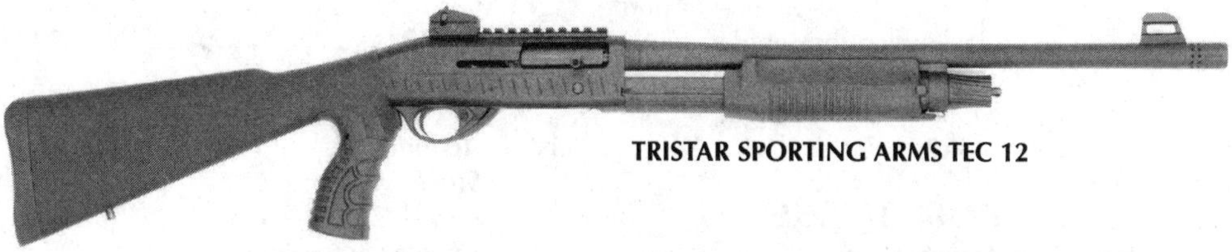

TRISTAR SPORTING ARMS TEC 12

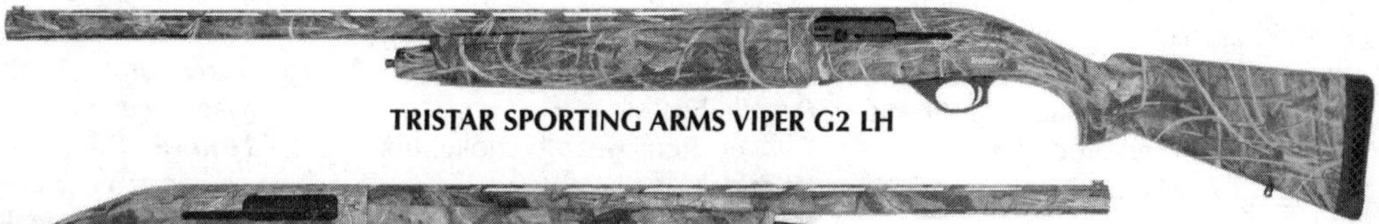

TRISTAR SPORTING ARMS VIPER G2 LH

TRISTAR SPORTING ARMS VIPER G2 YOUTH CAMO

UTAS

UTAS UTS-15 BLACK

UTS-15 BLACK

Action: Pump
Stock: Polymer
Barrel: 18.5 in.
Chokes: N/A
Weight: 6 lb. 15 oz.
Bore/ Gauge: 12
Magazine: 15 shells
Features: Corrosion-resistant, satin-nickel plating that is black-chromed
MSRP $1250

Weatherby

WEATHERBY PA-08 SYNTHETIC SLUG GUN COMBO

WEATHERBY PA-08 TR

WEATHERBY PA-08 TURKEY

WEATHERBY PA-08 UPLAND

PA-08 SYNTHETIC SLUG GUN COMBO

Action: Pump
Stock: Synthetic
Barrel: 24 in., 28 in.
Chokes: Interchangeable tubes (IC, M, F)
Weight: 7 lb. 4 oz.
Bore/Gauge: 12
Magazine: 4+1 or 5+1 shells
Features: Lightweight and durable injection-molded synthetic stock; comes with 28 in. field barrel and 24 in. rifled barrel with cantilever scope mount base; swivel studs; aircraft-grade aluminum alloy action; chrome-plated bolt in operating action
MSRP $549

PA-08 TR

Action: Pump
Stock: Synthetic
Barrel: 18.5 in.
Chokes: Cylinder
Weight: 6 lb.–6 lb. 8 oz.
Bore/Gauge: 12, 20
Magazine: None
Features: Dual-action-bar pump; black, injection-molded synthetic composite stock; black metal finish; white blade front sight
MSRP $399

PA-08 TURKEY

Action: Pump
Stock: Synthetic with Mothwing Spring Mimicry camo
Barrel: 22 in.
Chokes: Removeable choke tube (F)
Weight: 6 lb. 12 oz.
Bore/Gauge: 12
Magazine: 4+1 or 5+1 shells
Features: Dependable dual action bar system; features Mothwing Spring Mimicry camouflage pattern; special "dipping" process adheres camo directly to all stock components; swivel studs included; chrome-lined barrels
MSRP $429

PA-08 UPLAND

Action: Pump
Stock: Walnut
Barrel: 26 in., 28 in.
Chokes: Screw in tubes (IC, M, F)
Weight: 6 lb. 8 oz.–7 lb. 4 oz.
Bore/Gauge: 12, 20
Magazine: None
Features: Walnut stock with gloss finish; gloss black finish on metalwork; vented top dissipates heat and aids in target acquisition; chrome-lined barrels
MSRP $449

WEATHERBY PA-459 TR

WEATHERBY PA-08 UPLAND SLUG GUN COMBO

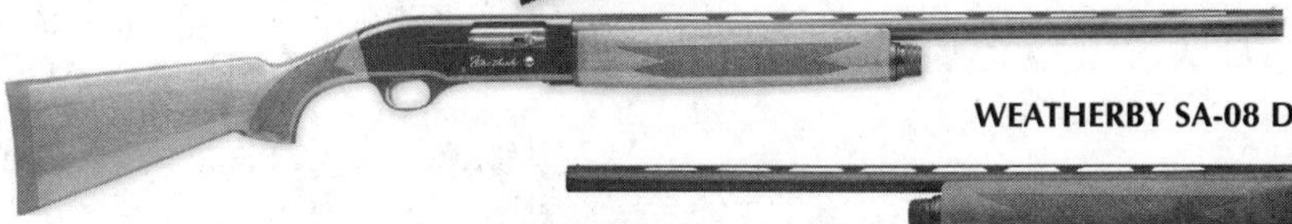

WEATHERBY SA-08 DELUXE

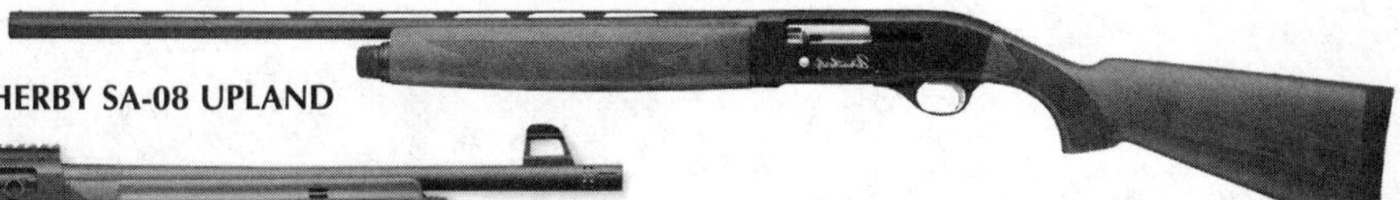

WEATHERBY SA-08 UPLAND

WEATHERBY SA-459 TR

WEATHERBY SA-459 TURKEY

PA-08 UPLAND SLUG GUN COMBO

Action: Pump
Stock: Walnut
Barrel: 24 in., 28 in.
Chokes: Interchangeable tubes (IC, M, F)
Weight: 7 lb. 4 oz.
Bore/Gauge: 12
Magazine: 4+1 or 5+1 shells
Features: Walnut stock with gloss finish; receiver with 28 in. field barrel is gloss black for a distinctive look; 24 in. rifled barrel with cantilever scope mount base in matte black; swivel studs; aircraft-grade aluminum alloy action; chrome-plated bolt in operating action
MSRP. $629

PA-459 TR

Action: Pump
Stock: Synthetic
Barrel: 18.5 in.
Chokes: Extended Ported Cylinder
Weight: 5 lb. 12 oz.
Bore/ Gauge: 20
Magazine: 5+1 or 4+1 rounds
Features: Short length of pull (13.5 in.) and ergonomic buttstock; chrome-lined barrel; adjustable rear LPA-style ghost ring sight; matte black metalwork; swivel studs; also available in 12 gauge
MSRP. $499

SA-08 DELUXE

Action: Semiautomatic
Stock: Walnut
Barrel: 26 in., 28 in.
Chokes: Screw in tubes (IC, M, F)
Weight: 6 lb.–6 lb. 12 oz.
Bore/Gauge: 12, 20
Magazine: None
Features: Walnut stock with high–gloss finish and metalwork; vented top rib dissipates heat and aids in target acquisition; dual valve system
MSRP. $829

SA-08 UPLAND

Action: Semiautomatic
Stock: Walnut
Barrel: 26 in., 28 in.
Chokes: Screw-in tubes (IC, M, F)
Weight: 6 lb.–6 lb. 12 oz.
Bore/Gauge: 12, 20
Magazine: None
Features: Walnut stock with satin finish; matte black finish on metalwork; vented top rib dissipates heat and aids in target acquisition; dual valve system
MSRP. $799

SA-459 TR

Action: Semiautomatic
Stock: Synthetic
Barrel: 18.5 in.
Chokes: Ported cylinder choke tube
Weight: 6 lb.–6 lb. 8 oz.
Bore/Gauge: 12, 20
Magazine: 5+1 shells
Features: Pistol grip stock with a rubber textured area; chrome-lined barrel; Picatinny rail for mounting scopes and optics; ghost ring style rear sight, front bead sight; black synthetic injection-molded stock is matched by black matte metal finishing
MSRP. $699

SA-459 TURKEY

Action: Gas-operated semiautomatic
Stock: Synthetic with Mothwing Spring Mimicry camo
Barrel: 21.25 in.
Chokes: Interchangeable tubes (X-F)
Weight: 6 lb. 4 oz.–6 lb. 12 oz.
Bore/Gauge: 12, 20
Magazine: 4+1 or 5+1 shells
Features: Trimmer forend for easier handling; swivel studs; Mil-Spec Picatinny rail for mounting optics; LPA-style ghost ring rear sight that is adjustable for windage and elevation; front blade sight with fiber optic insert; over-size hourglass-shaped bolt handle for quick and positive chambering; pistol grip stock
MSRP. $799

Weatherby

WEATHERBY WBY-X SA-459 BLACK REAPER TR

WBY-X SA-459 BLACK REAPER TR

Action: Semiautomatic
Stock: Synthetic
Barrel: 18.5 in.
Chokes: C
Weight: 6 lb.–6 lb. 8 oz.
Bore/Gauge: 12, 20
Magazine: 5 shells
Features: Picatinny rail; Proveil Reaper Black pattern on stock and forend; trimmer forend for easier handling; oversized hourglass bolt handle; swivel studs included
MSRP $749

Winchester Repeating Arms

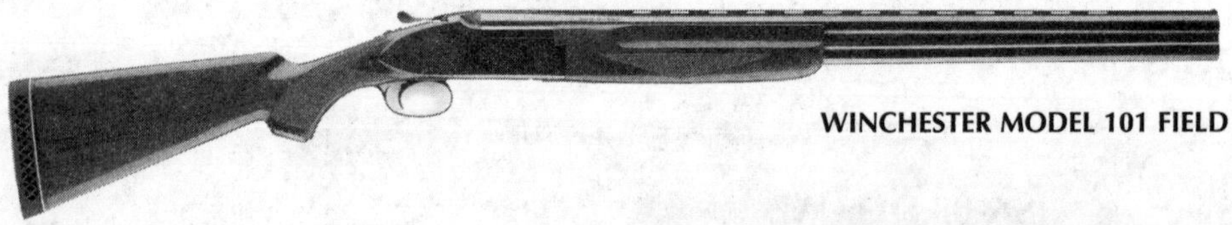

WINCHESTER MODEL 101 FIELD

WINCHESTER SUPER X PUMP BLACK SHADOW

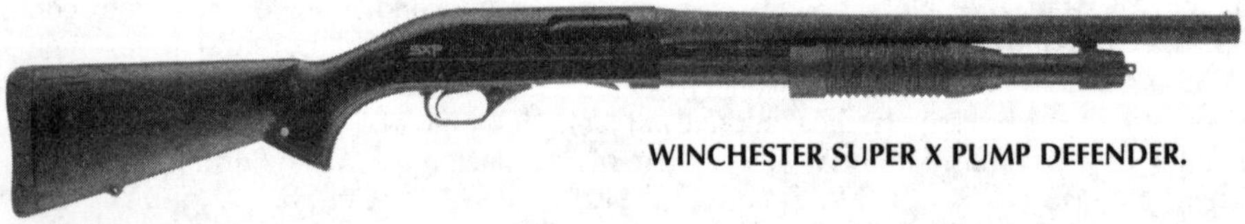

WINCHESTER SUPER X PUMP DEFENDER.

MODEL 101

Action: Over/under
Stock: Walnut
Barrel: 26 in., 28 in., 30 in., 32 in.
Chokes: Invector-Plus choke system, 3 tubes
Weight: 6 lb. 12 oz.–7 lb. 6 oz.
Bore/Gauge: 12
Magazine: 2 shells
Features: Solid brass bead front sight on Field; Truglo front sight on Sporting; deep relief receiver engraving; high-gloss grade II/III walnut stock; vented Pachmayr Decelerator pad with classic white line spacer
Field: $1900
Sporting: $2380

SUPER X PUMP BLACK SHADOW

Action: Pump
Stock: Synthetic
Barrel: 26 in., 28 in.
Chokes: Invector Plus
Weight: 6 lb. 12 oz.–7 lb.
Bore/Gauge: 12, 20
Magazine: 4 shells
Features: Hard chrome chamber and bores; drop-out trigger group for easy cleaning; synthetic stock with non-glare black matte finish on barrel and receiver
MSRP . . . . $380–$430

SUPER X PUMP DEFENDER

Action: Pump
Stock: Composite
Barrel: 18 in.
Chokes: Fixed cylinder choked barrel
Weight: 6 lb.–6 lb. 5 oz.
Bore/Gauge: 12, 20
Magazine: 5+1 shells
Features: Uses Foster-type slugs; non-glare metal surfaces with a tough black composite stock; deeply grooved forearm for control and stability
MSRP . . . . $350–$380

SHOTGUNS

Winchester Repeating Arms

WINCHESTER SUPER X PUMP TURKEY HUNTER

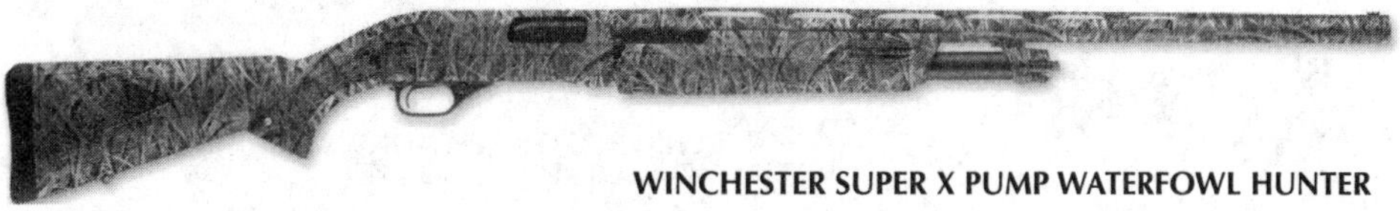

WINCHESTER SUPER X PUMP WATERFOWL HUNTER

WINCHESTER SX3 FIELD

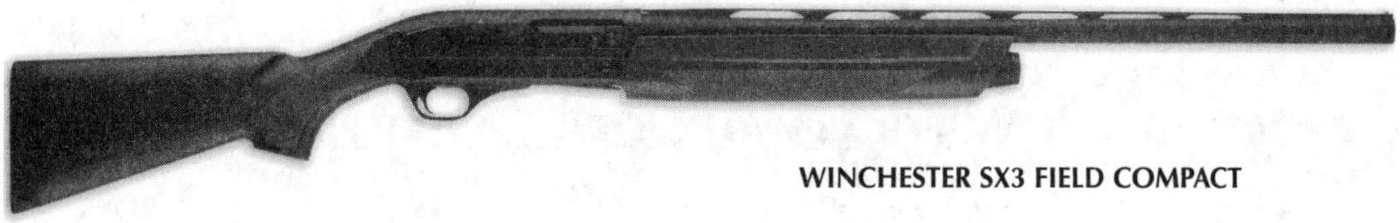

WINCHESTER SX3 FIELD COMPACT

SUPER X PUMP TURKEY HUNTER

Action: Pump
Stock: Synthetic
Barrel: 24 in.
Chokes: Invector Plus
Weight: 6 lb. 4 oz.–6 lb. 10 oz.
Bore/Gauge: 12, 20
Magazine: 4 shells
Features: Hard chrome chamber and bores; drop-out trigger group for easy cleaning; Invector Plus Extra-Full Turkey Choke Tube; crossbolt safety; Inflex technology recoil pad; synthetic stock with textured gripping surfaces in Mossy Oak Break-Up Infinity
MSRP . . . . $520–$550

SUPER X PUMP WATERFOWL HUNTER

Action: Pump
Stock: Synthetic
Barrel: 26 in., 28 in.
Chokes: Invector Plus
Weight: 6 lb. 8 oz.–7 lb.
Bore/Gauge: 12, 20
Magazine: 4 shells
Features: Hard chrome chamber and bores; drop-out trigger group for easy cleaning; synthetic stock with textured gripping surfaces in Mossy Oak Shadow Grass Blades
MSRP . . . . $460–$500

SUPER X3 FIELD

Action: Semiautomatic
Stock: Walnut
Barrel: 26 in., 28 in.
Chokes: Invector Plus
Weight: 6 lb. 6 oz.–6 lb. 14 oz.
Bore/Gauge: 12, 20
Magazine: 4 shells
Features: Satin oil finish walnut stock with classic cut checkering; matte black receivers in lightweight aluminum alloy; Invector Plus choke system
MSRP . . . .$1070–$1140

SUPER X3 FIELD COMPACT

Action: Semiautomatic
Stock: Walnut
Barrel: 24 in., 26 in., 28 in.
Chokes: Invector Plus
Weight: 6 lb. 4 oz.–6 lb. 14 oz.
Bore/Gauge: 12, 20
Magazine: 4 shells
Features: Stock dimensions trimmed for smaller-frame shooters and hunters with a 13-inch length of pull; satin oil finish walnut stock with classic cut checkering; matte black receivers in lightweight aluminum alloy
MSRP $1070

Winchester Repeating Arms

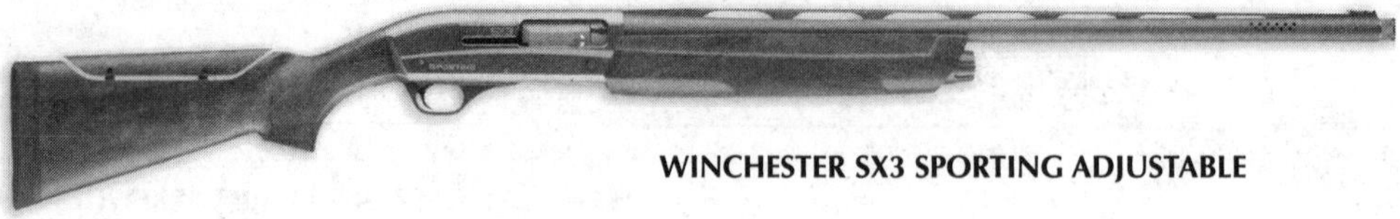

WINCHESTER SX3 SPORTING ADJUSTABLE

WINCHESTER REPEATING ARMS SUPER X3 WATERFOWL HUNTER

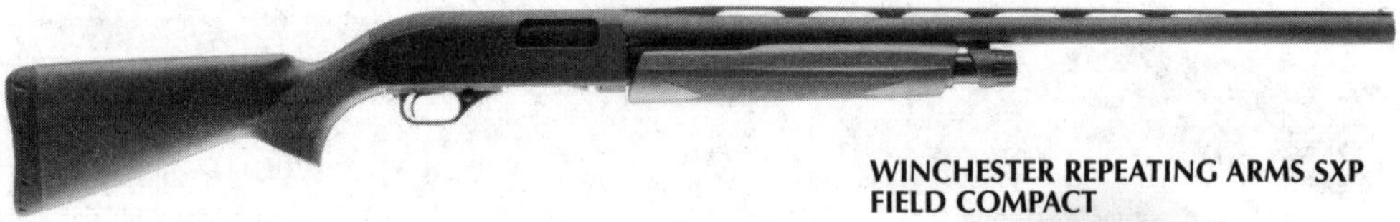

WINCHESTER REPEATING ARMS SXP FIELD COMPACT

SUPER X3 SPORTING ADJUSTABLE

Action: Semiautomatic
Stock: Walnut
Barrel: 28 in., 30 in., 32 in.
Chokes: Five extended signature choke tubes
Weight: 7 lb. 6 oz.–7 lb. 10 oz.
Bore/Gauge: 12
Magazine: holds up to 4 shells depending on shell size
Features: Aluminum-alloy receiver, and barrel; ventilated rib; buttstock features an adjustable comb; chrome-plated chamber and bore; Pachmayr decelerator recoil pad; molded red case included
MSRP. $1700

SUPER X3 WATERFOWL HUNTER

Action: Semiautomatic
Stock: Synthetic
Barrel: 26 in., 28 in.
Chokes: Invector-Plus tube
Weight: 6 lb. 10 oz.–7 lb. 2 oz.
Bore/Gauge: 12, 20
Magazine: None
Features: Mossy Oak Shadow Grass Blades; .742 Back-Bored technology; hard chrome chamber and bore; vent rib; TruGlo Long Bead fiber optic front sight; Active Valve Gas System; Quadra-Vent Ports; ambidextrous crossbolt safety
MSRP. . . . .$1140–$1199

SXP FIELD COMPACT

Action: Pump
Stock: Satin finish
Barrel: 24 in., 26 in., 28 in.
Chokes: Three Invector-Plus chokes
Weight: 6 lb. 4 oz.–6 lb. 10 oz.
Bore/ Gauge: 12, 20
Magazine: None
Features: Aluminum alloy receiver; matte black finish; hard chrome chamber and bore; Speed plug system; brass bead front sight; Inflex technology recoil pad
MSRP. . . . . $400–$430

HANDGUNS

298 Accu-Tek
298 American Derringer
300 American Tactical Imports
302 Arsenal Firearms
303 Arsenal Inc.
303 Auto-Ordnance
303 Beretta USA
305 Bersa
306 Boberg Arms
307 Bond Arms
308 Browning
310 Cabot Gun company
310 Century International Arms
310 Charter Arms
313 Chiappa Firearms
313 Christensen
314 Cimarron Firearms Co.
317 Citadel by Legacy Sports
317 Cobra
318 Colt's Manufacturing Company
320 Coonan Arms
320 CZ-USA (Ceska Zbrojovka)
323 Dan Wesson Firearms
324 Doubletap Defense llc
324 Eagle Imports
326 Ed Brown
327 E.M.F. Company
329 Entréprise Arms
329 European American Armory
330 FNH USA
331 Freedom Arms
331 Glock
334 Hämmerli
334 Heckler & Koch
336 Heritage Manufacturing
336 High Standard
337 Hi-Point Firearms
338 Kahr Arms
341 Kel-Tec
342 Kimber
345 Kriss USA
346 Magnum Research
347 MG Arms
347 MOA
347 Mossberg
348 Nighthawk Custom
349 North American Arms
351 Olympic Arms
351 Para USA
353 Remington Arms
355 Rock River Arms
355 Rossi
357 Ruger
361 Sig Sauer
365 Smith & Wesson
372 Sphinx (by Kriss)
372 Springfield Armory
375 Steyr Arms
375 STI International
378 Stoeger
379 Taurus
383 Taylor's & Co.
384 Thompson/Center
385 Traditions Firearms
385 Tristar Arms
386 Uberti
389 Walther
390 ZiP Factory

Accu-Tek

ACCU-TEK
AT-380 II

ACCU-TEK HC-380

AT-380 II

Action: Semiautomatic
Grips: Composite
Barrel: 2.8 in.
Sights: Target
Weight: 23.5 oz.
Caliber: .380 ACP
Capacity: 6+1 rounds
Features: Stainless steel construction; adjustable rear sight; one hand manual safety blocks; stainless steel magazine
MSRP. $289

HC-380

Action: Semiautomatic
Grips: Composite
Barrel: 2.8 in.
Sights: Target
Weight: 26 oz.
Caliber: .380 ACP
Capacity: 13 rounds
Features: Adjustable rear sight; black checkered grip; one-hand manual safety block; includes two magazines and cable lock
MSRP. $330

LT-380

Action: SA semiautomatic
Grips: Composite
Barrel: 2.8 in.
Sights: Adjustable rear sight
Weight: 15 oz.
Caliber: .380 ACP
Capacity: 6 rounds
Features: Aluminum frame; stainless steel slide; exposed hammer; manual safety; European type magazine release
MSRP. $324

ACCU-TEK
FIREARMS
LT-380

American Derringer

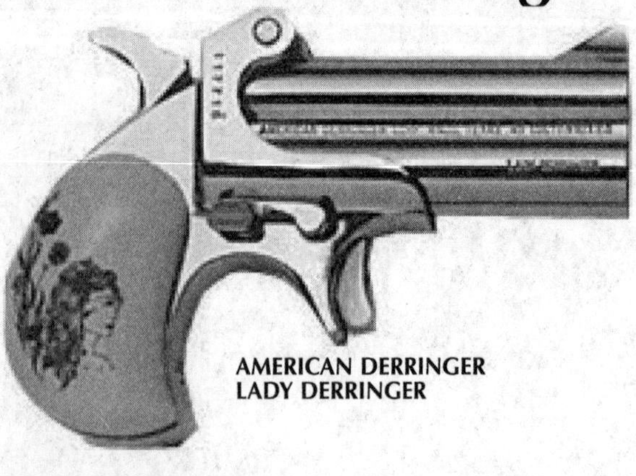

AMERICAN DERRINGER
LADY DERRINGER

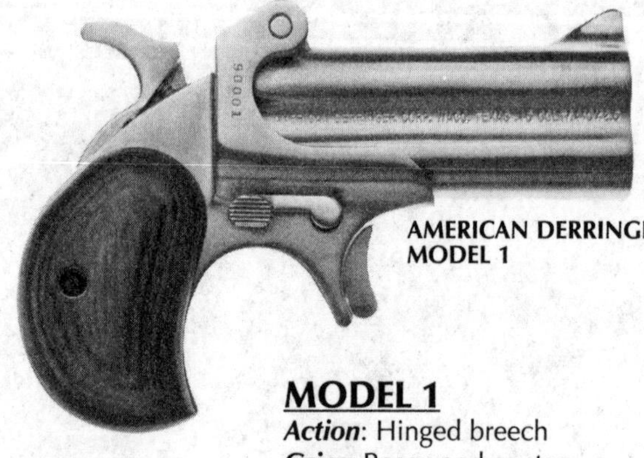

AMERICAN DERRINGER
MODEL 1

LADY DERRINGER

Action: Hinged breech
Grips: Camo, Pink, Scrimshaw
Barrel: 3 in.
Sights: Open, fixed
Weight: 15.5 oz.
Caliber: .38 Spl., .32 Mag.
Capacity: 2 rounds
Features: Lady Derringer Survivor Series in memory of breast cancer survivors; highly-polished brass or stainless steel frame; each pistol is handmade, custom serial numbers are available
Camo/Pink: $800

MODEL 1

Action: Hinged breech
Grips: Rosewood or stag
Barrel: 3 in.
Sights: Fixed, open
Weight: 15 oz.
Caliber: .45 Colt, .410
Capacity: 2 rounds
Features: Single-action; automatic barrel selection; manually operated hammer-block safety
MSRP. $670

American Derringer

AMERICAN DERRINGER
LM4 SIMMERLING

AMERICAN DERRINGER LM5

AMERICAN DERRINGER MODEL 4

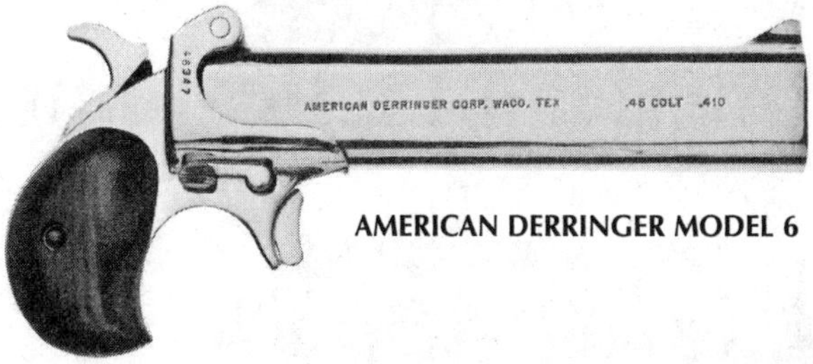

AMERICAN DERRINGER MODEL 6

AMERICAN DERRINGER MODEL 7

LM4 SIMMERLING

Action: Hinged breech
Grips: Mesquite, Rosewood, custom
Barrel: 2 in.
Sights: Open, fixed
Weight: 24 oz.
Caliber: .45 ACP
Capacity: 5 rounds
Features: Vest pocket pistol; first round carried in the chamber; only 1in. thick; stainless steel
MSRP. 3800

LM5

Action: Hinged breech
Grips: Rosewood
Barrel: 2 in.
Sights: Open, fixed
Weight: 15 oz.
Caliber: .25 ACP, .32 Mag.
Capacity: 4 (.32) or 5 (.25) rounds
Features: Stainless steel; cam lock safety
MSRP. $675

MODEL 4

Action: Hinged breech
Grips: Rosewood
Barrel: 4.1 in
Sights: Fixed open
Weight: 16.5 oz.
Caliber: .375 Mag., 357 Max., .45-70 Govt.,
.45 Colt/.410, .44 Mag.
Capacity: 2 rounds
Features: Satin or high polish stainless steel finish; single-action; automatic barrel selection; manually operated hammer-block type safety
MSRP. $725

MODEL 6

Action: Hinged breech
Grips: Rosewood, walnut, black
Barrel: 6 in.
Sights: Fixed open
Weight: 21 oz.
Caliber: .357 Mag., .45 ACP, .45 Colt/.410
Capacity: 2 rounds
Features: Satin or high polish stainless steel finish; single-action; automatic barrel selection; manually operated hammer-block type safety
MSRP. $825

MODEL 7 LIGHTWEIGHT & ULTRA LIGHTWEIGHT

Action: Hinged breech
Grips: Blackwood
Barrel: 3 in.
Sights: Fixed open
Weight: 7.5 oz.
Caliber: .44 Special, .380 ACP, .38 Special, .32 Mag./.32 S&W Long, .22LR, .22 Mag.
Capacity: 2 rounds
Features: Grey matte finish; single-action; automatic barrel selection; manually operated hammer-block type safety
MSRP. . . . . $670–$775

American Derringer

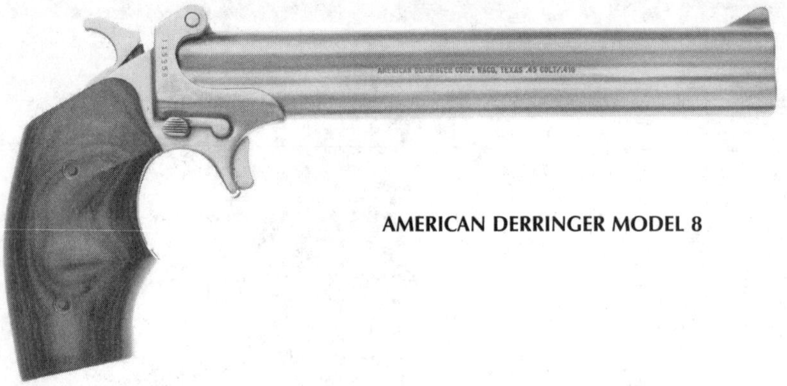

AMERICAN DERRINGER MODEL 8

MODEL 8

Action: Hinged breech
Grips: Rosewood, walnut, black
Barrel: 6 in.
Sights: Optional Adco red dot scope
Weight: 24 oz.
Caliber: .357 Mag., .45 ACP, .45 Colt/.410
Capacity: 2 rounds
Features: Satin or high polish stainless steel finish; single-action; automatic barrel selection; manually operated hammer-block type safety
MSRP. $875

American Tactical Imports

AMERICAN TACTICAL IMPORTS FX 45 1911 GI

AMERICAN TACTICAL IMPORTS FX 45 1911 MILITARY

AMERICAN TACTICAL IMPORTS FX 1911 THUNDERBOLT

FX 1911 GI

Action: Semiautomatic
Grips: Mahogany
Barrel: 4.25 in.
Sights: Fixed
Weight: 33.5 oz.
Caliber: .45 ACP
Capacity: 7+1 rounds
Features: Steel parts; black matte military-style fixed front and rear sights; military-style slide stop and thumb safety, solid mahogany grip panels
MSRP. $460

FX 1911 MILITARY

Action: Semiautomatic
Grips: Mahogany
Barrel: 5 in.
Sights: Fixed
Weight: 37 oz.
Caliber: .45 ACP
Capacity: 7+1 rounds
Features: Steel parts; black matte military-style fixed front and rear sights; military-style slide stop and thumb safety, solid mahogany grip panels
MSRP. $460

FX 1911 THUNDERBOLT

Action: Semi-automatic
Grips: Mahogany
Barrel: 5 in.
Sights: Fixed
Weight: 37 oz.
Caliber: .45 ACP
Capacity: 8+1 rounds
Features: Picatinny rail; steel parts; Solid mahogany grips
MSRP. $858

American Tactical Imports

AMERICAN TACTICAL IMPORTS FX 1911 TITAN

AMERICAN TACTICAL IMPORTS FX THUNDERBOLT STAINLESS

AMERICAN TACTICAL IMPORTS GSG 1911 PISTOL

AMERICAN TACTICAL IMPORTS GSG 922

GSG 922

Action: Semiautomatic
Grips: Plastic
Barrel: 3.2 in.
Sights: Click-adjustable target
Weight: 31 oz.
Caliber: .22 LR
Capacity: 10 rounds
Features: Frame is constructed of Zamak-5 zinc alloy; loaded chamber indicator, grip safety, magazine safety, firing-pin-block, external hammer; optional AD OP's faux suppressor
MSRP $380

FX 1911 TITAN

Action: Semiautomatic
Grips: Mahogany
Barrel: 3.13 in.
Sights: Fixed
Weight: 30 oz.
Caliber: .45 ACP
Capacity: 7+1 rounds
Features: Carbon-steel construction or stainless-steel construction; two-stage recoil spring system; low-profile rear sights with a dovetailed front sight; military-style slide stop and thumb safety; bull barrel
MSRP: $610

FX THUNDERBOLT ENHANCED

Action: Semiautomatic
Grips: Mahogany
Barrel: 5 in.
Sights: Adjustable 3-dot combat sights
Weight: 37 oz.
Caliber: .45 ACP
Capacity: 8 +1 rounds
Features: Picatinny rail; ambidextrous safety; grip checkering; enhanced model has barrel porting for less recoil
MSRP $900

GSG 1911 PISTOL

Action: Semiautomatic
Grips: Classic wood (standard), or black polymer grips
Barrel: 5 in.
Sights: Fixed
Weight: 34.4 oz.
Caliber: .22LR
Capacity: 10 rounds
Features: Picatinny rail; faux suppressor optional
MSRP $300
Suppressor: $310

Arsenal Firearms

ARSENAL FIREARMS AF-1 STRIKE ONE

ARSENAL FIREARMS AF2011–A1 "BLACK MAGIC"

ARSENAL FIREARMS AF2011-A1 DOUBLE BARREL PISTOL

AF-1 STRIKE ONE

Action: Semiautomatic
Grips: 3D polymer
Barrel: 5 in.
Sights: Fixed or adjustable
Weight: 26.4 oz. (poly), 31.4 oz. (ergal)
Caliber: 9mm Para, 9mm IMI, .357 SIG, .40 S&W
Capacity: 17 rounds
Features: Geometric lock, semiautomatic hammerless pistol; short recoil, in-line barrel, patented locking block system; automatic safety; single-action only trigger; ambidextrous magazine release button; reinforced polymer or ergal light alloy frame in ordnance black, desert tan, and olive drab with 360 degree integral mini-skirt; underbarrel integral Picatinny rail; interchangeable back plate/sight, fixed or adjustable, or Micro-Dot ready; available with a Long Range Conversion
MSRP. . . . . Price on request

ARSENAL FIREARMS STRIKE ONE ERGAL

STRIKE ONE ERGAL

Action: Semiautomatic
Grips: Synthetic
Barrel: 5 in.
Sights: Fixed or adjustable
Weight: 31.4 oz.
Caliber: 9mm, 9x21 IMI, .357 SIG, .40 S&W
Capacity: 17 rounds
Features: Integral aluminum frame; hammerless pistol; available in anodized Electro Colors or high tech Hard Anodized finishes
MSRP. $3950

AF2011-A1 "BLACK MAGIC"

Action: Semiautomatic double barrel
Grips: Synthetic
Barrel: 5 in.
Sights: Fixed or adjustable
Weight: 65.3 oz.
Caliber: .38 Super Auto, .45 ACP
Capacity: 18 rounds
Features: First industrial double barrel semiautomatic pistol; single slide, single frame, single spur double hammer; single grip safety; single body double mainspring housing and single double cavity magazine floorplate (two single magazines); long and double magazine latch; most internal parts are interchangeable with standard 1911 replacement parts; can be ordered with two independent triggers and one sear group or with two triggers permanently joined and one or two sear groups; "all black" dress: the only non black features are the silver and black grip's AF crests and the white line rear sight
MSRP. $5799

AF2011-A1 DOUBLE BARREL PISTOL

Action: Semiautomatic double barrel
Grips: Steel, rubber, or walnut
Barrel: 4.9 in.
Sights: Fixed or adjustable
Weight: 65.3 oz.
Caliber: .45 ACP
Capacity: 18 rounds
Features: First industrial double barrel semiautomatic pistol; single slide, single frame, single spur double hammer; single grip safety; single body double mainspring housing and single double cavity magazine floorplate (two single magazines); long and double magazine latch; most internal parts are interchangeable with standard 1911 replacement parts; can be ordered with two independent triggers and one sear group or with two triggers permanently joined and one or two sear groups; deep blued mirror finish or 3400 Vickers surface hardness white ash nitrite coating
MSRP. . . . . $4400–$4950

Arsenal Inc.

ARSENAL INC. SAM7K

SAM7K

Action: Semiautomatic
Grips: Black polymer
Barrel: 10.5 in.
Sights: Peep rear
Weight: 128 oz.
Caliber: 7.62x39 Warsaw
Capacity: 5 rounds
Features: Milled receiver; short gas system; front sight block; gas block system; chrome-lined hammer-forged barrel; ambidextrous safety lever; scope rail; sling included
MSRP. $1199

Auto-Ordnance

AUTO-ORDNANCE 1911PKZSE

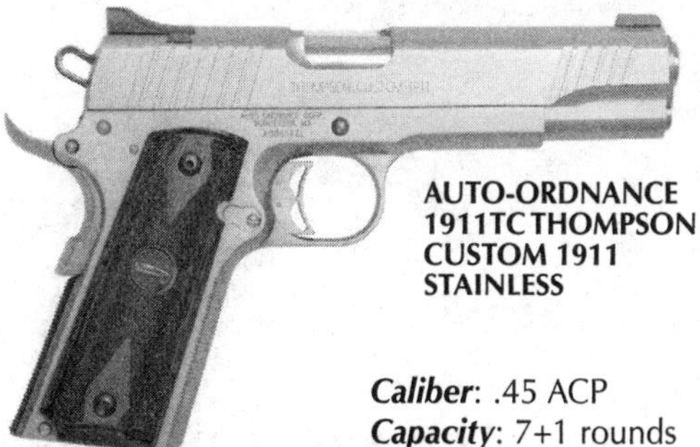

AUTO-ORDNANCE 1911TC THOMPSON CUSTOM 1911 STAINLESS

1911PKZSE

Action: Semiautomatic
Grips: Brown checkered plastic, checkered wood grips
Barrel: 5 in.
Sights: Blade front, rear drift adjustable sight
Weight: 39 oz.
Caliber: .45 ACP
Capacity: 7+1 rounds
Features: Single-action 1911 Colt design; WWII parkerized; stainless steel or blued metal finish
MSRP. $688

1911TC THOMPSON CUSTOM 1911 STAINLESS

Action: Semiautomatic
Grips: Checkered laminate
Barrel: 5 in.
Sights: Low-profile iron sights
Weight: 39 oz.
Caliber: .45 ACP
Capacity: 7+1 rounds
Features: Frames machined on high precision computerized machinery from a 420 stainless steel casting; slide is machined from a solid stainless steel billet utilizing specialized tooling to reduce set-up and refixturing; matte finish on slide and frame; front and rear sights are black with serrations; extended beavertail grip safety; extended magazine release
MSRP. $886

Beretta USA

BERETTA 21 BOBCAT

BERETTA 92A1

21 BOBCAT

Action: Semiautomatic
Grips: Plastic
Barrel: 2.4 in.
Sights: Fixed, open
Weight: 11.5 oz.
Caliber: .22LR, .25 ACP
Capacity: 7 or 8 rounds
Features: Double-action; tip-up barrel; stainless steel slide and barrel; alloy gray frame; other metal parts come in black or Inox finish
MSRP: $410

92A1

Action: Semiautomatic
Grips: Plastic
Barrel: 4.9 in.
Sights: 3-Dot System
Weight: 34.4 oz.
Caliber: 9mm, .40 S&W
Capacity: 12 or 17 rounds, restricted capacity 10 rounds
Features: Removable front sight; Picatinny rail, internal recoil buffer; captive recoil spring assembly
MSRP. $775

Beretta USA

BERETTA 92FS TYPE M9A1

BERETTA BU-9 NANO

BERETTA PICO .380

BERETTA 3032 TOMCAT

BERETTA M9 COMMERCIAL

92FS TYPE M9A1

Action: Semiautomatic
Grips: Plastic
Barrel: 4.9 in.
Sights: 3-Dot System
Weight: 33.9 oz.
Caliber: 9mm
Capacity: 15+1 rounds, restricted capacity 10+1 rounds
Features: Picatinny rail; magazine well bevel; sand-resistant magazine
MSRP $750

3032 TOMCAT

Action: Semiautomatic
Grips: Plastic
Barrel: 2.5 in.
Sights: Fixed, open
Weight: 14.5 oz.
Caliber: .32 ACP, .380 ACP
Capacity: 7+1 round
Features: Double-action; tip-up barrel latch; Inox has stainless steel slide and barrel; titanium alloy frame in black or gray; double- or single-trigger
Standard: $390
Inox: $485

BU-9 NANO

Action: Semiautomatic
Grips: Technopolymer
Barrel: 3.07 in.
Sights: 3-dot low profile
Weight: 17.67 oz.
Caliber: 9mm
Capacity: 6+1 rounds
Features: Interchangeable sights; ambidextrous magazine release button; serialized sub-chassis; patent-pending striker deactivator; technopolymer grip frame
MSRP . . . .
$450–$460

M9 COMMERCIAL

Action: Semiautomatic
Grips: Plastic
Barrel: 4.9 in.
Sights: Dot-and-Post system
Weight: 33.3 oz.
Caliber: 9mm
Capacity: 15 rounds, restricted capacity 10+1 rounds
Features: Has distinctive military style markings; chrome-lined bore; double-action; automatic firing pin block; ambidextrous manual safety; lightweight forged aluminum alloy frame w/ combat-style trigger guard
MSRP $675

PICO .380

Action: Semiautomatic
Grips: Technopolymer
Barrel: 2.7 in.
Sights: Front and rear adjustable
Weight: 11.5 oz.
Caliber: .380 ACP
Capacity: 6+1 rounds
Features: Stainless steel sub-chassis engraved with serial number; snag-free slide and frame; barrel can be replaced with a .32 ACP barrel; dovetail quick-change sights; frames available in flat dark earth, white, or purple
MSRP $400

Beretta USA

BERETTA PX4 STORM COMPACT

BERETTA PX4 STORM FULL SIZE

PX4 STORM COMPACT

Action: Semiautomatic
Grips: Plastic
Barrel: 3.2 in.
Sights: 3-Dot System
Weight: 27.3 oz.
Caliber: 9mm, .40 S&W
Capacity: 12 or 15 rounds; full size magazines 9mm: 17 or 20 rounds, .40 S&W: 14 or 17 rounds; restricted capacity 10 rounds
Features: Ambidextrous side stop lever; integral Picatinny rail; bruiton non-reflective black coating; visible automatic firing pin block
MSRP. $650

PX4 STORM FULL SIZE

Action: Semiautomatic
Grips: Plastic
Barrel: 4 in.
Sights: 3-Dot System
Weight: 27.7 oz.
Caliber: 9mm, .40 S&W, .45 ACP
Capacity: 14 or 17 rounds, restricted capacity 10 rounds
Features: Picatinny rail; innovative locked-breech with a rotating barrel system; visible automatic firing pin block; ambidextrous safety; reversible magazine release; available in Inox finish
MSRP. $650

BERETTA U22 NEOS

U22 NEOS

Action: Semiautomatic
Grips: Plastic
Barrel: 4.5 in., 6 in.
Sights: Target
Weight: 31.7–36.2 oz.
Caliber: .22LR
Capacity: 10+1 rounds
Features: Single-action; removable colored grip inserts; deluxe model features adjustable trigger, replaceable sights; optional 7.5 in. barrel
Standard:. $325
Inox: $350

Bersa

BERSA BP CC 9

BERSA THUNDER 40 ULTRA COMPACT PRO

BP CC 9

Action: Short reset DAO
Grips: Integral to frame
Barrel: 3.3 in.
Sights: Interchangeable front and rear
Weight: 21.5 oz.
Caliber: 9mm, .40 S&W
Capacity: 6+1 or 8+1 rounds
Features: Bersa polymer concealed carry; high impact polymer frame; Picatinny rail, polygonal rifling, and loaded chamber indicator; ambidextrous magazine release; striker fired; micro-polished bore with sharp, deep rifling; 3-dot sight system; integral locking system; automatic firing pin safety; matte black or duotone finish
MSRP. . . . . $430–$440

THUNDER 9 ULTRA COMPACT PRO

Action: Semiautomatic
Grips: Black polymer
Barrel: 3.25 in.
Sights: 3-Dot system
Weight: 23 oz.
Caliber: 9mm
Capacity: 10+1 or 13+1 rounds
Features: Picatinny rail; precision machined lightweight alloy; ambidextrous safety; lifetime service contract; integral locking system; anatomically designed polymer grips; double-action; available in matte or duotone finish
Matte: $492
Duotone:. $501

Bersa

THUNDER 40 ULTRA COMPACT PRO

Action: Semiautomatic
Grips: Black polymer
Barrel: 3.25 in.
Sights: 3-Dot system
Weight: 23 oz.
Caliber: .40 S&W
Capacity: 10+1 rounds
Features: Picatinny rail; precision machined lightweight alloy; ambidextrous safety; lifetime service contract; integral locking system; anatomically designed polymer grips; double-action; available in matte or duotone finish
Matte: $492
Duotone: $501

THUNDER 45 ULTRA COMPACT PRO

Action: Semiautomatic
Grips: Black polymer
Barrel: 3.6 in.
Sights: 3-Dot system
Weight: 27 oz.
Caliber: .45 ACP
Capacity: 7+1 rounds
Features: Double-action; Picatinny rail; precision machined lightweight alloy; ambidextrous safety; lifetime service contract; integral locking system; anatomically designed polymer grips; available in matte or duotone finish
Matte: $492
Duotone: $501

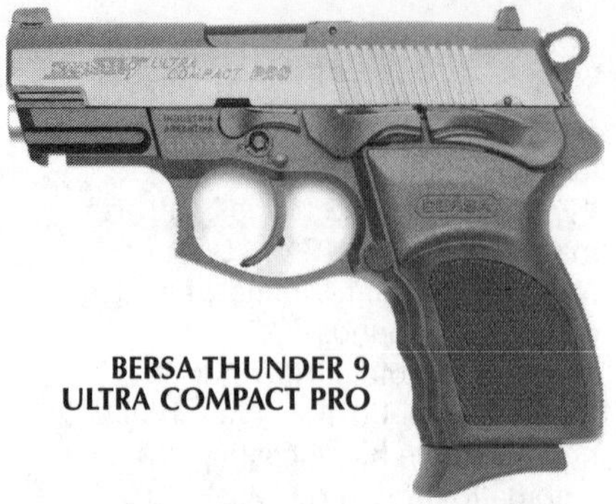

BERSA THUNDER 9 ULTRA COMPACT PRO

BERSA THUNDER 45 ULTRA COMPACT PRO

BERSA THUNDER 380

BERSA THUNDER 380 CONCEALED CARRY

THUNDER 380

Action: Semiautomatic
Grips: Black polymer
Barrel: 3.5 in.
Sights: 3-Dot system
Weight: 20 oz.
Caliber: .380 ACP
Capacity: 7+1 rounds
Features: Combat style trigger guard; extended slide release; micro-polished bore with sharp, deep rifling; integral locking system; available in matte, satin, nickel, or duotone finish
Matte: $320
Duotone: $320
Nickel: $341

THUNDER 380 CONCEALED CARRY

Action: Semiautomatic
Grips: Black polymer
Barrel: 3.2 in.
Sights: Blade front and notched-bar dovetailed rear
Weight: 16.4 oz.
Caliber: .380 ACP
Capacity: 8+1 rounds
Features: Extra low profile sights; combat style trigger guard; slim slide release; integral locking system
Matte: $335
Duotone: $345

Boberg Arms

XR-45S

Action: DAO semiautomatic
Grips: Synthetic
Barrel: 3.75 in.–4.6 in.
Sights: Fixed
Weight: 22 oz.
Caliber: .45 ACP, .45 ACP +P, .45 Super
Capacity: 6+1 rounds
Features: Utilizes Boberg Arms' patented reverse feed technology for reduced recoil; passive firing pin safety; dovetail sight; available in standard duotone, platinum, or onyx finishes
MSRP . . . . $1199–$1499

BOBERG ARMS R-45S

Bond Arms

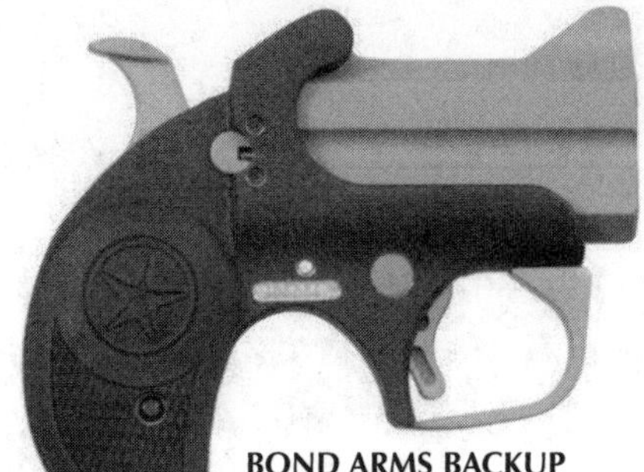
BOND ARMS BACKUP

BOND ARMS MINI

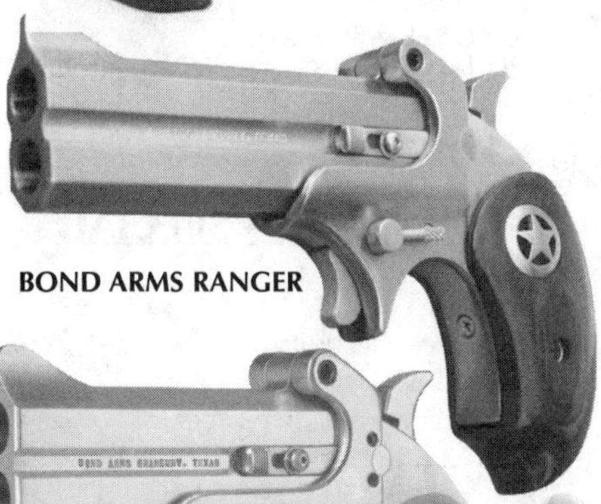
BOND ARMS RANGER

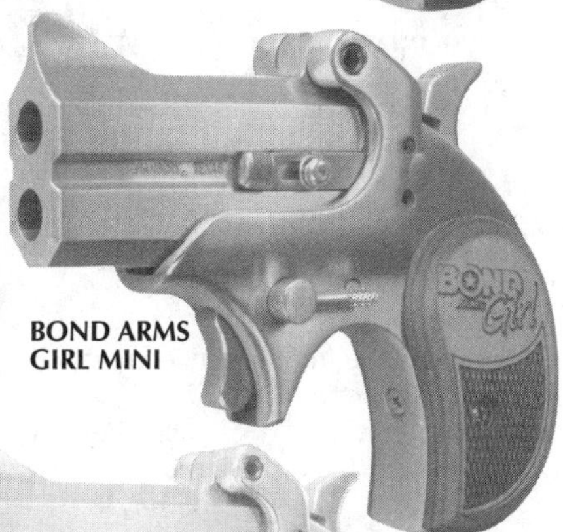
BOND ARMS GIRL MINI

BOND ARMS CENTURY 2000

BOND ARMS SNAKE SLAYER

BACKUP

Action: SA semiautomatic
Grips: Rubber
Barrel: 2.5 in.
Sights: Fixed
Weight: 18 oz.
Caliber: .357 Mag., .38 Spl., .40 S&W, .45 ACP, .45 Colt
Capacity: 2 rounds
Features: Interchangable barrels; rebounding hammer; retracting firing pins; crossbolt safety
MSRP $435

MINI

Action: SA
Grips: Rosewood or pink
Barrel: 2.5 in.
Sights: Blade front, fixed rear
Weight: 18 oz.–19 oz.
Caliber: .357 Mag./.38 Spl., .45 ACP, .45 Colt, .45 Glock Auto, .44 Spl., .44-40 Win., .40 S&W, 10mm, 9mm, .32 H&R Mag., .22LR, .22 Mag. (3 in. barrel .410/.45 LC with 2.5 in. chambers-rifled)
Capacity: 2 rounds
Features: The Bond Mini was developed as a special edition gun that is even easier to conceal and carry, but still packs the same power Bond Arms guns are known for; comes in two models the Mini .45 and the Girl Mini (.357/.38); Girl Mini has slightly smaller barrel included and pink grips
MSRP $418

RANGER

Action: SA
Grips: Black ash star
Barrel: 4.25 in.
Sights: Blade front and fixed rear
Weight: 23.5 oz.
Caliber: .357 Mag./.38 Spl., .45 ACP, .45 Colt, .45 Glock Auto, .44 Spl., .44-40 Win., .40 S&W, 10mm, 9mm, .32 H&R Mag., .22LR, .22 Mag.; .410/.45 LC with 3 in. chambers-rifled
Capacity: 2 rounds
Features: Interchangeable barrels; automatic extractor; retracting firing pins; crossbolt safety; spring-loaded cammed locking lever; stainless steel with satin polish finish
MSRP $673

CENTURY 2000

Action: SA
Grips: Custom laminated black ash or rosewood
Barrel: 3.5 in.
Sights: Blade front and fixed rear
Weight: 21 oz.
Caliber: .357 Mag./.38 Spl., .45 ACP, .45 Colt, .45 Glock Auto, .44 Spl., .44-40 Win., .40 S&W, 10mm, 9mm, .32 H&R Mag., .22LR, .22 Mag.; .410/.45 LC
Capacity: 2 rounds
Features: Interchangeable barrels; automatic extractor; rebounding hammer; retracting firing pins; crossbolt safety; spring-loaded cammed locking lever; trigger guard; stainless steel with satin polish finish
MSRP $435

SNAKE SLAYER

Action: SA
Grips: Extended custom rosewood
Barrel: 4.25 in.
Sights: Blade front and fixed rear
Weight: 22 oz.
Caliber: .357 Mag./.38 Spl., .45 ACP, .45 Colt, .45 Glock Auto, .44 Spl.,
.44-40 Win., .40 S&W, 10mm, 9mm, .32 H&R Mag., .22LR, .22 Mag.; .410/.45 LC with 3 in. chambers-rifled
Capacity: 2 rounds
Features: Interchangeable barrels; automatic extractor; rebounding hammer; retracting firing pins; crossbolt safety; spring-loaded cammed locking lever; trigger guard; stainless steel with satin polish finish
MSRP $519

Bond Arms

BOND ARMS SNAKE SLAYER IV

BOND ARMS TEXAS DEFENDER

BOND TEXAS RANGER - SPECIAL EDITION

SNAKE SLAYER IV

Action: SA
Grips: Extended custom rosewood
Barrel: 4.25 in.
Sights: Blade front and fixed rear
Weight: 23.5 oz.
Caliber: .357 Mag./.38 Spl., .45 ACP, .45 Colt, .45 Glock Auto, .44 Spl., .44–40 Win., .40 S&W, 10mm, 9mm, .32 H&R Mag., .22LR, .22 Mag.; .410/.45 LC with 3 in. chambers-rifled
Capacity: 2 rounds
Features: Automatic extractor; interchangeable barrels; rebounding hammer; retracting firing pins; crossbolt safety; spring-loaded cammed locking lever; trigger guard; stainless steel with satin polish finish
MSRP. $551

TEXAS DEFENDER

Action: SA
Grips: Custom laminated black ash or rosewood
Barrel: 3 in.
Sights: Blade front and fixed rear
Weight: 20 oz.
Caliber: 45 Colt/.410 Shot Shell (rifled), .357 Mag/.38 Spl, .357 Max, .45 ACP, .45 Colt, .45 Glock Auto, .44-40 Win., .40 S&W, 10mm, .32 H&R Mag., .22LR
Capacity: 2 rounds
Features: Interchangeable barrels; automatic extractor; rebounding hammer; retracting firing pins; crossbolt safety; spring-loaded cammed locking lever; trigger guard; stainless steel with satin polish finish
MSRP. $440

TEXAS RANGER - SPECIAL EDITION

Action: SA
Grips: Texas mesquite
Barrel: 4.25 in.
Sights: Blade front, fixed rear
Weight: 23.5 oz.
Caliber: .410/.45 LC, .357 Mag., .45 ACP, .45 Colt., .45 Glock Auto, .44 Spl., .44-40 Win., .40 S&W, 10mm, 9mm, .32 H&R Mag., .22LR, .22 Mag.
Capacity: 2 rounds
Features: Bond Arms has been chosen to represent the prestigious Texas Rangers in their historic 200th Anniversary; gun and knife grips are made from real Texas mesquite wood, the Texas Ranger Stars are handmade by Texas inmates in the Texas Department of Corrections, and it is gold engraved on the barrel; custom glass top display case included
MSRP. $1375

Browning

BROWNING 1911-22 A1

1911-22 A1

Action: Semiautomatic
Grips: Brown composite
Barrel: 4.25 in.
Sights: Fixed
Weight: 16 oz.
Caliber: 22LR
Capacity: 10+1 rounds
Features: Alloy frame in matte blued finish; stainless steel barrel block with matte blued finish; blowback action; single-action trigger; detachable magazine; manual thumb safety; grip safety
MSRP. $600

BROWNING 1911–22 A1 COMPACT DESERT TAN

BROWNING BUCK MARK CAMPER UFX

BROWNING BUCK MARK PLUS UDX

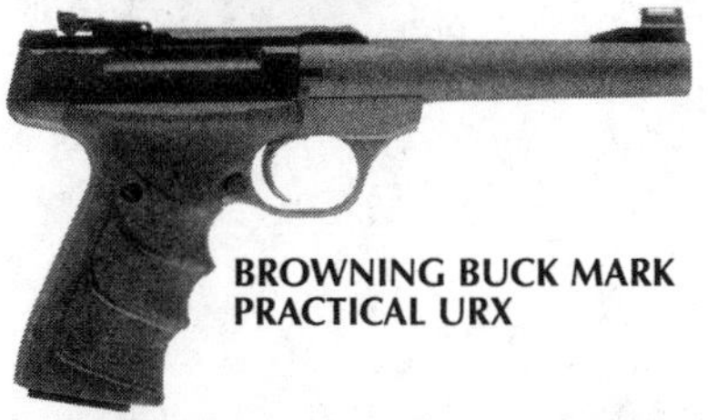

BROWNING BUCK MARK PRACTICAL URX

BROWNING BUCK MARK CAMPER

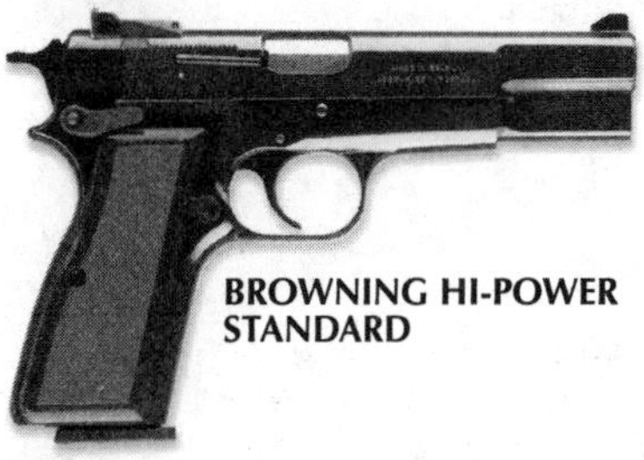

BROWNING HI-POWER STANDARD

1911-22 A1 COMPACT DESERT TAN

Action: Semiautomatic straight blowback
Grips: Synthetic
Barrel: 3.625 in.
Sights: Fixed
Weight: 13.5 oz.
Caliber: .22LR
Capacity: 10 rounds
Features: Machined aircraft-grade aluminum or polymer frame; large manual thumb safety and grip safety
MSRP $580

BUCK MARK CAMPER UFX

Action: Blowback
Grips: Overmolded Ultragrip FX
Barrel: 5.5 in.
Sights: Pro-Target adjustable
Weight: 34 oz.
Caliber: .22LR
Capacity: 10+1 rounds
Features: Built from aircraft-grade aluminum alloy; single-action trigger; target-crowned; large manual thumb safety; ambidextrous grip and slide release; available in blued or stainless finish
MSRP $390

BUCK MARK PLUS UDX

Action: Semiautomatic
Grips: Black laminated, or walnut Ultragrip DX ambidextrous
Barrel: 5.5–7.25 in.
Sights: Adjustable pro-target rear sight, Truglo/Marble fiber-optic front
Weight: 34 oz.
Caliber: 22LR
Capacity: 10+1 rounds
Features: Matte blued, polished barrel flats; blowback action; single-action trigger
Walnut: $540
Black laminated: $580

BUCK MARK PRACTICAL URX

Action: Semiautomatic
Grips: Ultragrip RX ambidextrous
Barrel: 5.5 in.
Sights: Pro-target adjustable rear; Truglo/Marble's fiber-optic front
Weight: 34 oz.
Caliber: .22LR
Capacity: 10+1 rounds
Features: Tapered bull barrel with matte blued finish; matte gray finish receiver
MSRP $440

BUCK MARK SERIES

Action: Semiautomatic
Grips: Composite, black
Barrel: 5.5–7.25 in.
Sights: Adjustable
Weight: 34–39 oz.
Caliber: .22LR
Capacity: 10+1 rounds
Features: Alloy, matte blued finish receiver; tapered barrel; blowback action; single-action trigger; URX ambidextrous grip in contour models; cocobolo, ambidextrous grip on hunter model; lite gray model has matte gray barrel finish and truglo/marble fiber-optic front sight
Camper UFX: $430
Stainless UFX: $430
Contour 5.5 URX: $550
Contour 7.25 URX:. $560
Hunter: $500
Lite Gray 5.5: $580

HI-POWER STANDARD

Action: Semiautomatic
Grips: Select walnut, cut checkering
Barrel: 4.6 in.
Sights: Low profile fixed or adjustable with ramped front post
Weight: 32 oz.
Caliber: 9mm
Capacity: 10+1 rounds
Features: Locked breech action; single-action trigger; ambidextrous thumb safety; extra magazine; steel, polished blued finish barrel
MSRP . . . .$1120–$1200

Cabot Gun Company

CABOT GUN COMPANY
AMERICAN JOE 1911

AMERICAN JOE 1911

Action: Semiautomatic
Grips: Aluminum
Barrel: 5 in.
Sights: Adjustable 2-dot rear
Weight: 40 oz.
Caliber: .45 ACP
Capacity: 8+1 rounds
Features: For this art gun crossing the rubicon between firearms and art, Cabot commissioned rock star designer Joe Faris to design art that represents Detroit and Americana, and the result is a limited edition run of a new iconic 1911, the American Joe; features top slide serrations; 420 stainless steel frame and slide; 20 LPI front strap checkering; tristar trigger
MSRP. $7450

Century International Arms

CENTURY INTERNATIONAL ARMS TP-9

TP-9

Action: DA semiautomatic
Grips: Polymer, interchangeable backstraps
Barrel: 4 in.
Sights: Adjustable 3-dot
Weight: 26.4 oz.
Caliber: 9mm
Capacity: 17+1 rounds
Features: Double-action striker-fired mechanism with de-cocking button; polymer frame and steel slide; modeled after S&W 99; available titanium, OD green, and desert finish
MSRP. $426

Charter Arms

.22 PATHFINDER

Action: DA revolver
Grips: Rubber; Crimson Trace lasergrips
Barrel: 2 in., 4 in., 5 in.
Sights: Fixed, adjustable rear on Target model
Weight: 19 oz.–20 oz.
Caliber: .22LR, .22 Mag.
Capacity: 6 rounds
Features: Stainless steel frame
Standard:. $379

CHARTER ARMS .22 PATHFINDER

Charter Arms

.32 H&R UNDERCOVERETTE

Action: DA revolver
Grips: Rubber; Crimson Trace lasergrips
Barrel: 2 in.
Sights: Fixed
Weight: 12 oz.–16 oz.
Caliber: .32 H&R
Capacity: 5 rounds
Features: Gun with less kick for women; standard or Crimson Trace grip; two-tone pink, stainless, gold & black, or lavender finish; high-grade cast aluminum revolver features
Pink Lady: $419
Lavender Lady: $419
SS Standard: $375

CHARTER ARMS .32 H&R UNDERCOVERETTE - PINK LADY

.38 CHIC LADY

Action: DA/SA, DAO revolver
Grips: Rubber
Barrel: 2 in.
Sights: Fixed
Weight: 12 oz.
Caliber: .38 Spl.
Capacity: 5 rounds
Features: High-polish stainless-steel pink anodized aluminum frame; comes in a faux alligator pink attaché case with high-polish stainless-steel trim; serrated front sight; quick-release cylinder
MSRP: $483

CHARTER ARMS .38 CHIC LADY DAO

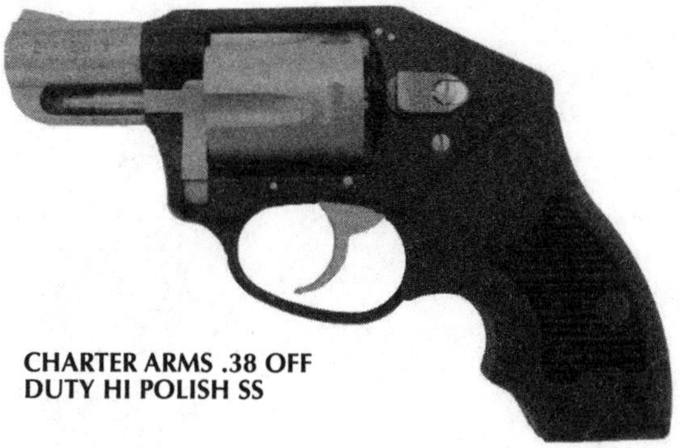

CHARTER ARMS .38 OFF DUTY HI POLISH SS

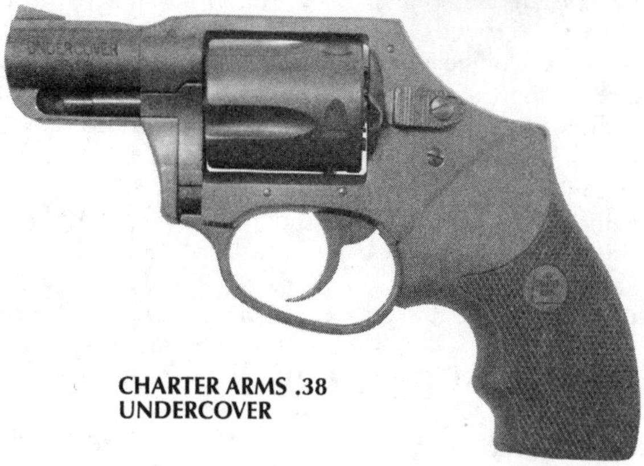

CHARTER ARMS .38 UNDERCOVER

.38 OFF DUTY HI POLISH SS

Action: DA revolver
Grips: Crimson Trace lasergrip
Barrel: 2 in.
Sights: Serrated front, rear notch
Weight: 12 oz.
Caliber: .38 Spl. +P
Capacity: 5 rounds
Features: High-polish stainless-steel finish; matte black frame; off duty model has internal DA hammer; Undercover Lite has external standard hammer
Off Duty: $436
Crimson: $651

.38 UNDERCOVER

Action: DA revolver
Grips: Checkered compact rubber or Crimson Trace lasergrips
Barrel: 2 in.
Sights: Fixed
Weight: 16 oz.
Caliber: .38 Spl. +P
Capacity: 5 rounds
Features: Stainless steel frame; blued, stainless, tiger & black, OD green & black, grey/SS finishes; DAO available; Crimson Trace grips available; compact and lightweight, this revolver is ideal for concealed carry situations; 3-point cylinder lock-up
Blue/Black: $352
SS: $388

Charter Arms

CHARTER ARMS .38 UNDERCOVER LITE

.38 UNDERCOVER LITE

Action: DA revolver
Grips: Rubber, compact
Barrel: 2 in.
Sights: Fixed
Weight: 12 oz.
Caliber: .38 Spl. +P
Capacity: 5 rounds
Features: Frame is constructed from aircraft-grade aluminum and steel; traditional spurred hammer; optional DAO (double action trigger); many finishes and special editions available
Black DAO: $419
Alum. Standard: $397
Red or Black & SS: $414

.38 UNDERCOVER ON DUTY

Action: DA revolver
Grips: Rubber; Crimson Trace lasergrips
Barrel: 2 in.
Sights: Fixed
Weight: 12 oz.
Caliber: .38 Spl. +P
Capacity: 5 rounds
Features: Unique hammer block design; constructed of heat-treated aluminum; allows single-action and double-action operations while minimizing the risk of snagging the hammer on clothing; standard or Crimson Trace grip
Standard: $402
Crimson Trace: $649

.44 SPECIAL BULLDOG

Action: DA revolver
Grips: Rubber; Crimson Trace lasergrips
Barrel: 2.5 in., 4 in. or 5 in. in target model
Sights: Fixed, adjustable rear on Target model
Weight: 21 oz.
Caliber: .44 Spl.
Capacity: 5 rounds
Features: Stainless steel frame; optional DAO trigger; standard hammer; stainless or blued finish
Blued STD: $409
SS STD: $422
DAO: . . . . $426–$469
Target Bulldog: $475
Crimson: $690

.357 MAG. PUG

Action: DA revolver
Grips: Rubber; Crimson Trace lasergrips
Barrel: 2.2 in., 4 in., 5 in.
Sights: Fixed, adjustable rear on Target model
Weight: 23 oz.
Caliber: .357 Mag.
Capacity: 5 rounds
Features: Traditional spurred hammer and full-size grips; optional Crimson Trace grip; stainless steel frame; blued and stainless finish
Standard: $388
Crimson: $609
Stainless: $402
SS DAO: $395

RIMLESS REVOLVER PITBULL

Action: DA/SA revolver
Grips: Rubber, neoprene
Barrel: 2.2 in., 2.3 in.
Sights: Fixed
Weight: 20 oz.–22 oz.
Caliber: 9mm, .40 S&W
Capacity: 5 or 6 rounds
Features: Dual coil spring assembly; stainless steel frame; 9mm has spurred hammer, .40 S&W has standard hammer
9mm: $502
.40: $489

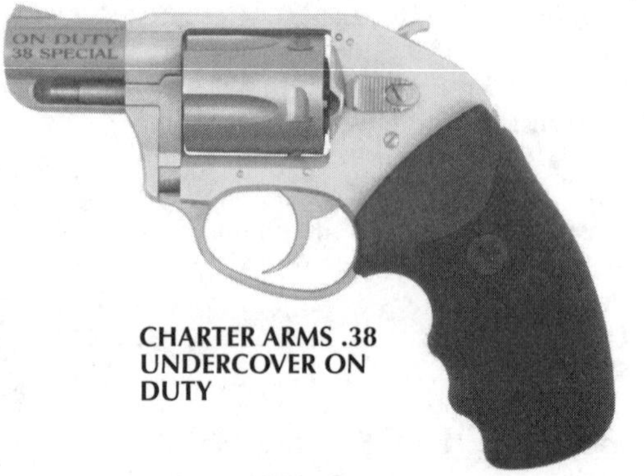

CHARTER ARMS .38 UNDERCOVER ON DUTY

CHARTER ARMS .44 SPECIAL BULLDOG

CHARTER ARMS .357 MAG. PUG

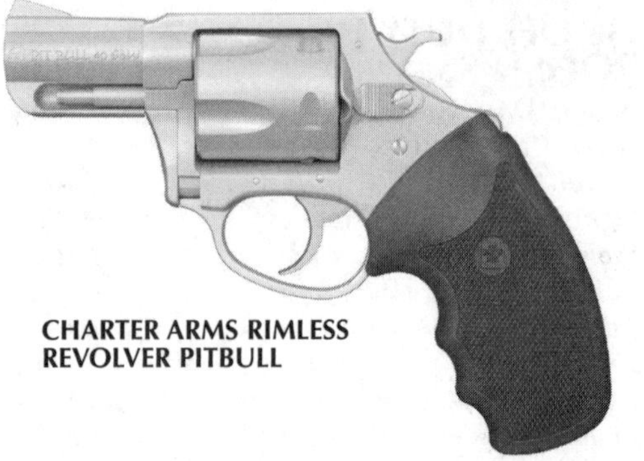

CHARTER ARMS RIMLESS REVOLVER PITBULL

Chiappa Firearms

CHIAPPA FIREARMS MC 14

MC 14

Action: Semiautomatic
Grips: Rubber
Barrel: 3.82 in.
Sights: Fixed
Weight: 24 oz.
Caliber: .380 ACP
Capacity: 13 rounds
Features: Short recoil; single or double action
MSRP $449

RHINO REVOLVER

Action: Revolver
Grips: Wood
Barrel: 6 in.
Sights: Front blade; adjustable rear
Weight: 37 oz.
Caliber: .357, .40 S&W, 9mm, 9x21
Capacity: 6 rounds
Features: Rhino barrel is aligned with the bottom most chamber, which lowers the center of gravity and yields a centerline of the bore more in line with the shooter's arm allowing for the most natural "point ability" while engaging a target; reduces both recoil and muzzle flip which insures subsequent shots are on target faster; frame available in chrome, black, or gold finish
MSRP . . . .$849–$1079

CHIAPPA FIREARMS
RHINO REVOLVER

CHIAPPA FIREARMS
SAA 17-10

SAA 17-10

Action: SA revolver
Grips: Plastic
Barrel: 7.5 in.
Sights: Adjustable
Weight: 34 oz.
Caliber: .17 HMR
Capacity: 10 rounds
Features: Black frame
MSRP $236

Christensen

TACTICAL COMMANDER

Action: Semiautomatic
Grips: Synthetic
Barrel:
Sights: Fixed
Weight: 38.1 oz.
Caliber: .45 ACP
Capacity: N/A
Features: Tritium night sights; Picatinny rail; optional threaded barrel, carbon fiber grips, and ambidextrous thumb safety
MSRP . . . . N/A

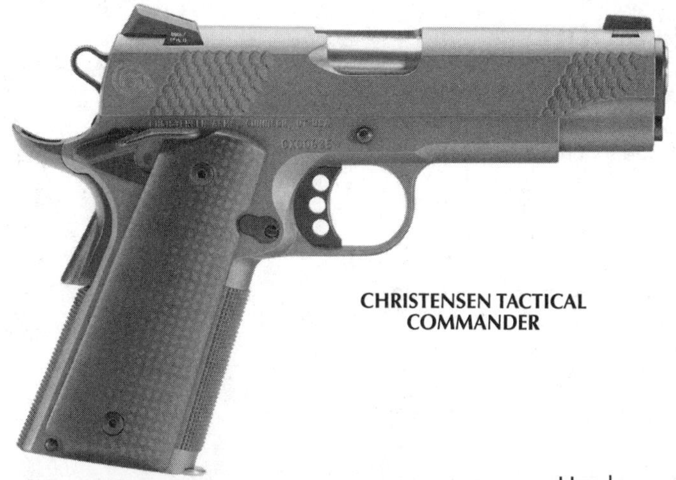

CHRISTENSEN TACTICAL
COMMANDER

Cimarron Firearms Co.

CIMARRON 1872 OPEN TOP NAVY

CIMARRON 1911 .45 ACP

1872 OPEN TOP NAVY

Action: SA revolver
Grips: Walnut
Barrel: 4.75 in., 5.5 in., 7.5 in.
Sights: Fixed, open
Weight: 40 oz.
Caliber: .44 Spl.; .44 Colt, .44 Russian, .45 Schofield, .45 Colt, .38 Colt, .38 Spl.
Capacity: 6 rounds
Features: Forged, color case-hardened frame; Army or Navy grip; charcoal blued, standard blued, or original barrel finish
MSRP $519

1911 .45 ACP

Action: Semiautomatic
Grips: Walnut
Barrel: 5 in.
Sights: Open, fixed
Weight: 39.52 oz.
Caliber: .45 ACP
Capacity: 8+1 rounds
Features: Next generation of firearm widely used in the First World War. Correct historical markings; diamond checkered walnt grips; nickel, polished high luster blued, and standard parkerized finish; optional World War I-style lanyard magazine
MSRP . . . . $541–$677

1911 WILD BUNCH COMBO

Action: Semiautomatic
Grips: Diamond checkered walnut
Barrel: 5 in.
Sights: Fixed
Weight: 39.52 oz.
Caliber: .45 ACP
Capacity: 8+1 rounds
Features: Correct historical markings; the original 1911 frame with a Type 1 smooth mainspring housing; combo includes the 1911 in polished blue finish and the Tanker shoulder holster, a reproduction of the rig used by William Holden in the movie The Wild Bunch
MSRP $842

CIMARRON 1911 WILD BUNCH COMBO

BISLEY MODEL

Action: SA revolver
Grips: Walnut
Barrel: 4.75 in., 5.5 in., 7.5 in.
Sights: Fixed, open
Weight: 42–45 oz.
Caliber: .45 LC, .44 Spl., .44 WCF, .357 Mag.
Capacity: 6 rounds
Features: Reproduction of the original Colt Bisley; forged, color case-hardened frame; blued, charcoal blued, or nickel finish
MSRP $615

CIMARRON BISLEY MODEL

Cimarron Firearms Co.

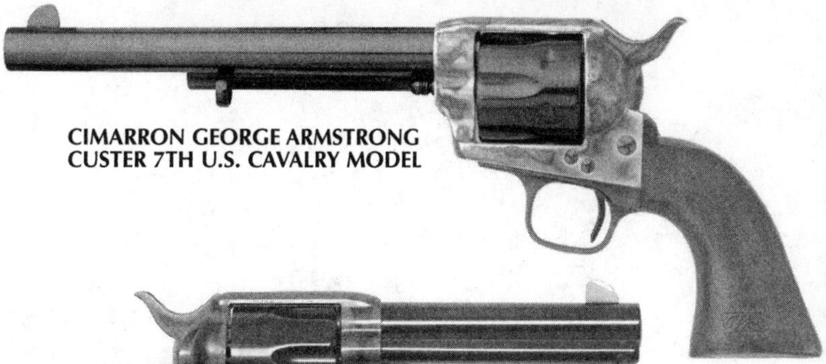
CIMARRON GEORGE ARMSTRONG CUSTER 7TH U.S. CAVALRY MODEL

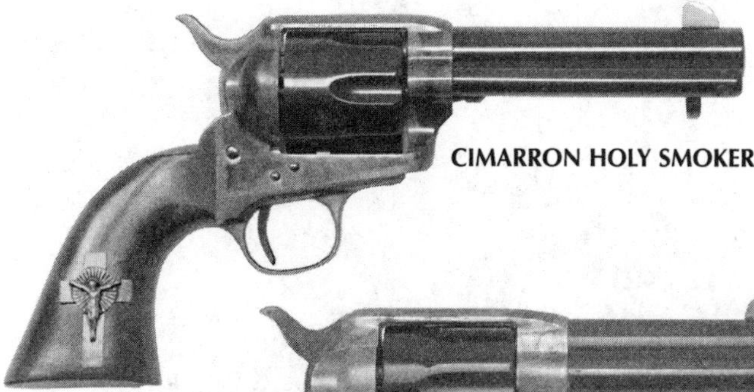
CIMARRON HOLY SMOKER

CIMARRON LIGHTNING

CIMARRON MAN WITH NO NAME

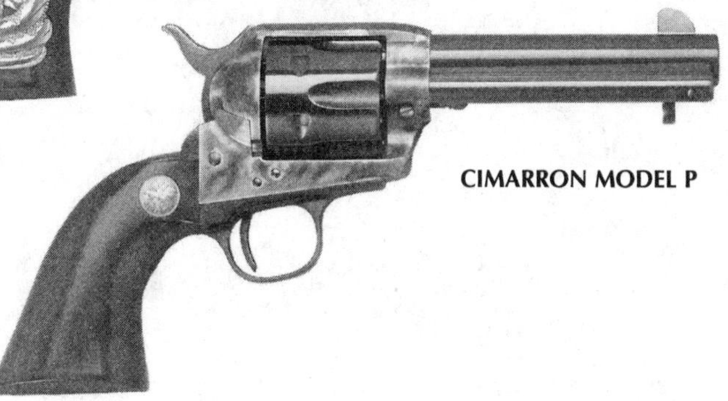
CIMARRON MODEL P

GEORGE ARMSTRONG CUSTER 7TH U.S. CAVALRY MODEL

Action: SA revolver
Grips: Walnut
Barrel: 7.5 in.
Sights: Fixed, open
Weight: 4.4 oz.
Caliber: .45 LC
Capacity: 6 rounds
Features: Old model case-hardened with 7th Cavalry markings; made with one piece of walnut with OWA (Ainsworth) Cartouche; blued, charcoal blued or nickel barrel finish
MSRP . . . . $590–$727

HOLY SMOKER

Action: SA revolver
Grips: Walnut
Barrel: 4.75 in.
Sights: Open, fixed
Weight: 36 oz.
Caliber: .45 Colt
Capacity: 6 rounds
Features: Revolver made famous in *3:10 to Yuma* film; standard blued finish; case-hardened pre-war frame; gold-plated sterling silver cross inlayed on both sides of one-piece walnut grip
MSRP $774

LIGHTNING

Action: SA revolver
Grips: Walnut
Barrel: 3.5 in., 4.75 in., 5.5 in., 6.5 in.
Sights: Fixed, open
Weight: 28.5–30.75 oz.
Caliber: .38 Spl., .22LR, .41 Colt, .32-20 Win./.32 H&R Dual Cylinder
Capacity: 6 rounds
Features: Forged, pre-war color case-hardened frame; charcoal blued, standard blued, or original barrel finish; walnut stock smooth or checkered
MSRP . . . .$532–$649

MAN WITH NO NAME

Action: SA revolver
Grips: Walnut
Barrel: 4.75 in., 5.5 in.
Sights: Open, fixed
Weight: 42.56 oz.–44.16 oz.
Caliber: .45 Colt
Capacity: 6 rounds
Features: Model P in .45 Colt; sterling silver snake on both sides of walnut grip; conversion version available in .38 Special/.38 Colt
MSRP . . . .$774–$818

MODEL P

Action: SA revolver
Grips: Walnut
Barrel: 4.75 in., 5.5 in., 7.5 in.
Sights: None
Weight: 44 oz.
Caliber: 32 WCF, .38 WCF, .357 Mag., .44 WCF, .44 Special, .45 LC, .45 LC/.45 ACP Dual Cylinder
Capacity: 6 rounds
Features: Fashioned after the 1873 Colt SAA; standard blued, charcoal blued, or original finish; available in old model or pre-war (new) model
MSRP $714

Cimarron Firearms Co.

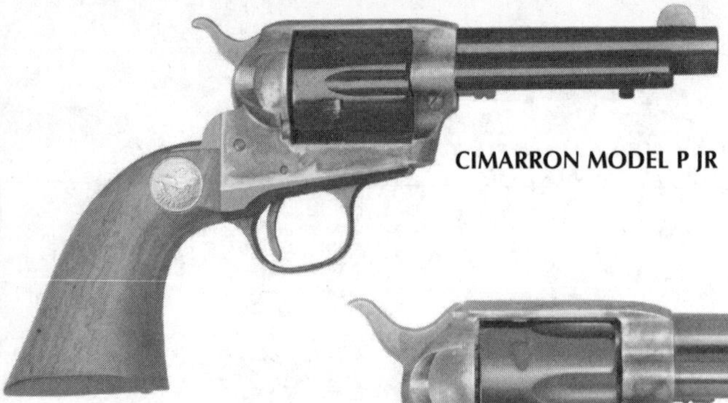

CIMARRON MODEL P JR

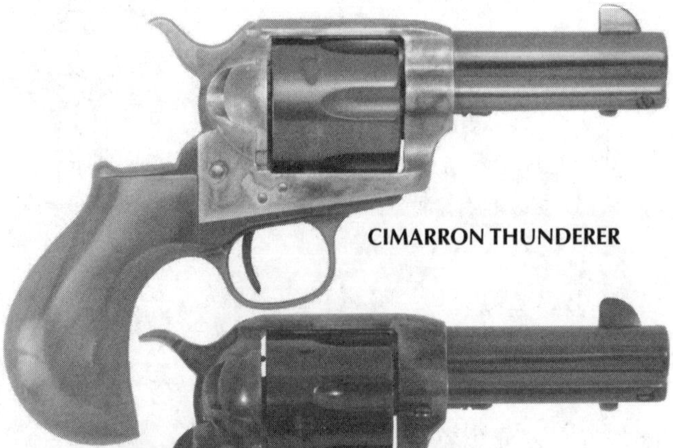

CIMARRON THUNDERER

CIMARRON THUNDERSTORM

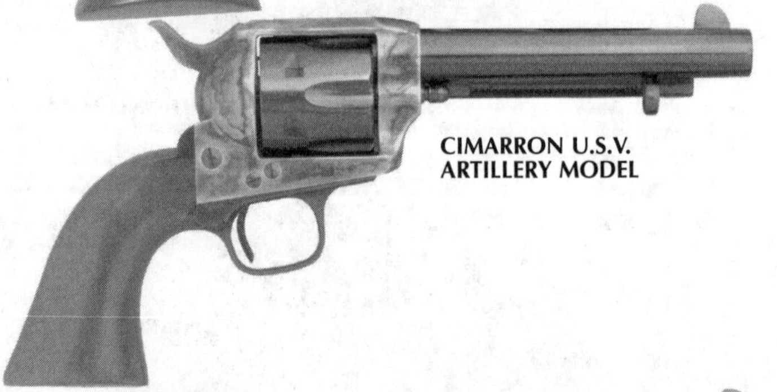

CIMARRON U.S.V. ARTILLERY MODEL

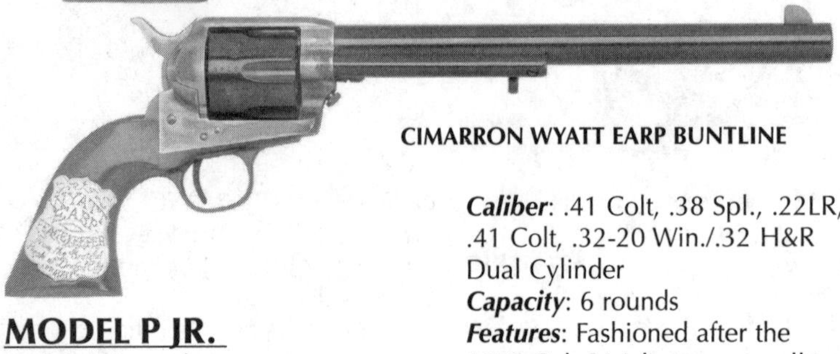

CIMARRON WYATT EARP BUNTLINE

MODEL P JR.

Action: SA revolver
Grips: Walnut
Barrel: 3.5 in., 4.75 in., 5.5 in.
Sights: Fixed, open
Weight: 35.2 oz.
Caliber: .41 Colt, .38 Spl., .22LR, .41 Colt, .32-20 Win./.32 H&R Dual Cylinder
Capacity: 6 rounds
Features: Fashioned after the 1873 Colt SAA but on a smaller scale; color case-hardened frame; blue, charcoal blue, or nickel finish
MSRP. . . . . $451–$601

THUNDERER

Action: SA revolver
Grips: Walnut, ivory, mother of pearl or black hard rubber
Barrel: 3.5 in. w/ ejector, 4.75 in., 5.5 in., 7.5 in.
Sights: Fixed, open
Weight: 38–43.60 oz.
Caliber: .45 LC, .44 Spl., .44 WCF, .357 Mag., .45 LC/.45 ACP Dual Cylinder
Capacity: 6 rounds
Features: Designed in 1990 by Cimarron founder & president "Texas Jack" Harvey; forged, color case-hardened frame; blued, charcoal blued or nickel finish
MSRP. . . . . $561–$699

THUNDERSTORM

Action: SA revolver
Grips: Walnut
Barrel: 3.5 in., 4.75 in.
Sights: Front, rear
Weight: 35.7 oz.–39.68 oz.
Caliber: .45 Colt, .357 Mag./.38 Spl.
Capacity: 6 rounds
Features: Checkered grips; stainless steel or standard blued finishes; wide front sights and deep rear notch; smooth action and hand-knurled hammer; available in Model P or Thunderer versions
MSRP. . . . . $753–$948

U.S.V. ARTILLERY MODEL

Action: SA revolver
Grips: Walnut
Barrel: 5.5 in.
Sights: Fixed, open
Weight: 40 oz.
Caliber: .45 LC
Capacity: 6 rounds
Features: Old model case-hardened with U.S. Artillery markings; stock is a solid piece of walnut with RAC Cartouche; blued, charcoal blued, or original finish
MSRP. . . . . $590–$605

WYATT EARP BUNTLINE

Action: SA revolver
Grips: Walnut
Barrel: 10 in.
Sights: Open, fixed
Weight: 43.04 oz.
Caliber: .45 LC
Capacity: 6 rounds
Features: Revolver made famous in the film *Tombstone*; old model case-hardened; walnut grip hand cast in solid sterling silver and hand inlaid into stock; standard blued or original finish
MSRP. . . . . $857–$883

Citadel by Legacy Sports

M-1911

Action: Semiautomatic
Grips: Full size or compact, wood or Hogue synthetic grips
Barrel: 3.5 in., 5 in.
Sights: Fixed
Weight: 33.6–37.6 oz.
Caliber: 9mm, .45 ACP, .38 Super
Capacity: 7 or 8 rounds
Features: Available in compact and full sized models; matte black, brush nickel, or polished nickel finish; optional Hogue wrap around grip in black, green, or sand; comes with lockable, hard plastic case
MSRP . . . . $591–$681

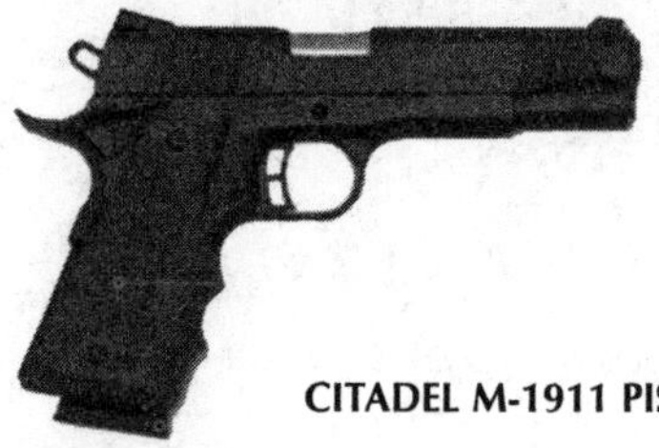

CITADEL M-1911 PISTOLS

M-1911 .22 G.I.

Action: SA semiautomatic
Grips: Wood
Barrel: 5 in.
Sights: G.I. standard
Weight: 33.6 oz.
Caliber: .22LR
Capacity: 10 rounds
Features: Alloy and steel parts; standard G.I. sights; two-piece wooden grip panels
MSRP $310

CITADEL M-1911 .22 G.I.

M-1911 .22 TAC

Action: SA semiautomatic
Grips: Rubber
Barrel: 5 in.
Sights: Fiber optic
Weight: 33.6 oz.
Caliber: .22LR
Capacity: 10 rounds
Features: Fixed barrel and blowback action; alloy and steel parts; one-piece wrap around rubber grip from Hogue; fiber optic front and rear sights; two magazines
MSRP $349

CITADEL M-1911 .22 TAC

Cobra

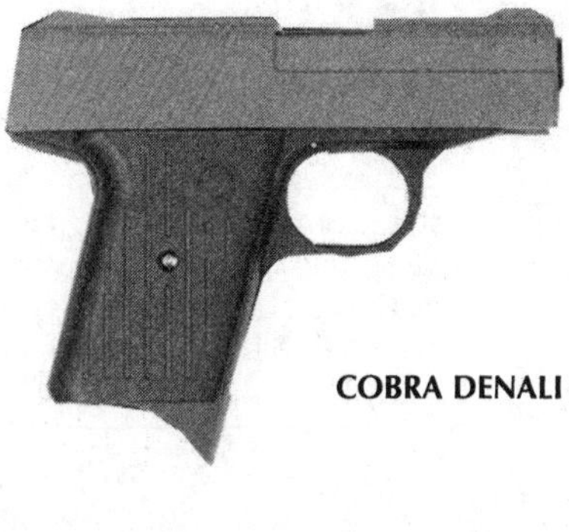

COBRA DENALI SERIES

DENALI SERIES

Action: SA semiautomatic
Grips: Synthetic
Barrel: 2.8 in.
Sights: Fixed
Weight: 17 oz.
Caliber: .380 ACP
Capacity: 5 rounds
Features: Compact, lightweight, and easily concealed; features a durable polymer frame with a pushbutton magazine release; available in black, tactical tan, satin, and OD green Cerakote finishes
MSRP $139

Colt's Manufacturing Company

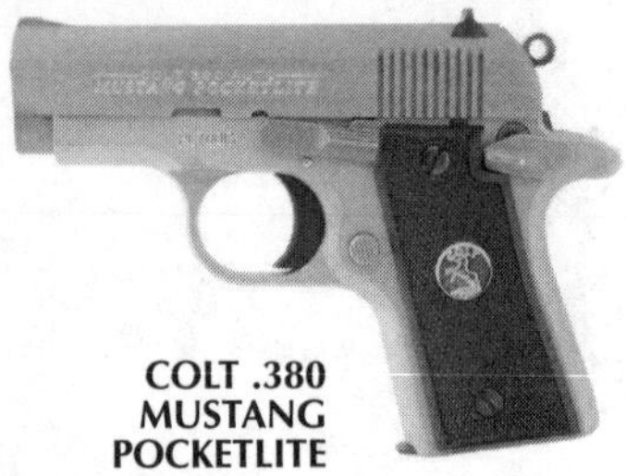
COLT .380 MUSTANG POCKETLITE

COLT .380 MUSTANG POCKETLITE (POLYMER)

COLT 1991 SERIES

.380 MUSTANG POCKETLITE

Action: SA semiautomatic
Grips: Composite
Barrel: 2.75 in.
Sights: High-profile
Weight: 12.5 oz.
Caliber: .380 ACP
Capacity: 6+1 rounds
Features: Aluminum alloy frame with a CNC-machined stainless steel slide and barrel; thumb safety and firing-pin-block safety; solid aluminum trigger; lowered ejection port; electroless nickeled aluminum receiver
MSRP . . . . $499–$599

.380 MUSTANG POCKETLITE (POLYMER)

Action: SA semiautomatic
Grips: Polymer
Barrel: 2.75 in.
Sights: Fixed
Weight: 11.8 oz.
Caliber: .380 ACP
Capacity: 6 rounds
Features: Polymer grip frame with tactical grip profile; texturing on front and back straps; front and rear dovetail sights; aluminum alloy frame also available
MSRP . . . . $499–$599

1991 SERIES

Action: Semiautomatic
Grips: Rosewood or composite
Barrel: 5 in.
Sights: Fixed
Weight: 39 oz.
Caliber: .45 ACP
Capacity: 7+1 rounds
Features: Beveled magazine well; single- and double-action; carbon steel, aluminum alloy, or stainless steel frame; standard or beavertail grip safety; blued, black anodized, brushed stainless steel, bright stainless steel frame finish
MSRP . . . . $799–$1499

DEFENDER

Action: Semiautomatic
Grips: Rubber finger-grooved
Barrel: 5 in.

COLT DEFENDER

Sights: White dot carry front and rear
Weight: 30 oz.
Caliber: .45 ACP
Capacity: 7+1 rounds
Features: Beveled magazine well; black skeletonized aluminum trigger; Series 80 firing system; beavertail grip and standard thumb safety; stainless steel slide, Teflon coated receiver; aluminum alloy frame
MSRP $973

COLT GOLD CUP TROPHY

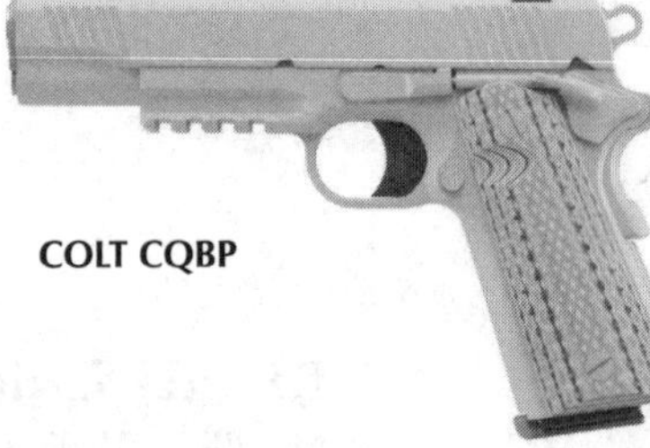
COLT CQBP

GOLD CUP SERIES

Action: Semiautomatic
Grips: Black composite
Barrel: 5 in.
Sights: Dovetail front, adjustable rear
Weight: 39 oz.
Caliber: .45 ACP
Capacity: 8+1 rounds
Features: Beveled magazine well; beavertail grip safety; black wrap around grips; wide aluminum 3-Hole trigger adjustable for over travel; stainless steel frame finish and material; enhanced hammer
MSRP . . . . $1249–$1299

CLOSE QUARTERS BATTLE PISTOL (CQBP)

Action: Semiautomatic
Grips: Composite
Barrel: 5 in.
Sights: Novak 3-dot night sights
Weight: 40 oz.
Caliber: .45 ACP
Capacity: 7 rounds
Features: Desert Tan Cerakoted stainless steel receiver and slide; serrated mainspring housing with lanyard loop; enhanced hammer; Colt tactical ambidextrous safety lock; National Match barrel; Picatinny rail
MSRP $2149

Colt's Manufacturing Company

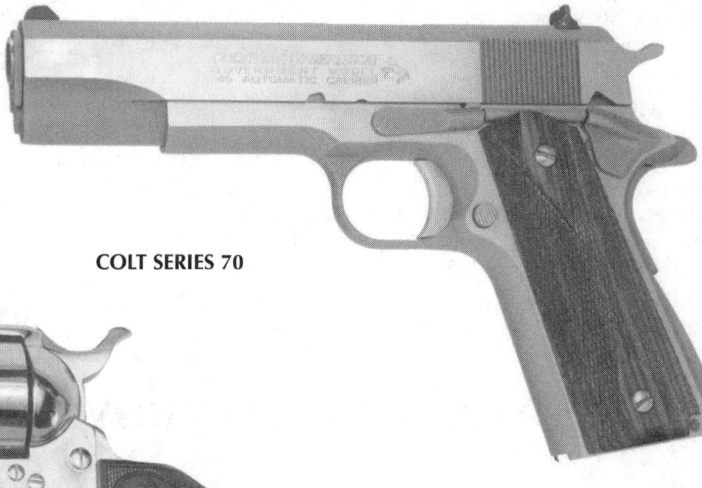

COLT SERIES 70

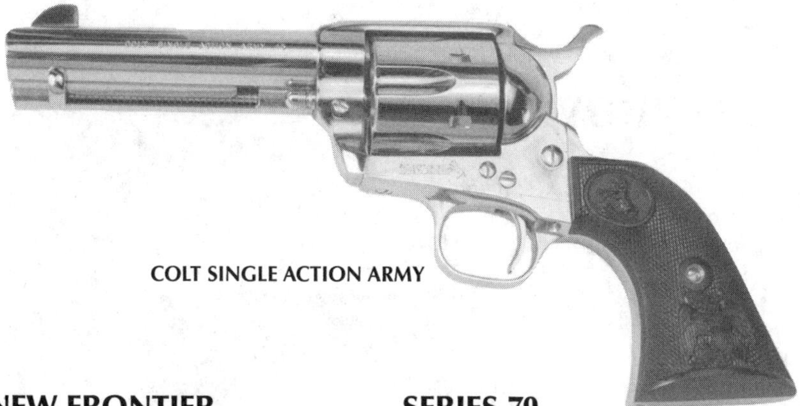

COLT SINGLE ACTION ARMY

NEW FRONTIER

Action: SA revolver
Grips: Walnut stock with gold medallions
Barrel: 4.75 in., 5.5 in., 7.5 in.
Sights: Ramp style front; adjustable rear
Weight: 46 oz.
Caliber: .357 Mag., .44 Spl., .45 Colt
Capacity: 6 rounds
Features: Royal blued barrel and cylinder; flat top case colored frame
MSRP. $1528

RAIL GUN

Action: Semiautomatic
Grips: Double diamond rosewood or blackened rosewood
Barrel: 5 in.
Sights: White dot, Novak rear
Weight: 39 oz.
Caliber: .45 ACP
Capacity: 8+1 rounds
Features: Stainless steel, blackened receiver and brushed slide, blackened receiver and slide frame finish options; stainless steel frame material; Colt upswept beavertail with palm swell; enhanced hammer; Picatinny rail; National Match barrel; single-slide tactical thumb safety
MSRP. . . . . $1198–$1284

SERIES 70

Action: Semiautomatic
Grips: Double diamond rosewood
Barrel: 5 in.
Sights: Fixed
Weight: 39 oz.
Caliber: .45 ACP
Capacity: 7+1 rounds
Features: Spur hammer; single-action; blued or brushed steel finish; carbon steel or stainless steel frame; short steel trigger; original series 70 firing system with titanium firing pin
Blued: . . . .$899–$1299
Brushed Steel: $979

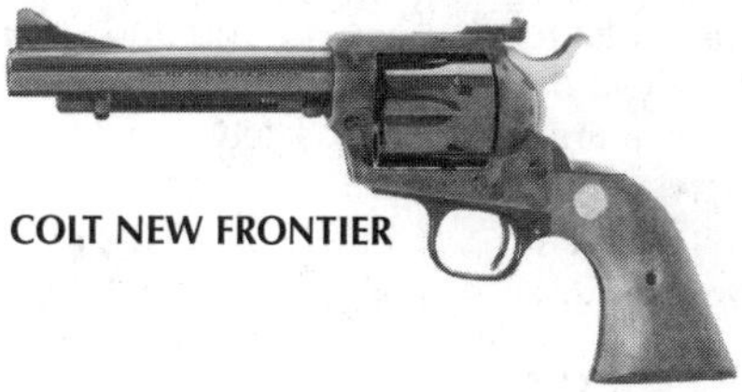

COLT NEW FRONTIER

SINGLE ACTION ARMY

Action: SA revolver
Grips: Black composite eagle
Barrel: 4.75 in., 5.5 in., 7.5 in.
Sights: Fixed
Weight: 46 oz.
Caliber: .32-20 Win., .38 Spl., .38-40 Win., .357 Mag., .44-40 Win., .45 Colt
Capacity: 6 rounds
Features: Case-colored frame; transfer bar; second generation style cylinder bushing; features 175th anniversary rollmark; blued or nickel finish
MSRP. . . . .$1349–$1551

COLT RAIL GUN

Coonan Arms

COONAN COMPENSATED CLASSIC

Action: Semiautomatic
Grips: Smooth black walnut
Barrel: 5 in.
Sights: Dovetail front and rear
Weight: 42 oz.
Caliber: .357 Mag.
Capacity: 7+1 rounds
Features: Coonan Classic with compensator barrel; recoil operated; extended slide catch and thumb lock; custom carry case
MSRP. $1495
Compensator: $1625

COONAN COMPENSATED CLASSIC

CZ-USA (Ceska Zbrojovka)

75 B

Action: Semiautomatic
Grips: Plastic
Barrel: 4.6 in.
Sights: Fixed, 3-dot system
Weight: 35.2 oz.
Caliber: .40 S&W, 9mm
Capacity: .40 S&W: 10 rounds, 9mm: 16 rounds
Features: Steel frame; high capacity double column magazines; hammer forged barrels; ergonomic grip and controls; double-action or single-action; firing pin block safety; black polycoat finish
.40 S&W: $625
9mm: $612

75 B OMEGA

Action: DA/SA semiautomatic
Grips: Plastic
Barrel: 4.6 in.
Sights: Fixed
Weight: 35 oz.
Caliber: 9mm Luger
Capacity: 16 rounds
Features: Manual safety; firing pin block; three-dot sighting system
MSRP. $544

75 COMPACT

Action: Semiautomatic
Grips: Plastic
Barrel: 3.8 in.
Sights: Fixed, 3-dot system
Weight: 32.48 oz.
Caliber: 9mm Luger
Capacity: 14 rounds
Features: Black polycoat, dual tone, satin nickel frame finishes; manual safety; steel frame; high capacity double column magazines; hammer forged barrels
Black polycoat: $544

75 SP-01

Action: Semiautomatic
Grips: Rubber
Barrel: 4.6 in.
Sights: 3-Dot tritium night
Weight: 38.4 oz.
Caliber: 9mm Luger
Capacity: 18 rounds
Features: Based upon the Shadow Target; decocking lever; safety stop on hammer; firing pin safety; steel frame
MSRP. $680

75 SP-01 ACCU-SHADOW

Action: SA/DA semiautomatic
Grips: Thin aluminum
Barrel: 4.6 in.
Sights: Fiber optic front, HAJO rear
Weight: 38.4 oz.
Caliber: 9mm
Capacity: 18+1 rounds
Features: The Accu-Bushing system holds the barrel with much more precision; pistols returned test groups substantially less than 3 inches at 50 yards (using Fiocci 124 JHP); competition hammer; lighter springs; stainless steel guide rod and polished internals; short-reset disconnector is used to greatly reduce trigger reset between shots; fiber optic front and HAJO serrated target rear (adjustable for height, also drift adjustable for windage)
MSRP. $1715

CZ 75 B

CZ–USA 75 B OMEGA

CZ 75 COMPACT

CZ 75 SP-01

CZ-USA 75 SP-01 ACCU-SHADOW

CZ-USA (Ceska Zbrojovka)

CZ 75 TS CZECHMATE

CZ 75 SP-01
SHADOW TARGET

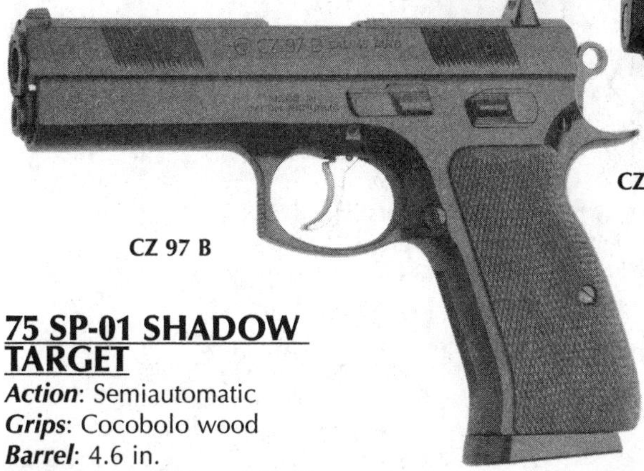

CZ 97 B

CZ 2075 RAMI

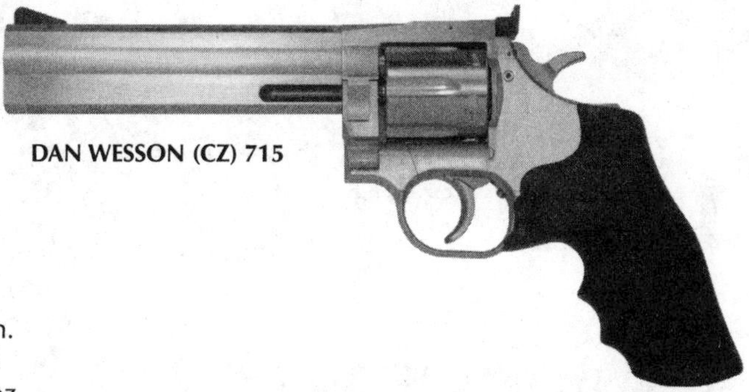

DAN WESSON (CZ) 715

75 SP-01 SHADOW TARGET

Action: Semiautomatic
Grips: Cocobolo wood
Barrel: 4.6 in.
Sights: Competition style, fiber optic
Weight: 38.4 oz.
Caliber: 9mm
Capacity: 18 rounds
Features: Single- or double-action; manual safety; steel frame; TRT rear sight; competition springs; CZ custom stainless guide rod
MSRP $1361

75 TS CZECHMATE

Action: Semiautomatic
Grips: Aluminum
Barrel: 5.4 in.
Sights: Fixed, C-more red dot
Weight: 48 oz.
Caliber: 9mm
Capacity: 20 or 26 rounds
Features: Built upon a modified version of the CZ 75 TS frame; interchangeable parts allow the user to quickly configure the gun for both roles; features a single-action trigger mechanism; red-dot sight; includes spare barrel; includes three 20-round magazines and one 26-round magazine; all-steel pistol is finished in black matte
MSRP $3317

97 B

Action: Semiautomatic
Grips: Plastic
Barrel: 4.8 in.
Sights: Fixed
Weight: 40 oz.
Caliber: .45 ACP
Capacity: 10 rounds
Features: Manual safety; cold hammer-forged barrel; single- or double-action
Black polycoat: $707
Glossy blued: $734

2075 RAMI

Action: Semiautomatic
Grips: Rubber
Barrel: 3 in.
Sights: Fixed
Weight: 25.6 oz.
Caliber: .40 S&W, 9mm Luger
Capacity: .40 S&W: 7 or 9 rounds, 9mm: 14 rounds
Features: Operates in selective DA and SA mode depending on shooter's preferences; firing pin block; manual safety; double-stack magazine; black polycoat alloy frame; cold hammer forged
.40 S&W: $633
9mm Luger: $614

DAN WESSON (CZ) 715

Action: DA semiautomatic
Grips: Rubber
Barrel: 6 in.
Sights: Fixed
Weight: 46 oz.
Caliber: .357 Mag.
Capacity: 6 rounds
Features: Adjustable target rear sight; six inch heavy barrel with ventilated rib; stainless steel construction
MSRP $1168

CZ-USA (Ceska Zbrojovka)

DAN WESSON (CZ)
GUARDIAN

DAN WESSON (CZ)
CHAOS

CZ P-01

CZ–USA P-07

CZ–USA P-09

DAN WESSON (CZ) CHAOS

Action: SA semiautomatic
Grips: Synthetic
Barrel: 5 in.
Sights: Adjustable
Weight: 51 oz.
Caliber: 9mm Luger
Capacity: 21 rounds
Features: Ambidextrous thumb safety; grip safety; double-stack magazine; Picatinny rail; fiber optic sights
MSRP $3829

DAN WESSON (CZ) GUARDIAN

Action: SA semiautomatic
Grips: Wood
Barrel: 4.25 in.
Sights: Fixed
Weight: 29 oz.
Caliber: 9mm Luger, .38 Super, .45 ACP
Capacity: 8 (.45 ACP) or 9 rounds
Features: Ambidextrous thumb safety; grip safety; fixed night sights
MSRP . . . . $1558–$1619

P-01

Action: Semiautomatic
Grips: Rubber
Barrel: 3.8 in.
Sights: Fixed
Weight: 28.8 oz.
Caliber: 9mm Luger
Capacity: 14 rounds
Features: Decocking lever; safety stop on hammer; firing pin safety; black polycoat frame finish; black or pink grips; single- or double-action
MSRP $627

P-07

Action: DA/SA semiautomatic
Grips: Synthetic
Barrel: 3.8 in.
Sights: Fixed
Weight: 27 oz.
Caliber: 9mm Luger, .40 S&W
Capacity: 12 or 15 rounds
Features: Ambidextrous safety or decocker; firing pin block
MSRP . . . . $510–$524

P-09

Action: DA/SA semiautomatic
Grips: Synthetic
Barrel: 4.53 in. or 5.23 in. (suppressor model)
Sights: Fixed
Weight: 30 oz.
Caliber: 9mm Luger, .40 S&W
Capacity: 15 (.40 S&W) or 19 rounds
Features: Ambidextrous safety or decocker; firing pin block; available in 9mm Luger suppressor ready and 9mm Flat Dark Earth with night sights models
MSRP . . . . $530–$544

Dan Wesson Firearms

DAN WESSON ECO

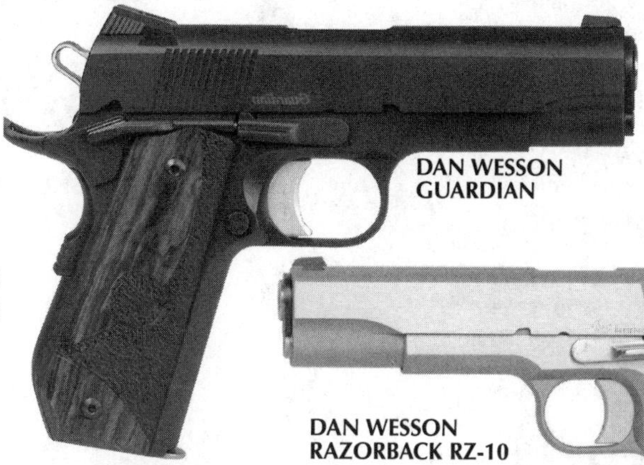
DAN WESSON GUARDIAN

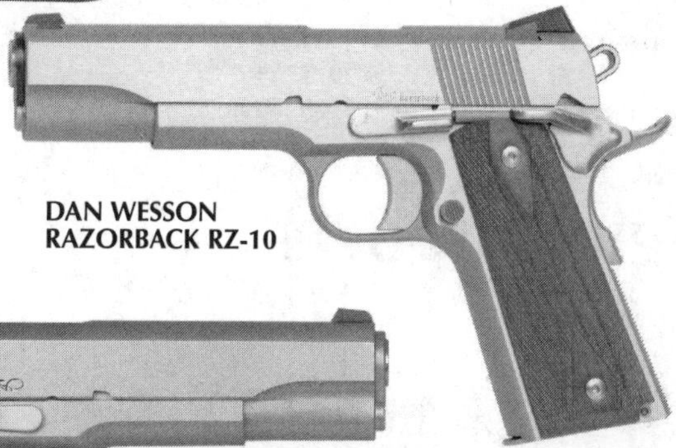
DAN WESSON RAZORBACK RZ-10

DAN WESSON VALOR

DAN WESSON SPECIALIST

ECO

Action: SA semiautomatic
Grips: Composite
Barrel: 3.5 in.
Sights: Fixed tritium
Weight: 25 oz.
Caliber: 9mm, .45 ACP
Capacity: 7+1 rounds
Features: Single-stack Officer's size 1991; aluminum alloy frame; undercut trigger guards; 25 lpi checkering; mainspring housing is aluminum with 25 lpi checkering; Ed Brown high rise grip safety; forged steel slide; tritium night sights with tactical ledge rear sight; flush cut ramped bull barrel with target crown
9mm: $1623
.45 ACP: $1662

GUARDIAN

Action: SA semiautomatic
Grips: Stippled shadow
Barrel: 4.25 in.
Sights: Novak low mount style, night
Weight: 28.8 oz.
Caliber: .45 ACP, 9mm
Capacity: 8 rounds
Features: Bobtail alloy frame; aluminum alloy frame; commander length barrel; finished in matte black with tritium sights
.45: $1619
9mm: $1558

RAZORBACK RZ-10

Action: SA semiautomatic
Grips: Diamond-checkered cocobolo
Barrel: 5 in.
Sights: Fixed
Weight: 38.4 oz.
Caliber: 10mm
Capacity: 9 rounds
Features: Razorback is back in 2012 in limited quantities; serrated Clark-style target rib; 1911 model; stainless steel frame; manual thumb safety, grip safety
MSRP $1350

SPECIALIST

Action: SA semiautomatic
Grips: G10 VZ Operator II grips
Barrel: 5 in.
Sights: Fixed tritium
Weight: 37 oz.
Caliber: .45 ACP
Capacity: 8+1 rounds
Features: Full size single-stack pistol; matte stainless steel or black Duty finishes; forged slide and frame; Clark-style serrated rib with tritium dual-colored night sights stacked in a straight eight-type pattern; tactical ledge rear sight with single rear amber dot and green front with white target ring; Picatinny rail; undercut trigger guard with 25 lpi front strap checkering; ambidextrous thumb safety; two magazines with bumper pads included
SS: $1701
Black: $2012

VALOR

Action: SA semiautomatic
Grips: Slim line G10
Barrel: 5 in.
Sights: Heinie Ledge straight eight night
Weight: 35.2 oz.
Caliber: .45 ACP
Capacity: 8 rounds
Features: Matte black duty receiver finish; manual thumb safety; forged stainless steel frame
SS: $1701
Black: $2012

Doubletap Defense LLC

DOUBLETAP

Action: DAO semiautomatic
Grips: Synthetic
Barrel: 3 in.
Sights: Front blade
Weight: 12 oz.–14 oz.
Caliber: .45 ACP, 9mm
Capacity: 2+2 rounds
Features: Titanium frame with a MIL-STD finish that resists corrosion; integral grips house additional two spare rounds; ported barrel reduces muzzle flip and recoil; ambidextrous thumb latch to eject spent rounds; quick-change interchangable barrels; comes with one barrel and you can purchase extra conversion kits
Aluminum:. . . . . $499–$569
Titanium:. . . . . $729–$799
Conversion kits:. . . . . $199–$269

DOUBLETAP DEFENSE LLC DOUBLETAP

Eagle Imports

EAGLE IMPORTS MAC 1911 BOBCUT

MAC 1911 BOBCUT

Action: SA semiautomatic
Grips: Hardwood
Barrel: 4.25 in.
Sights: Adjustable rear, dovetail front
Weight: 34.58 oz.
Caliber: .45 ACP
Capacity: 8+1 rounds
Features: 4140 steel frame and hammer forged slide; fully adjustable Novak-type rear sight; dovetail front sight with fiber optic; flared and lowered ejection port; enhanced beavertail grip safety; skeletal hammer; combat trigger; stippled front strap serration; throated forged steel barrel
Deep Blue:. $902
Hard Chrome: $978

EAGLE IMPORTS MAC 1911 BULLSEYE

MAC 1911 BULLSEYE

Action: SA semiautomatic
Grips: Hardwood
Barrel: 6 in.
Sights: Adjustable rear, dovetail front
Weight: 46.91 oz.
Caliber: .45 ACP
Capacity: 8+1 rounds
Features: The largest of the MAC 1911 pistol line; 4140 steel frame and hammer forged slide; fully adjustable Bomar-type rear sight; dovetail front sight; flared and lowered ejection port; enhanced beavertail grip safety; skeletal hammer; combat trigger; checkered front strap serration; ramped match grade bull barrel
Deep Blue:. $1219
Hard Chrome: $1294

MAC 1911 CLASSIC

Action: SA semiautomatic
Grips: Hardwood
Barrel: 5 in.
Sights: Adjustable rear, dovetail front
Weight: 40.56 oz.
Caliber: .45 ACP
Capacity: 8+1 rounds
Features: 4140 steel frame and hammer forged slide; fully adjustable bomar-type rear sight; dovetail front sight with fiber optic; flared and lowered ejection port; enhanced beavertail grip safety; skeletal hammer; combat trigger; checkered front strap serrations; ramped match grade bull barrel
Deep Blue: $1045
Hard Chrome: $1120

EAGLE IMPORTS MAC 1911 CLASSIC

SPS PANTERA

Action: SA semiautomatic
Grips: Glass-filled nylon polymer
Barrel: 5 in.
Sights: Adjustable rear, dovetail front
Weight: 36.68 oz.
Caliber: .45 ACP
Capacity: 12+1 rounds
Features: IPSC Standard or Open Competition ready; fully adjustable Bomar-type rear sight, dovetail front sight with fiber optic; light weight polymer trigger; wide front and rear slide serrations; ambidextrous thumb safety; black chrome finish
MSRP $1895

EAGLE IMPORTS SPS PANTERA

SPS VISTA LONG AND SHORT

Action: SA semiautomatic
Grips: Glass-filled nylon polymer
Barrel: 5 in., 5.5 in.
Sights: Sight mount included
Weight: 41.62 oz.–43.38 oz.
Caliber: 9mm (Short), .38 Super (Long)
Capacity: 21 rounds
Features: Hammer forged steel slide; scope mount for C-MORE optical sight included; checkered front strap serration; ramped match grade threaded barrel; wide magwell; black chrome finish
MSRP $2450

EAGLE IMPORTS SPS VISTA LONG AND SHORT

Ed Brown

ED BROWN CLASSIC CUSTOM

ED BROWN EXECUTIVE CARRY

ED BROWN EXECUTIVE ELITE

ED BROWN KOBRA

ED BROWN KOBRA CARRY LIGHTWEIGHT

CLASSIC CUSTOM

Action: Semiautomatic
Grips: Cocobolo wood
Barrel: 5 in.
Sights: Adjustable rear, cross dovetail front
Weight: 40 oz.
Caliber: .45 ACP
Capacity: 7+1 rounds
Features: Single-action; single-stack government model frame; special mirror finished side; two-piece guide rod for smoother cycling and easier disassembly; stainless or blued finish
MSRP. $3695

EXECUTIVE CARRY

Action: Semiautomatic
Grips: Checkered cocobolo wood
Barrel: 4.25 in.
Sights: Fixed, night
Weight: 35 oz.
Caliber: .45 ACP
Capacity: 7+1 rounds
Features: Frame modified with an innovative Ed Brown Bobtail; stainless or blued frame finish with stainless, black or blued slide finish; fixed dovetail 3-dot night sights with high visibility white outlines
MSRP. $3145

EXECUTIVE ELITE

Action: Semiautomatic
Grips: Checkered cocobolo wood
Barrel: 5 in.
Sights: Fixed, night
Weight: 38 oz.
Caliber: .45 ACP
Capacity: 7+1 rounds
Features: Single-stack government model frame; matte finished slide for low glare, with traditional square cut serrations on rear of slide only; blued or stainless finish
MSRP. $2895

KOBRA

Action: Semiautomatic
Grips: Cocobolo wood
Barrel: 5 in.
Sights: Fixed, night
Weight: 38 oz.
Caliber: .45 ACP
Capacity: 7+1 rounds
Features: Single-stack government model frame; John Browning traditional design; exclusive snakeskin treatment on forestrap and mainspring housing; matte finished slide for low glare; 3-dot night sights with high visibility white outlines; blued or stainless finish
MSRP. $2695

KOBRA CARRY LIGHTWEIGHT

Action: Semiautomatic
Grips: Cocobolo wood
Barrel: 4.25 in.
Sights: Fixed dovetail front night with high visibility white outlines
Weight: 27 oz.
Caliber: .45 ACP
Capacity: 7+1 rounds
Features: Lightweight aluminum frame and Bobtail housing; all other components are steel; exclusive snakeskin treatment on forestrap and housing; matte finished Gen III coated slide for low glare
MSRP. $3320

Ed Brown

ED BROWN SIGNATURE EDITION

SIGNATURE EDITION

Action: Semiautomatic
Grips: Cocobolo wood
Barrel: 5 in.
Sights: Adjustable rear, cross dovetail front
Weight: 40 oz.
Caliber: .45 ACP
Capacity: 7+1 rounds
Features: The Ed Brown Signature Edition is based on the timeless Classic Custom pistol, with hand relief engraving by our master engraver; single stack government model frame; special mirror finished slide; 50 lpi serrations on back of slide to match serrated adjustable sight; hand relief engraved package; adjustable rear sight buried deep into slide; cross dovetail front sight; blued metal parts
MSRP. $7695

ED BROWN SPECIAL FORCES CARRY

SPECIAL FORCES CARRY

Action: Semiautomatic
Grips: Double diamond checkered Cocobolo wood
Barrel: 4.25 in.
Sights: Fixed dovetail 3-dot night sights
Weight: 35 oz.
Caliber: .45 ACP
Capacity: 7 rounds
Features: Commander model slide, single stack Bobtail frame; chainlink treatment on forestrap; Bobtail housing; slide coated with Gen III low glare protection; high visibility white outlines for sights; available stainless finish
MSRP. $2945

E.M.F. Company

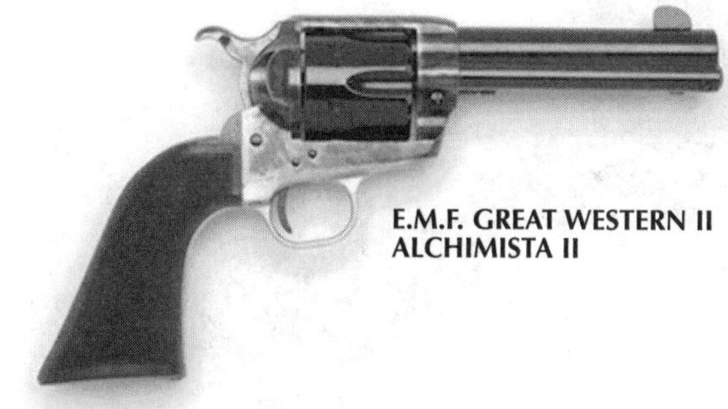

E.M.F. GREAT WESTERN II ALCHIMISTA II

GREAT WESTERN II ALCHIMISTA II

Action: SA revolver
Grips: Walnut
Barrel: 4.75 in., 5.5 in.
Sights: Fixed
Weight: 33.6 oz.
Caliber: .357 Mag., .45 LC
Capacity: 6 rounds
Features: Standard case-hardening; stainless steel; checkered walnut grips; express grips available
MSRP. $680

GREAT WESTERN II ALL BLUE "PALADIN"

Action: Revolver
Grips: Ultra Ivory
Barrel: 3.5 in., 5.5 in., 7.5 in.
Sights: Fixed
Weight: N/A
Caliber: .45 LC
Capacity: 6 rounds
Features: Single action; all blued barrel, cylinder, and frames as seen in Hollywood westerns
MSRP. $560

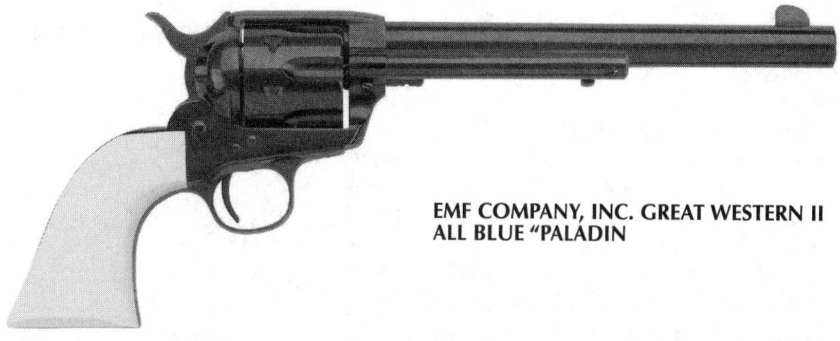

EMF COMPANY, INC. GREAT WESTERN II ALL BLUE "PALADIN

E.M.F. Company

EMF COMPANY, INC. GREAT WESTERN II BUNTLINE

GREAT WESTERN II BUNTLINE

Action: Revolver
Grips: Walnut or Ultra Stag
Barrel: 12 in.
Sights: Fixed
Weight: N/A
Caliber: .45 LC
Capacity: 6 rounds
Features: Deep color case hardened finish; first version was designed by Colt for Ned Buntline
MSRP $580

E.M.F. GREAT WESTERN II CALIFORNIAN

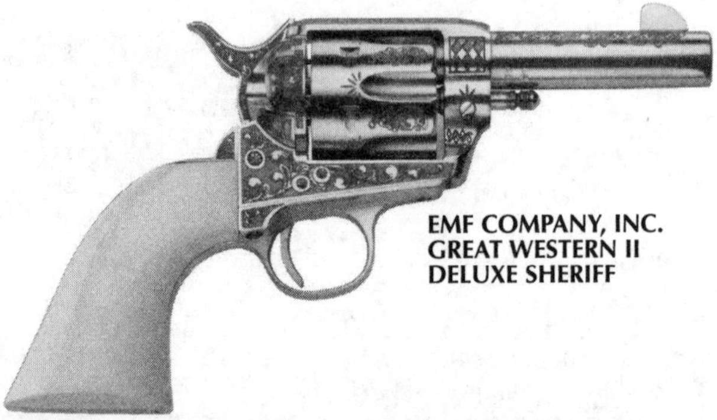

EMF COMPANY, INC. GREAT WESTERN II DELUXE SHERIFF

GREAT WESTERN II CALIFORNIAN

Action: SA revolver
Grips: Walnut
Barrel: 4.75 in., 5.5 in., 7.5 in.
Sights: Fixed
Weight: 48 oz.
Caliber: .22LR, .357 Mag., .44 Mag., .44-40 Win., .45 LC
Capacity: 6 rounds
Features: Standard case-hardening; steel frame
MSRP $545

GREAT WESTERN II DELUXE SHERIFF

Action: Revolver
Grips: Ultra Ivory
Barrel: 3 in.
Sights: Fixed
Weight: N/A
Caliber: .357 Mag., 45 LC
Capacity: 6 rounds
Features: Manufactured in Italy; stainless steel with factory laser engraving
MSRP $800

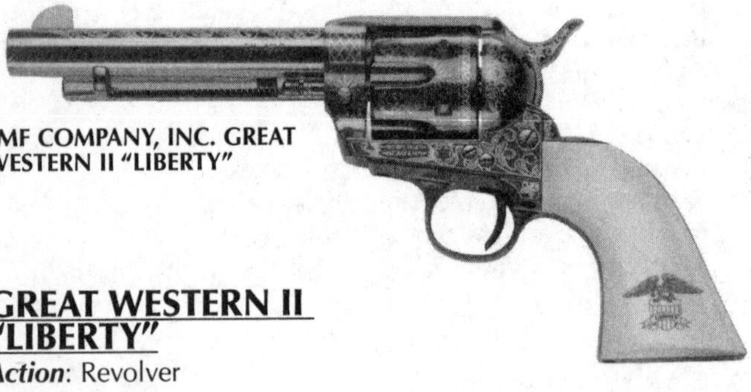

EMF COMPANY, INC. GREAT WESTERN II "LIBERTY"

GREAT WESTERN II "LIBERTY"

Action: Revolver
Grips: Ultra Ivory
Barrel: 4.75 in., 5.5 in.
Sights: Fixed
Weight: N/A
Caliber: .357 Mag., .45 LC
Capacity: 6 rounds
Features: Manufactured in Italy; all blued barrel, cylinder, and frame; factory laser engraved
MSRP $630

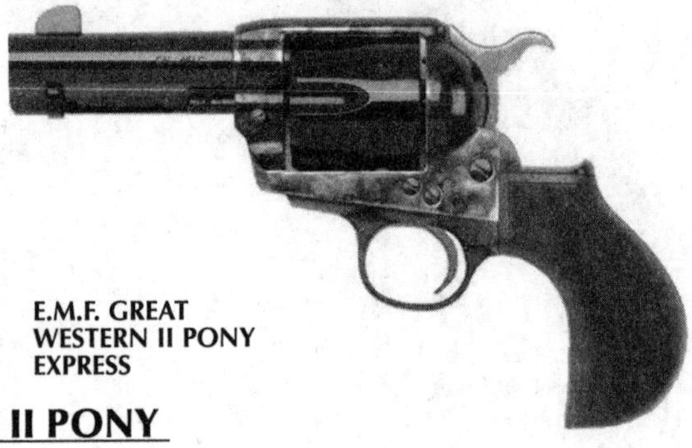

E.M.F. GREAT WESTERN II PONY EXPRESS

GREAT WESTERN II PONY EXPRESS

Action: SA revolver
Grips: Walnut express grips
Barrel: 3.5 in.
Sights: Fixed
Weight: 32 oz.
Caliber: .357 Mag., .45 LC
Capacity: 6 rounds
Features: Case-hardened steel; checkered walnut express grips; turned down hammer
MSRP . . . . $625–$820

Entréprise Arms

ENTRÉPRISE ARMS ELITE

ENTRÉPRISE ARMS MEDALIST

ELITE

Action: Semiautomatic
Grips: Composite
Barrel: 3.25 in., 4.25 in., or 5 in.
Sights: Fixed
Weight: 36–40 oz.
Caliber: .45 ACP
Capacity: 10 or 14 rounds
Features: Three Hi-visible dot sight; black oxide finish; extended thumb lock; match grade disconnector with polished contact points; hardened steel magazine release; adjustable anti-lash match trigger
MSRP $699

MEDALIST

Action: Semiautomatic
Grips: Composite
Barrel: 5 in.
Sights: Fixed
Weight: 40 oz.
Caliber: .40 Cal., .45 ACP
Capacity: 10 or 14 rounds
Features: Wide body frame; adjustable Anti-lash match trigger; High Ride beavertail grip safety; 4140 Chromoly steel firing pin; match extractor
MSRP . . . . $979–$1099

European American Armory

EUROPEAN AMERICAN ARMORY BOUNTY HUNTER

EUROPEAN AMERICAN ARMORY WITNESS - POLYMER

EUROPEAN AMERICAN ARMORY WITNESS COMPACT - STEEL

EUROPEAN AMERICAN ARMORY WITNESS HUNTER TANFOGLIO

BOUNTY HUNTER

Action: SA revolver
Grips: Walnut
Barrel: 4.5 in., 6.75 in., 7.5 in.
Sights: Fixed, open
Weight: 39–41 oz.
Caliber: .44 Mag., .22LR/.22 WMR, 45 LC
Capacity: 6 or 8 rounds
Features: Transfer bar safety; steel or alloy frame; blued, silver, case color, or blued/ivory finish
Nickel: . . . . $380–$515
Blued: . . . . $343–$480
Case Color: . . . . $478–$482

WITNESS

Action: Semiautomatic
Grips: Rubber
Barrel: 4.5 in.
Sights: 3-Dot
Weight: 33 oz.
Caliber: 9mm, .38 Super, .40 S&W, 10mm, .45 ACP, .45 ACP/.22 or 9mm/.22 combo
Capacity: 10+1, 15+1, or 17+1 rounds
Features: Wonder finish, windage adjustable sight; double- or single-action; polymer or steel frame; integral accessory rail
Polymer: $571
Steel: $646
Combo: $752

WITNESS COMPACT

Action: Semiautomatic
Grips: Rubber
Barrel: 3.6 in.
Sights: Adjustable
Weight: 30 oz.
Caliber: 9mm, .38 Super, .40 S&W, 10mm, .45 ACP
Capacity: 8+1, 12+1, or 14+1 rounds
Features: Wonder finish, windage adjustable sight; double- or single-action; polymer or steel frame; integral accessory rail; blued finish
Polymer: $571
Steel: $607

WITNESS HUNTER TANFOGLIO

Action: Semiautomatic
Grips: Rubber
Barrel: 6 in.
Sights: Dovetail front
Weight: 41 oz.
Caliber: 10mm, .45 ACP
Capacity: 10+1 or 15+1 rounds
Features: Single-action with over travel stop; extended manual safety; super sight; cone barrel, slide lockup; checkered non-slip frame; drilled and tapped for scope mount; auto-firing pin block
MSRP $1293

FNH USA

FNH FN FIVE-SEVEN SERIES

FNH FNS-9

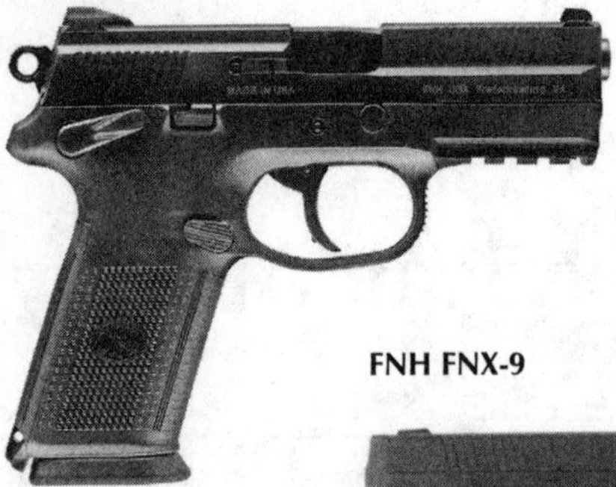

FNH FNX-9

FNH FNX-45

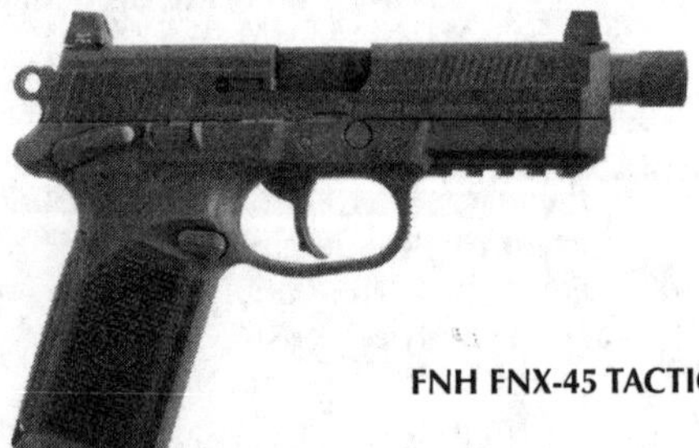

FNH FNX-45 TACTICAL

FN FIVE-SEVEN SERIES

Action: SA semiautomatic
Grips: Plastic
Barrel: 4.8 in.
Sights: Adjustable 3-dot
Weight: 20.8 oz.
Caliber: 5.7x28mm
Capacity: 10 or 20 round magazines
Features: Integrated accessory rail for mounting tactical lights or lasers; reversible magazine button; ambidextrous manual safety levers; hammer-forged, chrome lined barrel; choice of adjustable three-dot target sights or fixed C-More Systems; available with matte black, olive drab green, or flat dark earth
MSRP $1349

FNS-9/FNS-40

Action: DA semiautomatic
Grips: Polymer
Barrel: 4 in.
Sights: Night sights
Weight: 25.2 oz.
Caliber: 9mm, .40 S&W
Capacity: 17 (FNS-9) or 14 (FNS-40) rounds
Features: Striker-fired semiautomatic; manual safety levers; stainless steel slide in matte black or silver finish; external extractor with loaded chamber indicator; three-dot night sights; hammer-forged stainless steel barrel; black polymer frame; fully ambidextrous
MSRP $599
Night Sights: $649

FNX-9/FNX-40

Action: Semiautomatic
Grips: Interchangeable backstraps with lanyard eyelets
Barrel: 4 in.
Sights: 3-Dot system
Weight: 21.9 oz. (9mm), 24.4 oz. (.40)
Caliber: 9mm, .40 S&W
Capacity: 17 (9mm) or 14 (.40 S&W) rounds
Features: Ergonomic polymer black frame with low bore axis; checkered and ribbed grip panels; stainless steel slide and hammer-forged stainless barrel; DA/SA ambidextrous operating controls
MSRP . . . . $699–$749

FNX-45

Action: DA/SA Semiautomatic
Grips: Interchangeable backstraps with lanyard eyelets
Barrel: 4.5 in.
Sights: Fixed 3-dot
Weight: 33.2 oz.
Caliber: .45 ACP
Capacity: 15 rounds
Features: Polymer frame with stainless steel barrel; external extractor with loaded chamber indicator; front and rear cocking serrations; Picatinny rail; manual, ambidextrous safety; available in black or flat dark earth
MSRP $824

FNX-45 TACTICAL

Action: DA/SA semiautomatic
Grips: Textured polymer
Barrel: 5.3 in.
Sights: High-profile night sights
Weight: 33.6 oz.
Caliber: .45 ACP
Capacity: 15 rounds
Features: Stainless steel slide; external extractor with loaded chamber indicator; high-profile combat night sights; red-dot sight optional; hammer-forged stainless steel barrel; flat dark earth or black polymer frame; Picatinny rail; fully ambidextrous
MSRP $1399

Freedom Arms

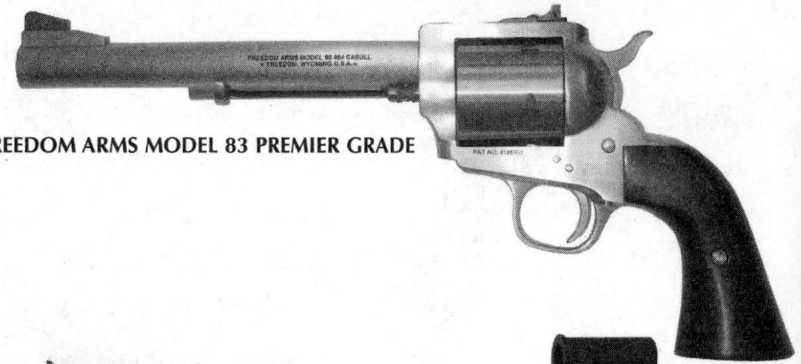

FREEDOM ARMS MODEL 83 PREMIER GRADE

MODEL 83 PREMIER GRADE

Action: SA revolver
Grips: Hardwood
Barrel: 4.75 in., 6 in., 7.5 in., 10 in.
Sights: Fixed or adjustable
Weight: 52.5 oz.
Caliber: .500 Wyoming Express, .475 Linebaugh, .454 Casull, .44 Rem. Mag., .41 Rem. Mag., .357 Mag.
Capacity: 5 rounds
Features: Adjustable sight models are drilled and tapped for scope mounts; stainless steel, brush finish and impregnated hardwood grips
MSRP . . . . $2587–$2686

FREEDOM ARMS MODEL 83 RIMFIRE

MODEL 83 RIMFIRE

Action: SA revolver
Grips: Hardwood
Barrel: 10 in.
Sights: Adjustable
Weight: 55.5 oz.
Caliber: .22LR match grade chambers
Capacity: 5 rounds
Features: Drilled and tapped for scope mounts; stainless steel frame; matte finish
MSRP $2487

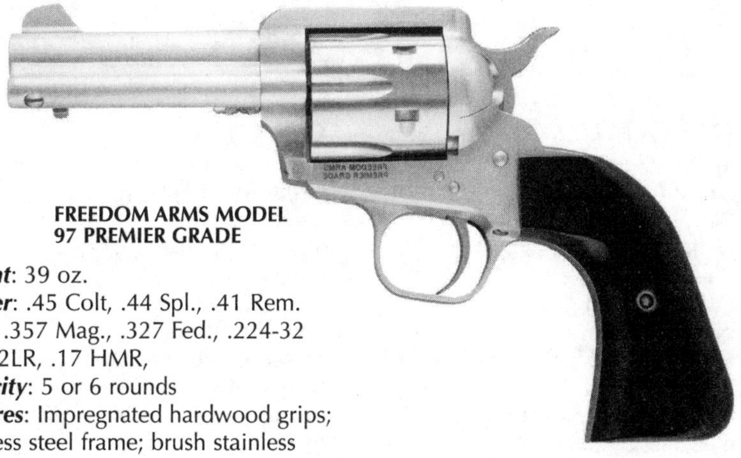

FREEDOM ARMS MODEL 97 PREMIER GRADE

MODEL 97 PREMIER GRADE

Action: SA revolver
Grips: Laminated hardwood
Barrel: 4.5 in., 5.5 in., 7.5 in., or 10 in.
Sights: Adjustable or fixed
Weight: 39 oz.
Caliber: .45 Colt, .44 Spl., .41 Rem. Mag., .357 Mag., .327 Fed., .224-32 FA, .22LR, .17 HMR,
Capacity: 5 or 6 rounds
Features: Impregnated hardwood grips; stainless steel frame; brush stainless finish
MSRP . . . . $2178–$2706

Glock

GLOCK COMPACT G19

GLOCK COMPETITION G34

COMPACT PISTOLS G19, G23, G32, G38

Action: Semiautomatic
Grips: Composite
Barrel: 4.02 in.
Sights: Fixed
Weight: 20.11–24.16 oz.
Caliber: 9mm, .40 S&W, .45 GAP, .380 Auto, .357 Mag.
Capacity: 8, 10, 13, 15 rounds
Features: Trigger safety; double-action
MSRP . . . . $614–$621

COMPETITION G34, G35

Action: Semiautomatic
Grips: Synthetic
Barrel: 5.32 in.
Sights: Adjustable
Weight: 22.92–24.5 oz.
Caliber: 9mm, .40 S&W
Capacity: 15, 17 rounds
Features: Safe action system; hexagonal barrel; right handed; extended barrel
MSRP $679

Glock

GLOCK G20 GEN4

GLOCK G21 GEN4

GLOCK G30S

GLOCK G29 GEN4

GLOCK G32 GEN4

GLOCK G33 GEN4

G20 GEN4

Action: Semiautomatic
Grips: Textured polymer
Barrel: 4.61 in.
Sights: 3-dot fixed sights
Weight: 27.51 oz.
Caliber: 10mm
Capacity: 15 rounds
Features: Full-size polymer frame; multiple backstrap frame with reduced short-frame trigger mechanism housing; three grip options; Rough Textured Frame; reversible magazine release catch; dual recoil spring
MSRP $687

G21 GEN4

Action: DAO semiautomatic
Grips: Synthetic
Barrel: 4.61 in.
Sights: Fixed
Weight: 26.28 oz.
Caliber: .45 ACP
Capacity: 13+1 rounds
Features: The GLOCK Pistol that validates the .45 ACP cartridge and its 100 year history by providing all the necessities for superb accuracy and functionality; dual recoil spring assembly and adjustable backstraps offer increased shooting comfort and control
MSRP $687

G29 GEN4

Action: Semiautomatic
Grips: Textured polymer
Barrel: 3.78 in.
Sights: 3-dot fixed sights
Weight: 24.34 oz.
Caliber: 10mm
Capacity: 10 rounds
Features: Subcompact polymer frame; trigger safety; multiple backstrap frame with reduced short-frame trigger mechanism housing; three grip options; Rough Textured Frame; reversible magazine release catch; dual recoil spring
MSRP $687

G30S

Action: Semiautomatic
Grips: Textured polymer
Barrel: 3.78 in.
Sights: White-dot front, white-outlines rear
Weight: 20.28 oz.
Caliber: .45 ACP
Capacity: 10 rounds
Features: "Slim"model built with the "Short Frame" Glock 30SF; polymer frame; dual recoil spring assembly; accessory rail; cold-hammer-forged barrel with octagonal rifling
MSRP $637

G32 GEN4

Action: DAO semiautomatic
Grips: Synthetic
Barrel: 4.02 in.
Sights: Fixed
Weight: 21.52 oz.
Caliber: .357 SIG
Capacity: 13+1 rounds
Features: The G32 is the size of the old .38 compacts with the magnum performance of the .357 SIG round without the felt recoil and 10/13/14 shots ready to fire when fully loaded
MSRP $649

G33 GEN4

Action: Semiautomatic
Grips: Textured polymer
Barrel: 3.43 in.
Sights: 3-dot fixed sights
Weight: 19.75 oz.
Caliber: .357 SIG
Capacity: 9 rounds
Features: Subcompact polymer frame; trigger safety; multiple backstrap frame with reduced short-frame trigger mechanism housing; three grip options; Rough Textured Frame; reversible magazine release catch; dual recoil spring
MSRP $599

Glock

GLOCK G34 GEN4

GLOCK G41 GEN4

GLOCK G42

GLOCK GEN4 G26

GLOCK STANDARD G17

GLOCK SUBCOMPACT G26

GLOCK SUBCOMPACT SLIMLINE G36

G34 GEN4

Action: DAO semiautomatic
Grips: Synthetic
Barrel: 5.31 in.
Sights: Fixed
Weight: 22.9 oz.
Caliber: 9mm
Capacity: 10, 17, 19 rounds
Features: This "Tactical/Practical" GLOCK 9mm is the G17 extended to the overall length of the Government Model 1911 pistols
MSRP. $729

G41 GEN4

Action: Semiautomatic
Grips: Synthetic
Barrel: 5.31 in.
Sights: Fixed
Weight: 27 oz.
Caliber: .45 ACP
Capacity: 13 rounds
Features: Safe Action system
MSRP. $729

G42

Action: Semiautomatic
Grips: Synthetic
Barrel: 3.25 in.
Sights: Fixed
Weight: 13.76 oz.
Caliber: .38 ACP
Capacity: 6 rounds
Features: Safe Action system
MSRP. $480

GEN4 G26, G27

Action: Semiautomatic
Grips: Synthetic
Barrel: 3.46 in.
Sights: Fixed or adjustable
Weight: 19.75 oz.
Caliber: 9mm, .40 S&W
Capacity: 15 rounds
Features: Rough textured frame; interchangeable backstrap system; two magazine-release catches for ambidextrous operation; dual-recoil spring system replaces the original single spring model
Fixed Sights: $649
Adjustable: $667
Steel: $671

STANDARD PISTOL G17, G20, G21, G22, G31, G37

Action: Semiautomatic
Grips: Composite
Barrel: 4.49 in.
Sights: Fixed
Weight: 22.04–27.68 oz.
Caliber: 9mm, .40 S&W, 10mm Auto, .45 GAP, .45 ACP, .380 ACP, .357 SIG
Capacity: 10, 13, 15, 17 rounds
Features: Double action; safe action trigger system; G20 model has recoil-damping Glock hi-tech polymer
MSRP. . . . . $599–$637

SUBCOMPACT PISTOLS G26, G27, G29, G30, G33,G39

Action: Semiautomatic
Grips: Composite
Barrel: 3.46–3.78 in.
Sights: Fixed
Weight: 18.66–24.69 oz.
Caliber: 9mm, .40 S&W, 10mm Auto, .45 GAP, .45 ACP, .380 ACP, .357 SIG
Capacity: 6, 9, 10 rounds
Features: Trigger safety; double-action
MSRP. . . . . $599–$637

SUBCOMPACT SLIMLINE PISTOL G36

Action: Semiautomatic
Grips: Synthetic
Barrel: 3.78 in.
Sights: Fixed
Weight: 20.11 oz.
Caliber: .45 ACP
Capacity: 6 rounds
Features: Safe action system; single stack magazine for slim grip
MSRP. $637

Hämmerli

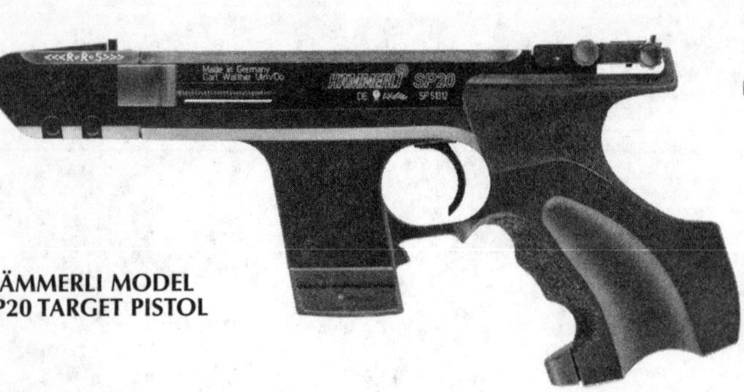

HÄMMERLI MODEL SP20 TARGET PISTOL

HÄMMERLI MODEL X-ESSE LONG

MODEL SP20 TARGET PISTOL

Action: Semiautomatic
Grips: Synthetic
Barrel: 4.86 in.
Sights: Target
Weight: 41 oz.
Caliber: .22LR, .32 S&W
Capacity: 5 rounds
Features: Front end magazine; counterweight with new recoil reduction system; various grip sizes
MSRP $1531

MODEL X-ESSE

Action: Semiautomatic
Grips: Composite
Barrel: 4.5 in., 5.9 in.
Sights: Adjustable
Weight: 27.9–31 oz.
Caliber: .22LR
Capacity: 10 rounds
Features: Single-action, two-stage trigger; universal hi-grip
MSRP $787

Heckler & Koch

HK45

Action: Semiautomatic
Grips: Polymer
Barrel: 4.53 in.
Sights: Fixed
Weight: 31 oz.
Caliber: .45 ACP
Capacity: 10 rounds
Features: DA/SA with control lever; integral Picatinny rail; ambidextrous controls with dual slide releases; modified Browning linkless recoil operating system; polygonal rifling; open square notch rear sight with contrast points; low profile drift adjustable three-dot sights
MSRP . . . . $1199–$1399

HECKLER & KOCH HK45

HECKLER & KOCH HK45 COMPACT TACTICAL

HK45 COMPACT TACTICAL

Action: DA/SA semiautomatic
Grips: Textured polymer
Barrel: 4.57 in.
Sights: 3-dot
Weight: 29.12 oz.
Caliber: .45 ACP
Capacity: 10 rounds
Features: Proprietary internal mechanical recoil reduction system; O-ring barrel; cold-hammer-forged barrel
MSRP . . . . $1399–$1499

HK45 TACTICAL

Action: Semiautomatic
Grips: Polymer with finger grooves
Barrel: 5.16 in.
Sights: 3-dot tritium night sights
Weight: 31.7 oz.
Caliber: .45 ACP
Capacity: 10 rounds
Features: Polymer frame; recoil-operated with modified Browning locking system; threaded barrel; Picatinny rail; key-based HK Lock-Out system; nine different trigger firing modes; available in black, tan, and green
MSRP . . . . $1399–$1499

HECKLER & KOCH HK45 TACTICAL

Heckler & Koch

HECKLER & KOCH MARK 23

HECKLER & KOCH P30

HECKLER & KOCH P30 L

HECKLER & KOCH P2000

HECKLER & KOCH USP COMPACT

HECKLER & KOCH USP

MARK 23

Action: Semiautomatic
Grips: Polymer
Barrel: 5.9 in.
Sights: 3-Dot
Weight: 39.4 oz.
Caliber: .45 ACP
Capacity: 12+1 rounds
Features: Threaded O-ring barrel with polygonal bore profile; match grade trigger; one piece machined steel slide; frame mounted decocking lever and separate ambidextrous safety lever; HK recoil reduction system; ambidextrous magazine release lever
MSRP $2299

P30

Action: Semiautomatic
Grips: Polymer
Barrel: 3.86 in.
Sights: Fixed
Weight: 26.08 oz.
Caliber: 9mm, .40 S&W
Capacity: 15 rounds
Features: Corrosion proof fiber-reinforced polymer frame; multiple trigger firing modes; HK recoil reduction system; blued finish; Picatinny rail; ambidextrous magazine release levers and side release
MSRP $1099

P30 L

Action: Semiautomatic
Grips: Polymer
Barrel: 4.4 in.
Sights: Fixed
Weight: 27.5 oz.
Caliber: 9mm, .40 S&W
Capacity: 10, 13, or 15 rounds
Features: Interchangeable backstraps and side panel grips in small, medium, and large sizes; ambidextrous slide and magazine releases levers; integral Picatinny rail; modular design allows DA trigger or DA/SA system, with a decocking button
MSRP $1149

P2000 & P2000 SK

Action: Semiautomatic
Grips: Polymer
Barrel: 3.26–3.66 in.
Sights: 3-Dot
Weight: 23.8–25.9 oz.
Caliber: 9mm, .40 S&W, .357 SIG
Capacity: 9–13 rounds
Features: LEM trigger system; double-action; pre-cock hammer; ambidextrous magazine release and interchangeable grip straps; mounting rail
P2000: $999
P2000 SK: $1049

USP

Action: Semiautomatic
Grips: Polymer
Barrel: 4.25–4.41 in.
Sights: 3-Dot
Weight: 27.2–31.36 oz.
Caliber: 9mm, .40 S&W, .45 ACP
Capacity: 12, 13, 15 rounds
Features: Browning-type action with a patented recoil reduction system; double and single action modes; available in nine trigger/firing mode configurations; fiber-reinforced polymer frame; blued finish; ambidextrous magazine release trigger
MSRP . . . . $979–$1149

USP COMPACT

Action: Semiautomatic
Grips: Polymer
Barrel: 3.58–3.80 in.
Sights: Fixed
Weight: 25.6–28.2 oz.
Caliber: 9mm, .40 S&W, .45 ACP
Capacity: 8, 12, 13 rounds
Features: Corrosion proof fiber-reinforced polymer frame; ambidextrous magazine release lever; grooved target triggers; can be converted to any of nine trigger firing modes
MSRP . . . . $999–$1199

Heritage Manufacturing

ROUGH RIDER BIG BORE

Action: SA revolver
Grips: Cocobolo wood
Barrel: 4.5 in., 5.5 in., 7.5 in.
Sights: Fixed, open
Weight: 38 oz.
Caliber: .357 SIG, .45 ACP
Capacity: 6 rounds
Features: Patterned after 1873 Colt; blued, nickel, stainless and blued/color-case-hardened finishes are available; frame mounted inertia firing pin and transfer bar
MSRP.................... $467

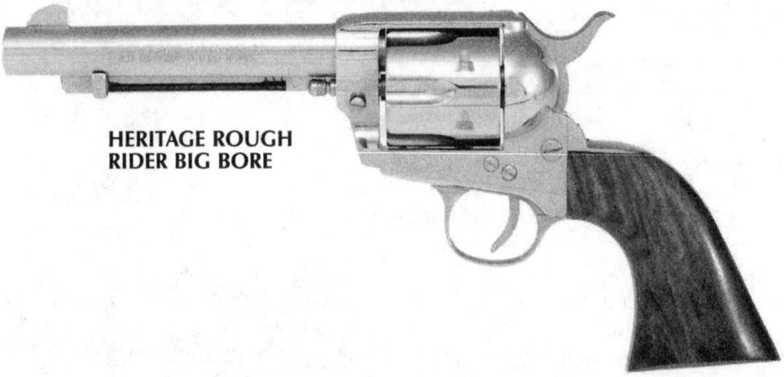

HERITAGE ROUGH RIDER BIG BORE

ROUGH RIDER SMALL BORE

Action: SA revolver
Grips: Cocobolo wood
Barrel: 3.5 in., 4.75 in., 6.5 in., 9 in.
Sights: Fixed
Weight: 31 oz.
Caliber: .22LR, .22 Mag.
Capacity: 6 rounds
Features: Machined barrel is micro-threaded; optional cocobolo grips include white mother of pearl, black mother of pearl, or green camo laminate grips; frame finish comes in smooth silver satin, deep matte black, low gloss black satin or case-hardened finish
MSRP................ $195–$350

HERITAGE ROUGH RIDER SMALL BORE

High Standard

OLYMPIC

Action: Semiautomatic
Grips: Cocobolo wood
Barrel: 5.5 in.
Sights: Adjustable
Weight: 44 oz.
Caliber: .22 Short
Capacity: 10+1 rounds
Features: Lightweight aluminum alloy slide; precision carbon steel frame; drilled and tapped for scopes; single-action
MSRP................... $1050

HIGH STANDARD OLYMPIC

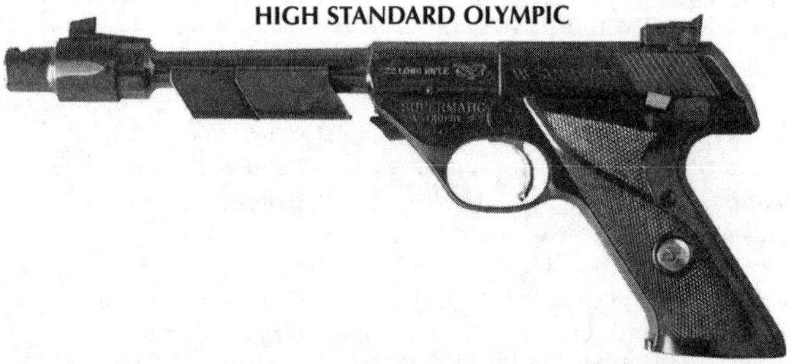

SUPERMATIC CITATION

Action: Semiautomatic
Grips: Walnut
Barrel: 5.5 in.
Sights: Adjustable
Weight: 44 oz.
Caliber: .22LR
Capacity: 10+1 rounds
Features: Durable parkerized finish and black epoxy-finished wood; ambidextrous grips; drilled and tapped for scopes
MSRP.................... $975

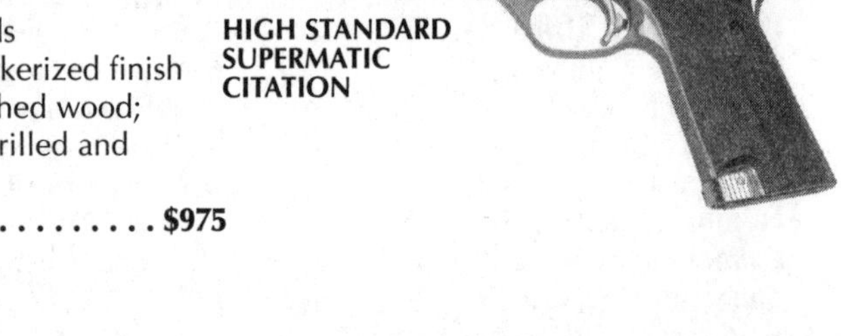

HIGH STANDARD SUPERMATIC CITATION

High Standard

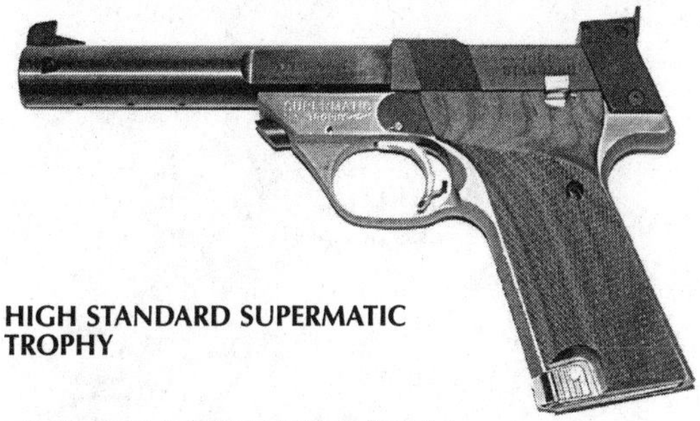

HIGH STANDARD SUPERMATIC TROPHY

HIGH STANDARD US MODEL 1911 CUSTOM

HIGH STANDARD VICTOR

SUPERMATIC TROPHY

Action: Semiautomatic
Grips: Walnut
Barrel: 5.5 in., 7.25 in.
Sights: Adjustable
Weight: 44 oz.–46 oz.
Caliber: .22LR
Capacity: 10+1 rounds
Features: Features gold plated components: trigger, safety, slide stop and magazine catch; adjustable trigger; checkered deluxe grips; blued finish
MSRP . . . .$1050–$1100

US MODEL 1911 CUSTOM

Action: Semiautomatic
Grips: Walnut
Barrel: 5 in.
Sights: Novak style adjustable
Weight: 40 oz.
Caliber: .45 ACP
Capacity: 7+1 rounds
Features: Beveled magazine well; match trigger with overtravel stop; available in stainless steel, blued or parkerized finish
MSRP $1150

VICTOR

Action: Semiautomatic
Grips: Walnut
Barrel: 4.5 in., 5.5 in.
Sights: Adjustable
Weight: 45 oz.
Caliber: .22LR
Capacity: 10+1 rounds
Features: Removable aluminum rib; drilled and tapped for scopes; optional slide conversion kit for .22 short; various customization options
MSRP $1050

Hi-Point Firearms

HI-POINT FIREARMS MODEL C-9 9MM

HI-POINT FIREARMS MODEL JHP45 ACP

HI-POINT FIREARMS MODEL CF-380

MODEL C-9 9MM

Action: Semiautomatic
Grips: Polymer
Barrel: 3.5 in.
Sights: 3-Dots adjustable
Weight: 29 oz.
Caliber: 9mm
Capacity: 8 or 10 rounds
Features: Polymer frame; last round lock open; quick on-off thumb safety; free trigger lock; free extra peep sight; black finish
MSRP $189

MODEL CF-380

Action: Semiautomatic
Grips: Polymer
Barrel: 3.5 in.
Sights: 3-Dots adjustable
Weight: 29 oz.
Caliber: .380 ACP
Capacity: 8 or 10 rounds
Features: High-impact polymer frame; black powder coat with chrome rail; durable, easy-grip finish; quick on-off thumb safety; free extra rear peep sight
MSRP $151

MODEL JHP45 ACP & JCP 40 S&W

Action: Semiautomatic
Grips: Polymer
Barrel: 4.5 in.
Sights: 3-Dots adjustable
Weight: 35 oz.
Caliber: .40 S&W, .45 ACP
Capacity: 10 rounds
Features: Polymer frame; quick on-off thumb safety; operations safety sheet; +P rated; free extra rear peep sight; free trigger lock; black finish; available with laserlyte laser and green slide
MSRP $199

Kahr Arms

KAHR ARMS CM9

KAHR ARMS CM40

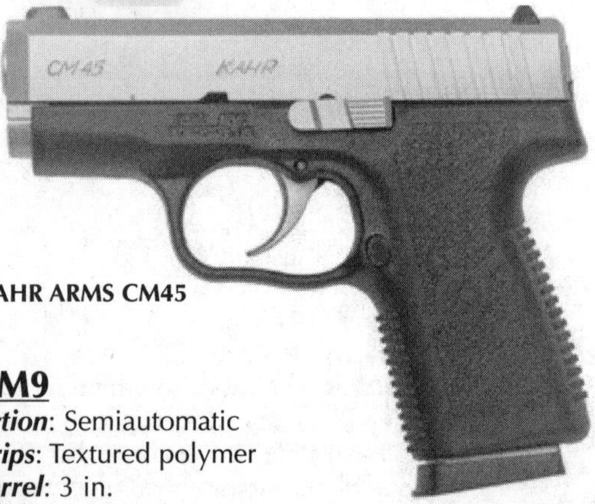

KAHR ARMS CM45

KAHR ARMS CT40

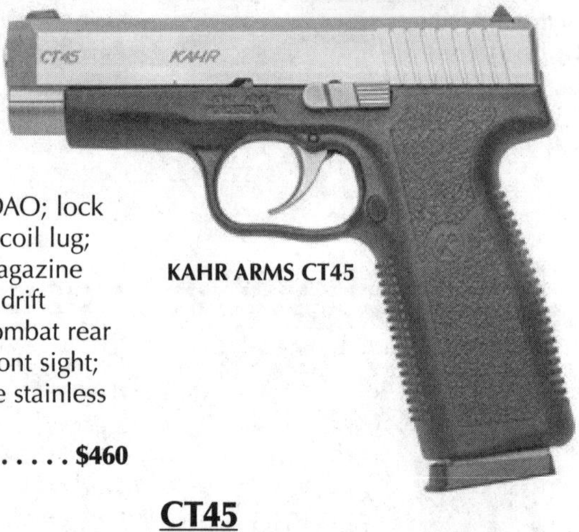

KAHR ARMS CT45

CM9

Action: Semiautomatic
Grips: Textured polymer
Barrel: 3 in.
Sights: Adjustable
Weight: 15.9 oz.
Caliber: 9mm
Capacity: 6+1 rounds
Features: Trigger cocking double-action; lock breech; Browning-type recoil lug; passive striker block; no magazine disconnect; drift adjustable, white bar-dot combat sights; black finish; matte stainless steel slide
MSRP. $460

CM40

Action: Semiautomatic
Grips: Textured polymer
Barrel: 3 in.
Sights: Adjustable
Weight: 17.7 oz.
Caliber: .40 S&W
Capacity: 5+1 rounds
Features: Trigger cocking DAO; lock breech; “Browning-type” recoil lug; passive striker block; no magazine disconnect; black polymer frame, matte stainless steel slide
MSRP. $460

CM45

Action: DAO semiautomatic
Grips: Synthetic
Barrel: 3.24 in.
Sights: Fixed
Weight: 17.3 oz.
Caliber: .45 ACP
Capacity: 5+1 rounds
Features: Trigger cocking DAO; lock breech; "Browning-type" recoil lug; passive striker block; no magazine disconnect; textured grips; drift adjustable white bar-dot combat rear sight; pinned in polymer front sight; black polymer frame, matte stainless steel slide
MSRP. $460

CT40

Action: DAO semiautomatic
Grips: Synthetic
Barrel: 4 in.
Sights: Fixed
Weight: 21.8 oz.
Caliber: .40 S&W
Capacity: 7+1 rounds
Features: Trigger cocking DAO; lock breech; "Browning-type" recoil lug; passive striker block; no magazine disconnect; textured grips; drift adjustable white bar-dot combat rear sight; pinned in polymer front sight; black polymer frame, matte stainless steel slide
MSRP. $449

CT45

Action: DAO semiautomatic
Grips: Synthetic
Barrel: 4.04 in.
Sights: Fixed
Weight: 23.7 oz.
Caliber: .45 ACP
Capacity: 7+1 rounds
Features: Trigger cocking DAO; lock breech; "Browning-type" recoil lug; passive striker block; no magazine disconnect; textured grips; drift adjustable white bar-dot combat rear sight; pinned in polymer front sight; black polymer frame, matte stainless steel slide
MSRP. $449

Kahr Arms

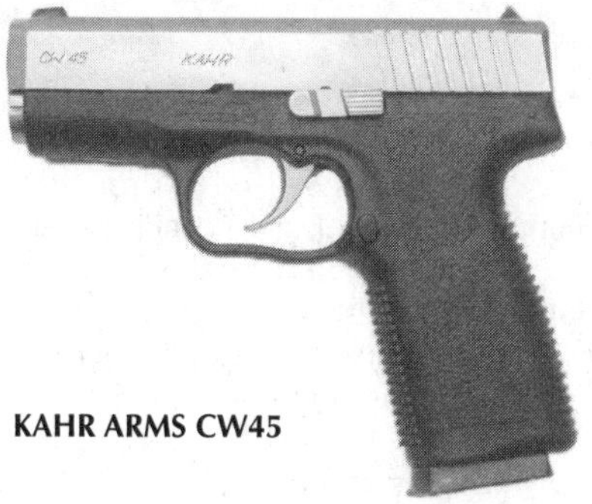

KAHR ARMS CW45

CW45

Action: Semiautomatic
Grips: Textured polymer
Barrel: 3.64 in.
Sights: Adjustable
Weight: 21.7 oz.
Caliber: .45 ACP
Capacity: 6+1 rounds
Features: Trigger cocking double-action; lock breech; Browning-type recoil lug; passive striker block; no magazine disconnect; drift adjustable, white bar-dot combat rear sight, pinned in polymer front sight; black finish; matte stainless steel slide
MSRP. $449

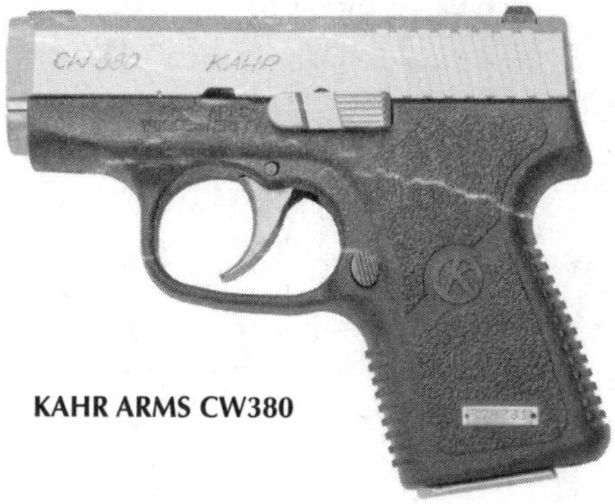

KAHR ARMS CW380

CW380

Action: DAO semiautomatic
Grips: Black polymer
Barrel: 2.58 in.
Sights: Adjustable white bar-dot combat rear, pinned in polymer front
Weight: 10.2 oz.
Caliber: .380 ACP
Capacity: 6+1 rounds
Features: Lock breech; modified Browning type recoil lug; "safe cam" action; conventional rifled barrel; metal-injection-molded slide stop lever; slide lock after last round; black and stainless matte finish
MSRP. $419

KAHR ARMS P9 SERIES

P9 SERIES

Action: Semiautomatic
Grips: Textured polymer
Barrel: 3.6 in.
Sights: Adjustable
Weight: 16.9 oz.
Caliber: 9mm
Capacity: 7+1 rounds
Features: Trigger cocking DAO; lock breech; Browning-type recoil lug; passive striker block; no magazine disconnect; black polymer frame; model available with external safety and LCI
MSRP. $762

KAHR ARMS P40 SERIES

P40 SERIES

Action: Semiautomatic
Grips: Textured polymer
Barrel: 3.6 in.
Sights: Adjustable
Weight: 18.7 oz.
Caliber: .40 S&W
Capacity: 6+1 rounds
Features: Trigger cocking DAO; lock breech; Browning-type recoil lug; passive striker block; no magazine disconnect; black polymer frame
P40: $762
P40 w/ Night Sights:. $883

Kahr Arms

P45 SERIES

Action: Semiautomatic
Grips: Textured polymer
Barrel: 3.54 in.
Sights: Adjustable
Weight: 18.5 oz.
Caliber: .45 ACP
Capacity: 5+1 or 6+1 rounds
Features: Trigger cocking DAO; lock breech; Browning-type recoil lug; passive striker block; no magazine disconnect; black polymer frame
P45: $829
P45 w/ Night Sights: $949
P45 Black: $880
P45 Black w/ Night sights: $999

P380 SERIES

Action: Semiautomatic
Grips: Textured polymer
Barrel: 2.5 in.
Sights: Adjustable
Weight: 11.27 oz.
Caliber: .380 ACP
Capacity: 6+1 rounds
Features: Trigger cocking DAO; Lock breech; Browning-type recoil lug; passive striker block; no magazine disconnect; black polymer frame, matte stainless steel slide; premium Lothar Walther match grade barrel; available in Black Rose and with night sights or LCI
MSRP $667

PM9 SERIES

Action: Semiautomatic
Grips: Textured polymer
Barrel: 3 in.
Sights: Adjustable
Weight: 15.9 oz.
Caliber: 9mm
Capacity: 6+1 or 7+1 rounds
Features: Trigger cocking DAO; lock breech; Browning-type recoil lug; passive striker block; no magazine disconnect; black polymer frame; available in Black Rose, with night sights, LCI, and an external safety
MSRP . . . . $810–$997

PM40 - EXTERNAL SAFETY & LCI

Action: Semiautomatic
Grips: Textured polymer
Barrel: 3 in.
Sights: Adjustable
Weight: 17.7 oz.
Caliber: .40 S&W
Capacity: 5+1 or 6+1 rounds
Features: Trigger cocking DAO; lock breech; "Browning-type" recoil lug; passive striker block; no magazine disconnect; black polymer frame, matte stainless steel slide; drift adjustable, white bar-dot combat sights (tritium night sights, Crimson Trace laser sight optional)
MSRP $810

PM45 SERIES

Action: Semiautomatic
Grips: Textured polymer
Barrel: 3.24 in.
Sights: Adjustable
Weight: 19.3 oz.
Caliber: .45 ACP
Capacity: 6+1 rounds
Features: Trigger cocking double action; lock breech; Browning-type recoil lug; passive striker block; no magazine disconnect; drift adjustable, white bar-dot combat sights; black polymer frame, matte blackened stainless steel slide; available with night sights or CT laser sight
MSRP $880

KAHR ARMS P45 BLACK WITH NIGHT SIGHTS

KAHR ARMS P380

KAHR ARMS PM9 SERIES

KAHR ARMS PM40 WITH EXTERNAL SAFETY & LCI

KAHR ARMS PM45

Kel-Tec

KEL-TEC P-3AT

KEL-TEC P-11

KEL-TEC P-32

KEL-TEC PF-9

KEL-TEC PMR-30

P-3AT

Action: Semiautomatic
Grips: Polymer
Barrel: 2.7 in.
Sights: Fixed
Weight: 8.3 oz.
Caliber: .380 ACP
Capacity: 6+1 rounds
Features: Double-action only; steel barrel and slide; aluminum frame; transfer bar
MSRP: $338

P-11

Action: Semiautomatic
Grips: Polymer
Barrel: 3.1 in.
Sights: Fixed
Weight: 14 oz.
Caliber: 9mm
Capacity: 10+1 rounds, optional 12 rounds
Features: Double-action only; steel barrel and slide; aluminum frame; locked breech; high-impact polymer DuPont grips
MSRP: $347

P-32

Action: Semiautomatic
Grips: Polymer
Barrel: 2.7 in.
Sights: Fixed
Weight: 6.6 oz.
Caliber: .32 ACP
Capacity: 7+1 rounds
Features: Steel barrel and slide; locked breech mechanism
MSRP: $325

PF-9

Action: Semiautomatic
Grips: Polymer
Barrel: 3.1 in.
Sights: Adjustable
Weight: 12.7 oz.
Caliber: 9mm
Capacity: 7+1 rounds
Features: Firing mechanism is double-action only with an automatic hammer block safety; grips available in black, grey, and olive drab; rear sight is a new design and is adjustable for windage
MSRP: $356

PMR-30

Action: SA Semiautomatic
Grips: Nylon
Barrel: 4.3 in.
Sights: Picatinny accessory rail under barrel
Weight: 13.6 oz.
Caliber: .22 WMR
Capacity: 30 rounds
Features: Blowback/locked breech system; lightweight but full sized; urethane recoil buffer; disassembles for cleaning with removal of one pin
MSRP: $455

Kimber

CLASSIC CARRY PRO

Action: SA semiautomatic
Grips: Bone
Barrel: 4 in.
Sights: Fixed low-profile, 3-dot
Weight: 35 oz.
Caliber: .45 ACP
Capacity: 8 rounds
Features: Deep charcoal blued finish; steel frame and slide; match grade bull barrel; serrated flat top slide; night sights; front strap checkering
MSRP $2056

COMPACT STAINLESS II

Action: Semiautomatic
Grips: Black synthetic double diamond
Barrel: 4 in.
Sights: Fixed, low profile
Weight: 27 oz.
Caliber: .45 ACP
Capacity: 7 rounds
Features: Full-length guide rod; aluminum frame in satin silver finish; steel Match Grade barrel; aluminum match grade trigger
MSRP $1052

CUSTOM II

Action: Semiautomatic
Grips: Black synthetic double diamond
Barrel: 5 in.
Sights: Fixed, low profile
Weight: 38 oz.
Caliber: .45 ACP
Capacity: 7 rounds
Features: Full-length guide rod; aluminum frame in matte black finish; steel Match Grade barrel; aluminum match grade trigger
MSRP $871

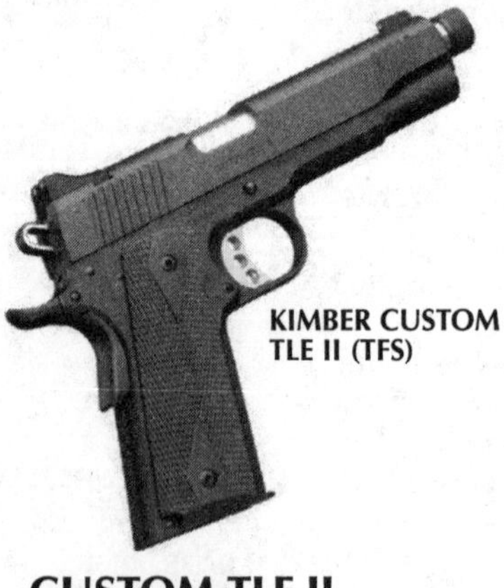

CUSTOM TLE II (TFS)

Action: Semiautomatic
Grips: Synthetic
Barrel: 5 in.
Sights: Fixed
Weight: 39 oz.
Caliber: .45 ACP, 9mm
Capacity: 7 rounds
Features: Threaded for suppression; Meprolight Tritium 3-dot night sight
MSRP $1153

CUSTOM TLE/RL II (TFS)

Action: Semiautomatic
Grips: Synthetic
Barrel: 5 in.
Sights: Fixed
Weight: 39 oz.
Caliber: .45 ACP, 9mm
Capacity: 7 rounds
Features: Threaded for suppression; Meprolight Tritium 3-dot night sight; Picatinny rail
MSRP $1326

ECLIPSE ULTRA II

Action: Semiautomatic
Grips: Laminated double diamond
Barrel: 3 in.
Sights: Meprolight Tritium 3-dot night, fixed
Weight: 38 oz.
Caliber: .45 ACP
Capacity: 7 rounds
Features: Full-length guide rod; stainless steel frame with brush polished finish; stainless steel slide; Match Grade steel barrel; aluminum Match Grade trigger
MSRP $1589

KIMBER GOLD MATCH II

KIMBER MASTER CARRY

KIMBER MICRO CARRY

KIMBER SAPPHIRE ULTRA II

KIMBER SOLO CARRY

KIMBER SOLO CDP (LG)

GOLD MATCH II

Action: Semiautomatic
Grips: Rosewood double diamond
Barrel: 5 in.
Sights: Kimber adjustable
Weight: 38 oz.
Caliber: .45 ACP
Capacity: 8 rounds
Features: Premium aluminum, Match Grade trigger; full length guide rod; steel frame with highly polished blued finish; stainless steel, Match Grade barrel
MSRP $1393

MASTER CARRY

Action: Semiautomatic
Grips: Crimson Trace Lasergrips
Barrel: 3in. (Ultra), 5 in.
Sights: Fixed low profile
Weight: 25 oz.–31 oz.
Caliber: .45 ACP
Capacity: 7 or 8 rounds
Features: Aluminum, round-heel frame; satin silver finish; dovetailed night sights; recessed slide-stop pin; serrated mainspring housing; stainless steel slide; available in a Custom model, Pro, or Ultra
MSRP $1568

MICRO CARRY

Action: Semiautomatic
Grips: Black synthetic or Rosewood, double diamond
Barrel: 2.75 in.
Sights: Fixed low profile
Weight: 13.4 oz.
Caliber: .380 ACP
Capacity: 6 rounds
Features: Aluminum frame; stainless steel barrel; dovetailed sights; single-side thumb safety; available in black, stainless, CDP, and CDP with Crimson Trace Lasergrips
MSRP $651
Stainless: $679
CDP: $951
CDP Lasergrips: $1210

SAPPHIRE ULTRA II

Action: SA semiautomatic
Grips: G-10 thin grips
Barrel: 3 in.
Sights: Tactical Wedge night sights
Weight: 25 oz.
Caliber: 9mm
Capacity: 8 rounds
Features: Highly-polished stainless steel slide and small parts are finished with bright blue PVD finish accented with fine engraving; blue/black ball-milled G-10 thin grips and short trigger; ambidextrous thumb safety; Tactical Wedge night sights
MSRP $1652

SOLO CARRY

Action: SA semiautomatic
Grips: Black synthetic checkered/smooth
Barrel: 2.7 in.
Sights: Fixed low profile
Weight: 17 oz.
Caliber: 9mm
Capacity: 6 rounds
Features: Aluminum finish frame; stainless steel barrel; single-action striker trigger
MSRP $815

SOLO CDP (LG)

Action: SA striker-fired
Grips: Synthetic, rosewood finish
Barrel: 2.7 in.
Sights: Fixed 3-dot night sights
Weight: 17 oz.
Caliber: 9mm
Capacity: 6, 8 rounds
Features: Single-action striker-fired trigger system; Crimson Trace Lasergrips; Carry Melt treatment to round endges; black KimPro II frame finish; checkering on front and back straps
MSRP $1223

Kimber

STAINLESS PRO RAPTOR II

Action: SA semiautomatic
Grips: Zebra wood, scale pattern
Barrel: 4 in.
Sights: Tactical wedge 3-dot
Weight: 35 oz.
Caliber: .45 ACP
Capacity: 8 rounds
Features: Stainless steel slide and frame with satin silver finish; Match Grade barrel; ambidextrous thumb safety; full-length guide rod
MSRP. $1434

STAINLESS PRO TLE II (LG)

Action: SA semiautomatic
Grips: Tactical gray double diamond, Crimson Trace lasergrips
Barrel: 4 in.
Sights: Meprolight tritium 3-dot night, fixed
Weight: 35 oz.
Caliber: .45 ACP
Capacity: 7 rounds
Features: Full-length guide rod; stainless steel frame with satin silver; Match Grade steel barrel; aluminum Match Grade trigger
MSRP. $1518

STAINLESS ULTRA TLE II

Action: SA semiautomatic
Grips: Tactical gray double diamond
Barrel: 3 in.
Sights: Meprolight tritium 3-dot night, fixed
Weight: 25 oz.
Caliber: .45 ACP
Capacity: 7 rounds
Features: Full-length guide rod; front strap checkering; aluminum frame with satin silver finish; steel match grade barrel; aluminum match grade trigger
MSRP. $1253

SUPER CARRY PRO

Action: SA SA semiautomatic
Grips: Micarta/ laminated rosewood
Barrel: 4 in.
Sights: Night, tritium
Weight: 28 oz.
Caliber: .45 ACP
Capacity: 8 rounds
Features: Ambidextrous thumb safety; carry melt; full-length guide rod; aluminum frame in satin silver; super carry serrations; high cut under trigger guard; steel Match Grade barrel; aluminum Match Grade trigger
MSRP. $1596

TACTICAL ENTRY II

Action: SA semiautomatic
Grips: Laminated double diamond, Kimber logo
Barrel: 5 in.
Sights: Meprolight tritium 3-dot night, fixed
Weight: 40 oz.
Caliber: .45 ACP
Capacity: 7 rounds
Features: Ambidextrous thumb safety; full-length guide rod; stainless steel frame and slide; matte gray Kim Pro II frame finish
**MSRP. . . . .
$1317**

ULTRA CARRY II

Action: SA semiautomatic
Grips: Black synthetic double diamond
Barrel: 3 in.
Sights: Fixed, low profile
Weight: 25 oz.
Caliber: .45 ACP
Capacity: 7 rounds
Features: Black matte finish; aluminum frame; steel slide; full-length guide rod
MSRP. $919

KIMBER STAINLESS PRO RAPTOR II

KIMBER STAINLESS PRO TLE II (LG)

KIMBER STAINLESS ULTRA TLE II

KIMBER TACTICAL ENTRY II

KIMBER SUPER CARRY PRO

KIMBER ULTRA CARRY II

Kimber

KIMBER ULTRA CDP II

KIMBER ULTRA CRIMSON CARRY II

KIMBER WARRIOR SOC

ULTRA CDP II

Action: Semiautomatic
Grips: Rosewood double diamond
Barrel: 3 in.
Sights: Meprolight tritium 3-dot night, fixed
Weight: 25 oz.
Caliber: .45 ACP
Capacity: 7 rounds
Features: Ambidextrous thumb safety; full-length guide rod; matte black Kim Pro frame finish; aluminum frame; stainless steel slide and barrel; Match Grade trigger
MSRP. 1331

ULTRA CRIMSON CARRY II

Action: SA semiautomatic
Grips: Rosewood double diamond, Crimson Trace lasergrips
Barrel: 3 in.
Sights: Fixed low profile
Weight: 25 oz.
Caliber: .45 ACP
Capacity: 7 rounds
Features: Full-length guide rod; aluminum frame in satin silver finish; steel Match Grade barrel; aluminum Match Grade trigger
MSRP. $1206

WARRIOR SOC

Action: Semiautomatic
Grips: Kimber G10
Barrel: 5 in.
Sights: Fixed tactical wedge tritium night sights, desert tan Crimson Trace Rail Master laser sight
Weight: 39 oz.
Caliber: .45 ACP
Capacity: 7 rounds
Features: Steel frame; front and rear slide serrations; Picatinny rail; ambidextrous thumb safety; checkered front strap; stainless steel barrel and bushing; beavertail grip; KimPro II dark green finish
MSRP. $1665

Kriss USA

SPHINX SDP COMPACT ALPHA

Action: DA/SA semiautomatic
Grips: Composite
Barrel: 3.7 in.
Sights: Fiber optic/tritium front, tritium rear
Weight: 27.5 oz.
Caliber: 9mm
Capacity: 15+1 rounds
Features: Upper frame machined from aeronautic-grade hard-anodized aluminum; integral recoil buffer; Picatinny rail; polymer lower frame; interchangeable grip sizes available; Defiance sights feature fiber optic/tritium day-night green front sight with tritium two-dot red rear sight; internal firing pin safety, drop safety, hammer safety, and integrated slide-position safety
MSRP. $1295

KRISS USA SPHINX SDP COMPACT ALPHA

Magnum Research

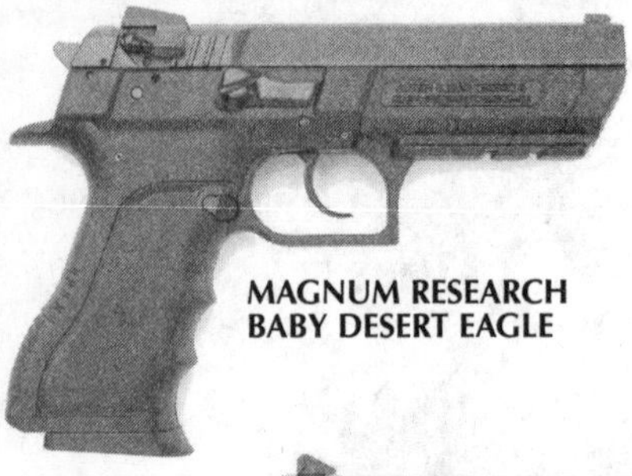

MAGNUM RESEARCH BABY DESERT EAGLE

MAGNUM RESEARCH BFR

MAGNUM RESEARCH DESERT EAGLE 1911

MAGNUM RESEARCH MARK XIX DESERT EAGLE

MAGNUM RESEARCH DESERT EAGLE 1911U "UNDERCOVER"

MAGNUM RESEARCH MR EAGLE

BABY DESERT EAGLE

Action: Semiautomatic
Grips: Plastic composite
Barrel: 3.64 in., 3.93 in., 4.52 in.
Sights: 3-Dot combat
Weight: 26.8–38.6 oz.
Caliber: 9mm, .40 S&W, .45 ACP
Capacity: 10, 12, 13, 15 rounds
Features: Black steel or polymer frame; slide safety; decocker; double and single action; polygonal rifling; Picatinny rail; available in full-size, compact, and semi-compact
Polymer: $646
Steel: $691

BFR (BIG FRAME REVOLVER)

Action: SA revolver
Grips: Rubber, optional wood
Barrel: 5 in., 6.5 in., 7.5 in., 10 in.
Sights: Adjustable rear, fixed front
Weight: 57.6–85 oz.
Caliber: Long Cylinder: .30-30 Win., .444 Marlin, .45 LC/.410, .45-70 Govt., .450 Marlin, .44 Mag., .460 S&W Mag., .500 S&W Mag.; Short Cylinder: .22 Hornet, .454 Casull, .480 Ruger/.475 Linebaugh, .50AE
Capacity: 5 rounds
Features: Both long and short-cylinder models are made of stainless steel; barrels are stress-relieved and cut rifled; current production revolvers are shipped with rubber grips and Weaver style scope mount
MSRP $1184

DESERT EAGLE 1911

Action: SA semiautomatic
Grips: Checkered wood
Barrel: 5 in., 4.3 in.
Sights: Fixed
Weight: 36 oz. (5 in. barrel), 32 oz. (4.3 in. barrel)
Caliber: .45 ACP
Capacity: 8 rounds
Features: Grip safety; extended thumb safety; blued finish
MSRP . . . . $831–$1120

DESERT EAGLE 1911U "UNDERCOVER"

Action: Semiautomatic
Grips: Wood
Barrel: 3 in.
Sights: Adjustable
Weight: 25.8 oz.
Caliber: .45 ACP
Capacity: 6+1 rounds
Features: Ultra lightweight frame made of aircraft grade aluminum alloy; 4140 high carbon steel slide; adjustable rear sight for windage and elevation
MSRP $946

MARK XIX DESERT EAGLE

Action: Semiautomatic
Grips: Plastic composite
Barrel: 6 in., 10 in.
Sights: Fixed combat
Weight: 62.4–71.4 oz.
Caliber: .357 Mag., .44 Mag., .50AE
Capacity: 7, 8, 9 rounds
Features: Gas operated; polygonal rifling; integral scope bases; many finishes available, including: black oxide, brushed/matte/polished chrome, bright/satin nickel, 24K gold, titanium gold, and titanium gold with tiger stripes
MSRP . . . . $1710–$2195

MR EAGLE

Action: Semiautomatic
Grips: Black polymer
Barrel: 4 in. (9mm), 4.15 in. (.40 S&W)
Sights: Adjustable rear, fixed front
Weight: 24.8 oz. (9mm), 26.4 oz. (.40 S&W)
Caliber: 9mm or .40 S&W
Capacity: 10, 15 rounds (9mm), 10, 11 rounds (.40 S&W)
Features: 6-groove filing; hammer forged barrel; full Picatinny rail; ergonomic polymer grip frame; four separate safety devices
MSRP $559

MG Arms

MG ARMS WRAITHE

WRAITHE

Action: Semiautomatic
Grips: Custom G10
Barrel: 4.5 in.
Sights: Night or fixed
Weight: 18 oz.–20 oz.
Caliber: .45 ACP, 9mm
Capacity: 8+1, 9+1 rounds
Features: Aluminum alloy bobtail frame; custom grip panels; high ride beavertail safety; two Wilson magazines included, available in olive drab, black or desert tan
MSRP $2750

MOA

MAXIMUM

Action: Hinged breech
Grips: Walnut
Barrel: 8.5 in., 10.5 in., 14 in.
Sights: Adjustable, open
Weight: 56–67 oz.
Caliber: most rifle chamberings from .22 Hornet to .375 H&H
Capacity: single-shot
Features: Falling block action; free floating barrel; multiple length barrels; receiver tapped for scope mounts
MSRP $1062

MOA MAXIMUM
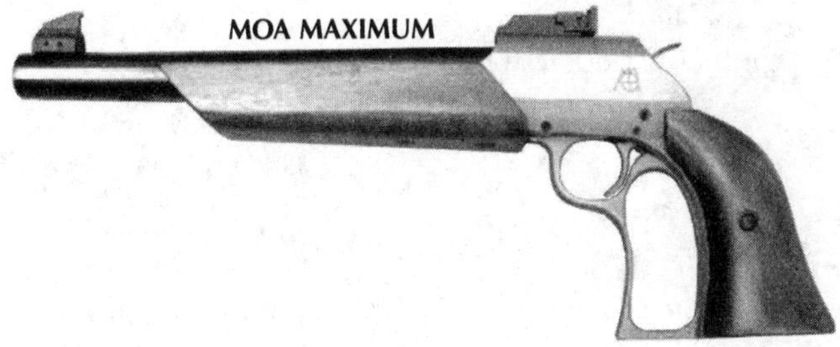

Mossberg

MOSSBERG 715P

715P

Action: Semiautomatic
Grips: Synthetic
Barrel: 6 in.
Sights: Adjustable
Weight: 48 oz.
Caliber: .22LR
Capacity: 11–26 rounds
Features: Muzzle brake; adjustable front and rear sights; blued finish; available with red dot sight and with Realtree Max-5 camo
MSRP . . . . $308–$447

Nighthawk Custom

NIGHTHAWK CUSTOM BOB MARVEL CUSTOM

BOB MARVEL CUSTOM

Action: Semiautomatic
Grips: Custom Mil Tac
Barrel: 4.25 in.
Sights: Novak tritium night sight front, tritium adjustable rear
Weight: 38 oz.
Caliber: 9mm, .45 ACP
Capacity: 8+1 rounds
Features: Incorporates new Nighthawk/Marvel Everlast Recoil System allowing for at least 10,000 rounds before a spring change is necessary and reduced recoil and muzzle flip
MSRP $3995

NIGHTHAWK CUSTOM GLOBAL RESPONSE PISTOL

NIGHTHAWK CUSTOM HEINIE SIGNATURE RECON

NIGHTHAWK CUSTOM T4

NIGHTHAWK CUSTOM T3

GLOBAL RESPONSE PISTOL (GRP)

Action: SA Semiautomatic
Grips: Micarta gator grips
Barrel: 5 in.
Sights: Night
Weight: 39 oz.
Caliber: .45 ACP, 10mm, 9mm
Capacity: 8 rounds
Features: 1911 design; Lanyard loop integrated into the mainspring housing; forged slide stop axle is cut flush with the frame; Heinie Slant-Pro Night Sights, Novak Low Mount Night Sights, or Novak Extreme Duty Adjustable Night Sights are standard; Perma Kote finish in black, sniper gray, green, coyote tan, titanium blued, and hard chrome
MSRP $2995

HEINIE SIGNATURE COMPACT, RECON

Action: Semiautomatic
Grips: Thin proprietary G10
Barrel: 4.25 in., 5 in.
Sights: Tritium front night sight, Heinie Slant-Pro Rear
Weight: 38 oz.–40 oz.
Caliber: 9mm, .45 ACP
Capacity: 7+1 or 8+1 rounds
Features: Features a proprietary thinned frame and mainspring housing that are scalloped to provide a positive grip without the abrasion felt from checkering; new G10 pattern grips are thinned to make concealed carry even easier, and feature a relieved area on the side to allow easy access to the magazine release
Compact: $3495
PDP: $3395
Recon: $3595

T3

Action: SA semiautomatic
Grips: G10 grips
Barrel: 4.25 in.
Sights: Heinie Straight Eight Slant-Pro, night
Weight: 40 oz.
Caliber: .45 ACP, 9mm
Capacity: 7 rounds
Features: Frame based on Officer model; extended magazine well; Heinie Slant-Pro Straight Eights Night Sights are standard; mainspring housing and rear of slide are horizontally serrated to match; top of slide serrated to reduce glare; Nighthawk Custom lightweight aluminum trigger that has been blacked-out using Perma Kote; available in black, gun metal grey, green coyote tan, titanium blued, and hard chrome Perma Kote or stainless steel model
MSRP $3350

T4

Action: Semiautomatic
Grips: Slim
Barrel: 3.8 in.
Sights: Fixed
Weight: 34.3 oz.
Caliber: 9mm
Capacity: 9 or 10 rounds
Features: Thinned aluminum frame and mainspring housing
MSRP $3395

NORTH AMERICAN ARMS .32 ACP GUARDIAN

.32 ACP GUARDIAN

Action: DAO semiautomatic
Grips: Polymer
Barrel: 2.5 in.
Sights: Fixed, open
Weight: 13.5 oz.
Caliber: .32 ACP
Capacity: 6+1 rounds
Features: Stainless steel; double action only; integral locking system safety; also available in .25 caliber
MSRP. $402

NORTH AMERICAN ARMS .380 ACP GUARDIAN

.380 ACP GUARDIAN

Action: DAO semiautomatic
Grips: Composite
Barrel: 2.49 in.
Sights: Fixed, open
Weight: 18.72 oz.
Caliber: .380 ACP
Capacity: 6+1 rounds
Features: Stainless steel; double action only; integral locking system safety
MSRP. $449

1860 EARL

Action: SA revolver
Grips: Rosewood
Barrel: 4 in. heavy octagonal
Sights: Bead front
Weight: 9.1 oz.
Caliber: .22 Mag.
Capacity: 5 rounds
Features: 1860s style mini revolver resembles 150-year-old percussion revolver; also available with 3 in. barrel
MSRP. $284

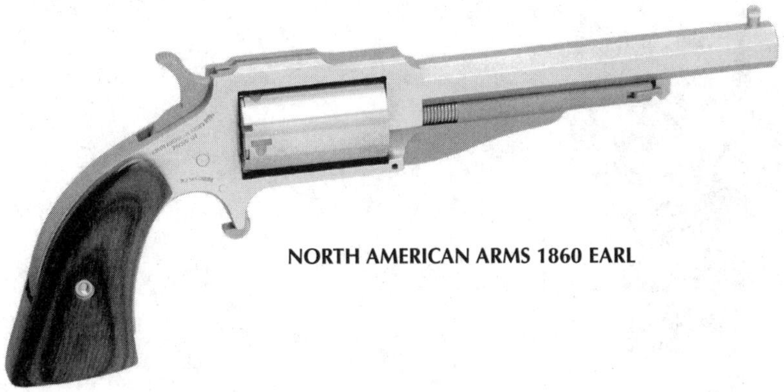

NORTH AMERICAN ARMS 1860 EARL

NORTH AMERICAN ARMS MINI MASTER SERIES REVOLVER

MINI MASTER SERIES REVOLVER

Action: SA revolver
Grips: Rubber
Barrel: 4 in.
Sights: Fixed or adjustable
Weight: 10.7 oz.
Caliber: .22LR, .22 Mag.
Capacity: 5 rounds
Features: Conversion cylinder or adjustable sights available
.22LR, .22 Mag.:. . . . . . . $284–$314
Conversion:. . . . . $319–$349

North American Arms

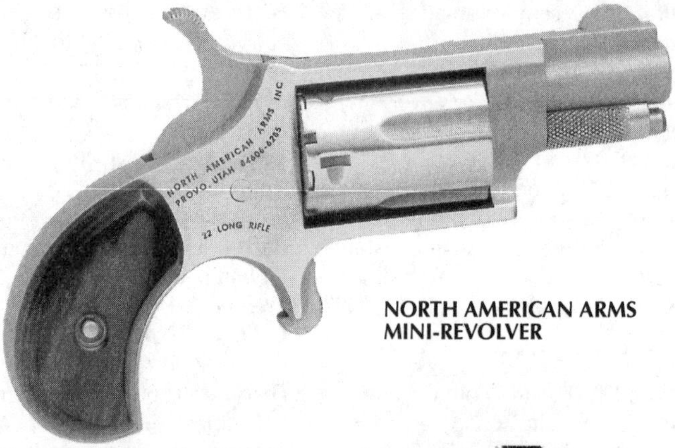

NORTH AMERICAN ARMS
MINI-REVOLVER

MINI-REVOLVER

Action: SA revolver
Grips: Laminated rosewood
Barrel: 1.2 in., 1.625 in.
Sights: Fixed, open
Weight: 4 oz.–6.2 oz.
Caliber: .22 Short, .22LR, .22 Mag.
Capacity: 5 rounds
Features: Features NAA's safety cylinder so mini-revolver can be carried fully loaded
.22: $209
.22LR: $209
.22 Mag: . . . . $219–$254

NORTH AMERICAN ARMS
PUG MINI-REVOLVER

PUG MINI-REVOLVER

Action: Revolver
Grips: Rubber
Barrel: 1 in.
Sights: Tritium and white dot
Weight: 6.4 oz.
Caliber: .22 Mag.
Capacity: 5 rounds
Features: Oversized pebble-textured rubber grips enable the handler to keep a firm grip
White dot sight: $314
Tritium sight: $334

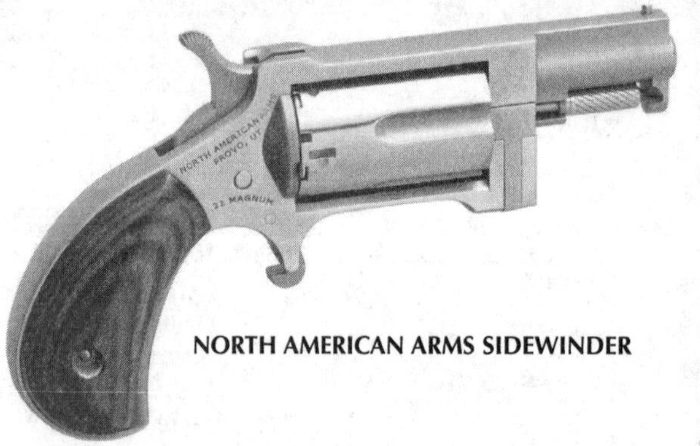

NORTH AMERICAN ARMS SIDEWINDER

SIDEWINDER

Action: Revolver
Grips: Laminated rosewood
Barrel: 1 in.
Sights: Stainless steel post
Weight: 6.7 oz.
Caliber: .22 Mag.
Capacity: 5 rounds
Features: Features NAA's safety cylinder; stainless steel frame; available .22LR conversion
MSRP $349

NORTH AMERICAN ARMS THE WASP

THE WASP

Action: SA revolver
Grips: Rubber pebble finish
Barrel: 1.125 in., 1.625 in.
Sights: Stainless post
Weight: 5.9 oz.–7.2 oz.
Caliber: .22 Mag.
Capacity: 5 rounds
Features: Stainless steel frame; vent rib barrel; skeleton hammer; .22LR conversion cylinders available; brushed sides, matte contours, black inlay
MSRP . . . . $249–$284

Olympic Arms

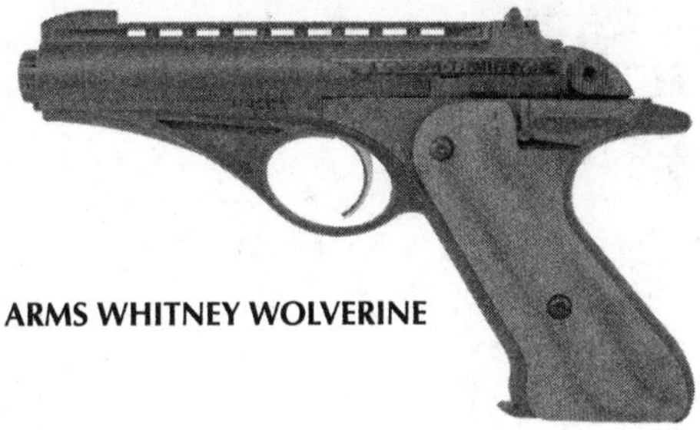

OLYMPIC ARMS WHITNEY WOLVERINE

WHITNEY WOLVERINE

Action: Semiautomatic
Grips: Black checkered
Barrel: 4.625 in.
Sights: Blade type front sight, dovetail rear sight
Weight: 19.2 oz.
Caliber: .22LR
Capacity: 10+1 rounds
Features: Revival of ray-gun style semiauto pistol; polymer frame; ventilated rib; thumb safety; available in black, pink, coyote brown, and desert tan
MSRP $294

Para USA

PARA BLACK OPS 14.45

PARA BLACK OPS RECON 9

PARA ELITE OFFICER CRIMSON TRACE

PARA ELITE

BLACK OPS 14.45

Action: Semiautomatic
Grips: Beavertail
Barrel: 5 in.
Sights: Trijicon 3-dot night sights
Weight: 41 oz.
Caliber: .45 ACP
Capacity: 14+1 rounds
Features: Stainless steel frame; oversized flared ejection port; ramped barrel; adjustable skeletonized trigger; black IonBond finish
MSRP $1299

BLACK OPS RECON 9

Action: Semiautomatic
Grips: Synthetic
Barrel: 4.25 in.
Sights: Fixed
Weight: 41 oz.
Caliber: 9mm
Capacity: 18+1 rounds
Features: Night sights; ambidextrous thumb safety; doublestack magazine
MSRP $1299

ELITE

Action: Semiautomatic
Grips: Beavertail
Barrel: 5 in.
Sights: 2-dot dovetail rear, green fiber optic front
Weight: 39 oz.
Caliber: .45 ACP
Capacity: 8+1 rounds
Features: Stainless steel frame; oversized flared ejection port; ramped barrel; adjustable skeletonized trigger; black IonBond PVD slide and frame
MSRP $949

ELITE OFFICER CRIMSON TRACE

Action: Semiautomatic
Grips: Synthetic
Barrel: 3.5 in.
Sights: Fixed
Weight: 32 oz.
Caliber: .45 ACP
Capacity: 7+1 rounds
Features: Fiber optic front sight; Crimson Trace laser grip
MSRP $1149

Para USA

EXECUTIVE CARRY

Action: Semiautomatic
Grips: VZ G10
Barrel: 3 in.
Sights: Trijicon night sights
Weight: 26 oz.
Caliber: .45 ACP
Capacity: 8+1 rounds
Features: Ed Brown Bobtail mainspring housing; lightweight aluminum frame; adjustable skeletonized trigger; two magazines included
MSRP. $1399

PARA EXECUTIVE CARRY

EXPERT

Action: Semiautomatic
Grips: Polymer
Barrel: 5 in.
Sights: Green fiber optic front; 2-dot combat rear
Weight: 39 oz.
Caliber: 9mm, .45 ACP
Capacity: 8+1 rounds
Features: Double-stack stainless steel frame; stainless match-grade barrel; adjustable skeletonized trigger; two magazines included
MSRP. $663

PARA EXPERT

LDA CARRY

Action: Semiautomatic
Grips: Polymer
Barrel: 3 in.
Sights: 2-dot combat rear, green fiber optic front
Weight: 30 oz.
Caliber: .45 ACP, 9mm
Capacity: 6+1 or 8+1 rounds
Features: Oversized, flared ejection port; steel frame and slide; beavertail grip safety; adjustable skeletonized trigger; black nitride finish available
MSRP. $1025

PARA LDA CARRY

LDA OFFICER CRIMSON TRACE

Action: Semiautomatic
Grips: Synthetic
Barrel: 3.5 in.
Sights: Fixed
Weight: 32 oz.
Caliber: 9mm, .45 ACP
Capacity: 7+1 (.45 ACP) or 8+1 rounds
Features: Night sights; Crimson Trace laser grip
MSRP. $1225

PARA LDA OFFICER CRIMSON TRACE

Para USA

PARA PRO COMP 9

PRO COMP 9

Action: Semiautomatic
Grips: Synthetic
Barrel: 5 in.
Sights: Adjustable
Weight: 40 oz.
Caliber: 9mm
Capacity: 9+1 rounds
Features: Adjustable rear, fiber optic front sights
MSRP. $1299

Remington Arms

REMINGTON MODEL 1911 R1

MODEL 1911 R1

Action: Semiautomatic
Grips: Double diamond walnut
Barrel: 5 in.
Sights: Fixed
Weight: 38.5 oz.
Caliber: .45 ACP
Capacity: 7 rounds
Features: Short trigger; double diamond walnut grips; modern enhancements include a lowered and flared ejection port; beveled magazine well; loaded chamber indicator; high-profile fixed sights in a three-white-dot pattern; match grade stainless-steel barrel; available in stainless steel
MSRP. $729
SS: $789

REMINGTON MODEL 1911 R1 CARRY

MODEL 1911 R1 CARRY

Action: Semiautomatic
Grips: Cocobolo wood
Barrel: 5 in.
Sights: Novak sights with tritium front night sight
Weight: 38.5 oz.
Caliber: .45 ACP
Capacity: 7 or 8 rounds
Features: De-horned forged carbon steel frame and de-horned carbon steel slide; beavertail grip safety with checkered memory bump; checkered front strap and mainspring housing; ambidextrous safety; satin black oxide finish
MSRP. $1299

REMINGTON 1911 R1 CARRY COMMANDER

1911 R1 CARRY COMMANDER

Action: Semiautomatic
Grips: Wood
Barrel: 4.25 in.
Sights: Fixed
Weight: 38.5 oz.
Caliber: .45 ACP
Capacity: 7+1 rounds
Features: Satin black oxide finish; beavertail grip safety with checkered memory bump; ambidextrous safety; Novak sights with Tritium front sight; Cocobolo grips
MSRP. $1299

Remington Arms

REMINGTON 1911 R1 CARRY COMMANDER CRIMSON TRACE

REMINGTON 1911 R1 COMMANDER

REMINGTON 1911 R1 ENHANCED CRIMSON TRACE

REMINGTON MODEL R51

1911 R1 CARRY COMMANDER CRIMSON TRACE

Action: Semiautomatic
Grips: Synthetic
Barrel: 4.25 in.
Sights: Fixed
Weight: 40 oz.
Caliber: .45 ACP
Capacity: 8+1 rounds
Features: Satin black oxide finish; beavertail grip safety with checkered memory bump; ambidextrous safety; Novak sights with Tritium front sight; Crimson Trace lasergrips
MSRP $1499

1911 R1 COMMANDER

Action: Semiautomatic
Grips: Wood
Barrel: 4.25 in.
Sights: Fixed
Weight: 38.5 oz.
Caliber: .45 ACP
Capacity: 7+1 rounds
Features: Oversized, flared ejection port; carbon steel frame and slide; 3-dot sights; GI style grip safety; GI style short trigger; black oxide finish; walnut double diamond grips
MSRP $729

1911 R1 ENHANCED CRIMSON TRACE

Action: Semiautomatic
Grips: Synthetic
Barrel: 5 in.
Sights: Adjustable
Weight: 40 oz.
Caliber: .45 ACP
Capacity: 8+1 rounds
Features: Satin black oxide finish; beavertail grip safety with checkered memory bump; ambidextrous safety; adjustable dovetailed rear sight with fiber optic front sight; Crimson Trace lasergrips
MSRP $940

MODEL R51

Action: Semiautomatic
Grips: Synthetic
Barrel: 3.4 in.
Sights: Adjustable
Weight: 22 oz.
Caliber: 9mm Luger
Capacity: 7+1 rounds
Features: Lightweight aluminum frame with rounded edges; dovetail drift-adjustable sights
MSRP $420

Remington Arms

REMINGTON
MODEL R51 CRIMSON TRACE

MODEL R51 CRIMSON TRACE

Action: Semiautomatic
Grips: Synthetic
Barrel: 3.4 in.
Sights: Adjustable
Weight: 22 oz.
Caliber: 9mm Luger
Capacity: 7+1 rounds
Features: Lightweight aluminum frame with rounded edges; dovetail drift-adjustable sights; Crimson Trace lasergrips
MSRP $609

HANDGUNS

Rock River Arms

ROCK RIVER ARMS
1911 POLY PISTOL

ROCK RIVER ARMS LAR-PDS PISTOL

1911 POLY PISTOL

Action: SA semiautomatic
Grips: Polymer
Barrel: 5 in.
Sights: Dovetail front and rear
Weight: 32.6 oz.
Caliber: .45 ACP
Capacity: 7 rounds
Features: Chromoly barrel; polymer frame and mainspring housing; steel frame insert; steel slide; parkerized finish on metal; RRA overmolded grips; aluminum speed trigger; beavertail grip safety; RRA dovetail front and rear sights
MSRP $925

LAR-PDS PISTOL

Action: Gas-operated semiautomatic
Grips: Hogue rubber
Barrel: 8 in. chromoly
Sights: Picatinny rail
Weight: 80 oz.
Caliber: 5.56 NATO
Capacity: 30 rounds
Features: A2 Flash Hider; aluminum tri-rail handguard; ambidextrous non-reciprocating charging handle
MSRP . . . . $1245–$1395

Rossi

ROSSI MODEL R352

MODEL R351 AND R352

Action: DA revolver
Grips: Rubber
Barrel: 2 in.
Sights: Fixed, open
Weight: 24 oz.
Caliber: .38 Spl., .38 Spl. +P
Capacity: 5 rounds
Features: Blued or stainless steel finish; checkered grips; forged steel frame
R35102: $391
R35202: $455

Rossi

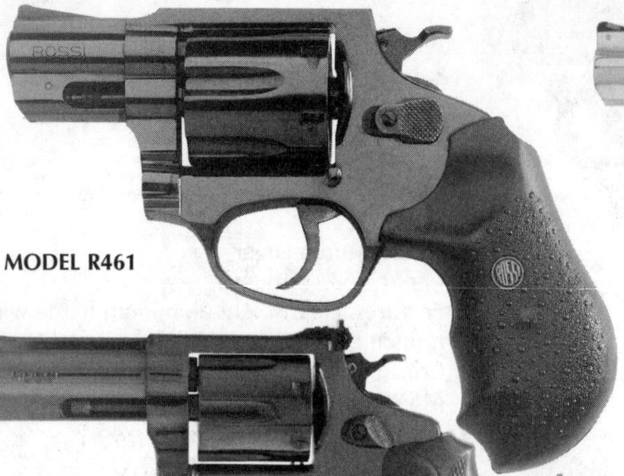

ROSSI MODEL R461

ROSSI MODEL R972

ROSSI MODEL R851

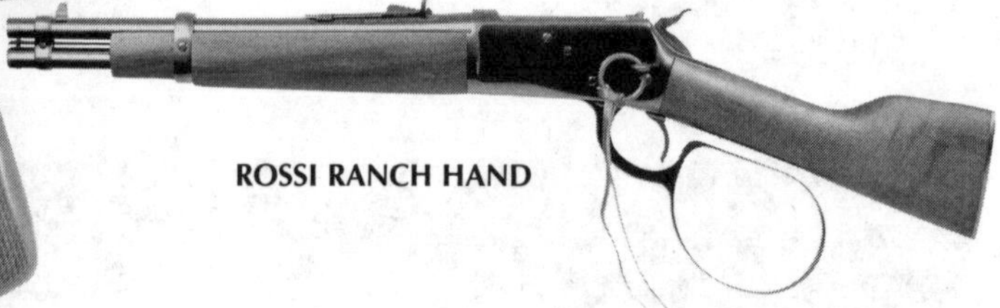

ROSSI RANCH HAND

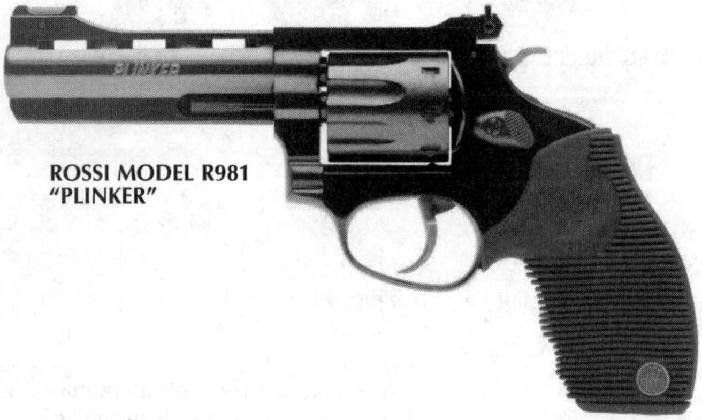

ROSSI MODEL R981 "PLINKER"

MODEL R851

Action: DA revolver
Grips: Rubber
Barrel: 4 in.
Sights: Adjustable
Weight: 32 oz.
Caliber: .38 Spl., .38 Spl. +P
Capacity: 6 rounds
Features: Adjustable rear sight; blued finish; forged steel frame
MSRP $391

MODEL R971 AND R972

Action: DA revolver
Grips: Rubber
Barrel: 4 in., 6 in.
Sights: Target
Weight: 35 oz.
Caliber: .357 Mag., .38 Spl.
Capacity: 6 rounds
Features: Stainless steel or blued finish; deep contoured finger grooves in the grip for solid grasp and comfort; frame forged from steel
Blued: $455
SS: $511

MODEL R981 "PLINKER"

Action: DA/SA revolver
Grips: Ribber
Barrel: 4 in.
Sights: Fixed red fiber optic front, adjustable rear
Weight: 29 oz.
Caliber: .22LR
Capacity: 8 rounds
Features: Alloy steel frame; key-based Taurus security system; transfer bar/hammer block safety; yoke detent system; blued finish
MSRP $408

RANCH HAND

Action: Lever-action repeating pistol
Grips: Walnut
Barrel: 12 in.
Sights: Gold-bead front w/adjustable buckhorn rear
Weight: 64 oz.
Caliber: .38 Spl./.357 Mag., .45 Colt, .44 Mag.
Capacity: 6 rounds
Features: Matte blued finish or blued case-hardened; Brazilian hardwood stock; oversize loop lever; investment-cast receiver
Blued: $597
Blued case-hardened: $661

MODEL R462 AND R461

Action: DA revolver
Grips: Rubber
Barrel: 2 in.
Sights: Fixed, open
Weight: 26 oz.
Caliber: .357 Mag.
Capacity: 6 rounds
Features: Blued or stainless steel finish; checkered grips; forged steel frame
R46102: $391
R46202: $455

Ruger

RUGER 22–45 LITE RIMFIRE

22/45 LITE RIMFIRE PISTOL

Action: SA semiautomatic
Grips: Black laminate
Barrel: 4.4 in.
Sights: Fixed front, adjustable rear
Weight: 23 oz.
Caliber: .22LR
Capacity: 10 rounds
Features: Aluminum upper, black anodized finish; stainless barrel sleeve; polymer grip frame; manual safety; loaded chamber indicator; magazine disconnect
MSRP. $375

RUGER 22/45 TARGET RIMFIRE PISTOL

22/45 TARGET RIMFIRE PISTOL

Action: SA semiautomatic
Grips: Checkered cocobolo wood
Barrel: 4 in., 5.5 in.
Sights: Adjustable rear
Weight: 31–33 oz.
Caliber: .22LR
Capacity: 10 rounds
Features: Replaceable panels; Zytel polymer frame; blued finish; classic 1911 style pistol
MSRP. . . . . $369–$415

RUGER BISLEY

BISLEY

Action: SA revolver
Grips: Hardwood
Barrel: 7.5 in.
Sights: Ramp front, adjustable rear
Weight: 48 oz.–50 oz.
Caliber: .44 Mag, .45 Colt
Capacity: 6 rounds
Features: Blued alloy steel frame; patented Ruger transfer bar mechanism and loading gate interlock; traditional western style hand-filling grip featuring rosewood grip panels; ramp front and precision adjustable rear sights
MSRP. $825

RUGER GP100

GP100

Action: DA revolver
Grips: Black hogue monogrip
Barrel: 3 in., 4.2 in., 6 in.
Sights: Ramp front, fixed or adjustable rear
Weight: 36 oz.–45 oz.
Caliber: .327 Fed Mag., .357 Mag.
Capacity: 6, 7 rounds
Features: Satin stainless or blued finish; stainless steel or alloy steel frame; cushioned rubber grip; transfer bar; triple-locking cylinder
MSRP. . . . . $ 725–$779

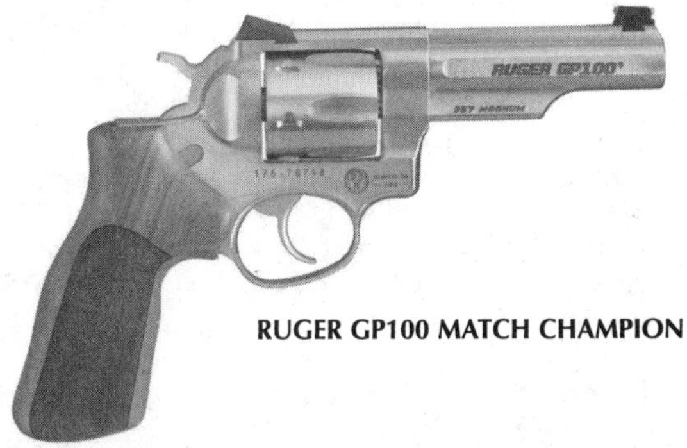

RUGER GP100 MATCH CHAMPION

GP100 MATCH CHAMPION

Action: DA revolver
Grips: Wood
Barrel: 4.2 in.
Sights: Fixed
Weight: 38 oz.
Caliber: .357 Mag.
Capacity: 6 rounds
Features: Fiber optic front, fixed rear sights; stainless steel
MSRP. $899

Ruger

RUGER LC9 9MM

RUGER LCP .380 ACP

RUGER LCP CENTERFIRE PISTOL

RUGER LCR

RUGER LC380

LC9 9MM

Action: Semiautomatic
Grips: Glass-filled nylon
Barrel: 3.12 in.
Sights: Adjustable 3-dot
Weight: 17.6 oz.
Caliber: 9mm Luger
Capacity: 7+1 rounds
Features: Alloy steel barrel and slide; blued finish; adjustable 3-dot/LaserMax CenterFire sights; black, high performance, glass-filled nylon grips
MSRP $449

LC380

Action: Semiautomatic
Grips: Black, glass-filled nylon
Barrel: 3.12 in.
Sights: Adjustable 3-dot
Weight: 17.2 oz.
Caliber: .380 ACP
Capacity: 7+1 rounds
Features: Hardened alloy steel slide; checkered grip frame; finger grip extension floorplate; three safeties and loaded chamber indicator; blued finish
MSRP . . . . $449 –$629

LCP .380 ACP

Action: Semiautomatic
Grips: Glass-filled nylon
Barrel: 2.75 in.
Sights: Crimson Trace/LaserMax
Weight: 9.9 oz.
Caliber: .380 ACP
Capacity: 6+1 rounds
Features: Alloy steel barrel and slide; blued finish; fixed/LaserMax CenterFire sights; black, high performance, glass-filled nylon grips
MSRP . . . . $389–$575

LCP CENTERFIRE PISTOL

Action: DA semiautomatic
Grips: Black, glass-filled nylon
Barrel: 2.75 in.
Sights: Fixed, optional Crimson Trace laserguard or LaserMax CenterFire
Weight: 9.4–10 oz.
Caliber: .380 ACP
Capacity: 6+1 rounds
Features: Blued, alloy slide and barrel; fixed front and rear sights are integral to the slide; hammer is recessed within the slide; factory-fitted trigger-guard-mounted laser available from LaserMaz and Crimson Trace
MSRP . . . . $389–$429
Crimson Trace: $575

LCR (LIGHTWEIGHT COMPACT REVOLVER)

Action: DA revolver
Grips: Hogue Tamer and Crimson Trace lasergrips
Barrel: 1.8 in.
Sights: U-Notch Integral rear
Weight: 13 oz.–17.1 oz.
Caliber: .22 Mag., .22LR, .38 Spl. +P, .357 Mag.
Capacity: 5, 6, 8 rounds
Features: Advanced target gray cylinder finish; option of replaceable, pinned ramp or XS standard dot tritium front sight
MSRP . . . . $545–$899

RUGER LCRX

RUGER NEW BEARCAT

RUGER MARK III HUNTER

RUGER SINGLE-SIX .17 HMR

RUGER MARK III STANDARD

RUGER SP101

LCRX

Action: DA/SA revolver
Grips: Rubber
Barrel: 1.875 in.
Sights: Fixed
Weight: 13.5 oz.
Caliber: .38 Spl. +P
Capacity: 5 rounds
Features: High-strength stainless steel cylinder features an Ionbond Diamondblack finish; Grip Peg allows a variety of grip styles to be installed; external hammer that allows for single-action mode; also available with Crimson Trace lasergrips
MSRP. $529

MARK III HUNTER

Action: SA semiautomatic
Grips: Brown or Target laminate
Barrel: 6.88 in.
Sights: Fiber optic front, adjustable rear
Weight: 41 oz.–43.7 oz.
Caliber: .22LR
Capacity: 10 rounds
Features: Stainless steel frame with satin finish; fluted bull barrel; visible loaded chamber indicator
MSRP. . . . . $699–$749

MARK III STANDARD

Action: semiautomatic
Grips: Checkered plastic
Barrel: 4.75 in., 6 in.
Sights: Open, adjustable
Weight: 35–37 oz.
Caliber: .22LR
Capacity: 10 rounds
Features: Steel frame with blued finish; loaded chamber indicator; manual safety; internal cylindrical bolt
MSRP. $399

NEW BEARCAT

Action: SA revolver
Grips: Hardwood
Barrel: 4.2 in.
Sights: Blade front, integral notch
Weight: 24 oz.
Caliber: .22LR
Capacity: 6 rounds
Features: Alloy steel with blued finish or stainless steel frame with satin stainless finish; decorative cylinder; transfer bar mechanism; features one piece frame reminiscent of old Remington Civil War-era revolvers
Alloy Steel: $589
SS: $639

SINGLE-SIX .17 HMR

Action: SA revolver
Grips: Black checkered hard rubber
Barrel: 6.5 in.
Sights: Ramp front, adjustable rear
Weight: 35 oz.
Caliber: .17 HMR
Capacity: 6 rounds
Features: Alloy steel frame with blued finish; transfer bar mechanism
MSRP. $589

SP101

Action: DA revolver
Grips: Black rubber
Barrel: 2.25 in., 3.06 in.
Sights: Fixed, windage adjustable
Weight: 25 oz.–30 oz.
Caliber: .357 Mag., .38 Spl.
Capacity: 5 or 6 rounds
Features: Stainless steel frame with satin finish; cushioned rubber grip; grip frame; transfer bar; triple-locking cylinder
MSRP. . . . . $679–$719

Ruger

RUGER SP101 .22LR

RUGER SR22
RIMFIRE PISTOL

RUGER SR45

RUGER SR9C

RUGER SR40

RUGER SR1911

SP101 .22LR

Action: DA revolver
Grips: Rubber, wood
Barrel: 4.2 in.
Sights: Fiber optic
Weight: 29.5 oz.
Caliber: .22LR
Capacity: 8 rounds
Features: Stainless steel frame with satin finish; cushioned rubber grip with engraved wood; grip frame; transfer bar; triple-locking cylinder
MSRP $719

SR9C

Action: DA semiautomatic
Grips: Black, glass-filled, nylon
Barrel: 3.4 in.
Sights: Adjustable 3-dot
Weight: 23.4 oz.
Caliber: 9mm Luger
Capacity: 10 or 17 rounds
Features: Compact version of SR9; black alloy or brushed stainless 6-groove rifling; high visibility sights; accessory mounting rail
MSRP $529

SR22 RIMFIRE PISTOL

Action: DA semiautomatic
Grips: Polymer
Barrel: 3.5 in.
Sights: Adjustable 3-dot
Weight: 17.5 oz.
Caliber: .22LR
Capacity: 10 rounds
Features: 3-dot sight system has fixed front sight and adjustable rear sight; polymer frame and two interchangeable rubberized grips; underside Picatinny rail; aluminum slide; ambidextrous manual thumb safety/decocking lever; ambidextrous magazine release
MSRP $415
Silver: $429
Threaded Barrel: $449

SR40

Action: semiautomatic
Grips: Black, high performance, glass-filled nylon
Barrel: 4.1 in.
Sights: Adjustable 3-dot
Weight: 27.25 oz.
Caliber: .40 S&W
Capacity: 10 or 15 rounds
Features: Glass-filled nylon frame; ambidextrous operating controls; trigger system and reversible; fully adjustable three-dot sights; integral accessory rail; backstraps are identical to SR9; Nitridox pro black or brushed stainless finish
MSRP $529

SR45

Action: Semiautomatic
Grips: Black, glass-filled nylon
Barrel: 4.5 in.
Sights: Adjustable 3-dot
Weight: 30.15 oz.
Caliber: .45 ACP
Capacity: 10+1 rounds
Features: Reversible backstrap; ambidextrous safety and magazine release; mouting rail; loaded chamber indicator; black nitride or brushed stainless finish
MSRP $529

SR1911

Action: Semiautomatic
Grips: Hardwood
Barrel: 4.25in., 5 in.
Sights: Windage adjustable Novak 3-dot
Weight: 36.4 oz.–39 oz.
Caliber: .45 ACP
Capacity: 7+1 or 8+1 rounds
Features: Checkered backstrap; stainless steel barrel and bushing; positive barrel lock-up; lightweight, aluminum, skeletonized trigger and hammer; beavertail grip safety; low-glare stainless finish
MSRP . . . . $859–$899

Ruger

RUGER SUPER BLACKHAWK

RUGER VAQUERO BLUED

RUGER SUPER REDHAWK

RUGER VAQUERO BISLEY

SUPER BLACKHAWK

Action: SA revolver
Grips: Hardwood
Barrel: 4.62 in., 5.5 in., 7.5 in., 10.5 in.
Sights: Ramp front, adjustable rear
Weight: 45–55 oz.
Caliber: .44 Mag
Capacity: 6 rounds
Features: Alloy steel or stainless steel frame; blued or satin stainless finish; transfer bar mechanism; western-style grip
MSRP. $769

SUPER REDHAWK

Action: DA revolver
Grips: Black Hogue Tamer monogrip
Barrel: 7.5 in., 9.5 in.
Sights: Ramp front, adjustable rear
Weight: 53 oz.–58 oz.
Caliber: .44 Mag., .454 Casull, .480 Ruger
Capacity: 6 rounds
Features: Satin stainless finish; triple-locking cylinder; integral scope system; corrosion-resistant; extended frame; dual chambering; transfer bar
MSRP. . . . .$1079–$1119

VAQUERO BISLEY

Action: SA revolver
Grips: Simulated ivory
Barrel: 5.5 in.
Sights: Fixed
Weight: 41 oz.–45 oz.
Caliber: .45 Colt, .357 Mag.
Capacity: 6 rounds
Features: Stainless steel frame with high-gloss stainless finish
MSRP. $835

VAQUERO BLUED

Action: SA revolver
Grips: Hardwood
Barrel: 4.62 in., 5.5 in.
Sights: Fixed
Weight: 40 oz.–43 oz.
Caliber: .45 Colt, .357 Mag.
Capacity: 6 rounds
Features: Blued finish alloy steel; reverse Indexing Pawl; ejector rod head; transfer bar mechanism; internal lock
MSRP. $769

Sig Sauer

SIG SAUER 1911 .22LR CAMO

SIG SAUER 1911 SPARTAN

1911 .22LR CAMO

Action: SAO semiautomatic
Grips: Polymer Camo
Barrel: 5 in.
Sights: Contrast sights
Weight: 34 oz.
Caliber: .22LR
Capacity: 10 rounds
Features: Lightweight metal frame and slide; low-profile sights; ambidextrous thumb safety; camo coating
MSRP. $518

1911 SPARTAN

Action: SAO semiautomatic
Grips: Hogue Spartan
Barrel: 5 in.
Sights: Low profile night sights
Weight: 41.6 oz.
Caliber: .45 ACP
Capacity: 8 rounds
Features: Oil-rubbed bronze Nitron finish; gold inlay engraving; 1911 design and ergonomic feel; ancient Greek inscription on slide and grip supposedly spoken by Spartan King Leonidas: "Molon labe," or "Come and take it"
MSRP. $1356

Sig Sauer

SIG SAUER 1911 TRADITIONAL

SIG SAUER P224 EQUINOX

SIG SAUER M11-A1

SIG SAUER MOSQUITO

SIG SAUER 1911 ULTRA TWO-TONE

SIG SAUER P220

1911 TRADITIONAL

Action: SA semiautomatic
Grips: Custom shop wood, aluminum, or polymer grips
Barrel: 4.2 in.
Sights: Novak Night, platinum elite model has adjustable combat night sights
Weight: 35.5 oz.
Caliber: .45 ACP
Capacity: 8 rounds
Features: Accessory rail; beavertail frame; checkered grip; match grade barrel, hammer/sear set and trigger; stainless finish on stainless model; nitron finish on TACOPS model
Compact stainless: $1142
Match Elite stainless: $1213
TACOPS: $1213

1911 ULTRA

Action: SA semiautomatic
Grips: Black diamondwood, rosewood
Barrel: 3.3 in.
Sights: Low-pro night sights
Weight: 28 oz.
Caliber: .45 ACP
Capacity: 6+1 rounds
Features: Smallest SIG 1911 yet; stainless slide over alloy frame; unique recoil system; 26 lpi front strap checkering; combine to make a very controllable and comfortable small .45; skeletonized trigger; two variants: Nitron (all black with black diamondwood grips) and Two-Tone (natural stainless slide over black hardcoat anodized aluminum frame; rosewood grips)
Nitron: $1142
Two-Tone: $1156

M11-A1

Action: DA/SA semiautomatic
Grips: Polymer
Barrel: 3.9 in.
Sights: Siglite night sights
Weight: 32 oz.
Caliber: 9mm
Capacity: 15 rounds
Features: Stainless steel slide; Short Reset Trigger; flush fit magazines; phosphate coated internals; Nitron slide finish; black hard anodized
MSRP . . . . $1149–$1220

MOSQUITO

Action: semiautomatic
Grips: Black polymer
Barrel: 3.9 in.
Sights: Adjustable rear
Weight: 24.6 oz.
Caliber: .22LR
Capacity: 10 rounds
Features: Integrated accessory rail; rugged blowback system; fixed barrel; superior ergonomic grip; internal locking device; slide mounted ambidextrous safety; blued slide finish; black polymer frame finish; other models available with various color schemes and features
MSRP . . . . $408 –$470

P220

Action: Semiautomatic
Grips: Polymer, laminated or custom shop wood
Barrel: 4.4 in.
Sights: Siglite night
Weight: 30.4 oz.–31.2 oz.
Caliber: 10mm, .45 ACP
Capacity: 8 rounds
Features: Nitron finish, light-weight alloy frame; accessory rail
Standard: $1015
Night Sights: $1108

P224

Action: SA/DA or DAO semiautomatic
Grips: Hogue, ergonomic
Barrel: 3.5 in.
Sights: Tritium, fiber optic, or night sights
Weight: 25.4 oz.
Caliber: 9mm, .40 S&W, .357 SIG
Capacity: 10+1, 11+1 rounds
Features: Classic SIG in a true sub-compact; 4 variants: SIG Anti-Snag (de-horned slide, ergonomic grips, night sights), Equinox (2-tone Nitron SS slide, Tru-Glo Tritium fiber optic front, SIGLITE rear, black diamondwood grips), Nickel (nickel slide and controls, Hogue grips, night sights), Extreme (Hogue black and gray Piranha grips, night sights)
Equinox: $1243
Extreme: $1170
Nickel: $1125
SAS: $1149

SIG SAUER P226

P226

Action: DA/SA Semiautomatic
Grips: One-piece ergo grip, extreme model features Hogue custom G10 grips, custom wood w/ SIG Medallion
Barrel: 4.4 in.
Sights: Contrast, Siglite night optional
Weight: 34 oz.–34.4 oz.
Caliber: 9mm, .357 SIG, .40 S&W
Capacity: 9mm: 10 or 15 rounds; .357 SIG: 10 or 12 rounds, .40 S&W: 10 or 12 rounds
Features: Black hard anodized frame finish; nitron slide finish; accessory rail; extreme model features SRT trigger and front cocking serrations
Standard:................$1015
Night Sights: $1108
Extreme: $1239
Elite SAO: $1243
Engraved:................$1289
Engraved Stainless: $1402

P226 MK25

Action: SA/DA semiautomatic
Grips: Polymer
Barrel: 4.4 in.
Sights: SIGLITE night sights
Weight: 34.4 oz.
Caliber: 9mm
Capacity: 10 or 15 rounds
Features: New designation of the Navy's P226 9mm variant issued to NSWG; still with phosphated internals; (three) 15 round magazines; classic two-piece polymer grips; anchor engraved on slide; Picatinny rail; actual UID scanable serial number label; packaged with FDE grip band and a certificate of authenticity
MSRP..................$1166

SIG SAUER P239

P227

Action: DA/SA semiautomatic
Grips: One-piece polymer
Barrel: 4.4 in.
Sights: Contrast or Siglite night sights
Weight: 32 oz.
Caliber: .45 ACP
Capacity: 10 rounds
Features: Full-size and carry lengths; double stack magazines; integral accessory rail; black hard anodized; Nitron slide finish
MSRP..................$1015
w/Night Sights:...........$1108

P229

Action: Semiautomatic
Grips: Black polymer factor grips
Barrel: 3.9 in.
Sights: Contrast, Siglite night optional
Weight: 32 oz.
Caliber: 9mm, .40 S&W, .357 SIG
Capacity: 9mm: 10, 13 rounds; .357 SIG: 10, 12 rounds, .40 S&W: 10, 12 rounds
Features: Black hard anodized frame finish; nitron slide finish; accessory rail
MSRP..................$1015
Night Sights: $1108

P238

Action: SA semiautomatic
Grips: Fluted polymer, Rosewood Tribal, Pearl, Tribal Engraved Aluminum, Hogue pink rubber
Barrel: 2.7 in.
Sights: Siglite night
Weight: 15.2 oz.
Caliber: .380 ACP (9mm Short)
Capacity: 6 rounds
Features: Nitron slide finish; beavertail style frame
MSRP.............. $679–$779

P239

Action: DA semiautomatic
Grips: Polymer, tactical model features black polymer factory grips
Barrel: 3.6 in., 4 in.
Sights: Contrast, Siglite night optional
Weight: 29.5 oz.
Caliber: 9mm, .40 S&W, .357 SIG
Capacity: 8 (9mm) or 7 rounds (.40 S&W, .357 SIG) rounds
Features: Black polymer factor grips; black hard anodized frame finish; nitron frame finish
Contrast Sights:...........$993
Night Sights: $1108
Tactical: $1176

SIG SAUER P226 MK25

SIG SAUER P227

SIG SAUER P229

SIG SAUER P238

Sig Sauer

P250 COMPACT

Action: Locked breech DAO semiauto
Grips: Interchangeable polymer
Barrel: 3.9 in.
Sights: Siglite Night
Weight: 25.1 oz.
Caliber: 9mm, .40 S&W, .45 ACP
Capacity: 9, 13, 15 rounds
Features: Interchangeable polymer grip shell with stainless insert; nitron slide finish; interchangeable grip sizes and calibers
Contrast: $466
Night Sights: $548

P290

Action: Semiautomatic
Grips: Black polymer
Barrel: 2.9 in.
Sights: Siglite or Contrast
Weight: 20.5 oz.
Caliber: 9mm
Capacity: 6+1 rounds
Features: Polymer frame; slide is machined from solid stainless-steel billet; interchangeable grips; features drift-adjustable Siglite sights or high-contrast black sight; available with Rainbow Titanium-Coated slide finish
MSRP . . . . $$513–$599

P320

Action: DAO semiautomatic
Grips: Synthetic
Barrel: 3.6 in.–4.7 in.
Sights: Fixed
Weight: 25 oz.–29.4 oz.
Caliber: .40 S&W, 9mm, .357 SIG, .45 ACP
Capacity: 10–17 rounds
Features: Quick and safe take-down with no tools or trigger manipulation required; double-dction striker fire operating system; SIGLITE night sights
MSRP $713

P938

Action: SA semiautomatic
Grips: Synthetic or wood
Barrel: 3 in.
Sights: SIGLITE night sights, TFO front on Equinox
Weight: 16 oz.
Caliber: 9mm, .40 S&W, .357 SIG
Capacity: 6+1, 7+1 rounds
Features: Ambi safety; SIG's most compact 9mm; initial offerings in 5 variants: Rosewood (nitron coated stainless slide over hard anodized alloy frame; rosewood grips), Blackwood (natural stainless slide over hard

SIG SAUER P250 COMPACT

SIG SAUER P290

SIG SAUER P250 2SUM SUBCOMPACT

SIG SAUER P938 BLACKWOOD

SIG SAUER P320

SIG SAUER XFIVE CLASSIC

SIG SAUER SP2022

anodized black alloy frame; black diamondwood grips), Extreme (nitron coated stainless slide over hard anodized alloy frame; Hogue G-10 piranha grips in black/gray), SAS (SIG anti-snag dehorned slide and frame; natural stainless slide over hard anodized black alloy frame; walnut stippled grips), Equinox (polished Nitron two-tone slide over hardcoat anodized frame; TFO front with SIGLITE rear; black diamondwood grips)
Black Aluminum: $846
Blackwood: $819
Equinox: $833
Extreme: $833
Rosewood: $805
SAS: $838

SP2022

Action: Semiautomatic
Grips: Polymer
Barrel: 3.9 in., 4.4 in.
Sights: Contrast, Siglite Night optional
Weight: 29 oz.
Caliber: 9mm, .40 S&W
Capacity: 10 or 15 rounds (9mm), 10 or 12 rounds (.40 S&W)
Features: Accessory rail; wear-resistant polymer frame; black polymer frame finish; nitron slide finish
MSRP $513
Night sights: $585
Nitron threaded barrel: $656

XFIVE CLASSIC

Action: SAO semiautomatic
Grips: Wood
Barrel: 5 in.
Sights: Adjustable
Weight: 45.7 oz.
Caliber: .40 S&W, 9mm
Capacity: 14 or 19 rounds
Features: Custom walnut grips; user-adjustable SAO trigger; fully adjustable target sights; aluminum jet funnel and magazine base; Picatinny rail; stainless steel frame and slide
MSRP $2679

Smith & Wesson

BODYGUARD 38

Action: DA revolver
Grips: Matte black synthetic
Barrel: 1.9 in.
Sights: Integrated Insight laser system
Weight: 4.3 oz.
Caliber: .38 S&W Spl. +P
Capacity: 5 rounds
Features: Stainless steel cylinder with PVD coating
MSRP $539

BODYGUARD 380

Action: DA semiautomatic
Grips: Polymer
Barrel: 2.75 in.
Sights: Stainless steel drift-adjustable front and rear
Weight: 11.85 oz.
Caliber: .380 ACP
Capacity: 6+1 rounds
Features: Manual thumb safety external takedown lever; external slide stop; barrel and slide stainless with Melonite finish; integrated Insight laser sighting system
MSRP . . . . $379–$449

CLASSIC M57

Action: DA N-frame revolver
Grips: Checkered square-butt walnut
Barrel: 6 in.
Sights: Pinned red ramp front, micro adjustable white outline rear;
Weight: 4.8 oz.
Caliber: .41 Mag.
Capacity: 6 rounds
Features: Bright blued or nickel finish; carbon steel frame; classic style thumbpiece; color case wide spur hammer; color case wide serrated target trigger
MSRP: $1009

CLASSIC M586

Action: SA/DA revolver
Grips: Wood
Barrel: 4 in., 6 in.
Sights: Adjustable
Weight: 40.9 oz.–46.3 oz.
Caliber: .357 Mag., .38 S&W Spl. +P
Capacity: 6 rounds
Features: Carbon steel frame and cylinder with blued finish; adjustable white outline rear sight and red ramp front sight; square-butt design; checkered wood grips
MSRP $839

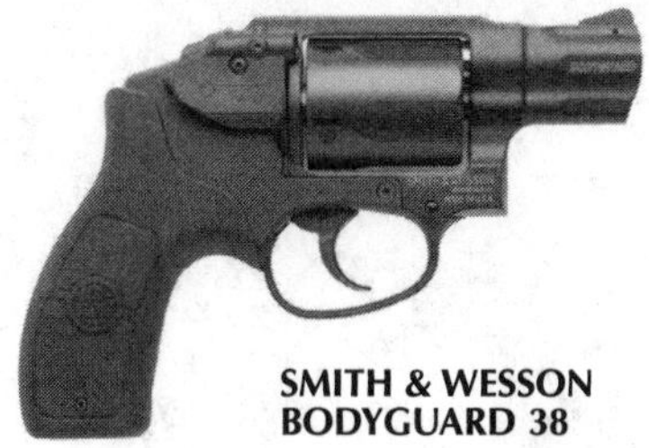

SMITH & WESSON BODYGUARD 38

SMITH & WESSON BODYGUARD 380

SMITH & WESSON CLASSIC M57

SMITH & WESSON CLASSIC M586

SMITH & WESSON GOVERNOR

SMITH & WESSON M10

GOVERNOR

Action: SA/DA revolver
Grips: Synthetic, Crimson Trace
Barrel: 2.75 in.
Sights: Fixed
Weight: 29.6 oz.
Caliber: .45 Colt, .45 ACP, .410
Capacity: 6 rounds
Features: Patented heat-treated scandium frame; PVD coated cylinder; dovetailed Tritium front night sight; fixed rear sight; matte black finish; optional factory-installed Crimson Trace Lasergrips
Standard: $869
Crimson Trace: $1119

M10

Action: SA/DA revolver
Grips: Wood
Barrel: 4 in.
Sights: Black blade, fixed
Weight: 36 oz.
Caliber: .38 S&W Spl. +P
Capacity: 6 rounds
Features: Carbon steel frame; carbon steel cylinder; blued finish; medium size frame; exposed hammer
MSRP $739

Smith & Wesson

SMITH & WESSON M27 CLASSIC

SMITH & WESSON M29

SMITH & WESSON M36

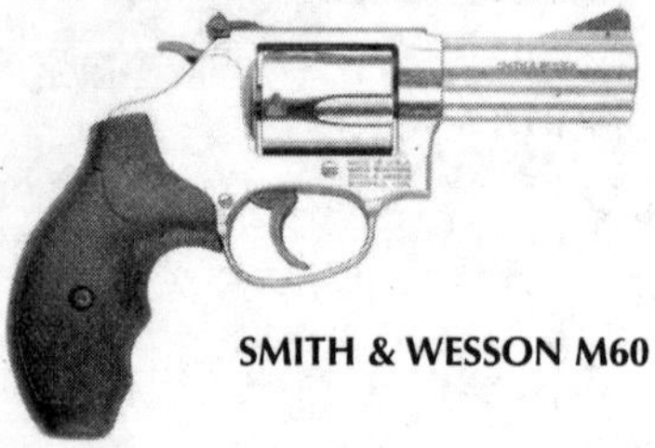

SMITH & WESSON M60

SMITH & WESSON M325 THUNDER RANCH

M27 CLASSIC

Action: SA/DA revolver
Grips: Checkered square butt walnut
Barrel: 4 in.
Sights: Pinned serrated ramp front; Micro adjustable with cross serrations
Weight: 48.5 oz.
Caliber: .357 Mag., .38 S&W Spl. +P
Capacity: 6 rounds
Features: Carbon steel frame; bright blued or blued finish
MSRP $1059

M29

Action: Revolver
Grips: Checkered square butt walnut; 6 in. model features Altamont Service walnut grips
Barrel: 4 in., 6.5 in.
Sights: Red ramp, micro adjustable rear
Weight: 48.5 oz.
Caliber: .44 Mag., .44 S&W Spl.
Capacity: 6 rounds
Features: Carbon steel frame with nickel finish, available blued
4 in.: $999
6.5 in.: $1169

M36

Action: Revolver
Grips: Wood
Barrel: 1.8 in.
Sights: Integral front, fixed rear
Weight: 19.5 oz.
Caliber: .38 S&W Spl. +P
Capacity: 5 rounds
Features: Small sized frame; exposed hammer; carbon steel frame and cylinder; blued or nickel finish; single or double action
MSRP $749

M60

Action: Revolver
Grips: Synthetic, wood
Barrel: 2.125 in., 3 in.
Sights: Black blade front, adjustable rear
Weight: 22.6 oz.–23.2 oz.
Caliber: .357 Mag., .38 S&W Spl. +P
Capacity: 5 rounds
Features: Satin stainless finish; single- or double-action; stainless steel fame and cylinder
MSRP $729

M325 THUNDER RANCH

Action: SA/DA revolver
Grips: Synthetic
Barrel: 4 in.
Sights: Interchangeable gold bead front; adjustable rear
Weight: 31 oz.
Caliber: .45 ACP
Capacity: 6 rounds
Features: Scandium alloy frame; stainless steel cylinder; matte black
MSRP $1329

SMITH & WESSON
M327

SMITH & WESSON
M327 TRR8

SMITH & WESSON M442

SMITH & WESSON M442
MACHINE ENGRAVED

M327

Action: Revolver
Grips: Wood
Barrel: 2 in.
Sights: Red ramp front, fixed rear
Weight: 21.4 oz.
Caliber: .357 Mag., .38 S&W Spl. +P
Capacity: 8 rounds
Features: Color case with overtravel stop; color case tear drop with pinned sear; large frame size; exposed hammer; matte black finish; scandium alloy frame and titanium alloy cylinder; polish button rifling; smooth double action with Wolff Mainspring
MSRP $1309

M327 TRR8

Action: SA/DA revolver
Grips: Synthetic
Barrel: 5 in.
Sights: Interchangeable front; adjustable V-notch rear
Weight: 35.3 oz.
Caliber: .357 Mag., .38 S&W Spl. +P
Capacity: 8 rounds
Features: Scandium alloy frame; stainless steel cylinder; matte black; large size frame; exposed hammer; equipment rails
MSRP $1329

M442

Action: DA revolver
Grips: Synthetic
Barrel: 1.87 in.
Sights: Integral front, fixed rear
Weight: 15 oz.
Caliber: .38 S&W Spl. +P
Capacity: 5 rounds
Features: Aluminum alloy frame; stainless steel cylinder; matte black finish; small size frame; internal hammer; cylinder cut for moon clips
MSRP $469

M442 MACHINE ENGRAVED

Action: DA revolver
Grips: Engraved wood
Barrel: 1.875 in.
Sights: Integral front, fixed rear
Weight: 15 oz.
Caliber: .38 S&W Spl. +P
Capacity: 5 rounds
Features: Aluminum alloy frame; stainless steel barrel/cylinder; matte black
MSRP $749

M460 XVR

Action: SA/DA revolver
Grips: Synthetic
Barrel: 10.5 in.
Sights: Interchangeable front, adjustable rear
Weight: 82.5 oz.
Caliber: .460 S&W Mag.
Capacity: 5 rounds
Features: Satin stainless finish; stainless steel frame and cylinder; X-Large size frame; exposed tear drop chrome hammer; .312 chrome trigger; multi-caliber capability: .454 Casull, .45 Colt; integral weaver base for optic mounting
MSRP $1369

SMITH & WESSON M460 XVR

Smith & Wesson

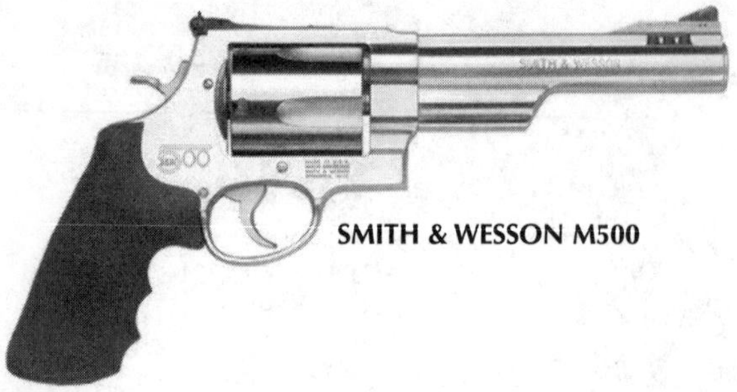

SMITH & WESSON M500

SMITH & WESSON M617

M500

Action: SA/DA revolver
Grips: Synthetic
Barrel: 6.5 in.
Sights: Red ramp front, adjustable white outline rear
Weight: 60.7 oz.
Caliber: .500 S&W Mag.
Capacity: 5 rounds
Features: Stainless steel frame and cylinder; satin stainless finish; integral compensator; internal lock; recoil tamed with effective muzzle compensator
MSRP $1299

M617

Action: SA/DA revolver
Grips: Synthetic
Barrel: 4 in.
Sights: Partridge front, adjustable rear
Weight: 38.9 oz.
Caliber: .22LR
Capacity: 10 rounds
Features: Stainless steel frame and cylinder with satin stainless finish; medium size frame with exposed hammer
MSRP $829

M625

Action: SA/DA revolver
Grips: Hogue combat laminate, red, white & blue
Barrel: 4 in.
Sights: Gold bead S&W interchangeable front; Black adjustable rear
Weight: 42 oz.
Caliber: .45 ACP
Capacity: 6 rounds
Features: Stainless steel frame and cylinder with satin stainless finish; deep cut broached rifling; chambered charge holes; PC trigger with stop
MSRP $1079

M625 JM

Action: SA/DA revolver
Grips: Jerry Miculek wood
Barrel: 4 in.
Sights: Gold bead partridge front, adjustable rear
Weight: 40.3 oz.
Caliber: .45 ACP
Capacity: 6 rounds
Features: Stainless steel frame and cylinder; matte stainless; large size frame; exposed hammer; Miculek style .265 wide grooved speed trigger; low reflection bead blast finish
MSRP $979

M627

Action: SA/DA revolver
Grips: Synthetic
Barrel: 5 in.
Sights: Interchangeable front; adjustable rear
Weight: 44 oz.
Caliber: .357 Mag., .38 S&W Spl. +P
Capacity: 8 rounds
Features: Stainless steel frame and cylinder; matte stainless; large size frame; exposed hammer
MSRP $1079

M629

Action: SA/DA revolver
Grips: Synthetic
Barrel: 7.5 in.
Sights: Red ramp, adjustable white outline
Weight: 44.3 oz.
Caliber: .44 Mag, .44 S&W Spl.
Capacity: 6 rounds
Features: Stainless steel frame and cylinder with satin stainless finish; exposed hammer
MSRP $1319

SMITH & WESSON M625

SMITH & WESSON M625 JM

SMITH & WESSON M627

SMITH & WESSON M629

Smith & Wesson

SMITH & WESSON M629 V-COMP

SMITH & WESSON M640

SMITH & WESSON M686

SMITH & WESSON M686 SSR

SMITH & WESSON M&P 9MM

SMITH & WESSON M&P40 COMPACT

SMITH & WESSON M&P45

M629 V-COMP

Action: SA/DA revolver
Grips: Synthetic
Barrel: 4 in.
Sights: Adjustable orange dovetail front, adjustable black rear
Weight: 40.3 oz.
Caliber: .44 Mag., .44 S&W Spl.
Capacity: 6 rounds
Features: Stainless steel frame and cylinder with matte finish; removable compensator and cap muzzle protector; chambered charge holes; ball detent lock-up; chromed hammer and trigger with overtravel stop
MSRP $1559

M640

Action: DA revolver
Grips: Synthetic
Barrel: 2.1 in.
Sights: Black blade front, fixed rear
Weight: 23 oz.
Caliber: .357 Mag., .38 S&W Spl. +P
Capacity: 5 rounds
Features: Stainless steel frame and cylinder; satin stainless finish; Pro Series
MSRP $839

M686

Action: Revolver
Grips: Synthetic
Barrel: 2.5 in.
Sights: Red ramp front, adjustable white outline rear
Weight: 34.7 oz.
Caliber: .357 Mag., .38 S&W Spl. +P
Capacity: 6 rounds
Features: Stainless steel frame and cylinder; satin stainless finish; exposed hammer; single- and double-action; built on L frame
MSRP $829

M686 SSR

Action: Revolver
Grips: Wood
Barrel: 4 in.
Sights: Interchangeable front, adjustable rear
Weight: 38.3 oz.
Caliber: .357 Mag., .38 S&W Spl. +P
Capacity: 6 rounds
Features: Stainless steel frame and barrel with satin finish; exposed hammer; chambered charge holes; bossed mainspring; ergonomic grip to force high-hand hold; custom barrel with recessed precision crown
MSRP $999

M&P 9MM

Action: Semiautomatic
Grips: Polymer
Barrel: 4.25 in.
Sights: Steel ramp dovetail mount front, steel Novak Lo-Mount Carry
Weight: 24 oz.
Caliber: 9mm
Capacity: 17+1 rounds
Features: Zytel polymer frame, stainless steel barrel/slide and structural components; optional tritium sights; black melonite finish
MSRP $569

M&P40 COMPACT

Action: Semiautomatic
Grips: Polymer
Barrel: 3.5 in.
Sights: White dot dovetail front; steel low profile carry rear
Weight: 21.9 oz.
Caliber: .40 S&W
Capacity: 10 rounds
Features: 3 interchangeable palm swell grip sizes; black melonite; thumb safety
MSRP $569

M&P45

Action: Semiautomatic
Grips: Polymer
Barrel: 4.5 in.
Sights: White dot dovetail front; steel low profile carry rear
Weight: 29.6 oz.
Caliber: .45 ACP
Capacity: 10+1 rounds
Features: Zytel polymer frame, stainless steel barrel/slide and structural components; black melonite finish; CA compliant; 3 interchangeable palm swell grip sizes
MSRP $599

Smith & Wesson

SMITH & WESSON
M&P BODYGUARD 380

SMITH & WESSON M&P
PRO SERIES C.O.R.E.
PISTOL

SMITH & WESSON MODEL 66

SMITH & WESSON
M&P R8

SMITH & WESSON M&P
SHIELD PISTOL

M&P BODYGUARD 380

Action: DA semiautomatic
Grips: Synthetic
Barrel: 2.75 in.
Sights: Adjustable
Weight: 11.85 oz.
Caliber: .38 ACP
Capacity: 6+1 rounds
Features: Stainless steel drift adjustable sights; ergonomic grip; high-strength polymer frame; external takedown lever and slide stop; manual thumb safety; double action fire control (2nd strike compatibility); stainless steel barrel and slide
MSRP. $379

M&P PRO SERIES C.O.R.E. PISTOL

Action: Striker Fire Double Action
Grips: Polymer
Barrel: 4.25 in., 5 in.
Sights: White dot dovetail front, fixed 2-dot rear
Weight: 24 oz.–26 oz.
Caliber: 9mm, .40 S&W
Capacity: 17+1, 15+1 rounds
Features: Competition Optics Ready Equipment; mounting platform on slide; engineered as a competition platform; polymer frame; ambidextrous operating controls; interchangeable back strap; Performance Center sear; Melonite finish
MSRP. $769

M&P R8

Action: SA/DA revolver
Grips: Polymer
Barrel: 5 in.
Sights: Interchangeable front, adjustable v-notch
Weight: 36.3 oz.
Caliber: .357 Mag., .38 S&W Spl. +P
Capacity: 8 rounds
Features: Single- or double-action; scandium alloy frame; stainless steel cylinder; integral accessory Picatinny style rail; precision barrel forcing cone
MSRP. $1329

M&P SHIELD PISTOL

Action: Striker Fired
Grips: Polymer
Barrel: 3.1 in.
Sights: White dot front, white 2-dot rear
Weight: 19 oz.
Caliber: 9mm, .40 S&W
Capacity: 6, 7, 8 rounds
Features: Slim, concealable, and lightweight defense firearm; high-strength polymer frame; Melonite coated; consistent 6.5 lb. trigger pull; loaded chamber indicator
MSRP. $449

MODEL 66

Action: DA/SA revolver
Grips: Synthetic
Barrel: 4.25 in.
Sights: Adjustable
Weight: 36.6 oz.
Caliber: .38 S&W Spl. +P, .357 Mag.
Capacity: 6 rounds
Features: Full top strap and barrel serration; ball-detent lock-up; two-piece barrel
MSRP. $849

Smith & Wesson

SMITH & WESSON MODEL 69

SMITH & WESSON MODEL 929

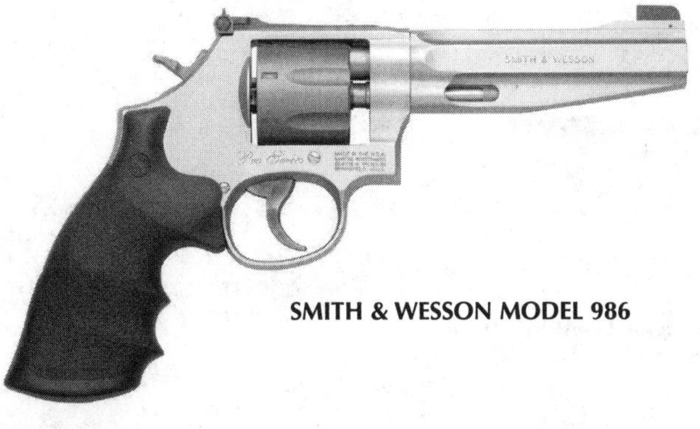

SMITH & WESSON MODEL 986

SMITH & WESSON SD9 VE

MODEL 69

Action: DA/SA revolver
Grips: Synthetic
Barrel: 4.25 in.
Sights: Adjustable
Weight: 37.2 oz.
Caliber: .44 Mag., .44 Spl.
Capacity: 5 rounds
Features: Full top strap and barrel serration; ball-detent lock-up; two-piece barrel
MSRP $849

MODEL 929

Action: DA/SA revolver
Grips: Synthetic
Barrel: 6.5 in.
Sights: Adjustable
Weight: 44.2 oz.
Caliber: 9mm
Capacity: 8 rounds
Features: Removable compensator; titanium cylinder; Jerry Miculek signature; chrome teardrop hammer; chrome trigger with stop
MSRP $1189

MODEL 986

Action: DA/SA revolver
Grips: Synthetic
Barrel: 5 in.
Sights: Adjustable
Weight: 34.9 oz.
Caliber: 9mm
Capacity: 7 rounds
Features: Titanium, fluted cylinder; precision crowned barrel; cylinder cut for moonclips
MSRP $1149

SD9 VE AND SD40 VE

Action: Striker Fired
Grips: Textured polymer
Barrel: 4 in.
Sights: White dot front, fixed 2-dot rear
Weight: 22.7 oz.
Caliber: 9mm, .40 S&W
Capacity: 10+1, 14+1, 16+1 rounds
Features: Lightweight polymer frame; front and rear slide serrations; Self Defense Trigger; ergonomic grip; Picatinny rail; two-tone finish
MSRP $389

Sphinx (by Kriss)

SDP COMPACT BLACK

Action: DA/SA semiautomatic
Grips: Synthetic
Barrel: 3.7 in.
Sights: Fixed
Weight: 29.27 oz.
Caliber: 9mm
Capacity: 10+1 or 15+1 rounds
Features: Hard anodized aluminum frame; Picatinny rail; ambidextrous decocking lever and magazine release; threaded barrel available
MSRP. $1395

SPHINX SDP COMPACT BLACK

Springfield Armory

SPRINGFIELD ARMORY 1911 RANGE OFFICER

SPRINGFIELD ARMORY EMP

1911 RANGE OFFICER

Action: Semiautomatic
Grips: Cocobolo
Barrel: 5 in.
Sights: Adjustable
Weight: 41 oz.
Caliber: 9mm
Capacity: 9 rounds
Features: Competition ready 1911 without the recoil of a .45 caliber round
MSRP. $977

EMP (ENHANCED MICRO PISTOL)

Action: Semiautomatic
Grips: Thin line cocobolo wood, G10
Barrel: 3 in.
Sights: Fixed low profile combat rear, dovetail
Weight: 26 oz.–33 oz.
Caliber: 9mm, .40 S&W
Capacity: 3–9 (9mm) or 3–8 (.40 S&W) rounds
Features: Forged stainless steel, satin finish; dual spring recoil system with full length guide rod
MSRP. . . . . $1249–$1320

LIGHTWEIGHT CHAMPION OPERATOR

Action: Semiautomatic
Grips: Cocobolo wood
Barrel: 4 in.
Sights: Fixed low profile combat rear, dovetail
Weight: 31 oz.
Caliber: .45 ACP
Capacity: 2–7 rounds
Features: Stainless steel match grade, fully supported ramped bull barrel; long aluminum Match Grade trigger; forged aluminum alloy with integral accessory rail; black hard coat anodized; dual spring with full length guide rod
MSRP. $1050

SPRINGFIELD ARMORY LIGHTWEIGHT CHAMPION OPERATOR

Springfield Armory

SPRINGFIELD ARMORY MIL-SPEC FULL SIZE STAINLESS

MIL-SPEC FULL SIZE STAINLESS

Action: Semiautomatic
Grips: Cocobolo wood and black plastic
Barrel: 5 in.
Sights: Fixed combat, 3-dot
Weight: 39 oz.
Caliber: .45 ACP
Capacity: 2–7 rounds
Features: Forged stainless steel, matte rounds with polished flats; GI style recoil system; available Parkerized finish
MSRP . . . . $719–$819

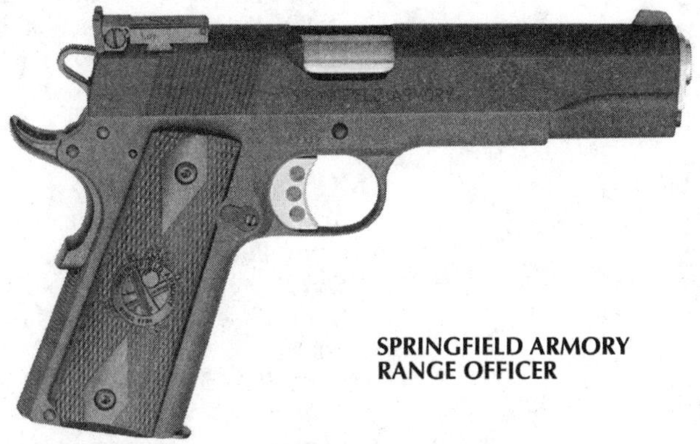

SPRINGFIELD ARMORY RANGE OFFICER

RANGE OFFICER

Action: Semiautomatic
Grips: Cocobolo wood
Barrel: 5 in.
Sights: Low profile adjustable target
Weight: 40 oz.
Caliber: .45 ACP
Capacity: 2–7 rounds
Features: Standard guide rod; forged steel frame with blued finish; stainless Match Grade barrel
MSRP $899

SPRINGFIELD ARMORY TRP

TRP (TACTICAL RESPONSE PISTOL)

Action: Semiautomatic
Grips: G10 composite
Barrel: 5 in.
Sights: Front tritium 3-dot, fixed low profile combat rear, dovetail
Weight: 42 oz.
Caliber: .45 ACP
Capacity: 2–7 rounds
Features: Forged steel frame with black armory kote; two piece full length guide rod; wide-mouth magazine well; tuned trigger; available in Armory Kote, Light Rail Armory Kote, and stainless
MSRP $1646

SPRINGFIELD ARMORY XD (M)

XD (M)

Action: DA semiautomatic
Grips: Polymer
Barrel: 3.8 in., 4.5 in. Match Grade
Sights: 3-dot
Weight: 27.5 oz.–32 oz.
Caliber: 9mm, .40 S&W, .45 ACP
Capacity: 19 (9mm), 16 (.40 S&W) or 13 (.45 ACP) rounds
Features: "M" features include carrying case, two magazines, paddle holster, magi loader, double magi pouch and three interchangeable backstraps and two magazines; "all-terrain" texture and deep slide serrations are standard
9mm: . . . . $681–$744
.40 S&W: . . . . $681–$744
.45 ACP: . . . . $709–$771

Springfield Armory

SPRINGFIELD ARMORY
XD (M) COMPACT

SPRINGFIELD
ARMORY XD-S

SPRINGFIELD ARMORY
XDS 4.0

XD (M) COMPACT

Action: Semiautomatic
Grips: Synthetic
Barrel: 3.8 in., 5.25 in.
Sights: Fiber optic front, adjustable rear
Weight: 27 oz.–32 oz.
Caliber: 9mm, .45 ACP, .40 S&W
Capacity: 13, 19 rounds
Features: A handgun with improved accuracy, lessened recoil, faster shot recovery and greater sight radius of its newly enhanced performance; lightening cut in the slide reduces reciprocating mass which allows for faster cycling and allows a larger variety of loads to be used
MSRP . . . . $689–$751

XD-S

Action: DAO semiautomatic
Grips: Polymer
Barrel: 3.3 in.
Sights: Steel dovetail rear, fiber optic front
Weight: 21.5 oz.
Caliber: .45 ACP
Capacity: 5+1 rounds
Features: Slim contour, single stack frame; Ultra Safety Assurance trigger system; loaded chamber indicator; fail-safe disassembly; Picatinny rail system; Mould-Tru backstraps; Melonite finish
MSRP . . . . $499–$593

XDS 4.0

Action: Semiautomatic
Grips: Synthetic
Barrel: 4 in.
Sights: Fixed
Weight: 25 oz.
Caliber: 9mm
Capacity: 9 or 10 rounds
Features: X-Tension magazine available; fiber optic front and dovetail rear sights
MSRP . . . . $599–$669

Steyr Arms

STEYR ARMS C9-A1

STEYR L-A1

C9-A1

Action: Striker-fired semiautomatic
Grips: Textured polymer
Barrel: 3.6 in.
Sights: Fixed triangular/trapezoid
Weight: 25.6 oz.
Caliber: 9mm
Capacity: 17+1 rounds
Features: Polymer frame; trigger, internal striker, internal gun-lock safeties; polygonal rifling; black matte Mannox finish; Picatinny rail
MSRP. $560

L-A1

Action: Semiautomatic
Grips: Synthetic
Barrel: 4.5 in.
Sights: Fixed triangular/trapezoid
Weight: 28.6 oz.
Caliber: 9mm, .40 S&W
Capacity: 12 or 17 rounds
Features: Rectangular sights with or without Trilux, match sights; full size service pistol; matte finish
From $560

STI International

STI INTERNATIONAL APEIRO

APEIRO

Action: Semiautomatic
Grips: STI patented modular polymer
Barrel: 5 in.
Sights: Dawson fiber optic front mounted on barrel, STI adjustable rear
Weight: 39 oz.
Caliber: 9mm, .40 S&W, .45 ACP
Capacity: 11+1, 14+1, 17+1 rounds
Features: Full length stainless steel bar stock slide features STI's unique sabertooth rear cocking serrations; Schuemann barrel; STI recoil master; STI long curved trigger; blued finish with two toned blued/stainless steel slide
MSRP. $2699

STI INTERNATIONAL DUTY ONE SERIES

DUTY ONE SERIES

Action: Semiautomatic
Grips: STI patented modular polymer
Barrel: 3 in., 4.37 in., 5.11 in.
Sights: STI Ramped front, Tactical Adjustable Rear Sight
Weight: 31.6 oz.–37.2 oz.
Caliber: 9mm, .40 S&W, .45 ACP
Capacity: 8, 9 rounds
Features: STI government frame; integral tactical rail; ambidextrous thumb safeties and beavertail grip safety; lowered and flared ejection port; STI RecoilMaster guide rod system; front and rear serrations; blued matte finish
MSRP. . . . . $1499–$1599

STI International

STI INTERNATIONAL
EAGLE 5.0

STI INTERNATIONAL
EDGE

STI INTERNATIONAL
EXECUTIVE

STI INTERNATIONAL
LAWMAN 4

EAGLE 5.0

Action: Semiautomatic
Grips: STI patented modular polymer
Barrel: 5 in.
Sights: STI front, STI adjustable rear
Weight: 35.2 oz.
Caliber: 9mm, .357 SIG, .38 Super, .40 S&W, .45 ACP
Capacity: 11+1, 14+1, 17+1 rounds
Features: Stainless STI grip, ambi thumb, ramped bull barrel; STI patented modular steel frame; STI rear serrations; blued finish
MSRP . . . . $2099–$2199

EDGE

Action: Semiautomatic
Grips: STI patented modular polymer with aluminum mag well
Barrel: 5 in.
Sights: STI front, STI adjustable rear
Weight: 37.6 oz.
Caliber: 9mm, .38 Super, .40 S&W, .45 ACP
Capacity: 11+1, 14+1, 17+1 rounds
Features: STI fully supported, ramped bull barrel; stainless STI grip and ambi slided thumb; STI recoil master guide rod; blued finish
MSRP $2199

EXECUTIVE

Action: Semiautomatic
Grips: STI patented modular polymer with stainless mag well
Barrel: 5 in.
Sights: Dawson fiber optic front, STI adjustable rear
Weight: 39.2 oz.
Caliber: .40 S&W
Capacity: 14+1 rounds
Features: Stainless STI grip, ambi thumb, ramped bull barrel; STI patented modular steel, long wide frame; STI rear serrations; blued finish
MSRP $2599

LAWMAN FAMILY

Action: Semiautomatic
Grips: G10 Mycarta grip panels
Barrel: 3.24 in., 4.26 in., 5.11 in.
Sights: STI ramped front, tactical adjustable rear
Weight: 23.8 oz.–38.9 oz.
Caliber: 9mm, .45 ACP
Capacity: 6+1 rounds
Features: Forged aluminum frame; carbon steel slide; blue high rise beavertail grip safety and single sided thumb safety; available in traditional polished blue, two tone polymer light brown/coyote tan, and two tone black/olive drab
MSRP $1399

STI International

STI INTERNATIONAL RANGE MASTER

STI INTERNATIONAL TACTICAL FAMILY

STI INTERNATIONAL TACTICAL SS FAMILY

STI INTERNATIONAL TARGET MASTER

RANGE MASTER

Action: Semiautomatic
Grips: STI logo, checkered, cocobolo wood, standard thickness
Barrel: 5 in.
Sights: STI front, STI adjustable rear
Weight: 41.4 oz.
Caliber: 9mm, .45 ACP
Capacity: 8, 9 rounds
Features: STI long curved trigger; ramped bull barrel; STI polished stainless grip and ambi thumb; STI recoil master guide rod; matte blued finish
MSRP $1599

TACTICAL FAMILY

Action: Semiautomatic
Grips: Polymer
Barrel: 3.75 in., 4.26 in., 5.01 in.
Sights: STI ramped front, Novak style fixed rear
Weight: 30.1 oz.–34.2 oz.
Caliber: 9mm, .40 S&W, .45 ACP
Capacity: 11+1, 14+1, 17+1 rounds
Features: STI International's patented 2011 technology gives the STI Tactical more fire power advantage than 1911 tactical pistols without greatly increasing the size of the grip; less recoil felt; aluminum frame; light tactical rail milled into the dust cover of the frame; STI patented glass filled polymer modular grips; blued slide
MSRP . . . . $2099–$2299

TACTICAL SS FAMILY

Action: Semiautomatic
Grips: STI patented modular polymer
Barrel: 3.76 in., 4.26 in., 5 in.
Sights: STI Ramped front, STI Fixed Ledge Style Rear
Weight: 34.4 oz.–41.1 oz.
Caliber: 9mm, .40 S&W, .45 ACP
Capacity: 8+1 rounds
Features: Tactical line features in a traditional 1911 package; fully forged frames with Picatinny rail system; flat top slide with front and rear serrations; ambidextrous thumb safety and beavertail grip safety; blued matte finish
MSRP . . . . $1899–$1999

TARGET MASTER

Action: Semiautomatic
Grips: STI logo, checkered, cocobolo wood, standard thickness
Barrel: 6 in.
Sights: Aristocrat adjustable
Weight: 45.5 oz.
Caliber: 9mm, .45 ACP
Capacity: 8, 9 rounds
Features: STI long curved trigger; STI stainless grip and ambi sided thumb; STI two piece rail guide rod; matte blued finish
MSRP $1699

STI International

STI INTERNATIONAL
TROJAN 5.0

TROJAN 5.0

Action: Semiautomatic
Grips: STI logo, checkered, cocobolo wood, thin
Barrel: 5 in., 6 in.
Sights: STI front, STI adjustable rear
Weight: 36 oz.
Caliber: 9mm, .38 Super, .40 S&W, .45 ACP
Capacity: 8, 9 rounds
Features: STI standard blue grip and single-slided thumb safeties; STI one-piece steel guide rod; flat blued finish
MSRP . . . . $1299–$1399

Stoeger

STOEGER COUGAR

STOEGER COUGAR
COMPACT

COUGAR

Action: DA/SA semiautomatic
Grips: Black plastic
Barrel: 3.6 in.
Sights: White 3-dot
Weight: 32 oz.–32.6 oz.
Caliber: .45 ACP, .40 S&W, 9mm
Capacity: 8+1, 11+1, 15+1 rounds
Features: Ambidextrous safety; rotary-locking principal; available in a non-glare Bruniton silver steel slide with an anodized alloy matte-silver frame or two-tone style, featuring a matte Bruniton black steel slide combined with an anodized alloy matte-silver frame
MSRP. . . . . $469–$509

COUGAR COMPACT

Action: DA/SA semiautomatic
Grips: Black plastic
Barrel: 3.6 in.
Sights: Quick read 3-dot
Weight: 32 oz.
Caliber: 9mm
Capacity: 13+1 rounds
Features: Ambidextrous safety; rotary-locking principal; Bruniton matte black finish
MSRP. $469

Taurus

22BR

Action: Semiautomatic
Grips: Rosewood
Barrel: 2.75 in.
Sights: Fixed
Weight: 12.3 oz.
Caliber: .22LR
Capacity: 8+1 rounds
Features: Steel/alloy frame with blued finish; manual safety; tip-up barrel; Taurus security system
MSRP. $276

TAURUS 22BR

22/25 PLY

Action: DA semiautomatic
Grips: Polymer
Barrel: 2.3 in.
Sights: Fixed
Weight: 11.3 oz.
Caliber: .22LR, .25 ACP
Capacity: 8+1, 9+1 rounds
Features: Polymer/blued steel construction; blued steel finish; tip-up barrel
MSRP. . . . . $256–$276

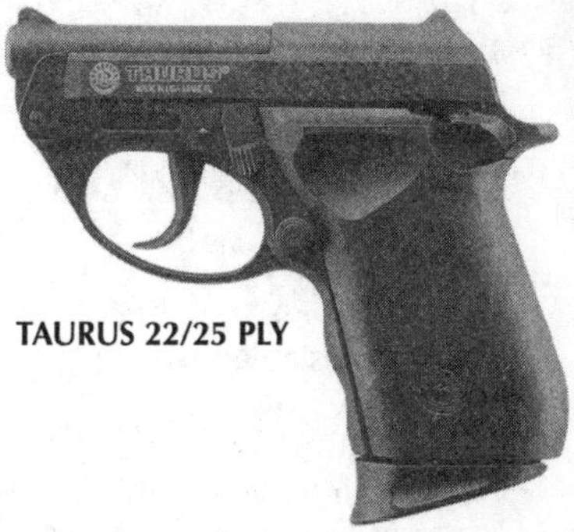

TAURUS 22/25 PLY

24/7 G2

Action: DA/SA semiautomatic
Grips: Checkered polymer with metallic inserts
Barrel: 4.2 in.
Sights: Low-profile, adjustable rear
Weight: 28 oz.
Caliber: 9mm, .40 S&W, .45 ACP
Capacity: 17+1 rounds (9mm), 15+1 rounds (.40 S&W), 12+1 rounds (.45 ACP)
Features: Blued or stainless steel; DA/SA trigger system; SA or DA only; contoured thumb rests; Picatinny rail; compact model available at same price
Blued: $528
Stainless: $543

TAURUS 24/7 G2

44

Action: Revolver
Grips: Soft rubber
Barrel: 4 in., 6.5 in., 8.4 in.
Sights: Fixed
Weight: 45–57 oz.
Caliber: .44 Mag.
Capacity: 6 rounds
Features: Transfer bar; ported barrel; matte stainless steel finish; double and single-action
4 in.: $726
6.5 in.: . . . . $741–$800
8.4 in.: . . . . $741–$800

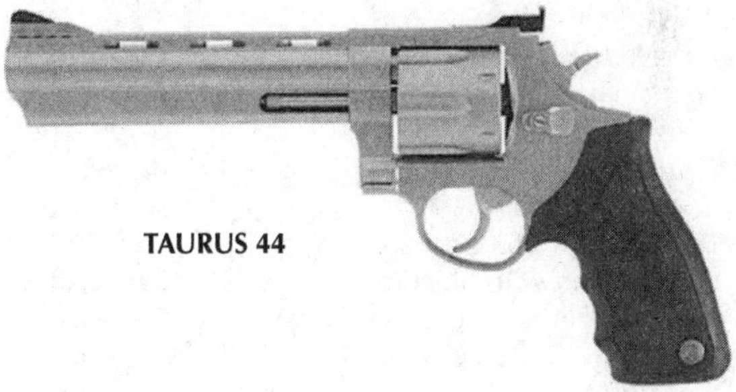

TAURUS 44

82

Action: Revolver
Grips: Rubber
Barrel: 4 in.
Sights: Fixed
Weight: 36.5 oz.
Caliber: .38 Spl. +P
Capacity: 6 rounds
Features: Transfer bar; steel construction with blued finish; single/double-action trigger
Blued: $472

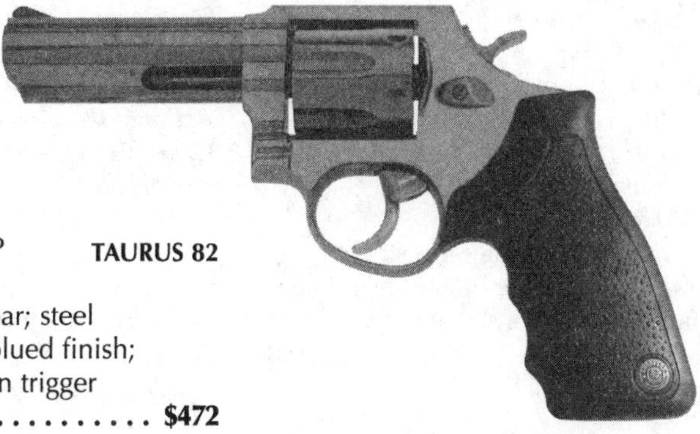

TAURUS 82

Taurus

92

Action: Semiautomatic
Grips: Checkered rubber
Barrel: 5 in.
Sights: Fixed-1 dot front, fixed-2 dots rear
Weight: 34 oz.
Caliber: 9mm
Capacity: 10+1 or 17+1 rounds
Features: Blued, stainless steel finish; steel/alloy construction; firing pin block, hammer decocker, manual safety
Blued: $638
Stainless: $653

.380 MINI REVOLVER

Action: Revolver
Grips: Rubber
Barrel: 1.75 in.
Sights: Adjustable rear
Weight: 15.5 oz.
Caliber: .380 ACP
Capacity: 5 rounds
Features: Double-action trigger; fully enclosed hammer; blued or matte stainless finish; bobbed hammer
Blued: $434
Stainless: $466

605

Action: Revolver
Grips: Rubber
Barrel: 2 in.
Sights: Fixed
Weight: 24 oz.
Caliber: .357 Mag
Capacity: 5 rounds
Features: Transfer bar safety; steel construction with blued or stainless finish; single-double action trigger
Blued: $356
Stainless: $371

608

Action: Revolver
Grips: Rubber
Barrel: 4 in., 6.5 in.
Sights: Fixed front, adjustable rear
Weight: 44 oz.–51 oz.
Caliber: .357 Mag
Capacity: 8 rounds
Features: Matte stainless steel finish; transfer bar; large frame; steel frame; Taurus security system; porting
MSRP: $688

TAURUS 92

TAURUS .380 MINI REVOLVER

TAURUS 605

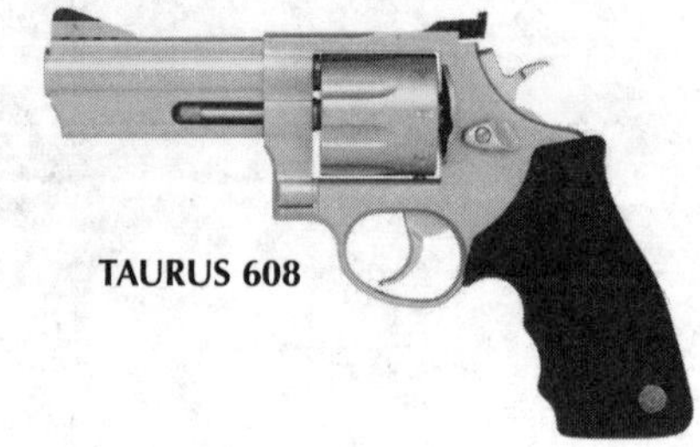

TAURUS 608

TAURUS 709 "SLIM"

709 "SLIM"

Action: Semiautomatic
Grips: Checkered polymer
Barrel: 3 in.
Sights: Fixed
Weight: 19 oz.
Caliber: 9mm
Capacity: 7+1 rounds
Features: Steel construction; blued or stainless finish; single- and double-action
Blued: $404
Stainless: $504

TAURUS 738 TCP

738 TCP

Action: DA semiautomatic
Grips: Checkered polymer
Barrel: 2.84 in.
Sights: Fixed
Weight: 10.2 oz.
Caliber: .380 ACP
Capacity: 6+1 rounds
Features: Titanium construction; compact frame; smooth trigger
MSRP $356

TAURUS 809

TAURUS 905

TAURUS JUDGE .45/.410

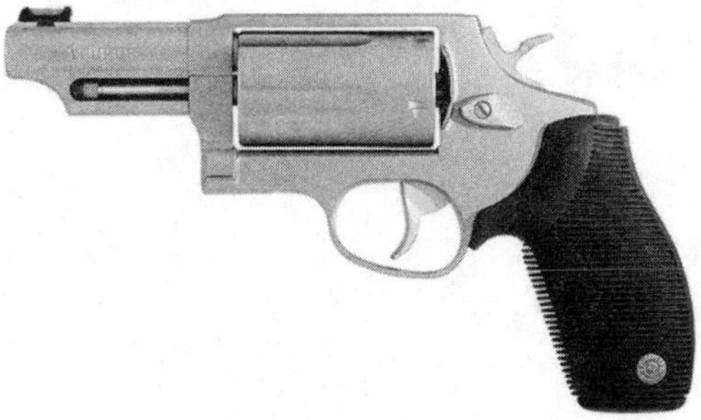

TAURUS RAGING BULL 444

809

Action: Semiautomatic
Grips: Checkered polymer
Barrel: 3.5 in., 4 in.
Sights: Fixed
Weight: 30.2 oz.
Caliber: 9mm
Capacity: 17+1 rounds
Features: Black Tennifer finish; smooth trigger type; strike-two capability.
MSRP. $487

905

Action: DA/SA revolver
Grips: Rubber
Barrel: 2 in.
Sights: Fixed
Weight: 22.2 oz.
Caliber: 9mm
Capacity: 5 rounds
Features: Blued finish; transfer bar; steel frame; porting; Taurus security system
Blued: $481
Stainless: $528
Stainless: $605

JUDGE .45/.410

Action: DA/SA revolver
Grips: Taurus rubber grips
Barrel: 3 in.
Sights: Red fiber optic, fixed
Weight: 29–36.8 oz.
Caliber: .45 Colt/.410
Capacity: 5 rounds
Features: Firing pin block, transfer bar safety; compact frame; matte stainless steel finish; steel construction
MSRP. . . . . $608–$653

RAGING BULL 444

Action: Revolver
Grips: Rubber w/cushioned insert
Barrel: 6.5 in., 8.38 in.
Sights: Partridge front, adjustable rear
Weight: 53 oz.–63 oz.
Caliber: .44 Mag.
Capacity: 6 rounds
Features: Steel construction with blued or stainless steel finish; transfer bar; dual lockup cylinder; porting; Taurus security system
Blued: $753
Stainless: $800

Taurus

TAURUS RAGING JUDGE MAGNUM

TAURUS TRACKER 992

TAURUS SLIM 740

TAURUS TRACKER SERIES

RAGING JUDGE MAGNUM

Action: DA/SA revolver
Grips: Rubber with soft cushion insert
Barrel: 3 in., 6.5 in.
Sights: Fiber optic front, fixed rear
Weight: 60.6 oz.–73 oz.
Caliber: .410/.45 Colt, .454 Casull
Capacity: 6 rounds
Features: Stainless steel finish; "Raging Bull" backstrap for added cushioning
MSRP $1038

SLIM 740

Action: DA/SA semiautomatic
Grips: Polymer metallic inserts
Barrel: 3.2 in.
Sights: Adjustable rear
Weight: 19 oz.
Caliber: .40 S&W
Capacity: 6+1 rounds
Features: Sub-compact pistol in blued, black Tenifer, or stainless steel; loaded chamber indicator; low-profile sights; short, crisp DA/SA trigger pull
Blued: $404
Stainless: $504

TRACKER 992

Action: SA/DA revolver
Grips: Taurus Ribber
Barrel: 4 in., 6.5 in.
Sights: Adjustable
Weight: 55 oz.
Caliber: .22LR
Capacity: 9 rounds
Features: The versatile Tracker 992 easily transforms from .22LR to .22 Magnum in seconds with its breakthrough removable cylinder; perfect for plinking, target practice, or varmint hunting
Blued: $591
Stainless: $627

TRACKER SERIES

Action: Revolver
Grips: Rubber with ribs
Barrel: 4 in., 4.5 in., 6.5 in.
Sights: Fixed front, adjustable rear
Weight: 28.8 oz.–46 oz.
Caliber: .17HMR, .22LR, .22 Mag., .357 Mag., .44 Mag.
Capacity: 5, 7, 9 rounds
Features: Matte stainless steel or blued finish; transfer bar; steel frame; porting
MSRP . . . . $555–$693

Taylor's & Co.

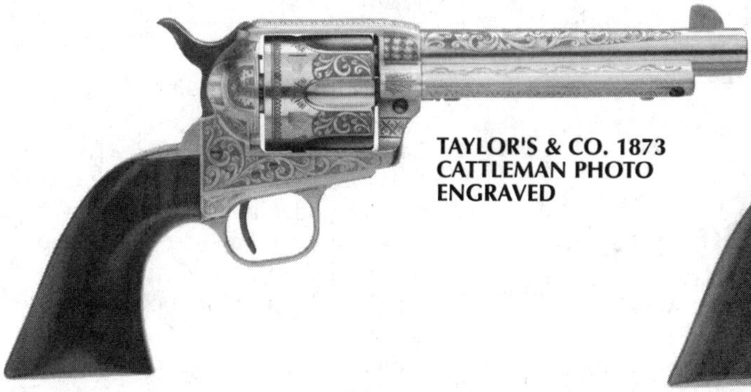

TAYLOR'S & CO. 1873 CATTLEMAN PHOTO ENGRAVED

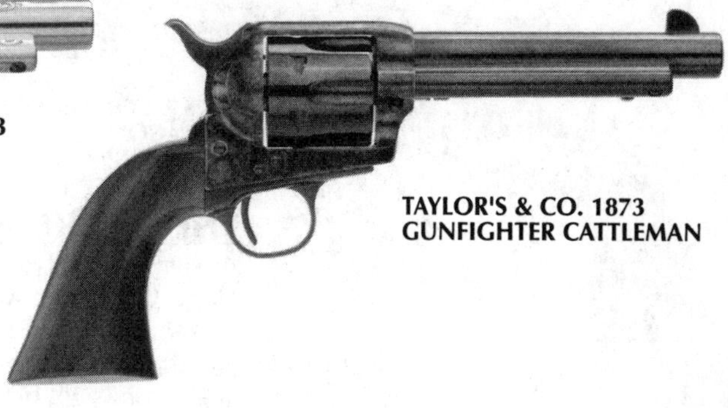

TAYLOR'S & CO. 1873 GUNFIGHTER CATTLEMAN

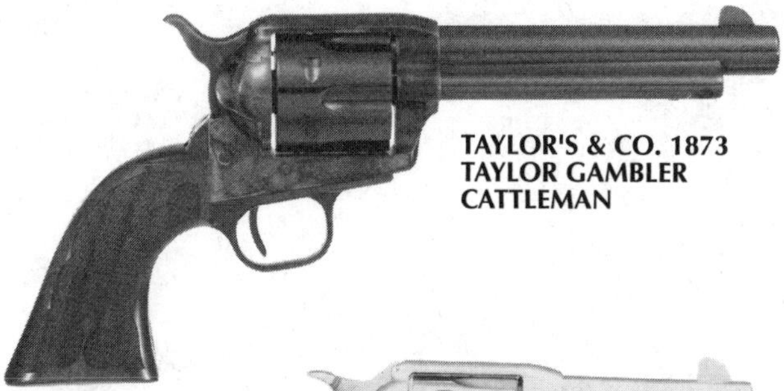

TAYLOR'S & CO. 1873 TAYLOR GAMBLER CATTLEMAN

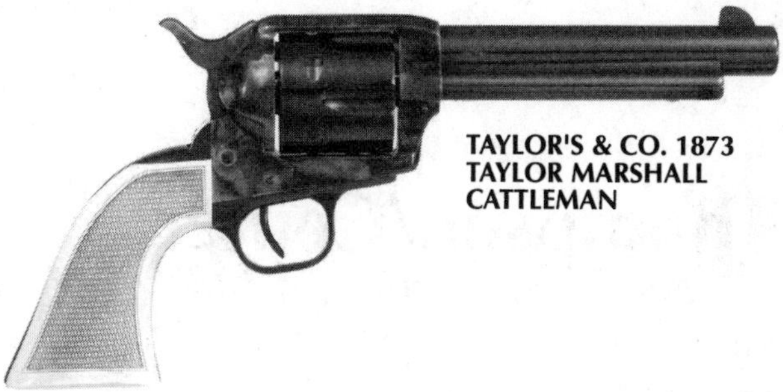

TAYLOR'S & CO. 1873 TAYLOR MARSHALL CATTLEMAN

TAYLOR'S & CO. RUNNIN' IRON

1873 CATTLEMAN PHOTO ENGRAVED

Action: SA revolver
Grips: Walnut
Barrel: 4.75 in., 5.5 in., 7.5 in.
Sights: Fixed
Weight: 2 lb. 4 oz.–3 lb. 6 oz.
Caliber: .357 Mag., .45 LC
Capacity: 6 rounds
Features: White, heat-treated steel finish with charcoal blued screws; laser-engraved and hand chased; forged frame
MSRP. . . . . $848–$875

1873 GUNFIGHTER CATTLEMAN

Action: SA revolver
Grips: Walnut
Barrel: 5.5 in.
Sights: Fixed
Weight: 2 lb. 5 oz.
Caliber: .357 Mag., .45 Colt
Capacity: 6 rounds
Features: Special Army-sized grip; steel trigger guard and backstrap; blued finish with case-hardened frame; forged frame
MSRP. . . . . $526–$560

1873 TAYLOR GAMBLER CATTLEMAN

Action: SA revolver
Grips: Walnut
Barrel: 5.5 in.
Sights: Fixed
Weight: 2 lb. 5 oz.
Caliber: .357 Mag., .45 Colt
Capacity: 6 rounds
Features: Fancy checkered walnut grip; blued color case-hardened forged frame
MSRP. $552

1873 TAYLOR MARSHALL CATTLEMAN

Action: SA revolver
Grips: White PVC
Barrel: 5.5 in.
Sights: Fixed
Weight: 2 lb. 5 oz.
Caliber: .45 Colt
Capacity: 6 rounds
Features: Checkered white PVC grip; blued color case-hardened forged frame
MSRP. $640

RUNNIN' IRON

Action: SA revolver
Grips: Checkered walnut
Barrel: 3.5 oz.–5.5 in.
Sights: Wider fixed, open
Weight: 39 oz.
Caliber: .45 Colt, .357 Mag.
Capacity: 6 rounds
Features: Designed for the sport of mounted shooting; offered in stainless or blued finish with low, wide hammer spur; checkered, one-piece gunfighter style grips in walnut or black polymer; wide trigger and extra clearance at front and rear of cylinder
Stainless: . . . . $743–$911
Blued: . . . . $579–$734

Taylor's & Co.

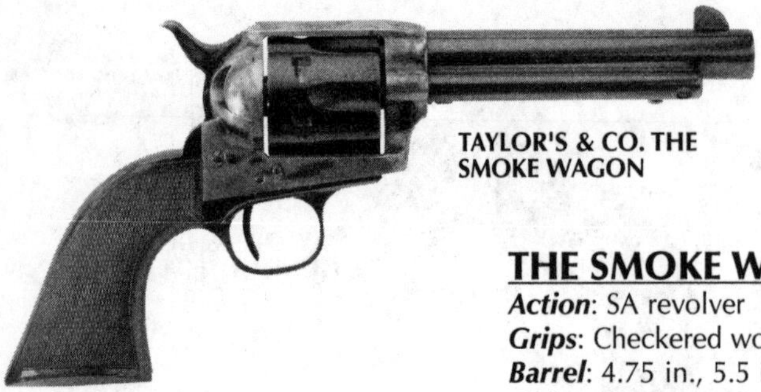

TAYLOR'S & CO. THE SMOKE WAGON

THE SMOKE WAGON

Action: SA revolver
Grips: Checkered wood
Barrel: 4.75 in., 5.5 in.
Sights: Open rear sight groove, wide angle front sight blade
Weight: 40 oz.
Caliber: .357 Mag., .45 Colt, .44-40 Win.
Capacity: 6 rounds
Features: Low profile hammer; deluxe edition model includes custom tuning, custom hammer and base pin springs; jig-cut positive angles on trigger and sears; wire bolt and trigger springs
Standard: $556
Deluxe: $711

Thompson/Center

ENCORE

Action: Single-shot, break open design
Grips: Walnut or rubber
Barrel: 12 in., 15 in.
Sights: Adjustable rear; ramp front blade
Weight: 68–72 oz.
Caliber: .204 Ruger, .223 Rem, .22-250 Rem., .243 Win., .25-06 Rem., .270 Win., 7mm-08 Rem., .308 Win., .30-06 Spfd., .45-70 Govt., .44 Rem. Mag., .45 Colt/.410, .17 HMR, .22LR, .460 S&W, .500 S&W
Capacity: 1 round
Features: Interchangeable barrels; button rifled; drilled and tapped for T/C scope mounts; adjustable trigger for overtravel; ambidextrous pistol grip with finger grooves and butt cap; matching forend; blued or stainless steel finish; patented automatic hammer block with bolt interlock
MSRP $779

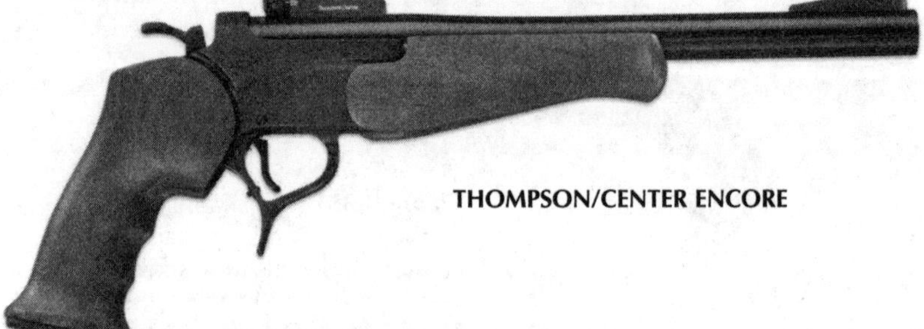

THOMPSON/CENTER ENCORE

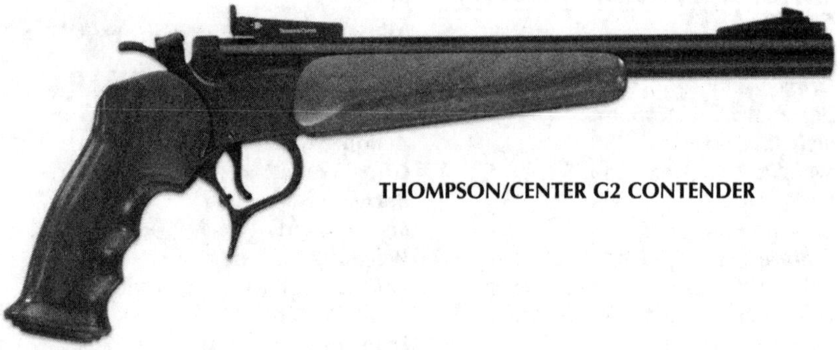

THOMPSON/CENTER G2 CONTENDER

G2 CONTENDER

Action: Single shot, break open design
Grips: Walnut or rubber
Barrel: 12 in., 14 in.
Sights: Adjustable rear; ramp front blade
Weight: 56–60 oz.
Caliber: .22LR Match, .357 Mag., .44 Rem. Mag., .45 Colt/410 Vent Rib, .223 Rem., .17 HMR, .204 Ruger, .22 Hornet, 6.8 mm Rem., 7-30 Waters, .45-70 Govt., .30-30 Win.
Capacity: 1 round
Features: .45/410 models include removable choke tube and wrench; stainless steel or walnut frame; manual firing pin selector; button rifled; drilled and tapped for T/C scope mounts
MSRP $729

Traditions Firearms

TRADITIONS FIREARMS FRONTIER

TRADITIONS FIREARMS RAWHIDE

FRONTIER SERIES

Action: SA revolver
Grips: Simulated ivory or walnut
Barrel: 4.75 in., 5.5 in., 7.5 in.
Sights: Front blade
Weight: N/A
Caliber: .357 Mag., .44 Mag., .45 Colt, .44-40 Win.
Capacity: 6 rounds
Features: 1873 single action revolvers; deep bluing and nickel frames and barrel or color case hardened frame, all polished to perfection; transfer bar safety system provides the highest lever of safety offered in an 1873 single action firearm
MSRP . . . . $529–$644

RAWHIDE SERIES

Action: SA revolver
Grips: Walnut
Barrel: 4.75 in., 5.5 in., 7.5 in.
Sights: Front blade
Weight: N/A
Caliber: .45 Colt, .357 Mag., .22LR, and .22LR/.22 Mag.
Capacity: 6 rounds
Features: Quality single action shooter features at an affordable price; matte black finish that provides excellent corrosion resistance; transfer bar system provides the highest level of safety offered in an 1873 single action
MSRP . . . . $459–$504

Tristar Arms

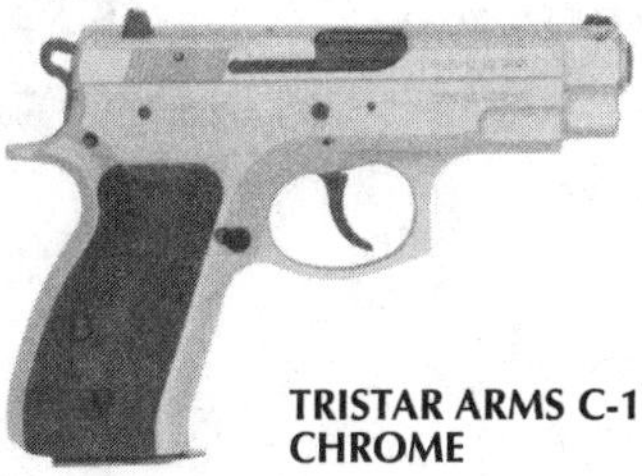

TRISTAR ARMS C-100 CHROME

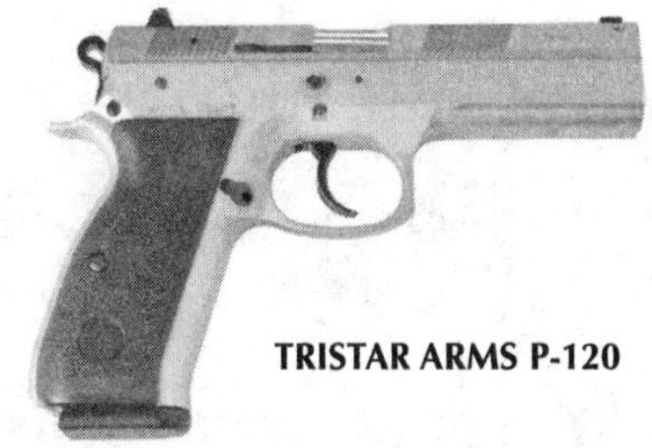

TRISTAR ARMS P-120

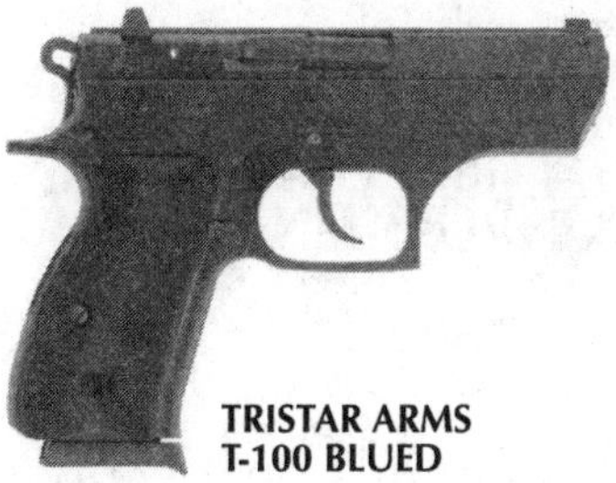

TRISTAR ARMS T-100 BLUED

C-100

Action: DA/SA semiautomatic
Grips: Polymer
Barrel: 3.9 in.
Sights: Rear dovetail, fixed front
Weight: 24.48 oz.–26.08 oz.
Caliber: 9mm, .40 S&W
Capacity: 11, 15 rounds
Features: Produced to NATO specs; rear snag-free dovetail sights; fixed blade front sight; black polycoat finish; black polymer checkered grips; includes two magazines and a hard plastic case
MSRP . . . . $459–$479

P-120

Action: DA/SA semiautomatic
Grips: Polymer
Barrel: 4.7 in.
Sights: Rear dovetail, fixed front
Weight: 29.9 oz.
Caliber: 9mm
Capacity: 17 rounds
Features: Originally created for military use; constructed from steel alloy; blued or chrome finish; rear snag-free dovetail sights; fixed blade front sight; includes two magazines, cleaning kit, gun lock, and a black carrying case
MSRP . . . . $489–$509

T-100

Action: DA/SA semiautomatic
Grips: Polymer
Barrel: 3.7 in.
Sights: Rear dovetail, fixed front
Weight: 26.24 oz.
Caliber: 9mm
Capacity: 15 rounds
Features: Compact pistol perfect for concealed carry; constructed from steel alloy; blued or chrome finish; rear snag-free dovetail sights; fixed blade front sight; includes two magazines, cleaning kit, gun lock, and a black carrying case
MSRP . . . . $459–$479

Uberti

UBERTI 1851 NAVY CONVERSION

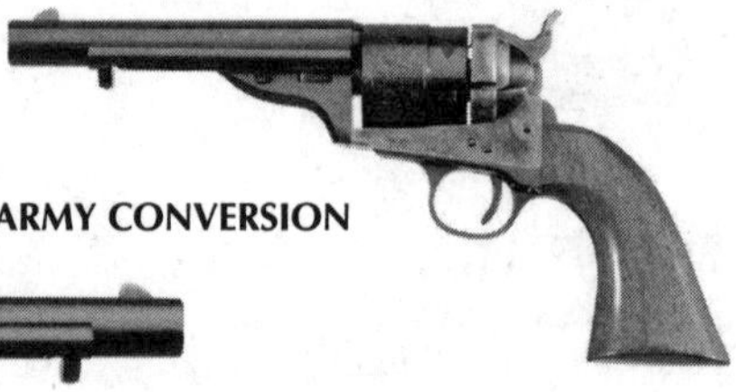

UBERTI 1860 ARMY CONVERSION

UBERTI 1871–1872 OPEN-TOP CONVERSION

UBERTI 1873 CATTLEMAN BIRD'S HEAD

UBERTI 1873 CATTLEMAN BISLEY

UBERTI 1873 .22LR

1851 NAVY CONVERSION

Action: SA revolver
Grips: Walnut
Barrel: 4.75 in., 5.5 in., 7.5 in.
Sights: Fixed, open
Weight: 42 oz.
Caliber: .38 Spl.
Capacity: 6 rounds
Features: Case-hardened frame octagonal barrel; brass backstrap and trigger guard; conversion revolver frames are retro-fitted with loading gates to accommodate metallic cartridges like the originals
MSRP $569

1860 ARMY CONVERSION

Action: SA revolver
Grips: Walnut
Barrel: 4.75 in., 5.5 in., 8 in.
Sights: Fixed, open
Weight: 42 oz.
Caliber: .38 Spl., .45 Colt
Capacity: 6 rounds
Features: Case-hardened frame; round barrel; steel backstrap and trigger guard; conversion revolver frames are retro-fitted with loading gates to accommodate metallic cartridges like the originals
MSRP $589

1871–1872 OPEN-TOP CONVERSION

Action: SA revolver
Grips: Walnut
Barrel: 4.75 in., 5.5 in., 7.5 in.
Sights: Fixed, open
Weight: 42 oz.
Caliber: .38 Spl., .45 Colt
Capacity: 6 rounds
Features: 1872 model has steel backstrap and trigger guard; 1871 model has brass backstrap and trigger guard; case-hardened frame; round barrel; blued finish conversion revolver frames are retro-fitted with loading gates to accommodate metallic cartridges like the originals
1871: $539
1872: $569

1873 BIRD'S HEAD

Action: SA revolver
Grips: Walnut
Barrel: 3.5 in., 4.75 in., 5.5 in.
Sights: Fixed, open
Weight: 35 oz.
Caliber: .45 Colt, .357 Mag.
Capacity: 6 rounds
Features: Case-hardened frame; steel backstrap and trigger guard; blued finish; bird head shape grip
MSRP $569

1873 BISLEY

Action: SA revolver
Grips: Bisley target style walnut
Barrel: 4.75 in., 5.5 in., 7.5 in.
Sights: Fixed, open
Weight: 40 oz.
Caliber: .45 Colt, .357 Mag.
Capacity: 6 rounds
Features: Case-hardened frame; steel backstrap and trigger guard; blued finish; fluted barrel
MSRP $609

1873 CATTLEMAN .22LR

Action: SA revolver
Grips: Walnut
Barrel: 4.75 in., 5.5 in., 7.5 in.
Sights: Fixed, open
Weight: 36.8 oz.
Caliber: .22LR
Capacity: 6 and 12 round models
Features: Ideal for cowboy-action shooting practice; light recoil; six-shot comes with brass or steel backstrap and trigger guard; available in six- or twelve-shot; case-hardened frame; blued finish
MSRP . . . . $509–$569

Uberti

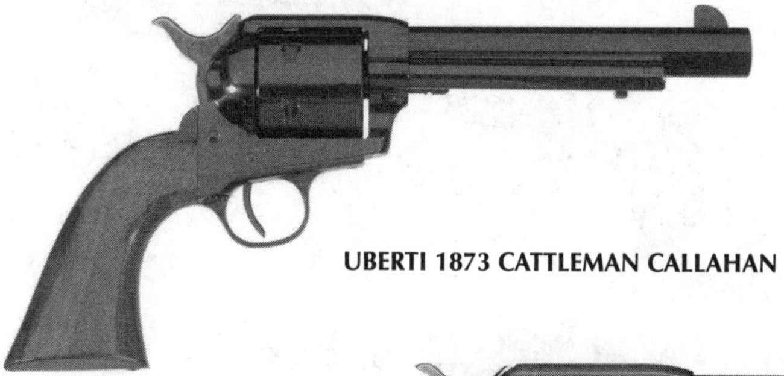

UBERTI 1873 CATTLEMAN CALLAHAN

UBERTI 1873 CATTLEMAN CHISHOLM

UBERTI 1873 CATTLEMAN DESPERADO

UBERTI 1873 CATTLEMAN MATCHING SET

1873 CATTLEMAN CALLAHAN

Action: SA revolver
Grips: Walnut, black or mother-of-pearl synthetic
Barrel: 4.75 in., 6 in., 7.5 in.
Sights: Fixed
Weight: 42 oz.
Caliber: .44 Mag.
Capacity: 6 rounds
Features: Blued, stainless, case-hardened or Old West finish; target model has angled front target sight and adjustable notched rear blade sight
MSRP $629

1873 CATTLEMAN CHISHOLM

Action: SA revolver
Grips: Checkered walnut
Barrel: 4.75 in., 5.5 in.
Sights: Fixed, open
Weight: 37 oz.
Caliber: .45 Colt
Capacity: 6 rounds
Features: Complete matte finished steel; fluted barrel
MSRP $559

1873 CATTLEMAN DESPERADO

Action: SA revolver
Grips: Bison horn style
Barrel: 4.75 in., 5.5 in.
Sights: Fixed, open
Weight: 37 oz.
Caliber: .45 Colt
Capacity: 6 rounds
Features: Full nickel-plated steel; fluted barrel
MSRP $829

1873 CATTLEMAN MATCHING SETS

Action: SA revolver
Grips: Walnut
Barrel: 5.5 in.
Sights: Fixed, open
Weight: 37 oz.
Caliber: .45 Colt, .357 Mag
Capacity: 6 rounds
Features: Fluted barrel; blued case-hardened frame; steel backstrap; trigger guard; the set shares matching serial numbers; also available in nickel and ivory-style grip
Walnut: . . . . $1079 per set
Cody ivory style: . . . . $1659 per set

Uberti

UBERTI 1873 EL PATRÓN COWBOY MOUNTED SHOOTER (CMS)

UBERTI 1873 HORSEMAN

UBERTI 1873 SA CATTLEMAN

UBERTI 1873 STALLION TARGET

UBERTI 1875 FRONTIER

UBERTI 1890 SA POLICE REVOLVER

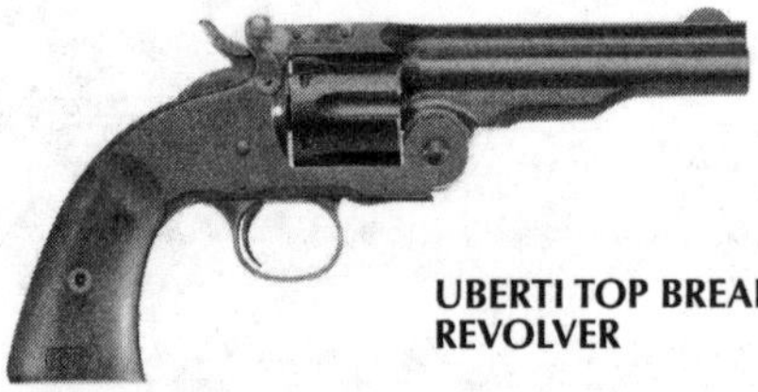

UBERTI TOP BREAK REVOLVER

1873 EL PATRÓN COWBOY MOUNTED SHOOTER (CMS)

Action: SA revolver
Grips: Checkered walnut
Barrel: 3.5 in., 4 in.
Sights: EasyView
Weight: 37 oz.
Caliber: .45 Colt, .357 Mag.
Capacity: 6 rounds
Features: Blued or stainless steel finish; optional case-hardened frame; fluted barrel; fitted with U.S.-made Wolff springs; numbered cylinders
Blued: $649
Stainless steel: $789

1873 HORSEMAN

Action: SA revolver
Grips: Walnut
Barrel: 4.75 in., 5.5 in., 7.5in.
Sights: Fixed, open
Weight: 36.8 oz.
Caliber: .45 Colt, .357 Mag., .22 LR
Capacity: 6 rounds
Features: Transfer-bar safety system; coil main spring; wider trigger; case-hardened frame; blued finish
MSRP . . . . $549–$579

1873 SINGLE-ACTION CATTLEMAN

Action: SA revolver
Grips: Walnut
Barrel: 4.75 in., 5.5 in., 7.5 in.
Sights: Fixed, open
Weight: 37 oz.
Caliber: .45 Colt, .44-40 Win., .357 Mag.
Capacity: 6 rounds
Features: Case-hardened frame; brass or steel backstrap and trigger guard; blued, nickel or stainless steel finish; fluted barrel
MSRP . . . . $509–$699

1873 STALLION/STALLION TARGET

Action: SA revolver
Grips: Walnut
Barrel: 4.75 in., 5.5 in.
Sights: Fixed, open
Weight: 32 oz.
Caliber: .22LR, .22LR/Mag
Capacity: 6 or 10 round
Features: Case-hardened frame; brass or steel backstrap and trigger guard; blued finish; fluted barrel
MSRP . . . . $449–$599

1875 OUTLAW & FRONTIER

Action: SA revolver
Grips: Walnut
Barrel: 5.5 in. (Frontier), 7.5 in.
Sights: Fixed, open
Weight: 40–45 oz.
Caliber: .45 Colt
Capacity: 6 rounds
Features: Case-hardened or full nickel plated steel frame; steel backstrap and trigger guard; fluted barrel
Outlaw: $559
Outlaw Nickel: $659
Frontier: $559

1890 SINGLE ACTION POLICE REVOLVER

Action: SA revolver
Grips: Walnut with lanyard ring
Barrel: 5.5 in.
Sights: Fixed, open
Weight: 42 oz.
Caliber: .45 Colt, .357 Mag.
Capacity: 6 rounds
Features: Blued steel frame, backstrap and trigger guard; fluted barrel
MSRP $579

TOP BREAK REVOLVERS

Action: SA revolver
Grips: Walnut or pearl-style
Barrel: 3.5 in., 5 in., 7 in.
Sights: Fixed, open
Weight: 40 oz.
Caliber: .45 Colt, .38 Spl., .44-40 Win.
Capacity: 6 rounds
Features: Full nickel plated steel or blued steel frame and blackstrap; case-hardened trigger guard; fluted barrel
Pearl-style grip: $1429
Walnut grip: $1079

Walther

WALTHER CCP
(CONCEALED CARRY PISTOL)

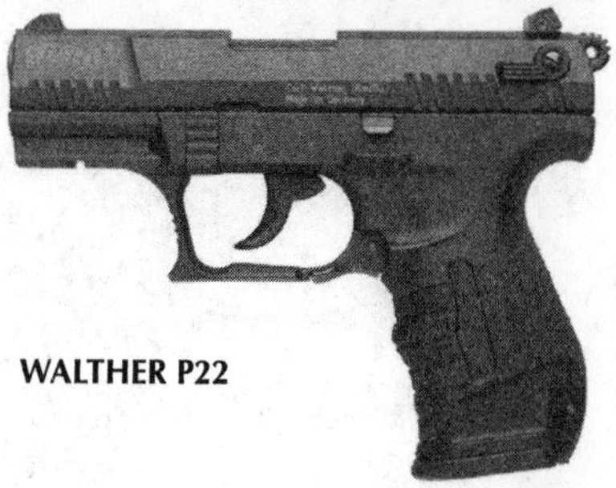

WALTHER P22

WALTHER P99AS
COMPACT

WALTHER PPK/S .22

WALTHER P99AS

CCP (CONCEALED CARRY PISTOL)

Action: Semiautomatic
Grips: Synthetic
Barrel: 3.54 in.
Sights: Adjustable
Weight: 22.33 oz.
Caliber: 9mm
Capacity: 8+1 rounds
Features: Available in black or stainless steel; interchangeable front sight with white dot; adjustable rear sight; reversible magazine release
MSRP................$469–$489

P22

Action: DA/SA semiautomatic
Grips: Polymer
Barrel: 3.42 in., 5 in.
Sights: 3-dot adjustable low-profile
Weight: 17.6 oz. (3.42 in. barrel), 21.3 oz. (5 in. barrel)
Caliber: .22LR
Capacity: 10 rounds
Features: Threaded barrel, interchangeable with target barrel; loaded chamber indicator; external slide stop; 3 safeties; two magazine styles; ergonomic grip; ambidextrous magazine release lever; available with integrated laser-set; available in black, nickel, and military finish
MSRP................$319–$339

P99AS

Action: DA semiautomatic
Grips: Black polymer frame and grips
Barrel: 4 in. stainless steel with Tenifer finish
Sights: Front and rear tritium night
Weight: 24 oz.–25.6 oz.
Caliber: 9mm, .40 S&W
Capacity: 15 (9mm) or 12 (.40 S&W) rounds
Features: The first pistol with a firing pin block combines advantages of a traditional DA pull with SA trigger and a decocking button safety integrated into slide, allowing users the ability to decock the striker, preventing inadvertent firing in both DA and SA mode
From:....................$629

P99AS COMPACT

Action: Striker-fired semiautomatic
Grips: Polymer
Barrel: 3.5 in.
Sights: 3-dot adjustable low-profile
Weight: 20.8 oz.–22.4 oz.
Caliber: 9mm, .40 S&W
Capacity: 10 (9mm) or 8 (.40 S&W) rounds
Features: Flat-bottom magazine buttplate, finger rest magazine buttplate; molded with a Weaver-style rail; interchangeable backstraps; hammerless striker system and integral safety devices come standard
From:....................$629

PPK AND PPK/S

Action: DA/SA semiautomatic
Grips: Polymer
Barrel: 3.3 in.
Sights: Fixed, open

WALTHER PKK/S

Weight: 22.4 oz. (PPK), 24 oz. (PPK/S)
Caliber: .380 ACP
Capacity: 6 (PPK) or 7 (PPK/S) rounds
Features: Firing pin safety; manual safety with decocking function; double- and single-action trigger; extended beaver tail; nickel plated or blued finish
MSRP................$399–$429

PPK/S .22

Action: DA/SA semiautomatic
Grips: Polymer
Barrel: 3.3 in.
Sights: Fixed, open
Weight: 24 oz.
Caliber: .22LR
Capacity: 10 rounds
Features: Manual safety; top strap waved to reduce glare; internal slide stop; iconic PPK/S frame; beaver tail extension; nickel plated or black finish
MSRP............... $399–$429

Walther

WALTHER PPQ M2

WALTHER PPS

PPQ M2

Action: Striker-fired semiautomatic
Grips: Polymer
Barrel: 4 in., 4.1 in., 4.6 in., 5 in.
Sights: 3-dot adjustable low-profile
Weight: 24 oz. (9mm), 25.6 oz. (.40 S&W)
Caliber: 9mm, 9mm (Navy SD), .40 S&W
Capacity: 15 (9mm), 15/17 (9mm Navy SD) or 11 (.40 S&W) rounds
Features: Quick defense trigger; three safeties; ergonomic grip with checkered trigger guard; ambidextrous slide stop and magazine release button; Tenifer coated slide and barrel with matte finish
MSRP. . . . . $649–$749

PPS (POLICE PISTOL SLIM)

Action: Striker-fired semiautomatic
Grips: Black polymer
Barrel: 3.2 in.
Sights: 3-dot low profile contoured
Weight: 20.8 oz.
Caliber: 9mm, 40 S&W
Capacity: 6 or 8 rounds (9mm), 5 or 7 rounds (.40 S&W)
Features: Ambidextrous magazine release; loaded chamber and cocking indicators; small and large backstrap; trigger safety; Walther QuickSafe safety
MSRP. $599

PPX

Action: Hammer fire action autoloader
Grips: Polymer
Barrel: 4 in., 4.6 in. (9MM SD)
Sights: 3-dot adjustable low-profile
Weight: 27.2 oz.
Caliber: 9mm, 9mm (SD), .40 S&W
Capacity: 16 rounds (9mm), 14 rounds (.40 S&W)

WALTHER PPX

Features: Constant 6.5 lb. trigger pull; three safeties; ergonomic grip; ambidextrous slide stop and reversible push button magazine release; loaded chamber viewport; Mil-Std-1913 Picatinny accessory mounting rail; Tenifer coated slide and barrel; available in black and stainless
MSRP. . . . . $449–$499

ZiP Factory

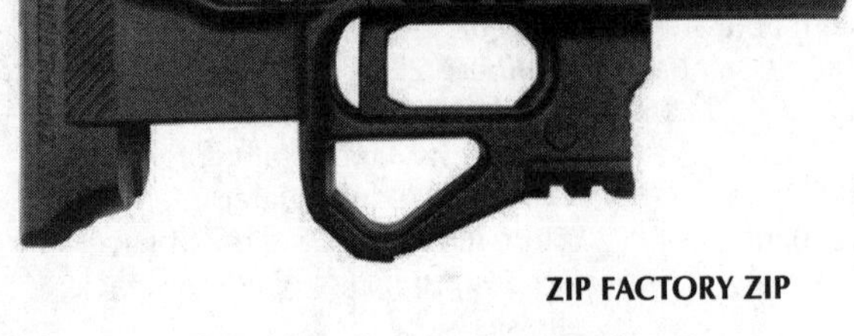

ZIP FACTORY ZIP

ZIP

Action: SA striker fired
Grips: Polymer, checkered
Barrel: 5.25 in.
Sights: Fixed, open
Weight: 15.2 oz.
Caliber: .22LR
Capacity: N/A
Features: Modular firearm system built on a polymer frame; configurations include striker-fired gun as a pistol or short barreled rifle; features an accessory rail; accepts Ruger 10/22-style magazines; available in black, gray, coyote tan, and blue
MSRP. . . . . $200–$230

BLACK POWDER

Connecticut Valley Arms (CVA)

CVA ACCURA MR

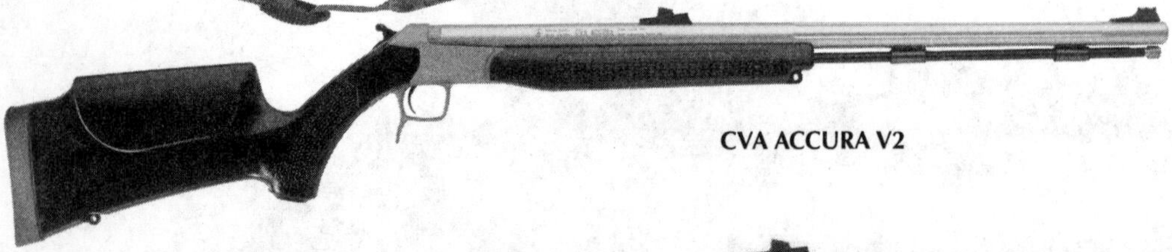

CVA ACCURA V2

CONNECTICUT VALLEY ARMS
ACCURA V2 NORTHWEST

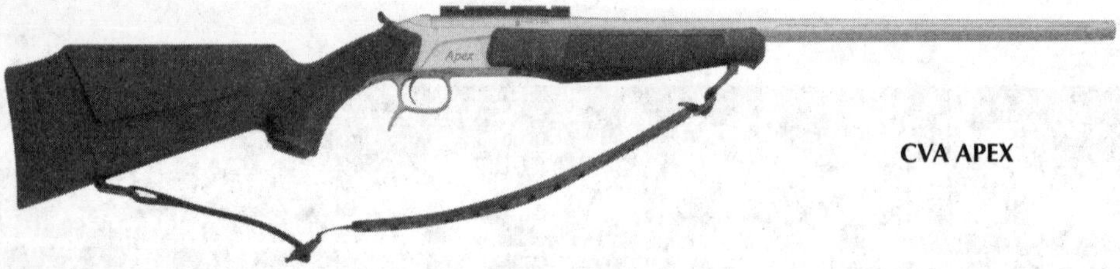

CVA APEX

ACCURA MR

Lock: Break-action in-line
Stock: Synthetic
Barrel: 25 in.
Sights: Scope mount
Weight: 6 lb. 6 oz.
Bore/Caliber: .50
Features: Aluminum frame; quick release breech plug; trigger guard actuated breeching action; Bergara barrel; neutral center of gravity trigger; premium SoftTouch stock with rubber grip panels; WeatherGuard barrel finish on the stainless steel barrel; Realtree Max-1 or black stock finishes; Quake Claw sling included; DuraSight Dead-On scope mount
MSRP. . . . . $480–$613

ACCURA V2

Lock: Break-action muzzleloading
Stock: Composite stock in standard or thumbhole
Barrel: 27 in.
Sights: DuraSight fiber optic
Weight: 7 lb. 5 oz.
Bore/Caliber: .45 or .50
Features: 416 stainless Bergara barrel; quick-release breech plug; CrushZone recoil pad; drilled and tapped for scope mount; SoftTouch coating and rubber grip panels; Quake Claw sling
MSRP. . . . . $464–$596

ACCURA V2 NORTHWEST

Lock: Break-action muzzleloading
Stock: Synthetic
Barrel: 27 in.
Sights: Fiber optics
Weight: 7 lb. 5 oz.
Bore/Caliber: .50
Features: Meets open-breech/ignition requirements of Idaho, Oregan, and Washington; CrushZone recoil pad; quick release breech plug
MSRP. $600

APEX

Lock: Hinged breech muzzleloading
Stock: Synthetic
Barrel: 27 in.
Sights: DuraSight rail mount
Weight: 8 lb.
Bore/Caliber: .45, .50
Features: Multibarrel interchangeable rifle system; ambidextrous buttstock; 416 stainless steel Bergara barrels; quick-release breech plug; Quake Claw sling; CrushZone recoil pad; available in black or Realtree APG camo; also available in centerfire models
MSRP. . . . . $615–$695

Connecticut Valley Arms (CVA)

CVA BUCKHORN

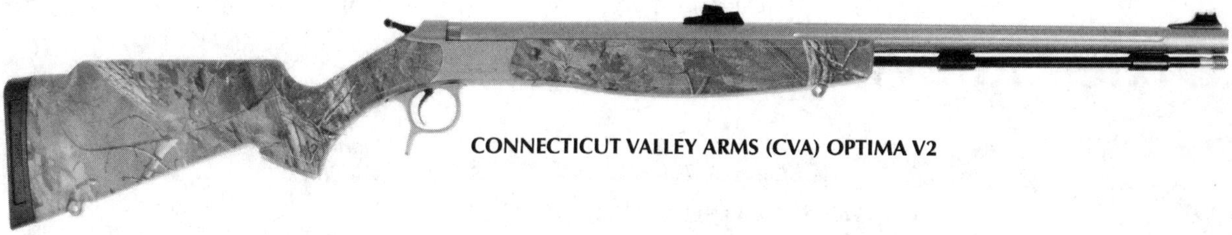

CONNECTICUT VALLEY ARMS (CVA) OPTIMA V2

CONNECTICUT VALLEY ARMS OPTIMA V2 NORTHWEST

CVA WOLF

BUCKHORN

Lock: In-line
Stock: Solid composite
Barrel: 24 in.
Sights: DuraSight fiber optic
Weight: 6 lb. 5 oz.
Bore/Caliber: .50
Features: 209 ignition; bullet guiding muzzle; DuraSight all-metal fiber optic sights; solid composite stock in black, with molded-in grip panels and sling swivel studs; CrushZone recoil pad; thumb-actuated safety; drilled and tapped for scope mounts
MSRP. $166

OPTIMA V2

Lock: Break-action muzzleloading
Stock: Realtree Xtra Green or black
Barrel: 26 in.
Sights: Fiber optic sights or mount
Weight: 6 lb. 10 oz.
Bore/Caliber: .50
Features: Modeled on the Accura V2; stainless steel barrel; quick release breech plug; 100 percent ambidextrous stock; includes DuraSight Dead-On scope mount and ramrod
Realtree: . . . .$376–$409
SS/Black: . . . . $317–$328
Blued/Black:. . . . . $225–$315

OPTIMA V2 NORTHWEST

Lock: Break-action muzzleloading
Stock: Synthetic
Barrel: 26 in.
Sights: Fiber optics
Weight: 6 lb. 10 oz.
Bore/Caliber: .50
Features: Meets open-breech/ignition requirements of Idaho, Oregan, and Washington; CrushZone recoil pad; quick release breech plug
MSRP. $380

WOLF

Lock: Break-action in-line
Stock: Synthetic
Barrel: 24 in.
Sights: DuraSight fiber optic; includes 3–9x40mm duplex scope
Weight: 6 lb. 4 oz.
Bore/Caliber: .50
Features: Bullet-guiding muzzle; new tool-free QR breech plug system; ambidextrous compact or standard stock in black or camo; CrushZone recoil pad; reversible hammer spur; blued barrel
MSRP. . . . . $224–$309

Connecticut Valley Arms (CVA)

CONNECTICUT VALLEY ARMS
WOLF NORTHWEST

WOLF NORTHWEST

Lock: Break-action muzzleloading
Stock: Synthetic
Barrel: 24 in.
Sights: Fiber optics
Weight: 6 lb. 4 oz.
Bore/Caliber: .50
Features: Meets open-breech/ignition requirements of Idaho, Oregan, and Washington; CrushZone recoil pad; quick release breech plug
MSRP $265

Dixie Gun Works

DIXIE GUN WORKS 1853 ENFIELD THREE-BAND

DIXIE GUN WORKS SHARPS
1859 MILITARY CARBINE

DIXIE GUN WORKS SPANISH MUSKET

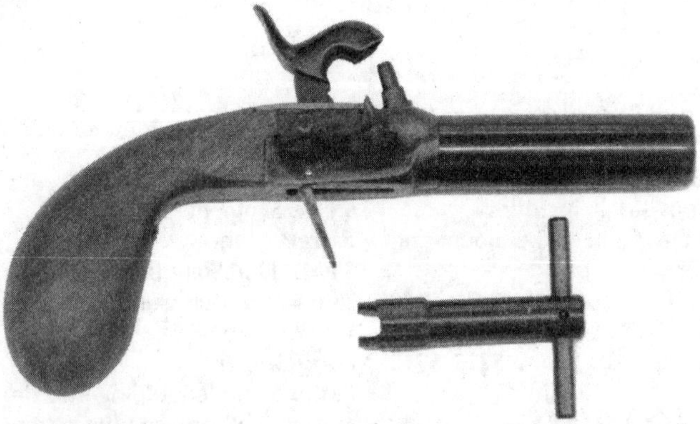

DIXIE GUN WORKS PEDERSOLI SCREW BARREL PISTOL

1853 ENFIELD THREE-BAND RIFLE MUSKET

Lock: Traditional caplock
Stock: Walnut
Barrel: 39 in.
Sights: Fixed
Weight: 10 lb. 4 oz.
Bore/Caliber: .58
Features: Color case-hardened lock; single trigger; single swivels; steel ramrod
MSRP . . . . $750–$1200

SHARPS 1859 MILITARY CARBINE

Lock: Dropping block
Stock: Walnut
Barrel: 22 in.
Sights: Adjustable open
Weight: 8 lb.
Bore/Caliber: .54
Features: Steel furniture; color case-hardened; single trigger; single barrel band; saddle bar with ring
MSRP $1400

SPANISH MUSKET

Lock: Flintlock muzzleloading
Stock: Full, European walnut 56 in.
Barrel: 44.75 in.
Sights: Steel stud front
Weight: 10 lb.
Bore/Caliber: .68 round ball
Features: Brass buttplate, trigger guard, and barrel bands; bright steel sideplates; steel ramrod
MSRP $1400

PEDERSOLI SCREW BARREL PISTOL

Lock: Traditional caplock
Stock: European walnut
Barrel: 3 in.
Sights: None
Weight: 12 oz.
Bore/Caliber: .44
Features: Color case-hardened lock; single folding trigger; combination nipple/barrel wrench included
MSRP $195

E.M.F. Company

E.M.F. 1851 NAVY

E.M.F. 1851 NAVY SHERIFF

E.M.F. 1858 REMINGTON ARMY REVOLVER

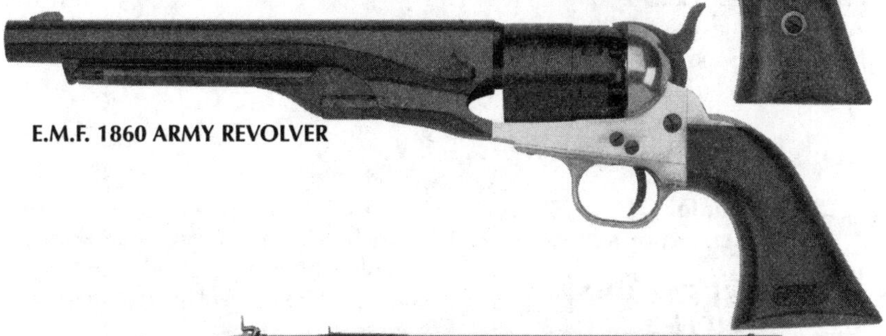
E.M.F. 1860 ARMY REVOLVER

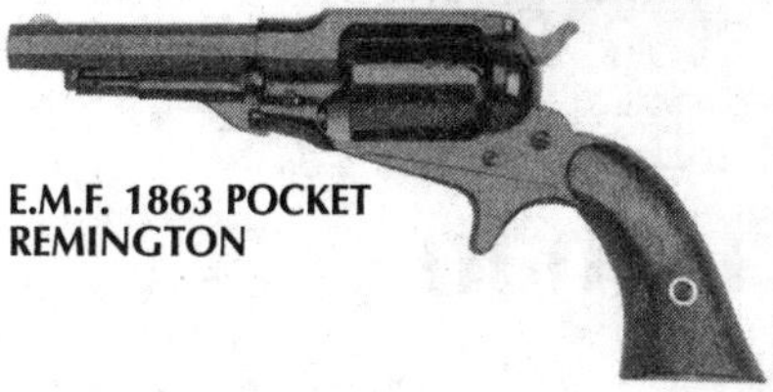
E.M.F. 1863 POCKET REMINGTON

E.M.F. MISSOURI RIVER HAWKEN

1851 NAVY

Lock: Caplock revolver
Stock: Walnut
Barrel: 7.5 in.
Sights: Fixed
Weight: 40 oz.
Bore/Caliber: .36, .44
Features: Brass, case-hardened stainless steel frame; blued barrel optional
Brass:....................$220
Case-hardened:............$240

1851 NAVY SHERIFF

Lock: Caplock revolver
Stock: Walnut
Barrel: 5.5 in.
Sights: None
Weight: 32 oz.
Bore/Caliber: .44
Features: Brass, case-hardened stainless steel frame; blued barrel optional
Brass:....................$250
Case-hardened:............$260

1858 REMINGTON ARMY REVOLVER

Lock: Caplock revolver
Stock: Walnut
Barrel: 8 in.
Sights: Fixed
Weight: 40 oz.
Bore/Caliber: .44
Features: Brass or stainless steel frame; blued barrel optional
Brass:....................$225
Blued:....................$290
Stainless:................$490

1860 ARMY REVOLVER

Lock: Caplock revolver
Stock: Walnut
Barrel: 8 in.
Sights: Fixed
Weight: 41.6 oz.
Bore/Caliber: .44
Features: Case-hardened frame; blued barrel
Brass:....................$270
Steel:....................$290

1863 POCKET REMINGTON

Lock: Caplock revolver
Stock: Walnut
Barrel: 3.5 in.
Sights: Fixed
Weight: 21 oz.
Bore/Caliber: .36
Features: Steel frame, blued barrel
MSRP....................$295

MISSOURI RIVER HAWKEN BY PEDERSOLI

Lock: Caplock muzzleloading
Stock: Maple or walnut
Barrel: 30 in.
Sights: Open
Weight: 9 lb. 4 oz.
Bore/Caliber: .45, .50
Features: Replica percussion rifle; available in maple or walnut stock in rust brown color finish; barrel features an octagonal cross-section; case-hardened color lock; equipped with a double-set trigger
Maple:..................$1360
Walnut:.................$1355

E.M.F. Company

KENTUCKY FLINTLOCK PISTOL

Lock: Flintlock
Stock: Walnut
Barrel: 10.375 in.
Sights: Fixed
Weight: 37 oz.
Bore/Caliber: .45, .50
Features: Classic American pistol during the American Revolution and a favorite of pioneers; case-hardened frame; octagonal rifled blued barrel, polished brass fittings
.45: $375
.50: $395

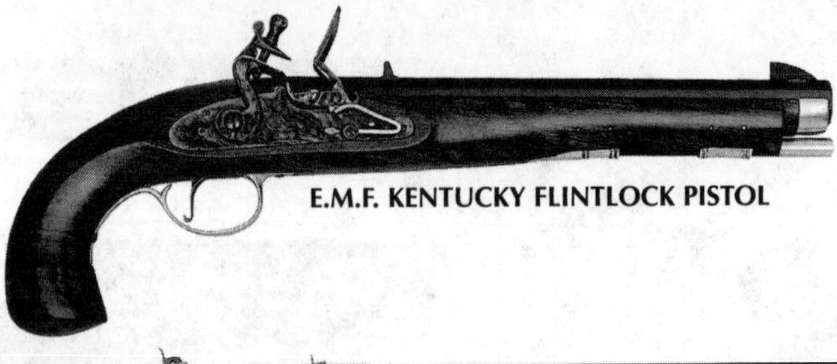

E.M.F. KENTUCKY FLINTLOCK PISTOL

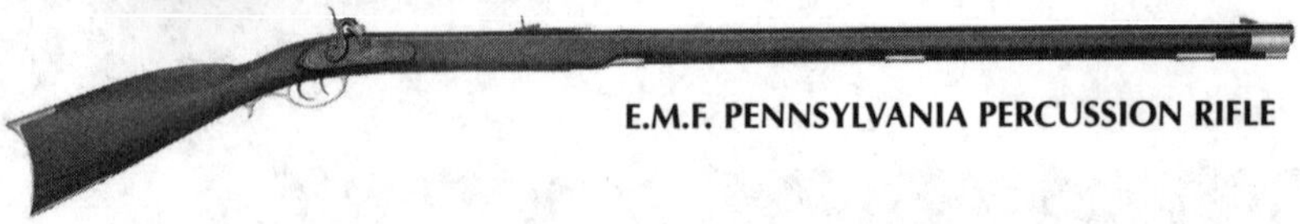

E.M.F. PENNSYLVANIA PERCUSSION RIFLE

PENNSYLVANIA PERCUSSION RIFLE

Lock: Caplock
Stock: Walnut
Barrel: 41.625 in.
Sights: Adjustable
Weight: 7 lb. 11 oz.
Bore/Caliber: .45
Features: Reproduction of the American rifles used by Pennsylvania hunters; evolved from the German Jaeger hunting rifle; adjustable rear and front sights; case-hardened frame; double set trigger; rust brown octagonal barrel; polished brass fitting
MSRP $1035

Lyman

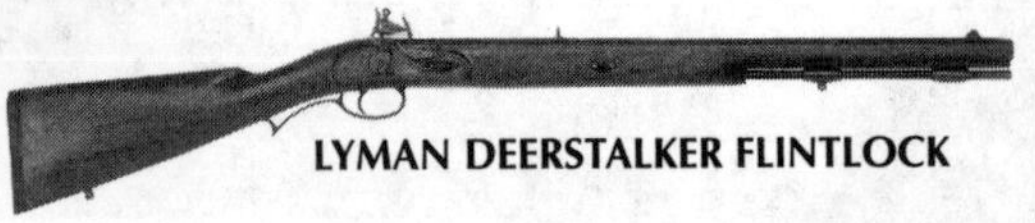

LYMAN DEERSTALKER FLINTLOCK

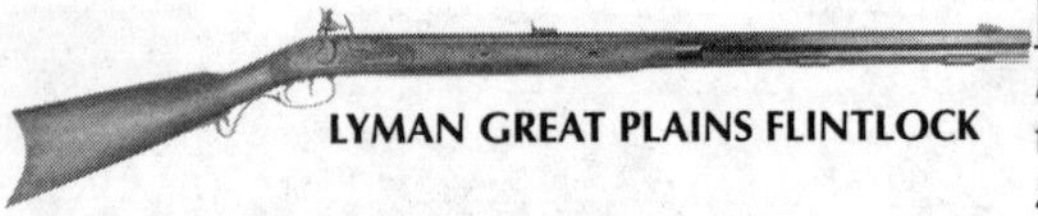

LYMAN GREAT PLAINS FLINTLOCK

LYMAN MUSTANG BREAKAWAY 209 MAGNUM

LYMAN PLAINS PISTOL

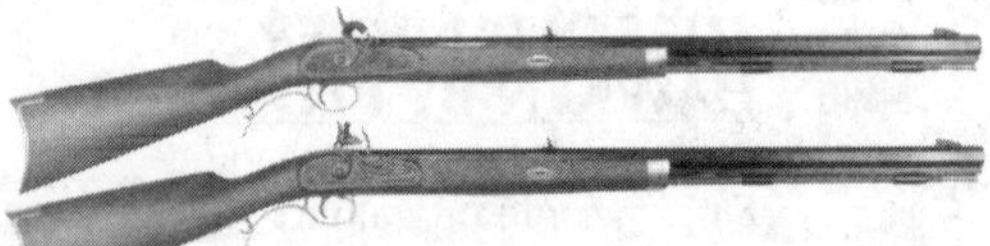

LYMAN TRADE RIFLE

DEERSTALKER RIFLE

Lock: Traditional cap or flint
Stock: Walnut
Barrel: 24 in.
Sights: Fiber optic front and rear
Weight: 10 lb. 6 oz.
Bore/Caliber: .50, .54
Features: Quiet single trigger; metal blackened to avoid glare; black rubber recoil pad; left-hand available
Flintlock: . . . . . $615–$655
Percussion: . . . $565–$670

GREAT PLAINS RIFLE

Lock: Traditional cap or flint
Stock: Walnut
Barrel: 32 in.
Sights: Adjustable open
Weight: 11 lb. 10 oz.
Bore/Caliber: .50, .54
Features: Double-set triggers; Hawken style percussion "snail" with clean-out screw; separate ramrod entry thimble and nose cap; reliable coil-spring lock with correct lock plate; left-hand available
Flintlock: . . . . . $830–$840
Percussion: . . . $770–$810

MUSTANG BREAKAWAY 209 MAGNUM

Lock: In-line
Stock: Hardwood
Barrel: 26 in.
Sights: Fiber optic front and rear
Weight: 11 lb.
Bore/Caliber: .50
Features: Pachmayr "Decelerator" recoil pad; comes drilled and tapped for Weaver style bases; hammerless; removable, stainless breech plug and easy takedown; "magnetized" primer retention system
MSRP $580

PLAINS PISTOL

Lock: Traditional caplock
Stock: Walnut
Barrel: 6 in.
Sights: Fixed
Weight: 3 lb. 2 oz.
Bore/Caliber: .50, .54
Features: Blackened iron furniture; polished brass trigger guard and ramrod tips; hooked patent breech takes down quickly for easy cleaning; thimble is recessed into the rib; detachable belt hook; spring-loaded trigger
Plains Pistol: $410
Kit: $350

TRADE RIFLE

Lock: Traditional cap or flint
Stock: Walnut
Barrel: 28 in.
Sights: Adjustable open
Weight: 10 lb. 13 oz.
Bore/Caliber: .50, .54
Features: Brass furniture; originally developed for the early Indian fur trade
Flintlock: $620
Percussion: $565

New Ultra Light Arms

MODEL 209 MUZZLELOADER

Action: Bolt
Stock: Kevlar/graphite composite
Barrel: 24 in.
Sights: None
Weight: 4 lb. 14 oz.
Caliber: .45, .50
Magazine: None
Features: Adjustable Timney trigger; positive primer extraction; button-rifled barrel; Kevlar/graphite stock comes in various

NEW ULTRA LIGHT ARMS MODEL 209

colors; recoil pad; sling swivels; ULA scope mounts; hard case; optional black powder
MSRP **$1800**

Pedersoli

1763 LEGER (1766) CHARLEVILLE

Action: Dropping block
Stock: Walnut
Barrel: 44.7 in.
Sights: Open
Weight: 10 lb. 2 oz.
Caliber: .69
Magazine: None
Features: Creedmoor sight; tunnel front sight; replica of French infantry musket
MSRP **$1506**

BAKER STYLE COACH GUN

Lock: Caplock
Stock: Walnut
Barrel: 11.25 in.
Sights: None
Weight: 5 lb. 12 oz.
Bore/Caliber: 12 Ga.
Features: Single trigger back action, side-by-side shotgun; reproduces a gun made by London gunsmith Ezekiel Baker in 1850; case-hardened locks
MSRP **$945**

BOUTET 1ER EMPIRE

Lock: Flintlock
Stock: Hardwood
Barrel: 10 in.
Sights: Fixed
Weight: 2 lb. 14 oz.
Bore/Caliber: .45
Features: Napoleon often wrote with flattering appreciation about the style and prestige of the Boutet guns, which Pedersoli now proudly introduces with fine checkering on the sides; metal buttplate; ramrod has a horn tip; single set trigger; on the lock two lines are engraved with MANUF RE/a Versailles.
MSRP **$2200**

COOK & BROTHER ARTILLERY CARBINE

Lock: Caplock
Stock: Walnut
Barrel: 24 in.
Sights: None
Weight: 6 lb. 10 oz.
Bore/Caliber: .58
Features: Inspired by English model guns; originally produced by Cook & Brother beginning in 1861; brass garnitures; blued barrel; case-hardened lock
MSRP **$1055**

DERRINGER PHILADELPHIA

Lock: Flintlock
Stock: Walnut
Barrel: 3.06 in.
Sights: None
Weight: 8.6 oz.
Bore/Caliber: .45
Features: Reproduction of the popular pocket pistols originally manufactured by John Henry Derringer; brass furniture; case-hardened lock; original markings on the lock: Derringer/ Philadelphia
MSRP **$505**

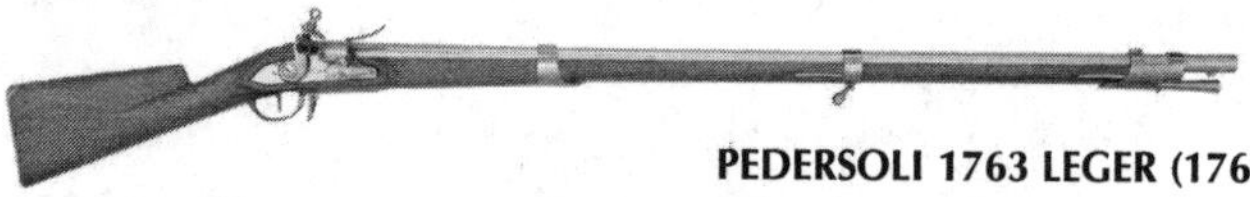

PEDERSOLI 1763 LEGER (1766) CHARLEVILLE

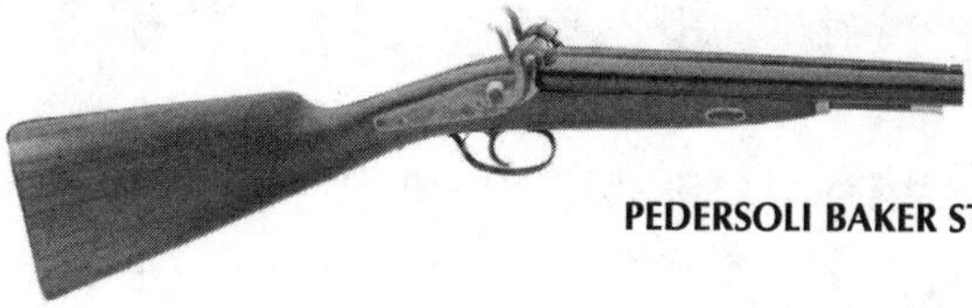

PEDERSOLI BAKER STYLE COACH GUN

PEDERSOLI BOUTET 1ER EMPIRE

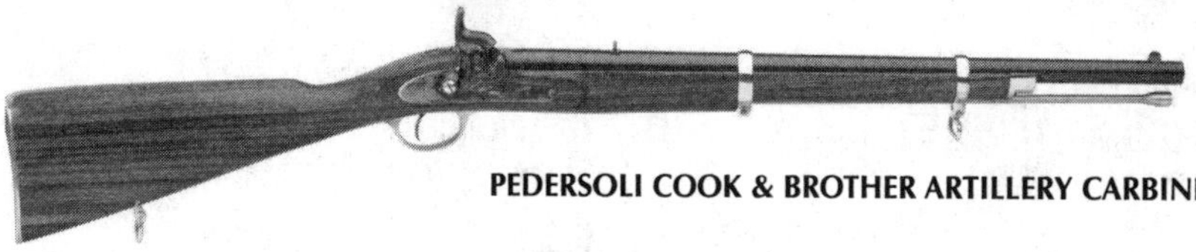

PEDERSOLI COOK & BROTHER ARTILLERY CARBINE

PEDERSOLI DERRINGER PHILADELPHIA

Pedersoli

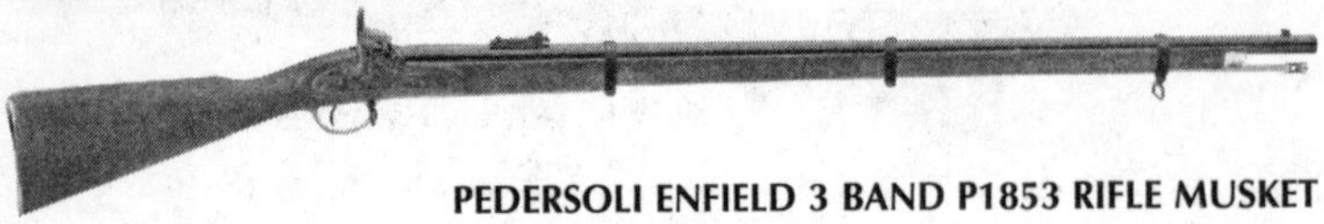

PEDERSOLI ENFIELD 3 BAND P1853 RIFLE MUSKET

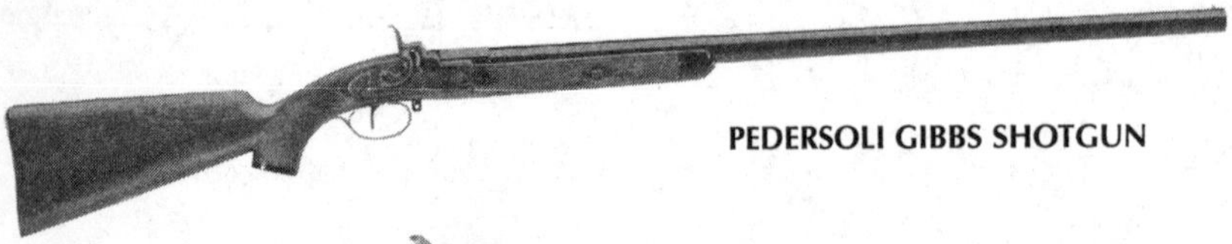

PEDERSOLI GIBBS SHOTGUN

PEDERSOLI HOWDAH HUNTER PISTOL

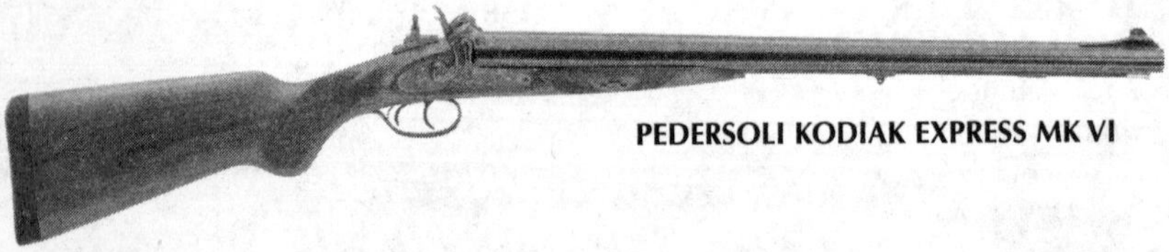

PEDERSOLI KODIAK EXPRESS MK VI

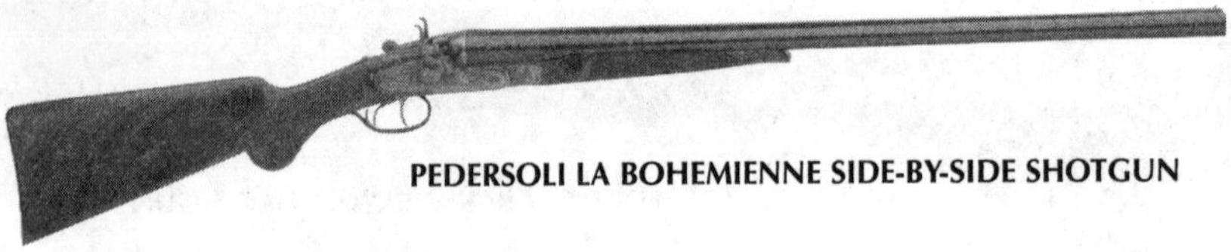

PEDERSOLI LA BOHEMIENNE SIDE-BY-SIDE SHOTGUN

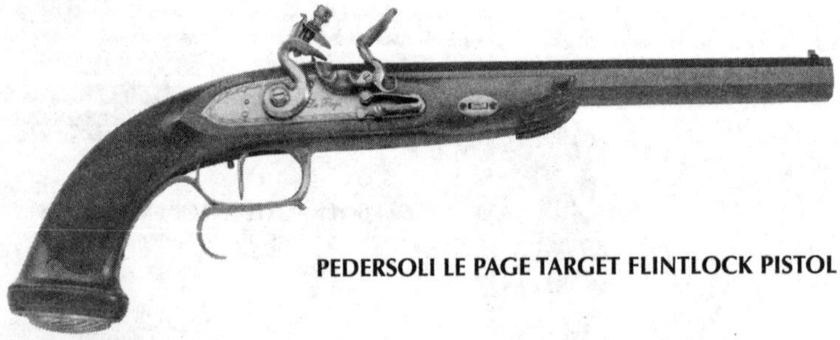

PEDERSOLI LE PAGE TARGET FLINTLOCK PISTOL

ENFIELD 3 BAND P1853 RIFLE MUSKET

Lock: Caplock
Stock: Walnut
Barrel: 39 in.
Sights: Adjustable rear
Weight: 8 lb. 13 oz.
Bore/Caliber: .577
Features: Ladder rear sight with a slider assembled on a base with steps; steel barrel bands; brass furniture; ramrod tip is shaped with characteristic jag slot; barrel is blued and lock case-hardened
MSRP. $1210

GIBBS SHOTGUN

Lock: Caplock
Stock: Walnut
Barrel: 32.3 in.
Sights: None
Weight: 8 lb. 9 oz.
Bore/Caliber: 12 Ga.
Features: Octagonal to round barrel; case-hardened color-finished lock; grip and forend caps with ebony inserts; pistol grip stock
MSRP. $1514

HOWDAH HUNTER PISTOL

Lock: Caplock
Stock: Walnut
Barrel: 11.25 in.
Sights: None
Weight: 5 lb. 1 oz.
Bore/Caliber: 20 Ga., .50, .58
Features: Engraved locks with wild animal scenes; case-hardened color finish; checkered walnut pistol grip with steel butt cap
MSRP. $821

KODIAK EXPRESS MK VI

Lock: Breechloading
Stock: Hardwood
Barrel: 24.25 in.
Sights: Creedmore
Weight: 10 lb. 2 oz.
Bore/Caliber: .50, .54, .58
Features: A very manageable gun, perfectly balanced; particularly suitable for wild boar hunting; practical rubber buttplate; half pistol grip stock; equipped with ghost sights
MSRP. $1388

LA BOHEMIENNE SIDE-BY-SIDE SHOTGUN

Lock: Hinged breech muzzleloading
Stock: Checkered walnut
Barrel: 28 in.
Chokes: cyl/mod choke tubes
Weight: 7 lb.
Bore/Caliber: 12 Ga.
Features: Rust brown finish barrel; interchangeable chokes; color case-hardened frame; hand-engraved locks
MSRP. $2050

LE PAGE TARGET FLINTLOCK PISTOL

Lock: Traditional flintlock
Stock: Walnut
Barrel: 10.5 in.
Sights: Adjustable
Weight: 2 lb. 10 oz.
Bore/Caliber: .44, .45
Features: Smoothbore .45 available; adjustable single-set trigger; brightly polished lock with a roller frizzen spring
MSRP. $1230

Pedersoli

PEDERSOLI MAMELOUK

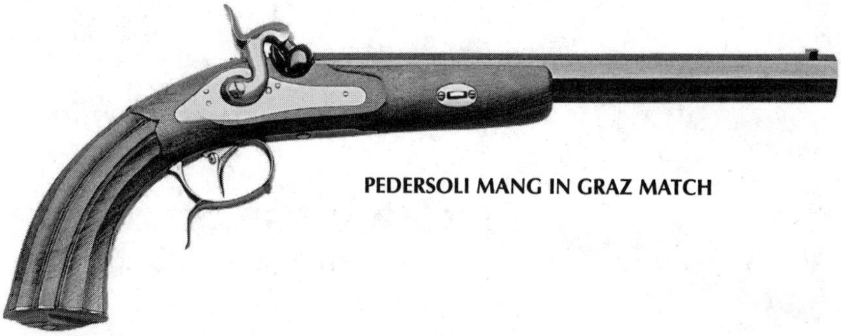

PEDERSOLI MANG IN GRAZ MATCH

PEDERSOLI MISSISSIPPI U.S. MODEL 1841

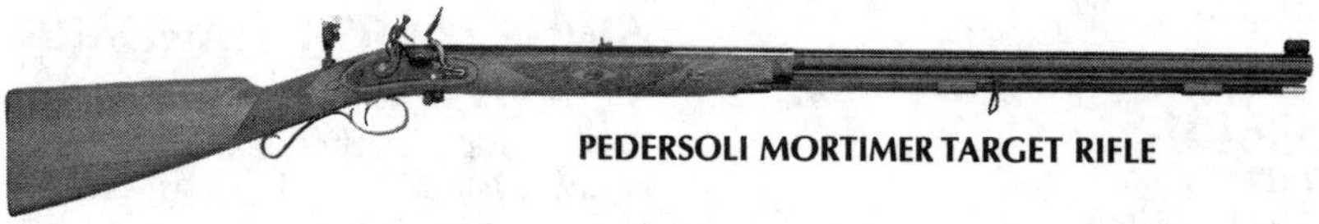

PEDERSOLI MORTIMER TARGET RIFLE

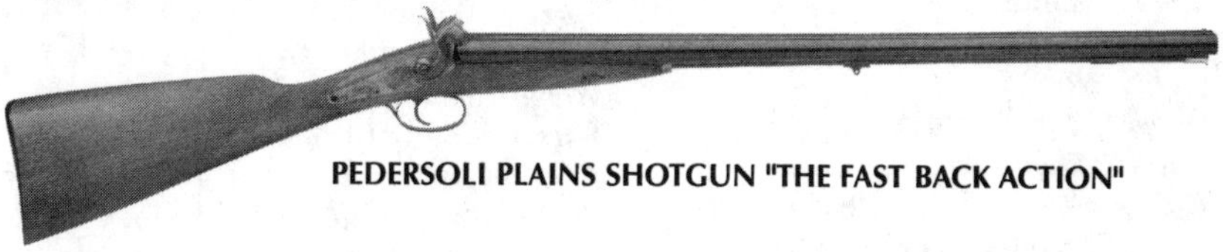

PEDERSOLI PLAINS SHOTGUN "THE FAST BACK ACTION"

PEDERSOLI RICHMOND 1862, TYPE III

MAMELOUK

Lock: Flintlock
Stock: Hardwood
Barrel: 7.6 in.
Sights: Fixed
Weight: 1 lb. 10 oz.
Bore/Caliber: N/A
Features: Like all the firearms equipping Napoleon's Imperial Guards, the Mameluke pistols were made at the Manufacture of Versailles under the technical management of Nicolas-Noël Boutet; the trigger guard, buttcap, screw washers of the lock, and ramrod tip are brass
MSRP. $978

MANG IN GRAZ MATCH

Lock: Traditional caplock
Stock: Walnut
Barrel: 11.4 in.
Sights: Fixed
Weight: 2 lb. 10 oz.
Bore/Caliber: .38, .44
Features: Fluted grip; octagonal, rifled barrel in brown rust finish; adjustable single set trigger; breech plug shows a typical mask of the period; barrel and tang enriched with gold inlays
MSRP. $1750

MISSISSIPPI U.S. MODEL 1841

Lock: Caplock
Stock: Walnut
Barrel: 33 in.
Sights: Open rear
Weight: 9 lb. 8 oz.
Bore/Caliber: .54, .58
Features: Considered the best-looking ordnance rifle of its period; brass furniture; browned barrel; notched rear sight; case-hardened lock; ramrod with brass tip
MSRP. $1261

MORTIMER TARGET RIFLE

Lock: Flintlock
Stock: English-style European walnut
Barrel: 36.4 in.
Sights: Target
Weight: 10 lb. 2 oz.
Bore/Caliber: .54
Features: Case-colored lock; stock has cheekpiece and hand checkering; 7-groove barrel
MSRP. $1758

PLAINS SHOTGUN "THE FAST BACK ACTION"

Lock: Caplock
Stock: Walnut
Barrel: 27.5 in., 28.5 in.
Sights: None
Weight: 7 lb. 5 oz.–7 lb. 8 oz.
Bore/Caliber: 12, 20 Ga.
Features: Single trigger; side-by-side shotgun; fast second shot, thanks to back action lock reducing minor residues of black powder in lock parts
MSRP. $1191

RICHMOND 1862, TYPE III

Lock: Caplock
Stock: Walnut
Barrel: 39.75 in.
Sights: None
Weight: 9 lb. 14 oz.
Bore/Caliber: .58
Features: Manufactured based on the U.S. 1855 Model with the Maynard tape ignition system; except for the lock's profile, the brass buttplate, and the stock nose cap, the gun's appearance resembles the U.S. Model 1861
MSRP. $1261

Pedersoli

PEDERSOLI SPRINGFIELD MODEL 1861 U.S.

PEDERSOLI SWISS MATCH STANDARD FLINTLOCK

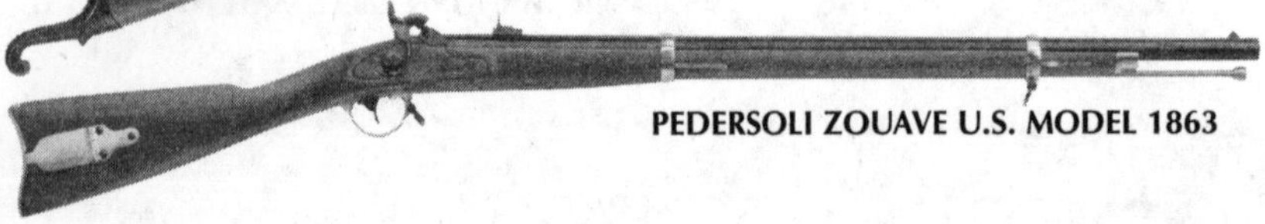

PEDERSOLI ZOUAVE U.S. MODEL 1863

PEDERSOLI TYRON TARGET STANDARD RIFLE

SPRINGFIELD MODEL 1861 U.S.

Lock: Caplock
Stock: Walnut
Barrel: 40 in.
Sights: None
Weight: 9 lb. 14 oz.
Bore/Caliber: .58
Features: More efficient than earlier smooth bored muskets used by both sides in the American Civil War; satin finish barrel; stock with three bands; coin-colored finish on the steel furniture
MSRP $1253

SWISS MATCH STANDARD FLINTLOCK

Lock: Traditional flintlock
Stock: Walnut
Barrel: 30.8 in.
Sights: Adjustable
Weight: 16 lb. 5 oz.
Bore/Caliber: .40
Features: Octagonal conical profile barrel with rust brown finish; lock is case-hardened; steel ramrod; double-set trigger; steel hook buttplate
MSRP $3191

TYRON TARGET STANDARD RIFLE

Lock: Traditional caplock
Stock: Walnut
Barrel: 36.4 in.
Sights: Adjustable open
Weight: 9 lb. 11 oz.
Bore/Caliber: .45, .50, .54
Features: Creedmoor version with aperture sight available
MSRP $1098

ZOUAVE U.S. MODEL 1863

Lock: Caplock
Stock: Hardwood
Barrel: 33 in.
Sights: Front, rear
Weight: 9 lb. 4 oz.
Bore/Caliber: .58
Features: Intended for the U.S. Artillery Department and never distributed to any Civil War army division; features brass furnitures; ramrod with a tulip tip; three-leaf rear sight; two sling swivels; the lock shows the Eagle stamp and the U.S. letters in front of the hammer
MSRP $1241

Remington

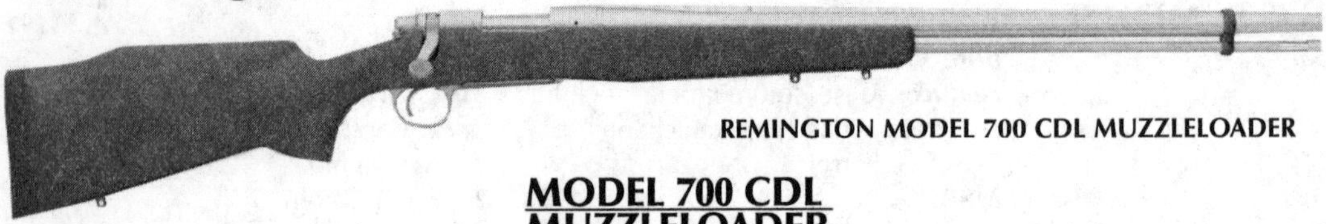

REMINGTON MODEL 700 CDL MUZZLELOADER

MODEL 700 CDL MUZZLELOADER

Lock: Bolt-action
Stock: Synthetic
Barrel: 26 in.
Sights: None
Weight: 8 lb. 8 oz.
Bore/Caliber: .50
Features: Fluted barrel; handles up to 200-grain magnum charges
MSRP $1295

Shiloh Rifle

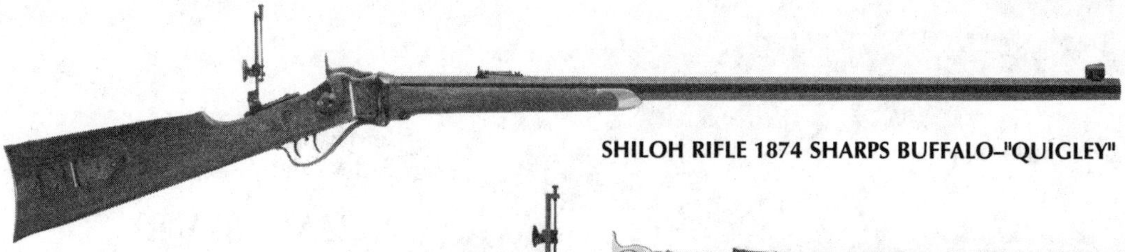

SHILOH RIFLE 1874 SHARPS BUFFALO–"QUIGLEY"

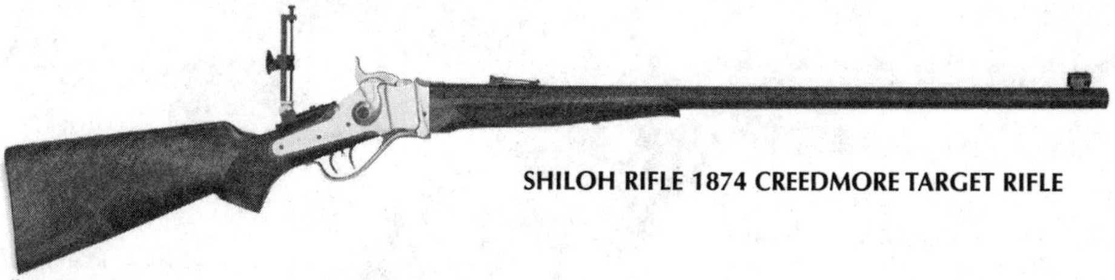

SHILOH RIFLE 1874 CREEDMORE TARGET RIFLE

SHILOH RIFLE 1877 #1 SHILOH ENGLISH RIFLE

1874 SHARPS BUFFALO–"QUIGLEY"

Lock: Falling block
Stock: Walnut
Barrel: 34 in.
Sights: Semi buckhorn rear, midrange vernier tang, #111 globe aperture front
Weight: 12 lb. 8 oz.
Bore/Caliber: .45-70 Govt. or .45-110
Features: Military buttstock; patchbox; heavy octagonal barrel; pewter tip; Hartford collars; double set triggers; antique or standard color finish; gold inlay initials in gold oval
MSRP $3464

1874 CREEDMORE TARGET RIFLE

Lock: Blackpowder cartridge
Stock: Walnut
Barrel: 32 in.
Sights: V aiming rear; blade front
Weight: 9 lb.
Bore/Caliber: All popular black powder cartridges from .38-55 to .50-90
Features: Pistol grip; single trigger; AA finish on American black walnut; polished barrel; octagon barrel; pewter tip
MSRP $2960

1877 #1 SHILOH ENGLISH RIFLE

Lock: Muzzleloading
Stock: Wood
Barrel: 26 in.–34 in.
Sights: Adjustable
Weight: N/A
Bore/Caliber: .38-55, .40-50BN, .40-50ST, .40-65, .40-70ST, .40-70BN, .40-90BN, .45-70, .45-90, .45-100
Features: Standard pistol grip; standard forearm; standard color cased; full or semi buckhorn rear sight; blade front sight; single trigger
MSRP $2250

Taylor's & Co.

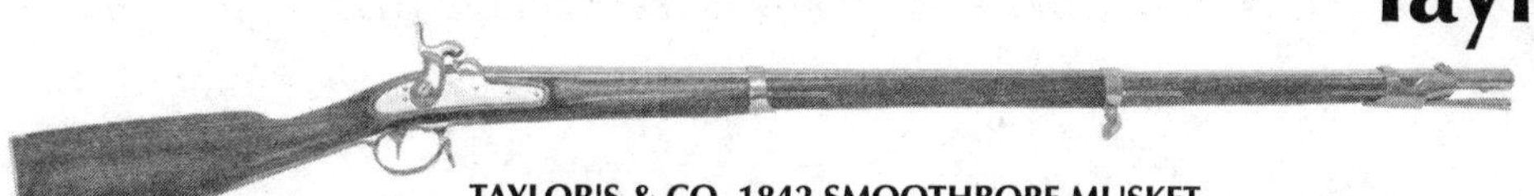

TAYLOR'S & CO. 1842 SMOOTHBORE MUSKET

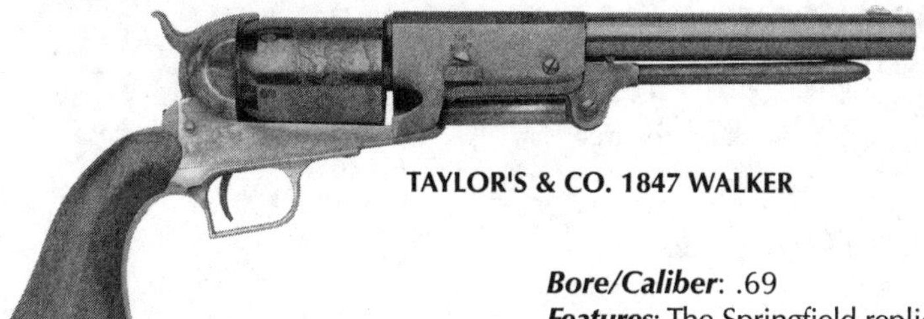

TAYLOR'S & CO. 1847 WALKER

1842 SMOOTHBORE MUSKET

Lock: Caplock
Stock: Walnut
Barrel: 42 in.
Sights: Military style
Weight: 9 lb. 12 oz.
Bore/Caliber: .69
Features: The Springfield replica has all the features of the original, including a one-piece, oil-finished walnut stock; original-style barrel bands; and completely interchangeable parts; the percussion lock has a V-style mainspring; features the lock with stamping noting 1842 and Springfield; NSSA approved, with certificate of authenticity and a brass medallion featuring the model and serial number
MSRP . . . . $896–$952

1847 WALKER

Lock: Caplock revolver
Stock: Walnut
Barrel: 9 in.
Sights: Fixed
Weight: 4 lb. 12 oz.
Bore/Caliber: .44
Features: Blued finish; round barrel
MSRP $439

Taylor's & Co.

TAYLOR'S & CO. 1848 DRAGOONS

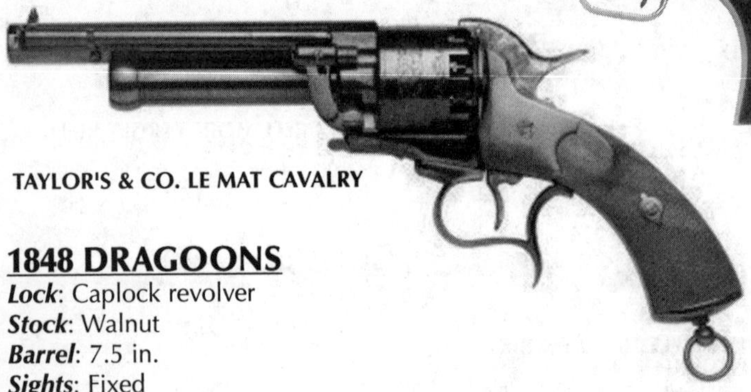

TAYLOR'S & CO. LE MAT CAVALRY

1848 DRAGOONS

Lock: Caplock revolver
Stock: Walnut
Barrel: 7.5 in.
Sights: Fixed
Weight: 4 lb.–4 lb. 14 oz.
Bore/Caliber: .44
Features: First used by the U.S. Army's Mounted Rifles 1st Cavalry in 1833 and they went on to see considerable use during the 1850 and during the Civil War; blued finish; six-round capacity

1st Model: $433
2nd Model: $433
3rd Model:. $433

LE MAT CAVALRY

Lock: Caplock revolver
Stock: Walnut
Barrel: 8 in.
Sights: Fixed
Weight: 5 lb.
Bore/Caliber: .44 or 20 Ga.
Features: Blued steel finish; nine-shot .44 caliber revolver with a 20 Ga. single-shot barrel was a favorite among Confederate cavalry troops; case-hardened hammer and trigger; lanyard ring; trigger guard with spur
MSRP $1203

Thompson/Center

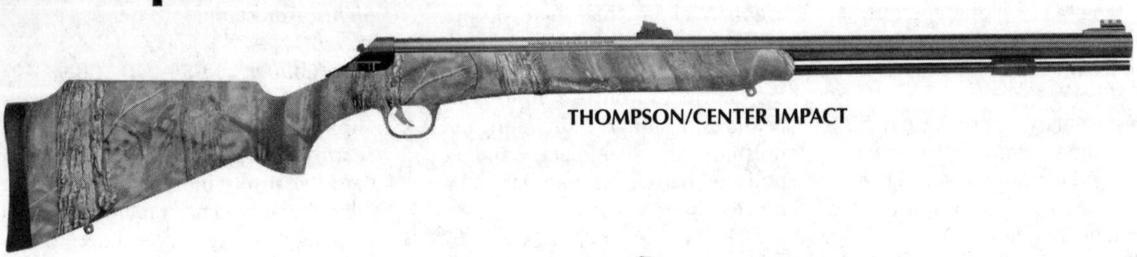

THOMPSON/CENTER IMPACT

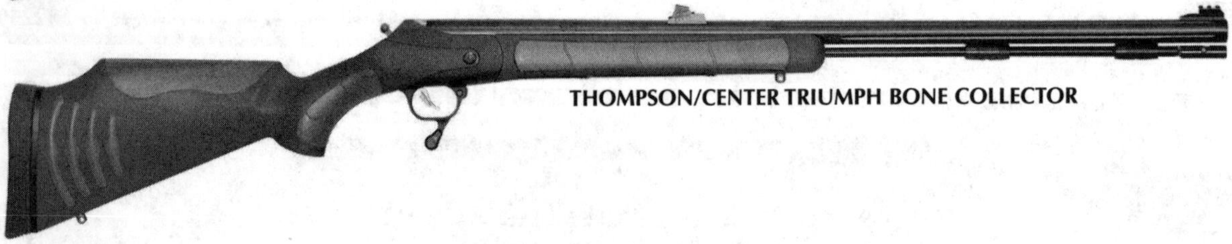

THOMPSON/CENTER TRIUMPH BONE COLLECTOR

IMPACT

Lock: Hinged breech muzzleloading
Stock: Black or LongLeaf camo
Barrel: 28 in.
Sights: Fiber optic
Weight: 6 lb. 8 oz.
Bore/Caliber: .50
Features: Triple lead thread breech plug; 1-inch adjustable buttstock
MSRP . . . . $263–$324

TRIUMPH BONE COLLECTOR

Lock: In-line
Stock: Composite, black or Realtree AP HD camo
Barrel: 28 in.
Sights: Adjustable fiber optic
Weight: 6 lb. 8 oz.
Bore/Caliber: .50
Features: Blued, stainless, and weather shield finish; speed breech XT
MSRP . . . . $638–$720

TRADITIONS FIREARMS 1851 NAVY REVOLVER

1851 NAVY REVOLVER

Lock: Caplock revolver
Stock: Walnut
Barrel: 7.5 in.
Sights: Fixed
Weight: 2 lb. 8 oz.
Bore/Caliber: .44
Features: Octagonal barrel and lever-style loader; brass, antiqued, or old silver frame and guard
Brass:.................... $244
Steel:.................... $274

TRADITIONS FIREARMS 1858 ARMY REVOLVER

1858 ARMY REVOLVER

Lock: Caplock
Stock: Walnut
Barrel: 8 in.
Sights: Fixed
Weight: 2 lb. 12 oz.
Bore/Caliber: .44
Features: Octagonal barrel and lever style loader; steel, brass, or stainless steel frame and guard; top strap and post sights
Steel:....................$359
Brass:....................$289
SS:......................$566

TRADITIONS FIREARMS 1860 ARMY REVOLVER

1860 ARMY REVOLVER

Lock: Caplock
Stock: Simulated ivory, walnut
Barrel: 8 in.
Sights: Fixed
Weight: 2 lb. 12 oz.
Bore/Caliber: .44
Features: Blued barrel; steel frame; brass guard; hammer/blade sights
Walnut/Steel:..............$319
Walnut/Brass:..............$269
Ivory/Nickel: $389

TRADITIONS FIREARMS BUCKSTALKER

BUCKSTALKER

Lock: Break-action muzzleloading
Stock: Synthetic
Barrel: 24 in.
Sights: Tru-Glo fiber optics
Weight: 7 lb. 8 oz.
Bore/Caliber: .50
Features: Dual safety system; nickel guard coating; synthetic black or G1 Vista camo stock; nickel or blued finish barrel; Monte Carlo stock; drilled and tapped for a scope; sling swivel studs
MSRP............... $219–$369

Traditions Firearms

TRADITIONS FIREARMS DEERHUNTER RIFLE

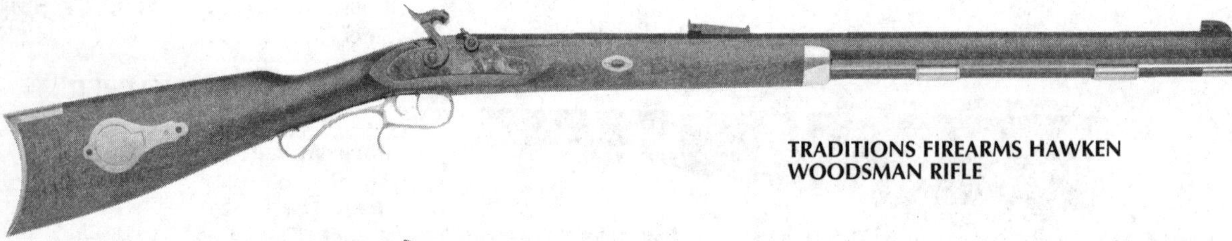

TRADITIONS FIREARMS HAWKEN WOODSMAN RIFLE

TRADITIONS FIREARMS KENTUCKY PISTOL

BLACK POWDER

DEERHUNTER RIFLE

Lock: Traditional cap or flint
Stock: Synthetic or hardwood
Barrel: 24 in.
Sights: Lite Optic adjustable
Weight: 6 lb.
Bore/Caliber: .32, .50, .54
Features: Octagonal performance barrels; blued or nickel barrel finish; percussion models are drilled and tapped to accept scope mounts; non-slip recoil pad; stock comes in black synthetic, Mossy Oak Tree Stand camo, or hardwood
MSRP. . . . . $269–$419

HAWKEN WOODSMAN RIFLE

Lock: Traditional cap or flint
Stock: Hardwood
Barrel: 28 in.
Sights: Adjustable rear hunting
Weight: 7 lb. 13 oz.
Bore/Caliber: .50
Features: Hooked breech for easy barrel removal; double-set triggers in an oversized glove-fitting trigger guard; inletted solid brass patch box; left-hand model available; octagonal blued barrel
Flint: $519
Percussion: $479

KENTUCKY PISTOL

Lock: Traditional caplock
Stock: Hardwood
Barrel: 10 in.
Sights: Fixed
Weight: 2 lb. 8 oz.
Bore/Caliber: .50
Features: Brass furniture; case-colored sidelock and brass ramrod thimble
MSRP. $244

TRADITIONS FIREARMS PENNSYLVANIA RIFLE

TRADITIONS FIREARMS PURSUIT ULTRALIGHT

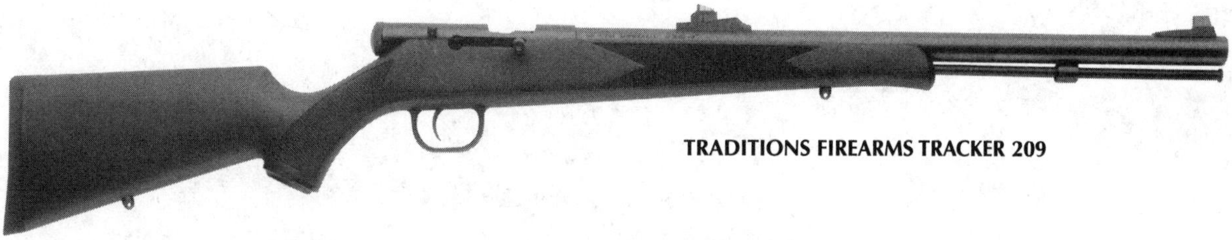

TRADITIONS FIREARMS TRACKER 209

PENNSYLVANIA RIFLE

Lock: Traditional cap or flint
Stock: Walnut
Barrel: 20 in.
Sights: Adjustable primitive style rear
Weight: 8 lb. 8 oz.
Bore/Caliber: .50
Features: Brass stock inlay ornamentation and toe plate; cheekpiece; solid brass patch box
Percussion: $794
Flint: $824

PURSUIT ULTRALIGHT

Lock: Hinged breech muzzleloading
Stock: Black synthetic, Reaper Buck camo, or MO Infinity camo
Barrel: 28 in.
Sights: Metal fiber optic
Weight: 5 lb. 2 oz.
Bore/Caliber: .50
Features: Accelerator breech plug; drilled and tapped for scopes; 209 shotgun primer ignition; black synthetic with blued or CeraKote finish; speed load system; fluted barrel; 3–9x40 scope available
MSRP . . . . $329–$539

TRACKER 209

Lock: In-line
Stock: Synthetic, camo
Barrel: 22 in.
Sights: Light optic adjustable
Weight: 6 lb. 8 oz.
Bore/Caliber: .50
Features: Removable 209 primer ignition; projectile alignment system; in-line bolt with a quiet thumb safety; removable breech plug system; rugged synthetic ramrod
MSRP $184

Traditions Firearms

TRADITIONS FIREARMS
TRAPPER PISTOL

TRAPPER PISTOL

Lock: Traditional cap or flint
Stock: Hardwood
Barrel: 9.75 in.
Sights: Primitive-style adjustable rear
Weight: 2 lb. 14 oz.
Bore/Caliber: .50
Features: Octagonal blued barrel; double set triggers
MSRP. . . . . $325–$362

TRADITIONS FIREARMS
VORTEK PISTOL - HARDWOOD

TRADITIONS FIREARMS
VORTEK ULTRALIGHT LDR

TRADITIONS FIREARMS VORTEK ULTRALIGHT

TRADITIONS FIREARMS
VORTEK STRIKERFIRE

VORTEK PISTOL

Lock: Hinged breech muzzleloading
Stock: Select hardwood, Realtree AP camo, Reaper Buck camo
Barrel: 13 in.
Sights: Fixed open
Weight: 3 lb. 4 oz.
Bore/Caliber: .50
Features: 209 primer ignition, accelerator breech plug; CeraKote finish on frame and barrel
MSRP: . . . . $324–$469

VORTEK STRIKERFIRE

Lock: Break-action muzzleloading
Stock: Soft Touch synthetic
Barrel: 28 in.
Sights: Fiber optic
Weight: N/A
Bore/Caliber: .50
Features: This patent-pending rifle takes in-line muzzleloaders to the next level by taking away the external hammer and using an internal StrikerFire System; to cock the gun, simply slide the striker button forward until it locks and fire; the recessed decocking buttons allows for quick and quiet de-cocking of the firearm and the gun is also equipped with an automatic de-cocking mechanism—when the gun is opened, it is automatically de-cocked; also includes: two-stage trigger; CeraKote finish; Realtree Xtra or black stock
MSRP: . . . .$493–$649

VORTEK ULTRALIGHT

Lock: Hinged breech muzzleloading
Stock: Synthetic black Hogue overmold, Realtree AP camo, or Reaper Buck camo
Barrel: 28 in.
Sights: Fixed, green
Weight: 6 lb. 4 oz.
Bore/Caliber: .50
Features: Drop-out trigger assembly; recoil pad; 3-pound factory trigger; frame and barrel have CeraKote finish
MSRP. . . . . $449–$634

VORTEK ULTRALIGHT LDR

Lock: Hinged breech muzzleloading
Stock: Synthetic, Reaper Buck camo
Barrel: 30 in.
Sights: Drilled and tapped for scopes
Weight: 6 lb. 13 oz.
Bore/Caliber: .50
Features: The only break-action muzzleloader with a 30-in. barrel on the market; accelerator breech plug; LT-1 alloy frame with Premium CeraKote finish; ultralight chromoly tapered, fluted barrel; Hogue comfort grip overmolding; Soft Touch camo stocks
MSRP. . . . . $479–$629

UBERTI 1847 WALKER

UBERTI 1848 DRAGOON

UBERTI 1849 POCKET REVOLVER

UBERTI 1851 NAVY REVOLVER

1847 WALKER

Lock: Caplock revolver
Stock: Walnut
Barrel: 9 in.
Sights: Fixed, open
Weight: 4 lb. 8 oz.
Bore/Caliber: .44
Features: Case-hardened frame, steel backstrap, brass trigger guard; blued finish
MSRP. $459

1848 DRAGOON

Lock: Caplock revolver
Stock: Walnut
Barrel: 7.5 in.
Sights: Fixed, open
Weight: 4 lb. 2 oz.
Bore/Caliber: .44
Features: Case-hardened frame; steel or brass backstrap and trigger guard; engraved
MSRP. . . . . $449–$459

1849 POCKET REVOLVER

Lock: Caplock revolver
Stock: Walnut
Barrel: 4 in.
Sights: Fixed, open
Weight: 1 lb. 8 oz.
Bore/Caliber: .31
Features: Case-hardened frame; brass backstrap and trigger guard; blued octagonal barrel; engraved
MSRP. $369

1851 NAVY REVOLVER

Lock: Caplock revolver
Stock: Walnut
Barrel: 7.5 in.
Sights: Fixed, open
Weight: 2 lb. 10 oz.
Bore/Caliber: .36
Features: Color case-hardened frame; oval or squareback trigger guard; brass or steel backstrap and trigger guard; octagonal barrel (Leech-Rigdon model has round barrel)
MSRP. $379

Uberti

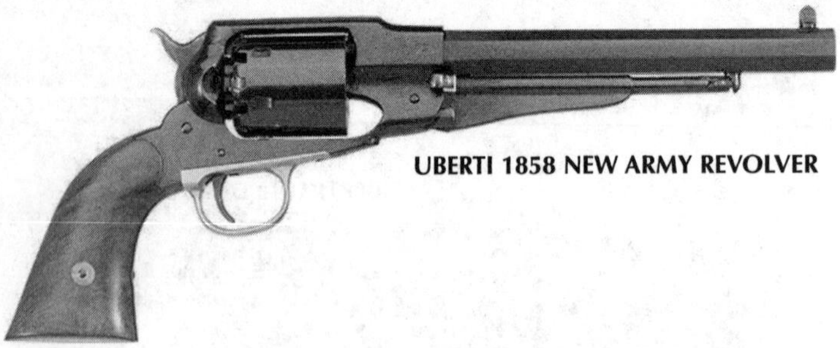

UBERTI 1858 NEW ARMY REVOLVER

1858 NEW ARMY REVOLVER

Lock: Caplock revolver
Stock: Walnut
Barrel: 8 in.
Sights: Fixed, open
Weight: 2 lb. 11 oz.
Bore/Caliber: .44
Features: Blued or stainless steel frame and backstrap; brass trigger guard; octagonal barrel
Blued: $369
Stainless Steel:. $459

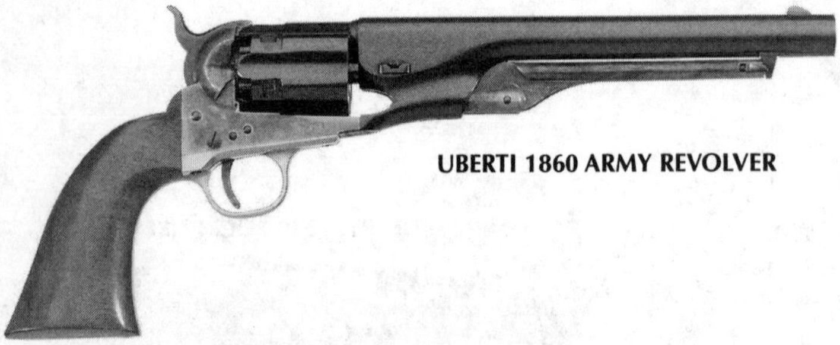

UBERTI 1860 ARMY REVOLVER

1860 ARMY REVOLVER

Lock: Caplock revolver
Stock: Walnut
Barrel: 7.5 in.
Sights: Fixed, open
Weight: 2 lb. 10 oz.
Bore/Caliber: .44
Features: Case-hardened frame, steel backstrap, brass trigger guard; blued, round barrel
MSRP: $369

UBERTI 1861 NAVY REVOLVER

1861 NAVY REVOLVER

Lock: Caplock revolver
Stock: Walnut
Barrel: 7.5 in.
Sights: Fixed, open
Weight: 2 lb. 10 oz.
Bore/Caliber: .36
Features: Case-hardened frame, steel or brass backstrap and trigger guard
MSRP $369

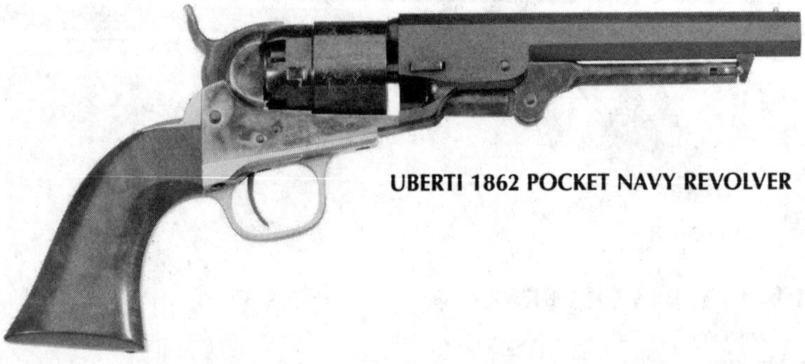

UBERTI 1862 POCKET NAVY REVOLVER

1862 POCKET NAVY REVOLVER

Lock: Caplock revolver
Stock: Walnut
Barrel: 5.5 in., 6.5 in.
Sights: Fixed, open
Weight: 1 lb. 11 oz.
Bore/Caliber: .36
Features: Case-hardened frame; brass backstrap and trigger guard; octagonal, blued barrel
MSRP $369

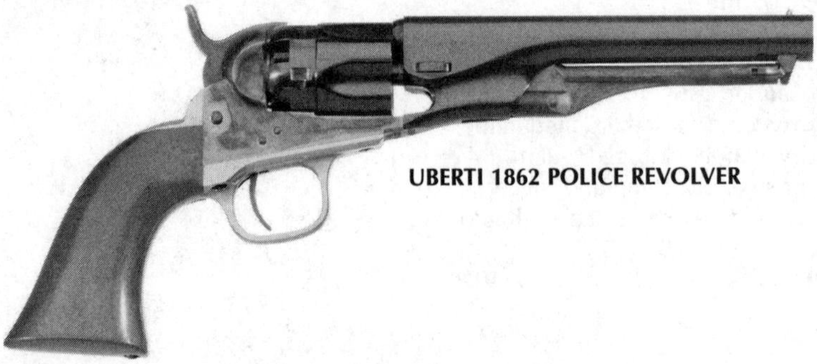

UBERTI 1862 POLICE REVOLVER

1862 POLICE REVOLVER

Lock: Caplock revolver
Stock: Walnut
Barrel: 5.5 in., 6.5 in.
Sights: Fixed, open
Weight: 1 lb. 10 oz.
Bore/Caliber: .36
Features: Case-hardened frame; brass backstrap and trigger guard; fluted round barrel
MSRP $389

OPTICS

SCOPES

410 Alpen Optics
411 Barska
412 British Small Arms Co. (BSA)
413 Burris
448 Schmidt & Bender
451 Simmons
452 Steiner
453 Swarovski Optik
454 Tangent Theta

SIGHTS

462 Aimpoint
462 Browning
463 Burris
464 Bushnell Performance Optics

SCOPES

Alpen Optics

APEX XP AR MODEL 4065

Weight: 15 oz.
Length: 10.7 in.
Power: 1–6X
Obj. Dia.: 24mm
Main Dia.: 30mm
Exit Pupil: 12.5–4mm
Field of View: 108–18 ft @ 100 yds
Twilight Factor: 4.9–12
Eye Relief: 3.75 in.
Features: AR-BDC reticle; water- and fogproof; fully multi-coated; fast focus eyepiece; matte black; zero adj. W/E
MSRP $998

ALPEN APEX XP AR MODEL 4065

APEX XP AR IRD MODEL 4069

Weight: 15 oz.
Length: 10.7 in.
Power: 1–6X
Obj. Dia.: 24mm
Main Dia.: 30mm
Exit Pupil: 12.5–4mm
Field of View: 108–18 ft @ 100 yds
Twilight Factor: 4.9–12
Eye Relief: 3.75 in.
Features: AR-BDC reticle; water- and fogproof; fully multi-coated; fast focus eyepiece; matte black; zero adj. W/E; illuminated red center dot
MSRP $1073

ALPEN APEX XP AR IRD MODEL 4069

OPTICS

APEX XP MODEL 4052 3–9X40MM

Weight: 14 oz.
Length: 12.5 in.
Power: 3–9X
Obj. Dia.: 40mm
Main Dia.: 1 in.
Exit Pupil: 13–4.5mm
Field of View: 35–12 ft @ 100 yds
Twilight Factor: 10.95–18.97
Eye Relief: 3.5 in.
Features: Fully multi-coated lens; WBDC-A reticle; matte black finish; fast-focus; side focus adjust; illuminated red-dot reticle
MSRP $500

ALPEN APEX XP MODEL 4052 3–9X40MM

Alpen Optics

APEX XP MODEL 4058 6–24X50MM

Weight: 24 oz.
Length: 15.5 in.
Power: 6–24X
Obj. Dia.: 50mm
Main Dia.: 30mm
Exit Pupil: 8–2mm
Field of View: 16–4 ft @ 100 yds
Twilight Factor: 17.3–34.6
Eye Relief: 3.5 in.
Features: Matte black; WBDC-TACT reticle available; also in 1.5–6x42, and in red-dot illuminated-reticle 1.5–6x42, 2.5–10x50, and 4–16x56; 6–24x50 and the 4–16x56 have 1/8 MOA adjustment increments, while the others have 1/4 MOA
MSRP $718

ALPEN APEX XP MODEL 4058 6–24X50MM

KODIAK MODEL 2060 3.5–10X50MM

Weight: 21 oz.
Length: 13.2 in.
Power: 3.5–10X
Obj.Dia.: 50mm
Main Dia.: 1 in.
Exit Pupil: 13.5–4.9mm
Field of View: 35–12 ft @ 100 yds
Twilight Factor: 13.2–22.4
Eye Relief: 3 in.
Features: Multi-coated optical design; oversized zero-reset windage and
elevation dials adjustable in 1/4 MOA
(1/8 MOA in the 6–24x50) clicks; AccuPlex Tapered duplex-style reticle; fast-focus eye piece; matte black; also in 1.5–4x32, 3–9x32, 4x32, 3–9x40, 4–12x40, and 6–24x50
MSRP: $235

ALPEN KODIAK MODEL 2060 3.5–10X50MM

Barska

AR6 1–6X24MM

Weight: 17.6 oz.
Length: 11 in.
Power: 1–6X
Obj. Dia.: 24mm
Main Dia.: 30mm
Exit Pupil: 4–11mm
Field of View: 75.78–12.79 ft @ 100 yds
Twilight Factor: 4.9–12
Eye Relief: 3.7 in.
Features: Water- and fogproof; red or green illuminated reticle; dual cantilever ring scope mount, flip-up scope caps
MSRP $240

BARSKA AR6 1–6X24MM

British Small Arms Co. (BSA)

BRITISH SMALL ARMS CO. 17 SUPERMAG SERIES 4.5–14X44MM

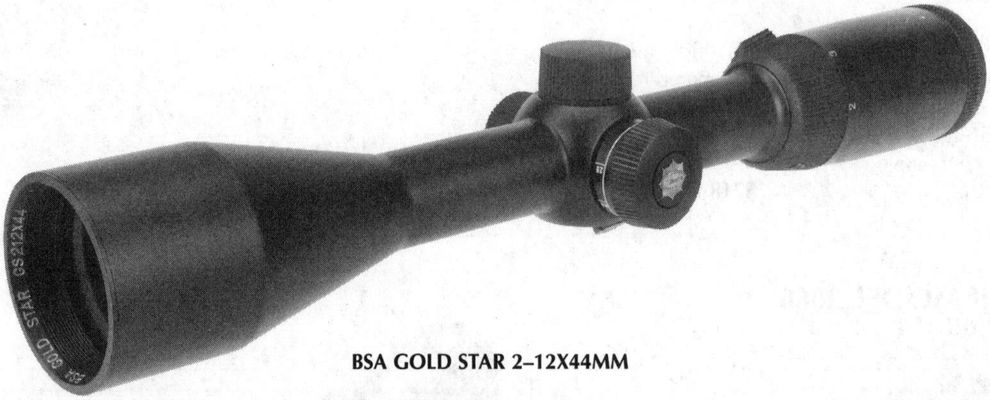

BSA GOLD STAR 2–12X44MM

BSA MAJESTIC DX 4–16X44MM

17 SUPERMAG SERIES 4.5–14X44MM

Weight: 21.7 oz.
Length: 13.9 in.
Power: 4.5–14X
Obj. Dia.: 44mm
Main Dia.: 1 in.
Exit Pupil: 6.6–2.3mm
Field of View: 16.6–4.8 ft @ 100 yds
Twilight Factor: 14.07–24.82
Eye Relief: 4 in.
Features: Shock-, water-, and fogproof; adjustable parallax; red, green, or blue glass-etched reticle; designed for use with .17 WSM; 6–24x44 also available
MSRP. . . . . $140–$160

GOLD STAR 2–12X44MM

Weight: 18 oz.
Length: 13.15 in.
Power: 2–12X
Obj.Dia.: 44mm
Main Dia.: 1 in.
Exit Pupil: 22–3.6mm
Field of View: 60–10 ft @ 100 yds
Twilight Factor: 9.38–22.98
Eye Relief: 4 in.
Features: The Gold Star line of riflescopes represent the pinnacle of BSA performance optics, exceptional clarity and resolution; 6x zoom system; perfected optical design; EZ Hunter reticle; precision W/E adjustment; side parallax available on some models
MSRP. $140

MAJESTIC DX 4–16X44MM

Weight: 17.6 oz.
Length: 12.66 in.
Power: 4–16X
Obj. Dia.: 44mm
Main Dia.: 1 in.
Exit Pupil: 8–4mm
Field of View: 45–7.3 ft @ 100 yds
Twilight Factor: 13.27–26.53
Eye Relief: 4 in.
Features: Newly redesigned one piece tube; fully multi-coated optics; ballistic compensating EZ Hunter reticle; 92 percent light transmission; fast-focus eyepiece
MSRP. $120

Burris

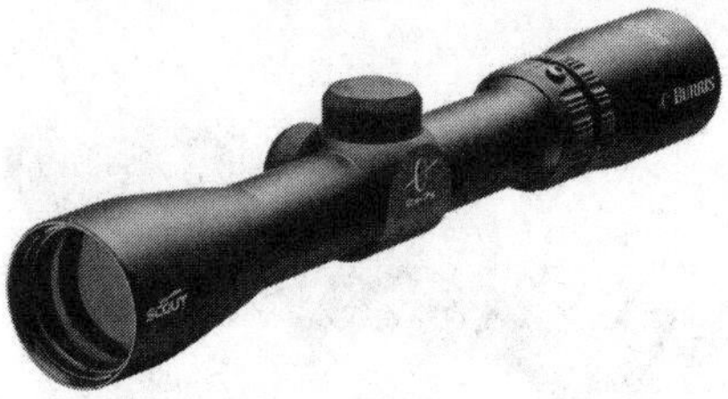

BURRIS 2X–7X SCOUT SCOPE

BURRIS AR RIFLESCOPE 4.5–14X42MM

BURRIS C4 RIFLESCOPE 4.5X–14X42MM

BURRIS DROPTINE RIFLESCOPE 4.5–14X42MM

BURRIS ELIMINATOR III 4X–16X50MM

2X–7X SCOUT SCOPE

Weight: 13 oz.
Length: 9.7 in.
Power: 2–7X
Obj. Dia.: 32mm
Main Dia.: 1 in.
Exit Pupil: 16–4.6mm
Field of View: 21–7 ft @ 100 yds
Twilight Factor: 8–15
Eye Relief: 11–21 in.
Features: Ballistic Plex reticle; fully multi-coated; variable power; low mounting capabilities; black matte finish
MSRP. . . . .$299–$479

AR RIFLESCOPE 4.5–14X42MM

Weight: 18 oz.
Length: 13 in.
Power: 4.5–14X
Obj. Dia.: 42mm
Main Dia.: 1 in.
Exit Pupil: 9–3mm
Field of View: 22–7.5 ft @ 100 yds
Twilight Factor: 13.75–24.25
Eye Relief: 3.1 in.–3.8 in.
Features: Shock-, water-, and fogproof; nitrogen filled; C4 Wind MOA reticle; adjustable parallax; anti-reflection device included; 5.56 and 7.62 calibrated custom clickers included
MSRP. $479

C4 RIFLESCOPE 4.5X–14X42MM

Weight: 18 oz.
Length: 12.2 in.
Power: 4.5–14X
Obj. Dia.: 42mm
Main Dia.: 1 in.
Exit Pupil: 9–3mm
Field of View: 23–8 ft @ 100 yds
Twilight Factor: 13.7–24.2
Eye Relief: 3.2–3.9 in.
Features: Custom knob to match elevation adjustment and a specified catridge and bullet; index matched Hi-Lume multi-coatings; ergonomic power rings; black matte finish; available in 3x–9x40 and 4.5–14x42 in both 1-in. and 30mm tubes
MSRP. . . . .$449–$749

DROPTINE RIFLESCOPE 4.5–14X42MM

Weight: 18 oz.
Length: 13 in.
Power: 4.5–14X
Obj. Dia.: 42mm
Main Dia.: 1 in.
Exit Pupil: 9–3mm
Field of View: 22–7.5 ft @ 100 yds
Twilight Factor: 13.75–24.25
Eye Relief: 3.1 in.–3.8 in.
Features: Shock-, water-, and fogproof; nitrogen filled; multi-coated lenses; Ballistic Plex reticle or G2B Mil-Dot reticle; adjustable parallax; 2–7x35, 3–9x40, and 3–9x50 also available
MSRP. . . . .$179–$299

ELIMINATOR III 4X–16X50MM

Weight: 26 oz.
Length: 15.75 in.
Power: 4–16X
Obj. Dia.: 50mm
Main Dia.: 39mm
Exit Pupil: 12.5–3.1mm
Field of View: 25–7 ft @ 100 yds
Twilight Factor: 14.1–28.3
Eye Relief: 3.5–4 in.
Features: Laser rangefinder with wind compensation; range of 1,200+ yards; accurate at any magnification; ergonomic activation buttons; parallax adjustment 50 yards-infinity; black matte finish; fully multi-coated
MSRP. . . . . $1559–$1799

Burris

BURRIS FULLFIELD E1
3–9X40MM ILLUMINATED

BURRIS MTAC 4.5–14X42MM

BURRIS MSR RIFLESCOPE 4.5–14X42MM

FULLFIELD E1 3–9X40MM ILLUMINATED

Weight: 12 oz.
Length: 11.4 in.
Power: 3–9X
Obj. Dia.: 40mm
Main Dia.: 1 in.
Exit Pupil: 17–5mm
Field of View: 45–13 ft @ 100 yds
Twilight Factor: 10.95–18.97
Eye Relief: 3.1–4.1 in.
Features: A series of cascading dots to the left and right of the reticle help compensate for crosswinds. The dots represent a 10 mph crosswind (+/- 1.5-in. at 400 yds) for most hunting cartridges. For a 5 mph crosswind, halve the distance between dot and reticle. For 20 mph crosswind, simply double the distance. Also available in 2–7x35, 3–9x50, 4.5–14x42, and 6.5–20x50
MSRP. . . . . **$239–$599**

MSR RIFLESCOPE 4.5–14X42MM

Weight: 18 oz.
Length: 13 in.
Power: 4.5–14X
Obj. Dia.: 42mm
Main Dia.: 1 in.
Exit Pupil: 9–3mm
Field of View: 22–7.5 ft @ 100 yds
Twilight Factor: 13.75–24.25
Eye Relief: 3.1–3.8 in.
Features: Shock-, water-, and fog-proof; nitrogen filled; multi-coated lenses; Ballistic Plex reticle; adjustable parallax; 3–9x40 also available
MSRP. . . . . **$239–$323**

MTAC 4.5–14X42MM

Weight: 17.6 oz.
Length: 13 in.
Power: 4.5–14X
Obj. Dia.: 42mm
Main Dia.: 30mm
Exit Pupil: 24–6mm
Field of View: 22–7.5 ft @ 100 yds
Twilight Factor: 13.75–24.25
Eye Relief: 3.1–3.8 in.
Features: For long-range tactical shooting; adjustable parallax; feature-rich G2B Mil-Dot reticle for precise aiming, distance measurement, holdover, and hold off; new MTAC Mil-Rad knobs with finger-adjustable/resettable dials for windage and elevation; also available in 1–4x24, 1.5–6x40, 3.5–10x42, 6.5–20x50
MSRP. . . . . **$479–$839**

BURRIS PREDATOR QUEST RIFLESCOPE 4.5–14X42MM

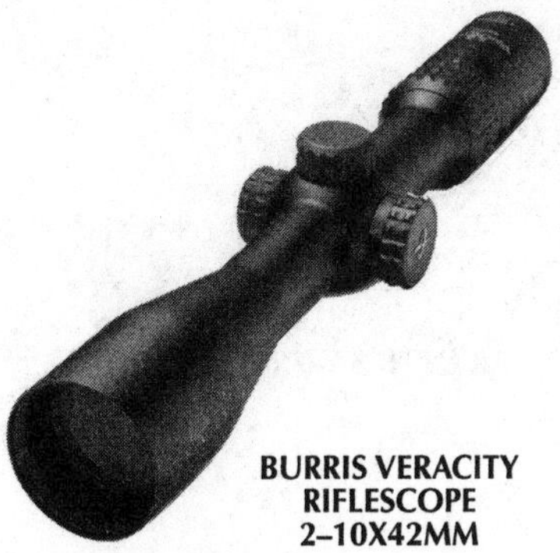

BURRIS VERACITY RIFLESCOPE 2–10X42MM

BURRIS XTR II 1–5X24MM

BURRIS XTR II 2–10X42MM

PREDATOR QUEST RIFLESCOPE 4.5–14X42MM

Weight: 18 oz.
Length: 13 in.
Power: 4.5–14X
Obj. Dia.: 42mm
Main Dia.: 1 in.
Exit Pupil: 9–3mm
Field of View: 22–7.5 ft @ 100 yds
Twilight Factor: 13.75–24.25
Eye Relief: 3.1 in.–3.8 in.
Features: Shock-, water-, and fog-proof; nitrogen filled; Hi-Lume multi-coated lenses; Ballistic Plex E1 reticle (illuminated optional); adjustable parallax; anti-reflection device included; camo or matte black; 2–7x35 and 3–9x40 also available
MSRP . . . . $275–$419

VERACITY RIFLESCOPE 2–10X42MM

Weight: 22.7 oz.
Length: 13.5 in.
Power: 2–10X
Obj. Dia.: 42mm
Main Dia.: 30mm
Exit Pupil: 21–4.2mm
Field of View: 52–10.5 ft @ 100 yds
Twilight Factor: 9.17–20.49
Eye Relief: 3.5 in.–4.25 in.
Features: Shock-, water-, and fog-proof; nitrogen filled; Ballistic E1 FFP MOA reticle with PTC technology; E1 Hunter knobs; parallax adjustment; 3–15x50, 4–20x50, and 5–25x50 also available
MSRP . . . . $719–$1079

XTR II 2–10X42MM

Weight: 22.7 oz.
Length: 13.5 in.
Power: 2–10X
Obj. Dia.: 42mm
Main Dia.: 34mm
Exit Pupil: 12–4.2mm
Field of View: 52–10.5 ft @ 100 yds
Twilight Factor: 9.17–20.49
Eye Relief: 3.5 in.–4.25 in.
Features: Shock-, water-, and fog-proof; nitrogen filled; Hi-Lume multi-coated lenses; Zero Click Stop technology; G2B Mil-Dot illuminated FFP reticle; adjustable parallax; 3–15x50, 4–20x50, 5–25x50, and 8–40x50 also available
MSRP . . . . $959–$1499

Bushnell Performance Optics

BUSHNELL AR OPTICS 2–7X32MM RIMFIRE

BUSHNELL AR OPTICS 1–4X24MM THROW DOWN PCL

BUSHNELL AR OPTICS 3–12X40MM

BUSHNELL AR OPTICS 4.5–18X40MM

AR OPTICS 1–4X24MM THROW DOWN PCL

Weight: 17.3 oz.
Length: 3.6 in.
Power: 1–4X
Obj. Dia.: 24mm
Main Dia.: 30mm
Exit Pupil: 13–6mm
Field of View: 110–36 ft @ 100 yds
Twilight Factor: 4.9–9.8
Eye Relief: 3.6 in.
Features: Optional illuminated BTR-1 reticle; first focal plane; Throw Down PCL lever for power changes; fully multi-coated optics; holdovers out to 500 yds; target turrets; matte finish
MSRP $281

AR OPTICS 2–7X32MM RIMFIRE

Weight: 19.6 oz.
Length: 11.3 in.
Power: 2–7X
Obj. Dia.: 32mm
Main Dia.: 1 in.
Exit Pupil: 13.5–4.6mm
Field of View: 50–17 ft @ 100 yds
Twilight Factor: 8–15
Eye Relief: 3.7 in.
Features: Target turrets; Drop Zone 22 LR BDC reticle; fully multi-coated optics; matte finish
MSRP $210

AR OPTICS 3–12X40MM

Weight: 21.3 oz.
Length: 12 in.
Power: 3–12X
Obj. Dia.: 40mm
Main Dia.: 1 in.
Exit Pupil: 13.7–3.7mm
Field of View: 33–11 ft @ 100 yds
Twilight Factor: 11–21.9
Eye Relief: 3.7 in.
Features: Target turrets; side parallax adjustment; Drop Zone 223 BDC reticle; second focal plane; fully multi-coated optics; 600 yard range; matte finish
MSRP $281

AR OPTICS 4.5–18X40MM

Weight: 21.5 oz.
Length: 12.4 in.
Power: 4.5–18X
Obj. Dia.: 40mm
Main Dia.: 1 in.
Exit Pupil: 8.6–2.3mm
Field of View: 22–7.3 ft @ 100 yds
Twilight Factor: 13.4–26.8
Eye Relief: 3.7 in.
Features: Target turrets; side parallax adjustment; Drop Zone 223 BDC reticle; second focal plane; fully multi-coated optics; 600 yard range; matte finish
MSRP $350

Bushnell Performance Optics

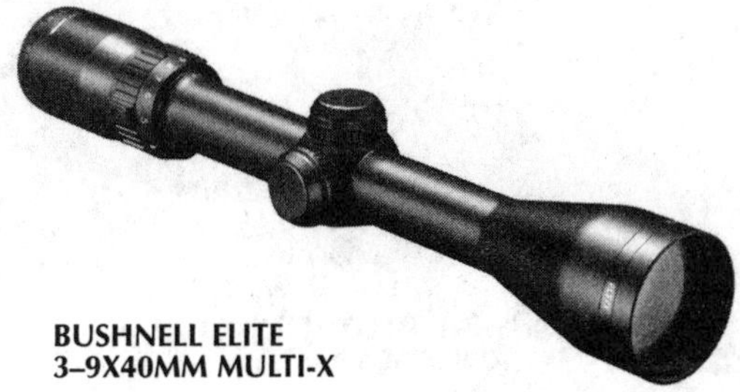

BUSHNELL ELITE
3–9X40MM MULTI-X

BUSHNELL ELITE 6500
2.5–16X50MM MIL-DOT

BUSHNELL ELITE
TACTICAL 1–8.5X24MM

BUSHNELL ELITE TACTICAL
HUNTER 3–12X40MM

ELITE 3–9X40MM MULTI-X

Weight: 13 oz.
Length: 12.6 in.
Power: 3–9X
Obj.Dia.: 40mm
Main Dia.: 1 in.
Exit Pupil: 13.3–4.44mm
Field of View: 33.8–11.5 ft @ 100 yds
Twilight Factor: 10.95–18.97
Eye Relief: 3.4 in.
Features: Bushnell's "Ultra Wide Band Coating"; lenses treated with moisture shedding RainGuard HD; fingertip windage and elevation adjustments are audible and resettable and in ¼ MOA increments; also in 1.25–4x24, 2.5–10x40, 2.5–10x50, 4–16x40 Multi-X, 4–16x40 DOA 600, 4–16x50, 6–24x40 Mil-Dot, 6–24x40 Multi-X, 8–32x40 Multi-X, 2–7x32, 3–10x40, 3–9x40 (Gloss/Silver), 3–9x40 FireFly, 3–9x40 DOA 600, 3–9x50 Multi-X, 3–9x50 DOA 600, 3–9x50 FireFly
MSRP $424

ELITE 6500 2.5–16X50MM MIL-DOT

Weight: 21 oz.
Length: 13.5 in.
Power: 2.5–16X
Obj.Dia.: 50mm
Main Dia.: 30mm
Exit Pupil: 20–3.12mm
Field of View: 42–7 ft @ 100 yds
Twilight Factor: 11.18–28.28
Eye Relief: 3.9 in.
Features: Lenses with 60-layer "Ultra Wide Band Coating"; 91 percent total light transmission through the scope; RainGuard HD; windage and elevation adjustments in ¼ MOA audible increments; also in 1.25–8x32, 2.5–16x42 Fine Multi-X, 2.5–16x42 Mil-Dot,
2.5–16x50 FMX, 4.5–30x50 DOA 600, 4.5–30x50 Fine Multi-X, 4.5–30x50 Mil-Dot
MSRP $1071

ELITE TACTICAL 1–8.5X24MM

Weight: 23 oz.
Length: 10.2 in.
Power: 1–8.5X
Obj. Dia.: 24mm
Main Dia.: 34mm
Exit Pupil: 13.2–3.2mm
Field of View: 105–14 ft @ 100 yds
Twilight Factor: 4.9–14.3
Eye Relief: 3.5 in.
Features: Illuminated BTR-2 reticle; first focal plane; .1 Mil click value; eleven brightness settings; T-Lok turrets; black matte finish
MSRP $3253

ELITE TACTICAL HUNTER 3–12X40MM

Weight: 24.4 oz.
Length: 13.4 in.
Power: 3–12X
Obj. Dia.: 40mm
Main Dia.: 30mm
Exit Pupil: 12.1–3.7mm
Field of View: 34.8–8.96 ft @ 100 yds
Twilight Factor: 10.95–21.91
Eye Relief: 3.74 in.
Features: Front focal plane; RainGuard HD coating makes water and fog bead up and roll off lens surfaces; fully multi-coated lenses
MSRP $1500

Bushnell Performance Optics

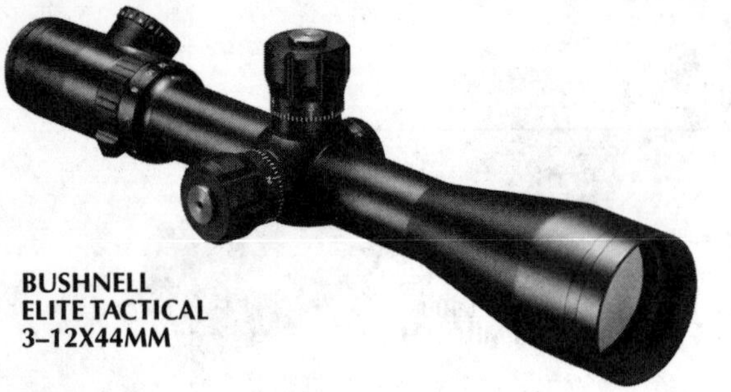

BUSHNELL
ELITE TACTICAL
3–12X44MM

BUSHNELL ELITE TACTICAL
4.5–30X50MM XRS

BUSHNELL
ELITE TACTICAL
6–24X50MM

BUSHNELL ELITE TACTICAL ERS
3.5–21X50MM

ELITE TACTICAL 3–12X44MM

Weight: 24.4 oz.
Length: 13 in.
Power: 3–12X
Obj.Dia.: 44mm
Main Dia.: 30mm
Exit Pupil: 14.66–3.66mm
Field of View: 36–10 ft @ 100 yds
Twilight Factor: 11.48–22.97
Eye Relief: 3.75 in.
Features: Tactical treatment of Elite 6500 riflescope; tactical target-adjustment turrets and non-glare black-matte finish as well as "blacked-out" cosmetics for concealment; Bushnell "Ultra Wide Band Coating" optics; RainGuard HD coating; illuminated and non-illuminated Mil-Dot reticles; also in 10x44, 2.5–16x42, 4.5–30x50, 5–15x40, 6–24x50 Mil-Dot, 6–24x50 Illuminated Mil-Dot
MSRP $1364

ELITE TACTICAL 4.5–30X50MM XRS

Weight: 37 oz.
Length: 10.2 in.
Power: 4.5–30X
Obj. Dia.: 50mm
Main Dia.: 34mm
Exit Pupil: 9–1.7mm
Field of View: 24–3.6 ft @ 100 yds
Twilight Factor: 15–38.7
Eye Relief: 3.7 in.
Features: T-Lok locking target turrets; Z-Lok zero stop; G2 reticle; first focal plane; side parallax adjustment; .1 Mil clicks, 10 Mils/rev; blacked-out finish
MSRP $3253

ELITE TACTICAL 6–24X50MM

Weight: 27 oz.
Length: 13.5 in.
Power: 6–24X
Obj.Dia.: 50mm
Main Dia.: 30mm
Exit Pupil: 7.5–2.1mm
Field of View: 17.5–4.5 ft @ 100 yds
Twilight Factor: 17.32–24
Eye Relief: 4 in.
Features: Exceptional brightness and extended-range magnification with side parallax; RainGuard HD; fully multi-coated optics; ultra-strong, one-piece tube; .1 Mil click value; 3-in. sunshade; side parallax adjustment; available in Mil-Dot, Illuminated Mil-Dot, G2, and Illuminated BTR-Mil reticles
MSRP $1523

ELITE TACTICAL ERS 3.5–21X50MM

Weight: 35 oz.
Length: 13 in.
Power: 3.5–21X
Obj. Dia.: 50mm
Main Dia.: 34mm
Exit Pupil: 10–2.4mm
Field of View: 26–5 ft @ 100 yds
Twilight Factor: 13.2–32.4
Eye Relief: 3.7 in.
Features: T-Lok locking turrets; Z-Lok zero stop; G2 reticle; first focal plane; side parallax adjustment; .1 Mil click, 10 rev; available in matte black or flat dark earth finishes
MSRP $2976

ELITE TACTICAL 10X40MM MIL-DOT

Weight: 15.9 oz.
Length: 11.5 in.
Power: 10X
Obj.Dia.: 40mm
Main Dia.: 1 in.
Exit Pupil: 4mm
Field of View: 11–3.7 ft @ 100 yds
Twilight Factor: 20
Eye Relief: 3.5 in.
Features: Fixed-power target scope with Mil-Dot reticle and target turret; RainGuard HD; ultra wide band coating; fully multi-coated optics; blacked-out finish; target turrets
MSRP. $391

ELITE TACTICAL HDMR AND DMR 3.5–21X50MM

Weight: 32.5 oz.
Length: 13.2 in.
Power: 3.5–21X
Obj. Dia.: 50mm
Main Dia.: 34mm
Exit Pupil: 10.4–2.4mm
Field of View: 25.3 ft @ 100 yds
Twilight Factor: 13.23–21.21
Eye Relief: 3.74 in.
Features: Part of the Bushnell extended range riflescope (ERS) family designed to give tactical marksmen a powerful optic that works equally well in short or extended range shooting applications; available with the Horus H59 and TreMor 2 reticles, and the Elite Tactical DMR features the G2DMR and Mil-Dot reticles.
MSRP. $2183

BUSHNELL ELITE TACTICAL 10X40MM MIL-DOT

BUSHNELL ELITE TACTICAL HDMR AND DMR 3.5–21X50MM

BUSHNELL LEGEND ULTRA HD 1.75–5X32MM

BUSHNELL TROPHY XLT 3–9X40MM MIL-DOT

LEGEND ULTRA HD 1.75–5X32MM DOA 200

Weight: 13 oz.
Length: 10.25 in.
Power: 1.75–5X
Obj. Dia.: 32mm
Main Dia.: 30mm
Exit Pupil: 18.2–6.4mm
Field of View: 49–17 ft @ 100 yds
Twilight Factor: 7.48–12.65
Eye Relief: 4.5 in.
Features: The perfect scope for medium range hunting with a shotgun; RainGuard HD; fully multi-coated optics; ultra-strong, one-piece tube; parallax set at 75 yds; waterproof, fogproof, and shockproof; fast-focus eyepiece; also in 1.75–5x32 Multi-X/DOA Crossbow, 3–9x40 Multi-X/DOA 600, 3–9x50 Multi-X/DOA 600, 4.5–14x44 Multi-X/Mil-Dot
MSRP. $379

TROPHY XLT 3–9X40MM MIL-DOT

Weight: 14.1 oz.
Length: 11.9 in.
Power: 3–9X
Obj.Dia.: 40mm
Main Dia.: 1 in.
Exit Pupil: 13.3–4.4mm
Field of View: 40–13 ft @ 100 yds
Twilight Factor: 10.95–18.97
Eye Relief: 4 in.
Features: 91percent total light transmission; one-piece tube with integrated saddle; ¼ MOA fingertip windage and elevation adjustments with range of adjustment of 80 MOA; Butler Creek flip-up scope covers; some scopes available in gloss, matte, silver, or camo finishes; also in 3–9x40 DOA 250, 3–9x40 DOA 600, 3–9x40 Multi-X, 3–9x40 Circle-X, 3–9x50, 4–12x40 DOA 600, 4–12x40 Multi-X, 1–4x24, 1.5–6x42, 1.5–6x44, 3–12x56, 1.75–4x32, 2–6x32, 2–7x36 DOA Crossbow, 2–7x36 DOA 200, 3–9x40 DOA 200, 6–18x50
MSRP. $205

Bushnell Performance Optics

TROPHY XLT CROSSBOW SCOPE 2–7X36MM

Weight: 14.3 oz.
Length: 13 in.
Power: 2–7X
Obj.Dia.: 36mm
Main Dia.: 1 in.
Exit Pupil: 13.3–4.4mm
Field of View: 33–11 ft @ 100 yds
Twilight Factor: 8.5–15.9
Eye Relief: 5 in.
Features: One-piece tube with an integrated mounting saddle; Butler Creek flip-up caps; 91 percent light transmission; DOA Crossbow reticle; ¼ MOA fingertip windage and elevation adjustments allow for extended-range shooting out to 60 yards
MSRP $228

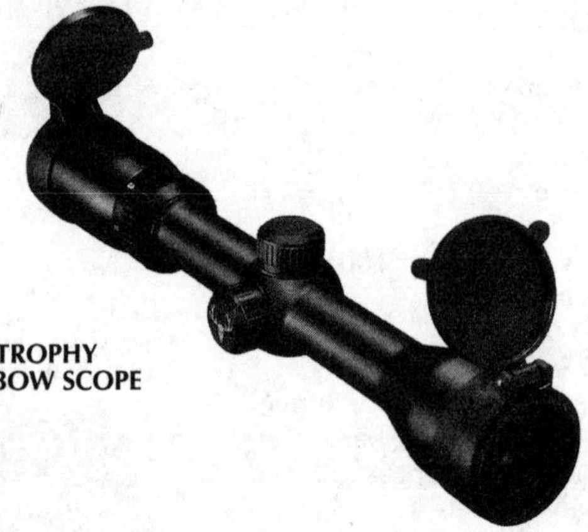

BUSHNELL TROPHY XLT CROSSBOW SCOPE 2–7X36MM

Cabela's

30MM TACTICAL CLASSIC 6–18X50MM EXT SF

Weight: 17.5 oz.
Length: 13.23 in.
Power: 6–18X
Obj.Dia.: 50mm
Main Dia.: 30mm
Exit Pupil: 8.33–2.77mm
Field of View: 15.88–5.24 ft @ 100 yds
Twilight Factor: 17.32–30
Eye Relief: 4 in.
Features: Tactical-grade 30mm tube; Guidetech broadband lens technology; machined to military-grade tolerances; low-profile turrets with ⅛ MOA click windage and elevation adjustments; hard-blasted anodized finish and moisture- and dust-repelling lenses; also in 2.5–10x50 and 8–32x50SF with both EXT and Duplex reticles
MSRP $440

CABELA'S 30MM TACTICAL CLASSIC 6–18X50MM EXT SF

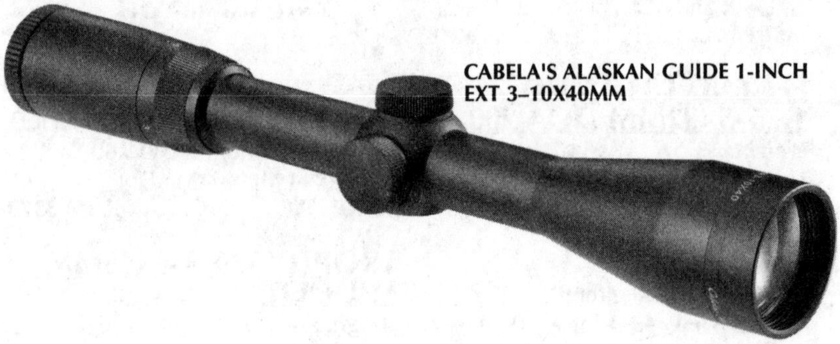

CABELA'S ALASKAN GUIDE 1-INCH EXT 3–10X40MM

ALASKAN GUIDE 1-INCH EXT 3–10X40MM

Weight: 13.5 oz.
Length: 12.8 in.
Power: 3–10X
Obj.Dia.: 40mm
Main Dia.: 1 in.
Exit Pupil: 13.33–4mm
Field of View: 33.65–10.48 ft @ 100 yds
Twilight Factor: 10.95–20
Eye Relief: 3.75 in.
Features: EXT—"extended range"; "Guidetech" broadband lens coating technology; one-piece tube; components machined to military-grade tolerances; low-profile turrets with ¼ MOA click windage and elevation adjustments; hard-blasted anodized finish for durability and corrosion resistance; moisture- and dust-repelling lenses; also in 4–12x44SF, 6–18x50SF EXT, and 3–10x40, 4–12x44SF, and 6–18x50SF
MSRP $270

OPTICS

Cabela's

CABELA'S EURO RIFLESCOPE DUPLEX 3–9X42MM

CABELA'S POWDERHORN MUZZLELOADER 3–10X40MM

EURO RIFLESCOPE DUPLEX 3–9X42MM

Weight: 16 oz.
Length: 12.4 in.
Power: 3–9X
Obj.Dia.: 42mm
Main Dia.: 1 in.
Exit Pupil: 14–4.66mm
Field of View: 36.3–12.1 ft @ 100 yds
Twilight Factor: 11.22–19.44
Eye Relief: 3.75 in.
Features: CNC machined from a single billet of aircraft-aluminum; ELOX (electrolytic oxidation) anodization for a reduced-glare black matte, abrasion-resistant finish; fully multi-coated lenses; fast-focus eyepieces; elevation and windage turrets are finger adjustable in ¼ MOA clicks; also with EXT reticle, and in 4–12x50 and 6–18x50 with EXT and Duplex reticles
MSRP. $450

LEVER ACTION 3–9X40MM

Weight: 14.64 oz.
Length: 13 in.
Power: 3–9X
Obj.Dia.: 40mm
Main Dia.: 1 in.
Exit Pupil: 13.33–4.44mm
Field of View: 30.55–9.6 ft @ 100 yds
Twilight Factor: 10.95–18.97
Eye Relief: 5.5 in.
Features: Ballistic glass reticles specifically engineered for use with a particular Hornady LEVERevolution round; tube is machined aluminum and lenses are multi-coated; windage and elevation are adjustable in ¼ MOA clicks; .30-30 Winchester Reticle (also in .308 Marlin, .338 Marlin Express, .444 Marlin, .35 Rem., and .45-70 Govt. reticles)
MSRP. $120

POWDERHORN MUZZLELOADER 3–10X40MM

Weight: 11.6 oz.
Length: 12.2 in.
Power: 3–10X
Obj.Dia.: 40mm
Main Dia.: 1 in.
Exit Pupil: 13.33–4mm
Field of View: 31.5–10.5 ft @ 100 yds
Twilight Factor: 10.95–20
Eye Relief: 3.75 in.
Features: Ballistic reticle regulated to match bullet drop; when the scope is sighted in at 100 yards at 10X, the next bar down is calibrated for a drop at 150 yards and the lowest bar down for 250 yards; loading data is based on the 250-grain saboted bullet and 150 grains of Triple Se7en FFg powder; hand-turn ¼ MOA click adjustments; also in silver and camo
MSRP. $100

RIMFIRE RIFLESCOPE 3–9X40MM

Weight: 13.4 oz.
Length: 12 in.
Power: 3–9X
Obj.Dia.: 40mm
Main Dia.: 1 in.
Exit Pupil: 13.33–4.44mm
Field of View: 37.7–12.4 ft @ 100 yds
Twilight Factor: 10.95–18.97
Eye Relief: 4 in.
Features: For hunting, target shooting, or plinking with a rimfire rifle; parallax-free at 50 yards; multi-coated glass optics; extended eye relief and an expanded exit pupil; low-profile windage and elevation turrets; Duplex reticle; also in 4x32
MSRP. $80

CABELA'S LEVER ACTION 3–9X40MM

CABELA'S RIMFIRE RIFLESCOPE 3–9X40MM

Carl Zeiss Sports Optics

CONQUEST HD5 2–10X42MM

Weight: 17.5 oz.
Length: 13.19 in.
Power: 2–10X
Obj. Dia.: 50mm
Main Dia.: 25.4mm
Exit Pupil: 10.6–4.2mm
Field of View: 52–10 ft @ 100 yds
Twilight Factor: 6.5–20.5
Eye Relief: 3.5 in.
Features: Versatile in close encounters from cover to mid-range; parallax free to 100 yds; available in z-Plex reticle, Rapid-Z 600, or standard hunting turrets; matte finish
MSRP . . . . $978–$1056

CONQUEST HD5 3–15X42MM

Weight: 18.4 oz.
Length: 13.8 in.
Power: 3–15X
Obj. Dia.: 50mm
Main Dia.: 25.4mm
Exit Pupil: 10–2.8mm
Field of View: 35–7 ft @ 100 yds
Twilight Factor: 9.5–25.1
Eye Relief: 3.5 in.
Features: Mid- to long-range; low profile; parallax adjustment; Z-Plex reticle; hunting turret or lockable target turret; available Rapid-Z 600 or 800 reticle for hunting turret; most versatile of HD5 line; matte finish
MSRP . . . .$1089–$1222

CONQUEST HD5 3–15X50MM

Weight: 24.7 oz.
Length: 13.78 in
Power: 3–15X
Obj. Dia.: 50mm
Main Dia.: 1 in.
Exit Pupil: 10–3.3mm
Field of View: 34.1–6.8 ft @ 100 yds
Twilight Factor: 12.25–27.39
Eye Relief: 3.5 in.
Features: Rear focal plane; water resistant; nitrogen filled
MSRP . . . . $1144–$1278

CONQUEST HD5 5–25X50MM

Weight: 26.6 oz.
Length: 14 in.
Power: 5–25X
Obj. Dia.: 60mm
Main Dia.: 25.4mm
Exit Pupil: 8.5–2mm
Field of View: 21–4.2 ft @ 100 yds
Twilight Factor: 14.5–35.4
Eye Relief: 3.5 in.
Features: Mid- to extra-long range; wide magnification range provide flexibility; side parallax adjustment; Z-Plex reticle with lockable target turret, Rapid-Z 800 with hunting turret, Rapid-Z 1000 with lockable target turret, or Rapid-Z Varmint reticle and hunting turret; matte finish
MSRP . . . . $1333–$1444

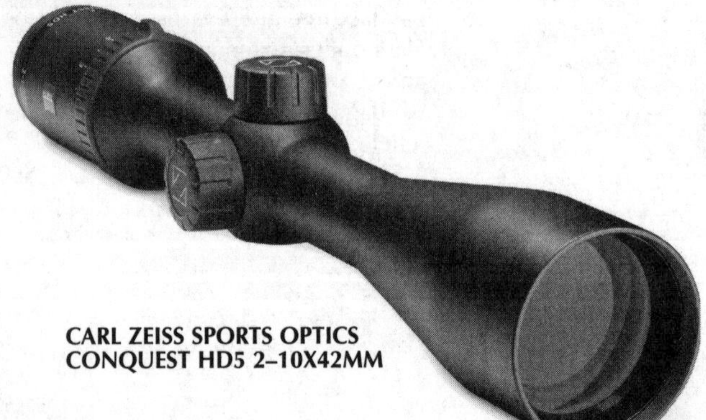

CARL ZEISS SPORTS OPTICS
CONQUEST HD5 2–10X42MM

CARL ZEISS CONQUEST HD5 3–15X50MM

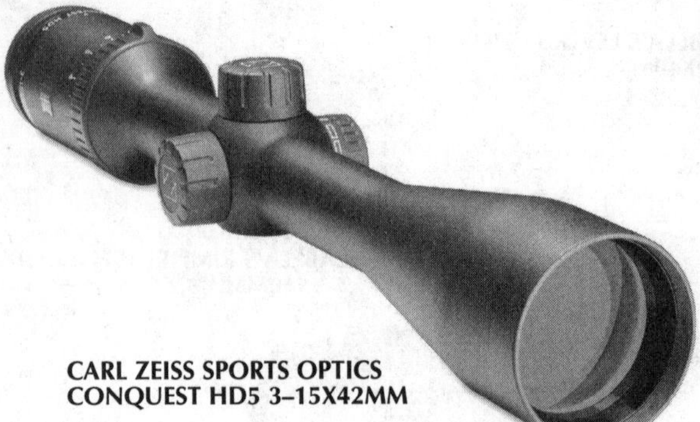

CARL ZEISS SPORTS OPTICS
CONQUEST HD5 3–15X42MM

CARL ZEISS SPORTS OPTICS
CONQUEST HD5 5–25X50MM

OPTICS

Carl Zeiss Sports Optics

CARL ZEISS SPORTS OPTICS TERRA 3X 3–9X42MM

CARL ZEISS TERRA 3X 3–9X50MM

CARL ZEISS VICTORY VARIPOINT 1.1–4X24MM T*

CARL ZEISS VICTORY DIAVARI 6–24X72MM T* FL

TERRA 3X 3–9X42MM

Weight: 14.8 oz.
Length: 12.4 in.
Power: 3–9X
Obj. Dia.: 42mm
Main Dia.: 25.4mm
Exit Pupil: 13.8–4.6mm
Field of View: 35.9–12.3 ft @ 100 yds
Twilight Factor: 11.2–19.4
Eye Relief: 3.5 in.
Features: MC anti-reflective coatings; standard Z-Plex or RZ 600 and 800 ballistic reticles available; all-purpose scope; larger objective for better low light situations; waterproof; matte finish
MSRP . . . . $444–$499

TERRA 3X 3–9X50MM

Weight: 17.5 oz.
Length: 13.2 in.
Power: 3–9X
Obj. Dia.: 50mm
Main Dia.: 1 in.
Exit Pupil: 12.4–4.16mm
Field of View: 34.8–11.3 ft @ 100 yds
Twilight Factor: 12.25–21.21
Eye Relief: 3.55 in.
Features: Water resistant; nitrogen filled; available with Z-Plex reticle, or RZ6 or RZ8 ballistic reticles; 4–12x50 also available
MSRP . . . . $500–$555

VICTORY DIAVARI 6–24X72MM T* FL

Weight: 37.39 oz.
Length: 14.9 in.
Power: 6–24X
Obj.Dia.: 72mm
Main Dia.: 34mm
Exit Pupil: 12–3mm
Field of View: 18.3–5.1 ft @ 100 yds
Twilight Factor: 16.9–41.6
Eye Relief: 3.5 in.
Features: FL glass objective and LotuTec coating; two ballistic-compensation options—BDC Ballistic Turret and Rapid Z Ballistic reticle; designed for tactical marksmen, varmint or predator hunters, and long-range hunters and shooters; parallax compensation and ¼ MOA lockable windage and elevation turrets; available with illumination
MSRP . . . . $3222–$3333

VICTORY HT 1.1–4X24MM

Weight: 15.5 oz.
Length: 11.37 in.
Power: 1.1–4X
Obj. Dia.: 30mm
Main Dia.: 30mm
Exit Pupil: 14.8mm
Field of View: 114–31.5 ft @ 100 yds
Twilight Factor: 3.1–9.8
Eye Relief: 3.54 in.
Features: With its large exit pupil and wide field of view on low power, this smallest VICTORY HT is perfect for any shooting requiring extremely fast target acquisition; the new reticle #54 with the fine cross on the illuminated dot allows you to shoot with confidence, even when the illuminated red-dot is turned off; also available with reticle #60; LotuTec coating
MSRP . . . . $2556–$2667

Carl Zeiss Sports Optics

VICTORY HT 2.5–10X50MM

Weight: 20.2 oz.
Length: 13.66 in.
Power: 3–12X
Obj. Dia.: 63mm
Main Dia.: 30mm
Exit Pupil: 14.9–4.7mm
Field of View: 37.5–25.9 ft @ 100 yds
Twilight Factor: 8.5–25.9
Eye Relief: 3.54 in.
Features: The largest of the VICTORY HT line, this 3–12x56 model makes targets visible in the very last of shooting light; the combination of the advanced HT glass, high-performance 56mm objective lens, the super-fine illuminated dot, and ASV+ turret option makes this scope deadly accurate at any distance, in any light; LotuTec lens coating
MSRP . . . . $2000–$2833

VICTORY VARIPOINT 1.1–4X24MM T*

Weight: 15.87 oz.
Length: 11.8 in.
Power: 1.1–4X
Obj.Dia.: 24mm
Main Dia.: 30mm
Exit Pupil: 14.8–6mm
Field of View: 108–31 ft @ 100 yds
Twilight Factor: 3.1–9.9
Eye Relief: 3.5 in.
Features: Illuminated red-dot reticle for fast target acquisition; LotuTec "hydrophobic" lens coating; also in 1.5–6x42 T*, 2.5–10x50 T*
MSRP $3000

VICTORY VARIPOINT 3–12X56MM T*

Weight: 21.34 oz.
Length: 14 in.
Power: 3–12X
Obj.Dia.: 56mm
Main Dia.: 30mm
Exit Pupil: 14.7–4.7mm
Field of View: 37.5–10.5 ft @ 100 yds
Twilight Factor: 8.5–25.9
Eye Relief: 3.5 in.
Features: The large objective lens of the Victory Varipoint 3–12x56 T* is traditional for European scopes that are often used from shooting towers in low light
MSRP $3222

CARL ZEISS VICTORY VARIPOINT 3–12X56MM T*

CARL ZEISS VICTORY HT 1.1–4X24MM

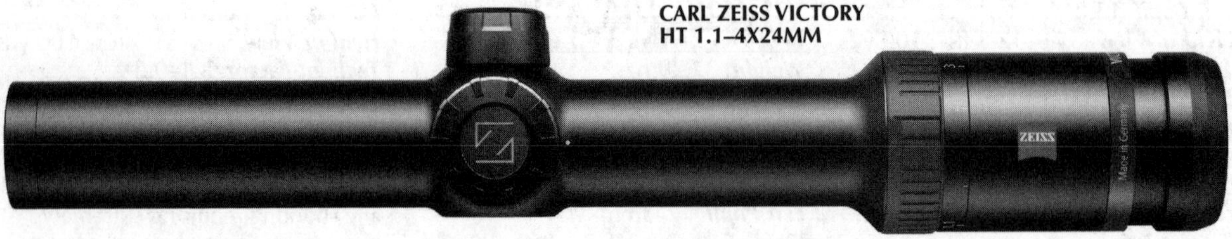

CARL ZEISS VICTORY HT 2.5–10X50MM

Kahles

KAHLES HELIA C 2.5–10X50MM

KAHLES K16I 1–6X24MM

KAHLES K15I 1–5X24MM

HELIA C 2.5–10X50MM

Weight: 17.3 oz.
Length: 12.8 in.
Power: 2.5–10X
Obj. Dia.: 50mm
Main Dia.: 30mm
Exit Pupil: 18.6–4.6mm
Field of View: 45–12.9 ft @ 100 yds
Twilight Factor: 7.8–22.4
Eye Relief: 3.54 in.
Features: Front focal plane; lightweight; extreme light transmission; edge to edge clarity; unprecedented field of view
MSRP $1399

K15I 1–5X24MM

Weight: 16.9 oz.
Length: 10.9 in.
Power: 1–5X
Obj. Dia.: 24mm
Main Dia.: 30mm
Exit Pupil: 9.65–4.83mm
Field of View: 127–24 ft @ 100 yds
Twilight Factor: 4.9–10.95
Eye Relief: 3.74 in.
Features: Rear focal plane; illuminated; integrated magnification throw lever allows for instant magnification changes even in the most adverse environmental conditions
MSRP $1990

K16I 1–6X24MM

Weight: 16.9 oz.
Length: 10.9 in.
Power: 1–6X
Obj. Dia.: 24mm
Main Dia.: 30mm
Exit Pupil: 9.65–3.81mm
Field of View: 127–20.1 ft @ 100 yds
Twilight Factor: 4.9–12
Eye Relief: 3.74 in.
Features: Rear focal plane; illuminated; integrated magnification throw lever allows for instant magnification changes even in the most adverse environmental conditions
MSRP $2350

Kahles

KAHLES K624I 6–24X56MM

KAHLES K1050 10–50X56MM

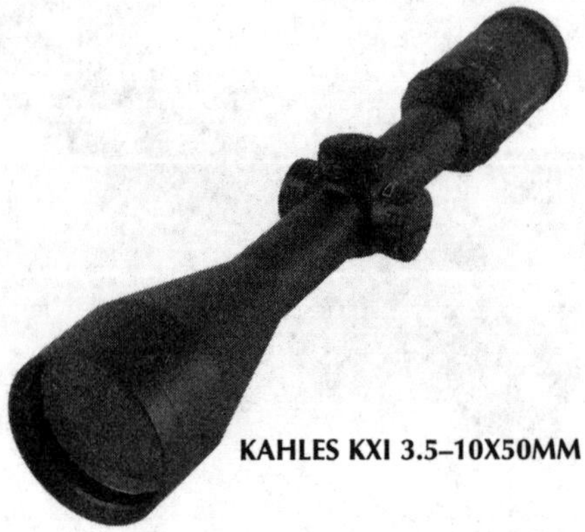

KAHLES KXI 3.5–10X50MM

OPTICS

K624I 6–24X56MM

Weight: 33.5 oz.
Length: 15.9 in.
Power: 6–24X
Obj. Dia.: 56mm
Main Dia.: 34mm
Exit Pupil: 9.3–2.3mm
Field of View: 20–5.1 ft @ 100 yds
Twilight Factor: 18.33–36.66
Eye Relief: 3.54 in.
Features: Front focal plane; illuminated; adjustable parallax; specifically engineered for long range precision
MSRP. $2870

K1050 10–50X56MM

Weight: 31.4 oz.
Length: 16.9 in.
Power: 10–50X
Obj. Dia.: 56mm
Main Dia.: 30mm
Exit Pupil: 15.1–5mm
Field of View: 9.5–2 ft @ 100 yds
Twilight Factor: 23.66–52.92
Eye Relief: 3.75 in.
Features: Rear focal plane; adjustable parallax; ultra-precise 1/8 MOA adjustments constructed of hardened steel
MSRP. $2450

KXI 3.5–10X50MM

Weight: 16.6 oz.
Length: 12.6 in.
Power: 3.5–10X
Obj. Dia.: 50mm
Main Dia.: 1 in.
Exit Pupil: 16.6–4.1mm
Field of View: 33.6–12 ft @ 100 yds
Twilight Factor: 12–22.2
Eye Relief: 3.54 in.
Features: Designed for the American hunter; rear focal plane; illuminated
MSRP. $1443

KONUS KONUSHOT 4X32MM

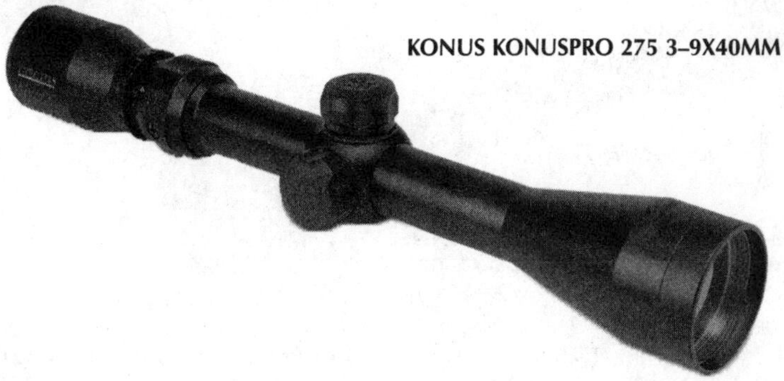

KONUS KONUSPRO 275 3–9X40MM

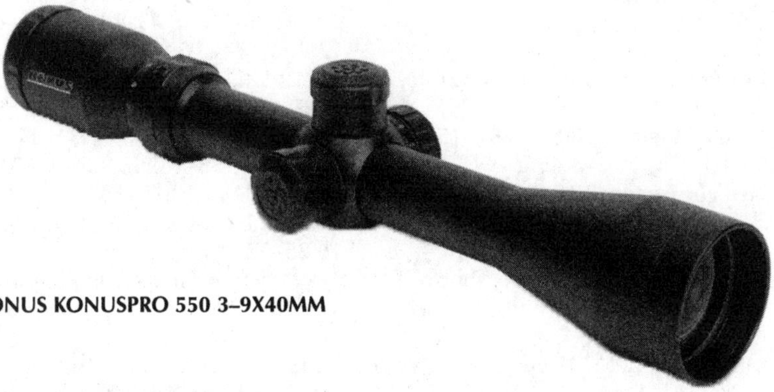

KONUS KONUSPRO 550 3–9X40MM

KONUSHOT SERIES

Weight: 12.6 oz., 11.2 oz., 13.7 oz.
Length: 12.2 in., 12.2 in., 13.3 in.
Power: 4X, 3–9X, 3–12X
Obj. Dia.: 32mm, 32mm, 40mm
Main Dia.: 1 in.
Exit Pupil: 8mm, 10.7–3.9mm, 13.3–3.3mm
Field of View @ 100 Yds: 25.5 ft, 33.54–11.56 ft, 27.4–6.9 ft
Twilight Factor: 11.31, 9.8–16.97, 10.95–21.91
Eye Relief: 3.4 in., 3 in., 3 in.
Features: Shock-, water-, and fogproof; nitrogen filled
MSRP $80

KONUSPRO 275 SERIES

Weight: 14.4 oz., 23.8 oz.
Length: 12.2 in., 12.9 in.
Power: 3–9X, 3–10X
Obj. Dia.: 40mm, 44mm
Main Dia.: 1 in.
Exit Pupil: 10–4.4mm, 14.7–4.4mm
Field of View @ 100 Yds: 35.1–10.8 ft
Twilight Factor: 10.95–18.97, 11.49–20.98
Eye Relief: 3 in.
Features: Rear focal plane; shock-, water-, and fogproof; nitrogen filled; designed specifically for muzzleloaders
MSRP $180

KONUSPRO 550 SERIES

Weight: 14.1 oz., 14.4 oz., 22.9 oz.
Length: 12.4 in., 12.2 in., 15.5 in.
Power: 3–9X, 3–9X, 4–16X
Obj. Dia.: 40mm, 40mm, 50mm
Main Dia.: 1 in.
Exit Pupil: 10–4.4mm, 10–4.4mm, 10–3.1mm
Field of View @ 100 Yds: 36.9–12.3 ft, 36.9–12.3 ft, 23.4–5.87 ft
Twilight Factor: 10.95–18.97, 10.95–18.97, 14.14–28.28
Eye Relief: 3 in.
Features: Rear focal plane; shock-, water-, and fogproof; nitrogen filled; illuminated reticle dots
MSRP $210

Konus

KONUS KONUSPRO M-30 4.5–16X40MM

KONUS KONUSPRO PLUS 3–12X50MM

KONUS KONUSPRO RIFLESCOPES 3–10X44MM

KONUS KONUSPRO T-30 3–9X30MM

KONUSPRO M-30 SERIES

Weight: 17.6 oz., 28.2 oz., 35.2 oz., 28.2 oz., 28.9 oz., 31.7 oz., 31.7 oz.
Length: 10.8 in., 14.1 in., 16.4 in., 15.2 in., 16.4 in., 17.6 in., 18.4 in.
Power: 1–4X, 2.5–10X, 3–12X, 4.5–16X, 6.5–25X, 8.5–32X, 10–40X
Obj. Dia.: 24mm, 52mm, 56mm, 40mm, 44mm, 52mm, 52mm
Main Dia.: 30mm
Exit Pupil: 12–6mm, 12.7–2.5mm, 12.7–4.7mm, 8.9–2.5mm, 6.8–1.8mm, 6.1–1.6mm, 5.2–1.4mm
Field of View @ 100 Yds: 100–25 ft, 40–11 ft, 32–8.5 ft, 23–6.5 ft, 17–4.5 ft, 13–3.3 ft, 11–2.8 ft
Twilight Factor: 4.9–9.8, 11.4–22.8, 12.96–25.92, 13.42–25.3, 16.91–33.17, 21–40.79, 22.8–45.61
Eye Relief: 3.9 in., 3.5 in., 3.9 in., 3.9–3.4 in., 3.9–3.4 in., 3.9–3.4 in., 3.4 in.
Features: Rear focal plane; shock-, water-, and fogproof; nitrogen filled; illuminated reticle; level bubble; adjustable parallax
MSRP $620

KONUSPRO PLUS SERIES

Weight: 23.2 oz., 24.3 oz., 25.7 oz.
Length: 12.2 in., 13.8 in., 16.06 in.
Power: 1.5–6X, 3–12X, 6–24X
Obj. Dia.: 44mm, 50mm, 50mm
Main Dia.: 30mm, 1 in., 1 in.
Exit Pupil: 18–7.3mm, 16.6–42mm, 8.3–2.1mm
Field of View @ 100 Yds: 64–15.7 ft, 31.4–8.1 ft, 16.2–4.45 ft
Twilight Factor: 8.12–16.25, 12.25–24.49, 17.32–34.64
Eye Relief: 3.9 in., 3 in., 3.4 in.
Features: Rear focal plane; shock-, water-, and fogproof; nitrogen filled; illuminated reticle
MSRP $330

KONUSPRO RIFLESCOPES SERIES

Weight: 11.6 oz., 10.4 oz., 16 oz., 14.8 oz., 12 oz., 17 oz., 17.2 oz., 15.8 oz., 18 oz., 17.6 oz., 19 oz., 213 oz.
Length: 10.9 in., 9.4 in., 12 in., 11.8 in., 11.8 in., 12.4 in., 12.9 in., 12.5 in., 13.6 in., 12.9 in., 14 in., 15.5 in.
Power: 2.5X, 4X, 4X, 1.5–5X, 2–7X, 3–9X, 3–9X, 3–9X, 3–9X, 3–10X, 3–12X, 6–24X
Obj. Dia.: 32mm, 32mm, 32mm, 32mm, 32mm, 32mm, 40mm, 40mm, 50mm, 44mm, 50mm, 44mm
Main Dia.: 1 in.
Exit Pupil: 12.8mm, 8mm, 8mm, 21.3–6.4mm, 8–4mm, 10.6–3.5mm, 3.3–4.4mm, 3.3–4.4mm, 16.7–5.5mm, 14.7–4.4mm, 16.7–4.2mm, 7.4–2mm
Field of View @ 100 Yds: 37 ft, 29 ft, 29.2 ft, 60–20 ft, 43–12.6 ft, 32.4–12.4 ft, 38–12.5 ft, 32.4–12.4 ft, 38–12.5 ft, 35–10.8 ft, 31–7.8 ft, 16.5–4.1 ft
Twilight Factor: 8.94, 11.31, 11.31, 6.93–12.65, 8–14.97, 9.8–16.97, 10.95–18.97, 10.95–18.97, 12.25–21.21, 11.49–20.98, 12.25–24.5, 16.25–32.5
Eye Relief: 4.9 in., 4.5 in., 3.4 in., 2.9 in., 3 in., 2.9 in., 3 in., 3 in., 3 in., 3 in., 2.9 in., 2.9 in.
Features: Shock-, water-, and fogproof; nitrogen filled; 3–9x50mm available with a 30mm main tube
MSRP $200

KONUSPRO T-30 SERIES

Weight: 18.6 oz., 18.6 oz., 20.8 oz.
Length: 9.1 in., 9.8 in., 10.4 in.
Power: 3–9X, 3–12X, 3–12X
Obj. Dia.: 40mm, 44mm, 50mm
Main Dia.: 30mm
Exit Pupil: 9.8–4.4mm, 9.4–3.7mm, 11–2.7mm
Field of View @ 100 Yds: 36.7–12.3 ft, 36.7–9.1 ft, 22.9–5.7 ft
Twilight Factor: 10.95–18.97, 11.49–22.98, 12.25–24.5
Eye Relief: 3.5 in.
Features: Rear focal plane; shock-, water-, and fogproof; nitrogen filled; illuminated reticle
MSRP $80

Kruger Optical

TACDRIVER T4I 2.5–10X50MM

KRUGER TACDRIVER T4I 2.5–10X50MM

Weight: 24 oz.
Length: 13 in.
Power: 2.5–10X
Obj. Dia.: 50mm
Main Dia.: 30mm
Exit Pupil: 5–12mm
Field of View: 38–10.5 ft @ 100 yds
Twilight Factor: 11.18–23.36
Eye Relief: 3.25 in.
Features: These scopes are equipped with proprietary illuminated glass-etched reticles with multiple brightness levels for low-light target engagement; the easy-to-operate 4x magnification system provides a solid zoom range for target acquisition at various distances; also available in 1–4x24, 1.5–5x32, 6–24x50, and 10–40x56
MSRP $400

Leatherwood/Hi-Lux

CLOSE MEDIUM RANGE (CMR) 1–4X24MM

Weight: 16.5 oz.
Length: 10.2 in.
Power: 1–4X
Obj.Dia.: 24mm
Main Dia.: 30mm
Exit Pupil: 11.1–6mm
Field of View: 94.8–26.2 ft @ 100 yds
Twilight Factor: 4.89–9.79
Eye Relief: 3 in.
Features: Zero-locking turrets; large external target-style windage and elevation adjustment knobs; power-ring extended lever handle for power change; CMR ranging reticle for determining range and also BDC hold over value good for .223, .308, and other calibers; green or red illuminated reticle; turrets adjustable in ½ MOA clicks
MSRP . . . . $399–$559

LEATHERWOOD/HI-LUX CMR 1–4X24MM

M1000 AUTO RANGING TRAJECTORY (ART) 2.5–10X44MM

LEATHERWOOD/HI-LUX M-1000 ART 2.5–10X44MM

Weight: 25.2 oz.
Length: 13.2 in.
Power: 2.5–10X
Obj.Dia.: 44mm
Main Dia.: 1 in.
Exit Pupil: 10.2–4mm
Field of View: 47.2–11.9 ft @ 100 yds
Twilight Factor: 10.5–21
Eye Relief: 3.1 in.
Features: Compensates for the bullet drop automatically by using an external cam system; can be calibrated for most centerfire rifle cartridges–from .223 to .50 BMG; comes with mount and rings; "No-Math Mil-Dot" reticle
MSRP $459

Leatherwood/Hi-Lux

LEATHERWOOD/HI-LUX M40 3–9X40MM

LEATHERWOOD/HI-LUX M73G4 2.5X16MM

LEATHERWOOD/HI-LUX MALCOLM 8X USMC SNIPER SCOPE

LEATHERWOOD/HI-LUX TOBY BRIDGES MUZZLELOADING

M40 3–9X40MM

Weight: 16.2 in.
Length: 12.5 in.
Power: 3–9X
Obj. Dia.: 40mm
Main Dia.: 1 in.
Exit Pupil: 13.3–4.4mm
Field of View: 37.7–12.6 ft @ 100 yds
Twilight Factor: 10.95–18.97
Eye Relief: 3.25 in.
Features: Built with the same ranging system that Marine Corps snipers relied on in Vietnam, only improved; auto-range system and BDC reticle; fully multi-coated lenses; military flip-up lens covers
MSRP $419

M73G4 2.5X16MM

Weight: 11.8 in.
Length: 8.3 oz.
Power: 2.5X
Obj. Dia.: 16mm
Main Dia.: ¾ in.
Exit Pupil: 4mm
Field of View: 24.9 ft @ 100 yds
Twilight Factor: 6.33
Eye Relief: 3.54 in.
Features: Built to bring the vintage sniper rifle competition shooter a top quality scope that surpasses the quality of the WWII originals used on the M1903A4 sniper rifles; modern erector tube and quality multi-coated lenses for superior light transmission; offers a minimum total of 60 MOA with either windage or elevation when those adjustments are at center
MSRP $359

MALCOLM 8X USMC SNIPER SCOPE

Weight: 25.4 oz.
Length: 22.1 in.
Power: 8X
Obj. Dia.: 31mm
Main Dia.: .75 in.
Exit Pupil: 4.2mm
Field of View: 11 ft @ 100 yds
Twilight Factor: 15.75
Eye Relief: 3.15 in.
Features: Fully multi-coated lens; fine cross reticle; elevation and wind adjustment ¼ MOA per click at the mounts
MSRP $549

TOBY BRIDGES SERIES HIGH PERFORMANCE MUZZLELOADING 3–9X40MM MATTE BLACK

Weight: 15.8 oz.
Length: 12.5 in.
Power: 3–9X
Obj.Dia.: 40mm
Main Dia.: 1 in.
Exit Pupil: 13.3–4.4mm
Field of View: 39–13 ft @ 100 yds
Twilight Factor: 10.9–19
Eye Relief: 3.25 in.
Features: The TB/ML scope is designed for in-line ignition muzzleloaders and saboted bullets. It offers multiple reticles for shooting at ranges out to 250 yards.
MSRP $179

TOP ANGLE SERIES

Weight: 39.8 oz.
Length: 17.2 in.
Power: 7–30X
Obj.Dia.: 50mm
Main Dia.: 30mm
Exit Pupil: 6.9–2.3mm
Field of View: 10.6–3.5 ft @ 100 yds
Twilight Factor: 18.70–38.72
Eye Relief: 3.33 in.
Features: Larger diameter turret housing offers additional windage-elevation adjustment in ¼ MOA clicks; top-angle objective lens focus rather than adjustment on the objective lens bell; and Mil-Dot reticle for determining range; also in 3–12x50 and 4–16x50
MSRP . . . . $299–$449

LEATHERWOOD/HI-LUX TOP ANGLE SERIES

W. M. MALCOLM SERIES LONG 6X32 INCH

Weight: 32.5 oz.
Length: 30.5 in.
Power: 6X
Obj.Dia.: 16mm
Main Dia.: .75 in.
Exit Pupil: 5.8mm
Field of View: 10 ft @ 100 yds
Twilight Factor: 9.79
Eye Relief: 4 in.
Features: A modern copy of the Model 1855 W. Malcolm riflescopes; early-style mounts for scoping original and replica 19th century breechloading rifles (Sharps, rolling block, high wall, etc.) or late period long-range percussion muzzleloading bullet rifles; ¾-in. (steel) scope tube; interchangeable front extension tubes to mount on rifles with barrels of 30 to 34 inches; also in 3x17-in. and 6x18-in. short Malcolms
MSRP $439

LEATHERWOOD/HI-LUX WM. MALCOLM SERIES LONG 6X32 INCH

Leica

ERI 3–12X50MM RIFLESCOPE

Weight: 21.9 oz.
Length: 13.4 in.
Power: 3–12X
Obj. Dia.: 50mm
Main Dia.: 30mm
Exit Pupil: 14.9–4.1mm
Field of View: 35–10 ft @ 100 yds
Twilight Factor: 12.2–24.5
Eye Relief: 4 in.
Features: Illuminated reticle; four reticle options; optional rapid reticle adjustment; matte finish
MSRP . . . .$1629–$2199

LEICA ERI 3–12X50MM RIFLESCOPE

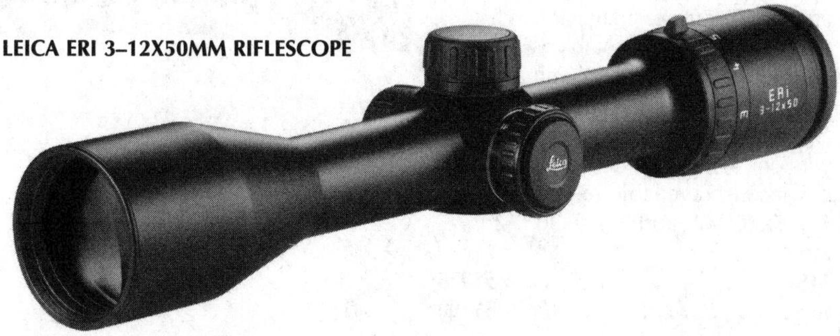

Leupold & Stevens

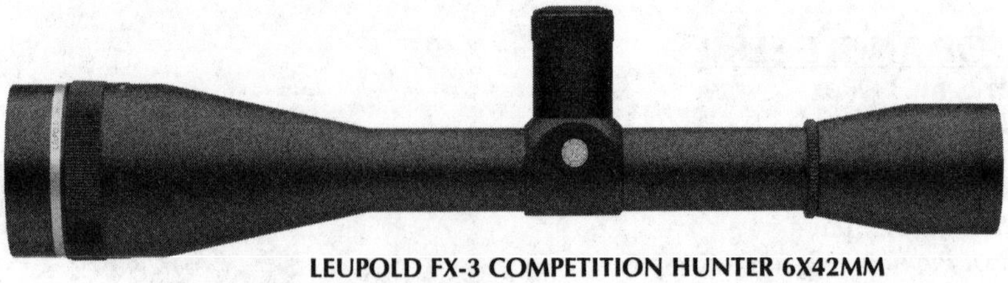

LEUPOLD FX-3 COMPETITION HUNTER 6X42MM

FX-3 COMPETITION HUNTER 6X42MM

Weight: 15 oz.
Length: 12.2 in.
Power: 6X
Obj.Dia.: 42mm
Main Dia.: 1 in.
Exit Pupil: 7mm
Field of View: 17.3 ft @ 100 yds
Twilight Factor: 15.87
Eye Relief: 4.4 in.
Features: Fixed-power riflescope; Xtended Twilight Lens System; DiamondCoat 2; blackened lens edges; windage and elevation adjustments are ¼ MOA; also available in 12x40 AO, 25x40 AO, 30x40 AO, and 6x42
MSRP. $500

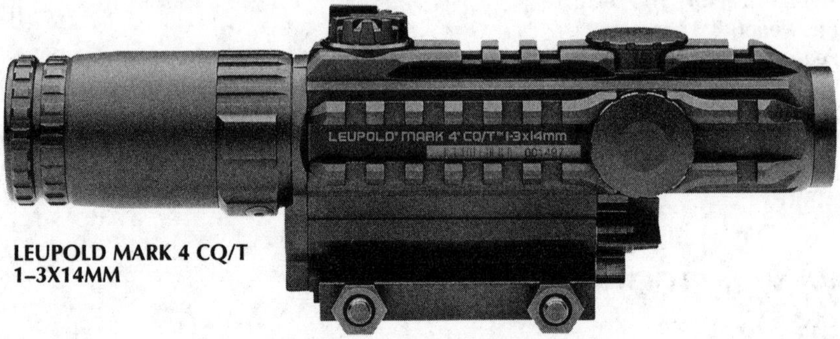

LEUPOLD MARK 4 CQ/T 1–3X14MM

MARK 4 CQ/T 1–3X14MM

Weight: 17.5 oz.
Length: 8.8 in.
Power: 1–3X
Obj.Dia.: 30mm
Main Dia.: 2.9 in.
Exit Pupil: 30–10mm
Field of View: 112–41 ft @ 100 yds
Twilight Factor: 3.74–6.48
Eye Relief: 2.8–2 in.
Features: Close Quarters/Tactical (CQ/T) riflescope combines a red dot at close range with a variable-power optic; Circle Dot reticle is visible with or without illumination or batteries; eleven reticle-illumination settings; slotted ½ MOA click adjustments for windage and elevation
MSRP. $1375

MARK 4 MR/T 2.5–8X36MM M1

Weight: 16 oz.
Length: 11.33 in.
Power: 2.5–8X
Obj.Dia.: 36mm
Main Dia.: 30mm
Exit Pupil: 14.4–4.5mm
Field of View: 35.5–13.6 ft @ 100 yds
Twilight Factor: 9.48–16.97
Eye Relief: 3.7–3 in.
Features: Xtended Twilight Lens System and DiamondCoat 2; M1 dials are ¼ MOA for windage and elevation; finger-adjustable with audible, tactile clicks; illuminated Mil-Dot, Tactical Milling Reticle (TMR),and non-illuminated TMR versions available; flip-open lens covers; also available in 1.5–5x20, 1.5–5x20 M2, and 2.5–8x36 M2 models
MSRP. $1375
IR: $1190

LEUPOLD MARK 4 MR/T 2.5–8X36MM M1

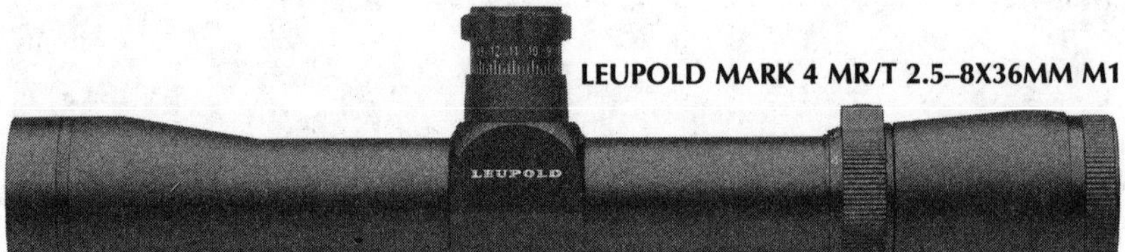

OPTICS

Leupold & Stevens

LEUPOLD MARK 6
1–6X20MM

LEUPOLD MARK 6
3–18X44MM

LEUPOLD MARK AR 3–9X40MM T2

LEUPOLD VX-3 3.5–10X40MM CDS

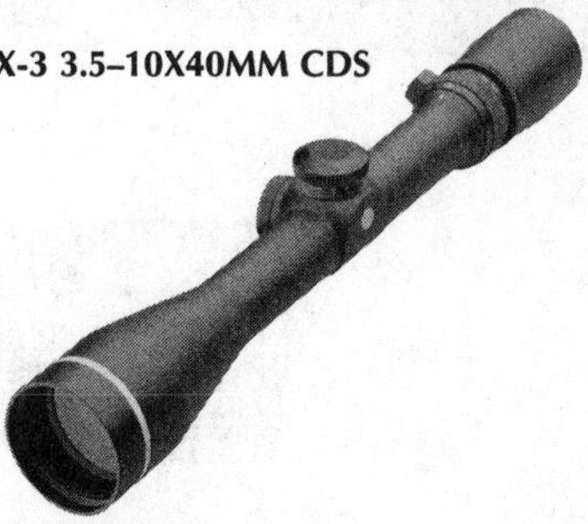

LEUPOLD RIFLEMAN 3–9X40MM

LEUPOLD VX-2 3–9X40MM

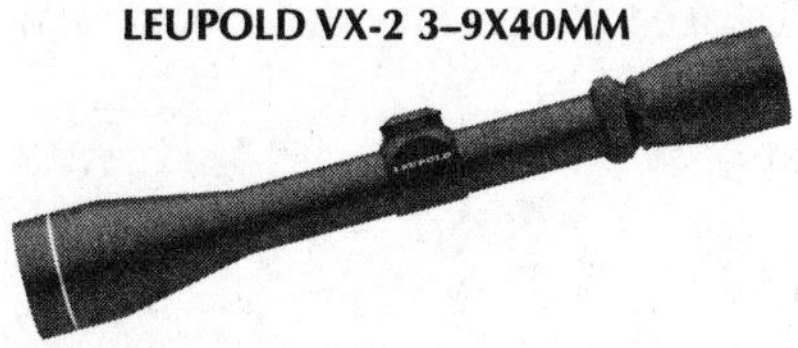

MARK 6 1–6X20MM

Weight: 17 oz.
Length: 10.3 in.
Power: 1–6X
Obj. Dia.: 20mm
Main Dia.: 1.34 in.
Exit Pupil: 10.2–3.3mm
Field of View: 103.2–17.4 ft @ 100 yds
Twilight Factor: 4.5–11
Eye Relief: 3.7 in.
Features: Xtended Twilight Lens System with Diamond Coat 2; illuminated front focal plane reticles; zerolock adjustments with available BDC; waterproof; fogproof; matte finish
MSRP. $2750

MARK 6 3–18X44MM

Weight: 23.6 oz.
Length: 11.9 in.
Power: 3–18X
Obj. Dia.: 44mm
Main Dia.: 1.34 in.
Exit Pupil: 10.3–2.4mm
Field of View: 36.8–6.3 ft @ 100 yds
Twilight Factor: 11.5–28.1
Eye Relief: 3.8–3.9 in.
Features: Xtended Twilight Lens System with Diamond Coat 2; M5B2 Autolocking Pinch & Turn; Elevation Zero Stop with Revolution Indicator; factory or custom quick change BDC rings available; waterproof; matte finish
MSRP. $2750

MARK AR 3–9X40MM T2

Weight: 12.5 oz.
Length: 12.4 in.
Power: 3–9X
Obj.Dia.: 40mm
Main Dia.: 1 in.
Exit Pupil: 13.33–4.44mm
Field of View: 32.3–14.0 ft @ 100 yds
Twilight Factor: 10.95–18.97
Eye Relief: 4.7–3.7 in.
Features: Multi-coated 4 lens system; ½ MOA T2 elevation adjustment includes a pre-engraved Bullet Drop Compensation (BDC) dial to match the ballistics of most 55-grain loads, including the .223 Rem. and 5.56 NATO; large power selector dial with aggressive knurling; also available in 1.5–4x20, 4–12x40 AO T2, and 6–18x40 AO T1 models
Duplex reticle:. $375

RIFLEMAN 3–9X40MM

Weight: 12.6 oz.
Length: 12.33 in.
Power: 3–9X
Obj.Dia.: 40mm
Main Dia.: 1 in.
Exit Pupil: 12–4.7mm
Field of View: 329–131 ft @ 1000 yds
Twilight Factor: 10.95–18.97
Eye Relief: 4.2–3.7 in.
Features: Fully coated lenses for excellent low light brightness; durable waterproof construction; also in 2–7x33, 4–12x40, and 3–9x50
MSRP. $275

VX-2 3–9X40MM

Weight: 12 oz.
Length: 12.4 in.
Power: 3–9X
Obj.Dia.: 40mm
Main Dia.: 1 in.
Exit Pupil: 12–4.6mm
Field of View: 323–140 ft @ 1000 yds
Twilight Factor: 10.95–18.97
Eye Relief: 4.7–3.7 in.
Features: Multi-coated 4 Lens System for 92 percent light transmission; coin click ¼ MOA windage and elevation dials; also in 1–4x20, 4–12x40 AO, 6–18x40 AO and Target, 3–9x50, 4–12x50
MSRP. . . . . $375–$440

VX-3 3.5–10X40MM CDS

Weight: 12.6 oz.
Length: 12.66 in.
Power: 3.5–10X
Obj.Dia.: 40mm
Main Dia.: 1 in.
Exit Pupil: 12.1–4.1mm
Field of View: 298–110 ft @ 1000 yds
Twilight Factor: 11.83–20
Eye Relief: 4.4–3.5 in.
Features: X-Tended Twilight Lens System; ¼ MOA windage and elevation dials; Diamond Coat 2 external lens coatings; dual spring erector assembly; available CDS dial options and illuminated reticles; also in 1.5–5x20, 1.5–5x20 IR, 1.75–6x32, 2.5–8x36, 4.5–14x40, 4.5–14x40 CDS, 4.5–14x40 SF, 4.5–14x40 AO, 6.5–20x40 AO, 6.5–20x40 EFR, 6.5–20x40 SF, 3.5–10x50, 3.5–10x50 CDS, 3.5–10x50 IR, 4.5–14x50, 4.5–14x50 SF, 4.5–14x50 SF IR, 6.5–20x50 SF Target, and
8.5–23x50 SF Target
MSRP. . . . . $625–$690

Leupold & Stevens

LEUPOLD VX6 3–18X50MM

LEUPOLD VX-6 ILLUMINATED 2–12X42MM

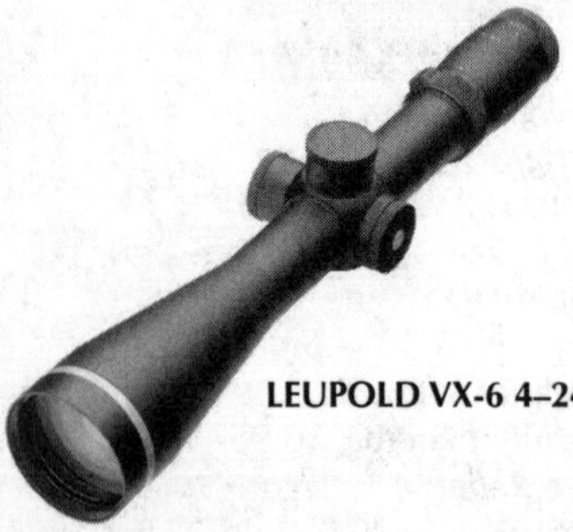

LEUPOLD VX-6 4–24X52MM SIDE FOCUS

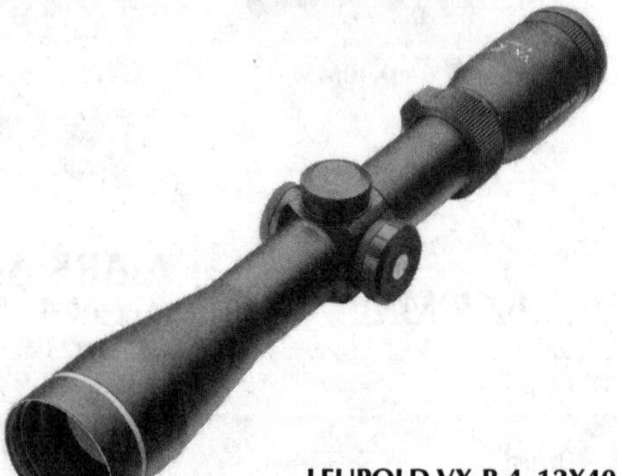

LEUPOLD VX-R 4–12X40MM CDS

VX6 3–18X50MM

Weight: 20.7 oz.
Length: 13.5 in.
Power: 3–18X
Obj. Dia.: 50mm
Main Dia.: 1.18 in.
Exit Pupil: 10–2.4mm
Field of View: 75.9–13.7 ft @ 100 yds
Twilight Factor: 12.2–30
Eye Relief: 3.7 in.
Features: Xtended Twilight lens; Diamond Coat 2 and Edge Blackened Lenses; lead-free optical design; Motion Sensor Technology (MST); FIREDOT illumination; waterproof; fogproof; matte finish
From:. . . . . $1500–$1750

VX-6 4–24X52MM SIDE FOCUS

Weight: 24.3 oz.
Length: 14.3 in.
Power: 4–24X
Obj. Dia.: 52mm
Main Dia.: 34mm
Exit Pupil: N/A
Field of View: 28–5 ft @ 100 yds
Twilight Factor: 14.42–35.33
Eye Relief: 3.7 in.
Features: Shock-, water-, and fog-proof; DiamondCoat 2 lens coating; 7–42x56 Side Focus CDS also available
MSRP. . . . . $1750–$1875

VX-6 ILLUMINATED 2–12X42MM

Weight: 17.8 oz.
Length: 12.5 in.
Power: 2–12X
Obj. Dia.: 42mm
Main Dia.: 30mm
Exit Pupil: 10–3.5mm
Field of View: 112–20.3 ft @ 100 yds
Twilight Factor: 9.17–22.45
Eye Relief: 3.8 in.
Features: Quantum optical system with Xtended Twilight lens coatings; 7 reticle styles include Duplex, Boone & Crockett, Illum. Duplex, Illum. LR Duplex, and Illum. German #4 Dot; also available in 1–6x24, 3–18x44, 3018x50, 4–24x52
MSRP. $1375

VX-R 4–12X40MM CDS

Weight: 15.1 oz.
Length: 12.4 in.
Power: 4–12X
Obj.Dia.: 40mm
Main Dia.: 30mm
Exit Pupil: 8.6–3.3mm
Field of View: 21.5–10 ft @ 100 yds
Twilight Factor: 14.2–23.1
Eye Relief: 3.7 in.
Features: Fire Dot reticle system with fiber optic technology; DiamondCoat lens coatings; finger click adjustments; index matched lens system; proprietary Motion Sensor Technology
MSRP. . . . .$750–$815

Lucid

LUCID 6–24X50MM ADVANTAGE RIFLE SCOPE

LUCID 4–16X44MM "CROSS OVER OPTIC"

6–24X50MM ADVANTAGE RIFLE SCOPE

Weight: 24.5 oz.
Length: 15.5 in.
Power: 6–24X
Obj. Dia.: 50mm
Main Dia.: 30mm
Exit Pupil: 8.3–2mm
Field of View: 16.5–4.3 ft @ 100 yds
Twilight Factor: 17.32–34.64
Eye Relief: 4.25–3.25 in.
Features: Sniper-style rifle scope with the new L5 reticle; multi-coated lenses; 1/8 MOA turret click value; water-, fog-, and shockproof; matte black finish; available in STRELOK
MSRP. $449

4–16X44MM "CROSS OVER OPTIC"

Weight: 18 oz.
Length: 13.25 in.
Power: 4–16X
Obj. Dia.: 44mm
Main Dia.: 34mm
Exit Pupil: 11–3mm
Field of View: 25.5–8.5 ft @ 100 yds
Twilight Factor: 13.27–8
Eye Relief: 4.25 in.–3.25 in.
Features: Shock-, water-, and fogproof; adjustable parallax; etched-glass reticle
MSRP. $419

Meopta

MEOPTA MEOSTAR R1 RD 1.5–6X42MM

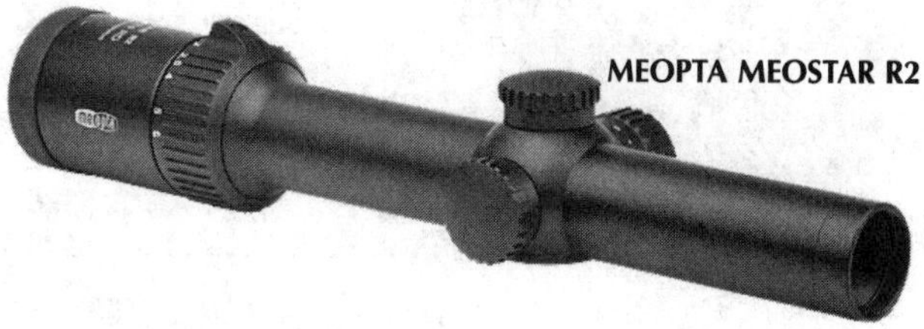

MEOPTA MEOSTAR R2 1–6X24MM

MEOSTAR R1 SERIES

Weight: 18.87 oz., 20.6 oz., 15.87 oz., 21.87 oz., 18.27 oz., 24.16 oz.
Length: 12.09 in., 13.54 in., 13.03 in., 14.37 in., 12.91 in., 15.16 in..
Power: 1–4X, 1.5–6X, 3–10X, 3–12X, 4–12X, 4–16X
Obj. Dia.: 22mm, 42mm, 50mm, 56mm, 40mm, 44mm
Main Dia.: 30mm
Exit Pupil: 13.5–5.5mm, 14.8–7mm, 16.7–5mm, 14.8–4.6mm, 10–3.3mm, 11–2.8mm
Field of View: @ 100 Yds: 117.78–28.22 ft, 73.49–22.31 ft, 43.64–13.12 ft, 36–11.15 ft, 33.14–11.15 ft, 16–4.46 ft
Twilight Factor: 4.69–9.38, 7.94–15.88, 12.25–22.36, 12.96–25.92, 12.65–21.91, 13.27–26.53
Eye Relief: 3.31–3.47 in., 3.23–3.74 in., 3.15–3.23 in., 3.03–3.27 in., 3.58–3.15 in., 3.94–3.15 in.
Features: Water- and fogproof; illuminated reticle; adjustable parallax; optional illuminated reticle also available
MSRP. $1595

MEOSTAR R2 SERIES

Weight: 17.64 oz., 20.32 oz., 21.02 oz., 22.93 oz.
Length: 11.69 in. 3.31–3.47 in., 3.23–3.74 in., 3.15–3.23 in., 3.03–3.27 in., 3.58–3.15 in., 3.94–3.15 in.
Power: 1–6X, 1.7–10X, 2–12X, 2.5–15X
Obj. Dia.: 24mm , 42mm, 50mm, 56mm
Main Dia.: 30mm
Exit Pupil: 11–4mm, 11.1–4.2mm, 11.2–4.3mm, 11–3.73mm
Field of View: @ 100 Yds: 121.72–20.34 ft, 71.85–12.14 ft, 61–10.17 ft, 48.56–8.2 ft
Twilight Factor: 4.9–12, 8.45–20.49, 10–24.5, 11.83–28.98
Eye Relief: 3.54 in., 3.54 in., 3.86–3.7 in., 3.86–3.74 in., 3.54 in.
Features: Water- and fogproof; illuminated reticle also available
MSRP. $1667

Meopta

MEOPTA MEOTAC 1–4X22MM

MEOTAC SCOPE SERIES

Weight: 19.4 oz., 28.22 oz.
Length: 9.76 in., 15.16 in.
Power: 1–4X, 4–16X
Obj. Dia.: 22mm, 44mm
Main Dia.: 30mm
Exit Pupil 13.5–5.5mm, 11–2.8mm
Field of View: @ 100 Yds: 67–17.22 ft, 27.89–7.87 ft
Twilight Factor: 4.69–9.38, 13.27–26.53
Eye Relief: 3.19–3.46 in., 3.94–13.15 in.
Features: Shock-, water-, and fog-proof; illuminated reticle, adjustable parallax available
MSRP $1150

Millett Optics

MILLETT DMS 1–4X24MM

MILLETT(DMS) 1–6X24MM

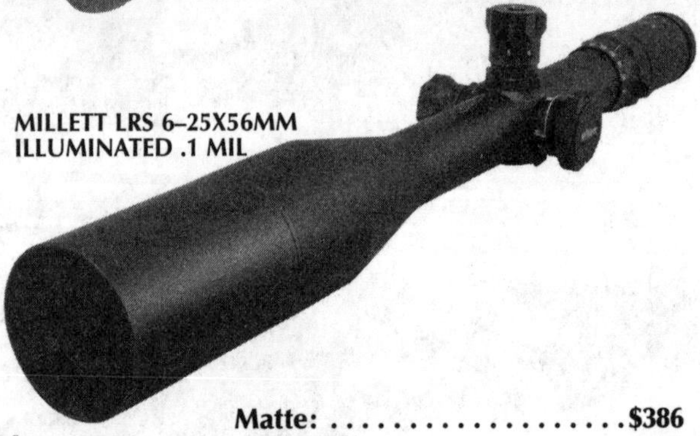

MILLETT LRS 6–25X56MM ILLUMINATED .1 MIL

DMS 1–4X24MM

Weight: 18 oz.
Length: 11.8 in.
Power: 1–4X
Obj.Dia.: 24mm
Main Dia.: 30mm
Exit Pupil: 24–6mm
Field of View: 90–23 ft @ 100 yds
Twilight Factor: 4.89–9.79
Eye Relief: 3.5 in.
Features: Designated Marksman Riflescope (DMS) features a Donut Dot illuminated reticle; "donut" subtending 18 MOA for ranges as close as three meters; illuminated dot 1 MOA for medium to extended ranges out to 500 yards; available in matte or ATAC finish; 1–6x24 available
Matte: $386
ATAC: $430

DESIGNATED MARKSMAN SCOPE (DMS) 1–6X24MM

Weight: 20.7 oz.
Length: 10.5 in.
Power: 1–6X
Obj. Dia.: 24mm
Main Dia.: 30mm
Exit Pupil: 46.99–11.75mm
Field of View: 90–23 ft @ 100 yds
Twilight Factor: 4.9–12
Eye Relief: 3.5 in.
Features: Fully multi-coated; illuminated reticle; matte black finish
MSRP $386

LRS 6–25X56MM ILLUMINATED .1 MIL

Weight: 35 oz.
Length: 18 in.
Power: 6–25X
Obj.Dia.: 56mm
Main Dia.: 35mm
Exit Pupil: 9.33–2.24mm
Field of View: 45–17 ft @ 100 yds
Twilight Factor: 18.33–37.41
Eye Relief: 3 in.
Features: For extreme-duty and extended-range for calibers such as the .50 BMG and .338 Lapua; one-piece tube; precision controls with 140 MOA range of adjustment; several glass-etched Mil-DotBar reticle and click value configurations; available in a matte or A-TACS finish; also in 6–25x56 Mil-DotBar Reticle .25 or .1 Click Value, 6–25x56 Illuminated Mil-DotBar Reticle A-TACS or Matte Finish
MSRP $752

Millett Optics

TRS 4–16X50MM .1 MIL

Weight: 29.5 oz.
Length: 16.4 in.
Power: 4–16X
Obj.Dia.: 50mm
Main Dia.: 30mm
Exit Pupil: 12.5–3.12mm
Field of View: 29–8 ft @ 100 yds
Twilight Factor: 14.14–28.28
Eye Relief: 3.5 in.
Features: Mil-DotBar reticle system functions as a standard Mil-Dot with the addition of a thin line for easier alignment for rangefinding and holdover; illuminated reticle is green and adjustable; scope has side-focus parallax adjustment knob; also in fixed 10x50 model and several 4–16x50 models finished in either matte or A-TACS
MSRP $500

MILLETT TRS 4–16X50MM .1 MIL

Minox

MINOX ZA 5 HD SERIES 1.2–6X24MM

MINOX ZA 5 HD SF TAC SERIES 5–25X56MM

MINOX ZA 5I HD SERIES 1.2–6X24MM

ZA 5 HD SERIES 1.2–6X24MM

Weight: 12.5 oz.
Length: 10.23 in.
Power: 1.2–6X
Obj. Dia.: 24mm
Main Dia.: 30mm
Exit Pupil: 13.3–4mm
Field of View: 81.2–16.2 ft @ 100 yds
Twilight Factor: 5.37–12
Eye Relief: 3.98 in.
Features: Rear focal plane; waterproof; adjustable parallax (on SF versions); 2–10x40, 2–10x50, 3–15x42 SF, 3–15x50 SF, 3–15x56 SF, and 5–25x56 SF also available
MSRP . . . . $589–$959

ZA 5 HD SF TAC SERIES 5–25X56MM

Weight: 23.1 oz.
Length: 15 in.
Power: 5–25X
Obj. Dia.: 56mm
Main Dia.: 30mm
Exit Pupil: 10–2.2mm
Field of View: 19.5–3.9 ft @ 100 yds
Twilight Factor: 16.73–37.42
Eye Relief: 3.98 in.
Features: Rear focal plane; waterproof; adjustable parallax (on SF versions); illuminated tactical reticle; 1.2–6x24 and 3–15x50 SF also available
MSRP . . . . $899–$1099

ZA 5I HD SERIES 1.2–6X24MM

Weight: 12.5 oz.
Length: 10.23 in.
Power: 1.2–6X
Obj. Dia.: 24mm
Main Dia.: 30mm
Exit Pupil: 13.3–4mm
Field of View: 81.2–16.2 ft @ 100 yds
Twilight Factor: 5.37–12
Eye Relief: 3.98 in.
Features: Rear focal plane; waterproof; adjustable parallax (on SF versions); illuminated tactical reticle; 2–10x50, 3–15x50 SF, 3–15x56 SF, and 5–25x56 SF also available
MSRP . . . . $689–$1039

Minox

MINOX ZE 5I 1–5X24MM

MINOX ZE 5I 2–10X50MM

MINOX ZE 5I 3–15X56MM

MINOX ZE 5I 5–25X56MM

ZE 5I 1–5X24MM

Weight: 16.9 oz.
Length: 11.2 in.
Power: 1–5X
Obj. Dia.: 24mm
Main Dia.: 30mm
Exit Pupil: 11.4–4.8mm
Field of View: 110.6–23.1 ft @ 100 yds
Twilight Factor: 4.9–11
Eye Relief: 3.94 in.
Features: Illuminated central red-dot with eleven brightness settings; automatic shut down to conserve battery; German A4, BDC, and Dot reticles available; finished with Minox's M* coating; waterproof; shockproof; Z-rail mount
MSRP. $1649

ZE 5I 2–10X50MM

Weight: 22.9 oz.
Length: 13.2 in.
Power: 2–10X
Obj. Dia.: 50mm
Main Dia.: 30mm
Exit Pupil: 11.4–5.1mm
Field of View: 55.2–11.5 ft @ 100 yds
Twilight Factor: 10–22.4
Eye Relief: 3.94 in.
Features: Illuminated central red-dot with eleven brightness settings; automatic shut down to conserve battery; German A4, BDC, and Dot reticles available; finished with Minox's M* coating; waterproof; shockproof; Z-rail mount
MSRP. $1849

ZE 5I 3–15X56MM

Weight: 26.1 oz.
Length: 14.6 in.
Power: 3–15x
Obj. Dia.: 56mm
Main Dia.: 30mm
Exit Pupil: 11.4–3.8mm
Field of View: 36.3–7.6 ft @ 100 yds
Twilight Factor: 13–29
Eye Relief: 3.94 in.
Features: Illuminated central red-dot with eleven brightness settings; automatic shut down to conserve battery; German A4, BDC, and Dot reticles available; finished with Minox's M* coating; waterproof; shockproof; Z-rail mount
MSRP. $1949

ZE 5I 5–25X56MM

Weight: 27.9 oz.
Length: 16.9 in.
Power: 5–25X
Obj. Dia.: 56mm
Main Dia.: 30mm
Exit Pupil: 10.9–2.5mm
Field of View: 21.6–4.5 ft @ 100 yds
Twilight Factor: 16.7–37.4
Eye Relief: 3.94 in.
Features: Illuminated central red-dot with eleven brightness settings; automatic shut down to conserve battery; German A4, BDC, and Dot reticles available; finished with Minox's M* coating; waterproof; shockproof; Z-rail mount
MSRP. $2049

Minox

MINOX ZP TAC SERIES 1–8X24MM

MINOX ZV 3 SERIES 3–9X40MM

ZP TAC SERIES 1–8X24MM

Weight: 24.5 oz.
Length: 11.6 in.
Power: 1–8X
Obj. Dia.: 24mm
Main Dia.: 34mm
Exit Pupil: 10.3–3mm
Field of View: 112.5–14.4 ft @ 100 yds
Twilight Factor: 4.9–13.86
Eye Relief: 3.5 in.
Features: Front focal plane; illuminated reticle; shock-, water-, and fog-proof; 3–15x50 and 5–25x56 also available
MSRP . . . . .Starting at $2899

ZV 3 SERIES 3–9X40MM

Weight: 13.6 oz.
Length: 12.2 in.
Power: 3–9X
Obj. Dia.: 40mm
Main Dia.: 1 in.
Exit Pupil: 13.3–4.4mm
Field of View: 35.4–11.5 ft @ 100 yds
Twilight Factor: 10.95–18.97
Eye Relief: 3.8 in.
Features: Fully multi-coated lenses; lightweight aluminum body; nitrogen filled and waterproof; available with a Plex or BDC reticle; 3–9x50 and 4.5–14x44 also available
MSRP . . . .$269–$349

Nightforce Optics, Inc.

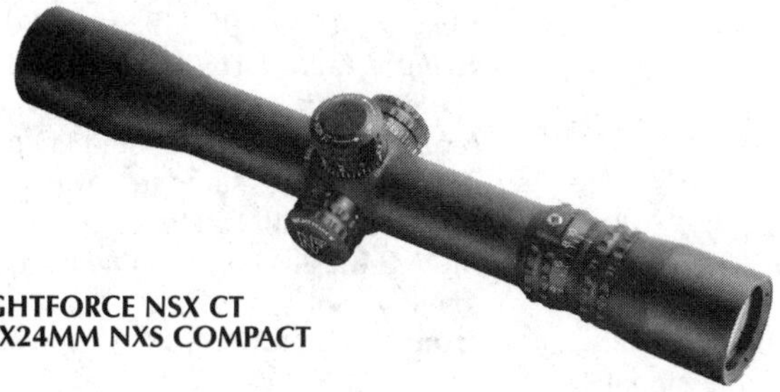

NIGHTFORCE NSX CT 1–4X24MM NXS COMPACT

NIGHTFORCE CT 2.5–10X32MM NXS COMPACT

NXS COMPACT 1–4X24MM

Weight: 17 oz.
Length: 8.8 in.
Power: 1–4X
Obj.Dia.: 24mm
Main Dia.: 30mm
Exit Pupil: 1–6mm
Field of View: 100–25 ft @ 100 yds
Twilight Factor: 4.89–9.79
Eye Relief: 3.5 in.
Features: Ideal for the hunter pursuing dangerous or running game at close quarters; low profile complements big bore bolt action and double rifles; as quick as open sights yet vastly more precise; shooter can keep both eyes open for instant target acquisition in high-stress situations
MSRP $1370
ZeroStop: $1561

NXS COMPACT 2.5–10X32MM

Weight: 19 oz.
Length: 12 in.
Power: 2.5–10X
Obj.Dia.: 32mm
Main Dia.: 30mm
Exit Pupil: 13.3–3.3mm
Field of View: 44–11 ft @ 100 yds
Twilight Factor: 8.94–17.88
Eye Relief: 3.4 in.
Features: Lightweight, low profile; provides low-light performance that exceeds most optics with much larger objective lenses; large exit pupil for fast target acquisition and no parallax or focusing issues; available with the Nightforce Velocity 600 yard reticle, which provides precise shot placement to 600 yards
MSRP $1465
ZeroStop: . . . .$1659–$1744

Nightforce Optics, Inc.

NIGHTFORCE, B.E.A.S.T.
5–25X56MM

NIGHTFORCE NXS COMPACT 2.5–10X42MM

NIGHTFORCE NXS 3.5–15X50MM

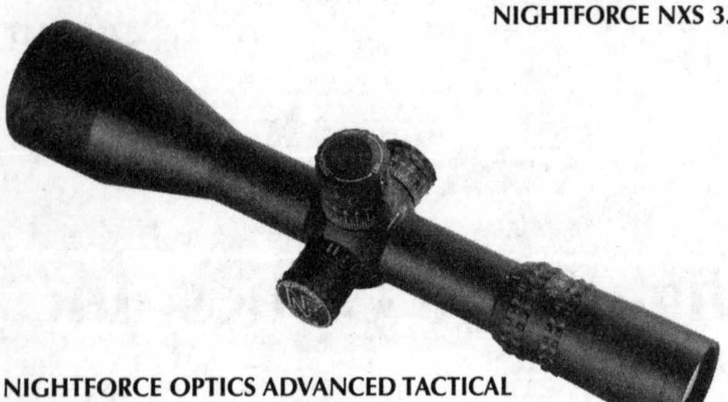

NIGHTFORCE OPTICS ADVANCED TACTICAL RIFLESCOPE (ATACR) 5–25X56MM

COMPACT 2.5–10X42MM

Weight: 20.5 oz.
Length: 11.9 in.
Power: 2.5–10
Obj. Dia.: 42mm
Main Dia.: 30mm
Exit Pupil: 15.5–4.4mm
Field of View: 44–11 ft @ 100 yds
Twilight Factor: 10.25–20.49
Eye Relief: 3.5 in.
Features: Illuminated reticle; adjustable paralax; available reticles: IHR, MOAR, MIL-DOT, Velocity 600 (LV, MV, HV), MIL-R
MSRP. $1800

NXS 3.5–15X50MM

Weight: 30 oz.
Length: 14.8 in.
Power: 3.5–15X
Obj.Dia.: 50mm
Main Dia.: 30mm
Exit Pupil: 14.3–3.6mm
Field of View: 27.6–7.3 ft @ 100 yds
Twilight Factor: 13.22–27.38
Eye Relief: 3.9 in.
Features: Excellent choice for all-around hunting and professional shooters; low mounting profile; full 110 MOA of internal adjustment; available with ¼ MOA and .1 Mil-Radian adjustments; offered with Nightforce's patented ZeroStop, which provides an instant return to the shooter's chosen zero point under any conditions
MSRP. $1655
ZeroStop: . . . . $1853–$1942

ADVANCED TACTICAL RIFLESCOPE (ATACR) 5–25X56MM

Weight: 38 oz.
Length: 14.3 in.
Power: 5–25X
Obj. Dia.: 56mm
Main Dia.: 34mm
Exit Pupil: 10.52–2.28mm
Field of View: 17.96–4.92 ft @ 100 yds
Twilight Factor: 16.7–37.4
Eye Relief: 3.54 in.
Features: Fully multi-coated ED glass; ZeroStop comes standard; available in MOAR and MIL-R reticles; 120 MOA/34.9Mils elevation adjustment; matte finish
From:. $2400

B.E.A.S.T. 5–25X56MM

Weight: 39 oz.
Length: 15.37 in.
Power: 5–25X
Obj. Dia.: 56mm
Main Dia.: 34mm
Exit Pupil: 8.3–2.3mm
Field of View: 18.7–4.92 ft @ 100 yds
Twilight Factor: 16.7–37.4
Eye Relief: 3.35–3.54 in.
Features: First focal plane precision; Nightforce Digillum illumination; 90 percent + light transmission; i4F intelligent four-function elevation control, ZeroStop system; XtremeSpeed adjustments; available with MIL-R, MOAR, MD2.0, TReMoR, and H59 reticles; matte finish
From:. . . . . $3400–$3900

Nightforce Optics, Inc.

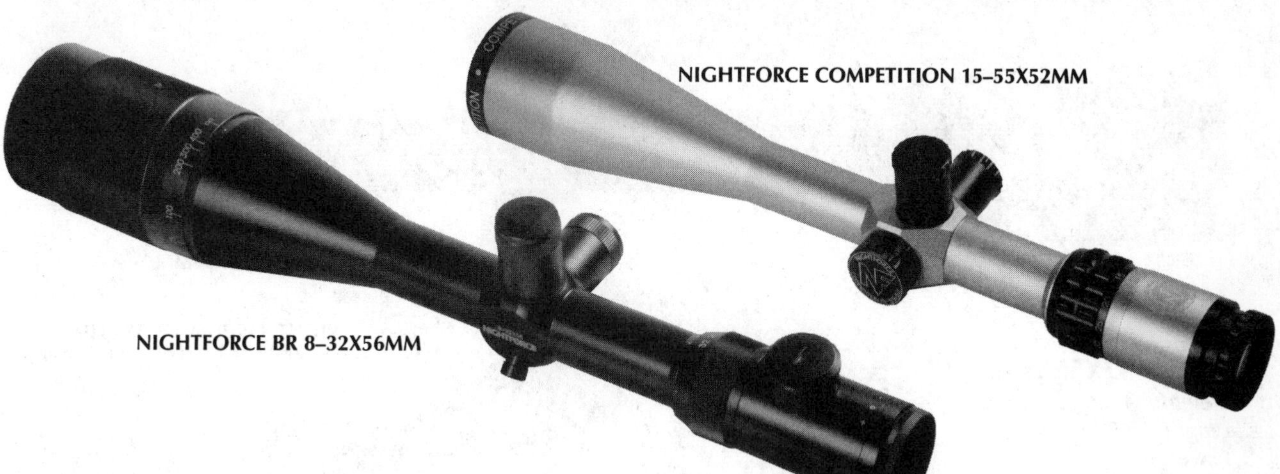

NIGHTFORCE COMPETITION 15–55X52MM

NIGHTFORCE BR 8–32X56MM

NIGHTFORCE NXS 5.5–22X56MM

NIGHTFORCE NXS 5.5–22X50MM

BENCHREST 8–32X56MM

Weight: 36 oz.
Length: 16.6 in.
Power: 8–32X
Obj.Dia.: 56mm
Main Dia.: 30mm
Exit Pupil: 5.6–1.7mm
Field of View: 9.4–3.1 ft @ 100 yds
Twilight Factor: 21.16–42.33
Eye Relief: 2.9 in.
Features: Superior resolution; adjustable objective allows extra-fine focus for parallax adjustment from 25 yards to infinity; target adjustments are calibrated in true 1/8 click) MOA values, and can be re-indexed to zero after sighting in; eyepiece allows for fast reticle focusing and a glass-etched illuminated reticle, with eight different reticles
MSRP. $1326

COMPETITION 15–55X52MM

Weight: 27.87 oz.
Length: 16.2 in.
Power: 15–55X
Obj. Dia.: 52mm
Main Dia.: 30mm
Exit Pupil: 3.54–.93mm
Field of View: 6.91–1.83 ft @ 100 yds
Twilight Factor: 27.9–53.5
Eye Relief: 3.15 in.
Features: ED glass; 92 percent light transmission; fast-focus European-style eyepiece; side parallax adjustment; available with CTR-1 or DDR reticles; available in matte and silver
From: $2400

NSX 5.5–22X50MM

Weight: 31 oz.
Length: 15.1 in.
Power: 5.5–22X
Obj.Dia.: 50mm
Main Dia.: 30mm
Exit Pupil: 9.1–2.3mm
Field of View: 17.5–4.7 ft @ 100 yds
Twilight Factor: 16.58–33.16
Eye Relief: 3.8 in.
Features: Originally developed for the U.S. military's extreme long range shooting and hard target interdiction; 100 MOA of elevation travel make it ideal for use on the .50 BMG, allowing accurate shots to 2000 yards and beyond; slim profile, easily adaptable to a wide range of mounting systems
MSRP. $1821
ZeroStop: . . . . $2020–$2107

NSX 5.5–22X56MM

Weight: 32 oz.
Length: 15.2 in.
Power: 5.5–22X
Obj.Dia.: 56mm
Main Dia.: 30mm
Exit Pupil: 10.2–2.5mm
Field of View: 17.5–4.7 ft @ 100 yds
Twilight Factor: 17.54–35.09
Eye Relief: 3.9 in.
Features: Advanced field tactical riflescope for long-range applications; maximum clarity and resolution across the entire magnification range, exceptional low-light performance; available with ZeroStop technology and 1/8 and 1/4 MOA or .1 Mil-Radian adjustments
MSRP. $1821
ZeroStop: . . . . $2020–$2107

Nightforce Optics, Inc.

NIGHTFORCE NXS 8–32X56MM

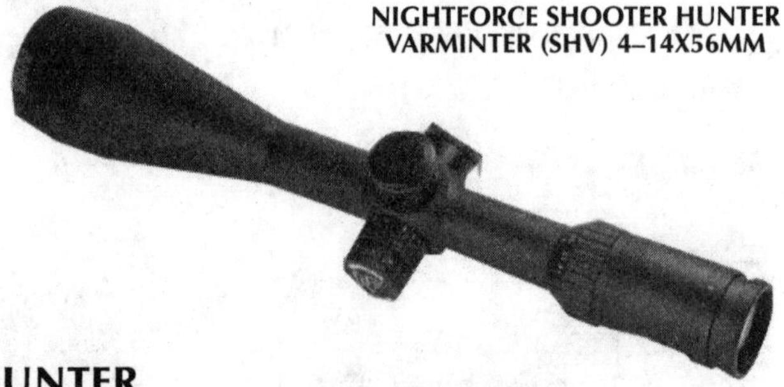

NIGHTFORCE SHOOTER HUNTER VARMINTER (SHV) 4–14X56MM

NSX 8–32X56MM

Weight: 34 oz.
Length: 15.9 in.
Power: 8–32X
Obj.Dia.: 56mm
Main Dia.: 30mm
Exit Pupil: 7–1.8mm
Field of View: 12.1–3.1 ft @ 100 yds
Twilight Factor: 21.16–42.33
Eye Relief: 3.8 in.
Features: For long-range hunting, competition, and target shooting; choice of five different reticles for the shooter's chosen application; offered with .125 MOA, .250 MOA or .1 Mil-Radian Hi-Speed adjustments; ZeroStop also available
MSRP. $1958
ZeroStop: . . . .$2157–$2244

SHOOTER HUNTER VARMINTER (SHV) SERIES

Weight: 20.8 oz., 26.9 oz., 29.1 oz.
Length: 11.6 in., 14.8 in., 15.2 in.
Power: 3–10X, 4–14X, 5–20X
Obj. Dia.: 42mm, 56mm, 56mm
Main Dia.: 30mm
Exit Pupil: 10.7–4.4mm, 12–3.6mm, 8.7–2.5mm
Field of View @ 100 Yds: 34.9–11 ft, 24.9–7.3 ft, 17.9–5 ft
Twilight Factor: 11.22–20.49, 14.97–28, 16.73–33.47
Eye Relief: 3.5 in., 3.15–3.54 in., 3.15–3.54 in.
Features: Rear focal plane; available in illuminated version
MSRP. . . . .$995–$1195

Nikko Stirling

NIKKO STIRLING TARGEMASTER SERIES 10–50X60MM

TARGEMASTER SERIES

Weight: 23.6 oz., 25 oz., 27.2 oz., 30.3 oz.
Length: 14.6 in., 15.3 in., 16.7 in., 17.3 in.
Power: 4–16X, 5–20X, 6–24X, 10–50X
Obj. Dia.: 44mm, 50mm, 56mm, 60mm
Main Dia.: 30mm
Exit Pupil: N/A
Field of View: @ 100 Yds: 26.4–6.6 ft, 21.6–5.4 ft, 15.6–3.9 ft, 9.2–1.9 ft
Twilight Factor: 13.27–26.53, 15.81–31.62, 18.33–36.66, 24.49–54.77
Eye Relief: 3.5 in.–3.9 in.
Features: Adjustable parallax; ETE Mirolux coated lenses; illuminated reticle
MSRP. . . . . $199–$299

Nikon

NIKON BOLT XR 3X32MM

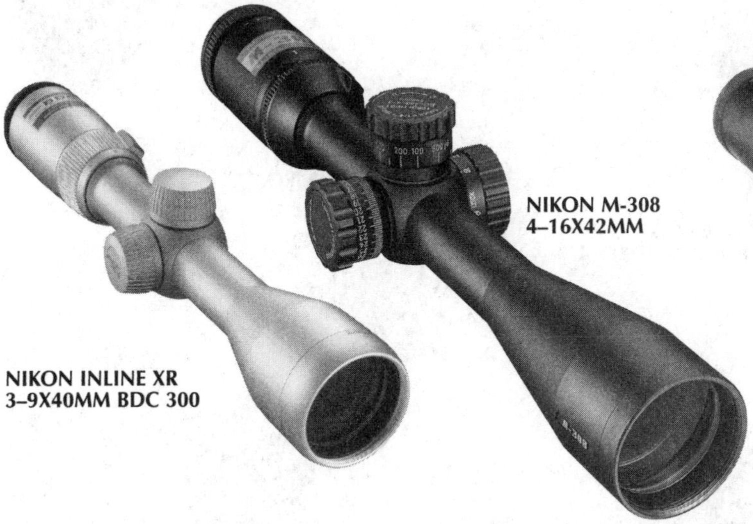

NIKON INLINE XR
3–9X40MM BDC 300

NIKON M-308
4–16X42MM

NIKON MONARCH 3
2.5–10X42MM NIKOPLEX

BOLT XR 3X32MM

Weight: 11.2 oz.
Length: 8.1 in.
Power: 3–32X
Obj.Dia.: 32mm
Main Dia.: 1 in.
Exit Pupil: 10.7mm
Field of View: 35.6 ft @ 100 yds
Twilight Factor: 9.79
Eye Relief: 3.4 in.
Features: 3x Nikon optics; large ocular; quick focus eye-piece with ±4 diopter adjustment; BDC 60 reticle offers aiming points out to 60 yards based upon velocity of approximately 305 fps; ¼ inch at 20 yards adjustments with a 150 MOA adjustment range (at 100 yards); parallax-free at 20 yards
MSRP $160

INLINE XR 3–9X40MM BDC 300

Weight: 13.8 oz.
Length: 11.3 in.
Power: 3–9X
Obj. Dia.: 40mm
Main Dia.: 1 in.
Exit Pupil: 4.4–13.3mm
Field of View: 8.4–25.2 ft @ 100 yds
Twilight Factor: 11–19
Eye Relief: 5 in.
Features: Long range muzzleloader; BDC 300 reticle; ¼ MOA adjustments; Spring-Loaded Zero-Reset Turrets; silver finish; waterproof; fogproof; shockproof
From: $220

M-308 4–16X42MM

Weight: 19 oz.
Length: 13.5 in.
Power: 4–16X
Obj. Dia.: 42mm
Main Dia.: 1 in.
Exit Pupil: 10.5–2.6mm
Field of View: 25.2–6.3 ft @ 100 yds
Twilight Factor: 12.96–25.92
Eye Relief: 4–3.7 in.
Features: Available with the all-new BDC 800 reticle or Nikoplex reticle with Rapid Action Turrets; developed specifically for the trajectory of the .308 Win./7.62 NATO round with 168-grain hollow point boat-tail Match bullet; Ultra ClearCoat optical system; Eye Box technology; smooth zoom control
MSRP $430

MONARCH 3 2.5–10X42MM NIKOPLEX

Weight: 16.6 oz.
Length: 12.6 in.
Power: 2.5–10X
Obj.Dia.: 42mm
Main Dia.: 1 in.
Exit Pupil: 16.8–4.2mm
Field of View: 40.3–10.1 ft @ 100 yds
Twilight Factor: 10.24–20.49
Eye Relief: 4.0–3.8 in.
Features: Enhanced ring spacing for mounting on rifles including magnum-length actions; see-through "ballistic circle" BDC reticle available; Ultra ClearCoat optical system; customized with accessory target-style windage and elevation adjustment knobs and caps; available in 2–8x30, 3–12x42, 4–16x42, 5–20x44, 2.5–10x50, 4–16x50, 6–24x50, and 8–32x50, in matte and silver with ED glass, SF Mil-Dot, and fine crosshair with dot
MSRP $400

Nikon

NIKON MONARCH 3 1–4X20MM BDC

NIKON MONARCH 3 4–16X42MM SIDE FOCUS MILDOT

NIKON P-300 BLK 2–7X32MM BDC SUPERSUB

NIKON PROSTAFF 3–9X40MM NIKOPLEX

OPTICS

MONARCH 3 1–4X20MM BDC

Weight: 12.2 oz.
Length: 10.35 in.
Power: 1–4X
Obj. Dia.: 20mm
Main Dia.: 1 in.
Exit Pupil: 5–20mm
Field of View: 23.1–92.9 ft @ 100 yds
Twilight Factor: 4.5–8.9
Eye Relief: 4 in.
Features: BDC reticle; designed for big game hunting; Spot On Ballistic Match technology; Spring Loaded Instant Zero-Reset Turrets; quick-focus eyepiece; enhanced mount ring spacing; waterproof; fogproof
MSRP $280

MONARCH 3 4–16X42MM SIDE FOCUS MILDOT

Weight: 19 oz.
Length: 13.5 in.
Power: 4–16X
Obj. Dia.: 42mm
Main Dia.: 1 in.
Exit Pupil: 2.6–10.5mm
Field of View: 6.3–25.2 ft @ 100 yds
Twilight Factor: 13–25.9
Eye Relief: 4 in.
Features: Mildot reticle; Max Adj. 40 MOA; waterproof; fogproof; Spring Loaded Instant Zero-Reset Turrets; Spot On Ballistic Match technology; Monarch 3 Eyebox technology; matte finish
MSRP $470

P-300 BLK 2–7X32MM BDC SUPERSUB

Weight: 16.1 oz.
Length: 11.5 in.
Power: 2–7X
Obj. Dia.: 32mm
Main Dia.: 1 in.
Exit Pupil: 4.6–16mm
Field of View: 12.7–44.5 ft @ 100 yds
Twilight Factor: 8–15
Eye Relief: 3.8 in.
Features: BDC SuperSub reticle; optimized for use with supersonic and subsonic ammo; Max Adj. 80 MOA; waterproof; fogproof; matte black
MSRP $200

PROSTAFF 3–9X40MM NIKOPLEX

Weight: 15 oz.
Length: 12.4 in.
Power: 3–9X
Obj.Dia.: 40mm
Main Dia.: 1 in.
Exit Pupil: 13.3–4.4mm
Field of View: 33.8–11.3 ft @ 100 yds
Twilight Factor: 10.95–18.97
Eye Relief: 3.6–3.6 in.
Features: ¼ MOA hand-turn reticle adjustments with "Zero-Reset" turrets; quick-focus eyepiece; also in 2–7x32–and in Shotgun Hunter with BDC 200 reticle and 3–9x50 in silver, RealTree APG, and with BDC reticle
MSRP $180

NIKON PROSTAFF 5
2.5–10X50MM MATTE BDC

NIKON PROSTAFF 5
3.5–14X50MM ILLUMINATED
NIKOPLEX

NIKON PROSTAFF
TARGET EFR 3–9X40MM

PROSTAFF 5 2.5–10X50MM MATTE BDC

Weight: 18 oz.
Length: 13.7 in.
Power: 2.5–10X
Obj. Dia.: 50mm
Main Dia.: 1 in.
Exit Pupil: 5–20mm
Field of View: 9.9–40.4 ft @ 100 yds
Twilight Factor: 11.2–22.4
Eye Relief: 4 in.
Features: Hand-turn reticle adjustments with Spring-Loaded Zero-Reset turrets; BDC reticle; multi-coated optics; Max Adj. 70 MOA; waterproof; fogproof; parallax setting
MSRP $330

PROSTAFF 5 3.5–14X50MM ILLUMINATED NIKOPLEX

Weight: 19.9 oz.
Length: 14.3 in.
Power: 3.5–14X
Obj. Dia.: 50mm
Main Dia.: 1 in.
Exit Pupil: 2.9–14.3mm
Field of View: 7.2–28.6 ft @ 100 yds
Twilight Factor: 13.2–26.5
Eye Relief: 4 in.
Features: Illuminated reticle; hand-turn reticle adjustments with Spring-Loaded Zero-Reset turrets; waterproof; fogproof; parallax adjustment; matte finish
MSRP $580

PROSTAFF TARGET EFR 3–9X40MM

Weight: 15.7 oz.
Length: 12.5 in.
Power: 3–9X
Obj. Dia.: 40mm
Main Dia.: 1 in.
Exit Pupil: 13.3–4.4mm
Field of View: 16.9–5.7 ft @ 50 yds
Twilight Factor: 10.95–18.97
Eye Relief: 3.6–3.6 in.
Features: Designed and engineered for .22LR, air rifle, and other applications where the versatility of focusing at extended ranges is desired; new Nikon Precision Reticle featuring a fine crosshair with dot; adjustable objective lens that allows parallax adjustments; large ocular with quick focus eyepiece; zero-reset turrets
MSRP $190

Pentax Imaging Co.

PENTAX LIGHTSEEKER XL 4–16X44MM

LIGHTSEEKER XL 4–16X44MM
Weight: 23 oz.
Length: 14 in.
Power: 4–16X
Obj.Dia.: 44mm
Main Dia.: 1 in.
Exit Pupil: 11–2.8mm
Field of View: 24–8 ft @ 100 yds
Twilight Factor: 9.4–26.5
Eye Relief: 3.5–4 in.
Features: Finger-adjustable windage and elevation turrets; "European-style" eyepieces; also in 3–9x40 and 2.5–10x50, and with P and Twilight Plex reticles
MSRP $439

Redfield

REDFIELD BATTLEZONE 3–9X42MM

BATTLEZONE SERIES
Weight: 14.8 oz., 29.8 oz.
Length: 12.4 in., 14.5 in.
Power: 3–9X, 6–18X
Obj. Dia.: 42mm, 44mm
Main Dia.: 1 in.
Exit Pupil: 14.2–14.9mm, 7.6–2.5mm
Field of View @ 100 Yds: 32.9–11.4 ft, 19.2–6 ft
Twilight Factor: 11.2–19, 16.25–28.14
Eye Relief: 3.5 in.
Features: Pop-up resettable ¼ MOA finger-click adjustments; BDC dials; TAC-MOA Reticle Matches Adjustments; waterproof; fogproof; shockproof; Redfield Lifetime Warranty; matte finish
From: . . . . $200–$240

REDFIELD BATTLEZONE TAC.22 2–7X34MM

BATTLEZONE TAC.22 2–7X34MM
Weight: 13.6 oz.
Length: 11.3 in.
Power: 2–7X
Obj. Dia.: 34mm
Main Dia.: 1 in.
Exit Pupil: 16.2–4.8mm
Field of View: 43.1–13.2 ft @ 100 yds
Twilight Factor: 8.25–15.43
Eye Relief: 3.5 in.
Features: Shock-, water-, and fogproof; nitrogen filled; multi-coated lens
MSRP $240

REDFIELD REVENGE 3–9X42MM

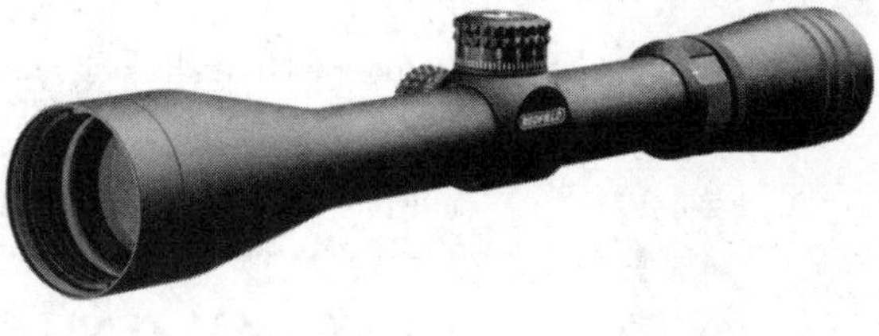

REDFIELD REVOLUTION/TAC 3–9X40MM

REDFIELD REVOLUTION 3–9X40MM

REVENGE SERIES

Weight: 13.6 oz., 14.8 oz., 17.1 oz., 15.3 oz., 29.8 oz.
Length: 11.3 in., 12.4 in., 12.4 in., 14.1 in., 14.5 in.,
Power: 2–7X, 3–9X, 3–9X, 4–12X, 6–18X
Obj. Dia.: 34mm, 42mm, 52mm, 42mm, 44mm
Main Dia.: 1 in.
Exit Pupil: 16.2–4.8mm, 14.2–4.9mm, 17.6–6.1mm, 11.1–3.5mm, 7.6–2.5mm
Field of View:@ 100 Yds: 43.1–13.2 ft, 32.9–11.4 ft, 32.7–11.5 ft, 24.6–7.9 ft, 19.2–6 ft
Twilight Factor: 8.25–15.43, 11.23–19.44, 12.49–21.63, 12.96–22.45, 16.25–28.14
Eye Relief: 3.5 in.
Features: Built-in optical rangefinder means you never need to take your eye off the target; flexible magnification range; available with 4-Plex, Accu-Ranger Hunter, and Accu-Ranger Sabot reticles
MSRP . . . . $175–$350

REVOLUTION SERIES

Weight: 11.1 oz., 12.6 oz., 14.5 oz., 13.1 oz.
Length: 11 in., 12.3 in., 12.4 in., 12.3 in.
Power: 2–7X, 3–9X, 3–9X, 4–12X
Obj. Dia.: 33mm, 40mm, 50mm, 40mm
Main Dia.: 1 in.
Exit Pupil: N/A
Field of View @ 100 Yds: 43.2–17.3 ft, 32.9–13.1 ft, 33–13.1 ft, 19.9–9.4 ft
Twilight Factor: 8.12–15.2, 10.95–18.97, 12.25–21.21, 12.65–21.91
Eye Relief: 3.7–4.2 in., 3.7–4.2 in., 3.7–4.2 in., 3.7–4.9 in.
Features: Black matte finish and either a 4-Plex or Accu-Range reticle; Illuminator Lens System with premium lenses and vapor-deposition multi-coatings; Accu-Trac windage and elevation adjustment system has resettable stainless steel 1/4 MOA finger click adjustments; "Rapid Target Acquisition" (RTA) lockable eyepiece
4-Plex: . . . . $250–$315
Accu-Range: . . . . $265–$325

REVOLUTION/TAC 3–9X40MM

Weight: 12.6 oz.
Length: 12.3 in.
Power: 3–9X
Obj. Dia.: 40mm
Main Dia.: 1 in.
Exit Pupil: 12.1–4.7mm
Field of View: 32.9–13.1 ft @ 100 yds
Twilight Factor: 10.95–18.97
Eye Relief: 3.7 in.–4.2 in.
Features: Shock-, water-, and fogproof; nitrogen filled; vapor deposited, multi-coated illuminator lens system
MSRP $350

Schmidt & Bender

SCHMIDT & BENDER 1.1–4X20MM SHORT-DOT LOCKING POLICE MARKSMAN

1.1–4X20MM PM SHORT-DOT LOCKING POLICE MARKSMAN

Weight: 20.11 oz.
Length: 10.6 in.
Power: 1.1–4X
Obj.Dia.: 20mm
Main Dia.: 30mm
Exit Pupil: 14–5mm
Field of View: 96–30 ft @ 100 yds
Twilight Factor: 4.69–8.94
Eye Relief: 3.5 in.
Features: Includes locking turrets and CQB reticle; M855, 75 gr. TAP, and M118LR calibration rings standard; also in 1.5–6x20 and 1–8x24 Short Dots and 1.1–4x24 PM Zenith Short-Dot LE
MSRP $2879

1.5–6X42MM ZENITH FLASH-DOT

Weight: 21.52 oz.
Length: 12.33 in.
Power: 1.5–6X
Obj.Dia.: 42mm
Main Dia.: 30mm
Exit Pupil: 28–7mm
Field of View: 60–19.5 ft @ 100 yds
Twilight Factor: 4.2–15.9
Eye Relief: 3.5 in.
Features: Flash-Dot reticle in the center of the crosshairs performs like front bead sight on shotgun when illuminated; Flash Dot can also be shut off; click values on the windage and elevation adjustments
are ½ MOA on the 1.1–4x24 and ⅓ MOA on the rest; also in 1.1–4x24, 1–8x24, 3–12x50, and 2.5–10x56 with Flash Dot and in 1.1–4x24, 1.5–6x42, 1–8x24, 3–12x50, and 2.5–10x56 with non-illuminated reticle
MSRP . . . . $2469–$2559

SCHMIDT & BENDER 1.5–6X42MM ZENITH FLASH-DOT

SCHMIDT & BENDER 2.5–10X40MM SUMMIT

SCHMIDT & BENDER 3–12X42MM KLASSIK

OPTICS

2.5–10X40MM SUMMIT

Weight: 16.8 oz.
Length: 13.2 in.
Power: 2.5–10X
Obj.Dia.: 40mm
Main Dia.: 1 in.
Exit Pupil: 16–4mm
Field of View: 40.4–12.3 ft @ 100 yds
Twilight Factor: 14–20
Eye Relief: 3.93 in.
Features: Built for the American market with its 1 inch tube; adjustments are ¼ MOA
MSRP $2059

3–12X42MM KLASSIK

Weight: 19.9 oz.
Length: 13.66 in.
Power: 3–12X
Obj.Dia.: 42mm
Main Dia.: 30mm
Exit Pupil: 3.5–14mm
Field of View: 31.5–11.4 ft @ 100 yds
Twilight Factor: 8.5–22.4
Eye Relief: 3.5 in.
Features: Enhanced model 3–12x42 Klassik designed for longer ranges; P3 reticle with bullet-drop compensated elevation knob; adjustments are in ⅓ MOA; third-turret parallax adjustment; also in 3–12x50 and 4–16x50
MSRP $2439

Schmidt & Bender

SCHMIDT & BENDER 3–12X50MM KLASSIK ILLUMINATED

SCHMIDT & BENDER 12.5–50X56MM FIELD TARGET

SCHMIDT & BENDER 4–16X42 POLICE MARKSMAN II/LP

3–12X50MM KLASSIK ILLUMINATED

Weight: 21.66 oz.
Length: 13.75 in.
Power: 3–12X
Obj.Dia.: 50mm
Main Dia.: 30mm
Exit Pupil: 4.2–14.4mm
Field of View: 33.3–11.4 ft @ 100 yds
Twilight Factor: 8.5–24.5
Eye Relief: 3.14 in.
Features: All of the Klassik variables have generous objectives for greater light transmission; variety of reticles in illuminated, non-illuminated, and varmint; also in illuminated-reticle 2.5–10x56 and 3–12x42, and in non-illuminated 2.5–10x40, 3–12x42, and 4–16x50
MSRP $2469

4–16X42MM POLICE MARKSMAN II/LP

Weight: 30.86 oz.
Length: 15.5 in.
Power: 4–16X
Obj.Dia.: 42mm
Main Dia.: 34mm
Exit Pupil: 10.5–2.6mm
Field of View: 22.5–7 ft @ 100 yds
Twilight Factor: 11.3–25.9
Eye Relief: 3.5 in.
Features: Color coded elevation turret; illuminated reticle and parallax adjustment; LP turret system features a color-coded elevation knob for instant reference to the elevation setting; also in 30mm 10x42 and 34mm 3–12x50 with non-IR, 34mm tube 4–16x42, 3–12x50, 3–20x50, 4–16x50, 5–25x56, and 12–50x56
MSRP $3459

6X42MM KLASSIK FIXED

Weight: 16.67 oz.
Length: 13.7 in.
Power: 6X
Obj.Dia.: 42mm
Main Dia.: 1 in.
Exit Pupil: 7mm
Field of View: 21 ft @ 100 yds
Twilight Factor: 15.8
Eye Relief: 3.14 in.
Features: Fixed 6-power magnification applicable to a wide range of hunting situation; windage and elevation adjustments are in 1/3 MOA increments.; classic European 8x56 configuration offers maximum light transmission; also in 10x42, 7x50, and 8x56
MSRP $1289

Schmidt & Bender

SCHMIDT & BENDER 6X42MM
KLASSIK FIXED

SIMMONS .22 MAG
3–9X32MM

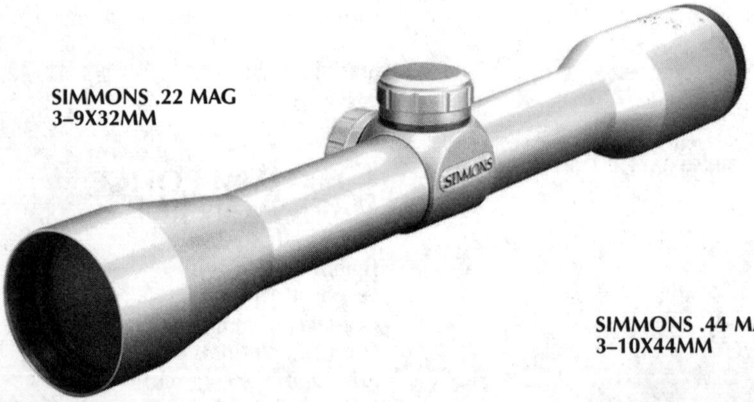

SIMMONS .44 MAG.
3–10X44MM

OPTICS

12.5–50X56MM FIELD TARGET

Weight: 40.56 oz.
Length: 16.4 in.
Power: 12.5–50X
Obj.Dia.: 56mm
Main Dia.: 30mm
Exit Pupil: 4.55–1.18mm
Field of View: 10.5–2.7 ft @ 100 yds
Twilight Factor: 26.5–53
Eye Relief: 2.75 in.
Features: High-magnification scope has a shallow depth of field, so the parallax side-focus wheel can be used as a reference for gauging the distance to the target and adjusting the trajectory; extra-large focus wheel to range distances from 7–70m; illuminated reticle with brightness settings adjustable from 1 to 11
MSRP $3619

.22 MAG 3–9X32MM

Weight: 10 oz.
Length: 12 in.
Power: 3–9X
Obj. Dia.: 32mm
Main Dia.: 1 in.
Exit Pupil: 10.7–3.6mm
Field of View: 31.4–10.5 ft @ 100 yds
Twilight Factor: 9.8–17
Eye Relief: 3.75 in.
Features: One piece tube construction; fully coated optics; waterproof; fogproof; shockproof; Truplex reticle; RF Rings with available Adjustable Objective; also available in 4x32; matte or silver finish
From: . . . . $57–$100

.44 MAG. 3–10X44MM

Weight: 11.3 oz.
Length: 12 in.
Power: 3–10X
Obj.Dia.: 44mm
Main Dia.: 1 in.
Exit Pupil: 14.66–4.4mm
Field of View: 33–9.4 ft @ 100 yds
Twilight Factor: 11.48–20.97
Eye Relief: 3.75 in.
Features: Wide field of view with brightness delivered via multi-coated optics; QTA (Quick Target Acquisition) eyepiece; TrueZero windage and elevation adjustment system; also in 4–12x44, 6–21x44, 6–24x44
MSRP . . . . $158–$250

Simmons

8-POINT 3–9X40MM

Weight: 10 oz.
Length: 13.125 in.
Power: 3–9X
Obj. Dia.: 40mm
Main Dia.: 1 in.
Exit Pupil: 10.7–3.6mm
Field of View: 31.4–10.5 ft @ 100 yds
Twilight Factor: 11–19
Eye Relief: 3.75 in.
Features: TrueZero fingertip adjustments; Quick Target Acquisition; fully coated optics; waterproof; fogproof; recoilproof; Truplex reticle; also available in 4x32, 3–9x32, and 3–9x50; matte finish
From: . . . . $50–$82

SIMMONS 8-POINT 3–9X40MM

SIMMONS PROHUNTER 3–9X40MM ILLUMINATED TRUPLEX RETICLE

SIMMONS PROSPORT 4–12X50MM

PROHUNTER 3–9X40MM ILLUMINATED TRUPLEX RETICLE

Weight: 10.8 oz.
Length: 12 in.
Power: 3–9X
Obj.Dia.: 40mm
Main Dia.: 1 in.
Exit Pupil: 13.33–4.44mm
Field of View: 31.4–11 ft @ 100 yds
Twilight Factor: 10.95–18.97
Eye Relief: 3.75 in.
Features: TrueZero windage and elevation adjustment system for a locked-in zero; raised tab on the power change ring for easy grip and surer adjustments; also in 4x32, 1.5–5x32, 3–9x40 TruPlex Reticle, 4x32, 2–6x32 Matte, 2–6x32 Silver
MSRP. . . . . $98–$195

PROSPORT 4–12X50MM

Weight: 14 oz.
Length: 13 in.
Power: 4–12X
Obj. Dia.: 50mm
Main Dia.: 1 in.
Exit Pupil: 12.5–4.2mm
Field of View: 23.8–8.2 ft @ 100 yds
Twilight Factor: 14.1–24.5
Eye Relief: 3.75 in.
Features: Adjustable Objective (AO); fully coated optics; TrueZero fingertip adjustments; Quick Target Acquisition eyepiece with Fast Focus; waterproof; fogproof; recoilproof; Truplex reticle; also available in 3–9x40, 3–9x50, 4–12x40 (AO), and 6–18x50 (AO); matte finish with silver or Realtree available for the 3–9x40 model
From:. . . . . $98–$174

Steiner

STEINER GS3 SERIES
2–10X42MM

STEINER MX5I SERIES
3–15X50MM

STEINER
NIGHTHUNTER
EXTREME SERIES
1–5X24MM

OPTICS

GS3 SERIES 2–10X42MM

Weight: 18 oz.
Length: 13.5 in.
Power: 2–10X
Obj. Dia.: 42mm
Main Dia.: 30mm
Exit Pupil: 16.8–4.2mm
Field of View: 52–10.5 ft @ 100 yds
Twilight Factor: 9.17–20.49
Eye Relief: 3.5 in.–4.25 in.
Features: Rear focal plane; water- and fog-proof; nitrogen filled; 3–15x50, 3–15x56, and 4–20x50 also available
MSRP. . . . . $920–$1150

MX5I SERIES 3–15X50MM

Weight: 32.5 oz.
Length: 14.2 in.
Power: 3–15X
Obj. Dia.: 50mm
Main Dia.: 34mm
Exit Pupil: 10.4–3.33mm
Field of View: 39.7–7.9 ft @ 100 yds
Twilight Factor: 12.25–27.39
Eye Relief: 3.54 in.
Features: Front focal plane; shock-, water-, and fogproof; nitrogen filled; adjustable parallax; rubber armoring; illuminated reticle; 1–5x24 and 5–25x56 also available
MSRP. . . . . $2990–$3700

NIGHTHUNTER EXTREME SERIES 1–5X24MM

Weight: 20.4 oz.
Length: 11.5 in.
Power: 1–5X
Obj. Dia.: 24mm
Main Dia.: 30mm
Exit Pupil: 11.5–4.8mm
Field of View: 108–21.5 ft @ 100 yds
Twilight Factor: 4.9–10.95
Eye Relief: 3.54 in.
Features: Rear focal plane; water- and fog-proof; nitrogen filled; illuminated reticle; rubber armoring; 1.6–8x42, 2–10x50, and 3–15x56 also available
MSRP. . . . . $2587–$3220

Swarovski Optik

Z3 3–10X42MM

Weight: 12.7 oz.
Length: 12.6 in.
Power: 3–10X
Obj.Dia.: 42mm
Main Dia.: 1 in.
Exit Pupil: 12.6–4.2mm
Field of View: 33–11.7 ft @ 1000 yds
Twilight Factor: 11.22–20.49
Eye Relief: 3.5 in.
Features: Z3 riflescopes have a 3x zoom factor and are the lightest riflescopes in the Swarovski Optik line; perfect fit for many of today's lightweight rifles; reticles for the Z3 include the 4A, Plex, BRX/BRH (3–10x and 4–12x), and ML in the 3–10x
MSRP $954

SWAROVSKI OPTIK Z3 3–10X42MM

Z5 5–25X52MM

Weight: 17.5 oz.
Length: 14.6 in.
Power: 5–25X
Obj.Dia.: 52mm
Main Dia.: 1 in.
Exit Pupil: 9.6–2.1mm
Field of View: 21.9–4.5 ft @ 100 yds
Twilight Factor: 16.12–36.05
Eye Relief: 3.75 in.
Features: The Z5 Riflescope line features a 5x zoom factor; a third parallax-adjustment turret; and long eye relief; with reticles available in #4, Plex, Fine in the 5–25x, and BRX/BRH; also available with the ballistic turrets; also in 3.5–18x44
MSRP $1777

SWAROVSKI OPTIK Z5 5–25X52MM

Z6I 5–30X50MM P

Weight: 22.6 oz.
Length: 15.67 in.
Power: 5–30X
Obj. Dia.: 48.2–50mm
Main Dia.: 30mm
Exit Pupil: 9.5–1.7mm
Field of View: 23.7–3.9 ft @ 100 yds
Twilight Factor: 14.1–38.7
Eye Relief: 3.74 in.
Features: New 2nd Generation scopes feature slimmer design that enables a clearer view of the controls and of the hunting situation; parallax turret also features a lock-in position at the 100 yds mark; more prominent ribbing on the magnification ring; 4A-1, 4W, Plex, and BRH reticles available; also available in 1–6x24, 1–6x24 BRT, 1–6x24 EE, 1.7–10x42, 2–12x50, 2.5–15x44 P, 2.5–15x56 P, 3–18x50 P
MSRP $3677

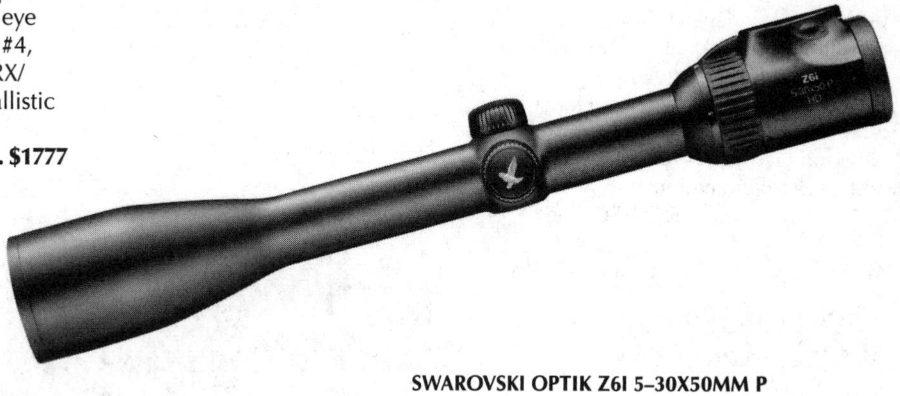
SWAROVSKI OPTIK Z6I 5–30X50MM P

Tangent Theta

TANGENT THETA PROFESSIONAL MARKSMAN SERIES 5–25X56MM

PROFESSIONAL MARKSMAN SERIES 5–25X56MM

Weight: 40.57 oz.
Length: 16.73 in.
Power: 5–25X
Obj. Dia.: 56mm
Main Dia.: 34mm
Exit Pupil: 11–2.3mm
Field of View: 7.6–1.6m @ 100m
Twilight Factor: 16.73–37.42
Eye Relief: 3.54 in.
Features: Water- and shockproof; adjustable parallax; illuminated reticle; 3–15x50 also available
MSRP . . . . $2998–$4250

Trijicon

ACCUPOINT 3–9X40MM

Weight: 13.4 oz.
Length: 12.4 in.
Power: 3–9X
Obj.Dia.: 40mm
Main Dia.: 1 in.
Exit Pupil: 13.3–4.4mm
Field of View: 6.45–2.15 ft @ 100 yds
Twilight Factor: 10.95–18.97
Eye Relief: 3.6 in.
Features: Tritium and fiber battery-free dual-illuminated; manual brightness adjustment override; quick-focus eyepiece; and windage and elevation adjustments; aircraft aluminum with black-matte finish; reticles include BAC Triangle, Standard Cross-Hair with Dot, Mil-Dot Cross-Hair with Dot, and German #4 in red, green, and amber illumination; also in 1–4x24, 1.25–4x24, 5–20x50, and 2.5–10x56
MSRP . . . . $975–$1599

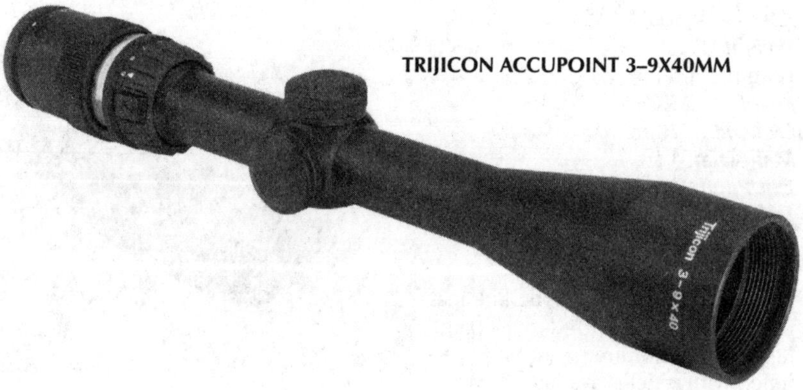

TRIJICON ACCUPOINT 3–9X40MM

OPTICS

ACOG CROSSBOW SCOPE 3X24MM XB

Weight: 5.89 oz.
Length: 5 in.
Power: 3X
Obj. Dia.: 24mm
Exit Pupil: 20–3mm
Field of View: 25.6 ft @ 100 yds
Twilight Factor: 8.49
Eye Relief: 1.4 in.
Features: The first truly high performance optic designed specifically for crossbows; lightest magnified crossbow optic; illuminated reticle accommodates speeds from 300–340 fps; bolt drop stadia lines out to 80 yds; Bad River Outdoors' patented deer/elk ranging capabilities; ability for ranging and hold-over, all in the field of view; fiber optics and tritium illumination
MSRP $1285

TRIJICON ACOG CROSSBOW SCOPE 3X24 XB

ACOG WITH 300 AAC BLACKOUT RETICLE 3X30MM

Weight: 11.64 oz.
Length: 6.1 in.
Power: 3X
Obj. Dia.: 30mm
Main Dia.: N/A
Exit Pupil: 10mm
Field of View: 19.3 ft @ 100 yds
Twilight Factor: 9.5
Eye Relief: 1.9 in.
Features: TA60 Mount; designed for law enforcement and military applications; 300 AAC Blackout Ballistic Reticle for subsonic and supersonic rounds; bullet drop compensator; Bindon Aiming Concept (BAC), fiber optics & tritium illuminated; available with amber, green, or red crosshair reticle
MSRP. $1407

TARS 3–15X50MM

Weight: 47 oz., 51 oz. with sunshade
Length: 13.9in, 16.9 in. with sunshade
Power: 3–15X
Obj. Dia.: 50mm
Main Dia.: 34mm
Exit Pupil: 16.8–3.3mm
Field of View: 37.5–7.5 ft @ 100 yds
Twilight Factor: 10.1–22.6
Eye Relief: 3.3 in.
Features: Tactical Advanced RifleScope is built for long-range shooting demands; multi-layer coated lenses; aircraft grade hard anodized aluminum; side-focus parallax compensation, powered by 1 CR2032 battery; constant eye relief; available with MOA, Duplex, JW MIL-Square reticles and MOA or MIL adjusters
MSRP. $4464

TRIJICON ACOG WITH 300 AAC BLACKOUT RETICLE 3X30MM

TRIJICON TARS 3–15X50MM

Trijicon

VCOG 1–6X24MM RIFLESCOPE

Weight: 23.2 oz.
Length: 10.05 in.
Power: 1–6X
Obj. Dia.: 24mm
Main Dia.: N/A
Exit Pupil: 10.4–3.8mm
Field of View: 95–15.9 ft @ 100 yds
Twilight Factor: 12
Eye Relief: 4 in.
Features: Designed and built in the U.S.; Mil Spec, hard-coat finish; 90 MOA of windage and elevation adjustment; fully multi-coated lenses; waterproof; seven different reticle choices, between centered crosshair and horseshoe/dot reticle; red illuminated reticle; six brightness settings; matte finish
MSRP. . . . . $2800–$3050

TRIJICON VCOG 1–6X24MM RIFLESCOPE

Truglo

TRUGLO TACTICAL IR 3–9X42MM

TACTICAL IR 3–9X42MM

Weight: 17.6 oz.
Length: 9.92 in.
Power: 3–9X
Obj. Dia.: 42mm
Main Dia.: 30mm
Exit Pupil: N/A
Field of View: 31–10.47 ft @ 100 yds
Twilight Factor: 11.23–19.44
Eye Relief: 3.46 in.–3.94 in.
Features: Two-color IR MilDot illuminated reticle; BDC can be calibrated to most .223 and .308 cartridges and accommodate targets up to 600 yards away
MSRP. $209

OPTICS

TRU-BRITE XTREME DUAL-COLOR TACTICAL COMPACT 4X32MM

Weight: 15.4 oz.
Length: 9.8 in.
Power: 4X
Obj. Dia.: 32mm
Main Dia.: 1 in.
Exit Pupil: N/A
Field of View: 20.79 ft @ 100 yds
Twilight Factor: 11.31
Eye Relief: 5.5 in.
Features: Illuminated reticle; fully coated lenses; durable, scratch-resistant, non-reflective matte finish
MSRP. $172

TRUGLO TRU-BRITE XTREME DUAL-COLOR TACTICAL COMPACT 4X32MM

U.S. Optics

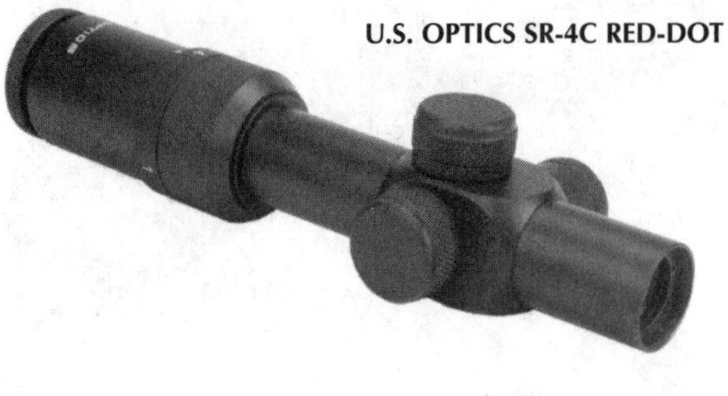

U.S. OPTICS SR-4C RED-DOT 1–4X

SR-4C RED-DOT 1–4X

Weight: 19.84 oz.
Length: 9.25 in.
Power: 1–4X
Obj. Dia.: N/A
Main Dia.: 30mm
Exit Pupil: N/A
Field of View: 110–33 ft @ 100 yds
Twilight Factor: N/A
Eye Relief: 3.7 in.
Features: Rear focal plane; illuminated reticle
MSRP $1999

Vortex

VORTEX CROSSFIRE II 30MM SERIES 3–12X56MM

VORTEX DIAMONDBACK HP SERIES 2–8X32MM

VORTEX RAZOR HD GEN II SERIES 4.5–27X56MM

CROSSFIRE II 30MM SERIES 3–12X56MM

Weight: 21.1 oz.
Length: 14.3 in.
Power: 3–12X
Obj. Dia.: 56mm
Main Dia.: 30mm
Exit Pupil: N/A
Field of View: 36.7–9.2 ft @ 100 yds
Twilight Factor: 12.96–25.92
Eye Relief: 3.5 in.
Features: Rear focal plane; shock-, water-, and fogproof; illuminated reticle; adjustable parallax; 1–4x24, 4–16x50, and 6–24x50 also available
MSRP . . . . $169–$349

DIAMONDBACK HP SERIES 2–8X32MM

Weight: 15.9 oz.
Length: 11.6 in.
Power: 2–8X
Obj. Dia.: 32mm
Main Dia.: 1 in.
Exit Pupil: N/A
Field of View: 41.9–12.2 ft @ 100 yds
Twilight Factor: 8–16
Eye Relief: 4.6 in.
Features: Rear focal plane; shock-, water-, and fogproof; adjustable parallax; 3–12x42 and 4–16x42 also available
MSRP . . . . $349–$429

RAZOR HD GEN II SERIES 4.5–27X56MM

Weight: 48.5 oz.
Length: 14.4 in
Power: 4.5–27X
Obj. Dia.: 56mm
Main Dia.: 34mm
Exit Pupil: N/A
Field of View: 25.3–4.4 ft @ 100 yds
Twilight Factor: 15.87–38.88
Eye Relief: 3.7 in.
Features: Front focal plane; shock-, water-, and fogproof; adjustable parallax; illuminated reticle; glass-etched reticle; 1–6x24 RFP and 3–18x50 also available
MSRP . . . . $1999–$3199

Vortex

VORTEX VIPER HS LR FFP SERIES 2.5–10X32MM

VORTEX HS LR RFP SERIES 4–16X44MM

VORTEX VIPER HS-T SERIES 6–24X50MM

VORTEX VIPER PST FFP SERIES 6–24X50MM

VORTEX VIPER PST RFP SERIES 1–4X24MM

VIPER HUNTING SHOOTING LONG RANGE (HS LR) FFP SERIES 2.5–10X32MM

Weight: 16.8 oz.
Length: 12.8 in.
Power: 2.5–10X
Obj. Dia.: 32mm
Main Dia.: 30mm
Exit Pupil: N/A
Field of View: 47–10.9 ft @ 100 yds
Twilight Factor: 8.94–17.89
Eye Relief: 4 in.
Features: Front focal plane; shock-, water-, and fogproof; adjustable parallax; 4–16x50 and 6–24x50 also available
MSRP . . . . $899–$999

VIPER HUNTING SHOOTING LONG RANGE (HS LR) RFP SERIES 4–16X44MM

Weight: 19.8 oz.
Length: 13.7 in.
Power: 4–16X
Obj. Dia.: 44mm
Main Dia.: 30mm
Exit Pupil: N/A
Field of View: 27.4–7.4 ft @ 100 yds
Twilight Factor: 13.27–26.53
Eye Relief: 4 in.
Features: Rear focal plane; shock-, water-, and fogproof; adjustable parallax; 4–16x50 also available
MSRP . . . . $649–$699

VIPER HUTING SHOOTING TACTICAL (HS-T) SERIES 6–24X50MM

Weight: 22.6 oz.
Length: 15.5 in.
Power: 6–24X
Obj. Dia.: 50mm
Main Dia.: 30mm
Exit Pupil: N/A
Field of View: 17.8–5.1 ft @ 100 yds
Twilight Factor: 17.32–34.64
Eye Relief: 4 in.
Features: Rear focal plane; shock-, water-, and fogproof; adjustable parallax; 4–16x44 also available
MSRP . . . . $669–$739

VIPER PRECISION SHOOTING TACTICAL (PST) FFP SERIES 6–24X50MM

Weight: 23.4 oz.
Length: 15.5 in.
Power: 6–24X
Obj. Dia.: 50mm
Main Dia.: 30mm
Exit Pupil: N/A
Field of View: 17.8–5.1 ft @ 100 yds
Twilight Factor: 17.32–34.64
Eye Relief: 4 in.
Features: Front focal plane; shock-, water-, and fogproof; adjustable parallax; illuminated reticle; glass-etched reticle; 2.5–10x32 and 4–16x50 also available
MSRP . . . . $899–$1049

VIPER PRECISION SHOOTING TACTICAL (PST) RFP SERIES 1–4X24MM

Weight: 16.2 oz.
Length: 9.7 in.
Power: 1–4X
Obj. Dia.: 24mm
Main Dia.: 30mm
Exit Pupil: N/A
Field of View: 98–27.5 ft @ 100 yds
Twilight Factor: 4.9–14.7
Eye Relief: 4 in.
Features: Rear focal plane; shock-, water-, and fogproof; illuminated reticle; adjustable parallax on some models; 2.5–10x44, 4–16x50, and 6–24x50 also available
MSRP . . . . $599–$849

40/44 3–10X44MM

Weight: 13.93 oz.
Length: 12.09 in.
Power: 3–10X
Obj.Dia.: 44mm
Main Dia.: 1 in.
Exit Pupil: 14.7–4.4mm
Field of View: 33.5–10.3 ft @ 100 yds
Twilight Factor: 11.49–20.98
Eye Relief: 3 in.
Features: Ballistic-X reticle on some models; one-piece tube construction; aspherical lens system on some models; also available in 2.8–10x44, 3–9x40, 3.8–12x44, 4–12x44, 6.5–20x44; silver finish on some models
MSRP . . . . $211–$332

40/44 SHOTGUN & MUZZLELOADER

Weight: 14–24 oz.
Length: 10.31–13.31 in.
Power: 2–7X
Obj.Dia.: 32mm
Main Dia.: 1 in.
Exit Pupil: 15–5.4mm
Field of View: 44.7–12.7 ft @ 100 yds
Twilight Factor: 8–14.97
Eye Relief: 3.5 in.
Features: Weaver's dedicated shotgun and muzzleloader scopes are engineered specifically for these firearms and give hunters maximum performance out of short to medium-range guns
MSRP . . . . $186–$196

CLASSIC HANDGUN 2.5–8X28MM

Weight: 9.1 oz.
Length: 9.29 in.
Power: 2.5–8X
Obj.Dia.: 28mm
Main Dia.: 1 in.
Exit Pupil: 11.2–3.5mm
Field of View: 11–4.5 ft @ 100 yds
Twilight Factor: 8.37–14.97
Eye Relief: 24.53 in.
Features: Handguns demand a scope that is built to withstand the brutal pounding from today's most powerful revolvers and single-shot pistols. Designed for the tremendous recoil of 1,000 rounds from a .454 Casull revolver; black or silver; also in 1.5–4x20, 2x28, and 4x28.
MSRP . . . . $268–$387

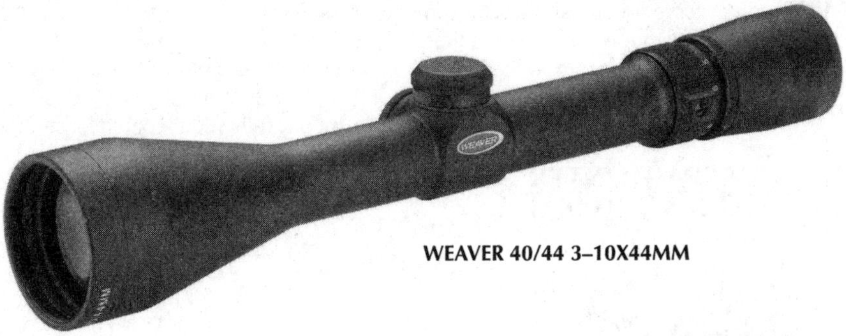

WEAVER 40/44 3–10X44MM

WEAVER 40/44 SHOTGUN & MUZZLELOADER

WEAVER CLASSIC HANDGUN 2.5–8X28MM

Weaver

CLASSIC K-SERIES 4X28MM

Weight: 14.2 oz.
Length: 9.17 in.
Power: 4X
Obj.Dia.: 38mm
Main Dia.: 1 in.
Exit Pupil: 7mm
Field of View: 8.5 ft @ 100 yds
Twilight Factor: 12.33
Eye Relief: 9.45 in.
Features: Crafted from a one-piece aircraft-grade aluminum tube; built to take heavy recoil punishment and hold zero to 10,000 rounds from a .375 H&H magnum rifle; presents a consistent field of view that's perfect for open field hunting and are among the easiest scopes any instinctive shooter will ever use; also in 4x38, 6x38, 8x56
MSRP . . . . $245–$522

CLASSIC RIMFIRE 3–9X32MM

Weight: 12 oz.
Length: 11.5 in.
Power: 3–9X
Obj.Dia.: 28mm
Main Dia.: 1 in.
Exit Pupil: 10.6mm
Field of View: 33.2–11 ft @ 100 yds
Twilight Factor: 9.17–15.87
Eye Relief: 3.58 in.
Features: Variable and fixed power models; non-glare lenses that produce edge-sharp, low-light brightness; rugged, aircraft-grade, one-piece aluminum construction; parallax is set at 50 yards; also in 2.5–7x28 (matte, silver) and 4x28
MSRP . . . . $222–$413

GRAND SLAM 3–12X50MM

Weight: 16.6 oz.
Length: 12.6 in.
Power: 3–12X
Obj. Dia.: 50mm
Main Dia.: 1 in.
Exit Pupil: 13.6–4.2mm
Field of View: 32.7–8.4 ft @ 100 yds
Twilight Factor: 12.2–24.5
Eye Relief: 3.19–3.46 in.
Features: 4x magnification ranges; ground, fully multi-coated lenses; fogproof; side focus parallax adjustments on select models; multiple reticle options; available in 2–8x36, 3–12x42, and 4–16x44; matte finish
MSRP . . . . $599–$880

KASPA HUNTER SERIES 3–9X40MM

Weight: 11.5 oz.
Length: 12.4 in.
Power: 3–9X
Obj. Dia.: 40mm
Main Dia.: 1 in.
Exit Pupil: 13–4.4mm
Field of View: 32.6–11 ft @ 100 yds
Twilight Factor: 10.95–18.97
Eye Relief: 4.37 in.–3.81 in.
Features: Fogproof; nitrogen purged; illuminated Dual-X reticle; 4–16x44 also available
MSRP . . . . $158–$215

KASPA TACTICAL 1–4X24MM

Weight: N/A
Length: 10.5 in.
Power: 1–4X
Obj. Dia.: 24mm
Main Dia.: 30mm
Exit Pupil: 6–13mm
Field of View: 27–109 ft @ 100 yds
Twilight Factor: 4.9–9.8
Eye Relief: 3.54–4 in.
Features: Illuminated Dual-X reticle; tactical 30mm tube; 1/4 MOA adjustments; fully multi-coated lenses; fogproof; matte finish
MSRP $361

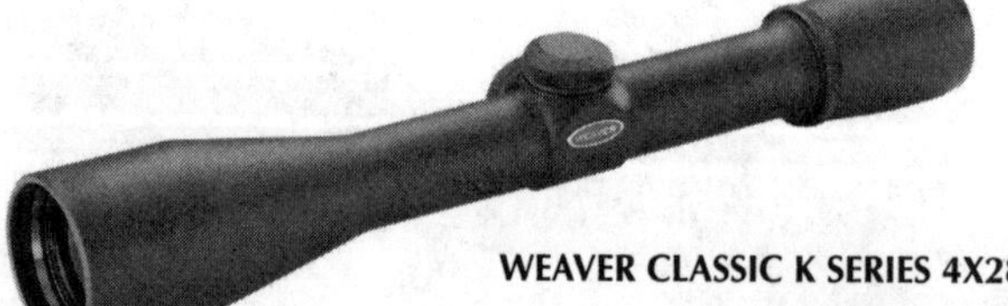

WEAVER CLASSIC K SERIES 4X28MM

WEAVER GRAND SLAM 3–12X50MM

WEAVER CLASSIC RIMFIRE 3–9X32MM

WEAVER KASPA TACTICAL 1–4X24MM

WEAVER KASPA HUNTER SERIES 3–9X40MM

WEAVER KASPA TACTICAL SERIES 2.5–10X50MM

WEAVER KASPA TACTICAL SERIES 3–12X44MM

KASPA TACTICAL SERIES 2.5–10X50MM

Weight: 25.04 oz.
Length: 12.79 in.
Power: 2.5–10X
Obj. Dia.: 50mm
Main Dia.: 30mm
Exit Pupil: 20–5mm
Field of View: 37.3 ft @ 100 yds
Twilight Factor: 11.18–22.36
Eye Relief: 3.74–3.15 in.
Features: Rugged one-piece tube construction; nitrogen purged to eliminate internal fogging; fully multi-coated lenses; crisp ¼-inch MOA adjustments; Dual-X, Ballistic-X, TBX, and Tactical Mil-Dot reticles on various models; also in 1x20, 1.5–6x32, 2.5–10x44, 2–7x32, 309x40, 3–12x44, 3–12x50, 4–16x44
MSRP $355

KASPA TACTICAL SERIES 3–12X44MM

Weight: 24.3 oz.
Length: 12.99 in.
Power: 3–12X
Obj. Dia.: 44mm
Main Dia.: 30mm
Exit Pupil: 14.6–3.7mm
Field of View: 31.4–7.9 ft @ 100 yds
Twilight Factor: 11.49–22.98
Eye Relief: 3.74 in.
Features: Front focal plane; fogproof; nitrogen purged; illuminated reticle; side focus
MSRP . . . . $281–$373

SUPER SLAM 4–20X50MM

Weight: 24 oz.
Length: 13.31 in.
Power: 4–20X
Obj.Dia.: 50mm
Main Dia.: 1 in.
Exit Pupil: 10.5–2.44mm
Field of View: 24.5–4.9 ft @ 100 yds
Twilight Factor: 14.14–31.62
Eye Relief: 3.98 in.
Features: Line of premier riflescopes designed for the serious big game hunter and shooter; side focus adjustable parallax; pull-up turrets; also in 1–5x24, 2–10x42, 2–10x50, 3–15x42, 3–15x50; in silver or matte black; EBX or Dual-x reticle available
MSRP . . . .$969–$1040

WEAVER SUPER SLAM 4–20X50MM

WEAVER TACTICAL 1–5X24MM

TACTICAL 1–5X24MM

Weight: 14.46 oz.
Length: 10.31 in.
Power: 1–5X
Obj.Dia.: 24mm
Main Dia.: 30mm
Exit Pupil: 11.4–4.9mm
Field of View: 100–19.9 ft @ 100 yds
Twilight Factor: 4.9–10.95
Eye Relief: 4.25 in.
Features: Rugged riflescopes designed specifically for tactical applications; extra hard coating on exterior lenses; first focal plane reticles; side focus parallax adjustment; reset-to-zero turrets; one-piece tube construction; also in 3–15x50 and 4–20x50; Mil-Dot, CIRT, and EMDR reticles on some scopes
MSRP $1197

Aimpoint

2 MOA MICRO H-1 AND T-1

Weight: 3 oz.
Length: 2.4 in.
Power: 1X
Features: High quality compact red-dot sight; sealed design ensures that no foreign matter will come between the emitter and the lens; can be mounted on nearly any individual weapon platform including: pistols, carbines, personal defense weapons, and sub-machineguns; also available in 4 MOA red-dot
H-1: . . . . $617–$709
T-1:. . . . . $681–$801

PATROL RIFLE OPTIC (PRO)

Weight: 7.8 oz.
Length: 5.1 in.
Power: 1X
Features: Parallax free optic; 2 MOA dot for accurate target engagement at all distances; four night vision settings and six daylight settings; modular QRP2 mount includes removable spacer that indexes the sight at optimal height for co-witness, with the standard iron sights on AR15/M16/M4 carbine style weapons
MSRP $424

AIMPOINT 2 MOA MICRO H-1

9000SC

Weight: 7.4 oz.
Length: 6.3 in.
Obj. Dia.: 38mm
Features: Ideal for short length action rifles, semi-automatic firearms, and magnum handguns; ACET technology for longer battery life; available in 2 or 4 MOA dot sizes; two-ring configuration for mounting; waterproof; matte finish
From: . . . . $436–$653

AIMPOINT PATROL RIFLE OPTIC

AIMPOINT 9000SC

Browning

BROWNING 2–1 HUNTING SIGHTS

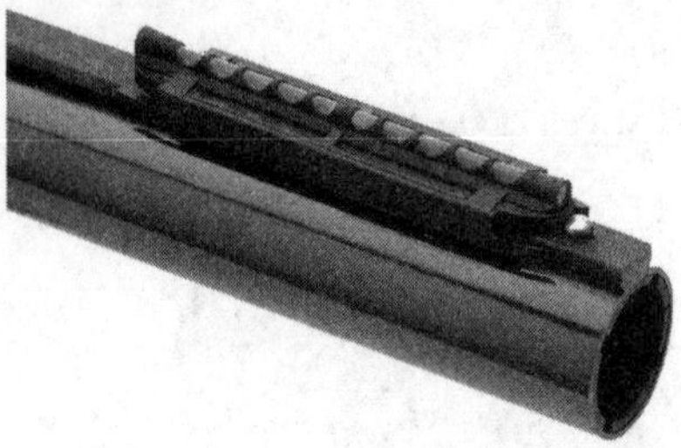

2–1 HUNTING SIGHTS

Features: Magnetic base attaches to shotgun rib; features both red and green LitePipes; comes with both round and triangular LitePipe systems; designed for guns with narrow ribs
MSRP $39

BROWNING BUCK MARK REFLEX SIGHT

BUCK MARK REFLEX SIGHT

Weight: N/A
Power: 1X
Field of View: 47 ft @ 100 yds
Eye Relief: Unlimited
Features: The Buck Mark has an aluminum housing, four red reticle patterns, a seven-position brightness rheostat powered by a lithium battery, and mounts on a standard Weaver-styled base
MSRP $88

BURRIS AR–1X PRISM

AR–1X PRISM

Weight: 13.2 oz.
Length: 4 in.
Power: 1X
Field of View: 75 ft @ 100 yds
Eye Relief: 3.5 in.
Features: Ballistic CQ 1X red, green, or black reticle; lens covers; night vision compatible
MSRP . . . . $335–$539

AR-536

Weight: 18.75 oz.
Length: 5.75 in.
Power: 5X
Obj. Dia.: 36mm
Field of View: 20 ft @ 100 yds
Eye Relief: 2.5–3.5 in.
Features: Ballistic/CQTM lighted reticle; 600 yard range; multi-coated lenses; adjustable diopter; three Picatinny rail mounting points; black matte finish; max adj. 60 MOA; one-year warranty
MSRP . . . . $479–$659

FASTFIRE III RED-DOT REFLEX SIGHT

Weight: 0.9 oz.
Power: 1.07X
Features: Upgraded features such as windage and elevation adjustments that don't require a special tool; 3 or 8 MOA Dot; power button with three levels of brightness; low battery warning indicator and see-through protective cap; ideally suited for use on pistols and AR-15s where fast target acquisition is desired, the FastFire red-dot sight will also match up well with carbines, lever guns, and shotguns; available picatinny mount
MSRP . . . . $287–$299

BURRIS AR-536

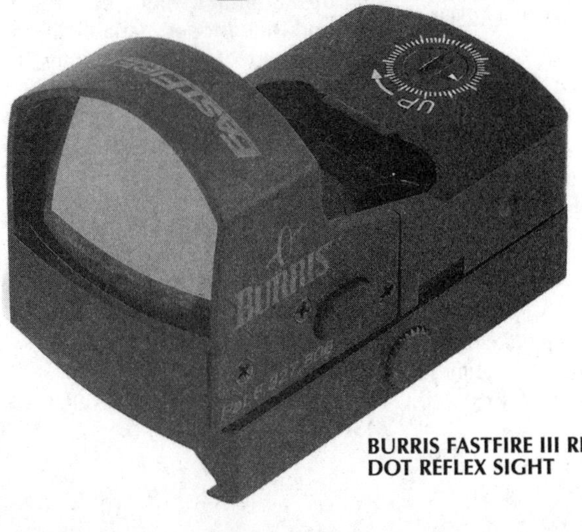

BURRIS FASTFIRE III RED-DOT REFLEX SIGHT

Bushnell Performance Optics

BUSHNELL 2X MP ELECTRONIC SIGHT

2X MP ELECTRONIC SIGHT

Weight: 15.6 oz.
Length: 6.75 in.
Power: 2X
Obj. Dia.: 32mm
Exit Pupil: 32mm
Field of View: 44 ft @ 100 yds
Eye Relief: Unlimited
Features: With the ability to display the T-dot reticle in green during low light and red during bright light, the 2X MP offers the versatility shooters demand from electronic sights. With two power magnification and multi-coated optics, the sight is ideal for acquiring close- to mid-range targets.
MSRP **$341**

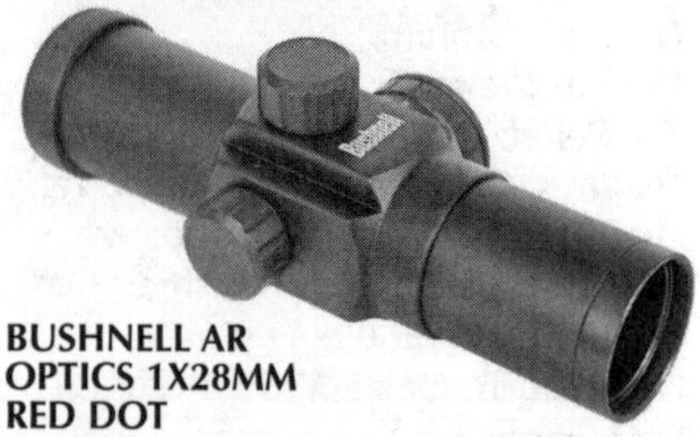

BUSHNELL AR OPTICS 1X28MM RED DOT

AR OPTICS 1X28MM RED DOT

Weight: 6 oz.
Length: 5.5 in.
Power: 1X
Obj. Dia.: 28mm
Exit Pupil: 28mm
Field of View: 68 ft @ 100 yds
Eye Relief: unlimited
Features: 6 MOA red dot sight; eleven brightness settings; tactical rings for variably mounts and heights; matte finish
MSRP: **$117**

BUSHNELL FIRST STRIKE RED DOT

BUSHNELL ELITE 1 MILE ARC

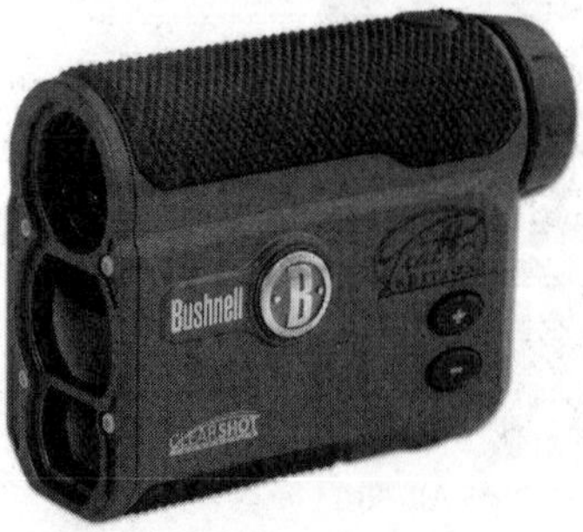

BUSHNELL THE TRUTH WITH CLEARSHOT

OPTICS

ELITE 1 MILE ARC

Weight: 12.1 oz.
Power: 7X
Obj. Dia.: 26mm
Range: 5–1760 yd
Features: Waterproof; built-in tripod mount; fully multi-coated lenses
MSRP **$599**

SCOUT DX 1000

Weight: 6.6 oz.
Power: 6X
Features: Built-in inclinometer; ARC Bow and Rifle Modes; Variable Sight-in; range up to 1,000 yds; diopter adjustment; waterproof; compatible with magnetic attachment system; available in black or RealTree AP
MSRP **$477**

THE TRUTH WITH CLEARSHOT

Weight: 6 oz.
Power: 4X
Obj. Dia.: 28mm
Range: 7–850 yd
Features: Rainproof and pocket-sized
MSRP **$280**

BUSHNELL SCOUT DX 1000

FIRST STRIKE RED DOT

Weight: 2.1 oz.
Length: 2.4 in.
Field of View: unlimited
Eye Relief: unlimited
Features: 5 MOA red dot reticle; multi-coated optics; self-regulating brightness; integrated mount; waterproof; fogproof; shockproof; matte finish
MSRP **$209**

Bushnell Performance Optics

BUSHNELL TRS-25 HIRISE

TRS-25 HIRISE

Weight: 6.3 oz.
Length: 2.4 in.
Power: 1X
Obj. Dia.: 25mm
Exit Pupil: 22mm
Field of View: unlimited
Eye Relief: unlimited
Features: 3 MOA red dot reticle; eleven brightness settings; multi-coated; waterproof; fogproof; shockproof; riser block; matte finish
MSRP **$171**

Cabela's

CABELA'S TACTICAL RED DOT SIGHT

CABELA'S TACTICAL REFLEX SIGHT

TACTICAL RED DOT SIGHT

Features: Bullet-drop-compensating reticle; reticle features three selectable colors; five adjustable brightness settings; multi-coated optics for low-light shooting; waterproof; shockproof; runs up to 300 hours on one battery
MSRP **$300**

TACTICAL REFLEX SIGHT

Features: Automatically turns on when cap is lifted; automatic reticle-brightness control; multi-coated optics with 5 MOA center-dot reticle; waterproof; shockproof; mounts to any Picatinny rail; runs for up to 300 hours on one battery
MSRP **$150**

Carl Zeiss Sports Optics

CARL ZEISS VICTORY COMPACT POINT SIGHT

VICTORY COMPACT POINT SIGHT

Weight: 2.64 oz.
Length: 2.28 in.
Power: 1.05X
Features: LotuTec coating; single button on/off and five level brightness; 25 percent wider than conventional reflex sites for natural viewing with both eyes; Blaser integrated mount allows mounting directly on barrel while standard mount allows mounting on Picatinny/Weaver rail
Standard: **$578**
Blaser: **$800**

CARL ZEISS Z-POINT

Z-POINT (RED DOT REFLEX SIGHT)

Weight: 5.65 oz.
Length: 2.5 in.
Power: 1X
Features: Acquisition sight for shotguns, rifles, and handguns; dual-source illuminated: a solar cell for daylight hours and battery power for dark; red dot automatically adapts to brightness of surroundings and can be regulated manually; available for Weaver or Picatinny mounts
MSRP **$667**

EOTech

EOTECH HOLOGRAPHIC HYBRID SIGHT

HOLOGRAPHIC HYBRID SIGHT (HHS)

Power: 3.25X
Eye Relief: 2.2 in.
Features: The HHS kits combine the speed of the EXPS holographic weapon sight and the extended range versatility of the new 3.25x G33 magnifier; includes the night vision compatible EXPS3–4 HWS with the four-dot reticle calibrated for shooting at 0–300, 400, 500 and 600 meters; includes the EXPS2–2 and non-night vision compatible sight with a two-dot reticle for fast action targeting
MSRP $1079

EOTECH MODEL 512 LASER BATTERY CAP

MODEL 512 LASER BATTERY CAP

Weight: 12.6 oz.
Length: 5.4 in.
Power: 1X
Field of View: N/A
Twilight Factor:
Eye Relief: N/A
Features: Submersible to 10 feet; twenty daylight settings; fully adjustable windage and elevation
MSRP $729

EOTECH MODEL 552 LASER BATTERY CAP

MODEL 552 LASER BATTERY CAP

Weight: 13.4 oz.
Length: 5.4 in.
Power: 1X
Field of View: N/A
Eye Relief: N/A
Features: Submersible to 33 feet; twenty daylight settings, ten additional settings for Gen I through III+ night vision devices; fully adjustable windage and elevation
MSRP $979

EOTECH XPS2-300 BLACKOUT

XPS2-300 BLACKOUT

Weight: 8 oz.
Length: 3.5 in.
Power: 1X
Field of View: 90 ft @ 100 yds
Eye Relief: Unlimited
Features: Two dot ballistic drop reticle for either subsonic or supersonic rounds; mounts to 1-in. Weaver or Picatinny rail; repeatable to within 1 MOA when remounting; runs 600 continuous hours; 65 MOA Ring with two 1 MOA aiming dots; waterproof to 10 ft; fogproof; 20 brightness settings; anti-glare coating
MSRP $549

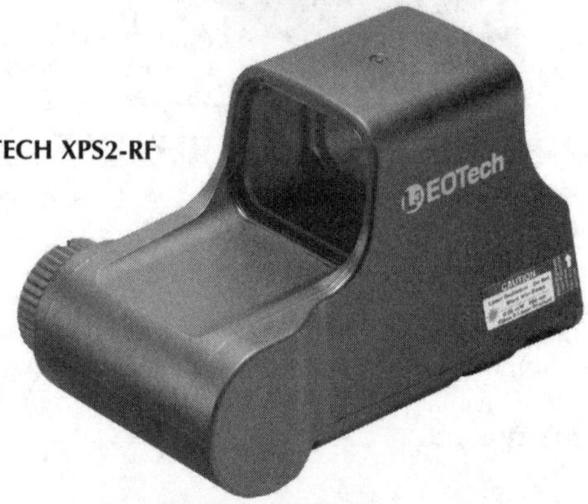

EOTECH XPS2-RF

XPS2-RF

Weight: 7 oz.
Length: 3.5 in.
Power: 1X
Eye Relief: Unlimited
Features: Holographic sight specifically for the rimfire rifle; integrated $^{3}/_{8}$-in. dovetail mount (not compatible with 1-in. Weaver or Picatinny rails); lightweight for smaller platforms; single transverse 123 battery to reduce sight length; shortened base; this model is only intended and warranted for calibers .22LR or smaller
MSRP $405

EOTech

EOTECH XPS2-Z
ZOMBIE STOPPER

XPS2-Z ZOMBIE STOPPER

Features: 20 brightness settings; 600 hours of run time on one battery; 65 MOA ring with 1 MOA aiming dot; cool biohazard tails to kill zombies deader
MSRP $579

Halo Optics

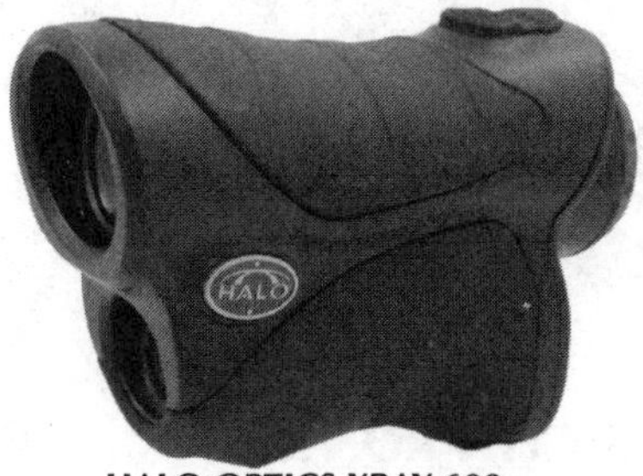

HALO OPTICS XRAY 600

HALO OPTICS XRAY 900

HALO OPTICS XRT

XRAY 600

Weight: 5.3 oz.
Power: 6X
Obj. Dia.: 23mm
Range: up to 600 yd
Features: Water resistent; Angle Intelligence compensation technology
MSRP $165

XRAY 900

Weight: N/A
Power: 9X
Obj. Dia.: N/A
Range: up to 900 yd
Features: Water resistent; Angle Intelligence compensation technology
MSRP $220

XRT

Weight: 8 oz.
Power: 6X
Obj. Dia.: 24mm
Range: up to 500 yd
Features: Water resistent; anti-fog
MSRP $132

Konus

KONUS SIGHTPRO ATOMIC 2.0

KONUS SIGHTPRO ATOMIC QR

KONUS SIGHTPRO FISSION 2.0

KONUS SIGHTPRO PTS1

KONUS SIGHTPRO TR

SIGHTPRO ATOMIC 2.0

Weight: 3.8 oz.
Length: 2.4 in.
Power: 1X
Field of View: 76 ft @ 100 yds
Eye Relief: N/A
Features: Illuminated reticle dots; fits both Picatinny and Weaver rails
MSRP $180

SIGHTPRO ATOMIC QR

Weight: 6.5 oz.
Length: 2.5 in.
Power: 1X
Field of View: N/A
Eye Relief: N/A
Features: Illuminated reticle dots; fits both Picatinny and Weaver rails
MSRP $230

SIGHTPRO FISSION 2.0

Weight: 1.76 oz.
Length: 1.7 in.
Power: 1X
Field of View: 115 ft @ 100 yds
Eye Relief: N/A
Features: Illuminated reticle dots; fits both Picatinny and Weaver rails
MSRP $180

SIGHTPRO PTS1

Weight: 14.1 oz.
Length: 12.2 in.
Power: 3X
Obj. Dia.: 32mm
Field of View: 36.6 ft @ 100 yds
Eye Relief: 4.5 in.
Features: Shock-, water-, and fog-proof; illuminated reticle dots; fits both Picatinny and Weaver rails
MSRP $400

SIGHTPRO TR

Weight: 13 oz.
Length: 4.75 in.
Power: 1X
Field of View: N/A
Eye Relief: N/A
Features: Illuminated reticle dots; four different reticle patterns
MSRP $220

Leica

RANGEMASTER CRF 1000-R

Weight: 7.8 oz.
Length: 4.4 in.
Power: 7X
Obj. Dia.: 24mm
Field of View: 345 ft @ 100 yds
Features: Starter model; basic ballistic funtionality; measures linear and horizontal distance; integrated diopter compensation; automatic brightness control; LED display; angle-of-inclination display
MSRP. $600

LEICA RANGEMASTER CRF 1000-R

LEICA RANGEMASTER CRF 1600-B

RANGEMASTER CRF 1600-B

Weight: 8.1 oz.
Length: 4.4 in.
Power: 7X
Obj. Dia.: 24mm
Field of View: 345 ft @ 100 yds
Features: Point-of-aim correction, angle, temperature, and barometric pressure readings; ABC intelligent ballistics program; LED display; range up to 1600 yds; waterproof
MSRP. $800

Leatherwood/Hi-Lux

LEATHERWOOD/ HI-LUX TAC-DOT

TAC-DOT

Weight: 2.1 oz.
Length: 2.5 in.
Power: 1X
Obj. Dia.: 21x16mm
Field of View: 30x22 ft @ 100 yds
Eye Relief: N/A
Features: Elevation and windage adjustments are 50 MOA per revolution; special illumination circuit is designed to control the illuminated dot size in a consistent shape and size; dot size is 4 MOA; light sensor will control the brightness of the dot automatically based on the light situation
MSRP. $130

Leupold & Stevens

DELTAPOINT REFLEX SIGHT

Weight: 0.6 oz.
Length: 1.66 in.
Features: For use on handguns, shotguns, and AR-style rifles; includes numerous mounting options; an aspheric lens, motion activation, auto-brightness sensor, locking elevation and windage adjustment system, and a magnesium housing; 7.5 MOA Delta and 3.5 MOA Dot reticles available
Cross-Slot mount: $500
Other mounts:. $565

PRISMATIC HUNTING 1X14MM

Weight: 12 oz.
Length: 4.5 in.
Power: 1X
Main Dia.: 30mm
Field of View: 83 ft @ 100 yds
Eye Relief: 3 in.
Features: Fast target acquisition of a non-magnifying red-dot sight with a wide field of view; etched-glass reticle that is visible with or without illumination; ½ MOA finger-adjustable windage and elevation dials; focusing eyepiece; black matte finish or dark earth anodized finish and with Circle Plex or DCD reticles
MSRP $625

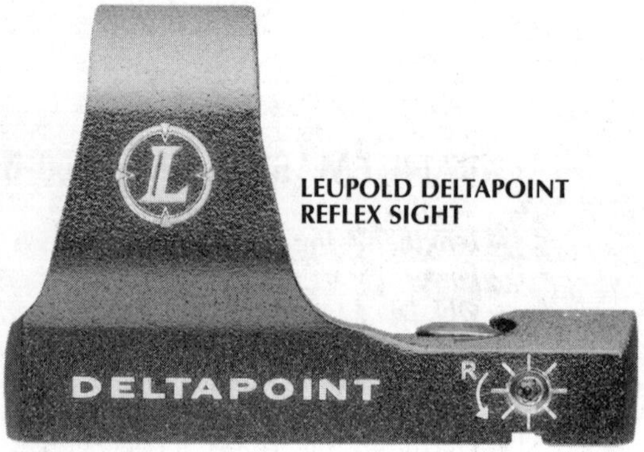

LEUPOLD DELTAPOINT REFLEX SIGHT

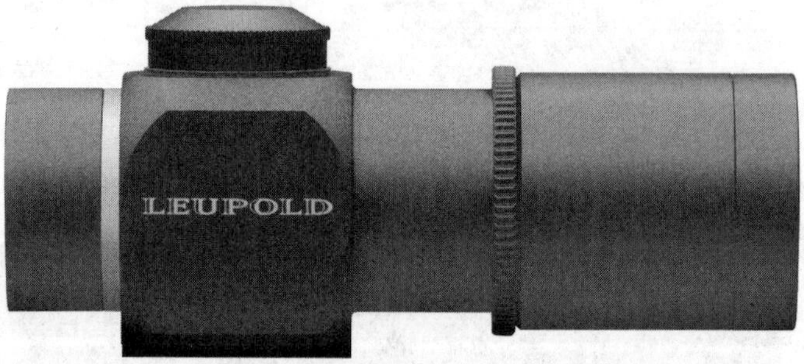

LEUPOLD PRISMATIC HUNTING 1X14MM

OPTICS

Lucid

LUCID HD7 RED DOT SIGHT

HD7 RED DOT SIGHT

Weight: 13 oz.
Length: 5.5 in.
Power: 1X
Obj.Dia.: 34mm
Field of View: 44 ft @ 100 yds
Eye Relief: Unlimited
Features: Third generation unit; integral Picatinny rail and reversible mounting pins for bullpup-style firearms; manual and a Auto-bBrightness with twelve brightness settings; four operator-selectable reticles based on a 2 MOA dot with ½ MOA click adjustments; parallax free, it is powered by one AAA battery; the frame is cast aluminum armored in chemical rubber and is available with a 2x screw-in eyepiece; available in tan
MSRP $249

Lucid

LUCID M7 MICRO RED DOT

M7 MICRO RED DOT

Weight: 4.6 oz.
Obj. Dia.: 21mm
Field of View: 48 ft @ 100 yds
Eye Relief: Unlimited
Features: 2 MOA dot 25 MOA circle reticle; auto brightness sensor; auto shut off; seven brightness levels; capped and leashed turrets; ½ MOA adjustments; parallax free; waterproof; fogproof; shockproof; cast aluminum; Limited Lifetime Warranty
MSRP $229

Meopta

MEOPTA MEOSIGHT III

MEOSIGHT III

Weight: 1.29 oz.
Length: 1.8 in.
Power: 1X
Field of View: N/A
Eye Relief: N/A
Features: Picatinny quick release mount; illuminated reticle; ideal for handguns, shotguns, and tactical weapons
MSRP $459

Millet Optics

SP SERIES RED DOT

Features: Precision-click adjustments; dot intensity control with eleven settings; waterproof; shockproof; available with 1 in. or 30mm tube; available 3 MOA dot, 5 MOA dot, and 3, 5, 8, 10 MOA, multi dot; available in matte or silver
MSRP . . . . $80–$110

MILLETT OPTICS SCOPES (BUSHNELL) SP SERIES RED DOT

Nikon

NIKON ACULON AL11

ACULON AL11

Weight: 4.4 oz.
Power: 6X
Obj. Dia.: 20mm
Range: 6–550 yd
Features: Ultra-compact for improved portability; multilayered lens coatings for higher light transmittance
MSRP. $170

PROSTAFF 7 LASER RANGEFINDER

Weight: 5.8 oz.
Length: 4.4 in.
Power: 6X
Obj. Dia.: 21mm
Exit Pupil: 3.5mm
Field of View: 11–600 yds
Eye Relief: 0.7 in.
Features: Multi-coated optics; waterproof; fogproof; Tru Target Technology; switchable display; Nikon's ID Technology; angle compensation
MSRP. $300

NIKON PROSTAFF 7 LASER RANGEFINDER

Pedersoli

ENGLISH REAR SIGHT, MODEL USA 428

Features: Rear sight with convex base, with two adjustable and folding leaves
From:. $140

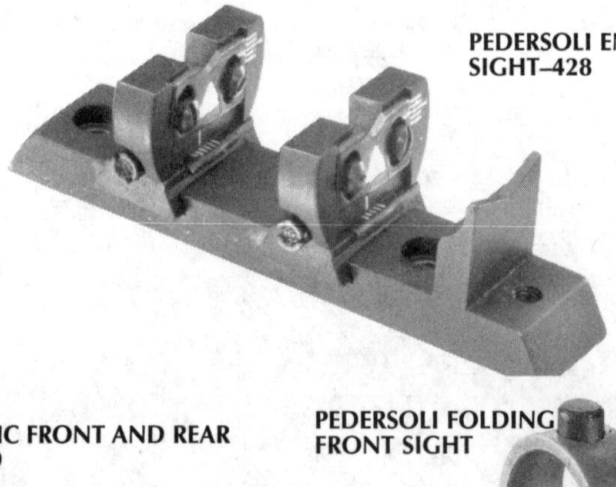

PEDERSOLI ENGLISH REAR SIGHT–428

FIBER OPTIC FRONT AND REAR SIGHT, MODEL USA 409

Features: Front sight and rear sight set for muzzleloading rifles (Model 410 for breechloaders); front sight with dovetail base; rear sight with base for octagonal barrel
From:. $125

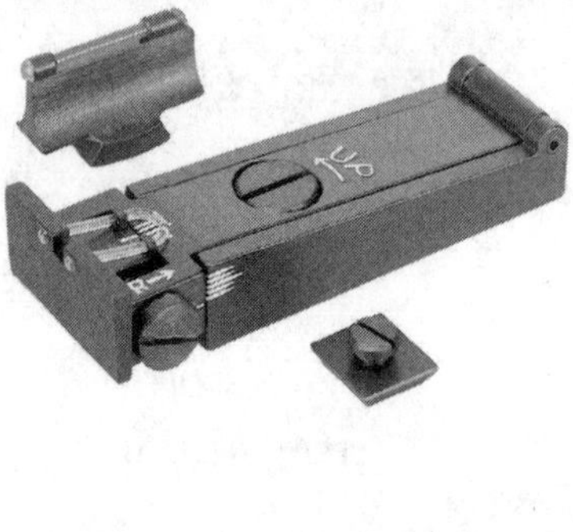

FIBER OPTIC FRONT AND REAR SIGHT–409

FOLDING FRONT SIGHT

Features: Globe sight for long-range when raised, or fold down for built-in blade for close range; ball/detent locking mechanism; 3/8-in. dovetail base; ½-in. high
From:. $69

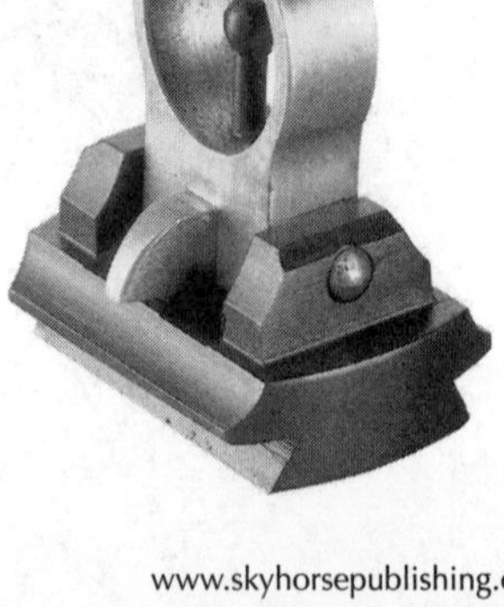

PEDERSOLI FOLDING FRONT SIGHT

Pedersoli

"GHOST" TANG SIGHT USA 422

Features: A tang sight inspired by some models in use in the 1800s, economic, functional, and useful for hunting; adjustable in elevation and windage; can fit several gun types; small eye piece ring enables a quick, instinctive aim at the target; when quickly shouldering the rifle, the open ring provides a clear sight picture with low light condition; distance between the two mounting holes is 1 ¾-in.

From:. $75

"SOULE TYPE" MIDDLE RANGE SET, MODEL USA 170

Features: Wooden-box set including Soule XL Middle Range Sight; tunnel front sight with a micrometric screw for windage adjustment, spirit level, and fifteen interchangeable inserts; professional "Hadley Style" eyepiece with eight varying diameter viewing holes, depending on available light, on a rotating disk which can be selected without disassembling or loosening the eyepiece, and a rubber ring on the eyepiece; six interchangeable glass bubbles (spirit level) with different colors for varying light conditions; 3-in. elevation adjustment

From:. $549

SPIRIT LEVEL TUNNEL SIGHT ADJUSTABLE WITH 12 INSERTS SET, MODEL USA 425

Features: Spirit level tunnel sight with micrometer adjustment for windage, equipped with twelve interchangeable inserts

From:. . . . . $30–$150

PEDERSOLI U.S. MODEL 1879 SPRINGFIELD TRAPDOOR REAR SIGHT–473

150 UNIVERSAL CREEDMOOR SIGHT, MIDDLE AND LONG RANGE, MODELS USA 465 AND 430

Features: Tang sight with elevation and windage adjustment in the eye piece; for long-distance target shooting both with muzzle-loading and breech-loading rifles; 2.1875–2.3125-in. between two mounting holes; 2- and 3-in. elevation adjustments

From:. . . . . $163–$271

U.S. MODEL 1879 SPRINGFIELD TRAPDOOR REAR SIGHT, MODEL USA 473

Features: Sometimes referred to as "Buckhorn" style; used on Trapdoor rifles from 1874 until superseded by Buffington style in 1884; side ramps are graduated to 500 yds and the ladder to 1500 yds; slide has windage adjustment

From:. $140

PEDERSOLI UNIVERSAL CREEDMOOR SIGHT–430

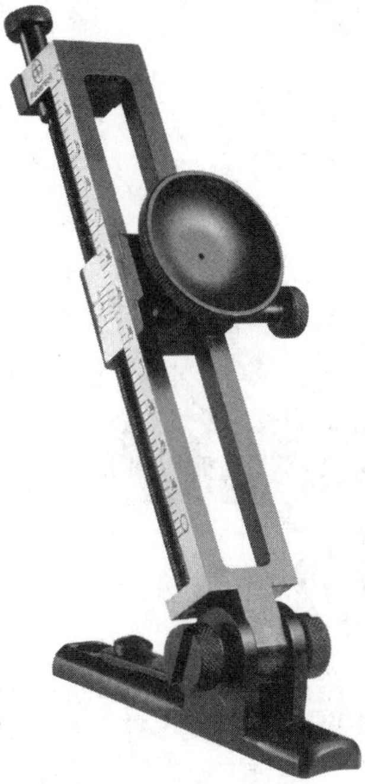

PEDERSOLI "GHOST" TANG SIGHT USA 422

PEDERSOLI "SOULE TYPE" MIDDLE RANGE SET-170

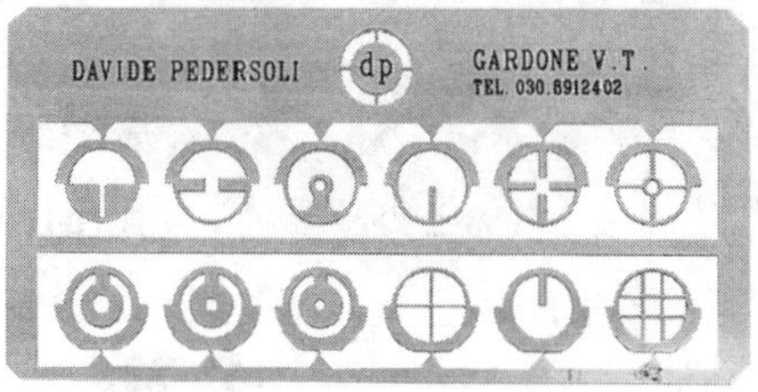

PEDERSOLI SPIRIT LEVEL TUNNEL SIGHT ADJUSTABLE–425

Pentax Imaging Co.

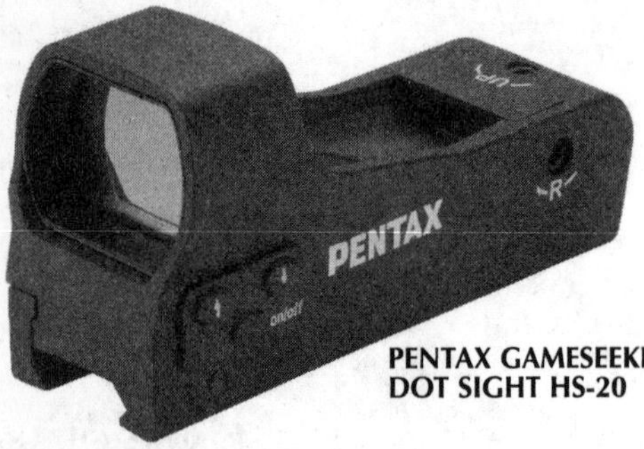

PENTAX GAMESEEKER DOT SIGHT HS-20

PENTAX GAMESEEKER DOT SIGHT RD-10

GAMESEEKER DOT SIGHT HS-20

Weight: 3.4 oz.
Length: 3.9 in.
Power: 1X
Field of View: 55–50 ft @ 100 yds
Features: 5 MOA dot with 11 brightness settings and 72 hours of continuous battery use; continuous, non-click adjustments; Weaver-style mounting system
MSRP $59

GAMESEEKER DOT SIGHT RD-10

Weight: 7.07 oz.
Length: 3.8 in.
Power: 1X
Obj.Dia.: 30mm
Main Dia.: 39mm
Field of View: 54 ft @ 100 yds
Features: Reflex sight with a 4 MOA dot; 11 brightness settings; 72 hours continuous battery life; continuous windage and elevation adjustments; Weaver-style mounting system
MSRP $69

Redfield by Leupold

REDFIELD ACCELERATOR

REDFIELD COUNTERSTRIKE 1X30MM TACTICAL RED DOT

ACCELERATOR

Weight: 1 oz.
Length: 1.92 in.
Power: 1X
Field of View: N/A
Eye Relief: N/A
Features: Shock- and waterproof; perfect for shotguns, rifles, and handguns; compatible with both Picatinny or Weaver-style rails or mounts
MSRP $199

COUNTERSTRIKE 1X30MM TACTICAL RED DOT

Weight: 14.8 oz.
Length: 5.9 in.
Power: 1X
Obj. Dia.: 30mm
Exit Pupil: 30mm
Eye Relief: Unlimited
Features: Coin-click ½ MOA adjustments; tethered adjustment covers; 4 MOA red/green dot; auto shut off; up to 5,000 hour battery life; waterproof; fogproof; shockproof; Redfield "No Excuses" warranty
From: $180

Trijicon

TRIJICON GLOCK SUPPRESSOR BRIGHT & TOUGH NIGHT SIGHTS

TRIJICON RMR ADJUSTABLE LED RM06

TRIJICON SRS 1X38

GLOCK SUPPRESSOR BRIGHT & TOUGH NIGHT SIGHTS

Features: Three-dot iron sights; shock-resistant design; increase night-fire accuracy by as much as 5x; fits the 17, 17L, 19, 22, 23, 24, 26, 27, 33, 34, 35, 38, and 39 Glock Models; available in black or white outline, with a green, orange, or yellow tritium lamp

MSRP. . . . . $44–$173

RMR ADJUSTABLE LED RM06

Weight: 1.2 oz.
Length: 1.77 in.
Power: 1X
Features: LED sight powered by standard CR2032 battery; rugged forged aluminum; adjusters with audible clicks allow for quick windage and elevation adjustments; eight brightness settings; reticle can be manually adjusted; also in Dual-Illuminated RMR with 13.0 MOA dot, 7.0 MOA dot, 9.0 MOA dot, and triangle-reticle RMR LED with 3.25 MOA dot and 6.5 MOA dot
MSRP: $708

SRS (SEALED REFLEX SIGHT) 1X38

Weight: 13.8 oz.
Length: 3.75 in.
Power: 1X
Obj. Dia.: 38mm
Features: Body length of only 3.75 inches virtually eliminates the "tube effect" common with other, competitive red-dot sights; field of view provides no obstruction to shooters; LED 1.75 MOA aiming point with 10 brightness settings; SRS powered by solar panel and AA battery; parallax free objective lens; available in Colt-Style flattop mount or Quick Release flattop mount
MSRP: . . . . $1350–$1425

Truglo

TRUGLO TRITON 30MM TRI-COLOR TACTICAL RED DOT

TRITON 30MM TRI-COLOR TACTICAL RED DOT

Weight: 6.4 oz.
Length: 5.2 in.
Power: 1X
Obj. Dia.: 30mm
Field of View: N/A
Eye Relief: N/A
Features: Weaver style mount; multi-coated lenses; tri-color illuminated reticle
MSRP. $160

OPTICS

Vortex

VORTEX SPARC II

VORTEX SPITFIRE PRISM

VORTEX STRIKEFIRE II CANTILEVER

SPARC II

Weight: 5.9 oz.
Length: 3.1 in.
Power: 1X
Field of View: N/A
Eye Relief: N/A
Features: Shock-, water-, and fogproof; illuminated red dot
MSRP **$259**

SPITFIRE PRISM

Weight: 12.2 oz.
Length: 5.5 in.
Power: 3X
Field of View: 31.5 ft @ 100 yds
Eye Relief: 2.8 in.
Features: Shock-, water-, and fogproof; illuminated red dot; 1X available
MSRP . . . . **$399–$449**

STRIKEFIRE II CANTILEVER

Weight: 7.2 oz.
Length: 5.6 in.
Power: 1X
Field of View: N/A
Eye Relief: N/A
Features: Shock-, water-, and fogproof; illuminated red dot; red/green dot cantilever and low mount models available
MSRP **$239**

OPTICS

Weaver

WEAVER MICRO DOT SIGHT

MICRO DOT SIGHT

Weight: 2.8 oz.
Length: 1.9 in.
Power: 1X
Eye Relief: Unlimited
Features: 4 MOA red dot reticle; matte finish; mounts to most firearms; adjustable brightness
MSRP **$108**

478 Barnes Bullets
478 Black Hills Ammunition
479 Brenneke USA
480 CCI Ammunition
482 Cor-Bon
483 ENVIRON-Metal
484 Federal Fusion Ammunition
485 Federal Premium Ammunition
490 Fiocchi USA
492 GECO
492 Hornady
495 Jarrett Rifles
495 Kynoch Ammunition
496 Lapua
496 Magtech Ammunition
497 Norma Ammunition
498 Nosler
499 PMC Ammunition
500 Remington Ammunition
505 Rottweil
505 RUAG Swiss P
506 Sig Sauer
506 Weatherby
506 Winchester Ammunition

MUZZLELOADING BULLETS

514 Barnes Bullets
515 Harvester
515 Hornady
516 Knight Rifles
516 PowerBelt
517 Thompson/Center

BULLETS

518 Barnes Bullets
522 Berger Bullets
524 Hornady Bullets
530 Lapua
531 Nosler Bullets
534 Sierra Bullets
538 Speer Bullets
542 Swift Bullets
544 Woodleigh Bullets

Barnes Bullets

TAC-XPD AMMUNITION

Features: Loaded with Barnes TAC-XP bullets, the all-copper construction and very large, deep hollow-point cavity expand, penetrate, and perform consistently and optimally for personal and home defense
Available in: .357 Mag., .380 ACP, 9mm Luger +P, .40 S&W, .45 ACP +P
Box 20: . . . . $23–$28

VOR-TX AMMUNITION

Features: Provides maximum tissue and bone destruction, pass-through penetration, and devastating energy transfer; multiple grooves in the bullet's shank reduce pressure and improve accuracy; bullets open instantly on contact causing the nose to peel back into four sharp-edged copper petals destroying tissue, bone, and vital organs for a quick, humane kill; handgun, Safari, and rifle lines.
Available in: rifle line: .223 Rem., 5.56 NATO, .243 Win., .22-250 Rem., .25-06 Rem., .260 Rem., .270 Win., .280 Rem., .270 WSM, 7mm–08 Rem., 7mm Rem. Mag., 7x64 Brenneke, .30-30 Win., .308 Win., .30-06 Spfd., .300 WSM, .300 Win. Mag., .300 RUM, .300 Weatherby Mag., .300 BLK, 8x57 Mauser, .338 Lapua (280 gr.), .338 Win. Mag., .338 Lapua Mag., .35 Whelen, 9.3x62 Mauser, .45-70 Govt.; Safari line: .357 H&H, .416 Rem. Mag., .416 Rigby, .458 Win. Mag., .458 Lott, .470 NE, .500 NE; handgun line: 10mm ACP, .375 Mag., .41 Rem. Mag., .44 Rem. Mag, .45 Colt, .454 Casull
MSRP . . . . $23–$166

BARNES BULLETS TAC-XPD AMMUNITION

BARNES BULLETS VOR-TX AMMUNITION

Black Hills Ammunition

Rifle Ammunition

BLACK HILLS GOLD

Features: Coupling the finest components in the industry with bullets by Barnes, these lead-free non-toxic rounds set a new standard for high-performance hunting ammunition
Available in: .22–250 Rem., .243 Win., .25-06 Rem., .260 Rem., .270 Win., 6.5-284 Norma, 7mm Rem. Mag., .300 Win. Mag., .308 Win., .30-06 Spfd., .338 Lapua
Box 20: . . . . $32–$57

FACTORY NEW RIFLE

Features: Coupling the finest components in the industry with bullets by manufacturers such as Hornady, Barnes, and Nosler, these rounds set a new standard for high-performance hunting ammunition; certain calibers available in Molycoat
Available in: .223 Rem., .308 Win. Match, .300 Win. Mag., .338 Lapua, .338 Norma Mag. , .300 Whisper, 5.56 NATO
Box 20, 50: . . . . $30–$130

REMANUFACTURED

Features: Ammunition designed with the practice shooter in mind, with incredible accuracy for a great price point; the same ammunition used by the U.S. Army Marksmanship Unit in 600 yd matches; has the capability to produce 2-in. groups at 300m
Available in: .223 Rem. (also in Molycoat), .40 S&W
Box 50: . . . . $28–$42

BLACK HILLS FACTORY NEW RIFLE

Black Hills Ammunition

Handgun Ammunition

BLACK HILLS COWBOY ACTION

COWBOY ACTION

Features: Designed to meet the needs of cowboy-action pistol shooters with its new virgin brass and premium-quality hard-cast bullets; velocities are moderate to provide low recoil and excellent accuracy
Available in: .32 H&R, .32-20 Win., .38 LC, .38 Spl., .38-40 Win., .44-40 Win., .44 Russian, .44 Spl., .44 Colt, .45 Schofield, .45 Colt, .38-55 Win., .357 Mag.
Box 50:. . . . . $31–$39

FACTORY NEW HANDGUN

Features: Used by the U.S. Military in all four branches for its reliability
Available in: .32 H&R Mag., .380 ACP, 9mm Luger, .38 Spl., .357 Mag., .40 S&W, .44 Mag., .45 ACP
Box 20:. . . . . $13–$26

Brenneke USA

Shotgun Ammunition
Slugs

28 GAUGE SLUGS

Features: The moderate recoil makes the 28 Ga. a perfect slug for young hunters who will be introduced to slug shooting; 28 Ga. is a multi-talent: small game, home defense, and all around shooting
Available in: 28 Ga. ($2^3/_4$ in.)
Box 5:. . . . . $10–$12

BLACK MAGIC MAGNUM AND SHORT MAGNUM

Features: The Black Magic Magnum and Black Magic Short Magnum are two of the most powerful cartridges available on the market, offering tremendous knockdown power up to 100/60 yds; clean speed coating reduces lead fouling inside the barrel by almost 100 percent
Available in: 12 Ga. ($2^3/_4$ in.), 12 Ga. (3 in.)
Box 5:. . . . . $10–$13

CLASSIC MAGNUM

Features: Invented by Wilhelm Brenneke in 1898, the classic is the ancestor of all modern shotgun slugs; this state-of-the-art slug provides long-range stopping power, consistently flat trajectories, and a patented B.E.T. wad column
Available in: 12 Ga. ($2^3/_4$ in.), 16 Ga. ($2^3/_4$ in.)
Box 5:. . . . . $9–$10

CLOSE ENCOUNTER

Features: The .410 Close Encounter is the perfect choice if you are a fan of $2^1/_2$-in. .410/.45 revolvers. They are powerful without having bad recoil, and they have an incredible frontal area and the legendary Brenneke penetration
Available in: .410 ($2^1/_2$ in.)
Box 5:. . . . . $7–$9

BRENNEKE CLOSE ENCOUNTER

AMMUNITION

Brenneke USA

HEAVY FIELD SHORT MAGNUM GREEN LIGHTNING

Features: The original "Emerald" slug with patented B.E.T wad and famous stopping power; for all barrel types; range up to 100 yds.
Available in: 12 Ga., 20 Ga. (2¾ in.)
Box 5:. $10

K.O. SABOT

Features: One of the most affordable sabots on the market, it offers 58 percent more frontal area than standard .50 cal. slugs, resulting in massive energy transfer; deep penetration, expansion up to .9 in.; range up to 100 yds
Available in: 12 Ga. (2¾ in.), 12 Ga. (3 in.)
Box 5:. $14

K.O. SLUG

Features: The KO is an improved Foster-type slug with excellent penetration; range up to 60 yds; for all barrel types
Available in: 12 Ga. (2¾ in.)
Box 5:. $6

MAGNUM CRUSH

Features: Delivers a force of more than 3.800 ft/lbs, weighs a full 1 ½ oz. / 666 gr. and the flat trajectory is ideal for bigger game; special coating to reduce lead fouling and broad ribs for optimum groove engagement
Available in: 12 Ga. (3 in.)
Box 5:. $12

SUPERSABOT

Features: Has a movable core, lead free construction and an effective range up to more than 100 yds; mushrooms up to 1-in.
Available in: 12 Ga. (2¾ in.), 12 Ga. (3 in.)
Box 5:. $19

BRENNEKE USA MAGNUM CRUSH

BRENNEKE K.O. SABOT

BRENNEKE HEAVY FIELD SHORT MAGNUM GREEN LIGHTNING SLUGS

CCI Ammunition

Rifle Ammunition

.22 LONG RANGE AR TACTICAL

Features: This load is designed specifically for AR-style guns being offered in .22 Long Rifle chambering; rounds get excellent accuracy including 1.5-in. at 100 yds for ten-shot groups; this target bullet has a copper-plated round nose for smooth feeding; CCI case, priming, and bullet lube combined with clean-burning powder; 375 rounds per box
Available in: .22 Long Rifle (40 gr.)
From:. $25

GREEN TAG

Features: Our first and still most-popular match rimfire product; tight manufacturing and accuracy specs mean you get the consistency and accuracy that the unforgiving field of competition demands; the rimfire match ammo leaves the muzzle sub-sonic which means no buffeting in the transonic zone; clean-burning propellants keep actions cleaner. Sure-fire CCI priming; reusable plastic box with dispenser lid
Available in: .22 LR (40 gr. lead round nose)
From:. $20

HMR TNT

Features: A 17-gr. Speer TNT hollow point answers requests from varmint hunters and gives explosive performance over the .17's effective range; clean-burning propellants keep actions cleaner; sure-fire CCI priming; reusable plastic box with dispenser lid
Available in: .17 HMR (17 gr. TNT hollow point)
MSRP. $17

LONG HV AND SHORT HV

Features: Designed for rimfire guns that require .22 Long and .22 Short ammunition; clean-burning propellants keep actions cleaner; sure-fire CCI priming; reusable plastic box with dispenser lid
Available in: .22 Short (29 gr. solid lead bullet), .22 Short (27 gr. hollow point bullet), .22 Long (29 gr. solid lead bullet)
MSRP. . . . . $10–$11

QUIET-22

Features: Ideal for bolt-action and single shot .22LR rifles (and perfectly safe in semiautomatics), this new reduced report cartridge generates ¼ the perceived noise level of standard velocity .22LR
Available in: .22LR
From: . . . . N/A

SELECT .22LR

Features: The .22 Long Rifle Select is built for semiautomatic competition; reliable operation, accuracy, and consistency make Select an ideal choice for competition shooters
Available in: .22LR
MSRP. $17

SUPPRESSOR 22 LONG RIFLE

Features: Subsonic velocity of 970 fps minimizes sound signature through suppressed firearms; HP bullet; consistent function in semiautomatic firearms; clean-burning powders
Available in: .22LR
Box 50:. $6

Handgun and Rifle Ammunition

.22 WIN. MAG. MAXI MAG

Features: A favorite of varmint shooters; 40 gr. TMJ flat nose at 1875 fps, or 40 gr. jacketed HP at 1875 fps; both loads give over 1400 fps from a 6-in. revolver; clean-burning propellants keep actions cleaner; sure-fire CCI priming; reusable plastic box with dispenser lid
Available in: .22 Win. Mag.
MSRP. $14

MINI-MAG. HV

Features: CCI's first rimfire product and still the most popular; Mini-Mag. hollow points are high-velocity products and offer excellent all-around performance for small game and varmints; clean-burning propellants keep actions cleaner; sure-fire CCI priming; reusable plastic box with dispenser lid
Available in: .22 LR (40 gr. gilded round nose or 36 gr. gilded lead hollow point)
From:. $9

V-MAX 17 MACH 2

Features: The 17 Mach 2 is a .22LR CCI Stinger case necked down to hold a .17 caliber bullet; CCI loads a super accurate 17 gr. polymer-tipped bullet, and drives it 60 percent faster than a .22 LR 40 gr. hollow point; the loaded cartridge is no longer than a .22LR, greatly expanding the gun actions that can accommodate .17 caliber rimfire cartridges; reusable fifty-count plastic box that protects and dispenses five cartridges at a time
Available in: .17 Mach 2 (V-Max also available in .17 HMR and .22 Mag. RF)
MSRP. $10

PISTOL MATCH

Features: Designed expressly for high-end semiautomatic match pistols; singe-die tooling and great care in assembly lets you wring the last bit of accuracy from your precision pistol; clean-burning propellants keep actions cleaner; sure-fire CCI priming; reusable plastic box with dispenser lid
Available in: .22LR (40 gr. lead round nose bullet)
From:. $10

CCI MINI-MAG. HV

CCI GREEN TAG

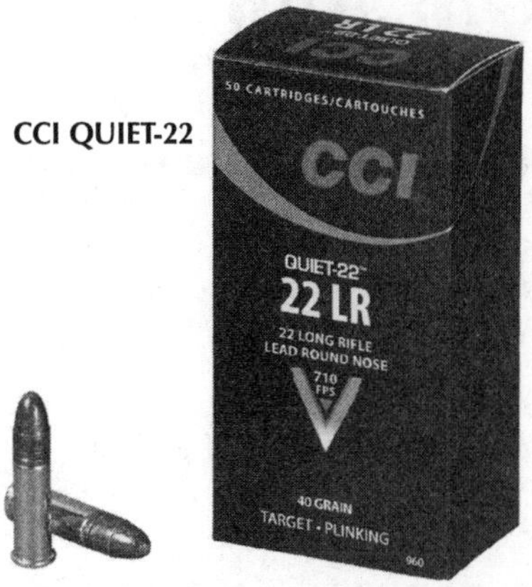

CCI QUIET-22

CCI AMMUNITION SUPPRESSOR 22 LONG RIFLE

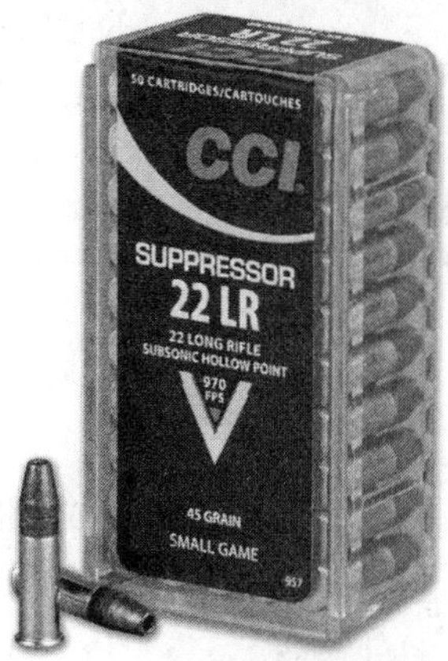

CCI V-MAX 17 MACH 2

CCI Ammunition

TROY LANDRY SIGNATURE SERIES

Features: Gator-tested performance endorsed by Troy Landry; clean-burning propellants; reliable cycling; sure-fire CCI priming; the Mini-Mag is a 36 gr., copper-plated hollow point and travels at 1,260 fps; the Maxi-Mag is a 40 gr., jacketed hollow point and travels at 1,875 fps
Available in: .22LR Mini-Mag; .22 WMR Maxi-Mag
.22LR Box 300: $27
.22 WMR Box 200: $48

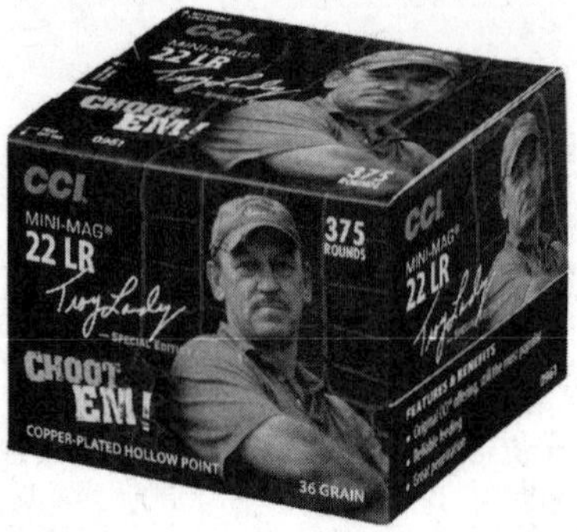

CCI AMMUNITION TROY LANDRY SIGNATURE SERIES

Cor-Bon

Rifle Ammunition

.457 WWG

Features: Cor-Bon Ammunition and Wild West Guns teamed up to offer the best in a lever gun big game cartridge
Available in: .457 WWG (350 gr., 405 gr., 460 gr.)
From: . . . . $57–$82

DPX RIFLE

Features: This is an optimum load for Law Enforcement; lead-free projectile; reduced recoil due to lighter weight projectile; deep penetration on soft tissue 12–17-in.
Available in: .223 Rem., .22-250 Rem., .243 Win., .25-06 Rem., .257 Wby. Mag., 6.5-284 Norma, .260 Rem., 6.8mm Rem. SPC, 7.62x39 Warsaw, .270 Win., .270 Wby. Mag., .270 WSM, 7mm RUM, 7mm WSM, 7mm Rem. Mag., .284 Win., .30 Carbon, .308 Win., .30-06 Spfd., .300 Win. Mag., .300 RUM, .300 WSM, .30–30 Win., .338 Win. Mag., .338 Lapua, .338 RUM, .340 Wby. Mag., .375 H&H Mag., .375 RUM, .416 Rigby, .444 Marlin, .45-70 Govt., .458 Win. Mag., .458 SOCOM
Box 20: . . . . $35–$254

EXPEDITION HUNTER

Features: Available with modern DPX lead free X-panding bullet or the legendary Woodleigh bullet; both field-tested and engineered specifically to take down thick-skinned and dangerous game with deep penetration
Available in: .375 Flanged, .375 H&H Mag., .416 Rem. Mag., .416 Rigby, .404 Jeffery, .458 Win. Mag., .458 Lott, .470 Nitro Express, .505 Gibbs, .577 Nitro Express
Box 10: . . . . $69–$187

GLASER SAFETY SLUG

Features: Although slug was originally designed for use by Sky Marshals on airplanes, today the slug is recommended for anyone concerned with over-penetration; uses a copper jacket and is filled with a compressed load of either #12 or #6 lead shot, then capped with a round polymer ball that enhances feeding and reloading
Available in: .25 ACP, .32 ACP, .32 NAA, .380 ACP, 9mm Makarov, 9mm Luger +P, .38 Super ACP, .38 Spl. Std., .38 Spl. +P, .357 SIG, .357 Mag., .40 S&W, 10mm Auto, .400 Corbon, .44 S&W Spl., .44 Mag., .45 ACP +P, .45 Colt +P, .223 Rem., 5.56 NATO, 7.62x39 Warsaw, .308 Win., .30-06 Spfd.
Box 6: . . . . $14–$32

HUNTER

Features: Bonded Core Soft Point ammunition retains optimum weight and integrity and provides reliable expansion coupled with deep penetration; features a heavy full-copper jacket enclosed in a hard linotype lead core; Hard Cast bullets are precision cast from hard linotype lead and have the flat, LBT nose design; both loads cause a through and through hole, penetrating the thickest hides and breaking the heaviest bone
Available in: .300 Whisper, 7.62x39 Warsaw, .357 Mag., 10mm Auto, .41 Rem. Mag., .44 Auto Mag., .44 Rem. Mag., .440 Corbon, .444 Marlin, .45 Colt +P, .45-70 Govt., .454 Casull, .460 Rowland, .460 S&W Mag., .475 Turnbull, .500 S&W Mag.
Box 12, 20: . . . . $38–$121

COR–BON AMMUNITION URBAN RESPONSE JHP

Features: Compatible with all AR-15/M-4 rifles with either .223 Rem. or 5.56 NATO chambers; high velocity, low penetration, and minimum hard surface ricochet; ideal self-defense load for close quarter urban environments
Available in: .223 Rem. (55 gr.)
Box 50: $64

COR-BON EXPEDITION HUNTER

COR-BON AMMUNITION URBAN RESPONSE JHP

Handgun Ammunition

DPX HANDGUN

Features: DPX is a solid copper hollowpoint bullet that combines the best of the lightweight high-speed JHPs and the heavyweight, deep-penetrating JHPs; the copper bullet construction allows it to conquer hard barriers like auto glass and steel while still maintaining its integrity
Available in: .32 ACP, 9x23mm Win., .380 ACP, 9mm Luger, 9mm Luger +P, .38 Super ACP +P, .38 Spl. +P, .357 SIG, .357 Mag., .40 S&W, 10mm ACP, .400 Corbon, .41 Rem. Mag., .44 S&W Special, .44 Rem. Mag., .45 GAP, .45 ACP Rim, .45 ACP, .45 ACP +P, .45 Colt +P, .454 Casull, .480 Ruger, .375 JDJ, .460 S&W Mag., .500 S&W Special, .500 S&W Mag.
Box 20:. . . . . $30–$96

DPX THUNDER RANCH AMMUNITION

Features: Teamed up with Thunder Ranch Training Center for exclusive ammunition package; Solid Copper X Bullet, deep penetrating, barrier blind, impressive expansion, and environmentally friendly
Available in: .38 Spl. +P (110 gr.), 9mm Luger (115 gr.), .357 Mag. (125 gr.), .40 S&W-140 gr.), .45 ACP +P (185 gr.)
Box 20:. . . . . $35–$43

GLASER POW'RBALL

Features: Designed for finicky feeding pistols, Pow'Rball is a great choice for your semiauto pistols or revolvers; reliable feeding and consistent reliable expansion; deeper soft tissue penetration; custom scored jacket; proprietary polymer ball and patented lead core
Available in: .32 ACP, .380 ACP, 9mm Makarov, 9mm Luger +P, 9x23mm Win., .38 Super +P, .38 Spl. +P, .357 SIG, .357 Mag, .40 S&W, 10mm ACP, .400 Corbon, .45 GAP, .45 ACP +P
Box 20:. . . . . $23–$32

Shotgun Ammunition

HEVI DUTY HOME DEFENSE

Features: Frangible, non-toxic, low recoil home defense load
Available in: 12 Ga. (2¾ in.) Shot sizes: 00, 4
Box 5:. . . . . $7–$8

HEVI-METAL TURKEY

Features: A layered load that combines premium steel shot with HEVI-Shot pellets; timeless testing of various shot load methods found layering to provide the most pellets on target and the best knockdown performance
Available in: 12 Ga. (3 in., 3½ in.), 20 Ga. (3 in.)
Box 5:. . . . . $10–$13

HEVI-SHOT CLASSIC DOUBLES

Features: Optimized for your fixed chokes and fine classic doubles; denser than steel but soft like lead which means you get deeper penetration; USFWS-approved non-toxic shot; 45 percent more on target pellets than steel; belted sphere for maximum pellet mass; buffered and nano-treated pellets for tight patterns; weather-resistant crimp
Available in: 12 Ga. (2¾ in., 3 in.), 16 Ga. (2¾ in.), 20 Ga. (2¾ in., 3 in.), .28 Ga. (2¾ in.), .410 (3 in.)
Box 10:. . . . . $31–$42

HEVI-SHOT DEAD COYOTE!

Features: With these HEVI-Shot T-shot loads, you can be deadly at ranges you never thought possible with a 12 gauge; the 3-in. load pounds out 50 perfectly round pellets at 1,350 fps. 10 percent heavier than lead, 54 percent denser than steel; every 50 rounds includes a dry-storage box.
Available in: 10 Ga. (3½ in.), 12 Ga. (2¾ in., 3 in., 3½ in.)
Box 5:. . . . . $20–$40

ENVIRON-METAL HEVI-METAL TURKEY

COR-BON AMMUNITION DPX THUNDER RANCH AMMUNITION

ENVIRON-METAL HEVI DUTY HOME DEFENSE

ENVIRON-METAL HEVI-SHOT DEAD COYOTE!

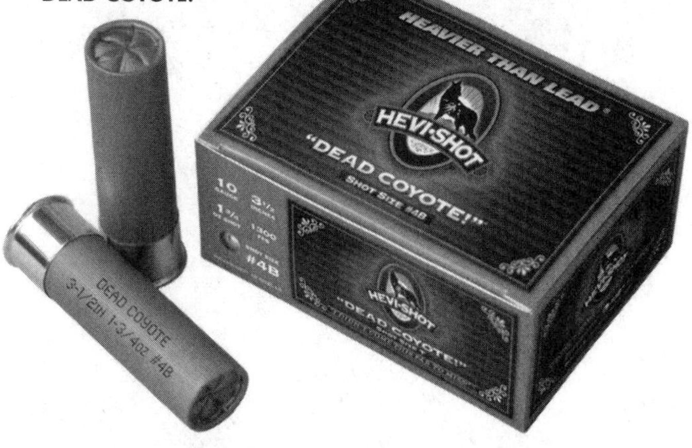

AMMUNITION

ENVIRON-Metal

HEVI-SHOT MAGNUM BLEND

Features: Put more lethal pellets in your pattern with a combination of No. 5, 6, and 7 HEVI-13 shot, and boost your lethal range by 14 to 17 percent; buffered and moly-coated pellets produce a denser pattern than conventional shot; HEVI-13 delivers 40 percent more knockdown energy and up to 40 percent longer range than lead shells

Available in: 12 Ga. (3 in.), 20 Ga. (3 in.)

Box 5:. . . . . $20–$38

SPEED BALL

Features: Speed Ball is an elastomeric ball in the base of the wad that accelerates pellets without boosting chamber pressures; an MV^2 pellet sits in the base of the shell with a HEVI-Shot layer on top, resulting in higher pellet counts in the 30-in. circle than you get with HEVI-Shot; nearly matches the lethal energy of HEVI-Shot, out to 60 yds (but far exceeds the energy of anything else)

Available in: 12 Ga. (3 in., 3½ in.) 20 Ga. (3 in.); Shot sizes: BB, 1, 3, 5

Box 5: . . . . $9–$15

ENVIRON-METAL SPEED BALL

Federal Fusion Ammunition

FUSION MSR

Features: Modern sporting rifles (MSRs) represent a very versatile class of firearms, handling a wide range of ammo and game, often built from the ground up and tricked out with accessories to match specific needs; all-new Fusion MSR loads provide that same degree of customization in ammunition

Available in: .223 Rem., .308 Win., .338 Fed., 6.8 SPC

Box 20:. . . . . $27–$38

FEDERAL FUSION FUSION MSR

FUSION RIFLE AMMO

Features: This specialized deer bullet electrochemically joins pure copper to an extreme pressure-formed core to ensure optimum performance. The result is high terminal energy on impact that radiates lethal shock throughout the target. This energy is optimized through mass weight retention, a top secretive tip-skiving process and superior bullet integrity.

Available in: .223 Rem., .22-250 Rem., .243 Win., .25-6 Rem., 6.5x55 Swedish, 6.8 SPC, .260 Rem., .270 Win., .270 WSM, 7mm-08 Rem., .280 Rem., 7mm Rem. Mag., 7mm WSM, 7.62x39 Warsaw, .30-30 Win., .308 Win., .30-06 Spfd., .300 Win. Mag., .300 WSM, .338 Fed., .338 Win. Mag., .35 Whelen, .375 H&H Mag., .416 Rigby, .416 Rem. Mag., .45-70 Govt., .458 Win. Mag., .458 Lott

Box 20:. . . . . $24–$60

FEDERAL FUSION RIFLE AMMO

Federal Fusion Ammunition

FUSION SHOTGUN SLUGS

Features: Fusion slugs have made shotgunners part of the next generation of deer hunters. Slug hunters can now find the same unequaled energy and deer devastation in their favorite rifled-barrel shotgun.
Available in: 12, 20 Ga. (2¾ in., 3 in.)
Box 5:. . . . . $11–$12

FUSION SP

Features: Real-world recoil can translate to inaccurate shooting and missed trophies, and because of this bullet weights and velocities have been developed to be lethal on whitetails, without pounding the shooter
Available in: .357 Mag., .41 Rem. Mag., .44 Rem. Mag., .454 Casull, .460 S&W, .500 S&W, 50 Action Express
Box 20:. . . . . $22–$50

Federal Premium Ammunition

Rifle Ammunition

CHAMPION .22LR FRESH FIRE PACK

Features: 325 36-grain copper-plated hollow-point cartridges in a tough, nitrogen-sealed can
Available in: .22LR
Box 50:. $26

FULL METAL JACKET BOAT-TAIL

Features: Accurate, non-expanding bullets; flat shooting trajectory, leaves small exit holes in game, and put clean holes in paper; smooth, reliable feeding into semiautomatics
Available in: .223 Rem., .308 Win., .30-06 Spfd. (American Eagle)
Box 20:. . . . . $12–$31

NOSLER PARTITION

Features: Bullet features a partitioned lead core and shank that allows the front half to mushroom while the rear core remains intact for deep penetration and stopping power
Available in: .223 Rem., .22-250 Rem., .243 Win., 6mm Rem., 257 Roberts +P, .25-06 Rem., .270 Win., .270 WSM, 7mm Mauser, 7mm-08 Rem., .280 Rem., 7mm Rem. Mag., .30-30 Win., .308 Win., .30-06 Spfd., 300 H&H Mag.
Box 20:. . . . . $29–$86

SIERRA MATCHKING BOAT-TAIL HP

Features: Long ranges are its specialty; excellent choice for everything from varmints to big game animals; tapered, boattail design provides extremely flat trajectories; higher downrange velocity for more energy at the point of impact; reduced wind drift
Available in: .223 Rem., 6.5x55 Swedish, .260 Rem., .308 Win., .30-06 Spfd., .300 Win. Mag., .338 Lapua Mag.
Box 20:. . . . . $30–$145

SOFT POINT

Features: Proven performer on small game and thin-skinned medium game; aerodynamic tip for a flat trajectory; exposed soft point expands rapidly for hard hits, even as velocity slows at longer ranges
Available in: .22 Hornet (V-Shok), .222 Rem., .223 Rem., .22-250 Rem., .243 Win., 6mm Rem., 6.5x55 Swedish, .270 Win., .270 WSM, .280 Rem., 7mm Rem. Mag., 7mm WSM, 7.62x39

FEDERAL PREMIUM CHAMPION .22LR FRESH FIRE PACK

AMMUNITION

Federal Premium Ammunition

Warsaw, .300 Savage, .308 Win., .30-06 Spfd., .300 WSM, .303 British, 8mm Mauser, .338 Fed. (Power-Shok, American Eagle), .375 H&H Mag. (Power-Shok)
Box 20: . . . . $20–$71

FEDERAL PREMIUM GUARD DOG HOME DEFENSE

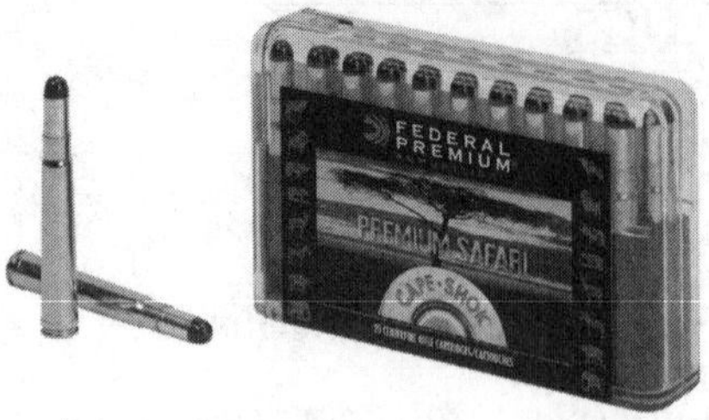

FEDERAL PREMIUM WOODLEIGH HYDRO SOLID

SOFT POINT FLAT NOSE

Features: Great for thick cover, it expands reliably and penetrates deep on light to medium game; flat nose prevents accidental discharge
Available in: .30-30 Win., .32 Win. Spl.
Box 20: . . . . $21–$38

SOFT POINT ROUND NOSE

Features: The choice in heavy cover; large exposed tip, good weight retention and specially tapered jacket provide controlled expansion
Available in: .270 Win., 7mm Mauser, .30 Carbine, .30-30 Win., .35 Rem.
Box 20: . . . . $21–$42

SPEER TNT GREEN

Features: Brings non-tox technology to the Federal Premium V-Shok varmint hunting line; a totally lead-free bullet that couples explosive expansion with match-grade accuracy
Available in: .22 Hornet, .222 Rem., .223 Rem., .22-250 Rem.
Box 20: . . . . $26–$57

TROPHY BONDED BEAR CLAW

Features: Ideal for medium to large dangerous game; jacket and core are 100 percent fusion-bonded for reliable bullet expansion from 25 yds to extreme ranges; bullet retains 95 percent of its weight for deep penetration; hard solid copper base tapering to a soft, copper nose section for controlled expansion
Available in: 7mm Rem. Mag., .30-06 Spfd., .300 Win. Mag., .388 Win. Mag., .35 Whelen (Vital-Shok), .375 H&H Mag., .416 Rigby, .416 Rem. Mag. (Cape-Shok), .45-70 Govt. (Vital-Shok), .458 Win. Mag., .458 Lott, .470 NE (Cape-Shok)
Box 20: . . . . $44–$246

TROPHY BONDED SLEDGEHAMMER

Features: Use it on the largest, most dangerous game in the world; Jack Carter design maximizes stopping power; bonded bronze solid with a flat nose that minimizes deflection off bone and muscle for a deep straight wound channel
Available in: .375 H&H Mag., .416 Rigby, .416 Rem. Mag., .458 Win. Mag., .458 Lott, .470 NE (Cape-Shok)
Box 20: . . . . $116–$268

TROPHY BONDED TIP

Features: Built on the Trophy Bonded Bear Claw platform to provide deep penetration and high weight retention; sleek profile, with tapered heel and translucent polymer tip; nickel-plated; available as component and in Federal loaded ammunition
Available in: .270 Win., .270 WSM, .270 Wby. Mag., 7mm-08 Rem., .280 Rem., 7mm Rem. Mag., 7mm WSM, 7mm Wby. Mag., 7mm STW, .308 Win., .30-06 Spfd., .300 H&H Mag., .300 Win. Mag., .300 WSM, .300 Wby. Mag., .300 Rem. Ultra Mag., .338 Federal, .338 Win. Mag.
Box 20: . . . . $44–$74

VITAL-SHOK TROPHY COPPER

Features: Tipped bullet cavity for consistent expansion across a broad range of velocities; grooved bullet shank for increased accuracy across a wider range of firearms; copper-alloy design that achieves up to 99 percent weight retention; nickel-plated case prevents corrosion and aids in easier, faster extraction from the chamber
Available in: .243 Win., .25-06 Rem., .270 Win., .270 WSM, 7mm-08 Rem., .280 Rem., 7mm Rem. Mag., 7mm WSM, .308 Win., .30-06 Spfd., .300 H&H, .300 Win. Mag., .300 WSM, .300 Wby. Mag., .300 Rem. Ultra Mag., .338 Fed., .338 Win. Mag.
Box 20: . . . . $34–$33

Federal Premium Ammunition

FEDERAL PREMIUM HST

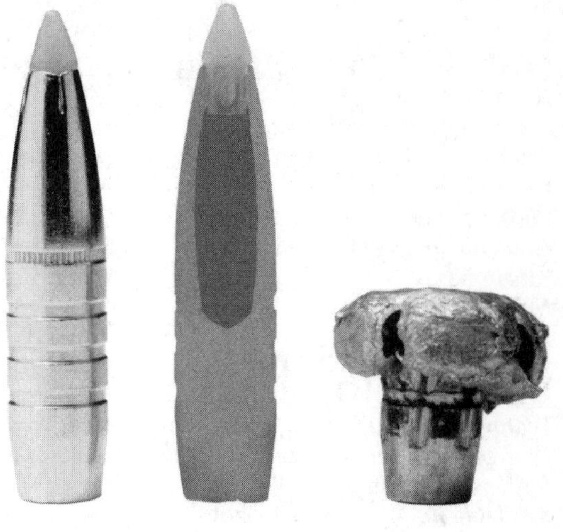

FEDERAL PREMIUM TROPHY BONDED TIP

WOODLEIGH HYDRO SOLID

Features: Provides safari hunters superb accuracy, consistent performance, and tremendous impact; special heavy jackets provide excellent weight retention, up to 100 percent for solids
Available in: 9.3x62 Mauser, 9.3x74 R, .370 Sako Mag. (Cape-Shok), .375 H&H Mag., .416 Rigby, .416 Rem. Mag., .458 Win. Mag., 458 Lott, .470 NE, .500 NE 3
Box 20:. . . . . $116–$268

Handgun Ammunition

CASTCORE

Features: Heavyweight, flat-nosed, hard cast-lead bullet that smashes through bone
Available in: .375 Mag., .41 Rem. Mag., .44 Rem. Mag. (Vital-Shok)
Box 20:. . . . . $33–$46

FULL METAL JACKET

Features: Good choice for range practice and reducing lead fouling in the barrel; jacket extends from the nose to the base, preventing bullet expansion and barrel leading; primarily as military ammunition for recreational shooting
Available in: .25 ACP, .32 ACP, .380 ACP, 5.7x28mm, 9mm Makarov, 9mm Luger, .38 Super +P, .357 SIG, .38 Spl., .40 S&W, 10mm ACP, .45 GAP, .45 ACP (American Eagle)
Box 50:. . . . . $18–$50

GUARD DOG HOME DEFENSE

Features: Protect your home and loved ones with a cartridge designed exclusively for home defense; packs the terminal performance that stops threats while reducing over-penetration through walls
Available in: 9mm Luger, .40 S&W, .45 ACP
Box 20:. . . . . $30–$33

HST

Features: Provides near 100 percent weight retention through most barriers; consistent expansion, optimum penetration, and superior terminal performance, it's specially designed hollow point won't plug while passing through a variety of barriers
Available in: 9mm Luger, .40 S&W, .45 ACP
Box 20:. . . . . $31–$34

HYDRA-SHOK JHP

Features: Unique center-post design delivers controlled expansion, and the notched jacket provides efficient energy transfer to penetrate barriers while retaining stopping power; deep penetration satisfies even the FBI's stringent testing requirements
Available in: .32 ACP, .327 Fed. Mag., .380 ACP, 9mm Luger, .38 Spl., .38 Spl. +P, .357 Mag., .40 S&W, 10mm ACP, .44 Rem. Mag., .45 GAP, .45 ACP (Premium Personal Defense)
Box 20:. . . . . $27–$44

JACKETED HOLLOW POINT

Features: Ideal personal defense round in revolvers and semiautomatics; quick, positive expansion; jacket ensures smooth feeding into autoloading firearms
Available in: .32 H&R Mag., 9mm Luger (Personal Defense), .38 Super +P (American Eagle), .357 SIG., .357 Mag. (Premium Personal Defense, Power-Shok), .40 S&W (Personal Defense), .41 Rem. Mag., .44 Rem. Mag. (Power-Shok, American Eagle), .45 ACP (Personal Defense)
Box 20:. . . . . $24–$53

LEAD ROUND NOSE

Features: Great training round for practicing at the range; 100 percent lead with no jacket; excellent accuracy and very economical
Available in: .32 S&W Long (Champion), .38 Spl. (American Eagle)
MSRP. . . . . $19–$29

Federal Premium Ammunition

LEAD SEMI-WADCUTTER
Features: Most popular all-around choice for target and personal defense, a versatile design that cuts clean holes in targets and efficiently transfers energy
Available in: .32 H&R Mag. (Champion)
MSRP $21

PREMIUM PERSONAL DEFENSE SHOT SHELLS
Features: The Judge from Taurus has emerged as a very popular handgun for Personal Defense.
Available in: .410 (2½ in.); Shot sizes: 000 Buck, 4
Box 20: $18

SEMI-WADCUTTER HP
Features: For both small game and personal defense; hollow point design promotes uniform expansion
Available in: .44 Spl., .45 Colt (Champion)
MSRP . . . . $28–$33

VITAL-SHOK TROPHY BONDED 10MM AUTO
Features: 180-grain Trophy Bonded JSP; 1275 fps muzzle velocity
Available in: 10mm Auto
Box 20: $40

Shotgun Ammunition

BLACK CLOUD FS STEEL
Available in: 10 Ga. (3½ in.), 12 Ga. (2¾ in., 3 in., 3½ in.), 20 Ga. (3 in.); Shot sizes: 2, 3, 4, BB, BBB
Box 25: . . . . $21–$36

BLACK CLOUD FS STEEL CLOSE RANGE
Features: Engineered to put more pellets on targets 20 to 30 yards away, achieves a full pattern within a very short distance; comprised of 100 percent Flitestopper Steel for the most lethal payload imaginable, produces more open and optimum patterns; crimp and primer sealed
Available in: 12 Ga., 20 Ga. (3 in.)
Box 25: . . . . $25–$28

BLACK CLOUD HIGH VELOCITY
Features: The Black Cloud High Velocity line pumps up the speed and lethal performance for waterfowl hunters everywhere.
Available in: 12 Ga. (3 in.); Shot Sizes: 3, 4
Box 25: $26

GAME-SHOK UPLAND GAME
Available in: 12, 16, 20 Ga. (2¾ in.); Shot sizes: 6, 8, 7.5
Box 25: . . . . $9–$12

GAME-SHOK UPLAND HEAVY FIELD
Available in: 12, 20 Ga. (2¾ in.); Shot sizes: 4, 5, 6, 7.5
Box 25: . . . . $10–$15

GAME-SHOK UPLAND GAME HI-BRASS
Available in: 12, 16, 20 Ga. (2¾ in.), .410 bore (2½ in., 3 in.); Shot sizes: 4, 5, 6, 7.5
Box 25: . . . . $18–$19

FEDERAL PREMIUM VITAL-SHOK TROPHY BONDED 10MM AUTO

FEDERAL PREMIUM BLACK CLOUD FS STEEL

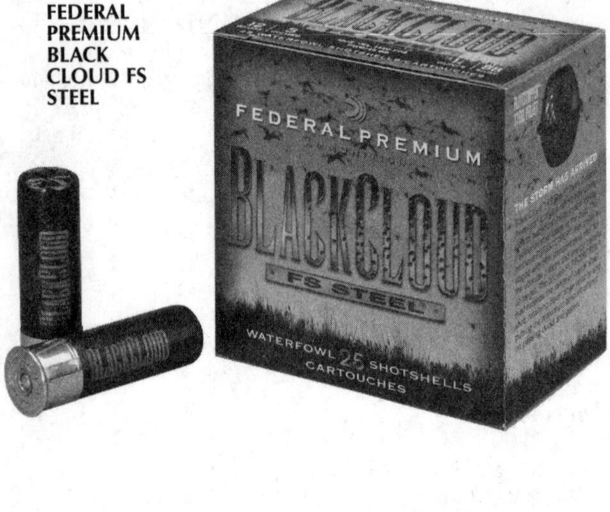

FEDERAL BLACK CLOUD FS STEEL CLOSE RANGE

Federal Premium Ammunition

GOLD MEDAL EXTRA-LITE PAPER (LR)

Features: Also available in plastic
Available in: 12 Ga. (2¾ in.); Shot sizes: 7.5, 8
Box 25:. $13

GOLD MEDAL-HANDICAP PAPER HV

Features: Also available in plastic
Available in: 12 Ga. (2¾ in.); Shot sizes: 7.5, 8
Box 25:. $13

GOLD MEDAL-INTERNATIONAL PAPER

Features: Also available in plastic (with Shot sizes: 7.5, 8)
Available in: 12 Ga. (2¾ in.); Shot sizes: 7.5
Box 25:. $13

GOLD MEDAL-PLASTIC

Features: Also available in paper (12 Ga., 2¾ in., Shot sizes: 7.5, 8, 9)
Available in: 12, 20, 28 Ga. (2¾ in.), .410 bore (2½ in.); Shot sizes: 7.5, 8, 8.5, 9
Box 25:. . . . . $12–$13

MAG-SHOK HEAVYWEIGHT TURKEY

Available in: 10 Ga. (3½ in.), 12 Ga. (2¾ in., 3 in., 3½ in.), 20 Ga. (2¾ in., 3 in.); Shot sizes: 5, 6, 7
Box 5:. . . . . $27–$41

MAG-SHOK HIGH VELOCITY LEAD WITH FLITECONTROL

Available in: 10 Ga. (3½ in.), 12 Ga. (2¾ in., 3 in., 3½ in.) 20 Ga. (3 in.); Shot sizes: 4, 5, 6
Box 10:. . . . . $14–$24

MAG-SHOK LEAD WITH FLITECONTROL

Available in: 12 Ga. (3 in., 3 ½ in.); Shot sizes: 4, 5, 6
Box 10:. . . . . $20–$24

PRAIRIE STORM - FS STEEL

Available in: 12, 20 Ga. (3 in.); Shot sizes: 3, 4
Box 25:. . . . . $24–$26

SPEED-SHOK WATERFOWL

Available in: 10 Ga. (3½ in.), 12 Ga. (2¾ in., 3 in., 3½ in.), 16 Ga. (2¾ in.), 20 Ga. (2¾ in., 3 in.); Shot sizes: 1, 2, 3, 4, 6, 7, BB, BBB, T
Box 25:. . . . . $13–$33

STRUT-SHOK TURKEY

Available in: 12 Ga. (3 in., 3½ in.); Shot sizes: 4, 5, 6
Box 10:. . . . . $12–$18

TOP GUN TARGET

Available in: 12 Ga., 20 Ga. (2¾ in.); Shot sizes: 7.5, 8, 9
Box 25:. $9

TOP GUN TARGET-STEEL

Available in: 12 Ga., 20 Ga. (2¾ in.); Shot size: 7
Box 25:. $11

TOP GUN TARGET-SUBSONIC

Available in: 12 Ga. (2¾ in.); Shot size: 7.5
Box 25:. $11

V-SHOK HEAVYWEIGHT COYOTE

Available in: 12 Ga. (3 in.); Shot size: BB
Box 5:. $29

WING-SHOK HIGH VELOCITY

Features: Pheasant and Quail Forever versions available
Available in: 12 Ga. (2¾ in., 3 in.), 28 Ga. (2¾ in.); Shot sizes: 4, 5, 6, 7, 7.5, 8
Box 25:. . . . . $21–$29

WING-SHOK MAGNUM

Available in: 10 Ga. (3½ in.), 12 Ga. (2¾ in., 3 in.), 16 Ga. (2¾ in.), 20 Ga. (2¾ in., 3 in.); Shot sizes: 2, 4, 5, 6, BB
Box 25:. . . . . $26–$72

Shotgun Ammunition Slugs

POWER-SHOK RIFLED SLUG

Features: Hollow point slug type
Available in: 10 Ga. (3½ in.), 12 Ga. (2¾ in., 3 in.), 16 Ga. (2¾ in.), 20 Ga. (2¾ in.), .410 (2½ in.)
Box 5:. . . . . $6–$13

POWER-SHOK SABOT

Features: Sabot hollow point slug type
Available in: 12 Ga., 20 Ga. (2¾ in.)
Box 5:. $9

FEDERAL PREMIUM PRAIRIE STORM - FS STEEL

AMMUNITION

Federal Premium Ammunition

VITAL-SHOK TROPHY COPPER SABOT SLUG

Features: A copper slug that incorporates some of the most advanced technology in the industry; better accuracy, less drop, manageable recoil (similar to a .30-06 Spfd.) and consistent penetration and expansion; unique two-part sabot design achieves accuracy through a clean launch and improved projectile support
Available in: 12 Ga., 20 Ga. (2¾ in., 3 in.)
Box 5: . . . . $15–$16

VITAL-SHOK TRUBALL RIFLED SLUG

Available in: 12, 20 Ga. (2¾ in., 3 in.)
Box 5:. . . . . $6–$7

FEDERAL PREMIUM VITAL-SHOK TRUBALL RIFLED SLUG

Fiocchi USA

Rifle Ammunition

EXTREMA RIFLE HUNTING LINE

Features: Combining the best bullets in the business with our precision-drawn brass cases gives you the best combination of value and performance; uses bullets like the Hornady SST, V Max, and Sierra Game King to provide a combination of accuracy, high ballistic coefficients, and reliable expansion
Available in: .222 Rem., .204 Ruger, .223 Rem., .22-50 Rem., .243 Win., 6.5x55 Swedish, .270 Win., .308 Win., .30-06 Spfd., .300 Win. Mag.
From:. . . . . $22–$52

SHOOTING DYNAMICS RIFLE LINE

Features: High-quality reloadable brass cases combined with quality full metal jacket, soft point, or flat soft point (for lever guns) make sure your shooting dollar goes further
Available in: .223 Rem., .22-250 Rem., .243 Win., .270 Win., .30-30 Win., .308 Win., .30-06 Spfd., .300 Win. Mag., 7.62x39 Warsaw
From:. . . . . $17–$56

Handgun Ammunition

COWBOY ACTION LINE

Features: Loaded with brass reloadable cases, noncorrosive primers, smokeless powders, and lead bullets coated with lube to reduce leading in the barrel; velocity is on par with what you would expect from period-correct ammo while keeping the recoil to a minimum for timed Cowboy Action competition and to reduce wear and tear on older guns
Available in: .32 S&W Long, .38 S&W Short, .38 S&W Spl., .357 Mag., .44 Spl., .44-40 Win., .45 Long Colt
From:. . . . . $37–$57

FIOCCHI SHOOTING DYNAMICS PISTOL LINE

AMMUNITION

Fiocchi USA

FIOCCHI GOLDEN PHEASANT SHOT SHELLS

FIOCCHI NICKEL PLATED BUCKSHOT

EXTREMA XTP HANDGUN LINE

Features: Combined with nickel-plated cases for positive feeding and extraction when you need it most, qualified primers and clean powders deliver the maximum performance for the ultimate hunting or self-defense application

Available in: .25 ACP, .32 ACP, .380 ACP, 9mm Luger, .38 Spl., .38 Spl.+P, .357 Mag., .40 S&W, .44 Rem. Mag., .45 ACP

From:. . . . . $22–$38

SHOOTING DYNAMICS PISTOL & REVOLVER LINE

Features: Combining quality brass cases with consistent primers, clean powders, and full metal jacket, jacketed hollow point, and soft point bullets in many calibers, Fiocchi loads bullets of the same weight to velocities that are comparable with high-quality defensive loads so you get realistic training-recoil impulse and point of aim/impact

Available in: .25 ACP, .32 ACP, .32 S&W Long, .380 ACP, 9mm Luger, 9mm Makarov, 9mm Steyr, 9x21 IMI, .38 Spl., .357 Mag., .38 Super Auto, .40 S&W, .44 Rem. Mag., .44 Spl., .45 ACP

From:. . . . . $20–$38

Shotgun Ammunition

EXACTA TARGET LOADS

Features: Specifically for competitive shooters; the Target Load Line is the offspring of a fifty year tradition of supporting the world of trap, skeet, and now sporting clays, FITASC, and Compaq

Available in: Steel: 12 Ga., 20 Ga. (2¾ in.), Shot size: 7; Helios: 12 Ga. (2¾ in.), Shot sizes: 7, 7.5

From:. . . . . $12–$13

GOLDEN PHEASANT LINE

Features: Golden Pheasant shot shells utilize a special hard, nickel-plated lead shot, based on Fiocchi's strict ballistic tolerances that ensure proven shot consistency and result in deeper penetration, longer ranges, and much tighter patterns

Available in: 12 Ga. (2¾ in., 3 in.), 16 Ga. (2¾ in.), 20, 28 Ga. (2¾ in., 3 in.); Shot sizes: 4, 5, 6, 7.5, 8, 9

From:. . . . . $22–$30

NICKEL PLATED BUCKSHOT

Features: Harder pellets from the nickel plating mean better patterns, better penetration, and no buffer needed

Available in: 12 Ga. (2¾ in.); Shot sizes: 00, 4

From:. . . . . $9–$10

OPTIMA SPECIFIC HIGH VELOCITY

Features: High brass hulls, one-piece shot cup and cushioned wads, and round shot pellets make sure you get the bang for your buck you have come to expect from Fiocchi

Available in: 12 Ga. (2¾ in., 3 in.), 16 Ga. (2¾ in.), 20 Ga. (2¾ in., 3 in.), 28 Ga. (2¾ in., 3 in.), .410 (3 in.); Shot sizes: 4, 5, 6, 7.5, 8, 9

From:. . . . . $15–$16

WATERFOWL STEEL HUNTING

Features: Treated steel pellets, the correct wad, and powders that perform in the cold conditions often encountered in waterfowl hunting deliver the kills a waterfowl hunter wants

Available in: 12 Ga. (2¾ in., 3 in.), 20 Ga. (3 in.); Shot sizes: T, BBB, BB, 1, 2, 3, 4, 5, 6

From:. . . . . $17–$24

GECO

Rifle Ammunition

Features: A range of bullets for training and all types of hunting situations worldwide; GECO offers four different bullet types to cover every hunting situation; GECO PLUS for shooting big game, GECO EXPRESS for the long distance shot, GECO SOFTPOINT as the real all-rounder, and GECO TARGET for accurate training; made in Germany, which means outstanding accuracy and reliable bullet performance
Available calibers: .223, 7x62-39, .243, .270 Win, .270 WSM, .300 Win. Mag, 30-06, .308 Win. 7mm Rem. Mag.
MSRP: . . . . $12-$35

Pistol Ammunition

Features: GECO offers 18 loads with cartridges in nine different calibers; these cover all relevant fields of application like precision shooting, dynamic sport disciplines, hunting, protection, and self-defense.
Available in: .32 ACP, .357 Mag., .38 Special, .38 Super Auto, .380 ACP, 9mm, .40, .45
MSRP: . . . . $16-$30
From: . . . . $29–$55

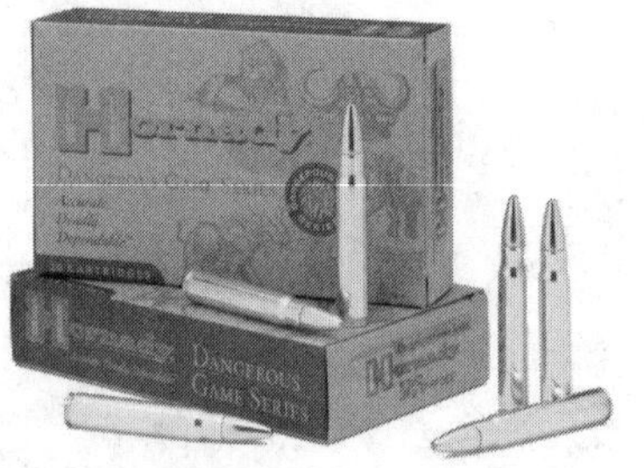

HORNADY DANGEROUS GAME

HORNADY AMERICAN WHITETAIL

Hornady

Rifle Ammunition

AMERICAN WHITETAIL

Features: Loaded with Hornady InterLock Bullets, optimized loads specifically for deer hunting, and select propellants for greater consistency
Available in: .243 Win., .25-06 Rem., .270 Win., 7mm-08 Rem., 7mm Rem. Mag, 30-30 Win., .308 Win., 30-06 Spfd., .300 Win. Mag
Box 20: . . . . $27–$29

CUSTOMLITE

Features: CustomLite ammunition is recommended for children, women, and anyone new to the game; offer minimum recoil and a reduced muzzle blast; often paired with SST and RN bullets
Available in: .243 Win, .270 Win., 7mm Rem. Mag., 7mm-08 Rem., .30-30 Win., .300 Win. Mag., .308 Win., .30-06 Spfd.
From: . . . . $29–$48

DANGEROUS GAME

Features: These bullets are among the largest offered by Hornady and feature the DGS (Dangerous Game Solid) and the DGX (Dangerous Game eXpanding); made with hard lead/antimony alloy cone and surrounded by a copper-clad steel jacket; straighter penetration comes from a flat meplat that creates more energy than traditional round bullets
Available in: 9.3x62 Mauser, 9.3x74R, .376 Steyr., .375 H&H, .375 Ruger, .450–400 Nitro Express, .404 Jeffrey, .416 Rem. Mag., .416 Ruger, .416 Rigby, .458 Win., .450 NE, .458 Lott, .470 NE, .500 NE
From: . . . . $68–$194

LEVEREVOLUTION

Features: LEVERevolution bullets travel at a speed of 250 fps and have a faster muzzle velocity than most other conventional lever gun loads; are unbelievably accurate and offer incomparable terminal performance; available in FTX and MonoFlex
Available in: .30-30 Win., .308 Marlin Express, .32 Win. Spl., .338 Marlin Express, .35 Rem., .357 Mag., .44 Mag., .444 Marlin, .45-70 Govt., .450 Marlin
From: . . . . $29–$55

MATCH

Features: Match bullets feature a boattail hollow point design that provides both accuracy and speed; these bullets' jackets feature near-zero wall thickness, which leads to uniformity throughout the jacket; case weight and internal capacity are also consistent throughout Match ammunition
Available in: .223 Rem., 6.5 Grendel, 6.5 Creedmoor, .308 Win., .30-06 Spfd., .300 Win. Mag., .338 Lapua, .50 BMG
From: . . . . $25–$121

SUPERFORMANCE

Features: Superformance bullets are 100–200 fps faster than any other traditional type of bullet on the market today. In addition to their speed, they also offer minimal recoil, muzzle blast, temperature sensativity, and inaccuracies; these bullets are versatile and can be paired with all types of firearms, including semiautomatics, lever guns, and pump actions
Available in: .223 Rem., .243 Win., .25-06 Rem., .257 Roberts +P, .270 Win., .280 Rem., .30 TC, .30-06 Spfd., .300 RCM., .300 Savage, .300 Win. Mag., .308 Win., .338 RCM, .338 Win. Mag., .35 Whelen, .375 H&H, .375 Ruger, .444 Marlin, .458 Win., 5.56 NATO, 6.5 Creedmoor, 6.5x55 Swedish, 6mm. Rem., 7mm Rem. Mag., 7mm-08 Rem., 7x57 Mauser
MSRP . . . . $31–$128

Hornady

Handgun Ammunition

COWBOY ACTION SHOOTING

Features: These swaged bullets flatten instead of fragment when they reach their targets; diamond knurling ensures that the entire surface of the bullet is well-lubed
Available in: .44-40 Win., .45 Colt
Box 20: . . . . $23–$25

CRITICAL DEFENSE

Features: Critical Defense bullets are custom-designed for individual loads, and their shiny silver nickel plating prevents bullet corrosion; Critical Defense ammunition is cannelured and crimped to avoid bullet setback, and clean burning and stable propellants reduce recoil
Available in: .410, .22 WMR, .32 NAA, 32 H&R Mag., 9x18mm Makarov, .380 ACP, 9mm Luger, .38 Spl., .357 SIG., .357 Mag., 40 S&W, 10mm ACP, .44 Spl., .44 Mag., .45 ACP, .45 Colt
From: . . . . $16–$33

CRITICAL DUTY

Features: Features FlexLock Bullets, crimped and nickel-plated cases, interlocking bands, and a core made of high-antimony lead; these bullets are among the top choices of law enforcement and military professionals and highly reliable
Available in: 45 ACP +P, 9mm, 9mm Luger +P, .40 S&W, .357 SIG
Box 20–25: . . . . $30–$32

LEVEREVOLUTION

Features: LEVERevolution bullets travel at a speed of 250 fps and are unbelievably accurate; these bullets feature Flex Tip Technology and should not be stored for long periods of time, as the tips may become deformed; deliver 40 percent more energy than traditional bullets
Available in: .357 Mag, .44 Mag, .45 Colt
From: . . . . $27–$29

Shotgun Ammunition

AMERICAN WHITETAIL SHOTGUN SLUGS

Features: InterLock ring that locks the core and jacket together to deliver controlled expansion combined with excellent weight retention, energy and accuracy; hollow point bullet design initiates rapid expansion upon impact; serrated lead core and jacket allow for even expansion at low velocities; tough lead alloy core; rigid polycarbonate sabot with exclusive buffer disc combine to open uniformly without compromising accuracy
Available in: 12 Ga. (2 ¾ in.)
Box 5: . . . . $11–$14

BUCKSHOT

Features: Buckshot ammunition is specially designed for unmodified semiauto and pump shotguns; made with Versatite wad technology, these reliable bullets offer a tight, accurate shot
Available in: 12 Ga. (2¾ in.)
Box 10: . . . . $16–$18

CUSTOM LITE SHOTGUN SLUGS

Features: Delivers 25 percent less recoil than standard loads; for rifled barrels only; FTX bullet improves ballistic coefficient and aids in expansion; lower recoil and muzzle blast while maintaining accuracy and effectiveness out to 150 yds; innovative sabot design enhances accuracy
Available in: 20 Ga. (2 ¾ in.)
Box 5: $16

HORNADY AMERICAN WHITETAIL SHOTGUN SLUGS

HORNADY CRITICAL DUTY

HORNADY CUSTOM LITE RIFLE AMMO

Hornady

HEAVY MAGNUM COYOTE

Features: Loaded with 1 ½ oz. of nickel plated lead shot in either a BB or 00 buckshot for close range predators; features Hornady Versatite wad for more impact on target; 1,300 fps
Available in: 12 Ga. (3 in., 00 buckshot or BB)
Box 10:. $18

HEAVY MAGNUM TURKEY

Features: Each 3-in., 12-ga. shotshell contains 1½ oz. of either #4, #5, or #6 nickel-plated lead; each 20-ga. shotshell is loaded with 1 3/8 oz. of #5 nickel-plated lead shot; loads don't require modified shotguns or specialized turkey chokes
Available in: 12 Ga. (3 in.), 20 Ga. (3 in.); Shot sizes: 4, 5, 6 nickel
Box 10:. $18

SST SLUGS

Features: Sharp points at the end of these slugs allow for faster and more accurate shooting; able to reach your target from an impressive 200 yards away; each shot delivers more than 1200 ft.-lbs. of energy; also available in Superperformance (SPF) Slugs
Available in: 12, 20 Ga. (2¾ in)
Box 5:. $16

Rimfire Ammunition

17 HMR

Features: The 17 HMR is one of the most accurate rimfire bullets ever made; polymer tip fragments rapidly and dramatically on impact, and its flat trajectory adds to its accuracy and consistency
Available in: .17 HMR
Box 50:. . . . . $17–$18

17 MACH2

Features: These V-MAX bullets are known for their rapid fragmentation and consistent accuracy; these bullets are made in America and hand inspected; paired with Varmint Express products, ignition is fast and easy
Available in: .17 Mach2
Box 50:. $10–12

22 WMR

Features: The .22 WMR guarantees accurate shooting from more than 125 feet; has a muzzle velocity of 2,200 fps and is one of the most requested products Hornady offers; available in 25, 30, and 45 gr.
Available in: .22 WMR
Box 50:. . . . . $16–$17

HORNADY HEAVY MAGNUM COYOTE

HORNADY SST SLUGS

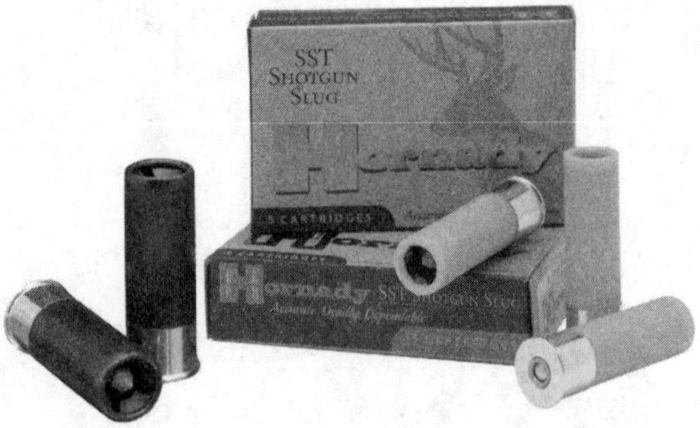

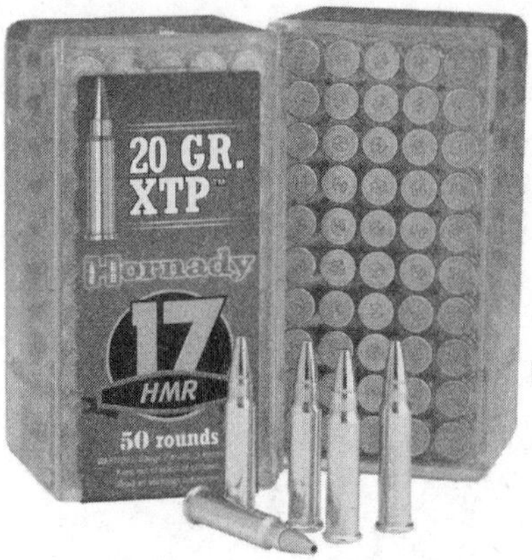

HORNADY 17 HMR

Jarrett Rifles

TROPHY AMMUNITION

Features: Jarrett's high-performance cartridges are in ten round boxes; cases are from Norma with Jarrett's headstamp
Available in: .243 Win., .270 Win., 7mm Rem. Mag., .30-06 Spfd., .300 WM, .300 Jarrett, .375 H&H, .416 Rem. Mag.
MSRP. . . . . $27–$76

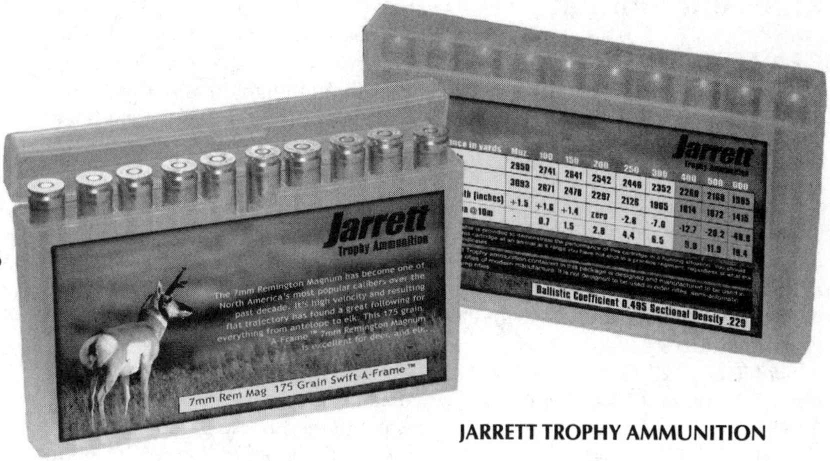

JARRETT TROPHY AMMUNITION

Kynoch Ammunition

KYNOCH RIFLE AMMUNITION

RIFLE AMMUNITION

Features: Kynoch hunting ammunition is now standardized on Woodleigh soft nosed and solid bullets, recognized world wide as the most reliable big game bullets currently manufactured; Kynamco offers virtually the whole range of classic British Nitro Express from its purpose-built factory
Available in: .300 Flanged, .303 British, .318 Westley Richards, 9.5x57 Mannlicher, .333 Jeffery Flanged, .350 Rigby, .400/.360 Westley Richards, .375 Flanged, .400 Purdey, .405 Win., .450/.400, .416 Rigby, .404 Jeffery, .425 Westley Richards, .450 NE, .450 No. 2 NE, .450 Rigby, .577/.450 Martini Henry, .500/.450 NE, .500/.465 NE, .470 NE, .475 No. 2 Eley, .475 No. 2 Jeffery, .476 Westley Richards, .505 Gibbs, .500 Jeffery, .500 NE, .577 NE, .600 NE, .700 NE
MSRP. . . . . $30–$250

Lapua

Rifle Ammunition

CENTERFIRE SPORT
Features: Lapua's extremely accurate target shooting cartridges are loaded with the best target bullets—Scenar, FMJBT, D46 and Lock Base; numerous world championships, Olympic championships, and other top competition gold medals, as well as many official world records in different disciplines, are shot with the Lapua cartridges
Available in: .222 Rem., .223 Rem., 6mm BR Norma, 6.5x47 Lapua, 6.5x55 Swedish, 7.62x39 Warsaw, .308 Win., .30-06 Spfd., 7.62x53R/54R, .338 Lapua Mag.
Box 50:. . . . . $88–$143

MEGA BULLETS
Features: Soft point bullet designed for big game hunting; lead core and copper jacket that are mechanically bonded together; long jacket protects core and prevents premature bullet expansion or breakage when bullet goes through light brush or grass cover; up to 97 percent weight retention
Available in: 6.5x55 Swedish, .308 Win., .30-06 Spfd., 7.62x53R/54R
Box 20:. . . . . $37–$62

NATURALIS
Features: Bullet mushrooming begins immediately on impact; bullet expands symmetrically and without shattering; gives a maximal shock effect to the hunted game; top premium copper bullet; retains up to 100 percent of its weight after the impact
Available in: 6.5x55 Swedish, .308 Win., .30-06 Spfd., .338 Lapua Mag.
Box 20:. . . . . $41–$94

LAPUA CENTERFIRE SPORT

LAPUA NATURALIS

Magtech Ammunition

Handgun Ammunition

CLEANRANGE
Features: CleanRange ammunition was developed to eliminate airborne lead and the need for lead retrieval at indoor ranges by using a state-of-the-art combination of high-tech, lead-free primers and specially designed Fully Encapsulated Bullets, a unique mix that eliminates lead and heavy metal exposure at the firing point.
Available in: .380 ACP, .38 Spl., .40 S&W, .45 ACP, 9mm Luger
Box 50:. . . . . $21–$32

COWBOY ACTION
Features: "Old West" Cowboy Action loads were developed specifically for cowboy action shooting ; these flat-nose bullets deliver reliable knockdown power that puts steel targets down on the first shot
Available in: .357 Mag., .38 Spl., .44-40 Win., .44 Spl., .45 Colt
Box 50:. . . . . $26–$34

FIRST DEFENSE
Features: Magtech First Defense rounds are designed with a 100 percent solid copper bullet, unlike traditional hollow points that contain a lead core covered by a copper jacket; First Defense solid copper bullets have no jacket to split or tear away, ensuring every round you fire meets its target with maximum impact and effectiveness
Available in: 9mm Luger, .38 Spl., .380 ACP, .357 Mag., .40 S&W, .45 ACP
Box 20:. . . . . $18–$27

GUARDIAN GOLD
Features: Thanks to its tremendous stopping power, deep penetration, awesome mushrooming, and dead-on accuracy, Guardian Gold is fast-becoming a favorite among those seeking reliable, affordable personal protection
Available in: 9mm Luger, .32 ACP, .38 Spl., .380 ACP, .357 Mag., .40 S&W, .45 ACP, .45 GAP
Box 20:. . . . . $13–$20

MAGTECH AMMUNITION

SPORT SHOOTING
Features: The 100 percent solid copper hollow-point projectile features a six-petal hollow-point specifically designed to deliver tight groups, superior expansion, virtually 100 percent weight retention, and increased penetration over jacketed lead-core bullets
Available in: .25 ACP, .308 Win., .32 ACP, .32 S&W, .32 S&W L, .357 Mag., .380 ACP, .38 Spl., .38 Spl. S, .38 Super Auto, .38 S&W, .40 S&W, .44-40 Win., .44 Rem. Mag., .454 Casull, .45 ACP, .45 GAP, .500 S&W, 9mm Luger
From:. . . . . $13–$47

Rifle Ammunition

AFRICAN PH

Features: Based on many generations of experience of reputable African Professional Hunters, this range of cartridges has been developed to optimize ballistic criteria such as bullet momentum, sectional density and deep, straight-line, bone-breaking penetration; loaded cartridges with Woodleigh softnose and solid bullets
Available in: .375 Flanged Mag. NE, .375 H&H Mag., .404 Jeffrey, .416 Rem. Mag., .416 Rigby, .500/.416 NE, .450 Rigby Rimless, .458 Lott, .470 NE, .500 Jeffrey, .500 NE 3, .505 Mag. Gibbs
Box 10: . . . . $74–$207

AMERICAN PH

Features: In the "American" style, this line of ammunition features lighter bullets, higher muzzle velocity, and longer average ranges
Available in: .223 Rem., .243 Win., .257 Roberts, 6.5 Jap, 6.5 Carcano, 6.5x55 Swedish, 6.5-284 Norma, .270 Win., .270 WSM; 7mm-08 Rem., .280 Rem., 7mm Rem. Mag, .308 Win., .30-06 Spfd., .308 Norma Magnum, .300 Win. Mag, .300 WSM, .300 RUM, 7.65 Arg, 7.7 Jap, .338 Win. Mag, 9.3x62 Mauser, 9.3x74R, .375 H&H Mag, .338 Lapua Mag, .257 Wby., .270 Wby., 7mm Wby., .300 Wby., .30-378 Wby., .340 Wby.
From: . . . . $45–$152

JAKTMATCH

Features: Target ammunition should have the same quality as your hunting cartridges; many hunters also use Jaktmatch to hunt birds and small game so there is no reason to distinguish between hunting and target cartridges; fired cases provide the reloader with a top quality product to reload
Available in: .222 Rem, .223 Rem, .22–250 Rem., 6mm Norma BR, 6XC, .243 Win., 6.5x55 Swedish, 6.5-284 Norma, .270 Win., .270 WSM, 7mm Rem. Mag., .308 Win, .30-06 Spfd., .300 WSM, .300 Win. Mag., .338 Win. Mag., .358 Norma Mag., 8x57 JS, 9.3x57, 9.3x62 Mauser
Box 10: . . . .$44.99–$57.99

KALAHARI

Features: The Kalahari is loaded with selected lots of powder to ensure the highest possible velocity, best possible ballistic coefficient, and lowest wind drift achievable at normal hunting ranges; bullet expansion is controlled and restricted–only the front third of the bullet will expand into six razor-edged petals, leaving the rear part of the bullet unimpeded, guaranteeing deep penetration
Available in: .270 Win., .270 WSM, .280 Rem., 7x64 Brenneke, 7mm Rem. Mag., .308 Win., .30–06 Spfd., .300 Win. Mag., .300 WSM
Box 20: . . . . $55–$79

ORYX

Features: The Oryx has a thin forward jacket with internal splitting zones; the bonding and the thicker rear jacket wall ensure a high residual weight after impact (often over 90 percent) and excellent penetration
Available in: .222 Rem., .223 Rem., .22–250 Rem., .220 Swift, 6mm Norma BR, 6XC, .243 Win., 6.5x55 Swedish, 6.5x284 Norma, .270 Wby., .270 Win., .270 WSM, .280 Rem., 7x57 R Mauser, 7x57 Mauser, 7x64 Brenneke, 7x65 R, 7mm Rem. Mag., 7mm Blaser Mag., 7.5x55 Swiss, .308 Win., .30-06 Spfd., .300 Win. Mag., .300 WSM, .300 Blaser Mag., .308 Norma Mag., .338 Blaser Mag., .338 Win. Mag., .35 Whelen, .358 Norma Mag., 8x57 JRS, 8x57 JS, 9.3x57, 9.3x62 Mauser, 9.3x74 R, .375 Blaser Mag., .375 H&H Mag.
Box 20: . . . . $45–$152

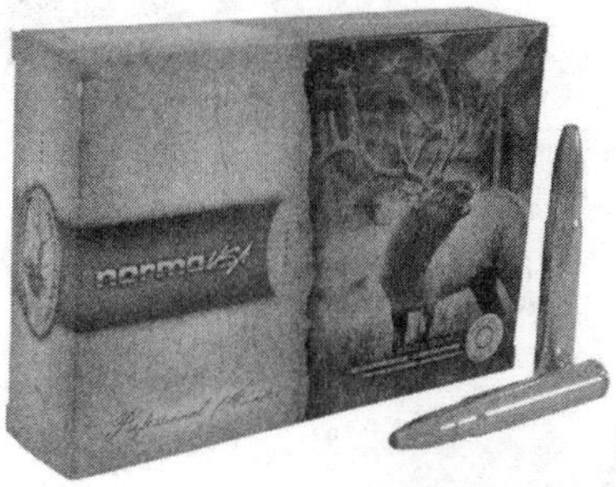

NORMA AMERICAN PH

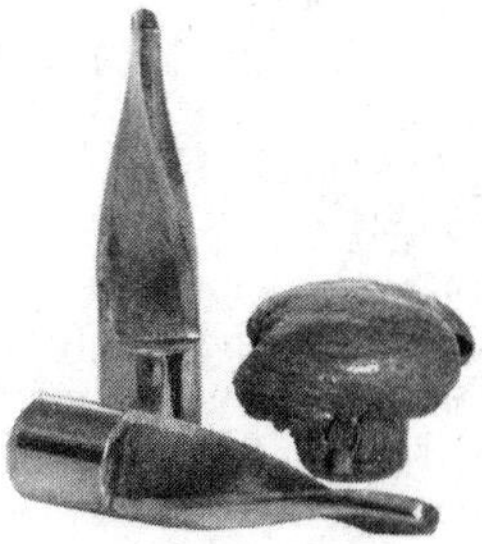

NORMA ORYX

NORMA KALAHARI

Nosler

Rifle Ammunition

MATCH GRADE

Features: Match Grade Ammunition consists of Nosler's precisely-designed Custom Competition bullet along with NoslerCustom Brass; each piece of brass is checked for correct length, neck-sized, chamfered, trued and flash holes are checked for proper alignment; powder charges are meticulously weighed and finished rounds are visually inspected and polished
Available in: .223 Rem., 300 BLK, .308 Win., .338 Lapua Mag., 6.5 Creedmoor, 6.5-284 Norma
Box 20: . . . . $24–$82

SAFARI

Features: Loaded with either the Partition or Nosler Solid and designed for the same point of impact with either bullet, Safari Ammunition provides the ultimate versatility for any dangerous game situation
Available in: Available in both Partition and Solid Dangerous Game: .375 Flanged, .375 H&H, .375 Ruger, .404 Jeffery, .416 Rem. Mag., .416 Rigby, .458 Lott, .458 Win. Mag., 9.3x62 Mauser; SD only: .470 NE, .500 Jeffery, .500 NE, .505 Gibbs; PT only: .500/.416 NE
Box 20: . . . . $109–$239

TROPHY GRADE HUNTING

Features: Manufactured to Nosler's strictest quality standards, Trophy Grade Ammunition uses Nosler Custom Brass and Nosler Bullets to attain optimum performance, no matter where your hunting trip takes you. Whether you want your ammunition loaded with AccuBond, Partition Ballistic Tip or, E-Tip, NoslerCustom Trophy Grade Ammunition will have the right load for the right game.
Available in: 243 Win., .25-06 Rem., .257 Roberts +P, .257 Wby., 6.5 Creedmoor, 6.5x55 Swedish, .260 Rem., 280 Rem., .260 Rem., 6.5-284 Norma, .264 Win. Mag., .270 Win., .270 WSM, 7mm-08 Rem., .280 Ack. Imp., 7mm SAUM, 7mm Rem. Mag., 7mm STW, 7mm RUM, 7x57 Mauser, 9.3x62 Mauser., 308 Win., .30–06 Spfd., .300 H&H Mag., .300 Win. Mag, .300 WSM, .300 SAUM, .300 RUM, .300 Wby., .325 WSM, .338 Lapua Mag., .338 RUM, .338 Win. Mag., .35 Whelen, .375 H&H, .375 H&H Mag., .375 Ruger
Box 20: . . . . $34–$105

TROPHY GRADE VARMINT

Features: Trophy Grade VARMINT Ammunition consists of the venerable Ballistic Tip VARMINT bullet or the frangible Ballistic Tip Lead Free along with NoslerCustom Brass
Available in: .204 Ruger, .223 Rem (35, 40 gr.), .22-250 Rem.
Box 20: . . . . $25–$33

VARMAGEDDON

Features: Featuring a highly accurate polymer tip or hollow point combined with flat base design, Varmageddon products were created for the high-volume varmint shooter who requires the utmost precision; loaded with Nosler Custom Brass, Varmageddon ammunition provides the highest levels of performance for any varmint hunter
Available in: .17 Rem., .22 Hornet, .204 Ruger, .221 Rem. Fireball, .222 Rem., .22-250 Rem., .223 Rem., .243 Win., 300 BLK, .308 Win.
Box 20: . . . . $20–$37

NOSLER SAFARI AMMUNITION

NOSLER TROPHY GRADE VARMINT AMMUNITION

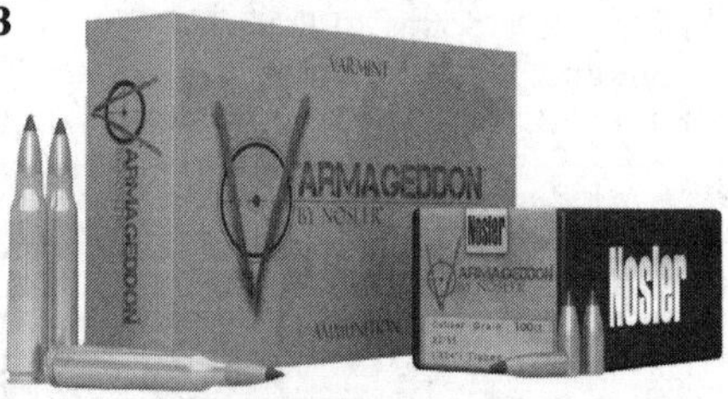

NOSLER VARMAGEDDON AMMUNITION & BULLETS

Handgun Ammunition

NOSLER DEFENSE HANDGUN

HANDGUN

Features: Bonded 'Performance' bullets for higher weight retention and maximum barrier penetration; either jacketed hollow point or polymer tipped configuration
Available in: 9mm Luger +P, .40 S&W, 45 ACP +P
MSRP . . . . $18–$24

PMC Ammunition

Rifle Ammunition

BRONZE LINE - RIFLE

Features: For shooters and hunters who appreciate affordable quality ammunition, the PMC Bronze Line offers reliable performance for every shooting application; Full Metal Jacket (FMJ) bullet types
Available in: .223 Rem, .308 Win., 7.62x39 Warsaw, .50
Box 20:. . . . . $8–$49

X-TAC

Features: PMC's exacting adherence to precise specifications of military and law enforcement organizations assures that X-TAC ammunition will perform perfectly in that fraction of a second when a serious threat arises and your life is on the line
Available in: 5.56 NATO
Box 20:. . . . . $9–$11

X-TAC MATCH

Features: X-TAC ammo performance comined with Sierra Bullets' ballistics, with a match grade .50-caliber bullet
Available in: .223 Rem., .308 Win.
Box 20:. . . . . $28–$40

Handgun Ammunition

BRONZE LINE - HANDGUN

Features: The same quality and dependability built into our Starfire ammunition is incorporated throughout our extensive line of PMC training ammunition and standard hollow point or soft point ammunition.
Available in: .25 ACP, .32 ACP, .380 ACP, .38 Spl., .38 Super +P, 9mm Luger, .357 Mag., 10mm ACP, .40 S&W, .44 S&W Spl., .44 Rem. Mag., .45 ACP
From:. . . . . $14–$39

GOLD LINE - STARFIRE

Features: The secret of Starfire's impressive performance lies in a unique, patented rib-and-flute hollow point cavity design; upon impact, the pre-notched jacket mouth begins to peel back, separating into five uniform copper petals and allowing expansion to begin
Available in: .380 ACP, .38 Spl. +P, .357 Mag., 9mm Luger, .40 S&W, .44 Rem. Mag., .45 ACP
From:. . . . . $13–$26

PMC BRONZE LINE - HANDGUN

PMC AMMUNITION X-TAC MATCH

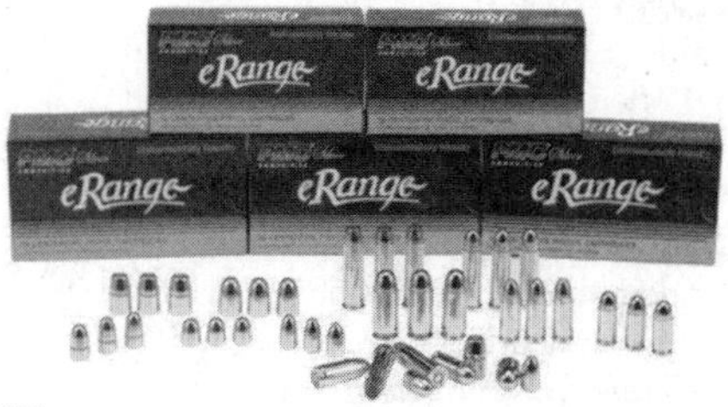

PMC SILVER LINE - ERANGE

SILVER LINE - ERANGE

Features: PMC's eRange environmentally friendly ammunition utilizes a reduced hazard primer that is the first of this type in the industry, an encapsulated metal jacket (EMJ) bullet which completely encloses the surface of the bullet core with precision made copper alloy, and powder with clean-burning characteristics and smooth fire for increased barrel life
Available in: .380 ACP, .38 Spl., .38 Spl. +P, .357 Mag., 9mm Luger, .40 S&W, .44 Rem., .45 ACP
From:. $27

Shotgun Ammunition

"ONE SHOT" HIGH VELOCITY PHEASANT LOADS

Features: These maximum velocity loads deliver a knockout punch of copper plating around extra-hard lead shots; specially designed plastic wads incorporate an innovative shot cup that ensures dense, uniform patterns needed to buckle late-season game birds and animals made fat by winter and wary by hunting pressure
Available in: 12, 20 Ga. (2¾ in., 3 in.); Shot sizes: 4, 5, 6, 7.5
From:. . . . . $25–$31

Remington Ammunition

Rifle Ammunition

REMINGTON AMMUNITION HOG HAMMER

.30 REM. AR

Features: A short, .30-caliber round whose 125-grain bullets match the speed of .308 150s, for hunting deer-size game with the AR-15 modular repeating rifle; ammo comes with Core-Lokt and AccuTip bullets (125 grains) and, in UMC loads, with full metal case (123 grains) bullets

Box 20:. . . . . $22–$45

300 AAC BLACKOUT

Features: A great 30-caliber solution for the R-15 platform. It matches the ballistic power of the 7.62x39 Warsaw, but at 300 meters has 16.7 percent more energy; optimal for sound and flash-suppressed fire, all in a low-recoiling package; features waterproofed primers, crimped and cannelured open-tip match bullets, and a low-drag design

Available in: 300 BLK

Box 20:. . . . . $25–$34

REMINGTON CORE-LOKT ULTRA BONDED

CORE-LOKT ULTRA BONDED

Features: The bonded bullet retains up to 95 percent of its original weight with maximum penetration and energy transfer; features a progressively tapered jacket design, the Core-Lokt Ultra Bonded bullet initiates and controls expansion nearly 2x

Available in: 7mm Rem. SA Ultra Mag., 7mm Rem. Ultra Mag., .300 Rem. SA Ultra Mag., .223 Rem., .243 Win., .25-06 Rem., .260 Rem., .270 Win., 7mm Rem. Mag., .30-06 Spfd., .300 Rem. Ultra Mag., .300 Win. Mag., .338 Win. Mag., .308 Win., 6.8mm Rem. SPC

Box 20:. . . . . $20–$92

REMINGTON AMMUNITION HYPERSONIC

HOG HAMMER

Features: Penetrating even the thickest-skinned pigs with a Barnes TSX Bullet at its heart, the all copper construction provides for 28 percent deeper penetration than standard lead-core bullets; offers near 100 percent weight-retention on-hog, while expanding rapidly to deliver devastating wound channels; utilizes a flash-suppressed propellant for nighttime or low light hunts, and uses nickel-plated cases for reliable feeding

Available in: 300 BLK, .223 Rem., .30 Rem. AR, .30–30 Win., .30–06 Spfd., .308 Win., .450 Bushmaster

Box 20:. . . . . $27–$41

HYPERSONIC

Features: Delivers more than just laser-flat trajectories and higher downrange energies due to its advanced bonded bullet design, Core-Lokt Ultra Bonded

Available in: .308 Win., 7mm Rem. Mag.

Box 20:. . . . . $27–$41

Remington Ammunition

MANAGED RECOIL

Features: Managed-Recoil Ammunition delivers Remington Field proven hunting performance out to 200 yards with half the recoil; bullets provide 2x expansion with over 75 percent weight retention on shots inside 50 yards and out to 200 yards.
Available in: .260 Rem., .270 Win., .30-06 Spfd., .300 Rem. Ultra Mag., .30-30 Win., .300 Win. Mag., 7mm Rem. Mag., 7mm-08 Rem., .308 Win.
Box 20:. . . . . $20–$41

PREMIER ACCUTIP

Features: Featuring precision-engineered polymer tip bullets designed for match-grade accuracy (sub MOA), Premier AccuTip offers an unprecedented combination of super-flat trajectory and deadly down-range performance
Available in: .30 Rem. AR, .300 BLK, .300 Rem. Ultra Mag., .270 WSM, .300 WSM, .223 Rem., .243 Win., .260 Rem., .270 Win., .280 Rem., 7mm Rem. Mag., .30-06 Spfd., .300 Win. Mag., .308 Win., 7mm-08 Rem.,
Box 20:. . . . . $20–$28

PREMIER MATCH

Features: Loaded with match-grade bullets, this ammunition employs special loading practices to ensure world-class performance and accuracy with every shot
Available in: .308 Win., .223 Rem., 6.8mm Rem. SPC, 300 BLK, .300 Win. Mag., .300 Rem. SA Ultra Mag.
Box 20:. . . . . $33–$39

Handgun Ammunition

GOLDEN SABER HPJ

Features: Designed for law enforcement and personal defense, the Golden Saber High Performance Jacket successfully combines match-type accuracy, deep penetration, maximum expansion, and near 100 percent weight retention. Cases nickel-plated for reliable feed, function, and extraction.
Available in: .357 Mag., .380 ACP, 9mm Luger +P, .38 Spl. +P, .40 S&W, .45 ACP +P
Box 25 . . . .$29

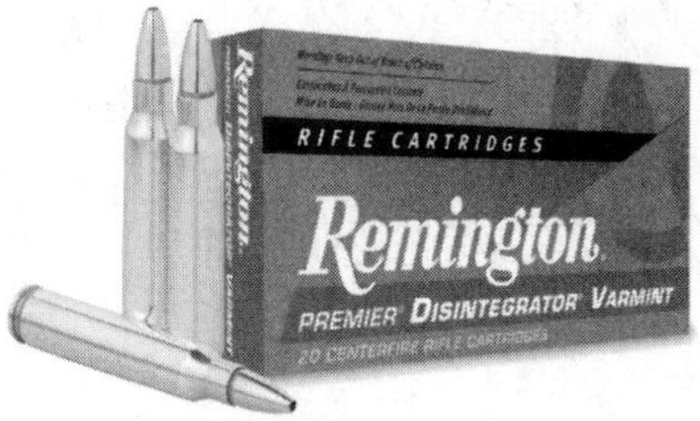

REMINGTON PREMIER DISINTEGRATOR VARMINT

REMINGTON AMMUNITION PREMIER ACCUTIP

REMINGTON GOLDEN SABER HPJ

Remington Ammunition

REMINGTON AMMUNITION
ULTIMATE DEFENSE COMPACT

ULTIMATE DEFENSE COMPACT

Features: Designed with the concealed carry permit holder in mind; delivers big gun terminal performance out of shorter barreled pistols and revolvers; engineered to provide optimal penetration and expansion at lower velocities for maximum stopping power
Available in: .38 Spl., .380 ACP, .40 S&W, .45 ACP, 9mm
Box 20:. $23

Rimfire Ammunition

.22 RIMFIRE TARGET

Features: Whether it's getting young shooters started, practice plinking, small-game hunting, or keeping match shooters scoring high, Remington's rimfire quality stands tall
Available in: .22LR
From:. . . . . $5–$10

MAGNUM RIMFIRE

Features: Premier Gold Box Rimfire ammunition features sleek AccuTip-V bullets; Magnum rimfire ammunition gives shooters the choice of either a Jacketed Hollow Point for quick expansion or a Pointed Soft Point for optimum penetration
Available in: .22 Win. Mag.
MSRP. $16

REMINGTON-ELEY COMPETITION RIMFIRE MATCH EPS

Features: Remington and Eley offer three grades of their premier .22 Long Rifle ammunition; this match grade load features Eley's innovative Tenex EPS-profile bullet—ideal for aspiring top class shooters and training at the highest level
Available in: .22LR
Box 50:. . . . . $11–$22

REMINGTON
TARGET-PREMIER
NITRO GOLD
SPORTING CLAYS

Shotgun Ammunition

TARGET-GUN CLUB TARGET

Features: Loaded with Gun Club Grade Shot, Premier STS Primers, and Power Piston One-Piece Wads, these high-quality shells receive the same care in loading as top-of-the-line Premier STS and Nitro .27 shells
Available in: 12, 20 Ga. (2¾ in.); Shot sizes: 7.5, 8, 9
Box 25:. $8

Remington Ammunition

TARGET-PREMIER NITRO 27 TARGET

Features: Designed specifically for back-fence trap and long-range sporting clays; delivers consistent handicap velocity and pattern uniformity; new, improved powder loading significantly reduces felt recoil while retaining high velocity; both factors allow avid trap shooters to stay fresh for the shoot off.
Available in: 12 Ga. (2¾ in.); Shot Sizes: 7.5, 8
From:....................$12

TARGET-PREMIER NITRO GOLD SPORTING CLAYS

Features: To meet the special demands of avid sporting clays shooters, Remington developed a new Premier Nitro Gold Sporting Clays target load, and at 1300 fps, the extra velocity gives you an added advantage for those long crossers—making target leads closer to normal for ultimate target-crushing satisfaction
Available in: 12, 28 Ga. (2¾ in.), .410 (2½ in.); Shot sizes: 7.5, 8
From:................ $12–$16

TARGET-PREMIER STS TARGET

Features: STS Target Loads have taken shot-to-shot consistency to a new performance level, setting the standard at all major skeet, trap, and sporting clays shooting across the country, while providing handloaders with unmatched reloading ease and hull longevity; available in most gauges, Premier STS shells are the most reliable, consistent, and reloadable shells you can shoot
Available in: 12, 20, 28 Ga. (2¾ in.), .410 (2½ in.); Shot sizes: 7.5, 8, 8.5, 9
From:................ $12–$16

TURKEY-NITRO MAG. BUFFERED MAGNUM

Features: The original buffered magnum shotshells from Remington, the shot charge is packed with a generous amount of shock-absorbing polymer buffering and surrounded by our patented Power Piston wad to protect the specially hardened shot all the way down the barrel for dense, even patterns and uniform shot strings
Available in: 12, 20 Ga. (2¾ in., 3 in.); Shot sizes: 2, 4, 6
Box 25:............... $26–$38

TURKEY-NITRO TURKEY BUFFERED

Features: These loads contain Nitro Mag. extra-hard lead shot that is as hard and round as copper-plated shot; will pattern as well as other copper-plated, buffered loads without the higher cost
Available in: 12 Ga. (2¾ in., 3 in., 3½ in.), 20 Ga. (3 in.); Shot sizes: 4, 5, 6
Box 10:................ $9–$17

TURKEY-PREMIER HIGH-VELOCITY MAGNUM COPPER-PLATED BUFFERED

Features: Utilizing a specially-blended powder recipe, Remington's advanced Power Piston one-piece wad, and hardened copper plated shot, these new high-velocity loads result in extremely dense patterns and outstanding knockdown power at effective ranges
Available in: 12 Ga. (3 in., 3½ in.); Shot sizes: 4, 5, 6
From:................ $18–$22

TURKEY-PREMIER MAGNUM COPPER-PLATED BUFFERED

Features: Premier Magnum Turkey Loads provide that extra edge to reach out with penetrating power and dense, concentrated patterns; the magnum-grade, Copper-Lokt shot is protected by our Power Piston wad and cushioned with special polymer buffering
Available in: 10 Ga. (3½ in.), 12 Ga. (2¾ in., 3 in., 3½ in.), 20 Ga. (3 in.).; Shot sizes: 4, 5, 6
Box 10:............... $13–$22

UPLAND-EXPRESS EXTRA LONG RANGE

Features: Long considered to be some of the best-balanced, best-patterning upland field loads available, our family of shotshells offer great selections for upland bird hunting; the hunter's choice for a wide variety of game-bird applications, from 12-gauge to .410 bore, with shot-size options ranging from BB's all the way down to 9s; suitable for everything from quail to farm predators
Available in: 12, 16, 20, 28 Ga. (2¾ in.), .410 (2½ in., 3 in.); Shot sizes: 2, 4, 5, 6, 7.5, 9
From:................ $16–$18

UPLAND-LEAD GAME

Features: For a wide variety of field gaming, these budget-stretching loads include the same quality components as other Remington shotshells, and are available in four different gauges to match up with your favorite upland shotguns
Available in: 12, 16, 20 Ga. (2¾ in.), .410 (2½ in.); Shot sizes: 6, 7.5, 8
From:................. $8–$16

UPLAND-NITRO PHEASANT

Features: Uses Remington's own Copper-Lokt copper-plated lead shot with high antimony content; hard shot stays rounder for truer flight, tighter patterns, and greater penetration; available in both high-velocity and magnum loadings
Available in: 12, 20 Ga. (2¾ in., 3 in.); Shot sizes: 4, 5, 6
From:................ $20–$23

UPLAND-PHEASANT

Features: For the broadest selection in game-specific Upland shotshells, Remington Upland Loads are the perfect choice with high-velocity and long-range performance for any pheasant hunting situation; standard high-base payloads feature Power Piston one-piece wads
Available in: 12, 16, 20 Ga. (2¾ in.); Shot sizes: 4, 5, 6, 7.5
From:................ $13–$17

Remington Ammunition

UPLAND-SHURSHOT HEAVY DOVE

Features: A sure bet for all kinds of upland game, ShurShot loads have earned the reputation as one of the best-balanced, best-pattering upland field loads available; shells combine an ideal balance of powder charge and shot payload to deliver effective velocities and near-perfect patterns with mild recoil for high-volume upland hunting situations
Available in: 12, 20 Ga. (2¾ in.); Shot sizes: 6, 7.5, 8
From:. $9

WATERFOWL-HYPERSONIC STEEL

Features: With unprecedented velocity and the highest downrange pattern energies ever achieved, Remington HyperSonic Steel takes lethality to new heights and lengths
Available in: 10 Ga. (3½ in.), 12 Ga. (3 in., 3½ in.), 20 Ga. (3 in.); Shot sizes: BB, BBB, 1, 2, 3, 4
From:. . . . . $24–$36

WATERFOWL-NITRO-STEEL HIGH-VELOCITY

Features: Greater hull capacity means heavier charges and larger pellets, which makes these loads ideal for large waterfowl; delivers denser patterns for greater lethality and is zinc plated to prevent corrosion
Available in: 10 Ga. (3½ in.), 12 Ga. (2¾ in., 3 in., 3½ in.), 16 Ga. (2¾ in.), 20 Ga. (2¾ in., 3 in.); Shot sizes: T, BBB, BB, 1, 2, 3, 4
From:. . . . . $21–$30

WATERFOWL-SPORTSMAN HI-SPEED STEEL

Features: Sportsman Hi-Speed Steel's sealed primer, high-quality steel shot, and consistent muzzle velocities combine to provide reliability in adverse weather, while delivering exceptional pattern density and retained energy; a high-speed steel load that is ideal for short-range high-volume shooting during early duck seasons or over decoys
Available in: 10 Ga. (3½ in.), 12 Ga. (2¾ in., 3 in., 3½ in.), 20 Ga. (2¾ in.); Shot sizes: BB, 1, 2, 3, 4, 6, 7
From:. . . . . $11–$29

Shotgun Ammunition–Buckshot

EXPRESS AND EXPRESS MAGNUM

Features: A combination of heavy cushioning behind the shot column and a granulated polymer buffering helps maintain pellet roundness for tight, even patterns
Available in: 12 (2¾ in., 3 in., 3½ in.), 20 Ga. (2¾ in.); Shot sizes: 000, 00, 0, 1, 3, 4
From:. . . . . $5–$12

EXPRESS MANAGED-RECOIL

Features: With less felt recoil than full velocity loads, Express Managed-Recoil Buckshot is an ideal close-range performer; less recoil means second shot recovery is quicker, allowing the user to get back on target more easily; loads are buffered for dense patterns, allowing for highly effective performance at up to 40 yards
Available in: 12 Ga. (2¾ in.); Shot size: 00
From:. $5

Shotgun Ammunition–Slugs

PREMIER ACCUTIP BONDED SABOT

Features: Guided by our new Power Port Tip, the AccuTip Bonded Sabot Slug delivers a degree of accuracy and terminal performance unmatched by any other we tested; yields over 95 percent weight retention thanks to its spiral nose cuts, bonded construction, and high-strength cartridge brass jacket; designed for fully-rifled barrels only
Available in: 12, 20 Ga. (2¾ in., 3 in.)
From:. . . . . $15–$17

REMINGTON WATERFOWL-HYPERSONIC STEEL

REMINGTON EXPRESS BUCKSHOT

Remington Ammunition

PREMIER CORE-LOKT ULTRA BONDED SABOT

Features: Ultra-high velocities deliver devastating on-game performance and the tightest groups (1.8-in.) of any shotgun slug with ultra-flat trajectories; patented spiral nose cuts ensure consistent 2x expansion over a wide range of terminal velocities; 385-grain bonded bullet yields near 100 percent weight retention; flattest shooting slug in existence—10 percent better than the nearest competition; designed for use in fully-rifled barrels only

Available in: 12, 20 Ga. (2¾ in.)

From: $23

SLUGGER HIGH VELOCITY

Features: This is the first high-velocity Foster-style lead slug which exits the barrel at 1800 fps, 13 percent faster than standard 1-oz. slugs; the ⅞ oz. Slugger High Velocity delivers 200 ft.-lbs. more energy at 50 yards with flatter trajectory on deer than standard 1-oz. slugs; designed for the avid deer hunter using smooth bore guns

Available in: 12 Ga. (2¾ in., 3 in.), 20 Ga. (2¾ in.)

From: . . . . $5–$7

SLUGGER MANAGED-RECOIL RIFLED

Features: Slugger Managed-Recoil Rifled Slugs offer remarkably effective performance but with 45 percent less felt recoil than full velocity Sluggers; with effective energy out of 80 yards, these 1-oz. slugs easily handle the majority of shotgun deer hunting ranges

Available in: 12 Ga. (2¾ in.)

From: $5

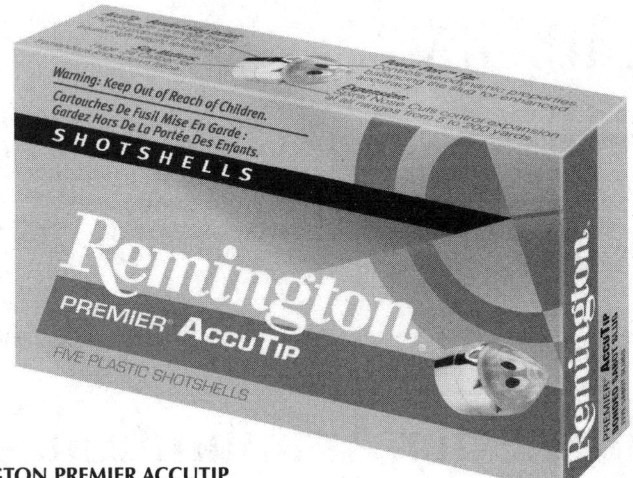

REMINGTON PREMIER ACCUTIP BONDED SABOT

SLUGGER RIFLED

Features: Remington redesigned their 12-gauge Slugger Rifled Slug for a 25 percent improvement in accuracy; at 1760 fps muzzle velocity, the 3-in. 12-gauge Magnum slug shoot 25 percent flatter than regular 12 gauge slugs

Available in: 12 Ga. (2¾ in., 3 in.), 16 Ga. (2¾ in.), 20 Ga. (2¾ in.), .410 (2½ in.)

From: . . . . $5–$7

Rottweil

SLUGS

Features: Everything from the powder to the pellets must be perfectly balanced to produce a shotshell that delivers the required performance. With Rottweil shotshells components and excellent quality control ensure that Rottweil shotgun cartridges not only perform, but perform safely: one expects no less from this renowned German manufacturer.

Available in: 12 Ga., 20 Ga.

MSRP: . . . . $5–$7

RUAG Swiss P

SNIPER AMMUNITION

Features: This family of rifle cartridges has been developed especially for snipers, refined down to the last detail for use by absolute professionals. All cartridges provide the same point of impact over the operative range. No adjustment is required if the combat situation demands a change of cartridge. All cartridges consistently achieve sub MoA accuracy (corresponding to approx. 1 inch at 100 yards). Even at long ranges the calibers .338 LM and .50 Browning maintain high velocities for maximum target effect. Due to tight manufacturing tolerances and quality control, constant ballistic values are guaranteed.

Available in: 5.56, .223, .50 cal., .308, .300 Win. Mag., .338 Lapua Ma.g, 4.6mmx30.

MSRP: . . . . N/A

Sig Sauer

ELITE PERFORMANCE

Features: Designed for personal defense, Elite Performance features a proprietary V-Crown stacked hollow point bullet; an additional smaller hollow point cavity behind the main cavity and V-shaped jackets skives and scores provides controlled, uniform expansion at all effective distances and velocities
Available in: .380 ACP, 9mm Luger, .357 Sig, .40 S&W, .45 ACP
Box 20:. . . . .$19–$25

SIG SAUER ELITE PERFORMANCE

Weatherby

WEATHERBY MAGNUM

Features: Weatherby Magnum cartridges are loaded with a variety of popular bullet types for a wide range of shooting purposes
Available in: .224, .240, .257, .270, 7mm, .300, .340, .30–378, .338–378, .375, .378, .416, .460
MSRP . . . . $37–$176

WEATHERBY MAGNUM

Winchester Ammunition

WINCHESTER AMMUNITION 17 WINCHESTER SUPER MAGNUM

WINCHESTER AMMUNITION AA TRAACKER

Rifle Ammunition

17 WINCHESTER SUPER MAGNUM

Features: A .27 caliber shellcase necked down to a .17 caliber bullet; surpasses the downrange velocity, energy, trajectory and wind bucking characteristics of both the .17 HMR and .22 WMR; loaded in the popular Winchester High Energy (HE) and High Velocity (HV) and Super-X brands; accommodates 20- and 25-grain polymer tipped bullets, plus a 20-grain JHP
Available in: .17 WSM
Box 50:. $15

AA TRAACKER

Features: Stay centered in the pattern all the way to the target; Shot-trap core design captures a portion of the shot to stabilize the wad; unique dove-tail petals allows the wad to spin-stabilize and track in the center of the pattern; available in bright orange for low light conditions and in black for bright light conditions
Available in: 12 Ga. (2 ¾ in.), 20 Ga. (2 ¾ in.)
Box 25:. $10

Winchester Ammunition

ACCUBOND CT

Features: Fully-bonded lead alloy core, high weight retention, pinpoint accuracy, boattail design, Lubalox coating/red polymer tip
Available in: .25-06 Rem., .25 WSSM, .270 Win., .270 WSM, .30-06 Spfd., .300 Win. Mag., .300 WSM, .325 WSM, .338 Win. Mag., .338 Lapua Mag., 7mm Rem. Mag., 7mm WSM
Box 20:. . . . . $33–$91

BALLISTIC SILVERTIP

Features: Solid-based boattail design delivers excellent long-range accuracy; in .22 calibers, the ballistic plastic polycarbonate Silvertip bullet initiates rapid fragmentation; in medium to larger calibers, special jacket contours extend range and reduce cross-wind drift; harder lead core ensures proper bullet expansion
Available in: .22-250 Rem., .223 Rem., .204 Ruger, .223 WSSM, .243 Win., .243 WSSM, .25-06 Rem., .25 WSSM, .270 Win., .270 WSM, .280 Rem., .300 Win. Mag., .30–06 Spfd., .300 WSM, .30–30 Win., .308 Win., .325 WSM, .338 Win. Mag., 7mm Rem. Mag., 7mm-08 Rem., 7mm WSM
Box 20:. . . . . $22–$60

BLIND SIDE

Features: Cube-shaped Hex Shot is designed to hit like high-velocity tumbling bricks creating massive wound channels, preventing over penetration, and maximizing energy deposit and knock-down shock within the bird; Hex Shot cube shots are "stacked" into the wad shot cup more efficiently to provide up to 15 percent more pellets per shell; "Diamond Cut Wad" has a diamond-shaped air-brake petal design that delivers consistent, bird-blasting patterns downrange; available in High Velocity Waterfoul, Magnum Waterfoul, and Magnum Pheasant
Available in: 12 Ga. (3 in., 3 ½ in.), 20 Ga. (3 in.)
Box 25:. . . . . $20–$27

E-TIP LEAD-FREE

Features: The E-Tip lead-free bullet is developed for big-game hunters and complies with current state non-toxic regulations; co-developed with Nosler, the bullet features an E2 energy expansion cavity, which promotes consistent upset, and is made of gliding metal instead of pure copper, which helps prevent barrel fouling
Available in: .270 WSM, .270 Win., .30-06 Spfd., .300 WSM, .300 Win. Mag., .308 Win., 7mm Rem. Mag.
Box 20: . . . . $43–$57

MATCH

Features: Combining proven Winchester technology with proven bullets, the hollow point boat tail design provides the precision match shooters demand; sleek bullet profile, large boattail and small hollow point maximizes long-range accuracy
Available in: .223 Rem., 5.56 NATO, 6.5 Creedmoor
Box:. . . . . $28–$92

PDX1 DEFENDER CENTERFIRE RIFLE

Features: Given the recent popularity of modern sporting rifles (MSR) among shooters and hunters, Winchester has designed a product using Split Core Technology (SCT) for personal defense; SCT technology, using a quick expansion front lead core and a deep driving bonded rear lead core, creates the ultimate .223 Rem. Home Defense load

WINCHESTER ACCUBOND CT

WINCHESTER AMMUNITION MATCH

WINCHESTER AMMUNITION BLIND SIDE

Available in: .223 Rem., .308 Win., 7.62x39 Warsaw
Box 20:. . . . . $30–$40

POWER MAX BONDED BULLETS

Features: Key features of the Super-X bullet include: protected hollow point PHP design, lead core bonded to jacket with proprietary process, massive frontal area of mushroom is more than double original diameter, lead remains bonded to jacket after impact
Available in: .223 Rem., .243 Win., .270 Win., .270 WSM, .30-06 Spfd., .300 WSM, .30-30 Win., .308 Win., .300 Win. Mag., .325 WSM. .338 Win. Mag., 7mm Rem. Mag., 7mm WSM
Box 20:. . . . . $20–$59

Winchester Ammunition

RAZOR BOAR XT

Features: Razor Boar XT is designed specifically for the rugged demands of boar hunting; drives through thick hide and bone to deliver lethal force; the lead-free bullet has a beveled profile and is made of solid gilding metal with a hollow point for delayed expansion on extremely tough wild hogs; flash suppressed powders make Razor Boar XT perfect for use in low light or after dark with night vision technology

Available in: .223 Rem., .270 Win., .30–06 Spfd., .308 Win., 7.62x39 Warsaw

Box 20: . . . . $27–$40

SUPER-X HOLLOW POINT

Available in: .204 Ruger, .218 Bee, .22 Hornet, .30-30 Win.

Box 20: . . . . $20–$59

SUPER-X HOLLOW SOFT POINT

Available in: .30 Carbine, .44 Rem. Mag.

Box 20: $24

SUPER-X JACKETED SOFT POINT

Available in: .357 Mag.

Box 50: $48

SUPER-X JHP

Available in: .45-70 Govt.

Box 20: $36

SUPER-X LEAD

Available in: .32-20 Win.

Box 50: $45

SUPER-X POSITIVE EXPANDING POINT

Available in: .25-06 Rem., .25 WSSM

Box 20: . . . . $33–$35

SUPER-X POWER CORE 95/5

Features: Start with a 95/5 copper alloy, integrate a highly engineered contoured cavity—and you have a new benchmark in lead-free big-game cartridges; features a devastating effective bullet with massive initial impact shock plus deep penetration and virtually 100 percent retained weight to assure maximum trauma to bone and vitals

Available in: .223 Rem., .243 Win., .270 Win., .270 WSM, .30-06 Spfd., .300 Win. Mag., .300 WSM, .30-30 Win., .308 Win., 7mm-08 Rem., 7mm Rem. Mag., 7mm WSM

Box 20: . . . . $28–$47

SUPER-X POWER-POINT

Available in: .22-250 Rem., .223 Rem., .223 WSSM, .243 Win., .243 WSSM, .257 Roberts +P, .264 Win. Mag., .270 Win., .270 WSM, .284 Win., .300 Savage, .30-06 Spfd., .300 WSM, .30–30 Win., .303 British, .30-40 Krag, .307 Win., .308 Win., .300 Win. Mag., .325 WSM, .32 Win. Spl., .338 Win. Mag., .356 Win., 35 Rem., .375 Win., 6mm Rem., 7mm-08 Rem., 7x57 Mauser, 7mm Rem. Mag., 7mm WSM, 8x57 Mauser, 6.5x55 Swede, 7.62x39mm

Box 20: . . . . $17–$60

SUPER-X SILVERTIP HOLLOW POINT

Available in: 44 Rem. Mag.

Box 20: $29

SUPER-X SOFT POINT

Available in: .22 Hornet, .25-20 Win., .25-35 Win., .38-40 Win., .38-55 Win., .44-40 Win., .458 Win.

Box 50: . . . . $46–$82

WIN3GUN SHOTGUN

Features: Built specifically for high-volume, fast-paced competition and time spent training at the range; available in #00 and #7.5 shot sizes

Available in: 12 Ga.

Box 5: . . . . $5–$8

VARMINT X

Features: Polymer tip, alloy jacket, lead core, and rapid fragmentation

Available in: .204 Ruger; .22-250 Rem.; .223 Rem.; .243 Win.

Box 20: . . . . $18–$27

XP3

Features: The XP3 bullet delivers precision accuracy, awesome knockdown power, and deep penetration all in one package—and it's as effective on thin-skinned game, like deer and antelope, as it is on tough game, like elk, moose, bear, and African animals, at short and long ranges

Available in: .243 Win., .243 WSSM, .270 WSM, .270 Win., .30-06 Spfd., .300 WSM, .300 Win. Mag., .308 Win., .325 WSM, 7mm Rem. Mag., 7mm WSM

Box 20: . . . . $42–$68

WINCHESTER AMMUNITION VARMINT X

WINCHESTER AMMUNITION WIN3GUN RIFLE

WINCHESTER RAZOR BOAR XT

Winchester Ammunition

Handgun Ammunition

DUAL BOND

Features: Dual Bond offers a large hollow point cavity, which provides consistent upsets at a variety of ranges and impact velocities; the heavy outer jacket is mechanically bonded to the inner bullet; inner bullet utilizes a proprietary bonding process for a combination of knockdown power, solid penetration, and significant tissue damage

Available in: .44 Rem. Mag., .454 Cassull, .460 S&W Mag., .500 S&W Mag.

Box 20: . . . . $38–$68

FULL METAL JACKET

Available in: .45 ACP, .38 Spl., 9mm Luger, .25 ACP, .38 Super Auto +P, .380 ACP, .40 S&W, .32 ACP, .45 GAP, 9mm Luger

From: . . . . $15–$33

LEAD FLATNOSE

Available in: .38 Spl., .44-40 Win., .44 S&W Spl., .45 Colt

Box 50: . . . . $34–$42

PDX1 DEFENDER

Features: The new Winchester Supreme Elite Bonded PDX1, which was chosen by the FBI as their primary service round, is engineered to maximize terminal ballistics, as defined by the demanding FBI test protocol, which simulates real-world threats

Available in: .357 Mag., .357 SIG, .380 ACP, .38 Spl., +P, .40 S&W, .45 Colt, .45 ACP, 9mm Luger +P, 9mm Luger

From: . . . . $18–$32

PLATINUM TIP HOLLOW POINT

Features: Patented notched reserve taper bullet jacket, plated heavy wall jacket, and two-part hollow point cavity for uniform bullet expansion, massive energy depot

Available in: .41 Rem. Mag., .44 Rem. Mag., .454 Casull, .500 S&W

Box 20: . . . . $31–$63

SUPER-X BLANK-BLACK POWDER

Available in: .32 S&W

Box 50: $34

SUPER-X BLANK-SMOKELESS

Available in: .38 Spl.

Box 50: $41

SUPER-X EXPANDING POINT

Available in: .25 ACP

Box 50: $41

SUPER-X HOLLOW SOFT POINT

Available in: .30 Carbine, .44 Rem. Mag.

Box 20: $24

SUPER-X JACKETED SOFT POINT

Available in: .357 Mag., .38 Spl.

Box 50: . . . . $26–$48

SUPER-X JHP

Available in: .357 Mag., .38 Spl. +P, .454 Casull, .45 Win. Mag., .460 S&W Mag.

Box 20: . . . . $35–$53

SUPER-X LEAD ROUND NOSE

Available in: .32 Short Colt, .32 S&W Long, .32 S&W, .38 Spl., .38 S&W, .44 S&W Spl., .45 Colt

From: . . . .
$37

SUPER-X LEAD SEMI-WAD CUTTER

Available in: .38 Spl.

Box 50: $37

WINCHESTER DUAL BOND

SUPER-X LEAD SEMI-WAD CUTTER HP

Available in: .38 Spl. +P

Box 50: $38

SUPER-X MATCH

Available in: .38 Spl. Super Match

Box 50: $34

SUPER-X SILVERTIP HOLLOW POINT

Available in: 10mm Auto, .32 ACP, .357 Mag., .380 ACP, .38 Super Auto +P, .38 Spl. +P, .38 Spl., .40 S&W, .41 Rem. Mag., .44 Rem. Mag., .44 S&W Spl., .45 ACP, .45 Colt, .45 GAP, 9x23 Win., 9mm Luger

Box 20, 50: . . . . $22–$55

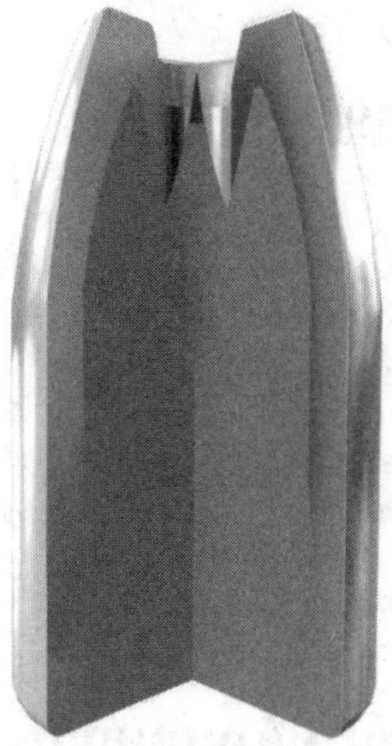

WINCHESTER PLATINUM TIP HOLLOW POINT

WINCHESTER SUPER-X SILVERTIP HOLLOW POINT

Winchester Ammunition

W TRAIN & DEFEND

Features: A straightforward solution for new shooters interested in training to become more proficient with their personal defense ammunition; ballistically-matched ammunition pairs range-ready TRAIN (T) rounds with threat-stopping, technologically-driven DEFEND (D) rounds, each designed for less felt recoil

Available in: .38 Spl., .380 ACP, .40 S&W, 9mm

Box 50 (Train): . . . . $16–$25

Box 20 (Defend): . . . . $18–$26

WIN3GUN PISTOL

Features: Built specifically for high-volume, fast-paced competition and time spent training at the range

Available in: .40 S&W, .45 ACP, 9mm

Box 50:. . . . . $17–$28

WIN1911

Features: Provides a choice of personal defense or training ammunition that has been matched for ballistic performance and engineered for the same feel and function; high-accuracy, ballistically matched full metal jacket and jacketed hollow point offerings make this an ideal ammunition choice

Available in: .45 ACP

Box 50:. . . . . $28–$40

Rimfire Ammunition

DEFENDER RIFLE

Features: Defender .223 Rem. features Split Core Technology, "SCT", designed to deliver massive initial trauma with ideal penetration to create the ultimate rifle load for personal defense; Defender 22 rimfire features a 40-gr. JHP jacketed hollow-point bullet and is designed to deliver the ideal personal defense combination of optimum penetration and maximum projectile expansion for maximum energy transfer

Available in: .22 Win. Mag., .223 Rem.

Box 50 . . . . $31

DYNA POINT - PLATED

Available in: .22 Win. Mag.

Box 250: $46

WINCHESTER AMMUNITION W TRAIN & DEFEND

WINCHESTER AMMUNITION WIN3GUN PISTOL

WINCHESTER AMMUNITION WIN1911

WINCHESTER AMMUNITION DEFENDER RIFLE

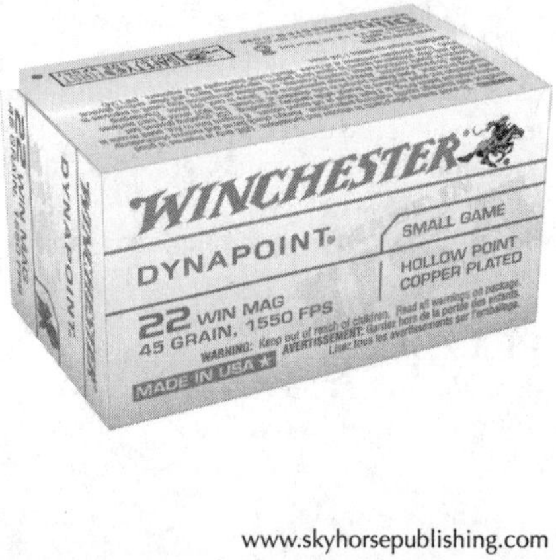

WINCHESTER DYNA POINT - PLATED

AMMUNITION

Winchester Ammunition

SUPER-X #12 SHOT
Available in: .22LR
Box 50:. $11

SUPER-X BLANK
Available in: .22 Short
Box 50: $9

SUPER-X FULL METAL JACKET
Available in: .22 Win. Mag.
Box 50: $11

SUPER-X JHP
Available in: .17 HMR, .17 Win. Super Mag., .22 Win. Mag.
Box 50, 250: . . . . $15–$57

SUPER-X LEAD HOLLOW POINT
Available in: .22LR
Box 100:. . . . .$8–$9

SUPER-X LEAD ROUND NOSE
Available in: .22LR, .22 Long, .22 Short
Box 100:. $7

SUPER-X LEAD ROUND NOSE, STANDARD VELOCITY
Available in: .22LR
Box 100:. . . . .$3–$6

SUPER-X POWER-POINT, LEAD HOLLOW POINT
Available in: .22LR
Box 50:. $4

XPERT LEAD HOLLOW POINT
Available in: .22LR
Box 500: $32

VARMINT HIGH ENERGY
Available in: .22LR, .22 Win. Mag., .17 WSM
Box 250, 500: . . . . $29–$155

VARMINT HIGH VELOCITY
Available in: .22 Win. Mag., .17 HMR, .17 WSM, .22LR
Box 500:. . . . .$136–$146

VARMINT LEAD FREE
Available in: .22 Mag., .22LR
Box 500:. $113

WILDCAT 22 LEAD ROUND NOSE
Available in: .22LR
Box 500: $26

Shotgun Ammunition–Loads

AA TARGET LOADS
Features: The hunter's choice for a wide variety of game bird applications, available in an exceptionally broad selection of loadings, from 12-gauge to .410 bore, with shot size options ranging from BBs all the way down to 9s—suitable for everything from quail to farm predators
Available in: 12, 20, 28 Ga. (2¾ in.), .410 (2½ in.); Shot sizes: 7.5, 8, 8.5, 9
Box 25:. . . . . $9–$11

AA TRAACKER
Features: Stay centered in the pattern all the way to the target; Shot-trap core design captures a portion of the shot to stabilize the wad; unique dove-tail petals allows the wad to spin-stabilize and track in the center of the pattern; available in bright orange for low light conditions and in black for bright light conditions
Available in: 12 Ga. (2 ¾ in.), 20 Ga. (2 ¾ in.)
Box 25:. $10

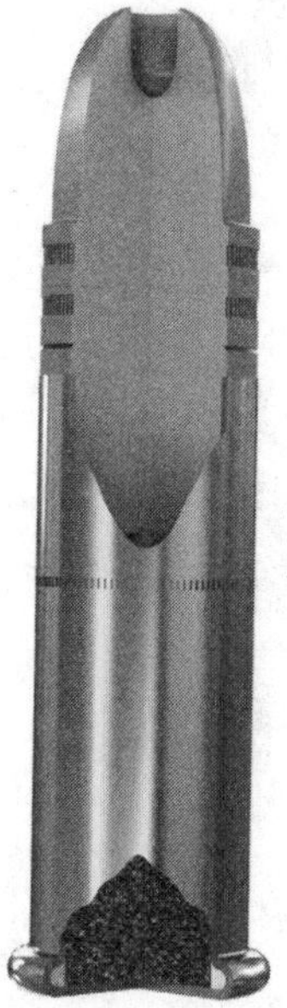

WINCHESTER VARMINT LEAD FREE

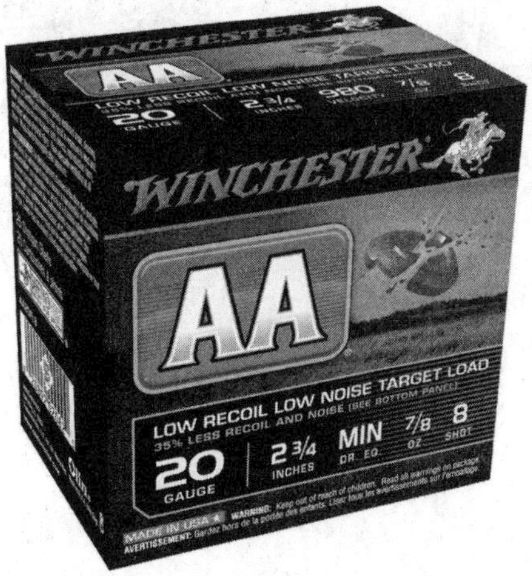

WINCHESTER AA FEATHERLITE

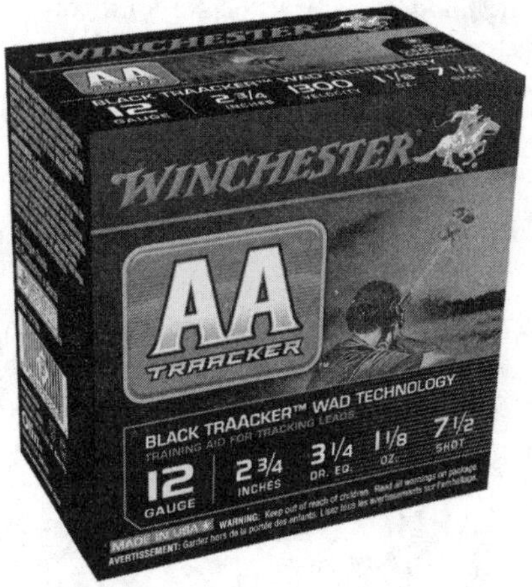

WINCHESTER AMMUNITION AA TRAACKER

Winchester Ammunition

BLIND SIDE
Features: Blind Side ammunition combines ground-breaking, stacked HEX Shot technology and the Diamond Cut Wad in the most deadly Winchester waterfowl load available. Loaded with 100 percent HEX Shot, you get more pellets on target, a larger kill zone, and more trauma inducing pellets than ever before, meaning quick kill shots
Available in: 12 Ga. (2¾ in., 3 in., 3½ in.), 20 Ga. (3 in.); Shot size: BB, 1, 2, 3, 5, 6
Box 25:. . . . . $20–$27

LONG BEARD XR
Features: Features Shot-Lok technology; offers the tightest patterns and longest shot capability of any traditional turkey load with twice the pellets in a 10-in. circle out to 60 yds
Available in: 12 Ga. (3 in., 3 ½ in.)
Box 10:. . . . . $18–$23

ROOSTER XR
Features: With Shot-Lok technology for deeper penetration and devastating terminal performance
Available in: 12 Ga. (2 ¾ in., 3 in.); Shot sizes: 4, 5, 6
Box 15:. . . . . N/A

SUPER TARGET LOADS
Available in: 12, 20 Ga. (2¾ in.); Shot sizes: 7, 7.5, 8, 9
Box 25:. $7

SUPER PHEASANT LOADS
Available in: 12 Ga. (2¾ in., 3 in.), 20 Ga. (3 in.); Shot sizes: 4, 5, 6
Box 25:. . . . . $19–$23

SUPER PHEASANT STEEL LOADS
Available in: 12 Ga. (3 in.); Shot size: 4
Box 25:. . . . . $20–$23

SUPER-X TRIALS AND BLANKS
Available in: 10 Ga. (2 7/8 in.), 12 Ga. (2¾ in.)
Box 25:. $20

SUPER-X TURKEY LOADS
Available in: 12 Ga. (2¾ in., 3 in.); Shot sizes: 4, 5, 6
Box 10: . . . . $9–$12

SUPER-X XPERT HI-VELOCITY STEEL LOADS
Available in: 12 Ga. (2¾ in., 3 in.), 20 Ga. (3 in.); Shot sizes: BB, 1, 2, 3, 4
Box 25:. . . . . $12–$18

SUPER-X XPERT STEEL LOADS
Available in: 12, 20, 28 Ga., .410 bore (2¾ in.); Shot sizes: 6, 7
Box 25:. $8

WIN3GUN SHOTGUN
Features: Built specifically for high-volume, fast-paced competition and time spent training at the range; available in #00 and #7.5 shot sizes
Available in: 12 Ga.
Box 5:. . . . . $5–$8

XTENDED RANGE HD COYOTE
Available in: 12 Ga. (3 in.); Shot size: B
Box 5: $15

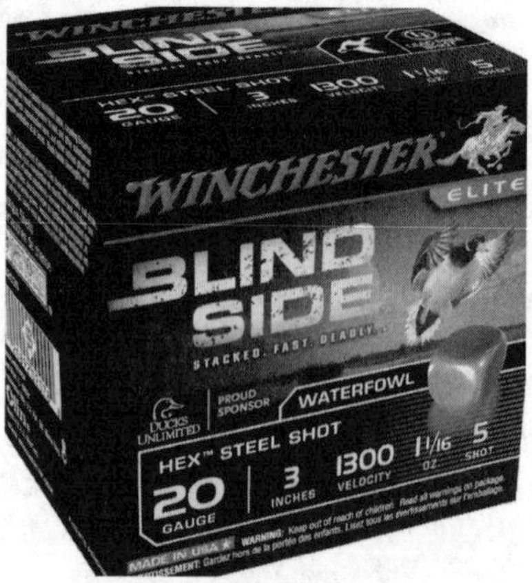

WINCHESTER BLIND SIDE

WINCHESTER AMMUNITION LONG BEARD XR

WINCHESTER AMMUNITION WIN3GUN SHOTGUN

WINCHESTER AMMUNITION ROOSTER XR

XTENDED RANGE HD TURKEY

Available in: 12 Ga. (2¾ in., 3 in., 3½ in.), 20 Ga. (3 in.); Shot sizes: 4, 5, 6
Box 10:................ $39–$44

XTENDED RANGE HD WATERFOWL

Available in: 12 Ga. (2¾ in., 3 in., 3½ in.), 20 Ga. (3 in.); Shot sizes: 2, 4, B
Box 10:.................. $$31

Shotgun Ammunition–Slugs

PDX1 12 AND BUCK

Features: The 12-gauge PDX1 Defender ammunition features a distinctive black hull, black oxide high-base head and three pellets of Grex buffered 00 plated buckshot nested on top of a 1 oz. rifled slug; an ideal, tight patterning personal defense load; slug/buckshot combination provides optimum performance at short and long ranges while compensating for aim error
Available in: 12 Ga. (2¾ in.)
Box 10:.................... $15

PDX1 DEFENDER SEGMENTING SLUG

Features: The uniquely designed slug segments into three pieces when fired into FBI protocol barriers such as bare, light cloth, and heavy cloth covered ballistic gelatin; the round is designed to compensate for aim error over traditional slugs.
Available in: 12 Ga. (2¾ in.), 20 Ga. (2¾ in.), .410 (2 in., 3 in.)
Box 10: $15

RACKMASTER RIFLED SLUGS

Features: The RackMaster system design consists of a hard-hitting lead nose and the innovative WinGlide rear projectile stabilizer, engineered specifically to improve in-bore alignment and enhance down-range accuracy; delivers high accuracy, hard-hitting knockdown performance to hunters shooting shotguns with either smooth bore, rifled choke tube or fully-rifled barrels
Available in: 12 Ga. (2¾ in., 3 in.), 20 Ga. (2¾ in.)
Box 5:.................. $7–$10

SUPER-X

Available in: 12, 20 Ga. (2¾ in., 3 in.), .410 (2½ in., 3 in.)
Box 5, 15:................ $5–$16

SUPER-X BUCKSHOT

Available in: 12 Ga. (2¾ in., 3 in., 3½ in.), 20 Ga. (2¾ in.), .410 (2½ in., 3 in.); Shot sizes: 4, 3, 1, 00, 000
Box 5:.................. $5–$14

XP3 SABOT SHOTGUN

Available in: 12 Ga. (2¾ in., 3 in.)
Box 5:................. $13–$15

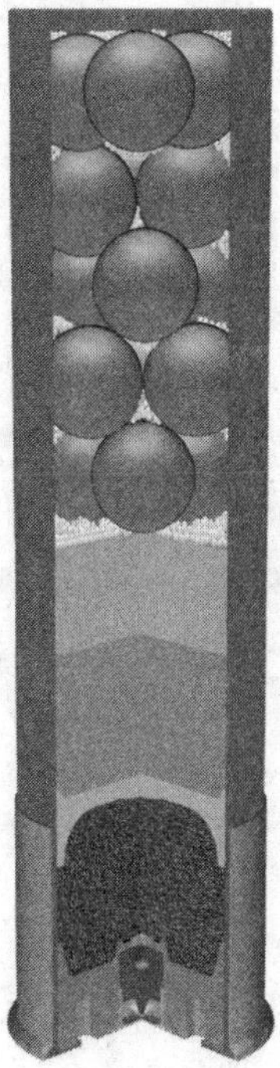

WINCHESTER SUPER-X BUCKSHOT

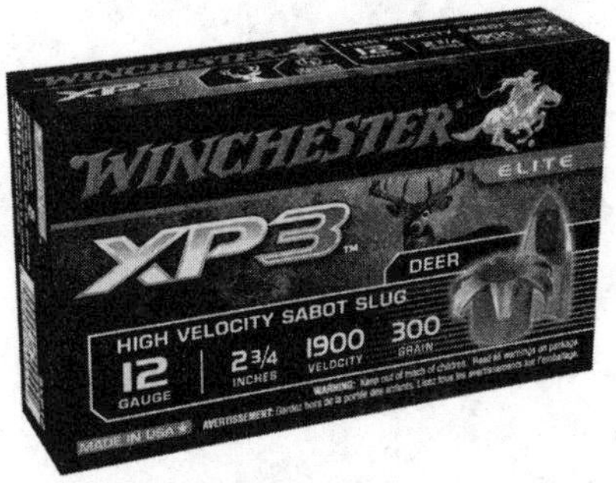

WINCHESTER XP3 SABOT SHOTGUN

WINCHESTER PDX1 DEFENDER SEGMENTING SLUG

MUZZLELOADING BULLETS

Barnes Bullets

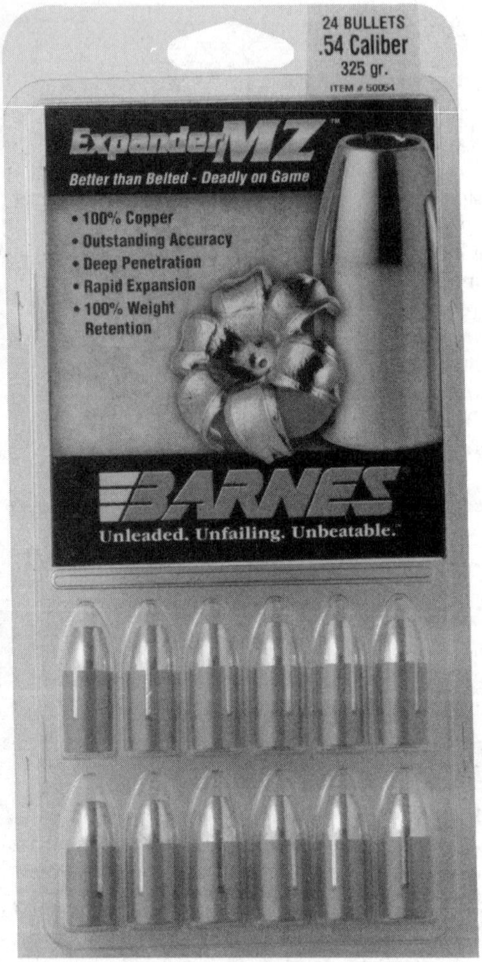

BARNES BULLETS EXPANDER MZ

EXPANDER MZ

Features: 100 percent copper with a large, hollow cavity; six copper petals with double-diameter expansion; full weight retention
Available in: .45 (195 gr.), .50 (250, 300 gr.), .54 (275, 325 gr.)
Box 15 or 24: . . . . $24–$39

SPIT-FIRE MZ

Features: A streamlined semi-spitzer give, boattail base and tack-driving accuracy; six razor-sharp copper petals create massive shock, deep penetration, and double-diameter expansion; retains virtually 100 percent of its original weight; available in 15 and 24-bullet packs
Available in: .50 (245, 285 gr.)
Box 15 or 24: . . . . $27–$36

SPIT-FIRE TMZ

Features: 100 percent copper boattail design with streamlined polymer tip for faster expansion; expands at 1050 fps.; remains intact at extreme velocities; redesigned sabot loads faster while retaining tight gas seal
Available in: .50 (250, 290 gr.)
Box 15 or 24: . . . . $26–$41

BARNES BULLETS SPIT-FIRE TMZ

BARNES BULLETS SPIT-FIRE MZ

Harvester

SABER TOOTH BELTED

Features: Copper-clad belted bullets in Harvester Crush Rib Sabot
Available in: .50 (250, 270, 300, 350 gr.)
MSRP $12

SCORPION FUNNEL POINT MAG

Features: Electroplated copper plating does not separate from lead core; loaded in Harvester Crush Rib Sabots
Available in: .50 (240, 260, 300 gr.); .54 (240, 260, 300 gr.)
MSRP . . . . $9–$12

SCORPION PT GOLD

Features: Scorpion PT Gold Ballistic Tip Bullets are electroplated with copper plating that does not separate from lead core; offers greater accuracy at longer ranges than a hollow point; 3 percent antimony makes the bullet harder than pure lead
Available in: .45 (240, 260, 300 gr.); .50 ((240, 260, 300 gr.)
MSRP . . . . $11–$21

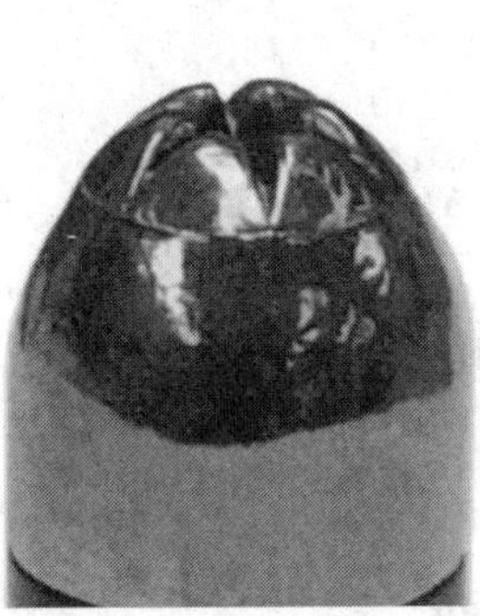

HARVESTER SABER TOOTH BELTED

HARVESTER SCORPION FUNNEL POINT MAG

HARVESTER SCORPION PT GOLD

Hornady

GREAT PLAINS - PA CONICAL

Features: Delivers greater accuracy and more knock-down power; PA bullets are prelubed with special knurled grooves on the bearing surface to hold the lubricant on the bullet—no need for a patch or sabot
Available in: .50 (240, 385 gr.); .54 (425 gr.)
MSRP . . . . $11–$15

HP/XTP BULLET/SABOT

Features: Hornady XTP bullet/sabot combination with controlled expansion XTP bullet
Available in: .50 cal. sabot with .44 (240 gr.) or .45 (240, 300 gr.) bullet
MSRP . . . . $13–$35

MONOFLEX ML

Features: Constructed with the Hornady Flex Tip and retaining 95 percent of its original weight, it's available in both a High Speed/Low Drag sabot and Lock-N-Load Speed Sabot
Available in: .50 cal. sabot with .45 cal. (250 gr.) bullet
Box 20: . . . . $16–$28

HORNADY GREAT PLAINS - PA CONICAL

HORNADY HP/XTP BULLET/SABOT

HORNADY MONOFLEX ML

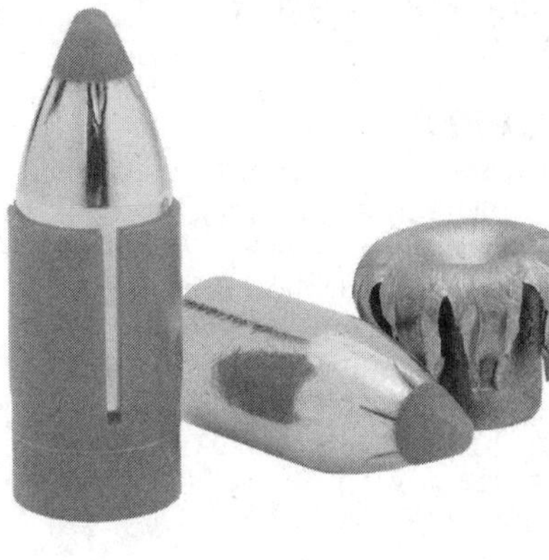

Knight Rifles

BLOODLINE BULLETS
Features: Individually machined, double knurled bullets for increased visual blood trails
Available in: .45 (185, 200 gr.); .50 (220, 250, 275, 300 gr.); .52 (220, 275, 300 gr., 350 gr.); .54 (325 gr.)
Box 20:. . . . . $20–$37

RED HOT BULLETS
Features: Saboted Barnes solid copper bullet with superior expansion
Available in: .45 (150 gr., 175 gr.); .50 (250, 300 gr., 350 gr.,); .52 (275, 350, 375 gr.)
MSRP. . . . .
$15–$29

SPITZER BOAT TAIL BULLETS
Features: Sabot loaded with Barnes Spit-Fire Boat-tail bullet; 18 pack
Available in: .50 (245 gr., 250 gr., 290 gr.)
MSRP. . . . . $20–$23

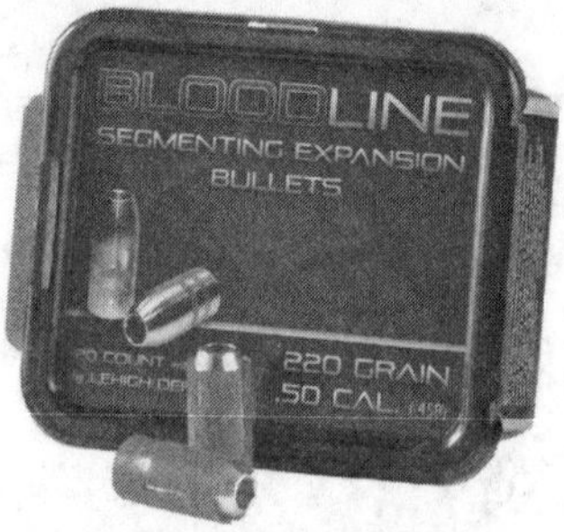

KNIGHT RIFLES BLOODLINE BULLETS

PowerBelt

POWERBELT AEROLITE

POWERBELT COPPER

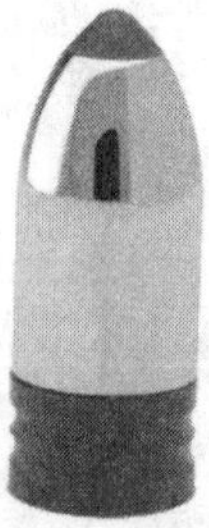

POWERBELT PLATINUM AEROTIP

POWERBELT PURE LEAD HOLLOW POINT

AEROLITE
Features: Designed specifically for use with standard 100-grain loads; AeroLite's shape is noticeably longer and more aerodynamic than other PowerBelts of similar weight; longer length is made possible by the massive hollow point cavity that is filled by an oversized polycarbonate point
Available in: .50 (250, 300 gr.)
MSRP. . . . . $33–$34

COPPER
Features: Thin copper plating reduces bore friction while allowing for optimal bullet expansion; available in four tip designs: Hollow Point, AeroTip, Flat Point, and Steel Tip
Available in: .45 (150 gr., 175, 195, 225, 275 gr.); .50 (223, 245, 295, 348, 405, 444 gr.); .54 (295, 348, 405, 444 gr., 250 gr., 290 gr.)
MSRP. . . . . $23–$70

PLATINUM AEROTIP
Features: Proprietary hard plating and aggressive bullet taper design for improved ballistic coefficient; large-size fluted gas check produces higher and more consistent pressures
Available in: .45 (223, 300 gr.); .50 (270, 300, 338 gr.)
MSRP. . . . . $31–$33

PURE LEAD
Features: Pure lead, available in four different grain weights in Hollow Point and 444 in Flat Point
Available in: .50 (295, 348, 405, 444 gr.); .54 (295, 348 , 405, 444 gr.)
MSRP. . . . . $23–$25

MAG EXPRESS SABOTS
Features: Mag Express Sabots separate from the projectile quickly; are preassembled with XTP bullets, but also available separately
Available in: .50 (240, 300 gr.); .54 (250 gr.)
Box 30:. . . . . $26–$28

MAXI-BALL

Features: An exceptionally accurate bullet and the preferred bullet for penetration needed for large game like elk; lubricating grooves (maxi wide grooves)
Available in: .50 (320, 370 gr.)
Box 20:. . . . . $27–$28

THOMPSON/CENTER MAXI-BALL

SHOCK WAVE SABOTS

Features: Polymer tip spire point bullet with sabot; incorporates harder lead core with walls interlocked with the jacket for maximum weight retention and expansion; available with spire point or bonded bullets
Available in: .45 (200 gr.); .50 (200, 250, 300 gr.)
Box 15:. . . . . $21–$31

THOMPSON/CENTER SHOCK WAVE SABOTS

SUPER 45 XR SABOTS

Features: Centerfire weight performance without the recoil, Super 45 XR sabots have a flatter trajectory, provide deep penetration, and nearly 2 times the expansion of its original diameter.
Available in: .45 (155, 180 gr.)
Box 30:. $27

THOMPSON/CENTER SUPER 45 XR SABOTS

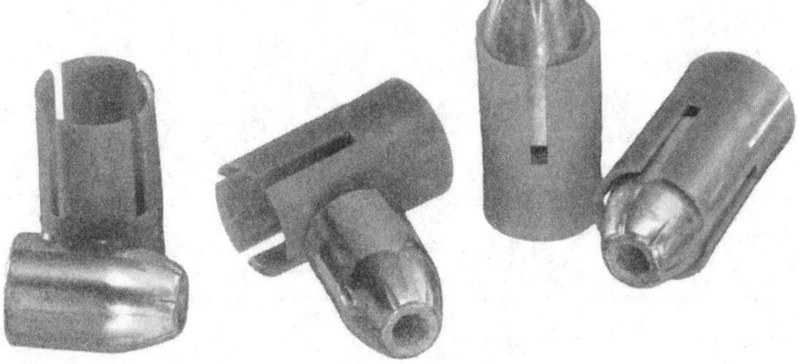

BULLETS

Barnes Bullets

Barnes continues to develop leading-edge products with a wide range of workability and functionality using an incredibly broad range of purpose-built components and ammunition. Barnes's most popular hunting bullets, the all-copper TSX line, also comes with a streamlined polymer tip. The Barnes Buster line can be used for both rifles and handguns.

Rifle Bullets

Banded Solids

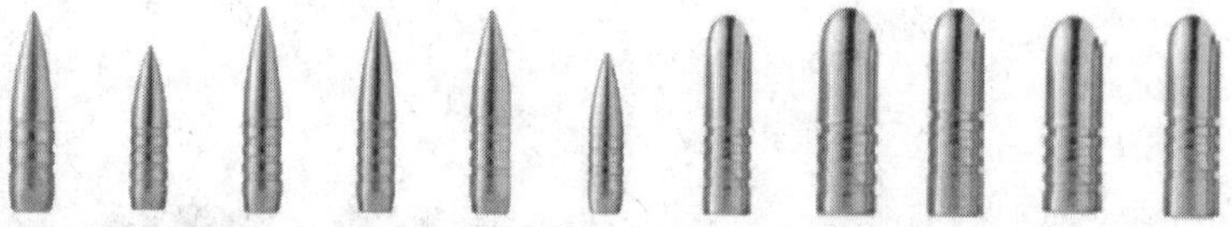

Caliber & Description	6MM S BT	25 S BT	6.5MM S BT	270 S BT	7MM S BT	30 S BT	338 RN	9.3MM RN	9.3MM RN	375 RN	375 RN
Diameter, Inches	.243	.257	.264	.277	.284	.308	.338	.366	.366	.375	.375
Weight, Grains	75	90	110	120	140	165	250	250	286	270	300
Density	.181	.195	.225	.223	.248	.248	.313	.267	.305	.274	.305
Ballistic Coefficient	.341	.325	.452	.438	.464	.438	.247	.214	.247	.207	.230
Catalog Number	24375	25793	26422	27763	28464	30816	33825	30466	30467	37512	37525

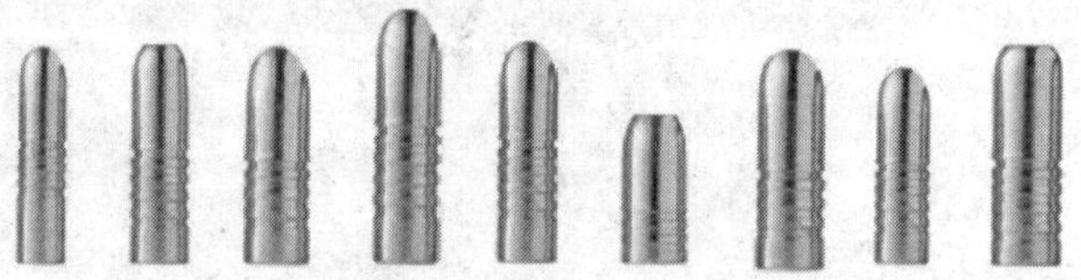

Caliber & Description	375 RN	450/400 FN	416 RN	416 RN	404 JEFF RN	458 SOCOM FN	458 RN	458 RN	470 NITRO FN
Diameter, Inches	.375	.410	.416	.416	.422	.458	.458	.458	.474
Weight, Grains	350	400	350	400	400	330	450	500	500
Density	.356	.340	.289	.330	.321	.226	.306	.341	.318
Ballistic Coefficient	.283	.292	.217	.261	.261	.191	.267	.394	.243
Catalog Number	37527	40935	30520	30526	30536	45861	45840	45855	30649

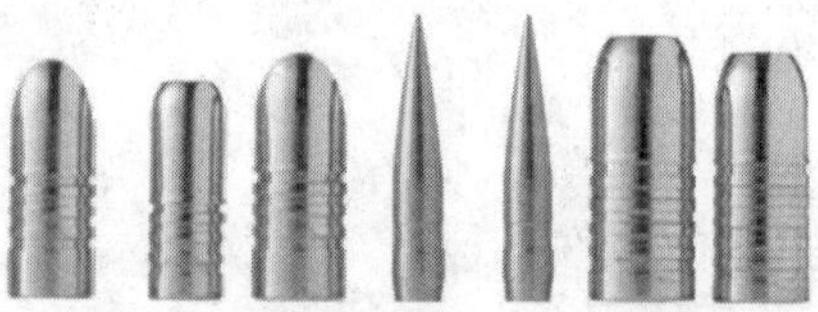

Caliber & Description	505 GIBBS RN	500 NITRO FN	500 JEFF RN	50 BMG BORE RIDER	50 BMG BORE RIDER	577 NITRO FN	600 NITRO FN
Diameter, Inches	.504	.509	.510	.510	.510	.583	.618
Weight, Grains	525	570	535	750	800	750	900
Density	.295	.314	.294	.412	.439	.315	.337
Ballistic Coefficient	.267	.243	-	1.070	1.095	.257	.380
Catalog Number	30685	30690	30694	30703	30707	30713	30714

LEGEND

Type of Bullet

- **BT** – Boattail
- **FB** – Flat Base
- **FN** – Flat Nose
- **RN** – Round Nose
- **S** – Spitzer
- **SP** – Soft Point
- **SS** – Semi-Spitzer

From: $30–$59

LEGEND

Type of Bullet

- **BT** – Boattail
- **FB** – Flat Base
- **FN** – Flat Nose
- **RN** – Round Nose
- **S** – Spitzer
- **SP** – Soft Point
- **SS** – Semi-Spitzer

Barnes Buster

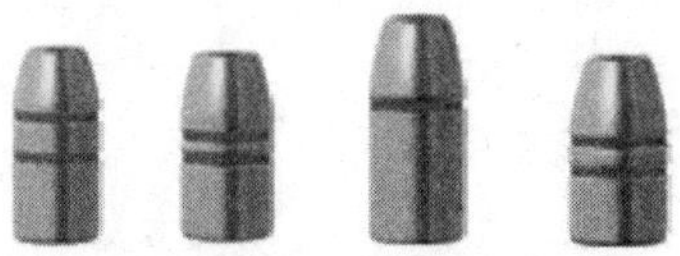

Caliber & Description	44 MAG. FN FB	454 CASULL FN FB	45/70 FN FB	500 S&W FN FB
Diameter, Inches	.429	.451	.458	.500
Weight, Grains	300	325	400	400
Density	.233	.228	.272	.229
Ballistic Coefficient	.241	.206	.242	.220
Catalog Number	30545	30572	30644	30672

Box 50: $50–$60

Barnes Original

Caliber & Description	348 WIN FN SP	348 WIN FN SP	375 WIN FN SP	38/55 FN SP	38/55 FN SP	"45/70 SSSP"	45/70 FN SP	45/70 SSSP	45/70 FN SP	50/110 WIN FN SP	50/110 WIN FN SP
Diameter, Inches	.348	.348	.375	.375	.377	.458	.458	.458	.458	.510	.510
Weight, Grains	220	250	255	255	255	300	300	400	400	300	450
Jckt.	.032	.032	.032	.032	.032	.032	.032	.032	.032	.032	.032
Density	.260	.295	.259	.259	.256	.204	.204	.272	.272	.165	.247
Ballistic Coefficient	.301	.327	.290	.290	.290	.291	.227	.389	.302	.183	.274
Catalog Number	30437	30438	30496	30498	30611	30612	30612	30613	30614	30682	30683

From: $20–$56

LRX Bullets

Caliber & Description	6.5MM BT	270 BT	7MM BT	7MM BT	30 BT	30 BT	338 LAPUA BT	338 LAPUA BT
Diameter, Inches	.264	.277	.284	.284	.308	.308	.338	.338
Weight, Grains	127	129	145	168	175	200	265	280
Density	.257	.240	.257	.257	.264	.301	.331	.350
Ballistic Coefficient	.468	.463	.486	.550	.508	.546	.575	.667
Catalog Number	30228	30262	30282	30284	30318	30374	30434	30432

Box 50: $37–$49

Match Burner Bullets

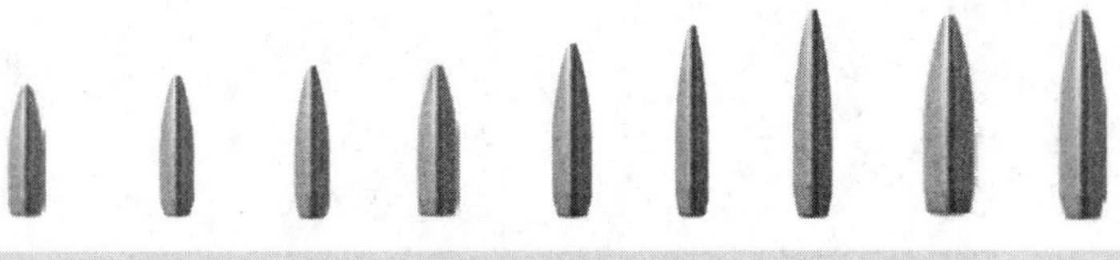

Caliber & Description	22 FB	22 BT	22 BT	6MM FB	6MM BT	6.5MM BT	7MM BT	"30 PALMA FB"	30 BT
Diameter, Inches	.224	.224	.224	.243	.243	.264	.284	.308	.308
Weight, Grains	52	69	85	68	105	140	171	155	175
Density	.148	.196	.242	.165	.254	.287	.303	.233	.264
Ballistic Coefficient	.224	.339	.410	.267	.511	.586	.645	.467	.521
Catalog Number	30160	30162	30164	30205	30206	30230	30285	30381	30385

Box 100: $20–$33

LEGEND

Type of Bullet

- **BT** – Boattail
- **FB** – Flat Base
- **FN** – Flat Nose
- **RN** – Round Nose
- **S** – Spitzer
- **SP** – Soft Point
- **SS** – Semi-Spitzer

Barnes Bullets

M/LE Reduced Ricochet, Limited Penetration (RRLP) Bullets

Caliber & Description	223/5.56 FB	6.8MM FB	30 FB	7.62X39 FB
Diameter, Inches	.224	.277	.308	.310
Weight, Grains	55	85	150	108
Density	.157	.158	.226	.161
Ballistic Coefficient	.225	.229	.357	.243
Catalog Number	80161	30252	30313	30390

From: $19–31

M/LE TAC-TX Bullets

Caliber & Description	300 AAC Blackout	6.5mm BT	6.5mm BT	6.8mm BT	30 FB	30 BT	338 BT	338 BT	458 SOCOM BT
Diameter, Inches	.308	.264	.264	.277	.308	.308	.338	.338	.458
Weight, Grains	110	100	120	95	110	168	225	265	300
Density	.166	.205	.246	.177	.166	.253	.281	.331	.204
Ballistic Coefficient	.289	-	.443	.292	.295	.470	.514	.575	.236
Catalog Number	30321	30236	30237	30253	30358	30359	30420	30419	30640

From: $34–$52

Multi-Purpose Green (MPG) Bullets

Caliber & Description	223 FB	6.8MM FB	30 FB	7.62X39 FB
Diameter, Inches	.224	.277	.308	.310
Weight, Grains	55	85	150	108
Density	.157	.158	.226	.161
Ballistic Coefficient	.225	.229	.357	.243
Catalog Number	30195	30249	30331	30388

From: $19–$31

LEGEND

Type of Bullet
- **BT** – Boattail
- **FB** – Flat Base
- **FN** – Flat Nose
- **RN** – Round Nose
- **S** – Spitzer
- **SP** – Soft Point
- **SS** – Semi-Spitzer

TSX Bullets

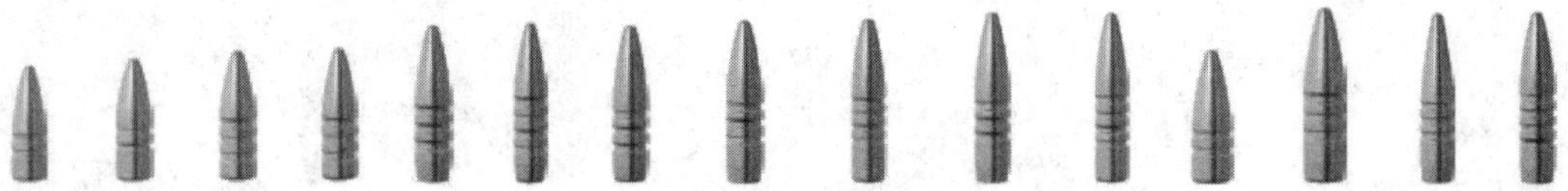

Caliber & Description	22 FB	22 FB	22 FB	22 FB	22 BT	22 BT	6MM BT	25 BT	25 FB	6.5MM BT	6.5MM FB	6.8MM FB	6.8MM BT	270 BT	270 BT
Diameter, Inches	.224	.224	.224	.224	.224	.224	.243	.257	.257	.264	.264	.277	.277	.277	.277
Weight, Grains	45	50	53	55	62	70	85	100	115	120	130	85	110	130	140
Density	.128	.142	.151	.157	.177	.199	.206	.216	.249	.246	.266	.158	.205	.242	.261
Ballistic Coefficient	.188	.197	.204	.209	.287	.314	.333	.336	.335	.381	.365	.246	.323	374	.404
Catalog Number	30176	30174	30180	30182	30190	30193	30212	30222	30224	30244	30246	30254	30260	30264	30266

Barnes Bullets

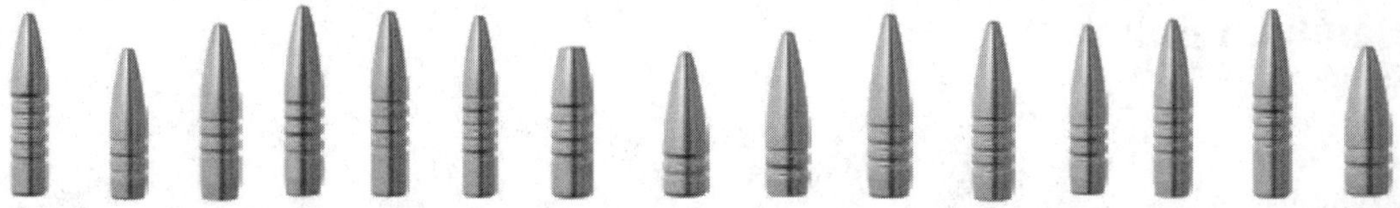

Caliber & Description	270 FB	7MM BT	7MM BT	7MM BT	7MM FB	7MM FB	30 FN FB	30 FB	30 BT	30 BT	30 BT	30 BT	30 BT	30 FB	7.62X39 BT
Diameter, Inches	.277	.284	.284	.284	.284	.284	.308	.308	.308	.308	.308	.308	.308	.308	.310
Weight, Grains	150	120	140	150	160	175	150	110	130	150	165	168	180	200	123
Density	.279	.213	.248	.266	.283	.310	.226	.166	.196	.226	.248	.253	.271	.301	.183
Ballistic Coefficient	.386	.349	.394	.408	.392	.417	.184	.264	.340	.369	.398	.404	.453	.423	.275
Catalog Number	30269	30287	30289	30293	30291	30294	30334	30341	30345	30347	30349	30351	30353	30356	30391

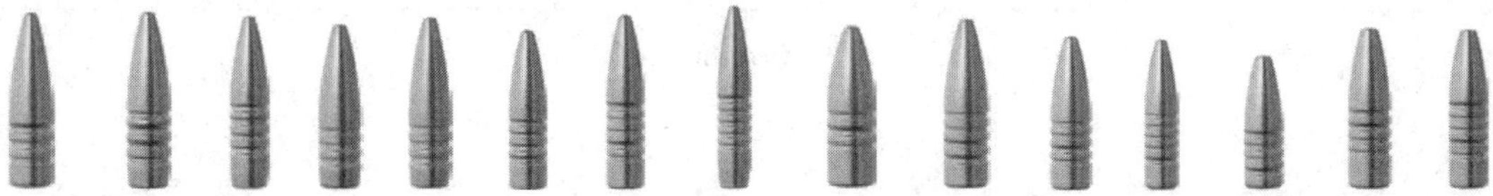

Caliber & Description	303/7.65MM FB	8MM BT	8MM BT	338 BT	338 BT	338 FB	338 FB	338 LAPUA BT	35 FB	35 FB	9.3MM FB	9.3MM FB	375 FB	375 FB	375 FB
Diameter, Inches	.311	.323	.323	.338	.338	.338	.338	.338	.358	.358	.366	.366	.375	.375	.375
Weight, Grains	150	180	200	185	210	225	250	285	200	225	250	286	235	270	300
Density	.222	.246	.274	.231	.263	.281	.313	.356	.223	.251	.267	.305	.239	.274	.305
Ballistic Coefficient	.322	.381	.421	.352	.404	.386	.425	.585	.284	.359	.361	.411	.270	.326	.357
Catalog Number	30393	30396	30398	30408	30410	30412	30415	30417	30455	30457	30469	30473	30486	30489	30491

Caliber & Description	375 FB	405 WIN FB	416 FB	416 FB	416 FB	404 JEFFREY FB	458 FB	458 FB	458 FB	458 FB	45/70 FN	45/70 FN	470 NITRO FB
Diameter, Inches	.375	.411	.416	.416	.416	.422	.458	.458	.458	.458	.458	.458	.474
Weight, Grains	350	300	300	350	400	400	300	350	450	500	250	300	500
Density	.356	.254	.248	.289	.330	.321	.204	.238	.306	.341	.170	.204	.318
Ballistic Coefficient	.425	.281	.298	.345	.392	.378	.234	.278	.369	.412	.136	.163	.363
Catalog Number	30494	30516	30527	30529	30532	30537	30615	30617	30619	30622	30629	30630	30647

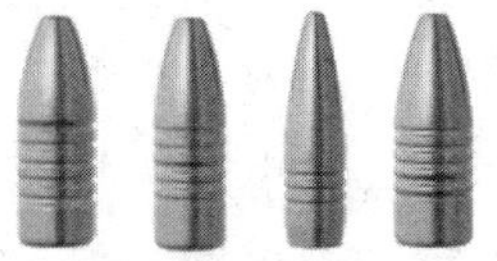

Caliber & Description	505 GIBBS FB	500 NITRO FB	50 BMG BT	577 NITRO FB
Diameter, Inches	.505	.509	.510	.583
Weight, Grains	525	570	647	750
Density	.294	.314	.355	.315
Ballistic Coefficient	.320	.369	.572	.402
Catalog Number	30688	30692	30700	30712

From: $19–$62

VARMIN-A-TOR

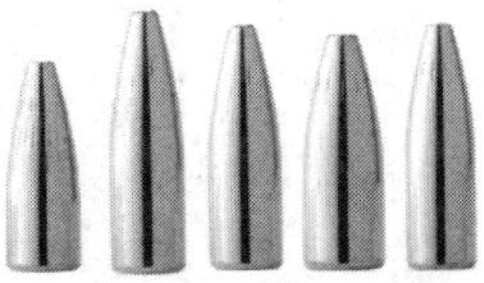

Caliber & Description	20 FB	22 FB	22 FB	6mm FB	6mm FB
Diameter, Inches	.204	.224	.224	.243	.243
Weight, Grains	32	40	50	58	72
Density	.110	.114	.142	.140	.174
Ballistic Coefficient	.159	.153	.192	.173	.208
Catalog Number	30092	30168	30178	30207	30210

From: $20–$23

VARMINT GRENADE

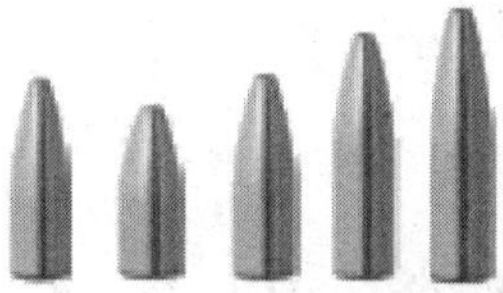

Caliber & Description	20 FB	22 HORNET FB	22 FB	223 FB	6MM FB
Diameter, Inches	.204	.224	.224	.224	.243
Weight, Grains	26	30	36	50	62
Density	.089	.085	.102	.142	.150
Ballistic Coefficient	.131	.101	.149	.183	.199
Catalog Number	30090	30170	30171	30198	30214

Box 100: $18–$59

Barnes Bullets

Handgun Bullets

M/LE TAC-XP Pistol Bullets

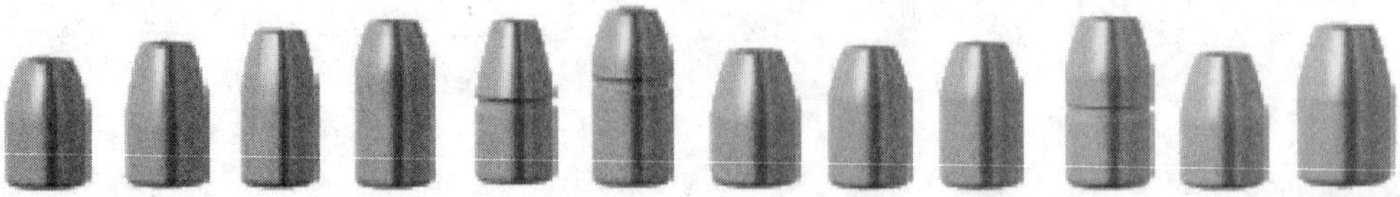

Caliber & Description	380 ACP	9MM	9MM	.357 SIG	38 SPL.	357 MAG.	10MM/40 S&W	10MM/40 S&W	10MM/40 S&W	44 SPL.	45 ACP/45 GAP	45 ACP
Diameter, Inches	.355	.355	.355	.355	.355	.357	.400	.400	.400	.429	.451	.451
Weight, Grains	80	95	115	125	110	125	125.	140	155	200	160	185
Density	.091	.108	.130	.142	.123	.140	.112	.125	.138	.155	.112	.130
Ballistic Coefficient	.107	.120	.167	.159	.156	.160	-	.128	.189	.138	.133	.167
Catalog Number	30440	30444	30442	30446	30449	30451	30500	30502	30504	30539	30550	30552

Box 40: $28–$49

XPB Pistol Bullets

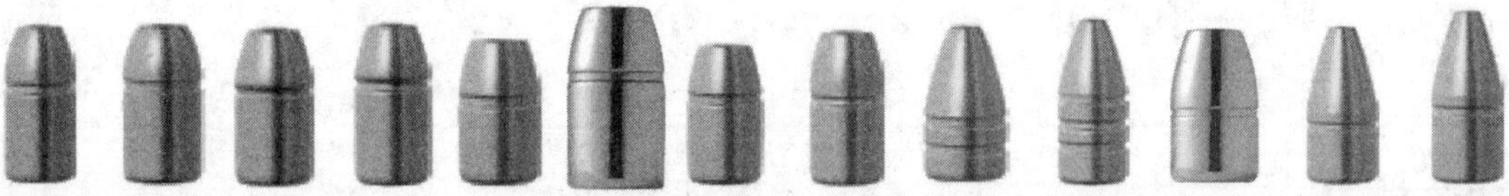

Caliber & Description	357 Mag.	41 Mag.	44 Mag.	44 Mag.	45 Colt	45 Colt	454 Casull	460 S&W	460 S&W	480 Ruger	500 S&W XPB	500 S&W XPB	500 S&W XPB
Diameter, Inches	.357	.410	.429	.429	.451	.451	.451	.451	.451	.475	.500	.500	.500
Weight, Grains	140	180	200	225	200	225	250	200	275	275	275	325	375
Density	.157	.153	.155	.175	.140	.158	.176	.140	.193	.174	.157	.186	.214
Ballistic Coefficient	.150	.126	.138	.166	-	.146	.141	.160	.215	.155	.141	.228	.261
Catalog Number	30453	30512	30541	30543	30556	30558	30562	30554	30548	30659	30663	30665	30667

Box 20: $16–$26

Berger Bullets

Famous for their superior performance in benchrest matches, Berger bullets also include hunting designs. From .17 to .30, all Bergers feature fourteen jackets with a wall concentricity tolerance of .0003. Lead cores are 99.9 percent pure and swaged in dies to within .0001 of a round. Berger's line includes several profiles: Match, Low Drag, Very Low Drag, Length Tolerant, and Maximum-Expansion, besides standard flat-base and boattail.

HUNTING

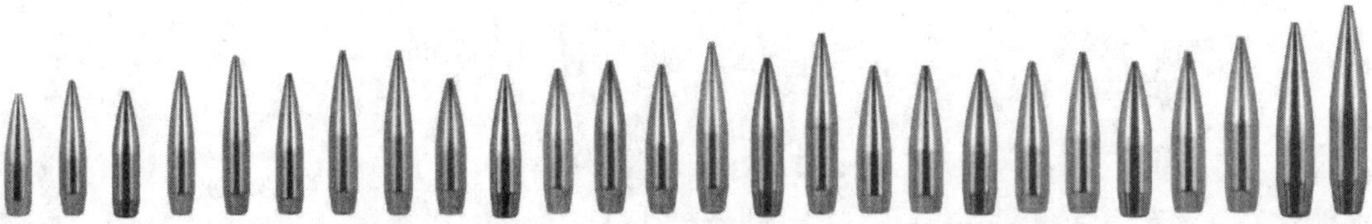

Caliber & Description	6mm VLD	6mm VLD	6mm	6mm VLD	6mm VLD	25 VLD"	6.5mm VLD	6.5mm VLD	270 VLD	270 Classic	270 VLD	270 VLD	7mm VLD	7mm VLD	7mm Classic	7mm VLD	30 VLD	30 VLD	30 Classic	30 VLD	30 VLD	30 Classic	30 VLD	30 VLD	338 Elite	338 Elite
Diameter, Inches	.243	.243	.243	.243	.243	.257	.264	.264	.277	.277	.277	.277	.284	.284	.284	.284	.308	.308	.308	.308	.308	.308	.308	.308	.338	.338
Weight, Grains	87	95	95	105	115	115	130	140	130	130	140	150	140	168	168	180	155	168	168	175	185	185	190	210	250	300
Density	.210	.230	-	.254	.278	.249	.266	.287	.241	-	.260	.279	.248	.298	-	.319	.233	.253	-	.264	.279	-	.286	.316	-	-
Ballistic Coefficient	.412	.480	.427	.532	.545	.466	.552	.612	.452	.497	.487	.531	.510	.617	.604	.659	.439	.473	.496	.498	.549	.547	.570	.631	.682	.818
Catalog Number	24524	24527	24570	24528	24530	25513	26503	26504	27501	27570	27502	27503	28503	28501	28570	28502	30508	30510	30570	30512	30513	30571	30514	30515	33554	33556

Box 100: $40–$91

Berger Bullets

Target

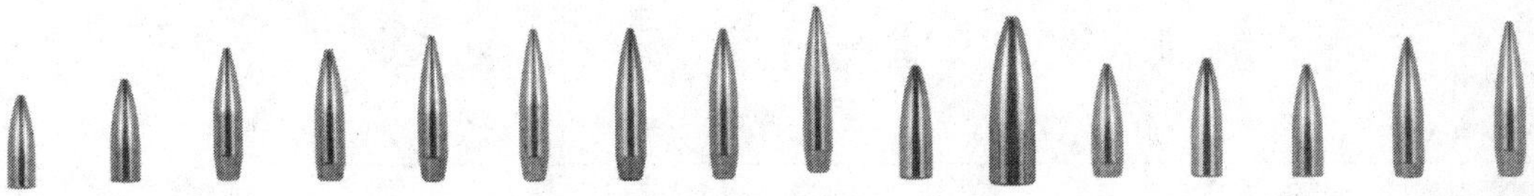

Caliber & Description	22 FBHP	22 FBHP	22 VLD	22 BTHP	22 VLD	22 VLD	22 VLD	22 LRBTHP	22 VLD	6mm FBHP	6mm BR	6mm BTHP	6mm FBHP	6mm FBHP	6mm BTHP	6mm VLD
Diameter, Inches	.224	.224	.224	.224	.224	.224	.224	.224	.224	.243	.243	.243	.243	.243	.243	.243
Weight, Grains	52	55	70	73	75	80	80.5	82	90	62	-	65	65	68	90	95
Density	.148	.157	.199	.208	.214	.228	.229	.233	.256	.150	-	.157	.157	.165	.218	.230
Ballistic Coefficient	.242	.262	.371	.343	.423	.445	.436	.444	.551	.253	.277	.270	.265	.280	.411	.480
Catalog Number	22408	22410	22418	22420	22421	22422	22427	22424	22423	24404	24407	24408	24409	24411	24425	24427

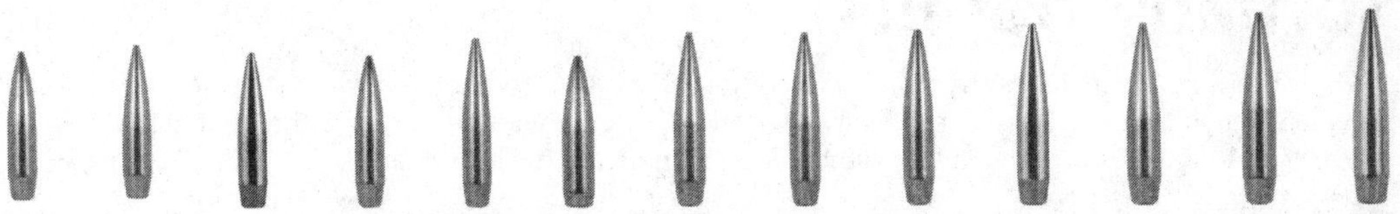

Caliber & Description	6mm BTHP	6mm VLD	6mm Hybrid	6mm BTHP	6mm VLD	6.5mm BTHP	6.5mm VLD	6.5mm VLD	6.5mm LRBTHP	6.5mm Hybrid	7mm VLD	7mm VLD	7mm Hybrid
Diameter, Inches	.243	.243	.243	.243	.243	.264	.264	.264	.264	.264	.284	.284	.284
Weight, Grains	105	105	105	108	115	120	130	140	140	140	168	180	180
Density	.254	.254	.254	.261	.278	.245	.266	.287	.287	.287	.298	.319	.319
Ballistic Coefficient	.493	.495	.547	.551	.545	.453	.552	.612	.592	.618	.617	.659	.674
Catalog Number	24428	24429	24433	24431	24430	26402	26403	26401	26409	26414	28401	28405	28407

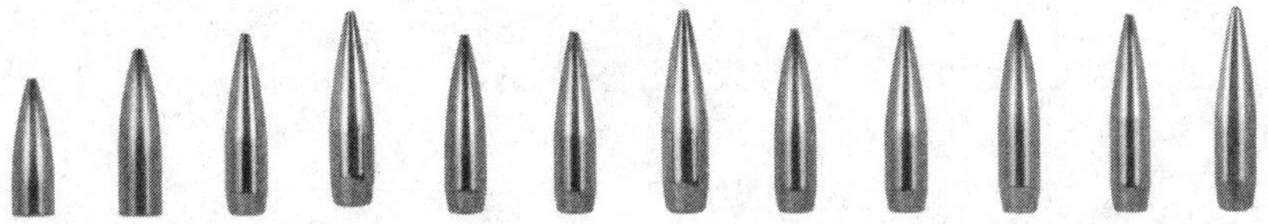

Caliber & Description	30 FBHP	30 FBHP	30 VLD	30 Hybrid	30 LRBTHP	30 VLD	30 Hybrid	30 LRBTHP	30 VLD	30 Juggernaut	30 VLD	30 Hybrid
Diameter, Inches	.308	.308	.308	.308	.308	.308	.308	.308	.308	.308	.308	.308
Weight, Grains	115	150	155	155	155.5	168	168	175	175	185	185	185
Density	.183	.226	.233	.233	.234	.253	.253	.264	.264	.279	.279	.279
Ballistic Coefficient	.296	.398	.439	.483	.464	.473	.519	.515	.498	.560	.549	.569
Catalog Number	30421	30407	30408	30426	30416	30410	30425	30420	30412	30418	30413	30424

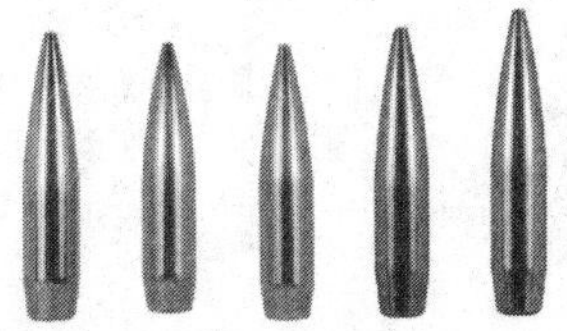

Caliber & Description	30 Hybrid	30 LRBTHP	30 VLD	30 Hybrid	30 Hybrid
Diameter, Inches	.308	.308	.308	.308	.308
Weight, Grains	200	210	210	215	230
Density	.301	.316	.316	-	-
Ballistic Coefficient	.624	.626	.631	.696	.743
Catalog Number	30427	30419	30415	30429	30430

Box 100: $31–$72

LEGEND

Type of Bullet

BT – Boattail
FB – Flat Base
HP – Hollow Point
LD – Low Drag
LR – Long Range
VLD – Very Low Drag

Berger Bullets

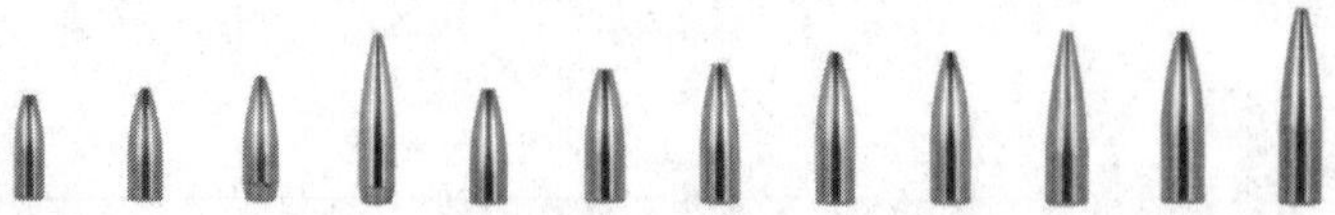

Varmint

Caliber & Description	17 FBHP	20 FBHP	20 BTHP	20 LRBTHP	22 FBHP	22 FBHP	22 FBHP	22 FBHP	22 FBHP	6mm LDHP	6mm FBHP	6mm LDHP
Diameter, Inches	.172	.204	.204	.204	.224	.224	.224	.224	.224	.243	.243	.243
Weight, Grains	25	35	40	55	40	52	55	60	64	69	80	88
Density	.121	.120	.137	.188	.114	.148	.157	.171	.182	.167	.194	.213
Ballistic Coefficient	.150	.176	.225	.381	.155	.197	.210	.278	.294	.291	.306	.391
Catalog Number	17308	20303	20304	20306	22303	22309	22311	22312	22316	24313	24321	24323

Box 100: $31–$64

Hornady Bullets

Hornady's product line includes over 300 bullets, ranging from .17 caliber all the way up to the .50 caliber A-MAX bullet for the .50 BMG. Hornady is always working to originate the next technological innovation. From prairie dogs to dangerous game, they have the perfect bullet to meet every hunting and shooting need.

Rifle Bullets

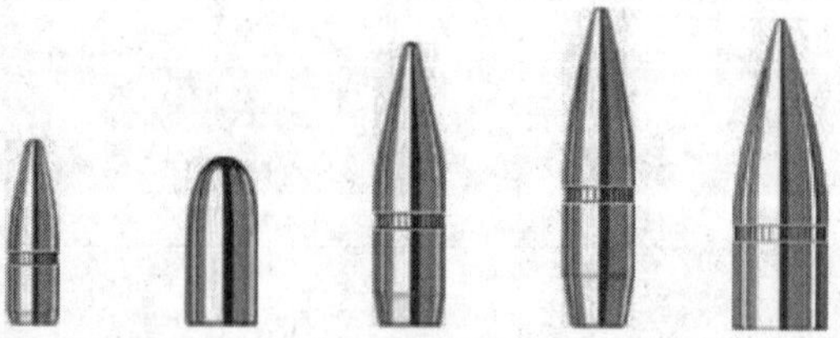

FMJ Bullets

Caliber & Description	22 FMJ-BT	30 FMJ	30 FMJ-BT	303 FMJ-BT	7.62 FMJ
Diameter, Inches	.224	.308	.308	.3105	.310
Weight, Grains	55	110	150	174	123
Density	.157	.166	.226	.255	.183
Ballistic Coefficient	.243	.178	.398	.470	.266
Catalog Number	2267	3017	3037	3131	3478

MSRP $19–$42

LEGEND

Type of Bullet

BT – Boat Tail
CT – Combat Target
FMJ – Full Metal Jacket
FP – Flat Point
HB – Hollow Base
L – Lead
RN – Round Nose
SP – Spire Point
SX – Super Explosive
SWC – Semi-Wadcutter
WC – Wadcutter

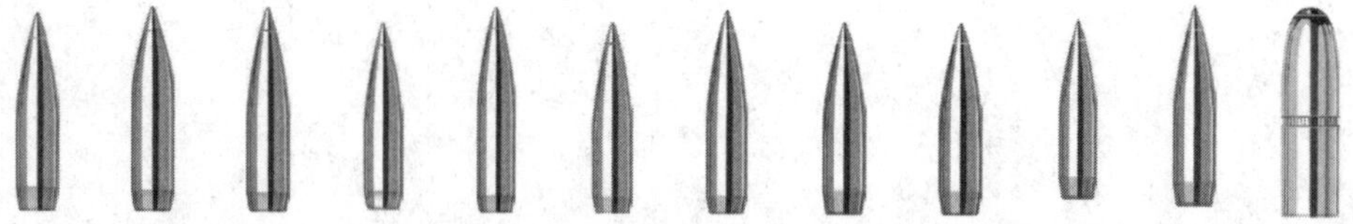

InterBond

Caliber & Description	6mm BT	25 BT	6.5mm BT	270 BT	270 BT	7mm BT	7mm BT	30 BT	30 BT	30 BT	338 BT	416 RN
Diameter, Inches	.243	.257	.264	.277	.277	.284	.284	.308	.308	.308	.338	.416
Weight, Grains	85	110	129	130	150	139	154	150	165	180	225	400
Density	.206	.238	.264	.242	.279	.246	.525	.226	.248	.271	.281	.330
Ballistic Coefficient	.395	.390	.485	.460	.525	.486	.273	.415	.447	.480	.515	.311
Catalog Number	24539	25419	26209	27309	27409	28209	28309	30309	30459	30709	33209	41659

MSRP $61–$89

Hornady Bullets

InterLock

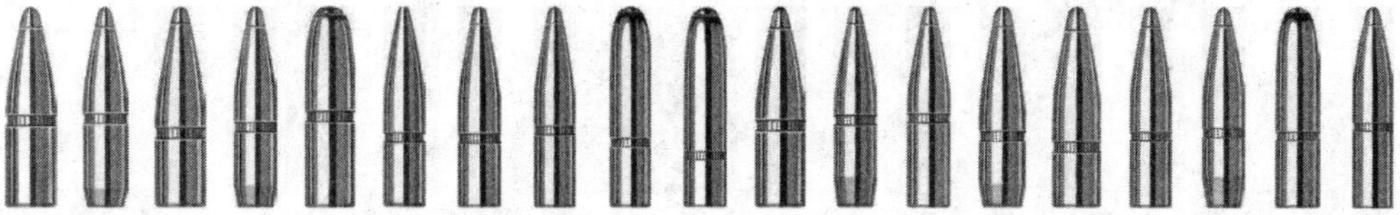

Caliber & Description	22 SP	6mm BT SP	25 SP	25 BTSP	25 RN	25 HP	6.5mm SP	6.5mm SP	6.5mm RN	6.5mm Carcano RN	270 SP	270 BTSP	270 SP	7mm BTSP	7mm SP	7mm SP	7mm BTSP	7mm RN	7mm SP
Diameter, Inches	.227	.243	.257	.257	.257	.257	.264	.264	.264	.268	.277	.277	.277	.284	.284	.284	.284	.284	.284
Weight, Grains	70	100	100	117	117	120	129	140	160	160	130	140	150	139	139	154	162	175	175
Density	.194	.242	.216	.253	.253	.260	.264	.287	.328	.321	.242	.261	.279	.246	.246	.273	.287	.310	.310
Ballistic Coefficient	.296	.405	.357	.391	.243	.394	.445	.465	.283	.275	.409	.486	.462	.453	.392	.433	.514	.285	.462
Catalog Number	2280	2453	2540	2552	2550	2560	2620	2630	2640	2645	2730	2735	2740	2825	2820	2830	2845	2855	2850

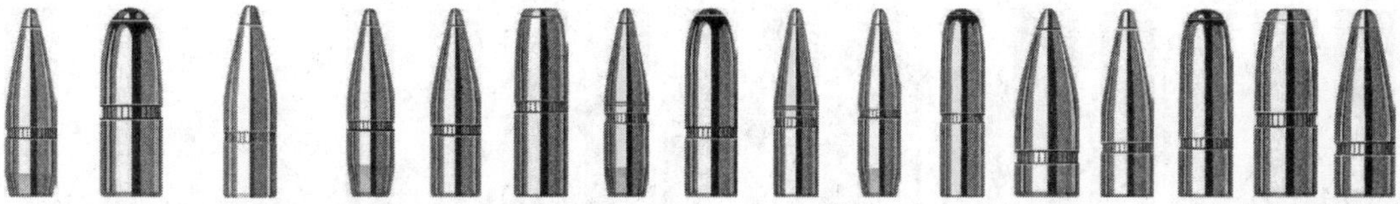

Caliber & Description	30 BTSP	30 RN	30 SP	30 BTSP	30 SP	30 FP	30 BTSP	30 RN	30 SP	30 BTSP	30 RN	7.62 SP	303 SP	303 RN	32 FP	8mm SP
Diameter, Inches	.308	.308	.308	.308	.308	.308	.308	.308	.308	.308	.308	.310	.312	.312	.321	.323
Weight, Grains	150	150	150	165	165	170	180	180	180	190	220	123	150	174	170	150
Density	.226	.226	.226	.248	.248	.256	.271	.271	.271	.286	.331	.183	.220	.255	.236	.205
Ballistic Coefficient	.349	.186	.338	.435	.387	.189	.452	.241	.425	.491	.300	.252	.361	.262	.249	.290
Catalog Number	3033	3035	3031	3045	3040	3060	3072	3075	3070	3085	3090	3140	3120	3130	3210	3232

LEGEND

Type of Bullet

- **BT** – Boat Tail
- **CT** – Combat Target
- **FMJ** – Full Metal Jacket
- **FP** – Flat Point
- **HB** – Hollow Base
- **L** – Lead
- **RN** – Round Nose
- **SP** – Spire Point
- **SX** – Super Explosive
- **SWC** – Semi-Wadcutter
- **WC** – Wadcutter

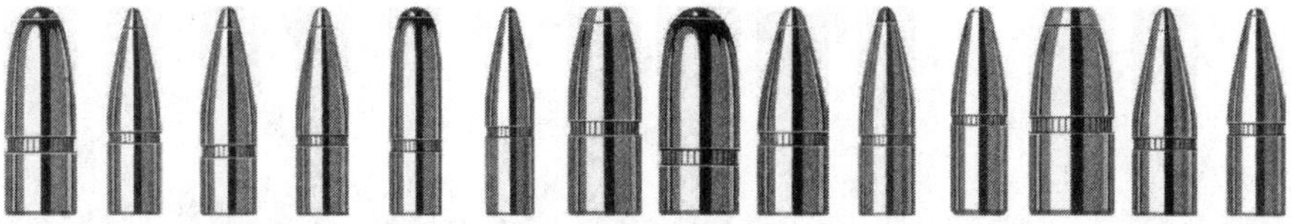

Caliber & Description	8mm RN	8mm SP	338 SP RP	338 SP RP	338 RN	338 SP RP	348 FP	35 RN	35 SP RP	35 SP RP	9.3 SP RP	375 FP	375 SP RP	375 SP RP
Diameter, Inches	.323	.323	.338	.338	.338	.338	.348	.358	.358	.358	.366	.375	.375	.375
Weight, Grains	170	195	200	225	250	250	200	200	200	250	286	220	225	270
Density	.233	.267	.250	.281	.313	.313	.236	.223	.223	.279	.305	.223	.229	.229
Ballistic Coefficient	.217	.410	.361	.397	.291	.431	.246	.195	.282	.375	.410	.217	.320	.380
Catalog Number	3235	3236	3310	3320	3330	3335	3410	3515	3510	3520	3560	3705	3706	3711

Hornady Bullets

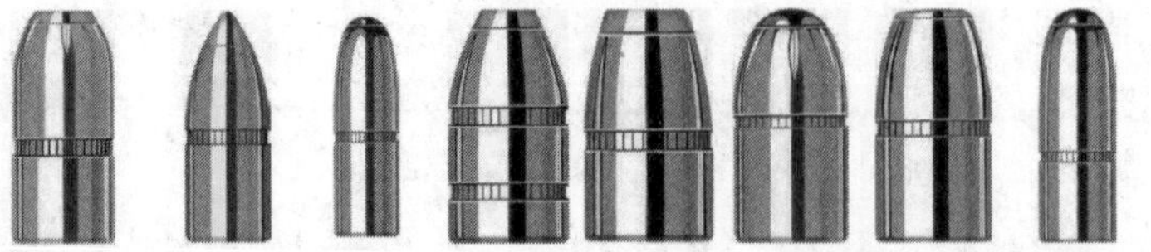

Caliber & Description	405 FP	405 SP	416 RN	44 FP	45 HP	45 FP	45 RN	45 RN
Diameter, Inches	.411	.411	.416	.430	.458	.458	.458	.458
Weight, Grains	300	300	400	265	300	350	350	500
Density	.251	.251	.330	.205	.204	.238	.238	.341
Ballistic Coefficient	.215	.250	.311	.186	.197	.195	.189	.287
Catalog Number	41050	41051	4165	4300	4500	4503	4502	4504

LEGEND

Type of Bullet

BT – Boat Tail
CT – Combat Target
FMJ – Full Metal Jacket
FP – Flat Point
HB – Hollow Base
L – Lead
RN – Round Nose
SP – Spire Point
SX – Super Explosive
SWC – Semi-Wadcutter
WC – Wadcutter

MSRP $29–$69

Match A-Max

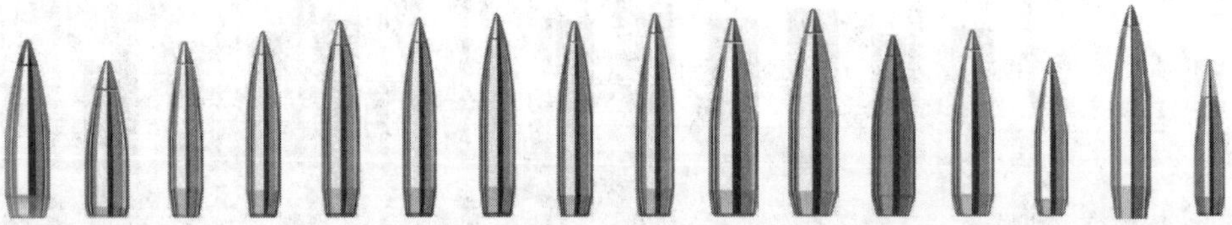

Caliber & Description	6.5mm	22	22	22	6mm	6.5mm	6.5mm	6.5mm	7mm	30	30	30 MOLY	30	30	338 BT	50
Diameter, Inches	.264	.224	.224	.224	.243	.264	.264	.264	.284	.308	.308	.308	.308	.308	.338	.510
Weight, Grains	100	52	75	80	105	120	123	140	162	155	168	168	178	208	285	750
Density	.246	.148	.214	.228	.254	.246	.252	.287	.287	.233	.253	.253	.268	.313	.356	.412
Ballistic Coefficient	.390	.247	.435	.453	.500	.465	.510	.585	.625	.435	.475	.475	.495	.325	720	1.050
Catalog Number	26101	22492	22792	22832	24562	26172	26171	26332	28402	30312	30502	30504	30712	30732	3338	5165

MSRP $26–$64

SST

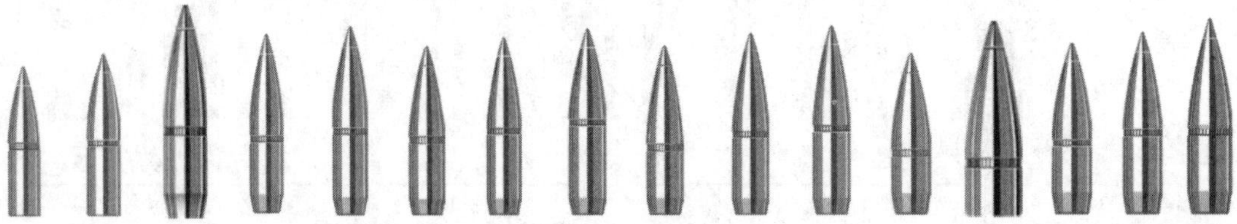

Caliber & Description	6mm	25	6.5mm	6.5mm	6.5mm	270	270	270	270	7mm SST	7mm SST	7mm SST	30	30	30	30
Diameter, Inches	.243	.257	.264	.264	.264	.277	.277	.277	.277	.284	.284	.284	.308	.308	.308	.308
Weight, Grains	95	117	123	129	140	120	130	140	150	139	154	162	125	150	150	165
Density	.230	.253	.252	.264	.287	.223	.242	.261	.279	.246	.273	.287	.185	.226	.226	.248
Ballistic Coefficient	.355	.390	.510	.485	.520	.400	.460	.495	.525	.486	.525	.550	.305	.415	.370	.447
Catalog Number	24532	25522	26173	26202	26302	2716	27302	27352	27402	28202	28302	28452	3019	30302	30303	30452

Hornady Bullets

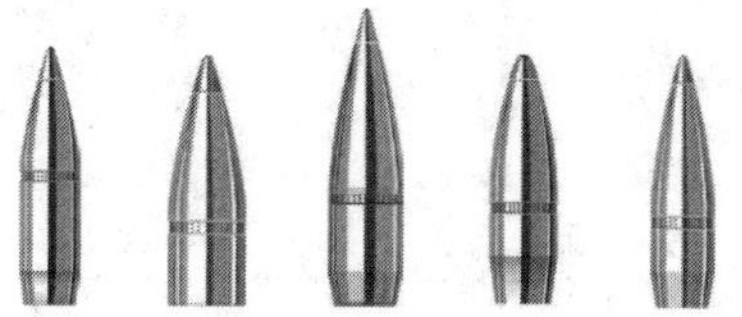

Caliber & Description	30	7.62	338	338	8mm BT
Diameter, Inches	.308	.310	.338	.338	
Weight, Grains	180	123	200	225	170
Density	.271	.183	.250	.281	.233
Ballistic Coefficient	.480	.260	.455	.515	.455
Catalog Number	30702	3142	33102	33202	3233

MSRP $40–$54

LEGEND

Type of Bullet

BT – Boat Tail
CT – Combat Target
FMJ – Full Metal Jacket
FP – Flat Point
HB – Hollow Base
L – Lead
RN – Round Nose
SP – Spire Point
SX – Super Explosive
SWC – Semi-Wadcutter
WC – Wadcutter

Traditional Varmint

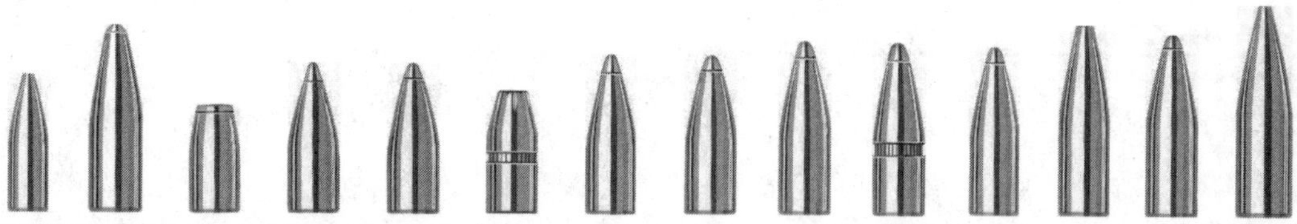

Caliber & Description	17 HP	20 SP	22 JET	22 Hornet	22 Hornet	22 HP BEE	22 SP	22 SP SX	22 SP	22 SP	22 SP SX	22 HP	22 SP	6mm HP
Diameter, Inches	.172	.204	.222	.223	.224	.224	.224	.224	.224	.224	.224	.224	.224	.243
Weight, Grains	25	45	40	45	45	45	50	50	55	55	55	60	60	75
Density	.121	.155	.116	.129	.128	.128	.142	.142	.157	.157	.157	.171	.171	.181
Ballistic Coefficient	.187	.245	.104	.202	.202	.108	.214	.214	.235	.235	.235	.271	.264	.294
Catalog Number	1710	22008	2210	2220	2230	2229	2245	2240	2265	2266	2260	2275	2270	2420

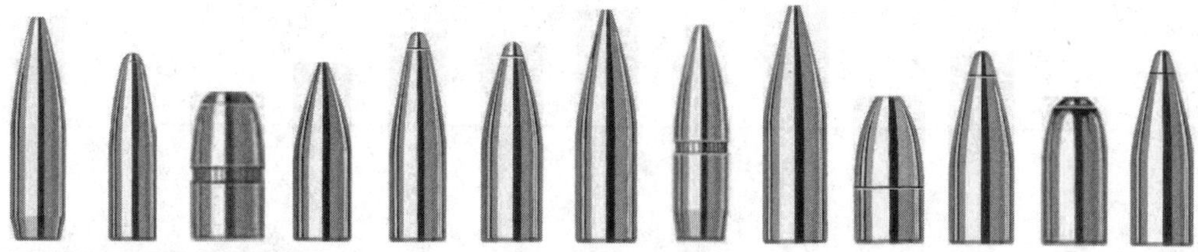

Caliber & Description	6mm BTHP	6mm SP	25 FP	25 HP	25 SP	270 SP	270 HP	270 BTHP	7mm HP	30 Short Jacket	30 SP	30 RN	30 SP
Diameter, Inches	.243	.243	.257	.257	.257	.277	.277	.277	.284	.308	.308	.308	.308
Weight, Grains	87	87	60	75	87	100	110	110	120	100	110	110	130
Density	.210	.210	.130	.162	.188	.186	.205	.205	.213	.151	.166	.166	.196
Ballistic Coefficient	.376	.327	.101	.257	.322	.307	.352	.360	.334	.152	.256	.150	.295
Catalog Number	2442	2440	2510	2520	2530	2710	2720	27200	2815	3005	3010	3015	3020

MSRP $18–$38

Hornady Bullets

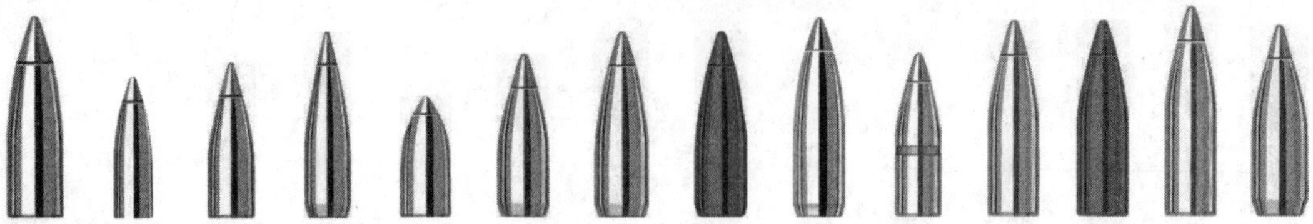

V-MAX

Caliber & Description	17	17	20	20	22	22	22	22 MOLY	22	22	22	22 MOLY	22	6mm
Diameter, Inches	.172	.172	.204	.204	.224	.224	.224	.224	.224	.224	.224	.224	.224	.243
Weight, Grains	20	25	32	40	35	40	50	50	53	55	55	55	60	58
Density	.097	.121	.110	.137	.100	.114	.142	.142	.151	.157	.157	.157	.171	.140
Ballistic Coefficient	.185	.230	.210	.275	.109	.200	.242	.242	.290	.255	.255	.255	.265	.250
Catalog Number	21710	17105	22004	22006	22252	22241	22261	22613	22265	22272	22271	22713	22281	22411

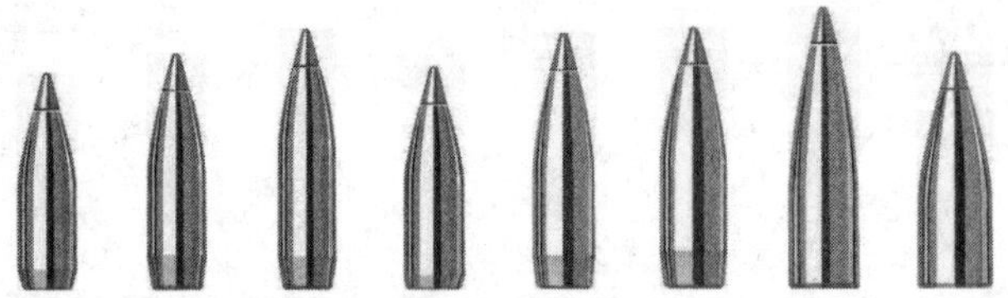

Caliber & Description	6mm	6mm	6mm	25	6.5mm	270	7mm	30
Diameter, Inches	.243	.243	.243	.257	.264	.277	.284	.308
Weight, Grains	65	75	87	75	95	110	120	110
Density	.157	.181	.210	.162	.195	.205	.213	.166
Ballistic Coefficient	.280	.330	.400	.290	.365	.370	.365	.290
Catalog Number	22415	22420	22440	22520	22601	22721	22810	23010

LEGEND

Type of Bullet

- **BT** – Boat Tail
- **CT** – Combat Target
- **FMJ** – Full Metal Jacket
- **FP** – Flat Point
- **HB** – Hollow Base
- **L** – Lead
- **RN** – Round Nose
- **SP** – Spire Point
- **SX** – Super Explosive
- **SWC** – Semi-Wadcutter
- **WC** – Wadcutter

MSRP $24–$38

Handgun Bullets

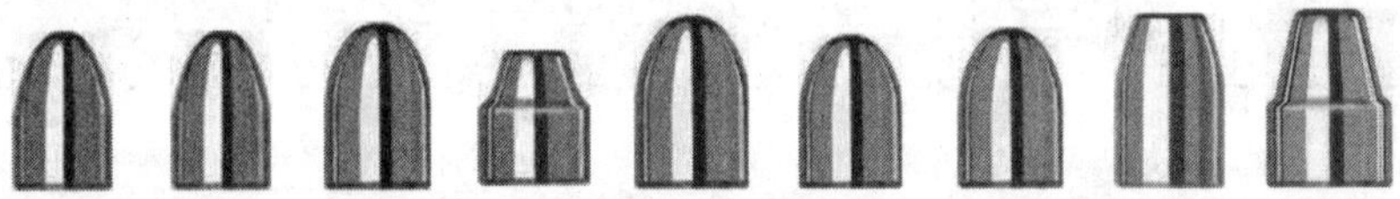

FMJ BULLETS

Caliber & Description	9mm FMJ-RN	9mm FMJ-RN	10mm FMJ- FP	45 SWC	45 FMJ-RN	9mm FMJ	9mm FMJ-RN	10mm FMJ-FP	45 FMJ-CT
Diameter, Inches	.355	.355	.400	.451	.451	.355	.355	.400	.451
Weight, Grains	115	124	180	185	230	100	147	200	200
Density	.130	.141	N/A	.130	.162	.141	.167	.179	.140
Ballistic Coefficient	.140	.145	N/A	.068	.184	.158	.212	.182	.115
Catalog Number	35557	355771	400471	45137	45177	35527B	35597B	40077B	45157B

MSRP $23–$33

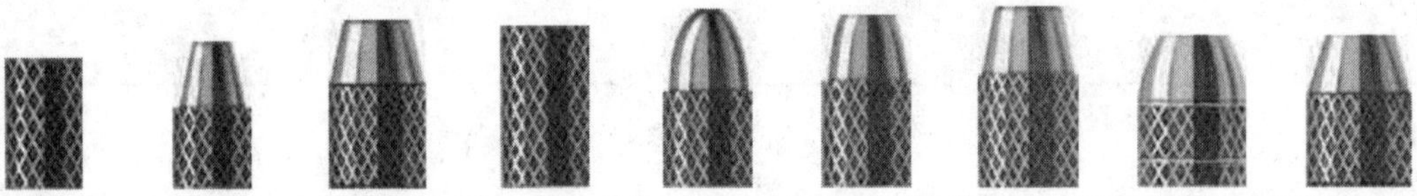

FRONTIER LEAD BULLETS

Caliber & Description	32 HBWC	32 SWC	38	38 HBWC	38 LRN	38 SWC	38 SWC HP	44 Cowboy	44 Cowboy
Diameter, Inches	.314	.314	.358	.358	.358	.358	.358	.427	.430
Weight, Grains	90	90	140	148	158	158	158	205	180
Density	.130	.130	.157	.165	.176	.176	.176	.161	.139
Ballistic Coefficient	.040	.096	.127	.047	.159	.135	.139	.123	.114
Catalog Number	10028	10008	10078	10208	10508	10408	10428	11208	11058

Frontier/ Lead Bullets (cont.)

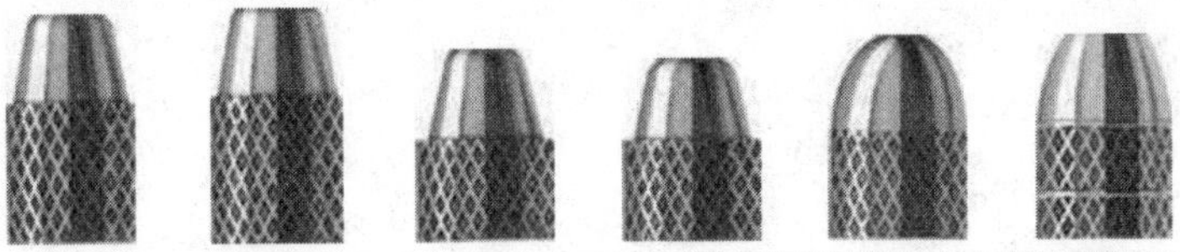

Caliber & Description	44 SWC	44 SWC HP	45 L-C/T	45 SWC	45 LRN	45 FP Cowboy
Diameter, Inches	.430	.430	.452	.452	.452	.454
Weight, Grains	240	240	200	200	230	255
Density	.185	.185	.140	.140	.162	.177
Ballistic Coefficient	.182	.204	.081	.070	.207	.117
Catalog Number	11108	11118	12208	12108	12308	12458

MSRP $32–$51

HAP Bullets

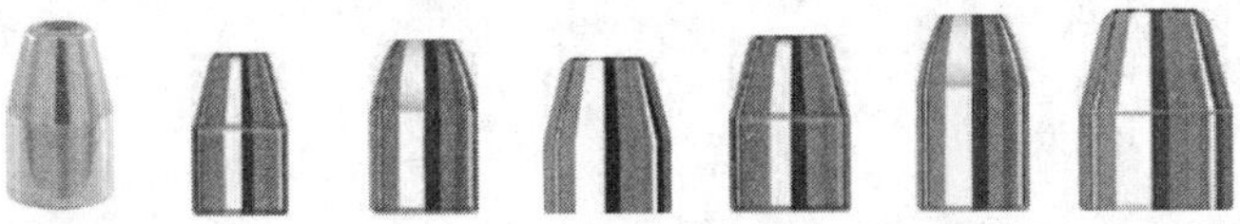

Caliber & Description	9mm	9mm	10mm	45	45	10mm	45
Diameter, Inches	.356	.356	.400	.451	.451	.400	.451
Weight, Grains	115	125	180	185	230	200	200
Density	.130	.141	.161	.130	.162	.179	.140
Ballistic Coefficient	.129	.158	.164	.139	.188	.199	151
Catalog Number	355281	355721	400421	451051	451611	40061B	45159B

MSRP $78–$139

LEGEND

Type of Bullet

BT – Boat Tail
CT – Combat Target
FMJ – Full Metal Jacket
FP – Flat Point
HB – Hollow Base
L – Lead
RN – Round Nose
SP – Spire Point
SX – Super Explosive
SWC – Semi-Wadcutter
WC – Wadcutter

XTP Bullets

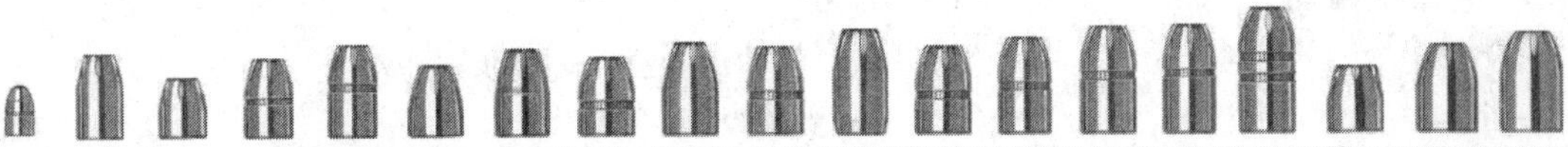

Caliber & Description	30 RN	30 HP	32 HP	32 HP	32 HP	9mm HP	9mm HP	38 HP	9mm HP	38 FP	9mm HP	38 HP	38 HP	38 FP	38 HP	38 HP	9x18mm HP	10mm HP	10mm HP
Diameter, Inches	.308	.309	.312	.312	.312	.355	.355	.357	.355	.357	.355	.357	.357	.357	.357	.357	.365	.400	.400
Weight, Grains	86	90	60	85	100	90	115	110	124	125	147	125	140	158	158	180	95	155	180
Density	.130	.136	.088	.125	.147	.102	.130	.123	.141	.140	.167	.140	.157	.177	.177	.202	.102	.138	.161
Ballistic Coefficient	.105	.115	.090	.145	.170	.099	.129	.131	.165	.148	.212	.151	.169	.199	.206	.230	.127	.137	.164
Catalog Number	3100	31000	32010	32050	32070	35500	35540	35700	35571	35730	35580	35710	35740	35780	35750	35771	36500	40000	40040

Caliber & Description	10mm HP	41 HP	44 HP	44 HP	44 HP	44 HP	45 HP	45 HP	45 HP	45	45 HP	45 HP	45	475 MAG	50	500 MAG	500 FP
Diameter, Inches	.400	.410	.430	.430	.430	.300	.451	.451	.451	.452	.452	.452	.452	.475	.500	.500	.500
Weight, Grains	200	210	180	200	240	300	185	200	230	240	250	300	300	325	300	350	500
Density	.179	.178	.139	.155	.185	.232	.130	.140	.162	.168	.175	.210	.210	.206	.171	.192	.275
Ballistic Coefficient	.199	.182	.138	.170	.205	.245	.139	.151	.188	.160	.146	.180	.200	.150	.120	.145	.185
Catalog Number	40060	41000	44050	44100	44200	44280	45100	45140	45160	45220	45200	45230	45235	47500	50101	50100	50105

MSRP $22–$61

Lapua

Rifle Bullets

Lapua precision bullets are made from the best raw materials and meet the toughest precision specifications. Each bullet is subject to visual inspection and tested with advanced measurement devices.

D46
Manufactured to the strictest tolerances for concentricity, uniformity of shape, and weight; 7.62mm (.308) available
Box 100: $50

D166
Superbly accurate FMJBT bullet for 7.62mm (.311) cartridges
Box 100: $52

FMJ
Ten rounds loaded with Lapua's .30 S374 8.0/123gr FMJ bullet from 100m can easily achieve groupings less than; 30mm .224, 6.5mm, 7.62mm (.308, .311) available
Box 100: . . . .$35–$44

HOLLOW POINT
This HPCE bullet cuts a clean and easily distinguishable hole in your target; with ten rounds (G477 in .308 Win.) fired at 100m, this bullet typically achieves groupings of under 25mm—sometimes even less than 15mm; 6mm also available
Box 100: $51

LOCK BASE
A distinctive Full Metal Jacket Boat Tail bullet that has many applications from sport shooting to battlefield; streamlined ballistic shape combined with patented base design; 7.62mm and .338 available
Box 100: . . . .$50–$77

MEGA
Soft point bullet with a protective copper jacket bullet at its best in the field and typically more than duplicates on impact; mechanical bonding locks the lead alloy in place; 6.5mm, 7.62mm, and 9.3mm available
Box 100: . . . .$52–$72

SCENAR
Scenar Hollow Point Boat Tail bullets have the IBS World Record in 600 yard Heavy Gun 5-shot group (.404") and hold the official world ISSF record of 600 out of 600 possible; also available in Coated Silver Jacket version; .244, 6mm, 6.5mm, 7.62mm, and .338 available
Box 100: . . . .$37–$88

SCENAR-L
A refinement in all manufacturing steps that has resulted in closer weight tolerances, tighter jacket wall concentricity standards, and greater uniformity in every dimension, including the gilding metal cup, lead wire and jacket forming, ending up to core-jacket assembly, boat tail pressing, and tipping ; 6mm, 6.5mm, 7mm, and 7.62mm (.308) available
Box 100: . . . .$49–$58

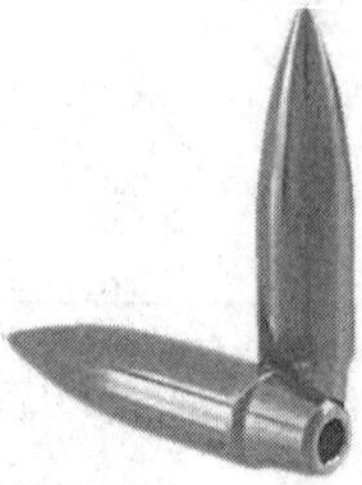
LAPUA D46

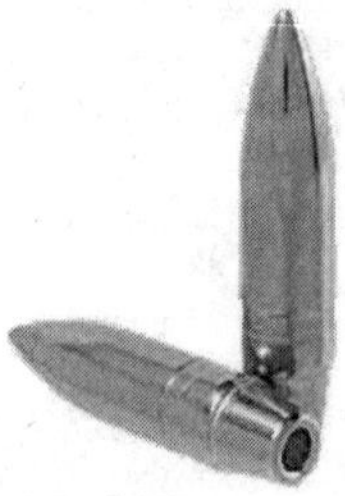
LAPUA D166

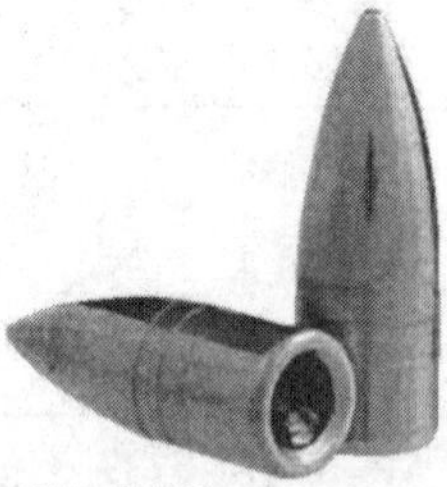
LAPUA FMJ S

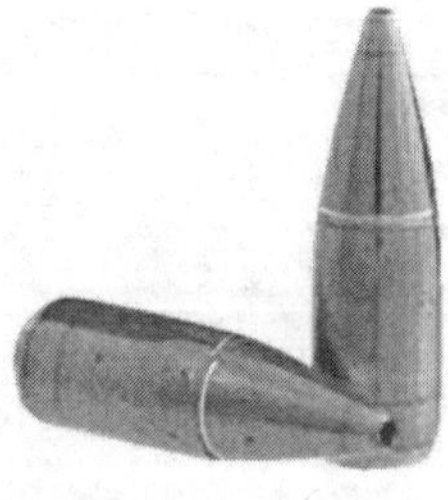
LAPUA HP

LAPUA LOCK BASE

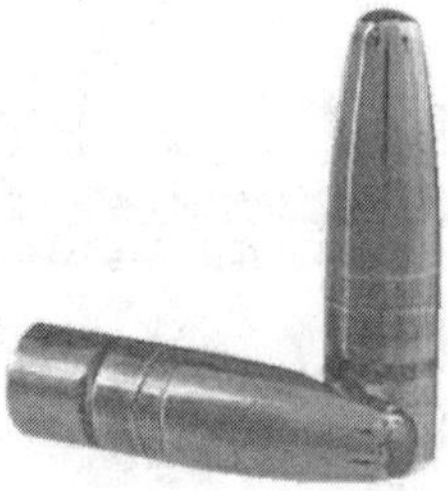
LAPUA MEGA

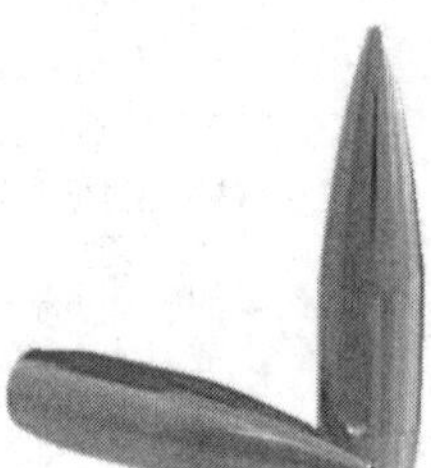
LAPUA SCENAR

LAPUA SCENAR-L

Nosler Bullets

Rifle Bullets

Accubond

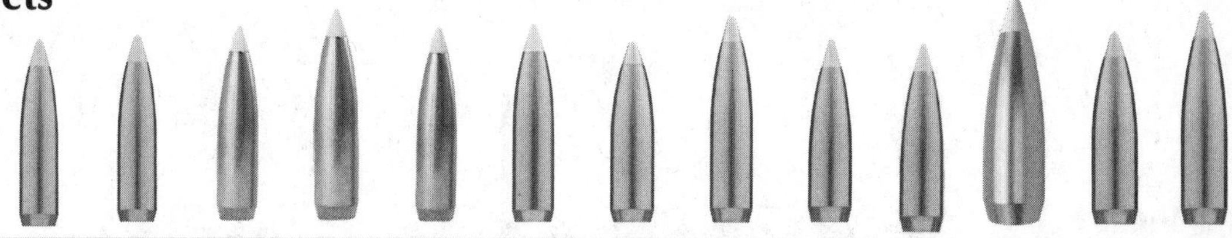

Caliber & Description	6mm S	25 SWT	6.5mm SWT	6.5mm	270 SWT	270 SWT	7mm SWT	7mm SWT	30 SWT	30 SWT	30 S	30 SWT	30 SWT
Diameter, inches	.243	.257	.264	.264	.277	.277	.277	.277	.284	.284	.308	.308	.308
Weight, Grains	90	110	130	140	100	110	130	140	140	160	125	150	165
Density	.218	.238	.266	.287	.186	.205	.242	.261	.248	.283	.188	.226	.248
Ballistic Coefficient	.376	.418	.488	.509	.323	.370	.435	.496	.485	.531	.366	.435	.475
Catalog Number	56357	53742	56902	57873	57845	54382	54987	54765	59992	54932	52165	56719	55602

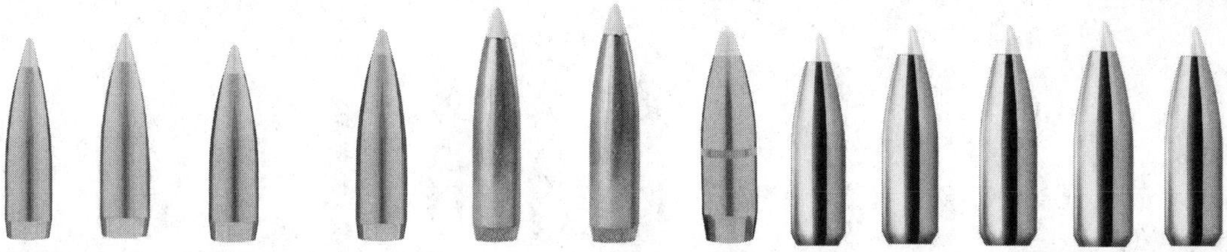

Caliber & Description	30 S	30 S	8mm S	338 S	338 S	338 S	338 S	338 S	35 Whelen S	35 Whelen S	9.3mm S	375 S	375 S
Diameter, inches	.308	.308	.323	.338	.338	.338	.338	.338	.358	.358	.366	.375	.375
Weight, Grains	180	200	200	180	200	225	250	300	200	225	250	260	300
Density	.271	.301	.274	.225	.250	.281	.313	.375	.223	.251	.267	.264	.305
Ballistic Coefficient	.507	.588	.450	.372	.414	.550	.575	.720	.365	.421	.494	.473	.485
Catalog Number	54825	54618	54374	57625	56382	54357	57287	54851	54425	50712	59756	54413	53662

Box 50, 100: $27–$63

Ballistic Tip Hunting

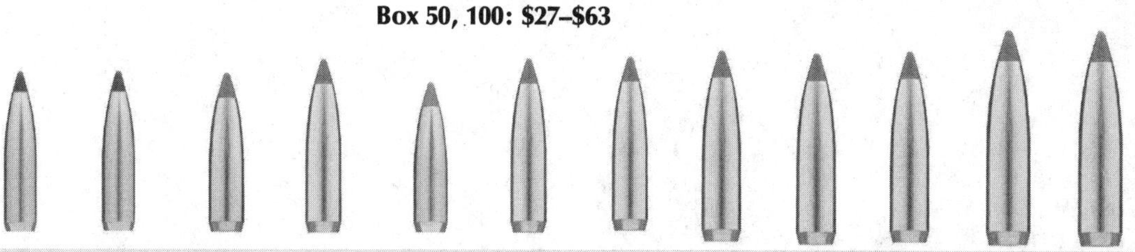

Caliber & Description	6mm S	6mm S	25 S	25 S	6.5mm S	6.5mm S	6.5mm S	270 S	270 S	270 S	7mm S	7mm S
Diameter, inches	.243	.243	.257	.257	.264	.264	.264	.277	.277	.277	.284	.284
Weight, Grains	90	95	100	115	100	120	140	130	140	150	120	140
Density	.218	.230	.216	.249	.205	.246	.287	.242	.261	.279	.213	.248
Ballistic Coefficient	.365	.379	.393	.453	.350	.458	.509	.433	.456	.496	.417	.485
Catalog Number	24090	24095	25100	25115	26100	26120	26140	27130	27140	27150	28120	28140

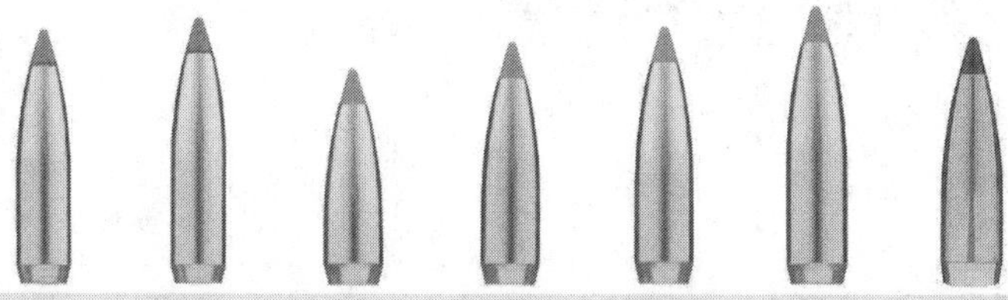

Caliber & Description	7mm S	30 S	30 S	30 S	30 S	30 S	8mm S
Diameter, inches	.284	.308	.308	.308	.308	.308	.323
Weight, Grains	150	125	150	165	168	180	180
Density	.266	.188	.226	.248	.253	.271	.247
Ballistic Coefficient	.493	.366	.435	.475	.490	.507	.394
Catalog Number	28150	30125	30150	30165	30168	30180	32180

Box 50: $17–$30

LEGEND

Type of Bullet
- BT – Boat Tail
- HP – Hollow Point
- J – Jacketed
- PP – Protected Point
- RN – Round Nose
- S – Spitzer
- SS – Semi Spitzer
- W – Whelen

Type of Tip
- PT – Purple Tip
- BT – Blue Tip
- BrT – Brown Tip
- BuT – Buckskin Tip
- GT – Green Tip
- GuT – Gunmetal Tip
- MT – Maroon Tip
- OT – Olive Tip
- RT – Red Tip
- SLT – Soft Lead Tip
- YT – Yellow Tip

Nosler Bullets

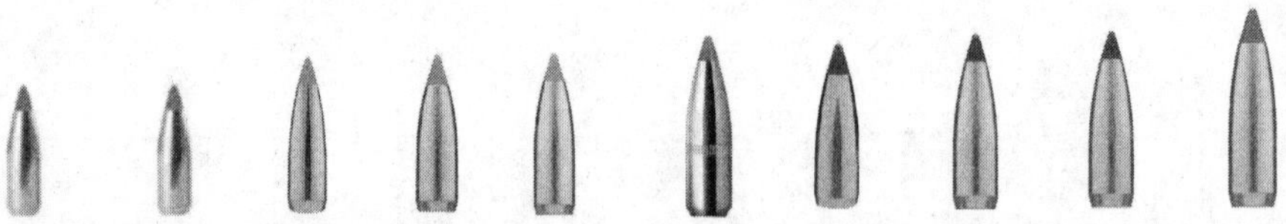

Ballistic Tip Varmint

Caliber & Description	204 S	204 S	22 S	22 S	22 S	22 S	6mm S	6mm S	6mm S	25 S
Diameter, inches	.204	.204	.224	.224	.224	.224	.243	.243	.243	.257
Weight, Grains	32	40	40	50	55	60	55	70	80	85
Density	.110	.137	.114	.142	.157	.171	.133	.169	.194	.184
Ballistic Coefficient	.206	.239	.221	.238	.27	.270	.276	.310	.329	.329
Catalog Number	35216	52111	39510	39522	39526	34992	24055	39532	24080	43004

Box 100: $23–$36

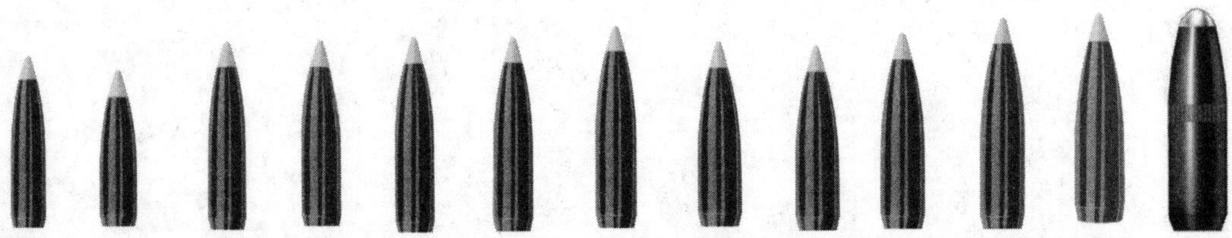

CT Ballistic Silvertip Hunting

Caliber & Description	6mm S	25 S	270 S	270 S	7mm S	7mm S	30 S	30 RN	30 S	30 S	8mm S	45-70 RN	338 S
Diameter, inches	.243	.257	.277	.277	.284	.284	.308	.308	.308	.308	.323	.458	.338
Weight, Grains	95	115	130	150	140	150	150	150	168	180	180	300	200
Density	.230	.249	.242	.279	.248	.266	.226	.226	.253	.271	.247	.204	.250
Ballistic Coefficient	.379	.453	.433	.496	.485	.493	.435	.232	.490	.507	.394	.191	.414
Catalog Number	51040	51050	51075	51100	51105	51110	51150	51165	51160	51170	51693	51834	51200

Box 50: $27

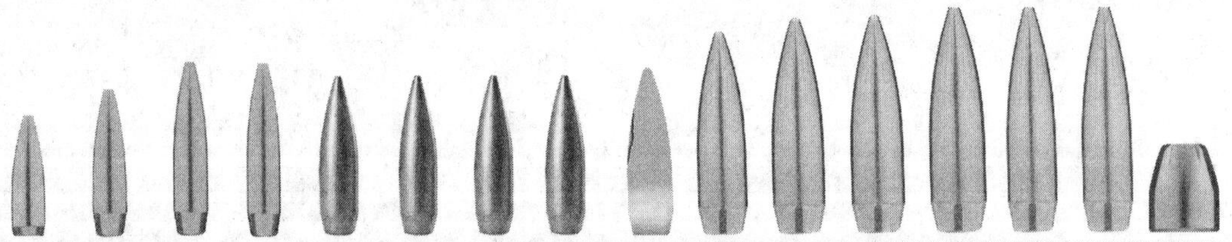

Custom Competition

Caliber & Description	22 HPBT	22 HPBT	22 HPBT	22 HPBT	6mm HPBT	6mm HPBT	6.5mm HPBT	6.5mm HPBT	6.8mm HPBT	7mm HPBT	30 HPBT	30 HPBT	30 HPBT	30 HPBT	30 HPBT	45 JHP
Diameter, Inches	.224	.224	.224	.224	.243	.243	.264	.264	.277	.284	.308	.308	.308	.308	.308	.451
Weight, Grains	52	69	77	80	105	107	123	140	115	168	140	155	168	175	190	185
Density	.148	.196	.219	.228	.254	.259	.252	.287	.214	.298	.211	.233	.253	.264	.286	.130
Ballistic Coefficient	.220	.305	.340	.415	.517	.525	.510	.529	.375	.520	.396	.450	.462	.505	.530	.142
Catalog Number	53294	17101	22421	25116	53614	49742	53415	26725	45357	53418	53152	53155	53164	53952	53412	44847

Box 100, 250: $19–$36

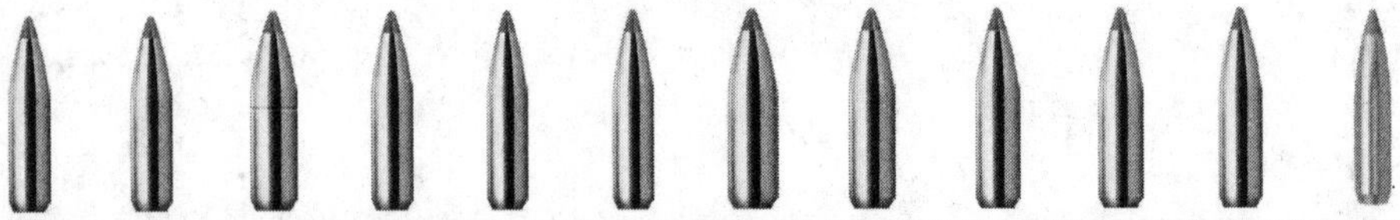

E-TIP

Caliber& Description	6mm S	25 S	6.8mm S	270 S	7mm S	7mm S	30 S	30 S	30 S	8mm S	338 S	6.5MM S
Diameter, Inches	.243	.257	.277	.277	.284	.284	.308	.308	.308	.323	.338	264
Weight, Grains	90	100	85	130	140	150	150	168	180	180	200	120
Density	.218	.216	.158	.242	.248	.266	.226	.253	.271	.246	.250	.246
Ballistic Coefficient	.403	.409	.273	.459	.489	.498	.469	.503	.523	.427	.425	.497
Catalog Number	59165	59456	59543	59298	59955	59426	59378	59415	59180	59265	59186	59765

Box 50: $29–$49

Nosler Bullets

Partition

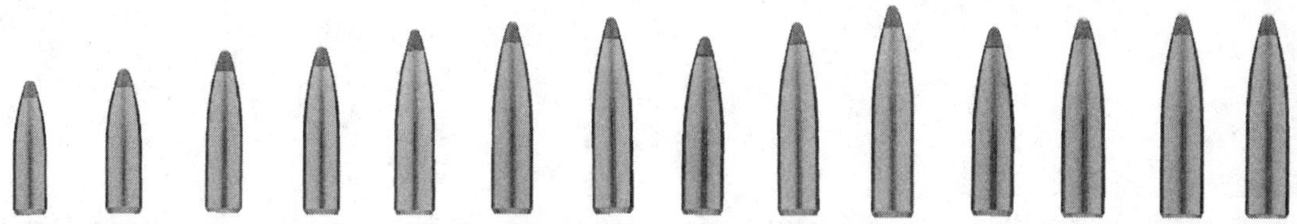

Caliber& Description	22 S	6mm S	6mm S	6mm S	25 S	25 S	25 S	6.5mm S	6.5mm S	6.5mm S	270 S	270 S	270 S	270 SS
Diameter, Inches	.224	.243	.243	.243	.257	.257	.257	.264	.264	.264	.277	.277	.277	.277
Weight, Grains	60	85	95	100	100	115	120	100	125	140	130	140	150	160
Density	.171	.206	.230	.242	.216	.249	.260	.205	.256	.287	.242	.261	.279	.298
Ballistic Coefficient	.228	.315	.365	.384	.377	.389	.391	.326	.4479	.490	.416	.432	.465	.434
Catalog Number	16316	16314	16315	35642	16317	16318	35643	16319	16320	16321	16322	35200	.16323	16324

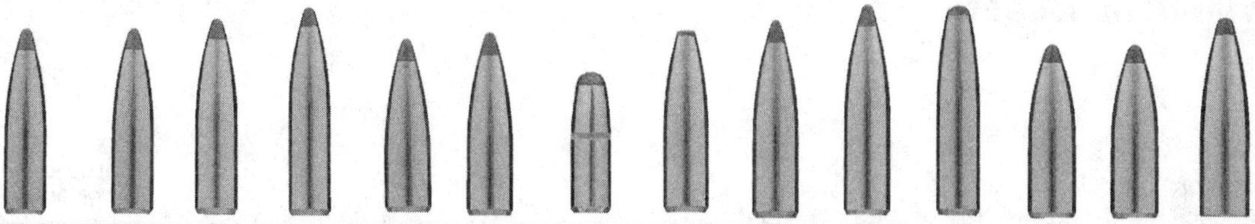

Caliber & Description	7mm S	7mm S	7mm S	7mm S	30 S	30 S	30 RN	30 PP	30 S	30 S	30 SS	8mm S	338 S	338 S
Diameter, Inches	.284	.284	.284	.284	.308	.308	.308	.308	.308	.308	.308	.323	.338	.338
Weight, Grains	140	150	160	175	150	165	170	180	180	200	220	200	210	225
Density	.248	.266	.283	.310	.226	.248	.256	.271	.271	.301	.331	.274	.263	.281
Ballistic Coefficient	.434	.456	.475	.519	.387	.410	.252	.361	.474	.481	.351	.426	.400	.454
Catalog Number	16325	16326	16327	35645	16329	16330	16333	25396	16331	35626	16332	35277	16337	16336

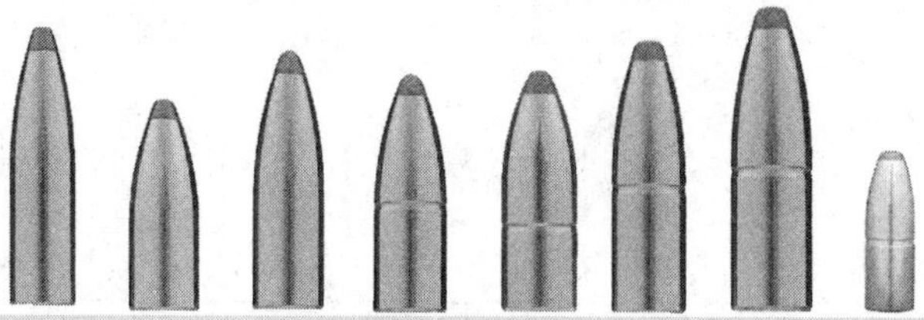

Caliber & Description	338 S	35 S	35 S	9.3mm S	375 S	375 S	416 S	458 PP
Diameter, Inches	.338	.358	.358	.366	.375	.375	.416	.458
Weight, Grains	250	225	250	286	260	300	400	500
Density	.313	.251	.279	.307	.264	.305	.330	.389
Ballistic Coefficient	.473	.430	.446	.482	.314	.398	.390	.341
Catalog Number	35644	44800	44801	44750	44850	44845	45200	44745

Box 25, 50: $26–$119

LEGEND

Type of Bullet		Type of Tip	
BT	– Boat Tail	**PT**	– Purple Tip
HP	– Hollow Point	**BT**	– Blue Tip
J	– Jacketed	**BrT**	– Brown Tip
PP	– Protected Point	**BuT**	– Buckskin Tip
RN	– Round Nose	**GT**	– Green Tip
S	– Spitzer	**GuT**	– Gunmetal Tip
SS	– Semi Spitzer	**MT**	– Maroon Tip
W	– Whelen	**OT**	– Olive Tip
		RT	– Red Tip
		SLT	– Soft Lead Tip
		YT	– Yellow Tip

Solid

Caliber & Description	9.3mm Solid	375 Solid	375 Solid	416 Solid	458 Solid	470 NE Solid
Diameter, Inches	.366	.375	.375	.416	.458	.474
Weight, Grains	286	260	300	400	500	500
Density	.305	.264	.305	.330	.341	.318
Ballistic Coefficient	.350	.254	.300	.289	.246	.237
Catalog Number	29825	29755	28451	23654	27452	28455

MSRP $70–$89

LEGEND

Type of Bullet			
BT	– Boattail	**J**	– Jacketed
FMJ	– Full Metal Jacket	**PP**	– Protected Point
		RN	– Round Nose
		S	– Spitzer

Nosler Bullets

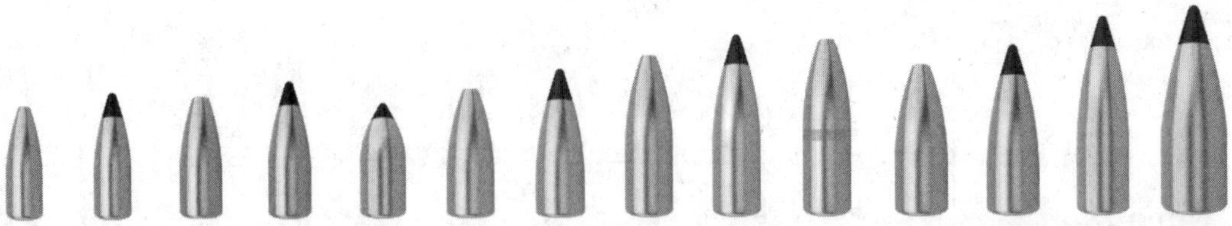

VARMAGEDDON

Caliber& Description	17 FBHP	17 FB Tipped	20 FBHP	20 FB Tipped	22 FB Tipped	22 FBHP	22 FB Tipped	22 FBHP	22 FB Tipped	22 FBHP	6mm FBHP	6mm FB Tipped	6mm FB Tipped	30 FB Tipped
Diameter, Inches	.172	.172	.204	.204	.224	.224	.224	.224	.224	.224	.243	.243	.243	.308
Weight, Grains	20	20	32	32	35	40	40	55	55	62	55	55	70	110
Density	.097	.097	.110	.110	.100	.114	.114	.157	.157	.176	.133	.133	.169	.166
Ballistic Coefficient	.119	.183	.131	.204	.120	.158	.211	.210	.218	.251	.192	.252	.334	.293
Catalog Number	17205	17210	17215	17220	36763	17225	17230	17235	17240	35631	17245	17250	26123	34057

Box 100, 250: $15–$25

Handgun Bullets

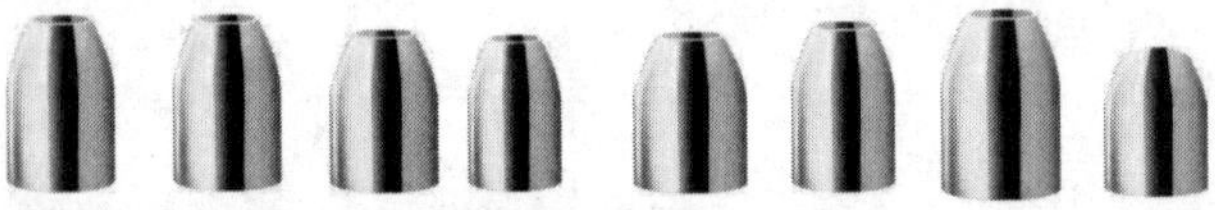

SPORTING PISTOL

Caliber & Description	9mm JHP	9mm JHP	10mm JHP	10mm JHP	10mm JHP	10mm JHP	45 JHP	45 FMJ
Diameter, Inches	.355	.355	.400	.400	.400	.400	.451	.451
Weight, Grains	115	124	135	150	180	200	230	230
Density	.109	.141	.093	.106	.161	.179	.1625	.162
Ballistic Coefficient	.130	.118	.121	.134	.147	.163	.175	.183
Catalog Number	44848	43123	44852	44860	44885	44952	44922	44964

Box 250: $42–$60

LEGEND

Type of Bullet

- **BT** – Boattail
- **FB** – Flat Base
- **FN** – Flat Nose
- **RN** – Round Nose
- **S** – Spitzer
- **SP** – Soft Point
- **SS** – Semi-Spitzer

SPORTING REVOLVER

Caliber & Description	38 JHP	41 JHP	44 JHP	44 JHP	44 JHP	44 JHP	45 Colt JHP
Diameter, Inches	.357	.410	.429	.429	.429	.429	.451
Weight, Grains	158	210	200	240	240	300	250
Density	.182	.170	.151	.173	.177	.206	.177
Ballistic Coefficient	.177	.178	155	.186	.186	.233	.176
Catalog Number	44841	43012	44846	44842	44868	42069	43013

Box 100, 250: $28–$58

Sierra Bullets

Rifle Bullets

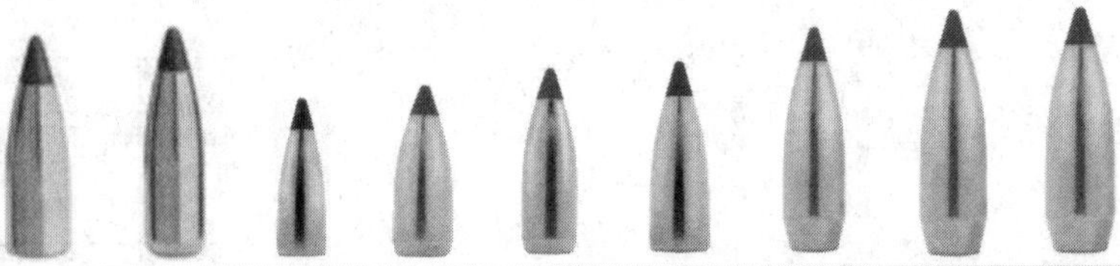

BLITZKING

Caliber & Description	20	20	224	224	224	6mm	6mm	257	257
Diameter, Inches	.204	.204	.224	.224	.224	.243	.243	.257	.257
Weight, Grains	32	39	40	50	55	55	70	70	90
Density	.110	.134	.114	.142	.157	.133	.169	.151	.195
Ballistic Coefficient	.221	.287	.196	.248	.185	.225	.299	.260	.388
Catalog Number	1032	1039	1440	1450	1455	1502	1507	1605	1616

From: $28–$34

Sierra Bullets

GameKing

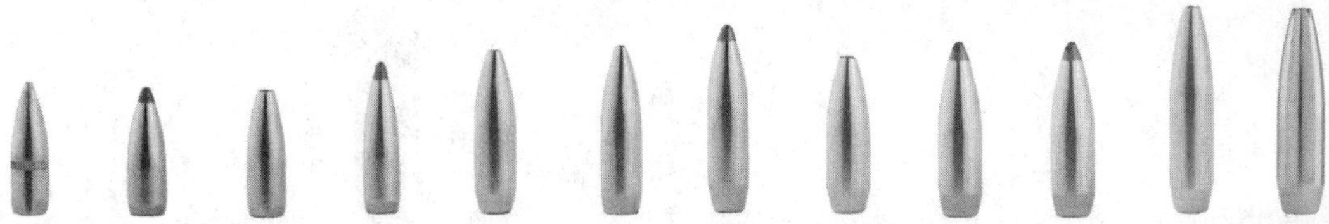

Caliber & Description	22 FMJBT	22 SBT	22 HPBT	22 SBT	6mm HPBT	6mm FMJBT	6mm SBT	25 HPBT	25 SBT	25 SBT	25 HPBT	6.5mm HPBT
Diameter, Inches	.224	.224	.224	.224	.243	.243	.243	.257	.257	.257	.257	.264
Weight, Grains	55	55	55	65	85	90	100	90	100	117	120	130
Density	.157	.257	.157	.185	.206	.218	.242	.195	.216	.253	.260	.266
Ballistic Coefficient	.272	.250	.185	.303	.282	.387	.430	.250	.355	.410	.350	.355
Catalog Number	1355	1365	1390	1395	1530	1535	1560	1615	1625	1630	1650	1728

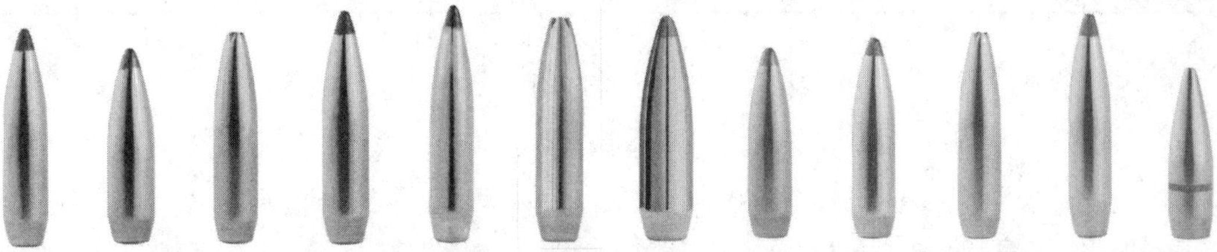

Caliber & Description	6.5mm SBT	270 SBT	270 HPBT	270 SBT	270 SBT	7mm HPBT	7mm SBT	7mm SBT	7mm SBT	7mm HPBT	7mm SBT	30 FMJBT
Diameter, Inches	.264	.277	.277	.277	.277	.284	.274	.284	.284	.284	.284	.308
Weight, Grains	140	130	140	140	150	140	140	150	160	160	175	150
Density	.287	.242	.261	.261	.279	.248	.248	.266	.283	.283	.310	.226
Ballistic Coefficient	.495	.436	.337	.457	.483	.375	.416	.436	.455	.384	.533	.408
Catalog Number	1730	1820	1835	1845	1840	1912	1905	1913	1920	1925	1940	2115

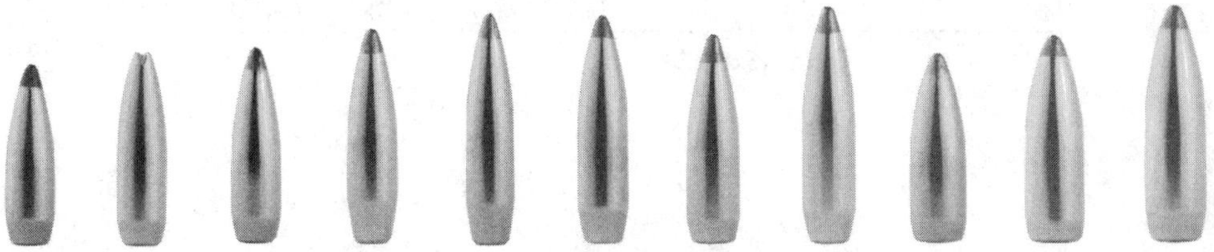

Caliber & Description	30 SBT	30 HPBT	30 SBT	30 SBT	30 SBT	8mm SBT	338 SBT	338 SBT	35 SBT	375 SBT	375 SBT
Diameter, Inches	.308	.308	.308	.308	.308	.323	.338	.338	.358	.375	.375
Weight, Grains	150	165	165	180	200	220	215	250	225	250	300
Density	.226	.248	.248	.271	.301	.301	.269	.313	.251	.254	.305
Ballistic Coefficient	.380	.363	.404	.501	.560	.521	.485	.565	.370	.353	.475
Catalog Number	2125	2140	2145	2160	2165	2420	2610	2600	2850	2950	3000

From: $21–$45

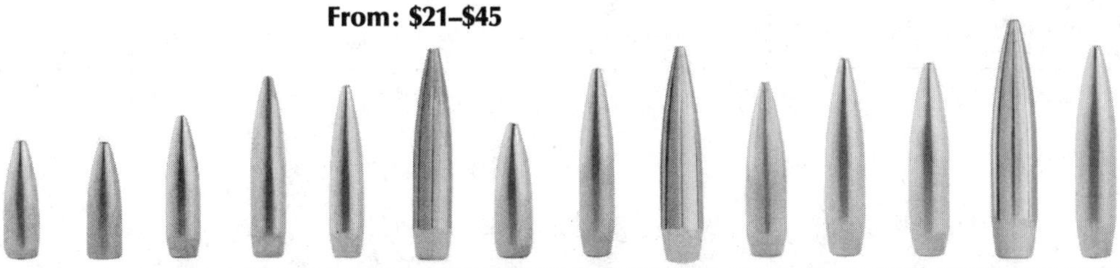

MatchKing

Caliber & Description	22 HPBT	22 HP	22 HPBT	22 HPBT	22 HPBT	22 HPBT	6mm HPBT	6mm HPBT	6mm HPBT	25 HPBT	6.5mm HPBT	6.5mm HPBT	6.5mm HPBT	6.5mm HPBT
Diameter, Inches	.224	.224	.224	.224	.224	.224	.243	.243	.243	.257	.264	.264	.264	.264
Weight, Grains	52	53	69	77	80	90	70	107	95	100	107	120	123	140
Density	.148	.151	.196	.219	.228	.256	.169	.259	.230	.216	.219	.246	.252	.287
Ballistic Coefficient	.225	.224	.301	.372	.420	.504	.259	.527	.480	.394	.430	.421	.510	.535
Catalog Number	1410	1400	1380	9377T	9390T	9290T	1505	1570	1537	1628	1715	1725	1727	1740

Sierra Bullets

MatchKing (cont.)

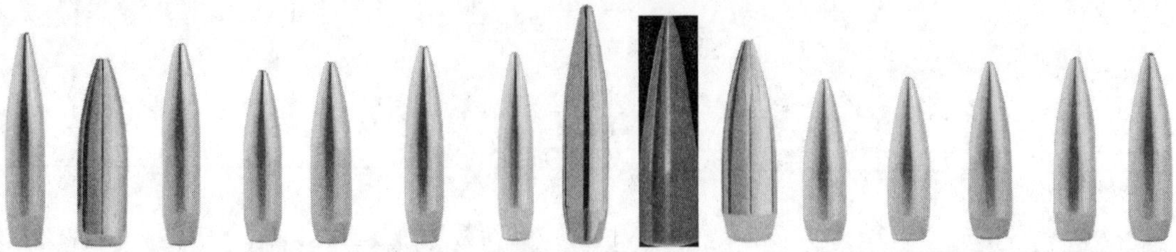

Caliber & Description	6.5mm HPBT	270 HPBT	270 HPBT	7mm HPBT	7mm HPBT	7mm HPBT	7mm HPBT	7mm HPBT	30 HP	30 HPBT	30 HPBT	30 HPBT	30 HPBT	30 HPBT	30 HPBT
Diameter, Inches	.264	.277	.277	.284	.284	.284	.284	.284	.308	.308	.308	.308	.308	.308	.308
Weight, Grains	142	115	135	130	150	168	175	180	125	135	150	155	168	175	180
Density	.291	.214	.251	.230	.266	.298	.310	.319	.188	.203	.226	.233	.253	.264	.271
Ballistic Coefficient	.595	.318	.488	.395	.429	.488	.608	.660	.349	.390	.417	.450	.462	.505	.475
Catalog Number	1742	1815	1833	1903	1915	1930	1975	1980	2121	2123	2190	2155	2200	2275	2220

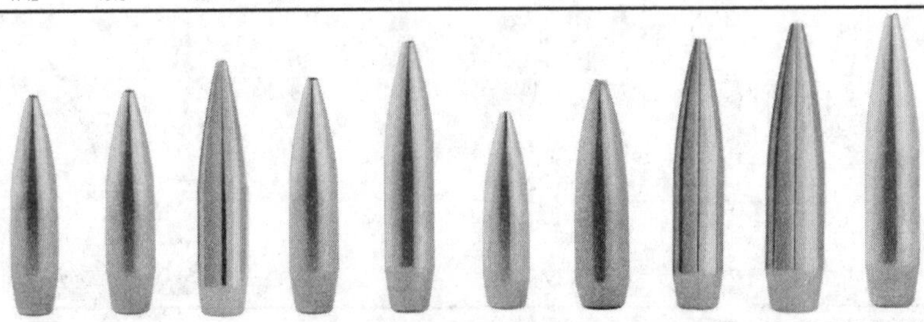

Caliber & Description	30 HPBT	30 HPBT	30 HPBT	30 HPBT	30 HPBT	303 HPBT	8mm HPBT	338 HPBT	338 HPBT	375 HPBT
Diameter, Inches	.308	.308	.308	.308	.308	.311	.323	.338	.338	.375
Weight, Grains	190	200	210	220	240	174	200	250	300	350
Density	.286	.301	.316	.331	.361	.257	.274	.313	.375	.355
Ballistic Coefficient	.533	.565	.645	.629	.711	.499	.520	.587	.768	.805
Catalog Number	2210	2230	9240T	2240	9245T	2315	2415	2650	9300T	9350T

LEGEND

BT – Boattail
FMJ – Full Metal Jacket
FN – Flat Nose
HC – Hollow Cavity
HP – Hollow Point
J – Jacketed
RN – Round Nose
S – Spitzer
SMP – Semi-Pointed
SP – Soft Point

From: $25–$54

Pro-Hunter

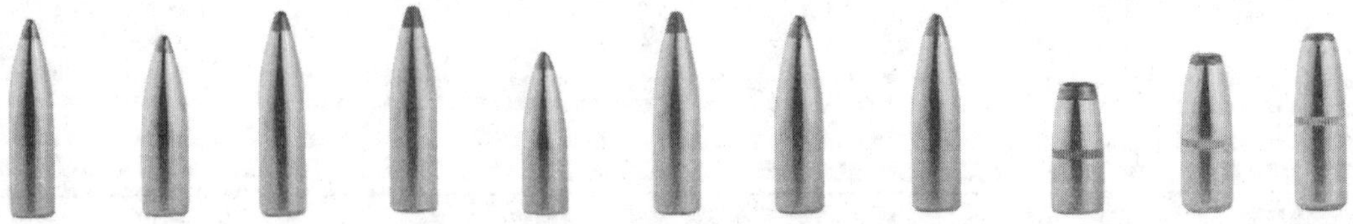

Caliber & Description	6mm S	25 S	25 S	6.5mm S	270 S	270 S	7mm S	7mm S	30 HP/FN	30 FN	30 FN
Diameter, Inches	.243	.257	.257	.264	.277	.277	.284	.284	.308	.308	.308
Weight, Grains	100	100	117	120	110	130	120	140	125	150	170
Density	.242	.216	.253	.246	.205	.242	.213	.248	.188	.226	.256
Ballistic Coefficient	.373	.330	.388	.356	.318	.370	.328	.377	.119	.185	.205
Catalog Number	1540	1620	1640	1720	1810	1830	1900	1910	2020	2000	2010

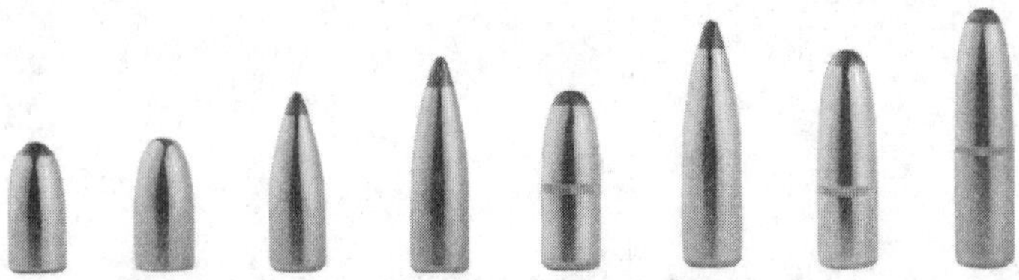

Caliber & Description	30 RN	30 FMJ	30 S	30 S	30 RN	30 S	30 RN	30 RN
Diameter, Inches	.308	.308	.308	.308	.308	.308	.308	.308
Weight, Grains	110	110	125	150	150	180	180	220
Density	.166	.166	.188	.226	.226	.271	.271	.331
Ballistic Coefficient	.144	.144	.279	.336	.200	.407	.240	.310
Catalog Number	2100	2105	2120	2130	2135	2150	2170	2180

PRO-HUNTER (CONT.)

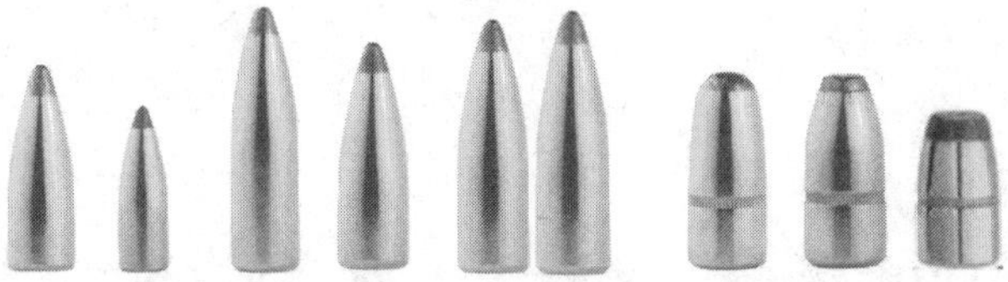

Caliber & Description	303 S	303 S	303 S	8mm S	8mm S	338 S	35 RN	375 FN	45-70 HP/FN
Diameter, Inches	.311	.311	.311	.323	.323	.338	.358	.375	.458
Weight, Grains	125	150	180	150	175	225	200	200	300
Density	.185	.222	.266	.205	.240	.281	.223	.203	.204
Ballistic Coefficient	.274	.344	.411	.336	.381	.462	.148	.195	.120
Catalog Number	2305	2300	2310	2400	2410	2620	2800	2900	8900

VARMINTER

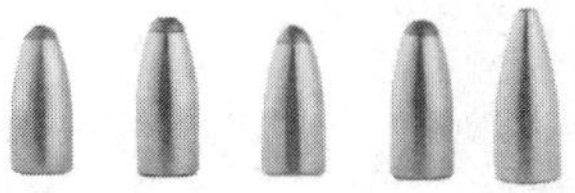

Caliber & Description	22 Hornet	22 Hornet	22 Hornet	22 Hornet	22 HP
Diameter, Inches	.223	.223	.224	.224	.224
Weight, Grains	40	45	40	45	40
Density	.115	.129	.114	.128	.114
Ballistic Coefficient	.117	.132	.116	.131	.155
Catalog Number	1100	1110	1200	1210	1385

From: $20–$37

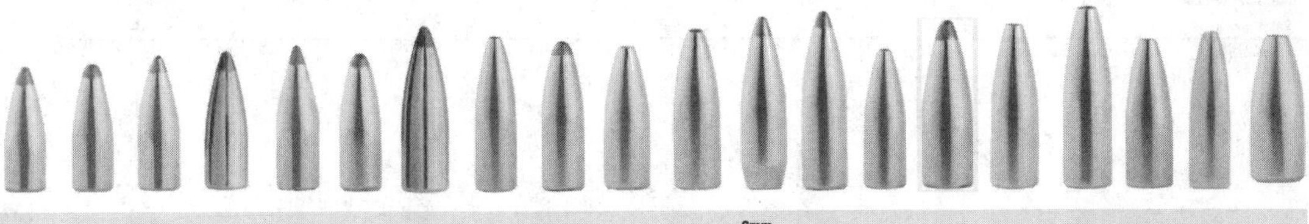

Caliber & Description	22 S	22 S	22 S	22 Blitz	22 Blitz	22 SMP	22 S	22 HP	22 SMP	6mm HP	6mm HP	6mm SBT Blitz	6mm S	25 HP	25 S	6.5mm HP	6.5mm HP	270 HP	7mm HP	30 HP
Diameter, Inches	.224	.224	.224	.224	.224	.224	.224	.224	.224	.243	.243	.243	.243	.257	.257	.264	.264	.277	.284	.308
Weight, Grains	45	50	50	50	55	55	55	60	63	60	75	80	85	75	87	85	100	90	100	110
Density	.128	.142	.142	.142	.157	.157	.157	.171	.179	.145	.181	.194	.206	.162	.188	.174	.205	.168	.177	.166
Ballistic Coefficient	.210	.192	.222	.222	.237	.204	.237	.246	.231	.182	.217	.319	.315	.189	.293	.225	.259	.195	.209	.177
Catalog Number	1310	1320	1330	1340	1345	1350	1360	1375	1370	1500	1510	1515	1520	1600	1610	1700	1710	1800	1895	2110

From: $20–$32

Handgun Bullets

SPORTS MASTER

Caliber & Description	30 RN	32 JHC	9mm JHP	9mm JHP	9mm JHP	38 JHP Blitz	38 JHP	38 JSP	38 JHP	38 JHC	38 JSP	10mm JHP	10mm JHP
Diameter, Inches	.308	.312	.355	.355	.355	.357	.357	.357	.357	.357	.357	.400	.400
Weight, Grains	85	90	90	115	125	110	125	125	140	158	158	135	150
Density	.128	.132	.102	.130	.142	.123	.140	.140	.157	.177	.177	.121	.134
Ballistic Coefficient	.102	.125	.095	.107	.124	.120	.133	.133	.0776	.100	.100	.105	.120
Catalog Number	8005	8030	8100	8110	8125	8300	8320	8310	8325	8360	8340	8425	8430

Caliber & Description	10mm JHP	10mm JHP	41 JHC	41 JHC	44 JHC	44 JHC	44 JHC	44 JSP	45 JHP	45 JHP	45 JHC	45 JSP	50 JHP	50 JSP
Diameter, Inches	.400	.400	.410	.410	.4295	.4295	.4295	.4295	.4515	.4515	.4515	.4515	.500	.500
Weight, Grains	165	180	170	210	180	210	240	300	185	230	240	300	350	400
Density	.147	.161	.144	.178	.139	.163	.186	.232	.130	.161	.168	.210	.200	.229
Ballistic Coefficient	.130	.140	.123	.165	.130	.160	.185	.230	.100	.145	.150	.192	.155	.185
Catalog Number	8445	8460	8500	8520	8600	8620	8610	8630	8800	8805	8820	8830	5350	5400

From: $22–$37

Speer Bullets

Rifle Bullets

Boat Tail Bullets

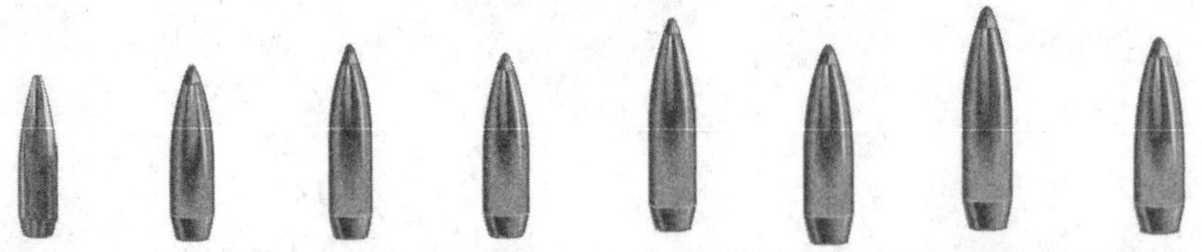

Caliber & Description	22 Match* HP	6mm SSP	6mm SSP	25 SHP	25 SSP	270 SSP	270 SSP	7mm SSP
Diameter, Inches	.224	.243	.243	.257	.257	.277	.277	.284
Weight, Grains	52	85	100	100	120	130	150	130
Density	.148	.206	.242	.216	.260	.242	.279	.230
Ballistic Coefficient	.253	.380	.446	.393	.480	.412	.489	.424
Catalog Number	1036	1213	1220	1408	1410	1458	1604	1624

*Match bullets are not recommended for use on game animals.

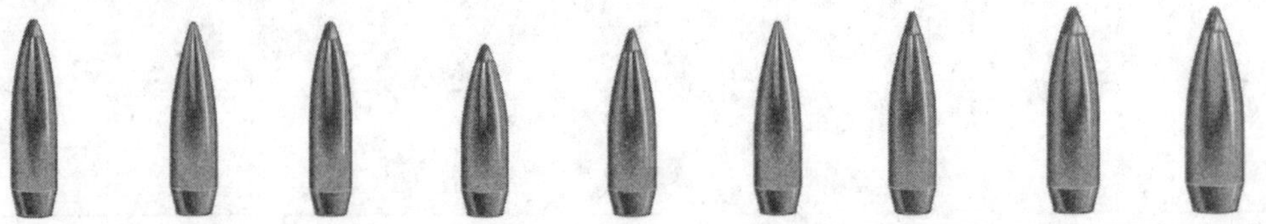

Caliber & Description	7mm SSP	7mm Match* HP	7mm SSP	30 SSP	30 SSP	30 Match* HP	30 SSP	338 SSP	375 SSP
Diameter, Inches	.284	.284	.284	.308	.308	.308	.308	.338	.375
Weight, Grains	145	145	160	150	165	168	180	225	270
Density	.257	.257	.284	.226	.248	.253	.271	.281	.274
Ballistic Coefficient	.472	.468	.519	.417	.520	.534	.545	.497	.478
Catalog Number	1628	1631	1634	2022	2034	2040	2052	2406	2472

*Match bullets are not recommended for use on game animals.

From: $27–$39

Grand Slam

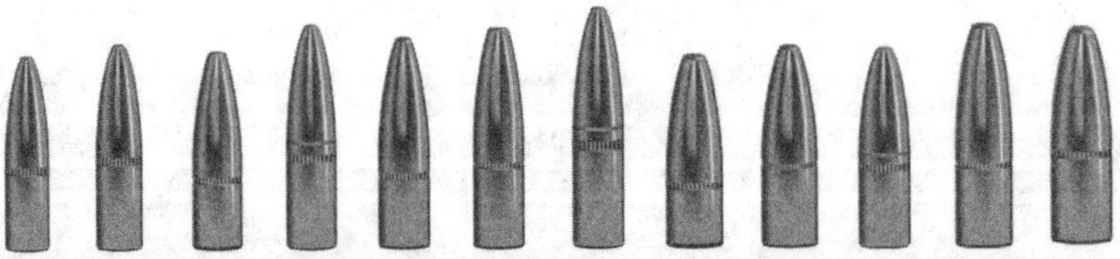

Caliber & Description	6mm SP	25 HCSP	270 HCSP	270 HCSP	7mm HCSP	7mm HCSP	7mm HCSP	30 HCSP	30 HCSP	30 HCSP	338 HCSP	375 HCSP
Diameter, Inches	.243	.257	.277	.277	.284	.284	.284	.308	.308	.308	.338	.375
Weight, Grains	100	120	130	150	145	160	175	150	165	180	250	285
Density	.242	.260	.242	.279	.257	.283	.310	.226	.248	.271	.313	.290
Ballistic Coefficient	.327	.356	.332	.378	.353	.389	.436	.295	.354	.374	.436	.354
Catalog Number	1222	1415	1465	1608	1632	1638	1643	2026	2038	2063	2408	2473

From: $31–$66

LEGEND

- **BT** – Boat Tail
- **FB** – Fusion Bonded
- **FMJ** – Full Metal Jacket
- **FN** – Flat Nose
- **GD** – Gold Dot®
- **HC** – Hot-Cor®
- **HP** – Hollow Point
- **L** – Lead
- **MHP™** – Molybdenum Disulfide Impregnated
- **S** – Spitzer
- **SS** – Semi-Spitzer
- **SB™** – For Short-Barrel Firearms
- **SP** – Soft Point
- **TMJ®** – Encased-Core Full Jacket
- **RN** – Round Nose
- **SWC** – Semi-Wadcutter
- **UC** – Uni-Cor®
- **WC** – Wadcutter

Speer Bullets

Hot-Cor Bullets*

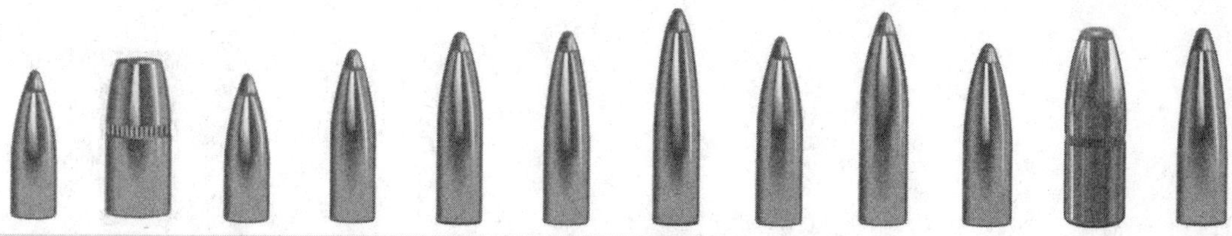

Caliber & Description	6mm SSP	25 SPFN	25 SSP	25 SSP	25 SSP	6.5mm SSP	6.5mm SSP	270 SSP	270 SSP	7mm SSP	7mm SPFN	7mm SSP
Diameter, Inches	.243	.257	.257	.257	.257	.264	.264	.277	.277	.284	.284	.284
Weight, Grains	90	75	87	100	120	120	140	130	150	130	130	145
Density	.218	.162	.188	.216	.260	.246	.287	.242	.279	.230	.230	.257
Ballistic Coefficient	.365	.135	.300	.334	.405	.392	.498	.383	.455	.394	.257	.416
Catalog Number	1217	1237	1241	1405	1411	1435	1441	1459	1605	1623	1625	1629

** Not recommended for lever-action rifles.*

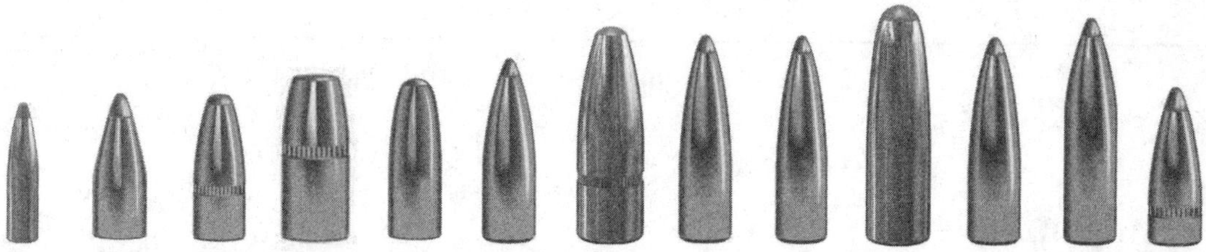

Caliber & Description	7mm SSP	30 Spire SP	30 FNSP	30 SPFN	30 RNSP	30 SSP	30 Mag-Tip	30 SSP	30 SSP	30 SPRN	30 SSP	30 SSP	7.62x39 SSP
Diameter, Inches	.284	.308	.308	.308	.308	.308	.308	.308	.308	.308	.308	.308	.310
Weight, Grains	160	110	130	150	150	150	150	165	170	180	180	200	123
Density	.283	.166	.196	.226	.226	.226	.226	.248	.256	.271	.271	.301	.183
Ballistic Coefficient	.504	.245	.213	.255	.235	.377	.301	.444	.298	.304	.441	.478	.283
Catalog Number	1635	1855	2007	2011	2017	2023	2025	2035	2041	2047	2053	2211	2213

** Not recommended for lever-action rifles.*

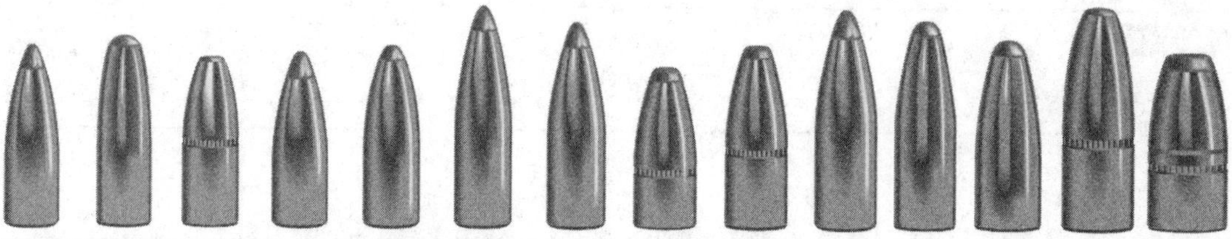

Caliber & Description	303 SSP	303 RNSP	32 FNSP	8mm SSP	8mm SSSP	8mm SSP	338 SSP	35 FNSP	35 FNSP	35 SSP	9.3mm SSSP	375 SSSP	416 Mag-Tip	45 FNSP
Diameter, Inches	.311	.311	.321	.323	.323	.323	.338	.358	.358	.358	.366	.375	.416	.458
Weight, Grains	150	180	170	150	170	200	200	180	220	250	270	235	350	350
Density	.222	.266	.236	.205	.233	.274	.250	.201	.245	.279	.288	.239	.289	.238
Ballistic Coefficient	.351	.299	.283	.343	.311	.440	.426	.236	.286	.422	.361	.301	.332	.218
Catalog Number	2217	2223	2259	2277	2283	2285	2405	2435	2439	2453	2459	2471	2477	2478

From: $20–$44

Jacketed HP Bullets

Caliber & Description	22 Hornet	45
Diameter, Inches	.224	.458
Weight, Grains	33	300
Density	.094	.204
Ballistic Coefficient	.080	.206
Catalog Number	1014	2482

From: $21–$36

Special Purpose Bullets*

Caliber & Description	30 SPRN	30 HP	45 SPFN
Diameter, Inches	.308	.308	.458
Weight, Grains	100	110	400
Density	.151	.166	.272
Ballistic Coefficient	.144	.128	.259
Catalog Number	1805	1835	2479

From: $20–$34

AMMUNITION

Speer Bullets

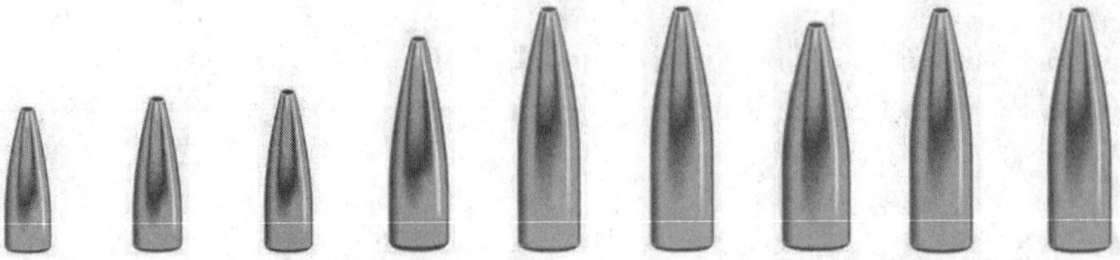

TNT
BULLETS

Caliber & Description	204 HP	22 HP	22 HP	6mm HP	25 HP	6.5mm HP	270 HP	7mm HP	30 HP
Diameter, Inches	.204	.224	.224	.243	.247	.264	.277	.284	.308
Weight, Grains	39	50	55	70	87	90	90	110	125
Density	.134	.142	.157	.169	.188	.184	.168	.195	.188
Ballistic Coefficient	.202	.228	.233	.279	.337	.281	.303	.384	.341
Catalog Number	1015	1030	1032	1206	1246	1445	1446	1616	1986

From: $20–$33

Handgun Bullets

GOLD DOT BULLETS

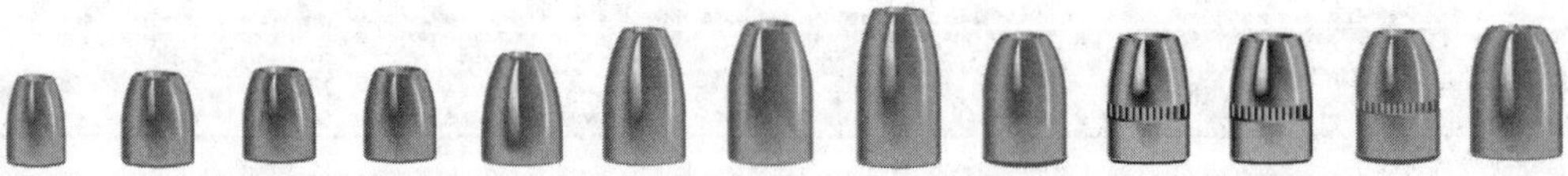

Caliber & Description	25 HP	32 Auto HP	327 Fed. Mag. HP	327 Fed. Mag. HP	380 Auto HP	9mm HP	9mm HP	9mm HP	357 SIG HP	38 Spl. HPSB	38 HPSB	357 Mag. HP	40/10mm HP
Diameter, Inches	.251	.312	.312	.312	.355	.355	.355	.355	.355	.357	.357	.357	.400
Weight, Grains	35	60	100	115	90	115	124	147	125	110	135	125	155
Density	.079	.088	.147	.168	.102	.130	.141	.167	.142	.123	.151	.177	.138
Ballistic Coefficient	.091	.118	.137	.180	.101	.125	.134	.164	.141	.117	.141	.140	.123
Catalog Number	3985	3986	3990	3988	3992	3994	3998	4002	4360	4009	4014	4012	4400

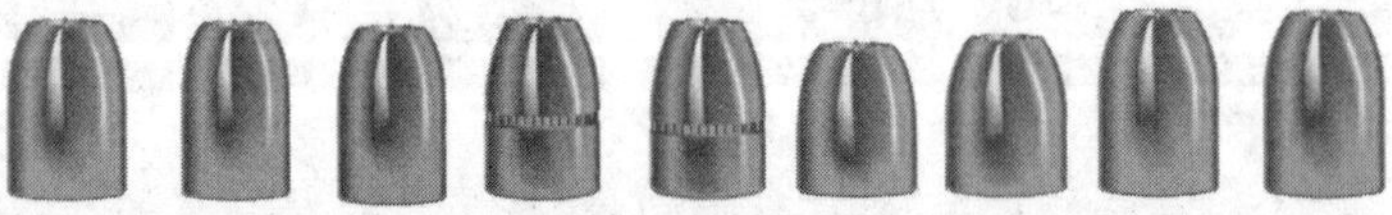

Caliber & Description	40/10mm HP	40/10mm HP	40/10mm HPSB	44 Spl. HP	44 Mag. HP	45 Auto HP	45 Auto HP	45 Auto HP	45 HPSB
Diameter, Inches	.400	.400	.400	.429	.429	.451	.451	.451	.451
Weight, Grains	165	180	180	.200	210	185	200	230	230
Density	.147	.161	.161	.155	.163	.130	.140	.162	.162
Ballistic Coefficient	.138	.143	.148	.145	.154	.109	.138	.143	.148
Catalog Number	4397	4406	4401	4427	4428	4470	4478	4483	4482

From: $22–$36

LEGEND

BT – Boat Tail
FB – Fusion Bonded
FMJ – Full Metal Jacket
FN – Flat Nose
GD – Gold Dot®
HC – Hot-Cor®
HP – Hollow Point
L – Lead
MHP™ – Molybdenum Disulfide Impregnated
S – Spitzer
SS – Semi-Spitzer
SB™ – For Short-Barrel Firearms
SP – Soft Point
TMJ® – Encased-Core Full Jacket
RN – Round Nose
SWC – Semi-Wadcutter
UC – Uni-Cor®
WC – Wadcutter

Speer Bullets

Jacketed Bullets

Caliber & Description	9mm Luger FN JSP	38 Spl./357 Mag. JHP	38 Spl./357 Mag. JSP	38 Spl./357 Mag. JHP	38 Spl./357 Mag. JHP	38 Spl./357 Mag. JHP	38 Spl./357 Mag. JSP
Diameter, Inches	.355	.357	.357	.357	.357	.357	.357
Weight, Grains	124	110	125	125	140	158	158
Density	.141	.123	.140	.140	.157	.177	.177
Ballistic Coefficient	.115	.113	.129	.129	.145	.163	.164
Catalog Number	3997	4007	4011	4013	4203	4211	4217

Caliber & Description	44 Mag. JSP	44 Mag. JSP	45 Colt/460 S&W JHP	45 Colt/460 S&W JSP	50 Action Express JHP
Diameter, Inches	.429	.429	.451	.451	.186
Weight, Grains	240	300	260	300	325
Density	.186	.233	.183	.211	.186
Ballistic Coefficient	.169	.213	.183	.199	.169
Catalog Number	4454	4463	4481	4485	4495

LEGEND

FN	– Flat Nose	**S**	– Spitzer
HB	– Hollow Base	**SP**	– Soft Point
HC	– Hot-Cor®	**SS**	– Semi-Spitzer
HP	– Hollow Point	**SWC**	– Semi-Wadcutter
J	– Jacketed	**WC**	– Wadcutter
RN	– Round Nose		

From: $18–$31

Lead Handgun Bullets

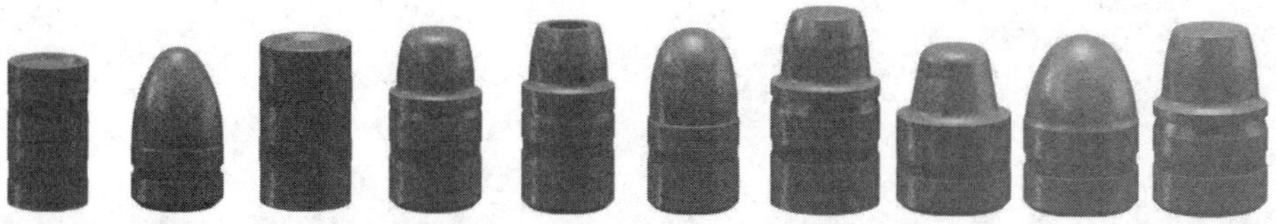

Caliber & Description	32 S&W HBWC	9mm Luger RN	38 HBWC	38 SWC	38 SWC HP	38 RN	44 SWC	45 Auto SWC	45 Auto RN	45 Colt SWC
Diameter, Inches	.314	.356	.358	.358	.358	.358	.430	.452	.452	.452
Weight, grains	98	125	148	158	158	158	240	200	230	250
Density	.142	.141	.165	.176	.176	.176	.185	.140	.161	.175
Ballistic Coefficient	.044	.155	.050	.123	.121	.170	.151	.078	.160	.117
Bulk Part No.	4600	4602	4618	4624	4628	4648	4661	4678	4691	4684
Bulk Count	1000	500	500	500	500	500	500	500	500	500

From: $46–$84

Swift Bullets

Rifle Bullets

The Scirocco II rifle bullet starts with a tough, pointed polymer tip that reduces air resistance, prevents tip deformation, and blends into the radius of its secant ogive nose section. The Scirocco II has a bonded core construction with a pure lead core encased in a tapered, progressively thickening jacket of pure copper. The Swift A-Frame bullet with its midsection wall of copper is less aerodynamic than the Scirocco, but it produces a broad mushroom while carrying almost all its weight through muscle and bone.

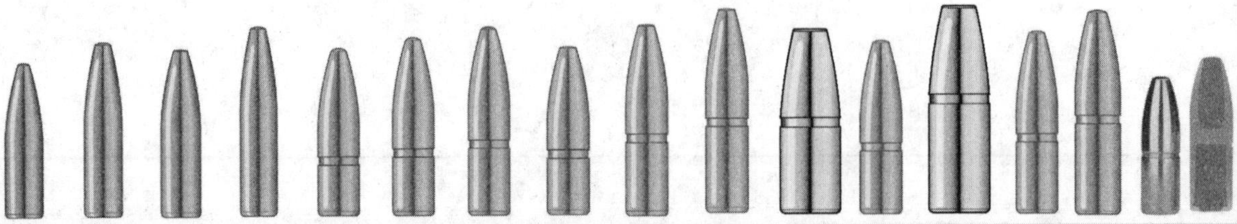

A-Frame

Caliber & Description	25 SS	25 SS	6.5mm SS	6.5mm SS	270 SS	270 SS	270 SS	7mm SS	7mm SS	7mm SS	30-30 FN	30 SS	30-30 FN	30 SS	30 SS	8mm SS	8mm SS
Diameter, Inches	.257	.257	.264	.264	.277	.277	.277	.284	.284	.284	.308	.308	.308	.308	.308	.323	.323
Weight, Grains	100	120	120	140	130	140	150	140	160	175	150	165	170	180	200	200	200
Density	.216	.260	.246	.287	.242	.261	.279	.248	.283	.310	.226	.248	.256	.271	.301	.274	.301
Ballistic Coefficient	.318	.382	.344	.401	.323	.414	.444	.335	.450	.493	.220	.367	.266	.400	.444	.357	.393

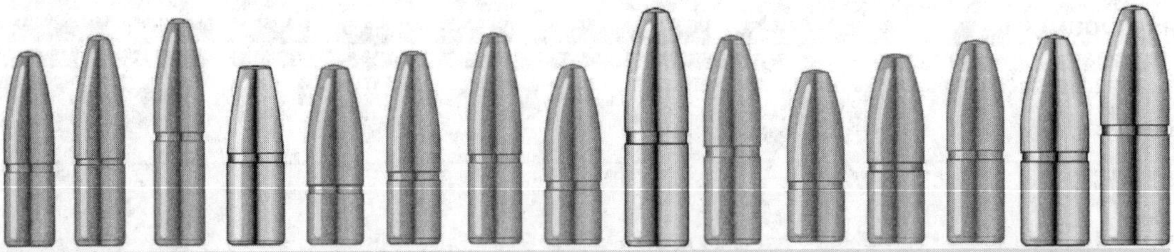

Caliber & Description	338 SS	338 SS	338 SS	348 FN	35 SS	35 SS	35 SS	9.3mm SS	9.3mm SS	9.3mm SS	375 SS	375 SS	375 SS	400 SS	400 SS
Diameter, Inches	.338	.338	.338	.348	.358	.358	.358	.366	.366	.366	.375	.375	.375	.410	.410
Weight, Grains	225	250	275	200	225	250	280	250	286	300	250	270	300	350	400
Density	.281	.313	.344	.236	.251	.279	.312	.267	.305	.320	.254	.274	.305	.297	.339
Ballistic Coefficient	.384	.427	.469	.245	.312	.347	.388	.285	.385	.342	.271	.349	.325	.321	.367

LEGEND

Type of Bullet

- **BT** – Boat Tail
- **CT** – Combat Target
- **FMJ** – Full Metal Jacket
- **FP** – Flat Point
- **HB** – Hollow Base
- **L** – Lead
- **RN** – Round Nose
- **SP** – Spire Point
- **SX** – Super Explosive
- **SWC** – Semi-Wadcutter
- **WC** – Wadcutter

Swift Bullets

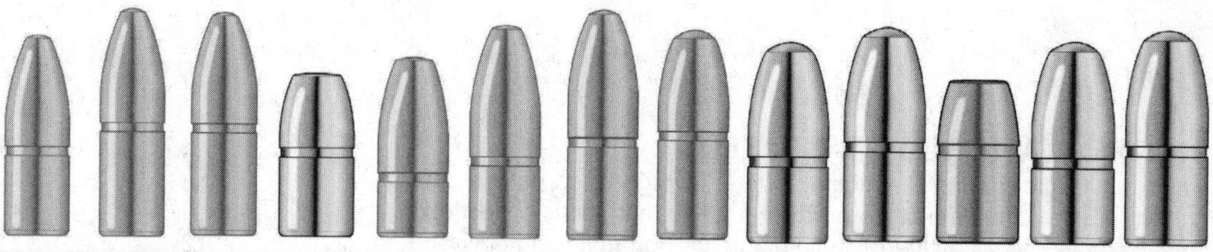

Caliber & Description	416 SS	416 SS	404 SS	45-70 FN	458 FN	458 SS	458 SS	470 RN	505 RN	505 RN	50 FN	500 RN	500 RN
Diameter, Inches	.416	.416	.423	.457	.458	.458	.458	.475	.505	.505	.509	.509	.509
Weight, Grains	350	400	400	350	400	450	500	500	535	570	450	535	570
Density	.289	.330	.319	.238	.272	.307	.341	.329	.300	.319	.247	.294	.313
Ballistic Coefficient	.321	.367	.375	.172	.258	.325	.361	.364	.285	.306	.180	.285	.306

MSRP $55–$115

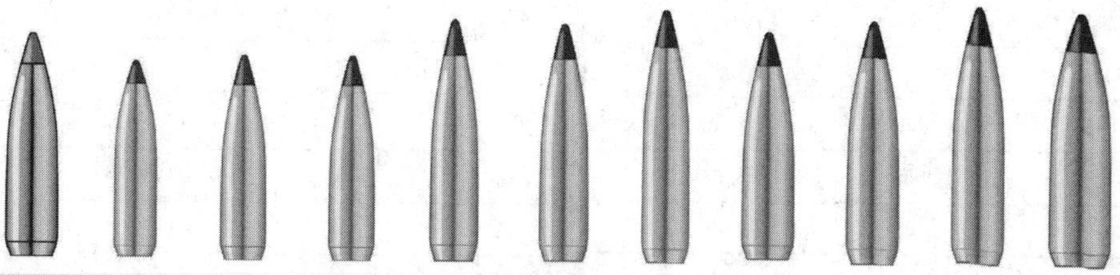

Scirocco

Caliber & Description	224 BTS	224 BTS	6mm BTS	25 BTS	6.5mm BTS	270 BTS	7mm BTS	30 BTS	30 BTS	30 BTS	338 BTS
Diameter, Inches	.224	.224	.243	.257	.264	.277	.284	.308	.308	.308	.338
Weight, Grains	62	75	90	100	130	130	150	150	165	180	210
Density	.177	.214	.218	.216	.266	.242	.266	.226	.248	.271	.263
Ballistic Coefficient	.307	.419	.419	.429	.571	.450	.515	.430	.470	.520	.507

MSRP $52–$69

LEGEND
- **BT** – Boattail
- **FN** – Flat Nose
- **HP** – Hollow Point
- **RN** – Round Nose
- **S** – Spitzer
- **SS** – Semi-Spitzer

Handgun Bullets

A-Frame Hunting Revolver Bullets

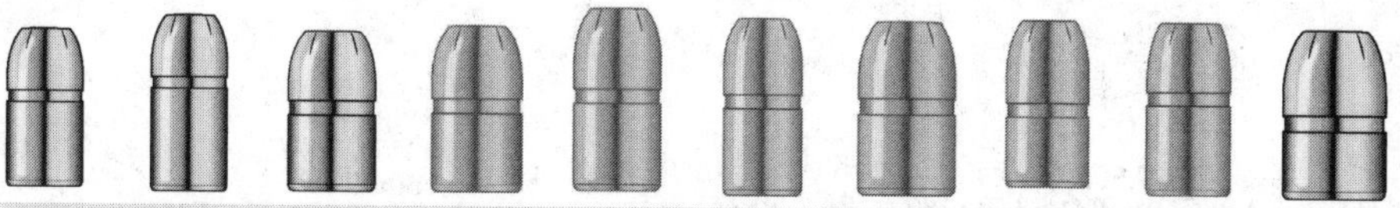

Caliber & Description	357 HP	357 HP	41 HP	44 HP	44 HP	44 HP	45 HP	45 HP	45 HP	50 HP
Diameter, Inches	.357	.357	.410	.430	.430	.430	.452	.452	.452	.499
Weight, Grains	158	180	210	240	280	300	265	300	325	325
Density	.177	.202	.178	.185	.216	.232	.185	.210	.227	.186
Ballistic Coefficient	.183	.189	.159	.119	.139	.147	.129	.153	.171	.135

MSRP $54

LEGEND
- **BT** – Boattail
- **FN** – Flat Nose
- **HP** – Hollow Point
- **RN** – Round Nose
- **S** – Spitzer
- **SS** – Semi-Spitzer

Woodleigh Bullets

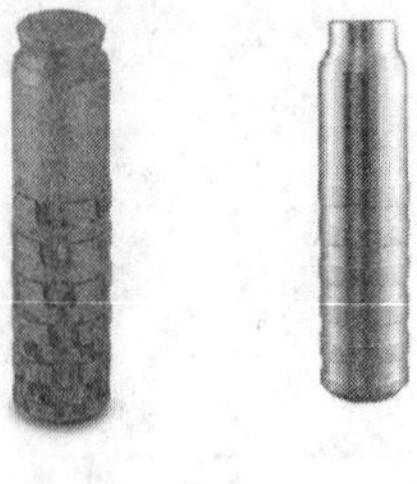

HYDROSTATICALLY STABILIZED

Hydrostatic stabilization is a method of producing pierced hollow bars to very precise concentricity to produce a bullet that resists deflection and achieves deep straight-line penetration. It's non-toxic and environmentally sensitive. It can be used in most nitro double and magazine rifles.

10–20 per box: $31–$80

Caliber	Diameter	"Weight, Grains"	Catalog Number
7mm	.284	140	H7mm
308	.308	150	H308A
308	.308	180	H308
303	.312	215	H303
8mm	.323	170	H8mm
338	.338	185	H338A
338	.338	225	H338
358	.358	225	H358
9.3	.366	232	H9.3A
9,3	.366	286	H9.3
375 Win.	.375	235	H375A
375	.375	300	H375
450/400 3"	.410	400	H450/400

Caliber	Diameter	"Weight, Grains"	Catalog Number
416	.416	400	H416
404 Jeffery	.422	400	H404
450	.458	325	H450BPE
45/70	.458	400	H45/70
458	.458	450	H458A
458	.458	480	H458
465	.468	480	H465
470	.474	500	H470
500	.510	570	H500
50 Alaskan	.510	400	H50 Alaskan
505	.505	525	H505
577	.585	750	H577

98% & 95% RETAINED WEIGHT 300 WIN MAG 180GR PP

458 X 500GN SN RECOVERED FROM BUFFALO

270 WIN 150GN PP 86% RETAINED WEIGHT

94% RETAINED WEIGHT 300 WIN MAG 180GR PP

500/465 RECOVERED FROM BUFFALO

Woodleigh Bullets

TRADITIONAL BULLETS

Fashioned from gilding-metal-clad steel 2mm thick, jackets on FMJ bullets are heavy at the nose for extra impact resistance. The jacket then tapers toward the base to assist rifling engraving. Woodleigh Weldcore Soft Nose bullets are made from 90/100 gilding metal (90 percent copper; 10 percent zinc) 1.6 mm thick.
50 per box: $36–$86

Caliber Diameter	Type	Weight, Grains	SD	BC	Catalog Number
6.5mm	PP SN	140	.287	.444	80
.264	PP SN	160	.328	.509	80A
	RN SN	160	.328	.285	80B
270 Win	PP SN	130	.242	.409	72
.277	PP SN	150	.279	.463	73
	PP SN	180	.334	.513	73A
7mm	PP SN	140	.248	.436	74
.284	PP SN	160	.283	.486	75
	PP SN	175	.310	.510	76
275 H&H	PP SN	160	.277	.474	77
.287	PP SN	175	.304	.509	78
308	PP SN	130	.189	.302	65I
.308	PP SN	150	.226	.310	65F
	PP SN	165	.248	.320	65A
	PP SN	180	.271	.376	65B
	RN SN	220	.331	.367	65C
	FMJ	220	.331	.359	65
30-30 .308	FN SN	150	.226	.246	65H
30-06 .308	PP SN	240	.361	.401	65G
300 Win. Mag.	PP SN	180	.271	.435	65D
.308	PP SN	200	.301	.450	65E
303 British	PP SN	174	.255	.362	68A
.312	RN SN	215	.316	.359	68
303/ 7.62x39mm .312	PP SN	130	.180	.295	68B
8mm	RN SN	196	.268	.315	64B
.323	RN SN	220	.301	.355	64C
	RN SN	250	.343	.403	64D
325 Win.	PP SN	200	.274	.406	64F
(8mm) .323	PP SN	220	.301	.448	64G
8x57 .318	RN SN	200	.283	.331	64E
318 WR	RN SN	250	.328	.420	63
.330	FMJ	250	.328	.364	64
333 Jeffery	RN SN	250	.322	.335	60
.333	RN SN	300	.386	.418	61
	FMJ	300	.386	.418	62
338 Fed	PP SN	180	.226	.361	56C
.338	PP SN	200	.251	.401	56D
33 Win. .338	FN SN	200	.246	.234	56E
338 Mag	PP SN	225	.281	.425	56A
.338	RN SN	250	.313	.332	56
	PP SN	250	.313	.431	56B
	FMJ	250	.313	.326	57
	RN SN	300	.375	.416	58
	FMJ	300	.375	.414	59
348 Win. .348	FN SN	250	.295	.281	348

Caliber Diameter	Type	Weight, Grains	SD	BC	Catalog Number
358	RN SN	225	.251	.263	51
.358	PP SN	225	.251	.372	51A
	FMJ	225	.251	.263	52
	RN SN	250	.279	.300	53
	PP SN	250	.279	.400	53A
	PP SN	275	.307	.450	53B
	RN SN	310	.346	.458	54
	FMJ	310	.346	.458	55
9.3	RN SN	250	.267	.281	47A
.366	PP SN	250	.267	.381	47C
	RN SN	286	.305	.321	47
	PP SN	286	.305	.396	47B
	FMJ	286	.305	.305	48
	RN SN	320	.341	.359	49
	PP SN	320	.341	.457	49A
	FMJ	320	.341	.341	50
375 Mag.	PP SN	235	.239	.310	42A
.375	RN SN	270	.274	.250	42
	PP SN	270	.274	.370	43A
	RN SN	300	.305	.277	44HD
	RN SN	300	.305	.277	44
	PP SN	300	.305	.380	45A
	FMJ	300	.305	.275	46
	RN SN	350	.356	.321	46B
	RN SN	350	.356	.323	46BHD
	PP SN	350	.356	.400	46C
	FMJ	350	.356	.307	46D
400 Purdey .405	RN SN	230	.200	.181	81
450/400 Nitro .408	RN SN	400	.344	.307	40A
450/400 Nitro .411	RN SN	400	.338	.307	40
450/400 Ruger .410	RN SN	400	.338	.307	40B
450/400 Ruger .408	FMJ	400	.344	.300	41A
.410 Ruger	FMJ	400	.338	.300	41
405 Win. .412	RN SN	300	.252	.194	71
416 Rigby	PP SN	340	.281	.330	39
.416	RN SN	410	.338	.307	37A
	FMJ	410	.338	.300	38
	RN SN	450	.371	.338	37B
	FMJ	450	.371	.330	38B"
416 Rem.	RN SN	400	.330	.305	37C
.416	FMJ	400	.330	.300	38C
	RN SN	450	.371	.338	37N
	FMJ	450	.371	.330	38N
404 Jeffery	RN SN	350	.281	.293	35
.422	RN SN	400	.321	.335	33A
	FMJ	400	.321	.330	34
	RN SN	450	.361	.360	33B
	FMJ	450	.361	.355	34B
10.75x68mm	RN SN	347	.277	.290	36
.423	FMJ	347	.277	.288	36A
444 Marlin .430	FN SN	280	.216	.186	444

Woodleigh Bullets

Caliber Diameter	Type	Weight, Grains	SD	BC	Catalog Number
425 WR .435	RN SN	410	.310	.222	31
	FMJ	410	.310	.221	32
11.2 Schuler .440	RN SN	401	.296	.325	67
458 Mag. .458	PP SN	400	.272	.340	30
	RN SN	480	.327	.328	24A
	FMJ	480	.327	.325	25A
	RN SN	500	.341	.310	26
	PP SN	500	.341	.378	26A
	FMJ	500	.341	.310	28
	RN SN	550	.375	.340	27
	FMJ	550	.375	.326	29
450 BPE .458	RN SN	350	.238	.250	30A
45/70 .458	FN SN	405	.276	.204	30B
	FN SN	300	.205	.196	30C
450 Nitro .458	RN SN	480	.327	.328	24
	FMJ	480	.327	.325	25
465 Nitro .468	RN SN	480	.313	.334	22
	FMJ	480	.313	.330	23
470 Nitro .474	RN SN	500	.318	.374	20
	FMJ	500	.318	.370	21
476 WR .476	RN SN	520	.328	.385	18
	FMJ	520	.328	.380	19
475 No. 2 .483	RN SN	480	.294	.309	15
	FMJ	480	.294	.300	16
475 No. 2 Jeffery .488	RN SN	500	.300	.315	13
	FMJ	500	.300	.300	14

Caliber Diameter	Type	Weight, Grains	SD	BC	Catalog Number
500 S&W MAG .500	FN SN	400	.229	.182	83
505 Gibbs .505	RN SN	525	.294	.345	11
	FMJ	525	.294	.340	12
	PP SN	600	.336	.360	11A
	FMJ	600	.336	.360	12A
500 Jeffery .510	RN SN	535	.294	.350	9
	PP SN	535	.294	.310	9A
	FMJ	535	.294	.340	10
	PP SN	600	.330	.350	10B
	FMJ	600	.330	.355	10A
500 BP .510	RN SN	440	.242	.255	8
50 Alaskan & 50/110 Win. .510	FN SN	500	.275	.219	82
500 Nitro .510	RN SN	450	.247	.257	06A
	RN SN	570	.313	.368	6
	FMJ	570	.313	.350	7
577 BP Express .585	RN SN	650	.271	.292	5
577 Nitro .585	RN SN	650	.271	.292	3A
	RN SN	750	.313	.346	3
577 Nitro .584	FMJ	650	.272	.292	4A
	FMJ	750	.314	.351	4
600 Nitro .620	RN SN	900	.334	.371	1
	FMJ	900	.334	.334	2
700 Nitro .700	RN SN	1000	.292	.340	A
	FMJ	1000	.292	.340	B

548 CENTERFIRE RIFLE BALLISTICS

548 .17 Hornet to .222 Remington
549 .222 Remington to .223 Remington
550 .223 Remington to 5.6x52 R
551 .22 PPC to .220 Swift
552 .220 Swift to .243 Winchester
553 .243 Winchester to .25-06 Remington
554 .25-06 Remington to 6.5x55 Swedish
555 6.5x55 Swedish to 6.5 Remington Magnum
556 6.5 Remington Magnum to .270 Winchester
557 .270 Winchester to .270 Winchester Short Magnum
558 .270 Winchester Short Magnum to 7mm-08 Remington
559 7mm-08 Remington to .280 Remington
560 .280 Remington to 7mm Remington Magnum
561 7mm Remington Magnum to 7mm Winchester Short Magnum
562 7mm Winchester Short Magnum to 7mm Remington Ultra Magnum
563 7.21 (.284) Firehawk to .30-30 Winchester
564 .30-30 Winchester to .308 Winchester
565 .308 Winchester to .308 Winchester
566 .308 Winchester to .30-06 Springfield
567 .30-06 Springfield to .30-06 Springfield
568 .30-06 Springfield to .300 Blackout
569 .300 H&H Magnum to .300 Winchester Magnum
570 .300 Winchester Magnum to .300 Remington Short Ultra Magnum
571 .300 Winchester Short Magnum to .300 Weatherby Magnum
572 .300 Weatherby Magnum to .303 British
573 .303 British to .338 Federal
574 .338 Marlin Express to .340 Weatherby Magnum
575 .340 Weatherby Magnum to .35 Remington
576 .35 Remington to 9.3x74 R
577 9.3x74 R to .375 Weatherby Magnum
578 .375 JRS to .416 Remington Magnum
579 .416 Rigby to .45-70 Government
580 .45-70 Government to .460 Weatherby Magnum
581 .460 Weatherby Magnum to .700 Nitro Express

582 LONG RANGE RIFLE

582 6.6 Creedmoor to .338 Lapua

583 RIMFIRE BALLISTICS

583 .22 to .17 Hornady Magnum Rimfire
584 .17 Hornady Magnum Rimfire to .22 Winchester Rimfire

585 CENTERFIRE HANDGUN BALLISTICS

585 .25 Auto to .32 S&W Long
586 .32 S&W Long to 9mm Luger
587 9mm Luger to .380 Auto
588 .380 Auto to .38 Special
589 .38 Special to .357 Magnum
590 .357 Magnum to .40 S&W
591 .40 S&W to .41 Remington magnum
592 .41 Remington Magnum to .45 Automatic (ACP)
593 .45 Automatic (ACP) to .45 GAP
594 .45 GAP to .500 Smith & Wesson

Centerfire Rifle Ballistics

Comprehensive Ballistics Tables for Currently Manufactured Sporting Rifle Cartridges

BALLISTICS

No more collecting catalogs and peering at microscopic print to find out what ammunition is offered for a cartridge, and how it performs relative to other factory loads! *Shooter's Bible* has assembled the data for you, in easy-to-read tables, by cartridge.

Data is taken from manufacturers' charts; your chronograph readings may vary. Listings are not intended as recommendations. For example, the data for the .44 Magnum at 400 yards shows its effective range is much shorter. The lack of data for a 285-grain .375 H&H bullet beyond 300 yards does not mean the bullet has no authority farther out. Besides ammunition, the rifle, sights, conditions and shooter ability all must be considered when contemplating a long shot. Accuracy and bullet energy both matter when big game is in the offing.

Barrel length affects velocity, and at various rates depending on the load. As a rule, figure 50 fps per inch of barrel, plus or minus, if your barrel is longer or shorter than 22 inches.

Bullets are given by make, weight (in grains) and type. Most type abbreviations are self-explanatory: BT=Boat-Tail, FMJ=Full Metal Jacket, HP=Hollow Point, SP=Soft Point—except in Hornady listings, where SP is the firm's Spire Point. TNT and TXP are trademarked designations of Speer and Norma. XLC identifies a coated Barnes X bullet. HE indicates a Federal High Energy load, similar to the Hornady LM (Light Magnum) and HM (Heavy Magnum) cartridges.

Arc (trajectory) is based on a zero range published by the manufacturer, from 100 to 300 yards. If a zero does not fall in a yardage column, it lies halfway between—at 150 yards, for example, if the bullet's strike is "+" at 100 yards and "-" at 200.

.17 HORNET TO .222 REMINGTON

.17 Hornet

CARTRIDGE BULLET	RANGE, YARDS:	0	100	200	300	400
Hornady 15.5 NXT SPF		0	100	200	300	400
	velocity, fps:	3860	2924	2159	1531	1108
	energy, ft-lb:	513	294	160	81	42
	arc, inches:	-1.5	+1.4	0	-9.1	-33.7
Hornady 20 V-MAX		0	100	200	300	400
	velocity, fps:	3650	3077	2574	2122	1721
	energy, ft-lb:	592	420	294	200	132
	arc, inches:	-1.5	+1.1	0	-6.4	-20.7

.17 Remington

CARTRIDGE BULLET	RANGE, YARDS:	0	100	200	300	400
Rem. 20 AccuTip BT	velocity, fps:	4250	3594	3028	2529	2081
	energy, ft-lb:	802	574	407	284	192
	arc, inches:		+1.3	+1.3	-2.5	-11.8
Rem. 20 Fireball	velocity, fps	4000	3380	2840	2360	1930
	energy, ft-lb	710	507	358	247	165
	arc, inches		+1.6	+1.5	-2.8	-13.5
Rem. 25 HP Power-Lokt	velocity, fps:	4040	3284	2644	2086	1606
	energy, ft-lb:	906	599	388	242	143
	arc, inches:		+1.8	0	-3.3	-16.6

.204 Ruger

CARTRIDGE BULLET	RANGE, YARDS:	0	100	200	300	400
Federal 32 Nosler Ballistic Tip	velocity, fps	4030	3465	2968	2523	2119
	arc, inches		+0.7	0	-4.7	-14.9
Federal 40 Ballistic Tip	velocity, fps:	3650	3200	2790	2420	2080
	energy, ft-lb:	1185	910	695	520	385
	arc, inches:		+1.0	0	-5.4	-16.9
Hornady 32 V-Max	velocity, fps:	4225	3632	3114	2652	2234
	energy, ft-lb:	1268	937	689	500	355
	arc, inches:		+0.6	0	-4.2	-13.4
Hornady 40 V-Max	velocity, fps:	3900	3451	3046	2677	2335
	energy, ft-lb:	1351	1058	824	636	485
	arc, inches:		+0.7	0	-4.5	-13.9
Rem. 32 AccuTip	velocity, fps:	4225	3632	3114	2652	2234
	Energy, ft-lb:	1268	937	689	500	355
	Arc, inches:		+0.6	0	-4.1	-13.1
Rem. 40 AccuTip	velocity, fps:	3900	3451	3046	2677	2336
	energy, ft-lb:	1351	1058	824	636	485
	arc, inches:		+0.7	0	-4.3	-13.2
Win. 32 Ballistic Silver Tip	velocity, fps	4050	3482	2984	2537	2132
	energy, ft-lb	1165	862	632	457	323
	arc, inches		+0.7	0	-4.6	-14.7
Win. 34 HP	velocity, fps:	4025	3339	2751	2232	1775
	energy, ft-lb:	1223	842	571	376	238
	arc, inches:		+0.8	0	-5.5	-18.1

.218 Bee

CARTRIDGE BULLET	RANGE, YARDS:	0	100	200	300	400
Win. 46 Hollow Point	velocity, fps:	2760	2102	1550	1155	961
	energy, ft-lb:	778	451	245	136	94
	arc, inches:		0	-7.2	-29.4	

.22 Hornet

CARTRIDGE BULLET	RANGE, YARDS:	0	100	200	300	400
Federal 30 Speer TNT	velocity, fps:	3150	2150	1390	990	830
	energy, ft-lb:	660	310	130	65	45
	arc, inches:		+3.3	0	-22.8	-78.7
Federal 45 JSP	velocity, fps:	2690	2100	1590	1210	1000
	energy, ft-lb:	725	440	255	145	100
	arc, inches:		+3.3	0	-17.6	-59.5
Hornady 35 V-Max	velocity, fps:	3100	2278	1601	1135	929
	energy, ft-lb:	747	403	199	100	67
	arc, inches:		+2.8	0	-16.9	-60.4
Rem. 35 AccuTip	velocity, fps:	3100	2271	1591	1127	924
	energy, ft-lb:	747	401	197	99	66
	arc, inches:		+1.5	-3.5	-22.3	-68.4
Rem. 45 Pointed Soft Point	velocity, fps:	2690	2042	1502	1128	948
	energy, ft-lb:	723	417	225	127	90
	arc, inches:		0	-7.1	-30.0	
Rem. 45 Hollow Point	velocity, fps:	2690	2042	1502	1128	948
	energy, ft-lb:	723	417	225	127	90
	arc, inches:		0	-7.1	-30.0	
Win. 34 Jacketed HP	velocity, fps:	3050	2132	1415	1017	852
	energy, ft-lb:	700	343	151	78	55.
	arc, inches:		0	-6.6	-29.9	
Win. 45 Soft Point	velocity, fps:	2690	2042	1502	1128	948.
	energy, ft-lb:	723	417	225	127	90
	arc, inches:		0	-7.7	-31.3	
Win. 46 Hollow Point	velocity, fps:	2690	2042	1502	1128	948.
	energy, ft-lb:	739	426	230	130	92
	arc, inches:		0	-7.7	-31.3	

.221 Remington Fireball

CARTRIDGE BULLET	RANGE, YARDS:	0	100	200	300	400
Rem. 50 AccuTip BT	velocity, fps:	2995	2605	2247	1918	1622
	energy, ft-lb:	996	753	560	408	292
	arc, inches:		+1.8	0	-8.8	-27.1

.222 Remington

CARTRIDGE BULLET	RANGE, YARDS:	0	100	200	300	400
Federal 40 Ballistic Tip	velocity, fps:	3450	2990	2570	2190	1840
	energy, ft-lb:	1055	790	585	425	300
	arc, inches:		+1.2	0	-6.5	-20.4

CARTRIDGE BULLET	RANGE, YARDS:	0	100	200	300	400
Federal 43 Speer TNT	velocity, fps:	3400	2750	2180	1680	1290
	energy, ft-lb:	1105	720	450	270	160
	arc, inches:		+1.6	0	-9.2	-31.4
Federal 50 Hi-Shok	velocity, fps:	3140	2600	2120	1700	1350
	energy, ft-lb:	1095	750	500	320	200
	arc, inches:		+1.9	0	-9.7	-31.6
Federal 55 FMJ boat-tail	velocity, fps:	3020	2740	2480	2230	1990
	energy, ft-lb:	1115	915	750	610	484
	arc, inches:		+1.6	0	-7.3	-21.5
Hornady 40 V-Max	velocity, fps:	3600	3117	2673	2269	1911
	energy, ft-lb:	1151	863	634	457	324
	arc, inches:		+1.1	0	-6.1	-18.9
Hornady 50 V-Max	velocity, fps:	3140	2729	2352	2008	1710
	energy, ft-lb:	1094	827	614	448	325
	arc, inches:		+1.7	0	-7.9	-24.4
Norma 50 Soft Point	velocity, fps:	3199	2667	2193	1771	
	energy, ft-lb:	1136	790	534	348	
	arc, inches:		+1.7	0	-9.1	
Norma 50 FMJ	velocity, fps:	2789	2326	1910	1547	
	energy, ft-lb:	864	601	405	266	
	arc, inches:		+2.5	0	-12.2	
Norma 62 Soft Point	velocity, fps:	2887	2457	2067	1716	
	energy, ft-lb:	1148	831	588	405	
	arc, inches:		+2.1	0	-10.4	
PMC 50 Pointed Soft Point	velocity, fps:	3044	2727	2354	2012	1651
	energy, ft-lb:	1131	908	677	494	333
	arc, inches:		+1.6	0	-7.9	-24.5
PMC 55 Pointed Soft Point	velocity, fps:	2950	2594	2266	1966	1693
	energy, ft-lb:	1063	822	627	472	350
	arc, inches:		+1.9	0	-8.7	-26.3
Rem. 50 Pointed Soft Point	velocity, fps:	3140	2602	2123	1700	1350
	energy, ft-lb:	1094	752	500	321	202
	arc, inches:		+1.9	0	-9.7	-31.7
Rem. 50 HP Power-Lokt	velocity, fps:	3140	2635	2182	1777	1432
	energy, ft-lb:	1094	771	529	351	228
	arc, inches:		+1.8	0	-9.2	-29.6
Rem. 50 AccuTip BT	velocity, fps:	3140	2744	2380	2045	1740
	energy, ft-lb:	1094	836	629	464	336
	arc, inches:		+1.6	0	-7.8	-23.9
Win. 40 Ballistic Silvertip	velocity, fps:	3370	2915	2503	2127	1786
	energy, ft-lb:	1009	755	556	402	283
	arc, inches:		+1.3	0	-6.9	-21.5
Win. 50 Pointed Soft Point	velocity, fps:	3140	2602	2123	1700	1350
	energy, ft-lb:	1094	752	500	321	202
	arc, inches:		+2.2	0	-10.0	-32.3

.222 Remington Magnum

CARTRIDGE BULLET	RANGE, YARDS:	0	100	200	300	400
Nosler 40 BT	velocity, fps:	3600	3140	2726	2347	2000
	energy, ft-lb:	1150	876	660	489	355
	arc, inches:	-1.5	+1.0	0	-5.7	-17.8
Nosler 50 BT	velocity, fps:	3340	2917	2533	2179	1855
	energy, ft-lb:	1238	945	712	527	382
	arc, inches:	-1.5	+1.3	0	-6.8	-20.9

.223 Remington

CARTRIDGE BULLET	RANGE, YARDS:	0	100	200	300	400
Black Hills 36 Varmint Grenade	velocity, fps:	w3750				
	energy, ft-lb:	1124				
	arc, inches:					
Black Hills 40 Nosler B. Tip	velocity, fps:	3600				
	energy, ft-lb:	1150				
	arc, inches:					
Black Hills 50 V-Max	velocity, fps:	3300				
	energy, ft-lb:	1209				
	arc, inches:					
Black Hills 52 Match HP	velocity, fps:	3300				
	energy, ft-lb:	1237				
	arc, inches:					
Black Hills 55 Softpoint	velocity, fps:	3250				
	energy, ft-lb:	1270				
	arc, inches:					
Black Hills 55 TSX	velocity, fps:	3200				
	energy, ft-lb:	1250				
	arc, inches:					
Black Hills 60 SP or V-Max	velocity, fps:	3150				
	energy, ft-lb:	1322				
	arc, inches:					
Black Hills 60 Partition	velocity, fps:	3150				
	energy, ft-lb:	1322				
	arc, inches:					
Black Hills 62 TSX	velocity, fps:	3100				
	energy, ft-lb:	1323				
	arc, inches:					
Black Hills 68 Heavy Match	velocity, fps:	2850				
	energy, ft-lb:	1227				
	arc, inches:					
Black Hills 69 OTM	velocity, fps:	2875				
	energy, ft-lb:	1266				
	arc, inches:					
Black Hills 69 Sierra MK	velocity, fps:	2850				
	energy, ft-lb:	1245				
	arc, inches:					
Black Hills 73 Berger BTHP	velocity, fps:	2750				
	energy, ft-lb:	1226				
	arc, inches:					
Black Hills 75 Heavy Match	velocity, fps:	2750				
	energy, ft-lb:	1259				
	arc, inches:					
Black Hills 77 Sierra MKing	velocity, fps:	2750				
	energy, ft-lb:	1293				
	arc, inches:					
Black Hills 77 Tipped	velocity, fps:	2750				
MatchKing	energy, ft-lb:	1293				
	arc, inches:					
Federal 40 Ballistic Tip	velocity, fps:	3700	3210	2770	2370	2010
	energy, ft-lb:	1215	915	680	500	360
	arc, inches:		+0.9	0	-5.5	-17.3
Federal 43 Speer TNT	velocity, fps:	3600	2920	2330	1810	1390
	energy, ft-lb:	1235	810	515	315	185
	arc, inches:		+1.3	0	-7.9	-27.1
Federal 50 Jacketed HP	velocity, fps:	3400	2910	2460	2060	1700
	energy, ft-lb:	1285	940	675	470	320
	arc, inches:		+1.3	0	-7.1	-22.7
Federal 50 Speer TNT HP	velocity, fps:	3300	2860	2450	2080	1750
	energy, ft-lb:	1210	905	670	480	340
	arc, inches:		+1.4	0	-7.3	-22.6
Federal 52 Sierra MatchKing	velocity, fps:	3300	2860	2460	2090	1760
BTHP	energy, ft-lb:	1255	945	700	505	360
	arc, inches:		+1.4	0	-7.2	-22.4
Federal 55 Hi-Shok	velocity, fps:	3240	2750	2300	1910	1550
	energy, ft-lb:	1280	920	650	445	295
	arc, inches:		+1.6	0	-8.2	-26.1
Federal 55 FMJ boat-tail	velocity, fps:	3240	2950	2670	2410	2170
	energy, ft-lb:	1280	1060	875	710	575
	arc, inches:		+1.3	0	-6.1	-18.3
Federal 55 Sierra GameKing	velocity, fps:	3240	2770	2340	1950	1610
BTHP	energy, ft-lb:	1280	935	670	465	315
	arc, inches:		+1.5	0	-8.0	-25.3
Federal 55 Trophy Bonded	velocity, fps:	3100	2630	2210	1830	1500
	energy, ft-lb:	1175	845	595	410	275
	arc, inches:		+1.8	0	-8.9	-28.7
Federal 55 Nosler Bal. Tip	velocity, fps:	3240	2870	2530	2220	1920
	energy, ft-lb:	1280	1005	780	600	450
	arc, inches:		+1.4	0	-6.8	-20.8
Federal 55 Sierra BlitzKing	velocity, fps:	3240	2870	2520	2200	1910
	energy, ft-lb:	1280	1005	775	590	445
	arc, inches:		+-1.4	0	-6.9	-20.9

Centerfire Rifle Ballistics

.223 REMINGTON TO 5.6X52 R

CARTRIDGE BULLET	RANGE, YARDS:	0	100	200	300	400
Federal 60 Partition	velocity, fps:	3160	2740	2350	2000	1680
	energy, ft-lb:	1330	1000	735	530	375
	arc, inches:		+1.6	0	-7.9	-24.8
Federal 62 FMJ	velocity, fps:	3020	2650	2310	2000	1710
	energy, ft-lb:	1225	970	735	550	405
	arc, inches:		+1.7	0	-8.4	-25.5
Federal 64 Hi-Shok SP	velocity, fps:	3090	2690	2325	1990	1680
	energy, ft-lb:	1360	1030	770	560	400
	arc, inches:		+1.7	0	-8.2	-25.2
Federal 69 Sierra MatchKing BTHP	velocity, fps:	3000	2720	2460	2210	1980
	energy, ft-lb:	1380	1135	925	750	600
	arc, inches:		+1.6	0	-7.4	-21.9
Hornady 40 V-Max	velocity, fps:	3800	3305	2845	2424	2044
	energy, ft-lb:	1282	970	719	522	371
	arc, inches:		+0.8	0	-5.3	-16.6
Hornady 53 Hollow Point	velocity, fps:	3330	2882	2477	2106	1710
	energy, ft-lb:	1305	978	722	522	369
	arc, inches:		+1.7	0	-7.4	-22.7
Hornady 55 V-Max	velocity, fps:	3240	2859	2507	2181	1891
	energy, ft-lb:	1282	998	767	581	437
	arc, inches:		+1.4	0	-7.1	-21.4
Hornady 75 BTHP Superformance Match	velocity, fps:	2930	2695	2471	2259	2057
	energy, ft-lb:	1430	1209	1017	850	705
	arc, inches:		+1.7	0	-7.4	-21.6
Hornady 55 TAP-FPD	velocity, fps:	3240	2854	2500	2172	1871
	energy, ft-lb:	1282	995	763	576	427
	arc, inches:		+1.4	0	-7.0	-21.4
Hornady 55 Urban Tactical	velocity, fps:	2970	2626	2307	2011	1739
	energy, ft-lb:	1077	842	650	494	369
	arc, inches:		+1.5	0	-8.1	-24.9
Hornady 60 Soft Point	velocity, fps:	3150	2782	2442	2127	1837
	energy, ft-lb:	1322	1031	795	603	450
	arc, inches:		+1.6	0	-7.5	-22.5
Hornady 60 TAP-FPD	velocity, fps:	3115	2754	2420	2110	1824
	energy, ft-lb:	1293	1010	780	593	443
	arc, inches:		+1.6	0	-7.5	-22.9
Hornady 60 Urban Tactical	velocity, fps:	2950	2619	2312	2025	1762
	energy, ft-lb:	1160	914	712	546	413
	arc, inches:		+1.6	0	-8.1	-24.7
Hornady 75 BTHP Match	velocity, fps:	2790	2554	2330	2119	1926
	energy, ft-lb:	1296	1086	904	747	617
	arc, inches:		+2.4	0	-8.8	-25.1
Hornacy 75 TAP-FPD	velocity, fps:	2790	2582	2383	2193	2012
	energy, ft-lb:	1296	1110	946	801	674
	arc, inches:		+1.9	0	-8.0	-23.2
Hornady 75 BTHP Tactical	velocity, fps:	2630	2409	2199	2000	1814
	energy, ft-lb:	1152	966	805	666	548
	arc, inches:		+2.0	0	-9.2	-25.9
PMC 40 non-toxic	velocity, fps:	3500	2606	1871	1315	
	energy, ft-lb:	1088	603	311	154	
	arc, inches:		+2.6	0	-12.8	
PMC 50 Sierra BlitzKing	velocity, fps:	3300	2874	2484	2130	1809
	energy, ft-lb:	1209	917	685	504	363
	arc, inches:		+1.4	0	-7.1	-21.8
PMC 52 Sierra HPBT Match	velocity, fps:	3200	2808	2447	2117	1817
	energy, ft-lb:	1182	910	691	517	381
	arc, inches:		+1.5	0	-7.3	-22.5
PMC 53 Barnes XLC	velocity, fps:	3200	2815	2461	2136	1840
	energy, ft-lb:	1205	933	713	537	398
	arc, inches:		+1.5	0	-7.2	-22.2
PMC 55 HP boat-tail	velocity, fps:	3240	2717	2250	1832	1473
	energy, ft-lb:	1282	901	618	410	265
	arc, inches:		+1.6	0	-8.6	-27.7
PMC 55 FMJ boat-tail	velocity, fps:	3195	2882	2525	2169	1843
	energy, ft-lb:	1246	1014	779	574	415
	arc, inches:		+1.4	0	-6.8	-21.1
PMC 55 Pointed Soft Point	velocity, fps:	3112	2767	2421	2100	1806
	energy, ft-lb:	1182	935	715	539	398
	arc, inches:		+1.5	0	-7.5	-22.9

CARTRIDGE BULLET	RANGE, YARDS:	0	100	200	300	400
PMC 64 Pointed Soft Point	velocity, fps:	2775	2511	2261	2026	1806
	energy, ft-lb:	1094	896	726	583	464
	arc, inches:		+2.0	0	-8.8	-26.1
PMC 69 Sierra BTHP Match	velocity, fps:	2900	2591	2304	2038	1791
	energy, ft-lb:	1288	1029	813	636	492
	arc, inches:		+1.9	0	-8.4	-25.3
Rem. 50 AccuTip BT	velocity, fps:	3300	2889	2514	2168	1851
	energy, ft-lb:	1209	927	701	522	380
	arc, inches:		+1.4	0	-6.9	-21.2
Rem. 55 Pointed Soft Point	velocity, fps:	3240	2747	2304	1905	1554
	energy, ft-lb:	1282	921	648	443	295
	arc, inches:		+1.6	0	-8.2	-26.2
Rem. 55 HP Power-Lokt	velocity, fps:	3240	2773	2352	1969	1627
	energy, ft-lb:	1282	939	675	473	323
	arc, inches:		+1.5	0	-7.9	-24.8
Rem. 55 AccuTip BT	velocity, fps:	3240	2854	2500	2172	1871
	energy, ft-lb:	1282	995	763	576	427
	arc, inches:		+1.5	0	-7.1	-21.7
Rem. 55 Metal Case	velocity, fps:	3240	2759	2326	1933	1587
	energy, ft-lb:	1282	929	660	456	307
	arc, inches:		+1.6	0	-8.1	-25.5
Remington 62 Core-Lokt Ultra Bonded	velocity, fps:	3100	2695	2324	1983	1676
	energy, ft-lb:	1323	1000	743	541	386
	arc, inches:		+1.7			
Rem. 62 HP Match	velocity, fps:	3025	2572	2162	1792	1471
	energy, ft-lb:	1260	911	643	442	298
	arc, inches:		+1.9	0	-9.4	-29.9
Rem. 69 BTHP Match	velocity, fps:	3000	2720	2457	2209	1975
	energy, ft-lb:	1379	1133	925	747	598
	arc, inches:		+1.6	0	-7.4	-21.9
Win. 40 Ballistic Silvertip	velocity, fps:	3700	3166	2693	2265	1879.
	energy, ft-lb:	1216	891	644	456	314
	arc, inches:		+1.0	0	-5.8	-18.4
Win. 45 JHP	velocity, fps:	3600				
	energy, ft-lb:	1295				
	arc, inches:					
Win. 50 Ballistic Silvertip	velocity, fps:	3410	2982	2593	2235	1907.
	energy, ft-lb:	1291	987	746	555	404
	arc, inches:		+1.2	0	-6.4	-19.8
Win. 53 Hollow Point	velocity, fps:	3330	2882	2477	2106	1770
	energy, ft-lb:	1305	978	722	522	369
	arc, inches:		+1.7	0	-7.4	-22.7
Win. 55 Pointed Soft Point	velocity, fps:	3240	2747	2304	1905	1554.
	energy, ft-lb:	1282	921	648	443	295
	arc, inches:		+1.9	0	-8.5	-26.7
Win. 55 Super Clean NT	velocity, fps:	3150	2520	1970	1505	1165
	energy, ft-lb:	1212	776	474	277	166
	arc, inches:		+2.8	0	-11.9	-38.9
Win. 55 FMJ	velocity, fps:	3240	2854			
	energy, ft-lb:	1282	995			
	arc, inches:					
Win. 55 Ballistic Silvertip	velocity, fps:	3240	2871	2531	2215	1923
	energy, ft-lb:	1282	1006	782	599	451
	arc, inches:		+1.4	0	-6.8	-20.8
Win. 64 Power-Point	velocity, fps:	3020	2656	2320	2009	1724
	energy, ft-lb:	1296	1003	765	574	423
	arc, inches:		+1.7	0	-8.2	-25.1
Win. 64 Power-Point Plus	velocity, fps:	3090	2684	2312	1971	1664
	energy, ft-lb:	1357	1024	760	552	393
	arc, inches:		+1.7	0	-8.2	-25.4
Winchester 69 BTHP Match	velocity, fps:	3060	2740	2442	2163	1902
	energy, ft-lb:	1434	1150	913	716	554
	arc, inches:		+1.6	0	-7.4	-22.4

5.6x52 R

CARTRIDGE BULLET	RANGE, YARDS:	0	100	200	300	400
Norma 71 Soft Point	velocity, fps:	2789	2446	2128	1835	
	energy, ft-lb:	1227	944	714	531	
	arc, inches:		+2.1	0	-9.9	

Centerfire Rifle Ballistics

.22 PPC TO .220 SWIFT

.22 PPC

CARTRIDGE BULLET	RANGE, YARDS:	0	100	200	300	400
A-Square 52 Berger	velocity, fps:	3300	2952	2629	2329	2049
	energy, ft-lb:	1257	1006	798	626	485
	arc, inches:		+1.3	0	-6.3	-19.1

.225 Winchester

CARTRIDGE BULLET	RANGE, YARDS:	0	100	200	300	400
Win. 55 Pointed Soft Point	velocity, fps:	3570	3066	2616	2208	1838.
	energy, ft-lb:	1556	1148	836	595	412
	arc, inches:		+2.4	+2.0	-3.5	-16.3

.224 Weatherby Magnum

CARTRIDGE BULLET	RANGE, YARDS:	0	100	200	300	400
Wby. 55 Pointed Expanding	velocity, fps:	3650	3192	2780	2403	2056
	energy, ft-lb:	1627	1244	944	705	516
	arc, inches:		+2.8	+3.7	0	-9.8

.22-250 Remington

CARTRIDGE BULLET	RANGE, YARDS:	0	100	200	300	400
Black Hills 50 Nos. Bal. Tip	velocity, fps:	3700				
	energy, ft-lb:	1520				
	arc, inches:					
Black Hills 60 Nos. Partition	velocity, fps:	3550				
	energy, ft-lb:	1679				
	arc, inches:					
Federal 40 Nos. Bal. Tip	velocity, fps:	4150	3610	3130	2700	2300
	energy, ft-lb:	1530	1155	870	645	470
	arc, inches:		+0.6	0	-4.2	-13.2
Federal 40 Sierra Varminter	velocity, fps:	4000	3320	2720	2200	1740
	energy, ft-lb:	1420	980	660	430	265
	arc, inches:		+0.8	0	-5.6	-18.4
Federal 43 Speer TNT	velocity, fps:	4000	3250	2650	2070	1590
	energy, ft-lb:	1530	1010	655	405	240
	arc, inches:		+0.9	0	-6.1	-20.8
Federal 55 Hi-Shok	velocity, fps:	3680	3140	2660	2220	1830
	energy, ft-lb:	1655	1200	860	605	410
	arc, inches:		+1.0	0	-6.0	-19.1
Federal 55 Sierra BlitzKing	velocity, fps:	3680	3270	2890	2540	2220
	energy, ft-lb:	1655	1300	1020	790	605
	arc, inches:		+0.9	0	-5.1	-15.6
Federal 55 Sierra GameKing	velocity, fps:	3680	3280	2920	2590	2280
BTHP	energy, ft-lb:	1655	1315	1040	815	630
	arc, inches:		+0.9	0	-5.0	-15.1
Federal 55 Trophy Bonded	velocity, fps:	3600	3080	2610	2190	1810.
	energy, ft-lb:	1585	1155	835	590	400.
	arc, inches:		+1.1	0	-6.2	-19.8
Hornady 35 NTX	velocity, fps:	4450	3736	3128	2598	2125
Superformance Varmint	energy, ft-lb:	1539	1085	761	524	351
	arc, inches:		+0.5	0	-4.1	-13.4
Hornady 40 V-Max	velocity, fps:	4150	3631	3147	2699	2293
	energy, ft-lb:	1529	1171	879	647	467
	arc, inches:		+0.5	0	-4.2	-13.3
Hornady 50 V-Max	velocity, fps:	3800	3349	2925	2535	2178
	energy, ft-lb:	1603	1245	950	713	527
	arc, inches:		+0.8	0	-5.0	-15.6
Hornady 50 V-Max	velocity, fps:	4000	3517	3086	2696	2337
Superformance Varmint	energy, ft-lb:	1776	1373	1057	807	606
	arc, inches:		+0.7	0	-4.3	-13.5
Hornady 53 Hollow Point	velocity, fps:	3680	3185	2743	2341	1974.
	energy, ft-lb:	1594	1194	886	645	459
	arc, inches:		+1.0	0	-5.7	-17.8
Hornady 55 V-Max	velocity, fps:	3680	3265	2876	2517	2183
	energy, ft-lb:	1654	1302	1010	772	582
	arc, inches:		+0.9	0	-5.3	-16.1
Hornady 60 Soft Point	velocity, fps:	3600	3195	2826	2485	2169
	energy, ft-lb:	1727	1360	1064	823	627
	arc, inches:		+1.0	0	-5.4	-16.3
Norma 53 Soft Point	velocity, fps:	3707	3234	2809	1716	
	energy, ft-lb:	1618	1231	928	690	
	arc, inches:		+0.9	0	-5.3	
PMC 50 Sierra BlitzKing	velocity, fps:	3725	3264	2641	2455	2103
	energy, ft-lb:	1540	1183	896	669	491
	arc, inches:		+0.9	0	-5.2	-16.2
PMC 50 Barnes XLC	velocity, fps:	3725	3280	2871	2495	2152
	energy, ft-lb:	1540	1195	915	691	514.
	arc, inches:		+0.9	0	-5.1	-15.9.
PMC 55 HP boat-tail	velocity, fps:	3680	3104	2596	2141	1737
	energy, ft-lb:	1654	1176	823	560	368
	arc, inches:		+1.1	0	-6.3	-20.2
PMC 55 Pointed Soft Point	velocity, fps:	3586	3203	2852	2505	2178
	energy, ft-lb:	1570	1253	993	766	579
	arc, inches:		+1.0	0	-5.2	-16.0
Rem. 50 AccuTip BT	velocity, fps:	3725	3272	2864	2491	2147
(also in EtronX)	energy, ft-lb:	1540	1188	910	689	512
	arc, inches:		+1.7	+1.6	-2.8	-12.8
Rem. 55 Pointed Soft Point	velocity, fps:	3680	3137	2656	2222	1832
	energy, ft-lb:	1654	1201	861	603	410
	arc, inches:		+1.9	+1.8	-3.3	-15.5
Rem. 55 HP Power-Lokt	velocity, fps:	3680	3209	2785	2400	2046.
	energy, ft-lb:	1654	1257	947	703	511
	arc, inches:		+1.8	+1.7	-3.0	-13.7
Rem. 60 Nosler Partition	velocity, fps:	3500	3045	2634	2258	1914
(also in EtronX)	energy, ft-lb:	1632	1235	924	679	488
	arc, inches:		+2.1	+1.9	-3.4	-15.5
Win. 40 Ballistic Silvertip	velocity, fps:	4150	3591	3099	2658	2257
	energy, ft-lb:	1530	1146	853	628	453
	arc, inches:		+0.6	0	-4.2	-13.4
Win. 50 Ballistic Silvertip	velocity, fps:	3810	3341	2919	2536	2182
	energy, ft-lb:	1611	1239	946	714	529.
	arc, inches:		+0.8	0	-4.9	-15.2
Win. 55 Pointed Soft Point	velocity, fps:	3680	3137	2656	2222	1832
	energy, ft-lb:	1654	1201	861	603	410
	arc, inches:		+2.3	+1.9	-3.4	-15.9
Win. 55 Ballistic Silvertip	velocity, fps:	3680	3272	2900	2558	2240
	energy, ft-lb:	1654	1307	1027	799	613
	arc, inches:		+0.9	0	-5.0	-15.4
Win. 64 Power-Point	velocity, fps:	3500	3086	2708	2360	2038
	energy, ft-lb:	1741	1353	1042	791	590
	arc, inches:		+1.1	0	-5.9	-18.0

.220 Swift

CARTRIDGE BULLET	RANGE, YARDS:	0	100	200	300	400
Federal 52 Sierra MatchKing	velocity, fps:	3830	3370	2960	2600	2230
BTHP	energy, ft-lb:	1690	1310	1010	770	575
	arc, inches:		+0.8	0	-4.8	-14.9
Federal 55 Sierra BlitzKing	velocity, fps:	3800	3370	2990	2630	2310.
	energy, ft-lb:	1765	1390	1090	850	650
	arc, inches:		+0.8	0	-4.7	-14.4
Federal 55 Trophy Bonded	velocity, fps:	3700	3170	2690	2270	1880
	energy, ft-lb:	1670	1225	885	625	430
	arc, inches:		+1.0	0	-5.8	-18.5
Hornady 40 V-Max	velocity, fps:	4200	3678	3190	2739	2329
	energy, ft-lb:	1566	1201	904	666	482
	arc, inches:		+0.5	0	-4.0	-12.9
Hornady 50 V-Max	velocity, fps:	3850	3396	2970	2576	2215.
	energy, ft-lb:	1645	1280	979	736	545
	arc, inches:		+0.7	0	-4.8	-15.1
Hornady 50 SP	velocity, fps:	3850	3327	2862	2442	2060.
	energy, ft-lb:	1645	1228	909	662	471
	arc, inches:		+0.8	0	-5.1	-16.1
Hornady 55 V-Max	velocity, fps:	3680	3265	2876	2517	2183
	energy, ft-lb:	1654	1302	1010	772	582
	arc, inches:		+0.9	0	-5.3	-16.1
Hornady 60 Hollow Point	velocity, fps:	3600	3199	2824	2475	2156
	energy, ft-lb:	1727	1364	1063	816	619
	arc, inches:		+1.0	0	-5.4	-16.3
Norma 50 Soft Point	velocity, fps:	4019	3380	2826	2335	
	energy, ft-lb:	1794	1268	887	605	
	arc, inches:		+0.7	0	-5.1	

Centerfire Rifle Ballistics

.220 Swift to .243 Winchester

CARTRIDGE BULLET	RANGE, YARDS:	0	100	200	300	400
Rem. 50 Pointed Soft Point	velocity, fps:	3780	3158	2617	2135	1710
	energy, ft-lb:	1586	1107	760	506	325
	arc, inches:		+0.3	-1.4	-8.2	
Rem. 50 V-Max boat-tail (also in EtronX)	velocity, fps:	3780	3321	2908	2532	2185
	energy, ft-lb:	1586	1224	939	711	530
	arc, inches:		+0.8	0	-5.0	-15.4
Win. 40 Ballistic Silvertip	velocity, fps:	4050	3518	3048	2624	2238.
	energy, ft-lb:	1457	1099	825	611	445
	arc, inches:		+0.7	0	-4.4	-13.9
Win. 50 Pointed Soft Point	velocity, fps:	3870	3310	2816	2373	1972
	energy, ft-lb:	1663	1226	881	625	432
	arc, inches:		+0.8	0	-5.2	-16.7

.223 WSSM

CARTRIDGE BULLET	RANGE, YARDS:	0	100	200	300	400
Win. 55 Ballistic Silvertip	velocity, fps:	3850	3438	3064	2721	2402
	energy, ft-lb:	1810	1444	1147	904	704
	arc, inches:		+0.7	0	-4.4	-13.6
Win. 55 Pointed Softpoint	velocity, fps:	3850	3367	2934	2541	2181
	energy, ft-lb:	1810	1384	1051	789	581
	arc, inches:		+0.8	0	-4.9	-15.1
Win. 64 Power-Point	velocity, fps:	3600	3144	2732	2356	2011
	energy, ft-lb:	1841	1404	1061	789	574
	arc, inches:		+1.0	0	-5.7	-17.7

6mm PPC

CARTRIDGE BULLET	RANGE, YARDS:	0	100	200	300	400
A-Square 68 Berger	velocity, fps:	3100	2751	2428	2128	1850
	energy, ft-lb:	1451	1143	890	684	516
	arc, inches:		+1.5	0	-7.5	-22.6

6x70 R

CARTRIDGE BULLET	RANGE, YARDS:	0	100	200	300	400
Norma 95 Nosler Bal. Tip	velocity, fps:	2461	2231	2013	1809	
	energy, ft-lb:	1211	995	810	654	
	arc, inches:		+2.7	0	-11.3	

.243 Winchester

CARTRIDGE BULLET	RANGE, YARDS:	0	100	200	300	400
Black Hills 55 Nosler B. Tip	velocity, fps:	3800				
	energy, ft-lb:	1763				
	arc, inches:					
Black Hills 95 Nosler B. Tip	velocity, fps:	2950				
	energy, ft-lb:	1836				
	arc, inches:					
Federal 70 Nosler Bal. Tip	velocity, fps:	3400	3070	2760	2470	2200
	energy, ft-lb:	1795	1465	1185	950	755.
	arc, inches:		+1.1	0	-5.7	-17.1
Federal 70 Speer TNT HP	velocity, fps:	3400	3040	2700	2390	2100
	energy, ft-lb:	1795	1435	1135	890	685
	arc, inches:		+1.1	0	-5.9	-18.0
Federal 80 Sierra Pro-Hunter	velocity, fps:	3350	2960	2590	2260	1950
	energy, ft-lb:	1995	1550	1195	905	675
	arc, inches:		+1.3	0	-6.4	-19.7
Federal 85 Sierra GameKing BTHP	velocity, fps:	3320	3070	2830	2600	2380
	energy, ft-lb:	2080	1770	1510	1280	1070
	arc, inches:		+1.1	0	-5.5	-16.1
Federal 85 Trophy Copper	velocity, fps:	3200	2950	2710	2480	2270
	energy, ft-lb:	1935	1640	1385	1160	970
	arc, inches:		+1.3	0	-6.0	-17.6
Federal 90 Trophy Bonded	velocity, fps:	3100	2850	2610	2380	2160.
	energy, ft-lb:	1920	1620	1360	1130	935
	arc, inches:		+1.4	0	-6.1	-19.2
Federal 100 Hi-Shok	velocity, fps:	2960	2700	2450	2220	1990
	energy, ft-lb:	1945	1615	1330	1090	880
	arc, inches:		+1.6	0	-7.5	-22.0
Federal 100 Sierra GameKing BTSP	velocity, fps:	2960	2760	2570	2380	2210
	energy, ft-lb:	1950	1690	1460	1260	1080
	arc, inches:		+1.5	0	-6.8	-19.8
Federal 100 Nosler Partition	velocity, fps:	2960	2730	2510	2300	2100
	energy, ft-lb:	1945	1650	1395	1170	975.
	arc, inches:		+1.6	0	-7.1	-20.9
Hornady 58 V-Max Superformance Varmint	velocity, fps:	3925	3465	3052	2676	2330
	energy, ft-lb:	1984	1546	1200	922	699
	arc, inches:		+0.7	0	-4.4	-13.8
Hornady 75 Hollow Point	velocity, fps:	3400	2970	2578	2219	1890
	energy, ft-lb:	1926	1469	1107	820	595
	arc, inches:		+1.2	0	-6.5	-20.3
Hornady 80 GMX Superformance	velocity, fps:	3425	3081	2763	2468	2190
	energy, ft-lb:	2084	1686	1357	1082	852
	arc, inches:		+1.1	0	-5.7	-17.1
Hornady 87 SST Custom Lite	velocity, fps:	2800	2574	2359	2155	1961
	energy, ft-lb:	1514	1280	1075	897	743
	arc, inches:		+1.9	0	-8.1	-23.8
Hornady 95 SST Superformance	velocity, fps:	3185	2908	2649	2404	2172
	energy, ft-lb:	2140	1784	1480	1219	995
	arc, inches:		+1.3	0	-6.3	-18.6
Hornady 100 BTSP	velocity, fps:	2960	2728	2508	2299	2099
	energy, ft-lb:	1945	1653	1397	1174	979
	arc, inches:		+1.6	0	-7.2	-21.0
Hornady 100 BTSP LM	velocity, fps:	3100	2839	2592	2358	2138
	energy, ft-lb:	2133	1790	1491	1235	1014
	arc, inches:		+1.5	0	-6.8	-19.8
Norma 80 FMJ	velocity, fps:	3117	2750	2412	2098	
	energy, ft-lb:	1726	1344	1034	782	
	arc, inches:		+1.5	0	-7.5	
Norma 100 FMJ	velocity, fps:	3018	2747	2493	2252	
	energy, ft-lb:	2023	1677	1380	1126	
	arc, inches:		+1.5	0	-7.1	
Norma 100 Soft Point	velocity, fps:	3018	2748	2493	2252	
	energy, ft-lb:	2023	1677	1380	1126	
	arc, inches:		+1.5	0	-7.1	
Norma 100 Oryx	velocity, fps:	3018	2653	2316	2004	
	energy, ft-lb:	2023	1563	1191	892	
	arc, inches:		+1.7	0	-8.3	
PMC 80 Pointed Soft Point	velocity, fps:	2940	2684	2444	2215	1999
	energy, ft-lb:	1535	1280	1060	871	709
	arc, inches:		+1.7	0	-7.5	-22.1
PMC 85 Barnes XLC	velocity, fps:	3250	3022	2805	2598	2401
	energy, ft-lb:	1993	1724	1485	1274	1088
	arc, inches:		+1.6	0	-5.6	16.3
PMC 85 HP boat-tail	velocity, fps:	3275	2922	2596	2292	2009
	energy, ft-lb:	2024	1611	1272	991	761
	arc, inches:		+1.3	0	-6.5	-19.7
PMC 100 Pointed Soft Point	velocity, fps:	2743	2507	2283	2070	1869
	energy, ft-lb:	1670	1395	1157	951	776
	arc, inches:		+2.0	0	-8.7	-25.5
PMC 100 SP boat-tail	velocity, fps:	2960	2742	2534	2335	2144
	energy, ft-lb:	1945	1669	1425	1210	1021
	arc, inches:		+1.6	0	-7.0	-20.5
Rem. 75 AccuTip BT	velocity, fps:	3375	3065	2775	2504	2248
	energy, ft-lb:	1897	1564	1282	1044	842
	arc, inches:		+2.0	+1.8	-3.0	-13.3
Remington 80 Copper Solid Tipped	velocity, fps:	3350	3011	2696	2403	2128
	energy, ft-lb:	1993	1610	1291	1025	894
	arc, inches:		+1.2	0	-6.1	-18.1
Rem. 80 Pointed Soft Point	velocity, fps:	3350	2955	2593	2259	1951
	energy, ft-lb:	1993	1551	1194	906	676
	arc, inches:		+2.2	+2.0	-3.5	-15.8
Rem. 80 HP Power-Lokt	velocity, fps:	3350	2955	2593	2259	1951
	energy, ft-lb:	1993	1551	1194	906	676
	arc, inches:		+2.2	+2.0	-3.5	-15.8
Rem. 90 Nosler Bal. Tip (also in EtronX) or Scirocco	velocity, fps:	3120	2871	2635	2411	2199
	energy, ft-lb:	1946	1647	1388	1162	966
	arc, inches:		+1.4	0	-6.4	-18.8
Rem. 95 AccuTip	velocity, fps:	3120	2847	2590	2347	2118
	energy, ft-lb:	2053	1710	1415	1162	946
	arc, inches:		+1.5	0	-6.6	-19.5
Rem. 100 PSP Core-Lokt (also in EtronX)	velocity, fps:	2960	2697	2449	2215	1993
	energy, ft-lb:	1945	1615	1332	1089	882
	arc, inches:		+1.6	0	-7.5	-22.1
Rem. 100 PSP boat-tail	velocity, fps:	2960	2720	2492	2275	2069
	energy, ft-lb:	1945	1642	1378	1149	950
	arc, inches:		+2.8	+2.3	-3.8	-16.6
Speer 100 Grand Slam	velocity, fps:	2950	2684	2434	2197	
	energy, ft-lb:	1932	1600	1315	1072	
	arc, inches:		+1.7	0	-7.6	-22.4

Centerfire Rifle Ballistics

.243 WINCHESTER TO .25-06 REMINGTON

CARTRIDGE BULLET	RANGE, YARDS:	0	100	200	300	400
Win. 55 Ballistic Silvertip	velocity, fps:	4025	3597	3209	2853	2525
	energy, ft-lb:	1978	1579	1257	994	779
	arc, inches:		+0.6	0	-4.0	-12.2
Win. 80 Pointed Soft Point	velocity, fps:	3350	2955	2593	2259	1951.
	energy, ft-lb:	1993	1551	1194	906	676
	arc, inches:		+2.6	+2.1	-3.6	-16.2
Win. 95 Ballistic Silvertip	velocity, fps:	3100	2854	2626	2410	2203
	energy, ft-lb:	2021	1719	1455	1225	1024
	arc, inches:		+1.4	0	-6.4	-18.9
Win. 95 Supreme Elite XP3	velocity, fps	3100	2864	2641	2428	2225
	energy, ft-lb	2027	1730	1471	1243	1044
	a rc, inches		+1.4	0	-6.4	-18.7
Win. 100 Power-Point	velocity, fps:	2960	2697	2449	2215	1993
	energy, ft-lb:	1945	1615	1332	1089	882
	arc, inches:		+1.9	0	-7.8	-22.6.
Win. 100 Power-Point Plus	velocity, fps:	3090	2818	2562	2321	2092
	energy, ft-lb:	2121	1764	1458	1196	972
	arc, inches:		+1.4	0	-6.7	-20.0

6mm Remington

CARTRIDGE BULLET	RANGE, YARDS:	0	100	200	300	400
Federal 80 Sierra Pro-Hunter	velocity, fps:	3470	3060	2690	2350	2040
	energy, ft-lb:	2140	1665	1290	980	735
	arc, inches:		+1.1	0	-5.9	-18.2
Federal 100 Hi-Shok	velocity, fps:	3100	2830	2570	2330	2100
	energy, ft-lb:	2135	1775	1470	1205	985
	arc, inches:		+1.4	0	-6.7	-19.8
Federal 100 Nos. Partition	velocity, fps:	3100	2860	2640	2420	2220
	energy, ft-lb:	2135	1820	1545	1300	1090
	arc, inches:		+1.4	0	-6.3	-18.7
Hornady 95 SST Superformance	velocity, fps:	3235	2955	2693	2445	2211
	energy, ft-lb:	2207	1842	1530	1261	1031
	arc, inches:		+1.3	0	-6.1	-18.0
Hornady 100 SP boat-tail	velocity, fps:	3100	2861	2634	2419	2231
	energy, ft-lb:	2134	1818	1541	1300	1088
	arc, inches:		+1.3	0	-6.5	-18.9
Hornady 100 SPBT LM	velocity, fps:	3250	2997	2756	2528	2311
	energy, ft-lb:	2345	1995	1687	1418	1186
	arc, inches:		+1.6	0	-6.3	-18.2
Rem. 75 V-Max boat-tail	velocity, fps:	3400	3088	2797	2524	2267
	energy, ft-lb:	1925	1587	1303	1061	856
	arc, inches:		+1.9	+1.7	-3.0	-13.1
Rem. 100 PSP Core-Lokt	velocity, fps:	3100	2829	2573	2332	2104.
	energy, ft-lb:	2133	1777	1470	1207	983
	arc, inches:		+1.4	0	-6.7	-19.8
Rem. 100 PSP boat-tail	velocity, fps:	3100	2852	2617	2394	2183.
	energy, ft-lb:	2134	1806	1521	1273	1058
	arc, inches:		+1.4	0	-6.5	-19.1
Win. 100 Power-Point	velocity, fps:	3100	2829	2573	2332	2104
	energy, ft-lb:	2133	1777	1470	1207	983
	arc, inches:		+1.7	0	-7.0	-20.4

.243 WSSM

CARTRIDGE BULLET	RANGE, YARDS:	0	100	200	300	400
Win. 55 Ballistic Silvertip	velocity, fps:	4060	3628	3237	2880	2550
	energy, ft-lb:	2013	1607	1280	1013	794
	arc, inches:		+0.6	0	-3.9	-12.0
Win. 95 Ballistic Silvertip	velocity, fps:	3250	3000	2763	2538	2325
	energy, ft-lb:	2258	1898	1610	1359	1140
	arc, inches:		+1.2	0	5.7	16.9
Win. 95 Supreme Elite XP3	velocity, fps	3150	2912	2686	2471	2266
	energy, ft-lb	2093	1788	1521	1287	1083
	arc, inches		+1.3	0	-6.1	-18.0
Win. 100 Power Point	velocity, fps:	3110	2838	2583	2341	2112
	energy, ft-lb:	2147	1789	1481	1217	991
	arc, inches:		+1.4	0	-6.6	-19.7

.240 Weatherby Magnum

CARTRIDGE BULLET	RANGE, YARDS:	0	100	200	300	400
Wby. 87 Pointed Expanding	velocity, fps:	3523	3199	2898	2617	2352
	energy, ft-lb:	2397	1977	1622	1323	1069
	arc, inches:		+2.7	+3.4	0	-8.4
Wby. 90 Barnes-X	velocity, fps:	3500	3222	2962	2717	2484
	energy, ft-lb:	2448	2075	1753	1475	1233
	arc, inches:		+2.6	+3.3	0	-8.0
Wby. 95 Nosler Bal. Tip	velocity, fps:	3420	3146	2888	2645	2414
	energy, ft-lb:	2467	2087	1759	1475	1229
	arc, inches:		+2.7	+3.5	0	-8.4
Wby. 100 Pointed Expanding	velocity, fps:	3406	3134	2878	2637	2408
	energy, ft-lb:	2576	2180	1839	1544	1287
	arc, inches:		+2.8	+3.5	0	-8.4
Wby. 100 Partition	velocity, fps:	3406	3136	2882	2642	2415
	energy, ft-lb:	2576	2183	1844	1550	1294
	arc, inches:		+2.8	+3.5	0	-8.4

.25-20 Winchester

CARTRIDGE BULLET	RANGE, YARDS:	0	100	200	300	400
Rem. 86 Soft Point	velocity, fps:	1460	1194	1030	931	858
	energy, ft-lb:	407	272	203	165	141
	arc, inches:		0	-22.9	-78.9	-173.0
Win. 86 Soft Point	velocity, fps:	1460	1194	1030	931	858.
	energy, ft-lb:	407	272	203	165	141
	arc, inches:		0	-23.5	-79.6	-175.9

.25-35 Winchester

CARTRIDGE BULLET	RANGE, YARDS:	0	100	200	300	400
Win. 117 Soft Point	velocity, fps:	2230	1866	1545	1282	1097
	energy, ft-lb:	1292	904	620	427	313
	arc, inches:		+2.1	-5.1	-27.0	-70.1

.250 Savage

CARTRIDGE BULLET	RANGE, YARDS:	0	100	200	300	400
Rem. 100 Pointed SP	velocity, fps:	2820	2504	2210	1936	1684.
	energy, ft-lb:	1765	1392	1084	832	630
	arc, inches:		+2.0	0	-9.2	-27.7
Win. 100 Silvertip	velocity, fps:	2820	2467	2140	1839	1569
	energy, ft-lb:	1765	1351	1017	751	547
	arc, inches:		+2.4	0	-10.1	-30.5

.257 Roberts

CARTRIDGE BULLET	RANGE, YARDS:	0	100	200	300	400
Federal 120 Nosler Partition	velocity, fps:	2780	2560	2360	2160	1970
	energy, ft-lb:	2060	1750	1480	1240	1030
	arc, inches:		+1.9	0	-8.2	-24.0
Hornady 117 SP boat-tail	velocity, fps:	2780	2550	2331	2122	1925
	energy, ft-lb:	2007	1689	1411	1170	963
	arc, inches:		+1.9	0	-8.3	-24.4
Hornady 117 SP boat-tail LM	velocity, fps:	2940	2694	2460	2240	2031
	energy, ft-lb:	2245	1885	1572	1303	1071
	arc, inches:		+1.7	0	-7.6	-21.8
Hornady 117 SST Superformance	velocity, fps:	2946	2707	2480	2265	2060
	energy, ft-lb:	2255	1903	1598	1332	1102
	arc, inches:		+1.6	0	-7.3	-21.4
Rem. 117 SP Core-Lokt	velocity, fps:	2650	2291	1961	1663	1404
	energy, ft-lb:	1824	1363	999	718	512
	arc, inches:		+2.6	0	-11.7	-36.1
Win. 117 Power-Point	velocity, fps:	2780	2411	2071	1761	1488
	energy, ft-lb:	2009	1511	1115	806	576.
	arc, inches:		+2.6	0	-10.8	-33.0

.25-06 Remington

CARTRIDGE BULLET	RANGE, YARDS:	0	100	200	300	400
Black Hills 100 Nos. Bal. Tip	velocity, fps:	3200				
	energy, ft-lb:	2273				
	arc, inches:					
Black Hills 100 Barnes XLC	velocity, fps:	3200				
	energy, ft-lb:	2273				
	arc, inches:					
Black Hills 115 Barnes X	velocity, fps:	2975				
	energy, ft-lb:	2259				
	arc, inches:					

Centerfire Rifle Ballistics

.25-06 REMINGTON TO 6.5X55 SWEDISH

CARTRIDGE BULLET	RANGE, YARDS:	0	100	200	300	400
Federal 90 Sierra Varminter	velocity, fps:	3440	3040	2680	2340	2030
	energy, ft-lb:	2365	1850	1435	1100	825
	arc, inches:		+1.1	0	-6.0	-18.3
Federal 100 Barnes XLC	velocity, fps:	3210	2970	2750	2540	2330
	energy, ft-lb:	2290	1965	1680	1430	1205
	arc, inches:		+1.2	0	-5.8	-17.0
Federal 100 Nosler Bal. Tip	velocity, fps:	3210	2960	2720	2490	2280
	energy, ft-lb:	2290	1940	1640	1380	1150.
	arc, inches:		+1.2	0	-6.0	-17.5
Federal 100 Trophy Copper	velocity, fps:	3210	2970	2740	2520	2310
	energy, ft-lb:	2290	1955	1665	1410	1185
	arc, inches:		+1.2	0	-5.9	-17.2
Federal 115 Nosler Partition	velocity, fps:	2990	2750	2520	2300	2100
	energy, ft-lb:	2285	1930	1620	1350	1120
	arc, inches:		+1.6	0	-7.0	-20.8
Federal 115 Trophy Bonded	velocity, fps:	2990	2740	2500	2270	2050
	energy, ft-lb:	2285	1910	1590	1310	1075
	arc, inches:		+1.6	0	-7.2	-21.1
Federal 117 Sierra Pro Hunt.	velocity, fps:	2990	2730	2480	2250	2030
	energy, ft-lb:	2320	1985	1645	1350	1100
	arc, inches:		+1.6	0	-7.2	-21.4
Federal 117 Sierra GameKing	velocity, fps:	2990	2770	2570	2370	2190
BTSP	energy, ft-lb:	2320	2000	1715	1465	1240
	arc, inches:		+1.5	0	-6.8	-19.9
Hornady 90 GMX	velocity, fps:	3350	3001	2679	2378	2098
Superformance	energy, ft-lb:	2243	1799	1434	1130	879
	arc, inches:		+1.2	0	-6.0	-18.3
Hornady 117 SP boat-tail	velocity, fps:	2990	2749	2520	2302	2096
	energy, ft-lb:	2322	1962	1649	1377	1141
	arc, inches:		+1.6	0	-7.0	-20.7
Hornady 117 SP boat-tail LM	velocity, fps:	3110	2855	2613	2384	2168
	energy, ft-lb:	2512	2117	1774	1476	1220
	arc, inches:		+1.8	0	-7.1	-20.3
Hornady 117 SST	velocity, fps:	3110	2862	2627	2405	2193
Superformance	energy, ft-lb:	2513	2127	1793	1502	1249
	arc, inches:		+1.4	0	-6.4	-18.9
PMC 100 SPBT	velocity, fps:	3200	2925	2650	2395	2145
	energy, ft-lb:	2273	1895	1561	1268	1019
	arc, inches:		+1.3	0	-6.3	-18.6
PMC 117 PSP	velocity, fps:	2950	2706	2472	2253	2047
	energy, ft-lb:	2261	1900	1588	1319	1088
	arc, inches:		+1.6	0	-7.3	-21.5
Rem. 100 PSP Core-Lokt	velocity, fps:	3230	2893	2580	2287	2014
	energy, ft-lb:	2316	1858	1478	1161	901
	arc, inches:		+1.3	0	-6.6	-19.8
Rem. 115 Core-Lokt Ultra	velocity, fps:	3000	2751	2516	2293	2081
	energy, ft-lb:	2298	1933	1616	1342	1106
	arc, inches:		+1.6	0	-7.1	-20.7
Rem. 120 PSP Core-Lokt	velocity, fps:	2990	2730	2484	2252	2032
	energy, ft-lb:	2382	1985	1644	1351	1100
	arc, inches:		+1.6	0	-7.2	-21.4
Speer 120 Grand Slam	velocity, fps:	3130	2835	2558	2298	
	energy, ft-lb:	2610	2141	1743	1407	
	arc, inches:		+1.4	0	-6.8	-20.1
Win. 85 Ballistic Silvertip	velocity, fps	3470	3156	2863	2589	2331
	energy, ft-lb:	2273	1880	1548	1266	1026
	arc, inches:		+1.0	0	-5.2	-15.7
Win. 90 Pos. Exp. Point	velocity, fps:	3440	3043	2680	2344	2034
	energy, ft-lb:	2364	1850	1435	1098	827
	arc, inches:		+2.4	+2.0	-3.4	-15.0
Win. 110 AccuBond CT	velocity, fps:	3100	2870	2651	2442	2243
	energy, ft-lb:	2347	2011	1716	1456	1228
	arc, inches:		+1.4	0	-6.3	-18.5
Win. 115 Ballistic Silvertip	velocity, fps:	3060	2825	2603	2390	2188
	energy, ft-lb:	2391	2038	1729	1459	1223
	arc, inches:		+1.4	0	-6.6	-19.2
Win. 120 Pos. Pt. Exp.	velocity, fps:	2990	2717	2459	2216	1987
	energy, ft-lb:	2382	1967	1612	1309	1053
	arc, inches:		+1.6	0	-7.4	-21.8

CARTRIDGE BULLET	RANGE, YARDS:	0	100	200	300	400

.25 Winchester Super Short Magnum

CARTRIDGE BULLET	RANGE, YARDS:	0	100	200	300	400
Win. 85 Ballistic Silvertip	velocity, fps:	3470	3156	2863	2589	2331
	energy, ft-lb:	2273	1880	1548	1266	1026
	arc, inches:		+1.0	0	-5.2	-15.7
Win. 110 AccuBond CT	velocity, fps:	3100	2870	2651	2442	2243.
	energy, ft-lb:	2347	2011	1716	1456	1228
	arc, inches:		+1.4	0	-6.3	-18.5
Win. 115 Ballistic Silvertip	velocity, fps:	3060	2844	2639	2442	2254
	energy, ft-lb:	2392	2066	1778	1523	1298
	arc, inches:		+1.4	0	-6.4	-18.6
Win. 120 Pos. Pt. Exp.	velocity, fps:	2990	2717	2459	2216	1987
	energy, ft-lb:	2383	1967	1612	1309	1053
	arc, inches:		+1.6	0	-7.4	-21.8

.257 Weatherby Magnum

CARTRIDGE BULLET	RANGE, YARDS:	0	100	200	300	400
Federal 115 Nosler Partition	velocity, fps:	3150	2900	2660	2440	
2220						
	energy, ft-lb:	2535	2145	1810	1515	1260
	arc, inches:		+1.3	0	-6.2	-18.4
Federal 115 Trophy Bonded	velocity, fps:	3150	2890	2640	2400	2180
	energy, ft-lb:	2535	2125	1775	1470	1210
	arc, inches:		+1.4	0	-6.3	-18.8
Wby. 87 Pointed Expanding	velocity, fps:	3825	3472	3147	2845	2563
	energy, ft-lb:	2826	2328	1913	1563	1269
	arc, inches:		+2.1	+2.8	0	-7.1
Wby. 100 Pointed Expanding	velocity, fps:	3602	3298	3016	2750	2500
	energy, ft-lb:	2881	2416	2019	1680	1388
	arc, inches:		+2.4	+3.1	0	-7.7
Wby. 115 Nosler Bal. Tip	velocity, fps:	3400	3170	2952	2745	2547
	energy, ft-lb:	2952	2566	2226	1924	1656.
	arc, inches:		+3.0	+3.5	0	-7.9
Wby. 115 Barnes X	velocity, fps:	3400	3158	2929	2711	2504
	energy, ft-lb:	2952	2546	2190	1877	1601
	arc, inches:		+2.7	+3.4	0	-8.1
Wby. 117 RN Expanding	velocity, fps:	3402	2984	2595	2240	1921
	energy, ft-lb:	3007	2320	1742	1302	956
	arc, inches:		+3.4	+4.31	0	-11.1
Wby. 120 Nosler Partition	velocity, fps:	3305	3046	2801	2570	2350
	energy, ft-lb:	2910	2472	2091	1760	1471
	arc, inches:		+3.0	+3.7	0	-8.9

6.53 (.257) Scramjet

CARTRIDGE BULLET	RANGE, YARDS:	0	100	200	300	400
Lazzeroni 85 Nosler Bal. Tip	velocity, fps:	3960	3652	3365	3096	2844
	energy, ft-lb:	2961	2517	2137	1810	1526
	arc, inches:		+1.7	+2.4	0	-6.0
Lazzeroni 100 Nosler Part.	velocity, fps:	3740	3465	3208	2965	2735
	energy, ft-lb:	3106	2667	2285	1953	1661.
	arc, inches:		+2.1	+2.7	0	-6.7

6.5x50 Japanese

CARTRIDGE BULLET	RANGE, YARDS:	0	100	200	300	400
Norma 156 Alaska	velocity, fps:	2067	1832	1615	1423	
	energy, ft-lb:	1480	1162	904	701	
	arc, inches:		+4.4	0	-17.8	

6.5x52 Carcano

CARTRIDGE BULLET	RANGE, YARDS:	0	100	200	300	400
Norma 156 Alaska	velocity, fps:	2428	2169	1926	1702	
	energy, ft-lb:	2043	1630	1286	1004	
	arc, inches:		+2.9	0	-12.3	

6.5x55 Swedish

CARTRIDGE BULLET	RANGE, YARDS:	0	100	200	300	400
Federal 140 Hi-Shok	velocity, fps:	2600	2400	2220	2040	1860
	energy, ft-lb:	2100	1795	1525	1285	1080
	arc, inches:		+2.3	0	-9.4	-27.2

Centerfire Rifle Ballistics

6.5X55 Swedish to 6.5 Remington Magnum

CARTRIDGE BULLET	RANGE, YARDS:	0	100	200	300	400
Federal 140 Trophy Bonded	velocity, fps:	2550	2350	2160	1980	1810
	energy, ft-lb:	2020	1720	1450	1220	1015
	arc, inches:		+2.4	0	-9.8	-28.4
Federal 140 Sierra MatchKg. BTHP	velocity, fps:	2630	2460	2300	2140	2000
	energy, ft-lb:	2140	1880	1640	1430	1235
	arc, inches:		+16.4	+28.8	+33.9	+31.8
Hornady 129 SP LM	velocity, fps:	2770	2561	2361	2171	1994
	energy, ft-lb:	2197	1878	1597	1350	1138
	arc, inches:		+2.0	0	-8.2	-23.2
Hornady 140 SP Interlock	velocity, fps	2525	2341	2165	1996	1836
	energy, ft-lb:	1982	1704	1457	1239	1048
	arc, inches:		+2.4	0	-9.9	-28.5
Hornady140 SP LM	velocity, fps:	2740	2541	2351	2169	1999
	energy, ft-lb:	2333	2006	1717	1463	1242
	arc, inches:		+2.4	0	-8.7	-24.0
Norma 120 Nosler Bal. Tip	velocity, fps:	2822	2609	2407	2213	
	energy, ft-lb:	2123	1815	1544	1305	
	arc, inches:		+1.8	0	-7.8	
Norma 139 Vulkan	velocity, fps:	2854	2569	2302	2051	
	energy, ft-lb:	2515	2038	1636	1298	
	arc, inches:		+1.8	0	-8.4	
Norma 140 Nosler Partition	velocity, fps:	2789	2592	2403	2223	
	energy, ft-lb:	2419	2089	1796	1536	
	arc, inches:		+1.8	0	-7.8	
Norma 156 TXP Swift A-Fr.	velocity, fps:	2526	2276	2040	1818	
	energy, ft-lb:	2196	1782	1432	1138	
	arc, inches:		+2.6	0	-10.9	
Norma 156 Alaska	velocity, fps:	2559	2245	1953	1687	
	energy, ft-lb:	2269	1746	1322	986	
	arc, inches:		+2.7	0	-11.9	
Norma 156 Vulkan	velocity, fps:	2644	2395	2159	1937	
	energy, ft-lb:	2422	1987	1616	1301	
	arc, inches:		+2.2	0	-9.7	
Norma 156 Oryx	velocity, fps:	2559	2308	2070	1848	
	energy, ft-lb:	2269	1845	1485	1183	
	arc, inches:		+2.5	0	-10.6	
PMC 139 Pointed Soft Point	velocity, fps:	2850	2560	2290	2030	1790
	energy, ft-lb:	2515	2025	1615	1270	985
	arc, inches:		+2.2	0	-8.9	-26.3
PMC 140 HP boat-tail	velocity, fps:	2560	2398	2243	2093	1949
	energy, ft-lb:	2037	1788	1563	1361	1181
	arc, inches:		+2.3	0	-9.2	-26.4
PMC 140 SP boat-tail	velocity, fps:	2560	2386	2218	2057	1903
	energy, ft-lb:	2037	1769	1529	1315	1126
	arc, inches:		+2.3	0	-9.4	-27.1
PMC 144 FMJ	velocity, fps:	2650	2370	2110	1870	1650
	energy, ft-lb:	2425	1950	1550	1215	945
	arc, inches:		+2.7	0	-10.5	-30.9
Rem. 140 PSP Core-Lokt	velocity, fps:	2550	2353	2164	1984	1814
	energy, ft-lb:	2021	1720	1456	1224	1023
	arc, inches:		+2.4	0	-9.8	-27.0
Speer 140 Grand Slam	velocity, fps:	2550	2318	2099	1892	
	energy, ft-lb:	2021	1670	1369	1112	
	arc, inches:		+2.5	0	-10.4	-30.6
Win. 140 Soft Point	velocity, fps:	2550	2359	2176	2002	1836
	energy, ft-lb:	2022	1731	1473	1246	1048.
	arc, inches:		+2.4	0	-9.7	-28.1

6.5 Grendel

CARTRIDGE BULLET	RANGE, YARDS:	0	100	200	300	400
Hornady 123 A-MAX	velocity, fps:	2590	2420	2256	2099	1948
	energy, ft-lb:	1832	1599	1390	1203	1037
	arc, inches:	-2.4	+1.8	0	-8.6	-25.1
Hornady 123 SST	velocity, fps:	2620	2449	2284	2126	1974
	energy, ft-lb:	1875	1638	1425	1234	1064
	arc, inches:	-2.4	+1.7	0	-8.4	-24.5

6.5 Creedmoor

CARTRIDGE BULLET	RANGE, YARDS:	0	100	200	300	400
Hornady 120 GMX	velocity, fps:	3050	2850	2659	2476	2300
	energy, ft-lb:	2479	2164	1884	1634	1410
	arc, inches:	-1.5	+1.4	0	-6.3	-18.3
Hornady 129 SST	velocity, fps:	2950	2756	2571	2394	2223
	energy, ft-lb:	2493	2176	1894	1641	1415
	arc, inches:	-1.5	+1.5	0	-6.8	-19.7
Hornady 140 A-MAX	velocity, fps:	2710	2557	2410	2267	2129
	energy, ft-lb:	2283	2033	1805	1598	1410
	arc, inches:	-1.5	+1.9	0	-7.9	-22.6
Nosler 140 BT	velocity, fps:	2550	2380	2217	2060	1910
	energy, ft-lb:	2021	1761	1527	1319	1134
	arc, inches:	-1.5	+2.3	0	-9.4	-27.0

.260 Remington

CARTRIDGE BULLET	RANGE, YARDS:	0	100	200	300	400
Federal 140 Sierra GameKing BTSP	velocity, fps:	2750	2570	2390	2220	2060
	energy, ft-lb:	2350	2045	1775	1535	1315
	arc, inches:		+1.9	0	-8.0	-23.1
Federal 140 Trophy Bonded	velocity, fps:	2750	2540	2340	2150	1970
	energy, ft-lb:	2350	2010	1705	1440	1210
arc, inches:		+1.9	0	-8.4	-24.1	
Rem. 120 Nosler Bal. Tip	velocity, fps:	2890	2688	2494	2309	2131
	energy, ft-lb:	2226	1924	1657	1420	1210
	arc, inches:		+1.7	0	-7.3	-21.1
Rem. 120 AccuTip	velocity, fps:	2890	2697	2512	2334	2163
	energy, ft-lb:	2392	2083	1807	1560	1340
	arc, inches:		+1.6	0	-7.2	-20.7
Rem. 125 Nosler Partition	velocity, fps:	2875	2669	2473	2285	2105.
	energy, ft-lb:	2294	1977	1697	1449	1230
arc, inches:		+1.71	0	-7.4	-21.4	
Rem. 140 PSP Core-Lokt (and C-L Ultra)	velocity, fps:	2750	2544	2347	2158	1979
	energy, ft-lb:	2351	2011	1712	1448	1217
	arc, inches:		+1.9	0	-8.3	-24.0
Speer 140 Grand Slam	velocity, fps:	2750	2518	2297	2087	
	energy, ft-lb:	2351	1970	1640	1354	
	arc, inches:		+2.3	0	-8.9	-25.8

6.5-284

CARTRIDGE BULLET	RANGE, YARDS:	0	100	200	300	400
Norma 120 Nosler Bal. Tip	velocity, fps:	3117	2890	2674	2469	
	energy, ft-lb:	2589	2226	1906	1624	
	arc, inches:		+1.3	0	-6.2	
Norma 140 Nosler Part.	velocity, fps:	2953	2750	2557	2371	
	energy, ft-lb:	2712	2352	2032	1748	
	arc, inches:		+1.5	0	-6.8	

6.5-284 Norma

CARTRIDGE BULLET	RANGE, YARDS:	0	100	200	300	400
Nosler 120 Ballistic Tip	velocity, fps:	3000	2792	2594	2404	2223
	energy, ft-lb:	2398	2077	1793	1540	1316
	arc, inches:	-1.5	+1.4	0	-6.6	-17.1
Nosler 125 PT	velocity, fps:	3000	2788	2585	2392	2207
	energy, ft-lb:	2497	2157	1855	1588	1352
	arc, inches:	-1.5	+1.5	0	-6.7	-19.5
Nosler 130 AccuBond	velocity, fps:	2900	2709	2526	2351	2182
	energy, ft-lb:	2427	2118	1842	1595	1374
	arc, inches:	-1.5	+1.5	0	-6.9	-18.4

6.5 Remington Magnum

CARTRIDGE BULLET	RANGE, YARDS:	0	100	200	300	400
Nosler 125 PT	velocity, fps:	3025	2811	2608	2414	2228
	energy, ft-lb:	2539	2194	1888	1617	1377
	arc, inches:	-1.5	+1.5	0	-6.6	-19.1

Centerfire Rifle Ballistics

6.5 REMINGTON MAGNUM TO .270 WINCHESTER

CARTRIDGE BULLET	RANGE, YARDS:	0	100	200	300	400
Rem. 120 Core-Lokt PSP	velocity, fps:	3210	2905	2621	2353	2102
	energy, ft-lb:	2745	2248	1830	1475	1177
	arc, inches:		+2.7	+2.1	-3.5	-15.5

.264 Winchester Magnum

CARTRIDGE BULLET	RANGE, YARDS:	0	100	200	300	400
Nosler 100 Ballistic Tip	velocity, fps:	3400	3105	2829	2569	2324
	energy, ft-lb:	2567	2141	1777	1465	1199
	arc, inches:	-1.5	+1.0	0	-5.5	-16.1
Nosler 130 AccuBond	velocity, fps:	3100	2900	2709	2527	2351
	energy, ft-lb:	2774	2428	2119	1843	1595
	arc, inches:	-1.5	+1.2	0	-6.0	-17.5
Rem. 140 PSP Core-Lokt	velocity, fps:	3030	2782	2548	2326	2114
	energy, ft-lb:	2854	2406	2018	1682	1389
	arc, inches:		+1.5	0	-6.9	-20.2
Win. 140 Power-Point	velocity, fps:	3030	2782	2548	2326	2114.
	energy, ft-lb:	2854	2406	2018	1682	1389
	arc, inches:		+1.8	0	-7.2	-20.8

6.8mm Remington SPC

CARTRIDGE BULLET	RANGE, YARDS:	0	100	200	300	400
Hornady 110 BTHP	velocity, fps:	2570	2332	2107	1895	1697
(16-in. barrel)	energy, ft-lb:	1613	1328	1084	877	703
	arc, inches:	-2.4	+2.0	0	-9.9	-29.5
Hornady 120 SST	velocity, fps:	2460	2250	2051	1863	1687
(16-in. barrel)	energy, ft-lb:	1612	1349	1121	925	758
	arc, inches:	-2.4	+2.3	0	-10.5	-31.1
Rem. 115 Open Tip Match	velocity, fps:	2800	2535	2285	2049	1828
(and HPBT Match)	energy, ft-lb:	2002	1641	1333	1072	853
	arc, inches:		+2.0	0	-8.8	-26.2
Rem. 115 Metal Case	velocity, fps:	2800	2523	2262	2017	1789
	energy, ft-lb:	2002	1625	1307	1039	817
	arc, inches:		+2.0	0	-8.8	-26.2
Rem. 115 Sierra HPBT	velocity, fps:	2775	2511	2263	2028	1809
(2005; all vel. @ 2775)	energy, ft-lb:	1966	1610	1307	1050	835
	arc, inches:		+2.0	0	-8.8	-26.2.
Rem. 115 CL Ultra	velocity, fps:	2775	2472	2190	1926	1683
	energy, ft-lb:	1966	1561	1224	947	723
	arc, inches:		+2.1	0	-9.4	-28.2

.270 Winchester

CARTRIDGE BULLET	RANGE, YARDS:	0	100	200	300	400
Black Hills 130 Nos. Bal. T.	velocity, fps:	2950				
	energy, ft-lb:	2512				
	arc, inches:					
Black Hills 130 Barnes XLC	velocity, ft-lb:	2950				
	energy, ft-lb:	2512				
	arc, inches:					
Federal 130 Barnes XLC	velocity, fps:	3060	2840	2620	2420	2220
And Triple Shock	energy, ft-lb:	2705	2320	1985	1690	1425
	arc, inches:		+1.4	0	-6.4	-18.9
Federal 130 Hi-Shok	velocity, fps:	3060	2800	2560	2330	2110
	energy, ft-lb:	2700	2265	1890	1565	1285
	arc, inches:		+1.5	0	-6.8	-20.0
Federal 130 Nosler Bal. Tip	velocity, fps:	3060	2840	2630	2430	2230
	energy, ft-lb:	2700	2325	1990	1700	1440
	arc, inches:		+1.4	0	-6.5	-18.8
Federal 130 Nos. Partition	velocity, fps:	3060	2830	2610	2400	2200
And Solid Base	energy, ft-lb:	2705	2310	19651665 1400		
	arc, inches:		+1.4	0	-6.5	-19.1
Federal 130 Sierra GameKing	velocity, fps:	3060	2830	2620	2410	2220
	energy, ft-lb:	2700	2320	1980	1680	1420
	arc, inches:		+1.4	0	-6.5	-19.0
Federal 130 Sierra Pro-Hunt.	velocity, fps:	3060	2830	2600	2390	2190
	energy, ft-lb:	2705	2305	1960	1655	1390
	arc, inches:	+1.4	0	-6.4	-19.0	
Federal 130 Trophy Bonded	velocity, fps:	3060	2810	2570	2340	2130
	energy, ft-lb:	2705	2275	1905	1585	1310
	arc, inches:		+1.5	0	-6.7	-19.8
Federal 130 Trophy	velocity, fps:	3060	2840	2630	2430	2240
Bonded Tip	energy, ft-lb:	2705	2330	2000	1710	1455
	arc, inches:		+1.4	0	-6.4	-18.7
Federal 140 Trophy Bonded	velocity, fps:	2940	2700	2480	2260	2060
	energy, ft-lb:	2685	2270	1905	1590	1315
	arc, inches:		+1.6	0	-7.3	-21.5
Federal 140 Trophy	velocity, fps:	2950	2740	2550	2360	2180
Bonded Tip	energy, ft-lb:	2705	2340	2015	1730	1475
	arc, inches:		+1.6	0	-6.9	-20.1
Federal 140 Tr. Bonded HE	velocity, fps:	3100	2860	2620	2400	2200.
	energy, ft-lb:	2990	2535	2140	1795	1500
	arc, inches:		+1.4	0	-6.4	-18.9
Federal 140 Nos. AccuBond	velocity, fps:	2950	2760	2580	2400	2230.
	energy, ft-lb:	2705	2365	2060	1790	1545
	arc, inches:		+1.5	0	-6.7	-19.6
Federal 150 Hi-Shok RN	velocity, fps:	2850	2500	2180	1890	1620
	energy, ft-lb:	2705	2085	1585	1185	870
	arc, inches:		+2.0	0	-9.4	-28.6
Federal 150 Sierra GameKing	velocity, fps:	2850	2660	2480	2300	2130
	energy, ft-lb:	2705	2355	2040	1760	1510
	arc, inches:		+1.7	0	-7.4	-21.4
Federal 150 Sierra GameKing	velocity, fps:	3000	2800	2620	2430	2260
HE	energy, ft-lb:	2995	2615	2275	1975	1700
	arc, inches:		+1.5	0	-6.5	-18.9
Federal 150 Nosler Partition	velocity, fps:	2850	2590	2340	2100	1880.
	energy, ft-lb:	2705	2225	1815	1470	1175
	arc, inches:		+1.9	0	-8.3	-24.4
Hornady 120 SST Custom Lite	velocity, fps:	2675	2288	1935	1619	1351
	energy, ft-lb:	1907	1395	998	699	486
	arc, inches:		+2.6	0	-12.0	-37.4
Hornady 130 GMX	velocity, fps:	3190	2975	2770	2575	2387
Superformance	energy, ft-lb:	2937	2554	2215	1913	1645
	arc, inches:		+1.2	0	-5.7	-16.8
Hornady 130 SST	velocity, fps:	3060	2845	2639	2442	2254
(or Interbond)	energy, ft-lb:	2700	2335	2009	1721	1467
	arc, inches:		+1.4	0	-6.6	-19.1
Hornady 130 SST LM	velocity, fps:	3215	2998	2790	2590	2400
(or Interbond)	energy, ft-lb:	2983	2594	2246	1936	1662
	arc, inches:		+1.2	0	-5.8	-17.0
Hornady 130 SST	velocity, fps:	3200	2984	2779	2583	2396
Superformance	energy, ft-lb:	2956	2570	2229	1926	1656
	arc, inches:		+1.2	0	-5.7	-16.7
Hornady 140 SP boat-tail	velocity, fps:	2940	2747	2562	2385	2214
	energy, ft-lb:	2688	2346	2041	1769	1524
	arc, inches:		+1.6	0	-7.0	-20.2
Hornady 140 SP boat-tail LM	velocity, fps:	3100	2894	2697	2508	2327.
	energy, ft-lb:	2987	2604	2261	1955	1684
	arc, inches:		+1.4	0	6.3	-18.3
Hornady 140 SST	velocity, fps:	3090	2894	2707	2568	2355
Superformance	energy, ft-lb:	2968	2604	2278	1986	1724
	arc, inches:		+1.3	0	-6.1	-17.6
Hornady 150 SP	velocity, fps:	2800	2684	2478	2284	2100
	energy, ft-lb:	2802	2400	2046	1737	1469
	arc, inches:		+1.7	0	-7.4	-21.6
Norma 130 SP	velocity, fps:	3140	2862	2601	2354	
	energy, ft-lb:	2847	2365	1953	1600	
	arc, inches:		+1.3	0	-6.5	
Norma 130 FMJ	velocity, fps:	2887	2634	2395	2169	
	energy, ft-lb:					
	arc, inches:		+1.8	0	-7.8	
Norma 150 SP	velocity, fps:	2799	2555	2323	2104	
	energy, ft-lb:	2610	2175	1798	1475	
	arc, inches:		+1.9	0	-8.3	
Norma 150 Oryx	velocity, fps:	2854	2608	2376	2155	
	energy, ft-lb:	2714	2267	1880	1547	
	arc, inches:		+1.8	0	-8.0	
PMC 130 Barnes X	velocity, fps:	2910	2717	2533	2356	2186
	energy, ft-lb:	2444	2131	1852	1602	1379
	arc, inches:		+1.6	0	-7.1	-20.4
PMC 130 SP boat-tail	velocity, fps:	3050	2830	2620	2421	2229
	energy, ft-lb:	2685	2312	1982	1691	1435
	arc, inches:		+1.5	0	-6.5	-19.0
PMC 130 Pointed Soft Point	velocity, fps:	2950	2691	2447	2217	2001
	energy, ft-lb:	2512	2090	1728	1419	1156
	arc, inches:		+1.6	0	-7.5	-22.1
PMC 150 Barnes X	velocity, fps:	2700	2541	2387	2238	2095
	energy, ft-lb:	2428	2150	1897	1668	1461
	arc, inches:		+2.0	0	-8.1	-23.1

.270 WINCHESTER TO .270 WINCHESTER SHORT MAGNUM

CARTRIDGE BULLET	RANGE, YARDS:	0	100	200	300	400
PMC 150 SP boat-tail	velocity, fps:	2850	2660	2477	2302	2134
	energy, ft-lb:	2705	2355	2043	1765	1516.
	arc, inches:		+1.7	0	-7.4	-21.4
PMC 150 Pointed Soft Point	velocity, fps:	2750	2530	2321	2123	1936
	energy, ft-lb:	2519	2131	1794	1501	1248
	arc, inches:		+2.0	0	-8.4	-24.6
Rem. 100 Pointed Soft Point	velocity, fps:	3320	2924	2561	2225	1916
	energy, ft-lb:	2448	1898	1456	1099	815
	arc, inches:		+2.3	+2.0	-3.6	-16.2
Rem. 115 PSP Core-Lokt mr	velocity, fps:	2710	2412	2133	1873	1636
	energy, ft-lb:	1875	1485	1161	896	683
	arc, inches:		+1.0	-2.7	-14.2	-35.6
Rem. 130 PSP Core-Lokt	velocity, fps:	3060	2776	2510	2259	2022
	energy, ft-lb:	2702	2225	1818	1472	1180
	arc, inches:		+1.5	0	-7.0	-20.9
Rem. 130 Bronze Point	velocity, fps:	3060	2802	2559	2329	2110
	energy, ft-lb:	2702	2267	1890	1565	1285
	arc, inches:		+1.5	0	-6.8	-20.0
Rem. 130 Swift Scirocco	velocity, fps:	3060	2838	2677	2425	2232
	energy, ft-lb:	2702	2325	1991	1697	1438
	arc, inches:		+1.4	0	-6.5	-18.8
Rem. 130 AccuTip BT	velocity, fps:	3060	2845	2639	2442	2254
	energy, ft-lb:	2702	2336	2009	1721	1467
	arc, inches:		+1.4	0	-6.4	-18.6
Rem. 140 Swift A-Frame	velocity, fps:	2925	2652	2394	2152	1923
	energy, ft-lb:	2659	2186	1782	1439	1150
	arc, inches:		+1.7	0	-7.8	-23.2
Rem. 140 PSP boat-tail	velocity, fps:	2960	2749	2548	2355	2171
	energy, ft-lb:	2723	2349	2018	1724	1465
	arc, inches:		+1.6	0	-6.9	-20.1
Rem. 140 Nosler Bal. Tip	velocity, fps:	2960	2754	2557	2366	2187
	energy, ft-lb:	2724	2358	2032	1743	1487
	arc, inches:		+1.6	0	-6.9	-20.0
Rem. 140 PSP C-L Ultra	velocity, fps:	2925	2667	2424	2193	1975
	energy, ft-lb:	2659	2211	1826	1495	1212
	arc, inches:		+1.7	0	-7.6	-22.5
Rem. 150 SP Core-Lokt	velocity, fps:	2850	2504	2183	1886	1618
	energy, ft-lb:	2705	2087	1587	1185	872
	arc, inches:		+2.0	0	-9.4	-28.6
Rem. 150 Nosler Partition	velocity, fps:	2850	2652	2463	2282	2108
	energy, ft-lb:	2705	2343	2021	1734	1480
	arc, inches:		+1.7	0	-7.5	-21.6
Speer 130 Grand Slam	velocity, fps:	3050	2774	2514	2269	
	energy, ft-lb:	2685	2221	1824	1485	
	arc, inches:		+1.5	0	-7.0	-20.9
Speer 150 Grand Slam	velocity, fps:	2830	2594	2369	2156	
	energy, ft-lb:	2667	2240	1869	1548	
	arc, inches:		+1.8	0	-8.1	-23.6
Win. 130 Power-Point	velocity, fps:	3060	2802	2559	2329	2110
	energy, ft-lb:	2702	2267	1890	1565	1285.
	arc, inches:		+1.8	0	-7.1	-20.6
Win. 130 Power-Point Plus	velocity, fps:	3150	2881	2628	2388	2161
	energy, ft-lb:	2865	2396	1993	1646	1348
	arc, inches:		+1.3	0	-6.4	-18.9
Win. 130 Silvertip	velocity, fps:	3060	2776	2510	2259	2022.
	energy, ft-lb:	2702	2225	1818	1472	1180
	arc, inches:		+1.8	0	-7.4	-21.6
Win. 130 Ballistic Silvertip	velocity, fps:	3050	2828	2618	2416	2224
	energy, ft-lb:	2685	2309	1978	1685	1428
	arc, inches:		+1.4	0	-6.5	-18.9
Win. 140 AccuBond	velocity, fps:	2950	2751	2560	2378	2203
	energy, ft-lb:	2705	2352	2038	1757	1508
	arc, inches:		+1.6	0	-6.9	-19.9
Win. 140 Fail Safe	velocity, fps:	2920	2671	2435	2211	1999
	energy, ft-lb:	2651	2218	1843	1519	1242
	arc, inches:		+1.7	0	-7.6	-22.3
Win. 150 Power-Point	velocity, fps:	2850	2585	2336	2100	1879
	energy, ft-lb:	2705	2226	1817	1468	1175
	arc, inches:		+2.2	0	-8.6	-25.0
Win. 150 Power-Point Plus	velocity, fps:	2950	2679	2425	2184	1957
	energy, ft-lb:	2900	2391	1959	1589	1276
	arc, inches:		+1.7	0	-7.6	-22.6
Win. 150 Partition Gold	velocity, fps:	2930	2693	2468	2254	2051
	energy, ft-lb:	2860	2416	2030	1693	1402
	arc, inches:		+1.7	0	-7.4	-21.6
Win. 150 Supreme Elite XP3	velocity, fps:	2950	2763	2583	2411	2245
	energy, ft-lb:	2898	2542	2223	1936	1679
	arc, inches:		+1.5	0	-6.9	-15.5

.270 WINCHESTER SHORT MAGNUM

CARTRIDGE BULLET	RANGE, YARDS:	0	100	200	300	400
Black Hills 140 AccuBond	velocity, fps:	3100				
	energy, ft-lb:	2987				
	arc, inches:					
Federal 130 Nos. Bal. Tip	velocity, fps:	3300	3070	2840	2630	2430
	energy, ft-lb:	3145	2710	2335	2000	1705
	arc, inches:		+1.1	0	-5.4	-15.8
Federal 130 Nos. Partition And Nos. Solid Base And Barnes TS	velocity, fps:	3280	3040	2810	2590	2380
	energy, ft-lb:	3105	2665	2275	1935	1635
	arc, inches:		+1.1	0	-5.6	-16.3
Federal 130 Trophy Copper	velocity, fps:	3280	3060	2850	2650	2460
	energy, ft-lb:	3105	2700	2345	2025	1745
	arc, inches:		+1.1	0	-5.4	-15.8
Federal 140 Nos. AccuBond	velocity, fps	3200	3000	2810	2630	2450
	energy, ft-lb:	3185	2795	2455	2145	1865
	arc, inches:		+1.2	0	-5.6	-16.2
Federal 140 Trophy Bonded	velocity, fps:	3130	2870	2640	2410	2200
	energy, ft-lb:	3035	2570	2160	1810	1500
	arc, inches:		+1.4	0	-6.3	18.7
Federal 140 Trophy Bonded Tip	velocity, fps:	3200	2980	2770	2580	2390
	energy, ft-lb:	3185	2765	2390	2060	1770
	arc, inches:		+1.2	0	-5.8	-16.7
Federal 150 Nos. Partition	velocity, fps:	3160	2950	2750	2550	2370
	energy, ft-lb:	3325	2895	2515	2175	1870
	arc, inches:		+1.3	0	-5.9	-17.0
Norma 130 FMJ	velocity, fps:	3150	2882	2630	2391	
	energy, ft-lb:					
	arc, inches:		+1.5	0	-6.4	
Norma 130 Ballistic ST	velocity, fps:	3281	3047	2825	2614	
	energy, ft-lb:	3108	2681	2305	1973	
	arc, inches:		+1.1	0	-5.5	
Norma 140 Barnes X TS	velocity, fps:	3150	2952	2762	2580	
	energy, ft-lb:	3085	2709	2372	2070	
	arc, inches:		+1.3	0	-5.8	
Norma 150 Nosler Bal. Tip	velocity, fps:	3280	3046	2824	2613	
	energy, ft-lb:	3106	2679	2303	1972	
	arc, inches:		+1.1	0	-5.4	
Norma 150 Oryx	velocity, fps:	3117	2856	2611	2378	
	energy, ft-lb:	3237	2718	2271	1884	
	arc, inches:		+1.4	0	-6.5	
Win. 130 Bal. Silvertip	velocity, fps:	3275	3041	2820	2609	2408
	energy, ft-lb:	3096	2669	2295	1964	1673
	arc, inches:		+1.1	0	-5.5	-16.1
Win. 140 AccuBond	velocity, fps:	3200	2989	2789	2597	2413
	energy, ft-lb:	3184	2779	2418	2097	1810
	arc, inches:		+1.2	0	-5.7	-16.5
Win. 140 Fail Safe	velocity, fps:	3125	2865	2619	2386	2165
	energy, ft-lb:	3035	2550	2132	1769	1457
	arc, inches:		+1.4	0	-6.5	-19.0
Win. 150 Ballistic Silvertip	velocity, fps:	3120	2923	2734	2554	2380.
	energy, ft-lb:	3242	2845	2490	2172	1886.
	arc, inches:		+1.3	0	-5.9	-17.2

Centerfire Rifle Ballistics

.270 WINCHESTER SHORT MAGNUM TO 7MM-08 REMINGTON

CARTRIDGE BULLET	RANGE, YARDS:	0	100	200	300	400
Win. 150 Power Point	velocity, fps:	3150	2867	2601	2350	2113
	energy, ft-lb:	3304	2737	2252	1839	1487
	arc, inches:		+1.4	0	-6.5	-19.4
Win. 150 Supreme Elite XP3	velocity, fps:	3120	2926	2740	2561	2389
	energy, ft-lb:	3242	2850	2499	2184	1901
	arc, inches:		+1.3	0	-5.9	-17.1

.270 Weatherby Magnum

CARTRIDGE BULLET	RANGE, YARDS:	0	100	200	300	400
Federal 130 Nosler Partition	velocity, fps:	3200	2960	2740	2520	2320
	energy, ft-lb:	2955	2530	2160	1835	1550
	arc, inches:		+1.2	0	-5.9	-17.3
Federal 130 Sierra GameKing BTSP	velocity, fps:	3200	2980	2780	2580	2400
	energy, ft-lb:	2955	2570	2230	1925	1655
	arc, inches:		+1.2	0	-5.7	-16.6
Federal 140 Trophy Bonded	velocity, fps:	3100	2840	2600	2370	2150.
	energy, ft-lb:	2990	2510	2100	1745	1440
	arc, inches:		+1.4	0	-6.6	-19.3
Federal 130 Trophy Bonded Tip	velocity, fps:	3200	2970	2760	2560	2360
	energy, ft-lb:	2955	2555	2200	1885	1610
	arc, inches:		+1.2	0	-5.9	-16.9
Wby. 100 Pointed Expanding	velocity, fps:	3760	3396	3061	2751	2462
	energy, ft-lb:	3139	2560	2081	1681	1346
	arc, inches:		+2.3	+3.0	0	-7.6
Wby. 130 Pointed Expanding	velocity, fps:	3375	3123	2885	2659	2444
	energy, ft-lb:	3288	2815	2402	2041	1724
	arc, inches:		+2.8	+3.5	0	-8.4
Wby. 130 Nosler Partition	velocity, fps:	3375	3127	2892	2670	2458.
	energy, ft-lb:	3288	2822	2415	2058	1744
	arc, inches:		+2.8	+3.5	0	-8.3
Wby. 140 Nosler Bal. Tip	velocity, fps:	3300	3077	2865	2663	2470.
	energy, ft-lb:	3385	2943	2551	2204	1896
	arc, inches:		+2.9	+3.6	0	-8.4
Wby. 140 Barnes X	velocity, fps:	3250	3032	2825	2628	2438
	energy, ft-lb:	3283	2858	2481	2146	1848
	arc, inches:		+3.0	+3.7	0	-8.7
Wby. 150 Pointed Expanding	velocity, fps:	3245	3028	2821	2623	2434
	energy, ft-lb:	3507	3053	2650	2292	1973
	arc, inches:		+3.0	+3.7	0	-8.7
Wby. 150 Nosler Partition	velocity, fps:	3245	3029	2823	2627	2439.
	energy, ft-lb:	3507	3055	2655	2298	1981
	arc, inches:		+3.0	+3.7	0	-8.

7-30 Waters

CARTRIDGE BULLET	RANGE, YARDS:	0	100	200	300	400
Federal 120 Sierra GameKing BTSP	velocity, fps:	2700	2300	1930	1600	1330.
	energy, ft-lb:	1940	1405	990	685	470
	arc, inches:		+2.6	0	-12.0	-37.6

7mm Mauser (7x57)

CARTRIDGE BULLET	RANGE, YARDS:	0	100	200	300	400
Federal 140 Sierra Pro-Hunt.	velocity, fps:	2660	2450	2260	2070	1890.
	energy, ft-lb:	2200	1865	1585	1330	1110
	arc, inches:		+2.1	0	-9.0	-26.1
Federal 140 Nosler Partition	velocity, fps:	2660	2450	2260	2070	1890.
	energy, ft-lb:	2200	1865	1585	1330	1110
	arc, inches:		+2.1	0	-9.0	-26.1
Federal 175 Hi-Shok RN	velocity, fps:	2440	2140	1860	1600	1380
	energy, ft-lb:	2315	1775	1340	1000	740
	arc, inches:		+3.1	0	-13.3	-40.1
Hornady 139 SP boat-tail	velocity, fps:	2700	2504	2316	2137	1965
	energy, ft-lb:	2251	1936	1656	1410	1192
	arc, inches:		+2.0	0	-8.5	-24.9
Hornady 139 SP Interlock	velocity, fps:	2680	2455	2241	2038	1846
	energy, ft-lb:	2216	1860	1550	1282	1052
	arc, inches:		+2.1	0	-9.1	-26.6
Hornady 139 SP boat-tail LM	velocity, fps:	2830	2620	2450	2250	2070
	energy, ft-lb:	2475	2135	1835	1565	1330
	arc, inches:		+1.8	0	-7.6	-22.1
Hornady 139 SP LM	velocity, fps:	2950	2736	2532	2337	2152.
	energy, ft-lb:	2686	2310	1978	1686	1429
	arc, inches:		+2.0	0	-7.6	-21.5
Hornady 139 SST Superformance	velocity, fps:	2760	2575	2397	2227	2063
	energy, ft-lb:	2351	2046	1774	1530	1314
	arc, inches:		+1.9	0	-7.9	-22.9
Norma 150 Soft Point	velocity, fps:	2690	2479	2278	2087	
	energy, ft-lb:	2411	2048	1729	1450	
	arc, inches:		+2.0	0	-8.8	
PMC 140 Pointed Soft Point	velocity, fps:	2660	2450	2260	2070	1890
	energy, ft-lb:	2200	1865	1585	1330	1110.
	arc, inches:		+2.4	0	-9.6	-27.3
PMC 175 Soft Point	velocity, fps:	2440	2140	1860	1600	1380
	energy, ft-lb:	2315	1775	1340	1000	740
	arc, inches:		+1.5	-3.6	-18.6	-46.8
Rem. 140 PSP Core-Lokt	velocity, fps:	2660	2435	2221	2018	1827
	energy, ft-lb:	2199	1843	1533	1266	1037
	arc, inches:		+2.2	0	-9.2	-27.4
Win. 145 Power-Point	velocity, fps:	2660	2413	2180	1959	1754
	energy, ft-lb:	2279	1875	1530	1236	990
	arc, inches:		+1.1	-2.8	-14.1	-34.4

7x57 R

CARTRIDGE BULLET	RANGE, YARDS:	0	100	200	300	400
Norma 150 FMJ	velocity, fps:	2690	2489	2296	2112	
	energy, ft-lb:	2411	2063	1756	1486	
	arc, inches:		+2.0	0	-8.6	
Norma 154 Soft Point	velocity, fps:	2625	2417	2219	2030	
	energy, ft-lb:	2357	1999	1684	1410	
	arc, inches:		+2.2	0	-9.3	
Norma 156 Oryx	velocity, fps:	2608	2346	2099	1867	
	energy, ft-lb:	2357	1906	1526	1208	
	arc, inches:		+2.4	0	-10.3	

7mm-08 Remington

CARTRIDGE BULLET	RANGE, YARDS:	0	100	200	300	400
Black Hills 140 AccuBond	velocity, fps:	2700				
	energy, ft-lb:					
	arc, inches:					
Federal 140 Nosler Partition	velocity, fps:	2800	2590	2390	2200	2020
	energy, ft-lb:	2435	2085	1775	1500	1265
	arc, inches:		+1.8	0	-8.0	-23.1
Federal 140 Nosler Bal. Tip And AccuBond	velocity, fps:	2800	2610	2430	2260	2100
	energy, ft-lb:	2440	2135	1840	1590	1360.
	arc, inches:		+1.8	0	-7.7	-22.3
Federal 140 Tr. Bonded HE	velocity, fps:	2950	2660	2390	2140	1900
	energy, ft-lb:	2705	2205	1780	1420	1120
	arc, inches:		+1.7	0	-7.9	-23.2
Federal 140 Trophy Copper	velocity, fps:	2800	2610	2440	2260	2100
	energy, ft-lb:	2435	2125	1845	1595	1370
	arc, inches:		+1.8	0	-7.7	-22.2
Federal 150 Sierra Pro-Hunt.	velocity, fps:	2650	2440	2230	2040	1860
	energy, ft-lb:	2340	1980	1660	1390	1150
	arc, inches:		+2.2	0	-9.2	-26.7
Hornady 120 SST Custom Lite	velocity, fps:	2675	2435	2207	1992	1790
	energy, ft-lb:	1907	1579	1298	1057	854
	arc, inches:		+2.2	0	-9.4	-27.5
Hornady 139 SP boat-tail LM	velocity, fps:	3000	2790	2590	2399	2216
	energy, ft-lb:	2777	2403	2071	1776	1515
	arc, inches:		+1.5	0	-6.7	-19.4
Norma 140 Ballistic ST	velocity, fps:	2822	2633	2452	2278	
	energy, ft-lb:	2476	2156	1870	1614	
	arc, inches:		+1.8	0	-7.6	
PMC 139 PSP	velocity, fps:	2850	2610	2384	2170	1969
	energy, ft-lb:	2507	2103	1754	1454	1197
	arc, inches:		+1.8	0	-7.9	-23.3
Rem. 120 Hollow Point	velocity, fps:	3000	2725	2467	2223	1992
	energy, ft-lb:	2398	1979	1621	1316	1058
	arc, inches:		+1.6	0	-7.3	-21.7
Rem. 140 PSP Core-Lokt	velocity, fps:	2860	2625	2402	2189	1988
	energy, ft-lb:	2542	2142	1793	1490	1228
	arc, inches:		+1.8	0	-7.8	-22.9
Rem. 140 PSP boat-tail	velocity, fps:	2860	2656	2460	2273	2094
	energy, ft-lb:	2542	2192	1881	1606	1363
	arc, inches:		+1.7	0	-7.5	-21.7

CARTRIDGE BULLET	RANGE, YARDS:	0	100	200	300	400
Rem. 140 AccuTip BT	velocity, fps:	2860	2670	2488	2313	2145
	energy, ft-lb:	2543	2217	1925	1663	1431
	arc, inches:		+1.7	0	-7.3	-21.2
Rem. 140 Nosler Partition	velocity, fps:	2860	2648	2446	2253	2068
	energy, ft-lb:	2542	2180	1860	1577	1330
	arc, inches:		+1.7	0	-7.6	-22.0
Speer 145 Grand Slam	velocity, fps:	2845	2567	2305	2059	
	energy, ft-lb:	2606	2121	1711	1365	
	arc, inches:		+1.9	0	-8.4	-25.5
Win. 140 Power-Point	velocity, fps:	2800	2523	2268	2027	1802.
	energy, ft-lb:	2429	1980	1599	1277	1010
	arc, inches:		+2.0	0	-8.8	-26.0
Win. 140 Power-Point Plus	velocity, fps:	2875	2597	2336	2090	1859
	energy, ft-lb:	2570	1997	1697	1358	1075
	arc, inches:		+2.0	0	-8.8	26.0
Win. 140 Fail Safe	velocity, fps:	2760	2506	2271	2048	1839
	energy, ft-lb:	2360	1953	1603	1304	1051
	arc, inches:		+2.0	0	-8.8	-25.9
Win. 140 Ballistic Silvertip	velocity, fps:	2770	2572	2382	2200	2026
	energy, ft-lb:	2386	2056	1764	1504	1276
	arc, inches:		+1.9	0	-8.0	-23.8

7x64 Brenneke

CARTRIDGE BULLET	RANGE, YARDS:	0	100	200	300	400
Federal 160 Nosler Partition	velocity, fps:	2650	2480	2310	2150	2000
	energy, ft-lb:	2495	2180	1895	1640	1415
	arc, inches:		+2.1	0	-8.7	-24.9
Norma 140 AccuBond	velocity, fps:	2953	2759	2572	2394	
	energy, ft-lb:	2712	2366	2058	1782	
	arc, inches:		+1.5	0	-6.8	
Norma 154 Soft Point	velocity, fps:	2821	2605	2399	2203	
	energy, ft-lb:	2722	2321	1969	1660	
	arc, inches:		+1.8	0	-7.8	
Norma 156 Oryx	velocity, fps:	2789	2516	2259	2017	
	energy, ft-lb:	2695	2193	1768	1410	
	arc, inches:		+2.0	0	-8.8	
Norma 170 Vulkan	velocity, fps:	2756	2501	2259	2031	
	energy, ft-lb:	2868	2361	1927	1558	
	arc, inches:		+2.0	0	-8.8	
Norma 170 Oryx	velocity, fps:	2756	2481	2222	1979	
	energy, ft-lb:	2868	2324	1864	1478	
	arc, inches:		+2.1	0	-9.2	
Norma 170 Plastic Point	velocity, fps:	2756	2519	2294	2081	
	energy, ft-lb:	2868	2396	1987	1635	
	arc, inches:		+2.0	0	-8.6	
PMC 170 Pointed Soft Point	velocity, fps:	2625	2401	2189	1989	1801
	energy, ft lb:	2601	2175	1808	1493	1224
	arc, inches:		+2.3	0	-9.6	-27.9
Rem. 175 PSP Core-Lokt	velocity, fps:	2650	2445	2248	2061	1883
	energy, ft-lb:	2728	2322	1964	1650	1378
	arc, inches:		+2.2	0	-9.1	-26.4
Speer 160 Grand Slam	velocity, fps:	2600	2376	2164	1962	
	energy, ft-lb:	2401	2006	1663	1368	
	arc, inches:		+2.3	0	-9.8	-28.6
Speer 175 Grand Slam	velocity, fps:	2650	2461	2280	2106	
	energy, ft-lb:	2728	2353	2019	1723	
	arc, inches:		+2.4	0	-9.2	-26.2

7x65 R

CARTRIDGE BULLET	RANGE, YARDS:	0	100	200	300	400
Norma 150 FMJ	velocity, fps:	2756	2552	2357	2170	
	energy, ft-lb:	2530	2169	1850	1569	
	arc, inches:		+1.9	0	-8.2	
Norma 156 Oryx	velocity, fps:	2723	2454	2200	1962	
	energy, ft-lb:	2569	2086	1678	1334	
	arc, inches:		+2.1	0	-9.3	
Norma 170 Plastic Point	velocity, fps:	2625	2390	2167	1956	
	energy, ft-lb:	2602	2157	1773	1445	
	arc, inches:		+2.3	0	-9.7	
Norma 170 Vulkan	velocity, fps:	2657	2392	2143	1909	
	energy, ft-lb:	2666	2161	1734	1377	
	arc, inches:		+2.3	0	-9.9	
Norma 170 Oryx	velocity, fps:	2657	2378	2115	1871	
	energy, ft-lb:	2666	2135	1690	1321	
	arc, inches:		+2.3	0	-10.1	

.284 Winchester

CARTRIDGE BULLET	RANGE, YARDS:	0	100	200	300	400
Win. 150 Power-Point	velocity, fps:	2860	2595	2344	2108	1886
	energy, ft-lb:	2724	2243	1830	1480	1185
	arc, inches:		+2.1	0	-8.5	-24.8

.280 Remington

CARTRIDGE BULLET	RANGE, YARDS:	0	100	200	300	400
Federal 140 Sierra Pro-Hunt.	velocity, fps:	2990	2740	2500	2270	2060
	energy, ft-lb:	2770	2325	1940	1605	1320
	arc, inches:		+1.6	0	-7.0	-20.8
Federal 140 Trophy Bonded	velocity, fps:	2990	2630	2310	2040	1730
	energy, ft-lb:	2770	2155	1655	1250	925
	arc, inches:		+1.6	0	-8.4	-25.4
Federal 140 Trophy	velocity, fps:	2950	2730	2520	2330	2140
Bonded Tip	energy, ft-lb:	2705	2320	1980	1680	1420
	arc, inches:		+1.6	0	-7.0	-20.6
Federal 140 Tr. Bonded HE	velocity, fps:	3150	2850	2570	2300	2050
	energy, ft-lb:	3085	2520	2050	1650	1310
	arc, inches:		+1.4	0	-6.7	-20.0
Federal 140 Nos. AccuBond	velocity, fps:	3000	2800	2620	2440	2260
And Bal. Tip	energy, ft-lb:	2800	2445	2130	1845	1590
And Solid Base	arc, inches:		+1.5	0	-6.5	-18.9
Federal 150 Hi-Shok	velocity, fps:	2890	2670	2460	2260	2060
	energy, ft-lb:	2780	2370	2015	1695	1420
	arc, inches:		+1.7	0	-7.5	-21.8
Federal 150 Nosler Partition	velocity, fps:	2890	2690	2490	2310	2130
	energy, ft-lb:	2780	2405	2070	1770	1510.
	arc, inches:		+1.7	0	-7.2	-21.1
Federal 150 Nos. AccuBond	velocity, fps	2800	2630	2460	2300	2150
	energy, ft-lb:	2785	2455	2155	1885	1645
	arc, inches:		+1.8	0	-7.5	-21.5
Federal 160 Trophy Bonded	velocity, fps:	2800	2570	2350	2140	1940
	energy, ft-lb:	2785	2345	1960	1625	1340
	arc, inches:		+1.9	0	-8.3	-24.0
Hornady 139 SPBT LMmoly	velocity, fps:	3110	2888	2675	2473	2280.
	energy, ft-lb:	2985	2573	2209	1887	1604
	arc, inches:		+1.4	0	-6.5	-18.6
Hornady 139 SST	velocity, fps:	3090	2891	2700	2518	2343
Superformance	energy, ft-lb:	2947	2579	2250	1957	1694
	arc, inches:		+1.3	0	-6.1	-17.7
Norma 156 Oryx	velocity, fps:	2789	2516	2259	2017	
	energy, ft-lb:	2695	2193	1768	1410	
	arc, inches:		+2.0	0	-8.8	
Norma 170 Plastic Point	velocity, fps:	2707	2468	2241	2026	
	energy, ft-lb:	2767	2299	1896	1550	
	arc, inches:		+2.1	0	-9.1	
Norma 170 Vulkan	velocity, fps:	2592	2346	2113	1894	
	energy, ft-lb:	2537	2078	1686	1354	
	arc, inches:		+2.4	0	-10.2	
Norma 170 Oryx	velocity, fps:	2690	2416	2159	1918	
	energy, ft-lb:	2732	2204	1760	1389	
	arc, inches:		+2.2	0	-9.7	
Rem. 140 PSP Core-Lokt	velocity, fps:	3000	2758	2528	2309	2102
	energy, ft-lb:	2797	2363	1986	1657	1373
	arc, inches:		+1.5	0	-7.0	-20.5
Rem. 140 PSP boat-tail	velocity, fps:	2860	2656	2460	2273	2094
	energy, ft-lb:	2542	2192	1881	1606	1363
	arc, inches:		+1.7	0	-7.5	-21.7
Rem. 140 Nosler Bal. Tip	velocity, fps:	3000	2804	2616	2436	2263
	energy, ft-lb:	2799	2445	2128	1848	1593
	arc, inches:		+1.5	0	-6.8	-19.0

Centerfire Rifle Ballistics

.280 REMINGTON TO 7MM REMINGTON MAGNUM

CARTRIDGE BULLET	RANGE, YARDS:	0	100	200	300	400
Rem. 140 AccuTip	velocity, fps:	3000	2804	2617	2437	2265
	energy, ft-lb:	2797	2444	2129	1846	1594
	arc, inches:		+1.5	0	-6.8	-19.0
Rem. 150 PSP Core-Lokt	velocity, fps:	2890	2624	2373	2135	1912
	energy, ft-lb:	2781	2293	1875	1518	1217
	arc, inches:		+1.8	0	-8.0	-23.6
Rem. 165 SP Core-Lokt	velocity, fps:	2820	2510	2220	1950	1701
	energy, ft-lb:	2913	2308	1805	1393	1060.
	arc, inches:		+2.0	0	-9.1	-27.4
Speer 145 Grand Slam	velocity, fps:	2900	2619	2354	2105	
	energy, ft-lb:	2707	2207	1784	1426	
	arc, inches:		+2.1	0	-8.4	-24.7
Speer 160 Grand Slam	velocity, fps:	2890	2652	2425	2210	
	energy, ft-lb:	2967	2497	2089	1735	
	arc, inches:		+1.7	0	-7.7	-22.4
Win. 140 Fail Safe	velocity, fps:	3050	2756	2480	2221	1977
	energy, ft-lb:	2893	2362	1913	1533	1216
	arc, inches:		+1.5	0	-7.2	-21.5
Win. 140 Ballistic Silvertip	velocity, fps:	3040	2842	2653	2471	2297
	energy, ft-lb:	2872	2511	2187	1898	1640
	arc, inches:		+1.4	0	-6.3	-18.4

.280 Ackley Improved

CARTRIDGE BULLET	RANGE, YARDS:	0	100	200	300	400
Nosler 140 AccuBond	velocity, fps:	3150	2947	2753	2567	2389
	energy, ft-lb:	3084	2700	2355	2048	1774
	arc, inches:	-1.5	+1.1	0	-5.0	-16.8
Nosler 150 ABLR	velocity, fps:	2930	2775	2626	2482	2342
	energy, ft-lb:	2858	2565	2297	2052	1827
	arc, inches:	-1.5	+1.5	0	-6.6	-18.7
Nosler 160 Partition	velocity, fps:	2950	2752	2562	2380	2206
	energy, ft-lb:	3091	2690	2332	2013	1729
	arc, inches:	-1.5	+1.5	0	-6.7	-19.4

7mm Remington Magnum

CARTRIDGE BULLET	RANGE, YARDS:	0	100	200	300	400
A-Square 175 Monolithic Solid	velocity, fps:	2860	2557	2273	2008	1771
	energy, ft-lb:	3178	2540	2008	1567	1219
	arc, inches:		+1.92	0	-8.7	-25.9
Black Hills 140 Nos. Bal. Tip	velocity, fps:	3150				
	energy, ft-lb:	3084				
	arc, inches:					
Black Hills 140 Barnes XLC	velocity, fps:	3150				
	energy, ft-lb:	3084				
	arc, inches:					
Black Hills 140 Nos. Partition	velocity, fps:	3150				
	energy, ft-lb:	3084				
	arc, inches:					
Federal 140 Nosler Bal. Tip And AccuBond	velocity, fps:	3110	2910	2720	2530	2360.
	energy, ft-lb:	3005	2630	2295	1995	1725
	arc, inches:		+1.3	0	-6.0	-17.4
Federal 140 Nosler Partition	velocity, fps:	3150	2930	2710	2510	2320
	energy, ft-lb:	3085	2660	2290	1960	1670
	arc, inches:		+1.3	0	-6.0	-17.5
Federal 140 Trophy Bonded	velocity, fps:	3150	2910	2680	2460	2250.
	energy, ft-lb:	3085	2630	2230	1880	1575
	arc, inches:		+1.3	0	-6.1	-18.1
Federal 140 Trophy Copper	velocity, fps:	3150	2950	2760	2570	2400
	energy, ft-lb:	3085	2705	2360	2055	1785
	arc, inches:		+1.3	0	-5.9	-16.9
Federal 150 Hi-Shok	velocity, fps:	3110	2830	2570	2320	2090
	energy, ft-lb:	3220	2670	2200	1790	1450
	arc, inches:		+1.4	0	-6.7	-19.9
Federal 150 Nosler Bal. Tip	velocity, fps:	3110	2910	2720	2540	2370
	energy, ft-lb:	3220	2825	2470	2150	1865
	arc, inches:		+1.3	0	-6.0	-17.4
Federal 150 Nos. Solid Base	velocity, fps:	3100	2890	2690	2500	2310
	energy, ft-lb:	3200	2780	2405	2075	1775
	arc, inches:		+1.3	0	-6.2	-17.8
Federal 150 Sierra GameKing BTSP	velocity, fps:	3110	2920	2750	2580	2410
	energy, ft-lb:	3220	2850	2510	2210	1930
	arc, inches:		+1.3 0	-5.9	-17.0	
Federal 150 Trophy Copper	velocity, fps:	3025	2830	2650	2470	2300
	energy, ft-lb:	3045	2675	2335	2035	1765
	arc, inches:		+1.4	0	-6.4	-18.4
Federal 160 Barnes XLC	velocity, fps:	2940	2760	2580	2410	2240
	energy, ft-lb:	3070	2695	2360	2060	1785
	arc, inches:		+1.5	0	-6.8	-19.6
Federal 160 Sierra Pro-Hunt.	velocity, fps:	2940	2730	2520	2320	2140
	energy, ft-lb:	3070	2640	2260	1920	1620
	arc, inches:		+1.6	0	-7.1	-20.6
Federal 160 Nosler Partition	velocity, fps:	2950	2770	2590	2420	2250.
	energy, ft-lb:	3090	2715	2375	2075	1800
	arc, inches:		+1.5	0	-6.7	-19.4
Federal 160 Nos. AccuBond	velocity, fps:	2950	2770	2600	2440	2280.
	energy, ft-lb:	3090	2730	2405	2110	1845
	arc, inches:		+1.5	0	-6.6	-19.1
Federal 160 Trophy Bonded	velocity, fps:	2940	2660	2390	2140	1900
	energy, ft-lb:	3070	2505	2025	1620	1280.
	arc, inches:		+1.7	0	-7.9	-23.3
Federal 165 Sierra GameKing BTSP	velocity, fps:	2950	2800	2650	2510	2370.
	energy, ft-lb:	3190	2865	2570	2300	2050
	arc, inches:		+1.5	0	-6.4	-18.4
Federal 175 Hi-Shok	velocity, fps:	2860	2650	2440	2240	2060
	energy, ft-lb:	3180	2720	2310	1960	1640
	arc, inches:		+1.7	0	-7.6	-22.1
Federal 175 Trophy Bonded	velocity, fps:	2860	2600	2350	2120	1900
	energy, ft-lb:	3180	2625	2150	1745	1400
	arc, inches:		+1.8	0	-8.2	-24.0
Hornady 139 SPBT	velocity, fps:	3150	2933	2727	2530	2341
	energy, ft-lb:	3063	2656	2296	1976	1692
	arc, inches:		+1.2	0	-6.1	-17.7
Hornady 139 SPBT HMmoly	velocity, fps:	3250	3041	2822	2613	2413
	energy, ft-lb:	3300	2854	2458	2106	1797
	arc, inches:		+1.1 0	-5.7	-16.6	
Hornady 139 SST (or Interbond)	velocity, fps:	3150	2948	2754	2569	2391
	energy, ft-lb:	3062	2681	2341	2037	1764
	arc, inches:		+1.1	0	-5.7	-16.7
Hornady 139 SST Custom Lite	velocity, fps:	2800	2613	2434	2262	2097
	energy, ft-lb:	2420	2108	1829	1579	1357
	arc, inches:		+1.8	0	-7.7	-22.2
Hornady 139 SST LM (or Interbond)	velocity, fps:	3250	3044	2847	2657	2475
	energy, ft-lb:	3259	2860	2501	2178	1890
	arc, inches:		+1.1	0	-5.5	-16.2
Hornady 139 SPBT HMmoly	velocity, fps:	3250	3041	2822	2613	2413
	energy, ft-lb:	3300	2854	2458	2106	1797.
	arc, inches:		+1.1	0	-5.7	-16.6
Hornady 154 Soft Point	velocity, fps:	3035	2814	2604	2404	2212
	energy, ft-lb:	3151	2708	2319	1977	1674
	arc, inches:		+1.3	0	-6.7	-19.3
Hornady 154 SST (or Interbond)	velocity, fps:	3035	2850	2672	2501	2337
	energy, ft-lb:	3149	2777	2441	2139	1867
	arc, inches:		+1.4	0	-6.5	-18.7
Hornady 162 SP boat-tail	velocity, fps:	2940	2757	2582	2413	2251
	energy, ft-lb:	3110	2735	2399	2095	1823
	arc, inches:		+1.6	0	-6.7	-19.7
Hornady 162 SST Superformance	velocity, fps:	3030	2856	2689	2527	2372
	energy, ft-lb:	3302	2933	2600	2298	2023
	arc, inches:		+1.4	0	-6.2	-17.8
Hornady 175 SP	velocity, fps:	2860	2650	2440	2240	2060.
	energy, ft-lb:	3180	2720	2310	1960	1640
	arc, inches:		+2.0	0	-7.9	-22.7
Norma 140 Nosler Bal. Tip	velocity, fps:	3150	2936	2732	2537	
	energy, ft-lb:	3085	2680	2320	2001	
	arc, inches:		+1.2	0	-5.9	
Norma 140 Barnes X TS	velocity, fps:	3117	2912	2716	2529	
	energy, ft-lb:	3021	2637	2294	1988	
	arch, inches:		+1.3	0	-6.0	
Norma 150 Scirocco	velocity, fps:	3117	2934	2758	2589	
	energy, ft-lb:	3237	2869	2535	2234	
	arc, inches:		+1.2	0	-5.8	
Norma 156 Oryx	velocity, fps:	2953	2670	2404	2153	
	energy, ft-lb:	3021	2470	2002	1607	
	arc, inches:		+1.7	0	-7.7	

Centerfire Rifle Ballistics

7MM REMINGTON MAGNUM TO 7MM WINCHESTER SHORT MAGNUM

CARTRIDGE BULLET	RANGE, YARDS:	0	100	200	300	400
Norma 170 Vulkan	velocity, fps:	3018	2747	2493	2252	
	energy, ft-lb:	3439	2850	2346	1914	
	arc, inches:		+1.5	0	-2.8	
Norma 170 Oryx	velocity, fps:	2887	2601	2333	2080	
	energy, ft-lb:	3147	2555	2055	1634	
	arc, inches:		+1.8	0	-8.2	
Norma 170 Plastic Point	velocity, fps:	3018	2762	2519	2290	
	energy, ft-lb:	3439	2880	2394	1980	
	arc, inches:		+1.5	0	-7.0	
PMC 140 Barnes X	velocity, fps:	3000	2808	2624	2448	2279
	energy, ft-lb:	2797	2451	2141	1863	1614
	arc, inches:		+1.5	0	-6.6	18.9
PMC 140 Pointed Soft Point	velocity, fps:	3099	2878	2668	2469	2279
	energy, ft-lb:	2984	2574	2212	1895	1614
	arc, inches:		+1.4	0	-6.2	-18.1
PMC 140 SP boat-tail	velocity, fps:	3125	2891	2669	2457	2255
	energy, ft-lb:	3035	2597	2213	1877	1580
	arc, inches:		+1.4	0	-6.3	-18.4
PMC 160 Barnes X	velocity, fps:	2800	2639	2484	2334	2189
	energy, ft-lb:	2785	2474	2192	1935	1703
	arc, inches:		+1.8	0	-7.4	-21.2
PMC 160 Pointed Soft Point	velocity, fps:	2914	2748	2586	2428	2276
	energy, ft-lb:	3016	2682	2375	2095	1840
	arc, inches:		+1.6	0	-6.7	-19.4
PMC 160 SP boat-tail	velocity, fps:	2900	2696	2501	2314	2135
	energy, ft-lb:	2987	2582	2222	1903	1620
	arc, inches:		+1.7	0	-7.2	-21.0
PMC 175 Pointed Soft Point	velocity, fps:	2860	2645	2442	2244	2957
	energy, ft-lb:	3178	2718	2313	1956	1644
	arc, inches:		+2.0	0	-7.9	-22.7
Remington 140 Copper Solid Tipped	velocity, fps:	3175	2964	2762	2570	2385
	energy, ft-lb:	3133	2730	2372	2053	1768
	arc, inches:		+1.4	0	-6.0	-17.6
Rem. 140 PSP Core-Lokt mr	velocity, fps:	2710	2482	2265	2059	1865
	energy, ft-lb:	2283	1915	1595	1318	1081
	arc, inches:		+1.0	-2.5	-12.8	-31.3
Rem. 140 PSP Core-Lokt	velocity, fps:	3175	2923	2684	2458	2243
	energy, ft-lb:	3133	2655	2240	1878	1564
	arc, inches:		+2.2	+1.9	-3.2	-14.2
Rem. 140 PSP boat-tail	velocity, fps:	3175	2956	2747	2547	2356
	energy, ft-lb:	3133	2715	2345	2017	1726
	arc, inches:		+2.2	+1.6	-3.1	-13.4
Rem. 150 AccuTip	velocity, fps:	3110	2926	2749	2579	2415
	energy, ft-lb:	3221	2850	2516	2215	1943
	arc, inches:		+1.3	0	-5.9	-17.0
Rem. 150 PSP Core-Lokt	velocity, fps:	3110	2830	2568	2320	2085
	energy, ft-lb:	3221	2667	2196	1792	1448
	arc, inches:		+1.3	0	-6.6	-20.2
Rem. 150 Nosler Bal. Tip	velocity, fps:	3110	2912	2723	2542	2367
	energy, ft-lb:	3222	2825	2470	2152	1867
	arc, inches:		+1.2	0	-5.9	-17.3
Rem. 150 Swift Scirocco	velocity, fps:	3110	2927	2751	2582	2419
	energy, ft-lb:	3221	2852	2520	2220	1948
	arc, inches:		+1.3	0	-5.9	-17.0
Rem. 160 Swift A-Frame	velocity, fps:	2900	2659	2430	2212	2006
	energy, ft-lb:	2987	2511	2097	1739	1430
	arc, inches:		+1.7	0	-7.6	-22.4
Rem. 160 Nosler Partition	velocity, fps:	2950	2752	2563	2381	2207
	energy, ft-lb:	3091	2690	2333	2014	1730
	arc, inches:		+0.6	-1.9	-9.6	-23.6
Rem. 175 PSP Core-Lokt	velocity, fps:	2860	2645	2440	2244	2057
	energy, ft-lb:	3178	2718	2313	1956	1644
	arc, inches:		+1.7	0	-7.6	-22.1
Speer 145 Grand Slam	velocity, fps:	3140	2843	2565	2304	
	energy, ft-lb:	3174	2602	2118	1708	
	arc, inches:		+1.4	0	-6.7	
Speer 175 Grand Slam	velocity, fps:	2850	2653	2463	2282	
	energy, ft-lb:	3156	2734	2358	2023	
	arc, inches:		+1.7	0	-7.5	-21.7
Win. 140 Fail Safe	velocity, fps:	3150	2861	2589	2333	2092
	energy, ft-lb:	3085	2544	2085	1693	1361
	arc, inches:		+1.4	0	-6.6	-19.5
Win. 140 Ballistic Silvertip	velocity, fps:	3100	2889	2687	2494	2310
	energy, ft-lb:	2988	2595	2245	1934	1659.
	arc, inches:		+1.3	0	-6.2	-17.9
Win. 140 AccuBond CT	velocity, fps:	3180	2965	2760	2565	2377
	energy, ft-lb:	3143	2733	2368	2044	1756
	arc, inches:		+1.2	0	-5.8	-16.9
Win. 150 Power-Point	velocity, fps:	3090	2812	2551	2304	2071
	energy, ft-lb:	3181	2634	2167	1768	1429
	arc, inches:		+1.5	0	-6.8	-20.2
Win. 150 Power-Point Plus	velocity, fps:	3130	2849	2586	2337	2102
	energy, ft-lb:	3264	2705	2227	1819	1472
	arc, inches:		+1.4	0	-6.6	-19.6
Win. 150 Ballistic Silvertip	velocity, fps:	3100	2903	2714	2533	2359
	energy, ft-lb:	3200	2806	2453	2136	1853
	arc, inches:		+1.3	0	-6.0	-17.5
Win. 160 AccuBond	velocity, fps:	2950	2766	2590	2420	2257
	energy, ft-lb:	3091	2718	2382	2080	1809
	arc, inches:		+1.5	0	-6.7	-19.4
Win. 160 Partition Gold	velocity, fps:	2950	2743	2546	2357	2176
	energy, ft-lb:	3093	2674	2303	1974	1682
	arc, inches:		+1.6	0	-6.9	-20.1
Win. 160 Fail Safe	velocity, fps:	2920	2678	2449	2331	2025
	energy, ft-lb:	3030	2549	2131	1769	1457
	arc, inches:		+1.7	0	-7.5	-22.0
Win. 175 Power-Point	velocity, fps:	2860	2645	2440	2244	2057
	energy, ft-lb:	3178	2718	2313	1956	1644
	arc, inches:		+2.0	0	-7.9	-22.7

7MM REMINGTON SHORT ULTRA MAGNUM

CARTRIDGE BULLET	RANGE, YARDS:	0	100	200	300	400
Rem. 140 PSP C-L Ultra	velocity, fps:	3175	2934	2707	2490	2283
	energy, ft-lb:	3133	2676	2277	1927	1620.
	arc, inches:		+1.3	0	-6.0	-17.7
Rem. 150 PSP Core-Lokt	velocity, fps:	3110	2828	2563	2313	2077
	energy, ft-lb:	3221	2663	2188	1782	1437
	arc, inches:		+2.5	+2.1	-3.6	-15.8
Rem. 160 Partition	velocity, fps:	2960	2762	2572	2390	2215
	energy, ft-lb:	3112	2709	2350	2029	1744
	arc, inches:		+2.6	+2.2	-3.6	-15.4
Rem. 160 PSP C-L Ultra	velocity, fps:	2960	2733	2518	2313	2117
	energy, ft-lb:	3112	2654	2252	1900	1592
	arc, inches:		+2.7	+2.2	-3.7	-16.2

7MM WINCHESTER SHORT MAGNUM

CARTRIDGE BULLET	RANGE, YARDS:	0	100	200	300	400
Federal 140 Nos. AccuBond	velocity, fps:	3250	3040	2840	2660	2470
	energy, ft-lb:	3285	2875	2515	2190	1900
	arc, inches:		+1.1	0	-5.5	-15.8
Federal 140 Nos. Bal. Tip	velocity, fps:	3310	3100	2900	2700	2520
	energy, ft-lb:	3405	2985	2610	2270	1975
	arc, inches:		+1.1	0	-5.2	15.2
Federal 150 Nos. Solid Base	velocity, fps:	3230	3010	2800	2600	2410
	energy, ft-lb:	3475	3015	2615	2255	1935
	arc, inches:		+1.3	0	-5.6	-16.3
Federal 150 Trophy Copper	velocity, fps:	3140	2940	2750	2570	2400
	energy, ft-lb:	3285	2885	2525	2205	1915
	arc, inches:		+1.3	0	-5.9	-16.9
Federal 160 Nos. AccuBond	velocity, fps:	3120	2940	2760	2590	2430
	energy, ft-lb:	3460	3065	2710	2390	2095
	arc, inches:		+1.3	0	-5.9	-16.8
Federal 160 Nos. Partition	velocity, fps:	3160	2950	2750	2560	2380.
	energy, ft-lb:	3545	3095	2690	2335	2015.
	arc, inches:		+1.2	0	-5.9	-16.9

Centerfire Rifle Ballistics

7MM WINCHESTER SHORT MAGNUM TO 7MM REMINGTON ULTRA MAGNUM

BALLISTICS

CARTRIDGE BULLET	RANGE, YARDS:	0	100	200	300	400
Federal 160 Barnes TS	velocity, fps:	2990	2780	2590	2400	2220
	energy, ft-lb:	3175	2755	2380	2045	1750
	arc, inches:		+1.5	0	-6.6	-19.4
Federal 160 Trophy Bonded	velocity, fps:	3120	2880	2650	2440	2230
	energy, ft-lb:	3460	2945	2500	2105	1765
	arc, inches:		+1.4	0	-6.3	-18.5
Federal 160 Trophy Bonded Tip	velocity, fps:	3000	2820	2640	2470	2310
	energy, ft-lb:	3195	2820	2480	2170	1895
	arc, inches:		+1.5	0	-6.4	-18.5
Win. 140 Bal. Silvertip	velocity, fps:	3225	3008	2801	2603	2414
	energy, ft-lb:	3233	2812	2438	2106	1812
	arc, inches:		+1.2	0	-5.6	-16.4
Win. 140 AccuBond CT	velocity, fps:	3225	3008	2801	2604	2415
	energy, ft-lb:	3233	2812	2439	2107	1812
	arc, inches:		+1.2	0	-5.6	-16.4
Win. 150 Power Point	velocity, fps:	3200	2915	2648	2396	2157
	energy, ft-lb:	3410	2830	23351911		1550
	arc, inches:		+1.3	0	-6.3	-18.6
Win. 160 AccuBond	velocity, fps:	3050	2862	2682	2509	2342
	energy, ft-lb:	3306	2911	2556	2237	1950
	arc, inches:		1.4	0	-6.2	-17.9
Win. 160 Fail Safe	velocity, fps:	2990	2744	2512	2291	2081
	energy, ft-lb:	3176	2675	2241	1864	1538
	arc, inches:		+1.6	0	-7.1	-20.8

7MM WEATHERBY MAGNUM

CARTRIDGE BULLET	RANGE, YARDS:	0	100	200	300	400
Federal 160 Nosler Partition	velocity, fps:	3050	2850	2650	2470	2290
	energy, ft-lb:	3305	2880	2505	2165	1865
	arc, inches:		+1.4	0	-6.3	-18.4
Federal 160 Sierra GameKing BTSP	velocity, fps:	3050	2880	2710	2560	2400
	energy, ft-lb:	3305	2945	2615	2320	2050
	arc, inches:		+1.4	0	-6.1	-17.4
Federal 160 Trophy Bonded	velocity, fps:	3050	2730	2420	2140	1880.
	energy, ft-lb:	3305	2640	2085	1630	1255
	arc, inches:		+1.6	0	-7.6	-22.7
Federal 160 Trophy Bonded Tip	velocity, fps:	3100	2910	2730	2560	2390
	energy, ft-lb:	3415	3015	2655	2330	2035
	arc, inches:		+1.3	0	-6.0	-17.2
Hornady 139 GMX Superformance	velocity, fps:	3300	3091	2891	2701	2519
	energy, ft-lb:	3361	2948	2580	2252	1958
	arc, inches:		+1.1	0	-5.2	-15.2
Hornady 154 Soft Point	velocity, fps:	3200	2971	2753	2546	2348.
	energy, ft-lb:	3501	3017	2592	2216	1885
	arc, inches:		+1.2	0	-5.8	-17.0
Hornady 154 SST (or Interbond)	velocity, fps:	3200	3009	2825	2648	2478
	energy, ft-lb:	3501	3096	2729	2398	2100
	arc, inches:		+1.2	0	-5.7	-16.5
Hornady 175 Soft Point	velocity, fps:	2910	2709	2516	2331	2154
	energy, ft-lb:	3290	2850	2459	2111	1803
	arc, inches:		+1.6	0	-7.1	-20.6
Wby. 139 Pointed Expanding	velocity, fps:	3340	3079	2834	2601	2380.
	energy, ft-lb:	3443	2926	2478	2088	1748
	arc, inches:		+2.9	+3.6	0	-8.7
Wby. 140 Nosler Partition	velocity, fps:	3303	3069	2847	2636	2434
	energy, ft-lb:	3391	2927	2519	2159	1841
	arc, inches:		+2.9	+3.6	0	-8.5
Wby. 150 Nosler Bal. Tip	velocity, fps:	3300	3093	2896	2708	2527
	energy, ft-lb:	3627	3187	2793	2442	2127
	arc, inches:		+2.8	+3.5	0	-8.2
Wby. 150 Barnes X	velocity, fps:	3100	2901	2710	2527	2352
	energy, ft-lb:	3200	2802	2446	2127	1842
	arc, inches:		+3.3	+4.0	0	-9.4
Wby. 154 Pointed Expanding	velocity, fps:	3260	3028	2807	2597	2397
	energy, ft-lb:	3634	3134	2694	2307	1964
	arc, inches:		+3.0	+3.7	0	-8.8
Wby. 160 Nosler Partition	velocity, fps:	3200	2991	2791	2600	2417
	energy, ft-lb:	3638	3177	2767	2401	2075.
	arc, inches:		+3.1	+3.8	0	-8.9
Wby. 175 Pointed Expanding	velocity, fps:	3070	2861	2662	2471	2288
	energy, ft-lb:	3662	3181	2753	2373	2034
	arc, inches:		+3.5	+4.2	0	-9.9

7MM DAKOTA

CARTRIDGE BULLET	RANGE, YARDS:	0	100	200	300	400
Dakota 140 Barnes X	velocity, fps:	3500	3253	3019	2798	2587
	energy, ft-lb:	3807	3288	2833	2433	2081
	arc, inches:		+2.0	+2.1	-1.5	-9.6
Dakota 160 Barnes X	velocity, fps:	3200	3001	2811	2630	2455
	energy, ft-lb:	3637	3200	2808	2456	2140
	arc, inches:		+2.1	+1.9	-2.8	-12.5

7MM STW

CARTRIDGE BULLET	RANGE, YARDS:	0	100	200	300	400
A-Square 140 Nos. Bal. Tip	velocity, fps:	3450	3254	3067	2888	2715
	energy, ft-lb:	3700	3291	2924	2592	2292
	arc, inches:		+2.2	+3.0	0	-7.3
A-Square 160 Nosler Part.	velocity, fps:	3250	3071	2900	2735	2576.
	energy, ft-lb:	3752	3351	2987	2657	2357
	arc, inches:		+2.8	+3.5	0	-8.2
A-Square 160 SP boat-tail	velocity, fps:	3250	3087	2930	2778	2631
	energy, ft-lb:	3752	3385	3049	2741	2460
	arc, inches:		+2.8	+3.4	0	-8.0
Federal 140 Trophy Bonded	velocity, fps:	3330	3080	2850	2630	2420
	energy, ft-lb:	3435	2950	2520	2145	1815
	arc, inches:		+1.1	0	-5.4	-15.8
Federal 150 Trophy Bonded	velocity, fps:	3250	3010	2770	2560	2350.
	energy, ft-lb:	3520	3010	2565	2175	1830
	arc, inches:		+1.2	0	-5.7	-16.7
Federal 160 Sierra GameKing BTSP	velocity, fps:	3200	3020	2850	2670	2530.
	energy, ft-lb:	3640	3245	2890	2570	2275
	arc, inches:		+1.1	0	-5.5	-15.7
Federal 160 Trophy Bonded Tip	velocity, fps:	3100	2910	2730	2560	2390
	energy, ft-lb:	3415	3015	2655	2330	2035
	arc, inches:		+1.3	0	-6.0	-17.2
Nosler 175 ABLR	velocity, fps:	2900	2760	2625	2493	2366
	energy, ft-lb:	3267	2960	2677	2416	2175
	arc, inches:	-1.5	+1.5	0	-6.6	-18.8
Rem. 140 PSP Core-Lokt	velocity, fps:	3325	3064	2818	2585	2364
	energy, ft-lb:	3436	2918	2468	2077	1737
	arc, inches:		+2.0	+1.7	-2.9	-12.8
Rem. 140 Swift A-Frame	velocity, fps:	3325	3020	2735	2467	2215
	energy, ft-lb:	3436	2834	2324	1892	1525
	arc, inches:		+2.1	+1.8	-3.1	-13.8
Speer 145 Grand Slam	velocity, fps:	3300	2992	2075	2435	
	energy, ft-lb:	3506	2882	2355	1909	
	arc, inches:		+1.2	0	-6.0	-17.8
Win. 140 Ballistic Silvertip	velocity, fps:	3320	3100	2890	2690	2499
	energy, ft-lb:	3427	2982	2597	2250	1941
	arc, inches:		+1.1	0	-5.2	-15.2
Win. 150 Power-Point	velocity, fps:	3250	2957	2683	2424	2181
	energy, ft-lb:	3519	2913	2398	1958	1584
	arc, inches:		+1.2	0	-6.1	-18.1
Win. 160 Fail Safe	velocity, fps:	3150	2894	2652	2422	2204
	energy, ft-lb:	3526	2976	2499	2085	1727
	arc, inches:		+1.3	0	-6.3	-18.5

7MM REMINGTON ULTRA MAGNUM

CARTRIDGE BULLET	RANGE, YARDS:	0	100	200	300	400
Nosler 175 ABLR	velocity, fps:	3040	2896	2756	2621	2490
	energy, ft-lb:	3590	3258	2952	2669	2409
	arc, inches:	-1.5	+1.3	0	-5.9	-16.9
Rem. 140 PSP Core-Lokt	velocity, fps:	3425	3158	2907	2669	2444
	energy, ft-lb:	3646	3099	2626	2214	1856
	arc, inches:		+1.8	+1.6	-2.7	-11.9
Rem. 140 Nosler Partition	velocity, fps:	3425	3184	2956	2740	2534
	energy, ft-lb:	3646	3151	2715	2333	1995
	arc, inches:		+1.7	+1.6	-2.6	-11.4
Rem. 160 Nosler Partition	velocity, fps:	3200	2991	2791	2600	2417
	energy, ft-lb:	3637	3177	2767	2401	2075
	arc, inches:		+2.1	+1.8	-3.0	-12.9

Centerfire Rifle Ballistics

7.21 (.284) FIREHAWK TO .30-30 WINCHESTER

7.21 (.284) Firehawk

CARTRIDGE BULLET	RANGE, YARDS:	0	100	200	300	400
Lazzeroni 140 Nosler Part.	velocity, fps:	3580	3349	3130	2923	2724
	energy, ft-lb:	3985	3488	3048	2656	2308
	arc, inches:		+2.2	+2.9	0	-7.0
Lazzeroni 160 Swift A-Fr.	velocity, fps:	3385	3167	2961	2763	2574
	energy, ft-lb:	4072	3565	3115	2713	2354
	arc, inches:		+2.6	+3.3	0	-7.8

7.5x55 Swiss

CARTRIDGE BULLET	RANGE, YARDS:	0	100	200	300	400
Norma 180 Soft Point	velocity, fps:	2651	2432	2223	2025	
	energy, ft-lb:	2810	2364	1976	1639	
	arc, inches:		+2.2	0	-9.3	
Norma 180 Oryx	velocity, fps:	2493	2222	1968	1734	
	energy, ft-lb:	2485	1974	1549	1201	
	arc, inches:		+2.7	0	-11.8	

7.62x39 Russian

CARTRIDGE BULLET	RANGE, YARDS:	0	100	200	300	400
Federal 123 Hi-Shok	velocity, fps:	2300	2030	1780	1550	1350
	energy, ft-lb:	1445	1125	860	655	500.
	arc, inches:		0	-7.0	-25.1	
Federal 124 FMJ	velocity, fps:	2300	2030	1780	1560	1360
	energy, ft-lb:	1455	1135	875	670	510
	arc, inches:		+3.5	0	-14.6	-43.5
PMC 123 FMJ	velocity, fps:	2350	2072	1817	1583	1368
	energy, ft-lb:	1495	1162	894	678	507
	arc, inches:		0	-5.0	-26.4	-67.8
PMC 125 Pointed Soft Point	velocity, fps:	2320	2046	1794	1563	1350
	energy, ft-lb:	1493	1161	893	678	505.
	arc, inches:		0	-5.2	-27.5	-70.6
Rem. 125 Pointed Soft Point	velocity, fps:	2365	2062	1783	1533	1320
	energy, ft-lb:	1552	1180	882	652	483
	arc, inches:		0	-6.7	-24.5	
Win. 123 Soft Point	velocity, fps:	2365	2033	1731	1465	1248
	energy, ft-lb:	1527	1129	818	586	425
	arc, inches:		+3.8	0	-15.4	-46.3

.30 Carbine

CARTRIDGE BULLET	RANGE, YARDS:	0	100	200	300	400
Federal 110 Hi-Shok RN	velocity, fps:	1990	1570	1240	1040	920
	energy, ft-lb:	965	600	375	260	210
	arc, inches:		0	-12.8	-46.9	
Federal 110 FMJ	velocity, fps:	1990	1570	1240	1040	920
	energy, ft-lb:	965	600	375	260	210
	arc, inches:		0	-12.8	-46.9	
Hornady 110 FTX (20-inch barrel)	velocity, fps:	2000	1601	1279	1067	
	energy, ft-lb:	977	626	399	278	
	arc, inches:		0	-12.9	-47.2	
Magtech 110 FMC	velocity, fps:	1990	1654			
	energy, ft-lb:	965	668			
	arc, inches:		0			
PMC 110 FMJ	(and RNSP)velocity, fps:	1927	1548	1248		
	energy, ft-lb:	906	585	380		
	arc, inches:		0	-14.2		
Rem. 110 Soft Point	velocity, fps:	1990	1567	1236	1035	923
	energy, ft-lb:	967	600	373	262	208
	arc, inches:		0	-12.9	-48.6	
Win. 110 Hollow Soft Point	velocity, fps:	1990	1567	1236	1035	923
	energy, ft-lb:	967	600	373	262	208
	arc, inches:		0	-13.5	-49.9	

.30 T/C Hornaday

CARTRIDGE BULLET	RANGE, YARDS:	0	100	200	300	400
Hornady 150	velocity, fps	3000	2772	2555	2348	
	energy, ft-lb	2997	2558	2176	1836	
	arc, inches	-1.5	+1.5	0	-6.9	
Hornady 165	velocity, fps	2850	2644	2447	2258	
	energy, ft-lb	2975	2560	2193	1868	
	arc, inches	-1.5	+1.7	0	-7.6	

.30-30 Winchester

CARTRIDGE BULLET	RANGE, YARDS:	0	100	200	300	400
Federal 125 Hi-Shok HP	velocity, fps:	2570	2090	1660	1320	1080
	energy, ft-lb:	1830	1210	770	480	320
	arc, inches:		+3.3	0	-16.0	-50.9
Federal 150 Hi-Shok FN	velocity, fps:	2390	2020	1680	1400	1180
	energy, ft-lb:	1900	1355	945	650	460
	arc, inches:		+3.6	0	-15.9	-49.1
Federal 170 Hi-Shok RN	velocity, fps:	2200	1900	1620	1380	1190
	energy, ft-lb:	1830	1355	990	720	535
	arc, inches:		+4.1	0	-17.4	-52.4
Federal 170 Sierra Pro-Hunt.	velocity, fps:	2200	1820	1500	1240	1060
	energy, ft-lb:	1830	1255	845	575	425
	arc, inches:		+4.5	0	-20.0	-63.5
Federal 170 Nosler Partition	velocity, fps:	2200	1900	1620	1380	1190
	energy, ft-lb:	1830	1355	990	720	535
	arc, inches:		+4.1	0	-17.4	-52.4
Hornady 150 Round Nose	velocity, fps:	2390	1973	1605	1303	1095
	energy, ft-lb:	1902	1296	858	565	399
	arc, inches:		0	-8.2	-30.0	
Hornady 160 Evolution	velocity, fps:	2400	2150	1916	1699	
	energy, ft-lb:	2046	1643	1304	1025	
	arc, inches:		+3.0	0.2	-12.1	
Hornady 170 Flat Point	velocity, fps:	2200	1895	1619	1381	1191
	energy, ft-lb:	1827	1355	989	720	535
	arc, inches:		0	-8.9	-31.1	
Norma 150 Soft Point	velocity, fps:	2329	2008	1716	1459	
	energy, ft-lb:	1807	1344	981	709	
	arc, inches:		+3.6	0	-15.5	
PMC 150 Starfire HP	velocity, fps:	2100	1769	1478		
	energy, ft-lb:	1469	1042	728		
	arc, inches:		0	-10.8		
PMC 150 Flat Nose	velocity, fps:	2300	1943	1627		
	energy, ft-lb:	1762	1257	881		
	arc, inches:		0	-7.8		
PMC 170 Flat Nose	velocity, fps:	2150	1840	1566		
	energy, ft-lb:	1745	1277	926		
	arc, inches:		0	-8.9		
Rem. 55 PSP (sabot) "Accelerator"	velocity, fps:	3400	2693	2085	1570	1187
	energy, ft-lb:	1412	886	521	301	172
	arc, inches:		+1.7	0	-9.9	-34.3
Rem. 150 SP Core-Lokt	velocity, fps:	2390	1973	1605	1303	1095
	energy, ft-lb:	1902	1296	858	565	399
	arc, inches:		0	-7.6	-28.8	
Rem. 170 SP Core-Lokt	velocity, fps:	2200	1895	1619	1381	1191
	energy, ft-lb:	1827	1355	989	720	535
	arc, inches:		0	-8.3	-29.9	
Rem. 170 HP Core-Lokt	velocity, fps:	2200	1895	1619	1381	1191.
	energy, ft-lb:	1827	1355	989	720	535
	arc, inches:		0	-8.3	-29.9	
Speer 150 Flat Nose	velocity, fps:	2370	2067	1788	1538	
	energy, ft-lb:	1870	1423	1065	788	
	arc, inches:		+3.3	0	-14.4	-43.7
Win. 150 Hollow Point	velocity, fps:	2390	2018	1684	1398	1177
	energy, ft-lb:	1902	1356	944	651	461
	arc, inches:		0	-7.7	-27.9	
Win. 150 Power-Point	velocity, fps:	2390	2018	1684	1398	1177
	energy, ft-lb:	1902	1356	944	651	461
	arc, inches:		0	-7.7	-27.9	
Win. 150 Silvertip	velocity,fps:	2390	2018	1684	1398	1177
	energy, ft-lb:	1902	1356	944	651	461
	arc, inches:		0	-7.7	-27.9	

Centerfire Rifle Ballistics

.30-30 WINCHESTER TO .308 WINCHESTER

CARTRIDGE BULLET	RANGE, YARDS:	0	100	200	300	400
Win. 150 Power-Point Plus	velocity, fps:	2480	2095	1747	1446	1209
	energy, ft-lb:	2049	1462	1017	697	487
	arc, inches:		0	-6.5	-24.5	
Win. 170 Power-Point	velocity, fps:	2200	1895	1619	1381	1191
	energy, ft-lb:	1827	1355	989	720	535.
	arc, inches:		0	-8.9	-31.1	
Win. 170 Silvertip	velocity, fps:	2200	1895	1619	1381	1191
	energy, ft-lb:	1827	1355	989	720	535
	arc, inches:		0	-8.9	-31.1	

.300 Savage

CARTRIDGE BULLET	RANGE, YARDS:	0	100	200	300	400
Federal 150 Hi-Shok	velocity, fps:	2630	2350	2100	1850	1630
	energy, ft-lb:	2305	1845	1460	1145	885
	arc, inches:		+2.4	0	-10.4	-30.9
Federal 180 Hi-Shok	velocity, fps:	2350	2140	1940	1750	1570
	energy, ft-lb:	2205	1825	1495	1215	985
	arc, inches:		+3.1	0	-12.4	-36.1
Hornady 150 SST	velocity, fps:	2740	2499	2272	2056	1852
	energy, ft-lb:	2500	2081	1718	1407	1143
	arc, inches:		+2.1	0	-8.8	-25.8
Rem. 150 PSP Core-Lokt	velocity, fps:	2630	2354	2095	1853	1631
	energy, ft-lb:	2303	1845	1462	1143	806.
	arc, inches:		+2.4	0	-10.4	-30.9
Rem. 180 SP Core-Lokt	velocity, fps:	2350	2025	1728	1467	1252
	energy, ft-lb:	2207	1639	1193	860	626
	arc, inches:		0	-7.1	-25.9	
Win. 150 Power-Point	velocity, fps:	2630	2311	2015	1743	1500
	energy, ft-lb:	2303	1779	1352	1012	749
	arc, inches:		+2.8	0	-11.5	-34.4

.307 Winchester

CARTRIDGE BULLET	RANGE, YARDS:	0	100	200	300	400
Win. 180 Power-Point	velocity, fps:	2510	2179	1874	1599	1362
	energy, ft-lb:	2519	1898	1404	1022	742
	arc, inches:		+1.5	-3.6	-18.6	-47.1

.30-40 Krag

CARTRIDGE BULLET	RANGE, YARDS:	0	100	200	300	400
Rem. 180 PSP Core-Lokt	velocity, fps:	2430	2213	2007	1813	1632.
	energy, ft-lb:	2360	1957	1610	1314	1064
	arc, inches, s:		0	-5.6	-18.6	
Win. 180 Power-Point	velocity, fps:	2430	2099	1795	1525	1298
	energy, ft-lb:	2360	1761	1288	929	673
	arc, inches, s:		0	-7.1	-25.0	

7.62x54R Russian

CARTRIDGE BULLET	RANGE, YARDS:	0	100	200	300	400
Norma 150 Soft Point	velocity, fps:	2953	2622	2314	2028	
	energy, ft-lb:	2905	2291	1784	1370	
	arc, inches:		+1.8	0	-8.3	
Norma 180 Alaska	velocity, fps:	2575	2362	2159	1967	
	energy, ft-lb:	2651	2231	1864	1546	
	arc, inches:		+2.9	0	-12.9	
Winchester 180 FMJ	velocity, fps:	2580	2401	2230	2066	1909
	energy, ft-lb:	2658	2304	1987	1706	1457
	arc, inches:	-1.5	+2.6	0	-9.6	-27.3
Winchester 180 SP	velocity, fps:	2625	2302	2003	1729	1485
	energy, ft-lb:	2751	2117	1603	1195	882
	arc, inches:	-1.5	+2.9	0	-11.6	-34.9

.308 Marlin Express

CARTRIDGE BULLET	RANGE, YARDS:	0	100	200	300	400
Hornady 160	velocity, fps	2660	2438	2226	2026	1836
	energy, ft-lb	2513	2111	1761	1457	1197
	arc, inches	-1.5	+3.0	+1.7	-6.7	-23.5
Hornady 140 MonoFlex	velocity, fps:	2800	2532	2279	2040	1818
	energy, ft-lb:	2437	1992	1614	1294	1027
	arc, inches:	-1.5	+2.0	0	-8.7	-25.8

.308 Winchester

CARTRIDGE BULLET	RANGE, YARDS:	0	100	200	300	400
Black Hills 150 Nosler B. Tip	velocity, fps:	2800				
	energy, ft-lb:	2611				
	arc, inches:					
Black Hills 165 Nosler B. Tip (and SP)	velocity, fps:	2650				
	energy, ft-lb:	2573				
	arc, inches:					
Black Hills 168 Barnes X (and Match)	velocity, fps:	2650				
	energy, ft-lb:	2620				
	arc, inches:					
Black Hills 175 Match	velocity, fps:	2600				
	energy, ft-lb:	2657				
	arc, inches:					
Black Hills 180 AccuBond	velocity, fps:	2600				
	energy, ft-lb:	2701				
	arc, inches:					
Federal 150 Barnes XLC	velocity, fps:	2820	2610	2400	2210	2030
	energy, ft-lb:	2650	2265	1925	1630	1370
	arc, inches:		+1.8 0	-7.8	-22.9	
Federal 150 FMJ Boat-Tail	velocity, fps:	2820	2620	2430	2250	2070
	energy, ft-lb:	2650	2285	1965	1680	1430
	arc, inches:		+1.8 0	-7.7	-22.4	
Federal 150 Hi-Shok	velocity, fps:	2820	2530	2260	2010	1770
	energy, ft-lb:	2650	2140	1705	1345	1050
	arc, inches:		+2.0	0	-8.8	-26.3
Federal 150 Nosler Bal. Tip.	velocity, fps:	2820	2610	2410	2220	2040
	energy, ft-lb:	2650	2270	1935	1640	1380
	arc, inches:		+1.8	0	-7.8	-22.7
Federal 150 Trophy Copper	velocity, fps:	2820	2630	2440	2260	2090
	energy, ft-lb:	2650	2295	1980	1700	1455
	arc, inches:		+1.8	0	-7.6	-22.2
Federal 155 Sierra MatchKg. BTHP	velocity, fps:	2950	2740	2540	2350	2170
	energy, ft-lb:	2995	2585	2225	1905	1620
	arc, inches:		+1.9	0	-8.9	-22.6
Federal 165 Sierra GameKing BTSP	velocity, fps:	2700	2520	2330	2160	1990
	energy, ft-lb:	2670	2310	1990	1700	1450
	arc, inches:		+2.0	0	-8.4	-24.3
Federal 165 Trophy Bonded	velocity, fps:	2700	2440	2200	1970	1760
	energy, ft-lb:	2670	2185	1775	1425	1135
	arc, inches:		+2.2	0	-9.4	-27.7
Federal 165 Tr. Bonded HE	velocity, fps:	2870	2600	2350	2120	1890
	energy, ft-lb:	3020	2485	2030	1640	1310
	arc, inches:		+1.8	0	-8.2	-24.0
Federal 168 Sierra MatchKg. BTHP	velocity, fps:	2600	2410	2230	2060	1890
	energy, ft-lb:	2520	2170	1855	1580	1340.
	arc, inches:		+2.1	0	+8.9	+25.9
Federal 180 Hi-Shok	velocity, fps:	2620	2390	2180	1970	1780
	energy, ft-lb:	2745	2290	1895	1555	1270
	arc, inches:		+2.3	0	-9.7	-28.3
Federal 180 Nosler Partition	velocity, fps:	2620	2430	2240	2060	1890
	energy, ft-lb:	2745	2355	2005	1700	1430.
	arc, inches:		+2.2	0	-9.2	-26.5
Federal 180 Nosler Part. HE	velocity, fps:	2740	2550	2370	2200	2030
	energy, ft-lb:	3000	2600	2245	1925	1645
	arc, inches:		+1.9	0	-8.2	-23.5
Federal 180 Sierra Pro-Hunt.	velocity, fps:	2620	2410	2200	2010	1820
	energy, ft-lb:	2745	2315	1940	1610	1330
	arc, inches:		+2.3	0	-9.3	-27.1
Federal 180 Trophy Bonded Tip	velocity, fps:	2620	2450	2280	2120	1960
	energy, ft-lb:	2745	2390	2070	1790	1535
	arc, inches:		+2.2	0	-8.9	-25.5
Hornady 110 TAP-FPD	velocity, fps:	3165	2830	2519	2228	1957
	energy, ft-lb:	2446	1956	1649	1212	935
	arc, inches:		+1.4	0	-6.9	-20.9
Hornady 110 Urban Tactical	velocity, fps:	3170	2825	2504	2206	1937
	energy, ft-lb:	2454	1950	1532	1189	916
	arc, inches:		+1.5	0	-7.2	-21.2

CARTRIDGE BULLET	RANGE, YARDS:	0	100	200	300	400
Hornady 125 SST Custom Lite	velocity, fps:	2675	2389	2121	1871	1642
	energy, ft-lb:	1986	1584	1248	971	748
	arc, inches:		+2.3	0	-10.1	-30.1
Hornady 150 SP boat-tail	velocity, fps:	2820	2560	2315	2084	1866
	energy, ft-lb:	2648	2183	1785	1447	1160
	arc, inches:		+2.0	0	-8.5	-25.2
Hornady 150 SP LM	velocity, fps:	2980	2703	2442	2195	1964
	energy, ft-lb:	2959	2433	1986	1606	1285
	arc, inches:	+1.6 0	-7.5	-22.2		
Hornady 150 SST (or Interbond)	velocity, fps:	2820	2593	2378	2174	1984
	energy, ft-lb:	2648	2240	1884	1574	1311
	arc, inches:		+1.9	0	-8.1	-22.9
Hornady 150 SST LM (or Interbond)	velocity, fps:	3000	2765	2541	2328	2127
	energy, ft-lb:	2997	2545	2150	1805	1506
	arc, inches:		+1.5	0	-7.1	-20.6
Hornady 155 A-Max	velocity, fps:	2815	2610	2415	2229	2051
	energy, ft-lb:	2727	2345	2007	1709	1448
	arc, inches:		+1.9	0	-7.9	-22.6
Hornady 155 TAP-FPD	velocity, fps:	2785	2577	2379	2189	2008
	energy, ft-lb:	2669	2285	1947	1649	1387
	arc, inches:		+1.9	0	-8.0	-23.3
Hornady 165 GMX Superformance	velocity, fps:	2750	2550	2358	2174	1999
	energy, ft-lb:	2771	2381	2037	1732	1464
	arc, inches:		+1.9	0	-8.2	-23.8
Hornady 165 SP boat-tail	velocity, fps:	2700	2496	2301	2115	1937
	energy, ft-lb:	2670	2283	1940	1639	1375
	arc, inches:		+2.0	0	-8.7	-25.2
Hornady 165 SPBT LM	velocity, fps:	2870	2658	2456	2283	2078
	energy, ft-lb:	3019	2589	2211	1877	1583
	arc, inches:		+1.7	0	-7.5	-21.8
Hornady 165 SST LM (or Interbond)	velocity, fps:	2880	2672	2474	2284	2103
	energy, ft-lb:	3038	2616	2242	1911	1620
	arc, inches:		+1.6	0	-7.3	-21.2
Hornady 168 BTHP Match	velocity, fps:	2700	2524	2354	2191	2035.
	energy, ft-lb:	2720	2377	2068	1791	1545
	arc, inches:		+2.0	0	-8.4	-23.9
Hornady 168 BTHP Match LM	velocity, fps:	2640	2630	2429	2238	2056
	energy, ft-lb:	3008	2579	2201	1868	1577
	arc, inches:		+1.8	0	-7.8	-22.4
Hornady 168 A-Max Match	velocity fps:	2620	2446	2280	2120	1972
	energy, ft-lb:	2560	2232	1939	1677	1450
	arc, inches:		+2.6	0	-9.2	-25.6
Hornady 168 A-Max	velocity, fps:	2700	2491	2292	2102	1921
	energy, ft-lb:	2719	2315	1959	1648	1377
	arc, inches:		+2.4	0	-9.0	-25.9
Hornady 168 TAP-FPD	velocity, fps:	2700	2513	2333	2161	1996
	energy, ft-lb:	2719	2355	2030	1742	1486
	arc, inches:		+2.0	0	-8.4	-24.3
Hornady 178 BTHP Match	velocity, fps:	2600	2436	2278	2125	1979
	energy, ft-lb:	2672	2345	2050	1785	1548
	arc, inches:		+2.2	0	-8.9	-25.5
Hornady 180 A-Max Match	velocity, fps:	2550	2397	2249	2106	1974
	energy, ft-lb:	2598	2295	2021	1773	1557
	arc, inches:		+2.7	0	-9.5	-26.2
Norma 150 Nosler Bal. Tip	velocity, fps:	2822	2588	2365	2154	
	energy, ft-lb:	2653	2231	1864	1545	
	arc, inches:		+1.6	0	-7.1	
Norma 150 Soft Point	velocity, fps:	2861	2537	2235	1954	
	energy, ft-lb:	2727	2144	1664	1272	
	arc, inches:		+2.0	0	-9.0	
Norma 165 TXP Swift A-Fr.	velocity, fps:	2700	2459	2231	2015	
	energy, ft-lb:	2672	2216	1824	1488	
	arc, inches:		+2.1	0	-9.1	

CARTRIDGE BULLET	RANGE, YARDS:	0	100	200	300	400
Norma 180 Plastic Point	velocity, fps:	2612	2365	2131	1911	
	energy, ft-lb:	2728	2235	1815	1460	
	arc, inches:		+2.4	0	-10.1	
Norma 180 Nosler Partition	velocity, fps:	2612	2414	2225	2044	
	energy, ft-lb:	2728	2330	1979	1670	
	arc, inches:		+2.2	0	-9.3	
Norma 180 Alaska	velocity, fps:	2612	2269	1953	1667	
	energy, ft-lb:	2728	2059	1526	1111	
	arc, inches:		+2.7	0	-11.9	
Norma 180 Vulkan	velocity, fps:	2612	2325	2056	1806	
	energy, ft-lb:	2728	2161	1690	1304	
	arc, inches:		+2.5	0	-10.8	
Norma 180 Oryx	velocity, fps:	2612	2305	2019	1755	
	energy, ft-lb:	2728	2124	1629	1232	
	arc, inches:		+2.5	0	-11.1	
Norma 200 Vulkan	velocity, fps:	2461	2215	1983	1767	
	energy, ft-lb:	2690	2179	1747	1387	
	arc, inches:		+2.8	0	-11.7	
PMC 147 FMJ boat-tail	velocity, fps:	2751	2473	2257	2052	1859
	energy, ft-lb:	2428	2037	1697	1403	1150
	arc, inches:		+2.3	0	-9.3	-27.3
PMC 150 Barnes X	velocity, fps:	2700	2504	2316	2135	1964
	energy, ft-lb:	2428	2087	1786	1518	1284
	arc, inches:		+2.0	0	-8.6	-24.7
PMC 150 Pointed Soft Point	velocity, fps:	2750	2478	2224	1987	1766
	energy, ft-lb:	2519	2045	1647	1315	1039
	arc, inches:		+2.1	0	-9.2	-27.1
PMC 150 SP boat-tail	velocity, fps:	2820	2581	2354	2139	1935
	energy, ft-lb:	2648	2218	1846	1523	1247.
	arc, inches:		+1.9	0	-8.2	-24.0
PMC 168 Barnes X	velocity, fps:	2600	2425	2256	2095	1940
	energy, ft-lb:	2476	2154	1865	1608	1379
	arc, inches:		+2.2	0	-9.0	-26.0
PMC 168 HP boat-tail	velocity, fps:	2650	2460	2278	2103	1936
	energy, ft-lb:	2619	2257	1935	1649	1399
	arc, inches:		+2.1	0	-8.8	-25.6
PMC 168 Pointed Soft Point	velocity, fps:	2559	2354	2160	1976	1803
	energy, ft-lb:	2443	2067	1740	1457	1212
	arc, inches:		+2.4	0	-9.9	-28.7
PMC 168 Pointed Soft Point	velocity, fps:	2600	2404	2216	2037	1866
	energy, ft-lb:	2476	2064	1709	1403	1142
	arc, inches:		+2.3	0	-9.8	-28.7
PMC 180 Pointed Soft Point	velocity, fps:	2550	2335	2132	1940	1760
	energy, ft-lb:	2599	2179	1816	1504	1238.
	arc, inches:		+2.5	0	-10.1	-29.5
PMC 180 SP boat-tail	velocity, fps:	2620	2446	2278	2117	1962
	energy, ft-lb:	2743	2391	2074	1790	1538
	arc, inches:		+2.2	0	-8.9	-25.4
Rem. 125 PSP C-L MR	velocity, fps:	2660	2348	2057	1788	1546
	energy, ft-lb:	1964	1529	1174	887	663
	arc, inches:		+1.1	-2.7	-14.3	-35.8
Rem. 150 PSP Core-Lokt	velocity, fps:	2820	2533	2263	2009	1774
	energy, ft-lb:	2648	2137	1705	1344	1048
	arc, inches:		+2.0	0	-8.8	-26.2
Rem. 150 PSP C-L Ultra	velocity, fps:	2620	2404	2198	2002	1818
	energy, ft-lb:	2743	2309	1930	1601	1320
	arc, inches:		+2.3	0	-9.5	-26.4
Rem. 150 Swift Scirocco	velocity, fps:	2820	2611	2410	2219	2037
	energy, ft-lb:	2648	2269	1935	1640	1381
	arc, inches:		+1.8	0	-7.8	-22.7
Rem. 165 AccuTip	velocity, fps:	2700	2501	2311	2129	1958.
	energy, ft-lb:	2670	2292	1957	1861	1401.
	arc, inches:		+2.0	0	-8.6	-24.8
Rem. 165 PSP boat-tail	velocity, fps:	2700	2497	2303	2117	1941.
	energy, ft-lb:	2670	2284	1942	1642	1379
	arc, inches:		+2.0	0	-8.6	-25.0
Rem. 165 Nosler Bal. Tip	velocity, fps:	2700	2613	2333	2161	1996
	energy, ft-lb:	2672	2314	1995	1711	1460
	arc, inches:		+2.0	0	-8.4	-24.3

Centerfire Rifle Ballistics

.308 WINCHESTER TO .30-06 SPRINGFIELD

CARTRIDGE BULLET	RANGE, YARDS:	0	100	200	300	400
Rem. 165 Swift Scirocco	velocity, fps:	2700	2513	2233	2161	1996
	energy, fps:	2670	2313	1994	1711	1459
	arc, inches:		+2.0	0	-8.4	-24.3
Rem. 168 HPBT Match	velocity, fps:	2680	2493	2314	2143	1979
	energy, ft-lb:	2678	2318	1998	1713	1460
	arc, inches:		+2.1	0	-8.6	-24.7
Rem. 180 SP Core-Lokt	velocity, fps:	2620	2274	1955	1666	1414
	energy, ft-lb:	2743	2066	1527	1109	799
	arc, inches:		+2.6	0	-11.8	-36.3
Rem. 180 PSP Core-Lokt	velocity, fps:	2620	2393	2178	1974	1782
	energy, ft-lb:	2743	2288	1896	1557	1269
	arc, inches:		+2.3	0	-9.7	-28.3
Rem. 180 Nosler Partition	velocity, fps:	2620	2436	2259	2089	1927.
	energy, ft-lb:	2743	2371	2039	1774	1485
	arc, inches:		+2.2	0	-9.0	-26.0
Speer 150 Grand Slam	velocity, fps:	2900	2599	2317	2053	
	energy, ft-lb:	2800	2249	1788	1404	
	arc, inches:		+2.1	0	-8.6	-24.8
Speer 165 Grand Slam	velocity, fps:	2700	2475	2261	2057	
	energy, ft-lb:	2670	2243	1872	1550	
	arc, inches:		+2.1	0	-8.9	-25.9
Speer 180 Grand Slam	velocity, fps:	2620	2420	2229	2046	
	energy, ft-lb:	2743	2340	1985	1674	
	arc, inches:		+2.2	0	-9.2	-26.6
Win. 150 Power-Point	velocity, fps:	2820	2488	2179	1893	1633
	energy, ft-lb:	2648	2061	1581	1193	888
	arc, inches:		+2.4	0	-9.8	-29.3
Win. 150 Power-Point Plus	velocity, fps:	2900	2558	2241	1946	1678
	energy, ft-lb:	2802	2180	1672	1262	938
	arc, inches:		+1.9	0	-8.9	-27.0
Win. 150 Partition Gold	velocity, fps:	2900	2645	2405	2177	1962
	energy, ft-lb:	2802	2332	1927	1579	1282.
	arc, inches:		+1.7	0	-7.8	-22.9
Win. 150 Ballistic Silvertip	velocity, fps:	2810	2601	2401	2211	2028
	energy, ft-lb:	2629	2253	1920	1627	1370.
	arc, inches:		+1.8	0	-7.8	-22.8
Win. 150 Fail Safe	velocity, fps:	2820	2533	2263	2010	1775
	energy, ft-lb:	2649	2137	1706	1346	1049
	arc, inches:		+2.0	0	-8.8	-26.2
Win. 150 Supreme Elite XP3	velocity, fps:	2825	2616	2417	2226	2044
	energy, ft-lb:	2658	2279	1945	1650	1392
	arc, inches:		+1.8	0	-7.8	-22.6
Win. 168 Ballistic Silvertip	velocity, fps:	2670	2484	2306	2134	1971
	energy, ft-lb:	2659	2301	1983	1699	1449
	arc, inches:		+2.1	0	-8.6	-24.8
Win. 168 HP boat-tail Match	velocity, fps:	2680	2485	2297	2118	1948
	energy, ft-lb:	2680	2303	1970	1674	1415
	arc, inches:		+2.1	0	-8.7	-25.1
Win. 180 Power-Point	velocity, fps:	2620	2274	1955	1666	1414
	energy, ft-lb:	2743	2066	1527	1109	799
	arc, inches:		+2.9	0	-12.1	-36.9
Win. 180 Silvertip	velocity, fps:	2620	2393	2178	1974	1782
	energy, ft-lb:	2743	2288	1896	1557	1269
	arc, inches:		+2.6	0	-9.9	-28.9

.30-06 Springfield

CARTRIDGE BULLET	RANGE, YARDS:	0	100	200	300	400
A-Square 180 M & D-T	velocity, fps:	2700	2365	2054	1769	1524
	energy, ft-lb:	2913	2235	1687	1251	928
	arc, inches:		+2.4	0	-10.6	-32.4
A-Square 220 Monolythic Solid	velocity, fps:	2380	2108	1854	1623	1424
	energy, ft-lb:	2767	2171	1679	1287	990
	arc, inches:		+3.1	0	-13.6	-39.9
Black Hills 150 Nosler B. Tip	velocity, fps:	2900				
	energy, ft-lb:	2770				
	arc, inches:					
Black Hills 165 Nosler B. Tip	velocity, fps:	2750				
	energy, ft-lb:	2770				
	arc, inches:					
Black Hills 168 Hor. Match	velocity, fps:	2700				
	energy, ft-lb:	2718				
	arc, inches:					
Black Hills 180 Barnes X	velocity, fps:	2650				
	energy, ft-lb:	2806				
	arc, inches:					
Black Hills 180 AccuBond	velocity, ft-lb:	2700				
	energy, ft-lb:					
	arc, inches:					
Federal 125 Sierra Pro-Hunt.	velocity, fps:	3140	2780	2450	2140	1850
	energy, ft-lb:	2735	2145	1660	1270	955
	arc, inches:		+1.5	0	-7.3	-22.3
Federal 150 Hi-Shok	velocity, fps:	2910	2620	2340	2080	1840
	energy, ft-lb:	2820	2280	1825	1445	1130
	arc, inches:		+1.8	0	-8.2	-24.4
Federal 150 Sierra Pro-Hunt.	velocity, fps:	2910	2640	2380	2130	1900
	energy, ft-lb:	2820	2315	1880	1515	1205
	arc, inches:		+1.7	0	-7.9	-23.3
Federal 150 Sierra GameKing BTSP	velocity, fps:	2910	2690	2480	2270	2070
	energy, ft-lb:	2820	2420	2040	1710	1430
	arc, inches:		+1.7	0	-7.4	-21.5
Federal 150 Nosler Bal. Tip	velocity, fps:	2910	2700	2490	2300	2110
	energy, ft-lb:	2820	2420	2070	1760	1485
	arc, inches:		+1.6	0	-7.3	-21.1
Federal 150 FMJ boat-tail	velocity, fps:	2910	2710	2510	2320	2150
	energy, ft-lb:	2820	2440	2100	1800	1535
	arc, inches:		+1.6	0	-7.1	-20.8
Federal 165 Sierra Pro-Hunt.	velocity, fps:	2800	2560	2340	2130	1920
	energy, ft-lb:	2875	2410	2005	1655	1360
	arc, inches:		+1.9	0	-8.3	-24.3
Federal 165 Sierra GameKing BTSP	velocity, fps:	2800	2610	2420	2240	2070.
	energy, ft-lb:	2870	2490	2150	1840	1580
	arc, inches:		+1.8	0	-7.8	-22.4
Federal 165 Sierra GameKing HE	velocity, fps:	3140	2900	2670	2450	2240.
	energy, ft-lb:	3610	3075	2610	2200	1845
	arc, inches:		+1.5	0	-6.9	-20.4
Federal 165 Nosler Bal. Tip	velocity, fps:	2800	2610	2430	2250	2080
	energy, ft-lb:	2870	2495	2155	1855	1585
	arc, inches:		+1.8	0	-7.7	-22.3
Federal 165 Trophy Bonded	velocity, fps:	2800	2540	2290	2050	1830.
	energy, ft-lb:	2870	2360	1915	1545	1230
	arc, inches:		+2.0	0	-8.7	-25.4
Federal 165 Tr. Bonded HE	velocity, fps:	3140	2860	2590	2340	2100
	energy, ft-lb:	3610	2990	2460	2010	1625.
	arc, inches:		+1.6	0	-7.4	-21.9
Federal 165 Trophy Copper	velocity, fps:	2800	2620	2450	2280	2120
	energy, ft-lb:	2870	2515	2190	1900	1645
	arc, inches:		+1.8	0	-7.6	-22.0
Federal 168 Sierra MatchKg. BTHP	velocity, fps:	2700	2510	2320	2150	1980
	energy, ft-lb:	2720	2350	2010	1720	1460
	arc, inches:		+16.2	+28.4	+34.1	+32.3
Federal 180 Barnes XLC	velocity, fps:	2700	2530	2360	2200	2040
	energy, ft-lb:	2915	2550	2220	1930	1670
	arc, inches:	+2.0	0	-8.3	-23.8	
Federal 180 Hi-Shok	velocity, fps:	2700	2470	2250	2040	1850
	energy, ft-lb:	2915	2435	2025	1665	1360
	arc, inches:		+2.1	0	-9.0	-26.4
Federal 180 Sierra Pro-Hunt. RN	velocity, fps:	2700	2350	2020	1730	1470
	energy, ft-lb:	2915	2200	1630	1190	860
	arc, inches:		+2.4	0	-11.0	-33.6
Federal 180 Nosler Partition	velocity, fps:	2700	2500	2320	2140	1970
	energy, ft-lb:	2915	2510	2150	1830	1550
	arc, inches:		+2.0	0	-8.6	-24.6

CARTRIDGE BULLET	RANGE, YARDS:	0	100	200	300	400
Federal 180 Nosler Part. HE	velocity, fps:	2880	2690	2500	2320	2150
	energy, ft-lb:	3315	2880	2495	2150	1845
	arc, inches:		+1.7	0	-7.2	-21.0
Federal 180 Sierra GameKing	velocity, fps:	2700	2540	2380	2220	2080
BTSP	energy, ft-lb:	2915	2570	2260	1975	1720
	arc, inches:		+1.9	0	-8.1	-23.1
Federal 180 Barnes XLC	velocity, fps:	2700	2530	2360	2200	2040.
	energy, ft-lb:	2915	2550	2220	1930	1670
	arc, inches:		+2.0	0	-8.3	-23.8
Federal 180 Sierra Pro-Hunt.	velocity, fps:	2700	2350	2020	1730	1470
RN	energy, ft-lb:	2915	2200	1630	1190	860
	arc, inches:		+2.4	0	-11.0	-33.6
Federal 180 Trophy Bonded	velocity, fps:	2700	2460	2220	2000	1800
	energy, ft-lb:	2915	2410	1975	1605	1290
	arc, inches:		+2.2	0	-9.2	-27.0
Federal 180 Tr. Bonded HE	velocity, fps:	2880	2630	2380	2160	1940
	energy, ft-lb:	3315	2755	2270	1855	1505
	arc, inches:		+1.8	0	-8.0	-23.3
Federal 180 Trophy	velocity, fps:	2700	2520	2350	2190	2030
Bonded Tip	energy, ft-lb:	2915	2540	2219	1910	1645
	arc, inches:		+2.0	0	-8.4	-23.9
Federal 200 Trophy Bonded	velocity, fps:	2540	2320	2120	1920	1740
	energy, ft-lb:	2865	2395	1990	1640	1345
	arc, inches:		+2.5	0	-10.1	-29.9
Federal 220 Sierra Pro-Hunt.	velocity, fps:	2410	2130	1870	1630	1420
RN	energy, ft-lb:	2835	2215	1705	1300	985
	arc, inches:		+3.1	0	-13.1	-39.3
Hornady 125 SST Custom Lite	velocity, fps:	2700	2412	2143	1891	1660
	energy, ft-lb:	2023	1615	1274	993	765
	arc, inches:		+2.3	0	-9.9	-29.5
Hornady 150 GMX	velocity, fps:	3080	2848	2628	2418	2218
Superformance	energy, ft-lb:	3159	2701	2300	1948	1639
	arc, inches:		+1.4	0	-6.4	-18.8
Hornady 150 SP	velocity, fps:	2910	2617	2342	2083	1843
	energy, ft-lb:	2820	2281	1827	1445	1131
	arc, inches:		+2.1	0	-8.5	-25.0
Hornady 150 SP LM	velocity, fps:	3100	2815	2548	2295	2058
	energy, ft-lb:	3200	2639	2161	1755	1410
	arc, inches:		+1.4	0	-6.8	-20.3
Hornady 150 SP boat-tail	velocity, fps:	2910	2683	2467	2262	2066.
	energy, ft-lb:	2820	2397	2027	1706	1421
	arc, inches:		+2.0	0	-7.7	-22.2
Hornady 150 SST	velocity, fps:	2910	2802	2599	2405	2219
(or Interbond)	energy, ft-lb:	3330	2876	2474	2118	1803
	arc, inches:		+1.5	0	-6.6	-19.3
Hornady 150 SST LM	velocity, fps:	3100	2860	2631	2414	2208
	energy, ft-lb:	3200	2724	2306	1941	1624
	arc, inches:		+1.4	0	-6.6	-19.2
Hornady 165 GMX	velocity, fps:	2940	2731	2532	2341	2158
Superformance	energy, ft-lb:	3167	2732	3248	2007	1706
	arc, inches:		+1.5	0	-7.0	-20.4
Hornady 165 SP boat-tail	velocity, fps:	2800	2591	2392	2202	2020
	energy, ft-lb:	2873	2460	2097	1777	1495
	arc, inches:		+1.8	0	-8.0	-23.3
Hornady 165 SPBT LM	velocity, fps:	3015	2790	2575	2370	2176
	energy, ft-lb:	3330	2850	2428	2058	1734
	arc, inches:		+1.6	0	-7.0	-20.1
Hornady 165 SST	velocity, fps:	2800	2598	2405	2221	2046
(or Interbond)	energy, ft-lb:	2872	2473	2119	1808	1534
	arc, inches:		+1.9	0	-8.0	-22.8
Hornady 165 SST LM	velocity, fps:	3015	2802	2599	2405	2219
	energy, ft-lb:	3330	2878	2474	2118	1803.
	arc, inches:		+1.5	0	-6.5	-19.3
Hornady 168 A-Max	velocity, fps:	2710	2523	2343	2171	2006
Garand Match	energy, ft-lb:	2739	2374	2048	1758	1501
	arc, inches:		+2.3	0	-8.6	-24.6
Hornady 168 HPBT Match	velocity, fps:	2790	2620	2447	2280	2120.
	energy, ft-lb:	2925	2561	2234	1940	1677.
	arc, inches:		+1.7	0	-7.7	-22.2
Hornady 180 SP	velocity, fps:	2700	2469	2258	2042	1846
	energy, ft-lb:	2913	2436	2023	1666	1362
	arc, inches:		+2.4	0	-9.3	-27.0
Hornady 180 SPBT LM	velocity, fps:	2880	2676	2480	2293	2114
	energy, ft-lb:	3316	2862	2459	2102	1786
	arc, inches:		+1.7	0	-7.3	-21.3

CARTRIDGE BULLET	RANGE, YARDS:	0	100	200	300	400
Norma 150 Nosler Bal. Tip	velocity, fps:	2936	2713	2502	2300	
	energy, ft-lb:	2872	2453	2085	1762	
	arc, inches:		+1.6	0	-7.1	
Norma 150 Soft Point	velocity, fps:	2972	2640	2331	2043	
	energy, ft-lb:	2943	2321	1810	1390	
	arc, inches:		+1.8	0	-8.2	
Norma 180 Alaska	velocity, fps:	2700	2351	2028	1734	
	energy, ft-lb:	2914	2209	1645	1202	
	arc, inches:		+2.4	0	-11.0	
Norma 180 Nosler Partition	velocity, fps:	2700	2494	2297	2108	
	energy, ft-lb:	2914	2486	2108	1777	
	arc, inches:		+2.1	0	-8.7	
Norma 180 Plastic Point	velocity, fps:	2700	2455	2222	2003	
	energy, ft-lb:	2914	2409	1974	1603	
	arc, inches:		+2.1	0	-9.2	
Norma 180 Vulkan	velocity, fps:	2700	2416	2150	1901	
	energy, ft-lb:	2914	2334	1848	1445	
	arc, inches:		+2.2	0	-9.8	
Norma 180 Oryx	velocity, fps:	2700	2387	2095	1825	
	energy, ft-lb:	2914	2278	1755	1332	
	arc, inches:		+2.3	0	-10.2	
Norma 180 TXP Swift A-Fr.	velocity, fps:	2700	2479	2268	2067	
	energy, ft-lb:	2914	2456	2056	1708	
	arc, inches:		+2.0	0	-8.8	
Norma 180 AccuBond	velocity, fps:	2674	2499	2331	2169	
	energy, ft-lb:	2859	2497	2172	1881	
	arc, inches:		+2.0	0	-8.5	
Norma 200 Vulkan	velocity, fps:	2641	2385	2143	1916	
	energy, ft-lb:	3098	2527	2040	1631	
	arc, inches:		+2.3	0	-9.9	
Norma 200 Oryx	velocity, fps:	2625	2362	2115	1883	
	energy, ft-lb:	3061	2479	1987	1575	
	arc, inches:		+2.3	0	-10.1	
PMC 150 X-Bullet	velocity, fps:	2750	2552	2361	2179	2005
	energy, ft-lb:	2518	2168	1857	1582	1339
	arc, inches:		+2.0	0	-8.2	-23.7
PMC 150 Pointed Soft Point	velocity, fps:	2773	2542	2322	2113	1916
	energy, ft-lb:	2560	2152	1796	1487	1222.
	arc, inches:		+1.9	0	-8.4	-24.6
PMC 150 SP boat-tail	velocity, fps:	2900	2657	2427	2208	2000
	energy, ft-lb:	2801	2351	1961	1623	1332
	arc, inches:		+1.7	0	-7.7	-22.5
PMC 150 FMJ	velocity, fps:	2773	2542	2322	2113	1916
	energy, ft-lb:	2560	2152	1796	1487	1222
	arc, inches:		+1.9	0	-8.4	-24.6
PMC 168 Barnes X	velocity, fps:	2750	2569	2395	2228	2067
	energy, ft-lb:	2770	2418	2101	1818	1565
	arc, inches:		+1.9	0	-8.0	-23.0
PMC 180 Barnes X	velocity, fps:	2650	2487	2331	2179	2034
	energy, ft-lb:	2806	2472	2171	1898	1652
	arc, inches:		+2.1	0	-8.5	-24.3
PMC 180 Pointed Soft Point	velocity, fps:	2650	2430	2221	2024	1839
	energy, ft-lb:	2807	2359	1972	1638	1351
	arc, inches:		+2.2	0	-9.3	-27.0
PMC 180 SP boat-tail	velocity, fps:	2700	2523	2352	2188	2030
	energy, ft-lb:	2913	2543	2210	1913	1646
	arc, inches:		+2.0	0	-8.3	-23.9
PMC 180 HPBT Match	velocity, fps:	2800	2622	2456	2302	2158
	energy, ft-lb:	3133	2747	2411	2118	1861
	arc, inches:		+1.8	0	-7.6	-21.7
Rem. 55 PSP (sabot)	velocity, fps:	4080	3484	2964	2499	2080
"Accelerator"	energy, ft-lb:	2033	1482	1073	763	528.
	arc, inches:		+1.4	+1.4	-2.6	-12.2
Rem. 125 PSP C-L MR	velocity, fps:	2660	2335	2034	1757	1509
	energy, ft-lb:	1964	1513	1148	856	632
	arc, inches:		+1.1	-3.0	-15.5	-37.4
Rem. 125 Pointed Soft Point	velocity, fps:	3140	2780	2447	2138	1853
	energy, ft-lb:	2736	2145	1662	1269	953.
	arc, inches:		+1.5	0	-7.4	-22.4
Rem. 150 AccuTip	velocity, fps:	2910	2686	2473	2270	2077
	energy, ft-lb:	2820	2403	2037	1716	1436
	arc, inches:		+1.8	0	-7.4	-21.5

Centerfire Rifle Ballistics

.30-06 SPRINGFIELD TO .300 BLACKOUT

CARTRIDGE BULLET	RANGE, YARDS:	0	100	200	300	400
Rem. 150 PSP Core-Lokt	velocity, fps:	2910	2617	2342	2083	1843
	energy, ft-lb:	2820	2281	1827	1445	1131
	arc, inches:		+1.8	0	-8.2	-24.4
Rem. 150 Bronze Point	velocity, fps:	2910	2656	2416	2189	1974
	energy, ft-lb:	2820	2349	1944	1596	1298
	arc, inches:		+1.7	0	-7.7	-22.7
Rem. 150 Nosler Bal. Tip	velocity, fps:	2910	2696	2492	2298	2112.
	energy, ft-lb:	2821	2422	2070	1769	1485
	arc, inches:		+1.6	0	-7.3	-21.1
Rem. 150 Swift Scirocco	velocity, fps:	2910	2696	2492	2298	2111
	energy, ft-lb:	2820	2421	2069	1758	1485
	arc, inches:		+1.6	0	-7.3	-21.1
Rem. 165 AccuTip	velocity, fps:	2800	2597	2403	2217	2039
	energy, ft-lb:	2872	2470	2115	1800	1523
	arc, inches:		+1.8	0	-7.9	-22.8
Rem. 165 PSP Core-Lokt	velocity, fps:	2800	2534	2283	2047	1825.
	energy, ft-lb:	2872	2352	1909	1534	1220
	arc, inches:		+2.0	0	-8.7	-25.9
Rem. 165 PSP boat-tail	velocity, fps:	2800	2592	2394	2204	2023
	energy, ft-lb:	2872	2462	2100	1780	1500
	arc, inches:		+1.8	0	-7.9	-23.0
Rem. 165 Nosler Bal. Tip	velocity, fps:	2800	2609	2426	2249	2080.
	energy, ft-lb:	2873	2494	2155	1854	1588
	arc, inches:		+1.8	0	-7.7	-22.3
Rem. 168 PSP C-L Ultra	velocity, fps:	2800	2546	2306	2079	1866
	energy, ft-lb:	2924	2418	1984	1613	1299
	arc, inches:		+1.9	0	-8.5	-25.1
Rem. 180 SP Core-Lokt	velocity, fps:	2700	2348	2023	1727	1466
	energy, ft-lb:	2913	2203	1635	1192	859
	arc, inches:		+2.4	0	-11.0	-33.8
Rem. 180 PSP Core-Lokt	velocity, fps:	2700	2469	2250	2042	1846
	energy, ft-lb:	2913	2436	2023	1666	1362
	arc, inches:		+2.1	0	-9.0	-26.3
Rem. 180 PSP C-L Ultra	velocity, fps:	2700	2480	2270	2070	1882
	energy, ft-lb:	2913	2457	2059	1713	1415
	arc, inches:		+2.1	0	-8.9	-25.8
Rem. 180 Bronze Point	velocity, fps:	2700	2485	2280	2084	1899.
	energy, ft-lb:	2913	2468	2077	1736	1441
	arc, inches:		+2.1	0	-8.8	-25.5
Rem. 180 Swift A-Frame	velocity, fps:	2700	2465	2243	2032	1833
	energy, ft-lb:	2913	2429	2010	1650	1343
	arc, inches:		+2.1	0	-9.1	-26.6
Rem. 180 Nosler Partition	velocity, fps:	2700	2512	2332	2160	1995
	energy, ft-lb:	2913	2522	2174	1864	1590
	arc, inches:		+2.0	0	-8.4	-24.3
Rem. 220 SP Core-Lokt	velocity, fps:	2410	2130	1870	1632	1422
	energy, ft-lb:	2837	2216	1708	1301	988
	arc, inches, s:		0	-6.2	-22.4	
Speer 150 Grand Slam	velocity, fps:	2975	2669	2383	2114	
	energy, ft-lb:	2947	2372	1891	1489	
	arc, inches:		+2.0	0	-8.1	-24.1
Speer 165 Grand Slam	velocity, fps:	2790	2560	2342	2134	
	energy, ft-lb:	2851	2401	2009	1669	
	arc, inches:		+1.9	0	-8.3	-24.1
Speer 180 Grand Slam	velocity, fps:	2690	2487	2293	2108	
	energy, ft-lb:	2892	2472	2101	1775	
	arc, inches:		+2.1	0	-8.8	-25.1
Win. 125 Pointed Soft Point	velocity, fps:	3140	2780	2447	2138	1853
	energy, ft-lb:	2736	2145	1662	1269	953
	arc, inches:		+1.8	0	-7.7	-23.0
Win. 150 Power-Point	velocity, fps:	2920	2580	2265	1972	1704
	energy, ft-lb:	2839	2217	1708	1295	967
	arc, inches:		+2.2	0	-9.0	-27.0
Win. 150 Power-Point Plus	velocity, fps:	3050	2685	2352	2043	1760
	energy, ft-lb:	3089	2402	1843	1391	1032
	arc, inches:		+1.7	0	-8.0	-24.3
Win. 150 Silvertip	velocity, fps:	2910	2617	2342	2083	1843
	energy, ft-lb:	2820	2281	1827	1445	1131
	arc, inches:		+2.1	0	-8.5	-25.0

CARTRIDGE BULLET	RANGE, YARDS:	0	100	200	300	400
Win. 150 Partition Gold	velocity, fps:	2960	2705	2464	2235	2019
	energy, ft-lb:	2919	2437	2022	1664	1358.
	arc, inches:		+1.6	0	-7.4	-21.7
Win. 150 Ballistic Silvertip	velocity, fps:	2900	2687	2483	2289	2103
	energy, ft-lb:	2801	2404	2054	1745	1473
	arc, inches:		+1.7	0	-7.3	-21.2
Win. 150 Fail Safe	velocity, fps:	2920	2625	2349	2089	1848
	energy, ft-lb:	2841	2296	1838	1455	1137
	arc, inches:		+1.8	0	-8.1	-24.3
Win. 165 Pointed Soft Point	velocity, fps:	2800	2573	2357	2151	1956
	energy, ft-lb:	2873	2426	2036	1696	1402
	arc, inches:		+2.2	0	-8.4	-24.4
Win. 165 Fail Safe	velocity, fps:	2800	2540	2295	2063	1846
	energy, ft-lb:	2873	2365	1930	1560	1249
	arc, inches:		+2.0	0	-8.6	-25.3
Win. 168 Ballistic Silvertip	velocity, fps:	2790	2599	2416	2240	2072
	energy, ft-lb:	2903	2520	2177	1872	1601
	arc, inches:		+1.8	0	-7.8	-22.5
Win. 180 Ballistic Silvertip	velocity, fps:	2750	2572	2402	2237	2080
	energy, ft-lb:	3022	2644	2305	2001	1728
	arc, inches:		+1.9	0	-7.9	-22.8
Win. 180 Power-Point	velocity, fps:	2700	2348	2023	1727	1466
	energy, ft-lb:	2913	2203	1635	1192	859
	arc, inches:		+2.7	0	-11.3	-34.4
Win. 180 Power-Point Plus	velocity, fps:	2770	2563	2366	2177	1997
	energy, ft-lb:	3068	2627	2237	1894	1594
	arc, inches:		+1.9	0	-8.1	-23.6
Win. 180 Silvertip	velocity, fps:	2700	2469	2250	2042	1846
	energy, ft-lb:	2913	2436	2023	1666	1362
	arc, inches:		+2.4	0	-9.3	-27.0
Win. 180 AccuBond	velocity, fps:	2750	2573	2403	2239	2082
	energy, ft-lb:	3022	2646	2308	2004	1732
	arc, inches:		+1.9	0	-7.9	-22.8
Win. 180 Partition Gold	velocity, fps:	2790	2581	2382	2192	2010
	energy, ft-lb:	3112	2664	2269	1920	1615
	arc, inches:		+1.9	0	-8.0	-23.2
Win. 180 Fail Safe	velocity, fps:	2700	2486	2283	2089	1904
	energy, ft-lb:	2914	2472	2083	1744	1450
	arc, inches:		+2.1	0	-8.7	-25.5
Win. 150 Supreme Elite XP3	velocity, fps:	2925	2712	2508	2313	2127
	energy, ft-lb:	2849	2448	2095	1782	1507
	arc, inches:		+1.6	0	-7.2	-20.8
Win. 180 Supreme Elite XP3	velocity, fps:	2750	2579	2414	2256	2103
	energy, ft-lb:	3022	2658	2330	2034	1768
	arc, inches:		+1.9	0	-7.8	-22.5

.300 Blackout (.300 Whisper)

CARTRIDGE BULLET	RANGE, YARDS:	0	100	200	300	400
Barnes 110 Tac/TX	velocity, fps:	2350	1810	1369		
	energy, ft-lb:	1349	800	458		
	arc, inches:	-1.5	-6.7	-55.5		
Black Hills 125 OTM	velocity, fps:	2200				
	energy, ft-lb:	1343				
	arc, inches					
Black Hills 220 OTM	velocity, fps:	1000				
	energy, ft-lb:	488				
	arc, inches					
Hornady 110 V-Max (16-inch barrel)	velocity, fps:	2375	2094	1834	1597	1389
	energy, ft-lb:	1378	1071	821	623	471
	arc, inches:		+3.20	0	-13.7	-41.0
Hornady 110 V-MAX	velocity, fps:	2375	2094	1834	1597	
	energy, ft-lb:	1378	1071	821	623	
	arc, inches:	-1.5	+3.2	0	-13.7	
Hornady 208 A-MAX	velocity, fps:	1020	987	959		
	energy, ft-lb:	480	450	424		
	arc, inches:	-1.5	0	-34.1		

.300 H&H MAGNUM TO .300 WINCHESTER MAGNUM

.300 H&H Magnum

CARTRIDGE BULLET	RANGE, YARDS:	0	100	200	300	400
Federal 180 Barnes TSX	velocity, fps:	2880	2680	2480	2290	2120
	energy, ft-lb:	3315	2860	2460	2105	1790
	arc, inches:	-1.5	+1.7	0	-7.3	-21.3
Federal 180 Nosler Partition	velocity, fps:	2880	2620	2380	2150	1930
	energy, ft-lb:	3315	2750	2260	1840	1480
	arc, inches:		+1.8 0	-8.0	-23.4	
Federal 180 Trophy Bonded Tip	velocity, fps:	2880	2700	2520	2350	2180
	energy, ft-lb:	3315	2900	2530	2200	1900
	arc, inches:		+1.6	0	-7.1	-20.6
Handload, 165 Sierra HP	velocity, fps:	3000	2784	2579	2382	2195
	energy, ft-lb:	3297	2840	2436	2079	1764
	arc, inches:	-1.5	+1.5	0	-6.7	-19.5
Handload, 190 Hornady	velocity, fps:	2800	2615	2437	2266	2102
	energy, ft-lb:	3307	2884	2505	2166	1864
	arc, inches:	-1.5	+1.8	0	-7.7	-22.1
Hornady 180 InterBond	velocity, fps:	2870	2678	2493	2316	2146
	energy, ft-lb:	3292	2865	2484	2144	1841
	arc, inches:	-1.5	+1.	0	-7.3	-21.0
Win. 180 Fail Safe	velocity, fps:	2880	2628	2390	2165	1952
	energy, ft-lb:	3316	2762	2284	1873	1523
	arc, inches:		+1.8 0	-7.9	-23.2	

.308 Norma Magnum

CARTRIDGE BULLET	RANGE, YARDS:	0	100	200	300	400
Norma 180 TXP Swift A-Fr.	velocity, fps:	2953	2704	2469	2245	
	energy, ft-lb:	3486	2924	2437	2016	
	arc, inches:		+1.6	0	-7.3	
Norma 180 Oryx	velocity, fps:	2953	2630	2330	2049	
	energy, ft-lb:	3486	2766	2170	1679	
	arc, inches:		+1.8	0	-8.2	
Norma 200 Vulkan	velocity, fps:	2903	2624	2361	2114	
	energy, ft-lb:	3744	3058	2476	1985	
	arc, inches:	0	+1.8	0	-8.0	
Nosler 180 AB	velocity, fps:	2975	2787	2608	2435	2269
	energy, ft-lb:	3536	3105	2718	2371	2058
	arc, inches:	-1.5	+1.5	0	-6.6	-19.1

.300 Winchester Magnum

CARTRIDGE BULLET	RANGE, YARDS:	0	100	200	300	400
A-Square 180 Dead Tough	velocity, fps:	3120	2756	2420	2108	1820
	energy, ft-lb:	3890	3035	2340	1776	1324
	arc, inches:		+1.6	0	-7.6	-22.9
Black Hills 180 Nos. Bal. Tip	velocity, fps:	3100				
	energy, ft-lb:	3498				
	arc, inches:					
Black Hills 180 Barnes X	velocity, fps:	2950				
	energy, ft-lb:	3498				
	arc, inches:					
Black Hills 180 AccuBond	velocity, fps:	3000				
	energy, ft-lb:	3597				
	arc, inches:					
Black Hills 190 Match	velocity, fps:	2950				
	energy, ft-lb:	3672				
	arc, inches:					
Federal 150 Sierra Pro Hunt.	velocity, fps:	3280	3030	2800	2570	2360.
	energy, ft-lb:	3570	3055	2600	2205	1860
	arc, inches:		+1.1	0	-5.6	-16.4
Federal 150 Trophy Bonded	velocity, fps:	3280	2980	2700	2430	2190
	energy, ft-lb:	3570	2450	2420	1970	1590
	arc, inches:		+1.2	0	-6.0	-17.9
Federal 165 Trophy Copper	velocity, fps:	3050	2860	2680	2500	2330
	energy, ft-lb:	3410	2995	2620	2290	1990
	arc, inches:		+1.4	0	-6.3	-18.0
Federal 180 Sierra Pro Hunt.	velocity, fps:	2960	2750	2540	2340	2160
	energy, ft-lb:	3500	3010	2580	2195	1860
	arc, inches:		+1.6	0	-7.0	-20.3
Federal 180 Barnes XLC	velocity, fps:	2960	2780	2600	2430	2260
	energy, ft-lb:	3500	3080	2700	2355	2050
	arc, inches:		+1.5	0	-6.6	-19.2
Federal 180 Trophy Bonded	velocity, fps:	2960	2700	2460	2220	2000
	energy, ft-lb:	3500	2915	2410	1975	1605
	arc, inches:		+1.6	0	-7.4	-21.9
Federal 180 Tr. Bonded HE	velocity, fps:	3100	2830	2580	2340	2110
	energy, ft-lb:	3840	3205	2660	2190	1790
	arc, inches:		+1.4	0	-6.6	-19.7
Federal 180 Nosler Partition	velocity, fps:	2960	2700	2450	2210	1990
	energy, ft-lb:	3500	2905	2395	1955	1585
	arc, inches:		+1.6	0	-7.5	-22.1
Federal 190 Sierra MatchKg. BTHP	velocity, fps:	2900	2730	2560	2400	2240
	energy, ft-lb:	3550	3135	2760	2420	2115
	arc, inches:		+12.9	+22.5	+26.9	+25.1
Federal 200 Sierra GameKing BTSP	velocity, fps:	2830	2680	2530	2380	2240
	energy, ft-lb:	3560	3180	2830	2520	2230
	arc, inches:		+1.7	0	-7.1	-20.4
Federal 200 Nosler Part. HE	velocity, fps:	2930	2740	2550	2370	2200
	energy, ft-lb:	3810	3325	2885	2495	2145
	arc, inches:		+1.6	0	-6.9	-20.1
Federal 200 Trophy Bonded	velocity, fps:	2800	2570	2350	2150	1950
	energy, ft-lb:	3480	2935	2460	2050	1690
	arc, inches:		+1.9	0	-8.2	-23.9
Hornady 150 SP boat-tail	velocity, fps:	3275	2988	2718	2464	2224
	energy, ft-lb:	3573	2974	2461	2023	1648
	arc, inches:		+1.2	0	-6.0	-17.8
Hornady 150 SST (and Interbond)	velocity, fps:	3275	3027	2791	2565	2352
	energy, ft-lb:	3572	3052	2593	2192	1842
	arc, inches:		+1.2	0	-5.8	-17.0
Hornady 150 SST Custom Lite	velocity, fps:	2800	2582	2375	2177	1988
	energy, ft-lb:	2611	2220	1878	1578	1316
	arc, inches:		+1.9	0	-8.0	-23.5
Hornady 165 SP boat-tail	velocity, fps:	3100	2877	2665	2462	2269.
	energy, ft-lb:	3522	3033	2603	2221	1887
	arc, inches:		+1.3	0	-6.5	-18.5
Hornady 165 SST	velocity, fps:	3100	2885	2680	2483	2296
	energy, ft-lb:	3520	3049	2630	2259	1930
	arc, inches:		+1.4	0	-6.4	-18.6
Hornady 180 SP boat-tail	velocity, fps:	2960	2745	2540	2344	2157
	energy, ft-lb:	3501	3011	2578	2196	1859
	arc, inches:		+1.9	0	-7.3	-20.9
Hornady 180 SST	velocity, fps:	2960	2764	2575	2395	2222
	energy, ft-lb:	3501	3052	2650	2292	1974
	arc, inches:		+1.6	0	-7.0	-20.1.
Hornady 180 SPBT HM	velocity, fps:	3100	2879	2668	2467	2275
	energy, ft-lb:	3840	3313	2845	2431	2068
	arc, inches:		+1.4	0	-6.4	-18.7
Hornady 190 BTHP Match	velocity, fps:	2930	2760	2596	2438	2286
	energy, ft-lb:	3717	3297	2918	2574	2262
	arc, inches:		+1.5	0	-6.7	-19.3
Hornady 190 SP boat-tail	velocity, fps:	2900	2711	2529	2355	2187
	energy, ft-lb:	3549	3101	2699	2340	2018
	arc, inches:		+1.6	0	-7.1	-20.4
Norma 150 Nosler Bal. Tip	velocity, fps:	3250	3014	2791	2578	
	energy, ft-lb:	3519	3027	2595	2215	
	arc, inches:		+1.1	0	-5.6	
Norma 150 Barnes TS	velocity, fps:	3215	2982	2761	2550	
	energy, ft-lb:	3444	2962	2539	2167	
	arc, inches:		+1.2	0	-5.8	
Norma 165 Scirocco	velocity, fps:	3117	2921	2734	2554	
	energy, ft-lb:	3561	3127	2738	2390	
	arc, inches:		+1.2	0	-5.9	
Norma 180 Soft Point	velocity, fps:	3018	2780	2555	2341	
	energy, ft-lb:	3641	3091	2610	2190	
	arc, inches:		+1.5	0	-7.0	
Norma 180 Plastic Point	velocity, fps:	3018	2755	2506	2271	
	energy, ft-lb:	3641	3034	2512	2062	
	arc, inches:		+1.6	0	-7.1	
Norma 180 TXP Swift A-Fr.	velocity, fps:	2920	2688	2467	2256	
	energy, ft-lb:	3409	2888	2432	2035	
	arc, inches:		+1.7	0	-7.4	

Centerfire Rifle Ballistics

.300 WINCHESTER MAGNUM TO .300 REMINGTON SHORT ULTRA MAGNUM

CARTRIDGE BULLET	RANGE, YARDS:	0	100	200	300	400
Norma 180 AccuBond	velocity, fps:	2953	2767	2588	2417	
	energy, ft-lb:	3486	3061	2678	2335	
	arc, inches:		+1.5	0	-6.7	
Norma 180 Oryx	velocity, fps:	2920	2600	2301	2023	
	energy, ft-lb:	3409	2702	2117	1636	
	arc, inches:		+1.8	0	-8.4	
Norma 200 Vulkan	velocity, fps:	2887	2609	2347	2100	
	energy, ft-lb:	3702	3023	2447	1960	
	arc, inches:		+1.8	0	-8.2	
Norma 200 Oryx	velocity, fps:	2789	2510	2248	2002	
	energy, ft-lb:	3455	2799	2245	1780	
	arc, inches:		+2.0	0	-8.9	
PMC 150 Barnes X	velocity, fps:	3135	2918	2712	2515	2327
	energy, ft-lb:	3273	2836	2449	2107	1803
	arc, inches:		+1.3	0	-6.1	-17.7
PMC 150 Pointed Soft Point	velocity, fps:	3150	2902	2665	2438	2222
	energy, ft-lb:	3304	2804	2364	1979	1644.
	arc, inches:		+1.3	0	-6.2	-18.3
PMC 150 SP boat-tail	velocity, fps:	3250	2987	2739	2504	2281
	energy, ft-lb:	3517	2970	2498	2088	1733
	arc, inches:		+1.2	0	-6.0	-17.4
PMC 180 Barnes X	velocity, fps:	2910	2738	2572	2412	2258
	energy, ft-lb:	3384	2995	2644	2325	2037
	arc, inches:		+1.6	0	-6.9	-19.8
PMC 180 Pointed Soft Point	velocity, fps:	2853	2643	2446	2258	2077
	energy, ft-lb:	3252	2792	2391	2037	1724
	arc, inches:		+1.7	0	-7.5	-21.9
PMC 180 SP boat-tail	velocity, fps:	2900	2714	2536	2365	2200
	energy, ft-lb:	3361	2944	2571	2235	1935
	arc, inches:		+1.6	0	-7.1	-20.3
PMC 180 HPBT Match	velocity, fps:	2950	2755	2568	2390	2219
	energy, ft-lb:	3478	3033	2636	2283	1968
	arc, inches:		+1.5	0	-6.8	-19.7
Rem. 150 PSP Core-Lokt	velocity, fps:	3290	2951	2636	2342	2068
	energy, ft-lb:	3605	2900	2314	1827	1859
	arc, inches:		+1.6	0	-7.0	-20.2
Rem. 150 PSP C-L MR	velocity, fps:	2650	2373	2113	1870	1646
	energy, ft-lb:	2339	1875	1486	1164	902
	arc, inches:		+1.0	-2.7	-14.3	-35.8
Rem. 150 PSP C-L Ultra	velocity, fps:	3290	2967	2666	2384	2120
	energy, ft-lb:	3065	2931	2366	1893	1496
	arc, inches:		+1.2	0	-6.1	-18.4
Rem. 180 AccuTip	velocity, fps:	2960	2764	2577	2397	2224
	energy, ft-lb:	3501	3053	2653	2295	1976
	arc, inches:		+1.5	0	-6.8	-19.6
Rem. 180 PSP Core-Lokt	velocity, fps:	2960	2745	2540	2344	2157
	energy, ft-lb:	3501	3011	2578	2196	1424
	arc, inches:		+2.2	+1.9	-3.4	-15.0
Rem. 180 PSP C-L Ultra	velocity, fps:	2960	2727	2505	2294	2093
	energy, ft-lb:	3501	2971	2508	2103	1751
	arc, inches:		+2.7	+2.2	-3.8	-16.4
Rem. 180 Nosler Partition	velocity, fps:	2960	2725	2503	2291	2089
	energy, ft-lb:	3501	2968	2503	2087	1744
	arc, inches:		+1.6	0	-7.2	-20.9
Rem. 180 Nosler Bal. Tip	velocity, fps:	2960	2774	2595	2424	2259.
	energy, ft-lb:	3501	3075	2692	2348	2039
	arc, inches:		+1.5	0	-6.7	-19.3
Rem. 180 Swift Scirocco	velocity, fps:	2960	2774	2595	2424	2259
	energy, ft-lb:	3501	3075	2692	2348	2039
	arc, inches:		+1.5	0	-6.7	-19.3
Rem. 190 PSP boat-tail	velocity, fps:	2885	2691	2506	2327	2156
	energy, ft-lb:	3511	3055	2648	2285	1961
	arc, inches:		+1.6	0	-7.2	-20.8

CARTRIDGE BULLET	RANGE, YARDS:	0	100	200	300	400
Rem. 190 HPBT Match	velocity, fps:	2900	2725	2557	2395	2239
	energy, ft-lb:	3547	3133	2758	2420	2115
	arc, inches:		+1.6	0	-6.9	-19.9
Rem. 200 Swift A-Frame	velocity, fps:	2825	2595	2376	2167	1970
	energy, ft-lb:	3544	2989	2506	2086	1722
	arc, inches:		+1.8	0	-8.0	-23.5
Speer 180 Grand Slam	velocity, fps:	2950	2735	2530	2334	
	energy, ft-lb:	3478	2989	2558	2176	
	arc, inches:		+1.6	0	-7.0	-20.5
Speer 200 Grand Slam	velocity, fps:	2800	2597	2404	2218	
	energy, ft-lb:	3481	2996	2565	2185	
	arc, inches:		+1.8	0	-7.9	-22.9
Win. 150 Power-Point	velocity, fps:	3290	2951	2636	2342	2068.
	energy, ft-lb:	3605	2900	2314	1827	1424
	arc, inches:		+2.6	+2.1	-3.5	-15.4
Win. 150 Fail Safe	velocity, fps:	3260	2943	2647	2370	2110
	energy, ft-lb:	3539	2884	2334	1871	1483
	arc, inches:		+1.3	0	-6.2	-18.7
Win. 165 Fail Safe	velocity, fps:	3120	2807	2515	2242	1985
	energy, ft-lb:	3567	2888	2319	1842	1445
	arc, inches:		+1.5	0	-7.0	-20.0
Win. 180 Power-Point	velocity, fps:	2960	2745	2540	2344	2157
	energy, ft-lb:	3501	3011	2578	2196	1859
	arc, inches:		+1.9	0	-7.3	-20.9
Win. 180 Power-Point Plus	velocity, fps:	3070	2846	2633	2430	2236
	energy, ft-lb:	3768	3239	2772	2361	1999
	arc, inches:		+1.4	0	-6.4	-18.7
Win. 180 Ballistic Silvertip	velocity, fps:	2950	2764	2586	2415	2250
	energy, ft-lb:	3478	3054	2673	2331	2023
	arc, inches:		+1.5	0	-6.7	-19.4
Win. 180 AccuBond	velocity, fps:	2950	2765	2588	2417	2253
	energy, ft-lb:	3478	3055	2676	2334	2028
	arc, inches:		+1.5	0	-6.7	-19.4
Win. 180 Fail Safe	velocity, fps:	2960	2732	2514	2307	2110
	energy, ft-lb:	3503	2983	2528	2129	1780
	arc, inches:		+1.6	0	-7.1	-20.7
Win. 180 Partition Gold	velocity, fps:	3070	2859	2657	2464	2280
	energy, ft-lb:	3768	3267	2823	2428	2078
	arc, inches:		+1.4	0	-6.3	-18.3
Win. 150 Supreme Elite XP3	velocity, fps:	3260	3030	2811	2603	2404
	energy, ft-lb:	3539	3057	2632	2256	1925
	arc, inches:		+1.1	0	-5.6	-16.2
Win. 180 Supreme Elite XP3	velocity, fps:	3000	2819	2646	2479	2318
	energy, ft-lb:	3597	3176	2797	2455	2147
	arc, inches:		+1.4	0	-6.4	-18.5

.300 Remington Short Ultra Magnum

CARTRIDGE BULLET	RANGE, YARDS:	0	100	200	300	400
Rem. 150 PSP C-L Ultra	velocity, fps:	3200	2901	2672	2359	2112
	energy, ft-lb:	3410	2803	2290	1854	1485
	arc, inches:		+1.3	0	-6.4	-19.1
Rem. 165 PSP Core-Lokt	velocity, fps:	3075	2792	2527	2276	2040
	energy, ft-lb:	3464	2856	2339	1828	1525
	arc, inches:		+1.5	0	-7.0	-20.7
Rem. 180 Partition	velocity, fps:	2960	2761	2571	2389	2214
	energy, ft-lb:	3501	3047	2642	2280	1959
	arc, inches:		+1.5	0	-6.8	-19.7
Rem. 180 PSP C-L Ultra	velocity, fps:	2960	2727	2506	2295	2094
	energy, ft-lb:	3501	2972	2509	2105	1753
	arc, inches:		+1.6	0	-7.1	-20.9
Rem. 190 HPBT Match	velocity, fps:	2900	2725	2557	2395	2239
	energy, ft-lb:	3547	3133	2758	2420	2115
	arc, inches:		+1.6	0	-6.9	-19.9

.300 Winchester Short Magnum

CARTRIDGE BULLET	RANGE, YARDS:	0	100	200	300	400
Black Hills 175 Sierra MKing	velocity, fps:	2950				
	energy, ft-lb:	3381				
	arc, inches:					
Black Hills 180 AccuBond	velocity, fps:	2950				
	energy, ft-lb:	3478				
	arc, inches:					
Federal 150 Nosler Bal. Tip	velocity, fps:	3200	2970	2755	2545	2345
	energy, ft-lb:	3410	2940	2520	2155	1830.
	arc, inches:		+1.2	0	-5.8	-17.0
Federal 160 Trophy Bonded Tip	velocity, fps:	3130	2910	2710	2510	2320
	energy, ft-lb:	3590	3110	2680	2305	1970
	arc, inches:		+1.3	0	-6.0	-17.6
Federal 165 Nos. Partition	velocity, fps:	3130	2890	2670	2450	2250
	energy, ft-lb:	3590	3065	2605	2205	1855.
	arc, inches:		+1.3	0	-6.2	-18.2
Federal 165 Nos. Solid Base	velocity, fps:	3130	2900	2690	2490	2290
	energy, ft-lb:	3590	3090	2650	2265	1920
	arc, inches:		+1.3	0	-6.1	-17.8
Federal 180 Barnes TS And Nos. Solid Base	velocity, fps:	2980	2780	2580	2400	2220
	energy, ft-lbs:	3550	3085	2670	2300	1970
	arc, inches:		+1.5	0	-6.7	-19.5
Federal 180 Grand Slam	velocity, fps:	2970	2740	2530	2320	2130
	energy, ft-lb:	3525	3010	2555	2155	1810
	arc, inches:		+1.5	0	-7.0	-20.5
Federal 180 Trophy Bonded	velocity, fps:	2970	2730	2500	2280	2080
	energy, ft-lb:	3525	2975	2500	2085	1725
	arc, inches:		+1.5	0	-7.2	-21.0
Federal 180 Nosler Partition	velocity, fps:	2975	2750	2535	2290	2126
	energy, ft-lb:	3540	3025	2570	2175	1825
	arc, inches:		+1.5	0	-7.0	-20.3
Federal 180 Nos. AccuBond	velocity, fps:	2960	2780	2610	2440	2280
	energy, ft-lb:	3500	3090	2715	2380	2075
	arc, inches:		+1.5	0	-6.6	-19.0
Federal 180 Hi-Shok SP	velocity, fps:	2970	2520	2115	1750	1430
	energy, ft-lb:	3525	2540	1785	1220	820
	arc, inches:		+2.2	0	-9.9	-31.4
Norma 150 FMJ	velocity, fps:	2953	2731	2519	2318	
	energy, ft-lb:					
	arc, inches:		+1.6	0	-7.1	
Norma 150 Barnes X TS	velocity, fps:	3215	2982	2761	2550	
	energy, ft-lb:	3444	2962	2539	2167	
	arc, inches:		+1.2	0	-5.7	
Norma 180 Nosler Bal. Tip	velocity, fps:	3215	2985	2767	2560	
	energy, ft-lb:	3437	2963	2547	2179	
	arc, inches:		+1.2	0	-5.7	
Norma 180 Oryx	velocity, fps:	2936	2542	2180	1849	
	energy, ft-lb:	3446	2583	1900	1368	
	arc, inches:		+1.9	0	-8.9	
Win. 150 Power-Point	velocity, fps:	3270	2903	2565	2250	1958
	energy, ft-lb:	3561	2807	2190	1686	1277
	arc, inches:		+1.3	0	-6.6	-20.2
Win. 150 Ballistic Silvertip	velocity, fps:	3300	3061	2834	2619	2414
	energy, ft-lb:	3628	3121	2676	2285	1941
	arc, inches:		+1.1	0	-5.4	-15.9
Win. 165 Fail Safe	velocity, fps:	3125	2846	2584	2336	2102
	energy, ft-lb:	3577	2967	2446	1999	1619
	arc, inches:		+1.4	0	-6.6	-19.6
Win. 180 Ballistic Silvertip	velocity, fps:	3010	2822	2641	2468	2301.
	energy, ft-lb:	3621	3182	2788	2434	2116
	arc, inches:		+1.4	0	-6.4	-18.6
Win. 180 AccuBond	velocity, fps:	3010	2822	2643	2470	2304
	energy, ft-lbs:	3622	3185	2792	2439	2121
	arc, inches:		+1.4	0	-6.4	-18.5
Win. 180 Fail Safe	velocity, fps:	2970	2741	2524	2317	2120
	energy, ft-lb:	3526	3005	2547	2147	1797
	arc, inches:		+1.6	0	-7.0	-20.5
Win. 180 Power Point	velocity, fps:	2970	2755	2549	2353	2166
	energy, ft-lb:	3526	3034	2598	2214	1875
	arc, inches:		+1.5	0	-6.9	-20.1
Win. 150 Supreme Elite XP3	velocity, fps:	3300	3068	2847	2637	2437
	energy, ft-lb:	3626	3134	2699	2316	1978
	arc, inches:		+1.1	0	-5.4	-15.8
Win. 180 Supreme Elite XP3	velocity, fps:	3010	2829	2655	2488	2326
	energy, ft-lb:	3621	3198	2817	2473	2162
	arc, inches:		+1.4	0	-6.4	-18.3

.300 Ruger Compact Magnum

CARTRIDGE BULLET	RANGE, YARDS:	0	100	200	300	400
Hornady 150 SST	velocity, fps:	3310	3065	2833	2613	2404
	energy, ft-lb:	3648	3128	2673	2274	1924
	arc, inches:	-1.5	+1.1	0	-5.4	-16.0
Hornady 165 GMX	velocity, fps:	3130	2911	2703	2504	2314
	energy, ft-lb:	3589	3105	2677	2297	1963
	arc, inches:	-1.5	+1.3	0	-6.1	-17.7
Hornady 180 SST	velocity, fps:	3040	2840	2649	2466	2290
	energy, ft-lb:	3693	3223	2804	2430	2096
	arc, inches:	-1.5	+1.4	0	-6.4	-18.5

.300 Weatherby Magnum

CARTRIDGE BULLET	RANGE, YARDS:	0	100	200	300	400
A-Square 180 Dead Tough	velocity, fps:	3180	2811	2471	2155	1863.
	energy, ft-lb:	4041	3158	2440	1856	1387
	arc, inches:		+1.5	0	-7.2	-21.8
A-Square 220 Monolythic Solid	velocity, fps:	2700	2407	2133	1877	1653
	energy, ft-lb:	3561	2830	2223	1721	1334
	arc, inches:		+2.3	0	-9.8	-29.7
Federal 180 Nosler Partition	velocity, fps:	3190	2980	2780	2590	2400
	energy, ft-lb:	4055	3540	3080	2670	2305
	arc, inches:		+1.2	0	-5.7	-16.7
Federal 180 Nosler Part. HE	velocity, fps:	3330	3110	2810	2710	2520
	energy, ft-lb:	4430	3875	3375	2935	2540
	arc, inches:		+1.0	0	-5.2	-15.1
Federal 180 Sierra GameKing BTSP	velocity, fps:	3190	3010	2830	2660	2490
	energy, ft-lb:	4065	3610	3195	2820	2480
	arc, inches:		+1.2	0	-5.6	-16.0
Federal 180 Trophy Bonded	velocity, fps:	3190	2950	2720	2500	2290
	energy, ft-lb:	4065	3475	2955	2500	2105
	arc, inches:		+1.3	0	-5.9	-17.5
Federal 180 Tr. Bonded HE	velocity, fps:	3330	3080	2850	2750	2410
	energy, ft-lb:	4430	3795	3235	2750	2320
	arc, inches:		+1.1	0	-5.4	-15.8
Federal 180 Trophy Copper	velocity, fps:	3100	2910	2740	2560	2400
	energy, ft-lb:	3840	3395	2990	2625	2300
	arc, inches:		+1.3	0	-6.0	-17.1
Federal 200 Trophy Bonded	velocity, fps:	2900	2670	2440	2230	2030
	energy, ft-lb:	3735	3150	2645	2200	1820
	arc, inches:		+1.7	0	-7.6	-22.2
Hornady 150 SST (or Interbond)	velocity, fps:	3375	3123	2882	2652	2434
	energy, ft-lb:	3793	3248	2766	2343	1973
	arc, inches:		+1.0	0	-5.4	-15.8
Hornady 165 GMX Superformance	velocity, fps:	3140	2921	2713	2515	2325
	energy, ft-lb:	3612	3126	2697	2317	1980
	arc, inches:		+1.3	0	-6.0	-17.5
Hornady 180 SP	velocity, fps:	3120	2891	2673	2466	2268.
	energy, ft-lb:	3890	3340	2856	2430	2055
	arc, inches:		+1.3	0	-6.2	-18.1
Hornady 180 SST	velocity, fps:	3120	2911	2711	2519	2335
	energy, ft-lb:	3890	3386	2936	2535	2180
	arc, inches:		+1.3	0	-6.2	-18.1
Rem. 180 PSP Core-Lokt	velocity, fps:	3120	2866	2627	2400	2184
	energy, ft-lb:	3890	3284	2758	2301	1905
	arc, inches:		+2.4	+2.0	-3.4	-14.9

Centerfire Rifle Ballistics

.300 WEATHERBY MAGNUM TO .303 BRITISH

CARTRIDGE BULLET	RANGE, YARDS:	0	100	200	300	400
Rem. 190 PSP boat-tail	velocity, fps:	3030	2830	2638	2455	2279
	energy, ft-lb:	3873	3378	2936	2542	2190.
	arc, inches:		+1.4	0	-6.4	-18.6
Rem. 200 Swift A-Frame	velocity, fps:	2925	2690	2467	2254	2052
	energy, ft-lb:	3799	3213	2701	2256	1870
	arc, inches:		+2.8	+2.3	-3.9	-17.0
Speer 180 Grand Slam	velocity, fps:	3185	2948	2722	2508	
	energy, ft-lb:	4054	3472	2962	2514	
	arc, inches:		+1.3	0	-5.9	-17.4
Wby. 150 Pointed Expanding	velocity, fps:	3540	3225	2932	2657	2399
	energy, ft-lb:	4173	3462	2862	2351	1916
	arc, inches:		+2.6	+3.3	0	-8.2
Wby. 150 Nosler Partition	velocity, fps:	3540	3263	3004	2759	2528
	energy, ft-lb:	4173	3547	3005	2536	2128
	arc, inches:		+2.5	+3.2	0	-7.7
Wby. 165 Pointed Expanding	velocity, fps:	3390	3123	2872	2634	2409
	energy, ft-lb:	4210	3573	3021	2542	2126
	arc, inches:		+2.8	+3.5	0	-8.5
Wby. 165 Nosler Bal. Tip	velocity, fps:	3350	3133	2927	2730	2542
	energy, ft-lb:	4111	3596	3138	2730	2367
	arc, inches:		+2.7	+3.4	0	-8.1
Wby. 180 Pointed Expanding	velocity, fps:	3240	3004	2781	2569	2366
	energy, ft-lb:	4195	3607	3091	2637	2237
	arc, inches:		+3.1	+3.8	0	-9.0
Wby. 180 Barnes X	velocity, fps:	3190	2995	2809	2631	2459
	energy, ft-lb:	4067	3586	3154	2766	2417
	arc, inches:		+3.1	+3.8	0	-8.7
Wby. 180 Bal. Tip	velocity, fps:	3250	3051	2806	2676	2503
	energy, ft-lb:	4223	3721	3271	2867	2504
	arc, inches:		+2.8	+3.6	0	-8.4
Wby. 180 Nosler Partition	velocity, fps:	3240	3028	2826	2634	2449
	energy, ft-lb:	4195	3665	3193	2772	2396
	arc, inches:		+3.0	+3.7	0	-8.6
Wby. 200 Nosler Partition	velocity, fps:	3060	2860	2668	2485	2308
	energy, ft-lb:	4158	3631	3161	2741	2366
	arc, inches:		+3.5	+4.2	0	-9.8
Wby. 220 RN Expanding	velocity, fps:	2845	2543	2260	1996	1751.
	energy, ft-lb:	3954	3158	2495	1946	1497
	arc, inches:		+4.9	+5.9	0	-14.6

.300 Dakota

CARTRIDGE BULLET	RANGE, YARDS:	0	100	200	300	400
Dakota 165 Barnes X	velocity, fps:	3200	2979	2769	2569	2377
	energy, ft-lb:	3751	3251	2809	2417	2070
	arc, inches:		+2.1	+1.8	-3.0	-13.2
Dakota 200 Barnes X	velocity, fps:	3000	2824	2656	2493	2336
	energy, ft-lb:	3996	3542	3131	2760	2423
	arc, inches:		+2.2	+1.5	-4.0	-15.2

.300 Pegasus

CARTRIDGE BULLET	RANGE, YARDS:	0	100	200	300	400
A-Square 180 SP boat-tail	velocity, fps:	3500	3319	3145	2978	2817
	energy, ft-lb:	4896	4401	3953	3544	3172
	arc, inches:		+2.3	+2.9	0	-6.8
A-Square 180 Nosler Part.	velocity, fps:	3500	3295	3100	2913	2734
	energy, ft-lb:	4896	4339	3840	3392	2988
	arc, inches:		+2.3	+3.0	0	-7.1
A-Square 180 Dead Tough	velocity, fps:	3500	3103	2740	2405	2095
	energy, ft-lb:	4896	3848	3001	2312	1753
	arc, inches:		+1.1	0	-5.7	-17.5

.300 Remington Ultra Magnum

CARTRIDGE BULLET	RANGE, YARDS:	0	100	200	300	400
Federal 180 Trophy Bonded	velocity, fps:	3250	3000	2770	2550	2340
	energy, ft-lb:	4220	3605	3065	2590	2180
	arc, inches:		+1.2	0	-5.7	-16.8
Federal 180 Trophy Copper	velocity, fps:	3150	2960	2780	2610	2440
	energy, ft-lb:	3965	3505	3090	2715	2380
	arc, inches:		+1.2	0	-5.8	-16.6
Federal 200 Partition	velocity, fps:	3070	2870	2680	2490	2320
	energy, ft-lb:	4185	3655	3180	2760	2380
	arc, inches:		+1.4	0	-6.2	-18.0
Rem. 150 Swift Scirocco	velocity, fps:	3450	3208	2980	2762	2556
	energy, ft-lb:	3964	3427	2956	2541	2175
	arc, inches:		+1.7	+1.5	-2.6	-11.2
Remington 165 Copper Solid	velocity, fps:	3250	3035	2821	2617	2422
	energy, ft-lb:	3893	3373	2916	2602	2390
	arc, inches:		+1.4	0	-5.8	-16.7
Rem. 180 Nosler Partition	velocity, fps:	3250	3037	2834	2640	2454
	energy, ft-lb:	4221	3686	3201	2786	2407
	arc, inches:		+2.4	+1.8	-3.0	-12.7
Rem. 180 Swift Scirocco	velocity, fps:	3250	3048	2856	2672	2495
	energy, ft-lb:	4221	3714	3260	2853	2487
	arc, inches:		+2.0	+1.7	-2.8	-12.3
Rem. 180 PSP Core-Lokt	velocity, fps:	3250	2988	2742	2508	2287
	energy, ft-lb:	3517	2974	2503	2095	1741
	arc, inches:		+2.1	+1.8	-3.1	-13.6
Rem. 200 Nosler Partition	velocity, fps:	3025	2826	2636	2454	2279
	energy, ft-lb:	4063	3547	3086	2673	2308
	arc, inches:		+2.4	+2.0	-3.4	-14.6

.30-378 Weatherby Magnum

CARTRIDGE BULLET	RANGE, YARDS:	0	100	200	300	400
Nosler 210 ABLR	velocity, fps:	3040	2907	2778	2653	2531
	energy, ft-lb:	4308	3940	3599	3282	2987
	arc, inches:	-1.5	+1.3	0	-5.8	-16.6
Wby. 165 Nosler Bal. Tip	velocity, fps:	3500	3275	3062	2859	2665
	energy, ft-lb:	4488	3930	3435	2995	2603
	arc, inches:		+2.4	+3.0	0	-7.4
Wby. 180 Nosler Bal. Tip	velocity, fps:	3420	3213	3015	2826	2645
	energy, ft-lb:	4676	4126	3634	3193	2797
	arc, inches:		+2.5	+3.1	0	-7.5
Wby. 180 Barnes X	velocity, fps:	3450	3243	3046	2858	2678.
	energy, ft-lb:	4757	4204	3709	3264	2865
	arc, inches:		+2.4	+3.1	0	-7.4
Wby. 200 Nosler Partition	velocity, fps:	3160	2955	2759	2572	2392.
	energy, ft-lb:	4434	3877	3381	2938	2541
	arc, inches:		+3.2	+3.9	0	-9.1

7.82 (.308) Warbird

CARTRIDGE BULLET	RANGE, YARDS:	0	100	200	300	400
Lazzeroni 150 Nosler Part.	velocity, fps:	3680	3432	3197	2975	2764
	energy, ft-lb:	4512	3923	3406	2949	2546.
	arc, inches:		+2.1	+2.7	0	-6.6
Lazzeroni 180 Nosler Part.	velocity, fps:	3425	3220	3026	2839	2661
	energy, ft-lb:	4689	4147	3661	3224	2831
	arc, inches:		+2.5	+3.2	0	-7.5
Lazzeroni 200 Swift A-Fr.	velocity, fps:	3290	3105	2928	2758	2594.
	energy, ft-lb:	4808	4283	3808	3378	2988
	arc, inches:		+2.7	+3.4	0	-7.9

7.65x53 Argentine

CARTRIDGE BULLET	RANGE, YARDS:	0	100	200	300	400
Norma 174 Soft Point	velocity, fps:	2493	2173	1878	1611	
	energy, ft-lb:	2402	1825	1363	1003	
	arc, inches:		+2.0	0	-9.5	
Norma 180 Soft Point	velocity, fps:	2592	2386	2189	2002	
	energy, ft-lb:	2686	2276	1916	1602	
	arc, inches:		+2.3	0	-9.6	

.303 British

CARTRIDGE BULLET	RANGE, YARDS:	0	100	200	300	400
Federal 150 Hi-Shok	velocity, fps:	2690	2440	2210	1980	1780
	energy, ft-lb:	2400	1980	1620	1310	1055
	arc, inches:		+2.2	0	-9.4	-27.6
Federal 180 Sierra Pro-Hunt.	velocity, fps:	2460	2230	2020	1820	1630
	energy, ft-lb:	2420	1995	1625	1315	1060
	arc, inches:		+2.8	0	-11.3	-33.2
Federal 180 Tr. Bonded HE	velocity, fps:	2590	2350	2120	1900	1700
	energy, ft-lb:	2680	2205	1795	1445	1160
	arc, inches:		+2.4	0	-10.0	-30.0
Hornady 150 Soft Point	velocity, fps:	2685	2441	2210	1992	1787
	energy, ft-lb:	2401	1984	1627	1321	1064
	arc, inches:		+2.2	0	-9.3	-27.4

CARTRIDGE BULLET	RANGE, YARDS:	0	100	200	300	400
Hornady 150 SP LM	velocity, fps:	2830	2570	2325	2094	1884.
	energy, ft-lb:	2667	2199	1800	1461	1185
	arc, inches:		+2.0	0	-8.4	-24.6
Hornady 174 BTHP	velocity, fps:	2430	2252	2082	1919	1765
	energy, ft-lb:	2281	1959	1674	1423	1204
	arc, inches:		+2.7	0	-10.7	-30.9
Norma 150 Soft Point	velocity, fps:	2723	2438	2170	1920	
	energy, ft-lb:	2470	1980	1569	1228	
	arc, inches:		+2.2	0	-9.6	
PMC 174 FMJ (and HPBT)	velocity, fps:	2400	2216	2042	1876	1720
	energy, ft-lb:	2225	1898	1611	1360	1143
	arc, inches:		+2.8	0	-11.2	-32.2
PMC 180 SP boat-tail	velocity, fps:	2450	2276	2110	1951	1799
	energy, ft-lb:	2399	2071	1779	1521	1294
	arc, inches:		+2.6	0	-10.4	-30.1
Rem. 180 SP Core-Lokt	velocity, fps:	2460	2124	1817	1542	1311
	energy, ft-lb:	2418	1803	1319	950	687
	arc, inches, s:		0	-5.8	-23.3	
Win. 180 Power-Point	velocity, fps:	2460	2233	2018	1816	1629
	energy, ft-lb:	2418	1993	1627	1318	1060
	arc, inches, s:		0	-6.1	-20.8	

7.7x58 Japanese Arisaka

CARTRIDGE BULLET	RANGE, YARDS:	0	100	200	300	400
Norma 174 Soft Point	velocity, fps:	2493	2173	1878	1611	
	energy, ft-lb:	2402	1825	1363	1003	
	arc, inches:		+2.0	0	-9.5	
Norma 180 Soft Point	velocity, fps:	2493	2291	2099	1916	
	energy, ft-lb:	2485	2099	1761	1468	
	arc, inches:		+2.6	0	-10.5	

.32-20 Winchester

CARTRIDGE BULLET	RANGE, YARDS:	0	100	200	300	400
Rem. 100 Lead	velocity, fps:	1210	1021	913	834	769
	energy, ft-lb:	325	231	185	154	131
	arc, inches:		0	-31.6	-104.7	
Win. 100 Lead	velocity, fps:	1210	1021	913	834	769
	energy, ft-lb:	325	231	185	154	131
	arc, inches:		0	-32.3	-106.3	

.32 Winchester Special

CARTRIDGE BULLET	RANGE, YARDS:	0	100	200	300	400
Federal 170 Hi-Shok	velocity, fps:	2250	1920	1630	1370	1180
	energy, ft-lb:	1910	1395	1000	710	520
	arc, inches:		0	-8.0	-29.2	
Hornady 165 FTX	velocity, fps:	2410	2145	1897	1669	
	energy, ft-lb:	2128	1685	1318	1020	
	arc, inches:	-1.5	+3.0	0	-12.8	
Rem. 170 SP Core-Lokt	velocity, fps:	2250	1921	1626	1372	1175
	energy, ft-lb:	1911	1393	998	710	521
	arc, inches:		0	-8.0	-29.3	
Win. 170 Power-Point	velocity, fps:	2250	1870	1537	1267	1082
	energy, ft-lb:	1911	1320	892	606	442
	arc, inches:		0	-9.2	-33.2	

8mm Mauser (8x57)

CARTRIDGE BULLET	RANGE, YARDS:	0	100	200	300	400
Federal 170 Hi-Shok	velocity, fps:	2360	1970	1620	1330	1120
	energy, ft-lb:	2100	1465	995	670	475
	arc, inches:		0	-7.6	-28.5	
Hornady 195 SP	velocity, fps:	2550	2343	2146	1959	1782
	energy, ft-lb:	2815	2377	1994	1861	1375
	arc, inches:		+2.3	0	-9.9	-28.8.
Hornady 195 SP (2005)	velocity, fps:	2475	2269	2074	1888	1714
	energy, ft-lb:	2652	2230	1861	1543	1271
	arc, inches:		+2.6	0	-10.7	-31.3
Norma 123 FMJ	velocity, fps:	2559	2121	1729	1398	
	energy, ft-lb:	1789	1228	817	534	
	arc, inches:		+3.2	0	-15.0	
Norma 196 Oryx	velocity, fps:	2395	2146	1912	1695	
	energy, ft-lb:	2497	2004	1591	1251	
	arc, inches:		+3	0	-12.6	
Norma 196 Vulkan	velocity, fps:	2395	2156	1930	1720	
	energy, ft-lb:	2497	2023	1622	1289	
	arc, inches:		3.0	0	-12.3	
Norma 196 Alaska	velocity, fps:	2395	2112	1850	1611	
	energy, ft-lb:	2714	2190	1754	1399	
	arc, inches:		0	-6.3	-22.9	
Norma 196 Soft Point (JS)	velocity, fps:	2526	2244	1981	1737	
	energy, ft-lb:	2778	2192	1708	1314	
	arc, inches:		+2.7	0	-11.6	
Norma 196 Alaska (JS)	velocity, fps:	2526	2248	1988	1747	
	energy, ft-lb:	2778	2200	1720	1328	
	arc, inches:		+2.7	0	-11.5	
Norma 196 Vulkan (JS)	velocity, fps:	2526	2276	2041	1821	
	energy, ft-lb:	2778	2256	1813	1443	
	arc, inches:		+2.6	0	-11.0	
Norma 196 Oryx (JS)	velocity, fps:	2526	2269	2027	1802	
	energy, ft-lb:	2778	2241	1789	1413	
	arc, inches:		+2.6	0	-11.1	
PMC 170 Pointed Soft Point	velocity, fps:	2360	1969	1622	1333	1123
	energy, ft-lb:	2102	1463	993	671	476
	arc, inches:		+1.8	-4.5	-24.3	-63.8
Rem. 170 SP Core-Lokt	velocity, fps:	2360	1969	1622	1333	1123
	energy, ft-lb:	2102	1463	993	671	476
	arc, inches:		+1.8	-4.5	-24.3	-63.8.
Win. 170 Power-Point	velocity, fps:	2360	1969	1622	1333	1123
	energy, ft-lb:	2102	1463	993	671	476
	arc, inches:		+1.8	-4.5	-24.3	-63.8

.325 WSM

CARTRIDGE BULLET	RANGE, YARDS:	0	100	200	300	400
Win. 180 Ballistic ST	velocity, fps:	3060	2841	2632	2432	2242
	energy, ft-lb:	3743	3226	2769	2365	2009
	arc, inches:		+1.4	0	-6.4	-18.7
Win. 200 AccuBond CT	velocity, fps:	2950	2753	2565	2384	2210
	energy, ft-lb:	3866	3367	2922	2524	2170
	arc, inches:		+1.5	0	-6.8	-19.8
Win. 220 Power-Point	velocity, fps:	2840	2605	2382	2169	1968
	energy, ft-lb:	3941	3316	2772	2300	1893
	arc, inches:		+1.8	0	-8.0	-23.3

8mm Remington Magnum

CARTRIDGE BULLET	RANGE, YARDS:	0	100	200	300	400
A-Square 220 Monolythic Solid	velocity, fps:	2800	2501	2221	1959	1718
	energy, ft-lb:	3829	3055	2409	1875	1442
	arc, inches:		+2.1	0	-9.1	-27.6
Nosler 180 BT	velocity, fps:	3200	2923	2662	2416	2183
	energy, ft-lb:	4092	3414	2832	2333	1905
	arc, inches:	-1.5	+1.3	0	-6.2	-18.4
Rem. 200 Swift A-Frame	velocity, fps:	2900	2623	2361	2115	1885
	energy, ft-lb:	3734	3054	2476	1987	1577
	arc, inches:		+1.8	0	-8.0	-23.9

.338 Federal

CARTRIDGE BULLET	RANGE, YARDS:	0	100	200	300	400
Federal 180 AccuBond	velocity, fps:	2830	2590	2350	2130	1930
	energy, ft-lb:	3200	2670	2215	1820	1480
	arc, inches:	-1.5	+1.8	0	-8.2	-23.9
Federal 185 Barnes TSX	velocity, fps:	2750	2500	2260	2030	1820
	energy, ft-lb:	3105	2560	2090	1695	1355
	arc, inches:	-1.5	+2.0	0	-8.9	-26.2
Federal 200 Tr. Bonded T	velocity, fps:	2630	2430	2240	2060	1890
	energy, ft-lb:	3070	2625	2230	1885	1580
	arc, inches:	-1.5	+2.2	0	-9.2	-26.3
Federal 210 Partition	velocity, fps:	2630	2410	2200	2010	1820
	energy, ft-lb:	3225	2710	2265	1880	1545
	arc, inches:	-1.5	+2.3	0	-9.4	-27.3

Centerfire Rifle Ballistics

.338 MARLIN EXPRESS TO .340 WEATHERBY MAGNUM

.338 Marlin Express

CARTRIDGE BULLET	RANGE, YARDS:	0	100	200	300	400
Hornady 200 FTX	velocity, fps:	2565	2365	2174	1992	`1820
	energy, ft-lb:	2922	2484	2099	1762	1471
	arc, inches:	-1.5	+3.0	+1.2	-7.9	-25.9

.338-06

CARTRIDGE BULLET	RANGE, YARDS:	0	100	200	300	400
A-Square 200 Nos. Bal. Tip	velocity, fps:	2750	2553	2364	2184	2011
	energy, ft-lb:	3358	2894	2482	2118	1796
	arc, inches:		+1.9	0	-8.2	-23.6
A-Square 250 SP boat-tail	velocity, fps:	2500	2374	2252	2134	2019
	energy, ft-lb:	3496	3129	2816	2528	2263
	arc, inches:		+2.4	0	-9.3	-26.0
A-Square 250 Dead Tough	velocity, fps:	2500	2222	1963	1724	1507
	energy, ft-lb:	3496	2742	2139	1649	1261
	arc, inches:		+2.8	0	-11.9	-35.5
Nosler 180 AB	velocity, fps:	2950	2698	2460	2234	2020
	energy, ft-lb:	3477	2909	2418	1994	1631
	arc, inches:	-1.5	+1.6	0	-7.4	-21.8
Nosler 225 AB	velocity, fps:	2600	2441	2287	2139	1997
	energy, ft-lb:	3376	2976	2614	2286	1992
	arc, inches:	-1.5	+2.2	0	-8.8	-25.3
Wby. 210 Nosler Part.	velocity, fps:	2750	2526	2312	2109	1916
	energy, ft-lb:	3527	2975	2403	2074	1712
	arc, inches:		+4.8	+5.7	0	-13.5

.338 Ruger Compact Magnum

CARTRIDGE BULLET	RANGE, YARDS:	0	100	200	300	400
Hornady 185 GMX	velocity, fps:	2980	2755	2542	2338	2143
	energy, ft-lb:	3647	3118	2653	2242	1887
	arc, inches:	-1.5	+1.5	0	-6.9	-20.3
Hornady 200 SST	velocity, fps:	2950	2744	2547	2358	2177
	energy, ft-lb:	3846	3342	2879	2468	2104
	arc, inches:	-1.5	+1.6	0	-6.9	-20.1
Hornady 225 SST	velocity, fps:	2750	2575	2407	2245	2089
	energy, ft-lb:	3778	3313	2894	2518	2180
	arc, inches:	-1.5	+1.9	0	-7.9	-22.7

.338 Winchester Magnum

CARTRIDGE BULLET	RANGE, YARDS:	0	100	200	300	400
A-Square 250 SP boat-tail	velocity, fps:	2700	2568	2439	2314	2193
	energy, ft-lb:	4046	3659	3302	2972	2669
	arc, inches:		+4.4	+5.2	0	-11.7
A-Square 250 Triad	velocity, fps:	2700	2407	2133	1877	1653
	energy, ft-lb:	4046	3216	2526	1956	1516
	arc, inches:		+2.3	0	-9.8	-29.8
Federal 200 Trophy Bonded Tip	velocity, fps:	2930	2720	2520	2320	2140
	energy, ft-lb:	3810	3280	2810	2395	2025
	arc, inches:		+1.6	0	-7.1	-20.7
Federal 210 Nosler Partition	velocity, fps:	2830	2600	2390	2180	1980
	energy, ft-lb:	3735	3160	2655	2215	1835
	arc, inches:		+1.8	0	-8.0	-23.3
Federal 225 Sierra Pro-Hunt.	velocity, fps:	2780	2570	2360	2170	1980
	energy, ft-lb:	3860	3290	2780	2340	1960
	arc, inches:		+1.9	0	-8.2	-23.7
Federal 225 Trophy Bonded	velocity, fps:	2800	2560	2330	2110	1900
	energy, ft-lb:	3915	3265	2700	2220	1800
	arc, inches:		+1.9	0	-8.4	-24.5
Federal 225 Tr. Bonded HE	velocity, fps:	2940	2690	2450	2230	2010
	energy, ft-lb:	4320	3610	3000	2475	2025
	arc, inches:		+1.7	0	-7.5	-22.0
Federal 225 Barnes XLC	velocity, fps:	2800	2610	2430	2260	2090
	energy, ft-lb:	3915	3405	2950	2545	2190
	arc, inches:		+1.8	0	-7.7	-22.2
Federal 250 Nosler Partition	velocity, fps:	2660	2470	2300	2120	1960
	energy, ft-lb:	3925	3395	2925	2505	2130.
	arc, inches:		+2.1	0	-8.8	-25.1
Federal 250 Nosler Part HE	velocity, fps:	2800	2610	2420	2250	2080
	energy, ft-lb:	4350	3775	3260	2805	2395
	arc, inches:		+1.8	0	-7.8	-22.5
Hornady 185 GMX Superformance	velocity, fps:	3080	2851	2633	2426	2228
	energy, ft-lb:	3897	3338	2848	2417	2038
	arc, inches:		+1.4	0	-6.4	-18.8
Hornady 200 SST Superformance	velocity, fps:	3030	2820	2620	2429	2246
	energy, ft-lb:	4077	3532	3049	2621	2240
	arc, inches:		+1.4	0	-6.5	-18.9
Hornady 225 Soft Point HM	velocity, fps:	2920	2678	2449	2232	2027
	energy, ft-lb:	4259	3583	2996	2489	2053
	arc, inches:		+1.8	0	-7.6	-22.0
Norma 225 TXP Swift A-Fr.	velocity, fps:	2740	2507	2286	2075	
	energy, ft-lb:	3752	3141	2611	2153	
	arc, inches:		+2.0	0	-8.7	
Norma 230 Oryx	velocity, fps:	2756	2514	2284	2066	
	energy, ft-lb:	3880	3228	2665	2181	
	arc, inches:		+2.0	0	-8.7	
Norma 250 Nosler Partition	velocity, fps:	2657	2470	2290	2118	
	energy, ft-lb:	3920	3387	2912	2490	
	arc, inches:		+2.1	0	-8.7	
PMC 225 Barnes X	velocity, fps:	2780	2619	2464	2313	2168
	energy, ft-lb:	3860	3426	3032	2673	2348.
	arc, inches:		+1.8	0	-7.6	-21.6
Rem. 200 Nosler Bal. Tip	velocity, fps:	2950	2724	2509	2303	2108
	energy, ft-lb:	3866	3295	2795	2357	1973
	arc, inches:		+1.6	0	-7.1	-20.8
Rem. 210 Nosler Partition	velocity, fps:	2830	2602	2385	2179	1983
	energy, ft-lb:	3734	3157	2653	2214	1834
	arc, inches:		+1.8	0	-7.9	-23.2
Rem. 225 PSP Core-Lokt	velocity, fps:	2780	2572	2374	2184	2003
	energy, ft-lb:	3860	3305	2815	2383	2004
	arc, inches:		+1.9	0	-8.1	-23.4
Rem. 225 PSP C-L Ultra	velocity, fps:	2780	2582	2392	2210	2036
	energy, ft-lb:	3860	3329	2858	2440	2071
	arc, inches:		+1.9	0	-7.9	-23.0
Rem. 225 Swift A-Frame	velocity, fps:	2785	2517	2266	2029	1808
	energy, ft-lb:	3871	3165	2565	2057	1633
	arc, inches:		+2.0	0	-8.8	-25.2
Rem. 250 PSP Core-Lokt	velocity, fps:	2660	2456	2261	2075	1898
	energy, ft-lb:	3927	3348	2837	2389	1999
	arc, inches:		+2.1	0	-8.9	-26.0
Speer 250 Grand Slam	velocity, fps:	2645	2442	2247	2062	
	energy, ft-lb:	3883	3309	2803	2360	
	arc, inches:		+2.2	0	-9.1	-26.2
Win. 200 Power-Point	velocity, fps:	2960	2658	2375	2110	1862
	energy, ft-lb:	3890	3137	2505	1977	1539
	arc, inches:		+2.0	0	-8.2	-24.3
Win. 200 Ballistic Silvertip	velocity, fps:	2950	2724	2509	2303	2108
	energy, ft-lb:	3864	3294	2794	2355	1972
	arc, inches:		+1.6	0	-7.1	-20.8
Win. 225 AccuBond	velocity, fps:	2800	2634	2474	2319	2170
	energy, ft-lb:	3918	3467	3058	2688	2353
	arc, inches:		+1.8	0	-7.4	-21.3
Win. 230 Fail Safe	velocity, fps:	2780	2573	2375	2186	2005
	energy, ft-lb:	3948	3382	2881	2441	2054
	arc, inches:		+1.9	0	-8.1	-23.4
Win. 250 Partition Gold	velocity, fps:	2650	2467	2291	2122	1960
	energy, ft-lb:	3899	3378	2914	2520	2134
	arc, inches:		+2.1	0	-8.7	-25.2

.340 Weatherby Magnum

CARTRIDGE BULLET	RANGE, YARDS:	0	100	200	300	400
A-Square 250 SP boat-tail	velocity, fps:	2820	2684	2552	2424	2299
	energy, ft-lb:	4414	3999	3615	3261	2935
	arc, inches:		+4.0	+4.6	0	-10.6
A-Square 250 Triad	velocity, fps:	2820	2520	2238	1976	1741
	energy, ft-lb:	4414	3524	2781	2166	1683
	arc, inches:		+2.0	0	-9.0	-26.8
Federal 225 Trophy Bonded	velocity, fps:	3100	2840	2600	2370	2150
	energy, ft-lb:	4800	4035	3375	2800	2310
	arc, inches:		+1.4	0	-6.5	-19.4

CARTRIDGE BULLET	RANGE, YARDS:	0	100	200	300	400
Wby. 200 Pointed Expanding	velocity, fps:	3221	2946	2688	2444	2213
	energy, ft-lb:	4607	3854	3208	2652	2174
	arc, inches:		+3.3	+4.0	0	-9.9
Wby. 200 Nosler Bal. Tip	velocity, fps:	3221	2980	2753	2536	2329
	energy, ft-lb:	4607	3944	3364	2856	2409
	arc, inches:		+3.1	+3.9	0	-9.2
Wby. 210 Nosler Partition	velocity, fps:	3211	2963	2728	2505	2293
	energy, ft-lb:	4807	4093	3470	2927	2452
	arc, inches:		+3.2	+3.9	0	-9.5
Wby. 225 Pointed Expanding	velocity, fps:	3066	2824	2595	2377	2170
	energy, ft-lb:	4696	3984	3364	2822	2352
	arc, inches:		+3.6	+4.4	0	-10.7
Wby. 225 Barnes X	velocity, fps:	3001	2804	2615	2434	2260
	energy, ft-lb:	4499	3927	3416	2959	2551
	arc, inches:		+3.6	+4.3	0	-10.3
Wby. 250 Pointed Expanding	velocity, fps:	2963	2745	2537	2338	2149
	energy, ft-lb:	4873	4182	3572	3035	2563
	arc, inches:		+3.9	+4.6	0	-11.1
Wby. 250 Nosler Partition	velocity, fps:	2941	2743	2553	2371	2197
	energy, ft-lb:	4801	4176	3618	3120	2678
	arc, inches:		+3.9	+4.6	0	-10.9

.330 Dakota

Dakota 200 Barnes X	velocity, fps:	3200	2971	2754	2548	2350
	energy, ft-lb:	4547	3920	3369	2882	2452
	arc, inches:		+2.1	+1.8	-3.1	-13.4
Dakota 250 Barnes X	velocity, fps:	2900	2719	2545	2378	2217
	energy, ft-lb:	4668	4103	3595	3138	2727
	arc, inches:		+2.3	+1.3	-5.0	-17.5

.338 Remington Ultra Magnum

Federal 210 Nosler Partition	velocity, fps:	3025	2800	2585	2385	2190
	energy, ft-lb:	4270	3655	3120	2645	2230
	arc, inches:		+1.5	0	-6.7	-19.5
Federal 250 Trophy Bonded	velocity, fps:	2860	2630	2420	2210	2020
	energy, ft-lb:	4540	3850	3245	2715	2260.
	arc, inches:		+0.8	0	-7.7	-22.6
Rem. 250 Swift A-Frame	velocity, fps:	2860	2645	2440	2244	2057
	energy, ft-lb:	4540	3882	3303	2794	2347
	arc, inches:		+1.7	0	-7.6	-22.1
Rem. 250 PSP Core-Lokt	velocity, fps:	2860	2647	2443	2249	2064
	energy, ft-lb:	4540	3888	3314	2807	2363
	arc, inches:		+1.7	0	-7.6	-22.0

.338 Norma Magnum

Black Hills 300 MatchKing	velocity, fps:	2725				
	energy, ft-lb:	4946				
	arc, inches					

.338 Lapua

Black Hills 250 Sierra MKing	velocity, fps:	2950				
	energy, ft-lb:	4831				
	arc, inches:					
Black Hills 300 Sierra MKing	velocity, fps:	2800				
	energy, ft-lb:	5223				
	arc, inches:					
Hornady 250 BTHP Match	velocity, fps:	2900	2761	2626	2495	2368
	energy, ft-lb:	4668	4230	3827	3455	3112
	arc, inches:		+1.5	0	-6.6	-18.8
Hornady 285 BTHP	velocity, fps:	2745	2616	2491	2369	2251
	energy, ft-lb:	4768	4331	3926	3552	3206
	arc, inches:	-1.5	+1.8	0	-7.4	-21.0

CARTRIDGE BULLET	RANGE, YARDS:	0	100	200	300	600
Lapua 250 Scenar	velocity, fps:	2970	2823	2680	2539	2141
	energy, ft-lb:	4896	4424	3985	3579	2545
	arc, inches:	-1.5	+3.0	+4.0	0	-47.0
Lapua 300 Scenar	velocity, fps:	2723	2600	2482	2367	2042
	energy, ft-lb:	4938	4504	4102	3731	2778
	arc, inches:	-1.5	+4.0	+5.0	0	-54.0

CARTRIDGE BULLET	RANGE, YARDS:	0	100	200	300	400
Nosler 225 AB	velocity, fps:	3000	2826	2659	2498	2342
	energy, ft-lb:	4495	3990	3532	3117	2741
	arc, inches:	-1.5	+1.4	0	-6.3	-18.3

.338-378 Weatherby Magnum

Wby. 200 Nosler Bal. Tip	velocity, fps:	3350	3102	2868	2646	2434
	energy, ft-lb:	4983	4273	3652	3109	2631
	arc, inches:	0	+2.8	+3.5	0	-8.4
Wby. 225 Barnes X	velocity, fps:	3180	2974	2778	2591	2410.
	energy, ft-lb:	5052	4420	3856	3353	2902
	arc, inches:	0	+3.1	+3.8	0	-8.9
Wby. 250 Nosler Partition	velocity, fps:	3060	2856	2662	2475	2297
	energy, ft-lb:	5197	4528	3933	3401	2927
	arc, inches:	0	+3.5	+4.2	0	-9.8

8.59 (.338) Titan

Lazzeroni 200 Nos. Bal. Tip	velocity, fps:	3430	3211	3002	2803	2613
	energy, ft-lb:	5226	4579	4004	3491	3033
	arc, inches:		+2.5	+3.2	0	-7.6
Lazzeroni 225 Nos. Partition	velocity, fps:	3235	3031	2836	2650	2471
	energy, ft-lb:	5229	4591	4021	3510	3052
	arc, inches:		+3.0	+3.6	0	-8.6
Lazzeroni 250 Swift A-Fr.	velocity, fps:	3100	2908	2725	2549	2379
	energy, ft-lb:	5336	4697	4123	3607	3143
	arc, inches:		+3.3	+4.0	0	-9.3

.338 A-Square

A-Square 200 Nos. Bal. Tip	velocity, fps:	3500	3266	3045	2835	2634
	energy, ft-lb:	5440	4737	4117	3568	3081
	arc, inches:		+2.4	+3.1	0	-7.5
A-Square 250 SP boat-tail	velocity, fps:	3120	2974	2834	2697	2565.
	energy, ft-lb:	5403	4911	4457	4038	3652
	arc, inches:		+3.1	+3.7	0	-8.5
A-Square 250 Triad	velocity, fps:	3120	2799	2500	2220	1958
	energy, ft-lb:	5403	4348	3469	2736	2128
	arc, inches:		+1.5	0	-7.1	-20.4.

.338 Excaliber

A-Square 200 Nos. Bal. Tip	velocity, fps:	3600	3361	3134	2920	2715
	energy, ft-lb:	5755	5015	4363	3785	3274
	arc, inches:		+2.2	+2.9	0	-6.7
A-Square 250 SP boat-tail	velocity, fps:	3250	3101	2958	2684	2553
	energy, ft-lb:	5863	5339	4855	4410	3998
	arc, inches:		+2.7	+3.4	0	-7.8
A-Square 250 Triad	velocity, fps:	3250	2922	2618	2333	2066
	energy, ft-lb:	5863	4740	3804	3021	2370
	arc, inches:		+1.3	0	-6.4	-19.2

.348 Winchester

Win. 200 Silvertip	velocity, fps:	2520	2215	1931	1672	1443.
	energy, ft-lb:	2820	2178	1656	1241	925
	arc, inches:		0	-6.2	-21.9	

.357 Magnum

Federal 180 Hi-Shok HP Hollow Point	velocity, fps:	1550	1160	980	860	770
	energy, ft-lb:	960	535	385	295	235
	arc, inches:		0	-22.8	-77.9	-173.8
Win. 158 Jacketed SP	velocity, fps:	1830	1427	1138	980	883
	energy, ft-lb:	1175	715	454	337	274
	arc, inches:		0	-16.2	-57.0	-128.3

.35 Remington

Federal 200 Hi-Shok	velocity, fps:	2080	1700	1380	1140	1000
	energy, ft-lb:	1920	1280	840	575	445
	arc, inches:		0	-10.7	-39.3	

Centerfire Rifle Ballistics

.35 Remington to 9.3x74 R

CARTRIDGE BULLET	RANGE, YARDS:	0	100	200	300	400
Hornady 200 Evolution	velocity, fps:	2225	1963	1721	1503	
	energy, ft-lb:	2198	1711	1315	1003	
	arc, inches:		+3.0	-1.3	-17.5	
Rem. 150 PSP Core-Lokt	velocity, fps:	2300	1874	1506	1218	1039
	energy, ft-lb:	1762	1169	755	494	359
	arc, inches:		0	-8.6	-32.6	
Rem. 200 SP Core-Lokt	velocity, fps:	2080	1698	1376	1140	1001
	energy, ft-lb:	1921	1280	841	577	445
	arc, inches:		0	-10.7	-40.1	
Win. 200 Power-Point	velocity, fps:	2020	1646	1335	1114	985
	energy, ft-lb:	1812	1203	791	551	431
	arc, inches:		0	-12.1	-43.9	

.356 Winchester

CARTRIDGE BULLET	RANGE, YARDS:	0	100	200	300	400
Win. 200 Power-Point	velocity, fps:	2460	2114	1797	1517	1284
	energy, ft-lb:	2688	1985	1434	1022	732
	arc, inches:		+1.6	-3.8	-20.1	-51.2

.358 Winchester

CARTRIDGE BULLET	RANGE, YARDS:	0	100	200	300	400
Hornady 200 SP	velocity, fps:	2475	2180	1906	1655	1434
	energy, ft-lb:	2720	2110	1612	1217	913
	arc, inches:	-1.5	+2.9	0	-12.6	-37.9
Win. 200 Silvertip	velocity, fps:	2490	2171	1876	1610	1379
	energy, ft-lb:	2753	2093	1563	1151	844
	arc, inches:		+1.5	-3.6	-18.6	-47.2

.35 Whelen

CARTRIDGE BULLET	RANGE, YARDS:	0	100	200	300	400
Federal 225 Trophy Bonded	velocity, fps:	2600	2400	2200	2020	1840
	energy, ft-lb:	3375	2865	2520	2030	1690.
	arc, inches:		+2.3	0	-9.4	-27.3
Hornady 200 SP	velocity, fps:	2910	2585	2283	2001	1742
	energy, ft-lb:	3760	2968	2314	1778	1347
	arc, inches:	-1.5	+1.9	0	-8.6	-25.9
Rem. 200 Pointed Soft Point	velocity, fps:	2675	2378	2100	1842	1606
	energy, ft-lb:	3177	2510	1958	1506	1145
	arc, inches:		+2.3	0	-10.3	-30.8
Rem. 250 Pointed Soft Point	velocity, fps:	2400	2197	2005	1823	1652
	energy, ft-lb:	3197	2680	2230	1844	1515
	arc, inches:		+1.3	-3.2	-16.6	-40.0

.350 Remington Magnum

CARTRIDGE BULLET	RANGE, YARDS:	0	100	200	300	400
Nosler 225 PT	velocity, fps:	2550	2349	2158	1976	1804
	energy, ft-lb:	3248	2758	2327	1951	1626
	arc, inches:	-1.5	+2.4	0	-9.9	-28.7

.358 Norma Magnum

CARTRIDGE BULLET	RANGE, YARDS:	0	100	200	300	400
A-Square 275 Triad	velocity, fps:	2700	2394	2108	1842	1653
	energy, ft-lb:	4451	3498	2713	2072	1668
	arc, inches:		+2.3	0	-10.1	-29.8
Norma 250 TXP Swift A-Fr.	velocity, fps:	2723	2467	2225	1996	
	energy, ft-lb:	4117	3379	2748	2213	
	arc, inches:		+2.1	0	-9.1	
Norma 250 Woodleigh	velocity, fps:	2799	2442	2112	1810	
	energy, ft-lb:	4350	3312	2478	1819	
	arc, inches:		+2.2	0	-10.0	
Norma 250 Oryx	velocity, fps:	2756	2493	2245	2011	
	energy, ft-lb:	4217	3451	2798	2245	
	arc, inches:		+2.1	0	-9.0	

.358 STA

CARTRIDGE BULLET	RANGE, YARDS:	0	100	200	300	400
A-Square 275 Triad	velocity, fps:	2850	2562	2292	2039	1764
	energy, ft-lb:	4959	4009	3208	2539	1899.
	arc, inches:		+1.9	0	-8.6	-26.1

9.3x57

CARTRIDGE BULLET	RANGE, YARDS:	0	100	200	300	400
Norma 232 Vulkan	velocity, fps:	2329	2031	1757	1512	
	energy, ft-lb:	2795	2126	1591	1178	
	arc, inches:		+3.5	0	-14.9	
Norma 232 Oryx	velocity, fps:	2362	2058	1778	1528	
	energy, ft-lb:	2875	2182	1630	1203	
	arc, inches:		+3.4	0	-14.5	
Norma 285 Oryx	velocity, fps:	2067	1859	1666	1490	
	energy, ft-lb:	2704	2188	1756	1404	
	arc, inches:		+4.3	0	-16.8	
Norma 286 Alaska	velocity, fps:	2067	1857	1662	1484	
	energy, ft-lb:	2714	2190	1754	1399	
	arc, inches:		+4.3	0	-17.0	

9.3x62

CARTRIDGE BULLET	RANGE, YARDS:	0	100	200	300	400
Federal 286 Swift A-Frame	velocity, fps:	2360	2150	1950	1760	1580
	energy, ft-lb:	3535	2930	2405	1960	1590
	arc, inches:		+2.9	0	-11.6	-31.0
Federal 286 TSX	velocity, fps:	2360	2160	1970	1790	
	energy, ft-lb:	3535	2965	2465	2035	
	arc, inches:	-1.5	+3.0	0	-12.0	
Federal 286 Woodleigh Hydro	velocity, fps:	2360	2050	1760	1510	
	energy, ft-lb:	3535	2665	1975	1445	
	arc, inches::	-1.5	+3.4	0	-14.7	
Hornady 286 SP-HP	velocity, fps:	2350	2155	1961	1778	
	energy, ft-lb:	3537	2949	2442	2008	
	arc, inches:	-1.5	+3.0	0	-12.1	
Norma 232 Oryx	velocity, fps:	2625	2294	1988	1708	
	energy, ft-lb:	3535	2700	2028	1497	
	arc, inches:	-1.5	+2.5	0	-11.4	
Norma 250 A-Frame	velocity, fps:	2625	2322	2039	1778	
	energy, ft-lb:	3826	2993	2309	1755	
	arc, inches:	-1.5	+2.5	0	-10.9	
Norma 286 Plastic Point	velocity, fps:	2362	2141	1931	1736	
	energy, ft-lb:	3544	2911	2370	1914	
	arc, inches:	-1.5	+3.1	0	-12.4	
Nosler 250 AccuBond	velocity, fps:	2550	2376	2208	2048	1894
	energy, ft-lb:	3609	3133	2707	2328	1992
	arc, inches:	-1.5	+2.3	0	-9.5	-27.2
Nosler 286 Partition	velocity, fps:	2350	2179	2015	1859	1711
	energy, ft-lb:	3506	3014	2578	2194	1859
	arc, inches:	-1.5	+2.9	0	-11.5	-33.1

9.3x64

CARTRIDGE BULLET	RANGE, YARDS:	0	100	200	300	400
A-Square 286 Triad	velocity, fps:	2700	2391	2103	1835	1602
	energy, ft-lb:	4629	3630	2808	2139	1631
	arc, inches:		+2.3	0	-10.1	-30.8

.370 Sako

CARTRIDGE BULLET	RANGE, YARDS:	0	100	200	300	400
Federal 286 TSX	velocity, fps:	2550	2370	2190	2020	1860
	energy, ft-lb:	4130	3555	3045	2595	2195
	arc, inches:	-1.5	+2.4	0	-9.6	-27.5

370 Sako Magnum

CARTRIDGE BULLET	RANGE, YARDS:	0	100	200	300	400
Federal 286 Swift A-Frame	velocity, fps:	2550	2330	2120	1920	1730
	energy, ft-lb:	4130	3440	2845	2330	1900
	arc, inches:		+2.5	0	-10.1	-30.0
Federal 286 TSX	velocity, fps:	2550	2370	2190	2020	1860
	energy, ft-lb:	4130	3555	3045	2595	2195
	arc, inches:		+2.4	0	-9.5	-27.5
Federal 286 Woodleigh Hydro Solid	velocity, fps:	2550	2230	1920	1650	1410
	energy, ft-lb:	4130	3145	2350	1730	1265
	arc, inches:		+2.8	0	-12.4	-37.5

9.3x74 R

CARTRIDGE BULLET	RANGE, YARDS:	0	100	200	300	400
A-Square 286 Triad	velocity, fps:	2360	2089	1844	1623	
	energy, ft-lb:	3538	2771	2157	1670	
	arc, inches:		+3.6	0	-14.0	
Federal 286 Swift A-Frame	velocity, fps:	2360	2150	1950	1760	1580
	energy, ft-lb:	3535	2930	2405	1960	1590
	arc, inches:		+2.9	0	-11.6	-31.0
Federal 286 TSX	velocity, fps:	2360	2160	1970	1790	1630
	energy, ft-lb:	3535	2965	2465	2035	1675
	arc, inches:		+2.9	0	-11.1	-29.9
Federal 286 Woodleigh Hydro Solid	velocity, fps:	2360	2050	1760	1510	1300
	energy, ft-lb:	3535	2665	1975	1445	1065
	arc, inches:		+3.4	0	-14.7	-45.0
Hornady 286	velocity, fps	2360	2136	1924	1727	1545
	energy, ft-lb	3536	2896	2351	1893	1516
	arc, inches	-1.5	0	-6.1	-21.7	-49.0
Norma 232 Vulkan	velocity, fps:	2625	2327	2049	1792	
	energy, ft-lb:	3551	2791	2164	1655	
	arc, inches:		+2.5	0	-10.8	
Norma 232 Oryx	velocity, fps:	2526	2191	1883	1605	
	energy, ft-lb:	3274	2463	1819	1322	
	arc, inches:		+2.9	0	-12.8	

Centerfire Rifle Ballistics

9.3X74 R TO .375 WEATHERBY MAGNUM

CARTRIDGE BULLET	RANGE, YARDS:	0	100	200	300	400
Norma 285 Oryx	velocity, fps:	2362	2114	1881	1667	
	energy, ft-lb:	3532	2829	2241	1758	
	arc, inches:		+3.1	0	-13.0	
Norma 286 Alaska	velocity, fps:	2362	2135	1920	1720	
	energy, ft-lb:	3544	2894	2342	1879	
	arc, inches:		+3.1	0	-12.5	
Norma 286 Plastic Point	velocity, fps:	2362	2135	1920	1720	
	energy, ft-lb:	3544	2894	2342	1879	
	arc, inches:		+3.1	0	-12.5	

.375 Winchester

CARTRIDGE BULLET	RANGE, YARDS:	0	100	200	300	400
Win. 200 Power-Point	velocity, fps:	2200	1841	1526	1268	1089
	energy, ft-lb:	2150	1506	1034	714	
	arc, inches:		0	-9.5	-33.8	

.375 Flanged

CARTRIDGE BULLET	RANGE, YARDS:	0	100	200	300	400
Nosler 300 PT	velocity, fps:	2400	2191	1993	1806	1632
	energy, ft-lb:	3836	3198	2646	2173	1775
	arc, inches:	-1.5	+2.9	0	-11.7	-34.0

.375 H&H Magnum

CARTRIDGE BULLET	RANGE, YARDS:	0	100	200	300	400
A-Square 300 SP boat-tail	velocity, fps:	2550	2415	2284	2157	2034
	energy, ft-lb:	4331	3884	3474	3098	2755
	arc, inches:		+5.2	+6.0	0	-13.3
A-Square 300 Triad	velocity, fps:	2550	2251	1973	1717	1496
	energy, ft-lb:	4331	3375	2592	1964	1491
	arc, inches:		+2.7	0	-11.7	-35.1
Federal 250 Trophy Bonded	velocity, fps:	2670	2360	2080	1820	1580
	energy, ft-lb:	3955	3100	2400	1830	1380
	arc, inches:		+2.4	0	-10.4	-31.7
Federal 270 Hi-Shok	velocity, fps:	2690	2420	2170	1920	1700
	energy, ft-lb:	4340	3510	2810	2220	1740
	arc, inches:		+2.4	0	-10.9	-33.3
Federal 300 Hi-Shok	velocity, fps:	2530	2270	2020	1790	1580
	energy, ft-lb:	4265	3425	2720	2135	1665
	arc, inches:		+2.6	0	-11.2	-33.3
Federal 300 Nosler Partition	velocity, fps:	2530	2320	2120	1930	1750
	energy, ft-lb:	4265	3585	2995	2475	2040
	arc, inches:		+2.5	0	-10.3	-29.9
Federal 300 Trophy Bonded	velocity, fps:	2530	2280	2040	1810	1610
	energy, ft-lb:	4265	3450	2765	2190	1725
	arc, inches:		+2.6	0	-10.9	-32.8
Federal 300 Tr. Bonded HE	velocity, fps:	2700	2440	2190	1960	1740
	energy, ft-lb:	4855	3960	3195	2550	2020
	arc, inches:		+2.2	0	-9.4	-28.0
Federal 300 Trophy Bonded	velocity, fps:	2530	2160	1820	1520	1280.
Sledgehammer Solid	energy, ft-lb:	4265	3105	2210	1550	1090
	arc, inches, s:		0	-6.0	-22.7	-54.6
Federal 300 TSX	velocity, fps:	2470	2240	2010	1800	1610
	energy, ft-lb:	4065	3325	2700	2170	1735
	arc, inches:		+2.7	0	-11.3	-33.6
Federal 300 Woodleigh	velocity, fps:	2500	2180	1880	1610	1380
Hydro Solid	energy, ft-lb:	4165	3160	2355	1735	1270
	arc, inches:		+2.9	0	-20.1	-46.3
Hornady 250 GMX	velocity, fps:	2890	2675	2471	2275	2088
Superformance	energy, ft-lb:	4636	3973	3388	2873	2421
	arc, inches:		+1.7	0	-7.4	-21.5
Hornady 270 SP HM	velocity, fps:	2870	2620	2385	2162	1957
	energy, ft-lb:	4937	4116	3408	2802	2296
	arc, inches:		+2.2	0	-8.4	-23.9
Hornady 300 FMJ RN HM	velocity, fps:	2705	2376	2072	1804	1560
	energy, ft-lb:	4873	3760	2861	2167	1621
	arc, inches:		+2.7	0	-10.8	-32.1
Norma 300 Soft Point	velocity, fps:	2549	2211	1900	1619	
	energy, ft-lb:	4329	3258	2406	1747	
	arc, inches:		+2.8	0	-12.6	
Norma 300 TXP Swift A-Fr.	velocity, fps:	2559	2296	2049	1818	
	energy, ft-lb:	4363	3513	2798	2203	
	arc, inches:		+2.6	0	-10.9	

CARTRIDGE BULLET	RANGE, YARDS:	0	100	200	300	400
Norma 300 Oryx	velocity, fps:	2559	2292	2041	1807	
	energy, ft-lb:	4363	3500	2775	2176	
	arc, inches:		+2.6	0	-11.0	
Norma 300 Barnes Solid	velocity, fps:	2493	2061	1677	1356	
	energy, ft-lb:	4141	2829	1873	1234	
	arc, inches:		+3.4	0	-16.0	
PMC 270 PSP	velocity, fps:					
	energy, ft-lb:					
	arc, inches:					
PMC 270 Barnes X	velocity, fps:	2690	2528	2372	2221	2076
	energy, ft-lb:	4337	3831	3371	2957	2582
	arc, inches:		+2.0	0	-8.2	-23.4
PMC 300 Barnes X	velocity, fps:	2530	2389	2252	2120	1993
	energy, ft-lb:	4263	3801	3378	2994	2644
	arc, inches:		+2.3	0	-9.2	-26.1
Rem. 270 Soft Point	velocity, fps:	2690	2420	2166	1928	1707
	energy, ft-lb:	4337	3510	2812	2228	1747
	arc, inches:		+2.2	0	-9.7	-28.7
Rem. 300 Swift A-Frame	velocity, fps:	2530	2245	1979	1733	1512
	energy, ft-lb:	4262	3357	2608	2001	1523
	arc, inches:		+2.7	0	-11.7	-35.0
Speer 285 Grand Slam	velocity, fps:	2610	2365	2134	1916	
	energy, ft-lb:	4310	3540	2883	2323	
	arc, inches:		+2.4	0	-9.9	
Speer 300 African GS	velocity, fps:	2609	2277	1970	1690	
Tungsten Solid	energy, ft-lb:	4534	3453	2585	1903	
	arc, inches:		+2.6	0	-11.7	-35.6
Win. 270 Fail Safe	velocity, fps:	2670	2447	2234	2033	1842
	energy, ft-lb:	4275	3590	2994	2478	2035
	arc, inches:		+2.2	0	-9.1	-28.7
Win. 300 Fail Safe	velocity, fps:	2530	2336	2151	1974	1806
	energy, ft-lb:	4265	3636	3082	2596	2173
	arc, inches:		+2.4	0	-10.0	-26.9

.375 Dakota

CARTRIDGE BULLET	RANGE, YARDS:	0	100	200	300	400
Dakota 270 Barnes X	velocity, fps:	2800	2617	2441	2272	2109
	energy, ft-lb:	4699	4104	3571	3093	2666
	arc, inches:		+2.3	+1.0	-6.1	-19.9
Dakota 300 Barnes X	velocity, fps:	2600	2316	2051	1804	1579
	energy, ft-lb:	4502	3573	2800	2167	1661
	arc, inches:		+2.4	-0.1	-11.0	-32.7

.375 Ruger

CARTRIDGE BULLET	RANGE, YARDS:	0	100	200	300	400
Hornady 250 GMX	velocity, fps:	2890	2675	2471	2275	2088
Superformance	energy, ft-lb:	4636	3973	3388	2873	2421
	arc, inches:		+1.7	0	-7.4	-21.5
Hornady 270 SP	velocity, fps:	2840	2600	2372	2156	1951
	energy, ft-lb:	4835	4052	3373	2786	2283
	arc, inches:	-1.5	+1.8	0	-8.0	-23.6
Hornady 300 Solid	velocity, fps	2660	2344	2050	1780	1536
	energy, ft-lb	4713	3660	2800	2110	1572
	arc, inches	-1.5	+2.4	0	-10.8	-32.6
Nosler 260 AB	velocity, fps:	2900	2703	2514	2333	2160
	energy, ft-lb:	4854	4217	3649	3143	2693
	arc, inches:	-1.5	+1.6	0	-7.1	-20.7

.375 Weatherby Magnum

CARTRIDGE BULLET	RANGE, YARDS:	0	100	200	300	400
A-Square 300 SP boat-tail	velocity, fps:	2700	2560	2425	2293	2166
	energy, ft-lb:	4856	4366	3916	3503	3125
	arc, inches:		+4.5	+5.2	0	-11.9
A-Square 300 Triad	velocity, fps:	2700	2391	2103	1835	1602
	energy, ft-lb:	4856	3808	2946	2243	1710
	arc, inches:		+2.3	0	-10.1	-30.8
Wby. 300 Nosler Part.	velocity, fps:	2800	2572	2366	2140	1963
	energy, ft-lb:	5224	4408	3696	3076	2541
	arc, inches:		+1.9	0	-8.2	-23.9

Centerfire Rifle Ballistics

.375 JRS TO .416 REMINGTON MAGNUM

BALLISTICS

.375 JRS

CARTRIDGE BULLET	RANGE, YARDS:	0	100	200	300	400
A-Square 300 SP boat-tail	velocity, fps:	2700	2560	2425	2293	2166.
	energy, ft-lb:	4856	4366	3916	3503	3125
	arc, inches:		+4.5	+5.2	0	-11.9
A-Square 300 Triad	velocity, fps:	2700	2391	2103	1835	1602
	energy, ft-lb:	4856	3808	2946	2243	1710
	arc, inches:		+2.3	0	-10.1	-30.8

.375 Remington Ultra Magnum

CARTRIDGE BULLET	RANGE, YARDS:	0	100	200	300	400
Nosler 260 AB	velocity, fps:	2950	2750	2560	2377	2202
	energy, ft-lb:	5023	4367	3783	3262	2799
	arc, inches:	-1.5	+1.6	0	-6.9	-19.9
Nosler 300 PT	velocity, fps:	2750	2524	2309	2105	1912
	energy, ft-lb:	5036	4244	3553	2953	2435
	arc, inches:	-1.5	+2.0	0	-8.5	-24.9
Rem. 270 Soft Point	velocity, fps:	2900	2558	2241	1947	1678
	energy, fps:	5041	3922	3010	2272	1689
	arc, inches:		+1.9	0	-9.2	-27.8
Rem. 300 Swift A-Frame	velocity, fps:	2760	2505	2263	2035	1822
	energy, fps:	5073	4178	3412	2759	2210
	arc, inches:		+2.0	0	-8.8	-26.1

.375 A-Square

CARTRIDGE BULLET	RANGE, YARDS:	0	100	200	300	400
A-Square 300 SP boat-tail	velocity, fps:	2920	2773	2631	2494	2360
	energy, ft-lb:	5679	5123	4611	4142	3710
	arc, inches:		+3.7	+4.4	0	-9.8
A-Square 300 Triad	velocity, fps:	2920	2596	2294	2012	1762
	energy, ft-lb:	5679	4488	3505	2698	2068
	arc, inches:		+1.8	0	-8.5	-25.5

.376 Steyr

CARTRIDGE BULLET	RANGE, YARDS:	0	100	200	300	400
Hornady 225 SP	velocity, fps:	2600	2331	2078	1842	1625
	energy, ft-lb:	3377	2714	2157	1694	1319
	arc, inches:		+2.5	0	-10.6	-31.4
Hornady 270 SP	velocity, fps:	2600	2372	2156	1951	1759
	energy, ft-lb:	4052	3373	2787	2283	1855
	arc, inches:		+2.3	0	-9.9	-28.9

.378 Weatherby Magnum

CARTRIDGE BULLET	RANGE, YARDS:	0	100	200	300	400
A-Square 300 SP boat-tail	velocity, fps:	2900	2754	2612	2475	2342
	energy, ft-lb:	5602	5051	4546	4081	3655
	arc, inches:		+3.8	+4.4	0	-10.0
A-Square 300 Triad	velocity, fps:	2900	2577	2276	1997	1747
	energy, ft-lb:	5602	4424	3452	2656	2034
	arc, inches:		+1.9	0	-8.7	-25.9
Wby. 270 Pointed Expanding	velocity, fps:	3180	2921	2677	2445	2225
	energy, ft-lb:	6062	5115	4295	3583	2968
	arc, inches:		+1.3	0	-6.1	-18.1
Wby. 270 Barnes X	velocity, fps:	3150	2954	2767	2587	2415
	energy, ft-lb:	5948	5232	4589	4013	3495
	arc, inches:		+1.2	0	-5.8	-16.7
Wby. 300 RN Expanding	velocity, fps:	2925	2558	2220	1908	1627.
	energy, ft-lb:	5699	4360	3283	2424	1764
	arc, inches:		+1.9	0	-9.0	-27.8
Wby. 300 FMJ	velocity, fps:	2925	2591	2280	1991	1725
	energy, ft-lb:	5699	4470	3461	2640	1983
	arc, inches:		+1.8	0	-8.6	-26.1

.38-40 Winchester

CARTRIDGE BULLET	RANGE, YARDS:	0	100	200	300	400
Win. 180 Soft Point	velocity, fps:	1160	999	901	827	
	energy, ft-lb:	538	399	324	273	
	arc, inches:		0	-23.4	-75.2	

.38-55 Winchester

CARTRIDGE BULLET	RANGE, YARDS:	0	100	200	300	400
Black Hills 255 FN Lead	velocity, fps:	1250				
	energy, ft-lb:	925				
	arc, inches:					
Win. 255 Soft Point	velocity, fps:	1320	1190	1091	1018	
	energy, ft-lb:	987	802	674	587	
	arc, inches:		0	-33.9	-110.6	

.41 Magnum

CARTRIDGE BULLET	RANGE, YARDS:	0	100	200	300	400
Win. 240 Platinum Tip	velocity, fps:	1830	1488	1220	1048	
	energy, ft-lb:	1784	1180	792	585	
	arc inches:		0	-15.0	-53.4	

.450/.400 Nitro Express

CARTRIDGE BULLET	RANGE, YARDS:	0	100	200	300	400
A-Square 400 Triad	velocity, fps:	2150	1910	1690	1490	
	energy, ft-lb:	4105	3241	2537	1972	
	arc, inches:		+4.4	0	-16.5	
Hornady 400 DGS, DGX	velocity, fps:	2050	1820	1609	1420	
	energy, ft-lb:	3732	2940	2298	1791	
	arc, inches:	-0.9	0	-9.7	-32.8	

.404 Jeffery

CARTRIDGE BULLET	RANGE, YARDS:	0	100	200	300	400
A-Square 400 Triad	velocity, fps:	2150	1901	1674	1468	1299
	energy, ft-lb:	4105	3211	2489	1915	1499
	arc, inches:		+4.1	0	-16.4	-49.1
Hornady 400 DGS, DGX	velocity, fps:	2300	2046	1809	1592	
	energy, ft-lb:	4698	3717	2906	2251	
	arc, inches:	-1.5	0	-6.9	-24.4	
Norma 450 Woodleigh SP	velocity, fps:	2150	2048	1949	1853	1760
	energy, ft-lb:	4620	4191	3795	3430	3096
	arc, inches:	-1.5	+.2	0	-2.5	-7.6

.405 Winchester

CARTRIDGE BULLET	RANGE, YARDS:	0	100	200	300	400
Hornady 300 Flatpoint	velocity, fps:	2200	1851	1545	1296	
	energy, ft-lb:	3224	2282	1589	1119	
	arc, inches:		0	-8.7	-31.9	
Hornady 300 SP Interlock	velocity, fps:	2200	1890	1610	1370	
	energy, ft-lb:	3224	2379	1727	1250	
	arc, inches:		0	-8.3	-30.2	

.416 Taylor

CARTRIDGE BULLET	RANGE, YARDS:	0	100	200	300	400
A-Square 400 Triad	velocity, fps:	2350	2093	1853	1634	1443
	energy, ft-lb:	4905	3892	3049	2371	1849
	arc, inches:		+3.2	0	-13.6	-39.8

.416 Hoffman

CARTRIDGE BULLET	RANGE, YARDS:	0	100	200	300	400
A-Square 400 Triad	velocity, fps:	2380	2122	1879	1658	1464
	energy, ft-lb:	5031	3998	3136	2440	1903
	arc, inches:		+3.1	0	-13.1	-38.7

.416 Remington Magnum

CARTRIDGE BULLET	RANGE, YARDS:	0	100	200	300	400
A-Square 400 Triad	velocity, fps:	2380	2122	1879	1658	1464
	energy, ft-lb:	5031	3998	3136	2440	1903
	arc, inches:		+3.1	0	-13.2	-38.7
Federal 400 Trophy Bonded	velocity, fps:	2400	2150	1920	1700	1500
Sledgehammer Solid	energy, ft-lb:	5115	4110	3260	2565	2005
	arc, inches:		0	-6.0	-21.6	-49.2
Federal 400 Trophy Bonded	velocity, fps:	2400	2180	1970	1770	1590
	energy, ft-lb:	5115	4215	3440	2785	2245
	arc, inches:		0	-5.8	-20.6	-46.9
Rem. 400 Swift A-Frame	velocity, fps:	2400	2175	1962	1763	1579
	energy, ft-lb:	5115	4201	3419	2760	2214
	arc, inches:		0	-5.9	-20.8	

.416 Rigby

CARTRIDGE BULLET	RANGE, YARDS:	0	100	200	300	400
A-Square 400 Triad	velocity, fps:	2400	2140	1897	1673	1478
	energy, ft-lb:	5115	4069	3194	2487	1940
	arc, inches:		+3.0	0	-12.9	-38.0
Federal 400 Trophy Bonded	velocity, fps:	2370	2150	1940	1750	1570
	energy, ft-lb:	4990	4110	3350	2715	2190
	arc, inches:		0	-6.0	-21.3	-48.1
Federal 400 Trophy Bonded Sledgehammer Solid	velocity, fps:	2370	2120	1890	1660	1460
	energy, ft-lb:	4990	3975	3130	2440	1895
	arc, inches:		0	-6.3	-22.5	-51.5
Federal 410 Woodleigh Weldcore	velocity, fps:	2370	2110	1870	1640	1440
	energy, ft-lb:	5115	4050	3165	2455	1895
	arc, inches:		0	-7.4	-24.8	-55.0
Federal 410 Solid	velocity, fps:	2370	2110	2870	1640	1440
	energy, ft-lb:	5115	4050	3165	2455	1895
	arc, inches:		0	-7.4	-24.8	-55.0
Hornady 400 DGX, DGS	velocity, fps:	2415	2156	1915	1691	
	energy, ft-lb:	5180	4130	3256	2540	
	arc, inches:	-1.5	0	-6.0	-21.6	
Norma 400 TXP Swift A-Fr.	velocity, fps:	2350	2127	1917	1721	
	energy, ft-lb:	4906	4021	3266	2632	
	arc, inches:		+3.1	0	-12.5	
Norma 400 Barnes Solid	velocity, fps:	2297	1930	1604	1330	
	energy, ft-lb:	4687	3310	2284	1571	
	arc, inches:		+3.9	0	-17.7	

.416 Ruger

CARTRIDGE BULLET	RANGE, YARDS:	0	100	200	300	400
Hornady 400 DGS, DGX	velocity, fps:	2400	2151	1917	1700	
	energy, ft-lb:	5116	4109	3264	2568	
	arc, inches:	-1.5	0	-6.0	-21.6	

.500/416 Nitro Express

CARTRIDGE BULLET	RANGE, YARDS:	0	50	100	150	200
Norma 450 Woodleigh SP	velocity, fps:	2100	1991	1886	1785	1688
	energy, ft-lb:	4408	3963	3556	3185	2849
	arc, inches:	-1.5	+.3	0	-2.7	-8.2

.416 Dakota

CARTRIDGE BULLET	RANGE, YARDS:	0	100	200	300	400
Dakota 400 Barnes X	velocity, fps:	2450	2294	2143	1998	1859
	energy, ft-lb:	5330	4671	4077	3544	3068
	arc, inches:		+2.5	-0.2	-10.5	-29.4

.416 Weatherby

CARTRIDGE BULLET	RANGE, YARDS:	0	100	200	300	400
A-Square 400 Triad	velocity, fps:	2600	2328	2073	1834	1624
	energy, ft-lb:	6004	4813	3816	2986	2343
	arc, inches:		+2.5	0	-10.5	-31.6
Wby. 350 Barnes X	velocity, fps:	2850	2673	2503	2340	2182
	energy, ft-lb:	6312	5553	4870	4253	3700
	arc, inches:		+1.7	0	-7.2	-20.9
Wby. 400 Swift A-Fr.	velocity, fps:	2650	2426	2213	2011	1820
	energy, ft-lb:	6237	5227	4350	3592	2941
	arc, inches:		+2.2	0	-9.3	-27.1
Wby. 400 RN Expanding	velocity, fps:	2700	2417	2152	1903	1676
	energy, ft-lb:	6474	5189	4113	3216	2493
	arc, inches:		+2.3	0	-9.7	-29.3
Wby. 400 Monolithic Solid	velocity, fps:	2700	2411	2140	1887	1656
	energy, ft-lb:	6474	5162	4068	3161	2435
	arc, inches:		+2.3	0	-9.8	-29.7

10.57 (.416) Meteor

CARTRIDGE BULLET	RANGE, YARDS:	0	100	200	300	400
Lazzeroni 400 Swift A-Fr.	velocity, fps:	2730	2532	2342	2161	1987
	energy, ft-lb:	6621	5695	4874	4147	3508
	arc, inches:		+1.9	0	-8.3	-24.0

.425 Express

CARTRIDGE BULLET	RANGE, YARDS:	0	100	200	300	400
A-Square 400 Triad	velocity, fps:	2400	2136	1888	1662	1465
	energy, ft-lb:	5115	4052	3167	2454	1906
	arc, inches:		+3.0	0	-13.1	-38.3

.44-40 Winchester

CARTRIDGE BULLET	RANGE, YARDS:	0	100	200	300	400
Rem. 200 Soft Point	velocity, fps:	1190	1006	900	822	756
	energy, ft-lb:	629	449	360	300	254
	arc, inches:		0	-33.1	-108.7	-235.2
Win. 200 Soft Point	velocity, fps:	1190	1006	900	822	756
	energy, ft-lb:	629	449	360	300	254
	arc, inches:		0	-33.3	-109.5	-237.4

.44 Remington Magnum

CARTRIDGE BULLET	RANGE, YARDS:	0	100	200	300	400
Federal 240 Hi-Shok HP	velocity, fps:	1760	1380	1090	950	860
	energy, ft-lb:	1650	1015	640	485	395
	arc, inches:		0	-17.4	-60.7	-136.0
Rem. 210 Semi-Jacketed HP	velocity, fps:	1920	1477	1155	982	880
	energy, ft-lb:	1719	1017	622	450	361
	arc, inches:		0	-14.7	-55.5	-131.3
Rem. 240 Soft Point	velocity, fps:	1760	1380	1114	970	878
	energy, ft-lb:	1650	1015	661	501	411
	arc, inches:		0	-17.0	-61.4	-143.0
Rem. 240 Semi-Jacketed Hollow Point	velocity, fps:	1760	1380	1114	970	878
	energy, ft-lb:	1650	1015	661	501	411
	arc, inches:		0	-17.0	-61.4	-143.0
Rem. 275 JHP Core-Lokt	velocity, fps:	1580	1293	1093	976	896
	energy, ft-lb:	1524	1020	730	582	490
	arc, inches:		0	-19.4	-67.5	-210.8
Win. 210 Silvertip HP	velocity, fps:	1580	1198	993	879	795
	energy, ft-lb:	1164	670	460	361	295
	arc, inches:		0	-22.4	-76.1	-168.0
Win. 240 Hollow Soft Point	velocity, fps:	1760	1362	1094	953	861
	energy, ft-lb:	1650	988	638	484	395
	arc, inches:		0	-18.1	-65.1	-150.3
Win. 250 Platinum Tip	velocity, fps:	1830	1475	1201	1032	931
	energy, ft-lb:	1859	1208	801	591	481
	arc, inches:		0	-15.3	-54.7	-126.6.

.444 Marlin

CARTRIDGE BULLET	RANGE, YARDS:	0	100	200	300	400
Rem. 240 Soft Point	velocity, fps:	2350	1815	1377	1087	941
	energy, ft-lb:	2942	1755	1010	630	472
	arc, inches:		+2.2	-5.4	-31.4	-86.7
Hornady 265 Evolution	velocity, fps:	2325	1971	1652	1380	
	energy, ft-lb:	3180	2285	1606	1120	
	arc, inches:		+3.0	-1.4	-18.6	
Hornady 265 FP LM	velocity, fps:	2335	1913	1551	1266	
	energy, ft-lb:	3208	2153	1415	943	
	arc, inches:		+ 2.0	-4.9	-26.5	
Hornady 265 InterLock FP	velocity, fps:	2400	1974	1601	1295	
	energy, ft-lb:	3389	2294	1508	987	
	arc, inches:		+3.8	0	-17.5	
Rem. 240 Soft Point	velocity, fps:	2350	1815	1377	1087	941
	energy, ft-lb:	2942	1755	1010	630	472
	arc, inches:		+2.2	-5.4	-31.4	-86.7

.45-70 Government

CARTRIDGE BULLET	RANGE, YARDS:	0	100	200	300	400
Black Hills 405 FPL	velocity, fps:	1250				
	energy, ft-lb:					
	arc, inches:					
Federal 300 Sierra Pro-Hunt. HP FN	velocity, fps:	1880	1650	1430	1240	1110
	energy, ft-lb:	2355	1815	1355	1015	810
	arc, inches:		0	-11.5	-39.7	-89.1
PMC 350 FNSP	velocity, fps:					
	energy, ft-lb:					
	arc, inches:					
Rem. 300 Jacketed HP	velocity, fps:	1810	1497	1244	1073	969
	energy, ft-lb:	2182	1492	1031	767	625
	arc, inches:		0	-13.8	-50.1	-115.7

Centerfire Rifle Ballistics

.45-70 GOVERNMENT TO .460 WEATHERBY MAGNUM

CARTRIDGE BULLET	RANGE, YARDS:	0	100	200	300	400
Rem. 405 Soft Point	velocity, fps:	1330	1168	1055	977	918
	energy, ft-lb:	1590	1227	1001	858	758
	arc, inches:		0	-24.0	-78.6	-169.4
Win. 300 Jacketed HP	velocity, fps:	1880	1650	1425	1235	1105
	energy, ft-lb:	2355	1815	1355	1015	810
	arc, inches:		0	-12.8	-44.3	-95.5
Win. 300 Partition Gold	velocity, fps:	1880	1558	1292	1103	988
	energy, ft-lb:	2355	1616	1112	811	651
	arc, inches:		0	-12.9	-46.0	-104.9.

.450 Bushmaster

CARTRIDGE BULLET	RANGE, YARDS:	0	100	200	300	400
Hornady 250 SST-ML	velocity, fps	2200	1840	1524	1268	
	energy, ft-lb	2686	1879	1289	893	
	arc, inches	-2.0	+2.5	-3.5	-24.5	

.450 Marlin

CARTRIDGE BULLET	RANGE, YARDS:	0	100	200	300	400
Hornady 325 FTX	velocity, fps:	2225	1887	1585	1331	
	energy, ft-lb:	3572	2569	1813	1278	
	arc, inches:	-1.5	+3.0	-2.2	-21.3	
Hornady 350 FP	velocity, fps:	2100	1720	1397	1156	
	energy, ft-lb:	3427	2298	1516	1039	
	arc, inches:		0	-10.4	-38.9	

.450 Nitro Express (3¼")

CARTRIDGE BULLET	RANGE, YARDS:	0	100	200	300	400
A-Square 465 Triad	velocity, fps:	2190	1970	1765	1577	
	energy, ft-lb:	4952	4009	3216	2567	
	arc, inches:		+4.3	0	-15.4	
Hornady 480 DGS, DGX	velocity, fps:	2150	1881	1635	1418	
	energy, ft-lb:	4927	3769	2850	2144	
	arc, inches:	-1.5	0	-8.4	-29.9	

.450 #2

CARTRIDGE BULLET	RANGE, YARDS:	0	100	200	300	400
A-Square 465 Triad	velocity, fps:	2190	1970	1765	1577	
	energy, ft-lb:	4952	4009	3216	2567	
	arc, inches:		+4.3	0	-15.4	

.458 Winchester Magnum

CARTRIDGE BULLET	RANGE, YARDS:	0	100	200	300	400
A-Square 465 Triad	velocity, fps:	2220	1999	1791	1601	1433
	energy, ft-lb:	5088	4127	3312	2646	2121
	arc, inches:		+3.6	0	-14.7	-42.5
Federal 350 Soft Point	velocity, fps:	2470	1990	1570	1250	1060
	energy, ft-lb:	4740	3065	1915	1205	870
	arc, inches:		0	-7.5	-29.1	-71.1
Federal 400 Trophy Bonded	velocity, fps:	2380	2170	1960	1770	1590
	energy, ft-lb:	5030	4165	3415	2785	2255
	arc, inches:		0	-5.9	-20.9	-47.1
Federal 500 Solid	velocity, fps:	2090	1870	1670	1480	1320
	energy, ft-lb:	4850	3880	3085	2440	1945
	arc, inches:		0	-8.5	-29.5	-66.2
Federal 500 Trophy Bonded	velocity, fps:	2090	1870	1660	1480	1310
	energy, ft-lb:	4850	3870	3065	2420	1915
	arc, inches:		0	-8.5	-29.7	-66.8
Federal 500 Trophy Bonded	velocity, fps:	2090	1860	1650	1460	1300
Sledgehammer Solid	energy, ft-lb:	4850	3845	3025	2365	1865
	arc, inches:		0	-8.6	-30.0	-67.8
Federal 510 Soft Point	velocity, fps:	2090	1820	1570	1360	1190
	energy, ft-lb:	4945	3730	2790	2080	1605
	arc, inches:		0	-9.1	-32.3	-73.9
Hornady 500 FMJ-RN HM	velocity, fps:	2260	1984	1735	1512	
	energy, ft-lb:	5670	4368	3341	2538	
	arc, inches:		0	-7.4	-26.4	
Norma 500 TXP Swift A-Fr.	velocity, fps:	2116	1903	1705	1524	
	energy, ft-lb:	4972	4023	3228	2578	
	arc, inches:		+4.1	0	-16.1	
Norma 500 Barnes Solid	velocity, fps:	2067	1750	1472	1245	
	energy, ft-lb:	4745	3401	2405	1721	
	arc, inches:		+4.9	0	-21.2	
Rem. 450 Swift A-Frame	velocity, fps:	2150	1901	1671	1465	1289
PSP	energy, ft-lb:	4618	3609	2789	2144	1659
	arc, inches:		0	-8.2	-28.9	
Speer 500 African GS	velocity, fps:	2120	1845	1596	1379	
Tungsten Solid	energy, ft-lb:	4989	3780	2828	2111	
	arc, inches:		0	-8.8	-31.3	
Speer African Grand Slam	velocity, fps:	2120	1853	1609	1396	
	energy, ft-lb:	4989	3810	2875	2163	
	arc, inches:		0	-8.7	-30.8	
Win. 510 Soft Point	velocity, fps:	2040	1770	1527	1319	1157
	energy, ft-lb:	4712	3547	2640	1970	1516
	arc, inches:		0	-10.3	-35.6	

.458 Lott

CARTRIDGE BULLET	RANGE, YARDS:	0	100	200	300	400
A-Square 465 Triad	velocity, fps:	2380	2150	1932	1730	1551
	energy, ft-lb:	5848	4773	3855	3091	2485
	arc, inches:		+3.0	0	-12.5	-36.4
Federal 500 TSX	velocity, fps:	2280	2090	1900	1730	1560
	energy, ft-lb:	5770	4825	4000	3305	2715
	arc, inches:	0	-6.4	-22.7	-50.7	
Hornady 500 RNSP or solid	velocity, fps:	2300	2022	1776	1551	
	energy, ft-lb:	5872	4537	3502	2671	
	arc, inches:		+3.4	0	-14.3	
Hornady 500 InterBond	velocity, fps:	2300	2028	1777	1549	
	energy, ft-lb:	5872	4535	3453	2604	
	arc, inches:		0	-7.0	-25.1	

CARTRIDGE BULLET	RANGE, YARDS:	0	50	100	150	200
Norma 500 Woodleigh SP	velocity, fps:	2100	1982	1868	1758	1654
	energy, ft-lb:	4897	4361	3874	3434	3039
	arc, inches:	-1.5	+.3	0	-2.8	-8.4

.450 Ackley

CARTRIDGE BULLET	RANGE, YARDS:	0	100	200	300	400
A-Square 465 Triad	velocity, fps:	2400	2169	1950	1747	1567
	energy, ft-lb:	5947	4857	3927	3150	2534
	arc, inches:		+2.9	0	-12.2	-35.8

.450 Rigby

CARTRIDGE BULLET	RANGE, YARDS:	0	50	100	150	200
Norma 550 Woodleigh SP	velocity, fps:	2100	1992	1887	1787	1690
	energy, ft-lb:	5387	4847	4352	3900	3491
	arc, inches:	-1.5	+.3	0	-2.7	-8.2

.460 Short A-Square

CARTRIDGE BULLET	RANGE, YARDS:	0	100	200	300	400
A-Square 500 Triad	velocity, fps:	2420	2198	1987	1789	1613
	energy, ft-lb:	6501	5362	4385	3553	2890
	arc, inches:		+2.9	0	-11.6	-34.2

.450 Dakota

CARTRIDGE BULLET	RANGE, YARDS:	0	100	200	300	400
Dakota 500 Barnes Solid	velocity, fps:	2450	2235	2030	1838	1658
	energy, ft-lb:	6663	5544	4576	3748	3051
	arc, inches:		+2.5	-0.6	-12.0	-33.8

.460 Weatherby Magnum

CARTRIDGE BULLET	RANGE, YARDS:	0	100	200	300	400
A-Square 500 Triad	velocity, fps:	2580	2349	2131	1923	1737
	energy, ft-lb:	7389	6126	5040	4107	3351
	arc, inches:		+2.4	0	-10.0	-29.4
Wby. 450 Barnes X	velocity, fps:	2700	2518	2343	2175	2013
	energy, ft-lb:	7284	6333	5482	4725	4050
	arc, inches:		+2.0	0	-8.4	-24.1

Centerfire Rifle Ballistics

.460 WEATHERBY MAGNUM TO .700 NITRO EXPRESS

CARTRIDGE BULLET	RANGE, YARDS:	0	100	200	300	400
Wby. 500 RN Expanding	velocity, fps:	2600	2301	2022	1764	1533.
	energy, ft-lb:	7504	5877	4539	3456	2608
	arc, inches:		+2.6	0	-11.1	-33.5
Wby. 500 FMJ	velocity, fps:	2600	2309	2037	1784	1557
	energy, ft-lb:	7504	5917	4605	3534	2690
	arc, inches:		+2.5	0	-10.9	-33.0

.500/.465

CARTRIDGE BULLET	RANGE, YARDS:	0	100	200	300	400
A-Square 480 Triad	velocity, fps:	2150	1928	1722	1533	
	energy, ft-lb:	4926	3960	3160	2505	
	arc, inches:		+4.3	0	-16.0	

.470 Nitro Express

CARTRIDGE BULLET	RANGE, YARDS:	0	100	200	300	400
A-Square 500 Triad	velocity, fps:	2150	1912	1693	1494	
	energy, ft-lb:	5132	4058	3182	2478	
	arc, inches:		+4.4	0	-16.5	
Federal 500 Trophy Bond	velocity, fps:	2150	1890	1660	1450	
(and Sledgehammer solid)	energy, ft-lb:	5130	3975	3045	2320	
	arc, inches:	-1.5	0	-9.4	-29.3	
Hornady 500 DGX, DGS	velocity, fps:	2150	1885	1643	1429	
	energy, ft-lb:	5132	3946	2998	2267	
	arc, inches:	-1.5	0	-8.9	-30.9	

CARTRIDGE BULLET	RANGE, YARDS:	0	50	100	150	200
Norma 500 Woodleigh	velocity, fps:	2100	2002	1906	1814	1725
(soft and solid)	energy, ft-lb:	4897	4449	4035	3654	3304
	arc, inches:	-1.5	+.3	0	-2.7	-8.0

.470 Capstick

CARTRIDGE BULLET	RANGE, YARDS:	0	100	200	300	400
A-Square 500 Triad	velocity, fps:	2400	2172	1958	1761	1553
	energy, ft-lb:	6394	5236	4255	3445	2678
	arc, inches:		+2.9	0	-11.9	-36.1

.475 #2

CARTRIDGE BULLET	RANGE, YARDS:	0	100	200	300	400
A-Square 480 Triad	velocity, fps:	2200	1964	1744	1544	
	energy, ft-lb:	5158	4109	3240	2539	
	arc, inches:		+4.1	0	-15.6	

.475 #2 Jeffery

CARTRIDGE BULLET	RANGE, YARDS:	0	100	200	300	400
A-Square 500 Triad	velocity, fps:	2200	1966	1748	1550	
	energy, ft-lb:	5373	4291	3392	2666	
	arc, inches:		+4.1	0	-15.6	

.495 A-Square

CARTRIDGE BULLET	RANGE, YARDS:	0	100	200	300	400
A-Square 570 Triad	velocity, fps:	2350	2117	1896	1693	1513
	energy, ft-lb:	6989	5671	4552	3629	2899
	arc, inches:		+3.1	0	-13.0	-37.8

.50 BMG

CARTRIDGE BULLET	RANGE, YARDS:	0	100	200	300	400
Hornady 750 A-Max	velocity, fps:	2815	2727	2641	2557	2474
	energy, ft-lb:	13,196	12,386	11,619	10,889	10,196
	arc, inches:		+1.4	0	-6.4	-18.2

.500 Nitro Express (3")

CARTRIDGE BULLET	RANGE, YARDS:	0	100	200	300	400
A-Square 570 Triad	velocity, fps:	2150	1928	1722	1533	
	energy, ft-lb:	5850	4703	3752	2975	
	arc, inches:		+4.3	0	-16.1	
Federal 570 TSX	velocity, fps:	2100	1890	1700	1520	1370
	energy, ft-lb:	5580	4530	3655	2935	2355
	arc, inches:	0	-8.4	-28.7	-64.2	
Hornady 570 DGX, DGS	velocity, fps:	2150	1881	1635	1419	
	energy, ft-lb:	5850	4477	3384	2547	
	arc, inches:	-.9	0	-9.0	-31.1	

CARTRIDGE BULLET	RANGE, YARDS:	0	50	100	150	200
Norma 570 Woodleigh SP	velocity, fps:	2100	2000	1903	1809	1719
	energy, ft-lb:	5583	5064	4585	4145	3742
	arc, inches:	-1.5	+.3	0	-2.7	-8.0
50 BMG						
Hornady 750 A-MAX	velocity, fps:	2815	2727	2641	2557	2474
	energy, ft-lb:	13196	12386	11619	10889	10196
	arc, inches:	-1.8	+1.4	0	-6.4	-18.2

.500 Jeffery

CARTRIDGE BULLET	RANGE, YARDS:	0	50	100	150	200
Norma 570 Woodleigh SP	velocity, fps:	2200	2097	1997	1901	1807
	energy, ft-lb:	6127	5568	5050	4573	4134
	arc, inches:	-1.5	+.2	0	-2.4	-7.1

.500 A-Square

CARTRIDGE BULLET	RANGE, YARDS:	0	100	200	300	400
A-Square 600 Triad	velocity, fps:	2470	2235	2013	1804	1620
	energy, ft-lb:	8127	6654	5397	4336	3495
	arc, inches:		+2.7	0	-11.3	-33.5

.505 Gibbs

CARTRIDGE BULLET	RANGE, YARDS:	0	100	200	300	400
A-Square 525 Triad	velocity, fps:	2300	2063	1840	1637	
	energy, ft-lb:	6166	4962	3948	3122	
	arc, inches:		+3.6	0	-14.2	

CARTRIDGE BULLET	RANGE, YARDS:	0	50	100	150	200
Norma 600 Woodleigh SP	velocity, fps:	2100	1998	1899	1803	1711
	energy, ft-lb:	5877	5319	4805	4334	3904
	arc, inches:	-1.5	+.3	0	-2.7	-8.1

.577 Nitro Express

CARTRIDGE BULLET	RANGE, YARDS:	0	100	200	300	400
A-Square 750 Triad	velocity, fps:	2050	1811	1595	1401	
	energy, ft-lb:	6998	5463	4234	3267	
	arc, inches:		+4.9	0	-18.5	

.577 Tyrannosaur

CARTRIDGE BULLET	RANGE, YARDS:	0	100	200	300	400
A-Square 750 Triad	velocity, fps:	2460	2197	1950	1723	1516
	energy, ft-lb:	10077	8039	6335	4941	3825
	arc, inches:		+2.8	0	-12.1	-36.0

.600 Nitro Express

CARTRIDGE BULLET	RANGE, YARDS:	0	100	200	300	400
A-Square 900 Triad	velocity, fps:	1950	1680	1452	1336	
	energy, ft-lb:	7596	5634	4212	3564	
	arc, inches:		+5.6	0	-20.7	

.700 Nitro Express

CARTRIDGE BULLET	RANGE, YARDS:	0	100	200	300	400
A-Square 1000 Monolithic Solid	velocity, fps:	1900	1669	1461	1288	
	energy, ft-lb:	8015	6188	4740	3685	
	arc, inches:		+5.8	0	-22.2	

Long Range Rifle

6.6 CREEDMOOR TO .338 LAPUA

6.6 Creedmoor

Cartridge Bullet	Range, yards:	0	400	600	800	1000
Nosler 140 HPBT	velocity, fps:	2550	2229	1932	1662	1426
	energy, ft-lb:	2021	1544	1160	859	632
	arc, inches:	-1.5	0	-26.7	-90.9	-205.9

.264 Winchester Magnum

Cartridge Bullet	Range, yards:	0	400	600	800	1000
Nosler 130 AccuBond	velocity, fps:	3100	2709	2350	2019	1718
	energy, ft-lb:	2773	2118	1594	1176	852
	arc, inches:	-1.5	0	-17.6	-60.6	-137.9

6.5-284 Norma

Cartridge Bullet	Range, yards:	0	400	600	800	1000
Nosler 129 AccuBond	velocity, fps:	2965	2633	2324	2036	1771
Long Range	energy, ft-lb:	2517	1985	1547	1188	899
	arc, inches:	-1.5	0	-18.7	-63.2	-141.6

.270 WSM

Cartridge Bullet	Range, yards:	0	400	600	800	1000
Nosler 150 AccuBond	velocity, fps:	2960	2661	2381	2118	1873
Long Range	energy, ft-lb:	2917	2358	1888	1495	1169
	arc, inches:	-1.5	0	-18.2	-61.1	-135.1

7mm Remington Magnum

Cartridge Bullet	Range, yards:	0	400	600	800	1000
Nosler 168 AccuBond	velocity, fps:	2880	2598	2333	2084	1851
Long Range	energy, ft-lb:	3093	2518	2030	1620	1278
	arc, inches:	-1.5	0	-19.2	-64.0	-141.0

7mm STW

Cartridge Bullet	Range, yards:	0	400	600	800	1000
Nosler 175 AccuBond	velocity, fps:	2900	2625	2366	2122	1893
Long Range	energy, ft-lb:	3267	2677	2175	1750	1393
	arc, inches:	-1.5	0	-18.8	-62.4	-137.1

7mm Remington Ultra Mag

Cartridge Bullet	Range, yards:	0	400	600	800	1000
Nosler 175 AccuBond	velocity, fps:	3040	2756	2490	2239	2002
Long Range	energy, ft-lb:	3590	2952	2409	1948	1558
	arc, inches:	-1.5	0	-16.9	-56.2	-123.5

.308 Winchester

Cartridge Bullet	Range, yards:	0	400	600	800	1000
Barnes 175 OTM						
velocity, fps:	2650	2318	2011	1730	1480	1272
energy, ft-lb:	2730	2089	1571	1163	852	629
arc, inches:	-1.5	0	-24.6	-83.8	-189. 9	-360.0

.300 WSM

Cartridge Bullet	Range, yards:	0	400	600	800	1000
Nosler 190 AccuBond	velocity, fps:	2875	2588	2319	2066	1830
Long Range	energy, ft-lb:	3486	2826	2269	1801	1413
	arc, inches:	-1.5	0	-19.3	-64.7	-142.7

.300 Winchester Magnum

Cartridge Bullet	Range, yards:	0	400	600	800	1000
Barnes 220 OTM						
velocity, fps:	2700	2420	2158	1912	1685	1481
energy, ft-lb:	3562	2862	2275	1786	1387	1072
arc, inches:	-1.5	0	-22.4	-74.7	-165.4	-305.3
Nosler 190 AccuBond	velocity, fps:	2870	2583	2314	2062	1826
Long Range	energy, ft-lb:	3474	2816	2260	1794	1407
	arc, inches:	-1.5	0	-19.4	-64.9	-143.3

.300 Weatherby Magnum

Cartridge Bullet	Range, yards:	0	400	600	800	1000
Nosler 210 AccuBond	velocity, fps:	2825	2575	2339	2115	1905
Long Range	energy, ft-lb:	3720	3092	2551	2087	1691
	arc, inches:	-1.5	0	-19.5	-64.6	-140.8

.300 Remington Ultra Mag

Cartridge Bullet	Range, yards:	0	400	600	800	1000
Nosler 210 AccuBond	velocity, fps:	2920	2665	2424	2196	1980
Long Range	energy, ft-lb:	3975	3311	2740	2248	1828
	arc, inches:	-1.5	0	-18.1	-60.0	-130.8

.30-378 Weatherby Magnum

Cartridge Bullet	Range, yards:	0	400	600	800	1000
Nosler 210 AccuBond	velocity, fps:	3040	2778	2531	2297	2076
Long Range	energy, ft-lb:	4308	3599	2987	2461	2009
	arc, inches:	-1.5	0	-16.6	-54.9	-119.7

.338 Remington Ultra Mag

Cartridge Bullet	Range, yards:	0	400	600	800	1000
Nosler 300 AccuBond	velocity, fps:	2600	2359	2131	1916	1716
	energy, ft-lb:	4502	3707	3026	2447	1963
	arc, inches:	-1.5	0	-23.6	-77.9	-170.2

.338 Lapua

Cartridge Bullet	Range, yards:	0	400	600	800	1000
Barnes 300 OTM						
velocity, fps:	2600	2375	2161	1958	1767	1591
energy, ft-lb:	4504	3757	3110	2554	2081	1687
arc, inches:	-1.5	0	-23.2	-76.4	-165.9	-300.1
Nosler 300 AccuBond	velocity, fps:	2650	2406	2176	1959	1755
	energy, ft-lb:	4677	3857	3154	2555	2053
	arc, inches:	-1.5	0	-22.6	-74.7	-163.1

Rimfire Ballistics

Rimfire cartridges have had a longer run than any centerfire you can name. Horace Smith and Daniel Wesson came up with the first successful .22 rimfires in the United States in 1857. Thirty years later the .22 Long Rifle arrived, courtesy of the J. Stevens Arms & Tool Company. It used 5 grains of black powder to drive a 40-grain bullet, shortly making the transition to smokeless in a case crimped on a heeled bullet. Remington produced the first modern high-speed load in 1930. Current .22 ammo includes myriad Long Rifle listings. The Long (essentially a Short bullet in a Long Rifle case), like the CB and WRF cartridges, is going the way of the dodo. The shot load of #12 "dust" has faded too, though it has dispatched many snakes, and was once hailed as just the ticket for barn mice and rats when you didn't want to perforate the boards. New rimfires have joined the versatile Long Rifle. The .22 WMR (Winchester Magnum Rimfire) came in 1959. More than four decades passed before Hornady necked down the WMR case to form the .17 HMR. A sibling on the CCI Stinger variation of the .22 LR appeared in 2004. Hornady dubbed it the .17 Mach 2. The newest .17, Winchester's Super Mag, arrived in 2013. The .17s and the .22 WMR feature jacketed hollowpoint and polymer-tipped bullets, just like centerfires.

This list is incomplete. For convenience (and given space constraints), it omits duplicate loads—those by the same manufacturer but under different labels). Units: velocity in feet per second, energy in foot-pounds, drop in inches.

.22 TO .17 HORNADY MAGNUM RIMFIRE

CARTRIDGE BULLET	LOAD	MUZZLE VEL./ENERGY	100-YD. VEL./ENERGY
.22			
CCI .22 CB Short	29-gr. RN	710/32	607/24
CCI .22 CB Long	29-gr. RN	710/32	607/24
CCI .22 Short	27-gr. HP	1105/73	868/45
CCI .22 Short	29-gr. RN	1080/75	857/47
CCI .22 Short	29-gr. Target RN	830/44	704/32
CCI .22 Long	29-gr. RN	1215/95	908/53
CCI .22 LR	21-gr. Short Range Green HP	1650/127	912/38
CCI .22 LR	31 gr. #12 birdshot	1000	
CCI .22 LR	32-gr. Stinger HP	1640/191	1066/81
CCI .22 LR	36-gr. HP	1260/127	1003/80
CCI .22 LR	40-gr. Tactical RN	1200/128	964/82
CCI .22 LR	40-gr. Mini-Mag RN	1235/135	998/88
CCI .22 LR	40-gr. Sub-sonic HP	1050/98	897/72
CCI .22 LR	40-gr. Velocitor HP	1435/183	1084/104
CCI .22 LR	40-gr. Small Game Bullet LFN	1235/135	992/87
CCI .22 LR	40-gr. Quiet-22 HP	710/45	640/36
CCI .22 LR	40-gr. Select RN	1200/128	964/82
CCI .22 LR	40-gr. Green Tag RN	1070/102	908/73
CCI .22 LR	45-gr. HP Suppressor	970/95	892/75
Federal .22 LR	25 gr. #12 birdshot		
Federal .22 LR	31-gr. Game-Shok HP	1430/140	1050/75
Federal .22 LR	36-gr. Champion HP	1260/125	1000/80
Federal .22 LR	38-gr. Game-Shok HP	1260/135	1010/85
Federal .22 LR	38-gr. Amer. Eagle HP	1260/135	1010/85
Federal .22 LR	40-gr. Prem. Gold Medal	1200/130	990/85
Federal .22 LR	40-gr. Game-Shok HP	1240/135	1010/90
Federal .22 LR	40-gr. Champion	1240/135	1010/90
Federal .22 LR	45-gr. Amer. Eagle Suppressed	1050/105	910/75
Lapua .22 LR	40-gr. Polar Biathlon	1106/109	914/74
Remington .22 Short	29-gr. RN	1095/77	903/52
Remington .22 LR	33-gr. CBee Low Noise HP	740/40	638/30
Remington .22 LR	33-gr. Yellow Jacket T. C.	1500/165	1075/85
Remington .22 LR	36-gr. Viper Truncated Cone	1410/159	1056/89
Remington .22 LR	36-gr. Cyclone HP	1280/131	1010/82
Remington .22 LR	38-gr. Sub-sonic HP	1050/93	901/69
Remington .22 LR	40-gr. Target	1150/117	976/85
Remington .22 LR	40-gr. Thunderbolt	1255/140	1017/92
Remington .22 LR	40-gr. Competition RN	1085/105	941/79
Winchester .22 Short	29-gr. RN	1095/77	903/52
Winchester .22 Long	29-gr. RN	770/38	681/30
Winchester .22 LR	31-gr. #12 birdshot	1000	
Winchester .22 LR	26-gr. Varmint LF HP	1650/157	1023/60
Winchester .22 LR	32-gr. Xpediter HP	1640/191	1078/83
Winchester .22 LR	29-gr. Super-X sub-sonic	770/38	681/30
Winchester .22 LR	36-gr. HP	1280/131	975/76
Winchester .22 LR	37-gr. Super-X HP	1280/135	1015/85
Winchester .22 LR	37-gr. Super Speed HP	1330/154	1038/88
Winchester .22 LR	37-gr. Varmint HE HP	1435/169	1080/96
Winchester .22 LR	40-gr. Super-X low-report	1065/101	922/76
Winchester .22 LR	40-gr. DynaPoint	1150/117	976/85
Winchester .22 LR	40-gr. M22 LRN Black	1255/140	1017/92
Winchester .22 LR	40-gr. Power-Point HP	1280/145	1001/89
Winchester .22 LR	40-gr. Super-X	1300/150	1038/96
Winchester .22 LR	40-gr. Hyper Speed HP	1435/183	1070/102
.17 Hornady Magnum Rimfire			
CCI .17 HMR	16-gr. TNT Green HP	2500/222	1642/96
CCI .17 HMR	17-gr. TNT JHP	2550/245	1757116
CCI .17 HMR	17-gr. Poly-Tip V-Max	2550/245	1915/138
CCI .17 HMR	20-gr. FMJ	2375/250	1776/140
CCI .17 HMR	20-gr. JSP	2375/250	1754/137
Federal .17 HMR	17-gr. Prem. V-Shok TNT JHP	2530/240	1800/125
Federal .17 HMR	17-gr. Prem. Hornady V-Max	2530/240	1880/135
Hornady .17 Mach 2	15.5-gr. NTX Lead-Free	2050/149	1450/75
Hornady .17 Mach 2	17-gr. V-Max	2100/166	1530/88

Rimfire Ballistics

.17 HORNADY MAGNUM RIMFIRE TO .22 WINCHESTER RIMFIRE

CARTRIDGE BULLET	LOAD	MUZZLE VEL./ENERGY	100-YD. VEL./ENERGY
Hornady .17 HMR	15.5-gr. NTX Lead-Free	2525/236	1829/119
Hornady .17 HMR	17-gr. V-Max	2550/245	1901/136
Hornady .17 HMR	20-gr. XTP	2375/250	1776/140
Remington.17 HMR	17-gr. AccuTip-V	2550/245	1901/136
Winchester .17 HMR	15.5-gr. Varmint LF NTX	2550/224	1901/124
Winchester .17 HMR	17-gr. Poly Tip V-Max	2550/245	1915/138
Winchester .17 HMR	20-gr. Super-X JHP	2375/250	1776/140

.22 Winchester Magnum Rimfire

CARTRIDGE BULLET	LOAD	MUZZLE VEL./ENERGY	100-YD. VEL./ENERGY
CCI .22 WMR	30 Maxi Mag HP + V	2200/322	1375/126
CCI .22 WMR	30 Poly-Tip V-Max	2200/322	1571/164
CCI .22 WMR	30 TNT JHP	2200/322	1405/131
CCI .22 WMR	30 TNT Green HP	2050/280	1317/116
CCI .22 WMR	40 Maxi Mag HP	1875/312	1319/155
CCI .22 WMR	40 Maxi Mag TMJ	1875/312	1366/166
CCI .22 WMR	40 GamePoint JSP	1875/312	1385/170
CCI .22 WMR	52 #12 birdshot	1000	
Federal .22 WMR	30-gr. Speer TNT HP	2200/320	1420/135
Federal .22 WMR	40-gr. FMJ	1880/315	1310/155
Hornady .22 WMR	30-gr. V-Max	2200/322	1421/134
Remington .22 WMR	33-gr. AccuTip-V	2000/293	1495/164
Remington .22 WMR	40-gr. JHP	1910/324	1350/162
Remington .22 WMR	40-gr. PSP	1910/324	1340/159
Winchester .22 WMR	28-gr. Varmint LF JHP	2200/301	1394/121
Winchester .22 WMR	30-gr. Varmint HV V-Max	2250/337	1490/148
Winchester .22 WMR	30-gr. Varmint HV JHP	2250/337	1450/140
Winchester .22 WMR	34-gr. Varmint HE JHP	2120/339	1437/156
Winchester .22 WMR	40-gr. Super-X JHP (and FMJ)	1910/324	1326/156
Winchester .22 WMR	45-gr. USA DynaPoint	1550/240	1147/131

.17 Winchester Super Mag.

CARTRIDGE BULLET	LOAD	MUZZLE VEL./ENERGY	100-YD. VEL./ENERGY
Winchester .17 Super Mag	20-gr. Varmint HV	3000/400	2504/278
Winchester .17 Super Mag	25-gr. Polymer Tip	2600/375	2230/276

.22 Winchester Rimfire

CARTRIDGE BULLET	LOAD	MUZZLE VEL./ENERGY	100-YD. VEL./ENERGY
CCI .22 WRF	45 JHP	1300/169	1013/103
Winchester .22 WRF	45 FN	1300/169	1023/105

Centerfire Handgun Ballistics

Data shown here is taken from manufacturers' charts; your chronograph readings may vary. Barrel lengths for pistol data vary, and depend in part on which pistols are typically chambered in a given cartridge. Velocity variations due to barrel length depend on the baseline bullet speed and the load. Velocity for the .30 Carbine, normally a rifle cartridge, was determined in a pistol barrel.

Listings are current as of February the year *Shooter's Bible* appears (not the cover year). Listings are not intended as recommendations. For example, the data for the .25 Auto gives velocity and energy readings to 100 yards. Few handgunners would call the little .25 a 100-yard cartridge.

Abbreviations: Bullets are designated by loading company, weight (in grains) and type, with these abbreviations for shape and construction: BJHP= brass-jacketed hollowpoint; FN=Flat Nose; FMC=Full Metal Case; FMJ=Full Metal Jacket; HP=Hollowpoint; L=Lead; LF=Lead-Free; +P=a more powerful load than traditionally manufactured for that round; RN=Round Nose; SFHP=Starfire (PMC) Hollowpoint; SP=Softpoint; SWC=Semi Wadcutter; TMJ=Total Metal Jacket; WC=Wadcutter; CEPP, SXT and XTP are trademarked designations of Lapua, Winchester and Hornady, respectively.

.25 AUTO TO .32 S&W LONG

.25 Auto

CARTRIDGE BULLET	RANGE, YARDS:	0	25	50	75	100
Federal 50 FMJ	velocity, fps:	760	750	730	720	700
	energy, ft-lb:	65	60	60	55	55
Hornady 35 JHP/XTP	velocity, fps:	900		813		742
	energy, ft-lb:	63		51		43
Magtech 50 FMC	velocity, fps:	760		707		659
	energy, ft-lb:	64		56		48
PMC 50 FMJ	velocity, fps:	754	730	707	685	663
	energy, ft-lb:	62				
Rem. 50 Metal Case	velocity, fps:	760		707		659
	energy, ft-lb:	64		56		48
Speer 35 Gold Dot	velocity, fps:	900		816		747
	energy, ft-lb:	63		52		43
Speer 50 TMJ (and Blazer)	velocity, fps:	760		717		677
	energy, ft-lb:	64		57		51
Win. 45 Expanding Point	velocity, fps:	815		729		655
	energy, ft-lb	66		53		42
Win. 50 FMJ	velocity, fps:	760		707		
	energy, ft-lb	64		56		

.30 Luger

CARTRIDGE BULLET	RANGE, YARDS:	0	25	50	75	100
Win. 93 FMJ	velocity, fps:	1220		1110		1040
	energy, ft-lb	305		255		225

7.62x25 Tokarev

CARTRIDGE BULLET	RANGE, YARDS:	0	25	50	75	100
PMC 93 FMJ	velocity and energy figures not available					

.30 Carbine

CARTRIDGE BULLET	RANGE, YARDS:	0	25	50	75	100
Win. 110 Hollow SP	velocity, fps:	1790		1601		1430
	energy, ft-lb	783		626		500

.32 Auto

CARTRIDGE BULLET	RANGE, YARDS:	0	25	50	75	100
Federal 65 Hydra-Shok JHP	velocity, fps:	950	920	890	860	830
	energy, ft-lb:	130	120	115	105	100
Federal 71 FMJ	velocity, fps:	910	880	860	830	810
	energy, ft-lb:	130	120	115	110	105
Hornady 60 JHP/XTP	velocity, fps:	1000		917		849
	energy, ft-lb:	133		112		96
Hornady 71 FMJ-RN	velocity, fps:	900		845		797
	energy, ft-lb:	128		112		100
Magtech 71 FMC	velocity, fps:	905		855		810
	energy, ft-lb:	129		115		103
Magtech 71 JHP	velocity, fps:	905		855		810
	energy, ft-lb:	129		115		103
PMC 60 JHP	velocity, fps:	980	849	820	791	763
	energy, ft-lb:	117				
PMC 70 SFHP	velocity, fps:	velocity and energy figures not available				
PMC 71 FMJ	velocity, fps:	870	841	814	791	763
	energy, ft-lb:	119				
Rem. 71 Metal Case	velocity, fps:	905		855		810
	energy, ft-lb:	129		115		97
Speer 60 Gold Dot	velocity, fps:	960		868		796
	energy, ft-lb:	123		100		84
Speer 71 TMJ (and Blazer)	velocity, fps:	900		855		810
	energy, ft-lb:	129		115		97
Win. 60 Silvertip HP	velocity, fps:	970		895		835
	energy, ft-lb	125		107		93
Win. 71 FMJ	velocity, fps:	905		855		
	energy, ft-lb	129		115		

.32 S&W

CARTRIDGE BULLET	RANGE, YARDS:	0	25	50	75	100
Rem. 88 LRN	velocity, fps:	680		645		610
	energy, ft-lb:	90		81		73
Win. 85 LRN	velocity, fps:	680		645		610
	energy, ft-lb	90		81		73

.32 S&W Long

CARTRIDGE BULLET	RANGE, YARDS:	0	25	50	75	100
Federal 98 LWC	velocity, fps:	780	700	630	560	500
	energy, ft-lb:	130	105	85	70	55
Federal 98 LRN	velocity, fps:	710	690	670	650	640
	energy, ft-lb:	115	105	100	95	90
Lapua 83 LWC	velocity, fps:	240		189*		149*
	energy, ft-lb:	154		95*		59*
Lapua 98 LWC	velocity, fps:	240		202*		171*
	energy, ft-lb:	183		130*		93*
Magtech 98 LRN	velocity, fps:	705		670		635
	energy, ft-lb:	108		98		88
Magtech 98 LWC	velocity, fps:	682		579		491
	energy, ft-lb:	102		73		52
Norma 98 LWC	velocity, fps:	787	759	732		683
	energy, ft-lb:	136	126	118		102
PMC 98 LRN	velocity, fps:	789	770	751	733	716
	energy, ft-lb:	135				
PMC 100 LWC	velocity, fps:	683	652	623	595	569
	energy, ft-lb:	102				
Rem. 98 LRN	velocity, fps:	705		670		635
	energy, ft-lb:	115		98		88

Centerfire Handgun Ballistics

.32 S&W LONG TO 9MM LUGER

CARTRIDGE BULLET	RANGE, YARDS:	0	25	50	75	100
Win. 98 LRN	velocity, fps:	705		670		635
	energy, ft-lb:	115		98		88

.32 Short Colt

CARTRIDGE BULLET	RANGE, YARDS:	0	25	50	75	100
Win. 80 LRN	velocity, fps:	745		665		590
	energy, ft-lb	100		79		62

.32-20

CARTRIDGE BULLET	RANGE, YARDS:	0	25	50	75	100
Black Hills 115 FPL	velocity, fps:	800				
	energy, ft-lb:					

.32 H&R Mag

CARTRIDGE BULLET	RANGE, YARDS:	0	25	50	75	100
Black Hills 85 JHP	velocity, fps	1100				
	energy, ft-lb	228				
Black Hills 90 FPL	velocity, fps	750				
	energy, ft-lb					
Black Hills 115 FPL	velocity, fps	800				
	energy, ft-lb					
Federal 85 Hi-Shok JHP	velocity, fps:	1100	1050	1020	970	930
	energy, ft-lb:	230	210	195	175	165
Federal 95 LSWC	velocity, fps:	1030	1000	940	930	900
	energy, ft-lb:	225	210	195	185	170
Hornady 80 FTX		0		50 yds.		100.
	velocity, fps:	1150		1039		963
	energy, ft-lb:	235		192		165

.38 Special Lite, 4"bbl

CARTRIDGE BULLET	RANGE, YARDS:	0	25	50	75	100
Hornady 90 FTX	velocity, fps:	1200		1037		938
	energy, ft-lb:	288		215		176

9mm Makarov

CARTRIDGE BULLET	RANGE, YARDS:	0	25	50	75	100
Federal 90 Hi-Shok JHP	velocity, fps:	990	950	910	880	850
	energy, ft-lb:	195	180	165	155	145
Federal 90 FMJ	velocity, fps:	990	960	920	900	870
	energy, ft-lb:	205	190	180	170	160
Hornady 95 JHP/XTP	velocity, fps:	1000		930		874
	energy, ft-lb:	211		182		161
PMC 100 FMJ-TC	velocity, fps:	velocity and energy figures not available				
Speer 95 TMJ Blazer	velocity, fps:	1000		928		872
	energy, ft-lb:	211		182		161

9x21 IMI

CARTRIDGE BULLET	RANGE, YARDS:	0	25	50	75	100
PMC 123 FMJ	velocity, fps:	1150	1093	1046	1007	973
	energy, ft-lb:	364				

9mm Luger

CARTRIDGE BULLET	RANGE, YARDS:	0	25	50	75	100
Black Hills 115 JHP	velocity, fps:	1150				
	energy, ft-lb:	336				
Black Hills 115 FMJ	velocity, fps:	1150				
	energy, ft-lb:	336				
Black Hills 115 JHP +P	velocity, fps:	1300				
	energy, ft-lb:	431				
Black Hills 115 EXP JHP	velocity, fps:	1250				
	energy, ft-lb:	400				
Black Hills 124 JHP +P	velocity, fps:	1250				
	energy, ft-lb:	430				
Black Hills 124 JHP	velocity, fps:	1150				
	energy, ft-lb:	363				
Black Hills 124 FMJ	velocity, fps:	1150				
	energy, ft-lb:	363				
Black Hills 147 JHP subsonic	velocity, fps:	975				
	energy, ft-lb:	309				
Black Hills 147 FMJ subsonic	velocity, fps:	975				
	energy, ft-lb:	309				
Federal 105 EFMJ	velocity, fps:	1225	1160	1105	1060	1025
	energy, ft-lb:	350	315	285	265	245
Federal 115 Hi-Shok JHP	velocity, fps:	1160	1100	1060	1020	990
	energy, ft-lb:	345	310	285	270	250
Federal 115 FMJ	velocity, fps:	1160	1100	1060	1020	990
	energy, ft-lb:	345	310	285	270	250
Federal 124 FMJ	velocity, fps:	1120	1070	1030	990	960
	energy, ft-lb:	345	315	290	270	255
Federal 124 Hydra-Shok JHP	velocity, fps:	1120	1070	1030	990	960
	energy, ft-lb:	345	315	290	270	255
Federal 124 TMJ TMF Primer	velocity, fps:	1120	1070	1030	990	960
	energy, ft-lb:	345	315	290	270	255
Federal 124 Truncated FMJ	velocity, fps:	1120	1070	1030	990	960
Match	energy, ft-lb:	345	315	290	270	255
Federal 124 Nyclad HP	velocity, fps:	1120	1070	1030	990	960
	energy, ft-lb:	345	315	290	270	255
Federal 124 FMJ +P	velocity, fps:	1120	1070	1030	990	960
	energy, ft-lb:	345	315	290	270	255
Federal 135 Hydra-Shok JHP	velocity, fps:	1050	1030	1010	980	970
	energy, ft-lb:	330	315	300	290	280
Federal 147 Hydra-Shok JHP	velocity, fps:	1000	960	920	890	860
	energy, ft-lb:	325	300	275	260	240
Federal 147 Hi-Shok JHP	velocity, fps:	980	950	930	900	880
	energy, ft-lb:	310	295	285	265	255
Federal 147 FMJ FN	velocity, fps:	960	930	910	890	870
	energy, ft-lb:	295	280	270	260	250
Federal 147 TMJ TMF Primer	velocity, fps:	960	940	910	890	870
	energy, ft-lb:	300	285	270	260	245
Hornady 115 JHP/XTP	velocity, fps:	1155		1047		971
	energy, ft-lb:	341		280		241
Hornady 124 JHP/XTP	velocity, fps:	1110		1030		971
	energy, ft-lb:	339		292		259
Hornady 124 TAP-FPD	velocity, fps:	1100		1028		967
	energy, ft-lb:	339		291		257
Hornady 147 JHP/XTP	velocity, fps:	975		935		899
	energy, ft-lb:	310		285		264
Hornady 147 TAP-FPD	velocity, fps:	975		935		899
	energy, ft-lb:	310		285		264
Lapua 116 FMJ	velocity, fps:	365		319*		290*
	energy, ft-lb:	500		381*		315*
Lapua 120 FMJ CEPP Super	velocity, fps:	360		316*		288*
	energy, ft-lb:	505		390*		324*
Lapua 120 FMJ CEPP Extra	velocity, fps:	360		316*		288*
	energy, ft-lb:	505		390*		324*
Lapua 123 HP Megashock	velocity, fps:	355		311*		284*
	energy, ft-lb:	504		388*		322*
Lapua 123 FMJ	velocity, fps:	320		292*		272*
	energy, ft-lb:	410		342*		295*
Lapua 123 FMJ Combat	velocity, fps:	355		315*		289*
	energy, ft-lb:	504		397*		333*
Magtech 115 JHP +P	velocity, fps:	1246		1137		1056
	energy, ft-lb:	397		330		285
Magtech 115 FMC	velocity, fps:	1135		1027		961
	energy, ft-lb:	330		270		235
Magtech 115 JHP	velocity, fps:	1155		1047		971
	energy, ft-lb:	340		280		240
Magtech 124 FMC	velocity, fps:	1109		1030		971
	energy, ft-lb:	339		292		259
Norma 84 Lead Free Frangible	velocity, fps:	1411				
(Geco brand)	energy, ft-lb:	371				
Norma 124 FMJ	velocity, fps:	1120				
(Geco brand)	energy, fps:	341				
Norma 123 FMJ	velocity, fps:	1099	1032	980		899
	energy, ft-lb:	331	292	263		221
Norma 123 FMJ	velocity, fps:	1280	1170	1086		972
	energy, ft-lb:	449	375	323		259

Centerfire Handgun Ballistics

9MM LUGER TO .380 AUTO

CARTRIDGE BULLET	RANGE, YARDS:	0	25	50	75	100
PMC 75 Non-Toxic Frangible	velocity, fps:	1350	1240	1154	1088	1035
	energy, ft-lb:	303				
PMC 95 SFHP	velocity, fps:	1250	1239	1228	1217	1207
	energy, ft-lb:	330				
PMC 115 FMJ	velocity, fps:	1157	1100	1053	1013	979
	energy, ft-lb:	344				
PMC 115 JHP	velocity, fps:	1167	1098	1044	999	961
	energy, ft-lb:	350				
PMC 124 SFHP	velocity, fps:	1090	1043	1003	969	939
	energy, ft-lb:	327				
PMC 124 FMJ	velocity, fps:	1110	1059	1017	980	949
	energy, ft-lb:	339				
PMC 124 LRN	velocity, fps:	1050	1006	969	937	908
	energy, ft-lb:	304				
PMC 147 FMJ	velocity, fps:	980	965	941	919	900
	enerby, ft-lb:	310				
PMC 147 SFHP	velocity, fps:	velocity and energy figures not available				
Rem. 101 Lead Free Frangible	velocity, fps:	1220		1092		1004
	energy, ft-lb:	334		267		226
Rem. 115 FN Enclosed Base	velocity, fps:	1135		1041		973
	energy, ft-lb:	329		277		242
Rem. 115 Metal Case	velocity, fps:	1135		1041		973
	energy, ft-lb:	329		277		242
Rem. 115 JHP	velocity, fps:	1155		1047		971
	energy, ft-lb:	341		280		241
Rem. 115 JHP +P	velocity, fps:	1250		1113		1019
	energy, ft-lb:	399		316		265
Rem. 124 JHP	velocity, fps:	1120		1028		960
	energy, ft-lb:	346		291		254
Rem. 124 FNEB	velocity, fps:	1100		1030		971
	energy, ft-lb:	339		292		252
Rem. 124 BJHP	velocity, fps:	1125		1031		963
	energy, ft-lb:	349		293		255
Rem. 124 BJHP +P	velocity, fps:	1180		1089		1021
	energy, ft-lb:	384		327		287
Rem. 124 Metal Case	velocity, fps:	1110		1030		971
	energy, ft-lb:	339		292		259
Rem. 147 JHP subsonic	velocity, fps:	990		941		900
	energy, ft-lb:	320		289		264
Rem. 147 BJHP	velocity, fps:	990		941		900
	energy, ft-lb:	320		289		264
Speer 90 Frangible	velocity, fps:	1350		1132		1001
	energy, ft-lb:	364		256		200
Speer 115 JHP Blazer	velocity, fps:	1145		1024		943
	energy, ft-lb:	335		268		227
Speer 115 FMJ Blazer	velocity, fps:	1145		1047		971
	energy, ft-lb:	341		280		241
Speer 115 FMJ	velocity, fps:	1200		1060		970
	energy, ft-lb:	368		287		240
Speer 115 Gold Dot HP	velocity, fps:	1200		1047		971
	energy, ft-lb:	341		280		241
Speer 124 FMJ Blazer	velocity, fps:	1090		989		917
	energy, ft-lb:	327		269		231
Speer 124 FMJ	velocity, fps:	1090		987		913
	energy, ft-lb:	327		268		230
Speer 124 TMJ-CF (and Blazer)	velocity, fps:	1090		989		917
	energy, ft-lb:	327		269		231
Speer 124 Gold Dot HP	velocity, fps:	1150		1030		948
	energy, ft-lb:	367		292		247
Speer 124 Gold Dot HP+P	velocity, ft-lb:	1220		1085		996
	energy, ft-lb:	410		324		273
Speer 147 TMJ Blazer	velocity, fps:	950		912		879
	energy, ft-lb:	295		272		252

CARTRIDGE BULLET	RANGE, YARDS:	0	25	50	75	100
Speer 147 TMJ	velocity, fps:	985		943		906
	energy, ft-lb:	317		290		268
Speer 147 TMJ-CF (and Blazer)	velocity, fps:	985		960		924
	energy, ft-lb:	326		300		279
Speer 147 Gold Dot	velocity, fps:	985		960		924
	energy, ft-lb:	326		300		279
Win. 105 Jacketed FP	velocity, fps:	1200		1074		989
	energy, ft-lb:	336		269		228
Win. 115 Silvertip HP	velocity, fps:	1225		1095		1007
	energy, ft-lb:	383		306		259
Win. 115 Jacketed HP	velocity, fps:	1225		1095		
	energy, ft-lb:	383		306		
Win. 115 FMJ	velocity, fps:	1190		1071		
	energy, ft-lb:	362		293		
Win. 115 EB WinClean	velocity, fps:	1190		1088		
	energy, ft-lb:	362		302		
Win. 124 FMJ	velocity, fps:	1140		1050		
	energy, ft-lb:	358		303		
Win. 124 EB WinClean	velocity, fps:	1130		1049		
	energy, ft-lb:	352		303		
Win. 147 FMJ FN	velocity, fps:	990		945		
	energy, ft-lb:	320		292		
Win. 147 SXT	velocity, fps:	990		947		909
	energy, ft-lb:	320		293		270
Win. 147 Silvertip HP	velocity, fps:	1010		962		921
	energy, ft-lb:	333		302		277
Win. 147 JHP	velocity, fps:	990		945		
	energy, ft-lb:	320		291		
Win. 147 EB WinClean	velocity, fps:	990		945		
	energy, ft-lb:	320		291		

9 x 23 Winchester

CARTRIDGE BULLET	RANGE, YARDS:	0	25	50	75	100
Win. 124 Jacketed FP	velocity, fps:	1460		1308		
	energy, ft-lb:	587		471		
Win. 125 Silvertip HP	velocity, fps:	1450		1249		1103
	energy, ft-lb:	583		433		338

.38 S&W

CARTRIDGE BULLET	RANGE, YARDS:	0	25	50	75	100
Rem. 146 LRN	velocity, fps:	685		650		620
	energy, ft-lb:	150		135		125
Win. 145 LRN	velocity, fps:	685		650		620
	energy, ft-lb:	150		135		125

.38 Short Colt

CARTRIDGE BULLET	RANGE, YARDS:	0	25	50	75	100
Rem. 125 LRN	velocity, fps:	730		685		645
	energy, ft-lb:	150		130		115

.38 Long Colt

CARTRIDGE BULLET	RANGE, YARDS:	0	25	50	75	100
Black Hills 158 RNL	velocity, fps:	650				
	energy, ft-lb:					

.380 Auto

CARTRIDGE BULLET	RANGE, YARDS:	0	25	50	75	100
Black Hills 90 JHP	velocity, fps:	1000				
	energy, ft-lb:	200				
Black Hills 95 FMJ	velocity, fps:	950				
	energy, ft-lb:	190				
Federal 90 Hi-Shok JHP	velocity, fps:	1000	940	890	840	800
	energy, ft-lb:	200	175	160	140	130
Federal 90 Hydra-Shok JHP	velocity, fps:	1000	940	890	840	800
	energy, ft-lb:	200	175	160	140	130
Federal 95 FMJ	velocity, fps:	960	910	870	830	790
	energy, ft-lb:	190	175	160	145	130
Hornady 90 JHP/XTP	velocity, fps:	1000		902		823
	energy, ft-lb:	200		163		135

Centerfire Handgun Ballistics

.380 AUTO TO .38 SPECIAL

CARTRIDGE BULLET	RANGE, YARDS:	0	25	50	75	100
Magtech 85 JHP + P	velocity, fps:	1082		999		936
	energy, ft-lb:	221		188		166
Magtech 95 FMC	velocity, fps:	951		861		781
	energy, ft-lb:	190		156		128
Magtech 95 JHP	velocity, fps:	951		861		781
	energy, ft-lb:	190		156		128
PMC 77 NT/FR	velocity, fps:	1200	1095	1012	932	874
	energy, ft-lb:	223				
PMC 90 FMJ	velocity, fps:	910	872	838	807	778
	energy, ft-lb:	165				
PMC 90 JHP	velocity, fps:	917	878	844	812	782
	energy, ft-lb:	168				
PMC 95 SFHP	velocity, fps:	925	884	847	813	783
	energy, ft-lb:	180				
Rem. 88 JHP	velocity, fps:	990		920		868
	energy, ft-lb:	191		165		146
Rem. 95 FNEB	velocity, fps:	955		865		785
	energy, ft-lb:	190		160		130
Rem. 95 Metal Case	velocity, fps:	955		865		785
	energy, ft-lb:	190		160		130
Rem. 102 BJHP	velocity, fps:	940		901		866
	energy, ft-lb:	200		184		170
Speer 88 JHP Blazer	velocity, fps:	950		920		870
	energy, ft-lb:	195		164		148
Speer 90 Gold Dot	velocity, fps:	990		907		842
	energy, ft-lb:	196		164		142
Speer 95 TMJ Blazer	velocity, fps:	945		865		785
	energy, ft-lb:	190		160		130
Speer 95 TMJ	velocity, fps:	950		877		817
	energy, ft-lb:	180		154		133
Win. 85 Silvertip HP	velocity, fps:	1000		921		860
	energy, ft-lb:	189		160		140
Win. 95 SXT	velocity, fps:	955		889		835
	energy, ft-lb:	192		167		147
Win. 95 FMJ	velocity, fps:	955		865		
	energy, ft-lb:	190		160		
Win. 95 EB WinClean	velocity, fps:	955		881		
	energy, ft-lb:	192		164		

.38 Special

CARTRIDGE BULLET	RANGE, YARDS:	0	25	50	75	100
Black Hills 125 JHP +P	velocity, fps:	1050				
	energy, ft-lb:	306				
Black Hills 148 HBWC	velocity, fps:	700				
	energy, ft-lb:					
Black Hills 158 SWC	velocity, fps:	850				
	energy, ft-lb:					
Black Hills 158 CNL	velocity, fps:	800				
	energy, ft-lb:					
Federal 110 Hydra-Shok JHP	velocity, fps:	1000	970	930	910	880
	energy, ft-lb:	245	225	215	200	190
Federal 110 Hi-Shok JHP +P	velocity, fps:	1000	960	930	900	870
	energy, ft-lb:	240	225	210	195	185
Federal 125 Nyclad HP	velocity, fps:	830	780	730	690	650
	energy, ft-lb:	190	170	150	130	115
Federal 125 Hi-Shok JSP +P	velocity, fps:	950	920	900	880	860
	energy, ft-lb:	250	235	225	215	205
Federal 125 Hi-Shok JHP +P	velocity, fps:	950	920	900	880	860
	energy, ft-lb:	250	235	225	215	205
Federal 125 Nyclad HP +P	velocity, fps:	950	920	900	880	860
	energy, ft-lb:	250	235	225	215	205
Federal 129 Hydra-Shok JHP+P	velocity, fps:	950	930	910	890	870
	energy, ft-lb:	255	245	235	225	215
Federal 130 FMJ	velocity, fps:	950	920	890	870	840
	energy, ft-lb:	260	245	230	215	205
Federal 148 LWC Match	velocity, fps:	710	670	630	600	560
	energy, ft-lb:	165	150	130	115	105
Federal 158 LRN	velocity, fps:	760	740	720	710	690
	energy, ft-lb:	200	190	185	175	170
Federal 158 LSWC	velocity, fps:	760	740	720	710	690
	energy, ft-lb:	200	190	185	175	170
Federal 158 Nyclad RN	velocity, fps:	760	740	720	710	690
	energy, ft-lb:	200	190	185	175	170
Federal 158 SWC HP +P	velocity, fps:	890	870	860	840	820
	energy, ft-lb:	280	265	260	245	235
Federal 158 LSWC +P	velocity, fps:	890	870	860	840	820
	energy, ft-lb:	270	265	260	245	235
Federal 158 Nyclad SWC-HP+P	velocity, fps:	890	870	860	840	820
	energy, ft-lb:	270	265	260	245	235
Hornady 125 JHP/XTP	velocity, fps:	900		856		817
	energy, ft-lb:	225		203		185
Hornady 140 JHP/XTP	velocity, fps:	825		790		757
	energy, ft-lb:	212		194		178
Hornady 140 Cowboy	velocity, fps:	800		767		735
	energy, ft-lb:	199		183		168
Hornady 148 HBWC	velocity, fps:	800		697		610
	energy, ft-lb:	210		160		122
Hornady 158 JHP/XPT	velocity, fps:	800		765		731
	energy, ft-lb:	225		205		188
Lapua 123 HP Megashock	velocity, fps:	355		311*		284*
	energy, ft-lb:	504		388*		322*
Lapua 148 LWC	velocity, fps:	230		203*		181*
	energy, ft-lb:	254		199*		157*
Lapua 150 SJFN	velocity, fps:	325		301*		283*
	energy, ft-lb:	512		439*		388*
Lapua 158 FMJLF	velocity, fps:	255		243*		232*
	energy, ft-lb:	332		301*		275*
Lapua 158 LRN	velocity, fps:	255		243*		232*
	energy, ft-lb:	332		301*		275*
Magtech 125 JHP +P	velocity, fps:	1017		971		931
	energy, ft-lb:	287		262		241
Magtech 148 LWC	velocity, fps:	710		634		566
	energy, ft-lb:	166		132		105
Magtech 158 LRN	velocity, fps:	755		728		693
	energy, ft-lb:	200		183		168
Magtech 158 LFN	velocity, fps:	800		776		753
	energy, ft-lb:	225		211		199
Magtech 158 SJHP	velocity, fps:	807		779		753
	energy, ft-lb:	230		213		199
Magtech 158 LSWC	velocity, fps:	755		721		689
	energy, ft-lb:	200		182		167
Magtech 158 FMC-Flat	velocity, fps:	807		779		753
	energy, ft-lb:	230		213		199
PMC 85 Non-Toxic Frangible	velocity, fps:	1275	1181	1109	1052	1006
	energy, ft-lb:	307				
PMC 110 SFHP +P	velocity, fps:	velocity and energy figures not available				
PMC 125 SFHP +P	velocity, fps:	950	918	889	863	838
	energy, ft-lb:	251				
PMC 125 JHP +P	velocity, fps:	974	938	906	878	851
	energy, ft-lb:	266				
PMC 132 FMJ	velocity, fps:	841	820	799	780	761
	energy, ft-lb:	206				
PMC 148 LWC	velocity, fps:	728	694	662	631	602
	energy, ft-lb:	175				
PMC 158 LRN	velocity, fps:	820	801	783	765	749
	energy, ft-lb:	235				
PMC 158 JSP	velocity, fps:	835	816	797	779	762
	energy, ft-lb:	245				

Centerfire Handgun Ballistics

.38 SPECIAL TO .357 MAGNUM

CARTRIDGE BULLET	RANGE, YARDS:	0	25	50	75	100
PMC 158 LFP	velocity, fps:	800		761		725
	energy, ft-lb:	225		203		185
Rem. 101 Lead Free Frangible	velocity, fps:	950		896		850
	energy, ft-lb:	202		180		162
Rem. 110 SJHP	velocity, fps:	950		890		840
	energy, ft-lb:	220		194		172
Rem. 110 SJHP +P	velocity, fps:	995		926		871
	energy, ft-lb:	242		210		185
Rem. 125 SJHP +P	velocity, ft-lb:	945		898		858
	energy, ft-lb:	248		224		204
Rem. 125 BJHP	velocity, fps:	975		929		885
	energy, ft-lb:	264		238		218
Rem. 125 FNEB	velocity, fps:	850		822		796
	energy, ft-lb:	201		188		176
Rem. 125 FNEB +P	velocity, fps:	975		935		899
	energy, ft-lb:	264		242		224
Rem. 130 Metal Case	velocity, fps:	950		913		879
	energy, ft-lb:	261		240		223
Rem. 148 LWC Match	velocity, fps:	710		634		566
	energy, ft-lb:	166		132		105
Rem. 158 LRN	velocity, fps:	755		723		692
	energy, ft-lb:	200		183		168
Rem. 158 SWC +P	velocity, fps:	890		855		823
	energy, ft-lb:	278		257		238
Rem. 158 SWC	velocity, fps:	755		723		692
	energy, ft-lb:	200		183		168
Rem. 158 LHP +P	velocity, fps:	890		855		823
	energy, ft-lb:	278		257		238
Speer 125 JHP +P Blazer	velocity, fps:	945		898		858
	energy, ft-lb:	248		224		204
Speer 125 Gold Dot +P	velocity, fps:	945		898		858
	energy, ft-lb:	248		224		204
Speer 158 TMJ +P (and Blazer)	velocity, fps:	900		852		818
	energy, ft-lb:	278		255		235
Speer 158 LRN Blazer	velocity, fps:	755		723		692
	energy, ft-lb:	200		183		168
Speer 158 Trail Blazer LFN	velocity, fps:	800		761		725
	energy, ft-lb:	225		203		184
Speer 158 TMJ-CF +P	velocity, fps:	900		852		818
(and Blazer)	energy, ft-lb:	278		255		235
Win. 110 Silvertip HP	velocity, fps:	945		894		850
	energy, ft-lb:	218		195		176
Win. 110 Jacketed FP	velocity, fps:	975		906		849
	energy, ft-lb:	232		201		176
Win. 125 Jacketed HP	velocity, fps:	945		898		
	energy, ft-lb:	248		224		
Win. 125 Jacketed HP +P	velocity, fps:	945		898		858
	energy, ft-lb:	248		224		204
Win. 125 Jacketed FP	velocity, fps:	850		804		
	energy, ft-lb:	201		179		
Win. 125 Silvertip HP + P	velocity, fps:	945		898		858
	energy, ft-lb:	248		224		204
Win. 125 JFP WinClean	velocity, fps:	775		742		
	energy, ft-lb:	167		153		
Win. 130 FMJ	velocity, fps:	800		765		
	energy, ft-lb:	185		169		
Win. 130 SXT +P	velocity, fps:	925		887		852
	energy, ft-lb:	247		227		210
Win. 148 LWC Super Match	velocity, fps:	710		634		566
	energy, ft-lb:	166		132		105
Win. 150 Lead	velocity, fps:	845		812		
	energy, ft-lb:	238		219		
Win. 158 Lead	velocity, fps:	800		761		725
	energy, ft-lb:	225		203		185
Win. 158 LRN	velocity, fps:	755		723		693
	energy, ft-lb:	200		183		168
Win. 158 LSWC	velocity, fps:	755		721		689
	energy, ft-lb:	200		182		167
Win. 158 LSWC HP +P	velocity, fps:	890		855		823
	energy, ft-lb:	278		257		238

.38-40

CARTRIDGE BULLET	RANGE, YARDS:	0	25	50	75	100
Black Hills 180 FPL	velocity, fps:	800				
	energy, ft-lb:					

.38 Super

CARTRIDGE BULLET	RANGE, YARDS:	0	25	50	75	100
Federal 130 FMJ +P	velocity, fps:	1200	1140	1100	1050	1020
	energy, ft-lb:	415	380	350	320	300
PMC 115 JHP	velocity, fps:	1116	1052	1001	959	923
	energy, ft-lb:	318				
PMC 130 FMJ	velocity, fps:	1092	1038	994	957	924
	energy, ft-lb:	348				
Rem. 130 Metal Case	velocity, fps:	1215		1099		1017
	energy, ft-lb:	426		348		298
Win. 125 Silvertip HP +P	velocity, fps:	1240		1130		1050
	energy, ft-lb:	427		354		306
Win. 130 FMJ +P	velocity, fps:	1215		1099		
	energy, ft-lb:	426		348		

.357 Sig

CARTRIDGE BULLET	RANGE, YARDS:	0	25	50	75	100
Federal 125 FMJ	velocity, fps:	1350	1270	1190	1130	1080
	energy, ft-lb:	510	445	395	355	325
Federal 125 JHP	velocity, fps:	1350	1270	1190	1130	1080
	energy, ft-lb:	510	445	395	355	325
Federal 150 JHP	velocity, fps:	1130	1080	1030	1000	970
	energy, ft-lb:	420	385	355	330	310
Hornady 124 JHP/XTP	velocity, fps:	1350		1208		1108
	energy, ft-lb:	502		405		338
Hornady 147 JHP/XTP	velocity, fps:	1225		1138		1072
	energy, ft-lb:	490		422		375
PMC 85 Non-Toxic Frangible	velocity, fps:	1480	1356	1245	1158	1092
	energy, ft-lb:	413				
PMC 124 SFHP	velocity, fps:	1350	1263	1190	1132	1083
	energy, ft-lb:	502				
PMC 124 FMJ/FP	velocity, fps:	1350	1242	1158	1093	1040
	energy, ft-lb:	512				
Rem. 104 Lead Free Frangible	velocity, fps:	1400		1223		1094
	energy, ft-lb:	453		345		276
Rem. 125 Metal Case	velocity, fps:	1350		1146		1018
	energy, ft-lb:	506		422		359
Rem. 125 JHP	velocity, fps:	1350		1157		1032
	energy, ft-lb:	506		372		296
Speer 125 TMJ (and Blazer)	velocity, fps:	1350		1177		1057
	energy, ft-lb:	502		381		307
Speer 125 TMJ-CF	velocity, fps:	1350		1177		1057
	energy, ft-lb:	502		381		307
Speer 125 Gold Dot	velocity, fps:	1375		1203		1079
	energy, ft-lb:	525		402		323
Win. 105 JFP	velocity, fps:	1370		1179		1050
	energy, ft-lb	438		324		257
Win. 125 FMJ FN	velocity, fps:	1350		1185		
	energy, ft-lb	506		390		

.357 Magnum

CARTRIDGE BULLET	RANGE, YARDS:	0	25	50	75	100
Black Hills 125 JHP	velocity, fps:	1500				
	energy, ft-lb:	625				
Black Hills 158 CNL	velocity, fps:	800				
	energy, ft-lb:					
Black Hills 158 SWC	velocity, fps:	1050				
	energy, ft-lb:					

Centerfire Handgun Ballistics

.357 MAGNUM TO .40 S&W

CARTRIDGE BULLET	RANGE, YARDS:	0	25	50	75	100
Black Hills 158 JHP	velocity, fps:	1250				
	energy, ft-lb:					
Federal 110 Hi-Shok JHP	velocity, fps:	1300	1180	1090	1040	990
	energy, ft-lb:	410	340	290	260	235
Federal 125 Hi-Shok JHP	velocity, fps:	1450	1350	1240	1160	1100
	energy, ft-lb:	580	495	430	370	335
Federal 130 Hydra-Shok JHP	velocity, fps:	1300	1210	1130	1070	1020
	energy, ft-lb:	490	420	370	330	300
Federal 158 Hi-Shok JSP	velocity, fps:	1240	1160	1100	1060	1020
	energy, ft-lb:	535	475	430	395	365
Federal 158 JSP	velocity, fps:	1240	1160	1100	1060	1020
	energy, ft-lb:	535	475	430	395	365
Federal 158 LSWC	velocity, fps:	1240	1160	1100	1060	1020
	energy, ft-lb:	535	475	430	395	365
Federal 158 Hi-Shok JHP	velocity, fps:	1240	1160	1100	1060	1020
	energy, ft-lb:	535	475	430	395	365
Federal 158 Hydra-Shok JHP	velocity, fps:	1240	1160	1100	1060	1020
	energy, ft-lb:	535	475	430	395	365
Federal 180 Hi-Shok JHP	velocity, fps:	1090	1030	980	930	890
	energy, ft-lb:	475	425	385	350	320
Federal 180 Castcore	velocity, fps:	1250	1200	1160	1120	1080
	energy, ft-lb:	625	575	535	495	465
Hornady 125 JHP/XTP	velocity, fps:	1500		1314		1166
	energy, ft-lb:	624		479		377
Hornady 125 JFP/XTP	velocity, fps:	1500		1311		1161
	energy, ft-lb:	624		477		374
Hornady 140 Cowboy	velocity, fps:	800		767		735
	energy, ft-lb:	199		183		168
Hornady 140 JHP/XTP	velocity, fps:	1400		1249		1130
	energy, ft-lb:	609		485		397
Hornady 158 JHP/XTP	velocity, fps:	1250		1150		1073
	energy, ft-lb:	548		464		404
Hornady 158 JFP/XTP	velocity, fps:	1250		1147		1068
	energy, ft-lb:	548		461		400
Lapua 150 FMJ CEPP Super	velocity, fps:	370		527*		303*
	energy, ft-lb:	664		527*		445*
Lapua 150 SJFN	velocity, fps:	385		342*		313*
	energy, ft-lb:	719		569*		476*
Lapua 158 SJHP	velocity, fps:	470		408*		359*
	energy, ft-lb:	1127		850*		657*
Magtech 158 SJSP	velocity, fps:	1235		1104		1015
	energy, ft-lb:	535		428		361
Magtech 158 SJHP	velocity, fps:	1235		1104		1015
	energy, ft-lb:	535		428		361
PMC 85 Non-Toxic Frangible	velocity, fps:	1325	1219	1139	1076	1025
	energy, ft-lb:	331				
PMC 125 JHP	velocity, fps:	1194	1117	1057	1008	967
	energy, ft-lb:	399				
PMC 150 JHP	velocity, fps:	1234	1156	1093	1042	1000
	energy, ft-lb:	512				
PMC 150 SFHP	velocity, fps:	1205	1129	1069	1020	980
	energy, ft-lb:	484				
PMC 158 JSP	velocity, fps:	1194	1122	1063	1016	977
	energy, ft-lb:	504				
PMC 158 LFP	velocity, fps:	800		761		725
	energy, ft-lb:	225		203		185
Rem. 110 SJHP	velocity, fps:	1295		1094		975
	energy, ft-lb:	410		292		232
Rem. 125 SJHP	velocity, fps:	1450		1240		1090
	energy, ft-lb:	583		427		330
Rem. 125 BJHP	velocity, fps:	1220		1095		1009
	energy, ft-lb:	413		333		283
Rem. 125 FNEB	velocity, fps:	1450		1240		1090
	energy, ft-lb:	583		427		330
Rem. 158 SJHP	velocity, fps:	1235		1104		1015
	energy, ft-lb:	535		428		361
Rem. 158 SP	velocity, fps:	1235		1104		1015
	energy, ft-lb:	535		428		361
Rem. 158 SWC	velocity, fps:	1235		1104		1015
	energy, ft-lb:	535		428		361
Rem. 165 JHP Core-Lokt	velocity, fps:	1290		1189		1108
	energy, ft-lb:	610		518		450
Rem. 180 SJHP	velocity, fps:	1145		1053		985
	energy, ft-lb:	542		443		388
Speer 125 Gold Dot	velocity, fps:	1450		1240		1090
	energy, ft-lb:	583		427		330
Speer 158 JHP Blazer	velocity, fps:	1150		1104		1015
	energy, ft-lb:	535		428		361
Speer 158 Gold Dot	velocity, fps:	1235		1104		1015
	energy, ft-lb:	535		428		361
Speer 170 Gold Dot SP	velocity, fps:	1180		1089		1019
	energy, ft-lb:	525		447		392
Win. 110 JFP	velocity, fps:	1275		1105		998
	energy, ft-lb:	397		298		243
Win. 110 JHP	velocity, fps:	1295		1095		
	energy, ft-lb:	410		292		
Win. 125 JFP WinClean	velocity, fps:	1370		1183		
	energy, ft-lb:	521		389		
Win. 145 Silvertip HP	velocity, fps:	1290		1155		1060
	energy, ft-lb:	535		428		361
Win. 158 JHP	velocity, fps:	1235		1104		1015
	energy, ft-lb:	535		428		361
Win. 158 JSP	velocity, fps:	1235		1104		1015
	energy, ft-lb:	535		428		361
Win. 180 Partition Gold	velocity, fps:	1180		1088		1020
	energy, ft-lb:	557		473		416

.40 S&W

CARTRIDGE BULLET	RANGE, YARDS:	0	25	50	75	100
Black Hills 155 JHP	velocity, fps:	1150				
	energy, ft-lb:	450				
Black Hills 165 EXP JHP	velocity, fps:	1150 (2005: 1100)				
	energy, ft-lb:	483				
Black Hills 180 JHP	velocity, fps:	1000				
	energy, ft-lb:	400				
Black Hills 180 JHP	velocity, fps:	1000				
	energy, ft-lb:	400				
Federal 135 Hydra-Shok JHP	velocity, fps:	1190	1050	970	900	850
	energy, ft-lb:	420	330	280	245	215
Federal 155 FMJ Ball	velocity, fps:	1140	1080	1030	990	960
	energy, ft-lb:	445	400	365	335	315
Federal 155 Hi-Shok JHP	velocity, fps:	1140	1080	1030	990	950
	energy, ft-lb:	445	400	365	335	315
Federal 155 Hydra-Shok JHP	velocity, fps:	1140	1080	1030	990	950
	energy, ft-lb:	445	400	365	335	315
Federal 165 EFMJ	velocity, fps:	1190	1060	970	905	850
	energy, ft-lb:	520	410	345	300	265
Federal 165 FMJ	velocity, fps:	1050	1020	990	960	935
	energy, ft-lb:	405	380	355	335	320
Federal 165 FMJ Ball	velocity, fps:	980	950	920	900	880
	energy, ft-lb:	350	330	310	295	280
Federal 165 Hydra-Shok JHP	velocity, fps:	980	950	930	910	890
	energy, ft-lb:	350	330	315	300	290
Federal 180 High Antim. Lead	velocity, fps:	990	960	930	910	890
	energy, ft-lb:	390	365	345	330	315
Federal 180 TMJ TMF Primer	velocity, fps:	990	960	940	910	890
	energy, ft-lb:	390	370	350	330	315
Federal 180 FMJ Ball	velocity, fps:	990	960	940	910	890
	energy, ft-lb:	390	370	350	330	315

Centerfire Handgun Ballistics

.40 S&W TO .41 REMINGTON MAGNUM

BALLISTICS

CARTRIDGE BULLET	RANGE, YARDS:	0	25	50	75	100
Federal 180 Hi-Shok JHP	velocity, fps:	990	960	930	910	890
	energy, ft-lb:	390	365	345	330	315
Federal 180 Hydra-Shok JHP	velocity, fps:	990	960	930	910	890
	energy, ft-lb:	390	365	345	330	315
Hornady 155 JHP/XTP	velocity, fps:	1180		1061		980
	energy, ft-lb:	479		387		331
Hornady 155 TAP-FPD	velocity, fps:	1180		1061		980
	energy, ft-lb:	470		387		331
Hornady 180 JHP/XTP	velocity, fps:	950		903		862
	energy, ft-lb:	361		326		297
Hornady 180 TAP-FPD	velocity, fps:	950		903		862
	energy, ft-lb:	361		326		297
Magtech 155 JHP	velocity, fps:	1025		1118		1052
	energy, ft-lb:	500		430		381
Magtech 180 JHP	velocity, fps:	990		933		886
	energy, ft-lb:	390		348		314
Magtech 180 FMC	velocity, fps:	990		933		886
	energy, ft-lb:	390		348		314
PMC 115 Non-Toxic Frangible	velocity, fps:	1350	1240	1154	1088	1035
	energy, ft-lb:	465				
PMC 155 SFHP	velocity, fps:	1160	1092	1039	994	957
	energy, ft-lb:	463				
PMC 165 JHP	velocity, fps:	1040	1002	970	941	915
	energy, ft-lb:	396				
PMC 165 FMJ	velocity, fps:	1010	977	948	922	899
	energy, ft-lb:	374				
PMC 180 FMJ/FP	velocity, fps:	985	957	931	908	885
	energy, ft-lb:	388				
PMC 180 SFHP	velocity, fps:	985	958	933	910	889
	energy, ft-lb:	388				
Rem. 141 Lead Free Frangible	velocity, fps:	1135		1056		996
	energy, ft-lb:	403		349		311
Rem. 155 JHP	velocity, fps:	1205		1095		1017
	energy, ft-lb:	499		413		356
Rem. 165 BJHP	velocity, fps:	1150		1040		964
	energy, ft-lb:	485		396		340
Rem. 180 JHP	velocity, fps:	1015		960		914
	energy, ft-lb:	412		368		334
Rem. 180 FN Enclosed Base	velocity, fps:	985		936		893
	energy, ft-lb:	388		350		319
Rem. 180 Metal Case	velocity, fps:	985		936		893
	energy, ft-lb:	388		350		319
Rem. 180 BJHP	velocity, fps:	1015		960		914
	energy, ft-lb:	412		368		334
Speer 105 Frangible	velocity, fps:	1380		1128		985
	energy, ft-lb:	444		297		226
Speer 155 TMJ Blazer	velocity, fps:	1175		1047		963
	energy, ft-lb:	475		377		319
Speer 155 TMJ	velocity, fps:	1200		1065		976
	energy, ft-lb:	496		390		328
Speer 155 Gold Dot	velocity, fps:	1200		1063		974
	energy, ft-lb:	496		389		326
Speer 165 TMJ Blazer	velocity, fps:	1100		1006		938
	energy, ft-lb:	443		371		321
Speer 165 TMJ	velocity, fps:	1150		1040		964
	energy, ft-lb:	484		396		340
Speer 165 Gold Dot	velocity, fps:	1150		1043		966
	energy, ft-lb:	485		399		342
Speer 180 HP Blazer	velocity, fps:	985		951		909
	energy, ft-lb:	400		361		330
Speer 180 FMJ Blazer	velocity, fps:	1000		937		886
	energy, ft-lb:	400		351		313
Speer 180 FMJ	velocity, fps:	1000		951		909
	energy, ft-lb:	400		361		330

CARTRIDGE BULLET	RANGE, YARDS:	0	25	50	75	100
Speer 180 TMJ-CF (and Blazer)	velocity, fps:	1000		951		909
	energy, ft-lb:	400		361		330
Speer 180 Gold Dot	velocity, fps:	1025		957		902
	energy, ft-lb:	420		366		325
Win. 140 JFP	velocity, fps:	1155		1039		960
	energy, ft-lb:	415		336		286
Win. 155 Silvertip HP	velocity, fps:	1205		1096		1018
	energy, ft-lb	500		414		357
Win. 165 SXT	velocity, fps:	1130		1041		977
	energy, ft-lb:	468		397		349
Win. 165 FMJ FN	velocity, fps:	1060		1001		
	energy, ft-lb:	412		367		
Win. 165 EB WinClean	velocity, fps:	1130		1054		
	energy, ft-lb:	468		407		
Win. 180 JHP	velocity, fps:	1010		954		
	energy, ft-lb:	408		364		
Win. 180 FMJ	velocity, fps:	990		936		
	energy, ft-lb:	390		350		
Win. 180 SXT	velocity, fps:	1010		954		909
	energy, ft-lb:	408		364		330
Win. 180 EB WinClean	velocity, fps:	990		943		
	energy, ft-lb:	392		356		

10 mm Auto

CARTRIDGE BULLET	RANGE, YARDS:	0	25	50	75	100
Federal 155 Hi-Shok JHP	velocity, fps:	1330	1230	1140	1080	1030
	energy, ft-lb:	605	515	450	400	360
Federal 180 Hi-Shok JHP	velocity, fps:	1030	1000	970	950	920
	energy, ft-lb:	425	400	375	355	340
Federal 180 Hydra-Shok JHP	velocity, fps:	1030	1000	970	950	920
	energy, ft-lb:	425	400	375	355	340
Federal 180 High Antim. Lead	velocity, fps:	1030	1000	970	950	920
	energy, ft-lb:	425	400	375	355	340
Federal 180 FMJ	velocity, fps:	1060	1025	990	965	940
	energy, ft-lb:	400	370	350	330	310
Hornady 155 JHP/XTP	velocity, fps:	1265		1119		1020
	energy, ft-lb:	551		431		358
Hornady 180 JHP/XTP	velocity, fps:	1180		1077		1004
	energy, ft-lb:	556		464		403
Hornady 200 JHP/XTP	velocity, fps:	1050		994		948
	energy, ft-lb:	490		439		399
PMC 115 Non-Toxic Frangible	velocity, fps:	1350	1240	1154	1088	1035
	energy, ft-lb:	465				
PMC 170 JHP	velocity, fps:	1200	1117	1052	1000	958
	energy, ft-lb:	543				
PMC 180 SFHP	velocity, fps:	950	926	903	882	862
	energy, ft-lb:	361				
PMC 200 TC-FMJ	velocity, fps:	1050	1008	972	941	912
	energy, ft-lb:	490				
Rem. 180 Metal Case	velocity, fps:	1150		1063		998
	energy, ft-lb:	529		452		398
Speer 200 TMJ Blazer	velocity, fps:	1050		966		952
	energy, ft-lb:	490		440		402
Win. 175 Silvertip HP	velocity, fps:	1290		1141		1037
	energy, ft-lb:	649		506		418

.41 Remington Magnum

CARTRIDGE BULLET	RANGE, YARDS:	0	25	50	75	100
Federal 210 Hi-Shok JHP	velocity, fps:	1300	1210	1130	1070	1030
	energy, ft-lb:	790	680	595	540	495
PMC 210 TCSP	velocity, fps:	1290	1201	1128	1069	1021
	energy, ft-lb:	774				
PMC 210 JHP	velocity, fps:	1289	1200	1127	1068	1020
	energy, ft-lb:	774				
Rem. 210 SP	velocity, fps:	1300		1162		1062
	energy, ft-lb:	788		630		526

Centerfire Handgun Ballistics

.41 REMINGTON MAGNUM TO .45 AUTOMATIC (ACP)

CARTRIDGE BULLET	RANGE, YARDS:	0	25	50	75	100
Win. 175 Silvertip HP	velocity, fps:	1250		1120		1029
	energy, ft-lb:	607		488		412
Win. 240 Platinum Tip	velocity, ft-lb:	1250		1151		1075
	energy, ft-lb:	833		706		616

.44 Colt

CARTRIDGE BULLET	RANGE, YARDS:	0	25	50	75	100
Black Hills 230 FPL	velocity, fps:	730				
	energy, ft-lb:					

.44 Russian

CARTRIDGE BULLET	RANGE, YARDS:	0	25	50	75	100
Black Hills 210 FPL	velocity, fps:	650				
	energy, ft-lb:					

.44 Special

CARTRIDGE BULLET	RANGE, YARDS:	0	25	50	75	100
Black Hills 210 FPL	velocity, fps:	700				
	energy, ft-lb:					
Federal 200 SWC HP	velocity, fps:	900	860	830	800	770
	energy, ft-lb:	360	330	305	285	260
Federal 250 CastCore	velocity, fps:	1250	1200	1150	1110	1080
	energy, ft-lb:	865	795	735	685	645
Hornady 180 JHP/XTP	velocity, fps:	1000		935		882
	energy, ft-lb:	400		350		311
Magtech 240 LFN	velocity, fps:	750		722		696
	energy, ft-lb:	300		278		258
PMC 180 JHP	velocity, fps:	980	938	902	869	839
	energy, ft-lb:	383				
PMC 240 SWC-CP	velocity, fps:	764	744	724	706	687
	energy, ft-lb:	311				
PMC 240 LFP	velocity, fps:	750		719		690
	energy, ft-lb:	300		275		253
Rem. 246 LRN	velocity, fps:	755		725		695
	energy, ft-lb:	310		285		265
Speer 200 HP Blazer	velocity, fps:	875		825		780
	energy, ft-lb:	340		302		270
Speer 200 Trail Blazer LFN	velocity, fps:	750		714		680
	energy, ft-lb:	250		226		205
Speer 200 Gold Dot	velocity, fps:	875		825		780
	energy, ft-lb:	340		302		270
Win. 200 Silvertip HP	velocity, fps:	900		860		822
	energy, ft-lb:	360		328		300
Win. 240 Lead	velocity, fps:	750		719		690
	energy, ft-lb	300		275		253
Win. 246 LRN	velocity, fps:	755		725		695
	energy, ft-lb:	310		285		265

.44 Remington Magnum

CARTRIDGE BULLET	RANGE, YARDS:	0	25	50	75	100
Black Hills 240 JHP	velocity, fps:	1260				
	energy, ft-lb:	848				
Black Hills 300 JHP	velocity, fps:	1150				
	energy, ft-lb:	879				
Federal 180 Hi-Shok JHP	velocity, fps:	1610	1480	1370	1270	1180
	energy, ft-lb:	1035	875	750	640	555
Federal 240 Hi-Shok JHP	velocity, fps:	1180	1130	1080	1050	1010
	energy, ft-lb:	740	675	625	580	550
Federal 240 Hydra-Shok JHP	velocity, fps:	1180	1130	1080	1050	1010
	energy, ft-lb:	740	675	625	580	550
Federal 240 JHP	velocity, fps:	1180	1130	1080	1050	1010
	energy, ft-lb:	740	675	625	580	550
Federal 300 CastCore	velocity, fps:	1250	1200	1160	1120	1080
	energy, ft-lb:	1040	960	885	825	775
Hornady 180 JHP/XTP	velocity, fps:	1550		1340		1173
	energy, ft-lb:	960		717		550
Hornady 200 JHP/XTP	velocity, fps:	1500		1284		1128
	energy, ft-lb:	999		732		565
Hornady 240 JHP/XTP	velocity, fps:	1350		1188		1078
	energy, ft-lb:	971		753		619
Hornady 300 JHP/XTP	velocity, fps:	1150		1084		1031
	energy, ft-lb:	881		782		708
Magtech 240 SJSP	velocity, fps:	1180		1081		1010
	energy, ft-lb:	741		632		623
PMC 180 JHP	velocity, fps:	1392	1263	1157	1076	1015
	energy, ft-lb:	772				
PMC 240 JHP	velocity, fps:	1301	1218	1147	1088	1041
	energy, ft-lb:	900				
PMC 240 TC-SP	velocity, fps:	1300	1216	1144	1086	1038
	energy, ft-lb:	900				
PMC 240 SFHP	velocity, fps:	1300	1212	1138	1079	1030
	energy, ft-lb:	900				
PMC 240 LSWC-GCK	velocity, fps:	1225	1143	1077	1025	982
	energy, ft-lb:	806				
Rem. 180 JSP	velocity, fps:	1610		1365		1175
	energy, ft-lb:	1036		745		551
Rem. 210 Gold Dot HP	velocity, fps:	1450		1276		1140
	energy, ft-lb:	980		759		606
Rem. 240 SP	velocity, fps:	1180		1081		1010
	energy, ft-lb:	721		623		543
Rem. 240 SJHP	velocity, fps:	1180		1081		1010
	energy, ft-lb:	721		623		543
Rem. 275 JHP Core-Lokt	velocity, fps:	1235		1142		1070
	energy, ft-lb:	931		797		699
Speer 240 JHP Blazer	velocity, fps:	1200		1092		1015
	energy, ft-lb:	767		636		549
Speer 240 Gold Dot HP	velocity, fps:	1400		1255		1139
	energy, ft-lb:	1044		839		691
Speer 270 Gold Dot SP	velocity, fps:	1250		1142		1060
	energy, ft-lb:	937		781		674
Win. 210 Silvertip HP	velocity, fps:	1250		1106		1010
	energy, ft-lb:	729		570		475
Win. 240 Hollow SP	velocity, fps:	1180		1081		1010
	energy, ft-lb:	741		623		543
Win. 240 JSP	velocity, fps:	1180		1081		
	energy, ft-lb:	741		623		
Win. 250 Partition Gold	velocity, fps:	1230		1132		1057
	energy, ft-lb:	840		711		620
Win. 250 Platinum Tip	velocity, fps:	1250		1148		1070
	energy, ft-lb:	867		732		635

.44-40

CARTRIDGE BULLET	RANGE, YARDS:	0	25	50	75	100
Black Hills 200 RNFP	velocity, fps:	800				
	energy, ft-lb:					
Hornady 205 Cowboy	velocity, fps:	725		697		670
	energy, ft-lb:	239		221		204
Magtech 225 LFN	velocity, fps:	725		703		681
	energy, ft-lb:	281		247		232
PMC 225 LFP	velocity, fps:	725		723		695
	energy, ft-lb:	281		261		242
Win. 225 Lead	velocity, fps:	750		723		695
	energy, ft-lb:	281		261		242

.45 Automatic (ACP)

CARTRIDGE BULLET	RANGE, YARDS:	0	25	50	75	100
Black Hills 185 JHP	velocity, fps:	1000				
	energy, ft-lb:	411				
Black Hills 200 Match SWC	velocity, fps:	875				
	energy, ft-lb:	340				
Black Hills 230 FMJ	velocity, fps:	850				
	energy, ft-lb:	368				

Centerfire Handgun Ballistics

.45 AUTOMATIC (ACP) TO .45 GAP

CARTRIDGE BULLET	RANGE, YARDS:	0	25	50	75	100
Black Hills 230 JHP	velocity, fps:	850				
	energy, ft-lb:	368				
Black Hills 230 JHP +P	velocity, fps:	950				
	energy, ft-lb:	460				
Federal 165 Hydra-Shok JHP	velocity, fps:	1060	1020	980	950	920
	energy, ft-lb:	410	375	350	330	310
Federal 165 EFMJ	velocity, fps:	1090	1045	1005	975	942
	energy, ft-lb:	435	400	370	345	325
Federal 185 Hi-Shok JHP	velocity, fps:	950	920	900	880	860
	energy, ft-lb:	370	350	335	315	300
Federal 185 FMJ-SWC Match	velocity, fps:	780	730	700	660	620
	energy, ft-lb:	245	220	200	175	160
Federal 200 Exp. FMJ	velocity, fps:	1030	1000	970	940	920
	energy, ft-lb:	470	440	415	395	375
Federal 230 FMJ	velocity, fps:	850	830	810	790	770
	energy, ft-lb:	370	350	335	320	305
Federal 230 FMJ Match	velocity, fps:	855	835	815	795	775
	energy, ft-lb:	375	355	340	325	305
Federal 230 Hi-Shok JHP	velocity, fps:	850	830	810	790	770
	energy, ft-lb:	370	350	335	320	300
Federal 230 Hydra-Shok JHP	velocity, fps:	850	830	810	790	770
	energy, ft-lb:	370	350	335	320	305
Federal 230 FMJ	velocity, fps:	850	830	810	790	770
	energy, ft-lb:	370	350	335	320	305
Federal 230 TMJ TMF Primer	velocity, fps:	850	830	810	790	770
	energy, ft-lb:	370	350	335	315	305
Hornady 185 JHP/XTP	velocity, fps:	950		880		819
	energy, ft-lb:	371		318		276
Hornady 200 JHP/XTP	velocity, fps:	900		855		815
	energy, ft-lb:	358		325		295
Hornady 200 HP/XTP +P	velocity, fps:	1055		982		925
	energy, ft-lb:	494		428		380
Hornady 200 TAP-FPD	velocity, fps:	1055		982		926
	energy, ft-lbs:	494		428		380
Hornady 230 FMJ/RN	velocity, fps:	850		809		771
	energy, ft-lb:	369		334		304
Hornady 230 FMJ/FP	velocity, fps:	850		809		771
	energy, ft-lb:	369		334		304
Hornady 230 HP/XTP +P	velocity, fps:	950		904		865
	energy, ft-lb:	462		418		382
Hornady 230 TAP-FPD	velocity, fps:	950		908		872
	energy, ft-lb:	461		421		388
Magtech 185 JHP +P	velocity, fps:	1148		1066		1055
	energy, ft-lb:	540		467		415
Magtech 200 LSWC	velocity, fps:	950		910		874
	energy, ft-lb:	401		368		339
Magtech 230 FMC	veloctiy, fps:	837		800		767
	energy, ft-lb:	356		326		300
Magtech 230 FMC-SWC	velocity, fps:	780		720		660
	energy, ft-lb:	310		265		222
PMC 145 Non-Toxic Frangible	velocity, fps:	1100	1045	999	961	928
	energy, ft-lb:	390				
PMC 185 JHP	velocity, fps:	903	870	839	811	785
	energy, ft-lb:	339				
PMC 200 FMJ-SWC	velocity, fps:	850	818	788	761	734
	energy, ft-lb:	321				
PMC 230 SFHP	velocity, fps:	850	830	811	792	775
	energy, ft-lb:	369				
PMC 230 FMJ	velocity, fps:	830	809	789	769	749
	energy, ft-lb:	352				
Rem. 175 Lead Free Frangible	velocity, fps:	1020		923		851
	energy, ft-lb:	404		331		281
Rem. 185 JHP	velocity, fps:	1000		939		889
	energy, ft-lb:	411		362		324
Rem. 185 BJHP	velocity, fps:	1015		951		899
	energy, ft-lb:	423		372		332
Rem. 185 BJHP +P	velocity, fps:	1140		1042		971
	energy, ft-lb:	534		446		388
Rem. 185 MC	velocity, fps:	1015		955		907
	energy, ft-lb:	423		375		338
Rem. 230 FN Enclosed Base	velocity, fps:	835		800		767
	energy, ft-lb:	356		326		300
Rem. 230 Metal Case	velocity, fps:	835		800		767
	energy, ft-lb:	356		326		300
Rem. 230 JHP	velocity, fps:	835		800		767
	energy, ft-lb:	356		326		300
Rem. 230 BJHP	velocity, fps:	875		833		795
	energy, ft-lb:	391		355		323
Speer 140 Frangible	velocity, fps:	1200		1029		928
	energy, ft-lb:	448		329		268
Speer 185 Gold Dot	velocity, fps:	1050		956		886
	energy, ft-lb:	453		375		322
Speer 185 TMJ/FN	velocity, fps:	1000		909		839
	energy, ft-lb:	411		339		289
Speer 200 JHP Blazer	velocity, fps:	975		917		860
	energy, ft-lb:	421		372		328
Speer 200 Gold Dot +P	velocity, fps:	1080		994		930
	energy, ft-lb:	518		439		384
Speer 200 TMJ/FN	velocity, fps:	975		897		834
	energy, ft-lb:	422		357		309
Speer 230 FMJ (and Blazer)	velocity, fps:	845		804		775
	energy, ft-lb:	363		329		304
Speer 230 TMJ-CF (and Blazer)	velocity, fps:	845		804		775
	energy, ft-lb:	363		329		304
Speer 230 Gold Dot	velocity, fps:	890		845		805
	energy, ft-lb:	405		365		331
Win. 170 JFP	velocity, fps:	1050		982		928
	energy, ft-lb:	416		364		325
Win. 185 Silvertip HP	velocity, fps:	1000		938		888
	energy, ft-lb:	411		362		324
Win. 185 FMJ FN	velocity, fps:	910		861		
	energy, ft-lb:	340		304		
Win. 185 EB WinClean	velocity, fps:	910		835		
	energy, ft-lb:	340		286		
Win. 230 JHP	velocity, fps:	880		842		
	energy, ft-lb:	396		363		
Win. 230 FMJ	velocity, fps:	835		800		
	energy, ft-lb:	356		326		
Win. 230 SXT	velocity, fps:	880		846		816
	energy, ft-lb:	396		366		340
Win. 230 JHP subsonic	velocity, fps:	880		842		808
	energy, ft-lb:	396		363		334
Win. 230 EB WinClean	velocity, fps:	835		802		
	energy, ft-lb:	356		329		

.45 GAP

CARTRIDGE BULLET	RANGE, YARDS:	0	25	50	75	100
Federal 185 Hydra-Shok JHP	velocity, fps:	1090	1020	970	920	890
And Federal TMJ	energy, ft-lb:	490	430	385	350	320
Federal 230 Hydra-Shok	velocity, fps:	880	870	850	840	820
And Federal FMJ	energy, ft-lb:	395	380	3760	355	345
Win. 185 STHP	velocity, fps:	1000		938		887
	energy, ft-lb:	411		361		323
Win. 230 JHP	velocity, fps:	880		842		
	energy, ft-lb:	396		363		

Centerfire Handgun Ballistics

.45 GAP TO .500 SMITH & WESSON

BALLISTICS

CARTRIDGE BULLET	RANGE, YARDS:	0	25	50	75	100
Win. 230 EB WinClean	velocity, fps:	875		840		
	energy, ft-lb:	391		360		
Win. 230 FMJ	velocity, fps:	850		814		
	energy, ft-lb:	369		338		

.45 Winchester Magnum

CARTRIDGE BULLET	RANGE, YARDS:	0	25	50	75	100
Win. 260 Partition Gold	velocity, fps:	1200		1105		1033
	energy, ft-lb:	832		705		616
Win. 260 JHP	velocity, fps:	1200		1099		1026
	energy, ft-lb:	831		698		607

.45 Schofield

CARTRIDGE BULLET	RANGE, YARDS:	0	25	50	75	100
Black Hills 180 FNL	velocity, fps:	730				
	energy, ft-lb:					
Black Hills 230 RNFP	velocity, fps:	730				
	energy, ft-lb:					

.45 Colt

CARTRIDGE BULLET	RANGE, YARDS:	0	25	50	75	100
Black Hills 250 RNFP	velocity, fps:	725				
	energy, ft-lb:					
Federal 225 SWC HP	velocity, fps:	900	880	860	840	820
	energy, ft-lb:	405	385	370	355	340
Hornady 255 Cowboy	velocity, fps:	725		692		660
	energy, ft-lb:	298		271		247
Magtech 250 LFN	velocity, fps:	750		726		702
	energy, ft-lb:	312		293		274
PMC 250 LFP	velocity, fps:	800		767		736
	energy, ft-lb:	355		331		309
PMC 300 +P+	velocity, fps:	1250	1192	1144	1102	1066
	energy, ft-lb:	1041				
Rem. 225 SWC	velocity, fps:	960		890		832
	energy, ft-lb:	460		395		346
Rem. 250 RLN	velocity, fps:	860		820		780
	energy, ft-lb:	410		375		340
Speer 200 FMJ Blazer	velocity, fps:	1000		938		889
	energy, ft-lb:	444		391		351
Speer 230 Trail Blazer LFN	velocity, fps:	750		716		684
	energy, ft-lb:	287		262		239
Speer 250 Gold Dot	velocity, fps:	900		860		823
	energy, ft-lb:	450		410		376
Win. 225 Silvertip HP	velocity, fps:	920		877		839
	energy, ft-lb:	423		384		352
Win. 255 LRN	velocity, fps:	860		820		780
	energy, ft-lb:	420		380		345
Win. 250 Lead	velocity, fps:	750		720		692
	energy, ft-lb:	312		288		266

.454 Casull

CARTRIDGE BULLET	RANGE, YARDS:	0	25	50	75	100
Federal 300 Trophy Bonded	velocity, fps:	1630	1540	1450	1380	1300
	energy, ft-lb:	1760	1570	1405	1260	1130
Federal 360 CastCore	velocity, fps:	1500	1435	1370	1310	1255
	energy, ft-lb:	1800	1640	1500	1310	1260
Hornady 240 XTP-MAG	velocity, fps:	1900		1679		1483
	energy, ft-lb:	1923		1502		1172
Hornady 300 XTP-MAG	velocity, fps:	1650		1478		1328
	energy, ft-lb:	1813		1455		1175
Magtech 260 SJSP	velocity, fps:	1800		1577		1383
	energy, ft-lb:	1871		1437		1104
Rem. 300 Core-Lokt Ultra	velocity, fps:	1625		1472		1335
	energy, ft-lb:	1759		1442		1187

CARTRIDGE BULLET	RANGE, YARDS:	0	25	50	75	100
Speer 300 Gold Dot HP	velocity, fps:	1625		1477		1343
	energy, ft-lb:	1758		1452		1201
Win. 250 JHP	velocity, fps:	1300		1151		1047
	energy, ft-lb:	938		735		608
Win. 260 Partition Gold	velocity, fps:	1800		1605		1427
	energy, ft-lb:	1871		1485		1176
Win. 260 Platinum Tip	velocity, fps:	1800		1596		1414
	eneryg, ft-lb:	1870		1470		1154
Win. 300 JFP	velocity, fps:	1625		1451		1308
	energy, ft-lb:	1759		1413		1141

.460 Smith & Wesson

CARTRIDGE BULLET	RANGE, YARDS:	0	25	50	75	100
Federal 275 Expander	velocity, fps:	1800		1640		1500
	energy, ft-lb:	1980		1650		1370
Federal 300 A-Frame	velocity, fps:	1750		1510		1300
	energy, ft-lb:	2040		1510		1125
Hornady 200 SST	velocity, fps:	2250		2003		1772
	energy, ft-lb:	2248		1395		1081
Win. 260 Supreme Part. Gold	velocity, fps	2000		1788		1592
	energy, ft-lb	2309		1845		2012

.475 Linebaugh

CARTRIDGE BULLET	RANGE, YARDS:	0	25	50	75	100
Hornady 400 XTP-MAG	velocity, fps:	1300		1179		1093
	energy, ft-lb:	1501		1235		1060

.480 Ruger

CARTRIDGE BULLET	RANGE, YARDS:	0	25	50	75	100
Federal 275 Expander	velocity, fps:	1350		1190		1080
	energy, ft-lb:	1115		870		710
Hornady 325 XTP-MAG	velocity, fps:	1350		1191		1076
	energy, ft-lb:	1315		1023		835
Hornady 400 XTP-MAG	velocity, fps:	1100		1027		971
	energy, ft-lb:	1075		937		838
Speer 275 Gold Dot HP	velocity, fps:	1450		1284		1152
	energy, ft-lb:	1284		1007		810
Speer 325 SP	velocity, fps:	1350		1224		1124
	energy, ft-lb:	1315		1082		912

.50 Action Express

CARTRIDGE BULLET	RANGE, YARDS:	0	25	50	75	100
Hornady 300 XTP/HP	velocity, fps:	1475		1251		1092
	energy, ft-lb:	1449		1043		795
Speer 300 Gold Dot HP	velocity, fps:	1550		1361		1207
	energy, ft-lb:	1600		1234		970
Speer 325 UCHP	velocity, fps:	1400		1232		1106
	energy, ft-lb:	1414		1095		883

.500 Smith & Wesson

CARTRIDGE BULLET	RANGE, YARDS:	0	25	50	75	100
Federal 275 Expander	velocity, fps:	1660		1440		1250
	energy, ft-lb:	1680		1255		950
Federal 325 A-Frame	velocity, fps:	1800		1560		1350
	energy, ft-lb:	2340		1755		1315
Hornady 350 XTP Mag	velocity, fps:	1900		1656		1439
	energy, ft-lb:	2805		2131		1610
Hornady 500 FP-XTP	velocity, fps:	1425		1281		1164
	energy, ft-lb:	2254		1823		1505
Win. 350 Super-X	velocity, fps	1400		1231		1106
	energy, ft-lb	1523		1178		951
Win. 400 Platinum Tip	velocity, fps:	1800		1647		1505
	energy, ft-lb:	2877		2409		2012

Directory of Manufacturers & Suppliers

Accu-Tek Firearms
Ontario, CA
www.accu-tekfirearms.com

Adcor Defense
Baltimore, MD
www.adcordefense.com

Advanced Armament
Lawrenceville, GA
www.advanced-armament.com

Aimpoint
Chantilly, VA
www.aimpoint.com

Airforce Airguns
Fort Worth, TX
www.airforceairguns.com

Alpen Optics
Rancho Cucamonga, CA
www.alpenoptics.com

American Derringer
Waco, TX
www.amderringer.com

American Tactical Imports
Rochester, NY
www.americantactical.us

Anderson Rifles
Hebron, KY
www.andersonrifles.com

ArmaLite, Inc.
Geneso, IL
www.armalite.com

Arsenal Firearms
Gardone val Trompia, Italy
www.arsenalfirearms.com

Arsenal Inc.
Las Vegas, NV
www.arsenalinc.com

Ashbury Precision Ordnance
Charlottesville, VA
www.ashburyprecisionordnance.com

Auto-Ordnance
Worcester, MA
www.auto-ordnance.com

AYA
Eibar, Spain
www.aya-fineguns.com

Barnes Bullets
Mona, UT
www.barnesbullets.com

Barrett
Murfreesboro, TN
www.barrett.net

Barska
Pomona, CA
www.barska.com

Beeman Precision Airguns
Santa Fe Springs, CA
www.beeman.com

Benelli USA
Pocomoke, MD
www.benelliusa.com

Beretta
Brescia, Italy
www.berettausa.com

Berger Bullets
Fullerton, CA
www.bergerbullets.com

Bernardelli
Brescia, Italy
www.bernardelli.com

Bersa
Wanamassa, NJ
www.bersa.com

Black Hills
Rapid City, SD
www.black-hills.com

Blaser
San Antonio , TX
www.blaser-usa.com

Boberg Arms Corp.
White Bear Lake, MN
www.barska.com

Bond Arms
Granbury, TX
www.bondarms.com

Brenneke USA
Clinton, IA
www.brennekeusa.com

Browning
Morgan, UT
www.browning.com

BSA Optics
Ft. Lauderdale, FL
www.bsaoptics.com

Burris
Greeley , CO
www.burrisoptics.com

Bushmaster
Madison, NC
www.bushmaster.com

Bushnell Outdoor Products
Overland Park, KS
www.bushnell.com

Cabela's, Inc.
Sidney, NE
www.cabelas.com

Cabot Gun Company
Cabot, PA
www.cabotgun.com

Caesar Guerini USA, Inc.
Cambridge, MD
www.gueriniusa.com

Carl Zeiss Sports Optics
North Chesterfield, VA
www.sportsoptics.zeiss.com

CCI Ammunition
Lewiston, ID
www.cci-ammunition.com

Century International Arms
Delray Beach, FL
www.centuryarms.com

Ceska Zbrojovka Arms (CZ)
Kansas City, KS
www.cz-usa.com

C&H Precision Weapons
LaBelle, FL
www.chpws.com

Charles Daly
Miami, FL
www.charlesdaly-us.com

Charter Arms
Shelton, CT
www.charterfirearms.com

Chiappa Firearms
Dayton, OH
www.chiappafirearms.com

Chipmunk Rifles
Milton, PA
www.chipmunkrifles.com

Christensen Arms
Gunnison, UT
www.christensenarms.com

Cimarron Firearms Co.
Fredericksburg, TX
www.cimarron-firearms.com

Citadel by Legacy Sports
see Legacy Sports

CMMG
Fayette, MO
www.cmmginc.com

Cobra Firearms
Salt Lake City, UT
www.cobrapistols.net

Colt Competition Rifle
Breckenridge, TX
www.coltcompetitionrifle.com

Colt's Manufacturing Company
Hartford, CT
www.coltsmfg.com

Connecticut Shotguns Mfg. Co.
New Britain, CT
www.connecticutshotgun.com

Connecticut Valley Arms (CVA)
Duluth, GA
www.cva.com

Coonan Inc.
Blaine, MN
www.coonaninc.com

Cooper Firearms
Stevensville, MT
www.cooperfirearms.com

CorBon / Glaser
Sturgis, SD
www.corbon.com

Crosman
Bloomfield, NY
www.crosman.com

Daisy
Rogers, AR
www.daisy.com

Dakota Arms
Sturgis, SD
www.dakotaarms.com

Dan Wesson Firearms Co.
Norwich, NY
www.cz-usa.com/products/by-brand/dan-wesson

Daniel Defense
Black Creek, GA
www.danieldefense.com

Del-Ton, Inc.
Elizabethtown, NC
www.del-ton.com

Dixie Gun Works
Union City, TN
www.dixiegunworks.com

DoubleTap Defense LLC
St. Louis, MO
www.doubletapdefense.com

DPMS Firearms
St. Cloud, MN
www.dpmsinc.com

Eagle Imports
Wanamassa, NJ
www.eagleimportsinc.com

Ed Brown Products, Inc.
Perry, MO
www.edbrown.com

EMF Company, Inc.
Santa Ana, CA
www.emf-company.com

Enterprise Arms
Irwindale, CA
www.entreprise.com

ENVIRON-Metal, Inc.
Sweet Home, OR
www.hevishot.com

EOTech
Ann Arbor, MI
www.eotech-inc.com

E.R. Shaw, Inc.
Bridgeville, PA
www.ershawbarrels.com

Escort by Legacy Sports
see Legacy Sports

European American Armory
Rockledge, FL
www.eaacorp.com

Excel Arms
Ontario, CA
www.excelarms.com

Fabarm
Brescia, Italy
www.fabarm.com

Fausti USA
Fredericksburg, VA
www.faustiusa.com

Federal Armament
Fort Smith, AZ
www.fedarm.com

Federal Premium Ammunition
Anoka, MN
www.federalpremium.com

Fiocchi
Ozark, MO
www.fiocchiusa.com

Flodman
Jarsta, Sweden
www.flodman.com

FNH USA
McLean, VA
www.fnhusa.com

Franchi USA
Pocomoke, MD
www.franchiusa.com

Freedom Arms
Freedom, WY
www.freedomarms.com

Gamo USA
Ft. Lauderdale, FL
www.gamousa.com

Glock, Inc.
Smyrna, GA
www.glock.com

Halo Optics
Grand Prarie, TX
www.halooptics.com

Hammerli
Ulm, Germany
www.haemmerli.info

Harvester Muzzleloading
Henderson, KY
www.harvestermuzzleloading.com

Heckler & Koch
Columbus, GA
www.hk-usa.com

Henry Repeating Arms
Bayonne, NJ
www.henryrepeating.com

Heritage Mfg., Inc.
Miami, FL
www.heritagemfg.com

High Standard
Houston, TX
www.highstandard.com

Hi-Point
Dayton, OH
www.hi-pointfirearms.com

Hornady Mfg., Co.
Grand Island, NE
www.hornady.com

Howa by Legacy Sports
see Legacy Sports

H-S Precision
Rapid City, SD
www.hsprecision.com

I.O., Inc.
Palm Bay, FL
www.ioinc.us

Ithaca Gun Company
Upper Sandusky, OH
www.ithacagun.com

J.G. Anschutz
Ulm, Germany
www.jga.anschuetz-sport.com

Jarrett Rifles
Jackson, SC
www.jarrettrifles.com

J. P. Sauer & Sohn Rifles
San Antonio, TX
www.jpsauer.us/firearms

Kahles
Guntramsdorf, Austria
www.kahles.at

Kahr Arms
Worcester, MA
www.kahr.com

Kel-Tec CNC Industries, Inc.
Cocoa, FL
www.keltecweapons.com

Kimber Mfg. Inc.
Elmsford, NY
www.kimberamerica.com

Directory of Manufacturers & Suppliers

Knight Rifles
Athens, TN
www.knightrifles.com

Konus
Miami, FL
www.konuspro.com/en

Krieghoff International, Inc.
Ottsville, PA
www.krieghoff.com

Kriss USA
Virginia Beach, VA
www.kriss-usa.com

Kruger Optical
Sisters, OR
www.krugeroptical.com

K-Var Corp.
Las Vegas, NV
www.k-var.com

Kynoch Ammunition
Englewood, CO
www.kynochusa.com

Lapua Bullets
Lapua, Finland
www.lapua.com

Lazzeroni Arms, Inc.
Tuscon, AZ
www.lazzeroni.com

Leatherwood/Hi-Lux Optics
Torrance, CA
www.hi-luxoptics.com
www.leatherwoodoptics.com

Legacy Sports International
Reno, NV
www.legacysports.com

Leica
Allendale, NJ
www.us.leica-camera.com/sport_optics

Les Baer Custom
LeClaire, IA
www.lesbaer.com

Leupold and Stevens
Beaverton, OR
www.leupold.com

Ljutic LLC
Yakima, Washington
www.Ljuticgun.com

Lucid
Riverton, WY
www.mylucidgear.com

Lyman Products
Middletown , CT
www.lymanproducts.com

Magnum Research
Pillager, MN
www.magnumresearch.com

Magtech Ammunition Company, Inc.
Lino Lakes, MN
www.magtechammunition.com

Marlin
Madison, NC
www.marlinfirearms.com

Marocchi Arms
Sarezzo, Italy
www.marocchiarms.com

MasterPiece Arms
Carrollton, GA
www.masterpiecearms.com

Maunz Match Rifles
Maumee, OH
www.maunzmatchrifles.com

Mauser
Isny, Germany
www.mauser.com

McMillian
Phoenix, AZ
www.mcmillanfirearms.com

Meopta
Hauppauge, NY
www.meoptasportsoptics.com/us

Merkel
Trussville, AL
www.merkel-usa.com

MG Arms
Spring, TX
www.mgarmsinc.com

Millet Sights
Overland Park, KS
www.millettsights.com

Minox
Germany
www.minox.com

M.O.A. Corporation
Sundance, WY
www.moaguns.com

Montana Rifle Company
Kalispell, MT
www.montanarifleco.com

Mossberg
North Haven, CT
www.mossberg.com

Nesika Firearms
Sturgis, SD
www.nesikafirearms.com

New Ultra Light Arms
Granville, WV
www.newultralight.com

Nightforce Optics, Inc.
Orofino, ID
www.nightforceoptics.com

Nighthawk Custom
Berryville, AR
www.nighthawkcustom.com

Nikko Stirling
Shanghai, China
www.nikkostirling.com

Nikon Sport Optics
Melville, NY
www.nikonsportoptics.com

Noreen Firearms
Belgrade, MT
www.onlylongrange.com

Norma
Amotfors, Sweden
www.norma-usa.com

North American Arms
Provo, UT
www.naaminis.com

Nosler
Bend, OR
www.nosler.com

Noveske
Grants Pass, OR
www.shopnoveske.com

Olympic Arms
Olympia, WA
www.olyarms.com

PARA USA, LLC
Pineville, NC
www.para-usa.com

Patriot Ordnance Factory
Phoenix, Arizona
www.pof-usa.com

Pedersoli & Co.
Brescia, Italy
www.davide-pedersoli.com

Pentax Ricoh Imaging
Denver, CO
www.pentaximaging.com/sports-optics

Perazzi
Azusa, CA
www.perazzi.it

P.M.C. Ammunition
Conroe, TX
www.pmcammo.com

Pointer by Legacy Sports
Reno, NV
www.legacysports.com

Powerbelt Bullets
Nampa, ID
www.powerbeltbullets.com

Primary Weapons Systems
Boise, ID
www.primaryweapons.com

PTR Industries
Aynor, SC
www.ptr91.com

Purdey
London, England
www.purdey.com

Redfield
Beaverton, OR
www.redfield.com

Remington Arms
Madison, NC
www.remington.com

Rifles, Inc.
Pleasanton, TX
www.riflesinc.com

Rock Island Armory
Pahrump, NV
us.armscor.com

Rock River Arms
Colona, IL
www.rockriverarms.com

Rossi
Miami, FL
www.rossiusa.com

Ruger
Newport, NH
www.ruger.com

Sako
Riihimaki, Finland
www.sako.fi

Savage Arms
Westfield, MA
www.Savagearms.com

Schmidt & Bender
Claremont, NH
www.schmidtundbender.de/en

Shiloh
Big Timber, MT
www.shilohrifle.com

Sierra Bullets
Sedalia, MO
www.sierrabullets.com

Sig Sauer
Exeter, NH
www.sigsauer.com

Simmons Optics
Overland Park, KS
www.simmonsoptics.com

Smith & Wesson
Springfield, MA
www.smith-wesson.com

Speer Bullets
Lewiston, ID
www.speer-bullets.com

Sphinx (by Kriss)
Interlaken, Switzerland
www.sphinxarms.com

Springfield Armory
Geneso, IL
www.springfield-armory.com

SRM Arms
Meridian, ID
www.srmarms.com

Stag Arms
New Britain, CT
www.stagarms.com

Steiner Division
Creeley, CO
www.steiner-binoculars.com

Steyr Arms
Trussville, AL
www.steyrarms.com

STI International, Inc.
Georgetown, TX
www.stiguns.com

Stoeger Industries
Pocomoke, MD
www.stoegerindustries.com

Swarovski Optik
Cranston, RI
www.swarovskioptik.com

Swift Bullets
Quinter, KS
www.swiftbullets.com

Szecsei & Fuchs
Windsor, Ontario, Canada
www.fuchs-fine-guns.com

Tactical Rifles
Zephyrhills, FL
www.tacticalrifles.net

Tangent Theta
Halifax, Nova Scotia, Canada
www.tangenttheta.com

Taurus
Miami, FL
www.taurususa.com

Taylor's & Co.
Winchester , VA
www.taylorsfirearms.com

Thompson/Center
Springfield, MA
www.tcarms.com

Traditions Firearms
Old Saybrook, CT
www.traditionsfirearms.com

Tikka T3
Riihimaki, Finland
www.tikka.fi

Trijicon
Wixom, Michigan
www.trijicon.com

Tristar Sporting Arms
North Kansas City, MO
www.tristarsportingarms.com

Troy Defense
West Springfield, MA
www.troydefense.com

Truglo
Richardson, TX
www.truglo.com

Turnbull Mfg. Co.
Bloomfield, NY
www.turnbullmfg.com

Uberti
Pocomoke, MD
www.uberti.com

U.S. Optics
Brea, CA
www.usoptics.com

UTAS USA
Des Plaines, IL
www.utas-usa.com

Volquartsen Custom
Carroll, IA
www.volquartsen.com

Vortex Optics
Middletown, WI
www.vortexoptics.com

Walther Arms, Inc.
Fort Smith, AR
www.waltherarms.com

Weatherby
Paso Robles, CA
www.weatherby.com

Weaver Optics
Anoka, MN
www.weaveroptics.com

Wild West Guns
Anchorage, AK
www.wildwestguns.com

Wilson Combat
Berryville, AR
www.wilsoncombat.com

Winchester Repeating Arms & Ammunition
East Alton, IL
www.winchester.com

Windham Weaponry
Windham, ME
www.windhamweaponry.com

Woodleigh Bullets
Murrabit, Australia
www.woodleighbullets.com.au

ZiP Factory
Jackson, WY
zipfactory.com

Gunfinder Index

RIFLES

ADCORE DEFENSE
A-556 Elite, 108

ADVANCED ARMAMENT CORP.
Multi Purpose Weapon (MPW), 108

AMERICAN TACTICAL
GSG MP-40 Carbine, 109
Omni Hybrid 5.56, 109
Omni Hybrid Maxx, 24

ANSCHÜTZ
1416 D HB, 109
1416 D HB Walnut Thumbhole, 109
1517, 109
1710, 110
1727F, 110
1770, 110
1780, 110
1827 Fortner Sprint, 110
1903 Target Small Bore Rifle, 110
1907 in 1914 Stock, 110
2013/690 with 2018 Precise Stock, 111
MSR RX 22, 111

ARMALITE
AR-10 3-Gun Rifle, 24
AR-10 A4 Carbine, 111
AR-10 Super S.A.S.S., 111
AR-10A Super SASS Carbine, 112
AR-30A1 Standard Rifle, 112
AR-30A1 Target Rifle, 112
AR-31, 113
AR-50A1 NM, 113
M-15 A4 Carbine, 113
SPR Mod 1 Carbine, 114

ARSENAL FIREARMS
Special Purpose Rifle (SPR-1), 114

ARSENAL, INC.
SAM7R, 114
SAM7UF, 114
SA RPK-3R, 115
SLR-104FR, 115
SLR-104UR, 115
SLR-106F, 115

ASHBURY PRECISION ORDNANCE
SPR-308, 24

AUTO-ORDNANCE
AOM150, 116
M1SB Thompson M1 SBR, 116
T1 Thompson 1927 A-1, 116
T1-C Thompson 1927 A-1 Commando, 116
T1SB Thompson 1927 A-1 SBR Short Barrel Rifle, 116
TM1 Thompson M1, 116

BARRETT
Model 82A1, 117
Model 95, 117
Model 98B, 117
Model 99, 117
M107A1, 117
MRAD, 117
REC7 Gen II, 117

BENELLI USA
R1, 118

BERETTA USA
ARX100, 118
CX4 Storm, 118

BLASER USA
K95 Stutzen Baronesse, 118
R8 Classic Sporter, 118
R8 Jaeger, 119
R8 Professional, 119
R8 Professional Success, 119
R93 Professional, 119
S2 Safari Double Rifle, 120

BROWNING
AB3 Hunter, 25
AB3 Composite Stalker, 120
BAR LongTrac Stalker, 120
BAR Safari, 120
BAR ShortTrac, 120
BAR ShortTrac Hog Stalker Realtree Max-1, 121
BAR ShortTrac, Left-Hand, 121
BLR Lightweight '81, 121
BLR Lightweight '81 Stainless Takedown, 121
BLR Lightweight Stainless, 122
BLR White Gold Medallion, 122
RMEF X-Bolt White Gold, 122
X-Bolt Eclipse Hunter, 122
X-Bolt Eclipse Target, 25
X-Bolt Eclipse Varmint, 25
X-Bolt Eclipse Varmint Stalker, 26
X-Bolt Hunter, 123
X-Bolt Medallion, 123
X-Bolt Micro Midas, 123
X-Bolt Stainless Stalker, 123
X-Bolt Stalker Carbon Fiber Fluted, 124
X-Bolt Varmint Special Stainless, 124

BUSHMASTER FIREARMS INTERNAT'L
300 AAC Blackout, 124
.308 Hunter, 124
.308 ORC, 124
.450 Rifle & Carbine, 125
ACR Basic Folder Combination, 125
ACR Designated Marksman Rifle, 125
A-TACS Predator, 125
C-22 Carbine, 26
M4 Type Carbines, 125
MOE 308 Enhanced ORC, 126
MOE 308 Mid-Length, 126
Predator, 126
Quad Rail A3, 126
Target Model Rifles, 126
Varminter, 127
XM-15 3-Gun Enhanced Carbine, 127
XM-15 Quick Response Carbine (QRC), 26

CENTURY INTERNATIONAL ARMS
Centurion 39 Sporter, 127
M70 Standard/Magnum, 128
M85 Mini Mauser, 128

C&H PRECISION
USMC M40A1, 128
USMC M40A3, 129
USMC M40A5, 129

CHIAPPA FIREARMS
AK-22, 129
Little Badger, 130
M1-22, 130
Model 39, 130

CHIPMUNK RIFLES
Chipmunk, 130

CHISTENSEN
CD-10 Designated Marksman Rifle, 131
CD-15 Recon, 131
VTAC-15, 27

CIMARRON FIREARMS
1860 Henry Civilian, 131
1873 Saddle Shorty, 131
1876 Centennial, 132
1876 Crossfire Carbine, 132
1876 N.W.M.P. (North West Mounted Police) Carbine, 132
1885 High Wall Sporting Rifle, 132
1886 Rifle, 132
Model 71 Boarbuster, 132
Model 71 Classic, 133
Pedersoli Sharps Business Rifle, 27

CITADEL BY LEGACY SPORTS
M1 9mm Carbine, 133

CMMG
MK47 Mutant AKM, 27
MK47 Mutant T, 28

COLT'S MANUFACTURING COMPANY
Competition Marksman CRX-16, 133
Competition Pro CRP-18, 133
LE901-16S, 134
LE6940, LE6920 Carbines, 134
M2012LT260G, 134
M2012LT308G, 134
M2012MT308T, 135
M2012SA308, 135

COLT COMPETITION
Colt "Marksman" Model CRX-16E, 28

CONNECTICUT VALLEY ARMS (CVA)
Apex, 135
Scout, 135

COOPER FIREARMS
Model 21, 136
Model 22, 136
Model 38, 136
Model 51, 136
Model 52, 136
Model 54, 137
Model 57M, 137
Stocks, 137

CZ-USA (CESKA ZBROJOVKA)
455 American, 138
455 American Synthetic Suppressor Ready, 138
455 FS, 138
455 Lux, 138
455 Tacticool Suppressor Ready, 138
455 Training, 29
455 Training Rifle, 138
455 Ultra Lux, 29
455 Varmint, 139
455 Varmint with SS Evolution Stock, 139
455 Varmint Precision Trainer, 139
455 Varmint Tacticool, 139
512 Rimfire Rifle, 139
527, 140
550, 140
550 Badlands, 140
550 (H.E.T) High Energy Tactical II, 140
550 Safari Magnum, 140
550 Sonoran, 141
550 Sonoran "Western Series", 29
550 Ultimate Hunting Rifle, 141
550 Varmint, 141
550 Varmint Tacticool, 141
557 Carbine, 141
557 Sporter, 141
557 Sporter Manners, 142
750 Sniper, 142

DAKOTA ARMS
Model 10, 142
Model 76 Classic, 142
Model 97, 142
Sharps, 142
Varminter, 143

DANIEL DEFENSE
DDM4v9, 143
DDM4v9 LW, 143
DDM4v9 S2W, 143
DDM4v11 Pro, 30

DEL-TON
DT Sport OR, 144
DTI Evolution, 144
DTI Extreme Duty 316, 30
Echo 316H OR, 144

DIXIE GUN WORKS
1873 Trapdoor Officer's Model by Pedersoli, 144
Kodiak Double Rifle by Pedersoli, 144

DPMS PANTHER ARMS
.22 Bull Barrel, 145
24 Special, 145
3G2, 145
6.8 Hunter, 145
A2 Classic, 146
AP4 Carbine, 146
Arctic Panther, 146
Carbine 16, 146
Compact Hunter, 146
DCM, 146
GII AP4, 30, 147
GII Bull, 32, 147
GII Hunter, 31, 147
GII MOE, 32, 147
GII Recon, 31, 148
GII SASS, 31, 148
Lite LR-308, 148
Lo-Pro Classic, 148
LR-204, 148
LR-243H, LR-243L, 149
LR-260/LR-65, 149
LR-308, 149
Prairie Panther Camo, 149
Recon, 149
REPR, 149
Sweet 16, Bull 20, Bull 24, 150
Tactical 16, 150

E.M.F. COMPANY
1866 "Yellowboy" Short Rifle, 150
Rossi 1892 Trapper Carbine, 150

E.R. SHAW
E.R. Shaw Mark VII Custom, 151

EXCEL ARMS
Accelerator Rifle, 151
X-5.7R, 151
X-22R Rifle, 151

FNH USA
Ballista, 152
FN15 1776, 32
FN15 Carbine, 152
FN15 Rifle, 152
FN SPR A5 XP, 152
FNAR Standard, 152
SCAR 17S Carbine, 152

HECKLER & KOCH
MR556A1, 153
MR762A1, 153
MR762A1 (LRP), 153

HENRY REPEATING ARMS
.30-30, 154
.45-70 Lever Action, 154
.45-70 Lever Action Octagon, 33
Big Boy, 154
Golden Boy Deluxe Engraved II, 154
Lever Action .22, 155
Lever Octagon Frontier, 155
Mare's Leg, 155
Mini Bolt Youth, 155
The Original Henry Rifle, 156
Pump Action Octagon, 156
U.S. Survival AR-7, 156
Varmint Express, 156

HIGH STANDARD
Enforcer, 157

HI-POINT FIREARMS
Model 995TS, 157
Model 4095TS, 33

HOWA BY LEGACY SPORTS
Classic Laminate Varminter, 157
Hogue Kryptek, 157
Hogue Ranchland Compact, 157
Hogue Zeiss Package, 158
Howa/Hogue Rifles, 158
Howa/Hogue or Talon Snowking, 158
Hogue Zeiss Package, 158
Howa/Hogue/Targetmaster Combo, 158
Howa Hunter Gameking Package, 158
Mini Action, 33

H-S PRECISION
HTR (Heavy Tactical Rifle), 159
PHR (Professional Hunter Rifle), 159
TTD (Tactical Take-Down Rifle), 159

I.O. INC.
M214, 159

JARRETT RIFLES
Beanfield, 160
Professional Hunter, 160
Shikar Series, 34
Wind Walker, 160

Gunfinder Index

J.P. SAUER & SOHN
S 101, 160
S 101 Artemis, 34
S 202 Classic Bolt Action Rifle, 161
S 303 Classic XT, 161
S 303 Elegance, 161
S 404, 34

KEL-TEC
RFB, 161
SUB-2000, 161

KIMBER
Model 84L Series, 162
Model 84M Adirondack, 162
Model 84M Classic, 162
Model 84M Longmaster, 162
Model 84M Series, 162
Model 8400 Advanced Tactical II, 163
Model 8400 Advanced Tactical SOC, 163
Model 8400 Patrol Tactical, 163
Model 8400 WSM, 163

KRIEGHOFF RIFLES
Classic Big Five, 164
Classic Standard, 164
Semprio, 164

KRISS USA
Vector Carbine Enhanced, 164
Vector SBR, 164

K-VAR
SGL 31-95, 165

LAZZERONI RIFLES
L2012LLT Long Magnum Lite, 165
L2012LSP-XTLR Long Magnum Sporter, 165
L2012LTH Long Magnum Thumbhole, 165

LES BAER CUSTOM
.308 Semi-Auto Match Rifle, 166
AR .223 Super Varmint, 166
Mid-Length Monolith .308 Semi-Auto SWAT Model, 166
Monolith .308 Semi-Auto SWAT, 167

MAGNUM RESEARCH
.22LR Barracuda Nutmeg, 35
.22WMR Barracuda Forest Camo, 35
MagnumLite Barracuda, 167
MagnumLite Ultra Barrel, 167
Mountain Eagle MagnumLite Graphite, 167

MARLIN
60, 168
70PSS, 168
336C, 168
336SS, 168
336XLR, 168
795, 168
1894 Cowboy, 169
1895GBL, 169
1895SBL, 169
Classic 1895, 169
Golden 39A, 169
XT-22, 170

MASTERPIECE ARMS
MPAR 6.8, 170
MPAR 556 Rifle, 170

MAUNZ
Model 007 Maunz Rifle, 170
Model 11 Manuz Sportsman Rifle, 35, 171
Model 77 Maunz Service Match Rifle, 171
Model 87 Maunz Match Rifle, 171
Model 97 Maunz Sportsman Carbine, 36, 171

MAUSER
M03 Expert, 172
M12 Hunting Rifle, 172

MCMILLAN
CS5, 172
Custom Hunting Rifles - Legacy, 172
Long Range Hunting Rifle, 172
TAC-50, 173
TAC-50 A1, 173
TAC-50 A1-R2, 173
TAC-338, 173

MERKEL
African Safari Series Double Rifle Model 140AE, 173
B3 Over-and-Under Rifle, 173
RX Helix Explorer, 174
RX Helix, 174
Side-by-Side Rifle 140, 174

MONTANA RIFLE
American Vantage Rifle (AVR), 174
Montana Marksman Rifle, 174
Seven Continent Rifle, 175

MOSSBERG
464 Lever-Action Rifle, 175
464 SPX, 175
702 Bantam Plinkster, 175
715T Tactical Flat Top, 175
802 Plinkster Bolt-Action, 176
817 Bolt-Action, 176
Blaze Series, 37
Blaze-47, 37
Duck Commander 715T, 176
MMR Hunter, 176
MVP Flex, 176
MVP LC (Light Chassis) Series, 37
MVP LR (Light Chassis) Series, 38
MVP Patrol, 177
MVP Scout, 38
MVP Series Predator, 177
MVP Series Varmint, 177
Patriot Series, 36

NESIKA
Long Range Hunter, 177
Sporter, 177
Tactical, 178

NEW ULTRA LIGHT ARMS
Model 20 Rimfire, 178
Model 20 Ultimate Mountain Rifle, 178

NOREEN
BN36, 178

NOSLER
M48 Heritage Magnum, 179
M48 Heritage Sporter, 179
M48 Patriot Magnum, 179
M48 Patriot Sporter, 179
Nosler Custom Rifle, 179

NOVESKE
Gen 3 Series, 180

OLYMPIC ARMS
Gamestalker, 180
Ultimate Magnum AR (UMAR), 180

PATRIOT ORDNANCE FACTORY
P15 Patriot, 180

PEDERSOLI
1874 Sharps Old West Maple, 181
1886 Sporting Rifle, 38
1886/71 Lever Action Stainless Steel, 39
Kodiak Mark IV, 181
Model 86/71 Lever Action Boarbuster, 181
Model 86/71 Lever Action Classic, 181
Model 86/71 Lever Action Wildbuster, 181
Rolling Block Mississippi Classic, 39
Rolling Block Target, 181
Sharps Little Betsy, 39

PRIMARY WEAPONS SYSTEMS
MK216, 182
MK220, 182

PTR INDUSTRIES
GEN 2 PTR-32, 40

PURDEY
Bolt Action Rifles, 182
Double Rifles, 182

REMINGTON ARMS
Model 552 BDL Speedmaster, 183
Model 572 BDL Fieldmaster, 183
Model 597, 183
Model 597 Heavy Barrel, 183
Model 597 Heavy Barrel A-TACS Camo, 183
Model 700 BDL, 184
Model 700 CDL, 184
Model 700 Long Range, 184
Model 700 Mountain SS, 184
Model 700 Sendero SF II, 185
Model 700 SPS, 185
Model 700 SPS Camo, 185
Model 700 SPS Tactical, 185
Model 700 SPS Tactical AAC-SD, 185
Model 700 SPS Varmint, 185
Model 700 SPS Wood Tech, 186
Model 700 Tactical Chassis, 186
Model 700 Target Tactical, 186
Model 700 VLS, 186
Model 700 VTR, 186
Model 750 Woodsmaster, 187
Model 770, 187
Model 770 Stainless Camo, 187
Model 783, 187
Model 7600, 188
Model 7600 Synthetic, 188
Model R-15 450 Bushmaster, 188
Model R-25 GII, 40
Model Seven CDL, 188
Model Seven Synthetic, 188

RIFLES INC.
Canyon, 189
Classic, 189
Lightweight Strata, 189
Master's Series, 189
Safari, 189

ROCK RIVER ARMS
LAR-6.8 Coyote Carbine, 190
LAR-6.8 X-1, 190
LAR-8 Predator HP, 190
LAR-8 X-1, 190
LAR-15 Delta CAR/Delta Mid-Length, 191
LAR-15 Hunter Series, 191
LAR-15LH LEF-T Coyote Rifle & Carbine, 191
LAR-15 R3 Competition Rifle, 192
LAR-15 X-1, 192
LAR-40 Mid-Length A4, 192
LAR-47 CAR A4, 192
LAR-47 Delta Carbine, 192
LAR-47 X-1, 40
LAR-300 AAC X-1, 41
LAR-458 CAR A4, 193
LAR-458 X-1, 193
LAR-PDS Carbine, 193

ROSSI
Circuit Judge, 193
Circuit Judge .44 Mag., 194
Circuit Judge Convertible, 194
Circuit Judge Tactical Synthetic, 194
Full Size Centerfire Matched Pair, 194
R92 .44-40, 194
R92 Carbine .45 Colt Stainless, 195
Rio Grande, 195
Single Shot Rifle, 195
Youth Size Centerfire Matched Pair, 195

RUGER
10/22 Carbine, 196
10/22 Collector's Series, 41
10/22 Takedown, 196
10/22 Target, 196
77/17, 196
77/22, 196
77/44, 197
American Rifle, 197
American Rifle Ranch, 41
AR-556, 42
Guide Gun with Muzzle Brake System, 197
Gunsite Scout Rifle, 197
Hawkeye FTW Predator, 42
M77 Hawkeye, 197
M77 Hawkeye Predator, 198
Mini-14 Ranch Rifle, 198
Mini-14 Tactical, 198
Mini-14 Target Rifle, 198
Mini Thirty Rifle, 198
No. 1 Light Sporter, 199
No. 1 Varminter, 199
SR-22, 199
SR-556, 199
SR-556VT, 199

SAKO
85 Bavarian, 200
85 Bavarian LH, 200
85 Black Bear, 200
85 Brown Bear, 200
85 Brown Bear XL, 201
85 Carbonlight, 42
85 Classic, 201
85 Finnlight, 201
85 Hunter LH, 201
85 Kodiak, 202
85 Long Range, 202
85 Safari, 202
85 Synthetic Black, 202
85 Varmint Laminated Stainless, 202
A7 Roughtech Pro, 203
A7 Roughtech Range, 203
Finnfire II, 203
TRG 22, 203
TRG M10, 43

SAVAGE ARMS
10 FCP-SR, 43
10 FLCP-SR, 43
11 Scout, 44
12 FCV, 44
12 Varmint Series BTCSS, 204
14/114 American Classic, 204
25 Lightweight Varminter, 204
25 Walking Varminter, 204
93 FV-SR Landry, 44
112 Magnum Target, 45
A17, 45
Axis, 204
Axis Heavy Barrel, 45
Axis XP Youth Camo, 204
B.Mag, 205
B.Mag Target, 46
Hunter Series 11/111 BTH, 205
Landry Rascal, 46
Law Enforcement Series 110 BA Left Hand Model, 205
Magnum Series 93 BRJ, 205
Mark II Series BTV, 205
Mark II Series FV-SR Landry, 46
Model 42 Youth, 47
Rascal Single Shot, 205
Semi-Automatic Series 64 F, 206
Specialty Series 11/111 Hog Hunter, 206
Specialty Series 11/111 Lady Hunter, 206
Specialty Series 11/111 Long Range Hunter, 206
Specialty Series 16/116 Bear Hunter, 207
Specialty Series Model 42, 207
Target Series 12 Bench Rest, 207
Weather Warrior Series 16/116 FCSS, 207

SIG SAUER RIFLES
SIG516 Carbon, 208
SIG516 Patrol, 208
SIG522 Commando, 208
SIG 556XI Russian, 208
SIG716 Patrol Rifle, 209
SIG M400, 209
SIG M400 Enhanced, 209

SMITH & WESSON
M&P10, 47, 209
M&P15, 210
M&P15-22 Rifle, 210
M&P15 300 Whisper, 210
M&P15 MOE Mid, 210
M&P15 PC, 210
M&P15 Sport, 211
M&P15T, 211

Gunfinder Index

M&P15 VTAC II, 211

SPRINGFIELD ARMORY
Loaded M1A, 47
M1A Socom 16, 212
National Match M1A, 212
Scout Squad, 212
Standard M1A, 213

STAG ARMS
Model 3G, 213
Model 8, 213
Model 8T, 213
Model 9, 48

STEYR ARMS
AUG/A3 SA USA, 214
Duett Hunting Combination Rifle Shotgun, 214
Classic, 214
Pro Hunter, 214
Scout, 215
SSG 08, 215

SZECSEI & FUCHS FINE GUNS
DBR Repeating Rifle, 215

TACTICAL RIFLES
Classic Sporter, 216
Special Purpose Grendel (SPG), 216
Tactical L.R., 216

TAURUS
CTG29 Carbine, 216
CTG240 Carbine, 217

TAYLOR'S & CO. FIREARMS
1860 Henry Lever Action Rifle, 217
1873 Rifle - Checkered Straight Stock, 217
1886 Ridge Runner, 48
1892 Alaskan Take-Down Model, 217
Lightning Slide Action Rifle, 217

THOMPSON/CENTER
Dimension, 218
Prohunter Predator, 218
Venture Compact, 48, 218
Venture Predator Snow, 218

TIKKA
T3 Compact, 219
T3 CTR, 219
T3 Hunter, 219
T3 Lite, 219
T3 Lite Adjustable, 220
T3 Sporter, 220

TROY DEFENSE
M7A1 PDW, 220

TURNBULL MFG. CO.
TAR-15, 220

UBERTI
1860 Henry Rifle, 221
1866 Yellowboy, 221
1871 Rolling Block Hunter Carbine, 221
1871 Rolling Block Hunter Rimfire, 221
1873 Competition, 221
1873 Rifle & Carbine, 222
1874 Cavalry Carbine Sharps, 222
1874 Sharps Rifle, 222
1876 Centennial, 222
1883 Burgess Rifle & Carbine, 222
1885 High-Wall Single-Shot, 223
Lightning, 223
Silverboy Lever Action, 223
Springfield Trapdoor Carbine, 223
Springfield Trapdoor Rifle, 223

VOLQUARTSEN CUSTOM
TF-17 & TF-22, 224

WALTHER
HK G36 Rimfire, 49

WEATHERBY
Mark V Accumark, 224
Mark V Accumark RC Rifle, 224
Mark V Deluxe, 225
Mark V Fibermark, 225
Mark V Lazermark, 225
Mark V Sporter, 225
Mark V Ultra Lightweight, 226
Mark V Ultramark, 226
Vanguard 2 Back Country, 226
Vanguard 2 Sporter, 226
Vanguard 2 Sporter DBM, 227
Vanguard 2 Synthetic, 227
Vanguard 2 Synthetic Package, 227
Vanguard 2 Synthetic DBM, 227
Vanguard 2 Varmint Special, 228
WBY-X Vanguard Volt, 49

WILSON COMBAT
.308 Super Sniper, 49
Recon Tactical, 228
Urban Super Sniper, 50

WINCHESTER REPEATING ARMS
Model 70 Alaskan, 228
Model 70 Coyote Light, 228
Model 70 Featherweight Compact, 228
Model 70 Safari Express, 229
Model 70 Ultimate Shadow, 229
Model 70 Ultimate Shadow Hunter SS, 229
Model 73 Short Rifle Case Hardened, 50
Model 73 Sporter Octagon Case Hardened, 50
Model 94 Carbine, 229
Model 94 Short Rifle, 229
Model 94 Sporter, 230
Model 94 Trails End Takedown, 230
Model 1873 Short Rifle, 230
Model 1885 Low Wall Hunter Rimfire Octagon, 230
Model 1886 Short Rifle, 230
XPR Bolt Action Rifle, 51

WINDHAM WEAPONRY
300 Blackout, 51

AIR RIFLES

AIRFORCE AIRGUNS
Condor, 232
Condor SS, 232
Edge, 232
Escape, 232
EscapeSS, 233
EscapeUL, 233
Talon, 233
Talon P, 233
Talon SS, 233
Texan, 52

ANSCHÜTZ
8001 Club, 234
8001 Junior, 234
8002 S2 ALU, 234
8002 S2 Black Air, 234
9003 Premium S2 Precise, 234
9003 Premium S2 Benchrest Precise, 234

BEEMAN PRECISION AIRGUNS
Bear Claw, 235
Elkhorn, 235
Grizzly X2 Dual Caliber, 235
Mach 12.5, 235
Predator, 235
RS2 Combo, 236
Silver Kodiak X2 DC, 236
Silver Panther, 236
Teton, 236
Wolverine Carbine, 236

CROSMAN
Benjamin Armada, 52
Benjamin Armada Magpul Edition, 52
Benjamin Bulldog .357 Trophy Game Hunting Air Rifle, 52
Benjamin Discovery, 237
Benjamin Titan NP, 237
Crosman Benjamin Trail NP2, 237
Challenger PCP, 237
Classic 2100, 237
Fury NP, 238
M4-177 Rifle, 238
Marauder, 238
MTR77NP, 238
Optimus, 239
Phantom 1000, 239
Pumpmaster 760, 239
Recruit, 239
Repeatair 1077, 239
Torrent SX, 239
TR77, 240
Vantage NP, 240
Varmint Power Pack, 240

DAISY
Avanti Model 853 Legend, 240
Avanti Model 887 Gold Medalist, 240
Powerline Model 880, 240
Powerline Model 901, 241
Powerline TargetPro 953, 241
Winchester M-14, 241
Winchester Model 77XS, 241
Winchester Model 1100SS, 241
Winchester Model 1250WS, 242

GAMO USA
Big Cat 1250, 242
Big Cat 1400, 242
Coyote PCP, 53
Little Cat, 242
Mach1 Pigman Edition, 53
Recon Whisper, 243
Varmint Hunter HP 177, 243
Whisper, 243
Whisper G2, 243
Whisper CFR, 243
Whisper Fusion Pro, 244

RWS
Model 34, 244
Model 48, 244
Model 54 Air King, 244
Model 350 Magnum, 244

STOEGER AIRGUNS
A30, 53
ATAC Suppressor, 245
X3-Tac, 53
X-5, 245
X-20 Suppressor, 245
X-50, 245

SHOTGUNS

AMERICAN TACTICAL
Cavalry SC Over/Under, 247

AYA (AGUIRRE Y ARANZABAL)
Adarra, 247
Centenary, 54
Imperial, 247
Model No. 4/53, 247
Model No. 37, 247

BENELLI
828U, 54
Cordoba ComforTech, 248
Ethos, 248
Legacy, 248
Legacy Sport, 248
M2 Field 12 Ga., 248
M2 Field 20 Ga., 248
M2 Field Compact, 249
Montefeltro Black Synthetic, 249
Nova Pump Tactical, 249
Performance Shop Super Black Eagle II Turkey Edition, 249
Sport II, 249
Super Black Eagle II, 249
SuperNova Field, 250
SuperSport, 250
Super Vinci, 250
Ultra Light, 250
Vinci, 250

BERETTA USA
486 Parallelo, 54
686 Silver Pigeon I, 251
687 Silver Pigeon V, 251
690 Field III, 55
692 Sporting, 251
1301 Competition, 251
1301 Tactical, 251
A300 Outlander, 252
A400 Xplor Action, 252
A400 Xplor Light 12 Ga., 252
A400 Xplor Unico, 252
A400 Xtreme, 253
DT11 Sporting, 253
SV10 Perennia I, 253
SV10 Perennia III 20 Ga., 253
SV10 Prevail I, 253

BERNARDELLI
Hemingway Deluxe, 254
Mega, 254
PA 12, 254
Riserva, 254

BLASER USA
F3 Sporting, 254

BROWNING
A5 Hunter, 255
A5 Stalker, 255
A-Bolt Shotgun Hunter, 255
A-Bolt Shotgun Stalker & Infinity Camo, 255
BPS Hunter, 255
BPS Micro Midas, 255
BPS Rifled Deer Hunter, 256
BPS Trap, 256
BT-99, 256
BT-99 Micro Midas, 256
Citori 725 Feather, 256
Citori 725 Field, 256
Citori 725 Pro Sporting with Pro Fit Adjustable Comb, 55
Citori 725 Pro Trap with Pro Fit Adjustable Comb, 55
Citori 725 Sporting, 257
Citori 725 Sporting Adjustable Comb, 257
Citori 725 Sporting Grade V, 56
Citori 725 Sporting Grade VII, 56
Citori 725 Trap Adjustable Comb, 257
Citori Lightning, 257
Citori Superlight Feather, 257
Citori XT Trap, 258
Cynergy Classic Trap Unsingle Combo with Adjustable Comb, 258
Cynergy Feather, 258
Cynergy Field, 258
Cynergy Micro Midas, 56
Cynergy Satin Field, 259
Cynergy Sporting, 259
Gold Light 10 Ga., 259
Maxus Hunter, 259
Maxus Sporting, 259
Maxus Sporting Golden Clays, 259
Maxus Stalker, 260
Maxus Ultimate, 260
Silver Hunter, 260
Silver Hunter Micro Midas, 260

CAESAR GUERINI
Challenger Ascent, 260
Ellipse, 260
Ellipse EVO, 261
Invictus I Sporting, 261
Magnus Sporting, 261
Maximum Impact, 261
Tempio Field Gun, 261
Woodlander, 261

CENTURY INTERNATIONAL ARMS
Catamount Fury II, 262

CHARLES DALY
Model 300 Home Defense LH, 262

CHIAPPA
204X Extractor, 262
C6 Youth, 263
C6-12 Youth, 57
M6, 263
Triple Crown, 263
Triple Threat, 263
X-Caliber, 263

Gunfinder Index

CIMARRON
1878 Coach Gun, 264
1881 Hammerless Shotgun, 264

CONNECTICUT SHOTGUN MFG. CO.
A-10 American, 264
CSMC Model 21, 57

CZ-USA (CESKA ZBROJOVKA)
612 Field, 264
612 HC-P, 265
612 Home Defense, 265
620 Big Game, 265
620 Youth, 265
712 Adjustable Length Stock, 265
712 G2, 57
712 Practical G2, 265
712 Target G2, 266
712 Utility G2, 266
720 ALS G2, 266
812 Waterfowl, 58
912 Semiauto, 266
Canvasback Gold, 267
Lady Sterling, 267
Redhead Premier, 58
Sharp-Tail, 58
Southpaw Sterling, 59
Sporter Standard Grade G2, 267
Sporter Standard Grade Adjustable Rib, 268
Super Scroll Combo Set, 268
Upland Sterling, 268
Upland Ultralight, 268
Wingshooter Elite, 59

ESCORT BY LEGACY SPORTS
AimGuard, MarineGuard Home Defense, 269
Extreme Magnum Semi-Auto, 269
Extreme and Supreme Left-Handed Actions, 269
Gladius Home Defense Shotgun, 269
M87, 59
Pump Action, 60
Silver Standard, 270
Silver Synthetic Shorty, 270
Youth 20 Gauge, 270

FABARM
Axis RS12 Sporting, 60
Axis RS12 Sporting Quick Release Rib (QRR), 60
Axis RS12 Trap, 61
Elos Deluxe, 270
L4S Series, 61
XLR5 Velocity FR Compact, 61

FAUSTI USA
Caledon, 271
Class, 271
Italyco, 62
Magnificent, 271

FEDERAL ARMAMENT
Uzkon BR-99, 271

FLODMAN GUNS
Flodman Shotgun, 272

FRANCHI
48 AL, 272
Affinity, 272
Affinity Compact, 272
Aspire, 272
Instinct L, 273
Instinct SL, 273
Intensity, 273

ITHACA GUN COMPANY
Deerslayer II, 274
Deerslayer III, 274
Model 37 Defense, 274
Model 37 Featherlight, 275
Model 37 Trap, 275
Model 37 Waterfowl, 275

KEL-TEC
KSG, 62

KRIEGHOFF
Model K-20, 275
Model K-20 Pro-Sporter, 275
Model K-80, 276
Model K-80 ACS, 276
Model KX-6, 276

LJUTIC
Adjustable Rib Mono Gun, 276
Mono Gun, 276
PRO 3, 276

MAROCCHI
FinnClassic 612, 277
Super SJ, 62

MERKEL
Model 47E, XXE, XXEL, 277
Model 303E, 277
Model 2000L, 277

MOSSBERG
500 Classic All-Purpose Field, 278
500 Flex All-Purpose Series, 278
500 Flex All-Purpose L Series, 63
500 Flex Hunting Series, 278
500 JIC Flex, 278
500 JIC Mariner, 279
500 L Series, 62
500 Magpul, 279
500 Slugster, 279
500 Super Bantam Slugster, 279
500 Super Bantam Turkey, 279
500 Turkey, 279
510 Mini All-Purpose, 280
510 Mini Camo, 280
535 ATS Thumbhole Turkey, 280
535 ATS Turkey Thug, 280
590 L Series, 63
590A1 Adjustable Tactical Tri-Rail 9 Shot, 280
590A1 L Series, 63
835 Ulti-Mag, 280
835 Ulti-Mag-Recoil Reduction System, 280
930 Duck Commander Signature, 280
935 Magnum Turkey, 281
Silver Reserve II Field, 281

PERAZZI
High Tech, 63
MX8 Sporting Clays, 281

POINTER BY LEGACY SPORTS
Break-Action, 64
Slug Combo, 64
Sporting Series, 281

PURDEY
Over and Under Gun, 282
Side-by-Side Game Gun, 282

REMINGTON
Model 11-87 Sportsman Field, 282
Model 870 Express, 282
Model 870 Express Magpul FDE, 283
Model 870 Pachmayr Pistol Grip, 283
Model 870 Express Super Magnum, 283
Model 870 Express Tactical, 283
Model 870 Express Tactical with Blackhawk! Special Ops II, 283
Model 870 Shurshot Synthetic, 283
Model 870 SP Marine Magnum, 284
Model 870 SPS Shurshot Synthetic, 284
Model 870 Wingmaster, 284
Model 870 Wingmaster Classic Trap, 284
Model 887 Nitro Mag Camo Combo, 284
Model 1100 50th Anniversary Limited Edition, 284
Model 1100 Classic Trap, 284
Model 1100 Competition Synthetic, 284
V3 Field Sport, 64
Versa Max, 285
Versa Max Competition Tactical, 285
Versa Max Sportsman, 285
Versa Max Tactical, 285
Versa Max Wood Tech, 285

ROSSI
Field Grade Shotgun, 286
Rifled Barrel Slug Gun, 286

RUGER
Red Label, 286

SAVAGE ARMS
Specialty Series 220 Standard, Youth, Camo, 286
Stevens 320 Field Grade Youth, 65
Stevens 320 Pump, 286
Stevens 350 Pump Security, 287
Stevens 555, 65

SRM ARMS
Gen 2 Model 1216, 287

STOEGER
Coach Gun, 287
Condor, 287
Condor Competition, 287
Condor Outback, 288
Double Defense Over/Under, 288
Double Defense Side-by-Side, 288
M3K 3-Gun, 65
Model 3000, 288
Model 3020, 288
Model 3500, 289
P350 Pump, 289
The Grand, 289
Uplander, 289

TAYLOR'S & CO.
1887 T-Series Pistol, 290
Wyatt Earp Shotgun, 290

THOMPSON/CENTER
Pro Hunter Turkey, 290

TRISTAR SPORTING ARMS
Cobra Field Pump, 290
Cobra Tactical Pump, 290
Hunter EX LT, 291
Raptor A-TAC, 291
Setter S/T, 291
TEC 12, 291
TSA Mag Black, 291
Viper G2 LH, 291
Viper G2 Youth, 66
Viper G2 Youth Camo, 291

UTAS
UTS-15 Black, 292

WEATHERBY
Element Deluxe, 66
Orion I, 66
PA-08 Synthetic Slug Gun Combo, 292
PA-08 TR, 292
PA-08 Turkey, 292
PA-08 Upland, 292
PA-08 Upland Slug Gun Combo, 293
PA-459 TR, 293
SA-08 Deluxe, 293
SA-08 Upland, 293
SA-459 TR, 293
SA-459 Turkey, 293
WBY-X SA-459 Black Reaper TR, 294

WINCHESTER REPEATING ARMS
Model 101, 294
Super X Pump Black Shadow, 294
Super X Pump Defender, 294
Super X Pump Turkey Hunter, 295
Super X Pump Waterfowl Hunter, 295
Super X3 Field, 295
Super X3 Field Compact, 295
Super X3 Sporting Adjustable, 296
Super X3 Waterfowl Hunter, 296
SXP Compact Field, 296

HANDGUNS

ACCU-TEK
AT-380 II, 298
HC-380, 298
LT-380, 298
AMERICAN DERRINGER
Lady Derringer, 298
Model 1, 298
LM4 Simmerling, 299
LM5, 299
Model 4, 299
Model 6, 299
Model 7 Lightweight & Ultra Lightweight, 299
Model 8, 300

AMERICAN TACTICAL IMPORTS
FX 1911 GI, 300
FX 1911 Military, 300
FX 1911 Thunderbolt, 300
FX 1911 Titan, 301
FX Thunderbolt Enhanced, 301
GSG 922, 301
GSG 1911 Pistol, 301

ANDERSON RIFLES
AM15-7.5 Pistol, 67

ARSENAL FIREARMS
AF-1 Strike One, 302
Strike One Ergal, 302
AF2011-A1 "Black Magic", 302
AF2011-A1 Double Barrel Pistol, 302

ARSENAL INC.
SAM7K, 303

AUTO-ORDNANCE
1911PKZSE, 303
1911TC Thompson Custom 1911 Stainless, 303

BERETTA USA
21 Bobcat, 303
92A1, 303
92FS Type M9A1, 304
3032 Tomcat, 304
BU-9 Nano, 304
M9 Commercial, 304
PICO .380, 304
PX4 Storm Compact, 305
PX4 Storm Full Size, 305
U22 Neos, 305

BERSA
BP40CC, 67
BP380CC, 67
BP CC 9, 305
Thunder 9 Ultra Compact, 305
Thunder 40 Ultra Compact, 306
Thunder 45 Ultra Compact, 306
Thunder 380, 306
Thunder 380 Concealed Carry, 306

BOBERG ARMS
XR-45S, 306

BOND ARMS
Backup, 307
Mini, 307
Ranger, 307
Century 2000, 307
Snake Slayer, 307
Snake Slayer IV, 308
Texas Defender, 308
Texas Ranger - Special Edition, 308

BROWNING
1911-22 A1, 308
1911-22 A1 Compact Desert Tan, 309
1911-380, 67
Buck Mark Camper UFX, 309
Buck Mark Plus UDX, 309
Buck Mark Practical URX, 309
Buck Mark Series, 309
Hi-Power Standard, 309

CABOT GUN COMPANY
American Joe 1911, 310

CENTURY INTERNATIONAL ARMS, INC.
TP-9, 310

CHARTER ARMS
.22 Pathfinder, 310
.32 H&R Undercoverette, 311
.38 Chic Lady, 311
.38 Off Duty High Polish, 311

Gunfinder Index

.38 Undercover, 311
.38 Undercover Lite, 312
.38 Undercover On Duty, 312
.44 Special Bulldog, 312
.357 Mag. Pug, 312
Pitbull 45 ACP, 68
Rimless Revolver Pitbull, 312

CHIAPPA
MC 14, 313
Rhino Revolver, 313
SAA 17-10, 313

CHRISTENSEN
Tactical Commander, 313

CIMARRON FIREARMS CO. INC.
1872 Open Top Navy, 314
1911 .45 ACP, 314
1911 Wild Bunch Combo, 314
Bisley Model, 314
Eliminator 8, 68
Eliminator C, 68
Eliminator TS, 68
Frontier, 69
George Armstrong Custer 7th U.S. Cavalry Model, 315
Holy Smoker, 315
Lightning, 315
Man with No Name, 315
Model P, 315
Model P Jr., 316
Thunderer, 316
Thunderstorm, 316
Titan Derringer, 316
U.S. V. Artillery Model, 316
Wyatt Earp Buntline, 316

CITADEL BY LEGACY SPORTS
M-1911, 317
M-1911 .22 G.I., 317
M-1911 .22 TAC, 317

COBRA
Denali Series, 317

COLT'S MANUFACTURING COMPANY
.380 Mustang Pocketlite, 318
.380 Mustang Pocketlite Polymer, 318
1991 Series, 318
Defender, 318
Gold Cup Series, 318
CQBP, 318
New Frontier, 319
Rail Gun, 319
Series 70, 319
Single Action Army, 319

COONAN
Compensated Classic, 320

CZ-USA (CESKA ZBROJOVKA)
75 B, 320
75 B Omega, 320
75 Compact, 320
75 SP-01, 320
75 SP-01 Accu-Shadow, 320
75 SP-01 Shadow Target, 321
75 SP-91 Shadow Target II, 69
75 TS Czechmate, 321
85 Bren PS1 Pistol, 69
85 Combat, 70
97 B, 321
1911 A1, 70
2075 Rami, 321
Scorpion EVO 3 S1 Pistol, 70

DAN WESSON FIREARMS
715, 321
Chaos, 322
Guardian, 322
P-01, 322
P-07, 322
P-09, 322
ECO, 323
Razorback RZ-10, 323
Specialist, 323
Valor, 323

DOUBLETAP DEFENSE LLC
DoubleTap, 324

EAGLE IMPORTS
MAC 1911 Bobcut, 324
MAC 1911 Bullseye, 324
MAC 1911 Classic, 325
SPS Pantera, 325
SPS Vista Long and Short, 325

ED BROWN
Classic Custom, 326
Executive Carry, 326
Executive Elite, 326
Kobra, 326
Kobra Carry Lightweight, 326
Signature Edition, 327
Special Forces Carry, 327

E.M.F. COMPANY
Great Western II Alchimista II, 327
Great Western II All Blue "Paladin", 327
Great Western II Buntline, 328
Great Western II Californian, 328
Great Western II Deluxe Sheriff, 328
Great Western II "Liberty", 328
Great Western II Pony Express, 328

ENTRÉPRISE ARMS
Elite, 329
Medalist, 329

EUROPEAN AMERICAN ARMORY
Bounty Hunter, 329
Witness, 329
Witness Compact, 329
Witness Hunter Tanfoglio, 329

FNH USA
FN Five-Seven Series, 330
FNS-9/FNS-40, 330
FNX-9/FNX-40, 330
FNX-45, 330
FNX-45 Tactical, 330

FREEDOM ARMS
Model 83 Premier Grade, 331
Model 83 Rimfire, 331
Model 97 Premier Grade, 331

GLOCK
Compact Pistols G19, G23, G32, G38, 331
Competition G34, G35, 331
G20 Gen4, 332
G21 Gen4, 332
G29 Gen4, 332
G30S, 332
G32 Gen4, 332
G33 Gen4, 332
G34 Gen4, 333
G40 Gen4, 71
G41 Gen4, 333
G42, 333
G43 Single Stack, 71
Gen4 G26, G27, 333
Standard Pistol G17, G20, G21, G22, G31, G37, 333
Subcompact Pistols G26, G27, G29, G30, G33, G39, 333
Subcompact Slimline Pistol G36, 333

HÄMMERLI
Model SP20 Target Pistol, 334
Model X-Esse, 334

HECKLER & KOCH
HK45, 334
HK45 Cerakote, 72
HK45 Compact Cerakote, 72
HK45 Compact Tactical, 334
HK45 Tactical, 334
Mark 23, 335
P30, 335
P30 L, 335
P30SK, 72
P2000 & P2000 SK, 335
USP, 335
USP Compact, 335
USP9 Tactical, 73
VP40, 73

HERITAGE MANUFACTURING
Rough Rider Big Bore, 336
Rough Rider Small Bore, 336

HIGH STANDARD
Olympic, 336
Supermatic Citation, 336
Supermatic Trophy, 337
US Model 1911 Custom, 337
Victor, 337

HI-POINT FIREARMS
Model C-9 9mm, 337
Model CF-380, 337
Model JHP45 ACP & JCP 40 S&W, 337

KAHR ARMS
CM9, 338
CM40, 338
CM45, 338
CT40, 338
CT45, 338
CT380, 73
CW45, 339
CW380, 339
P9 Series, 339
P40 Series, 339
P45 Series, 340
P380 Series, 340
PM9 Series, 340
PM40 - External Safety & LCI, 340
PM45 Series, 340

KEL-TEC
P-3AT, 341
P-11, 341
P-32, 341
PF-9, 341
PMR-30, 341

KIMBER
Classic Carry Pro, 342
Compact Stainless II, 342
Custom II, 342
Custom TLE II (TFS), 342
Custom TLE/RL II (TFS), 342
Eclipse Ultra II, 342
Gold Match II, 343
Master Carry, 343
Micro Carry, 343
Sapphire Ultra II, 343
Solo Carry, 343
Solo CDP (LG), 343
Stainless Pro Raptor II, 344
Stainless Pro TLE II (LG), 344
Stainless Ultra TLE II, 344
Super Carry Pro, 344
Tactical Entry II, 344
Ultra Carry II, 344
Ultra CDP II, 345
Ultra Crimson Carry II, 345
Warrior SOC, 345

KRISS USA
Sphinx SDP Compact Alpha, 345

MAGNUM RESEARCH
Baby Desert Eagle, 346
Baby Desert Eagle III Series, 75
BFR (Big Frame Revolver), 346
Desert Eagle .357 Magnum with Integral Muzzle Break, 75
Desert Eagle 1911, 346
Desert Eagle 1911CSS, 74
Desert Eagle 1911GSS, 74
Desert Eagle 1911U "Undercover", 346
Desert Eagle 1911USS, 74
Mark XIX Desert Eagle, 346
Micro Desert Eagle, 346
MR40 Eagle, 75
MR Eagle "Fast Action", 346

MG ARMS
Wraithe, 347

MOA
Maximum, 347

MOSSBERG
715P, 347

NIGHTHAWK CUSTOM
Bob Marvel Custom, 348
Global Response Pistol (GRP), 348
Heinie Signature Compact, Recon, 348
Predator T5, 76
T3 - The Ultimate Concealed Carry 1911, 348
T4, 348
War Hawk Compact, 76
War Hawk Government, 76
War Hawk Recon, 77

NORTH AMERICAN ARMS
.32 ACP Guardian, 349
.380 ACP Guardian, 349
1860 Earl, 349
Mini Master Series Revolver, 349
Mini-Revolver, 350
Pug Mini-Revolver, 350
Sidewinder, 350
The Wasp, 350

OLYMPIC ARMS
Whitney Wolverine, 351

PARA USA
Black Ops 14.45, 351
Black Ops Recon 9, 351
Elite, 351
Elite Officer Crimson Trace, 351
Executive Carry, 352
Expert, 352
LDA Carry, 352
LDA Officer Crimson Trace, 352
Pro Comp 9, 353

REMINGTON ARMS
Model 1911 R1, 353
Model 1911 R1 Carry, 353
Model 1911 R1 Carry Commander, 353
Model 1911 R1 Carry Commander Crimson Trace, 354
Model 1911 R1 Commander, 354
Model 1911 R1 Enhanced Crimson Trace, 354
Model R51, 354
Model R51 Crimson Trace, 355
Model RM380 Subcompact, 77

ROCK ISLAND ARMORY
Baby Rock Standard CS, 77
GI Standard FS Hi-Cap, 78
GI Standard MS, 78
PRO Match Ultra, 78
PRO Match Ultra HC, 79
TCM TAC Ultra FS, 79
TCM TAC Ultra MS, 79
TCM TAC Ultra MS HC, 80
XT 22 Magnum, 80

ROCK RIVER ARMS
1911 Poly Pistol, 355
LAR-PDS Pistol, 355

ROSSI
Model R351 and R352, 355
Model R462 and R461, 356
Model R851, 356
Model R971 and R972, 356
Model R981 "Plinker", 356
Model R98104, 80
Model R98106, 80
Ranch Hand, 356

RUGER
22/45 Lite Rimfire Pistol, 81, 357
22/45 Target Rimfire Pistol, 357
22 Charger Takedown, 81
Bisley, 357
GP100, 357
GP100 Match Champion, 81, 357
LC9 9mm, 82, 358

GUNFINDER INDEX

Gunfinder Index

LC380, 358
LCP .380 ACP, 358
LCP Centerfire Pistol, 358
LCP Custom, 82
LCR (Lightweight Compact Revolver), 82, 358
LCRX, 359
Mark III Hunter, 359
Mark III Standard, 359
New Bearcat, 359
Redhawk, 83
Single-Six .17 HMR, 359
SP101, 83, 359
SP101 .22LR, 360
SR9C, 360
SR22 Rimfire Pistol, 360
SR40, 360
SR45, 360
SR1911, 83, 360
Super Blackhaw, 361
Super Redhawk, 361
Vaquero Bisley, 361
Vaquero Blued, 361

SIG SAUER
1911 .22LR Camo, 361
1911 Spartan, 361
1911 Traditional, 362
1911 Ultra, 362
M11-A1, 362
Mosquito, 362
P210, 362
P220, 362
P224, 362
P226, 363
P226 MK25, 363
P227, 363
P229, 363
P232, 363
P238, 363
P239, 363
P250 Compact, 364
P250 2SUM, 364
P290, 364
P320, 364
P938, 364
SP2022, 364
XFive Classic, 364

SMITH & WESSON
Bodyguard 38, 365
Bodyguard 380, 365
Classic M57, 365
Classic M586, 365
Governor, 365
M10, 365
M27 Classic, 366
M29, 366
M36, 366
M60, 366
M325 Thunder Ranch, 366
M327, 367
M327 TRR8, 367
M442, 367
M442 Machine Engraved, 367
M460 XVR, 367
M460 XVR Bone Collector, 84
M500, 368
M617, 368
M625, 368
M625 JM, 368
M627, 368
M629, 368
M629 V-Comp, 369
M640, 369
M642 Lasermax Centerfire Laser, 84
M686, 369
M686 SSR, 369
M929, 369
M&P 9mm, 369
M&P9 Carbon Fiber Finish, 85
M&P9 SHIELD Crimson Trace Green Laserguard, 84
M&P40 Carbon Fiber Finish, 85
M&P40 Compact, 369
M&P45, 369
M&P Bodygaurd 380, 370
M&P Pro Series C.O.R.E. Pistols, 370
M&P R8, 370
Model 66, 370
Model 69, 371
Model 929, 371
Model 986, 371
SD9 VE and SD40 VE, 371

SPHINX BY KRISS
SDP Compact Black, 372

SPRINGFIELD ARMORY
1911 Loaded Black Operator, 85
1911 Marine Corps Operator, 86
1911 Range Officer, 372
1911 Range Officer Champion, 86
EMP (Enhanced Micro Pistol), 372
Lightweight Champion Operator, 372
Mil-Spec Full Size Stainless, 373
Range Officer, 373
TRP (Tactical Response Pistol), 373
XD (M), 373
XD (M) Compact, 374
XD Mod.2 Sub-Compact with Grip Zone, 86
XD-S, 374
XDS 4.0, 374

STEYR ARMS
C9-A1, 375
L-A1, 375

STI INTERNATIONAL
Apeiro, 375
Duty One Series, 375
DVC Open, 87
Eagle 5.0, 376
Edge, 376
Executive, 376
Lawman Family, 376
Rangemaster, 377
Tactical Family, 377
Tactical SS Family, 377
TargetMaster, 377
Trojan 5.0, 378

STOEGER
Cougar, 378
Cougar Compact, 378

TAURUS
22BR, 379
22/25 PLY, 379
24/7 G2, 379
44, 379
82, 379
92, 380
94/941, 380
.380 Mini Revolver, 380
605, 380
608, 380
709 "Slim", 380
738 TCP, 380
809, 381
905, 381
Curve, 87
Judge .45/.410, 381
Millennium G2, 87
Raging Bull 444, 381
Raging Judge Magnum, 382
Slim 740, 382
Tracker 992, 382
Tracker Series, 382

TAYLOR'S & CO.
1873 Cattleman Photo Engraved, 383
1873 Gunfighter Cattleman, 383
1873 Taylor Gambler Cattleman, 383
1873 Taylor Marshall Cattleman, 383
Runnin' Iron, 383
The Smoke Wagon, 384

THOMPSON/CENTER
Encore, 384
G2 Contender, 384

TRADITIONS FIREARMS
Frontier Series, 385
Rawhide Series, 385

TRISTAR ARMS
C-100, 385
P-100, 88
P-120, 385
T-100, 385

UBERTI
1851 Navy Conversion, 386
1860 Army Conversion, 386
1871–1872 Open-Top Conversion, 386
1873 Cattleman Bird's Head, 386
1873 Cattleman .22LR, 386
1873 Cattleman Bisley, 387
1873 Cattleman Callahan, 387
1873 Cattleman Chisholm, 387
1873 Cattleman Desperado, 387
1873 Cattleman Matching Sets, 387
1873 El Patrón Cowboy Mounted Shooter (CMS), 388
1873 Horseman, 388
1873 Single-Action Cattleman, 388
1873 Stallion/Stallion Target, 388
1875 Outlaw & Frontier, 388
1890 Single Action Police Revolver, 388
Top Break Revolvers, 388

WALTHER
CCP (Concealed Carry Pistol), 389
P22, 389
P99AS, 389
P99AS Compact, 389
PPK and PPK/S, 389
PPK/S .22, 389
PPQ M2, 390
PPS (Police Pistol Slim), 390
PPX, 390

WINDHAM WEAPONRY,
300 Blackout Pistol, 88

ZIP FACTORY
ZIP, 390

BLACK POWDER

CONNECTICUT VALLEY ARMS (CVA)
Accura MR, 392
Accura V2, 392
Accura V2 NW, 392
Apex, 392
Buckhorn, 393
Optima V2, 393
Optima V2 NW, 393
Wolf, 393
Wolf NW, 394

DIXIE GUN WORKS
1853 Enfield Three-Band Rifle Musket, 394
Sharps 1859 Military Carbine, 394
Spanish Musket, 394
Pedersoli Screw Barrel Pistol, 394

E.M.F. COMPANY
1851 Navy, 395
1851 Navy Sheriff, 395
1858 Remington Army Revolver, 395
1860 Army Revolver, 395
1863 Pocket Remington, 395
Missouri River Hawken by Pedersoli, 395
Kentucky Flintlock Pistol, 396
Pennsylvania Percussion Rifle, 396

LYMAN
Deerstalker Rifle, 396
Great Plains Rifle, 396
Mustang Breakaway 209 Magnum, 396
Plains Pistol, 396
Trade Rifle, 396

NEW ULTRA LIGHT ARMS
Model 209 Muzzleloader, 397

PEDERSOLI
1763 Leger (1766) Charleville, 397
Baker Style Coach Gun, 397
Boutet 1er Empire, 397
Cook & Brother Artillery Carbine, 397
Cook & Brother Rifle, 89
Derringer Philadelphia, 397
Enfield 3 Band P1853 Rifle Musket, 398
Gibbs Shotgun, 398
Hawken Hunter Rifle, 89
Howdah Hunter Pistol, 398
Kodiak Express MK VI, 398
La Bohemienne Side-by-Side Shotgun, 398
Le Page Target Flintlock Pistol, 398
Mamelouk, 399
Mang in Graz Match, 399
Mississippi U.S. Model 1841, 399
Mortimer Target Rifle, 399
Plains Shotgun "The Fast Back Action", 399
Richmond 1861, Type III, 399
Springfield Model 1861 U.S., 400
Swiss Match Standard Flintlock, 400
Traditional Hawken Target Rifle, 89
Tyron Target Standard Rifle, 400
Zouave US Model 1863, 400

REMINGTON
Model 700, 400

SHILOH RIFLE
1874 Sharps Buffalo - "Quigley", 401
1874 Target Creedmoor Rifle, 401
1877 #1 Shiloh English Rifle, 401

TAYLOR'S & CO.
1842 Smoothbore Musket, 401
1847 Walker, 401
1848 Dragoons, 402
Le Mat Cavalry, 402

THOMPSON/CENTER
Impact, 402
Triumph Bone Collector, 402

TRADITIONS FIREARMS
1851 Navy Revolver, 403
1858 Army Revolver, 403
1860 Army Revolver, 403
Buckstalker, 403
Deerhunter Rifle, 404
Hawken Woodsman Rifle, 404
Kentucky Pistol, 404
Pennsylvania Rifle, 405
Pursuit G4 Ultralight, 89
Pursuit Ultralight, 405
Tracker 209, 405
Trapper Pistol, 406
Vortek Pistol, 406
Vortek StrikerFire, 406
Vortek Ultralight, 406
Vortek Ultralight LDR, 406

UBERTI
1847 Walker, 407
1848 Dragoon, 407
1849 Pocket Revolvers, 407
1851 Navy Revolver, 407
1858 New Army Revolver, 408
1860 Army Revolver, 408
1861 Navy Revolver, 408
1862 Pocket Navy Revolver, 408
1862 Police Revolver, 408